# CONTENTS

**Cover Picture: Stapleford Park, Stapleford, Leicestershire (see page 296)**

# FOREWORD BY THE EDITOR

*People who use Johansens guides often ask why we never say anything critical about a hotel, an inn, a country house or a business meetings venue which we recommend. The answer is easy. If we knew anything bad to say about one of our selections we would not recommend it*

*We visit all establishments regularly and irregularly, overtly and covertly – our professional inspectors non-stop, the rest of us ad hoc; but the many thousands of you who use our guides are really the best guardians of quality. Our recommendations must be reliable, so keep sending us those freepost Guest Surveys which you find among the back-pages of our guides. They provide our inspectors with the first hint of any fall in standards, though, as you will be glad to read, the majority of Guest Surveys are entirely complimentary. In 'The Caterer & Hotelkeeper' a regular columnist recently said that a characteristic of Johansens guests is that "they come to enjoy themselves". Keep helping us to help you do just that – to have a good time!*

***Rodney Exton, Editor***

# KEY TO SYMBOLS

13 rms Total number of rooms

 MasterCard accepted

 Visa accepted

 American Express accepted

 Diners Club accepted

 Quiet location

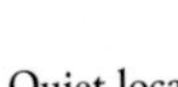

 Access for wheelchairs to at least one bedroom and public rooms

13 rms Nombre de chambres

 MasterCard accepté

 Visa accepté

 American Express accepté

 Diners Club accepté

 Un lieu tranquille

 Accès handicapé

 Anzahl der Zimmer

 MasterCard akzeptiert

 Visa akzeptiert

 American Express akzeptiert

 Diners Club akzeptiert

 Ruhige Lage

 Zugang für Behinderte

(The 'Access for wheelchairs' symbol (♿) does not necessarily indicate that the property fulfils National Accessible Scheme grading)

 Chef-patron

 20 Meeting/conference facilities with maximum number of delegates

 8 Children welcome, with minimum age where applicable

 Dogs accommodated in rooms or kennels

 At least one room has a four-poster bed

 Cable/satellite TV in all bedrooms

 Direct-dial telephone in all bedrooms

 No-smoking rooms (at least one no-smoking bedroom)

 Lift available for guests' use

 Air Conditioning

 Indoor swimming pool

 Outdoor swimming pool

 Tennis court at hotel

 Croquet lawn at hotel

 Fishing can be arranged

Golf course on site or nearby, which has an arrangement with hotel allowing guests to play

 Shooting can be arranged

 Riding can be arranged

Hotel has a helicopter landing pad

 Licensed for wedding ceremonies

 Chef-patron

 20 Salle de conférences – capacité maximale

 8 Enfants bienvenus

 Chiens autorisés

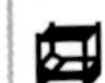 Lit à baldaquin

 TV câblée/satellite dans les chambres

 Téléphone dans les chambres

 Chambres non-fumeurs

 Ascenseur

 Climatisée

 Piscine couverte

 Piscine de plein air

 Tennis à l'hôtel

Croquet à l'hôtel

 Pêche

 Golf

 Chasse

 Équitation

Piste pour hélicoptère

 Cérémonies de noces

 Chef-patron

20 Konferenzraum-Höchstkapazität

 8 Kinder willkommen

 Hunde erlaubt

 Himmelbett

 Satellit-und Kabelfernsehen in allen Zimmern

 Telefon in allen Zimmern

 Zimmer für Nichtraucher

 Fahrstuhl

 Klimatisiert

 Hallenbad

 Freibad

 Hoteleigener Tennisplatz

 Krocketrasen

Angeln

 Golfplatz

 Jagd

 Reitpferd

Hubschrauberlandplatz

 Konzession für Eheschliessungen

Published by
Johansens, 175-179 St John Street, London EC1V 4RP
Tel: 0171-490 3090 Fax: 0171-490 2538
Find Johansens on the Internet at: http://www.johansen.com
E-Mail: admin@johansen.u–net.com

**Editor:** Rodney Exton

**Group Publisher:** Peter Hancock
**P.A. to Group Publisher:** Carol Sweeney

**Regional Inspectors:** Christopher Bond, Geraldine Bromley, Robert Bromley, Julie Dunkley, Susan Harangozo, Joan Henderson, Marie Iversen, Pauline Mason, John O'Neill, Mary O'Neill, Fiona Patrick, Brian Sandell

**Production Manager:** Daniel Barnett
**Production Controller:** Kevin Bradbrook
**Designer:** Michael Tompsett

**Copywriters:** Sally Sutton, Jill Wyatt, Norman Flack

**Sales and Marketing Manager:** Laurent Martinez
**Marketing Executive:** Samantha Lhoas
**Sales Executive:** Babita Sareen

**P.A. to Managing Director & regional editorial research:** Angela Franks

**Managing Director:** Andrew Warren

Johansens is a member company of Harmsworth Publishing Ltd, a subsidiary of the Daily Mail & General Trust plc

ISBN 1 86017 5015

Printed in England by St Ives plc
Colour origination by Graphic Facilities

Distributed in the UK and Europe by Johnsons International Media Services Ltd, London (direct sales) & Biblios PDS Ltd, West Sussex (bookstores). In North America by general sales agent: ETL Group, New York, NY (direct sales) and The Cimino Publishing Group, INC. New York (bookstores). In Australia and New Zealand by Bookwise International, Findon, South Australia.

# HOW TO USE THIS GUIDE

If you want to identify a Hotel whose name you already know, look for it in the Regional Indexes on pages 499–505.

If you want to find a Hotel in a particular area you can

- Turn to the Maps on page 14 and pages 490–496
- Search the Indexes on pages 499–505
- Look for the Town or Village where you wish to stay in the main body of the Guide. This is divided into Countries. Place names in each Country appear at the head of the pages in alphabetical order.

The Indexes list the Hotels by Countries and by Counties, they also show those with amenities such as wheelchair access, conference facilities, swimming, golf, etc. (Please note some recent Local Government Boundary changes).

The Maps cover all regions including London. Each Hotel symbol (a blue circle) relates to a Hotel in this guide situated in or near the location shown.

Red Triangles and Green Squares show the location of Johansens Recommended Inns and Johansens Recommended Country Houses & Small Hotels respectively. If you cannot find a suitable hotel near where you wish to stay, you may decide to choose one of these smaller establishments as an alternative. They are all listed by place names on pages 485–486.

On page 487 the names of Johansens Recommended Hotels – Europe are similarily shown in their separate countries, although as such they do not appear in this guide on any maps.

This year for the first time we are publishing Johansens Recommended Hotels and Inns – North America. This guide contains a selection of excellent places to stay in the United States, Canada and the Carribean. A list of hotels appears on page 489 of this guide

The prices, in most cases, refer to the cost of one night's accommodation, with breakfast, for two people. Prices are also shown for single occupancy. These rates are correct at the time of going to press but always should be checked with the hotel before you make your reservation.

All guides are obtainable from bookshops or by Johansens Freephone 0800 269397 or by using the order coupons on pages 509–512.

# INTRODUCTION

***One-man-conglomerate, Sir David Frost, talks to Sarah Tucker about his expectations of the hotels in which he stays...***

Anywhere where service is considered quite honourable, you'll find the service is usually exemplary. At Chewton Glen in the New Forest, for example, the staff are stunningly friendly and helpful. I have a tremendously good time there and it's a place where you find considerable peace and serenity.

Sometimes hotels mistakenly overdo the service. For example, in the States, I'm usually given two 'phone lines into my suite for business use. Several months ago I was on the 'phone to Paul McCartney. Having played telephone tag for three days, we had kept missing each other, we eventually managed to get together in New York on one of the 'phones when the other 'phone rang. Just like anyone would be, I was curious who was on the other line – so, wanting to know who it was, I asked Paul to wait while I answered the call. The voice on the line said 'Hello, Mr Frost, just calling to ask if you enjoyed your breakfast'. Checking to see if the customer is OK is a good thing – but there is a time and place for everything.

---

# JOHANSENS AWARDS FOR EXCELLENCE

The names of the winners of the 1998 Awards will be published in the 1999 editions of Johansens guides.
The winners of the 1997 Awards are listed below. They were presented with their certificates at the Johansens Annual Awards dinner, held at The Dorchester on 4th November 1996, by Jean Rozwadowski, Senior Vice-President and General Manager Europe, of MasterCard International.

**Johansens Country Hotel Award for Excellence**
*Marlfield House, Co. Wicklow, Ireland*

**Johansens City Hotel Award for Excellence**
*The Castle at Taunton, Somerset*

**Johansens Country House Award for Excellence**
*Balgonie Country House, Royal Deeside, Scotland*

**Johansens Inn Award for Excellence**
*The Manor Hotel, West Bexington, Dorset*

**Johansens London Hotel Award for Excellence**
*The Leonard, London W1*

**Johansens Most Excellent Value for Money Award**
*Appleton Hall, Appleton le Moors, N. Yorkshire*

**Johansens Most Excellent Service Award**
*Alexander House, Turner's Hill, W. Sussex*

**Johansens Most Excellent Restaurant Award**
*Freshmans Restaurant, Belbroughton, Worcestershire*

Candidates for awards derive from two main sources: from the thousands of Johansens guide users who send us Guest Gurvey Reports commending hotels, inns and country houses in which they have stayed and from our team of twelve regional inspectors who regularly visit all properties in our guides. Guest Survey Report forms can be found on pages 509–512. They are a vital part of our continuous process of assessment and they are the decisive factor in choosing the Value for Voney and the Most Excellent Service Awards.

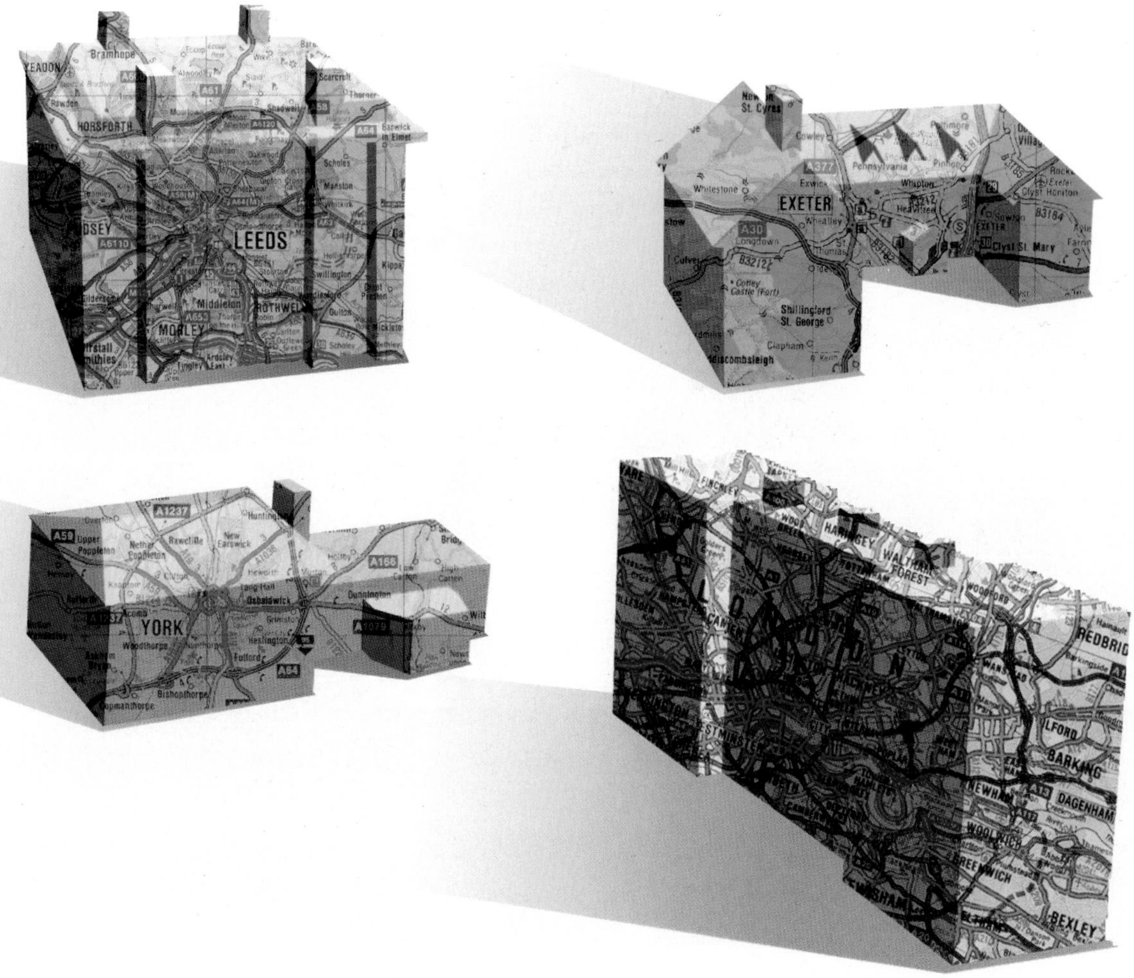

# INTRODUCTION

***From Marlfield House, Gorey, Co Wexford, Ireland***
***Winner of the 1997 Johansens Country Hotel Award***

We are very honoured to have been awarded the Johansens "Country Hotel Award". As one of its earliest featured hotels we have watched the Johansens Recommended Hotels guide develop into a very impressive publication containing most of the best hotels in Great Britain and Ireland and we are delighted to be part of it.

In the current climate of increasing competition and more discerning clients we are more determined than ever to keep up with industry changes and to maintain high standards of service. There is no room for complacency within either ourselves, as proprietors and managers, or our personnel, the staff whose dedication and teamwork are vital to the success of the hotel. Only continuous training and a lot of hard work will ensure that standards do not slip. We are as delighted to receive this Johansens award as we have been to receive all the awards presented to us over the last nineteen years.

Tourism from the UK to Ireland is increasing. Being on the east coast, Marlfield welcomes many guests coming to Ireland by ferry or by air from the UK every day. In fact, we had the same percentage of British as Irish guests staying with us in 1996, representing a significant increase on 1995. We know too that many of these guests come to us because of Johansens and we realise also that with the increasing world-wide distribution of Johansens guides we will be welcoming more and more Johansens guide readers not only from the British Isles but from all over Europe and North America.

***Mary, Ray and Margaret Bowe***

BRUT IMPÉRIAL
MOËT & CHANDON
Turning nature into art
MOËT & CHA

# INTRODUCTION

***From The Castle at Taunton, Taunton, Somerset***
***Winner of the 1997 Johansens Town and City Hotel of the Year Award***

During its long, distinguished, and often turbulent history, The Castle at Taunton has always been synonymous with good food, a good cellar and good service.

High standards of excellence require dedication at all levels and the "Johansens Town and City Hotel of the Year Award" is a tribute to all who are involved in this very special and unique operation. To work alongside enthusiastic, motivated staff is a great privilege especially those who make that extra effort when they least feel like it, despite the often punishing schedules the industry can at times dictate. There are many here at The Castle with this positive attitude, they make the hotel a special place and remain our greatest asset. On so many occasions immaculately presented hotels overlook what should be their main priority: training, supporting and valuing their staff.

At The Castle we achieve excellence by involving our staff as an integral part of any operational decision. A sense of ownership and a feeling of importance are vitally important, and the staff here at The Castle know they play a big part in a small company and they rise to every occasion with honours.

There is no doubt in my mind that a well run British hotel represents the finest hospitality in the world, a fact of which we in the industry should be very proud and should work hard to sustain.

***Andrew C Grahame***
***Director and General Manager***

# INTRODUCTION

*From Alexander House, Turner's Hill, West Sussex*
*Winner of the 1997 Johansens Most Excellent Service Award*

Alexander House was delighted to receive Johansens 'Most Excellent Service Award 1997'. We were elated that so many of our guests should have felt it necessary to praise our service in such a way that we should receive such a prestigious accolade and my heartfelt thanks go to those concerned.

Alexander House strives for excellence in a highly competitive market and to achieve such recognition from a quality publication like Johansens is surely proof that we are providing the customers with their every requirement.

The hotel has always been strongly committed to customer service. Although the house itself has only been in operation as a hotel for ten years, over that period the reputation of Alexander House has grown rapidly . This is a direct reflection upon the commitment of the staff at Alexander House – without their enthusiasm and dedication, awards such as this would not be received nor be for them so well deserved.

***Mark Godfrey***
***Resident Manager***

HILDON
WELL... DE GUSTIBUS NON EST DISPUTANDUM
& Friends
HILDON
NATURAL MINERAL WATER
ESTABLISHED
1986
HILDON
AN ENGLISH
NATURAL MINERAL WATER
OF EXCEPTIONAL TASTE
GENTLY CARBONATED
HILDON LTD.
Hildon House, Broughton, Hampshire SO20 8DG
☏ 01794-301 747, Fax 01794-301 718

# INTRODUCTION

*From The Leonard, London W1*
*Winner of the Most Excellent London Hotel Award 1997*

When our award was announced at Johansens annual dinner at The Dorchester we were taken by surprise, for the Leonard had been open for only ten months and to be placed above the other Johansens London hotels in the opinion of Johansens guests and judges was a great but unexpected honour.

In creating The Leonard, we set out to give people a hotel they looked forward to staying in and to provide service that was "un-stuffy", not pretentious. We have always believed that it is staff who make the hotel, and indeed this award confirms it. A large majority of the guest survey report forms reported that the staff were friendly, helpful and efficient. That is why we are where we are today. Our aim is for unpretentious friendly professionalism.

There is no doubt in many people's minds that London is "the" place to be, but it is important that we do not become complacent, remembering that there are hotels and restaurants in other big cities around the world that are all trying to attract customers. As we travel, we have become more and more impressed with the standards of service in all cities. We all have to create the edge and firmly believe that the Johansens guides are a continuous method of achieving excellence in many, many ways and communicating information to the future guests of our hotels.

***Bijan Daneshmand (Owner)***
***and Andrew Harris (General Manager)***

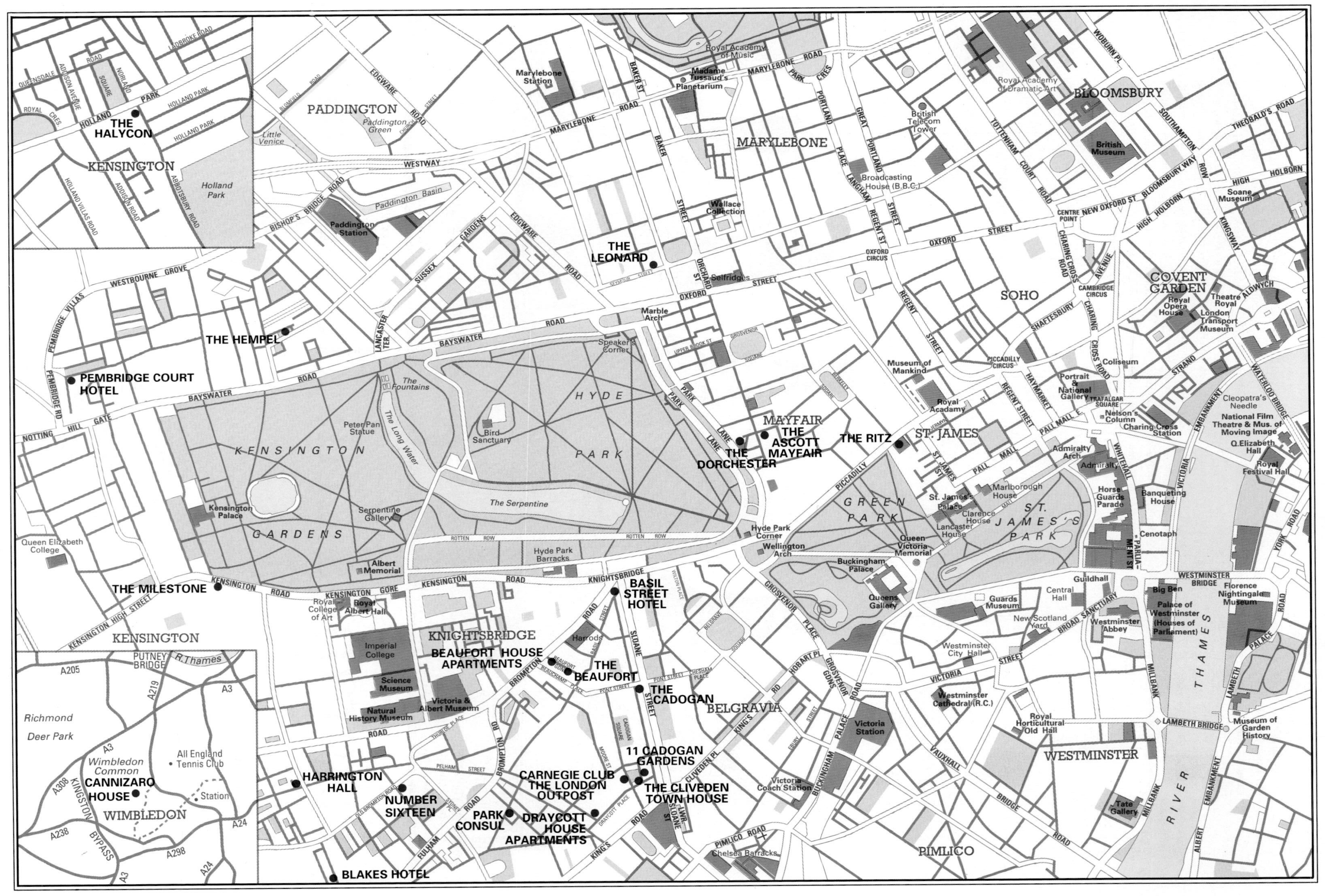
THE HALCYON
KENSINGTON
Holland Park
PADDINGTON
Paddington Green
Little Venice
Paddington Basin
Paddington Station
Marylebone Station
Royal Academy of Music
Madame Tussaud's Planetarium
MARYLEBONE
British Telecom Tower
Broadcasting House (B.B.C.)
Royal Academy of Dramatic Art
BLOOMSBURY
British Museum
Soane Museum
Wallace Collection
THE LEONARD
Selfridges
Marble Arch
SOHO
COVENT GARDEN
Theatre Royal
Royal Opera House
London Transport Museum
THE HEMPEL
PEMBRIDGE COURT HOTEL
Speaker's Corner
Museum of Mankind
Portrait & National Gallery
Coliseum
Cleopatra's Needle
National Film Theatre & Mus. of Moving Image
Q.Elizabeth Hall
Royal Festival Hall
The Fountains
The Long Water
Peter Pan Statue
KENSINGTON GARDENS
Bird Sanctuary
HYDE PARK
The Serpentine
MAYFAIR
THE ASCOTT MAYFAIR
THE DORCHESTER
THE RITZ
Royal Academy
ST. JAMES
Nelson's Column
Charing Cross Station
Admiralty Arch
Admiralty
Kensington Palace
Serpentine Gallery
Queen Elizabeth College
Albert Memorial
Hyde Park Barracks
Hyde Park Corner
Wellington Arch
GREEN PARK
St. James's Palace
Marlborough House
Clarence House
Lancaster House
ST. JAMES'S PARK
Queen Victoria Memorial
Buckingham Palace
Horse Guards Parade
Banqueting House
Cenotaph
THE MILESTONE
Royal College of Art
Royal Albert Hall
KENSINGTON
KNIGHTSBRIDGE
BASIL STREET HOTEL
Queens Gallery
Guards Museum
Central Hall
Guildhall
New Scotland Yard
Westminster Abbey
Big Ben
Palace of Westminster (Houses of Parliament)
Florence Nightingale Museum
THAMES
Imperial College
BEAUFORT HOUSE APARTMENTS
Harrods
THE BEAUFORT
THE CADOGAN
Westminster City Hall
Science Museum
Victoria & Albert Museum
Natural History Museum
BELGRAVIA
Victoria Station
Westminster Cathedral (R.C.)
Royal Horticultural Old Hall
Museum of Garden History
Richmond Deer Park
Wimbledon Common
All England Tennis Club
CANNIZARO HOUSE
Station
WIMBLEDON
PUTNEY BRIDGE
R.Thames
KINGSTON BYPASS
HARRINGTON HALL
NUMBER SIXTEEN
11 CADOGAN GARDENS
CARNEGIE CLUB THE LONDON OUTPOST
THE CLIVEDEN TOWN HOUSE
Victoria Coach Station
WESTMINSTER
PARK CONSUL
DRAYCOTT HOUSE APARTMENTS
Tate Gallery
RIVER
Chelsea Barracks
PIMLICO
BLAKES HOTEL

Tower Bridge and skyline

# Johansens Recommended Hotels & Apartments in London

*London recommendations represent a fine selection of full service hotels, town house hotels and apartments, from the grand to the petite.*

*Our choice is based on location, reputation, value for money and excellence, above all else.*

*The Johansens guest can be comfortably accommodated within easy reach of the principal shopping areas, museums, galleries, restaurants, theatres and Wimbledon!*

## LONDON

London is a city that lets you do whatever you want to do. A city where high fashion, new restaurants, superb theatre and entertainment are served up with lashings of history and pageantry. It is also a place full of surprises. So even if you have been to London many times before, there will always be something new to explore, or a hidden secret to discover...

For as the learned and famous Dr Samuel Johnson prophetically said: "When a man is tired of London, he is tired of life, for there is in London all that life can afford."

Everyone knows London's great historic sights, like the Tower of London, Trafalgar Square and Buckingham Palace. But when you come to the city, try to take time to visit its smaller, lesser known attractions. London has over 300 museums and galleries and numerous historic houses open to the public.

The Dulwich Picture Gallery is the oldest public art gallery (c. 1811) in the country. It was designed by Sir John Soane and contains a fine collection of over 300 old masters, including Gainsborough portraits and Canalettos. There is a programme of lectures and special exhibitions too.

In Camden, the Jewish Museum offers an insight into the Jewish way of life, its ceremonial art and history. Highlights include a magnificent synagogue ark, wedding rings and decorated marriage contracts.

Ranger's House in Blackheath was the home of the 4th Earl of Chesterfield, who retired to this 18th century villa after being rather too outspoken in politics. He became a prodigious collector of paintings and the house now contains a number of panelled rooms and rare 18th century furniture, together with a superb collection of Jacobean and Stuart portraits.

In October 1997, the BBC Visitor Centre opens to the public. Its mission is to show how the most famous broadcasting company in the world works. Guided tours are given around Broadcasting House, with the chance to see studios and archives and play with lots of 'hands-on' displays.

A brand new visitor attraction , the Commonwealth Experience, has been created within the Commonwelath Institute. With the aim of combining education and entertainment, the centre offers many innovative features including Heliride, an action packed helicopter 'flight'. Using the latest in simulator technology, the ride lurches visitors into the air in a dramatic helicopter adventure; while strapped into their seats, they swoop, dive and climb over Malaysia's fantastic scenery. More fun is to be had in Inter-active World, a 'hands-on' activity centre revealing natural phenomena across the Commonwealth.

The London Aquarium opened in County Hall in 1997 on the banks of the Thames. Constructed on three levels, visitors are able to observe many species never seen before in Britain. The highlights are twin tanks representing the Atlantic and Pacific Oceans. Piranha, octopus and sharks are among the hundreds of varieties of fish and sea-life display. A 'touch pool' allows children to get acquainted with some friendly stingrays.

Useful addresses:

**Dulwich Picture Gallery**
**College Road, Dulwich, London SE21**
**Tel: 0181 693 5254**

**Jewish Museum**
**Raymond Burton House**
**129-131 Albert Street, Camden**
**London NW1**
**Tel: 0171 284 1997**

**Rangers House**
**Chesterfield Walk, Blackheath**
**London SE10**
**Tel: 0181 853 0035**

**BBC Visitor Centre**
**Broadcasting House, Portland Place**
**London W1**
**Tel: 0171 580 4468**

**Commonwealth Experience at the Commonwealth Institute**
**Kensington High Street, London W8**
**Tel: 0171 603 4535**

**London Aquarium**
**County Hall Riverside Building**
**Waterloo, London SE1**
**Tel: 0171 967 8000**

Information supplied by:

**London Tourist Board and Convention Bureau (LTB)**
**26 Grosvenor Gardens**
**London SW1W ODU**

An information pack on London is available by writing to the above address.

LTB's Visitorcall* lines provide a comprehensive 24-hour information service on London.
0839 123 400 What's on this week
0839 123 480 Popular attractions
0839 123 483 Famous houses and gardens
*Visitorcall is charged at no more than 50p a minute, plus any hotel surcharge. NB These lines cannot be accessed outside the UK.

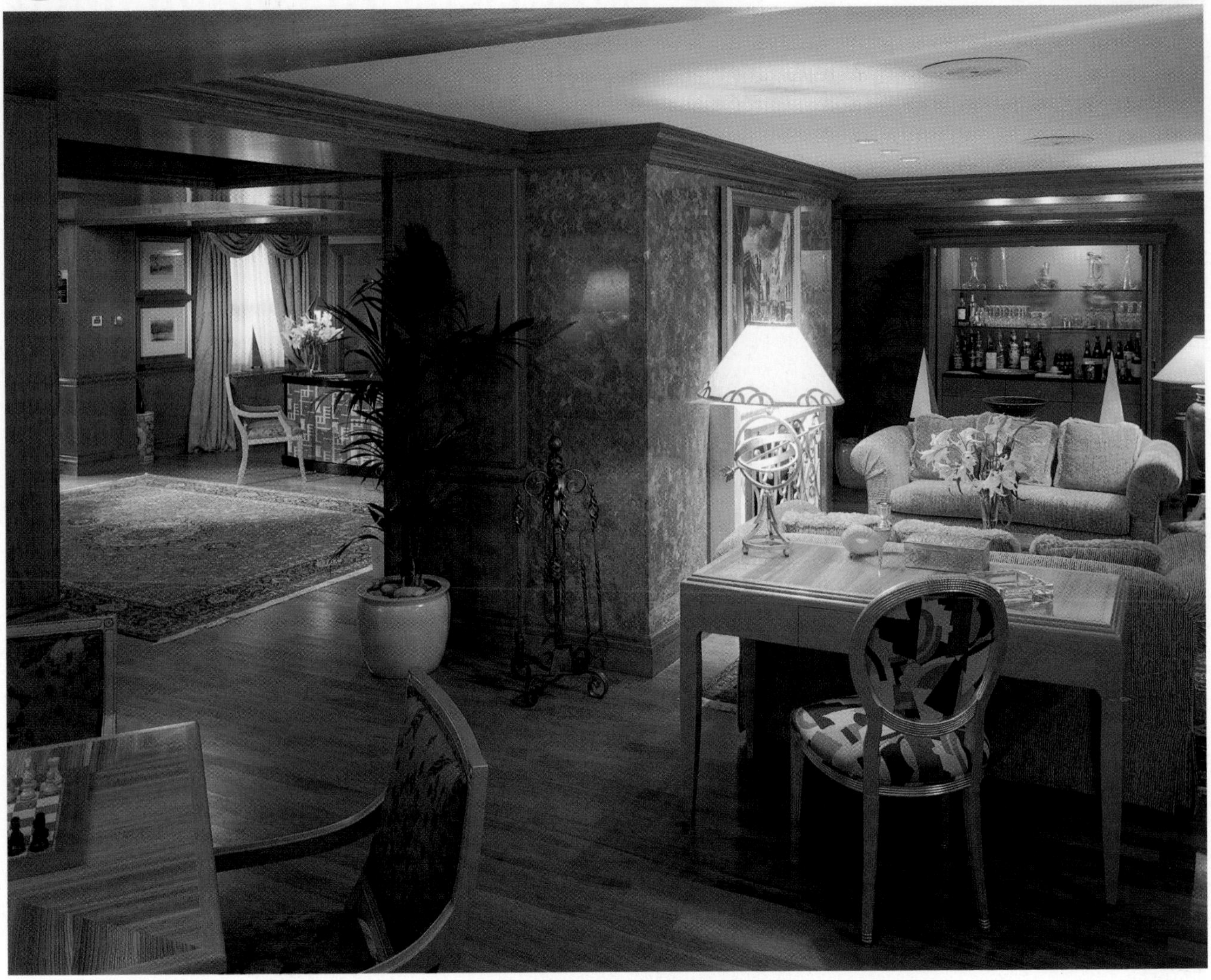

# THE ASCOTT MAYFAIR

49 HILL STREET, LONDON W1
TEL: 0171 499 6868 FAX: 0171 499 0705

This, the latest concept in city centre accommodation, offers all the benefits of a hotel and yet also privacy and space in what the brochure describes as "residences", with one, two or three bedrooms, in a spectacular art deco building. The apartments have a 24 hour concierge for security and assistance. A maid will be assigned to you for the full duration of your stay. There is no restaurant; however, a complimentary Continental breakfast is served on weekdays in The Terrace, overlooking the private gardens. There is an Honour Bar in The Club where guests can mingle or entertain. The Hothouse offers a gym, sauna, steamroom and solarium. The Business Service includes the use of a private boardroom. A marvellous kitchen is provided in each apartment with everything necessary for entertaining in the versatile lounge. The study area has fax and computer links. The sitting room is extremely comfortable and beautifully decorated. It has satellite television, a music system and video. The luxurious bedrooms have amazing en suite bathrooms, full of soft white towels. The Ascott is in the heart of London – Mayfair being close to all the major shopping centres and best restaurants, theatre-land and sightseeing. **Directions:** Hill Street is off Berkeley Square, near Green Park Underground Station. Price guide: 1 bed £164–£247 daily, £1,040–£1,565 weekly; 2 beds from £375daily–£2,365 weekly. (All rates are subject to VAT).

For hotel location, see map on page 14

# The Beaufort

**33 BEAUFORT GARDENS, KNIGHTSBRIDGE, LONDON SW3 1PP**
**TEL: 0171 584 5252 FAX: 0171 589 2834 E–MAIL: thebeaufort@nol.co.uk.**

The Beaufort offers the sophisticated traveller all the style and comfort of home – combining warm contempory colourings with the highest possible personal attention. The owner Diana Wallis (pictured below) believes that much of the success of the hotel is due to the charming, attentive staff – a feeling happily endorsed by guests. The Beaufort is situated in a quiet tree-lined square only 100 yards from Harrods and as guests arrive they are all greeted at the front door and given their own door key to come and go as they please. The closed front door gives added security and completes that feeling of home. All the bedrooms are individually decorated, with air conditioning and a great many extras such as shortbread, Swiss chocolates and brandy. The hotel owns a video and cassette library and is home to a magnificent collection of original English floral watercolours. Breakfast is brought to the bedroom – hot rolls and croissants, freshly squeezed orange juice and home-made preserves, tea and coffee. In the drawing room there is a 24-hour honour bar with complimentary champagne and between 4-5pm every day a free cream tea is served with scones, clotted cream and jam. The hotel is proud of its no tipping policy and is open all year. **Directions:** From the Harrods exit at Knightsbridge underground station take the third turning on the left. Price guide: Single £130; double/twin from £150; suites £240.

For hotel location, see map on page 14

# Basil Street Hotel

**BASIL STREET, LONDON SW3 1AH**
**TEL: 0171-581 3311 FAX: 0171-581 3693 – FROM USA CALL FREE: UTELL 1 800 448 8355**

The Basil feels more like an English home than a hotel. Privately owned by the same family for three generations, this traditional Edwardian hotel is situated in a quiet corner of Knightsbridge, on the threshold of London's most exclusive residential and shopping area. Harrods, Harvey Nichols and other famous stores are only minutes away. It is close to museums and theatres. The spacious public rooms are furnished with antiques, paintings, mirrors and *objets d'art*. The lounge, bar and dining room are on the first floor, reached by the distinctive staircase that dominates the front hall. Bedrooms, all individually furnished, vary in size, style and décor. The Hotel's Dining Room is an ideal venue either for unhurried, civilised lunch or dinner by candlelight with piano music. The Parrot Club, a lounge for the exclusive use of ladies, is a haven of rest in delightful surroundings. The Basil combines tradition and caring individual service with the comfort of a modern, cosmopolitan hotel. There is a discount scheme for regular guests, for weekends and stays of five nights or more. E-Mail: thebasil@aol.com **Directions:** Close to Pavilion Road car park. Basil Street runs off Sloane Street in the direction of Harrods. Near Knightsbridge underground and bus routes. Price guide: Single from £115; double/twin from £145; family room from £230. (Excluding VAT).

For hotel location, see map on page 14

# Beaufort House Apartments

45 BEAUFORT GARDENS, KNIGHTSBRIDGE, LONDON SW3 1PN
TEL: 0171 584 2600 FAX: 0171 584 6532 – USA CALL FREE: 1-800- 23-5463

Situated in Beaufort Gardens, a quiet tree-lined Regency cul-de-sac in the heart of Knightsbridge, 250 yards from Harrods, Beaufort House is an exclusive establishment comprising 22 self-contained fully serviced luxury apartments. All the comforts of a first-class hotel are combined with the privacy and discretion and the relaxed atmosphere of home. Accommodation ranges in size from an intimate one-bedroomed suite to a spacious, four-bedroomed apartment. Each apartment has been individually decorated in a contemporary style to a standard which is rigourously maintained. All apartments have direct dial telephones, personal safes, satellite TV and video systems. Most bedrooms benefit from en suite bathrooms and several have west facing balconies. The fully fitted and equipped kitchens include washers/dryers; many have dishwashers. A daily maid service is included at no additional charge. Full laundry/dry cleaning services are available. For your added security, a concierge is on call 24 hours a day, through whom taxis, theatre tickets, restaurant reservations and other services are also available. Executive support services are provided with confidentiality assured at all times. Complimentary membership to health and leisure facilities at Champney's Piccadilly is offered to all guests during their stay. **Directions:** Beaufort Gardens leads off Brompton road. Near Harrods and Knightsbridge Tube. Price Guide: £160–£408 per night (+VAT).

For hotel location, see map on page 14

# BLAKES HOTEL

33 ROLAND GARDENS, LONDON SW7 3PF

TEL: 0171 370 6701 FAX: 0171 373 0442 FROM USA CALL FREE: 1 800 926 3173

Created by Anouska Hempel, designer, hotelier and couturiere, Blakes is unique – a connoisseur's refuge. Each room has been individually designed, the colour schemes are daring, stunning and dramatic – black and mustard, rich cardinal reds, lavender, vanilla washes of tea rose and a room that is white on white on white offering style and elegance to the discerning traveller. "If ever dreams can become reality, then Blakes is where it will happen". The bedrooms and suites have been described as each being a fantasy. A full 24 hour room service is provided and if a guest is travelling on business the hotel will provide a room fax machine, full secretarial services and a courier service if required. Blakes intimate restaurant is recognised as one of the finest in the capital and is open until midnight. Breakfast, summer lunches and candlelit dinners can be enjoyed on the Garden Terrace which overlooks the private and secluded courtyard – an explosion of greenery all year round. The smart, fashionable shops of Brompton Cross are only a short stroll away through the leafy streets of South Kensington and Harrods can be reached by taxi in five minutes. **Directions:** Roland Gardens is a turning off Old Brompton Road. The nearest underground tube station is South Kensington. Price guide: Single £155; double/twin £190–£350; suite £540–£780.

50 rms MasterCard VISA AMERICAN EXPRESS M[22]

For hotel location, see map on page 14

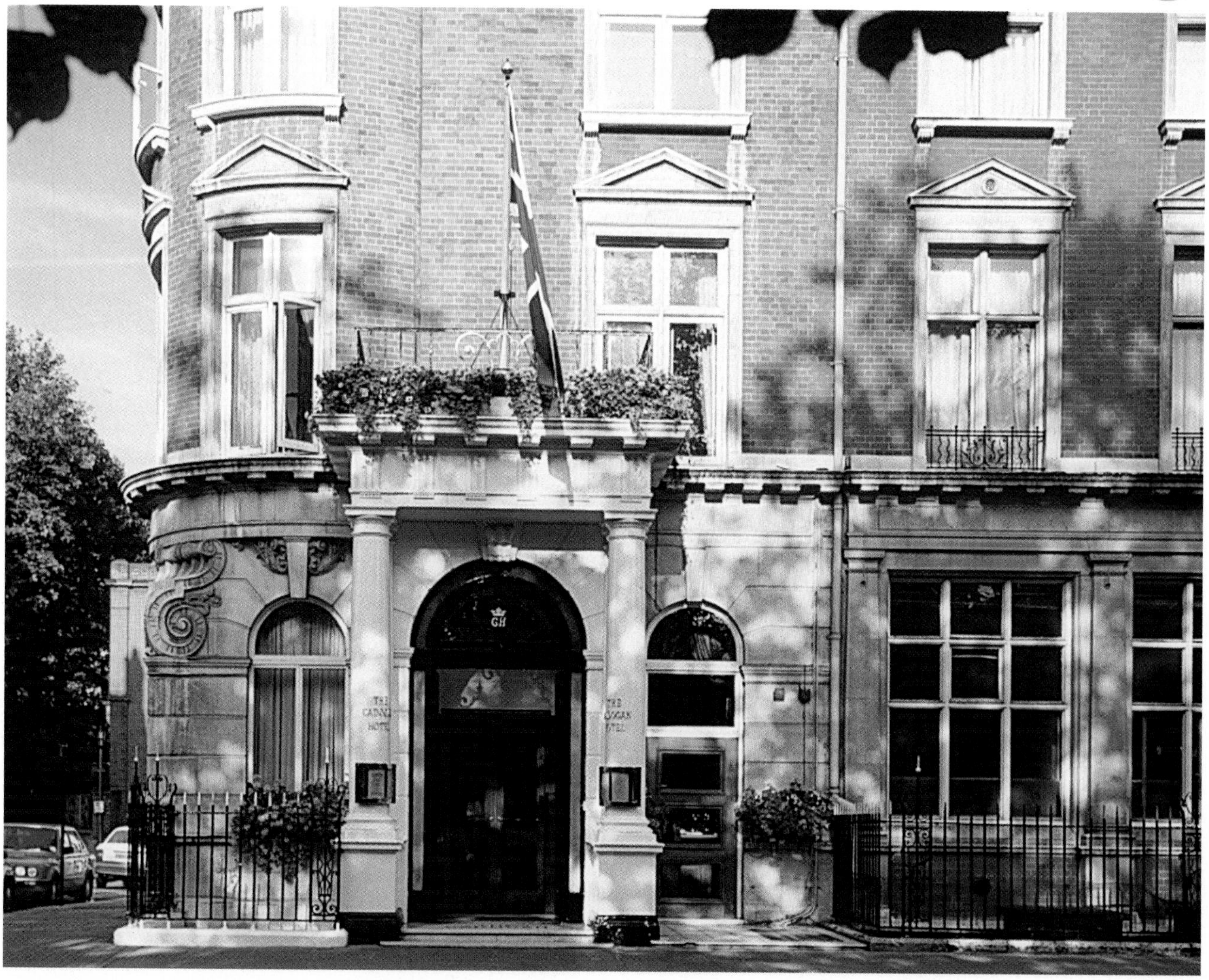

# THE CADOGAN

**SLOANE STREET, LONDON SW1X 9SG**

**TEL: 0171-235 7141 FAX: 0171-245 0994 E-MAIL: www.cadogan–hotel.com**

**FROM USA FAX TOLL FREE ON:** 800 260 8338 **CALL TOLL FREE Prima Hotels:** 800 447 7462; **Utell International 1800 44 UTELL**

The Cadogan is an imposing late-Victorian building in warm terracotta brick situated in a most desirable location in Sloane Street, Knightsbridge. It is well known for its association with Lillie Langtry, the 'Jersey Lily', actress and friend of King Edward VII, and her house in Pont Street now forms part of the hotel. Playwright and wit Oscar Wilde was a regular guest at The Cadogan. The Cadogan's elegant drawing room is popular for afternoon tea and the meals served in the air conditioned restaurant, which has 2 AA rosettes, combine imaginatively prepared food with value for money. The hotel has 65 comfortable bedrooms and suites equipped to the highest standards; several are air conditioned. The Langtry Rooms on the ground floor, once the famous actress's drawing room, make a delightful setting for private parties, wedding receptions and small meetings. The hotel is an excellent base for shopping trips being close to Harrods, Harvey Nichols and Peter Jones. Business visitors will find its central position and easy access make it a most acceptable place to stay when visiting London. **Directions:** The hotel is halfway along Sloane Street at the junction with Pont Street. Close to Knightsbridge and Sloane Square tubes. Price guide: Single £140–£190; double/twin £185–£215; studio/suite £265–£290.

For hotel location, see map on page 14

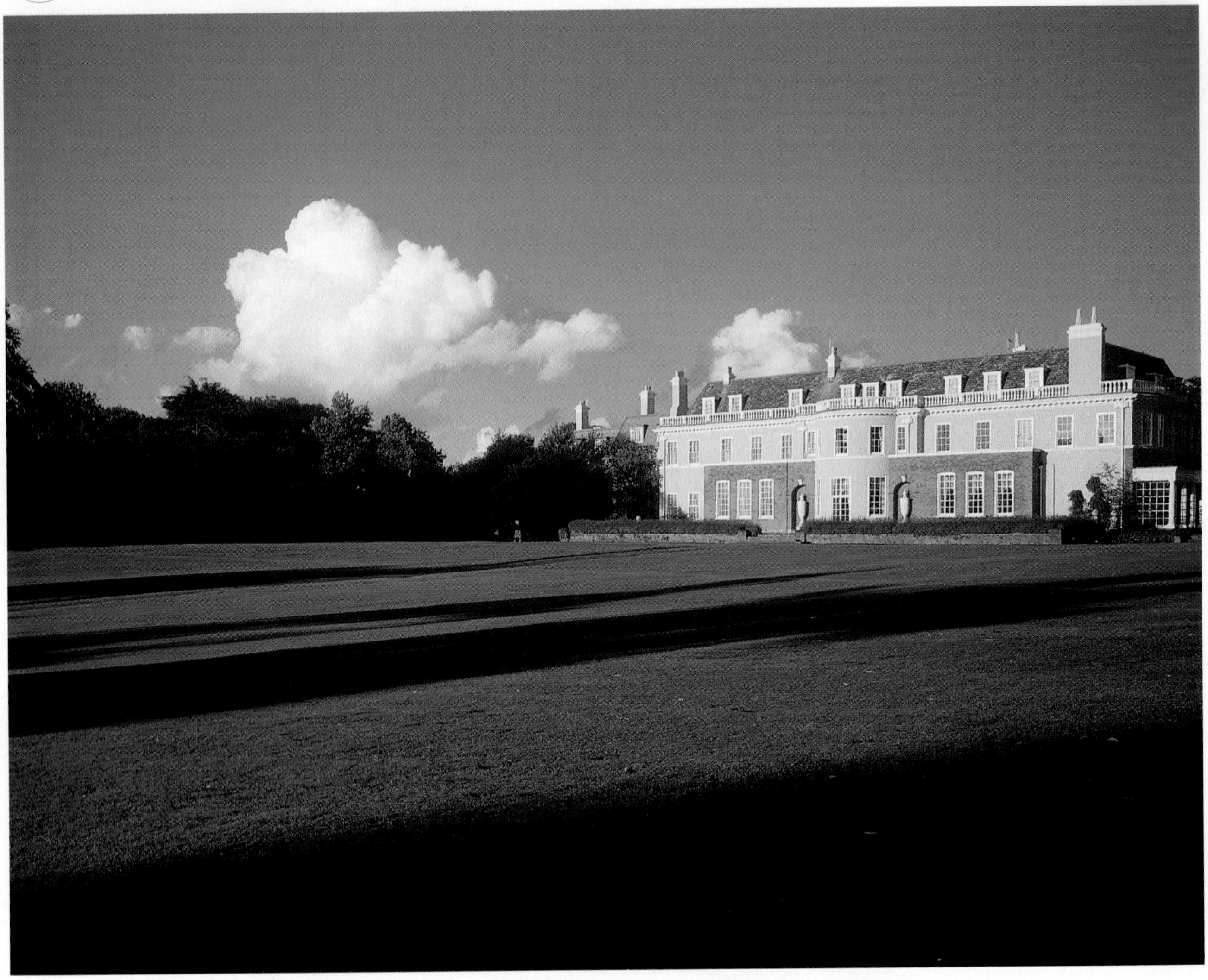

# CANNIZARO HOUSE

**WEST SIDE, WIMBLEDON COMMON, LONDON SW19 4UE**
**TEL: 0181 879 1464 FAX: 0181 879 7338**

Cannizaro House, an elegant Georgian Country House, occupies a tranquil position on the edge of Wimbledon Common, yet is only 20 minutes by train from central London. Cannizaro House has, throughout its history, welcomed royalty and celebrities such as George III, Oscar Wilde and William Pitt, and is now restored as a hotel which offers the very highest standards of hospitality. Winner of the AA's Courtesy and Care Award for London 1997. The 18th century is reflected in the ornate fireplaces and mouldings, gilded mirrors and many antiques. All the hotel's 46 bedrooms are individually designed, with many overlooking beautiful Cannizaro Park. Several intimate rooms are available for meetings and private dining, including the elegant Queen Elizabeth Room – a popular venue for Wedding Ceremonies. The newly refurbished Viscount Melville Room offers air-conditioned comfort for up to 100 guests. Ray Slade, General Manager of Cannizaro House for many years, ensures the high standards of excellence for which the hotel is renowned, are consistently met. The award-winning kitchen produces the finest modern and classical cuisine, complemented by an impressive list of wines. **Directions:** The nearest tube and British Rail station is Wimbledon. Price guide: Single £135–£145; double/twin from £155–£175; suite from £280–£395. Special weekend rates and celebratory packages available.

For hotel location, see map on page 14

# THE CLIVEDEN TOWN HOUSE

**26 CADOGAN GARDENS, LONDON SW3 2RP**

**TEL: 0171 730 6466 FAX: 0171 730 0263 FROM USA TOLL FREE 1 800 747 4942**

The Cliveden Town House offers the perfect balance of luxury, service, privacy and location. Tucked discreetly away in a tranquil, tree-lined garden square between Harrods and Kings Road it is at the very centre of fashionable London and is the epitome of stylish good taste and elegance. Like its gracious country cousin at Cliveden, one of England's most famous stately homes, The Cliveden Town House combines the grandeur of the past with the luxuries and conveniences of today, offering the sophisticated traveller all the exclusive comforts and ambience of a grand private residence. The Town House has enhanced its assured charm with the addition of nine more suites. Spacious, splendidly decorated rooms reminiscent of the Edwardian period combine with the highest possible 24-hour service and personal attention. The rooms and suites all have air conditioning, satellite television, stereo video, CD players, dedicated fax lines and voice mail. Nanny and baby sitting services can be arranged. Cliveden's standards of luxury can also be enjoyed at The Royal Crescent in Bath. The fashionable shops and first-class restaurants of Knightsbridge, Chelsea and Belgravia are within walking distance. West End theatres and the City are within easy reach. **Directions:** Nearest tube station is Sloane Square. Price guide: Single From £120; double/twin £210–£250; suite £310–£620.

For hotel location, see map on page 14

# THE DORCHESTER

**PARK LANE, MAYFAIR, LONDON W1A 2HJ**
**TEL: 0171 629 8888 FAX: 0171 409 0114 TELEX: 887704**

The Dorchester first opened its doors in 1931, offering a unique experience which almost instantly became legendary. Its reopening in November 1990 after an extensive refurbishment marked the renaissance of one of the world's grand hotels. Its history has been consistently glamorous; from the early days a host of outstanding figures has been welcomed, including monarchs, statesmen and celebrities. The architectural features have been restored to their original splendour and remain at the heart of The Dorchester's heritage. The 192 bedrooms and 52 suites have been luxuriously designed in a variety of materials, furnishings and lay-outs. All bedrooms are fully air-conditioned and have spectacular Italian marble bathrooms. There are rooms for non-smokers and some equipped for the disabled. In addition to The Grill Room, there is The Oriental Restaurant where the accent is on Cantonese cuisine. Specialised health and beauty treatments are offered in The Dorchester Spa with its statues, Lalique-style glass and water fountain. A series of meeting rooms, with full supporting services, is available for business clientèle. As ever, personalised care is a pillar of The Dorchester's fine reputation. **Directions:** Toward the Hyde Park Corner/Piccadilly end of Park Lane. Price guide excluding VAT: Single £240–£270; double/twin £270–£300; suite £400–£1,675.

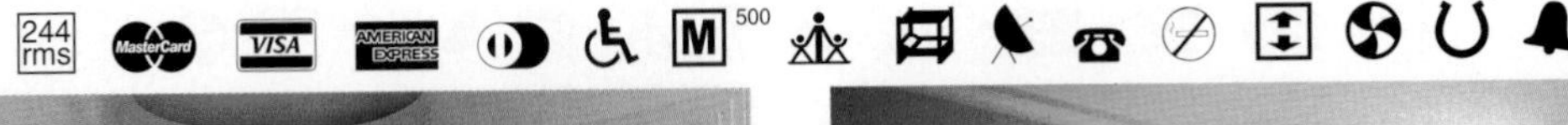

For hotel location, see map on page 14

# DRAYCOTT HOUSE APARTMENTS

**10 DRAYCOTT AVENUE, CHELSEA, LONDON SW3 3AA**

**TEL: 0171-584 4659 FAX: 0171-225 3694 E-MAIL: sales@draycotthouse.co.uk**

Draycott House stands in a quiet, tree-lined avenue in the heart of Chelsea. Housed in an attractive period building, the apartments have been designed in individual styles to provide the ideal surroundings for a private or business visit, combining comfort, privacy and security with a convenient location. All are spacious, luxury, serviced apartments, with three, two or one bedrooms. Some have private balconies, a roof terrace and overlook the private courtyard garden. Each apartment is fully equipped with all home comforts; cable television, video, radio/cassette, a private direct line for telephone/fax/answer machine. Complimentary provisions on arrival, milk and newspapers delivered. Daily maid service Monday to Friday. In-house laundry room and covered garage parking. Additional services, laundry and dry cleaning services. On request cars, airport transfers, catering, travel and theatre arrangements, child minders and an introduction to an exclusive health club. The West End is within easy reach. Knightsbridge within walking distance.Internet: http:/ www.Draycotthouse.co.uk **Directions:** Draycott House is situated on the corner of Draycott Avenue and Draycott Place, close to Sloane Square. Price guide: from £1037–£2522 +VAT per week: £164-£396 +VAT per night. Long term reservations may attract preferential terms. Contact: Jane Renton, General Manager.

For hotel location, see map on page 14

# THE HALCYON

81 HOLLAND PARK, LONDON W11 3RZ
TEL: 0171 727 7288 FAX: 0171 229 8516 E-MAIL: 101712.2063@CompuServe.COM

This small, exclusive hotel in Holland Park, winner of Johansens Most Excellent London Hotel Award 1996, offers an exceptional standard of accommodation and service. Essentially a large Town House, its architecture has been meticulously restored to the splendour of the Belle Epoque to take its place amongst the many imposing residences in the area. The generous proportions of the rooms, along with the striking individuality of their furnishings, creates the atmosphere of a fine country house. Each of the bedrooms and suites has been beautifully furnished and has every modern amenity. All have marble bathrooms and several boast a Jacuzzi. A splendid restaurant, opening onto a ornamental garden and patio, serves distinctive international cuisine complemented by a well chosen wine list. The adjoining bar provides a relaxing environment to enjoy a cocktail and meet with friends. The Halcyon prides itself on offering a superb service and ensuring guests' absolute comfort, privacy and security. Secretarial, Internet and fax facilities are all available. London's most fashionable shopping areas, restaurants and West End theatres are all easily accessible from The Halcyon. Directions: From Holland Park tube station, turn right. The Halcyon is on the left after the second set of traffic lights. Price guide: Single from £175; double/twin from £260; suite from £295.

43 rms · MasterCard · VISA · AMERICAN EXPRESS · M 12

For hotel location, see map on page 14

# HARRINGTON HALL

5-25 HARRINGTON GARDENS, LONDON SW7 4JW

TEL: 0171 396 9696 FAX: 0171 396 9090 E-MAIL: 101752.2030@compuserve.com

The original façade of late Victorian houses cleverly conceals a privately owned hotel of substantial proportions and contempory comfort. Harrington Hall offers 200 air-conditioned luxury bedrooms which have been most pleasantly furnished and equipped with an extensive array of facilities. A marble fireplace dominates the comfortable and relaxing Lounge Bar, where guests can enjoy a drink in pleasant surroundings. The restaurant's mixture of classical decoration and dramatic colour creates a delightful setting for the appreciation of fine cuisine. A choice of buffet or à la carte menu is available, both offering a tempting selection of dishes. Nine fully air conditioned conference and banqueting suites, with walls panelled in rich lacewood and solid cherry, provide a sophisicated venue for conferences, exhibitions or corporate hospitality. Harrington Hall also has a Business Centre for the exclusive use of its guests, along with a private Fitness Centre with multigym, saunas and showers. **Directions:** Harrington Hall is situated in the Royal Borough of Kensington and Chelsea, in Harrington Gardens south of the Cromwell Road, close to Gloucester Road underground station, two stops from Knightsbridge and Harrods. Price guide: Single £160; double £160; suites £195 (including VAT & service).

200 rms      250     

For hotel location, see map on page 14

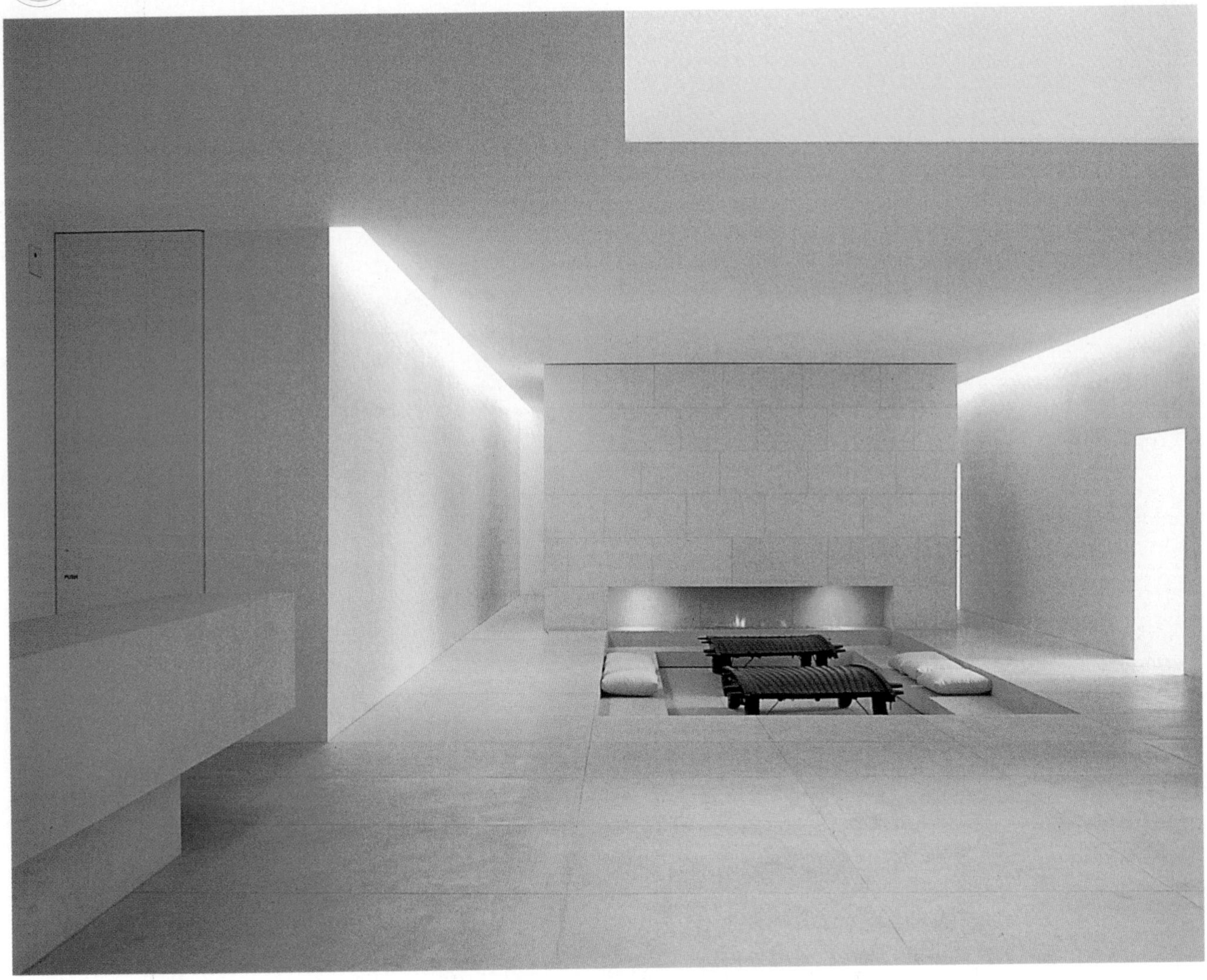

# THE HEMPEL

HEMPEL GARDEN SQUARE, 31-35 CRAVEN HILL GARDENS, LONDON W2 3EA
TEL: 0171 298 9000; FAX: 0171 402 4666

Designer Anouska Hempel has created The Hempel to be elegant, re-defining space for the traveller. Situated within easy reach of London's many attractions, the hotel with its immaculately preserved Georgian facade houses 47 individually designed rooms and fully serviced apartments. Influenced by the peace and simplicity of the Orient, the structure of Ancient Egypt with up to the minute technology from the Western World for the business connoisseur. The Hempel is innovative, monochromatic and full of surprises – tapwater that is lit at night, an open fire place that appears to float, a mix of light and shadow that can keep guests guessing how and pondering on just how this can all be real. The huge atrium within the lobby is astounding. A delicious mix of Italian-Thai and Japanese food, devised by Anouska Hempel is presented with style and flair in the I-Thai restaurant. Guests enjoying a pre-dinner drink in The Shadow Bar are surrounded by illusion and fantasy as The Hempel aims to take them out of this world and make their dreams a reality. **Directions:** The Hempel is situated in Lancaster gate with a short walk to Kensington Gardens and Hyde Park. Paddington railway station with Lancaster Gate and Queensway underground railway stations nearby. Price guide: Room/suite/apartment: from £220–£775 (excluding VAT)

For hotel location, see map on page 14

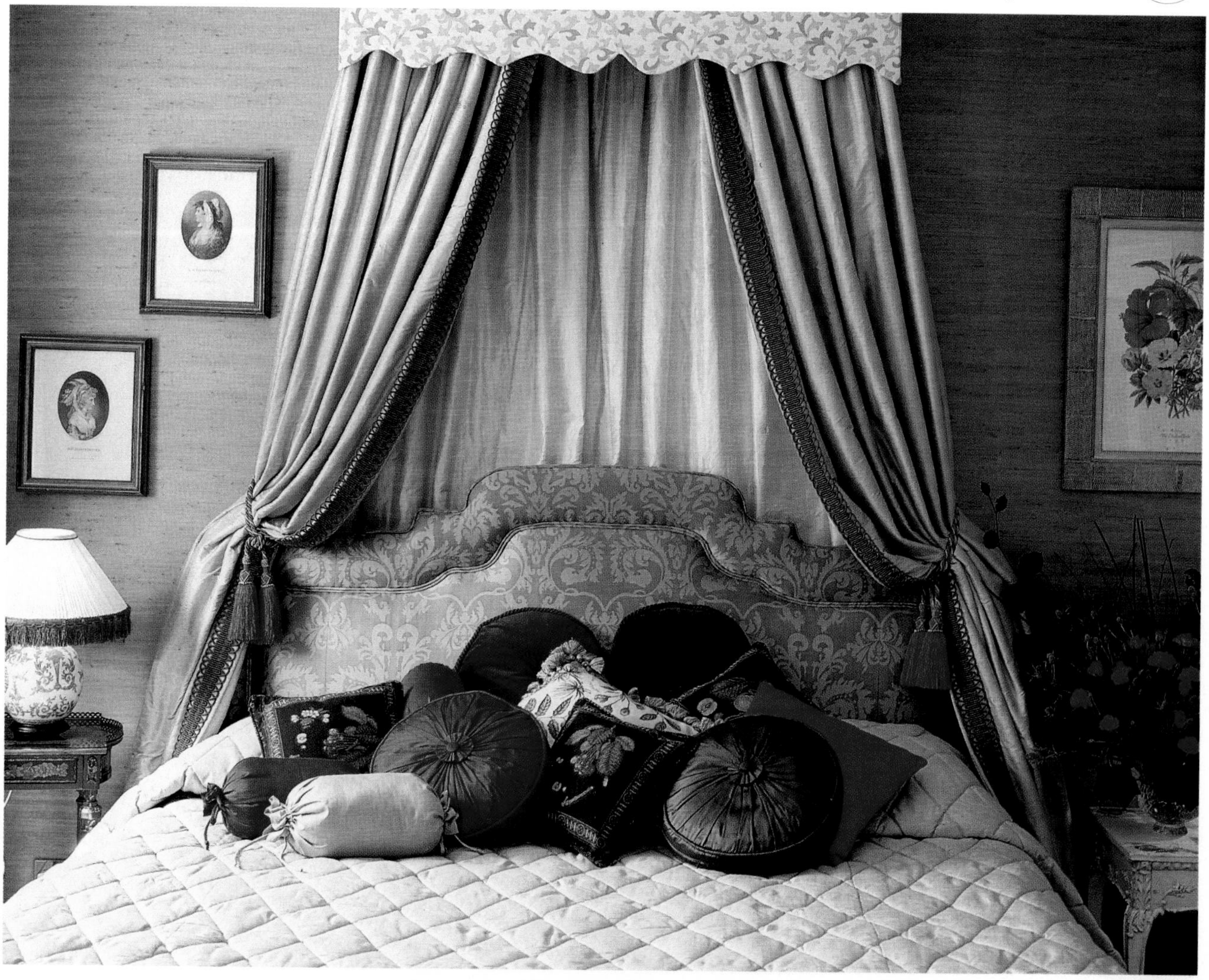

# The Leonard

**15 SEYMOUR STREET, LONDON W1H 5AA**

**TEL: 0171 935 2010 FAX: 0171 935 6700 E-MAIL: the.leonard@dial.pipex.com**

Four late 18th century Georgian town houses set the character of this exciting new property which opened in 1995 and has already proved to be extremely popular with Johansens guests, being winner of the Johansens Recommended London Hotel of the Year Award 1997. Imaginative reconstruction has created six rooms and twenty suites decorated individually to a very high standard. Wall coverings present striking colours, complemented by exquisite French furnishing fabrics creating a warm luxurious atmosphere. All rooms are fully air-conditioned and include a private safe, mini-bar, hi-fi system and provision for a modem/fax. Bathrooms are finished in marble and some of the larger suites have a butler's pantry or fully-equipped kitchen. For physical fitness and stress reductions there is a compact exercise room. "Can do" staff ensure that guests can enjoy the highest level of attention and service. Breakfast is available in the café bar and light meals are served throughout the day. 24-hour room service is also available. There are, of course, many good restaurants nearby. The Wallace Collection is just a short walk away and one of London's premier department stores, Selfridges, is round the corner in Oxford Street. **Directions:** The Leonard is on the south side of Seymour Street which is just north of Marble Arch and runs west off Portman Square. Car parking in Bryanston Street. Price guide: Double £170–£190; suites £230–£375.

For hotel location, see map on page 14

# THE LONDON OUTPOST OF THE CARNEGIE CLUB

69 CADOGAN GARDENS, LONDON SW3 2RB
TEL: 0171 589 7333 FAX: 0171 581 4958 E-MAIL: carnegie-londonoutpost@dial.pipex.com

This elite townhouse hotel is in a unique position in Knightsbridge – close to the prestigious shops and yet away from the bustle and noise in quiet Cadogan Gardens. It is a lovely building, and skilful restoration has transformed it into a beautiful residence where guests can relax and the staff will attend to their every need. Incidentally, it is not mandatory to be a member of the Carnegie Club to stay here. The Entrance Hall is graceful, with high ceilings, handsome paintings on the walls, antiques and bowls of flowers and this elegance is echoed in the Drawing Room, a peaceful retreat, the Library – perfect for pre-dinner drinks or a nightcap – and the convivial Snooker Room. The bedrooms are luxurious, with lovely drapes across the tall windows and comfortable period furniture. A drinks tray is on the table. Room service will deliver delicious light lunches, suppers and a traditional breakfast – although the latter can also be enjoyed in the attractive Conservatory. In the evening the staff will recommend good restaurants in walking distance. Theatre tickets can be booked, chauffeurs ordered or riding in Rotten Row can be arranged. Exclusive stores and fascinating musuems are all 'round the corner'. **Directions:** Sloane Square is the nearest underground station. Price guide (excluding VAT): Single £150; suite £235.

11 rms MasterCard VISA AMERICAN EXPRESS M 10

For hotel location, see map on page 14

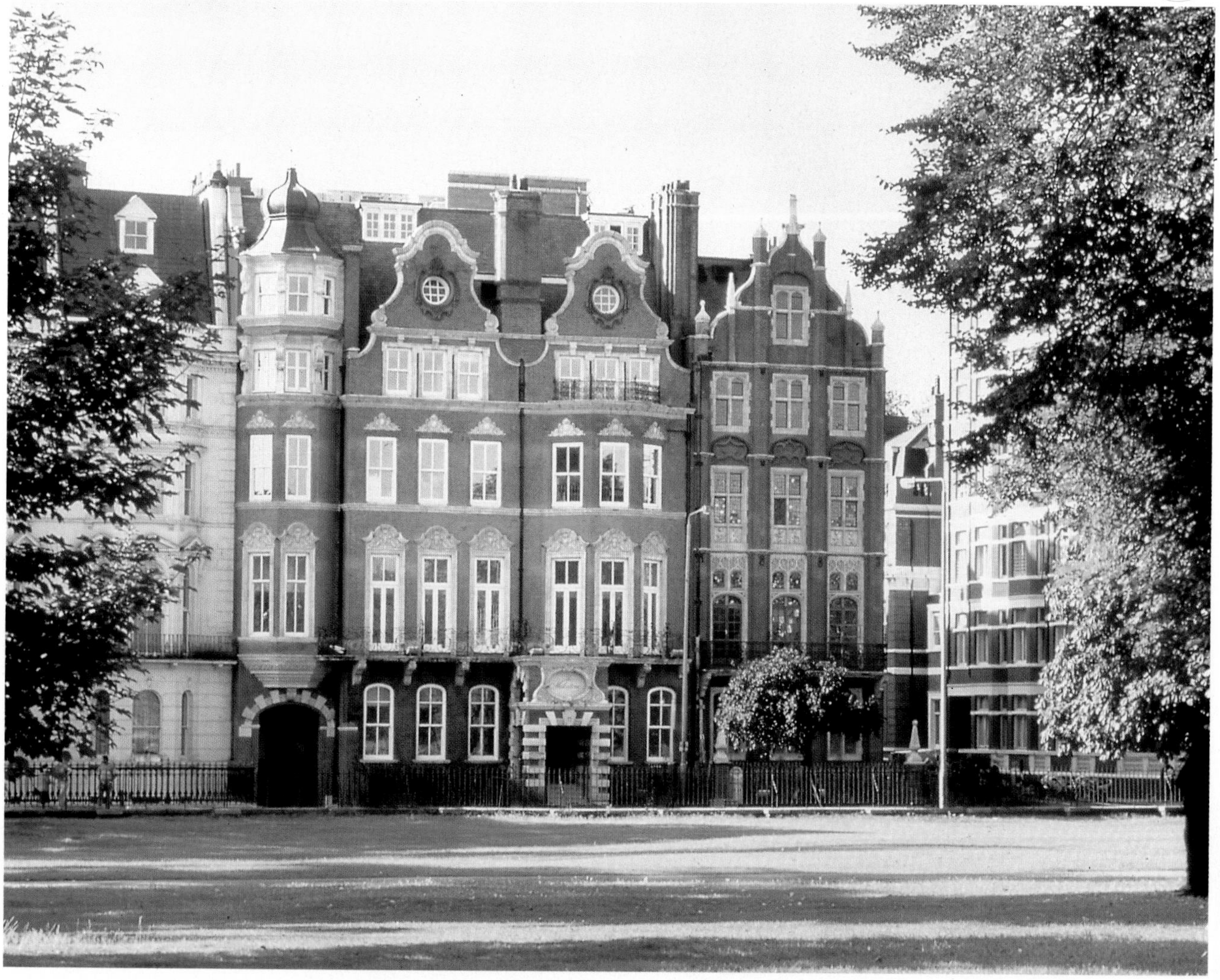

# THE MILESTONE

**1–2 KENSINGTON COURT, LONDON W8 5DL**

**TEL: 0171 917 1000 FAX: 0171 917 1010 FROM USA TOLL FREE 1 800 854 7092**

The beautifully appointed Milestone Hotel is situated opposite Kensington Palace with uninterrupted views over Kensington Gardens and the remarkable Royal parklands. A Victorian showpiece, this unique hotel has been carefully restored to its original splendour whilst incorporating every modern facility. The 53 bedrooms including 12 suites are all individually designed with antiques, elegant furnishings and some have private balconies. Guests may relax in the comfortable, panelled Park Lounge which, in company with all other rooms, provides a 24-hour service. The hotel's original Dining Room has an elaborately carved ceiling, original fireplace, ornate windows and an oratory, which can now be used for small private parties. The health and fitness centre offers guests the use of a solarium, spa bath, sauna and gymnasium. The traditional bar on the ground floor is an ideal place for meeting and entertaining friends. The Milestone is within walking distance of some of the finest shopping in Kensington and a little further away in Knightsbridge and is a short taxi ride to the West End, the heart of London's Theatreland. The Albert Hall and all the museums in Exhibition Road are nearby. **Directions:** At the end of Kensington High Street, at the junction with Princes Gate. Price guide: Single from £220; double/twin £270; suites from £330.

For hotel location, see map on page 14

# NUMBER ELEVEN CADOGAN GARDENS

**11 CADOGAN GARDENS, SLOANE SQUARE, KNIGHTSBRIDGE, LONDON SW3 2RJ**
**TEL: 0171 730 7000 FAX: 0171 730 5217**

Number Eleven Cadogan Gardens was the first of the exclusive private town house hotels in London and now, with the addition of its own in-house gymnasium and beauty rooms it continues to take the lead. Number Eleven remains traditional; no reception desk, no endless signing of bills, total privacy and security. It also offers the services you have a right to expect in the 1990s: round-the-clock room service, a chauffeur-driven Mercedes for airport collection and sightseeing, and a private room which can accommodate 12 for a meeting. Another attraction is the Garden Suite, with a large double bedroom and a spacious drawing room overlooking the gardens. The hotel occupies four stately Victorian houses tucked away between Harrods and Kings Road in a quiet, tree-lined square. Wood-panelled rooms, hung with oil-paintings, are furnished with antiques and oriental rugs in a traditional understated style. The fashionable shops and first-class restaurants of Knightsbridge, Chelsea and Belgravia are within easy walking distance. Theatre tickets can be arranged. **Directions:** Off Sloane Street. Nearest underground is Sloane Square. Price guide: Single from £120; double/twin from £160; suite from £270. (Excluding VAT)

For hotel location, see map on page 14

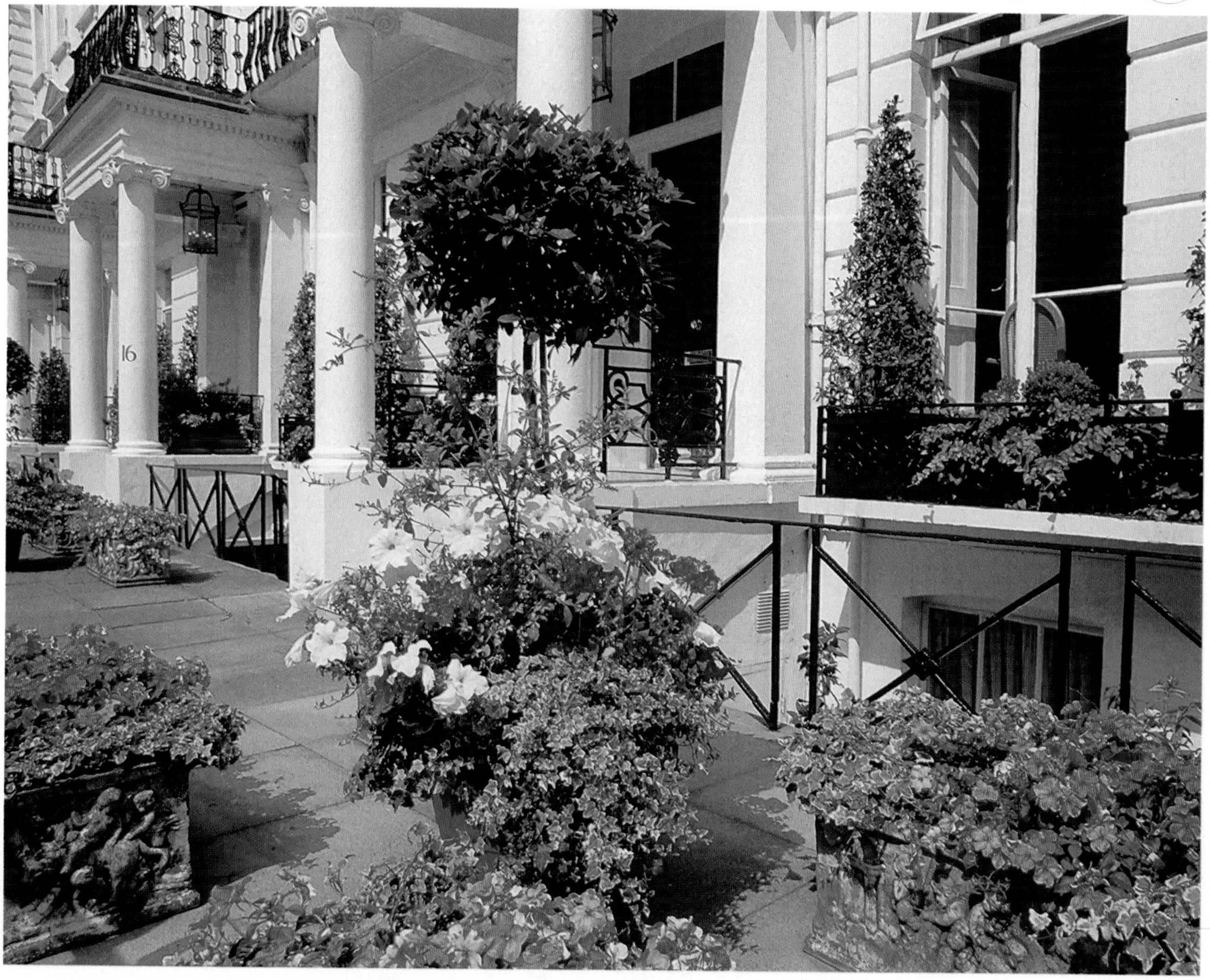

# NUMBER SIXTEEN

**16 SUMNER PLACE, LONDON SW7 3EG**

**TEL: 0171 589 5232 US TOLL FREE: 1800 592 5387 FAX: 0171 584 8615**

On entering Number Sixteen with its immaculate pillared façade visitors find themselves in an atmosphere of seclusion and comfort which has remained virtually unaltered in style since its early Victorian origins. The staff are friendly and attentive, regarding each visitor as a guest in a private home. The relaxed atmosphere of the library is the perfect place to pour a drink from the honour bar and meet friends or business associates. A fire blazing in the drawing room in cooler months creates an inviting warmth, whilst the conservatory opens on to a beautiful secluded walled garden which once again has won many accolades and awards for its floral displays. Each spacious bedroom is decorated with a discreet combination of antiques and traditional furnishings. The rooms are fully appointed with every facility that the discerning traveller would expect. A light breakfast is served in the privacy of guests' rooms and a tea and coffee service is available throughout the day. Although there is no dining room at Number Sixteen, some of London's finest restaurants are just round the corner. The hotel has membership of Aquilla Health and Fitness Club, 5 minutes away. The hotel is close to the West End, Knightsbridge and Hyde Park. **Directions:** Sumner Place is off Old Brompton Road near Onslow Square. South Kensington Tube Station is a 2 minute walk. Price guide: Single £80–£115; double/twin £150–£180; junior suite £190.

36 rms 12

For hotel location, see map on page 14

# PARK CONSUL HOTEL

**35 IXWORTH PLACE, CHELSEA, LONDON SW3 3QX**
**TEL: 0171 225 7500 FAX: 0171 225 7555**

Although situated near a busy residential area, the Park Consul Hotel is a luxuriously peaceful haven of charm, warmth and elegance. Its 1920s facade cleverly conceals a London town-house hotel of traditional spaciousness and comfort. The Park Consul offers 46 air-conditioned bedrooms and suites which have been pleasantly furnished to the highest standards and include an extensive array of quality fittings and facilities. There are mini-bars, modem points, personal safes and thick, soft robes in the bathrooms which have marble decor. One suite has a steam bath, Jacuzzi and fully-fitted kitchen. The hotel's main restaurant is in the delightful garden conservatory where the decoration, table accessories, plants and original paintings change with the seasons of the year. Imaginative breakfasts, luncheons, afternoon teas and seasonally adjusted excellent dinner menus are served here with grace and flair. Pre-dinner cocktails and late evening drinks can be enjoyed in the elegant drawingroom against a background of restful soft music and, in winter months, a glowing fireplace. London's most fashionable shopping areas, restaurants and West End theatres are within easy reach. **Directions:** Ixworth Place is the first road on the right after following Pelham Street into Sloane Avenue southeastward from South Kensington underground. Price guide: Single £125–£135; double/twin £155; suites £175–£225. (Exclusive of VAT)

46 rms MasterCard VISA AMERICAN EXPRESS M 100

For hotel location, see map on page 14

# PEMBRIDGE COURT HOTEL

**34 PEMBRIDGE GARDENS, LONDON W2 4DX**
**TEL: 0171 229 9977 FAX: 0171 727 4982**

This gracious Victorian town house has been lovingly restored to its former glory whilst providing all the modern facilities demanded by today's discerning traveller. The 20 rooms are individually decorated with pretty fabrics and the walls adorned with an unusual collection of framed fans and Victoriana. The Pembridge Court is renowned for the devotion and humour with which it is run. Its long serving staff and its two famous cats "Spencer" and "Churchill" assure you of an immensely warm welcome and the very best in friendly, personal service. Over the years the hotel has built up a loyal following amongst its guests, many of whom regard it as their genuine 'home from home' in London. Winner of the 1994 RAC Award for Best Small Hotel in the South East of England, the Hotel is situated in quiet tree-lined gardens just off Notting Hill Gate, an area described by Travel & Leisure magazine as 'one of the liveliest, most prosperous corners of the city. "The Gate" as is affectionately known, is certainly lively, colourful and full of life with lots of great pubs and restaurants and the biggest antiques market in the world at nearby Portobello Road. **Directions:** Pembridge Gardens is a small turning off Notting Hill Gate/Bayswater Road, just 2 minutes from Portobello Road Antiques Market. Price guide: Single £110–£140; double/twin £160–£170 (inclusive of both English breakfast & VAT)

20 rms MasterCard VISA AMERICAN EXPRESS

For hotel location, see map on page 14

# THE RITZ

**150 PICCADILLY, LONDON W1V 9DG**

**TEL: 0171 493 8181 FAX: 0171 493 2687 E-MAIL: enquire@theritzhotel.co.uk**

The Ritz is one of the world's legendary hotels and over the past 90 years it has welcomed countless monarchs, statesmen and celebrities. It is sumptuously decorated throughout in the style of Louis XVI and, being situated in the heart of London's West End overlooking Green Park, offers easy access to exclusive shopping areas, galleries, auction houses, theatres and all the excitements and attractions of the capital. Guests are surrounded by comfort and elegance. The Long Gallery leads to a series of grand rooms in which to see and be seen. No two bedrooms or suites are alike. Each has been individually decorated and all offer levels of comfort befitting a world class hotel of character and glamour. Service is excellent and attentive. The chandeliered and magnificently draped Ritz Restaurant with its internationally famous cuisine is one of the prettiest dining rooms in Europe, the Palm Court a delightful place to have afternoon tea and there are three private suites in which to hold special luncheons, dinners, receptions and meetings. Each has its own butler. At the heart of the hotel is the desk in the rotunda where the famed porters provide a 24-hour source of knowledge and service for guests and can arrange tennis, riding, golf, fishing and shooting if required. Directions: The Ritz is situated between Piccadilly Circus and Hyde Park Corner. Price guide (excluding VAT): Rooms/suites £225–£945.

131 rms MasterCard VISA AMERICAN EXPRESS M 50

For hotel location, see map on page 14

# Johansens Recommended Hotels in England

*Castles, cathedrals, museums, great country houses and the opportunity to stay in areas of historical importance, England has much to offer. Whatever your leisure interests, there's a network of more than 560 Tourist Information Centres throughout England offering friendly, free advice on places to visit, entertainment, local facilities and travel information.*

ENGLISH HERITAGE
**Keysign House**
**429 Oxford Street**
**London W1R 2HD**
**Tel: 0171 973 3396**
*Offers an unrivalled choice of properties to visit.*

HISTORIC HOUSES ASSOCIATION
**2 Chester Street**
**London SW1X 7BB**
**Tel: 0171 259 5688**
*Ensures the survival of historic houses and gardens in private ownership in Great Britain.*

THE NATIONAL TRUST
**36 Queen Anne's Gate**
**London SW1H 9AS**
**Tel: 0171 222 9251**
*Cares for more than 590,000 acres of countryside and over 400 historic buildings.*

## REGIONAL TOURIST BOARDS

CUMBRIA TOURIST BOARD
**Ashleigh**
**Holly Road**
**Windermere**
**Cumbria LA23 2AQ**
**Tel: 015394 44444**
*England's most beautiful lakes and tallest mountains reach out from the Lake District National Park to a landscape of spectacular coasts, hills and dales.*

EAST OF ENGLAND TOURIST BOARD
**Toppesfield Hall**
**Hadleigh**
**Suffolk IP7 5DN**
**Tel: 01473 822922**
*Cambridgeshire, Essex, Hertfordshire, Bedfordshire, Norfolk, Suffolk and Lincolnshire.*

HEART OF ENGLAND TOURIST BOARD
**Woodside**
**Larkhill Road**
**Worcester**
**Worcestershire WR5 2EZ**
**Tel: 01905 763436**
*Gloucestershire, Hereford & Worcester, Shropshire, Staffordshire, Warwickshire and West Midlands. Represents the districts of Cherwell and West Oxfordshire in the county of Oxfordshire.*

**Premier House**
**15 Wheeler Gate**
**Nottingham NG1 2NA**
**Tel: 0115 988 1778**
*Derbyshire, Leicestershire, Northamptonshire, Nottinghamshire and Rutland*

LONDON TOURIST BOARD
**26 Grosvenor Gardens**
**London SW1W ODU**
**Tel: 0171 730 3450**
*The Greater London area*
*(see page 15)*

NORTHUMBRIA TOURIST BOARD
**Aykley Heads**
**Durham DH1 5UX**
**Tel: 0191 375 3000**
*The Tees Valley, Durham, Northumberland and Tyne & Wear*

NORTH WEST TOURIST BOARD
**Swan House**
**Swan Meadow Road**
**Wigan Pier, Wigan**
**Lancashire WN3 5BB**
**Tel: 01942 821222**
*Cheshire, Greater Manchester, Lancashire, Merseyside and the High Peak District of Derbyshire*

SOUTH EAST ENGLAND TOURIST BOARD
**The Old Brew House**
**Warwick Park**
**Tunbridge Wells**
**Kent TN2 5TU**
**Tel: 01892 540766**
*East and West Sussex, Kent and Surrey*

SOUTHERN TOURIST BOARD
**40 Chamberlayne Road**
**Eastleigh**
**Hampshire SO5 5JH**
**Tel: 01703 620006**
*Eastern and Northern Dorset, Hampshire, Isle of Wight, Berkshire, Buckinghamshire and Oxfordshire*

WEST COUNTRY TOURIST BOARD
**60, St David's Hill**
**Exeter**
**Devon EX4 4SY**
**Tel: 01392 425426**
*Bath, Bristol, Cornwall and the Isles of Scilly, Devon, Dorset, Somerset and Wiltshire*

YORKSHIRE TOURIST BOARD
**312 Tadcaster Road**
**York YO2 2HF**
**Tel: 01904 707961**
*Yorkshire and Northern Lincolnshire*

# THE ELMS

**ABBERLEY, WORCESTERSHIRE WR6 6AT**
**TEL: 01299 896666 FAX: 01299 896804**

Built in 1710 by a pupil of Sir Christopher Wren and converted into a country house hotel in 1946, The Elms has achieved an international reputation for excellence spanning the past half century. Standing tall and impressively between Worcester and Tenbury Wells this fine Queen Anne mansion is surrounded by the beauties of the meadows, woodland, green hills, hop fields and orchards of cider apples and cherries of the Teme Valley whose river runs crimson when in flood from bankside soil tinged with red sandstone. Each of the hotel's 16 bedrooms has its own character, furnished with period antiques and having splendid views across the landscaped gardens and beyond to the beauty of the valley. There is a panelled bar and the elegant restaurant offers fine imaginative cuisine. The surrounding countryside offers opportunities for walking, fishing, shooting, golf and horseracing. Within easy reach are the attractions of the market town of Tenbury Wells, Witley Court, Bewdley and the ancient city of Worcester with its cathedral, county cricket ground and famous porcelain factory. **Directions:** From the M5, exit at junction 5 (Droitwich) or junction 6 (Worcester) then take the A443 towards Tenbury Wells. The Elms is two miles after Great Witley. Do not take the turning into Abberley village. Price guide: Single £75-£90; double/twin £110-£135.

For hotel location, see maps on pages 490-496

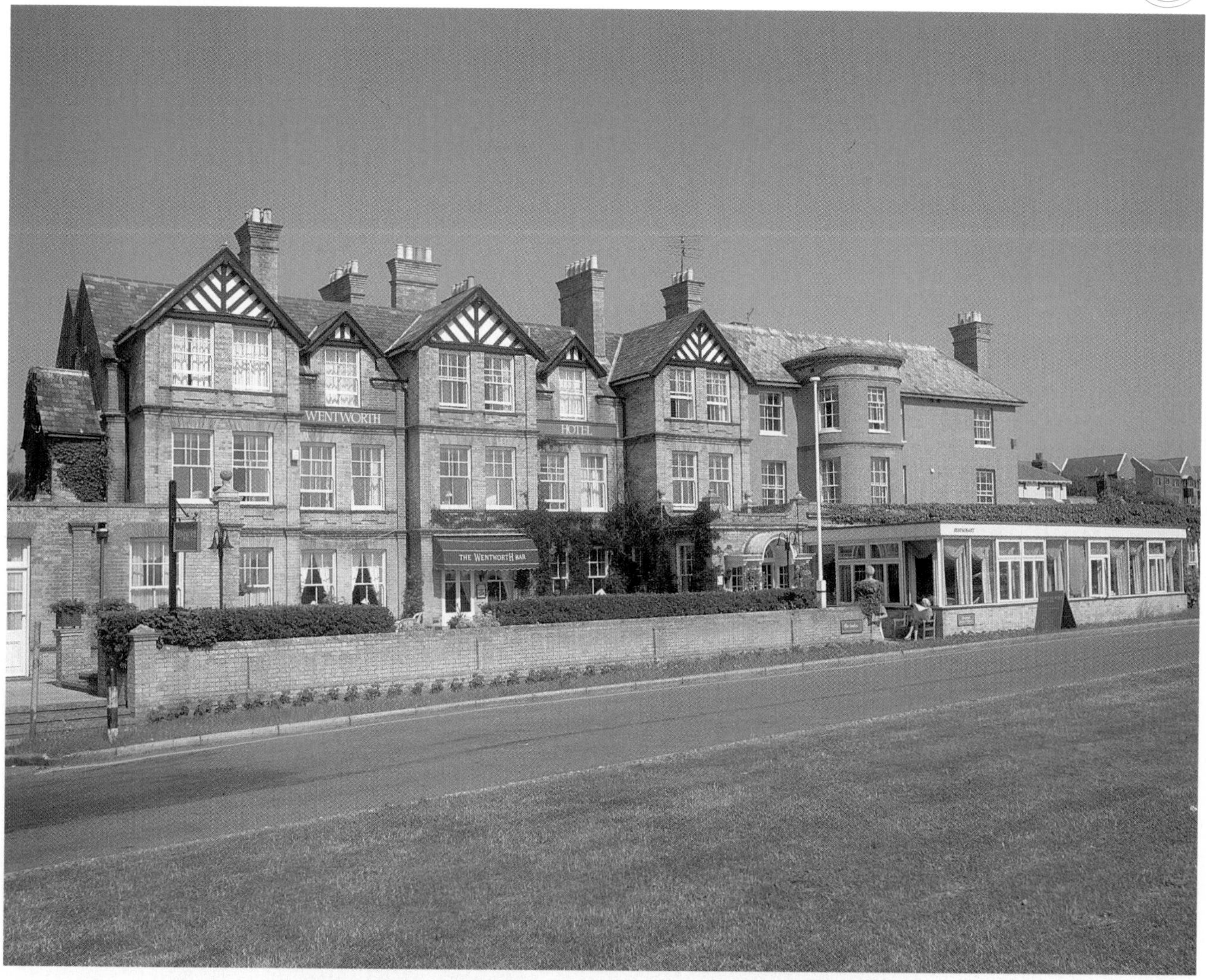

# WENTWORTH HOTEL

**WENTWORTH ROAD, ALDEBURGH, SUFFOLK IP15 5BD**
**TEL: 01728 452312 FAX: 01728 454343**

The Wentworth Hotel is ideally situated opposite the beach at Aldeburgh on Suffolk's unspoilt coast. Aldeburgh has maritime traditions dating back to the 15th century which are still maintained today by the longshore fishermen who launch their boats from the shore. It has also become a centre for music lovers: every June the Aldeburgh International Festival of Music, founded by the late Benjamin Britten, is held at Snape Maltings. Privately owned by the Pritt family since 1920, the Wentworth has established a reputation for comfort and service, good food and wine, for which many guests return year after year. Relax in front of an open fire in one of the hotel lounges, or sample a pint of the famous local Adnam's ales in the bar, which also serves meals. Many of the 38 elegantly furnished en suite bedrooms have sea views. The restaurant offers an extensive menu for both lunch and dinner and there is a comprehensive wine list. The garden terrace is the perfect venue for a light lunch *alfresco*. Nearby, the Minsmere Bird Sanctuary will be of interest to nature enthusiasts, while for the keen golfer, two of Britain's most challenging courses are within easy reach of the hotel at Aldeburgh and Thorpeness. Closed from December 27 to early new year. **Directions:** Aldeburgh is on A1094 just 7 miles from the A12 between Ipswich and Lowestoft. Price guide: Single £58; double/twin £105.

For hotel location, see maps on pages 490-496

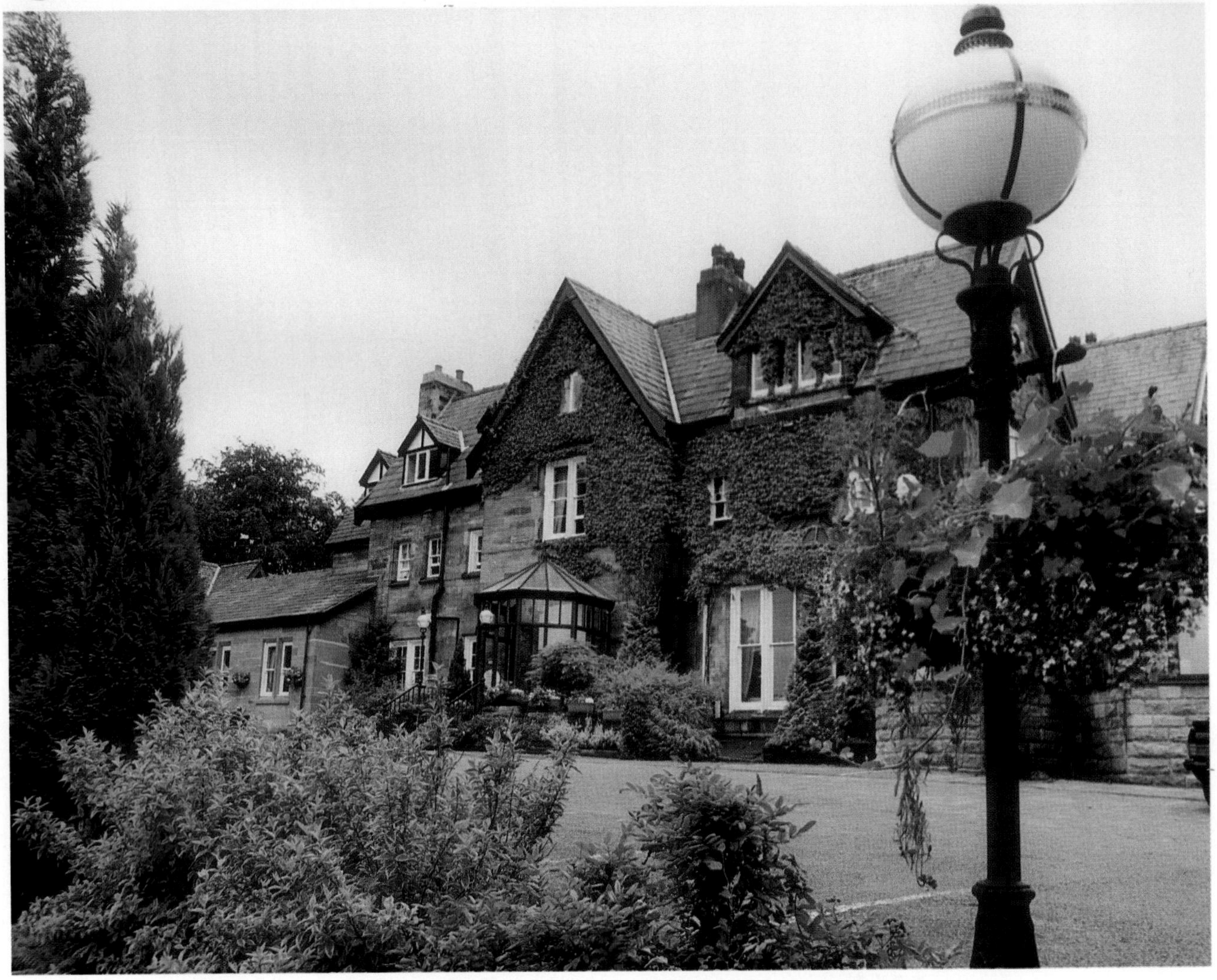

# THE ALDERLEY EDGE HOTEL

**MACCLESFIELD ROAD, ALDERLEY EDGE, CHESHIRE SK9 7BJ**
**TEL: 01625 583033 FAX: 01625 586343**

This privately owned award-winning hotel has 21 executive rooms and 11 de luxe rooms, each with a whirlpool bath, offering a choice of traditional decor or cottage-style accomodation. The restaurant is in the sumptuous conservatory with exceptional views and attention is given to the highest standards of cooking; fresh produce, including fish delivered daily, is provided by local suppliers. Specialities include hot and cold seafood dishes, puddings served piping hot from the oven, and a daily selection of unusual and delicious breads, baked each morning in the hotel bakery. The wine list features 100 champagnes and 600 wines. Special wine and champagne dinners are held monthly. In addition to the main conference room there is a suite of meeting and private dining rooms. The famous Edge walks are nearby, as are Tatton and Lyme Parks, Quarry Bank Mill and Dunham Massey. Manchester's thriving city centre is 15 miles away and the airport is a 20-minute drive. **Directions:** Follow M6 to M56 Stockport. Exit junction 6, take A538 to Wilmslow. Follow signs 1½ miles through to Alderley Edge. Turn left at the end of main shopping area on to Macclesfield Road (B5087) and the hotel is situated 200 yards on the right. From the M6 take junction 18 and follow signs for Holmes Chapel and Alderley Edge. Price guide: Single £95–£110; double £116–£160.

For hotel location, see maps on pages 490-496

# WHITE LODGE COUNTRY HOUSE HOTEL

**SLOE LANE, ALFRISTON, EAST SUSSEX BN26 5UR**
**TEL: 01323 870265 FAX: 01323 870284**

The White Lodge, an elegant Edwardian country house, has a perfect and peaceful position, looking down on Alfriston, one of the prettiest villages in the Sussex Downs. It stands in five acres of well tended grounds, surrounded by the verdant rolling countryside. Skilful modernisation has taken place, yet its old-world charm remains undisturbed, and a gentle ambience is created by gilt mirrors, fine period pieces, splendid flower arrangements and harmonious decorations, all appropriate to the age of the house. The handsome bedrooms, some with balconies, have magnificent views over the Downs. Graceful furniture, soft colours and attention to detail, anticipating the needs of seasoned travellers, ensures that guests will have a comfortable stay. The residents' lounges are relaxing, with delightful furnishings, tall windows and a tranquil atmosphere. Guests mingle in the convivial bar before dining in splendour in the Orchid Restaurant. Local fish is among the specialities on the menu. An additional pleasure is the extensive winelist. Glyndebourne is 20 minutes away. The area abounds with famous golf courses, castles and gardens. The joys of Eastbourne are nearby and France is between 2 and 4 hours away via the Newhaven Ferry. **Directions:** Alfriston is on the B2108 between the A27/A259. The hotel is accessed from the Market Cross via West Street. Price guide: Single from £50; double/twin £95–£135.

For hotel location, see maps on pages 490-496

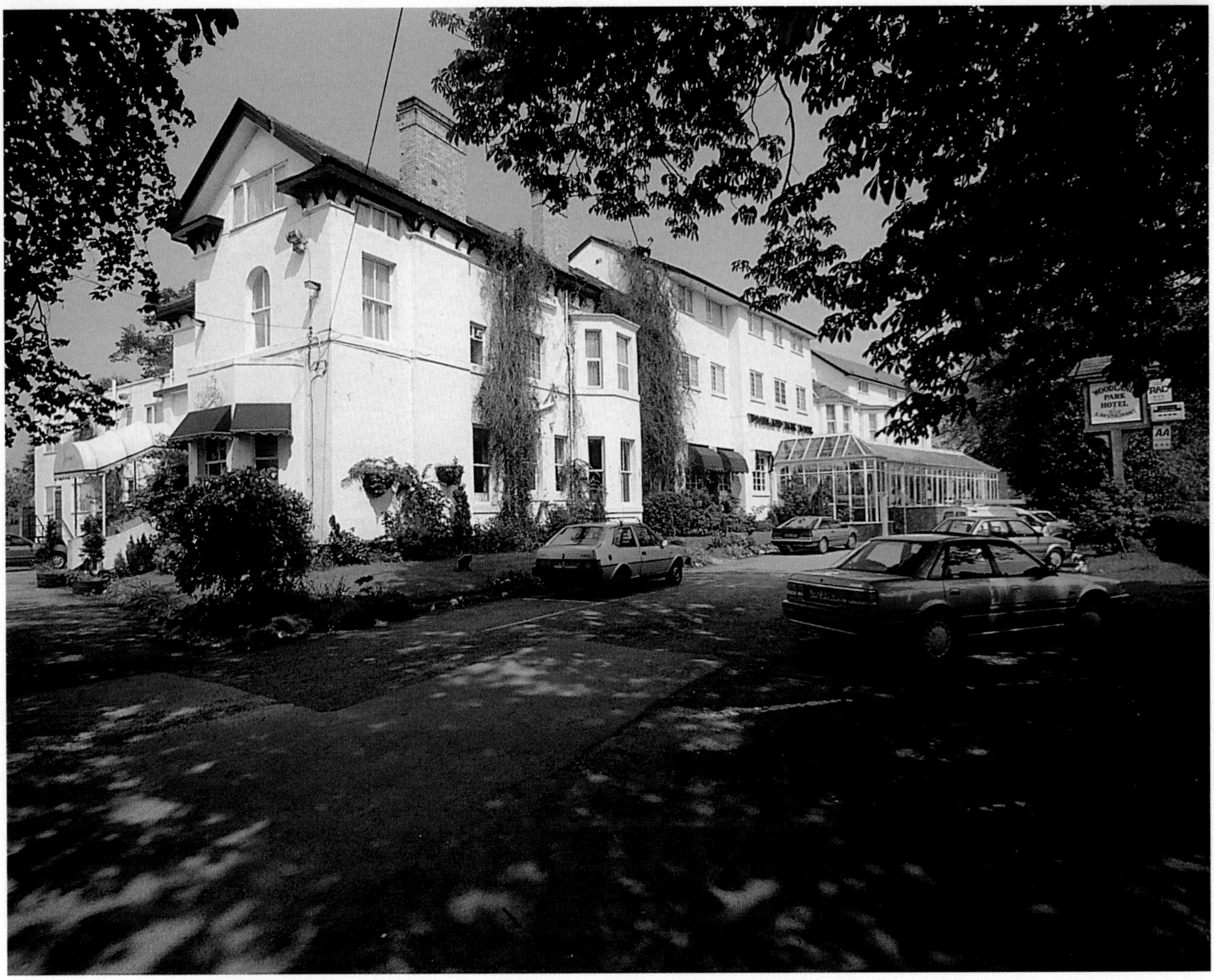

# Woodland Park Hotel

**WELLINGTON ROAD, TIMPERLEY, NR ALTRINCHAM, CHESHIRE WA15 7RG**
**TEL: 0161 928 8631 FAX: 0161 941 2821**

The Woodland Park Hotel is a delightful family owned hotel in a secluded residential area. Brian and Shirley Walker offer their guests a warm and friendly welcome, working as a team with their staff to ensure the highest standards of comfort and service. All the bedrooms are individually designed and furnished and some offer the added luxury of an aero spa bath. Guests are invited either to relax in the two comfortable lounges one of which is non-smoking or to enjoy an apéritif in the elegant conservatory adjoining the Terrace Restaurant. The restaurant offers a choice of Brasserie style menu or table d'hôte. The hotel has extensive facilities for business meetings, conferences and weddings. Manchester City Centre is about eight miles away and offers wonderful theatre productions and the famous China Town. The hotel is also a convenient base for visiting Tatton Park, Dunham Park and Capesthorne Hall and the many historical places of interest in Chester. Manchester International Airport is just four miles away. **Directions:** Leave the M56 at Junction 3 and take the A560 towards Altrincham. Turn right onto Wellington Road. Price guide: Single: £75–£98; double/twin £98–£120.

For hotel location, see maps on pages 490-496

# Amberley Castle

**AMBERLEY, NR ARUNDEL, WEST SUSSEX BN18 9ND**
**TEL: 01798 831992 FAX: 01798 831998**

Winner of the Johansens 1995 Country Hotel Award, Amberley Castle is over 900 years old and is set between the rolling South Downs and the peaceful expanse of the Amberley Wildbrooks. Its towering battlements give breathtaking views while its massive, 14th-century curtain walls and mighty portcullis bear silent testimony to its fascinating history. Resident proprietors, Joy and Martin Cummings, have transformed this medieval fortress into a unique country castle hotel. They offer a warm, personal welcome and their hotel provides the ultimate in contemporary luxury, while retaining an atmosphere of timelessness. Guests can choose from four-poster, twin four-poster or brass double-bedded rooms. Each room is individually designed and has its own Jacuzzi bath. The exquisite 12th-century Queen's Room Restaurant is the perfect setting for the creative cuisine of new head chef Simon Thyer and his team. Amberley Castle is a natural first choice for romantic or cultural weekends, sporting breaks or confidential executive meetings. It is ideally situated for opera at Glyndebourne, theatre at Chichester and racing at Goodwood and Fontwell. It is easily accessible from London and the major air and channel ports. **Directions:** Amberley Castle is on the B2139, off the A29 between Fontwell and Bury. Price guide: Single £100; double/twin £130–£300.

15 rms · MasterCard · VISA · AMERICAN EXPRESS · M 50 · 12

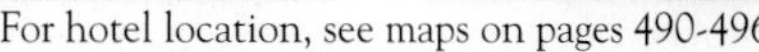

For hotel location, see maps on pages 490-496

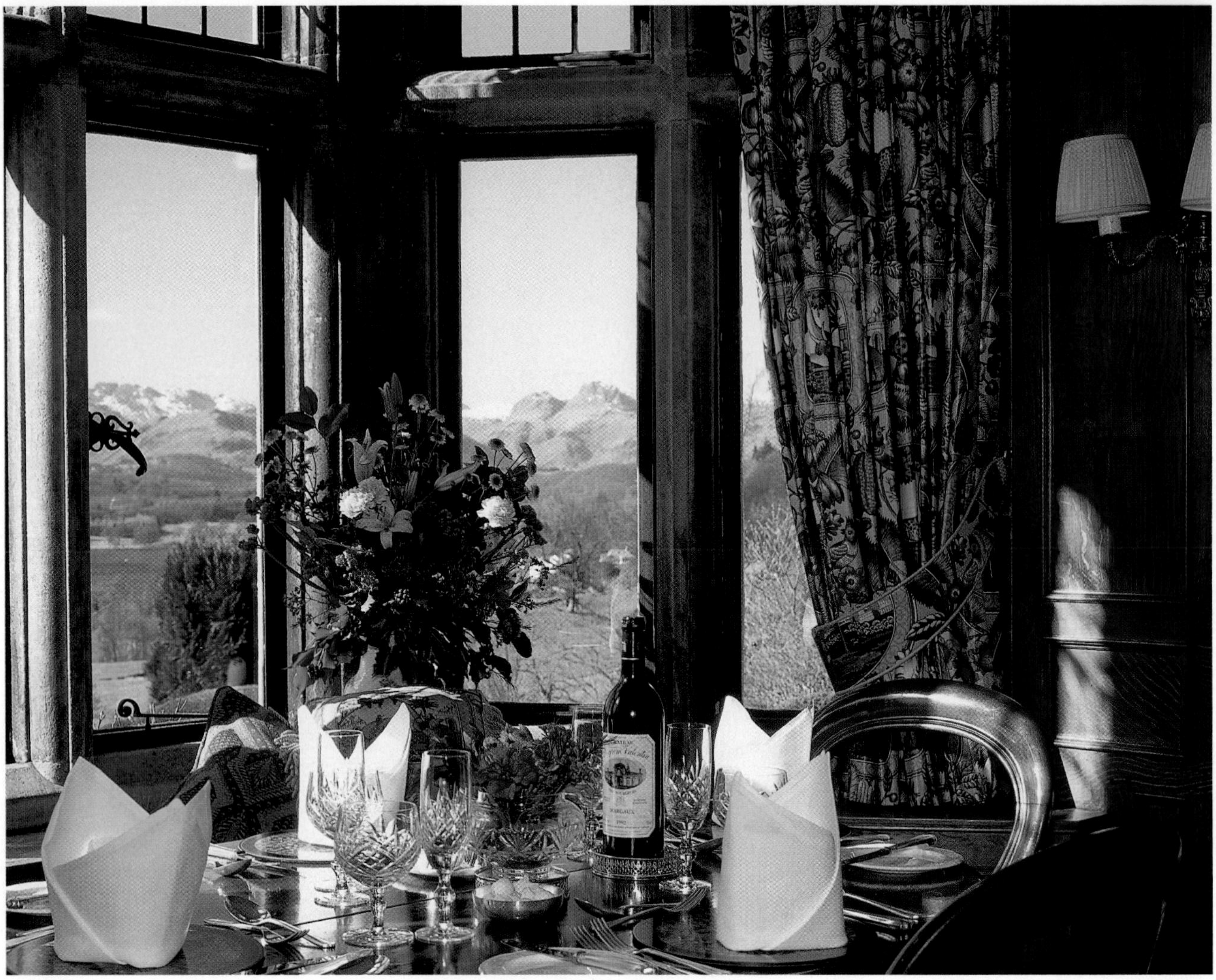

# HOLBECK GHYLL COUNTRY HOUSE HOTEL

**HOLBECK LANE, WINDERMERE, CUMBRIA LA23 1LU**
**TEL: 015394 32375 FAX: 015394 34743**

The saying goes that all the best sites for building a house in England were taken long before the days of the motor car. Holbeck Ghyll has one such prime position. It was built in the early days of the 19th century and is superbly located overlooking Lake Windermere and the Langdale Fells. Today this luxury hotel has an outstanding reputation and is managed personally and expertly by its proprietors, David and Patricia Nicholson. As well as being awarded the RAC Blue Ribbon and 3 AA Red Stars they are among an élite who have won an AA Courtesy and Care Award. The majority of bedrooms are large and have spectacular and breathtaking views. All are recently refurbished to a very high standard, are en suite and include decanters of sherry, fresh flowers, trouser presses, fluffy bathrobes and a lot more. The oak-panelled restaurant is a delightful setting for memorable dining and meals are classically prepared, with focus on flavours and presentation, while an extensive wine list reflects quality and variety. Awarded 3 AA Rosettes for food The hotel has an all-weather tennis court and a health spa with gym, sauna, steam room and treatment facilities. **Directions:** From Windermere, pass Brockhole Visitors Centre, then after 1/2 mile turn right into Holbeck Lane (signed Troutbeck). Hotel is 1/2 mile on left. Price guide (including dinner): Single from £85; double/twin £140–£220; suite £180–£240.

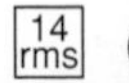

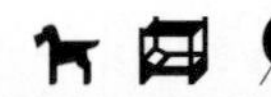

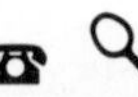

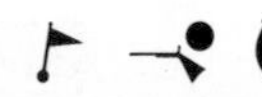

For hotel location, see maps on pages 490-496

# THE LANGDALE HOTEL & COUNTRY CLUB

**GREAT LANGDALE, NR AMBLESIDE, CUMBRIA LA22 9JD**
**TEL: 015394 37302 FAX: 015394 37694**

The Langdale Valley is in the heart of the Lake District National Park, an especially beautiful part of England, surrounded by the dramatic terrain that inspired the poet Wordsworth. The hotel is part of an imaginative complex, that is partly timeshare. Local stone has been used when renovating cottages, winning awards for its sensitivity to the environment. The pleasant bedrooms are both in the hotel and in cottages on the estate. They are comfortable and nearly all the bathrooms are de luxe – whirlpool baths etc. All today's anticipated extras are provided. Families are particularly welcome. Next to the hotel is the Country Club, with its many facilities. Formal meals are in the sophisticated Purdey's Restaurant, while informality is the keynote in the Terrace Restaurant and Cocktail Bar, with barbecues on the patio close to the water's edge. Children have their own menu. A stroll to Chapel Stile takes guests to Wainwright's Inn,authentically furnished, serving real ale and pub food. There is an indoor pool, squash, tennis, a nature trail to observe wild life and a health spa. Additionally visitors enjoy climbing, fishing, boat trips and exploring the fascinating countryside. **Directions:** M63J36, take A591 through Windermere. At Ambleside left onto A593, then B5343 at Skelwith Bridge, signposted Langdale. Price guide: Single £95–£115; double/twin £170–£190.

65 rms 100

For hotel location, see maps on pages 490-496

# NANNY BROW COUNTRY HOUSE HOTEL & RESTAURANT

**CLAPPERSGATE, AMBLESIDE, CUMBRIA LA22 9NF**
**TEL: 015394 32036 FAX: 015394 32450**

Away from the tourists visiting Ambleside at the northern end of Lake Windermere, a Victorian architect built Nanny Brow for himself on this magnificent site on Loughrigg Fell, looking across to the dramatic Langdale Pikes. and River Brathay In five acres of landscaped gardens. The house has been been lovingly converted into a comfortable contemporary hotel without losing its country house charm, winning many accolades for excellence. New arrivals appreciate the welcoming atmosphere of the lounge hall, filled with local antiques and bowls of flowers and find the drawingroom with its graceful furniture and log fires very restful. The pretty bedrooms, individually decorated, have been thoughtfully equipped with many extras. The romantic Garden Suites have balconies or patios outside the sittingrooms. Guests mingle in the inviting Library Bar, before dining by candlelight in the much acclaimed restaurant. The ever-changing five course menu demonstrates the chef's inspired rendition of traditional English dishes – and the cellar contains fine wines from round the world. The hotel offers private fishing, croquet, putting and spa facilities, with membership of a private leisure club. The hotel has its own sailing cruiser on Lake Windermere. **Directions:** From Ambleside A593 Coniston Road for 1 miles, finding Nanny Brow on the right. Price guide (including 5 course dinner): Single £65; double/twin £130–£150; suite £165–£185

18 rms M 30

For hotel location, see maps on pages 490-496

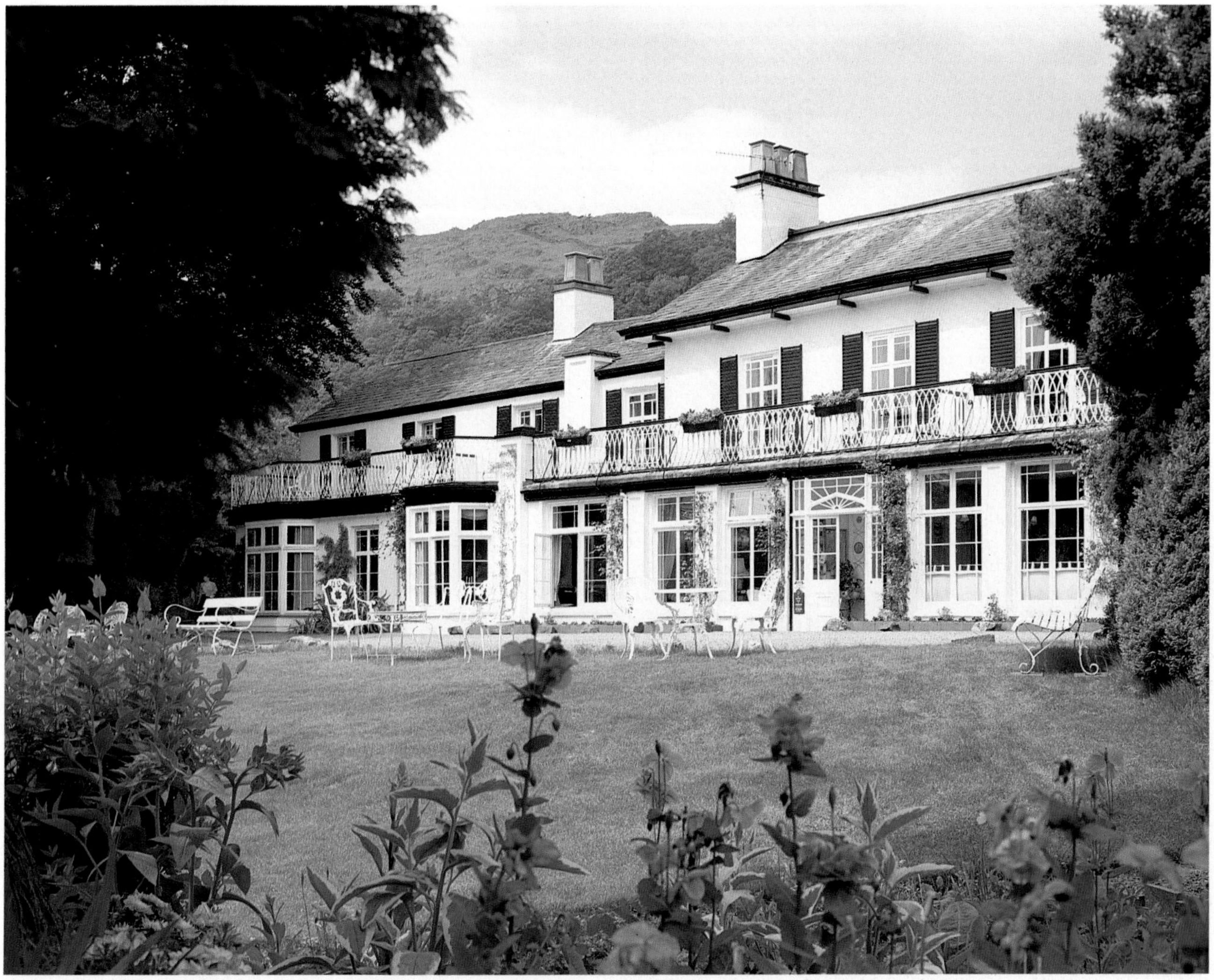

# Rothay Manor

**ROTHAY BRIDGE, AMBLESIDE, CUMBRIA LA22 0EH**
**TEL: 015394 33605 FAX: 015394 33607**

Situated half a mile from Lake Windermere, this Georgian listed building stands in 1½ acres of grounds. The bedrooms include three beautifully furnished suites, two of which are in the lodge beside the manor and afford an unusual measure of space and privacy. One suite is equipped for five people and designed with particular attention to the comfort of guests with disabilities: it has a ramp leading to the garden and a spacious shower. Care and consideration are evident throughout. The menu is varied and meals are prepared with flair and imagination to high standards, complemented by an interesting wine list. For health and fitness residents have free use of the nearby Low Wood Leisure Club, with swimming pool, sauna, steam room, Jacuzzi, squash, sunbeds and a health and beauty salon. Permits are available for fishing, while locally guests can play golf, arrange to go riding, take a trip on a steam railway or visit Wordsworth's cottage. Small functions can be catered for with ease. Closed 4 January to 7 February. Represented in the USA by Josephine Barr: 800-323 5463. Each winter a full programme of special breaks with reduced rates is offered, as well as music, silver and antiques, walking and painting holidays. **Directions:** ¾ mile from Ambleside on A593, the road to Coniston. Price guide: Single £79; double/twin £122–£137; suite £173.

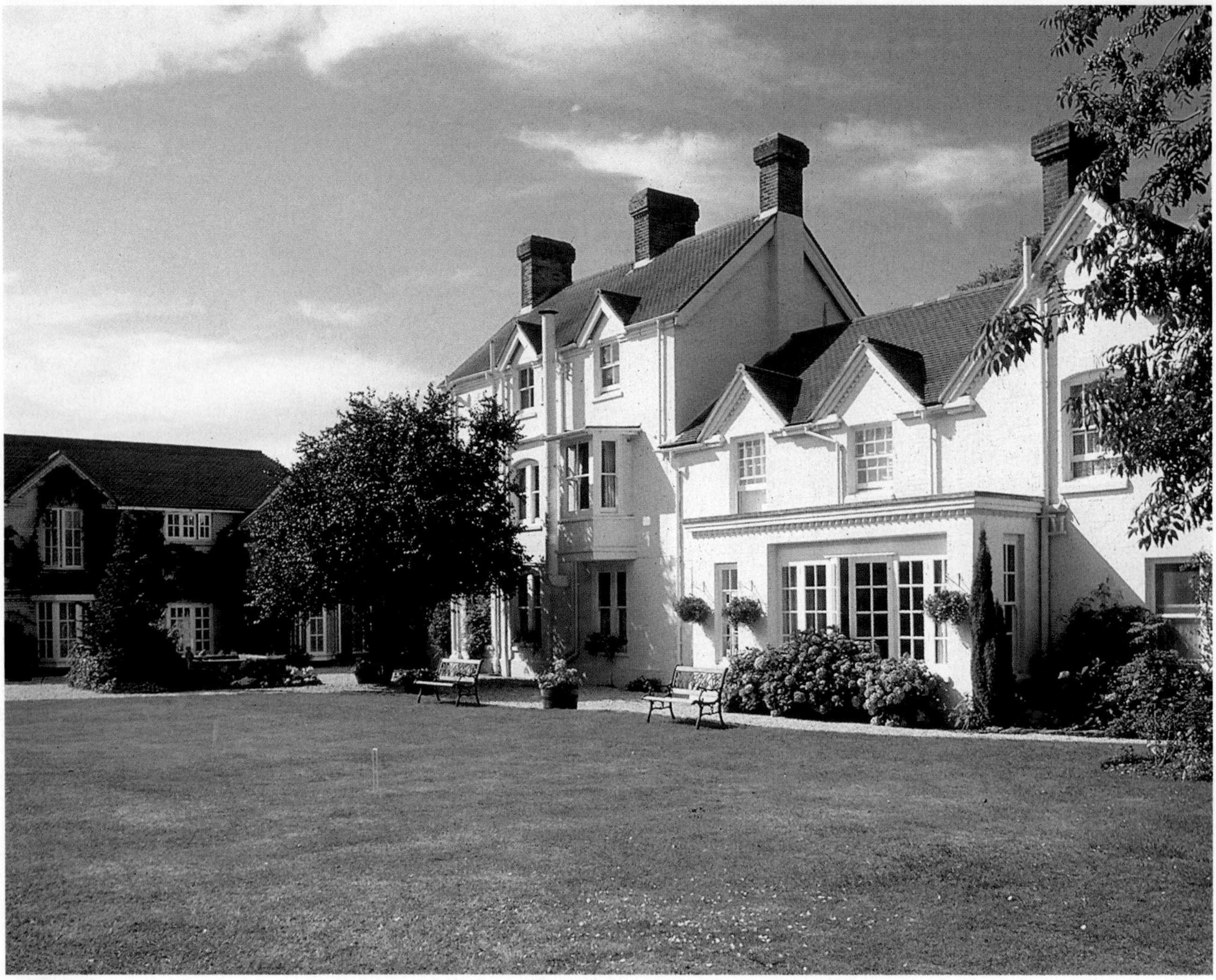

# ESSEBORNE MANOR

HURSTBOURNE TARRANT, ANDOVER, HAMPSHIRE SP11 0ER

TEL: 01264 736444 FAX: 01264 736725

Esseborne Manor is small and unpretentious, yet stylish. The present house was built at the end of the 19th century and carries the name used to record details of the local village in the *Domesday Book*. It is set in a pleasing garden amid the rich farmland of the North Wessex Downs in a designated area of outstanding natural beauty. Ian and Lucilla Hamilton, who manage the house, have established the restful atmosphere of a private country home where guests can unwind and relax. There are just 15 comfortable bedrooms, some reached via a courtyard. Two doubles and a delightful suite are in converted cottages with their own patio overlooking the main gardens. During the winter, a log fire glows in the sitting room, where guests can enjoy an apéritif before dinner. The pretty dining room reflects the importance the owners place upon service and good food. Chef Nick Watson creates imaginative menus from carefully selected, fresh seasonal produce. In the grounds there is a herb garden, an all-weather tennis court, a croquet lawn and plenty of good walking beyond. Nearby Newbury racecourse has a busy programme of steeplechasing and flat racing. Places to visit include Highclere Castle, Stonehenge, Salisbury, Winchester and Oxford. **Directions:** Midway between Newbury and Andover on the A343, 1½ miles north of Hurstbourne Tarrant. Price guide: Single £84–£95; double/twin £95–£135.

For hotel location, see maps on pages 490-496

# APPLEBY MANOR COUNTRY HOUSE HOTEL

ROMAN ROAD, APPLEBY-IN-WESTMORLAND, CUMBRIA CA16 6JB

TEL: 017683 51571 FAX: 017683 52888 E-MAIL: 100043.1561@compuserve.com

Surrounded by half a million acres of some of the most beautiful landscapes in England, sheltered by the mountains and fells of the Lake District, by the North Pennine Hills and Yorkshire Dales, in an area aptly known as Eden stands Appleby Manor, a friendly and relaxing hotel owned and run by the Swinscoe family. The high quality, spotlessly clean, bedrooms induce peaceful, undisturbed sleep. (Dogs are welcome only in The Coach House accommodation). The public areas are also restfully comfortable – the inviting lounges nicely warmed by log fires on cooler days, the cocktail bar luring guests with a choice of more than 70 malt whiskies and the restaurant offering an imaginative selection of tasty dishes and fine wines. The hotel pool, sauna, steam-room, Jacuzzi, solarium and games room keep indoor athletes happy. Locally there are outdoor sports: fishing, golf, riding, squash and, for the more venturesome, rambling on the fells. Appleby is an ideal base from which to visit the Lake District and an attractive stop-over on journeys north-south. **Directions:** From the South take junction 38 of the M6 and then the B6260 to Appleby (13 miles). Drive through the town to a T-junction, turn left, first right and follow road for two-thirds of a mile. Price guide: Single £69–£84; double/twin £98–£128.

For hotel location, see maps on pages 490-496

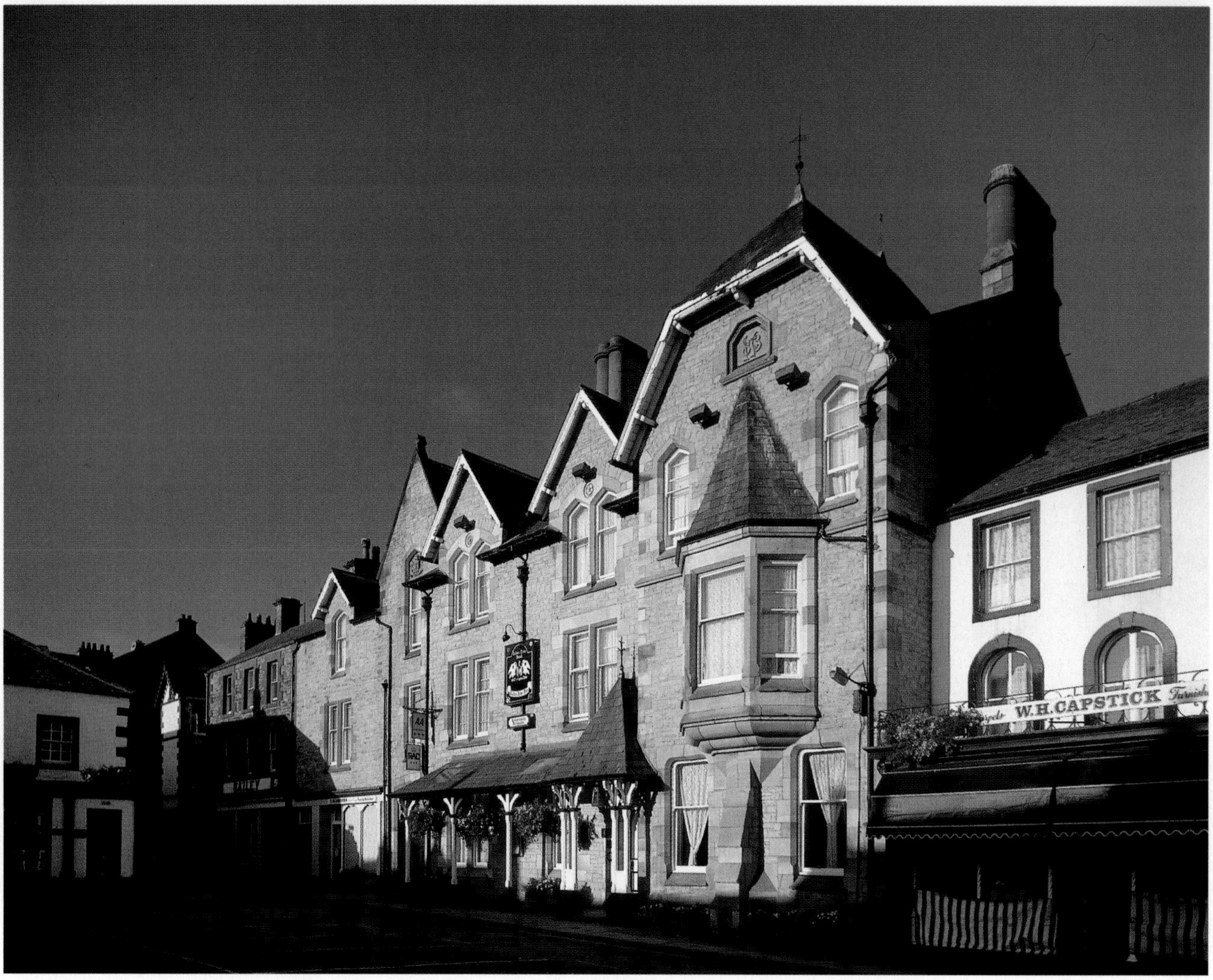

# Tufton Arms Hotel

**MARKET SQUARE, APPLEBY-IN-WESTMORLAND, CUMBRIA CA16 6XA**

**TEL: 017683 51593 FAX: 017683 52761**

This distinguished Victorian coaching inn, owned and run by the Milsom family, has been refurbished to provide a high standard of comfort. The bedrooms evoke the style of the 19th century, when the Tufton Arms became one of the premier hotels in Victorian England. The kitchen is run under the auspices of David Milsom, who spoils guests for choice with a gourmet dinner menu as well as a grill menu. The AA rosette and RAC Merit awarded restaurant is renowned for its fish dishes. Complementing the cuisine is an extensive wine list. There are conference and meeting rooms including the recently refurbished Hothfield Suite which can accommodate up to 100 people. 1995 RAC/Consort Hotel of the Year. RAC award for hospitality. Appleby, the historic county town of Westmorland, stands in splendid countryside and is ideal for touring the Lakes, Yorkshire Dales and Pennines. It is also a convenient stop-over en route to Scotland. Superb fishing for wild brown trout on a 24-mile stretch of the main River Eden, salmon fishing can be arranged on the lower reaches of the river. Shooting parties for grouse, duck and pheasant are a speciality. Appleby has an 18-hole moorland golf course. **Directions:** In centre of Appleby (bypassed by the A66), 38 miles west of Scotch Corner, 13 miles east of Penrith (M6 junction 40), 12 miles from M6 junction 38. Price guide: Single £60–£85; double/twin £90–£125; suite £140.

For hotel location, see maps on pages 490-496

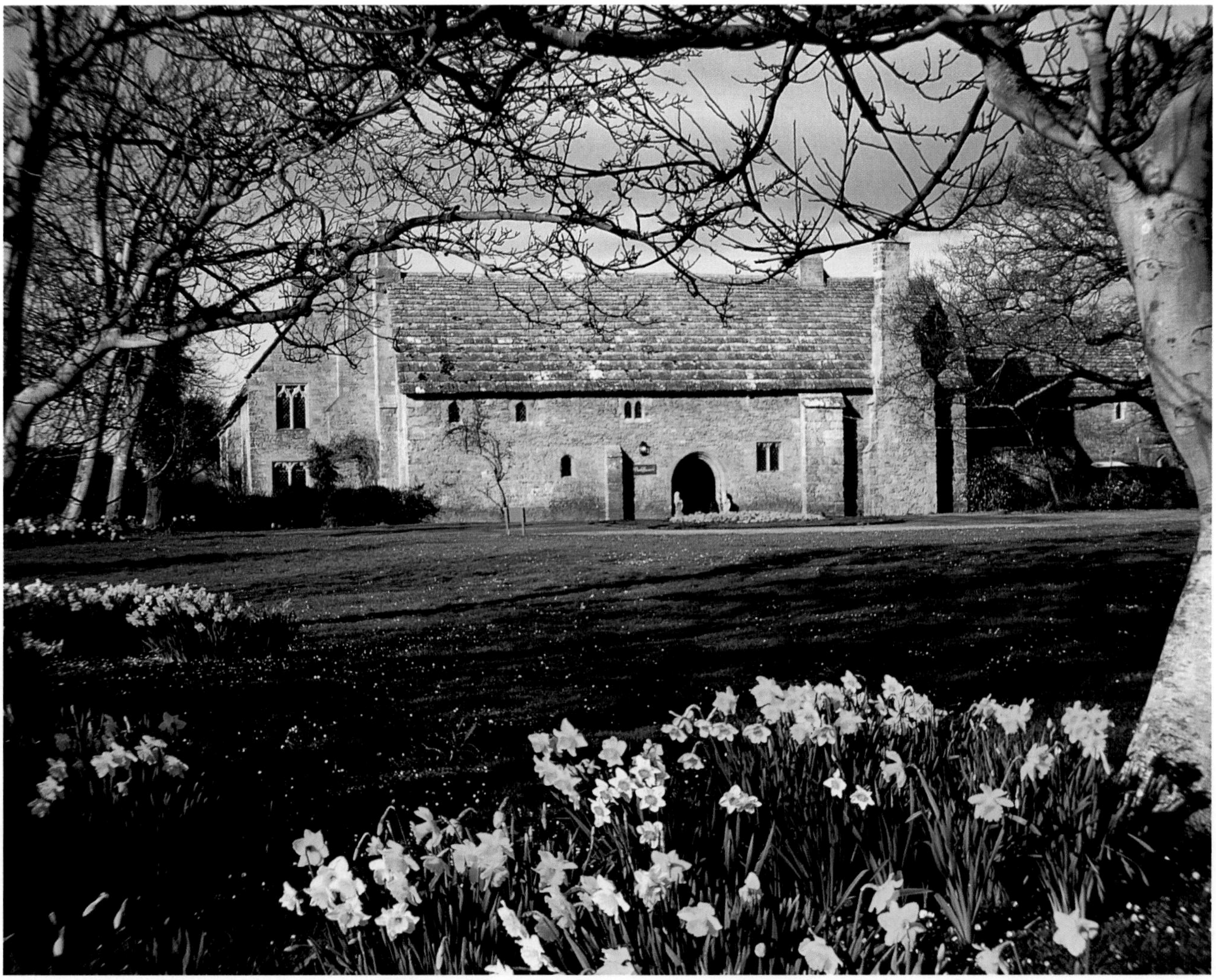

# BAILIFFSCOURT

**CLIMPING, WEST SUSSEX BN17 5RW**
**TEL: 01903 723511 FAX: 01903 723107**

Bailiffscourt is a perfectly preserved "medieval" house, built in the 1930s using authentic material salvaged from historic old buildings. Gnarled 15th century beams and gothic mullioned windows combine to recreate a home from the Middle Ages. Set in 22 acres of beautiful pastures and walled gardens, it provides guests with a wonderful sanctuary in which to relax or work. The bedrooms are all individually decorated and luxuriously furnished, with many offering four poster beds, open log fires and beautiful views over the surrounding countryside. The restaurant offers a varied menu and summer lunches can be taken alfresco in a rose-clad courtyard or the walled garden. A good list of well-priced wines accompanies meals. Private dining rooms are available for weddings, conferences and meetings, and companies can hire the hotel as their 'country house' for 2 or 3 days. Bailiffscourt, which is AA three rosettes and AA Courtesy & Care Award 1997 accredited, is surrounded by tranquil parkland with a golf practice area, outdoor pool and tennis courts. Climping Beach, 100 yards away, is ideal for windsurfing. Nearby are Arundel with its castle, Chichester and Goodwood. **Directions:** Three miles south of Arundel, off the A259. Price guide: Single £125; double from £130.

For hotel location, see maps on pages 490-496

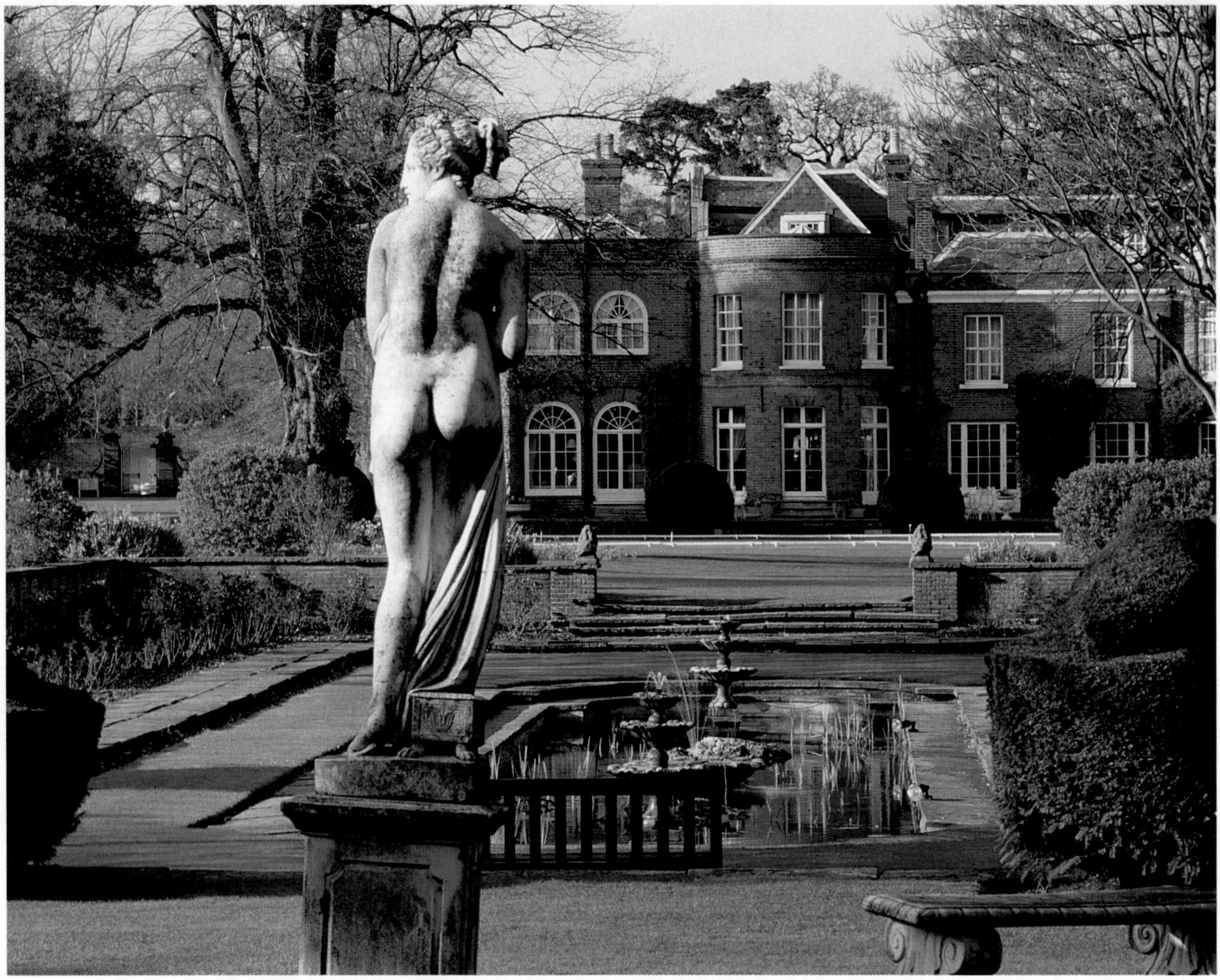

# The Royal Berkshire

**LONDON ROAD, SUNNINGHILL, ASCOT, BERKSHIRE SL5 0PP**
**TEL: 01344 23322 FAX: 01344 27100/01344 874240**

For over 100 years The Royal Berkshire was the home of the Churchill family. Now it is an elegant hotel, ideally located between Ascot racecourse and the Guards Polo Club. This Queen Anne mansion, built in 1705 by the Duke of Marlborough for his daughter, is set in 15 acres of gardens and woodlands. A wide range of leisure facilities including a croquet lawn, putting green, 2 tennis courts, indoor heated pool, squash court, Jacuzzi and sauna. The spacious interiors are smartly decorated in keeping with the country house retreat. Afternoon tea or drinks can be enjoyed in the drawing rooms or on the terrace with views across the lawns. The Stateroom restaurant has been recognised and awarded with an AA rosette. All dishes from the wonderful menu are carefully prepared with meticulous attention to presentation. A series of well-equipped function rooms, combined with easy accessibility from Heathrow and central London, makes The Royal Berkshire a popular venue for business events. For golfers, Sunningdale and Wentworth are all nearby. Royal Windsor and Eton are a short drive away. **Directions:** One mile from Ascot on the corner of A329 and B383. Nearest M25 exit is junction 13. Price guide: Midweek – Single from £149; double/twin £174. Weekend – Single from £64.50; double/twin 99; suites £149. Golf packages 2 nights – Single £218; double/twin £376.

For hotel location, see maps on pages 490-496

# CALLOW HALL

**MAPPLETON ROAD, ASHBOURNE, DERBYSHIRE DE6 2AA**
**TEL: 01335 343403 FAX: 01335 343624**

The approach to Callow Hall is up a tree-lined drive through the 44-acre grounds. On arrival visitors can take in the splendid views from the hotel's elevated position, overlooking the valleys of Bentley Brook and the River Dove. The majestic building and Victorian gardens have been restored by resident proprietors, David, Dorothy and their son, Anthony Spencer, who represent the fifth and sixth generations of hoteliers in the Spencer family. The famous local Ashboure mineral water and home-made biscuits greet guests in the spacious period bedrooms. Fresh local produce is selected daily for use in the kitchen, where the term 'home-made' comes into its own. Home-cured bacon, sausages, fresh bread, traditional English puddings and melt-in-the-mouth pastries are among the items prepared on the premises. Visiting anglers can enjoy a rare opportunity to fish for trout and grayling along a mile-long private stretch of the Bentley Brook, which is mentioned in Izaak Walton's *The Compleat Angler*. Callow Hall is ideally located for some of Englands finest stately homes. Closed at Christmas. **Directions:** Take the A515 through Ashbourne towards Buxton. At the Bowling Green Inn on the brow of a steep hill, turn left, then take the first right, signposted Mappleton, and the hotel is over the bridge on the right. Price guide: Single £73–£97.50; double/twin £110–£136.50; suite £170.

16 rms MasterCard VISA AMERICAN EXPRESS M 30

For hotel location, see maps on pages 490-496

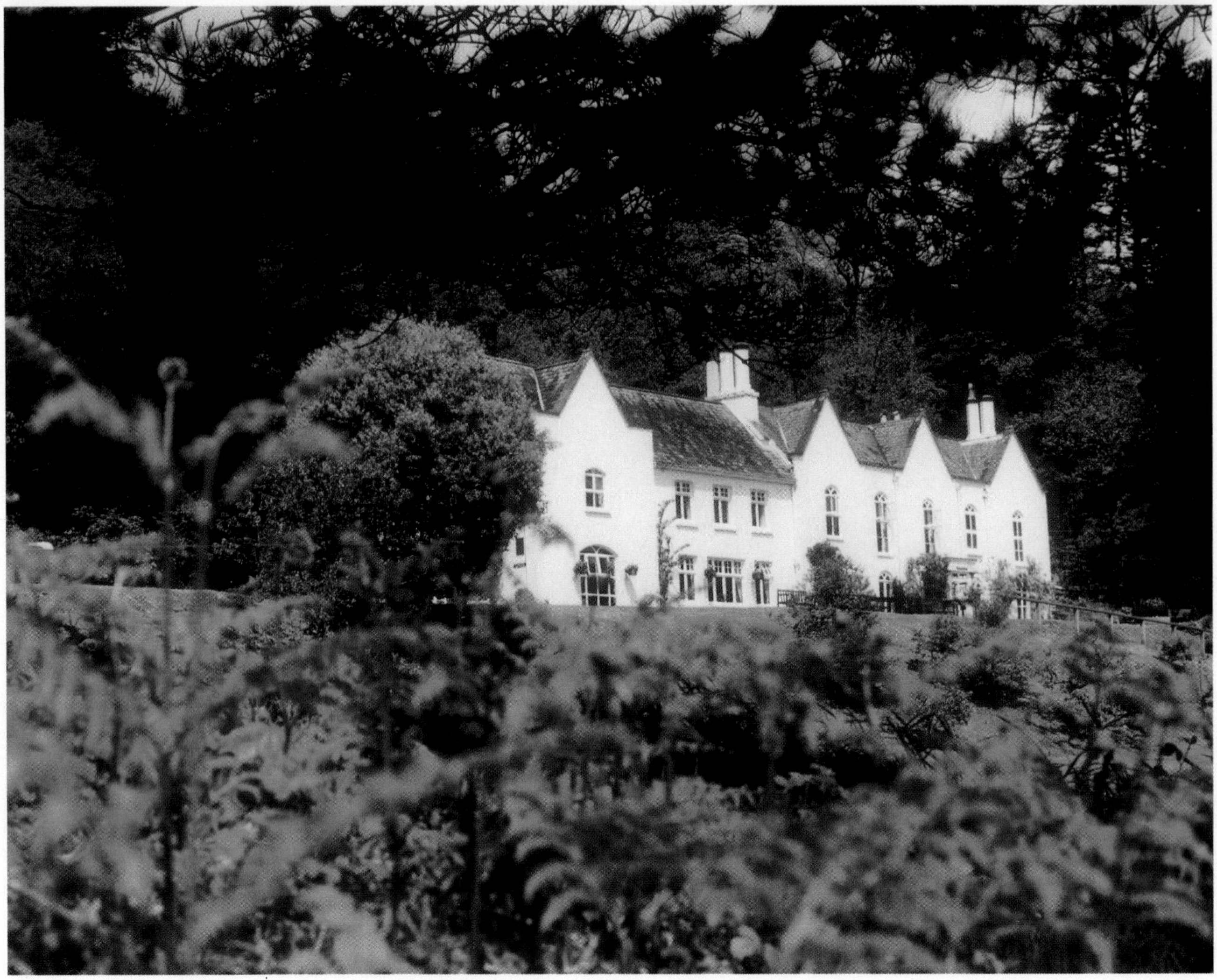

# HOLNE CHASE HOTEL AND RESTAURANT

**NR ASHBURTON, DEVON TQ13 7NS**

**TEL: 01364 631471 FAX: 01364 631453 E-MAIL: info@holne.chase.co.uk**

With sweeping lawns, and an outstanding position in over 70 acres of park and woodland inside Dartmoor National Park, Holne Chase is dedicated to relaxation. Its previous role as a 11th-century hunting lodge has become the hotel's theme for attracting visitors to traditional pursuits in a break from the bustle of everyday life. Fly-fishermen can enjoy the hotel's mile-long beat on the River Dart and driven shoots can be arranged in season. The hotel's stables have been converted to provide "Sporting Lodges" with sitting room and fire downstairs and bedroom suite upstairs. All the hotel's en suite bedrooms are individually furnished and many command spectacular views over the Dart Valley. A walled garden supplies the inviting restaurant, where Master Chef Wayne Pearson provides imaginative cuisine. Holne Chase is a good base for exploring Dartmoor's open moorland and wooded valleys. Picturesque villages and sandy beaches are within reach while Exeter, Plymouth and the English Riviera are just a short drive away. Canoeing, golf and riding can all be arranged. A member of Relais Du Silence, AA 3 Star, 3 Rosettes. **Directions:** Take the Ashburton turning off the A38 and follow the signs for Two Bridges. Holne Chase is on the right after the road crosses the River Dart. Price guide: Single £75; double/twin £115; suite £150.

For hotel location, see maps on pages 490-496

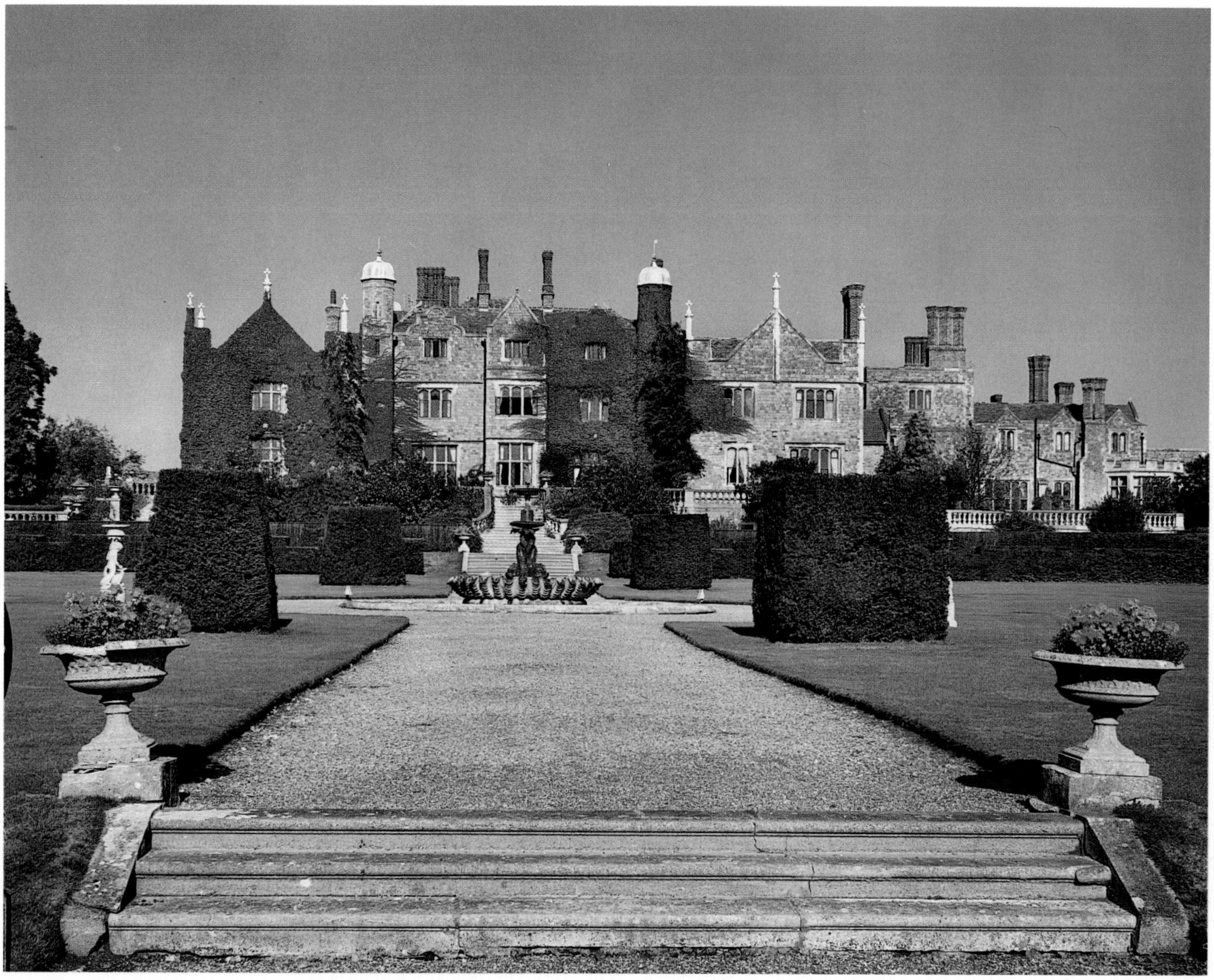

# EASTWELL MANOR

**BOUGHTON LEES, ASHFORD, KENT TN25 4HR**
**TEL: 01233 219955 FAX: 01233 635530**

In the midst of a 3,000-acre estate, set in 62 acres of lovely grounds, lies Eastwell Manor. It was once the home of Queen Victoria's second son, Prince Alfred, and his wife. The Queen and her elder son, later to become Edward VII, were frequent visitors here. The elegant bedrooms are named after past owners, lords, ladies and gentlemen, bearing witness to the hotel's rich history. Each room is individually and gracefully furnished and offers every modern comfort. Huge open fireplaces with stone mantles, carved panelling, leather Chesterfield sofas and fine antique furniture are features of the lounges, billiard room and bar. Modern British cuisine is served in the handsome wood panelled dining room, matched by an excellent cellar of carefully chosen wines. Guests are invited to take advantage of the hotel's tennis court and croquet lawn, while a variety of other leisure pursuits are available locally. The Manor is conveniently located for visiting the historic cathedral city of Canterbury, Leeds Castle and a number of charming market towns. It is also sited near to the Ashford stop for Eurostar. **Directions:** M20 junction 9. A28 towards Canterbury, then A251 signed Faversham. Hotel is three miles north of Ashford in the village of Boughton Lees. Price guide: Single £120–£160; double/twin £160–£210; suites £280–£300.

For hotel location, see maps on pages 490-496

# RIVERSIDE COUNTRY HOUSE HOTEL

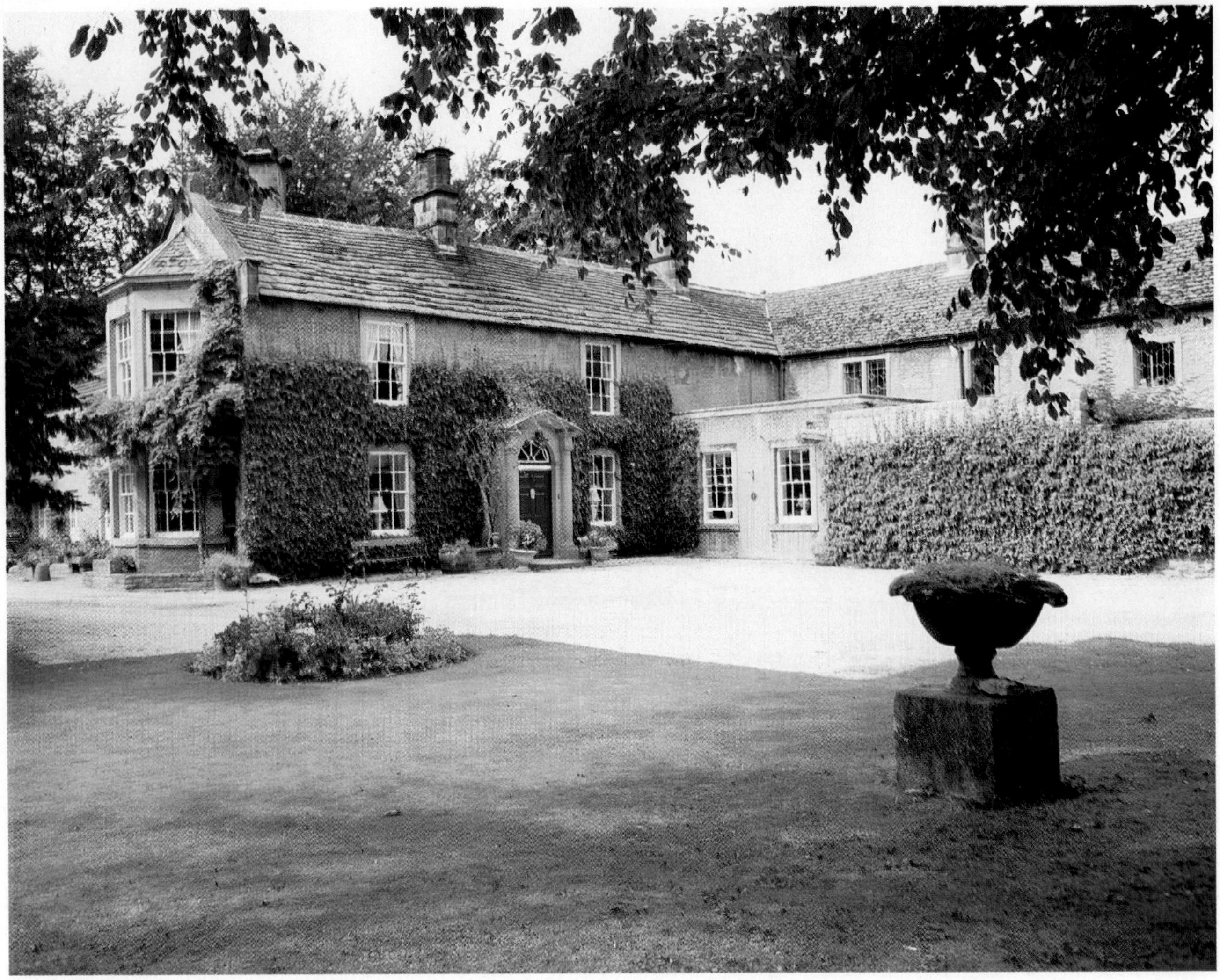

**ASHFORD-IN-THE-WATER, NR BAKEWELL, DERBYSHIRE DE45 1QF**
**TEL: 01629 814275 FAX: 01629 812873**

Ashford-in-the-Water lies in a limestone ravine of the River Wye in the Peak District National Park. In the centre of this picture-postcard village of quaint, stone-built cottages stands the Riverside Country House, a small ivy-clad Georgian mansion in an acre of mature garden and river frontage. Oak panelling and inglenook fireplaces in the lounge create a sense of warmth – an ideal place to chat or curl up with a book. Using seasonally available game and freshly caught fish in the AA 2 rosetted restaurant, master chefs create a series of exciting dishes. Dinner and fine wines are served at antique tables set with gleaming silver, sparkling crystal and illuminated by candle-light. Lunch is always available and the Terrace Room buttery is open all day for light meals. All the prettily decorated bedrooms, with hand-made soft furnishings, have private facilities. 3 star AA hotel. Ideally situated for Chatsworth, Haddon Hall and Hardwick Hall, the hotel is also convenient for the Derbyshire Dales, Lathkill and Dovedale. Bargain breaks are offered for two to five-night stays. **Directions:** 1½ miles north of Bakewell on the A6 heading towards Buxton. Ashford-in-the-Water lies on the right side of the river. The hotel is at the end of the village main street next to the Sheepwash Bridge. Price guide: Single £85–£150; double/twin £85–£150.

For hotel location, see maps on pages 490-496

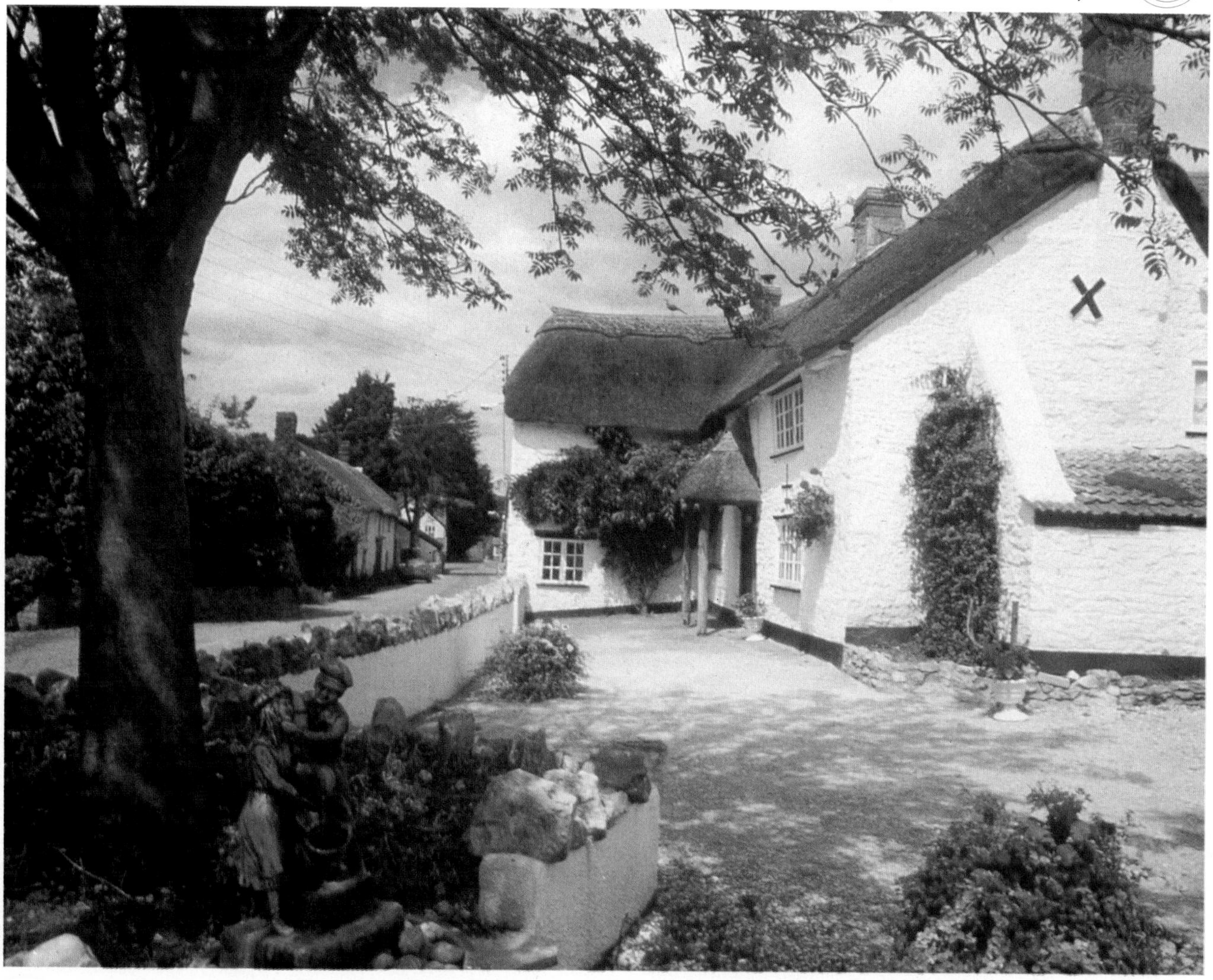

# TYTHERLEIGH COT HOTEL

**CHARDSTOCK, AXMINSTER, DEVON EX13 7BN**
**TEL: 01460 221170 FAX: 01460 221291**

Originally the village cider house, this 14th-century Grade II listed building has been skilfully converted into a spacious modern hotel, idyllically situated in the secluded village of Chardstock on the Devon/Dorset/Somerset borders. The bedrooms, converted from former barns and outbuildings, are all individually designed, some with four-poster or half-tester beds and double Jacuzzis. The beautifully designed award winning restaurant is housed in a Victorian-style conservatory, overlooking an ornamental lily pond with cascading fountain and wrought-iron bridge. Special house parties are held at Christmas and New Year and bargain break weekends can be arranged. The hotel has an outdoor heated swimming pool, sauna, solarium and mini-gym. Riding, tennis, golf and clay pigeon shooting can be arranged locally. The hotel is ideally located for guests to explore the varied landscape of the South West with many historic houses and National Trust properties nearby, such as Forde Abbey, Shute Barton and Parnham House. **Directions:** From Chard take A358 Axminster road; Chardstock signposted on right about 3 miles along. Price guide: Single £55; double/twin £98–£123.50.

For hotel location, see maps on pages 490-496

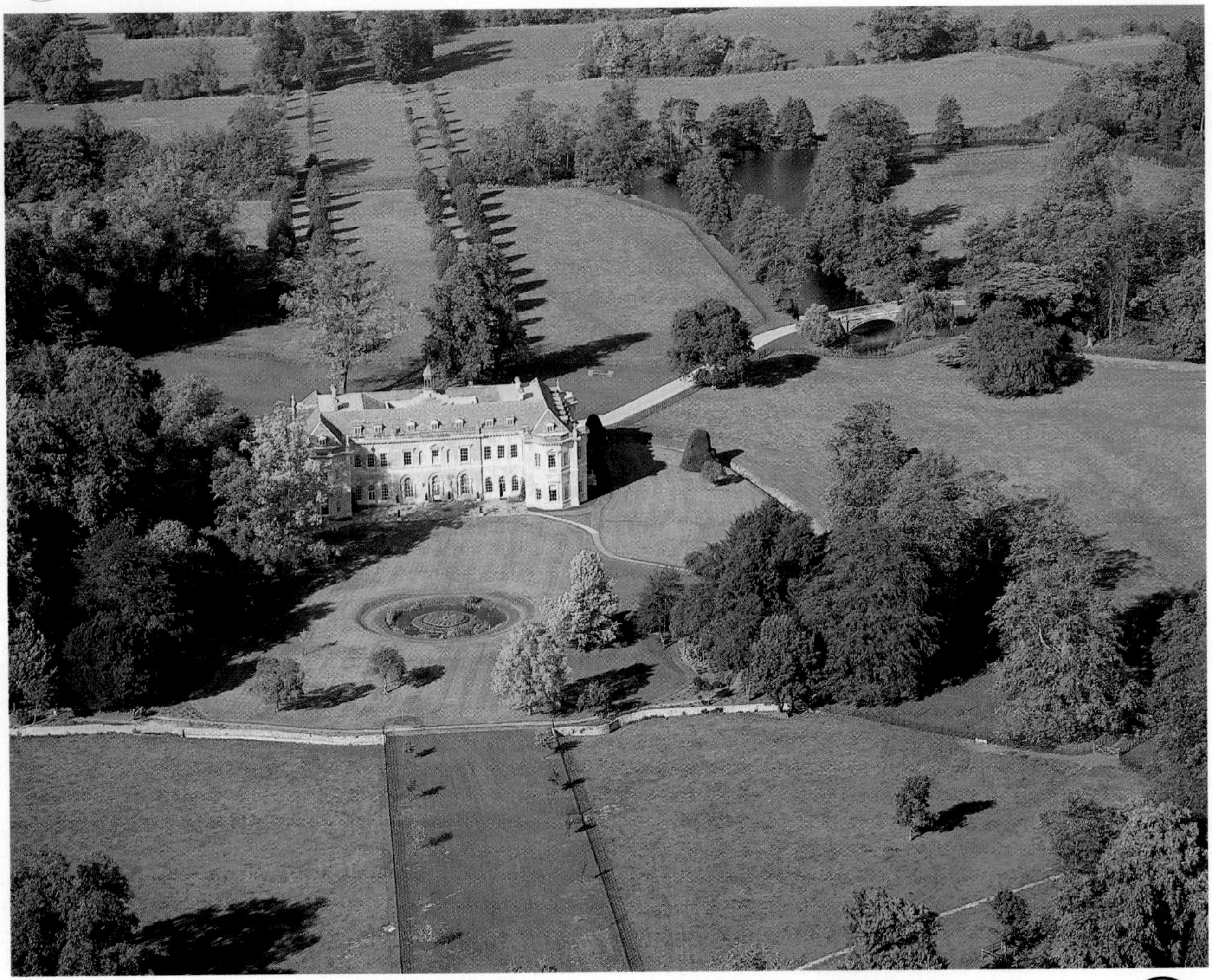

# HARTWELL HOUSE

**OXFORD ROAD, NR AYLESBURY, BUCKINGHAMSHIRE HP17 8NL**

**TEL: 01296 747444 FAX: 01296 747450 – FROM USA FAX FREE: 1 800 260 8338**

Standing in 90 acres of gardens and parkland landscaped by a contemporary of 'Capability' Brown, Hartwell House has both Jacobean and Georgian façades. This beautiful house, brilliantly restored by Historic House Hotels, was the residence in exile of King Louis XVIII of France from 1809 to 1814. The large ground floor reception rooms, with oak panelling and decorated ceilings, have antique furniture and fine paintings which evoke the elegance of the 18th century. There are 46 individually designed bedrooms and suites, some in the house and some in Hartwell Court, the restored 18th-century stables. The dining room at Hartwell is the setting for excellent food which is highly praised by guests. The Hartwell Spa adjacent to the hotel includes an indoor swimming pool, whirlpool spa bath, steam room, gymnasium, hairdressing and beauty salon. Situated in the Vale of Aylesbury, the hotel, which is a member of Relais & Chateaux, is only an hour from London and 20 miles from Oxford. Blenheim Palace, Waddesdon Manor and Woburn Abbey are nearby. Dogs are permitted only in the Hartwell Court bedrooms. **Directions:** On the A418 Oxford Road, 2 miles from Aylesbury. Price guide: Single £110–£140; double/twin £180–£300; suites £260–£500.

For hotel location, see maps on pages 490-496

# The Priory Hotel

HIGH STREET, WHITCHURCH, AYLESBURY, BUCKINGHAMSHIRE HP22 4JS
TEL: 01296 641239 FAX: 01296 641793

The Priory Hotel is a beautifully preserved, timber-framed house dating back to 1360. It is set in the picturesque conservation village of Whitchurch, which is about 5 miles north of Aylesbury. With its exposed timbers, leaded windows and open fires, it retains all its traditional character and charm – a refreshing alternative to the all-too-familiar chain hotels of today. All 11 bedrooms are individually furnished and many of them have four-poster beds. At the heart of the hotel is La Boiserie Restaurant, where classical French cuisine is served in intimate surroundings. An imaginative à la carte fixed-price menu is offered, including a range of seasonal dishes. Start, for example, with a rich terrine of partridge, wild mushrooms and pistachios, then perhaps choose marinated saddle of venison in Cognac butter sauce and garnished with truffles. Specialities include fresh lobster and flambé dishes. The self-contained conference suite can be used for private lunches, dinners and receptions. Among the places to visit locally are Waddesdon Manor, Claydon House, Stowe, Silverstone motor circuit and Oxford. Closed between Christmas and New Year's Eve; the restaurant, not the hotel, also closes on Sunday evenings. **Directions:** Situated on the A413 4 miles north of Aylesbury. Price guide: Single £60–£80; double/twin £95–£110; suite from £102.

For hotel location, see maps on pages 490-496

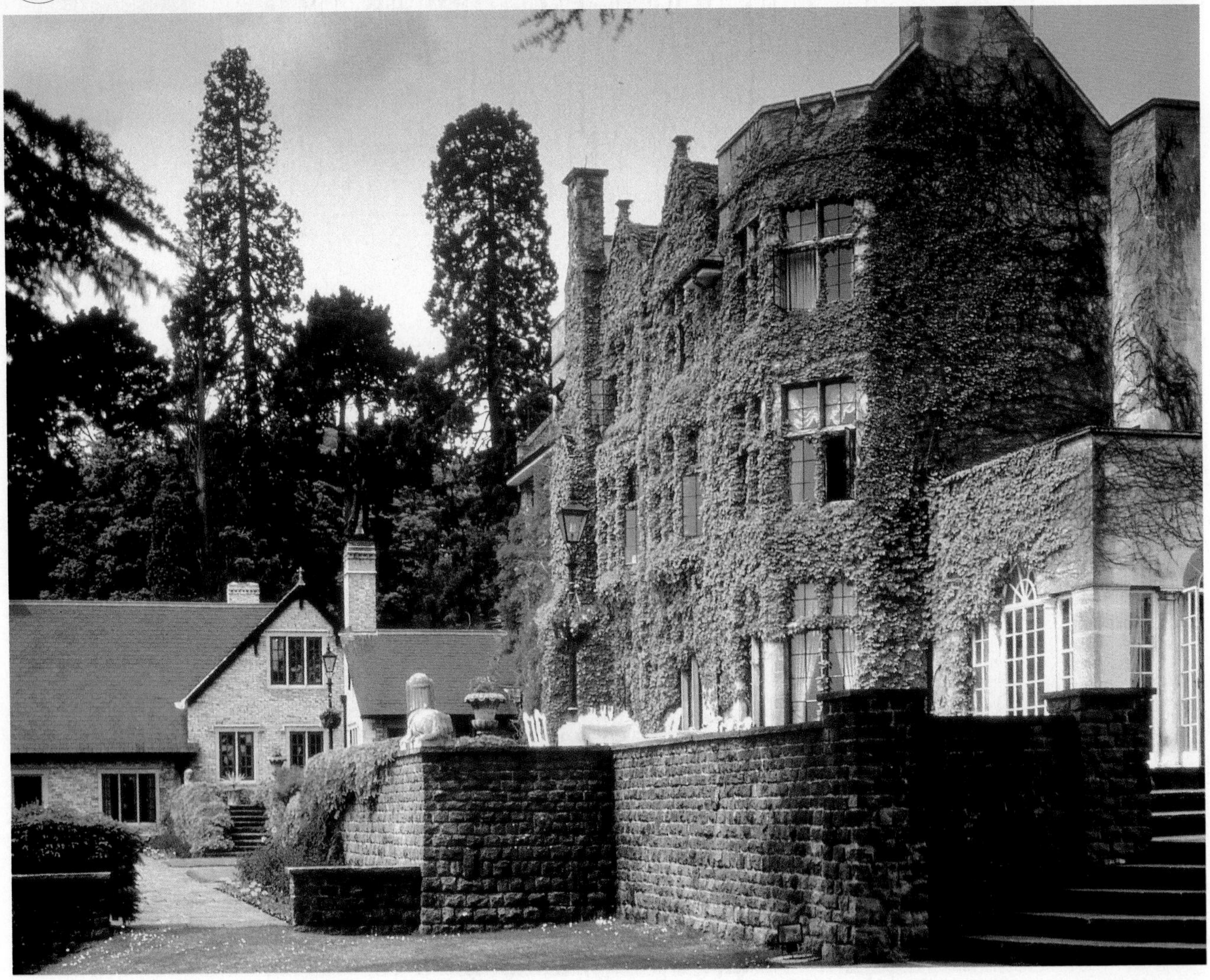

# PENNYHILL PARK HOTEL AND COUNTRY CLUB

**LONDON ROAD, BAGSHOT, SURREY GU19 5ET**
**TEL: 01276 471774 FAX: 01276 473217**

Bagshot has been a centre of hospitality since the early Stuart sovereigns James I and Charles I had a hunting lodge there. Pennyhill Park Hotel continues to uphold that tradition. Built in 1849, this elegant mansion reflects its journey through Victorian and Edwardian times while providing every modern amenity. The bedrooms are outstanding: no two are identical, and infinite care has been invested in creating practical rooms with distinctive features. Impeccable service is to be expected, as staff are trained to classical, Edwardian standards. Cuisine is served in the welcoming setting of the Latymer Restaurant, accompanied by a wine list that includes many rare vintages. Pennyhill is continually introducing new facilities that never fail to delight. Recreational facilities are available within the grounds, which span 120 acres and include landscaped gardens, a 9-hole golf course, a swimming pool and a three acre lake. Pennyhill Park is conveniently located only 27 miles from central London and not far from Heathrow, Windsor Castle, Ascot, Wentworth and Sunningdale. **Directions:** From the M3, exit 3, take A322 towards Bracknell. Turn left on to A30 signposted to Camberley. ¾ mile after Bagshot; turn right 50 yards past the Texaco garage. Price guide: Single from £135; double/twin £155–£210; suite from £285; apartments £400.

For hotel location, see maps on pages 490-496

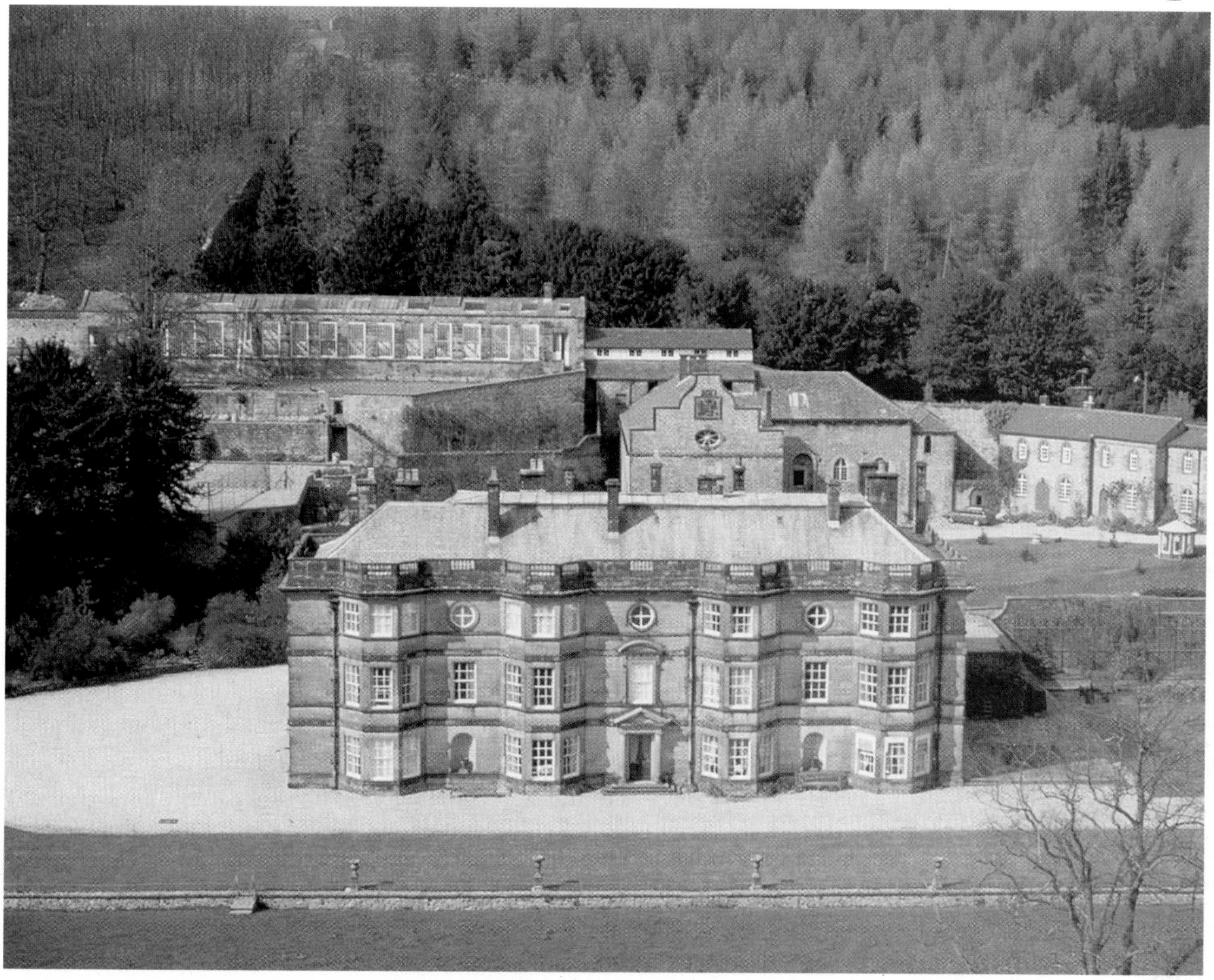

# HASSOP HALL

**HASSOP, NR BAKEWELL, DERBYSHIRE DE45 1NS**
**TEL: 01629 640488 FAX: 01629 640577**

The recorded history of Hassop Hall reaches back 900 years to the *Domesday Book*, to a time when the political scene in England was still dominated by the power struggle between the barons and the King, when the only sure access to that power was through possession of land. By 1643, when the Civil War was raging, the Hall was under the ownership of Rowland Eyre, who turned it into a Royalist garrison. It was the scene of several skirmishes before it was recaptured after the Parliamentary victory. Since purchasing Hassop Hall in 1975, Thomas Chapman has determinedly pursued the preservation of its outstanding heritage. Guests can enjoy the beautifully maintained gardens as well as the splendid countryside of the surrounding area. The bedrooms, some of which are particularly spacious, are well furnished and comfortable. A four-poster bedroom is available for romantic occasions. A comprehensive dinner menu offers a wide and varied selection of dishes, with catering for most tastes. As well as the glories of the Peak District, places to visit include Chatsworth House, Haddon Hall and Buxton Opera House. Christmas opening – details on application. **Directions:** From M1 exit 29 (Chesterfield), take A619 to Baslow, then A623 to Calver; left at lights to B6001. Hassop Hall is 2 miles on right. Price guide: Single £69–£89; double/twin £79–£99. Inclusive rates available on request.

For hotel location, see maps on pages 490-496

# HELLIDON LAKES HOTEL AND COUNTRY CLUB

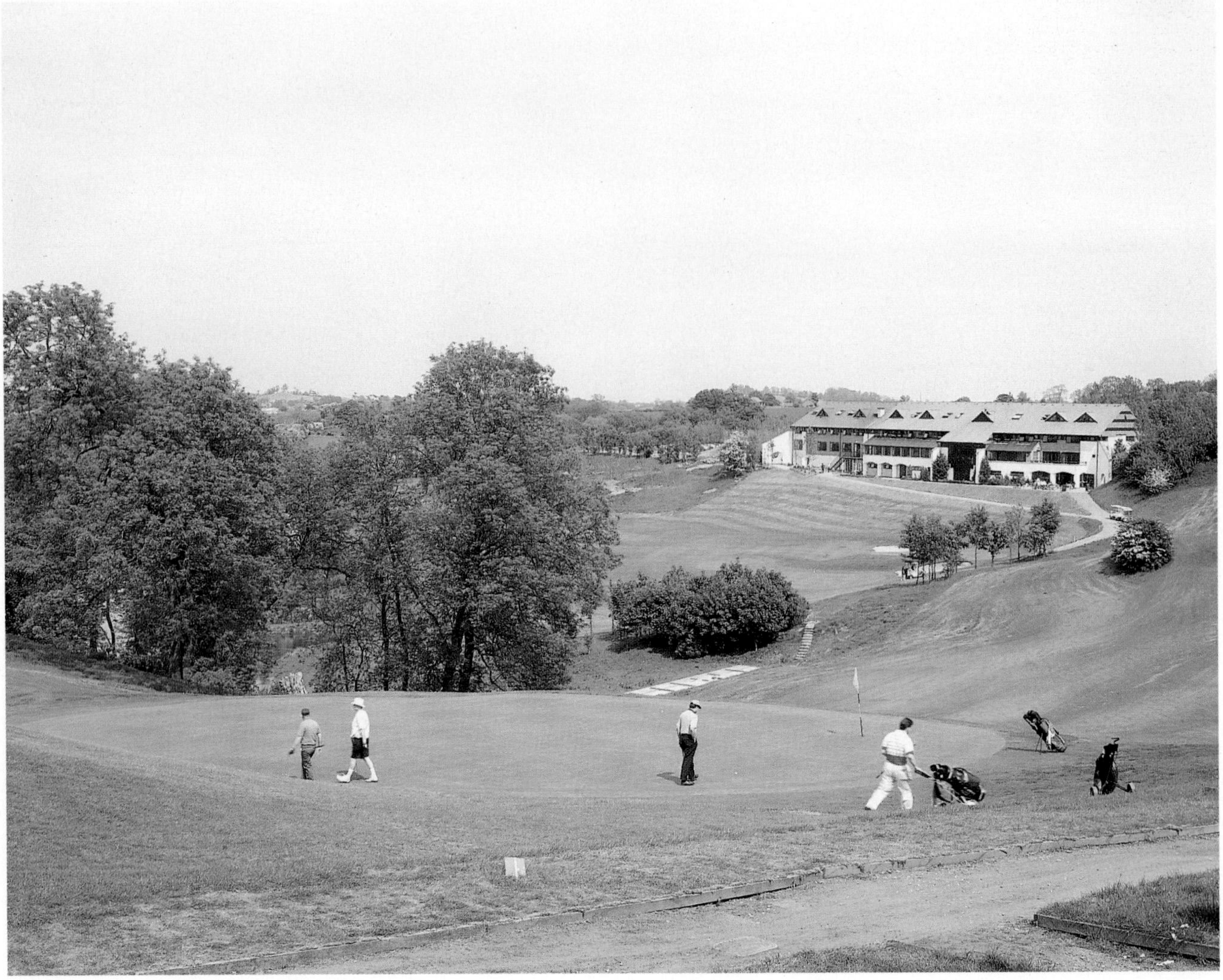

**HELLIDON, DAVENTRY, NORTHANTS NN11 6LN**
**TEL: 01327 262550 FAX: 01327 262559**

The Hellidon Lakes Hotel and Country Club is set against a background of beautiful rolling countryside, lakes and trees. It combines high standards of comfort with the personal service that only a small, luxury hotel can offer. The range of leisure facilities is extensive – as well as a 27-hole championship golf course, there is a covered driving range, putting green, fully-equipped gym, swimming pool, steam room and solarium. Four Qualified fitness and beauty staff are on hand to offer help and advice. Awarded 4 stars by the AA and an AA rosette awarded for food and wine, the hotel offers an excellent standard of accommodation in its tastefully furnished and well-equipped bedrooms. Guests have a choice of restaurants. The Lakes Restaurant offers superb à la carte and table d'hôte menus, while less formal dining is available in the Club Bar Restaurant which serves a full bar meal and tasty snacks. New reception and syndicate rooms have recently been added to the hotel's first class conference facilities which can cater for up to 180 delegates. Places of interest nearby include Stratford-upon-Avon, Leamington Spa and Newstead Abbey, a rare example of a medieval priory. **Directions:** From the M40 Junction 11 take the A361 to Charwelton, first left towards Priors Marston and second right towards Staverton. The hotel is on your left. Price guide: Single £89.50; double/twin £120; suite £115–£140.

For hotel location, see maps on pages 490-496

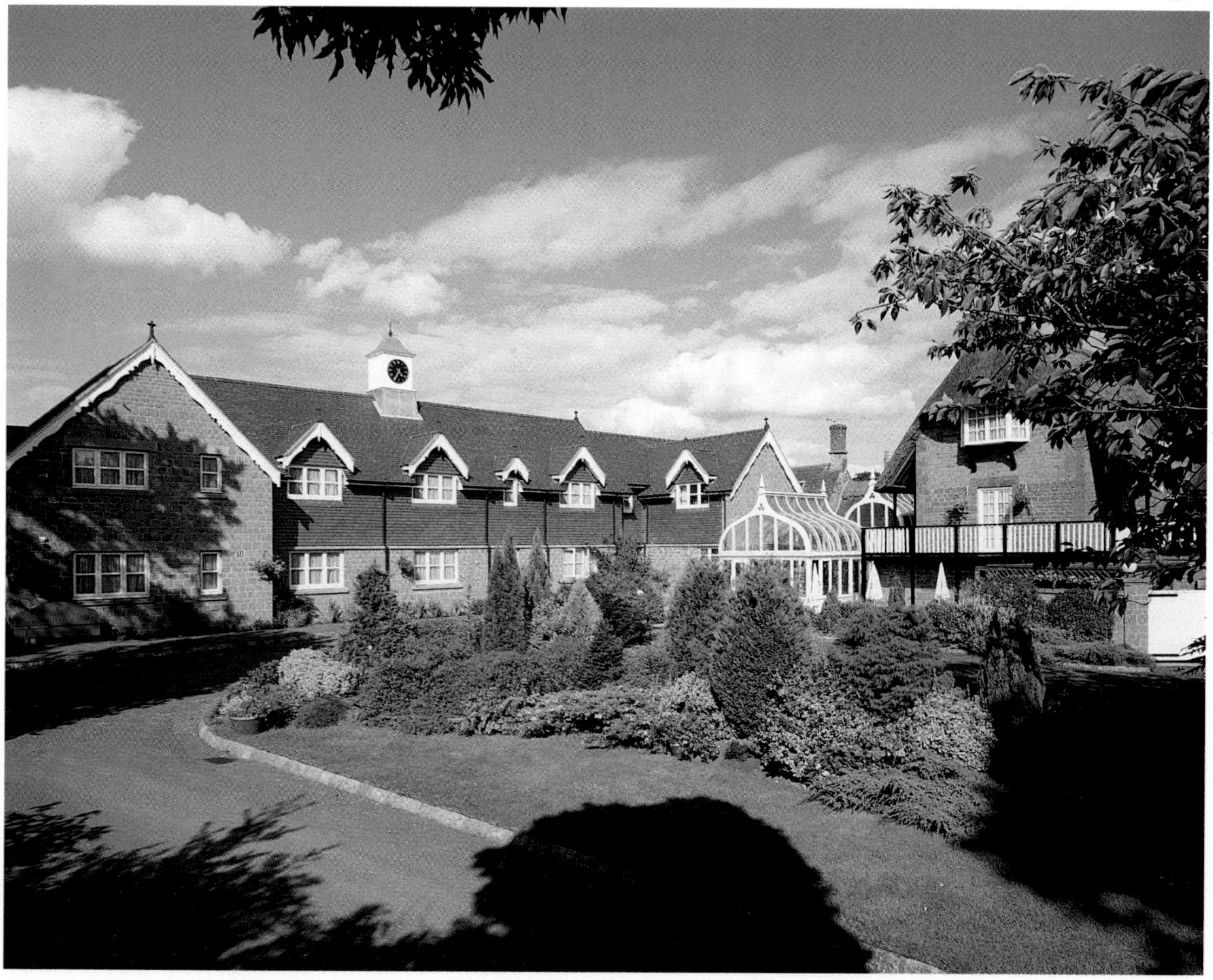

# WROXTON HOUSE HOTEL

**WROXTON ST MARY, NR BANBURY, OXFORDSHIRE OX15 6QB**
**TEL: 01295 730777 FAX: 01295 730800**

Built of honeyed local stone, Wroxton House has undergone a sensitive restoration linking three village houses, dating from the 17th century, with a delightful clocktower wing and conservatory lounge. The relaxing character of the hotel is created by the carefully selected staff, who combine attentive service with friendliness and informality. The spacious and bright lounges contain thoughtfully chosen furnishings, comfortable armchairs and a profusion of flowers and plants. The 32 en suite bedrooms have been individually decorated and the original timbers preserved in many of the older rooms. The classic English styles complement the deeply polished woods of the furniture. Guests may dine by candlelight in the intimate restaurant, where a traditional Cotswold atmosphere is evoked by original beams, inglenooks, carved oak recesses, horse brasses and pewter. The expertly prepared menus display a personal interpretation of classic British dishes which make imaginative use of the freshest local produce. Wroxton House Hotel is a popular choice with businessmen, as it offers good meeting facilities in a quiet setting. Golf and riding can be arranged locally. **Directions:** Easily reached via M40, Wroxton is two miles outside Banbury on the A422 Stratford-upon-Avon road. Price guide: Single £75–£85; double/twin £95–£125.

For hotel location, see maps on pages 490-496

In association with MasterCard 

# TYLNEY HALL

**ROTHERWICK, NR HOOK, HAMPSHIRE RG27 9AZ**
**TEL: 01256 764881 FAX: 01256 768141**

Arriving at this hotel in the evening with its floodlit exterior and forecourt fountain, you can imagine that you are arriving for a party in a private stately home. Grade II listed and set in 66 acres of ornamental gardens and parkland, Tylney Hall typifies the great houses of the past. Apéritifs are taken in the wood-panelled library bar; haute cuisine is served in the glass-domed Oak Room restaurant, complemented by conscientious service. The hotel holds 2 AA Rosettes for food and also AA 4 Red Stars. Extensive leisure facilities include indoor and outdoor heated swimming pools, multi-gym, sauna, tennis, croquet and snooker, while hot-air ballooning, archery, clay pigeon shooting, golf and riding can be arranged. Surrounding the hotel are wooded trails ideal for rambling or jogging. Functions for up to a hundred are catered for in the Tylney Suite or Chestnut Suite, while more intimate gatherings are held in one of the other ten private banqueting rooms. Tylney Hall is licensed to hold wedding ceremonies on site. The cathedral city of Winchester and Stratfield Saye House are nearby. **Directions:** M4, junction 11, towards Hook and Rotherwick – follow signs to hotel. M3, junction 5, 3rd exit, A287 towards Newnham – over A30 into Old School Road. Left for Newnham and right onto Ridge Lane. Hotel is on the left after one mile. Price guide: Single from £110; double/twin from £135; suite from £235.

For hotel location, see maps on pages 490-496

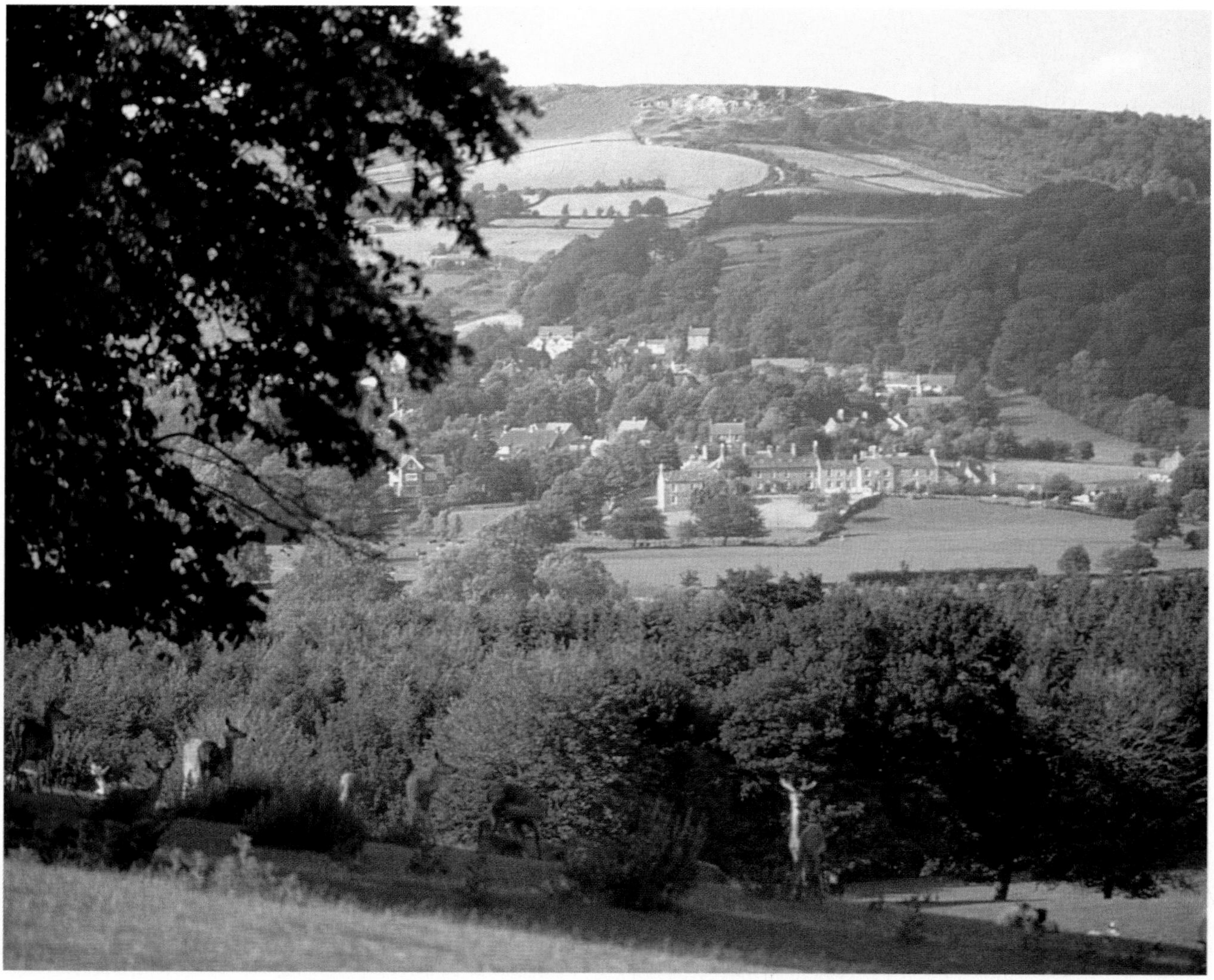

# Cavendish Hotel

**BASLOW, DERBYSHIRE DE45 1SP**
**TEL: 01246 582311 FAX: 01246 582312**

This enchanting hotel offers travellers an opportunity to stay on the famous Chatsworth Estate, close to one of England's greatest stately houses, the home of the Duke and Duchess of Devonshire. The hotel has a long history of its own – once known as the Peacock Inn on the turnpike road to Buxton Spa. When it became The Cavendish in 1975, the Duchess personally supervised the transformation, providing some of the furnishings from Chatsworth and her design talents are evident throughout. Guests have a warm welcome. before they are conducted to the luxurious bedrooms, all of which overlook the Estate. Harmonious colours, gorgeous fabrics and immense comfort prevail. Every imaginable extra is provided, from library books to bath robes. Breakfast is served until lunchtime – no rising at cockcrow – and informal meals are served from morning until bed-time in The Garden Room. At dusk you can sample cocktails and special whiskies in the bar before dining in the handsome restaurant with its imaginative menu and list of over 100 carefully selected wines. Climbing The Peak, exploring The Dales, fishing, golf and Sheffield's Crucible Theatre are among the many leisure pursuits near by. **Directions:** M1/J29, A617 to Chesterfield then A619 west to Baslow. Price guide (excluding breakfast): Single £84; double/twin £104.

For hotel location, see maps on pages 490-496

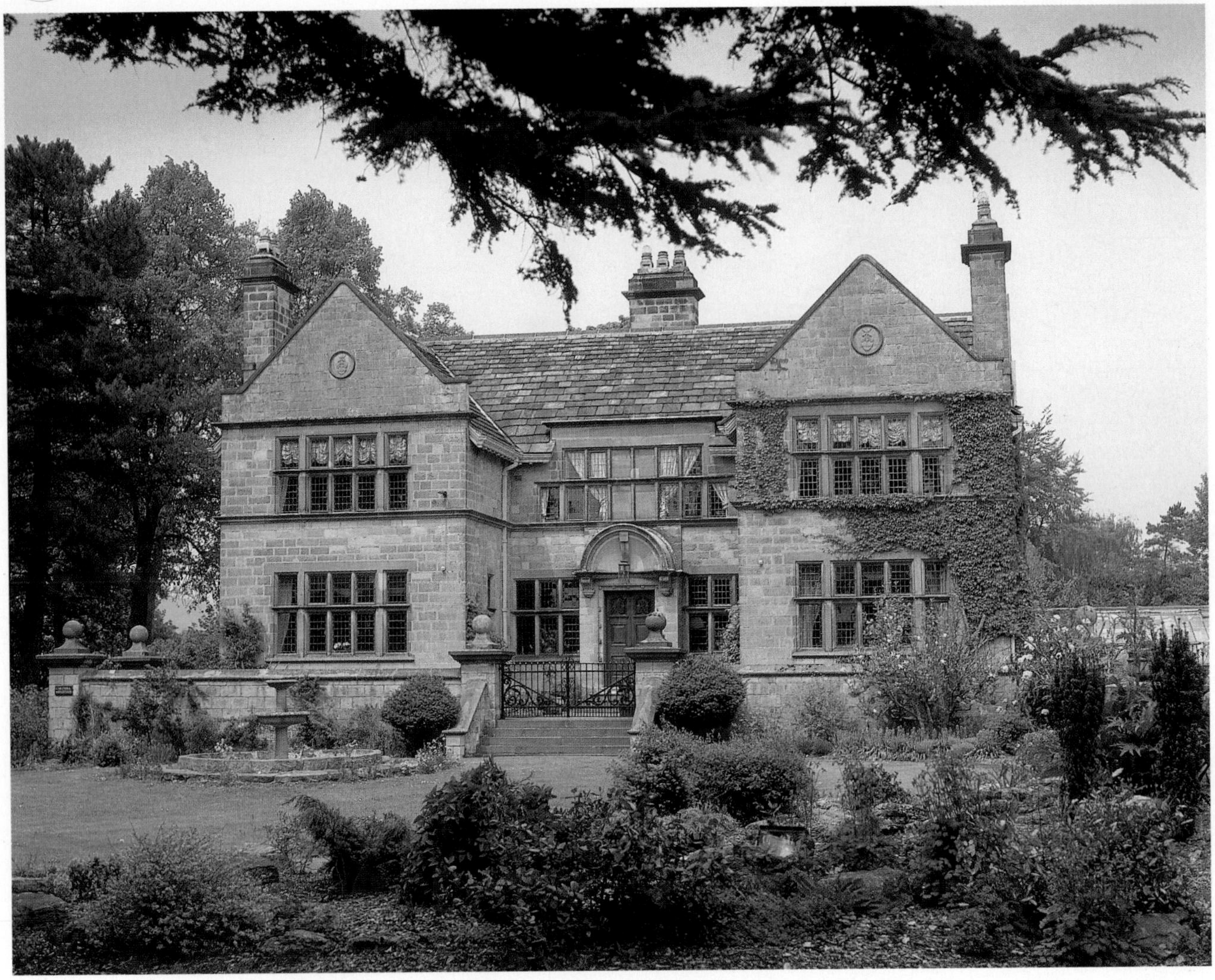

# FISCHER'S

## BASLOW HALL, CALVER ROAD, BASLOW, DERBYSHIRE DE45 1RR
## TEL: 01246 583259 FAX: 01246 583818

Situated on the edge of the magnificent Chatsworth Estate, Baslow Hall enjoys an enviable location surrounded by some of the country's finest stately homes and within easy reach of the Peak District's many cultural and historical attractions. Standing at the end of a winding chestnut tree-lined driveway, this fine Derbyshire manor house was tastefully converted by Max and Susan Fischer into an award winning country house hotel in 1989. Since opening Fischer's has consistently maintained its position as one of the finest establishments in the Derbyshire/South Yorkshire regions earning the prestigious Egon Ronay 'Restaurant of the Year' award in 1995. Whether you are staying in the area for private or business reasons, it is a welcome change to find a place that feels less like a hotel and more like a home combining comfort and character with an eating experience which is a delight to the palate. Max presides in the kitchen. His Michelin starred cuisine can be savoured either in the more formal main dining room or in 'Café Max' – where the emphasis is on more informal eating and modern tastes. Baslow Hall offers facilities for small conferences or private functions. Baslow is within 12 miles of the M1 motorway, Chesterfield and Sheffield. Fischer's is on the A623 in Baslow. Price guide: Single £80–£95; double/twin £95–£130; suite £130.

For hotel location, see maps on pages 490-496

# Bath Spa Hotel

**SYDNEY ROAD, BATH BA2 6JF**
**TEL: 01225 444424 FAX: 01225 444006**

Nestling in seven acres of mature grounds dotted with ancient cedars, formal gardens, ponds and fountains, the Bath Spa Hotel's elegant Grecian facade can only hint at the warmth, style, comfort and attentive personal service that awaits visitors. It is a handsome building in a handsome setting with antique furniture, richly coloured carpeting and well defined colour schemes lending an uplifting brightness throughout. This is particularly so in the individually decorated bedrooms whose bathrooms are luxuriously appointed in mahogany and marble. The Bath Spa offers all amenities that guests would expect of an RAC Five Star Hotel of the Year while retaining the character of a homely country house. Chef Jonathan Fraser's imaginative, contempory style is the primary inspiration for the award-winning cuisine served in the two restaurants. For relaxation there is a fully equipped health and leisure spa which includes a swimming pool, gymnasium and tennis court. Apart from the delights of Bath, there is motor racing at Castle Combe and hot air ballooning nearby. Directions: From the M4, exit at junction 18 and take A46 to Bath. Then join A4 signposted City Centre and at first traffic lights turn left following the signs for A36. Travel over Cleveland Bridge, turn right at mini roundabout and then take next left into Sydney Place. Price guide: Single From £129; double/twin from £149; suite from £329.

98 rms · MasterCard · VISA · AMERICAN EXPRESS · M 150

For hotel location, see maps on pages 490-496

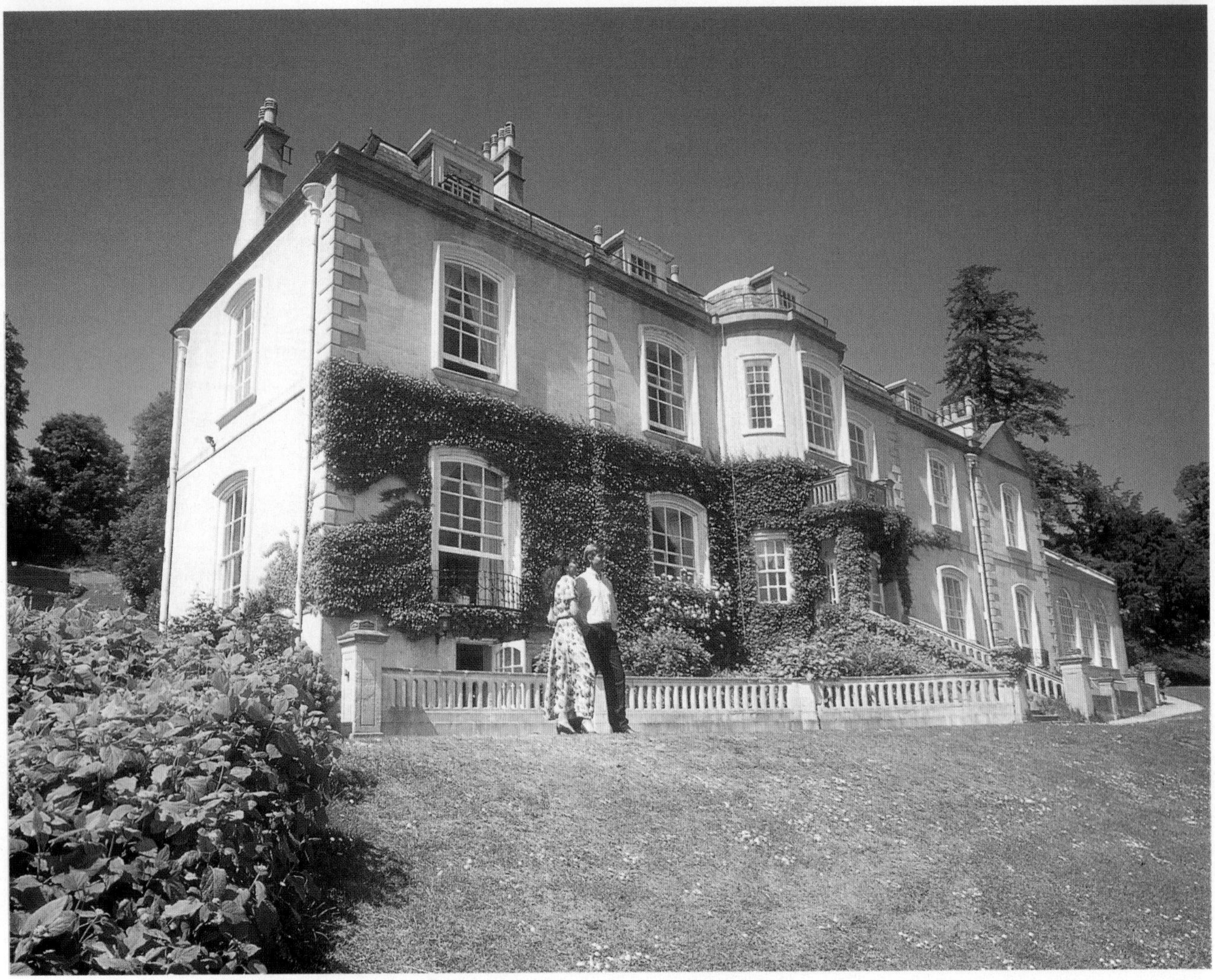

# COMBE GROVE MANOR HOTEL & COUNTRY CLUB

**BRASSKNOCKER HILL, MONKTON COMBE, BATH, SOMERSET BA2 7HS**
**TEL: 01225 834644 FAX: 01225 834961**

This is an exclusive 18th-century country house hotel situated two miles from the beautiful city of Bath. Built on the hillside site of a Roman settlement, Combe Grove Manor is set in 82 acres of private gardens and woodland, with magnificent views over the Limpley Stoke Valley. In addition to the Georgian Restaurant, which boast an exciting varied menu, there is a private dining room, plus a wine bar and restaurant with a terrace garden. After dinner guests may relax with drinks in the elegant drawing room or library. The bedrooms are lavishly furnished, all individually designed with en suite facilities, two of which have Jacuzzi baths. Within the grounds are some of the finest leisure facilities in the South West, including indoor and outdoor heated pools, hydrospa beds and steam room, four all-weather tennis courts, a 5-hole par 3 golf course and a two-tiered driving range. Guests may use the Nautilus gym, aerobics studio, saunas and solaria or relax in the Clarins beauty rooms where a full range of treatments are offered. Separate from the Manor House is the Garden Lodge which provides 31 rooms, with spectacular views and some have a private terrace. ETB 5 Crowns Highly Commended. AA 4 Stars. 2 Rosettes. **Directions:** Set south-east of Bath off the A36 near the University. Map can be supplied on request. Price guide: Single from £99; double/twin from £99; suite from £195.

For hotel location, see maps on pages 490-496

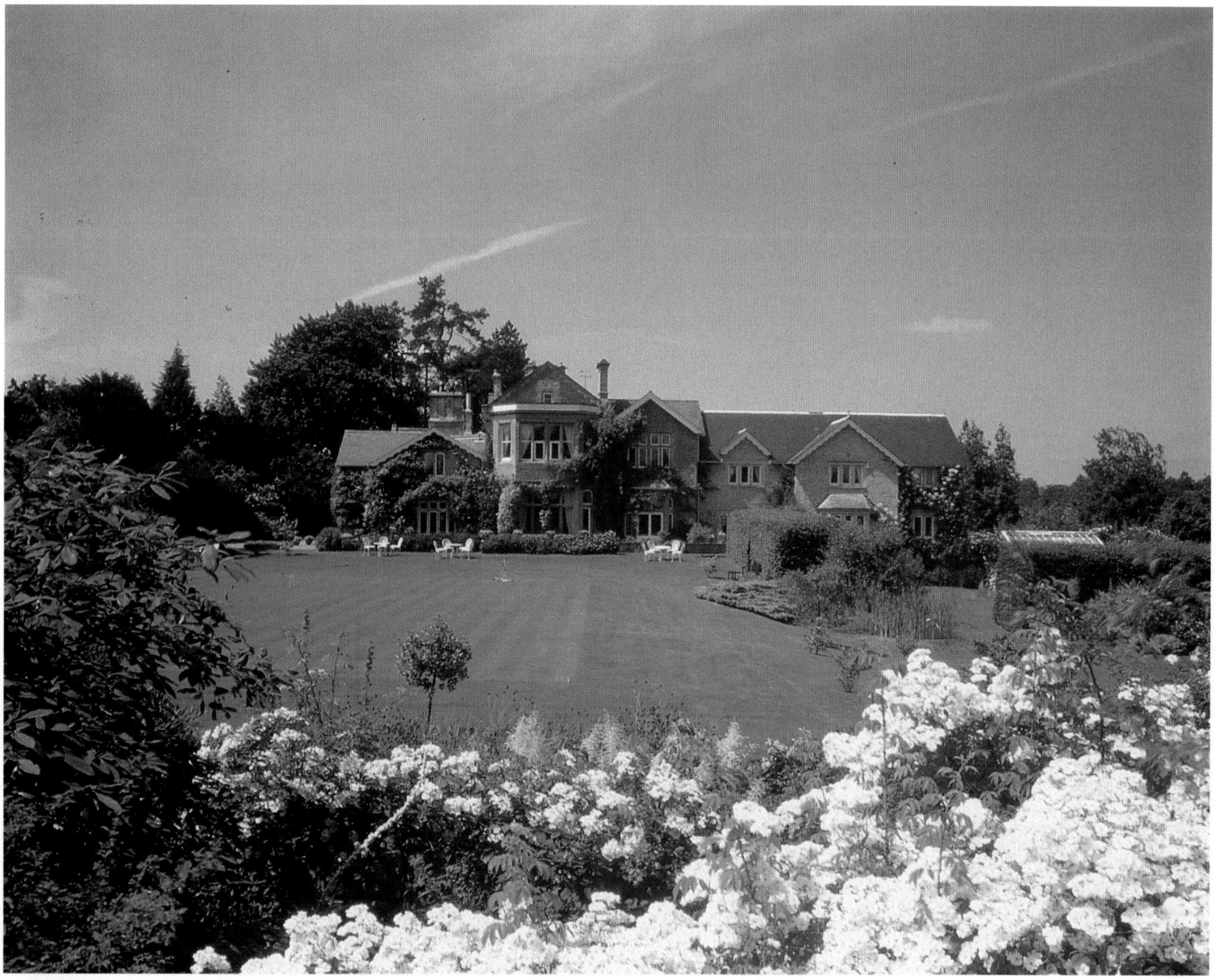

# HOMEWOOD PARK

**HINTON CHARTERHOUSE, BATH, SOMERSET BA3 6BB**
**TEL: 01225 723731 FAX: 01225 723820**

Standing amid 10 acres of beautiful grounds and woodland on the edge of Limpley Stoke Valley, a designated area of natural beauty is Homewood Park, one of Britain's finest privately-owned smaller country house hotels. This lovely 19th century building has an elegant interior, adorned with beautiful fabrics, antiques, oriental rugs and original oil paintings. Lavishly furnished bedrooms offer the best in comfort, style and privacy. Each of them has a charm and character of its own and all have good views over the Victorian garden. The outstanding cuisine has won the hotel an excellent reputation. The à la carte menu uses wherever possible produce both from local suppliers and from Homewood itself. A range of carefully selected wines, stored in the hotel's original mediaeval cellars, lies patiently waiting to augment lunch and dinner. Before or after a meal guests can enjoy a drink in the comfortable bar or drawing rooms, both of which have a log fire during the cooler months. The hotel is well placed for guests to enjoy the varied attractions of the wonderful city of Bath with its unique hot springs, Roman remains, superb Georgian architecture and American Museum. Further afield but within reach are Stonehenge and Cheddar caves. **Directions:** On the A36 six miles from Bath towards Warminster. Price guide: Single £95; double/twin £98–£195; suite from £235.

For hotel location, see maps on pages 490-496

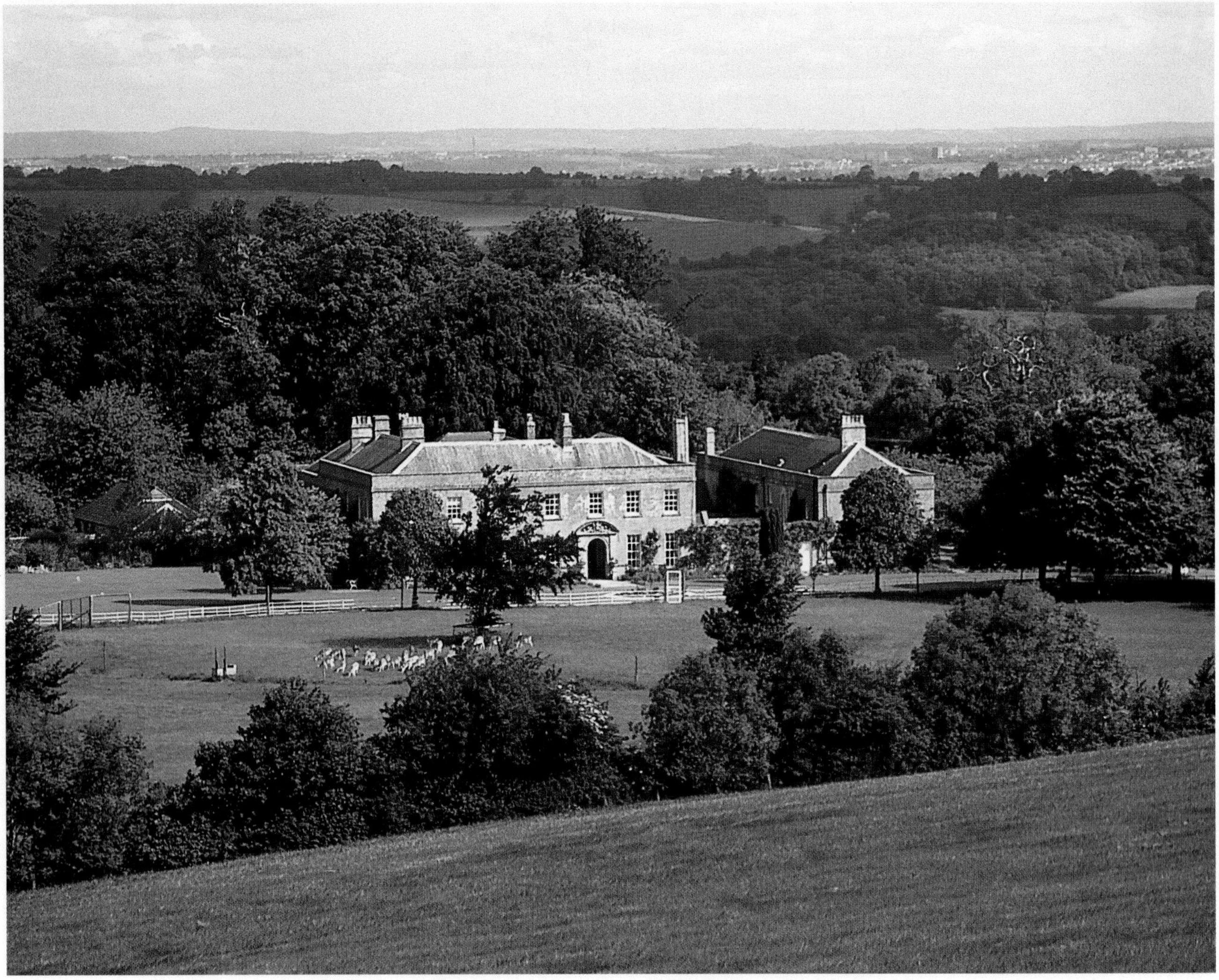

# HUNSTRETE HOUSE

**HUNSTRETE, CHELWOOD, NR BRISTOL, SOMERSET BS18 4NS**
**TEL: 01761 490490 FAX: 01761 490732**

In a classical English landscape on the edge of the Mendip Hills stands Hunstrete House. This unique hotel, surrounded by lovely gardens, is largely 18th century, although the history of the estate goes back to 963AD. Each of the bedrooms is individually decorated and furnished to a high standard, combining the benefits of a hotel room with the atmosphere of a charming private country house. Many offer uninterrupted views over undulating fields and woodlands. The reception areas exhibit warmth and elegance and are liberally furnished with beautiful antiques. Log fires burn in the hall, library and drawing room through the winter and on cooler summer evenings. The Terrace dining room looks out on to an Italianate, flower filled courtyard. A highly skilled head chef offers light, elegant dishes using produce from the extensive garden, along with the best of English meat and fish. The menu changes regularly and the hotel has an excellent reputation for the quality and interest of its wine list. In a sheltered corner of the walled garden there is a heated swimming pool for guests to enjoy. For the energetic, the all weather tennis court provides another diversion and there are riding stables in Hunstrete village, a five minute walk away. **Directions:** From Bath take the A4 towards Bristol and then the A368 to Wells. Price guide: Single from £115; double/twin from £120; suite from £250.

For hotel location, see maps on pages 490-496

# LUCKNAM PARK

COLERNE, NR BATH, WILTSHIRE SN14 8AZ
TEL: 01225 742777 FAX: 01225 743536 E-MAIL: compuservee-mail106312,3342

For over 250 years Lucknam Park has been a focus of fine society and aristocratic living, something guests will sense immediately upon their approach along the mile-long avenue lined with beech trees. Built in 1720, this magnificent Palladian mansion is situated just six miles from Bath on the southern edge of the Cotswolds. The delicate aura of historical context is reflected in fine art and antiques dating from the late Georgian and early Victorian periods. The Michelin-starred cuisine can be savoured in the elegant restaurant, at tables laid with exquisite porcelain, silver and glassware, accompanied with wines from an extensive cellar. Set within the walled gardens of the hotel is the Leisure Spa, comprising an indoor pool, sauna, solarium, steam room, whirlpool spa, gymnasium, beauty salon and snooker room. Numerous activities can be arranged on request, including hot-air ballooning, golf and archery. The Lucknam Park Equestrian Centre, which is situated on the estate, welcomes complete beginners and experienced riders, offers expert tuition from Heather Holgate and it takes liveries. Bowood House, Corsham Court and Castle Combe are all nearby. **Directions:** Fifteen minutes from M4, junctions 17 and 18, located between A420 and A4 near the village of Colerne. Price guide: Single from £130; double/twin from £190; suite from £355. (Room Only)

For hotel location, see maps on pages 490-496

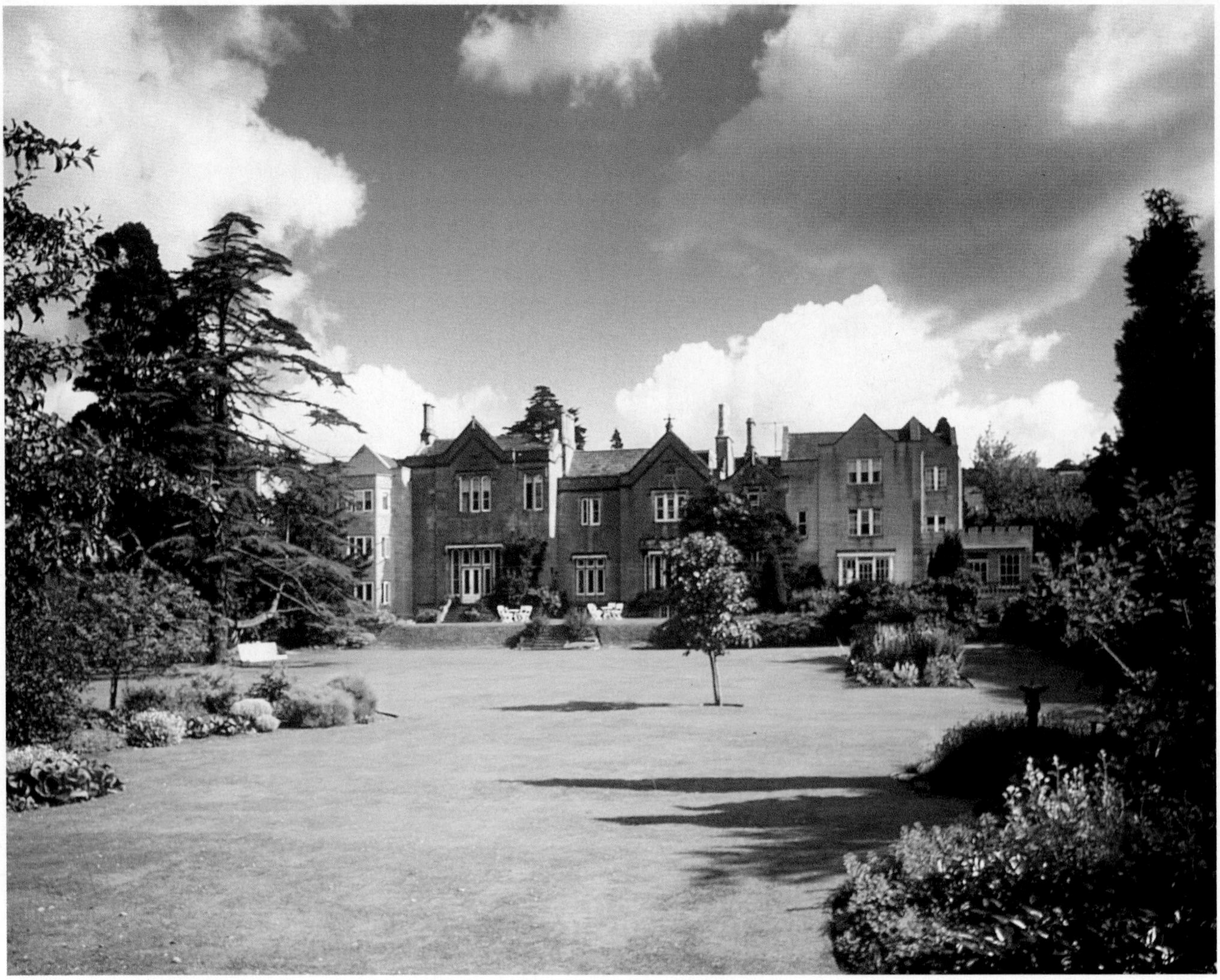

# THE PRIORY

**WESTON ROAD, BATH, SOMERSET BA1 2XT**

**TEL: 01225 331922 FAX: 01225 448276 E-MAIL: 106076.12658@compuserve.com**

Lying in the seclusion of landscaped grounds, The Priory Hotel is close to some of England's most famous and finest architecture. Within walking distance of Bath city centre, this Gothic-style mellow stone building dates from 1835, when it formed part of a row of fashionable residences on the west side of the city. Visitors will sense the luxury as they enter the hotel: antique furniture, plush rugs and *objets d'art* add interest to the two spacious reception rooms and the elegant drawing room. Well-defined colour schemes lend an uplifting brightness throughout, particularly in the tastefully appointed bedrooms. Chef Michael Collom's French classical style is the primary inspiration for the cuisine, served in three interconnecting dining rooms which overlook the garden. An especially good selection of wines can be recommended to accompany meals. Private functions can be accommodated both in the Drawing Room and the Orangery, with garden access an added bonus. The Roman Baths, Theatre Royal, Museum of Costume and a host of bijou shops offer plenty for visitors to see. **Directions:** Leave M4 at junction 18 to Bath on A46. Enter city on A4 London road and follow signs for Bristol. Turn right into Park Lane which runs through Royal Victoria Park. Then turn left into Weston Road. The hotel is on the left. Price guide: Single £120; double/twin £140–£230; junior suites £230.

For hotel location, see maps on pages 490-496

# THE QUEENSBERRY

RUSSEL STREET, BATH, SOMERSET BA1 2QF
TEL: 01225 447928 FAX: 01225 446065

When the Marquis of Queensberry commissioned John Wood to build this house in Russel Street in 1772, little did he know that 200 years hence guests would still be being entertained in these elegant surroundings. An intimate town house hotel, The Queensberry is in a quiet residential street just a few minutes' walk from Wood's other splendours – the Royal Crescent, Circus and Assembly Rooms. Bath is one of England's most beautiful cities. Regency stucco ceilings, ornate cornices and panelling combined with enchanting interior décor complement the strong architectural style. However, the standards of hotel-keeping have far outpaced the traditional surroundings, with high quality en suite bedrooms, room service and up-to-date office support for executives. The Olive Tree Restaurant is one of the leading restaurants in the Bath area. Proprietors Stephen and Penny Ross are thoroughly versed in offering hospitality and a warm welcome. Represented in America by Josephine Barr. The hotel is closed for one week at Christmas. **Directions:** From junction 18 of M4, enter Bath along A4 London Road. Turn sharp right up Lansdown Road, left into Bennett Street, then right into Russel Street opposite the Assembly Rooms. Price guide: Single £89–£110; double/twin £110–£190.

For hotel location, see maps on pages 490-496

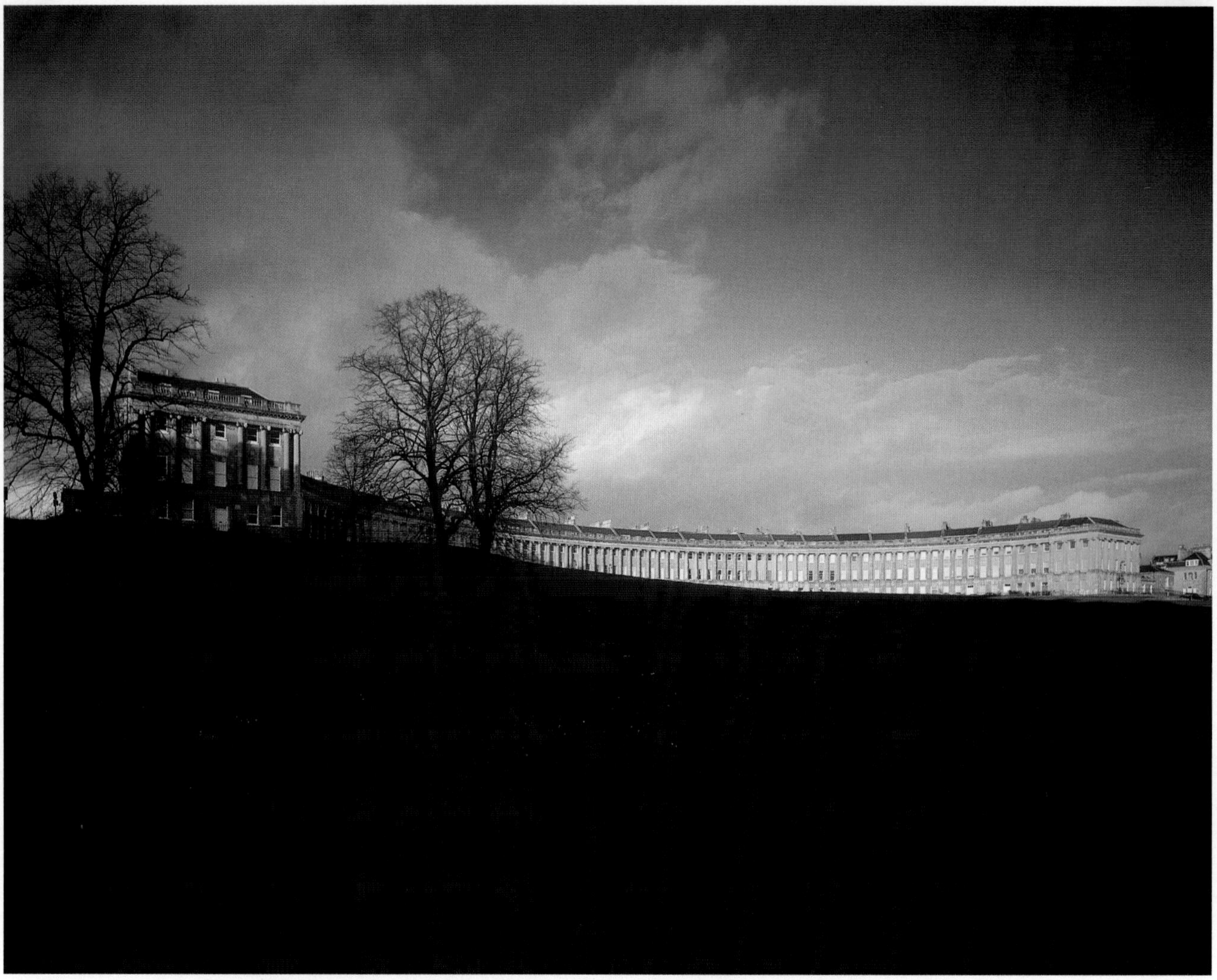

# THE ROYAL CRESCENT

**ROYAL CRESCENT, BATH, SOMERSET BA1 2LS**
**TEL: 01225 823333 FAX: 01225 339401**

The Royal Crescent Hotel, recently given a £2,000,000 restoration, is part of the Royal Crescent, a 500ft curve of 30 houses with identical façades. The Crescent was conceived in the latter part of the 18th century and is one of the greatest European architectural masterpieces. The hotel comprises the two central houses and within its beautiful gardens are The Pavilion, The Garden Villa and The Dower House. The bedrooms are individually decorated to please every taste and each is air-conditioned and has a private fax, voice mail, CD, TV, video and drinks tray. The hotel has two restaurants, their style is eclectic bringing tastes from around the world. Pimpernel's, the smaller more informal restaurant which offers an exceptional dining experience. The Dower House, a grill room with a relaxed atmosphere and garden outlook. This restaurant has received three AA rosettes and an Egon Ronay star. The hotel has peaceful conference facilities in the Royal Crescent Mews. As well as the delights of Bath, the Royal Crescent has acquired a hot air balloon and a 1923 river launch. **Directions:** Detailed directions are available from the hotel on booking. Price guide Single from £160; double/twin from £160; suites £330–£675.

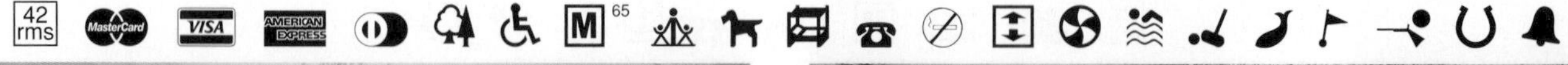

For hotel location, see maps on pages 490-496

# STON EASTON PARK

**STON EASTON, BATH, SOMERSET BA3 4DF**
**TEL: 01761 241631 FAX: 01761 241377 e-MAIL stoneaston@cityscape.co.uk**

The internationally renowned hotel at Ston Easton Park is a Grade I Palladian mansion of notable distinction. A showpiece for some exceptional architectural and decorative features of its period, it dates from 1739 and has recently undergone extensive restoration, offering a unique opportunity to enjoy the opulent splendour of the 18th century. A high priority is given to the provision of friendly and unobtrusive service. The hotel has won innumerable awards for its décor, service and food. Jean Monro, an acknowledged expert on 18th century decoration, supervised the design and furnishing of the interiors, complementing the original features with choice antiques, paintings and *objets d'art.* Fresh, quality produce, delivered from all parts of Britain, is combined with herbs and vegetables from the Victorian kitchen garden to create English and French dishes. To accompany the meal, a wide selection of rare wines and old vintages is stocked in the house cellars. The grounds, landscaped by Humphry Repton in 1793, consist of romantic gardens and parkland. The 17th century Gardener's Cottage, close to the main hotel on the wooded banks of the River Norr, provides private suite accommodation. A Relais et Châteaux member. **Directions:** Eleven miles south of Bath on the A37 between Bath and Wells. Price guide: Single £145; double/twin £185–£380.

21 rms MasterCard VISA AMERICAN EXPRESS M 35 7

For hotel location, see maps on pages 490-496

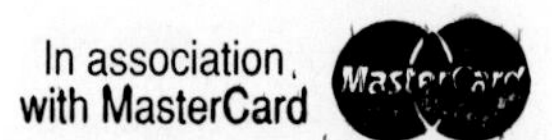

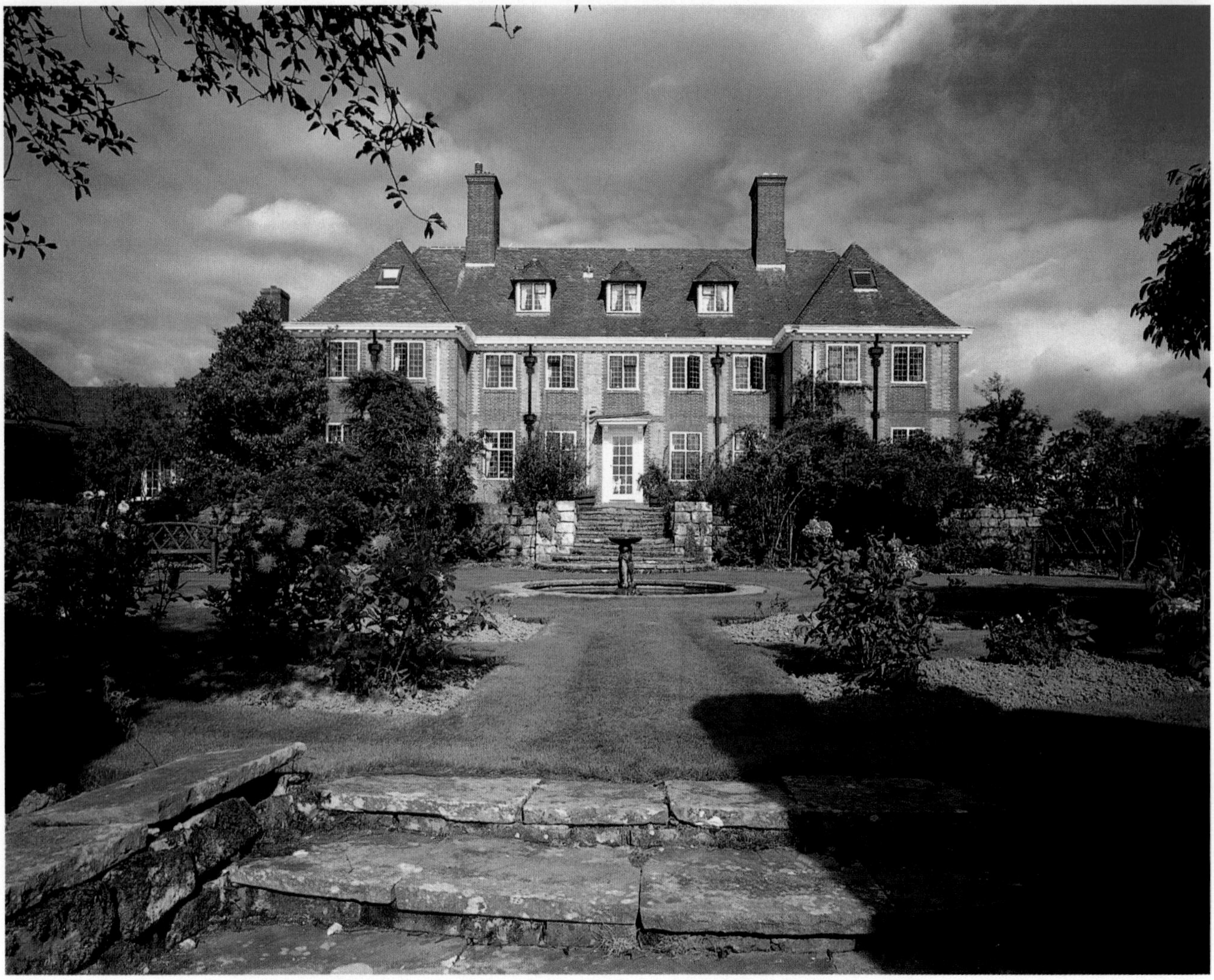

# NETHERFIELD PLACE

**NETHERFIELD HILL, BATTLE, EAST SUSSEX TN33 9PP**
**TEL: 01424 774455 FAX: 01424 774024**

Guests coming to Netherfield Place follow in the footsteps of William the Conqueror who landed nearby in 1066, but today they will be able to stay in style in this splendid country house, surrounded by 30 acres of verdant parkland and elegant gardens. Netherfield is an intimate hotel, with just fourteen spacious bedrooms – each differing from the next and decorated with period furniture and delicate chintz. The bathrooms are charmingly decorated with murals over the tubs. The pleasant lounge, next to the cocktail bar, is peaceful and comfortable, perfect for afternoon tea. On fine days guests may prefer refreshments on the terrace. the air fragrant from the colourful flowers and shrubs. Dining in the spacious restaurant is a pleasure – delicious dishes benefitting from the extensive kitchen garden with its many herbs, unusual fruits and vegetables. The wine list is reasonably priced. The famous Sissinghurst Gardens, and old towns – Rye Bodiam and Hastings – many with castles are close by. Active guests appreciate tennis, croquet and putting at the hotel, with excellent golf courses and trout fishing not far away. Brighton is 30 miles along the coast. Battle is convenient for Glyndebourne and day crossings to France. Directions: Leave M25 on A21, then taking A2100, finding hotel signed just north of Battle. Price guide: Single from £65; double/twin £105–£150.

14 rms · MasterCard · VISA · AMERICAN EXPRESS · M 50

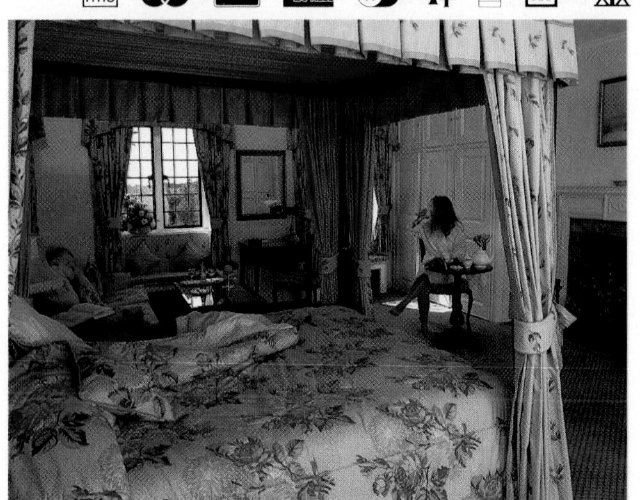

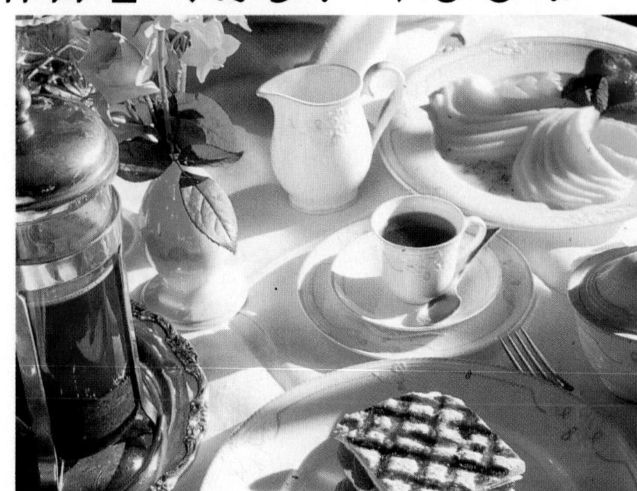

For hotel location, see maps on pages 490-496

# POWDERMILLS HOTEL

POWDERMILL LANE, BATTLE, EAST SUSSEX TN33 0SP
TEL: 01424 775511 FAX: 01424 774540

Situated outside the historic Sussex town famous for the 1066 battle, Powdermills is an 18th century listed country house which has been skilfully converted into an elegant hotel. Nestling in 150 acres of parks and woodland, the beautiful and tranquil grounds feature a 7-acre specimen fishing lake. Wild geese, swans, ducks, kingfishers and herons abound and a rare breed of Scottish sheep grazes nearby. Privately owned and run by Douglas and Julie Cowpland, the hotel has been carefully furnished with locally acquired antiques. On cooler days, log fires burn in the entrance hall and drawing room. The bedrooms – four with four-posters – are all individually furnished and decorated. The Orangery Restaurant has 2 AA rosettes and offers fine classical cooking by chef Paul Webbe. Guests may dine on the terrace in summer, looking out over the swimming pool and grounds. Light meals and snacks are available in the library. The location is ideal from which to explore the beautiful Sussex and Kent countryside and there are many villages and small towns in the area. **Directions:** From centre of Battle take the Hastings road south. After $^{1}/_{4}$ mile turn right into Powdermill Lane. After sharp bend, entrance is on right; cross over bridge and lakes to reach hotel. Price guide: Single from £70; double/twin £85–£150.

For hotel location, see maps on pages 490-496

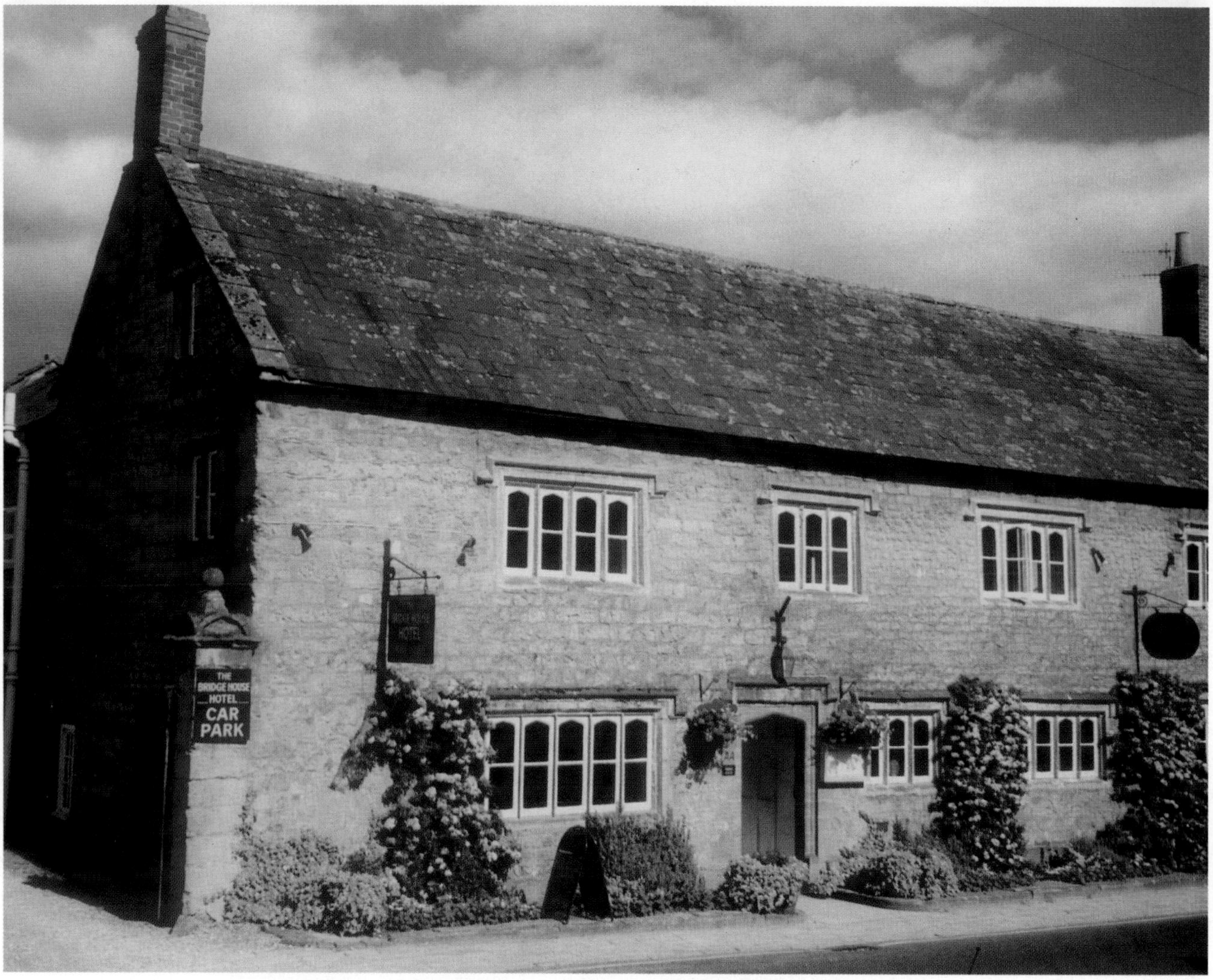

# BRIDGE HOUSE HOTEL

BEAMINSTER, DORSET DT8 3AY
TEL: 01308 862200 FAX: 01308 863700

This country town hotel, built of mellow stone, was once a priest's house and dates back to the 13th century. It is set in the heart of Beaminster, an old market town. In this charming hotel, enclosed by a beautiful walled garden, emphasis is placed on creating a relaxing atmosphere for guests and providing them with the highest standards of comfort without sacrificing the character of the surroundings. The warm stone, beams and large fireplaces combine with every modern day amenity to provide a pleasant environment which visitors will remember. Attractively decorated and furnished bedrooms include a colour television and tea and coffee making facilities. Four of them are on the ground floor and offer easy access. The pride of the house is its food, where attention to detail is evident. In the candle-lit Georgian dining room an imaginative menu offers dishes that make use of fresh produce from the local farms and fishing ports. Beaminster is convenient for touring, walking and exploring the magnificent Dorset countryside. Places of interest nearby include many fine houses and gardens. Several golf courses, fresh and salt water fishing, riding, sailing and swimming in the sea are all within reach. **Directions:** From M3 take A303 Crewkerne exit then A356 through Crewkerne, then A3066 to Beaminster. Hotel is 100 yds from town centre car park, on the left. Price guide Single £58–£76; twin/double £65–£107.

For hotel location, see maps on pages 490-496

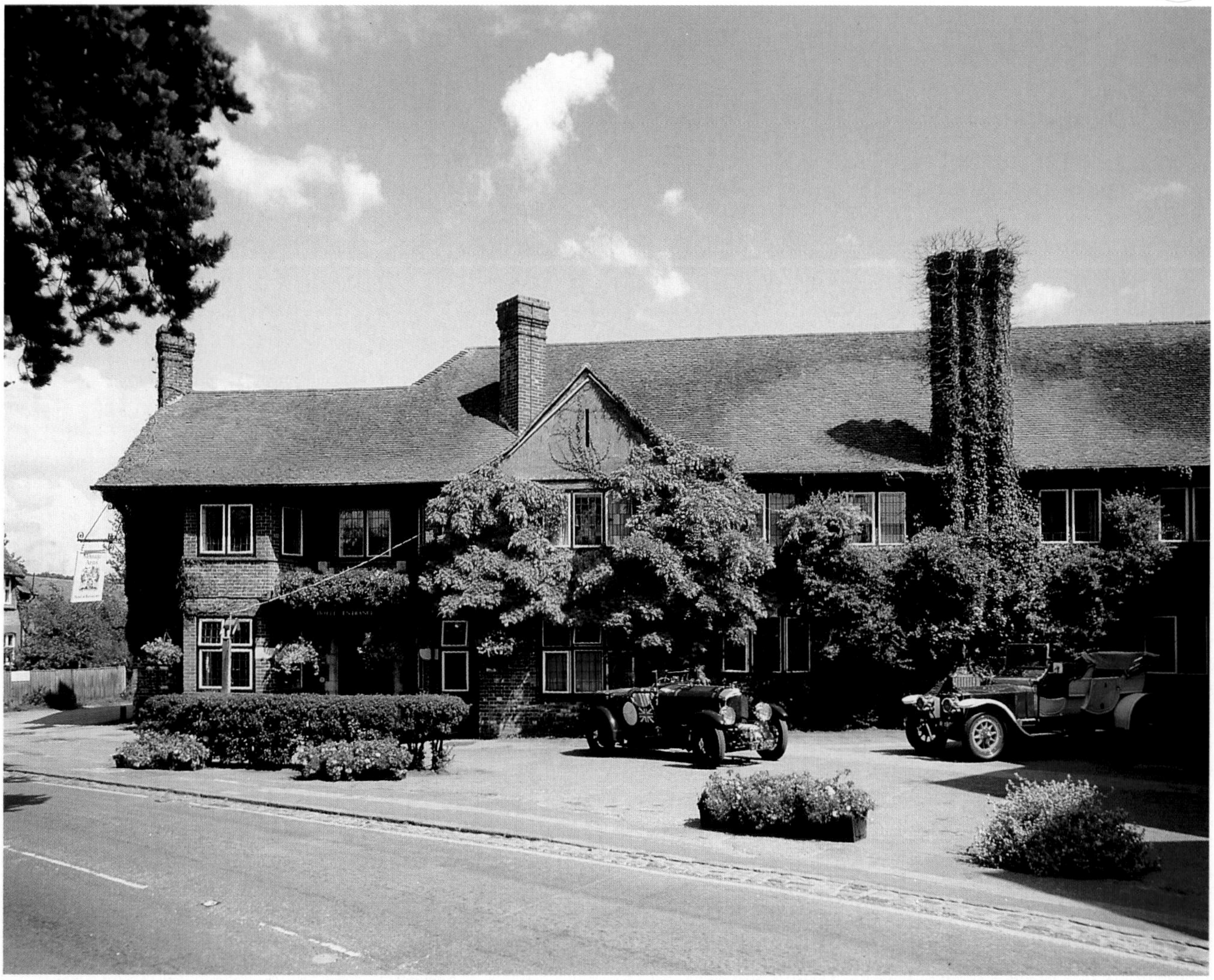

# THE MONTAGU ARMS HOTEL

## BEAULIEU, NEW FOREST, HAMPSHIRE S042 7ZL
## TEL: 01590 612324 FAX: 01590 612188

Situated at the head of the River Beaulieu in the heart of the New Forest, The Montagu Arms Hotel carries on a tradition of hospitality started 700 years ago. As well as being a good place for a holiday, the hotel is an ideal venue for small conferences. Each of the 24 bedrooms has been individually styled and many are furnished with four-poster beds. Choose from sumptuous suites, luxurious junior suites, superior and standard accommodation. All rooms are equipped with colour television, direct-dial telephones, radio and a trouser press. Dine in the oak-panelled restaurant overlooking the garden, where you can enjoy cuisine prepared by award-winning chef Simon Fennell. The menu is supported by an outstanding wine list. The hotel offers complimentary membership of an exclusive health club 6 miles away. Facilities there include a supervised gymnasium, large indoor ozone pool, Jacuzzi, steam room, sauna and beauty therapist. With much to see and do around Beaulieu why not hire a mountain bike? Visit the National Motor Museum, Exbury Gardens or Bucklers Hard, or walk for miles through the beautiful New Forest. Special tariffs are available throughout the year. **Directions:** The village of Beaulieu is well signposted and the hotel commands an impressive position at the foot of the main street. Price guide: Single £69.90–£119.90; double/twin £98.90–£129.90. Inclusive terms available

For hotel location, see maps on pages 490-496

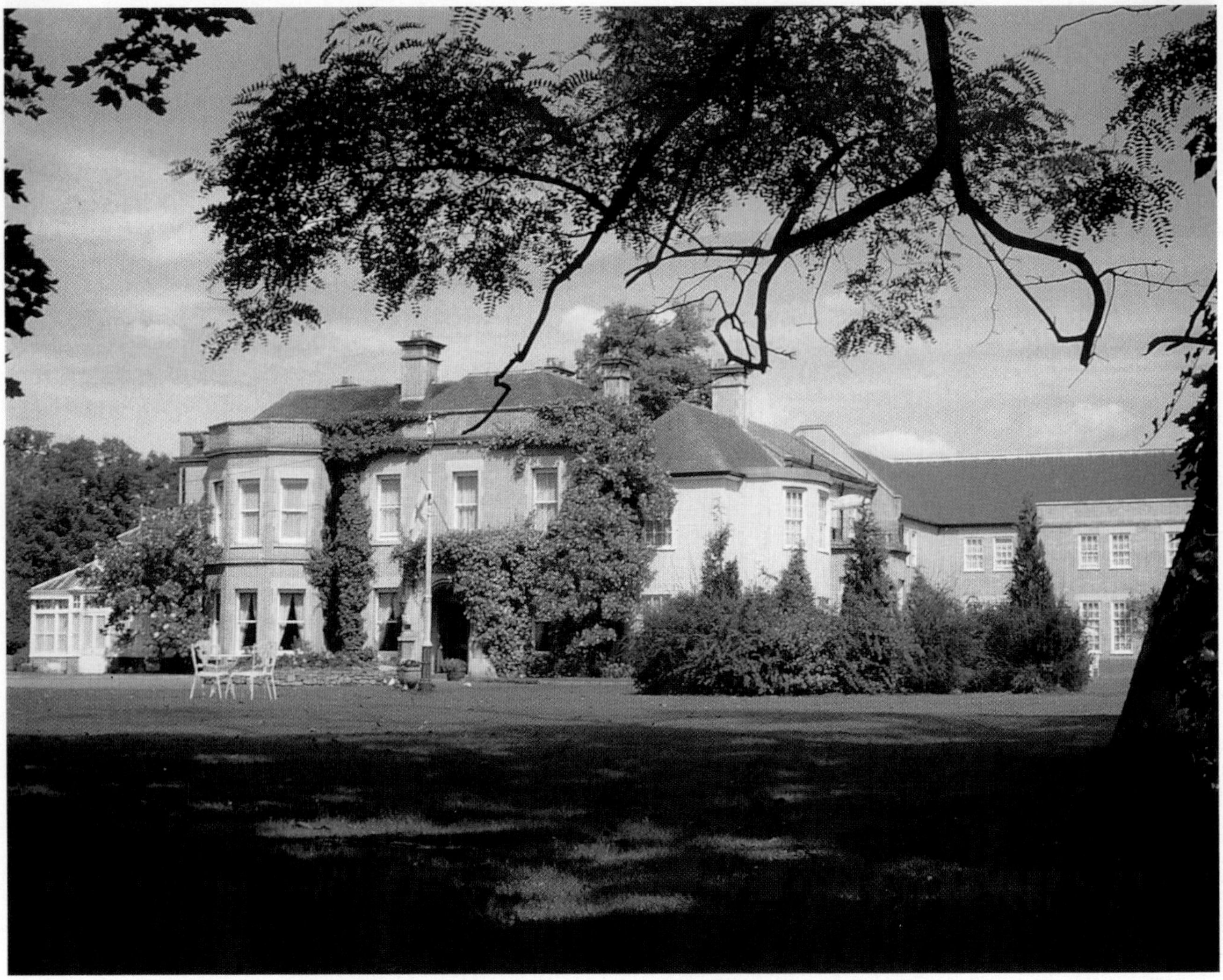

# WOODLANDS MANOR

**GREEN LANE, CLAPHAM, BEDFORD, BEDFORDSHIRE MK41 6EP**
**TEL: 01234 363281 FAX: 01234 272390**

Woodlands Manor is a secluded period manor house, set in acres of wooded grounds and gardens, only two miles from the centre of Bedford. The hotel is privately owned and a personal welcome is assured. In the public rooms, stylish yet unpretentious furnishings preserve the feel of a country house, with open fires in winter. The en suite bedrooms are beautifully decorated and have extensive personal facilities. All have views of the gardens and surrounding countryside. The elegantly proportioned restaurant, once the house's main reception room, provides an agreeable venue for dining. The menus balance English tradition with the French flair for fresh, light flavours, complemented by wines from well-stocked cellars. The private library is well suited to business meetings and intimate dinner parties. Woodlands Manor is conveniently located for touring: the historic centres of Ely, Cambridge and Oxford, all within easy reach, and stately homes such as Woburn Abbey and Warwick Castle are not far away. The hotel is two miles from the county town of Bedford, with its riverside park and the Bunyan Museum. Other places of interest nearby include the RSPB at Sandy and the Shuttleworth Collection of aircraft at Biggleswade. **Directions:** Clapham village is two miles north of the centre of Bedford. Price guide: Single £62.50–£85; double/twin ££85–£97.50.

For hotel location, see maps on pages 490-496

# Marshall Meadows Country House Hotel

**BERWICK-UPON-TWEED, NORTHUMBERLAND TD15 1UT**

**TEL: 01289 331133 FAX: 01289 331438**

Marshall Meadows can truly boast that it is England's most northerly hotel, just a quarter of a mile from the Scottish border, an ideal base for those exploring the rugged beauty of Northumberland. A magnificent Georgian mansion standing in 15 acres of woodland and formal gardens, Marshall Meadows today is a luxurious retreat, with a country house ambience – welcoming and elegant. This is not a large hotel, there are just nineteen bedrooms, each individually designed. Restful harmonious colour schemes, comfortable beds and the tranquillity of its surrounding ensure a good night's sleep! The lounge is delightful, with traditional easy chairs and sofas, overlooking the patio. Ideal for summer afternoon tea. The congenial "Duck & Grouse Bar" stocks forty whiskies and real ale. Marshall Meadows has three restaurants, "The Borderers", a traditional dining room, the candelit "Music Room" overlooking the sea and the intimate panelled "Gallery". Diners enjoy local game, fresh seafood and good wine. The manor has its own burn with a small waterfall, croquet and tennis Excellent golf and historic Berwick-on-Tweed are nearby. **Directions:** A1 heading North, take Berwick by-pass and at Meadow House roundabout, head towards Edinburgh. After 300 yards, turn right, indicated by white sign – hotel is at end of small side road. Price guide: Single £60; double/twin £80.

For hotel location, see maps on pages 490-496

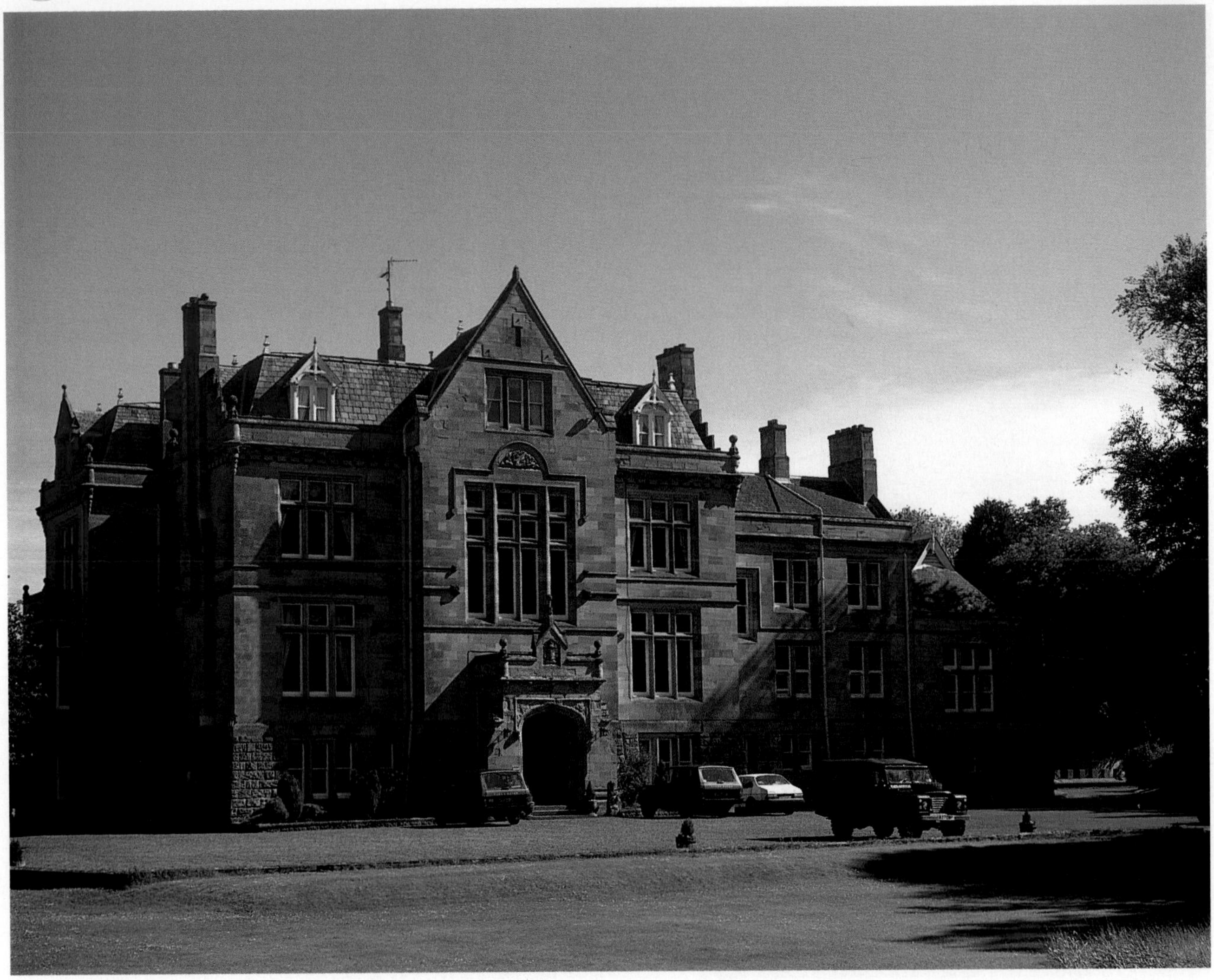

# TILLMOUTH PARK

**CORNHILL-ON-TWEED, NEAR BERWICK-UPON-TWEED, NORTHUMBERLAND TD12 4UU**
**TEL: 01890 882255 FAX: 01890 882540**

Designed by Charles Barry, the son of the famous Victorian architect of the Houses of Parliament in Westminster, Tillmouth Park offers the same warm welcome today as it did when it was an exclusive private country house. It is situated in a rich countryside farmland of deciduous woodland and moor. The generously sized bedrooms have been recently refurbished in a distinctive old fashioned style with period furniture, although all offer modern day amenities. The kitchen prides itself on traditional country fare, with the chef using fresh local produce to create imaginative and well presented dishes. The restaurant serves a fine table d'hôte menu, while the Bistro is less formal. Fresh salmon and game are always available with 24 hours' notice. A well chosen wine list and a vast selection of malt whiskies complement the cuisine. Tillmouth Park is an ideal centre for country pursuits including field sports, fishing, hill walking, shooting, riding, birdwatching and golf. For the spectator there is rugby, curling and horse racing during the season. Places of interest nearby include stately homes such as Floors, Manderston and Paxton. Flodden Field, Lindisfarne and Holy Island are all within easy reach and the coast is just 15 minutes away. **Directions:** Tillmouth Park is on the A698 Cornhill-on-Tweed to Berwick-on-Tweed road. Price guide: Single £80–£95; twin/double £115–£150.

For hotel location, see maps on pages 490-496

# THE SWAN HOTEL AT BIBURY

**BIBURY, GLOUCESTERSHIRE GL7 5NW**
**TEL: 01285 740695 FAX: 01285 740473**

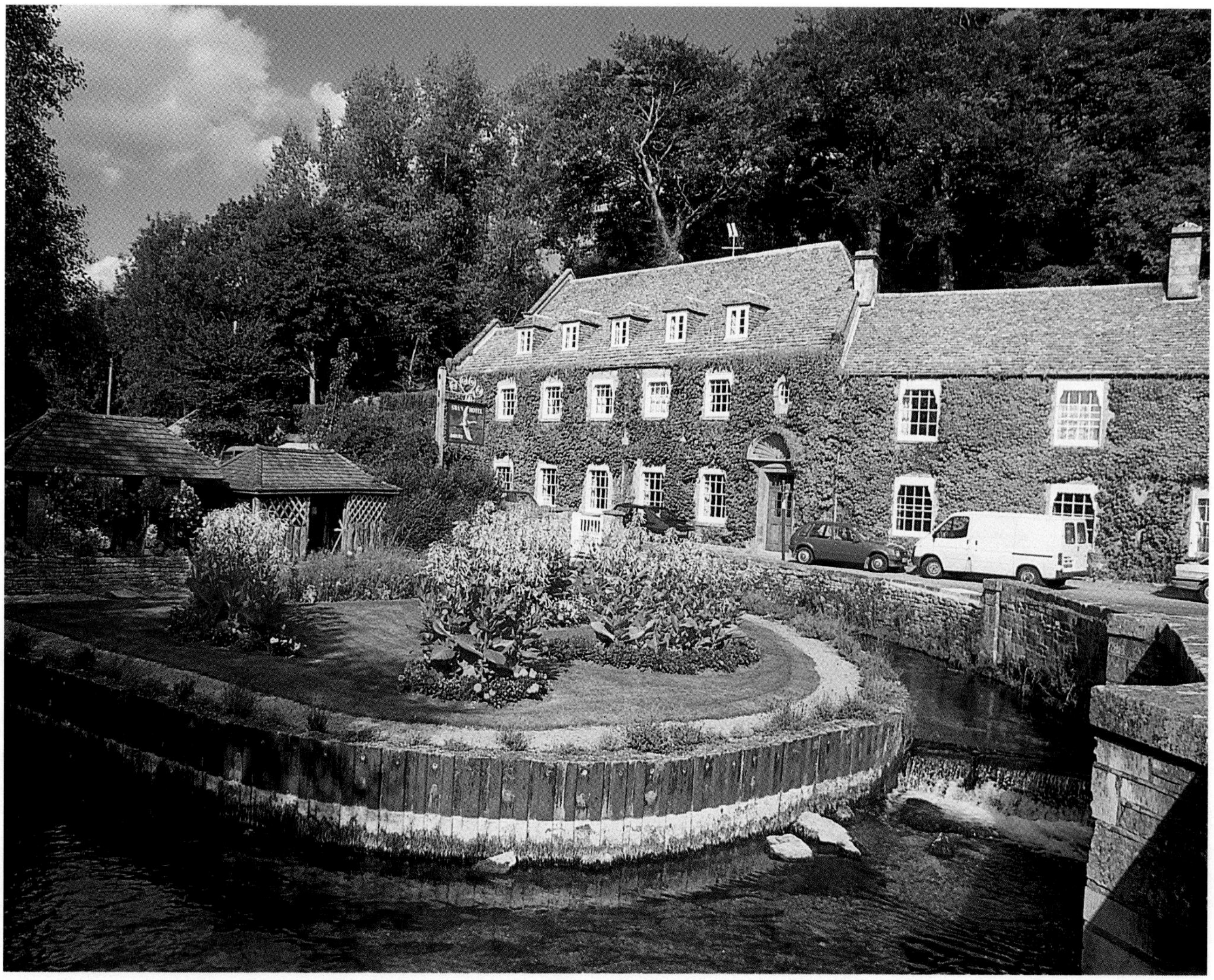

The Swan Hotel at Bibury in the South Cotswolds, a 17th century coaching inn, is a perfect base for both leisurely and active holidays which will appeal especially to motorists, fishermen and walkers. The hotel has its own fishing rights and a moated ornamental garden encircled by its own crystalline stream. Bibury itself is a delightful village, with its honey-coloured stonework, picturesque ponds, the trout filled River Coln and its utter lack of modern eyesores. The beautiful Arlington Row and its cottages are a vision of old England. When Liz and Alex Furtek acquired The Swan, they had the clear intention of creating a distinctive hotel in the English countryside which would acknowledge the needs of the sophisticated traveller of the 1990s. A programme of refurbishment and upgrading of the hotel and its services began with the accent on unpretentious comfort. Oak-panelling, plush carpets and sumptuous fabrics create the background for the fine paintings and antiques that grace the interiors. The 18 bedrooms are superbly appointed with luxury bathrooms and comfortable furnishings. Guests may dine in either the restaurant or the brasserie which serves meals all day. **Directions:** Bibury is signposted off A40 Oxford–Cheltenham road, on the left-hand side. Price guide: Single £86–£119; double/twin £115–£210.

For hotel location, see maps on pages 490-496

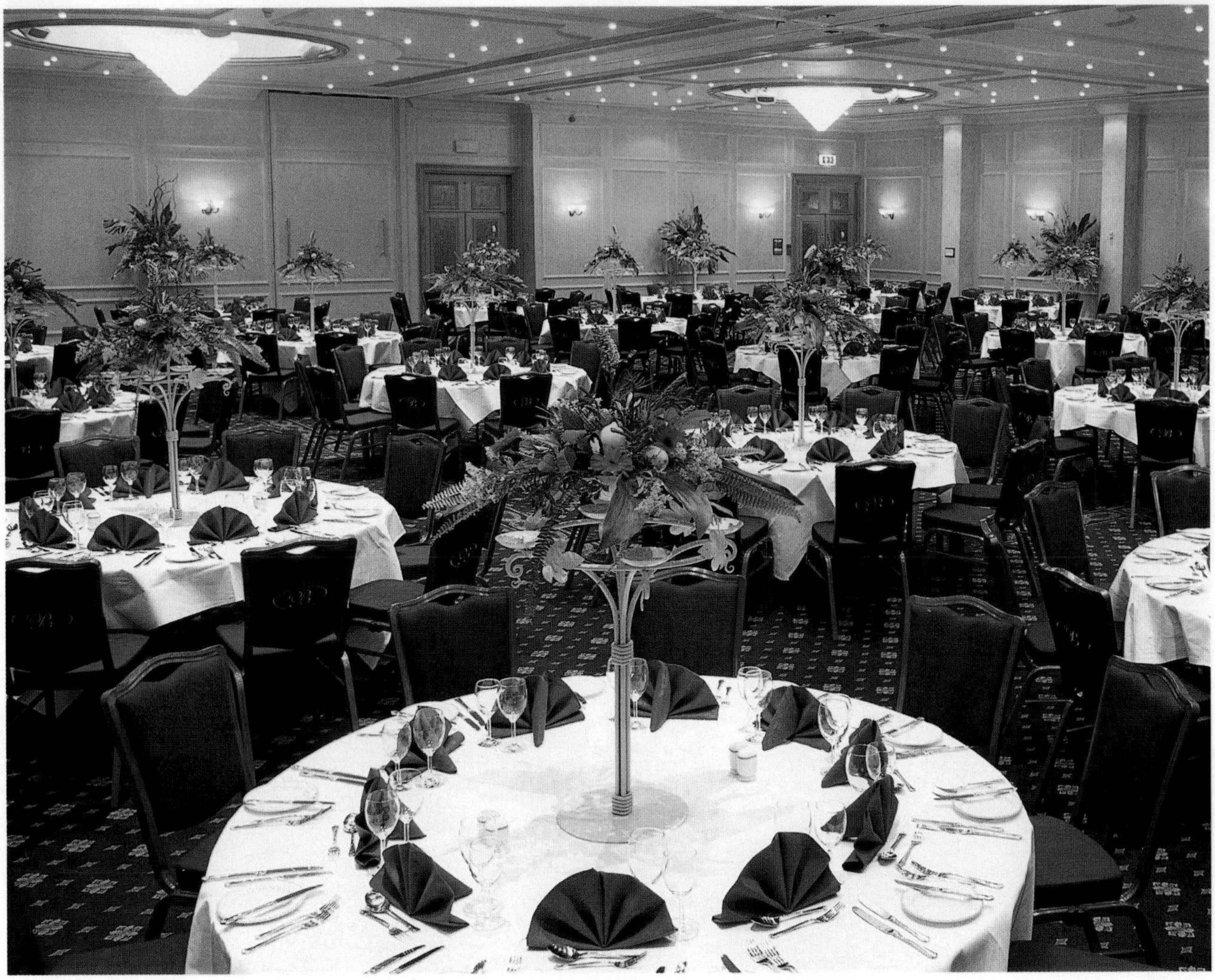

# The Burlington Hotel

**6 BURLINGTON ARCADE, 126 NEW STREET, BIRMINGHAM, WEST MIDLANDS B2 4JQ**
**TEL: 0121 643 9191 FAX: 0121 643 5075 E-MAIL: 100727.2760@compuserve.com**

The Burlington is a new hotel embodying the legendary old Midland Hotel which had played such an important role since its opening in 1871 The original handsome Victorian facade has not been destroyed, only embellished, while skilful restoration has retained much of the historic charm within. The new hotel is in Birmingham's pedestrianised City Centre, approached through an attractive arcade. It is focused on the commercial arena, with a strong emphasis on facilities for conferences and corporate activities. All bedrooms are pleasantly furnished, spacious, well equipped and comfortable, with the extras expected by today's traveller, including fax and modern links, electronic voice mail box and satellite TV. The bathrooms are well designed. On the first floor guests will find the delightful lounge – a peaceful retreat – the traditional bar and the splendid Victorian restaurant with its swathed windows, chandeliers and moulded ceilings. The fifth floor houses the leisure centre. The main function area is self contained, with its own entrance and foyer. Other rooms are ideal for seminars or board meetings. The Burlington is well placed for shopping, the Symphony Hall and just 15 minutes drive from the NEC. **Directions:** Close to New Street Station, 10 minutes from the airport, accessible from the M5, M6, M42. NCP parking. Price guide: Single £116; double/twin £137; suite £237

For hotel location, see maps on pages 490-496

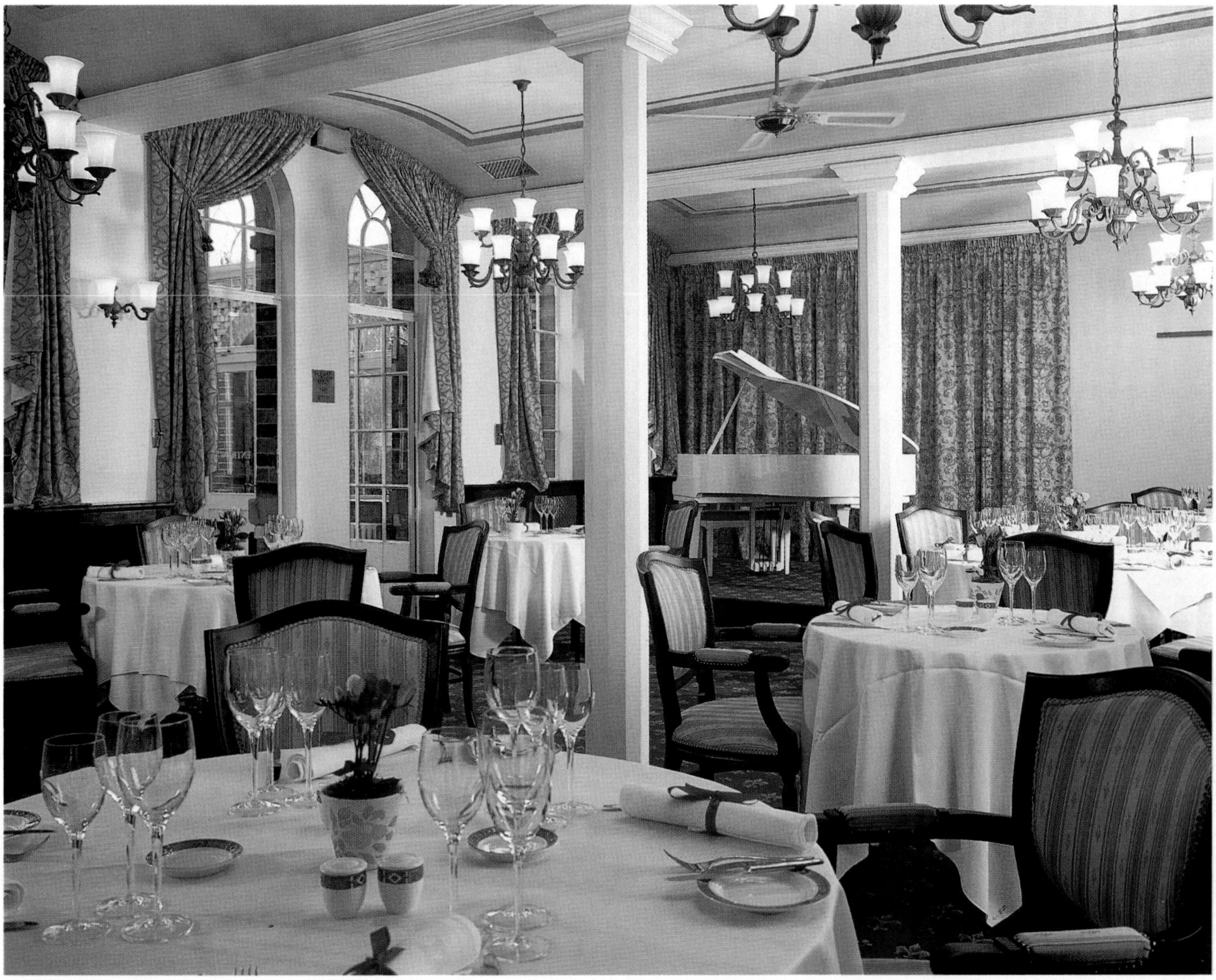

# THE MILL HOUSE HOTEL AND LOMBARD ROOM RESTAURANT

**180 LIFFORD LANE, KING'S NORTON, BIRMINGHAM B30 3NT**
**TEL: 0121 459 5800 FAX: 0121 459 8553**

Situated just 15 minutes away from the city of Birmingham, the Mill House offers the latest up-to-date hospitality to both the leisure guest and business visitor. Owners Anthony Davis and Anthony Morgan pride themselves on providing the highest standards of efficiency and service. Standing in landscaped terraced gardens complete with a small indoor heated swimming pool, the hotel provides luxuriously appointed accommodation. Each of the nine superb, beautifully decorated bedrooms has en suite marble bathrooms, colour television, mini bars, bath robes, mineral water and fresh fruit. Chef Anthony Morgan serves a tempting selection of English and continental specialities in the elegantly refurbished Lombard Room restaurant which is re-establishing its reputation as one of Birmingham's finest dining areas. Alternatively, guests can enjoy a light lunch or host a pre-dinner reception in the relaxing atmosphere of the spacious Victorian conservatory. Mill House also has excellent conference facilities for up to 20 delegates. **Directions:** From M42, exit at junction 3 onto A435 until Maypole Island, left King's Norton until the Poacher's Pocket, 2nd left Broadmeadow Lane just over bridge on left. Price guide: Single £95; double/twin £105; suite £125-£150. Special weekend breaks available.

For hotel location, see maps on pages 490-496

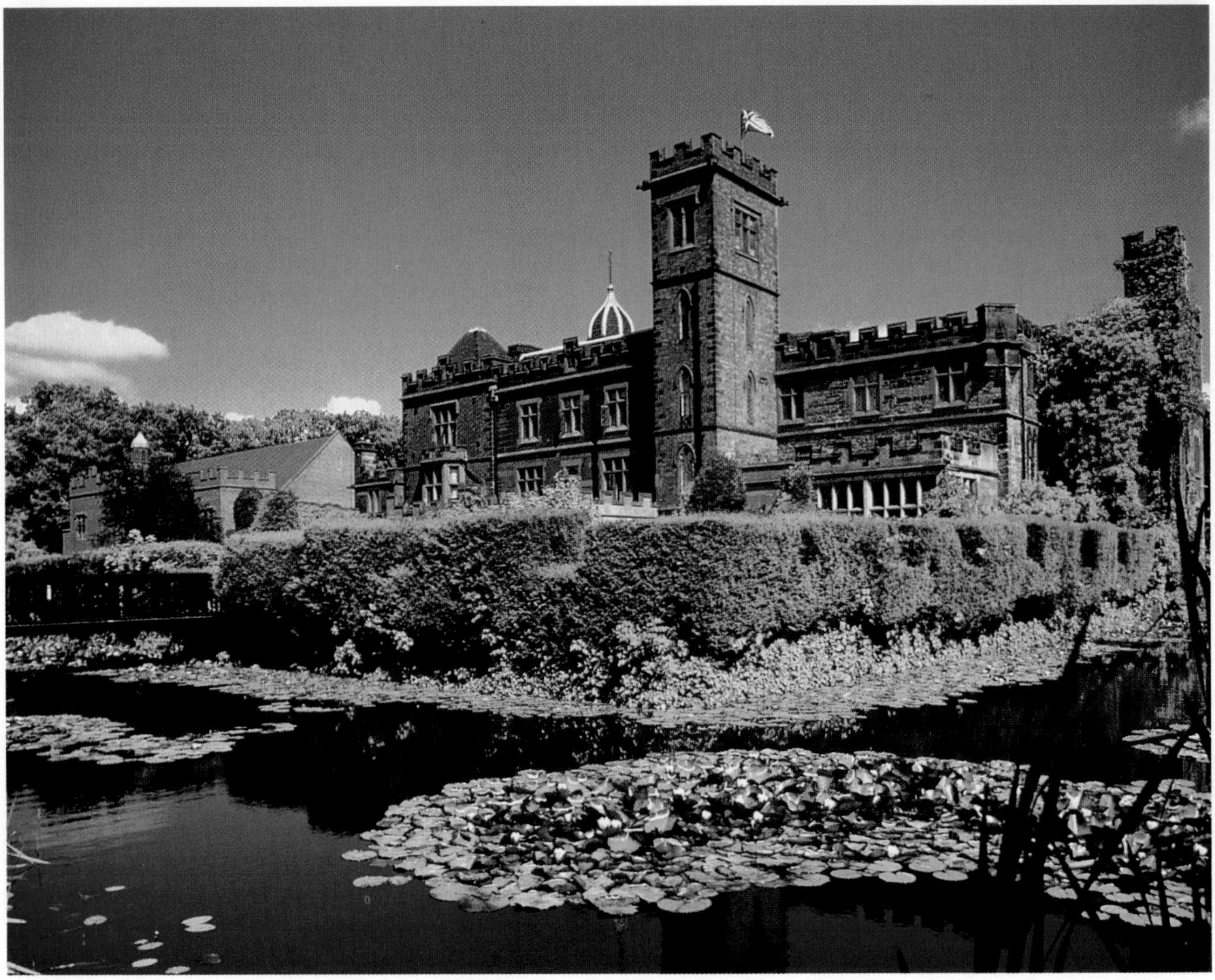

# NEW HALL

**WALMLEY ROAD, ROYAL SUTTON COLDFIELD, WEST MIDLANDS B76 1QX**
**TEL: 0121 378 2442 FAX: 0121 378 4637**

Set in 26 acres of private gardens and surrounded by a lily-filled moat, New Hall dates from the 12th century and is reputedly the oldest fully moated manor house in England. This prestigious hotel offers a warm welcome to both the discriminating business visitor and leisure guest. Much acclaimed, New Hall proudly holds the coveted RAC Blue Ribbon Award, for seven years, AA 4 Red stars and AA Inspectors' Hotel of the Year for England 1994. New Hall joins the elite band of De luxe Hotels with an Egon Ronay 80% rating, the highest in the West Midlands. The cocktail bar and adjoining drawing room overlook the terrace from which a bridge leads to the yew topiary, orchards and sunlit glades. Individually furnished bedrooms and suites offer every modern comfort and amenity with lovely views. A new 9-hole golf course is available for guests' use. Surrounded by a rich cultural heritage, New Hall is convenient for Lichfield Cathedral, Warwick Castle, Stratford-upon-Avon, the NEC and the ICC in Birmingham (only seven miles away). The Belfry Golf Centre is also nearby. Details of champagne weekend breaks, opera, ballet and wine weekends are available on request. **Directions:** From exit 9 of M42, follow A4097 (ignoring signs to A38 Sutton Coldfield). At B4148 turn right at the traffic lights. New Hall is one mile on the left. Price guide: Single £105–£135; double/twin £120–£165; suite £175–£300.

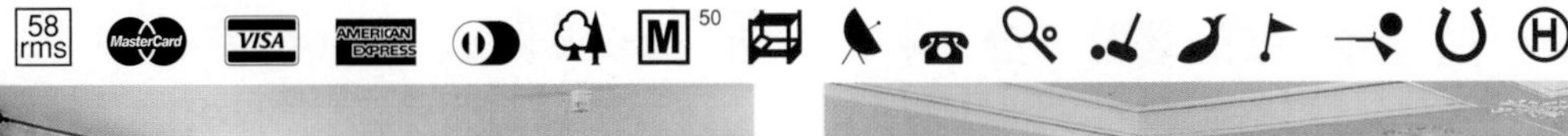

For hotel location, see maps on pages 490-496

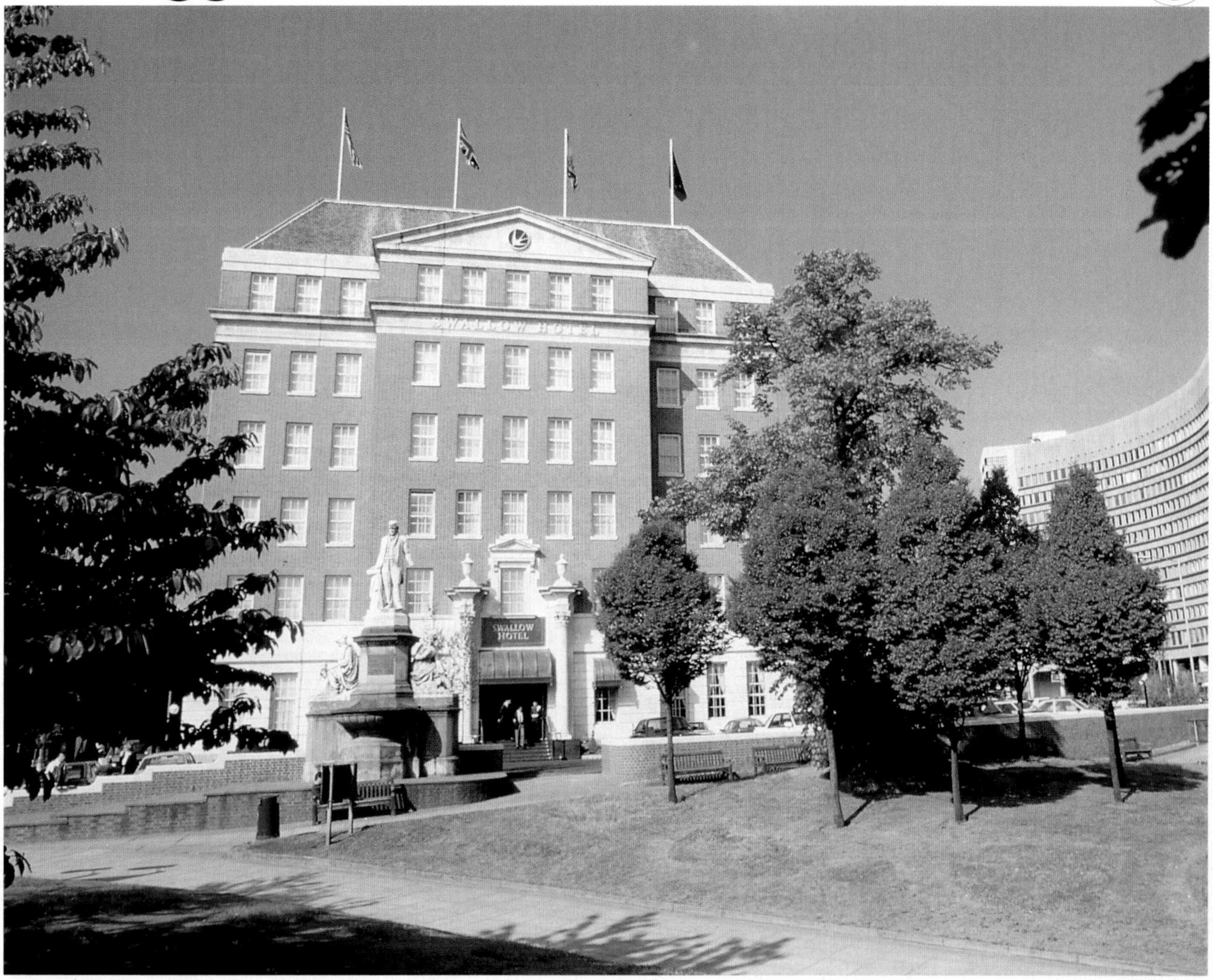

# The Swallow Hotel

12 HAGLEY ROAD, FIVEWAYS, BIRMINGHAM B16 8SJ
TEL: 0121 452 1144 FAX: 0121 456 3442

As soon as it opened, this very special hotel became the first in the Midlands to achieve five stars and since then it has won innumerable awards. These include the Caterer and Hotelkeeper's 'Hotel of the Year 1992', AA Courtesy and Care award and five AA Stars. Two of the most highly regarded other accolades have been received – English Tourist Board 'England for Excellence Award' 1993 (the Lanesborough in 1992 and the Chewton Glen in 1991) and more recently Johansens 'City Hotel of the Year' 1994. Awards, however, do not give the whole picture. The Swallow Hotel offers business and leisure travellers an oasis of calm and warm hospitality in a fascinating and culturally diverse city. Service and surroundings are quite outstanding. Ninety eight luxuriously comfortable bedrooms and suites offer all one would expect from a hotel of this calibre. Dining is memorable whether in the Sir Edward Elgar Restaurant or in Langtry's which warrant an Egon Ronay 'Star' and three AA Rosettes: traditional afternoon tea in the Drawing Room is a favourite indulgence with all guests. Nowhere is luxury more apparent than in the Swallow Leisure Club with its theme of Ancient Egypt – including hieroglyphics. **Directions:** Fiveways roundabout – junction 1 (M5) 5 miles, junction 6 (M6) 5½ miles. Price guide from: Single £140; double/twin £160; suite from £299.

98 rms

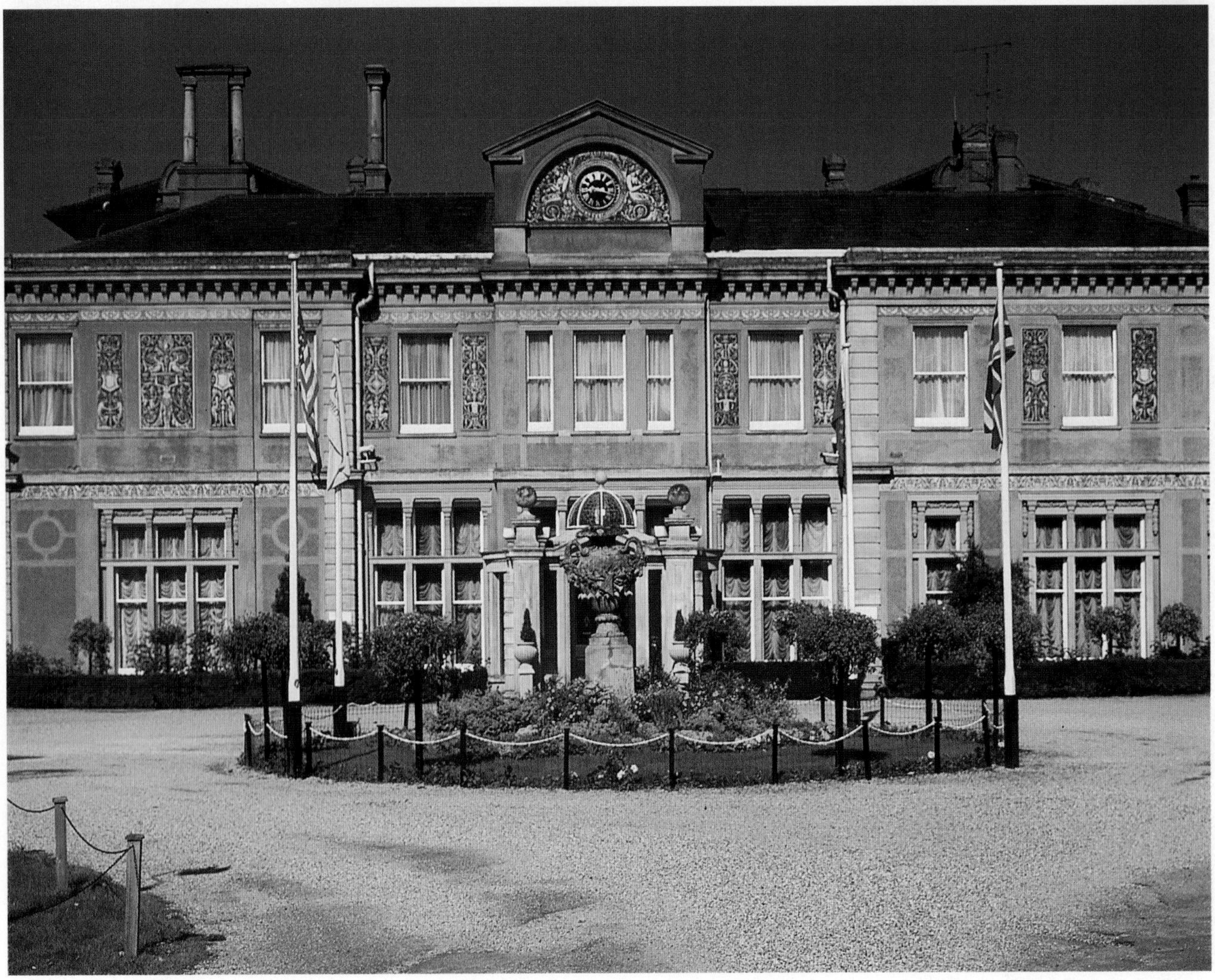

# DOWN HALL COUNTRY HOUSE HOTEL

**HATFIELD HEATH, NR BISHOP'S STORTFORD, HERTFORDSHIRE CM22 7AS**
**TEL: 01279 731441 FAX: 01279 730416 E-MAIL: 101703.2450@COMPUSERVE.COM**

Down Hall, a magnificent Italian-style mansion set in over 100 acres of woodland, park and landscaped gardens. The hotel is a splendid example of quality Victorian craftmanship, with superb attention to detail throughout. The well-proportioned bedrooms have antique-style inlaid mahogany furniture and brass chandeliers. Italian granite is an opulent feature of the luxurious en suite bathrooms. The public rooms feature fine furnishings, with high ceilings, crystal chandeliers and stunning views of the gardens. There are two restaurants, offering English and international cuisine, with a wide selection superb dishes. For conferences, there are 26 meeting rooms, including 16 purpose-built syndicate rooms. Indoor and outdoor leisure facilities include a heated pool, whirlpool, sauna, croquet and putting lawns, giant chess, tennis courts and a fitness trail. Down Hall is within easy access of London and of Stansted Airport. For excursions, Cambridge, Constable country and the old timbered village of Thaxted are all within a few miles. **Directions:** Exit at junction 7 of M11. Follow the A414 towards Harlow. At the 4th roundabout follow the B183 to Hatfield Heath. Bear right towards Matching Green and the hotel is 1.3 miles on the right. Price guide: Single £103; double/twin £144.

For hotel location, see maps on pages 490-496

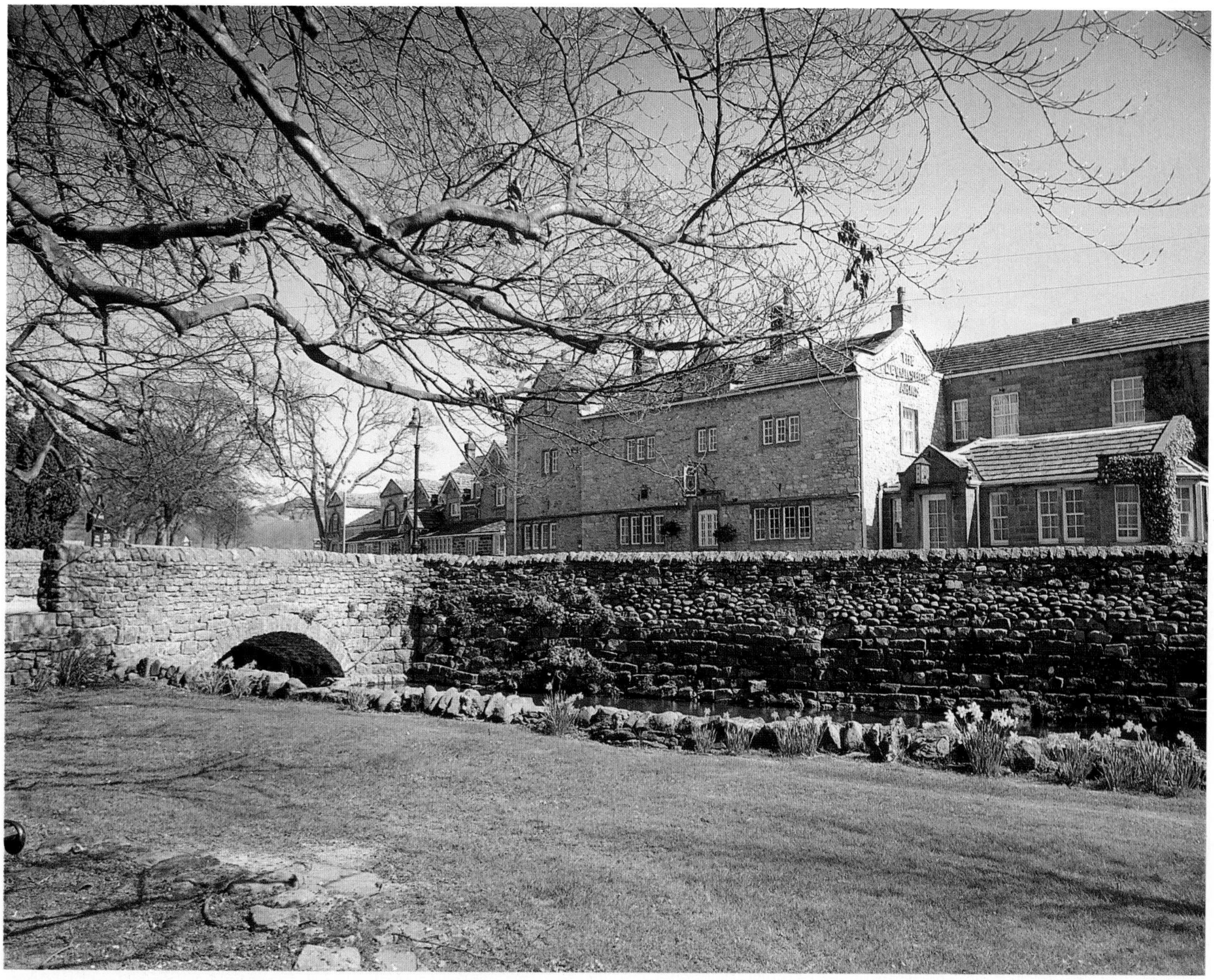

# THE DEVONSHIRE ARMS COUNTRY HOUSE HOTEL

**BOLTON ABBEY, SKIPTON, NORTH YORKSHIRE BD23 6AJ**
**TEL: 01756 710441 FAX: 01756 710564**

The Devonshire reflects its charming setting in the Yorkshire Dales: a welcome escape from a busy and crowded world, peace and quiet, beauty, and the perfect place to relax. The hotel is owned by the Duke and Duchess of Devonshire and is set in 12 acres of parkland on their Bolton Abbey estate, in the Yorkshire Dales National Park. Many antiques and paintings from Chatsworth in the public rooms and bedrooms (several of which are themed) add to the country house atmosphere, which is complemented by excellent service and an award-winning restaurant. As well as a wide choice of outdoor activities and themed or activity breaks, The Devonshire Club is adjacent to the hotel and offers a full range of leisure, health and beauty therapy facilities including: heated indoor swimming pool, steam room, sauna, spa bath, cold water plunge pool, high-powered sunbed, fully equipped gymnasium, beauty therapy rooms – staffed by "Clarins" trained therapists – health and relaxation treatments. In addition to the highest ETB rating (5 Crowns De Luxe), three AA Red Stars and two Rosettes the Devonshire is a member of 'Small Luxury Hotels of the World'. **Directions:** Off the A59 Skipton–Harrogate road at junction with the B6160. Price guide: Single £100–£170; double/twin £140–£220; suite £250–£275.

For hotel location, see maps on pages 490-496

# NORFOLK ROYALE HOTEL

**RICHMOND HILL, BOURNEMOUTH, DORSET BH2 6EN**
**TEL: 01202 551521 FAX: 01202 299729**

Bournemouth has long been a popular seaside resort and has not lost its unique character – The Norfolk Royale is a fine example of the elegant buildings that grace the town. It is a splendid Edwardian house, once the holiday home of the Duke of Norfolk, after whom it is named. Extensive restoration work throughout the hotel, while enhancing its comfort, has not eliminated the echoes of the past and new arrivals are impressed by the elegant furnishings and courtesy of the staff. Luggage is whisked away, cars are parked – life is instantly easier! The designs of the spacious bedrooms reflect consideration for lady travellers, non-smokers and the disabled. The rich fabrics of the delightful colour schemes contribute to their luxurious ambience. Guests relax in the lounge or attractive club bar, in summer enjoying the gardens or patio – all with waiter service – and delicious breakfasts, lunches and candle-lit dinners are served in the Orangery Restaurant, which has an excellent wine list. The good life includes the pleasures of a pool and spa while Bournemouth offers golf courses, tennis, water sports, a casino and theatre. It has a large conference and exhibition centre.Poole Harbour, The New Forest, Thomas Hardy country and long sandy beaches are nearby. **Directions:** From the M27, A31 & A338 find the hotel on the right, half way down Richmond Hill approaching the town centre. Price guide: Single £98–£105; double/twin £125–£165; suite £175–£330.

95 rms

For hotel location, see maps on pages 490-496

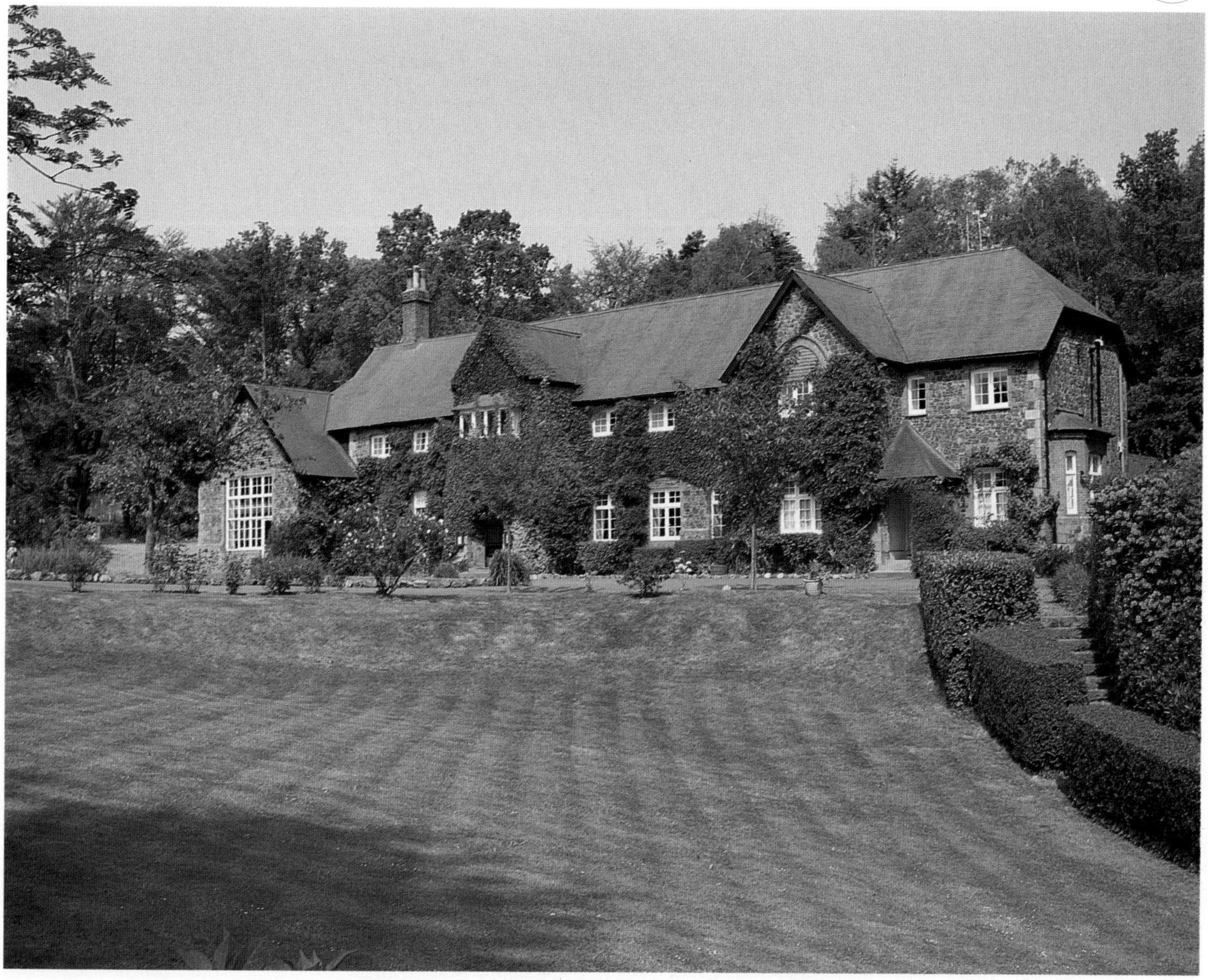

# THE EDGEMOOR

## HAYTOR ROAD, BOVEY TRACEY, SOUTH DEVON TQ13 9LE

**TEL: 01626 832466 FAX: 01626 834760 E-MAIL: edgemoor@btinternet.com**

Built in 1870, The Edgemoor Country House Hotel, owned and managed by Rod and Pat Day, stands in a peaceful location in two acres of grounds literally on the eastern boundary of the Dartmoor National Park. There are 12 charming bedrooms, two of which are on the ground floor. All have en suite bathrooms and some have four-poster beds. The public rooms look over the hotel grounds and provide comfortable and sophisticated surroundings in which guests enjoy their stay. In the restaurant, awarded 2 AA rosettes, chef Edward Elliott prepares modern English and French cuisine using local produce whenever possible. The wine list offers an interesting and varied selection. Children are welcome and a special high-tea is provided for them. With the hotel's close proximity to Dartmoor, walkers and naturalists are well catered for. Shooting, fishing and riding can be arranged locally. The Edgemoor is also a good touring base for the West Country. Worth a visit are Castle Drogo, Becky Falls and Haytor. **Directions:** On leaving the M5, join the A38 in the direction of Plymouth. At Drumbridges roundabout, take A382 towards Bovey Tracey. At the second roundabout turn left and, after approximately 1/2 mile, fork left at the sign for Haytor. Price guide: Single £46.50–£52.50; double/twin £75.95–£99.95.

For hotel location, see maps on pages 490-496

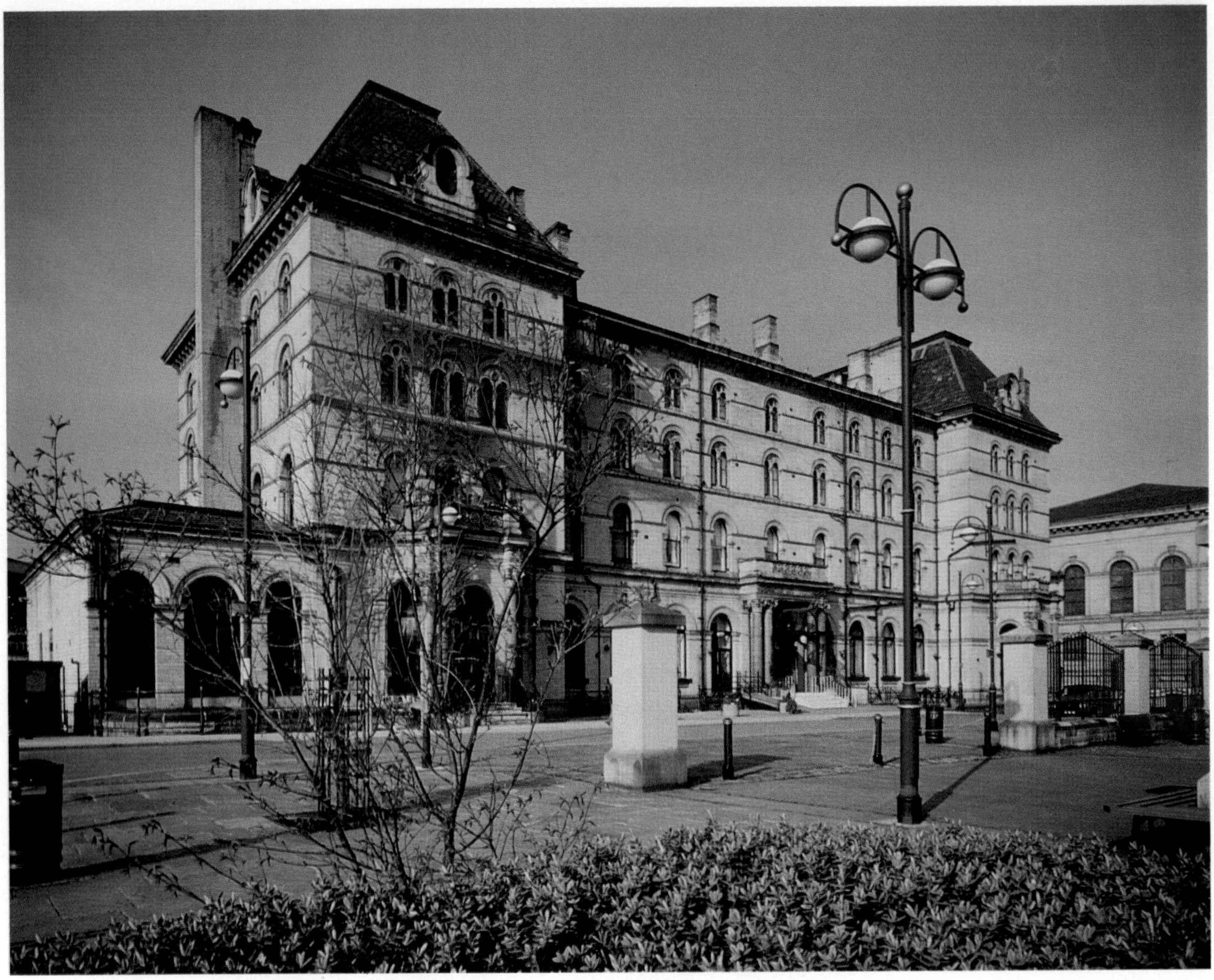

# The Victoria Hotel

**BRIDGE STREET, BRADFORD, WEST YORKSHIRE BD1 1JX**

**TEL: 01274 728706 FAX: 01274 736358**

Built as the showpiece of the Lancashire and Yorkshire railway in 1875, The Victoria has been totally restored and refreshed since its purchase in January 1995 by the owners of the award-winning 42 The Calls in Leeds. Emphasis has been placed on producing an outstandingly comfortable hotel, but with service scaled down to keep room rates substantially below other hotels with comparable comforts. The bedrooms all have stereos, video players, trouser presses, hairdryers and superb bathrooms with power showers. Vic and Bert's Restaurant is a modern interpretation of a Parisian Brasserie with a selection of dishes prepared under the supervision of Bradford's only Michelin starred chef. The excellent facilities include a small gym and sauna, The Pie Eyed Parrot Pub and a beautiful banqueting room for special events. Bradford is a base from which to visit Herriot country and the Brontë parsonage, whilst the world-famous National Museum of Film, Photography and Television and the Alhambra Theatre are within walking distance. **Directions:** From M62 take junction 26 onto the M606, then the A6177 and A64. At end of dual carriageway take right exit at roundabout to Hall Ings. Turn right at traffic lights and the hotel is on the left. Price guide: Single £69–£99; double/twin £69–£99; suites £99–£109. Exceptional rates for week-ends and Summer Breaks

For hotel location, see maps on pages 490-496

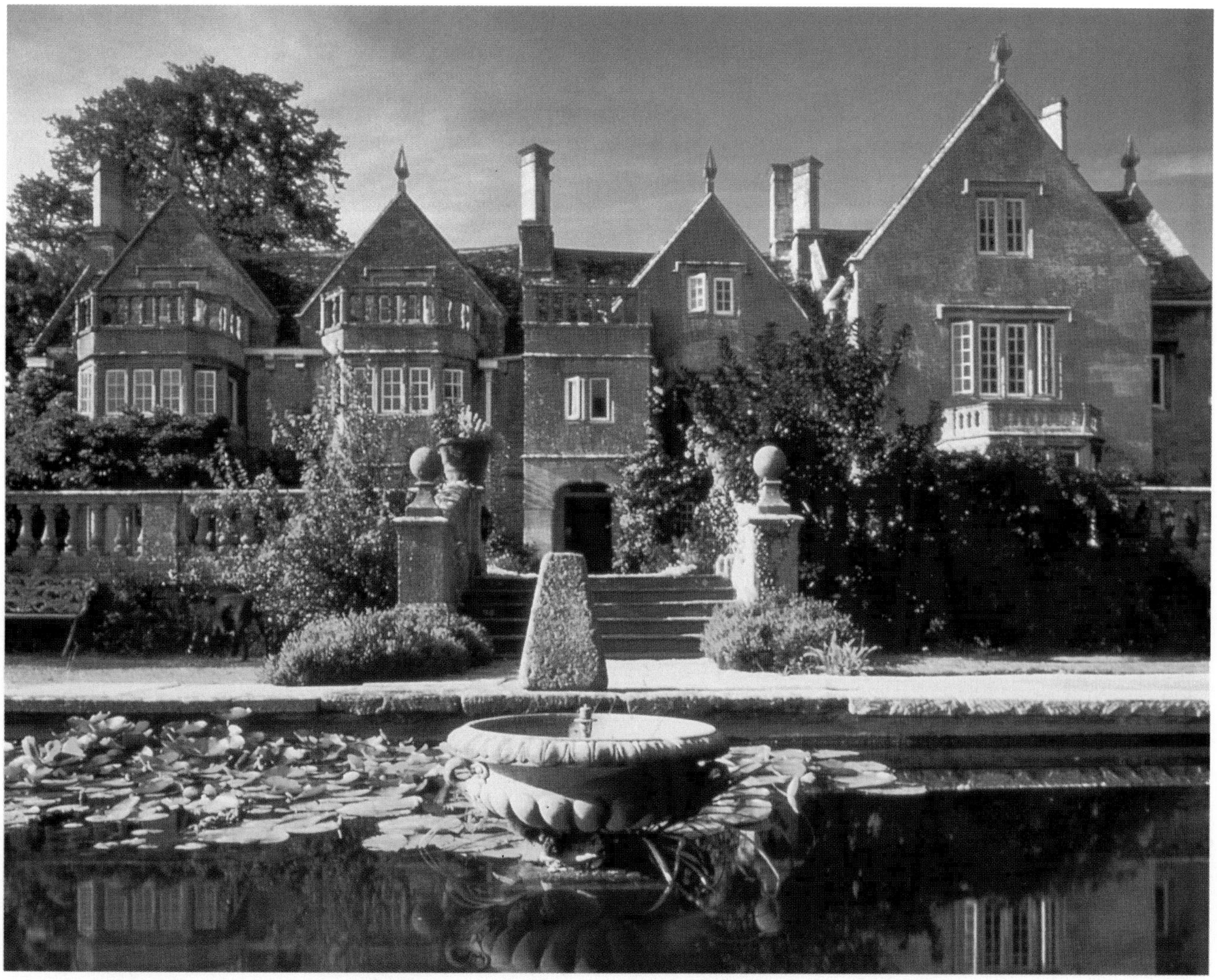

# WOOLLEY GRANGE

**WOOLLEY GREEN, BRADFORD-ON-AVON, WILTSHIRE BA15 1TX**
**TEL: 01225 864705 FAX: 01225 864059 E-MAIL: Woolley@cityscape.com.uk**

Woolley Grange is a 17th century Jacobean stone manor house set in 14 acres of formal gardens and paddocks. Standing on high ground, it affords southerly views of the White Horse at Westbury and beyond. Furnished with flair and an air of eccentricity, the interior décor and paintings echo the taste of owners Nigel and Heather Chapman. Woolley Grange has gained a reputation for outstanding cuisine. Using local farm produce and organically grown fruit and vegetables from the Victorian kitchen gardens, the chef has created a sophisticated style of country house food which aims to revive the focus on flavours. Children are particularly welcome; the owners have four of their own and they do not expect their young visitors to be 'seen but not heard'. In the Victorian coach house there is a huge games room and a well-equipped nursery with a full-time nanny available to look after guests' children 10am–6pm every day. A children's lunch and tea are provided daily. Nearby attractions include medieval Bradford-on-Avon, Georgian Bath, Longleat and prehistoric Stonehenge. Riding can be arranged. **Directions:** From Bath on A363, fork left at Frankleigh House after town sign. From Chippenham, A4 to Bath, fork left on B3109; turn left after town sign. Price guide: Single £90; double/twin £100–£150; Suite from £210–£225

For hotel location, see maps on pages 490-496

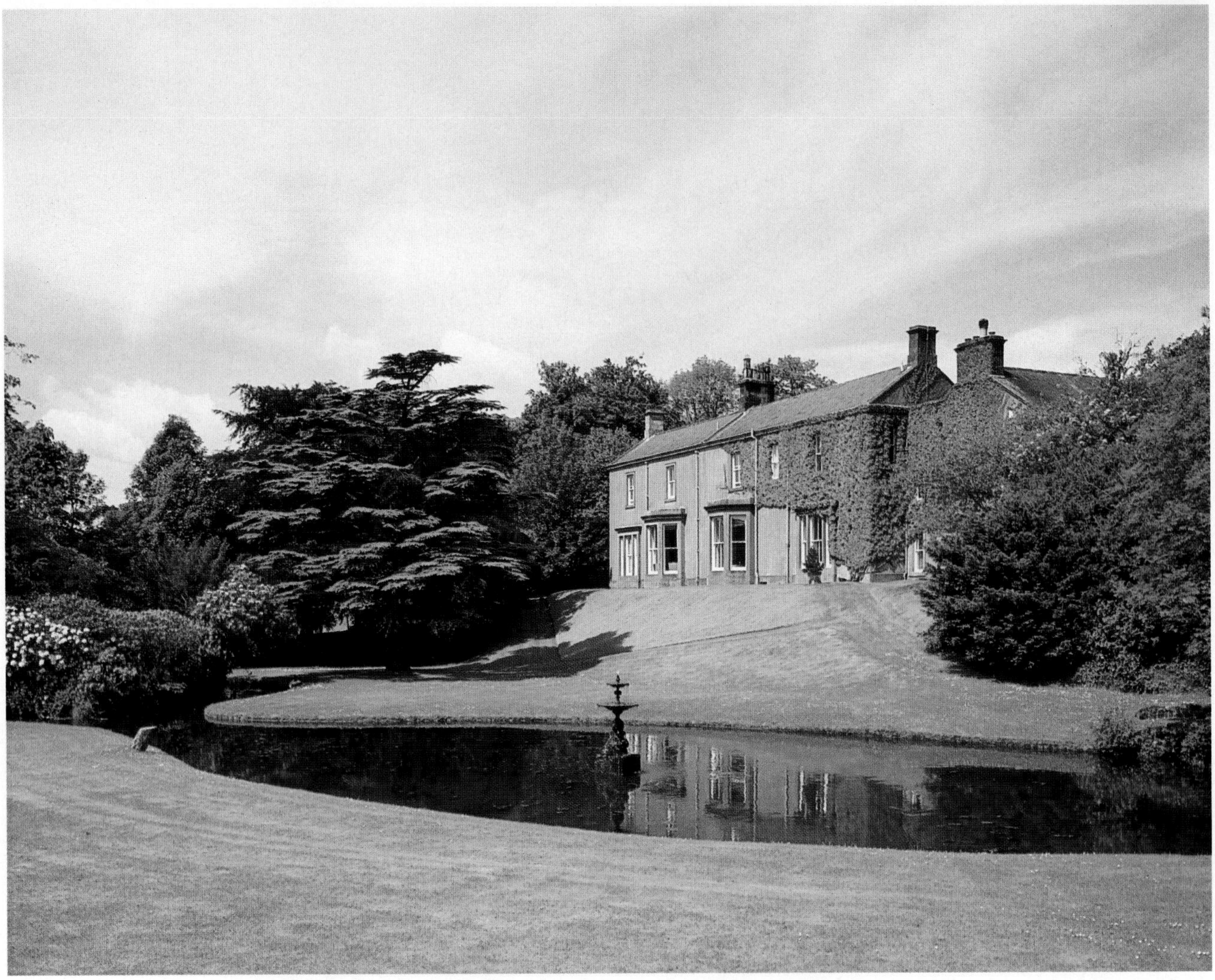

# FARLAM HALL HOTEL

**BRAMPTON, CUMBRIA CA8 2NG**
**TEL: 016977 46234 FAX: 016977 46683**

Farlam Hall was opened in 1975 by the Quinion and Stevenson families who over the years have managed to achieve and maintain consistently high standards of food, service and comfort. These standards have been recognised and rewarded by all the major guides and membership of Relais et Châteaux. This old border house, dating in parts from the 17th century, is set in mature gardens which can be seen from the elegant lounges and dining room, creating a relaxing and pleasing environment. The fine silver and crystal in the dining room complement the quality of the English country house cooking produced by Barry Quinion and his team of chefs. There are 12 individually decorated bedrooms varying in size and shape, some having Jacuzzi baths, one an antique four-poster bed, and there are two ground floor bedrooms. This area offers many different attractions: miles of unspoiled countryside for walking, eight golf courses within 30 minutes of the hotel, Hadrian's Wall, Lanercost Priory and Carlisle with its castle, cathedral and museum. The Lake District, Scottish Borders and Yorkshire Dales each make an ideal day's touring. Winter and spring breaks are offered. Closed Christmas. **Directions:** Farlam Hall is 2 1/2 miles east of Brampton on the A689, not in Farlam village. Price guide (including dinner): Single £110–£130; double/twin £200–£240.

12 rms

For hotel location, see maps on pages 490-496

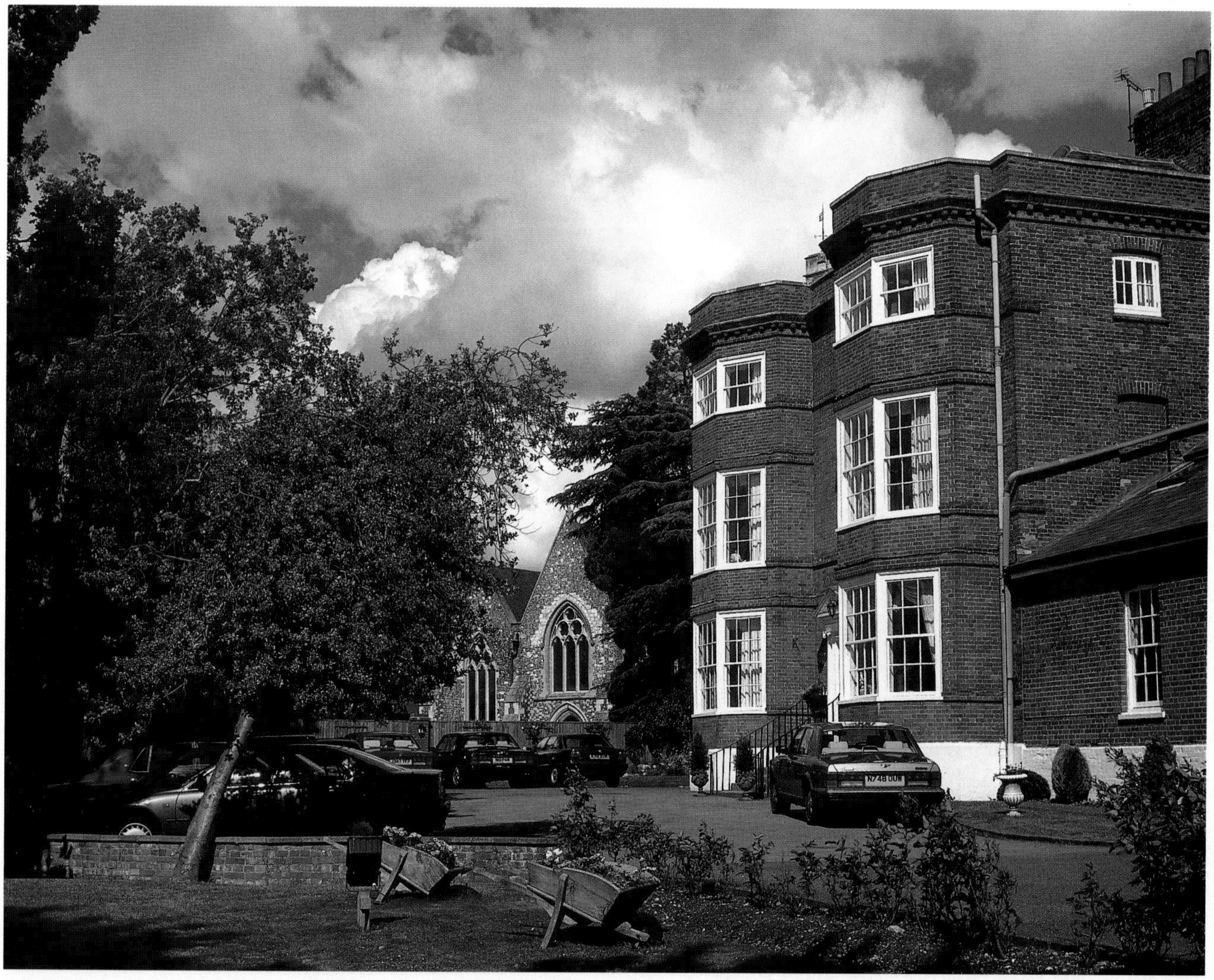

# Chauntry House Hotel And Restaurant

**HIGH STREET, BRAY, BERKSHIRE SL6 2AB**

**TEL: 01628 73991 FAX: 01628 773089**

Tucked between the local church and cricket club in the small, delightful Thames-side village of Bray, and a minutes walk to the famous Roux's Waterside Inn, Chauntry House is comfortable, friendly and has a plentiful supply of charm and character. With a spacious and secluded garden in which to lounge it is a fine example of an early 18th century country house: an ideal place to relax. The 15 en suite bedrooms are individually appointed in the best English designs and all have cable television, radio, direct dial telephones and tea and coffee making facilities. The public rooms offer comfort in the traditional country house manner and the welcoming drawing room, with an open fire for the winter months, is an ideal and comfortable environment in which to enjoy a pre-dinner aperitif. Modern English and Continental specialities with a distinctively oriental influence are served in the stylish restaurant. The hotel can accommodate conferences and meetings in an adjoining building for up to 30 delegates, boardroom style. Maidenhead, Royal Windsor, Eton, Henley, Ascot, Marlow, London and Heathrow Airport are within easy reach. Golf, fishing and riding can be arranged locally. **Directions:** From M4, exit at junction 8/9 and take A 308 (M) towards Maidenhead and Windsor. Then join B3028 to Bray village, just before M4 overhead bridge. Price guide: Single £90–£95; double/twin £120–£135.

For hotel location, see maps on pages 490-496

# MONKEY ISLAND HOTEL

**BRAY-ON-THAMES, MAIDENHEAD, BERKSHIRE SL6 2EE**
**TEL: 01628 23400 FAX: 01628 784732**

The name Monkey Island derives from the medieval Monk's Eyot. Circa 1723 the island was purchased by Charles Spencer, the third Duke of Marlborough, who built the fishing lodge now known as the Pavilion, and the fishing temple, both of which are Grade I listed buildings. The Pavilion's Terrace Bar, overlooking acres of riverside lawn, is an ideal spot for a relaxing cocktail, and the Pavilion Restaurant, perched on the island's narrowest tip with fine views upstream, boasts fine English cuisine, an award-winning cellar and friendly service. The River Room is suitable for weddings or other large functions, while the Regency-style boardroom is perfect for smaller parties. It is even possible to arrange exclusive use of the whole island for a truly memorable occasion. The Temple houses 25 comfortable bedrooms and suites, the Wedgwood Room, with its splendid ceiling in high-relief plaster, the octagonal Temple Room and gymnasium. Monkey Island is one mile downstream from Maidenhead, within easy reach of Royal Windsor, Eton, Henley and London. Closed from 26 December to mid-January. Weekend breaks from £75 p.p. **Directions:** Take A308 from Maidenhead towards Windsor; turn left following signposts to Bray. Entering Bray, go right along Old Mill Lane, which goes over M4; the hotel is on the left. Price guide: Single £70–£95; double/twin £95–£135; suites from £145.

For hotel location, see maps on pages 490-496

# TOPPS HOTEL

**17 REGENCY SQUARE, BRIGHTON, EAST SUSSEX BN1 2FG**

**TEL: 01273 729334 FAX: 01273 203679**

Quietly situated in Regency Square at the heart of Brighton, the Topps Hotel is only 2 minutes' walk from the sea and the Metropole Conference Centre, with the Lanes and Royal Pavilion nearby. This charming hotel offers an attractive alternative to the more anonymous large establishments in the vicinity and is under the personal supervision of resident proprietors, Paul and Pauline Collins. With its friendly welcome and efficient service, the Topps Hotel is certainly deserving of its name. The bedrooms are all elegantly appointed and every need of the discerning visitor has been anticipated. The hotel has long featured in our recommendations and remains unchallenged for value in Brighton. There is underground car parking below Regency Square. Brighton is often described as 'London-by-the-sea' – its urbane atmosphere and wide range of shops, clubs and theatres make it a popular town for pleasure-seeking visitors following the Georgian example of the Prince Regent. Glyndebourne, Arundel, Chichester and Lewes are within easy reach and London is only 52 minutes away by train. **Directions:** Regency Square is off King's Road (A259), opposite the West Pier. Price guide: Single from £45; double/twin £79–£109.

For hotel location, see maps on pages 490-496

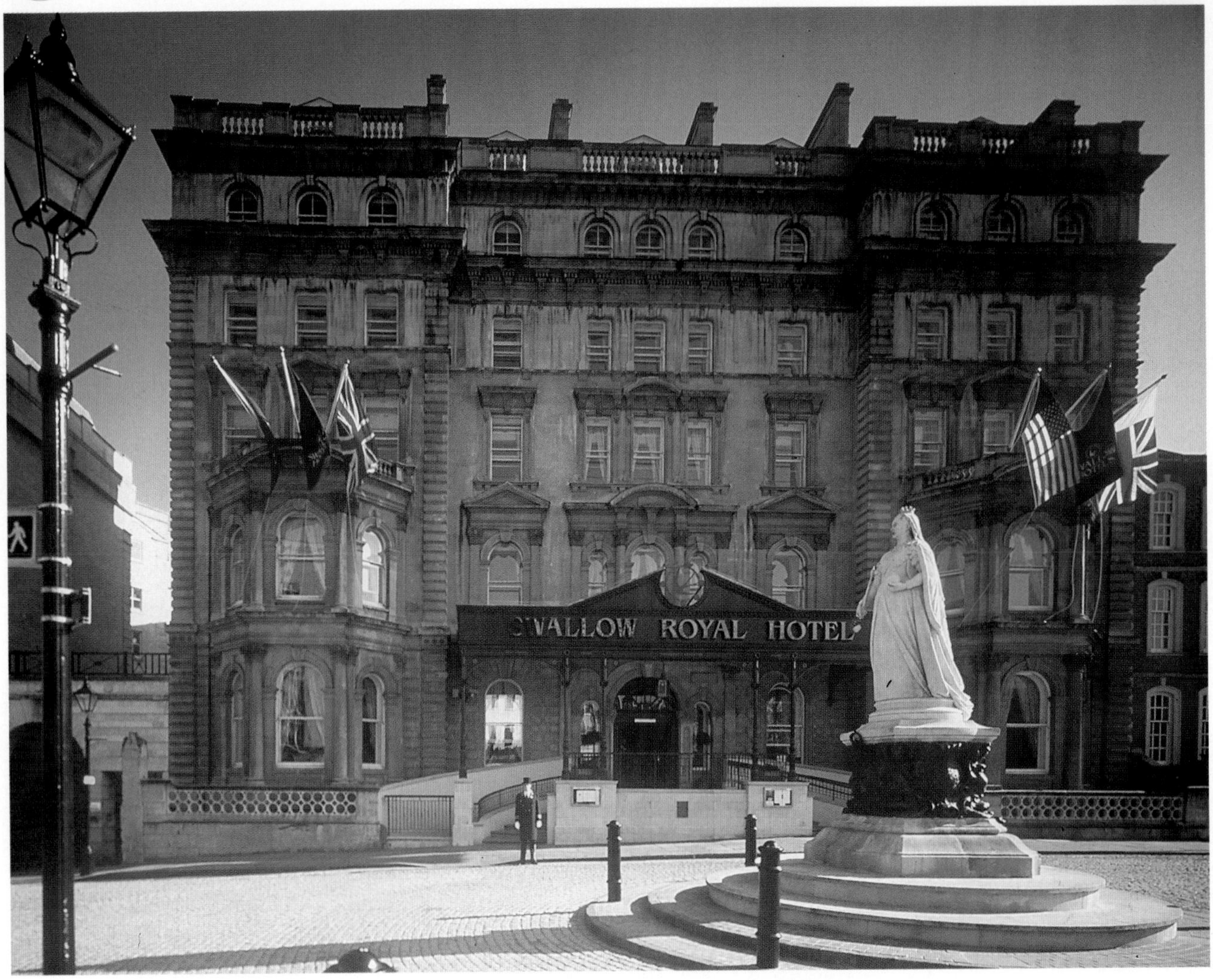

# Swallow Royal Hotel

**COLLEGE GREEN, BRISTOL BS1 5TA**
**TEL: 0117 9255200 FAX: 0117 9251515**

The Swallow Royal Hotel enjoys a central position near to Bristol Cathedral and overlooking College Green. It was much admired by Queen Victoria and Sir Winston Churchill and it survived Second World War bombs. Today it is restored to its former glory and is Bristol's leading luxury hotel. The warmest welcomes await guests, who are invited to savour the combined experience of Victorian elegance and modern day comfort. There are 242 rooms including 16 suites, all individually designed and furnished to the highest standards and many offer superb views over the city and harbour. Chef Giles Stonehouses overseas two restaurants; the imposing Victorian Palm Court with its spectacular glass roof or the less formal Terrace Restaurant overlooking Cathedral Square. Awarded 2 AA Rosettes. The Swallow Leisure Club, designed with Ancient Rome in mind, has handpainted murals, mosaics and Roman columns and offers an ideal environment for those seeking energetic pursuits or relaxation. Facilities include a heated indoor swimming pool, sauna, spa bath, steam room, sunbeds and fitness room. The hotel now has its own internal "pub" the Queen Vic where you can "surf the net" and watch sport on satellite TV. The hotel has its own car park. **Directions:** At the end of the M32 keep right and follow the signs for the City Centre. Price guide: Single from £115; double/twin from £135; suites £175–£350.

For hotel location, see maps on pages 490-496

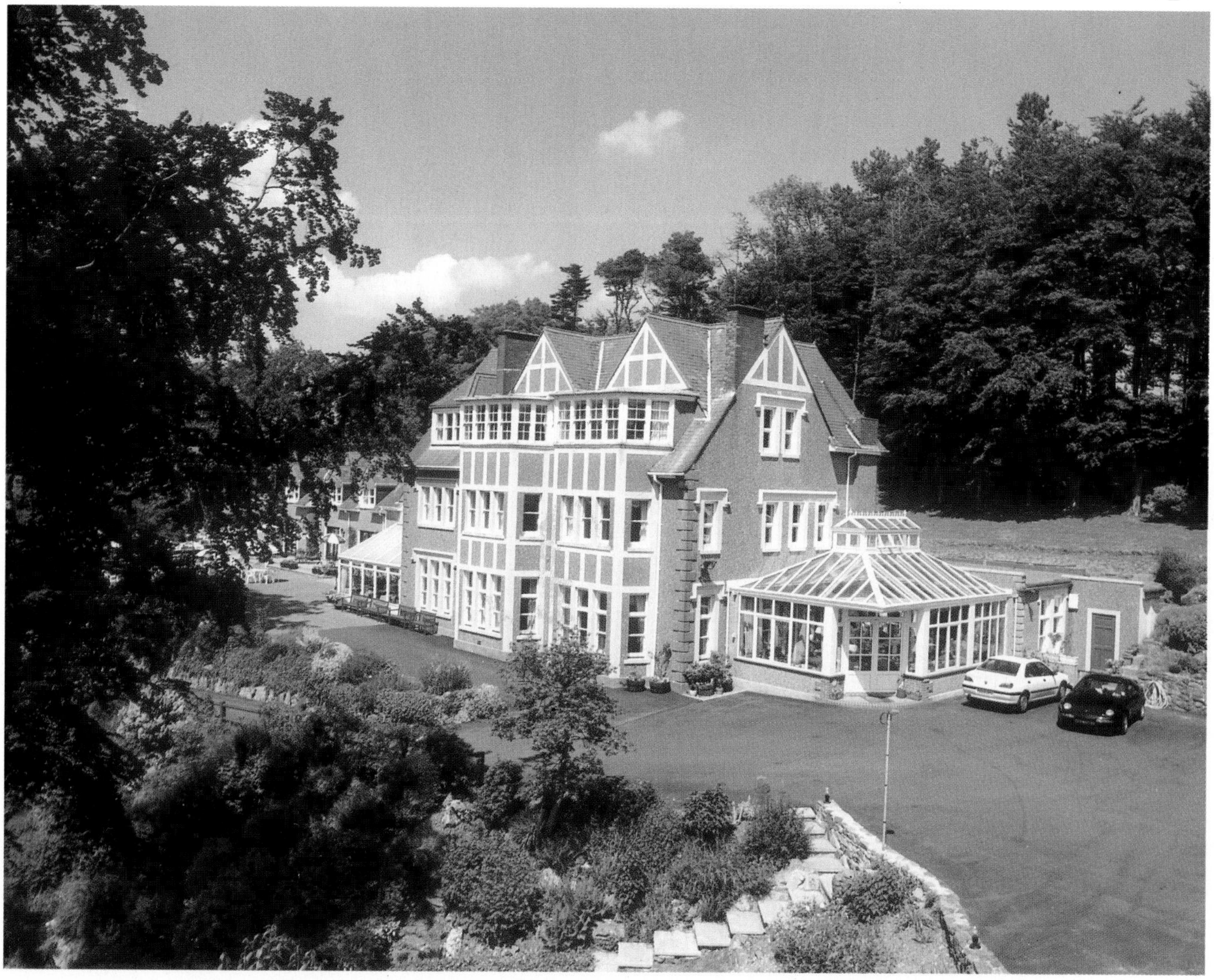

# DANESWOOD HOUSE HOTEL

**CUCK HILL, SHIPHAM, NR WINSCOMBE, SOMERSET BS25 1RD**
**TEL: 01934 843145 FAX: 01934 843824 E-MAIL: 101604.3531@COMPUSERVE.COM**

A small country house hotel, Daneswood House overlooks a leafy valley in the heart of the Mendip Hills – on a clear day, the views stretch as far as Wales. It was built by the Edwardians as a homeopathic health hydro and under the enthusiastic ownership of David and Elise Hodges it has been transformed into a charming hotel. Each bedroom is well furnished and individually decorated with striking fabrics. The honeymoon suite, with its king-sized bed, frescoed ceiling and antiques, is particularly comfortable. First-class cooking places equal emphasis on presentation and taste. Each dish is carefully prepared in a style that combines traditional English and French cooking. Awarded 2 AA Rosettes. During the summer, guests can dine alfresco and enjoy barbecued dishes such as Indonesian duck and baked sea bass with fennel and armagnac. There is a carefully selected wine list and a wide choice of liqueurs. The private conference lounge makes a quiet setting for meetings, while private functions can be catered for with ease. Cheddar Gorge is 2 miles away, and Wells, Glastonbury, Bristol and Bath are nearby. Guide dogs accommodated only. **Directions:** Shipham is signposted from A38 Bristol–Bridgwater road. Go through village towards Cheddar; hotel drive is on left leaving village. Price guide: Single £59–£72.50; double/twin £69.50–£89.50; suite £125.

For hotel location, see maps on pages 490-496

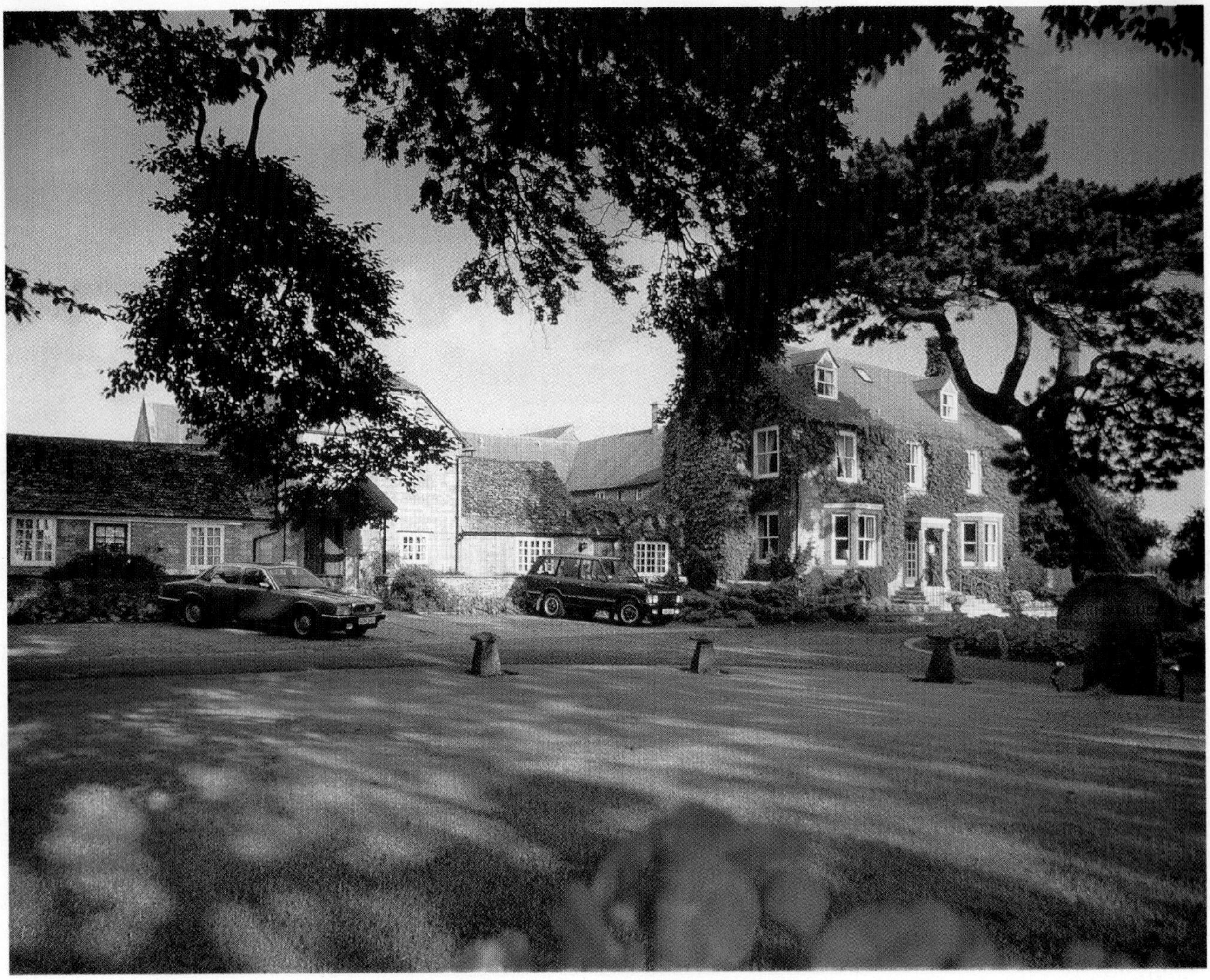

# DORMY HOUSE

## WILLERSEY HILL, BROADWAY, WORCESTERSHIRE WR12 7LF
## TEL: 01386 852711 FAX: 01386 858636

This former 17th-century farmhouse has been beautifully converted into a delightful hotel which retains much of its original character. With its oak beams, stone-flagged floors and honey-coloured local stone walls it imparts warmth and tranquillity. Dormy House provides a wealth of comforts for the most discerning guest. Each bedroom is individually decorated – some are furnished with four-poster beds – and suites are available. Head Chef, Alan Cutler, prepares a superb choice of menus and Tapestries Restaurant, expertly managed by Saverio Buchicchio, offers an extensive wine list includes many half bottles. The versatile Dormy Suite is an ideal venue for conferences, meetings or private functions – professionally arranged to individual requirements. The hotel has its own leisure facilities which include a games room, gym, sauna/steam, room, croquet lawn and putting green. Mountain bikes are available for hire. Broadway Golf Club is adjacent. The locality is idyllic for walkers. Stratford-upon-Avon, Cheltenham Spa, Hidcote Manor Garden and Sudeley Castle are all within easy reach. USA representative: Josephine Barr, 1-800-323-5463. Closed 2 days at Christmas. **Directions:** Hotel is ½ mile off A44 between Moreton-in-Marsh and Broadway. Taking the turning signposted Saintbury, the hotel is first on left past picnic area. Price guide: Single £65–£87; double/twin £130–£157.

49 rms · 200

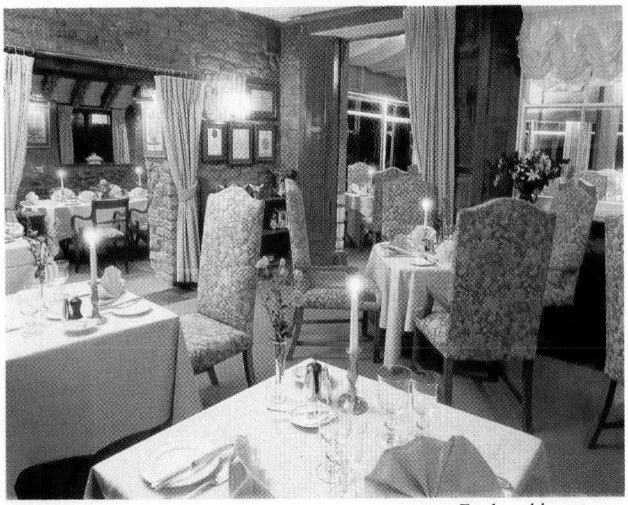

For hotel location, see maps on pages 490-496

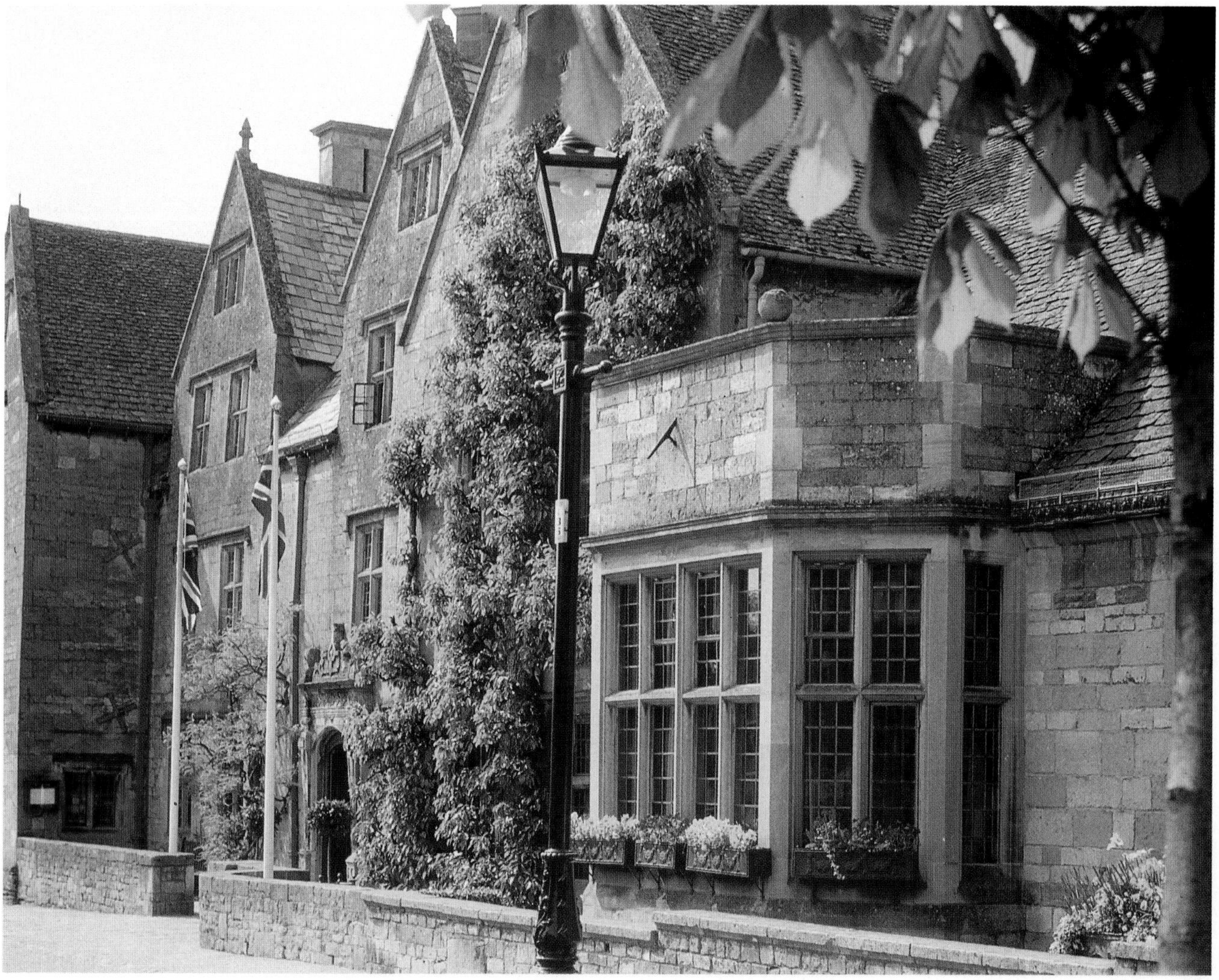

# THE LYGON ARMS

**BROADWAY, WORCESTERSHIRE WR12 7DU**

**TEL: 01386 852255 FAX: 01386 858611 E-MAIL: info@the-lygon-arms.co.uk**

The Lygon Arms, a magnificent Tudor building with numerous historical associations, stands in Broadway, acclaimed by many as 'the prettiest village in England', in the heart of the North Cotswolds. Over the years much restoration has been carried out, emphasising the outstanding period features, such as original 17th century oak panelling and an ancient hidden stairway. All the bedrooms are individually and tastefully furnished and offer guests every modern luxury, even telephone voice-mail, combined with the elegance of an earlier age. The Great Hall, complete with a 17th century minstrels' gallery, and the smaller private dining rooms provide a fine setting for a well-chosen and imaginative menu. Conference facilities including the state-of-the-art Torrington Room are available for up to 80 participants. Guests can enjoy a superb range of leisure amenities including all-weather tennis, indoor pool, gymnasium, billiard room, beauty salons, steam room, solarium and saunas. Golf can be arranged locally. The many Cotswold villages; Stratford-upon-Avon, Oxford and Cheltenham are nearby, while Broadway itself is a paradise for the antique collector. **Directions:** Set on the right-hand side of Broadway High Street on the A44 in the direction of London to Worcester. Price guide: Single from £90; double/twin from £155 including Continental breakfast, excluding VAT.

For hotel location, see maps on pages 490-496

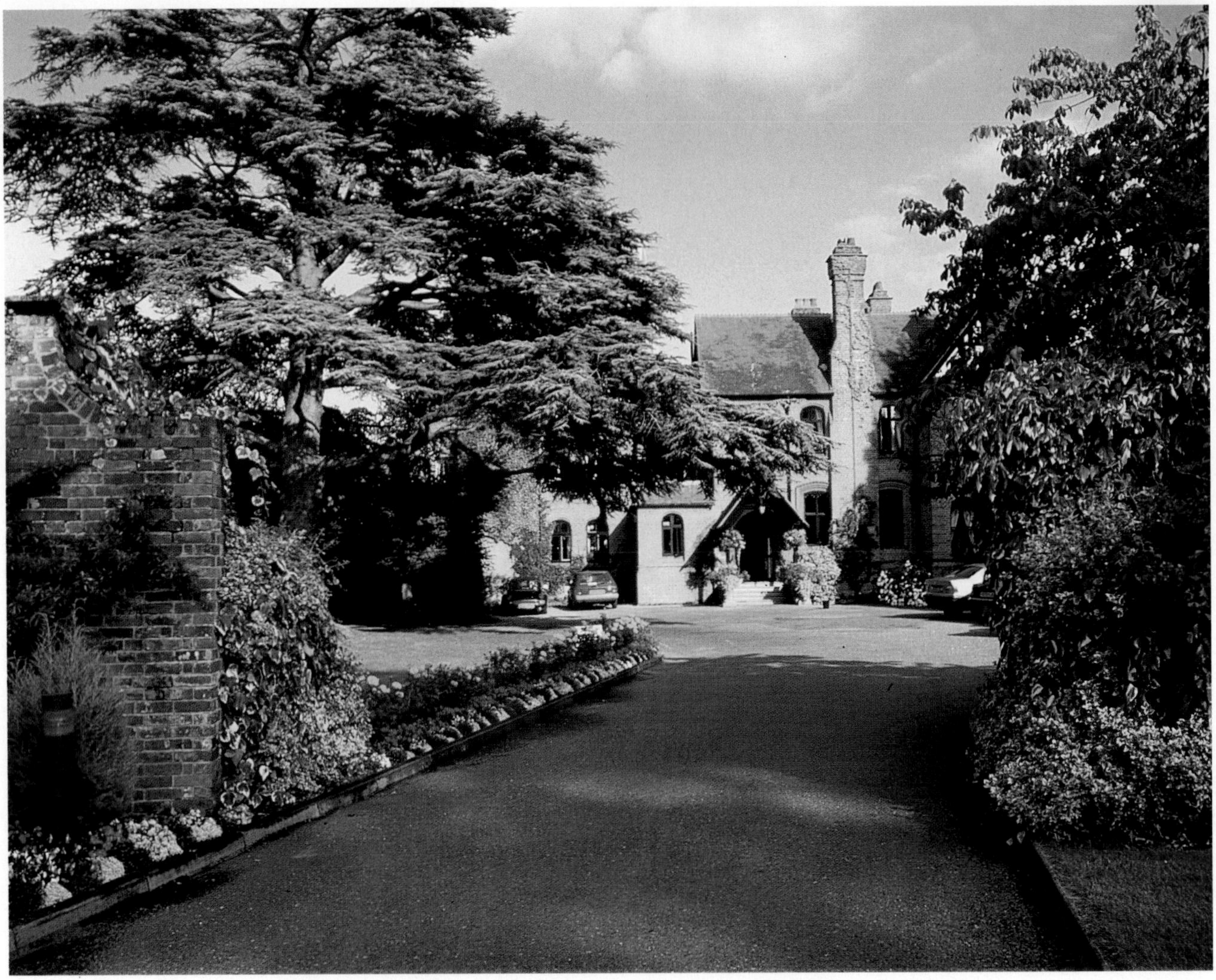

# Careys Manor Hotel

**BROCKENHURST, NEW FOREST, HAMPSHIRE SO42 7RH**
**TEL: 01590 623551 FAX: 01590 622799**

Careys Manor, an elegant country house, dates from 1888 and is built on the site of a royal hunting lodge used by Charles II. Situated in 5 acres of landscaped grounds and surrounded by glorious New Forest countryside, the hotel is proud of the personal welcome and care it extends to its visitors. The comfortably furnished bedrooms are appointed to the highest standards. In the Garden Wing, there is a choice of luxury bedrooms, some opening directly onto the lawns and others with a balcony overlooking the pretty gardens. The restaurant offers fine English and French cuisine, prepared and presented to gourmet standards. A prestigious sports complex comprises a large indoor swimming pool with Jacuzzi, sauna, solarium and a Turkish steam room. In addition, guests can work out in the professionally supervised gymnasium, where there is also a room for massage, sports injury and beauty treatments. Wind-surfing, riding and sailing can all be enjoyed locally, while Stonehenge, Beaulieu, Broadlands, Salisbury and Winchester are a short distance away. Business interests can be catered for – there are comprehensive self-contained conference facilities. **Directions:** From M27 junction 1, follow A337 to Lymington. Careys Manor is on the left after 30 mph sign at Brockenhurst. Price guide from: Single £73–£83; double/twin £119–£139; suite £169.

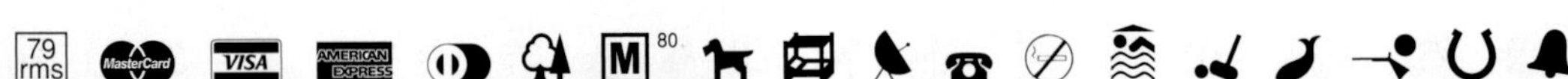

For hotel location, see maps on pages 490-496

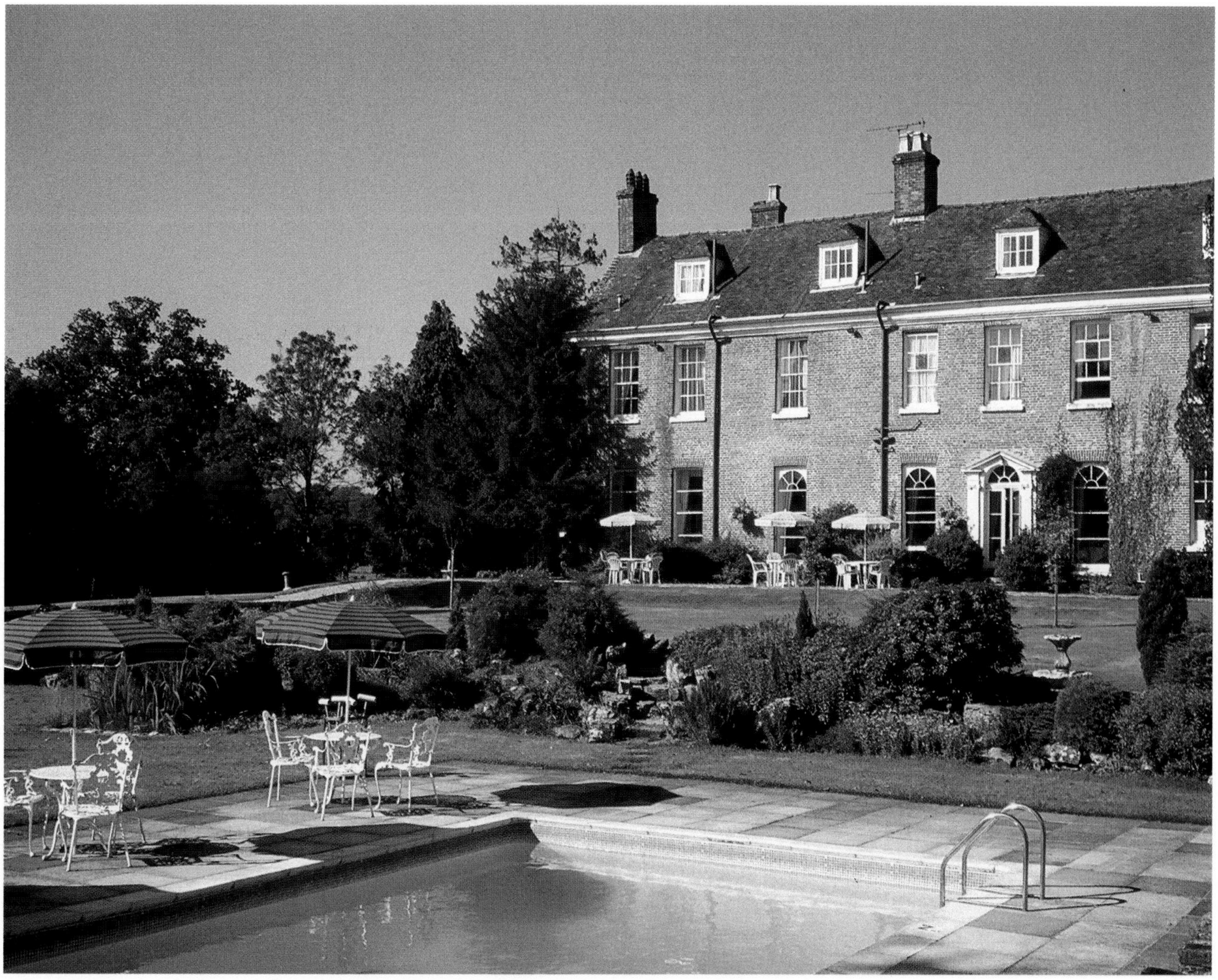

# NEW PARK MANOR

**LYNDHURST ROAD, BROCKENHURST, NEW FOREST, HAMPSHIRE SO42 7QH**
**TEL: 01590 623467 FAX: 01590 622268**

Escape from the crowds to one of the New Forest's finest country house hotels. A former hunting lodge of Charles II, the building is grade II listed and dates back to the 16th century. It stands in a very fine position a good distance from the road to Lyndhurst, the "capital" of the New Forest, where "Alice in Wonderland's" grave, and Rufus Stone are curiosities to be visited. The en-suite bedrooms are all individually decorated, keeping in mind the style and grandeur of the old manor; most offer superb views over the surrounding parklands with its wandering ponies and deer. Enjoy a romantic evening with fine wines and French influenced cuisine in the Stag Head Restaurant or relax with a good book from the library in front of the open log fire in the historic Rufus Bar. The New Forest suite creates a wonderful setting for all types of functions – tailor made to suit your personal requirements. For the more energetic New Park Manor offers riding from its own equestrian centre with BHS trained stable crew, a tennis court and an outdoor heated swimming pool. There is something for everyone so why not get away from it all and escape to the peace and tranquility, topped with service par excellence, of the New Park Manor? **Directions:** New Park Manor is 1/2 mile off the A337 between Lyndhurst and Brockenhurst easily reached from M27 via Cadnam. Price guide: Single from £85; double/twin £95–£180.

For hotel location, see maps on pages 490-496

# Rhinefield House Hotel

**RHINEFIELD ROAD, BROCKENHURST, HAMPSHIRE SO42 7QB**

**TEL: 01590 622922 FAX: 01590 622800**

Known locally as the 'jewel in the forest', at first sight the sheer grandeur of Rhinefield House surpasses all expectations. A hint of Italian Renaissance sweeps across ornamental gardens, with canals reflecting the mellow stonework. Lovingly restored to their original 1890s design, over 5,000 yew trees form the maze and formal parterres where a grass amphitheatre has been carved out of the western slopes for summer evening concerts. The interiors are equally impressive, the journey through the rooms is a voyage of discovery. Authentically created in the style of a Moorish Palace, the Alhambra Room has Islamic inscriptions, onyx pillars and mosaic flooring. Fine cuisine is served in the elegant Armada Restaurant – so called after its splendid carving depicting the Spanish Armada. An airy sun-lit conservatory and attractive bedrooms appointed in accordance with the style of the house all add to Rhinefield's appeal. The Grand Hall is a replica of Westminster Hall – an ideal setting for Balls, Society Weddings and stylish Banquets. A wide range of conference rooms and equipment is available for business events. Guests may unwind in the Atlantis Leisure Club with its plunge pool, solarium, sauna, steam room and gymnasium. Directions: A35 West from Lyndhurst and follow the signs to Christchurch. Price guide: Single from £95; double/twin from £130; suite from £160.

34 rms MasterCard VISA AMERICAN EXPRESS M 150

For hotel location, see maps on pages 490-496

# GRAFTON MANOR COUNTRY HOUSE HOTEL

PRIDE OF BRITAIN MEMBER

GRAFTON LANE, BROMSGROVE, WORCESTERSHIRE B61 7HA
TEL: 01527 579007 FAX: 01527 575221

Closely associated with many of the leading events in English history, Grafton Manor's illustrious past can be traced back to Norman times. Commissioned in 1567, the present manor is set in several acres of gardens leading to a lake. Modern comfort and style are combined with the atmosphere of an earlier age. Pot-pourri from the hotel's 19th-century rose gardens scents the rooms and over 100 herbs are grown in a unique, chessboard-pattern garden. All the herbs are in regular use in the restaurant kitchen, where Simon Morris aims to 'produce only the best' for guests. Preserves made from estate produce are on sale. Meals are served in the 18th-century dining room, the focal point of Grafton Manor. Damask-rose petal and mulberry sorbets are indicative of the inspired culinary style. Indian cuisine is Simon's award winning hobby and Asian dishes often complement the traditional English cooking. The fully equipped bedrooms have been meticulously restored and furnished, some with open fires on cooler evenings. Grafton Manor is ideally placed for Birmingham, the NEC and the International Conference Centre. It is an equally good base from which to explore the Worcestershire countryside. **Directions:** From M5 junction 5 proceed via A38 towards Bromsgrove. Bear left at first roundabout; Grafton Lane is first left after 1/2 mile. Price guide: Single £85; double/twin from £105; suite £150.

For hotel location, see maps on pages 490-496

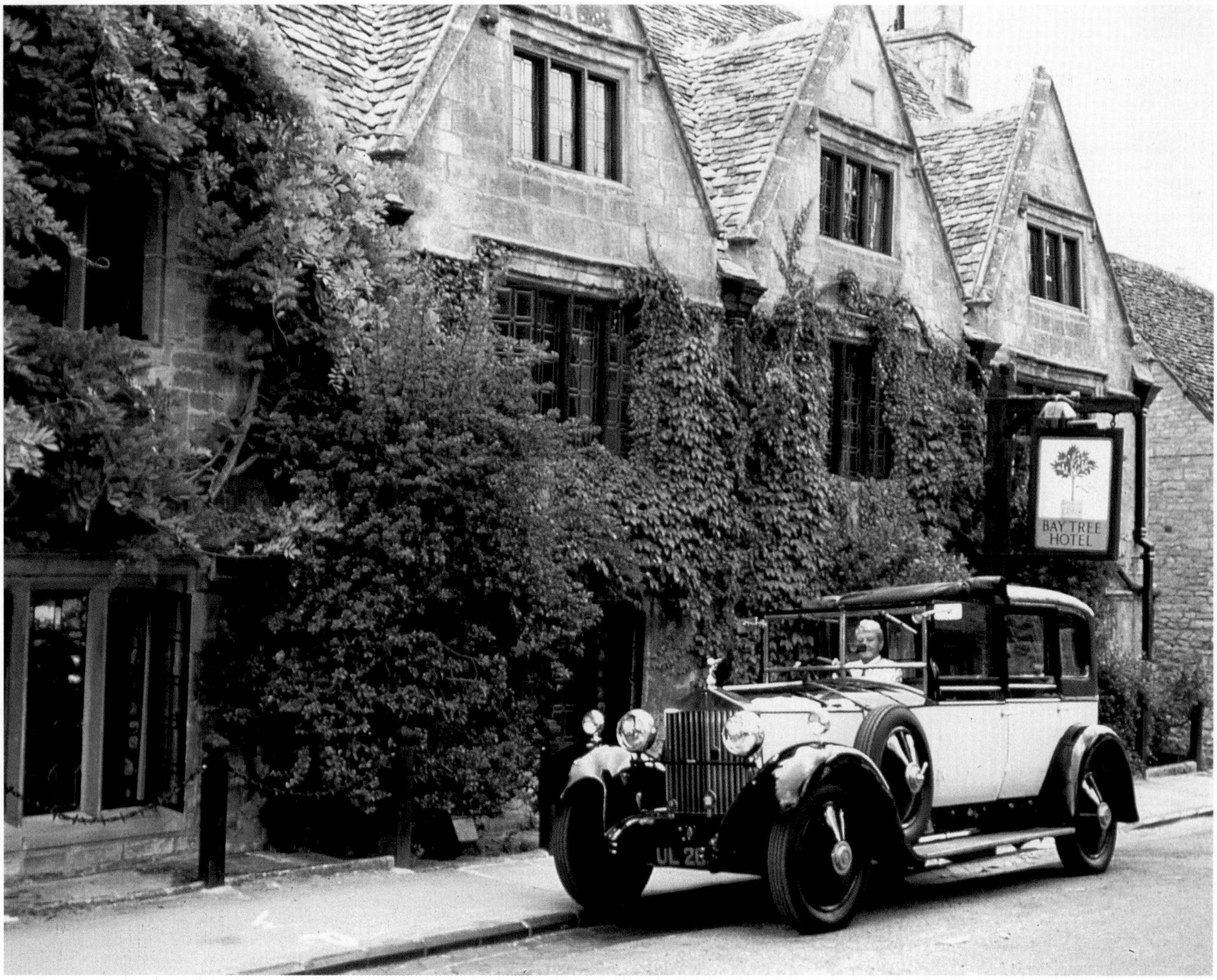

# THE BAY TREE HOTEL AND RESTAURANT

**SHEEP STREET, BURFORD, OXON OX18 4LW**
**TEL: 01993 822791 FAX: 01993 823008**

The Bay Tree has been expertly refurbished so that it retains all its Tudor splendour while offering every modern facility. The oak-panelled rooms have huge stone fireplaces, and a galleried staircase leads upstairs from the raftered hall. All the bedrooms are en suite, three of them furnished with four-poster beds and two of the five suites have half-tester beds. In the summer, you can relax in the delightful walled gardens, featuring landscaped terraces of lawn and flower beds. A relaxing atmosphere is enhanced by the staff's attentive service in the flagstoned dining room where the head chef's creative cuisine is complemented by a comprehensive selection of fine wines. Light meals are served in a country-style bar, while the conservatory lounge is the place to unwind and enjoy the view over the grounds. Burford, often described as the gateway to the Cotswolds, is renowned for its assortment of antique shops and the Tolsey Museum of local history. The Bay Tree Hotel makes a convenient base for day trips to Stratford-upon-Avon, Stow-on-the-Wold and Blenheim Palace. Golf, clay pigeon shooting and riding can be arranged locally. **Directions:** Burford is on the A40 between Oxford and Cheltenham. Proceed halfway down the hill into Burford, turn left into Sheep Street and The Bay Tree Hotel is 30 yards on your right. Price guide: Single £60–£80; double/twin £110–£115.

For hotel location, see maps on pages 490-496

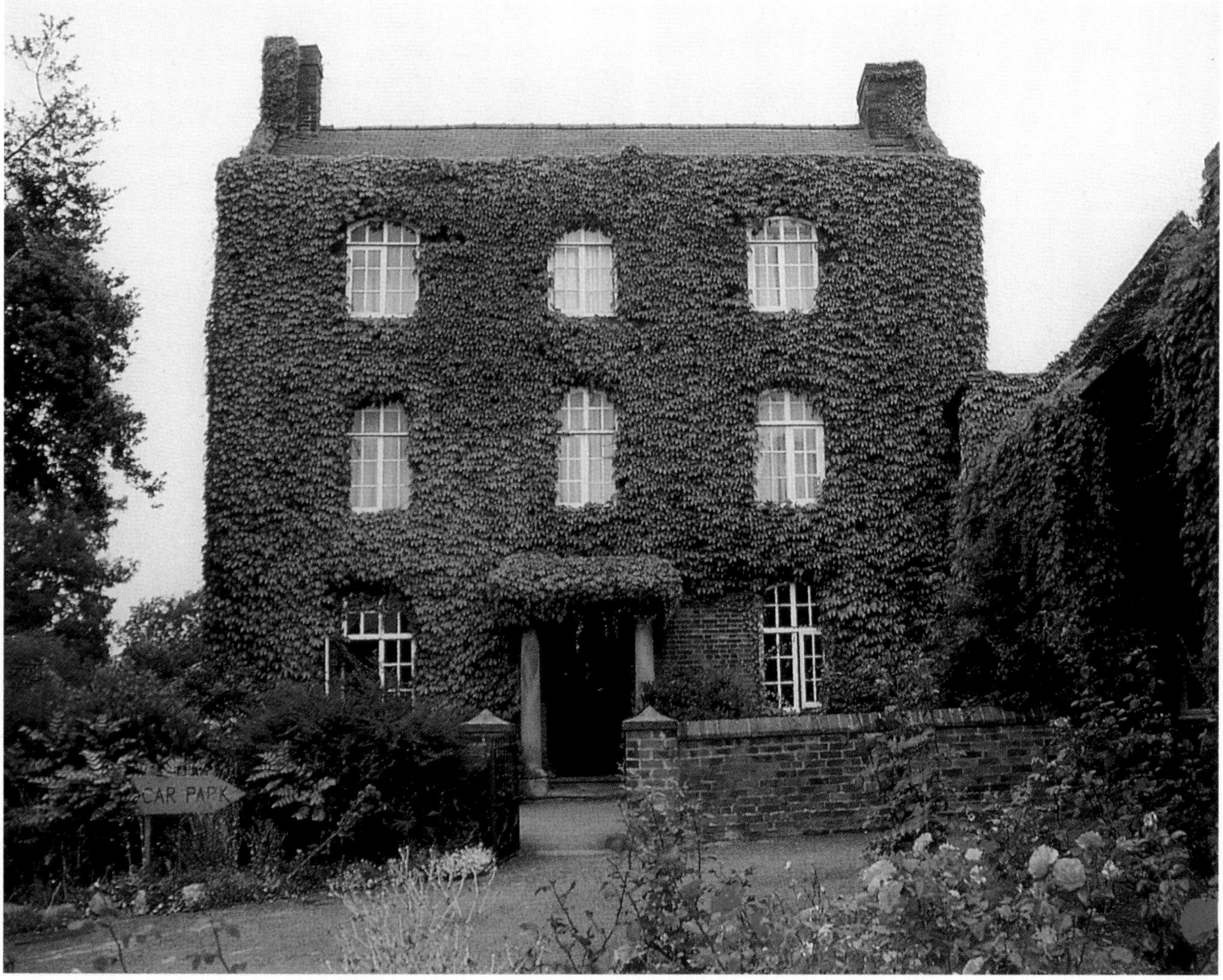

# The Brookhouse

**ROLLESTON-ON-DOVE, NR BURTON UPON TRENT, STAFFORDSHIRE DE13 9AA**
**TEL: 01283 814188 FAX: 01283 813644**

Originally built as a farmhouse in 1694, this attractive, ivy-clad William and Mary house stands in a tranquil position beside a gently flowing brook and lush gardens. Grade II listed, the building was converted into a hotel in 1976, and since then it has earned a reputation for its friendly service and hospitality. Of particular interest are the pretty bedrooms, with four-poster, half-tester or Victorian brass beds. The bedding is trimmed with Nottingham lace. Downstairs, the décor and antique furniture are in keeping with the cosy cottage style. In the restaurant, soft wall-lighting and candles create an intimate atmosphere, while polished wooden tables are set with silver and crystal. The food is of a consistently high quality. An extensive menu presents a wide choice to suit all tastes. Small private functions can be catered for: fax, photo-copying and secretarial services can be arranged for business meetings. Serious hikers and ramblers alike will find plenty of good walking in the nearby Derbyshire Dales and Peak District. Notable local attractions include the Shugborough Estate, Calke Abbey, The Bass Museum of Brewing, Haddon and Kedleston Halls. **Directions:** Rolleston is just outside Burton upon Trent between the A50 to Stoke-on-Trent and the A38 to Derby. Price guide: Single £69–£79; double/twin £89–£99.

For hotel location, see maps on pages 490-496

# THE ANGEL HOTEL

**BURY ST EDMUNDS, SUFFOLK IP33 1LT**
**TEL: 01284 753926 FAX: 01284 750092**

Immortalised by Charles Dickens as the hostelry where Mr Pickwick enjoyed an excellent roast dinner, The Angel Hotel is renowned for its first-class service to travellers, continuing the tradition since first becoming an inn in 1452. Visitors have the immediate impression of a hotel that is loved and nurtured by its owners. In the public rooms, guests will appreciate the carefully chosen ornaments and pictures, fresh flowers and log fires. Bedrooms are individually furnished and decorated and all have en suite bathrooms. The elegant dining room has been awarded 2 rosettes by the AA for excellent food and service. Overlooking the ancient abbey, the restaurant serves classic English cuisine, including local speciality dishes and succulent roasts. The Angel can offer a wide range of quality conference and banqueting facilities catering for private dinners, meetings and weddings from 10–120 persons. The hotel is within an hour of east coast ferry ports and 45 minutes from Stansted Airport. Nearby there is racing at Newmarket and several golf courses within easy reach. Bury St Edmunds is an interesting and historic market town and an excellent centre for touring East Anglia. **Directions:** The hotel is situated in the centre of the town. Price guide: Single from £62; double/twin from £72; suite from £100. Weekend rates £38 per person bed and breakfast.

For hotel location, see maps on pages 490-496

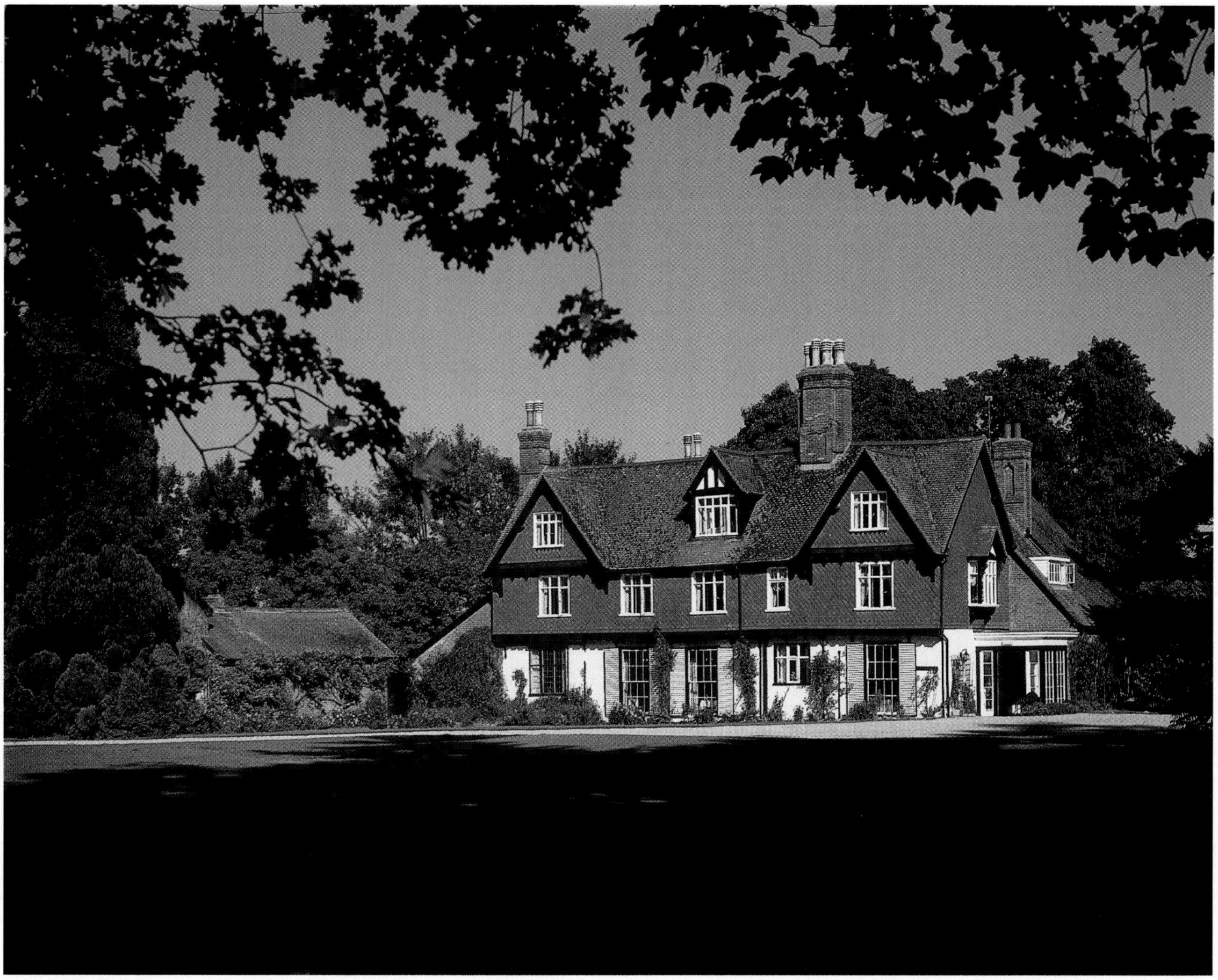

# RAVENWOOD HALL

**ROUGHAM, BURY ST EDMUNDS, SUFFOLK IP30 9JA**
**TEL: 01359 270345 FAX: 01359 270788**

Nestling within 7 acres of lovely lawns and woodlands deep in the heart of Suffolk lies Ravenwood Hall. Now an excellent country house hotel, this fine Tudor building dates back to 1530 and retains many of its original features. The restaurant, still boasting the carved timbers and huge inglenook from Tudor times, creates a delightfully intimate atmosphere in which to enjoy imaginative cuisine. The menu is a combination of adventurous and classical dishes, featuring some long forgotten English recipes. The Hall's extensive cellars are stocked with some of the finest vintages, along with a selection of rare ports and brandies. A cosy bar offers a less formal setting in which to enjoy some unusual snacks. Comfortable bedrooms are furnished with antiques, reflecting the historic tradition of the Hall, although each is equipped with every modern facility. A wide range of leisure facilities is available for guests, including a hard tennis court, a croquet lawn and heated swimming pool. There are golf courses and woodland walks to enjoy locally; hunting and shooting can be arranged. Places of interest nearby include the famous medieval wool towns of Lavenham and Long Melford; the historic cities of Norwich and Cambridge are within easy reach. **Directions:** 2 miles East of Bury St. Edmunds off the A14. Price guide: £59–£79; double/twin: £79–£109.

For hotel location, see maps on pages 490-496

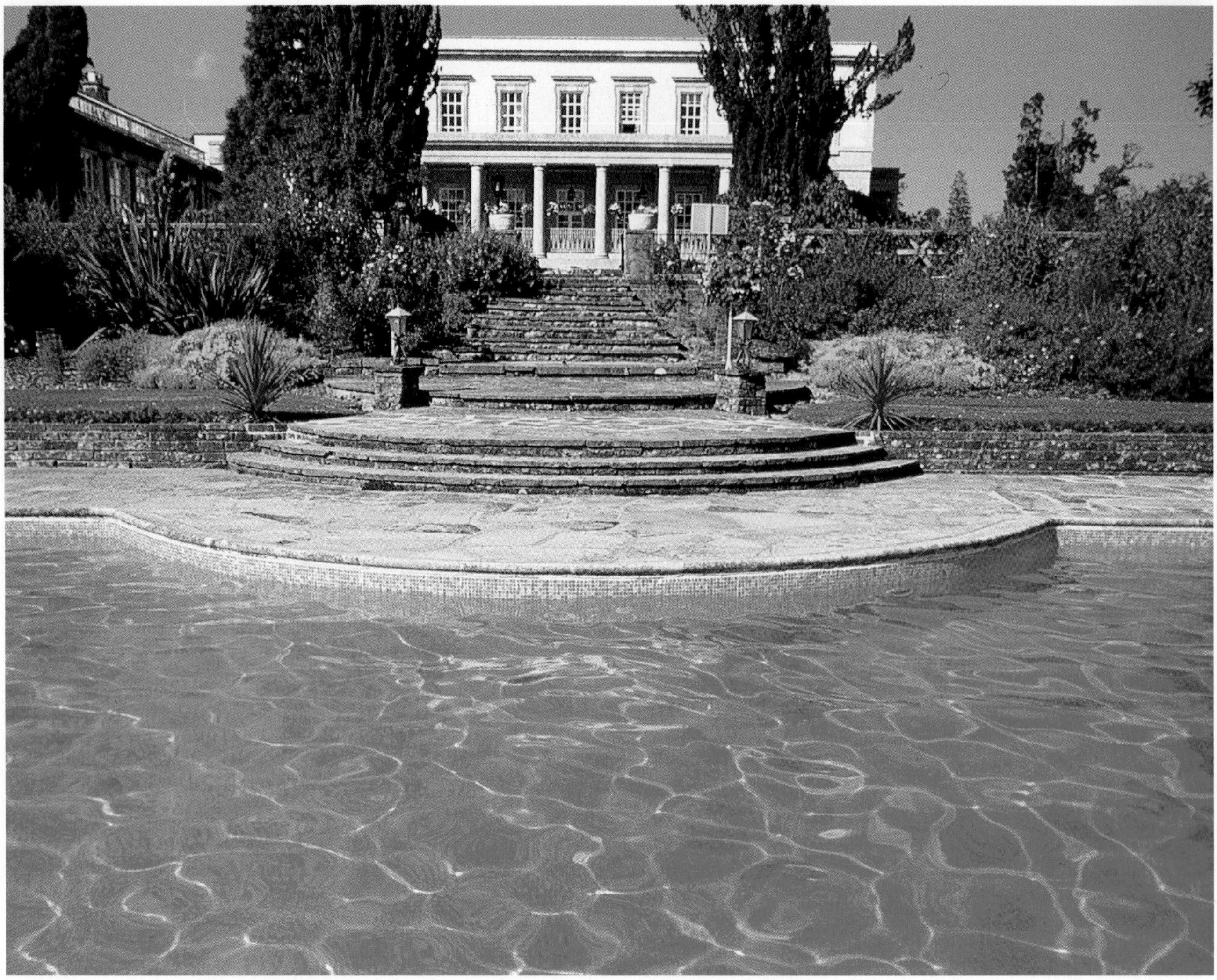

# Buxted Park Country House Hotel

**BUXTED, UCKFIELD, EAST SUSSEX TN22 4AY**
**TEL: 01825 732711 FAX: 01825 732770**

Buxted Park's rural environment, close to Ashdown Forest, provides a calm and peaceful atmosphere in which to relax. The attractive Georgian mansion, built in 1725, has recently been sympathetically restored to reclaim its former glory. Years ago, when Buxted was a private residence, Queen Victoria and Queen Mary were both regular visitors. There are 44 spacious bedrooms with all the amenities required for a comfortable stay. Most of them have superb views over the extensive grounds and undulating landscape. The Orangery Restaurant – a converted Victorian conservatory – provides elegant surrounding in which to enjoy the excellent food and fine wines. There are several salons which may also be used for meetings, as well as a grand Ballroom which opens out on the the Coat-of-Arms drawing room – ideal for pre-drinks for events in the Ballroom. Unique to the hotel is a 54 seater cinema with back projection. The hotel is justifiably proud of its Health Club which has a well-equipped gym, saunas, steam rooms, Jacuzzi and a lovely outdoor heated swimming pool, (open during the Summer). There is a snooker room, too. **Directions:** The entrance to the hotel is located on the A272, east of its junction with the A22. Price guide Single from £85; double/twin from £120; junior suites from £175. Two night leisure breaks include 4 course dinner for £72 per person per night.

For hotel location, see maps on pages 490-496

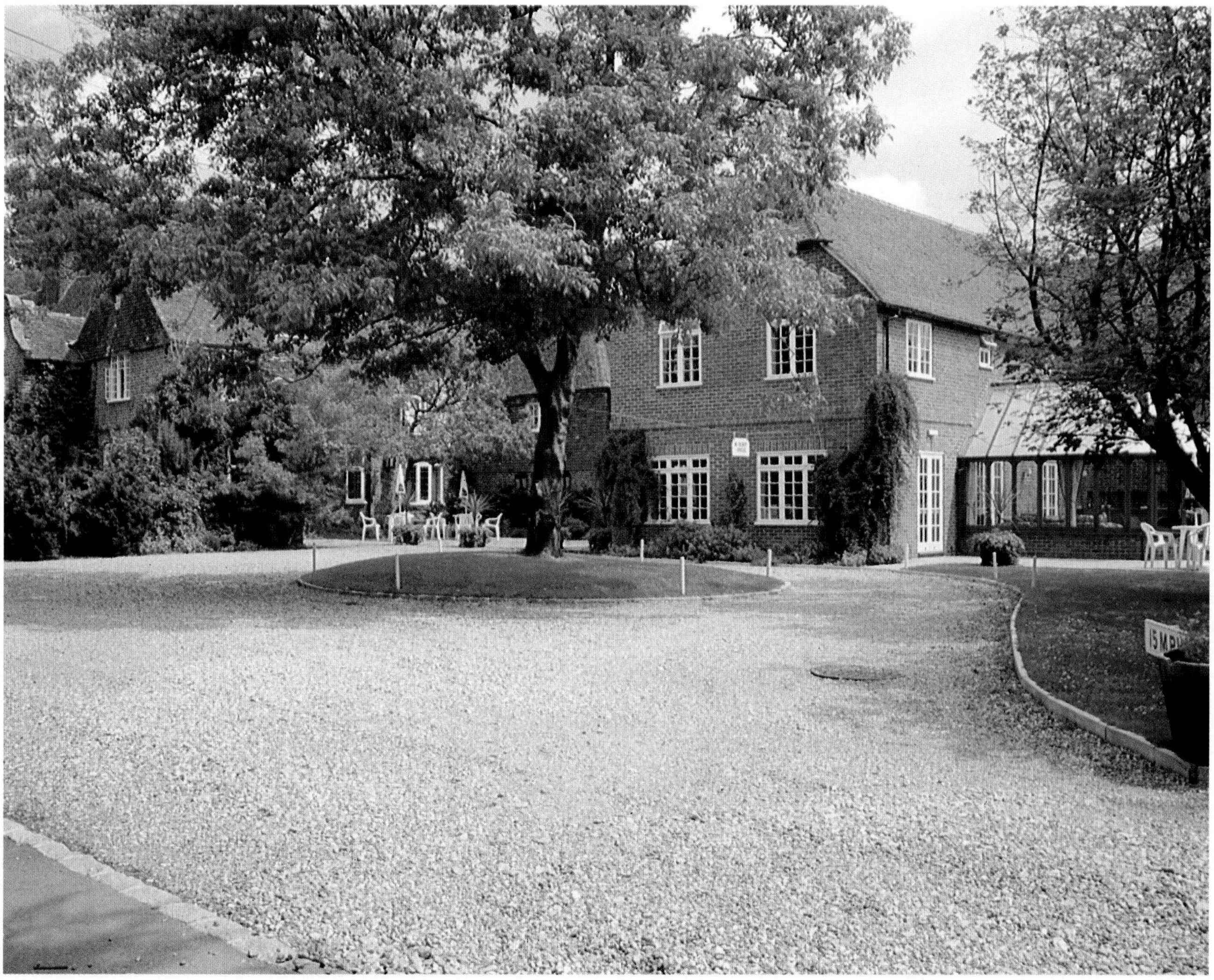

# HOWFIELD MANOR

**CHARTHAM HATCH, NR CANTERBURY, KENT CT4 7HQ**
**TEL: 01227 738294 FAX: 01227 731535**

At Howfield Manor great care has been taken to preserve a long tradition of hospitality dating back to 1181, while discreetly providing modern comforts. Originally part of the Priory of St Gregory, this historic country house is set in 5 acres of secluded grounds with a formal English rose garden. The hotel has an authentic priest hole and, in the Priory Bar, striking *trompe l'oeil* murals. Illuminated under the floor of the Old Well Restaurant is the ferned ancient well, which was the main source of water for the monks who lived here 800 years ago. A selection of wines and other refreshments nourishes today's visitors. Guests have the choice of an extensive range of menus to cater for every occasion – from an intimate à la carte meal for two to a gourmet dinner party in the self-contained conference and banqueting suite. The well-furnished bedrooms have been thoughtfully equipped. Located only 2 miles from the cathedral city of Canterbury, Howfield Manor makes an ideal base for touring this area and as a stopping-off point to and from the continent. Special weekend breaks are also available. **Directions:** From A2 London–Dover road, follow signs for Chartham Hatch after the Gate Service Station, then follow straight on for 2 1/4 miles. Hotel is on left at junction with A28. Price guide: Single £70; double/twin £90–£100.

For hotel location, see maps on pages 490-496

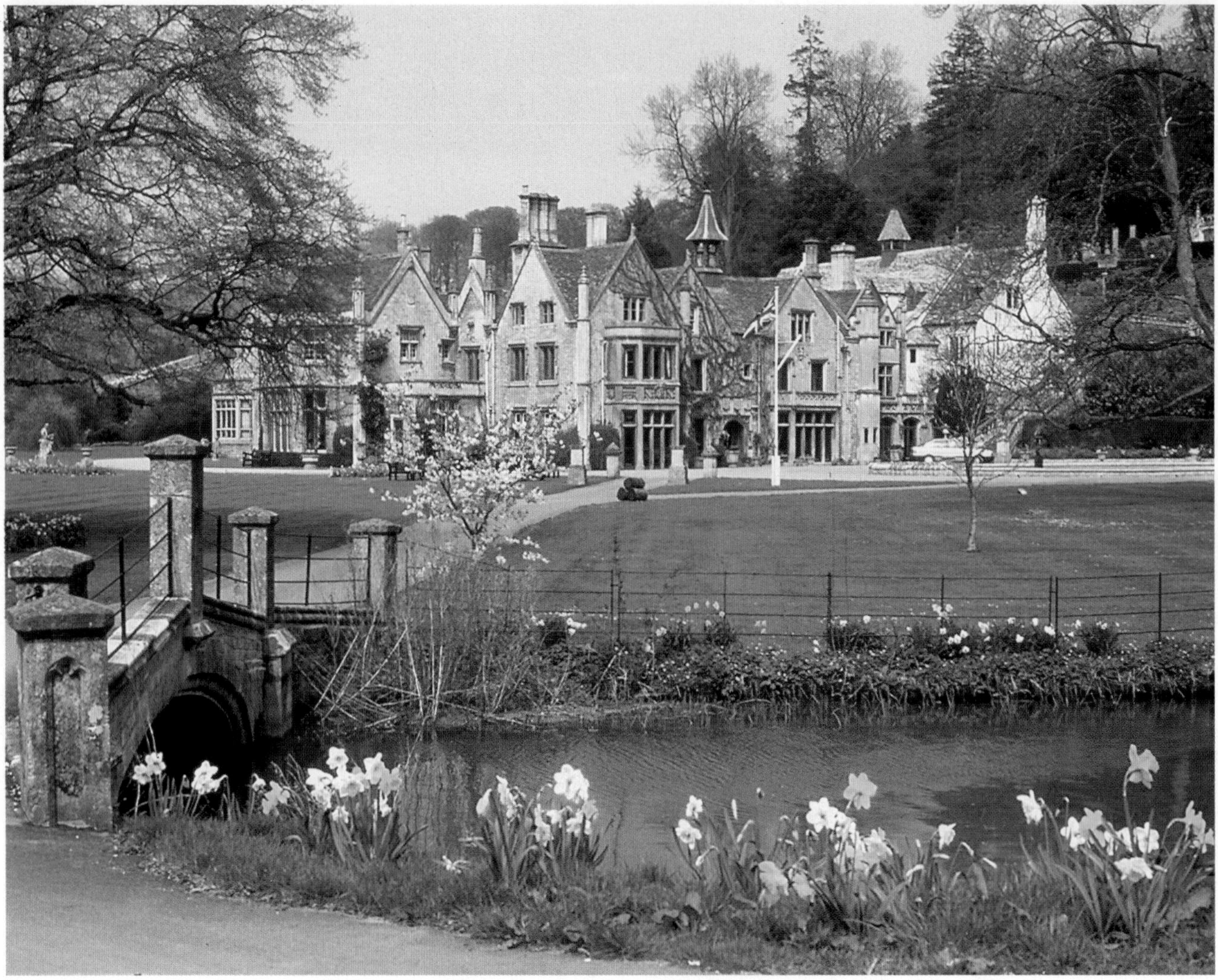

# THE MANOR HOUSE

**CASTLE COMBE, CHIPPENHAM, WILTSHIRE SN14 7HR**

**TEL: 01249 782206 FAX: 01249 782159 E-MAIL: enquiries@manor-house.co.uk.**

Nestling in the heart of one of England's prettiest villages deep in the Southern Cotswolds, the 14th century Manor House at Castle Combe is one of Britain's most architecturally beautiful and idyllically set country house hotels. Ivy clad stone walls and mullioned windows, oak panelling, log fires and antique furniture blend sympathetically with the individually designed bedrooms, many of which feature four poster beds, original beams and exposed walls. Designed by Peter Alliss and Clive Clark and set in 200 acres of woodland valley and downland, the 6340 yard par 73, championship golf course is one of the most spectacular and challenging courses in the South of England. Delightful walks in the surrounding countryside or a stroll through Castle Combe, unchanged for almost 200 years, is a magical experience. 26 acres of gardens and parkland, a gently flowing trout stream and the romance of a terraced Italian garden, The Manor House provides tranquillity in enchanting surroundings, together with a friendly atmosphere and award winning cuisine and hospitality. **Directions:** 15 minutes' drive from junctions 17 & 18 of the M4, or 20 minutes from the M5/M4 intersection. 12 miles from the beautiful Georgian city of Bath and only 2 hours drive from central London. Approached directly from A420 and B4039. Price guide: Single/double/twin from £100; suite from £235.

45 rms

For hotel location, see maps on pages 490-496

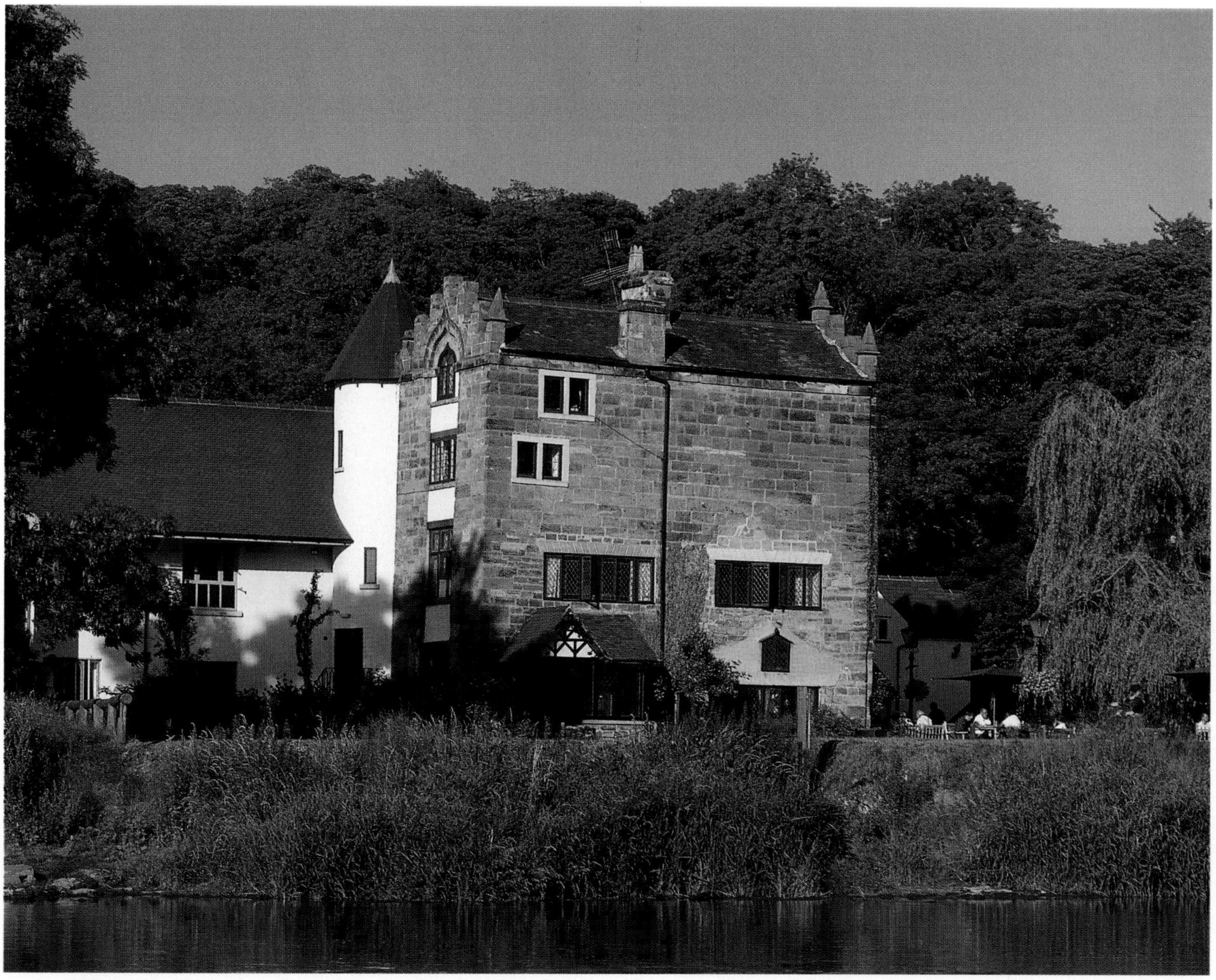

# THE PRIEST HOUSE ON THE RIVER

**KINGS MILLS, CASTLE DONINGTON, LEICESTERSHIRE DE74 2RR**
**TEL: 01332 810649 FAX: 01332 811141**

Magnificently situated on the banks of the River Trent, The Priest House is surrounded by 54 acres of mature unspoilt woodlands. Each of the bedrooms have been individually styled and the splendid Heron and Stocker suites are designed within the original Gothic Tower. Opening onto the private courtyard garden, the elegant library provides a perfect environment in which to read and relax. The traditional Waterside Inn offers a selection of real ales and is a popular venue for guests and non-residents alike, along with the Malt Bar which boasts over 50 different malt whiskies. The Mille Fleame Restaurant enjoys a growing reputation for the imaginative cuisine that it provides at both lunch and dinner, complemented by an excellent wine list. A number of spacious suites are available for banquets, receptions, weddings and private parties. A variety of leisure activities is available within the hotel, including clay pigeon shooting, coarse fishing and go-karting (all by arrangement). Places of interest nearby include Calke Abbey and Donington Park race circuit. An Arcadian Hotel. **Directions:** From M1, junction 24, follow signs for Donington Park then Castle Donington. At Castle Donington go left at traffic lights and follow road marked Kings Mills to the Priest House. Price guide: Single from £80, double/twin from £99; four-poster from £125; suite from £145.

For hotel location, see maps on pages 490-496

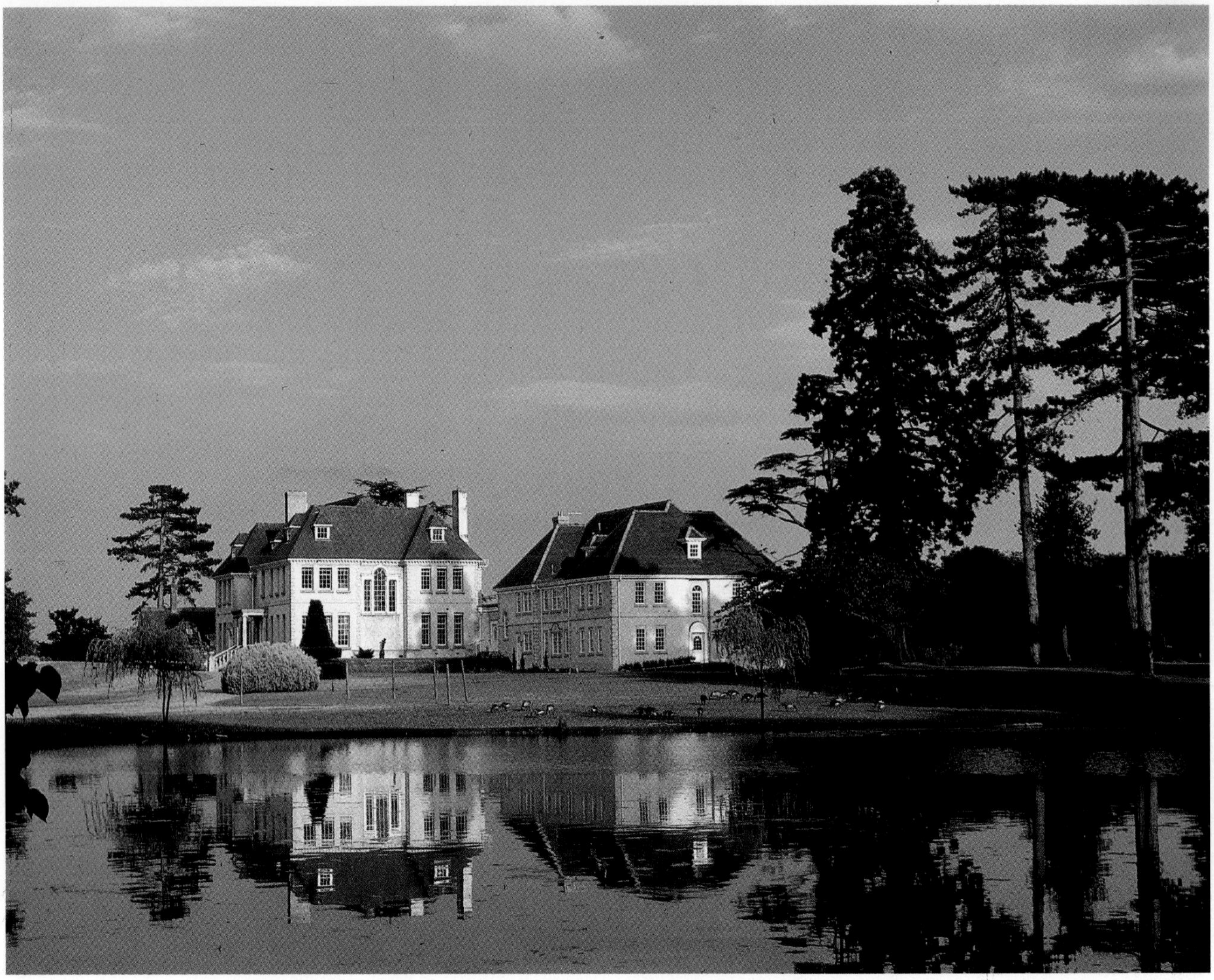

# BROCKENCOTE HALL

CHADDESLEY CORBETT, NR KIDDERMINSTER, WORCESTERSHIRE DY10 4PY

TEL: 01562 777876 FAX: 01562 777872

The Brockencote estate consists of 70 acres of landscaped grounds surrounding a magnificent hall. There are a gatehouse, half-timbered dovecote, lake, some fine European and North American trees and an elegant conservatory. The estate dates back over three centuries and the style of the building reflects the changes which have taken place in fashion and taste over the years. At present, the interior combines classical architectural features with contemporary creature comforts. As in most country houses, each of the bedrooms is different: all have their own character, complemented by tasteful furnishings and décor. The friendly staff provide a splendid service under the supervision of owners Alison and Joseph Petitjean. Head chef, Didier Philipot specialises in traditional French cuisine with occasional regional and seasonal specialities. Brockencote Hall is an ideal setting for those seeking peace and quiet in an unspoiled corner of the English countryside. Located a few miles south of Birmingham, it is convenient for business people and sightseers alike – it makes a fine base for touring historic Worcestershire. English Tourist Board – Silver award Hotel of the Year '95. **Directions:** Exit 4 from M5 or exit 1 from M42. Brockencote Hall is set back from the A448 at Chaddesley Corbett between Bromsgrove and Kidderminster. Price guide: Single £90; double/twin £120–£145.

For hotel location, see maps on pages 490-496

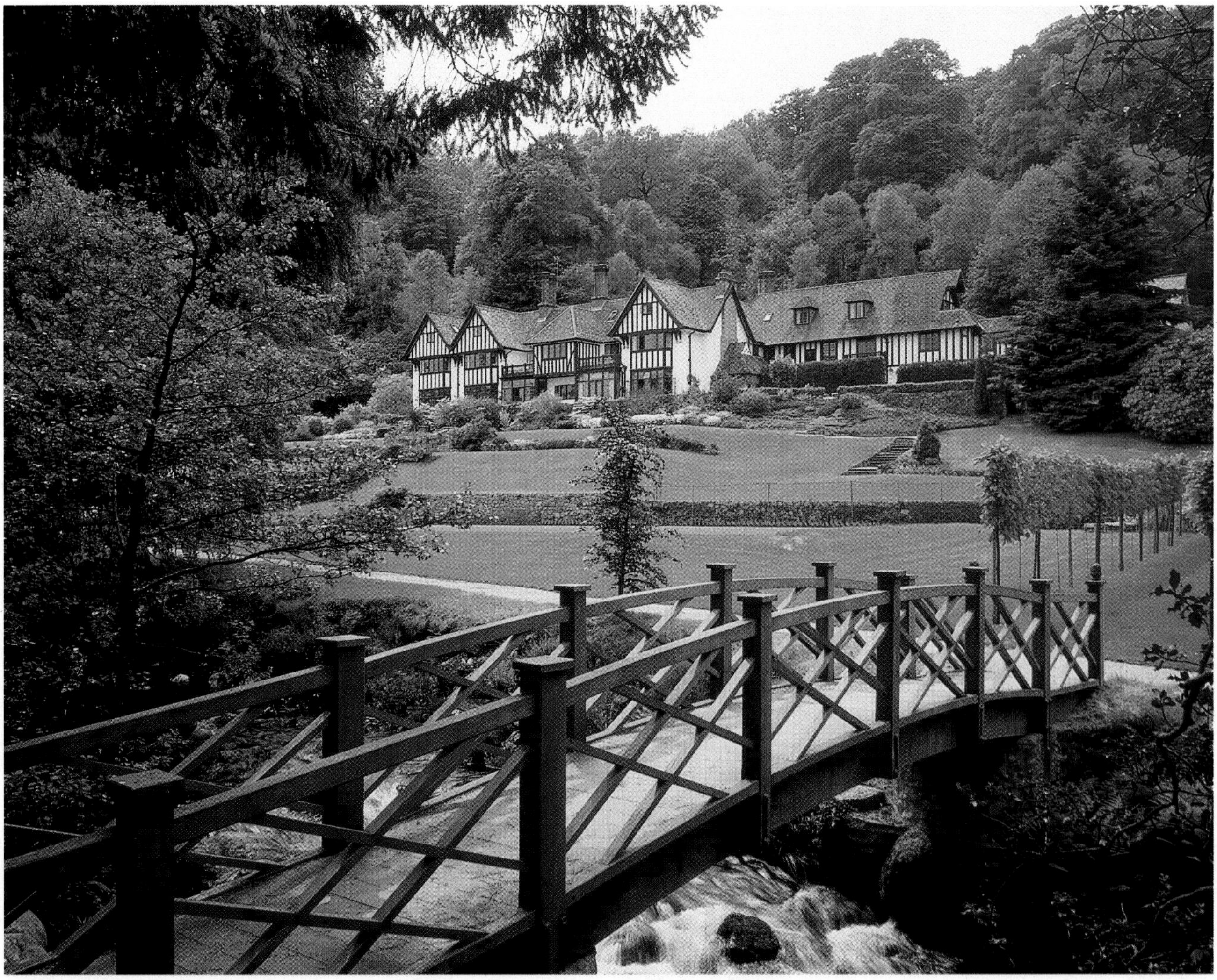

# GIDLEIGH PARK

**CHAGFORD, DEVON TQ13 8HH**

**TEL: 01647 432367 FAX: 01647 432574 E-MAIL: gidleighpark@gidleigh.co.uk**

Gidleigh Park enjoys an outstanding international reputation among connoisseurs for its comfort and gastronomy. It has collected a clutch of top culinary awards for its imaginative cuisine, and the Gidleigh Park wine list is one of the best in Britain. Service throughout the hotel is faultless. The en suite bedrooms – two of them in a converted chapel – are luxuriously furnished with antiques. The public rooms are elegantly appointed, and during the cooler months a fire burns merrily in the lounge's impressive fireplace. Set amid 45 secluded acres in the Teign Valley, Gidleigh Park is 1½ miles from the nearest public road. Two croquet lawns, an all-weather tennis court, a bowling lawn and a splendid water garden can be found in the grounds. A 250 yard long, par 27 putting course designed by Peter Alliss was opened in 1995. Guests can swim in the river or explore Dartmoor on foot or in the saddle. There are 14 miles of trout, sea trout and salmon fishing, as well as golf facilities nearby. Gidleigh Park is a Relais et Châteaux member. **Directions:** Approach from Chagford: go along Mill Street from Chagford Square. Fork right after 150 yards, cross into Holy Street at factory crossroads and follow lane for two miles. Price guide (including dinner): Single £220–£365; double/twin £335–£420.

For hotel location, see maps on pages 490-496

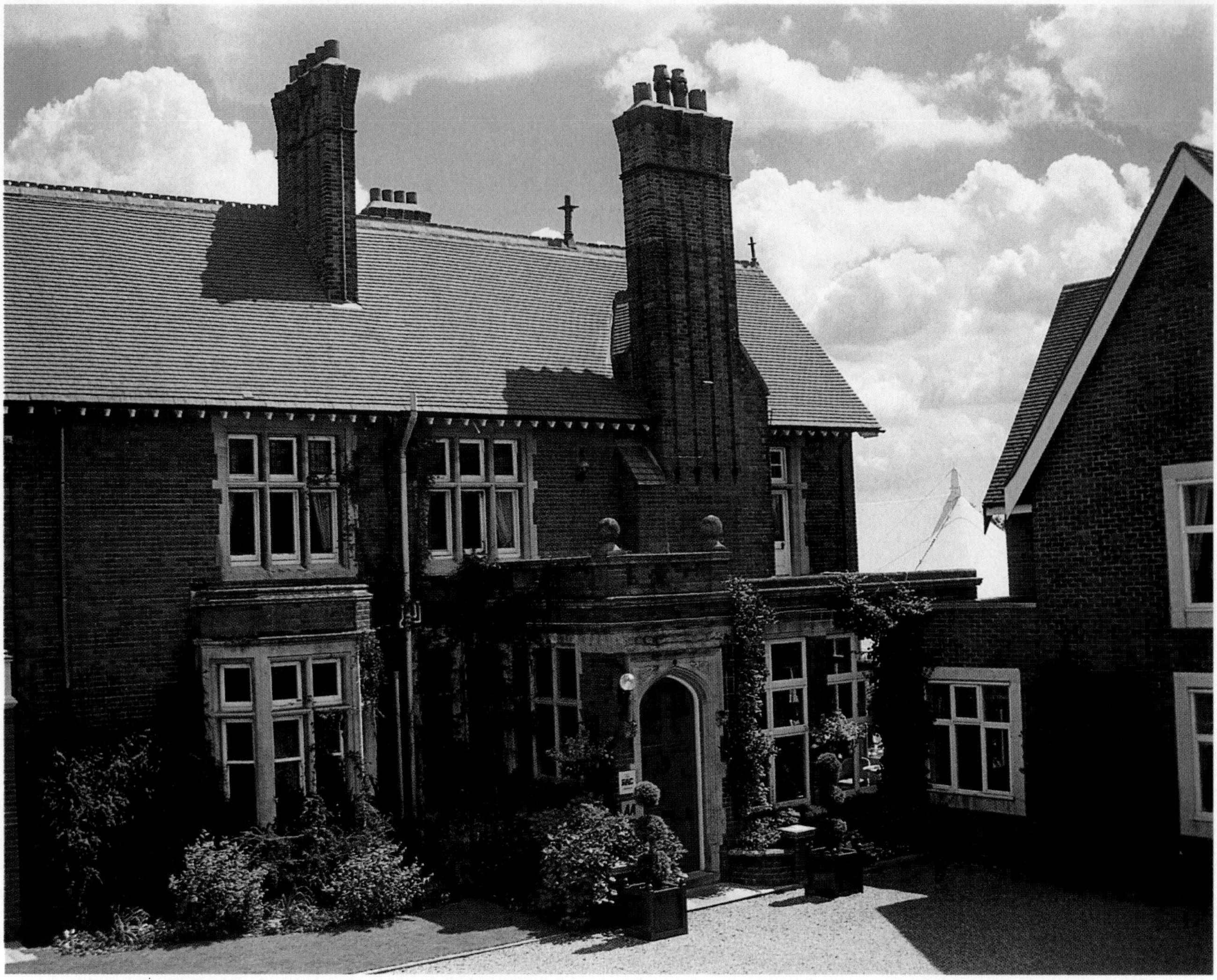

# PONTLANDS PARK COUNTRY HOTEL

**WEST HANNINGFIELD ROAD, GREAT BADDOW, NR CHELMSFORD, ESSEX CM2 8HR**
**TEL: 01245 476444 FAX: 01245 478393**

Pontlands Park is a fine Victorian mansion, originally built for the Thomasn-Foster family in 1879. It became a hotel in 1981. The Victorian theme is still much in evidence, tempered with the best of contemporary interior styling. Immaculate public rooms – the conservatory-style Garden Room, the Residents' Lounge with its deep sofas and the relaxed ambience of the Victorian bar – are designed with guests' comfort in mind. Beautifully furnished bedrooms have co-ordinated fabrics and well-defined colour schemes. Diners are offered a selection of imaginative menus, with fine wines and attentive service in our Conservatory Restaurant. Within the grounds, Trimmers Leisure Centre has indoor and outdoor swimming pools, Jacuzzis, saunas and a solarium. The Beauty Salon offers many figure-toning, hairstyling and beauty treatments. Meetings and private dinners from 2 to 100 guests can be accommodated, and functions for up to 200 guests can be held in the marquee. Closed 26 December to 3 January (but open for New Year's Eve). **Directions:** Pontlands Park is only about 30 miles from London. From A12 Chelmsford bypass take Great Baddow intersection (A130). Take first slip-road off A130 to Sandon/Great Baddow; bear left for Great Baddow, then first left for West Hanningfield Road. Price guide: Single £90; double/twin £120.

For hotel location, see maps on pages 490-496

# THE CHELTENHAM PARK HOTEL

**CIRENCESTER ROAD, CHARLTON KINGS, CHELTENHAM GL53 8EA**

**TEL: 01242 222021 FAX: 01242 254880/226935 E-MAIL: cheltenhampark@paramount-hotels.co.uk**

Nestling at the foot of the Cotswold Hills, just 2 miles south of the town centre, this splendid Georgian AA/RAC 4 Star hotel combines the character and style of its heritage with the comfort and efficiency of a modern luxury hotel. Colourful gardens, a natural lake and a gazebo enhance the atmosphere of elegance. All the bedrooms are en suite and comfortably furnished, many with scenic views. The Egon Ronay recommended Lakeside Restaurant, with its imaginative selection of international cuisine, carefully chosen menus and extensive wine list ensure that a meal is a memorable experience. Overlooking the lake to the golf course beyond, The Lilly Brook Bar and Terrace provide an ideal setting to enjoy morning coffee or an afternoon cocktail. The splendid Leisure Club includes a 15 metre indoor swimming pool, spa bath, steam room, sauna, solarium and health suite with cardio vascular and resistance gymnasiums. There are 7 conference rooms including a suite which can accommodate up to 350 delegates and a 10 further syndicate or small meeting rooms. Special weekend rates are available. **Directions:** From M5, exit at junction 11a. Follow A417 towards Cirencester/Birdlip. Straight over roundabout direction A436 Oxford. At 'T' junction, turn left direction Cheltenham, the hotel is on the left hand side just past the golf course. Price guide: Single from £90; double/twin from £120; suite from £180.

144 rms MasterCard VISA AMERICAN EXPRESS M 350

For hotel location, see maps on pages 490-496

# THE GREENWAY

**SHURDINGTON, CHELTENHAM, GLOUCESTERSHIRE GL51 5UG**
**TEL: 01242 862352 FAX: 01242 862780**

Set amidst gentle parkland with the rolling Cotswold hills beyond, The Greenway is an Elizabethan country house with a style that is uniquely its own – very individual and very special. Renowned for the warmth of its welcome, its friendly atmosphere and its immaculate personal service, The Greenway is the ideal place for total relaxation. The public rooms with their antique furniture and fresh flowers are elegant and spacious yet comfortable, with roaring log fires in winter and access to the formal gardens in summer. The 19 bedrooms all have private bathrooms and are individually decorated with co-ordinated colour schemes. Eleven of the rooms are located in the main house with a further eight rooms in the converted Georgian coach house immediately adjacent to the main building. The award winning conservatory dining room overlooks the sunken garden and lily pond, providing the perfect backdrop to superb cuisine of international appeal complemented by an outstanding selection of wines. Situated in one of Britain's most charming areas, The Greenway is well placed for visiting the spa town of Cheltenham, the Cotswold villages and Shakespeare country. **Directions:** On the outskirts of Cheltenham off the A46 Cheltenham–Stroud road, 2½ miles from the town centre. Price guide: Single £90; double/twin £135–£195.

For hotel location, see maps on pages 490-496

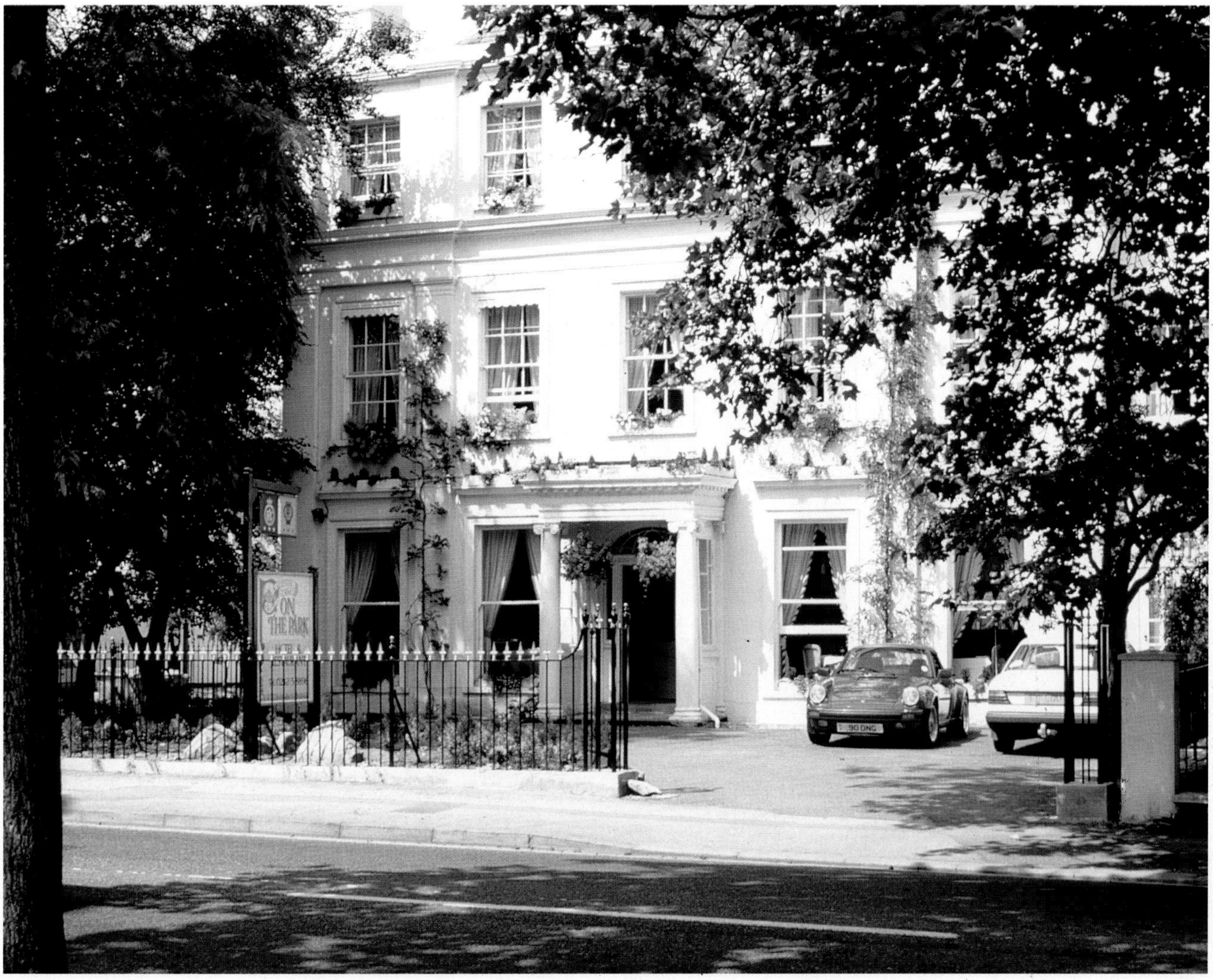

# HOTEL ON THE PARK

**EVESHAM ROAD, CHELTENHAM, GLOUCESTERSHIRE GL52 2AH**

**TEL: 01242 518898 FAX: 01242 511526**

Hotel On The Park is an exclusive AA three red-starred Town House Hotel situated in the elegant spa town of Cheltenham. It enjoys an envied position overlooking the beautiful Pittville Park. A classic example of a Regency villa, the atmosphere inside is one of warmth and sophistication, akin to that of a traditional country house. The 12 intimate and restful bedrooms are individually styled and furnished with antiques, offering everything that one would expect to find in a small, luxury hotel. Each room has a private bathroom en suite, colour satellite television, direct-dial telephone, hairdryer and refreshments. A board meeting room for 18 people is available. Guests can enjoy some of the best modern cooking on offer today in The Restaurant, where fresh produce is meticulously prepared with imagination and flair to produce well-balanced menus. The wine list has been carefully selected to offer something for all tastes. Cheltenham, with its Regency architecture, attractive promenade and exclusive shops, has plenty to offer visitors and is set in the heart of the Cotswolds. Cheltenham racecourse has a busy National Hunt programme. For details of terms during Gold Cup week, apply well in advance. Dogs accommodated by prior arrangement. **Directions:** Opposite Pittville Park, 5 minutes' walk from town centre. Price guide: Single from £74.50; double/twin from £91.50; suites from £121.50. Accomodation Only.

For hotel location, see maps on pages 490-496

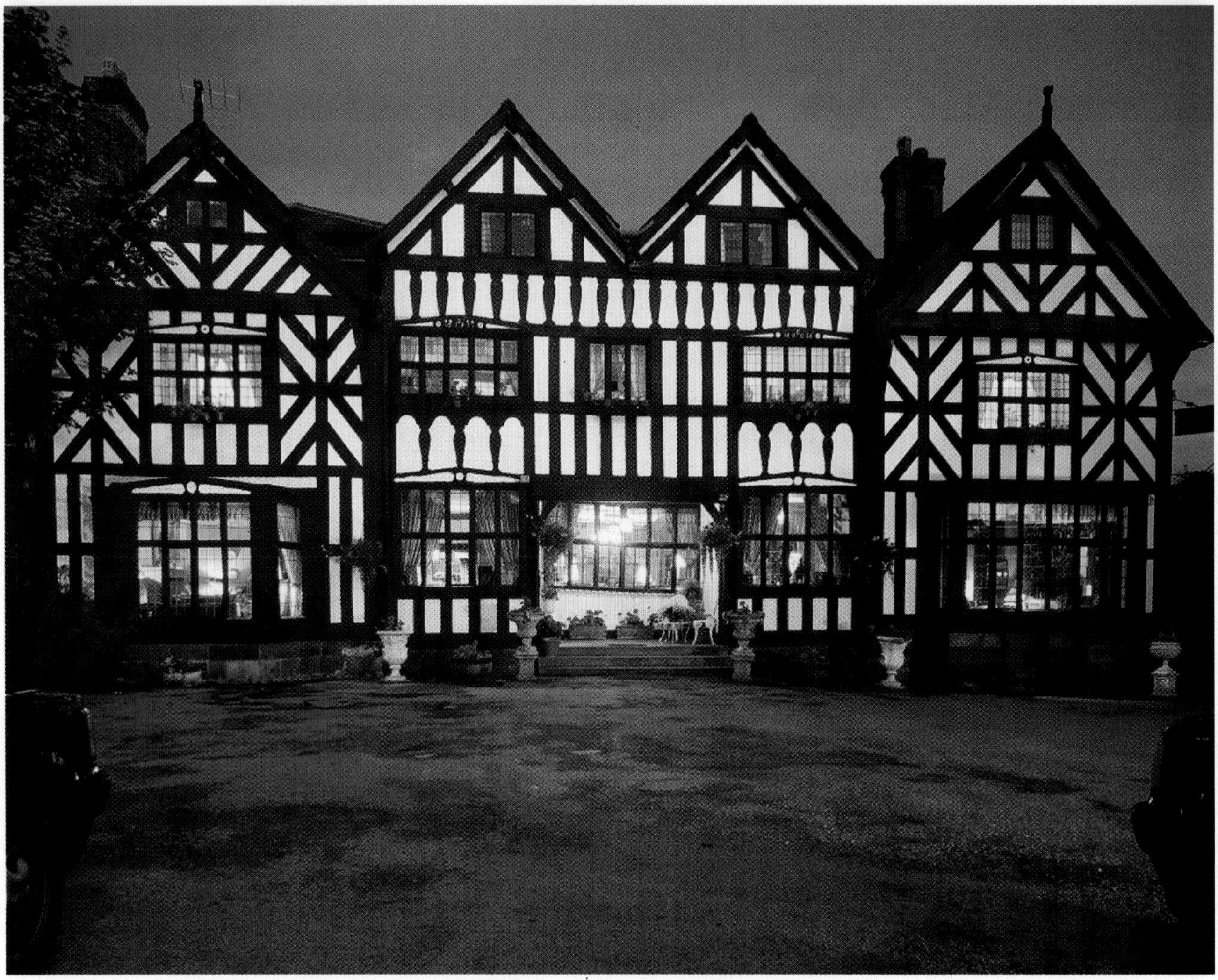

# BROXTON HALL COUNTRY HOUSE HOTEL

**WHITCHURCH ROAD, BROXTON, CHESTER, CHESHIRE CH3 9JS**
**TEL: 01829 782321 FAX: 01829 782330**

Built in 1671 by a local landowner, Broxton Hall is a black-and-white half-timbered building set in five acres of grounds and extensive gardens amid the rolling Cheshire countryside. The medieval city of Chester is eight miles away. The hotel provides every modern comfort while retaining the ambience of a bygone age. The reception area reflects the character of the entire hotel, with its magnificent Jacobean fireplace, plush furnishings, oak panelled walls and carved mahogany staircase. On cool evenings log fires are lit. The small but well-appointed bedrooms are furnished with antiques and have en suite bathrooms as well as every modern comfort. Overlooking the gardens, the restaurant receives constant praise from regular diners. French and English cuisine is served, using local game in season and freshly caught fish. There is an extensive wine list. Breakfast may be taken in the sunny conservatory overlooking the lawned gardens. The hotel is an ideal venue for business meetings and conferences. Broxton Hall is the perfect base from which to visit the North Wales coast and Snowdonia. There are a number of excellent golf courses nearby, and racecourses at Chester and Bangor-on-Dee. **Directions:** Broxton Hall is on the A41 Whitchurch–Chester road, eight miles between Whitchurch and Chester. Price guide: Single £60–£70; double/twin £70–£110.

For hotel location, see maps on pages 490-496

# THE CHESTER GROSVENOR

**EASTGATE, CHESTER CH1 1LT**
**TEL: 01244 324024 FAX: 01244 313246**

The Chester Grosvenor is in the heart of the historic city of Chester beneath the famous Queen Victoria Clock. The hotel is owned by the Duke of Westminster's Grosvenor Estate. It is renowned for its fabulous cuisine and has two restaurants – the Arkle and La Brasserie. The Arkle is an award winning gourmet restaurant, named after the famous racehorse Arkle. La Brasserie is an informal Parisian style restaurant which is open all day every day. The Chester Grosvenor has an extensive cellar with over 600 bins of fine wine. There are 85 bedrooms of which 11 are suites. All are beautifully appointed, fully air-conditioned with 24 hour room service provided and each room is equipped with all the amenities expected in a de luxe hotel awarded 5 AA Stars. The hotel has its own leisure suite with a multi-gymnasium, sauna and solarium and membership of an exclusive local country club which has indoor and outdoor swimming pools, tennis and squash. Adjacent are the famous Roman Walls and the Chester Rows with their boutiques and exclusive shops. A short stroll away is Chester Cathedral, Chester race course and the River Dee. **Directions:** In the centre of Chester on Eastgate. 24-hour NCP car parking – follow signs to Grosvenor Precinct Car Park. Price guide: Weekend break rate from £150 per double room per night. Single from £160; double/twin from £250; suites £400.

For hotel location, see maps on pages 490-496

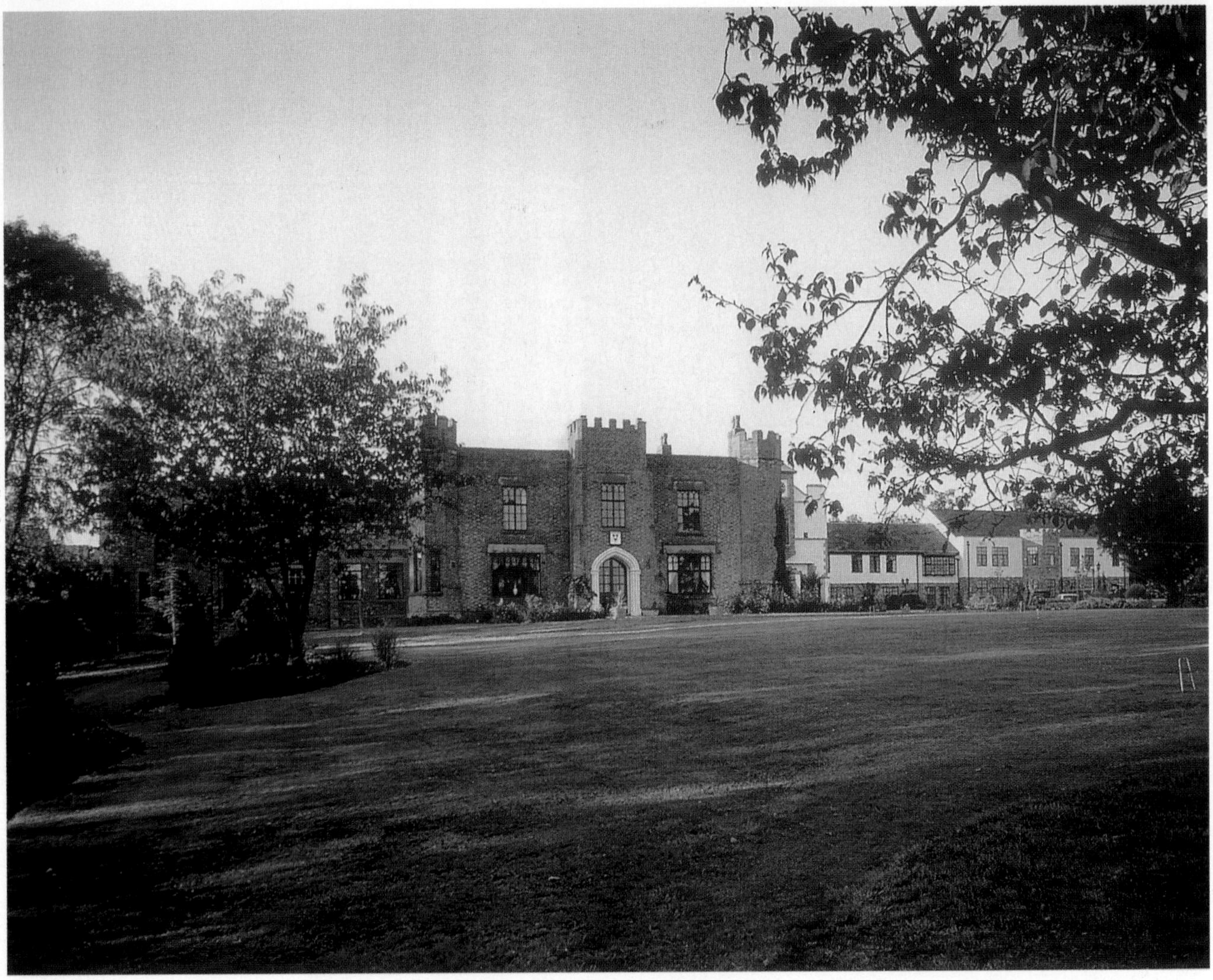

# Crabwall Manor

PARKGATE ROAD, MOLLINGTON, CHESTER, CHESHIRE CH1 6NE
TEL: 01244 851666 FAX: 01244 851400 E-MAIL: SALES@CRABWALL.U-NET.COM

Crabwall Manor can be traced back to Saxon England, prior to the Norman Conquest. The present Grade II listed manor at the heart of the hotel is believed to have originated from a Tudor farmhouse. Set in 11 acres of wooded parkland on the outer reaches of Chester, the hotel has achieved a fine reputation under the ownership of Carl Lewis. A relaxed ambience is enhanced by staff who combine attentive service with friendliness and care. Bathrobes and sherry are among the many extras to be found in the bedrooms and luxury suites. Brightly printed drapes and pastel shades lend a freshness to the décor of the spacious lounge and reception areas, while a log fire crackling away in the inglenook fireplace adds warmth. Chef Michael Truelove, formerly of The Box Tree Restaurant in Ilkley, introduces a classic French influence to traditional English dishes. Manchester and Liverpool Airports are 30 minutes away by road. Chester, the Wirral and North Wales are all easily accessible. **Directions:** Go to end of M56, ignoring signs to Chester. Follow signs to Queensferry and North Wales, taking the A5117 to the next roundabout. Left onto the A540, towards Chester for 2 miles. Crabwall Manor is on the right. Price guide: Single £90–£120; double/twin £105–£160; suite £190–£250. Weekend rates available. Internet: http://www.hotelnet.co.uk/crabwall

For hotel location, see maps on pages 490-496

# NUNSMERE HALL

TARPORLEY ROAD, OAKMERE, NORTHWICH, CHESHIRE CW8 2ES
TEL: 01606 889100 FAX: 01606 889055

Set in peaceful Cheshire countryside and surrounded on three sides by a lake, Nunsmere Hall epitomises the elegant country manor where superior standards of hospitality still exist. Wood panelling, antique furniture, exclusive fabrics, Chinese lamps and magnificent chandeliers evoke an air of luxury. The 32 bedrooms, with spectacular views of the lake and gardens, are beautifully appointed with king-size beds, comfortable breakfast seating and marbled bathrooms containing soft bathrobes and toiletries. The Brocklebank, Delamere and Oakmere business suites are air-conditioned, soundproofed and offer excellent facilities for boardroom meetings, private dining and seminars. The Restaurant has a reputation for fine food and uses only fresh seasonal produce. County Restaurant of the Year in the 1996 Good Food Guide. A snooker room is available and there are several championship golf courses nearby. Oulton Park racing circuit and the Cheshire Polo Club are next door. Golf pitch and putt is available in the grounds. Archery and Air rifle shooting by arrangement. Although secluded, Nunsmere is convenient for major towns and routes. AA 3 Red Star and Three Rosettes. **Directions:** Leave M6 at junction 18 northbound or 19 southbound, take A556 to Chester (approximately 12 miles). Turn left onto A49. Hotel is 1 mile on left. Price guide: Single £110; double/twin £150–£175; suite from £225.

32 rms MasterCard VISA AMERICAN EXPRESS M 58

For hotel location, see maps on pages 490-496

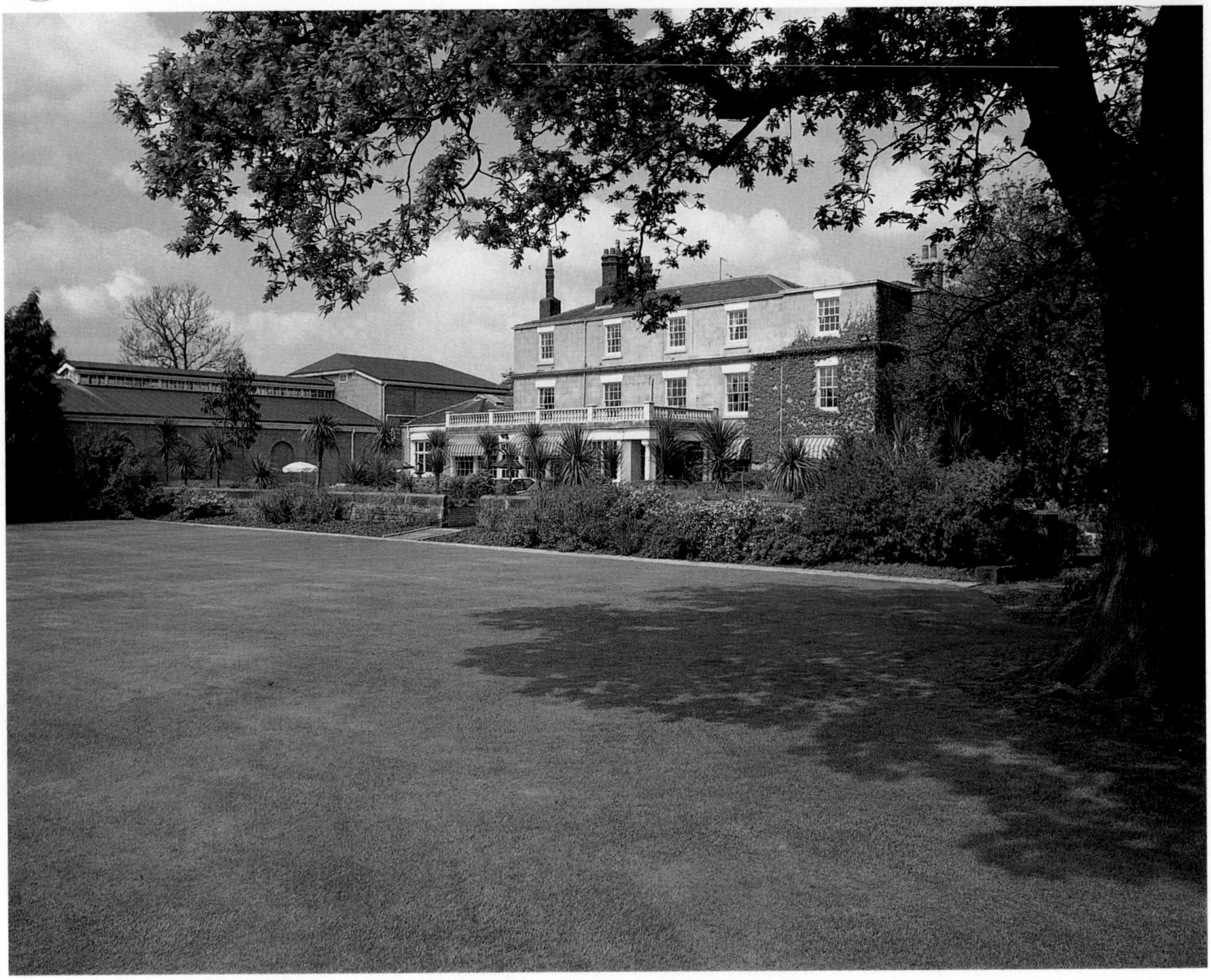

# ROWTON HALL HOTEL

WHITCHURCH ROAD, ROWTON, CHESTER, CHESHIRE CH3 6AD
TEL: 01244 335262 FAX: 01244 335464

Standing in eight acres of gardens and pastureland on the outskirts of the city of Chester, Rowton Hall enjoys far-reaching views across the Cheshire Plains to the Welsh hills. Built as a private residence in 1779, the hall is renowned for the informal country-house atmosphere which welcomes all its guests. It retains many original features, including a Robert Adam fireplace and superb carved staircase. The conservatory-style Hamilton Lounge, overlooking the garden, is the perfect place to enjoy morning coffee, afternoon tea or cocktails, while the Cavalier Bar is ideal for a lunchtime snack. The bedrooms are furnished with chintzy fabrics and all have en suite bathrooms. In the Langdale Restaurant, which has earned a first-class reputation, chef Roger Price's à la carte and table d'hôte menus can be sampled in elegant and restful surroundings. Fresh vegetables and herbs are supplied by the hall's kitchen garden. Hotel guests have complimentary use of Hamiltons Leisure Club – facilities include a swimming pool, multi-gym, sauna and solarium. There are five conference/meeting rooms accommodating up to 200. The hotel offers special weekend rates. **Directions:** From the centre of Chester, take the A41 towards Whitchurch. After three miles, turn right to Rowton village. The hotel is in the centre of the village. Price guide: Single £75–£78; double/twin £90–£95; four poster suite £98.

For hotel location, see maps on pages 490-496

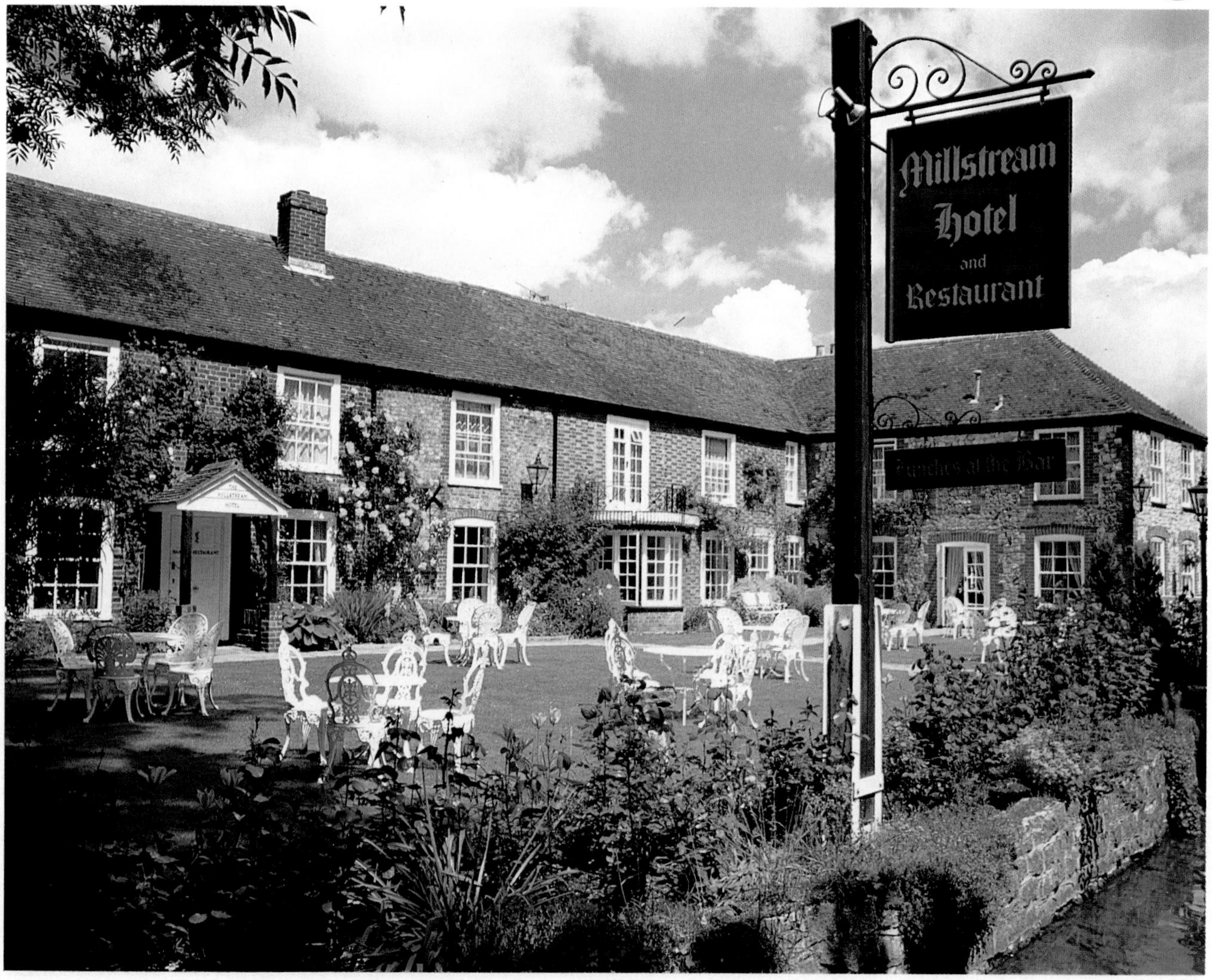

# THE MILLSTREAM HOTEL

**BOSHAM, NR CHICHESTER, WEST SUSSEX PO18 8HL**
**TEL: 01243 573234 FAX: 01243 573459**

A village rich in heritage, Bosham is depicted in the Bayeux Tapestry and is associated with King Canute, whose daughter is buried in the local Saxon church. Moreover, sailors from the world over navigate their way to Bosham, which is a yachtsman's idyll on the banks of Chichester Harbour. The Millstream consists of a restored 18th-century malthouse and adjoining cottages linked to The Grange, a small English manor house. Individually furnished bedrooms are complemented by chintz fabrics and pastel décor. Period furniture, a grand piano and bowls of freshly cut flowers feature in the drawing room. A stream meanders past the front of the delightful gardens, where traditional herbs are grown for use by the *chef de cuisine*. Whatever the season, care is taken to ensure that the composition and presentation of the dishes reflect high standards. An appetising luncheon menu is offered and includes local seafood specialities such as: dressed Selsey crab, home cured and smoked salmon and grilled fresh lemon sole. During the winter, good-value 'Hibernation Breaks' are available. **Directions:** From Chichester or Havant follow the A259 to Bosham. Price guide: Single £69–£75; double/twin £109–£112; suite £139–£145.

33 rms

For hotel location, see maps on pages 490-496

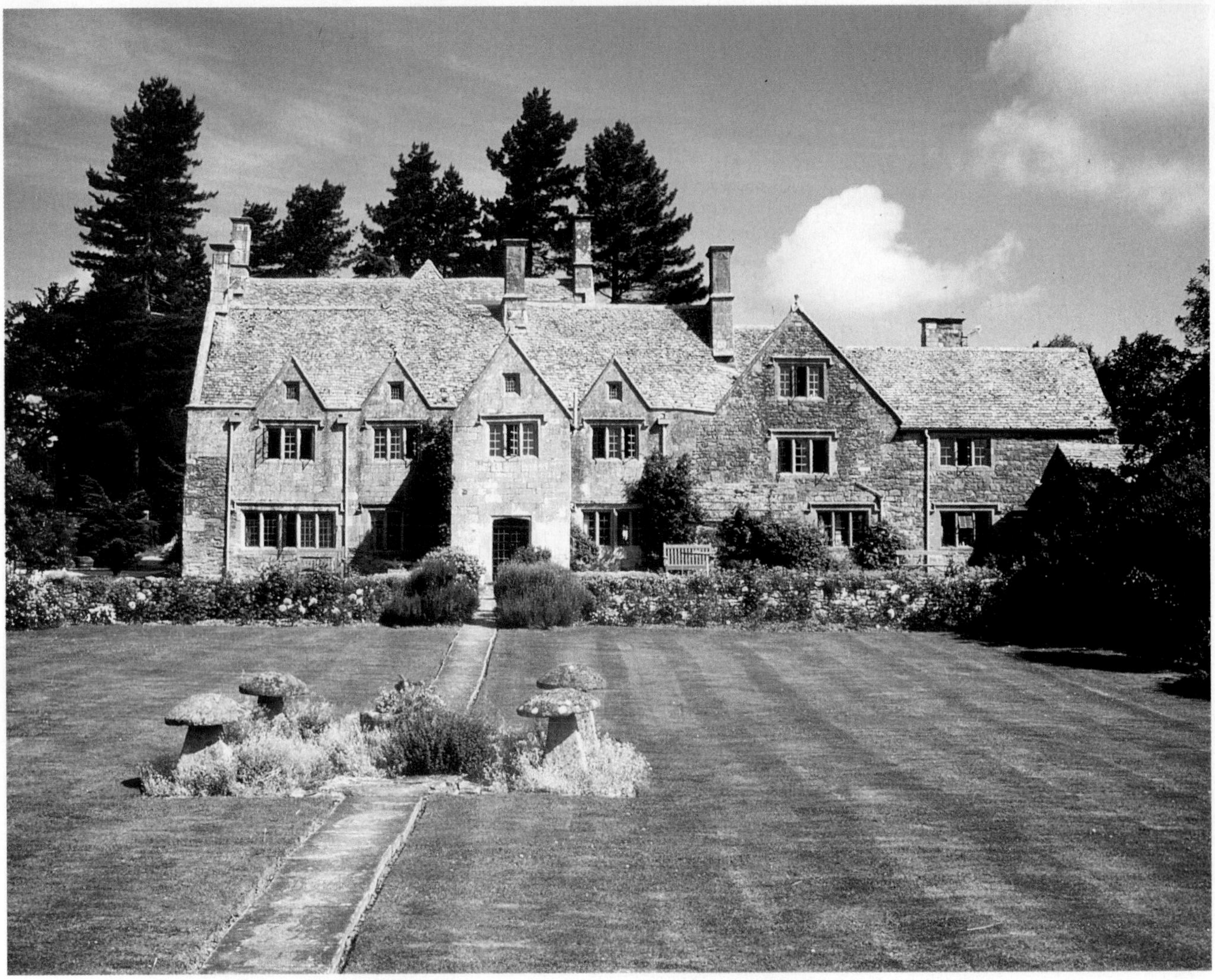

# CHARINGWORTH MANOR

**NR CHIPPING CAMPDEN, GLOUCESTERSHIRE GL55 6NS**
**TEL: 01386 593555 FAX: 01386 593353**

The ancient manor of Charingworth lies amid the gently rolling Cotswold countryside, just a few miles from the historic towns of Chipping Campden and Broadway. Beautiful old stone buildings everywhere recall the flourishing wool trade that gave the area its wealth. The 14th-century manor house overlooks its own 50-acre grounds and offers peace and enthralling views. Inside, Charingworth is a historic patchwork of intimate public rooms with log fires burning during the colder months. There are 26 individually designed bedrooms, all furnished with antiques and fine fabrics. Outstanding cuisine is regarded as being of great importance and guests at Charingworth are assured of imaginative dishes. Great emphasis is placed on using only the finest produce and the AA has awarded the cuisine two Rosettes. There is an all-weather tennis court within the grounds, while inside, a beautiful swimming pool, sauna, steam room, solarium and billiard room are available, allowing guests to relax and unwind. Warwick Castle, Hidcote Manor Gardens, Batsford Arboretum, Stratford-upon-Avon, Oxford and Cheltenham are all within easy reach. Short-break rates are available on request. **Directions:** Charingworth Manor is on the B4035 between Chipping Campden and Shipston-on-Stour. Price guide: (including full breakfast) Single from £95; double/twin from £159.

For hotel location, see maps on pages 490-496

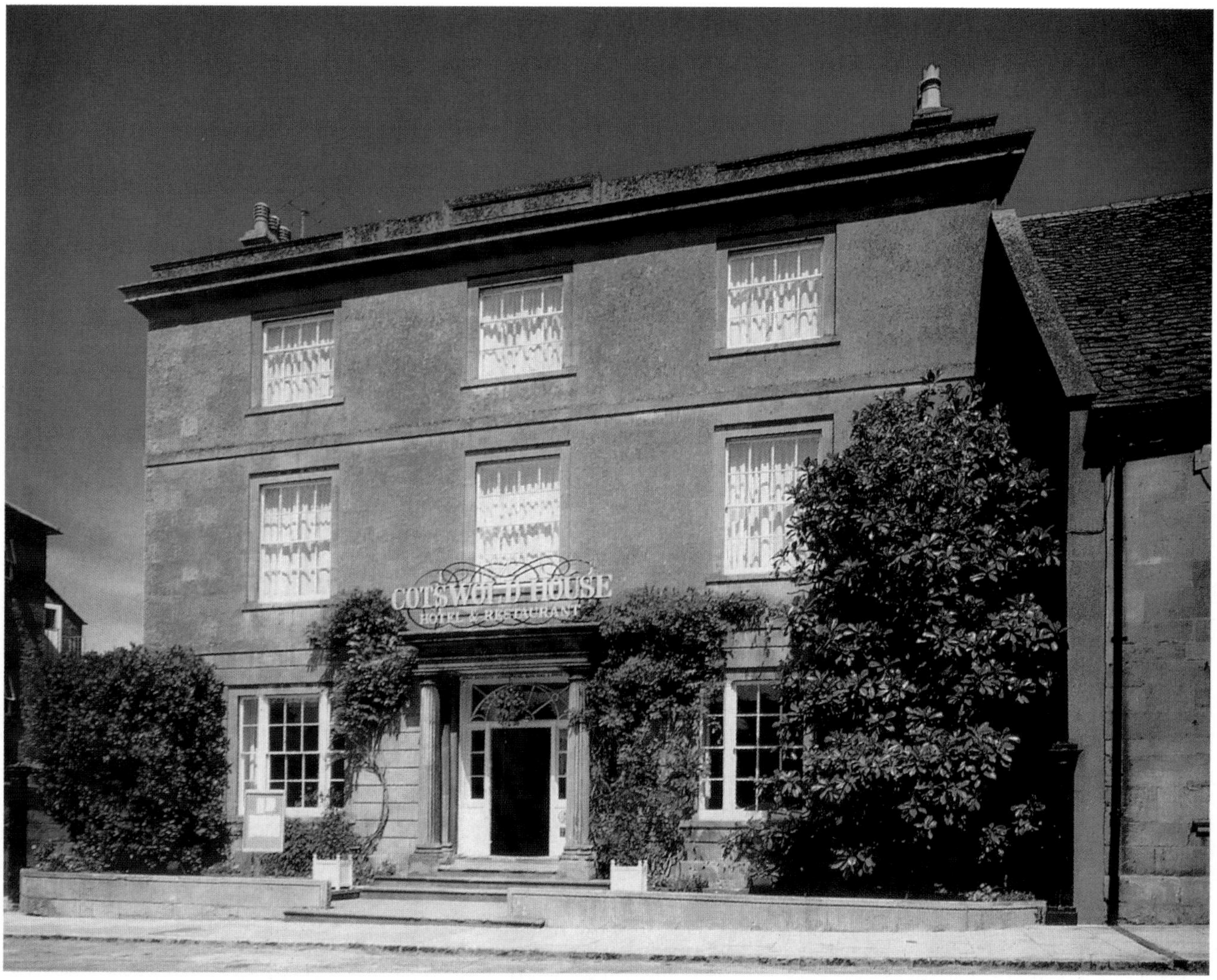

# The Cotswold House

HIGH STREET, CHIPPING CAMPDEN, GLOUCESTERSHIRE GL55 6AN

TEL: 01386 840330 FAX: 01386 840310

Chipping Campden is a nostalgic Cotswold town, unspoilt by the twentieth century, and Cotswold House is a splendid 17th century mansion facing the town square, impressive with colonnades flanking the front door and built in the lovely soft local stone. The interior has been sensitively decorated and modernised so there is no distraction from the graceful pillared archway and staircase. Lovely antiques, fine paintings, and fabrics reminiscent of the Regency era blend easily with comfortable sofas in the elegant drawing room. The bedrooms are very individual, with memorabilia appropriate to their theme, but all are peaceful, decorated in harmonious colours and have 'country house' style furnishings. Cotswold House is deservedly proud of its kitchen, which has won many accolades. The attractive Garden Room Restaurant has a splendid menu and a cellar book of 150 wines! Informal meals are in The Brasserie. Private functions and small conferences can be held in the secluded Courtyard Room. Guests enjoy exploring Chipping Campden's intriguing shops and alleyways, The hotel is a superb base for Cheltenham Races, Stratford-on-Avon, Oxford and visiting famous houses and gardens throughout the Cotswolds. **Directions:** Chipping Campden is 2 miles north-east of A44, on the B4081. The hotel has parking facilities. Price guide: Single from £55; double/twin from £110; four poster from £160.

For hotel location, see maps on pages 490-496

# THE PLOUGH AT CLANFIELD

**BOURTON ROAD, CLANFIELD, OXFORDSHIRE OX18 2RB**
**TEL: 01367 810222 FAX: 01367 810596**

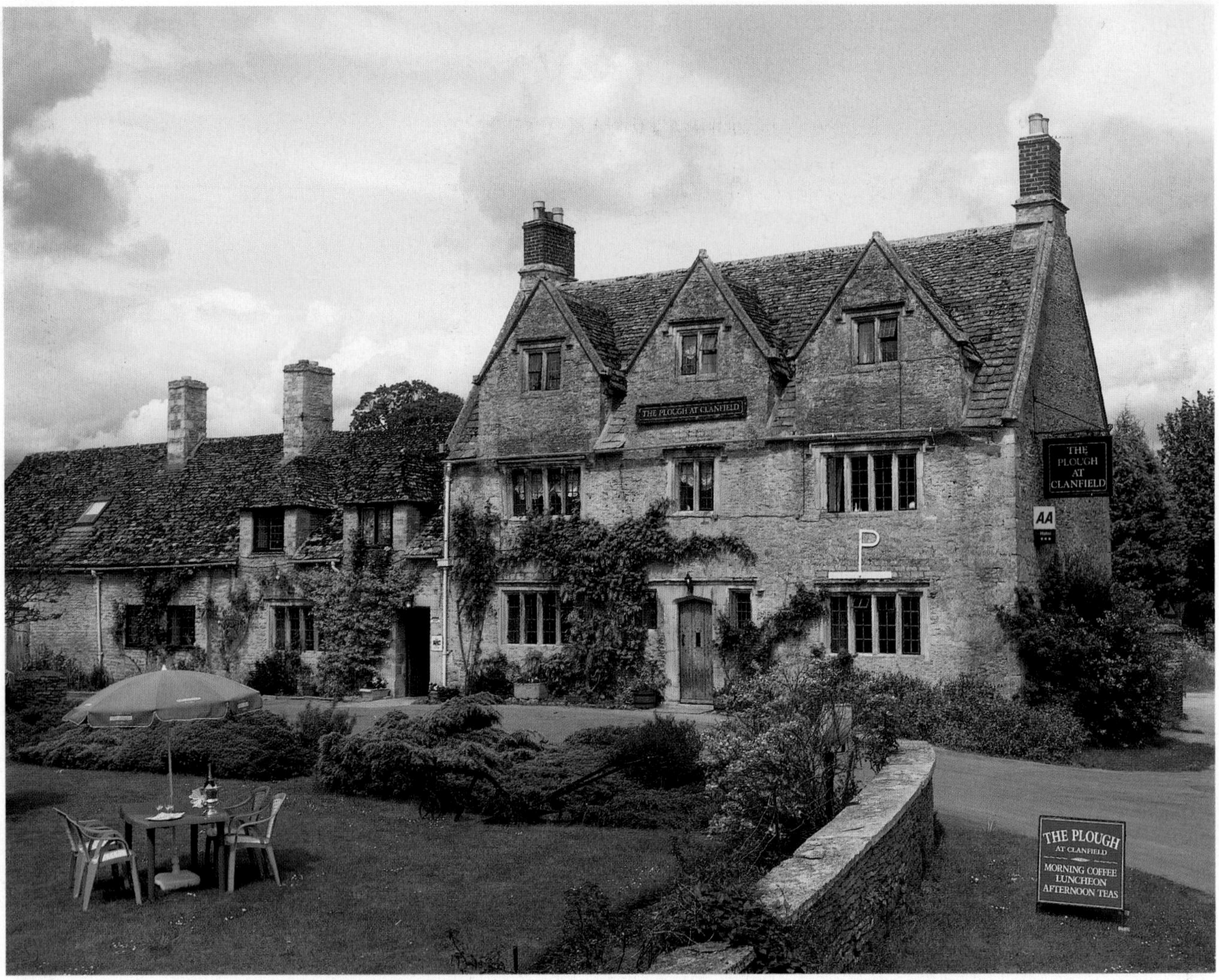

The Plough at Clanfield is an idyllic hideaway for the romantic at heart. Set on the edge of the village of Clanfield, typical of the Oxfordshire Cotswolds. The Plough dates from 1560 and is a fine example of well-preserved Elizabethan architecture. The hotel is owned and personally run by John and Rosemary Hodges, who have taken great care to preserve the charm and character of this historic building. Because there are only six bedrooms, guests can enjoy an intimate atmosphere and attentive, personal service. All the bedrooms are beautifully appointed to the highest standard and all have en suite bathrooms. At the heart of the hotel is the two AA Rosette Restaurant, regarded as one of the finest in the area. The cuisine is superbly prepared and impeccably served, with an interesting selection of wines. Two additional dining rooms are available for private entertaining. The hotel is an ideal base from which to explore the Cotswolds or the Thames Valley. There are many historic houses and gardens in the area, as well as racing at Newbury and Cheltenham. Hotel closed 27th, 28th & 29th December. **Directions:** The hotel is located on the edge of the village of Clanfield, at the junction of the A4095 and B4020, between the towns of Witney and Faringdon, some 15 miles to the west of the city of Oxford. Price guide: Single £70; Double £105–£120.

For hotel location, see maps on pages 490-496

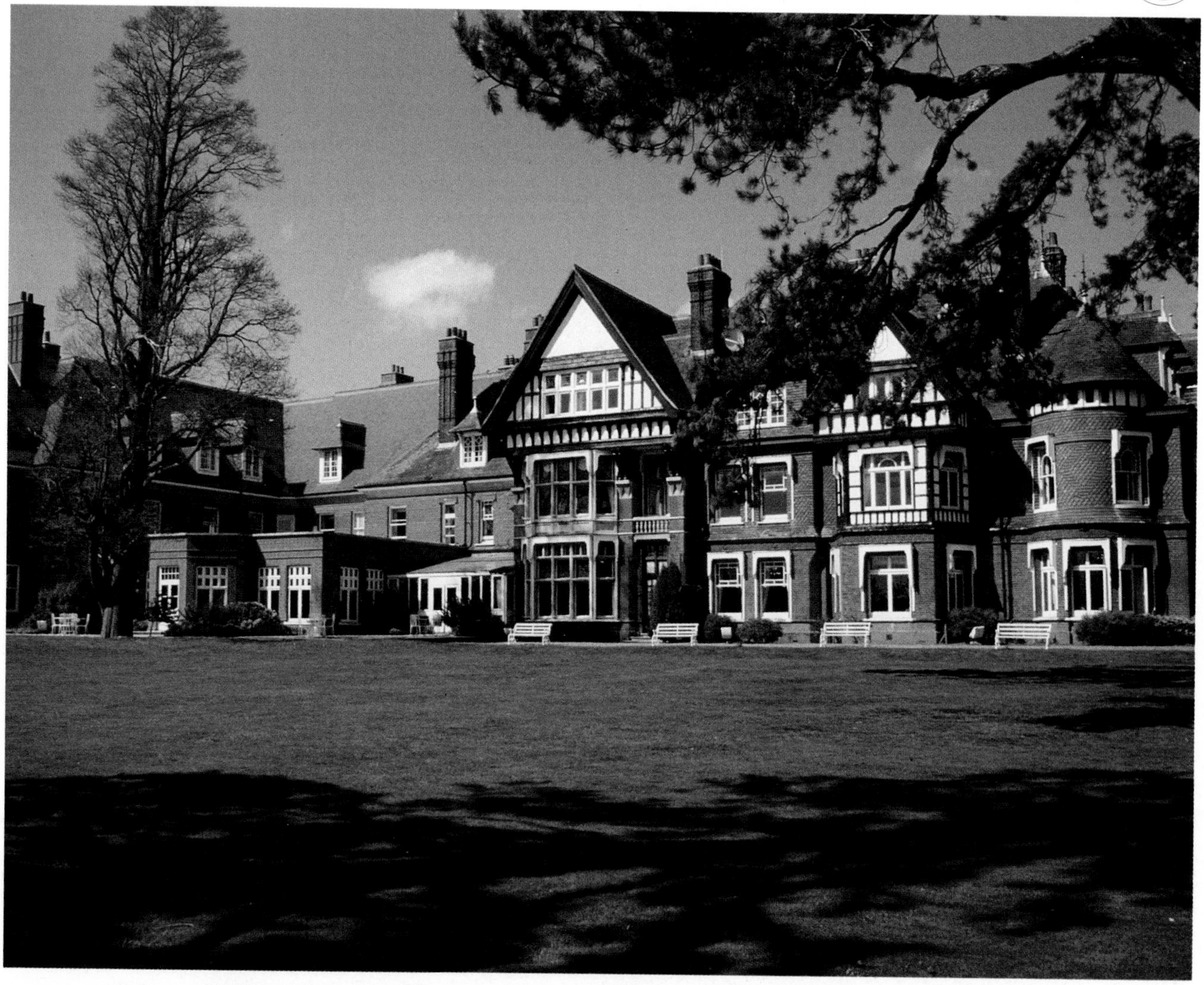

# WOODLANDS PARK HOTEL

**WOODLANDS LANE, STOKE D'ABERNON, COBHAM, SURREY KT11 3QB**
**TEL: 01372 843933 FAX: 01372 842704**

Set in 10 acres of parkland, Woodlands Park Hotel is an ideal location for touring the surrounding Surrey and Berkshire countryside or for those seeking a base on the edge of Greater London. At the turn of the century, the then Prince of Wales and the famous actress Lillie Langtry were frequent visitors to this splendid Victorian mansion. Well equipped en suite bedrooms retain an appealing Victorian theme and ambience, despite their having been refurbished to the highest modern standards. Each offers its guests luxury, comfort and every up to date amenity. The Oak Room Restaurant serves imaginative English and French cuisine in elegant surroundings, while Langtry's Bar and Brasserie, offering a daily blackboard menu and a wide selection of dishes from the speciality menu, is designed for those who prefer less formal dining. Small meeting rooms can be reached from the Grand Hall and can accommodate between 10 and 60 for private dinners or meetings, while the modern Prince of Wales Suite seats up to 280. Nearby are Wisley Gardens, Hampton Court and Brooklands Museum. Kempton Park, Epsom and Sandown are within a short distance for those who enjoy racing. An Arcadian Hotel. **Directions:** On the M25 take junction 9 or 10. The hotel is east of Cobham at Stoke d'Abernon on the A245. Price guide: Single £110–£125; twin/double £140–£155; suites £175–£200.

For hotel location, see maps on pages 490-496

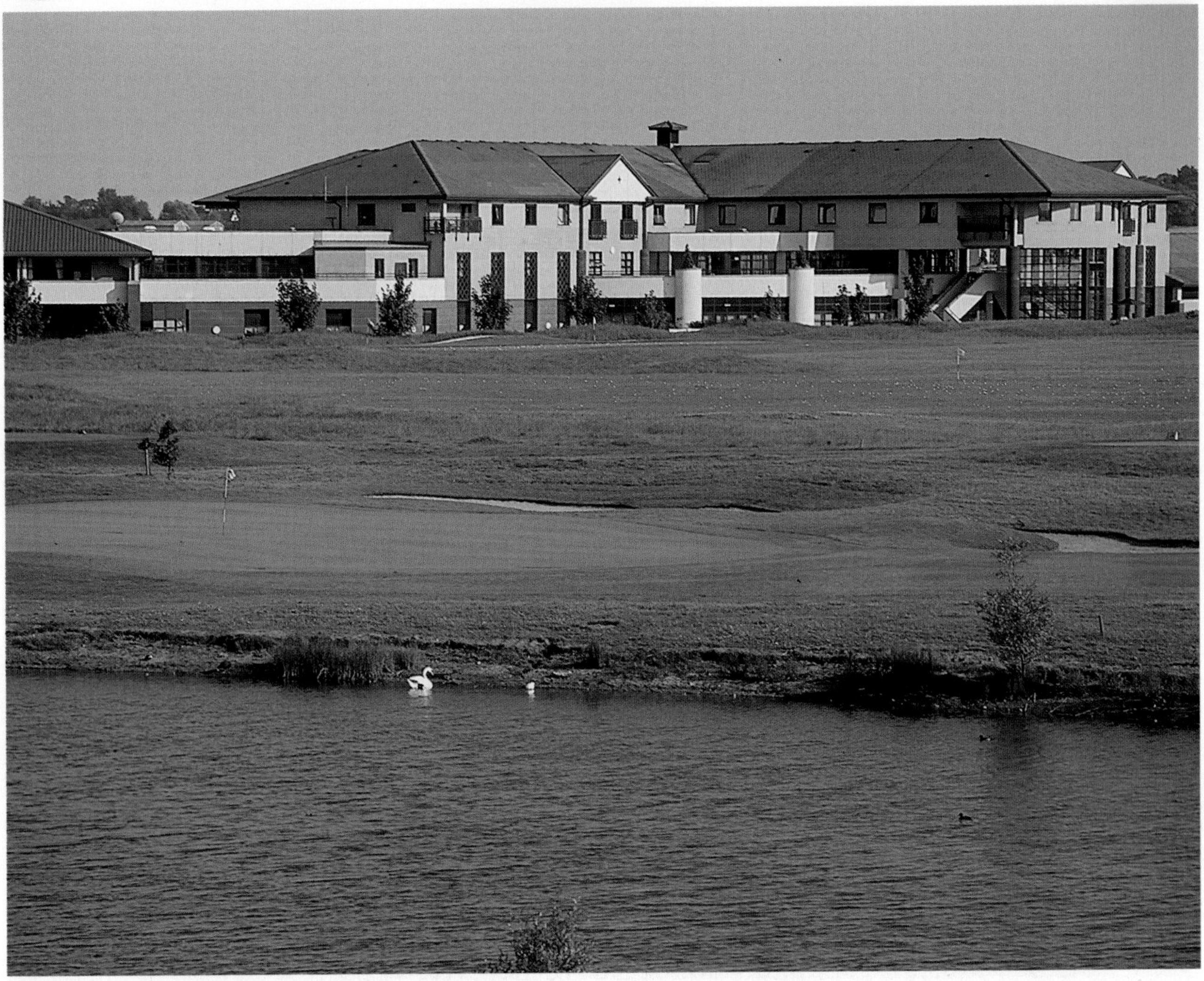

# FIVE LAKES HOTEL, GOLF & COUNTRY CLUB

**COLCHESTER ROAD, TOLLESHUNT KNIGHTS, MALDON, ESSEX CM9 8HX**
**TEL: 01621 868888 FAX: 01621 869696**

Set in 320 acres , Five Lakes is a superb 21st century hotel which combines the latest in sporting, leisure and health activities with state-of-the-art conference, meeting and banqueting facilities. The 114 bedrooms are furnished to a high standard and offer every comfort and convenience. With its two 18-hole courses – one of them, The Lakes, being a PGA European Tour course – the hotel is already recognised as one of East Anglia's leading golf venues. Guests are also invited to take advantage of the Championship standard indoor tennis; outdoor tennis; squash; indoor pool with Jacuzzi, steam and sauna; gymnasium; jogging trail; snooker and an outstanding health spa. There is a choice of restaurants, where good food is complemented by excellent service. Lounges and cocktail bars provide a comfortable environment in which to relax and enjoy a drink. Extensive facilities for conferences, meetings, exhibitions and functions include 18 rooms and a 3,500 sqm exhibition arena, suitable for over two thousand people. All rooms are air-conditioned or comfort-cooled, with 16 rooms having natural daylight. **Directions:** Approximately 36 miles from junction 28 of the M25 follow A12 towards Colchester and take B1024 at Kelvedon. Price guide: Single £85; double/twin £115–£135; suites £165.

For hotel location, see maps on pages 490-496

# THE WHITE HART HOTEL & RESTAURANT

**MARKET END, COGGESHALL, ESSEX CO6 1NH**
**TEL: 01376 561654 FAX: 01376 561789**

A historic, family-run hotel, The White Hart is situated in the Essex town of Coggeshall, where it has played an integral part for many years. In 1489 The White Hart became the town's meeting place when most of the adjoining Guildhall was destroyed by fire. Part of that original Guildhall now forms the residents' lounge, and features magnificent roof timbers hewn from sweet chestnut. Sympathetically restored throughout, the hotel has been comfortably appointed with much attention to detail. All the en suite bedrooms have been decorated with bright fabrics to reflect the hotel's colourful character. Heavily timbered and spacious, the restaurant enjoys a good reputation locally. The table d'hôte and à la carte menus feature a choice of Italian dishes with a particular emphasis on seafood and shellfish. Pasta is freshly made, and aromatic sauces and tender cuts of meat figure prominently on the menu. The hotel has recently received merit awards from the RAC for comfort and its restaurant, which already holds 2 AA rosettes and an Egon Ronay recommendedation. Coggeshall is noted for its antiques shops. It is also convenient for Colchester and Chelmsford and the ferry ports of Felixstowe and Harwich. **Directions:** Coggeshall is just off the A120 between Colchester and Braintree. From the A12 follow signs through Kelvedon, then take B1024. Price guide: Single £61.50; double/twin £97.

18 rms MasterCard VISA AMERICAN EXPRESS M 35

For hotel location, see maps on pages 490-496

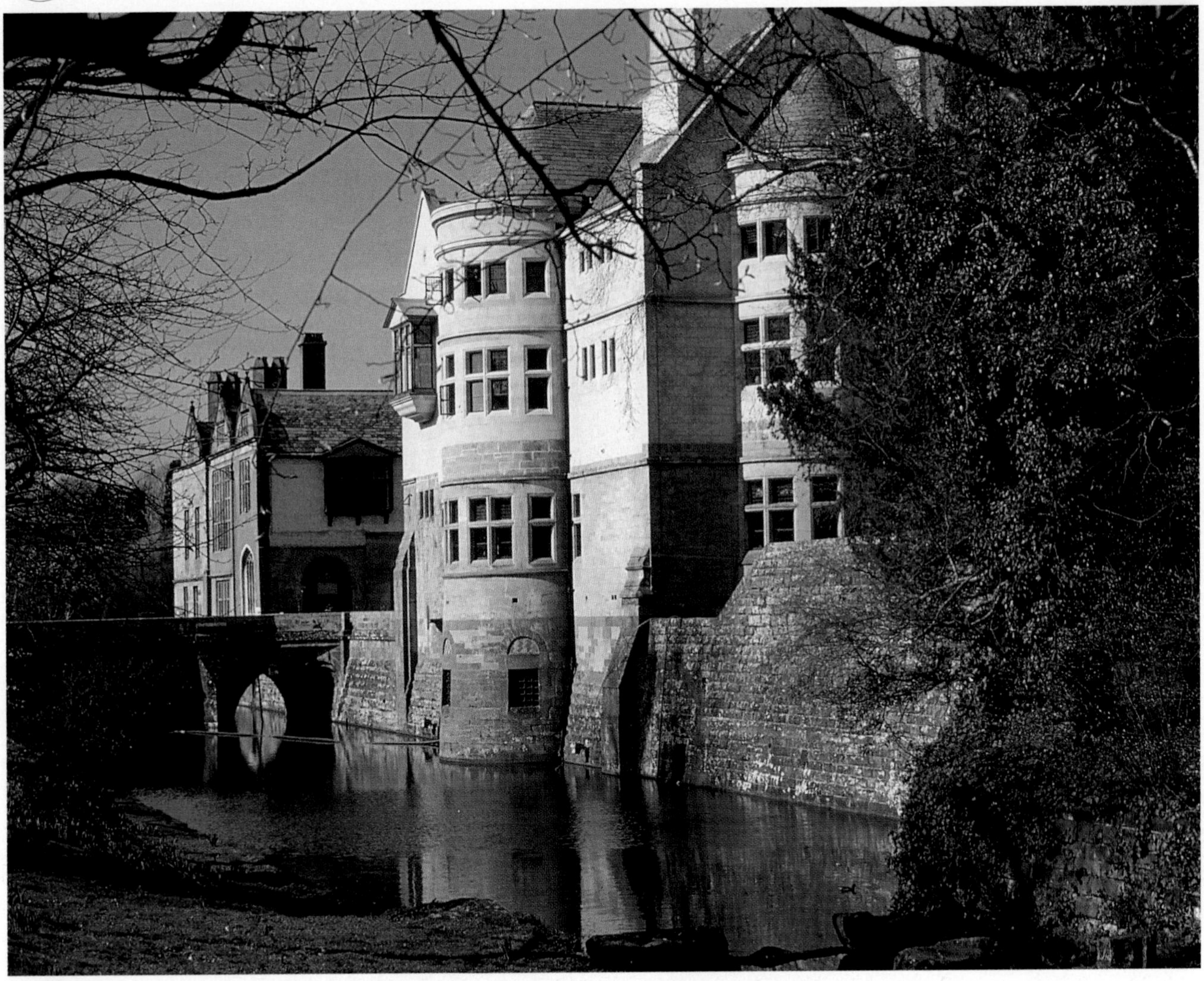

# COOMBE ABBEY

**BRINKLOW ROAD, BINLEY, WARWICKSHIRE CV3 2AB**
**TEL: 01203 450450 FAX: 01203 635101**

Coombe Abbey is approached by travelling along a lovely avenue of lime trees and chestnuts, crossing a moat and passing through a cloistered entrance. Originally a Cistercian Abbey dating back to the 11th century, this hotel lies in the heart of 500 acres of parkland and formal gardens. Deep colours, carefully selected fabrics and antique furnishing and lighting are all features of its restful bedrooms. Room designs, often eccentric or mischievous, include hidden bathrooms, four poster beds and the occasional hand painted Victorian bath in the centre of the room. Many bedrooms overlook the grounds with their splendid 80 acre lake. The restaurants and private dining rooms each have their individual charm and offer a variety of settings suitable for all occasions. Sophisticated and creative menus provide a good choice of delightful dishes and the service is attentive but never intrusive. The hotel is an ideal venue for conferences and weddings. Among the local attractions are Warwick Castle and Stratford and the surrounding area is excellent for walking and birdwatching. **Directions:** Leave the M40 at junction 15 and take the A46 towards Binley. Coombe Abbey is on the B4027. Price guide: Single £115–£125; twin/double £125–£295; suite £325.

For hotel location, see maps on pages 490-496

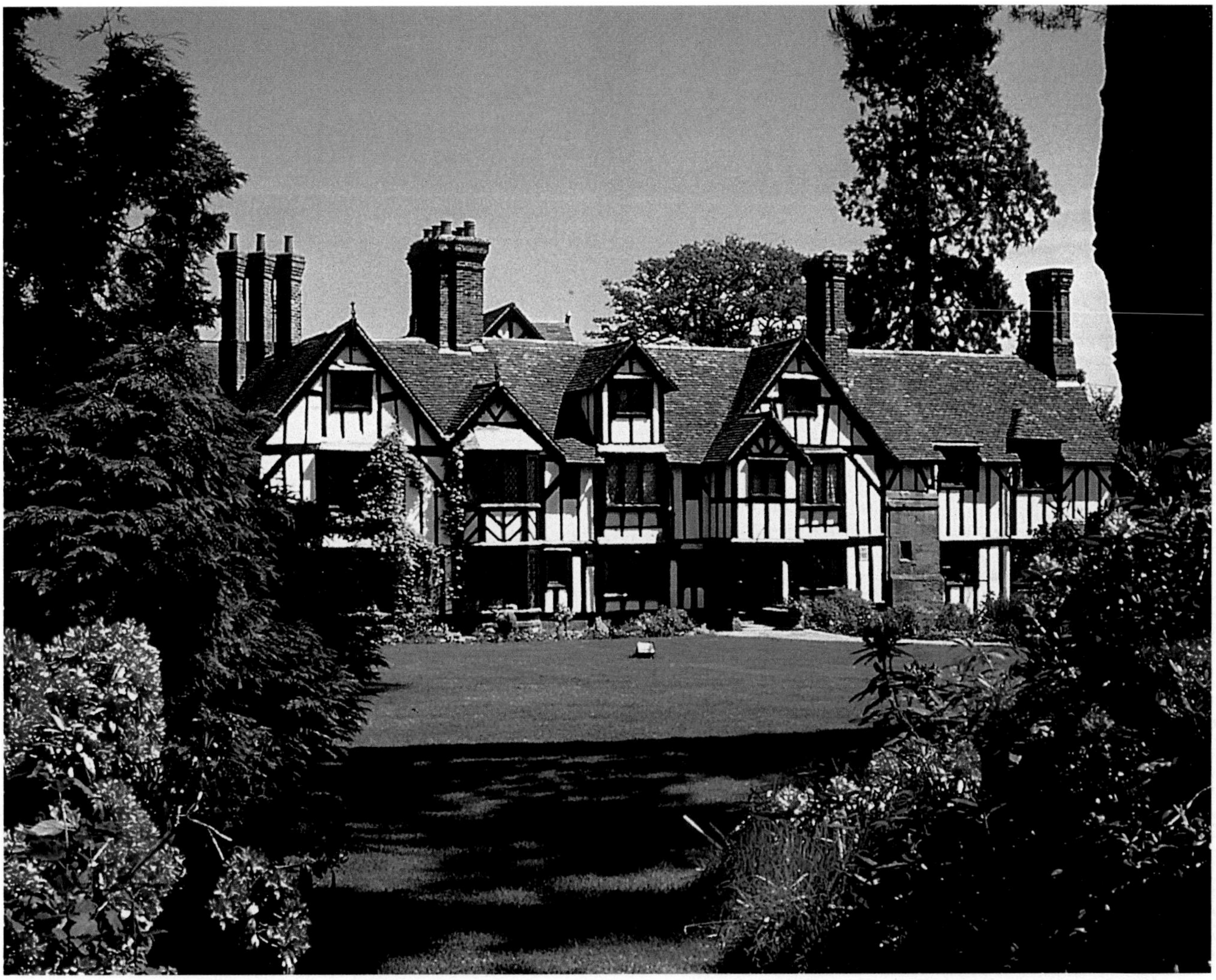

# NAILCOTE HALL

**NAILCOTE LANE, BERKSWELL, NR COVENTRY, WARWICKSHIRE CV7 7DE**
**TEL: 01203 466174 FAX: 01203 470720**

Nailcote Hall is a charming Elizabethan country house hotel set in 15 acres of gardens and surrounded by Warwickshire countryside. Built in 1640, the house was used by Cromwell during the Civil War and was damaged by his troops prior to the assault on Kenilworth Castle. Ideally located in the heart of England, Nailcote Hall is within 15 minutes' drive of the castle towns of Kenilworth and Warwick, Coventry Cathedral, Birmingham International Airport/Station and the NEC. Situated at the centre of the Midlands motorway network, Birmingham city centre, the ICC and Stratford-upon-Avon are less than 30 minutes away. Leisure facilities include indoor swimming pool, gymnasium, solarium and sauna. Outside there are all-weather tennis courts, petanque, croquet, a challenging 9-hole par-3 golf course and putting green (host to the Midland Professional Short Course Championship). In the intimate Tudor surroundings of the Oak Room restaurant, the chef will delight you with superb cuisine, while the cellar boasts an extensive choice of international wines. En suite bedrooms offer luxury accommodation, and elegant facilities are available for conferences, private dining and corporate hospitality. **Directions:** Situated 6 miles south of Birmingham International Airport/ NEC on the B4101 Balsall Common–Coventry road. Price guide: Single £125; double/twin £135; suite £155–£195.

For hotel location, see maps on pages 490-496

# CRATHORNE HALL HOTEL

CRATHORNE, NR YARM, NORTH YORKSHIRE TS15 0AR
TEL: 01642 700398 FAX: 01642 700814

Part of the Virgin group, Richard Branson's Crathorne Hall was the last great stately home built in the Edwardian era. Now a splendid country house hotel, it is set in 15 acres of woodland overlooking the River Leven and the Cleveland Hills. True to their original fashion, the interiors have elegant antique furnishings complementing the grand architectural style. There is no traffic to wake up to here: just the dawn chorus, all the comforts of a luxury hotel and, if desired, a champagne breakfast in bed. From a simple main course to a gastronomic dinner, the food is of the highest quality, complemented by a comprehensive wine list. Whether catering for conferences, product launches, wedding receptions or a quiet weekend for two, professional, courteous service is guaranteed. In the grounds guests can play croquet, follow the jogging trail or try clay pigeon shooting with a tutor on a layout designed to entertain the beginner and test the expert. Leisure activities such as clay shooting, golf, ballooning and racing circuit driving can be arranged. The Yorkshire Dales, Durham and York are nearby. **Directions:** From A19 Thirsk–Teesside road, turn to Yarm and Crathorne. Follow signs to Crathorne village; hotel is on left. Teesside Airport and Darlington rail station are both seven miles; a courtesy collection service is available. Price guide: Single £108–£130; double/twin £148–£210.

For hotel location, see maps on pages 490-496

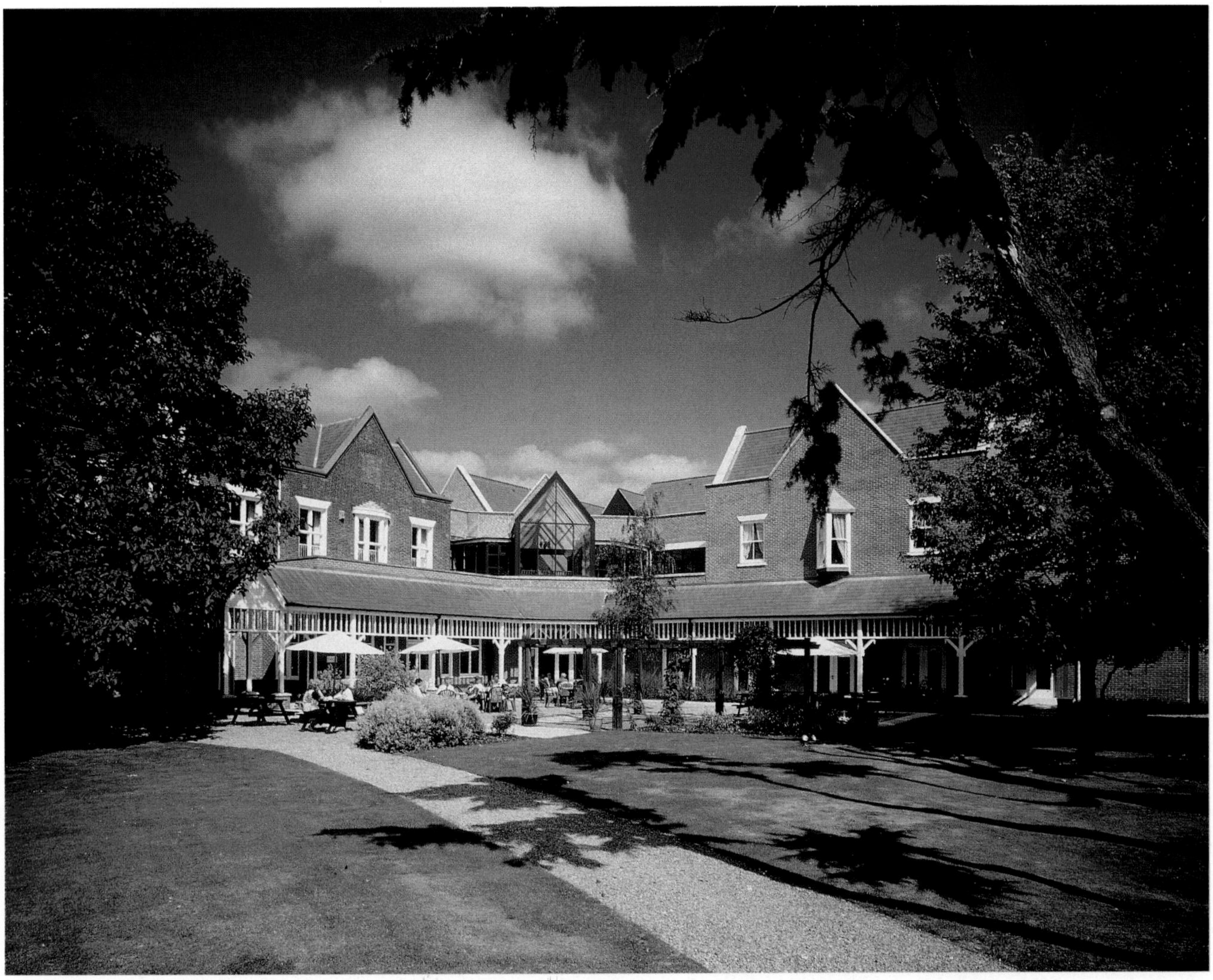

# Coulsdon Manor Hotel

**COULSDON COURT ROAD, COULSDON, NR CROYDON, SURREY CR5 2LL**

**TEL: 0181 668 0414 FAX: 0181 668 3118**

Coulsdon Manor enjoys a splendid location amid the peace and quiet of 140 acres of parkland, a large part of it laid down as a challenging 18-hole, par 70 golf course. Built in the 1850s the manor house has been faithfully restored and sympathetically extended. With fine furnishings, rich woodwork and impressive chandeliers Coulsdon Manor has a peaceful country house atmosphere and has been awarded 4 stars by the AA and RAC and two AA rosettes for its restaurant. Byrons Bar provides drinks and light meals throughout the day and guests can enjoy a pre-lunch or dinner drink in an elegant cocktail bar. All rooms have every modern facility. Many have views over the golf course. Business visitors are well catered for with five fully equipped conference rooms and six syndicate rooms. Coulsdon Manor has four all-weather tennis courts, four squash courts, racketball, a 1,000 sq ft gymnasium and sauna and steam rooms. 15 miles from Central London and within easy reach of Hever Castle and Chartwell. **Directions:** From M23/M25 junction 7 follow M23/A23 north and turn right after Coulsdon South Railway Station onto B2030 signposted Old Coulsdon and Caterham. After 1 mile turn left at the pond and continue until reaching Coulsdon Court Road on your right. Price guide: Single £98.50; double/twin £124–£144; suite £164.

# OCKENDEN MANOR

**OCKENDEN LANE, CUCKFIELD, WEST SUSSEX RH17 5LD**
**TEL: 01444 416111 FAX: 01444 415549**

Set in 9 acres of gardens in the centre of the Tudor village of Cuckfield on the Southern Forest Ridge, this hotel is an ideal base from which to discover Sussex and Kent, the Garden of England. First recorded in 1520, Ockenden Manor has become a hotel of great charm and character. The bedrooms all have their own individual identity: climb your private staircase to Thomas or Elizabeth, look out across the lovely Sussex countryside from Victoria's bay window or choose Charles, with its handsome four-poster bed. The restaurant, with its beautifully painted ceiling, is a dignified setting in which to enjoy acclaimed cuisine. 'Modern English' is how the chef describes his culinary style, offering an à la carte menu with a daily table d'hôte choice to include fresh seasonal produce and herbs from the hotel garden. An outstanding, extensive wine list offers, for example, a splendid choice of first-growth clarets. Spacious and elegantly furnished, the Ockenden Suite welcomes private lunch and dinner parties. A beautiful conservatory is attached to the Ockenden Suite, this opens on to the lawns, where marquees can be set up for summer celebrations. The gardens of Nymans, Wakehurst Place and Leonardslee are nearby, as is the opera at Glyndebourne. **Directions:** In the centre of Cuckfield on the A272. Less than 3 miles east of the A23. Price guide: Single from £89; double/twin from £170–£235.

For hotel location, see maps on pages 490-496

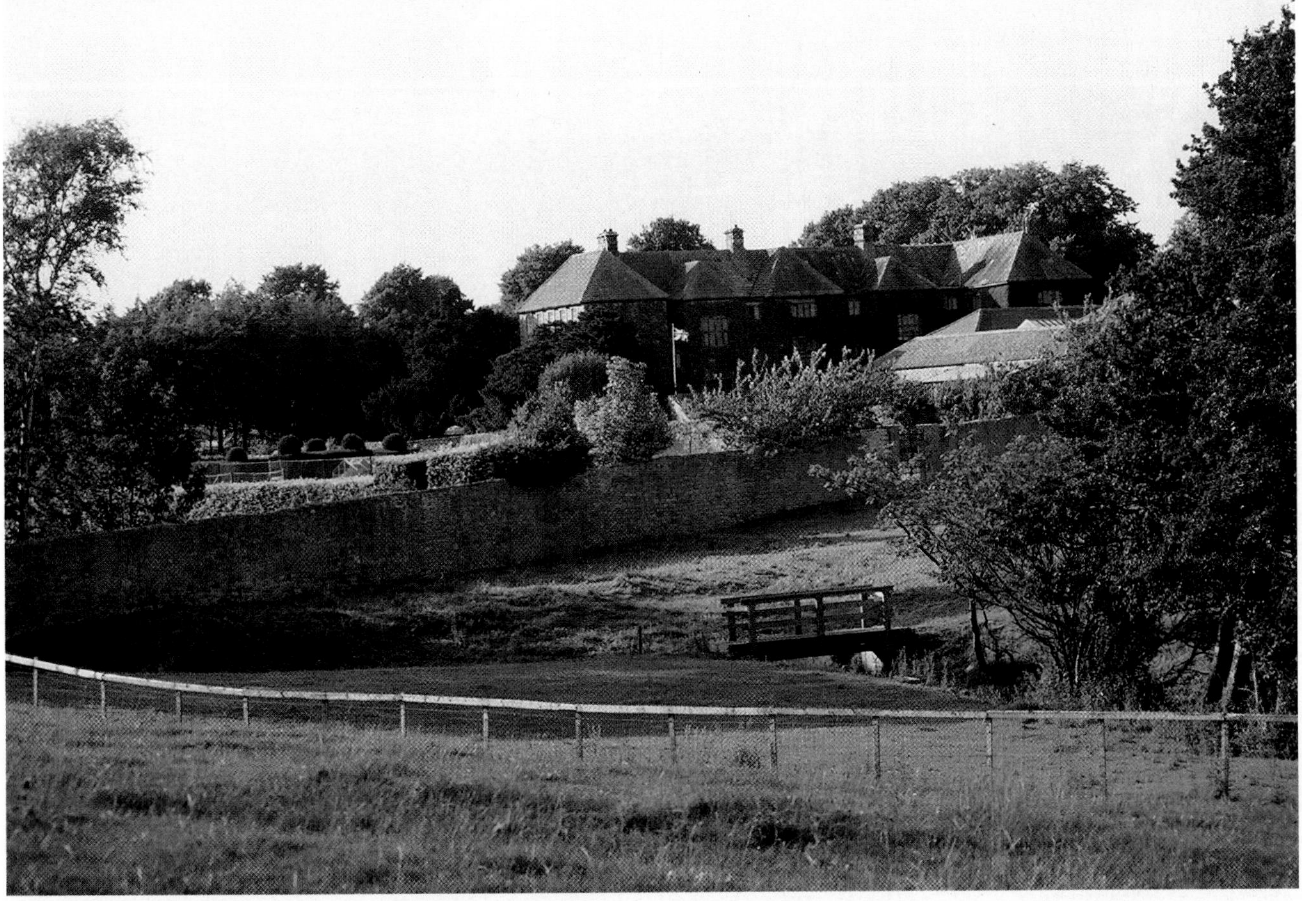

# HEADLAM HALL

HEADLAM, NR GAINFORD, DARLINGTON, COUNTY DURHAM DL2 3HA
TEL: 01325 730238 FAX: 01325 730790 E-MAIL: headlam@onyxnet.co.uk

This magnificent Jacobean mansion is set in four acres of formal gardens in the peaceful rolling countryside of lower Teesdale. Originally built in the 17th century, the hall has a rich history of ownership, being home to the Brocket family for some 150 years and more recently the residence of Lord Gainford. Since 1979 Headlam Hall has been owned and personally run by the Robinson family. The hotel has extensive facilities including a fishing water, hard tennis court, croquet lawn, a superb indoor pool, sauna and snooker room. All the bedrooms are furnished to a high standard and have Sky TV. The restaurant provides the best of traditional English and Continental cuisine. The main hall features a magnificent and original carved oak fireplace while the Georgian drawing room opens onto a stepped terrace overlooking the main lawn. There are four separate conference rooms including the Edwardian Suite holding up to 150 people. A free night's accommodation and champagne breakfast are provided for newly-weds holding their reception here. There are a number of excellent golf courses nearby and the regions main towns, cities and attractions are all within easy reach. Dogs by prior arrangement. **Directions:** Headlam is two miles north of Gainford off the A67 Darlington–Barnard Castle road. Price guide: Single £58–£70; double/twin £72–£85; suite £100.

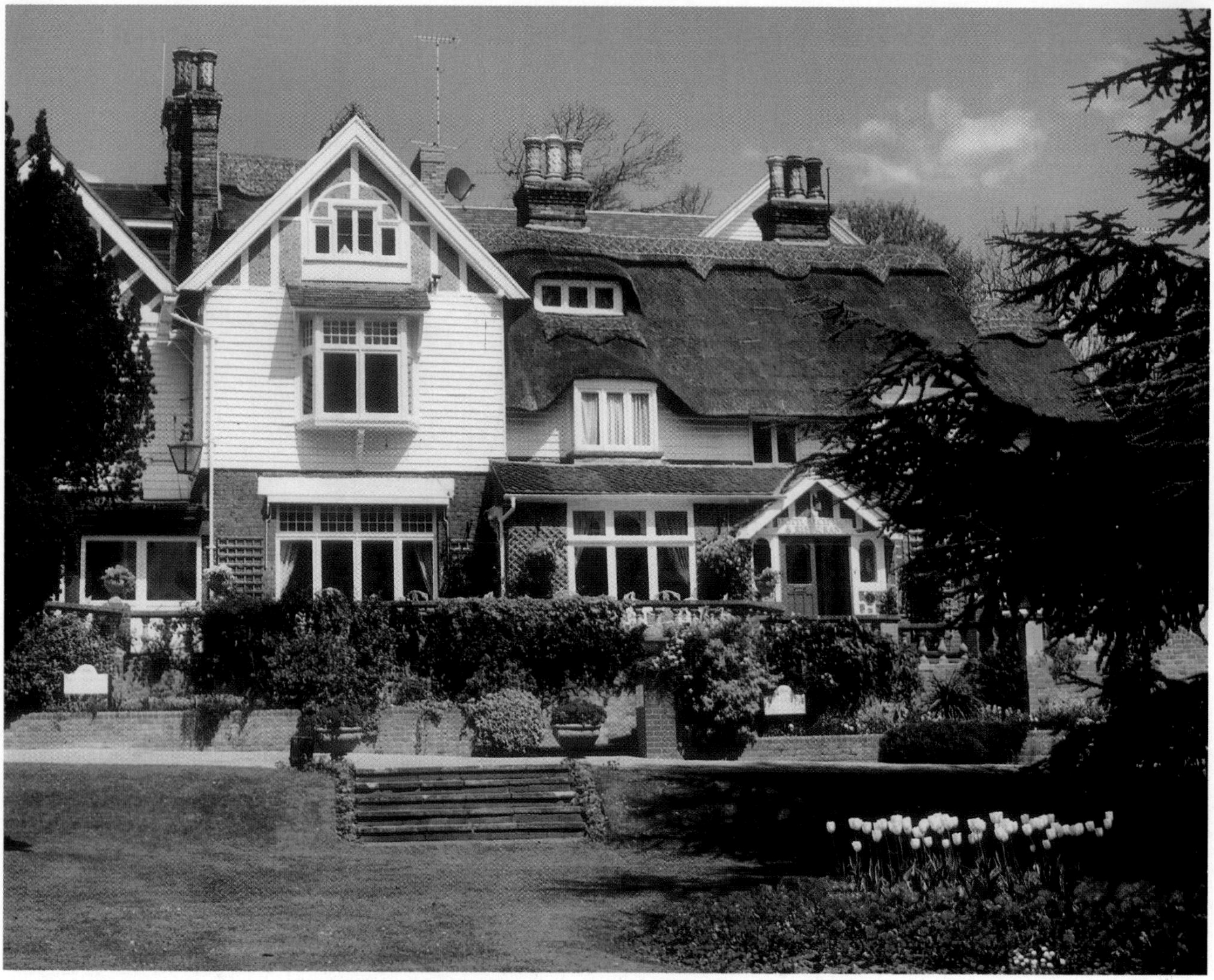

# ROWHILL GRANGE

## WILMINGTON, DARTFORD, KENT DA2 7QH
## TEL: 01322 615136 FAX: 01322 615137

An unexpected find on the outer edge of London bordering on the Kent countryside, Rowhill Grange nestles in nine acres of woodlands and mature gardens descending to a picturesque lake. A combination of top service and friendliness makes Rowhill Grange the perfect venue for everything from weekend breaks to special occasions such as weddings and anniversaries. All the luxurious bedrooms are named after flowers and boast individual character and decoration, with a full range of facilities available to ensure maximum comfort and convenience for guests. The à la carte Restaurant is supplemented with the delightful new Topiary Brasserie. From late spring and through the summer months guests may take dinner on the terrace, sharing a scenic view with the swans and ducks. For special occasions, business meetings or dinners the private oak panelled dining room is available. The Clockhouse Suite is a self contained functions annexe with a dining/dancing area, comfortable lounge and a bar. The new Utopia Health and Leisure Spa is outstanding with all the latest equipment for women and for men including the UK's first therapy pool of its kind. **Directions:** M20 junction 1/M25 junction 3. Take the B2173 into Swanley and B258 north at Superstore roundabout. After Hextable Green the entrance is almost immediately on the left. Price guide: Single £109–£139; double/twin £119–£159; suite £149–£169.

For hotel location, see maps on pages 490-496

# MAISON TALBOOTH

**STRATFORD ROAD, DEDHAM, COLCHESTER, ESSEX CO7 6HN**
**TEL: 01206 322367 FAX: 01206 322752**

In the north-east corner of Essex, where the River Stour borders with Suffolk, is the Vale of Dedham, an idyllic riverside setting immortalised in the early 19th century by the paintings of John Constable. One summer's day in 1952, the young Gerald Milsom enjoyed a 'cuppa' in the Talbooth tea room and soon afterwards took the helm at what would develop into Le Talbooth Restaurant. Business was soon booming and the restaurant built itself a reputation as one of the best in the country. In 1969 Maison Talbooth was created in a nearby Victorian rectory, to become, as it still is, a standard bearer for Britain's premier country house hotels. Indeed, in 1982 Gerald Milsom became the founder of the Pride of Britain group. With its atmosphere of opulence, Maison Talbooth has ten spacious guest suites which all have an air of quiet luxury. Every comfort has been provided. Breakfast is served in the suites. The original Le Talbooth Restaurant is about half a mile upstream on a riverside terrace reached by leisurely foot or courtesy car. It has recently been awarded the coveted Booker Sword of Excellence for quality,flair and renown. 'Which' Hotel of the Year for Essex. The hotel arranges special Constable tours. **Directions:** Dedham is about a mile from the A12 between Colchester and Ipswich. Price guide: Single £90–£130; double/twin £110–£170. Telephone for details of special short breaks. Exclusive use available.

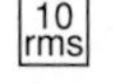

For hotel location, see maps on pages 490-496

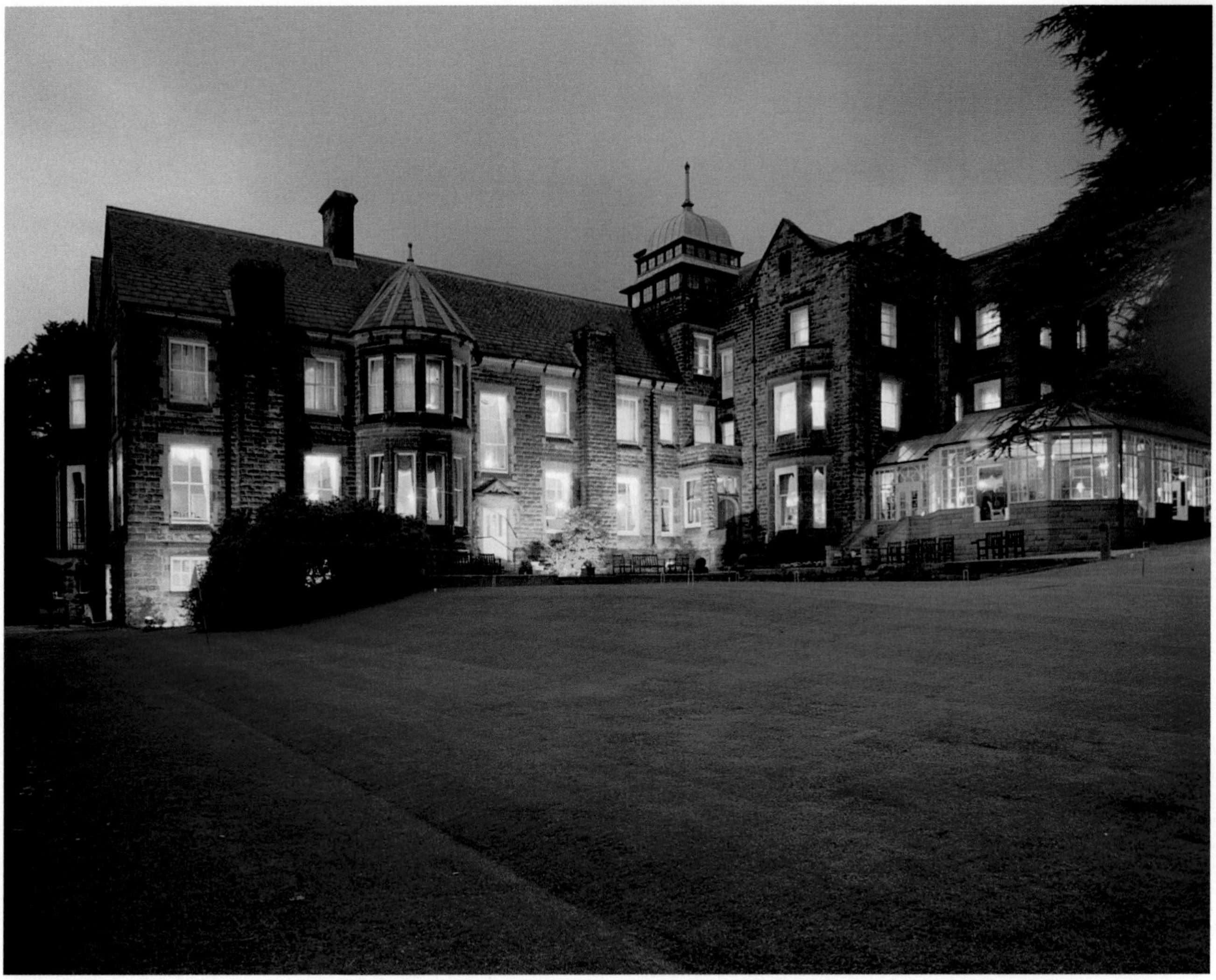

# MAKENEY HALL COUNTRY HOUSE HOTEL

**MAKENEY, MILFORD, DERBYSHIRE DE56 0RS**
**TEL: 01332 842999 FAX: 01332 842777**

Set in a restful location on the River Derwent, Makeney Hall is surrounded by over 6 acres of beautifully landscaped gardens just 10 minutes' drive from Derby, a historic city famous for its china, its silk and Rolls Royce. Built originally by the Strutt family this capacious and restful hotel, with its mid-Victorian features, offers guests a warm, distinctive welcome. The carefully chosen décor imparts an air of bygone comfort. Bedrooms in the main house are spacious and individually appointed and many overlook the gardens. A splendid covered courtyard gives access to a further eighteen new rooms. Guests dine in Lavinia's AA two rosetted restaurant, where expert cooking and fresh local produce create cuisine of the highest standard. The fare is British in flavour and a selection of fine wines is available. The hotel is now firmly established as one of Derbyshire's favourite, year-round venues for wedding ceremonies and receptions. Conference and Banqueting suites accommodate up to 130 visitors. Places of interest locally include the Derwent Valley – an area of outstanding natural beauty – the Peak District, the stately homes of Chatsworth and Haddon Hall, and Alton Towers. **Directions:** From M1 (exits 25 or 28) head for Derby and A38 northbound. Follow A6 (signposted Matlock). Makeney is signposted at Milford, 6 miles NW of Derby. Price guide: Double-twin: from £75; suite: from £140.

For hotel location, see maps on pages 490-496

# MICKLEOVER COURT

ETWALL ROAD, MICKLEOVER, DERBYSHIRE DE3 5XX
TEL: 01332 521234 FAX: 01332 521238

This luxurious modern hotel located in Derbyshire offers impressive bedrooms all pleasantly furnished each with a balcony and welcoming finishing touches such as fresh fruit, bathrobes, free 'in-house' movies and satellite television. Dining is an experience not to be missed, the award winning English Brasserie offers a delicious menu prepared with the finest and freshest local produce. The Italian Trattoria located in the atrium specialises in regional Italian dishes with a lively informal atmosphere. The Oasis Champagne Bar is the perfect place to enjoy a pre-dinner drink or perhaps just to relax with a night cap. Castaways Leisure Club has state-of-the-art gymnasium equipment, a large tropical pool, steam room, sauna, a coffee shop serving an all day snack menu and the '*Castaways*' hair and beauty salon. The hotel's extensive conference and banqueting facilities are extremely versatile and can accommodate up to 200 guests. Located around Derbyshire is a wide range of activities and country pursuits including golf, hot air ballooning, gliding, racing car tuition, clay pigeon shooting, water-skiing and riding. Places of interest nearby include Alton Towers, Uttoxeter Race Course and the Peak District. **Directions:** From M1 junction 28 follow signs to Derby. Ignore signs for city centre and take first exit for Mickleover. The hotel is on the right before the roundabout. Price guide: Single from £105; double/twin from £125.

For hotel location, see maps on pages 490-496

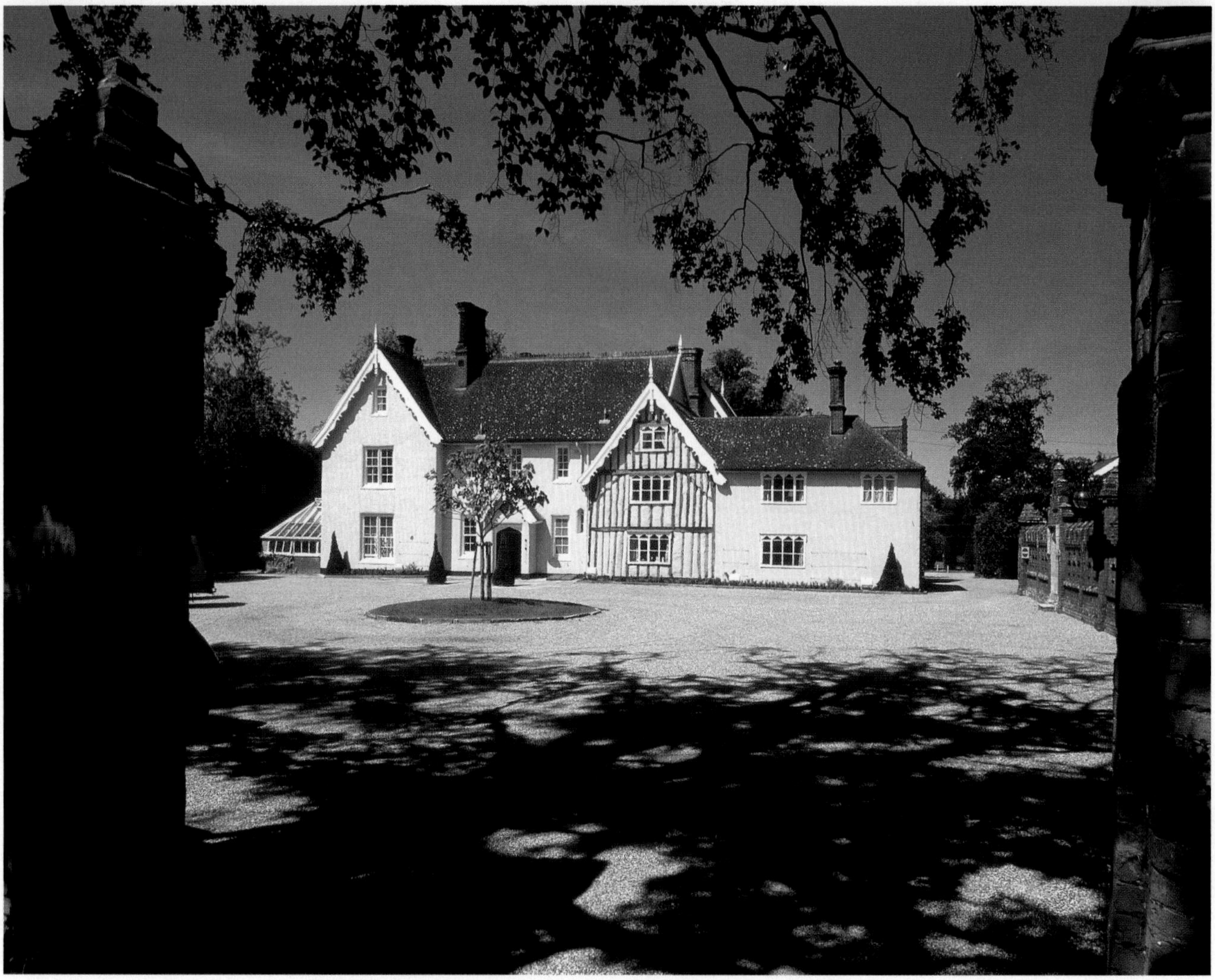

# Cornwallis Arms

**BROME, NR EYE, SUFFOLK IP23 8AJ**
**TEL: 01379 870326 FAX: 01379 870051**

A romantic, fairytale aura emanates from this former 16th century dower house as one approaches it along a leafy avenue bounded by a pretty ornamental lake and some of the finest yew topiary in England. Standing in 21 acres of parkland and gardens this compact country house with its sunny, cream-coloured facade, high twin peaks and tall, ornate chimneys is a historic reflection of three eras. It was built during Queen Elizabeth's reign for the Cornwallis family whose most unforunate member, Viscount Cornwallis, commanded the British forces who surrendered to George Washington. In Victorian times additions were made and in 1996 the hotel was extensively refurbished to include every modern facility. The beamed Tudor Bar, with original flagged floor, open fire and water well, is a comfortable area to enjoy a snack and real ales brewed by owners St Peter's Brewery. More formal meals are served in the elegant Oaksmere Restaurant and vine-draped conservatory. The en suite bedrooms are beautifully furnished and decorated in Tudor or Victorian style. Cornwallis Arms is an ideal base from which to visit Lavenham, Newmarket and Orford and Framlingham castles. Directions: From M11, exit junction 9 onto A11 or junction 14 onto A14 towards Bury St Edmunds. Then join A143 towards Diss and connect with A140 south. Price guide: Single £59.50-£75; double/twin £79.50-£95.

For hotel location, see maps on pages 490-496

# LUMLEY CASTLE HOTEL

**CHESTER-LE-STREET, COUNTY DURHAM DH3 4NX**
**TEL: 0191 389 1111 FAX: 0191 389 1881/0191 387 1437**

This magnificent 14th century castle offers an exciting blend of ancient history and modern convenience. The bedrooms are each individually styled and appointed to a high standard. The King James Suite is Lumley's hallmark of taste and distinction. The public areas of the hotel, amply supported by medieval pillars, captivate the attention and imagination of all visitors. The subdued lighting and hidden corridors enhance the exciting atmosphere that pervades this amazing building. The Black Knight Restaurant will please the most experienced palate. Lumley Castle's Medieval Memories special weekend breaks offer a magnificent 'get-away' opportunity. These include an evening at the award-winning Elizabethan Banquet, full of fun, feasting (5-course meal) and merriment. The sharp wit and musical talent of the Castle's entertainers in their striking costumery offer a night to remember. There are 25 golf courses within 25 minutes drive. The Riverside Health Club offers 'full'facilities for Hotel guests at a discounted rate. For the more serious minded, Lumley has a number of conference and meeting rooms which provide an unusual setting for business matters. **Directions:** From A1(M) northbound take A693/A167 to Chester-le-Street and Durham. At the second roundabout take first left to Lumley Castle. Price guide: Single £83–£145; double/twin £115–£160; suite £190.

62 rms · MasterCard · VISA · AMERICAN EXPRESS · M 150

For hotel location, see maps on pages 490-496

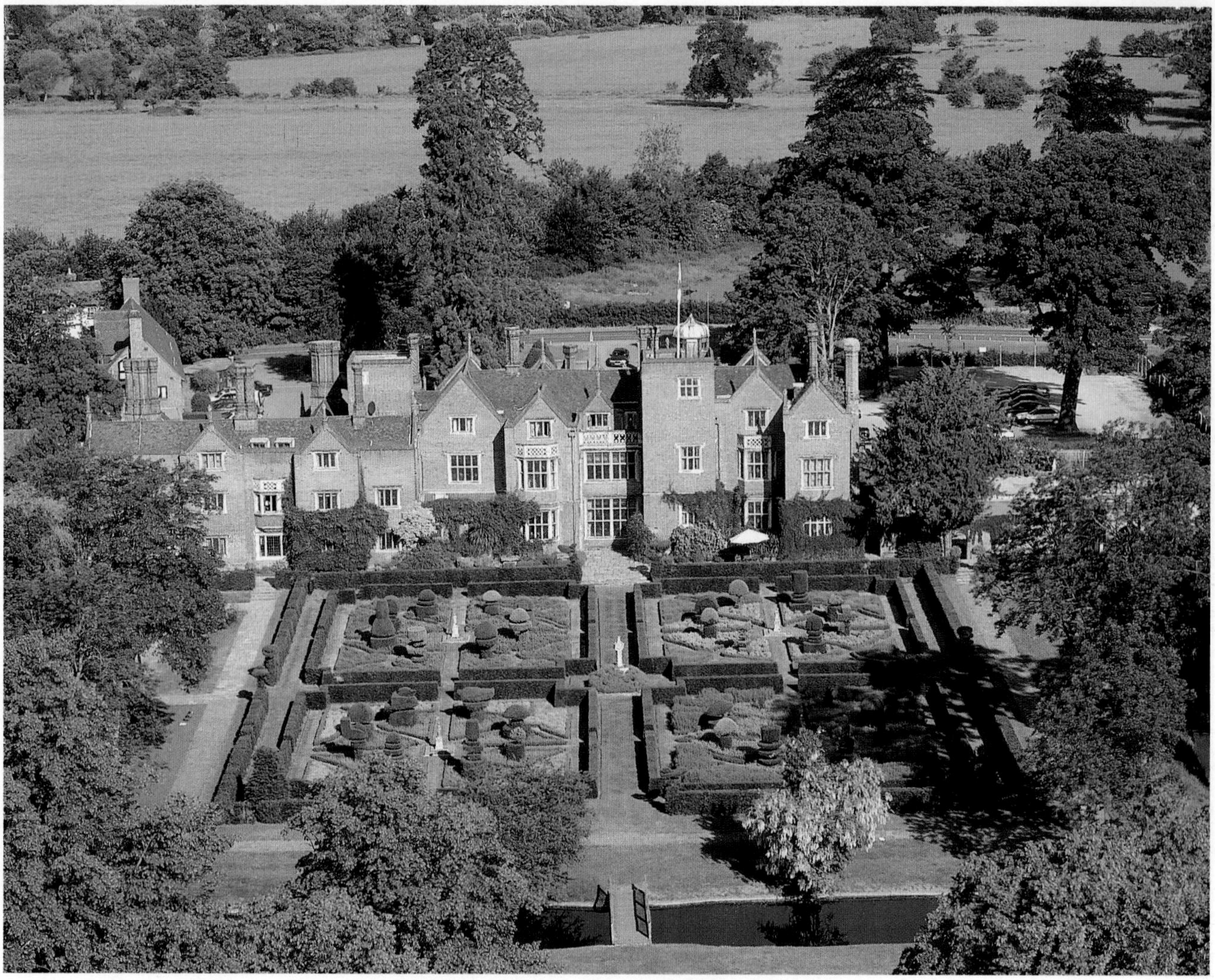

# Great Fosters

## STROUDE ROAD, EGHAM, SURREY TW20 9UR
## TEL: 01784 433822 FAX: 01784 472455

Probably built as a Royal Hunting lodge in Windsor Forest, very much a stately home since the 16th century, today Great Fosters is a prestigious hotel within half an hour of both Heathrow Airport and central London. Its past is evident in the mullioned windows, tall chimneys and brick finials, while the Saxon moat – crossed by a Japanese bridge – surrounds three sides of the formal gardens, complete with topiary, statuary and a charming rose garden. Within are fine oak beams and panelling, Jacobean chimney pieces, superb tapestries and a rare oakwell staircase leading to the Tower. Some of the guest rooms are particularly magnificent – one Italian styled with gilt furnishings and damask walls, others with moulded ceilings, beautiful antiques and Persian rugs. Guests relax in the bar, then enjoy good English and French cooking and carefully selected wines, either in the Tudor Dining Room or the Tithe Barn with its vaulted roof. Celebrations, meetings and weddings take place in the elegant Orangery and impressive Painted Hall, the ceiling a riot of exotic birds and animals. Great Fosters is close to polo in Windsor Great Park, racing at Ascot, golf at Wentworth, boating in Henley and pageantry at Windsor Castle, Runneymede and Hampton Court. **Directions:** M25/J13, head for Egham and watch for brown 'Historic Buildings' signs. Price guide: Single from £93; double/twin from £102.

For hotel location, see maps on pages 490-496

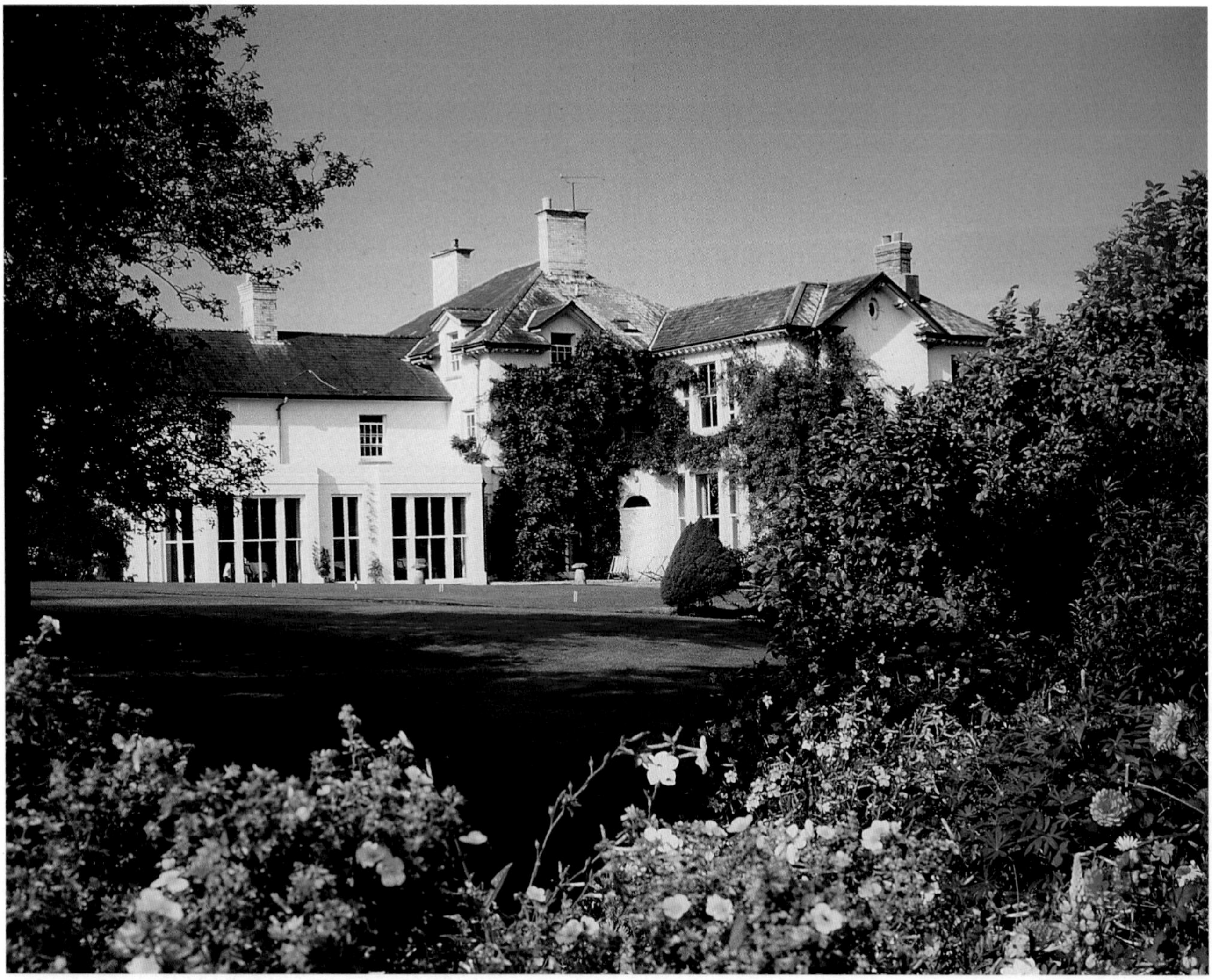

# SUMMER LODGE

SUMMER LANE, EVERSHOT, DORSET DT2 0JR
TEL: 01935 83424 FAX: 01935 83005

A charming Georgian building, idyllically located in Hardy country, the Summer Lodge was formerly the dower house of the Earls of Ilchester. Now it is a luxurious hotel where owners Nigel and Margaret Corbett offer their visitors a genuinely friendly welcome, encouraging them to relax as if in their own home. The bedrooms have views over the 4-acre sheltered gardens or overlook the village rooftops across the meadowland. In the dining room, with its French windows that open on to the garden, the cuisine is highly regarded. Fresh local produce is combined with the culinary expertise of chef Tim Ford to create a distinctive brand of English cooking. The unspoiled Dorset countryside and its coastline, 12 miles south, make for limitless exploration, and bring to life the setting of *Tess of the d'Urbevilles*, *The Mayor of Casterbridge*, *Far from the Madding Crowd* and the other Hardy novels. Many National Trust properties and gardens in the locality are open to the public. There are stables, golf courses and trout lakes nearby. **Directions:** The turning to Evershot leaves the A37 halfway between Dorchester and Yeovil. Once in the village turn left into Summer Lane and the hotel entrance is 150 yards on the right. Price guide: Single £115; double/twin £150–£225.

For hotel location, see maps on pages 490-496

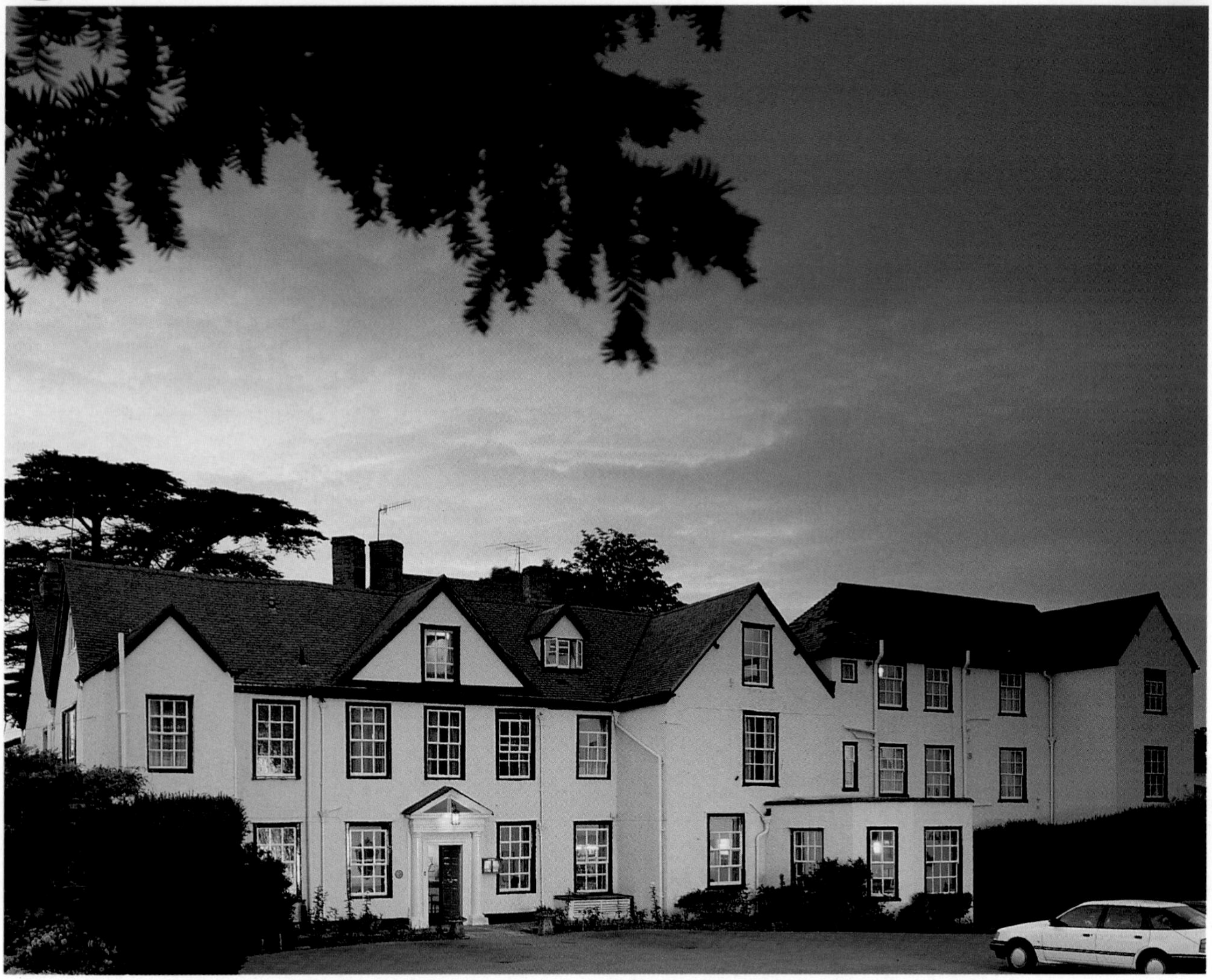

# THE EVESHAM HOTEL

**COOPERS LANE, OFF WATERSIDE, EVESHAM, WORCESTERSHIRE WR11 6DA**
**TEL: 01386 765566 RESERVATIONS: 0800 716969 FAX: 01386 765443**

It is the atmosphere at the Evesham Hotel that stays in the memory. Not remotely stuffy, it is totally efficient but completely relaxing in a sometimes unconventional manner. Originally a Tudor farmhouse, the hotel was extended and converted into a Georgian mansion house in 1810. Privately owned and managed by the Jenkinson family since the mid-1970s, guests can be assured of prompt, friendly service and a relaxed atmosphere. Each of the 40 en suite bedrooms is furnished complete with a teddy bear and a toy duck for the bath. The restaurant offers delicious cuisine from a very imaginative and versatile menu, accompanied by a somewhat unique "Euro-sceptic" wine list (everything but French and German!). The drinks selection is an amazing myriad. The indoor swimming pool has a seaside theme, and guests have access to squash and tennis at a nearby sports club. The peace of the 2½-acre garden belies the hotel's proximity to the town – a 5-minute walk away. In the gardens are six 300 year-old mulberry trees and a magnificent cedar of Lebanon, planted in 1809. The hotel is a good base from which to explore the Cotswolds, Stratford-upon-Avon and the Severn Valley. Closed at Christmas. **Directions:** Coopers Lane lies just off Waterside (the River Avon). Price guide: Single £60–£68; double/twin £88–£98.

For hotel location, see maps on pages 490-496

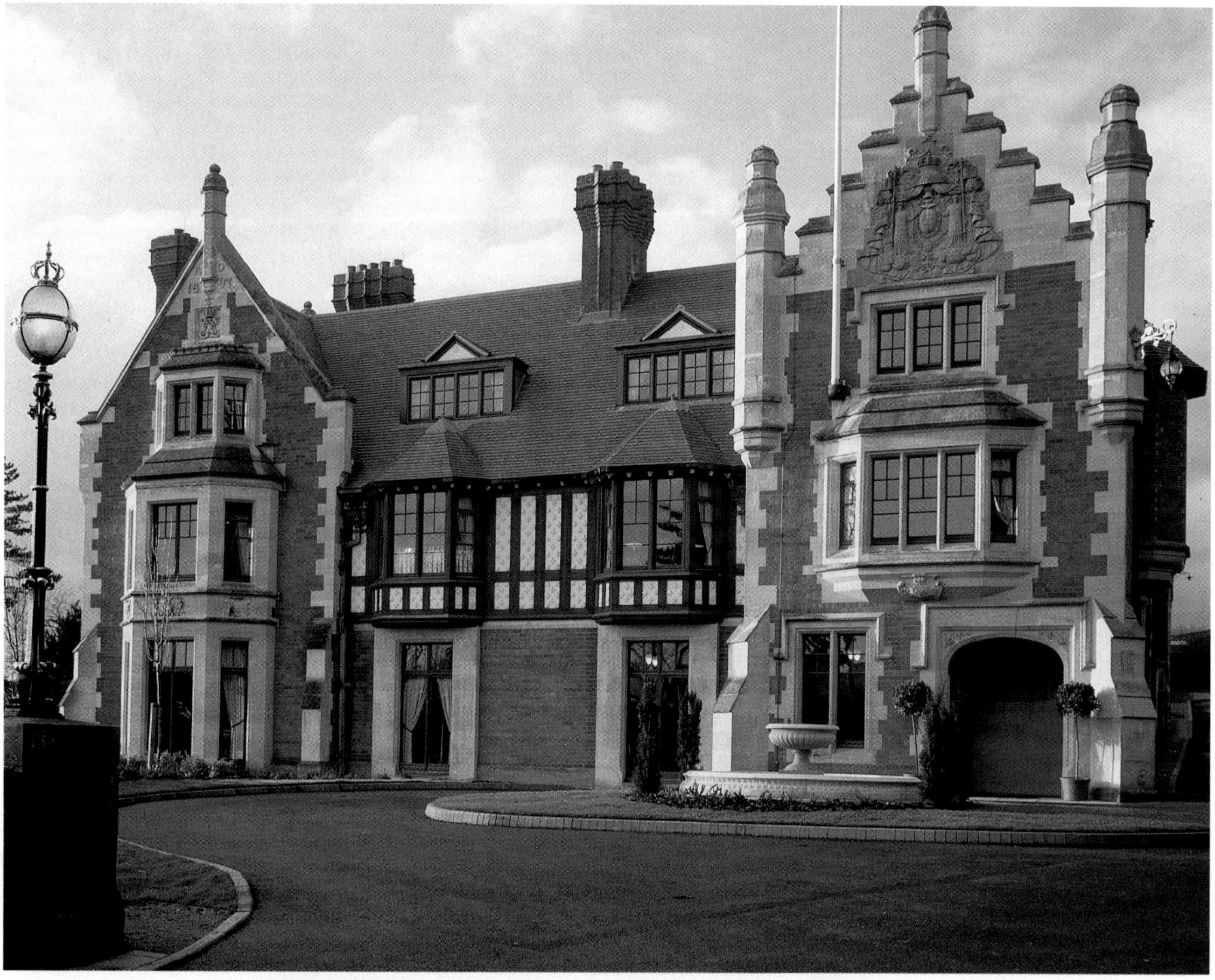

# WOOD NORTON HALL

**WOOD NORTON, EVESHAM, WORCESTERSHIRE WR11 4YB**

**TEL: 01386 420007 FAX: 01386 420190**

Wood Norton Hall is a glorious Grade 2 listed Victorian country house standing in 170 acres of beautiful Worcestershire countryside. A short drive from the historic market town of Evesham, 8 miles from Broadway and the Cotswold's with Stratford-upon-Avon only 15 miles away. French connections dating back to 1872 culminated in the wedding of the Princess Louise of Orleans and Prince Charles of Bourbon in 1907. Original fleur-de-lys carved oak panelling lines the walls, grand fireplaces, elegant furniture and beautiful tapestries add comfort and colour. Each of the 45 en suite rooms is furnished to the very highest standards. The ground floor public rooms reflect the grandeur of the Victorian era with voluptuous window drapes framing magnificent views to the Vale of Evesham and the River Avon. The award winning Duc's Restaurant, with its excellent but unobtrusive service, provides the perfect ambience to savour a fine culinary tradition and a small, intimate bar offers pre and post dining relaxation. Extensive leisure facilities include a swimming pool, billiard room, fitness suite, tennis, clay pigeon shooting and golf at a nearby championship course. **Directions:** Evesham is reached from M5 via junction 7 and then south east on A44, or via junction 9 and then north-east on A435. Price guide: Single from £70; double/twin from £140; suite from £140

For hotel location, see maps on pages 490-496

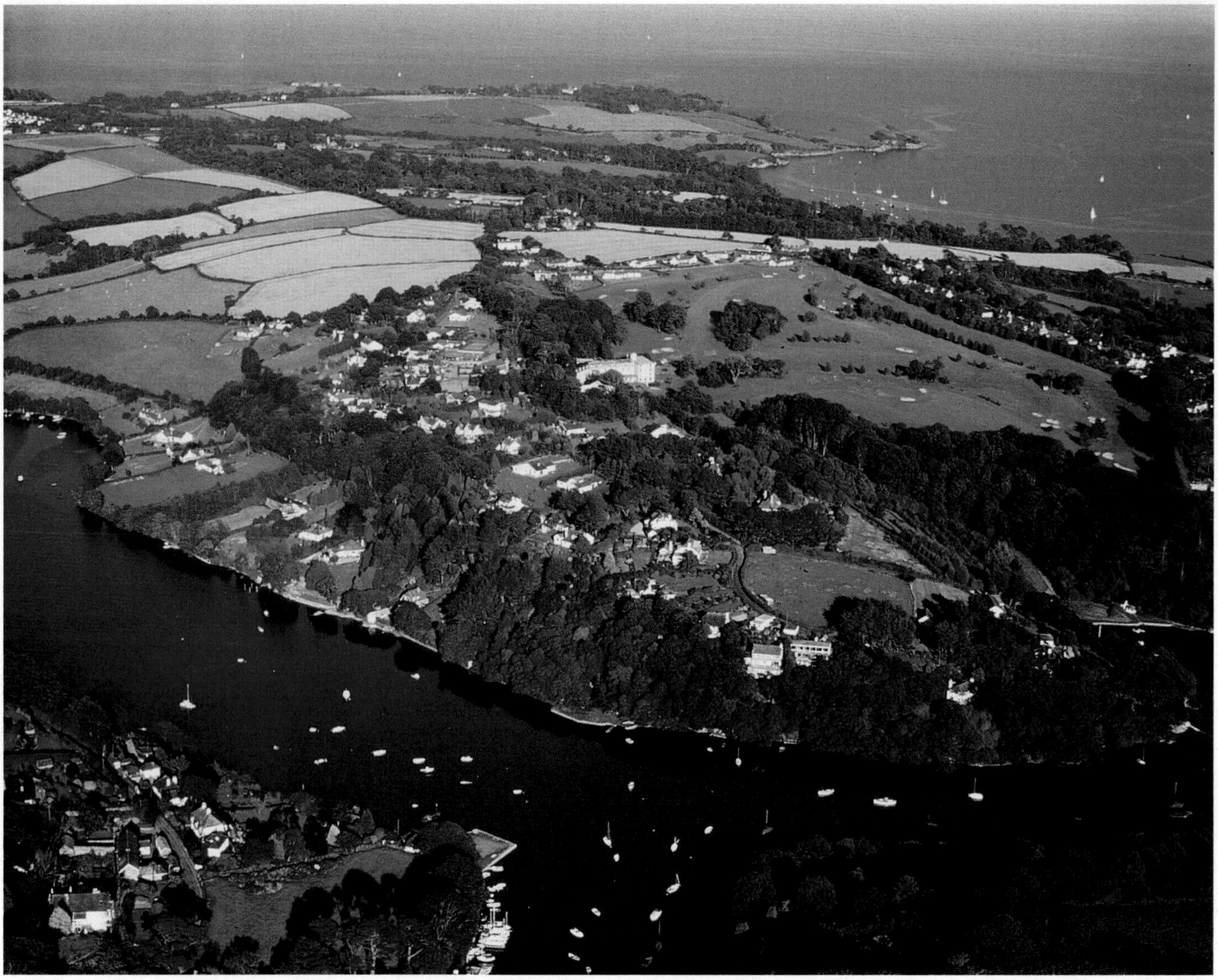

# Budock Vean Golf & Country House Hotel

**HELFORD RIVER, MAWNAN SMITH, FALMOUTH, CORNWALL TR11 5LG**

**TEL: 01326 250288 FAX: 01326 250892 RESERVATIONS: 01326 250230**

The elegant Budock Vean Golf and Country House Hotel is set in 65 acres of beautiful gardens and parklands, with a private foreshore leading to the Helford River. Most of the comfortably furnished bedrooms enjoy stunning views over the hotel's sub-tropical gardens, some have adjoining sitting rooms and all are well equipped with modern amenities. Keen appetites will be well satisfied by the variety of dishes offered on the hotel's excellent and original menus. Seafood, including local lobsters and oysters, is an obvious speciality. In addition to traditional food, there is a choice of dishes with an international flavour. The hotel has its own tennis courts, golf course and swimming pool and activities including watersports, horse riding, yachting, boating and fishing are all within easy reach of the hotel. Numerous places of interest nearby include the Seal Sanctuary at Gweek, several heritage sites, and many magnificent gardens and properties of the National Trust. **Directions:** Follow A39 to Falmouth, at Hillhead roundabout follow signs for Trebah Gardens and Mawnan Smith. Take the right at the Red Lion. Pass Trebah Gardens and the turning for Helford Passage – Budock Vean is on the left. Price guide (including dinner): Single £53–£89; double/twin/suites £106–£178.

For hotel location, see maps on pages 490-496

# MEUDON HOTEL

**MAWNAN SMITH, NR FALMOUTH, CORNWALL TR11 5HT**
**TEL: 01326 250541 FAX: 01326 250543**

Set against a delightfully romantic backdrop of densely wooded countryside between the Fal and Helford Rivers, Meudon Hotel is a unique, superior retreat: a luxury, family-run establishment which has its origins in two humble 17th century coastguards' cottages. The French name comes from a nearby farmhouse built by Napoleonic prisoners of war and called after their eponymous home village in the environs of Paris. Set in nearly nine acres of fertile gardens – laid out by landscape gardener 'Capability' Brown, and now coaxed annually into early bloom by the mild Cornish climate – Meudon is safely surrounded by 200 acres of beautiful National Trust land and the sea. All bedrooms are en suite and enjoy spectacular views over sub-tropical gardens. Many a guest is enticed by the cuisine to return: in the restaurant (or the gardens during warm weather), fresh seafood and kitchen garden produce is served with wines from a judiciously compiled list. There are opportunities locally for fishing, sailing and walking. Golf is free at nearby Falmouth Golf Club. **Directions:** From Truro A39 to Hillhead roundabout turn right and the hotel is four miles on the left. Price guide (including dinner): Single £100; double/twin £170; suite £240.

For hotel location, see maps on pages 490-496

# NANSIDWELL COUNTRY HOUSE

**MAWNAN SMITH, NR FALMOUTH, CORNWALL TR11 5HU**
**TEL: 01326 250340 FAX: 01326 250440 E-MAIL:BOMBEROB@aol.com**

Lying at the head of a wooded farmland valley running down to the sea, Nansidwell Country House is bounded by several acres of grounds between National Trust coastland and the Helford River. The house has five acres of sub-tropical gardens with Camellias coming out in December and also extraordinary banana trees, sometimes bearing tiny fruit. The philosophy of proprietors Jamie and Felicity Robertson is that their guests should experience the atmosphere of an amiable, well-run country house. That so many guests return each year is a credit to the hotel. The bedrooms are prettily furnished and offer every comfort. Chef Anthony Allcott places an emphasis on fresh, local produce, particularly seafood such as lobster, mussels and oysters. For the sports enthusiast, there are five 18-hole golf courses within a short drive, as well as sea fishing and reservoir trout fishing and the hotel has a tennis court. Windsurfing, sailing, riding and bowls can all be enjoyed in the vicinity and there is the natural beauty of Falmouth's great harbour, the Helford River and Frenchman's Creek. Closed 2 January to 1 February. Internet: BOMBEROB@aol.com **Directions:** Follow A39 to Falmouth. Then follow signs to Trebah and Glendurgan Gardens. At Mawnan Smith bear left at fork. Hotel entrance is on right. Price guide Single from £115; double/twin from £152 to include dinner and continental breakfast. Bed and breakfast rates available.

For hotel location, see maps on pages 490-496

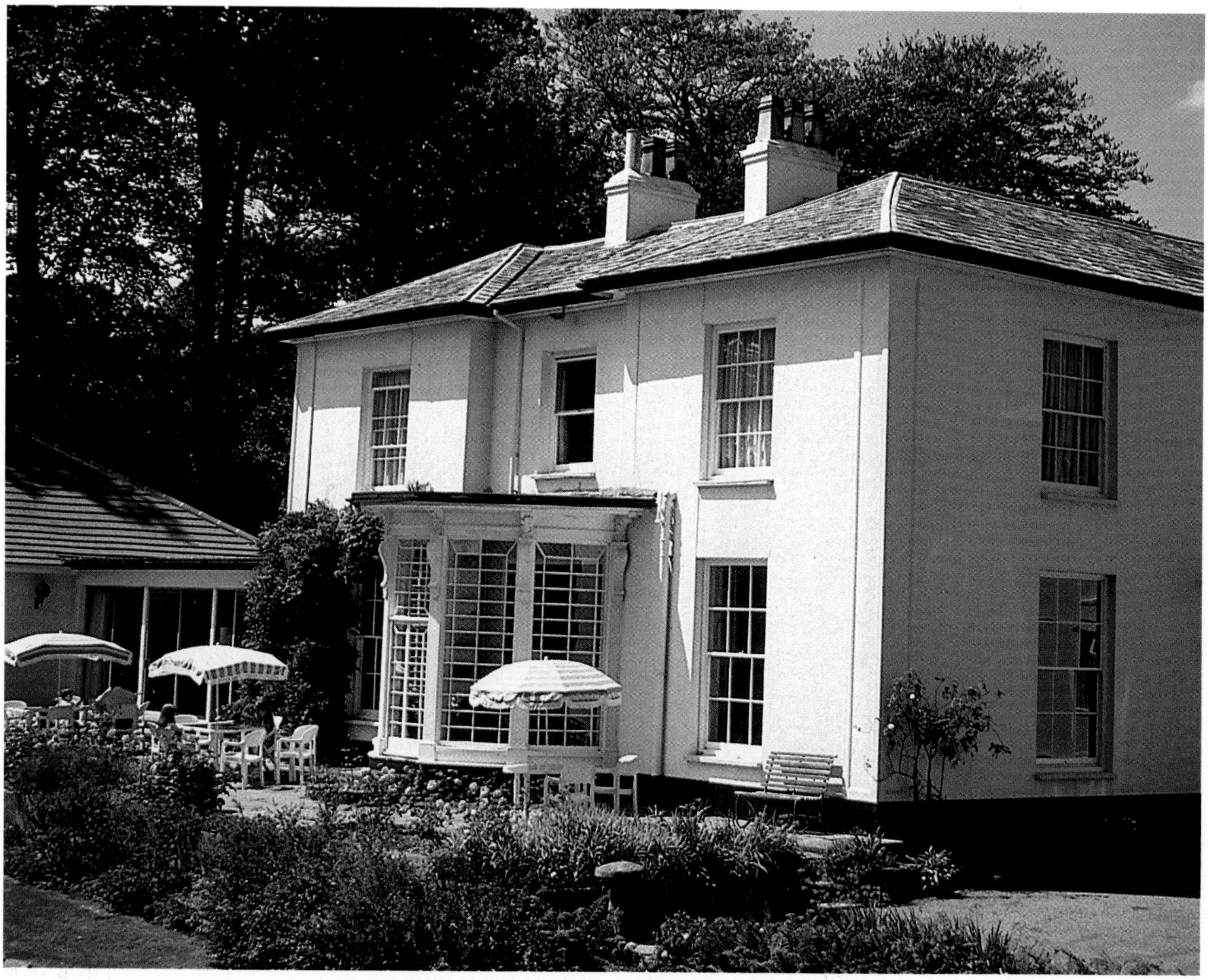

# PENMERE MANOR

**MONGLEATH ROAD, FALMOUTH, CORNWALL TR11 4PN**
**TEL: 01326 211411 FAX: 01326 317588**

Set in five acres of sub-tropical gardens and woodlands, this elegant Georgian country house is an oasis of gracious living and fine food. From arrival to departure the Manor's attentive staff ensure that guests have everything they need to enjoy their stay. Bedrooms offer every comfort and are furnished to maintain the country house ambience. The spacious Garden rooms are delightful. Each is named after a famous Cornish garden and has either king or queen size beds and a lounge area. The restaurant serves excellent international cuisine that includes an extensive lobster speciality menu. Light snacks and substantial lunchtime dishes are also provided in the bar which overlooks the garden and terrace. There is a heated outdoor swimming pool in the old walled garden and a splendid indoor pool, together with Jacuzzi spa, sauna, solarium and gym. Golfers can make use of the hotel's practice net and benefit from reduced green fees at Falmouth Golf Course. Cornish gardens, National Trust and English Heritage properties are within reach. Flambards Theme Park, Poldark Mine and Gweek Seal Sanctuary are less than ten miles away. Directions: From Truro follow the A39 towards Falmouth. Turn right at Hillhead roundabout and after 1 mile turn left into Mongleath Road. Price guide: Single £59; double/twin £85–£107.

For hotel location, see maps on pages 490-496

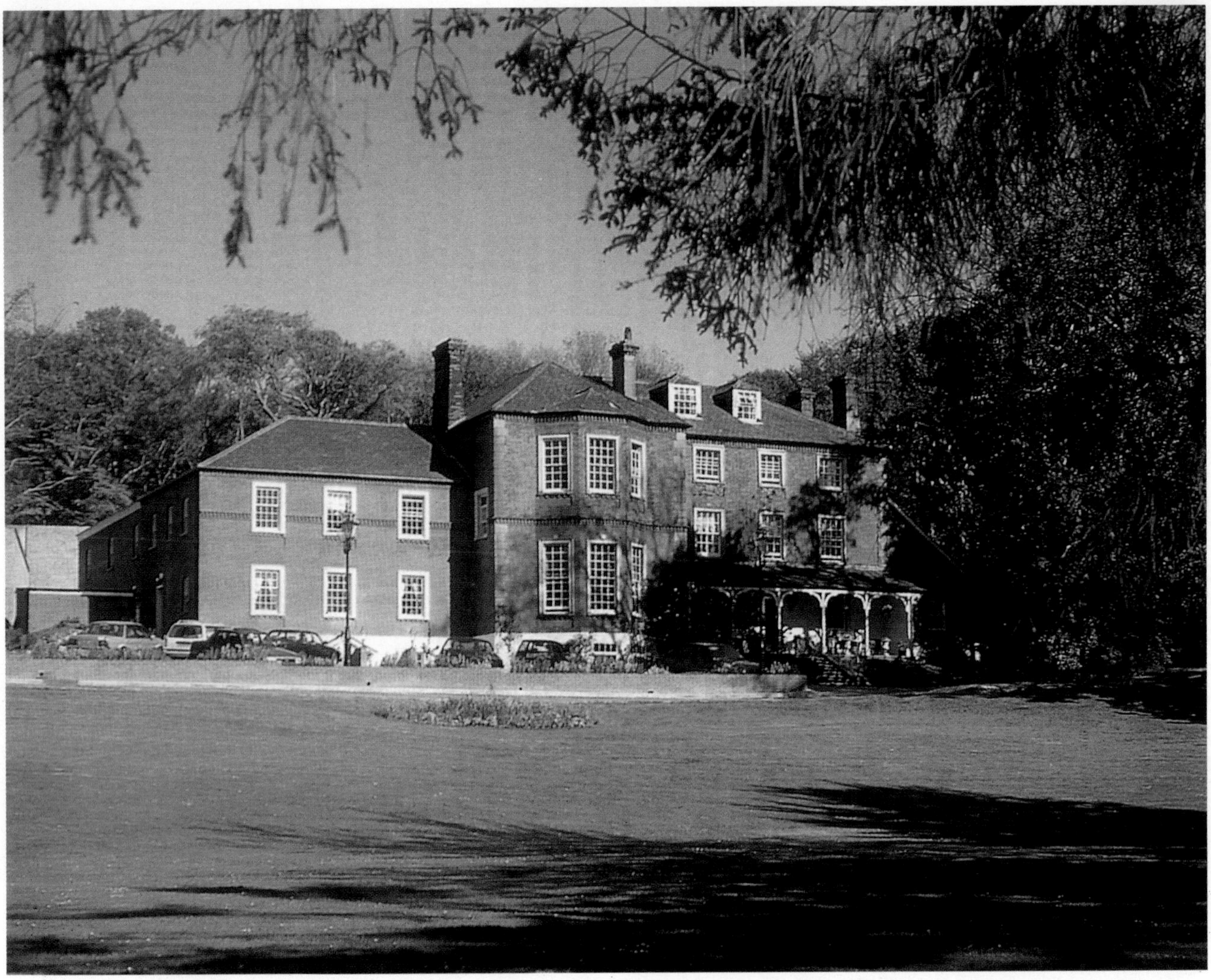

# BRANDSHATCH PLACE HOTEL

**FAWKHAM VALLEY ROAD, FAWKHAM, KENT DA3 8NQ**
**TEL: 01474 872239 FAX: 01474 879652**

Set amidst 12 acres of private parkland and gardens, Brandshatch Place is a distinguished Georgian residence built in 1806. Approached along an impressive tree-lined drive, it offers a peaceful getaway from London, only 20 miles to the south-east. The hotel is being carefully renovated to include every modern amenity, from banqueting and conference rooms to a fully equipped leisure club. Bedrooms are pleasantly decorated, 12 of which are located in the recently converted mews. Dine in the award-winning Hatchwood Restaurant where chefs create dishes of originality using only the best produce available. After your meal enjoy a relaxing drink in the restful bar. You are always welcome to use Fredericks, the sports and leisure complex with its indoor pool, three squash courts, supervised gymnasium, dance studio, hair and beauty salon, sauna, steam room, two solariums, snooker room and tennis courts. Business and private functions are easily accommodated in the eight meeting rooms. Of interest nearby, Eltham Palace and Lullingstone Roman Villa. An Arcadian Hotel. **Directions:** From M25 junction 3 follow A20 south, then signs to Fawkham Green, hotel is on the right about $^1/_2$ mile before Fawkham village. Price guide: Single: £89; double/twin £99–£145.

41 rms · 120

For hotel location, see maps on pages 490-496

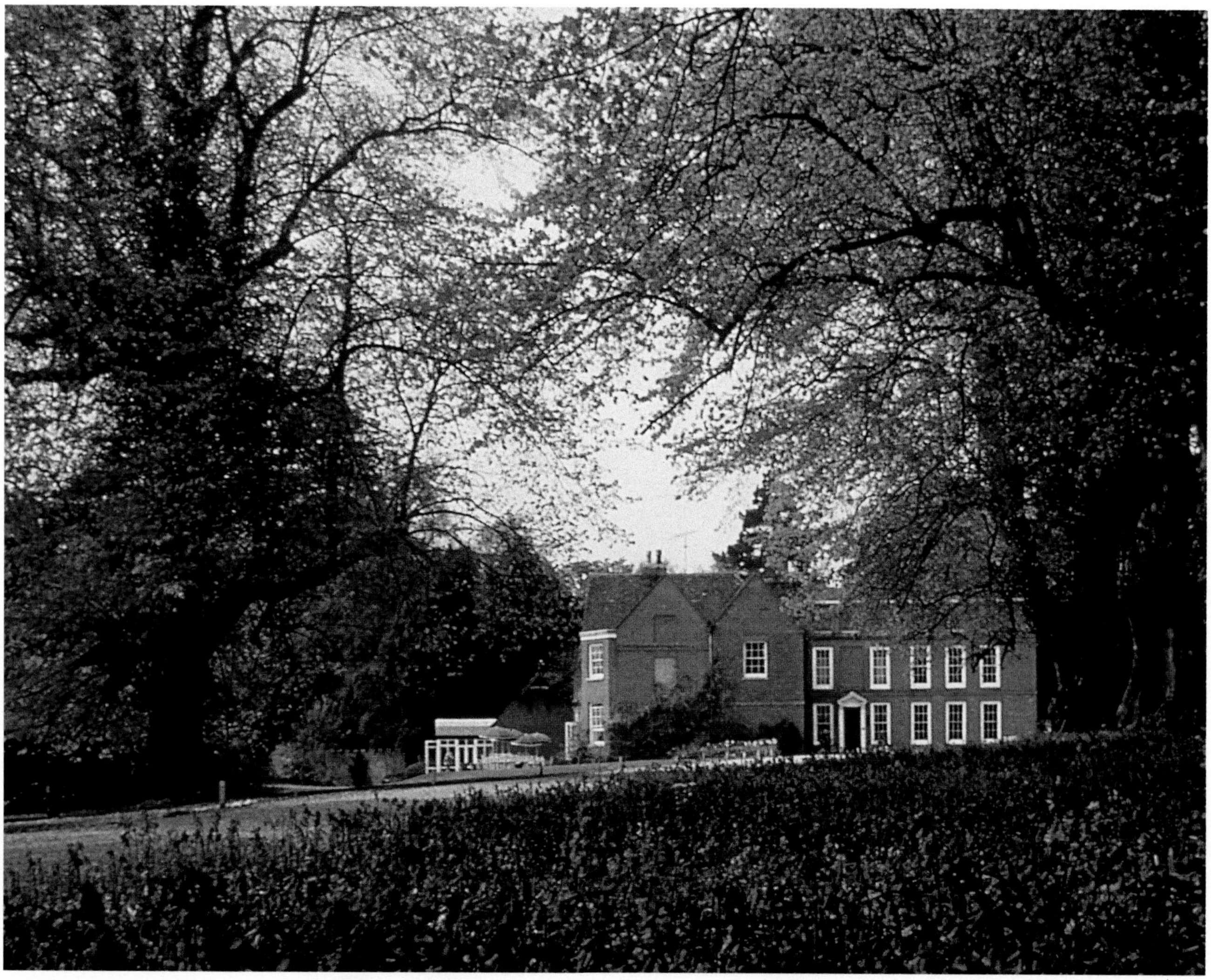

# FLITWICK MANOR

CHURCH ROAD, FLITWICK, BEDFORDSHIRE MK45 1AE
TEL: 01525 712242 FAX: 01525 718753

Flitwick Manor is a Georgian gem, classical in style, elegant in décor, comfortable in appointment, a country house hotel that remains true to the traditions of country house hospitality. Nestling in acres of glorious rolling parkland complete with lake, grotto and church, the manor has the intimacy and warmth that make it the ideal retreat for both pleasure and business. The fifteen bedrooms, with their distinctive characters and idiosyncrasies, add to the charm of the reception rooms: a soothing withdrawing room, a cosy library and pine panelled morning room, the latter two doubling up as both meeting and private dining rooms. Fine antiques and period pieces, easy chairs and inviting sofas, winter fires and summer flowers, they all blend effortlessly together to make a perfect whole. The restaurant is highly acclaimed by all the major food guides and indeed the AA, with its bestowal of three rosettes, rated Flitwick Manor as the county's best and amongst the top one hundred establishments in the country. Outside pleasures are afforded by the all-weather tennis court, croquet lawns and putting green as well as a range of local attractions such as Woburn Abbey and Safari Park. **Directions:** Flitwick is on the A5120 just north of the M1 junction 12. Price guide: Single £95–£190; double/twin/suite £125–£225. Special weekend rates available.

For hotel location, see maps on pages 490-496

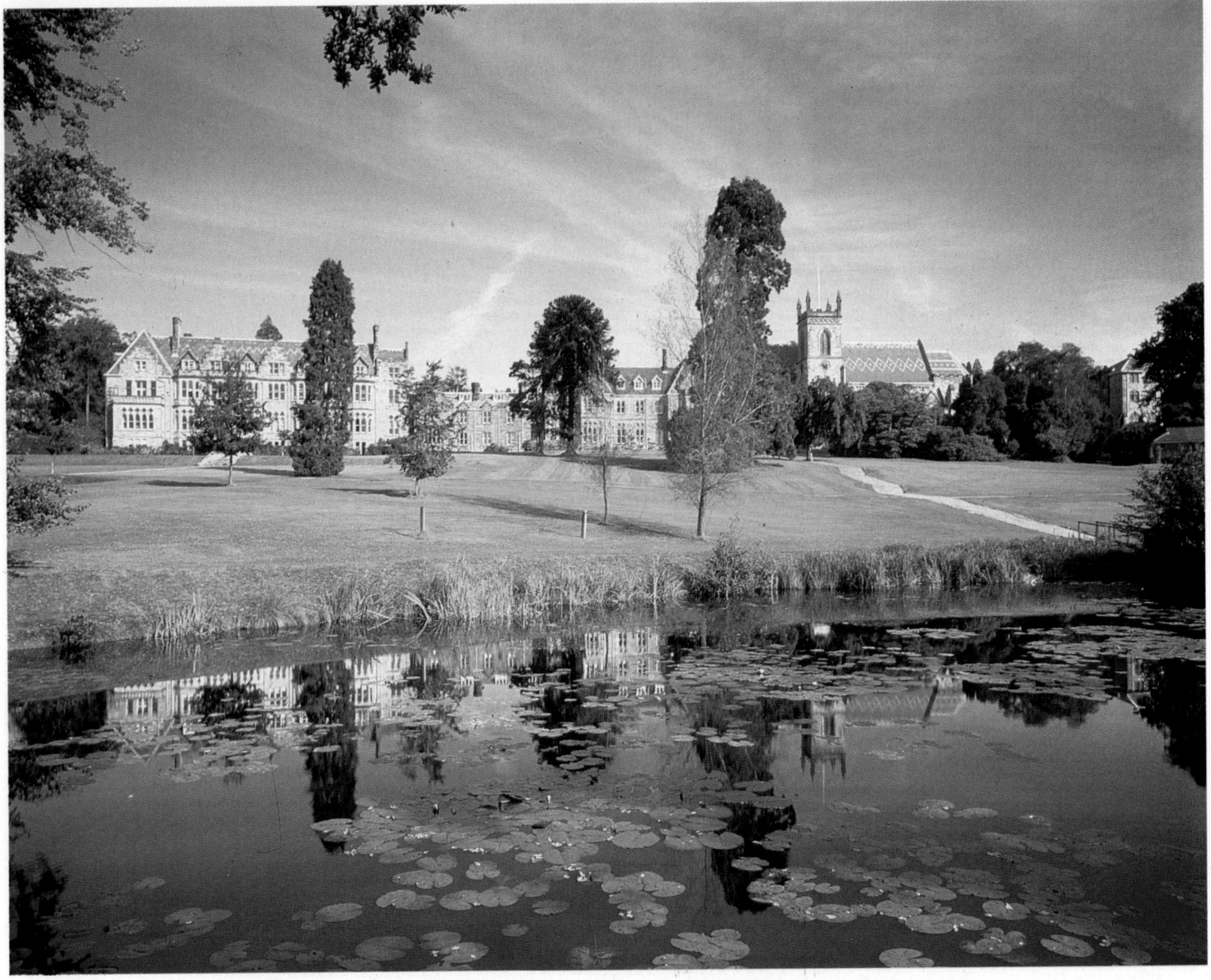

# ASHDOWN PARK HOTEL

WYCH CROSS, FOREST ROW, ASHDOWN FOREST, EAST SUSSEX RH18 5JR
TEL: 01342 824988 FAX: 01342 826206

Ashdown Park is a grand, rambling 19th century mansion overlooking almost 200 acres of landscaped gardens to the forest beyond. Built in 1867, the hotel is situated within easy reach of Gatwick Airport, London and the South Coast, and provides the perfect backdrop for every occasion, from a weekend getaway to a honeymoon or business convention. The hotel is subtly furnished throughout to satisfy the needs of escapees from urban stress. The 95 en suite bedrooms are beautifully decorated – several with elegant four-poster beds, all with up-to-date amenities. The Anderida restaurant offers a thoughtfully compiled menu and wine list, complemented by discreetly attentive service in soigné surroundings. Guests seeking relaxation can retire to the indoor pool and sauna, pamper themselves with a massage, before using the solarium, or visiting the beauty salon. Alternatively, guests may prefer to amble through the gardens and nearby woodland paths; the more energetic can indulge in tennis, squash pitch and putt, croquet or use the Fitness Studio and Beauty Therapy. There is also an indoor driving range, a lounge/bar and a 9-hole par 3 golf course with an outdoor driving range. **Directions:** East of A22 at Wych Cross on road signposted to Hartfield. Price guide: Single £105–£260; double/twin £130–£225; suite £285.

For hotel location, see maps on pages 490-496

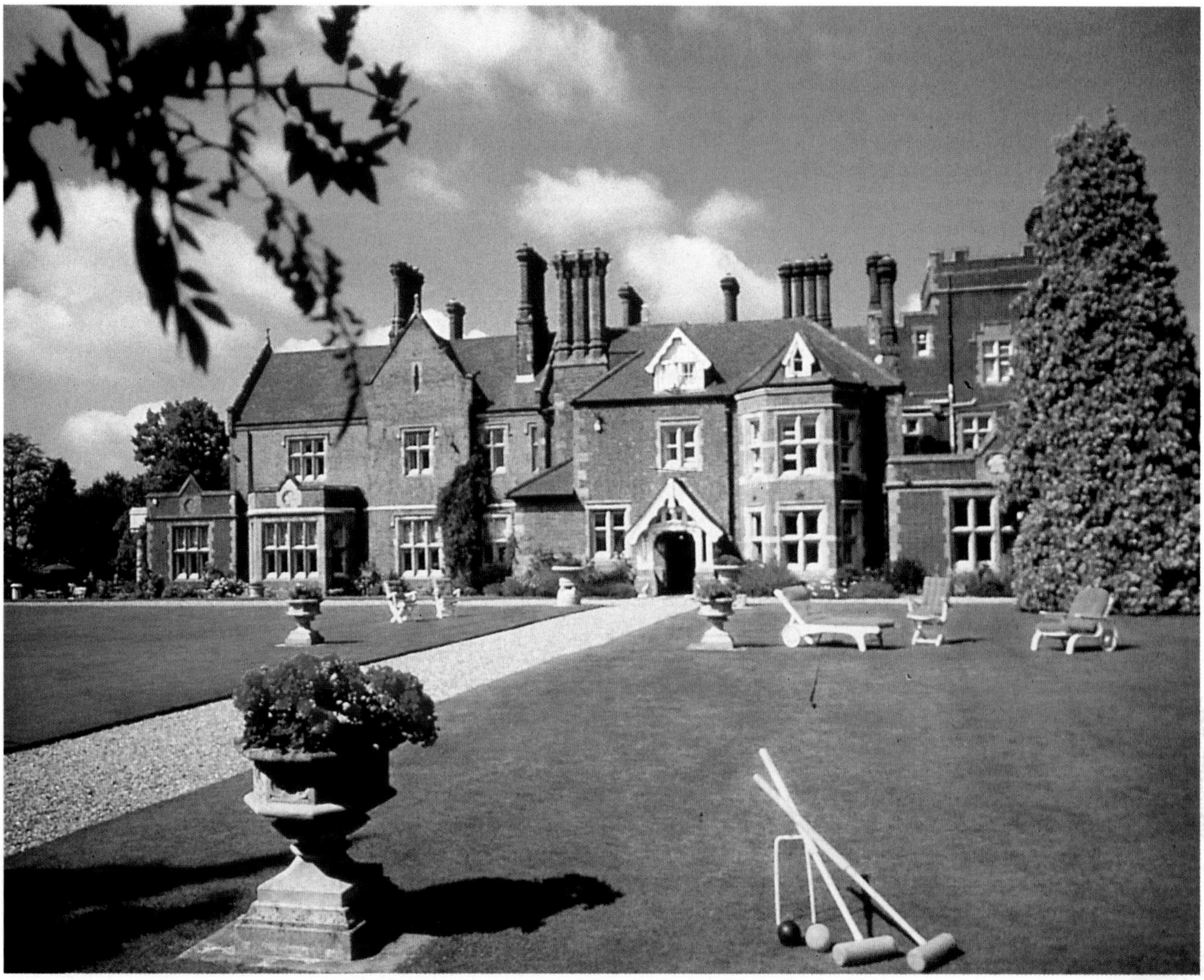

# ALEXANDER HOUSE

**TURNER'S HILL, WEST SUSSEX RH10 4QD**
**TEL: 01342 714914 FAX: 01342 717328**

Winner of Johansens 1997 Award for Most Excellent Service, Alexander House is a magnificent mansion with its own secluded 135 acres of park, including a gently sloping valley which forms the head of the River Medway. Records trace the estate from 1332 when a certain John Atte Fen made it his home. Alexander House is now a modern paragon of good taste and excellence. Spacious rooms throughout this luxurious hotel are splendidly decorated to emphasise their many original features and the bedrooms are lavishly furnished to the highest standards of comfort. The House is renowned for its delicious classic English and French cuisine, rare wines and vintage liqueurs. Music recitals and garden parties are among the events held here and there are good conference facilities available. Guests are invited to take part in activities including clay pigeon shooting, croquet, snooker and tennis. There is in addition a resident beautician. Courtesy transport can take guests to Gatwick Airport in under 15 minutes. Antique shops, National Trust properties, museums and the Royal Pavilion in Brighton are nearby. **Directions:** Alexander House lies on the B2110 road between Turner's Hill and East Grinstead, six miles from junction 10 of the M23 motorway. Price guide: Single £120–£170; double/twin £155–£195; suites £285.

For hotel location, see maps on pages 490-496

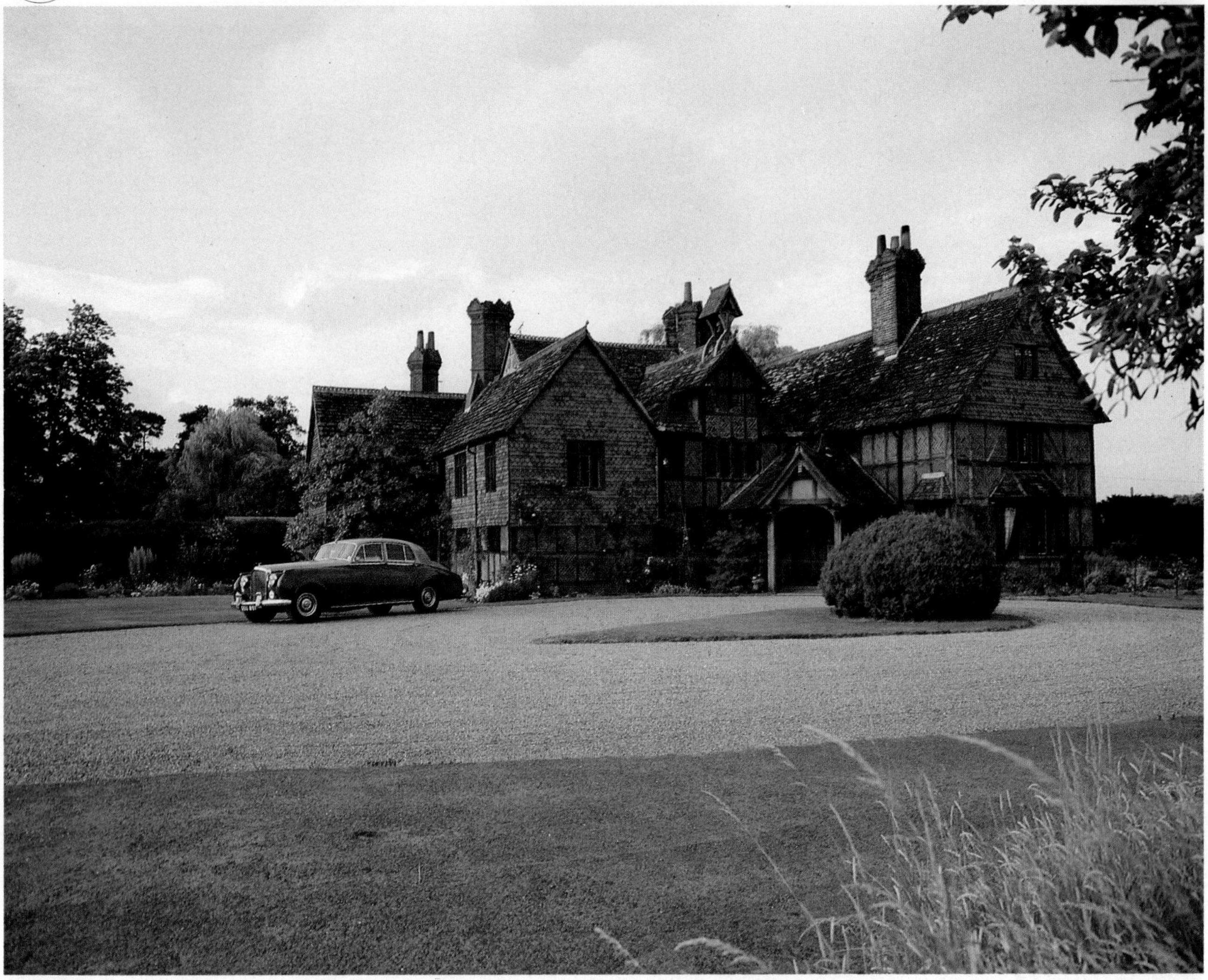

# LANGSHOTT MANOR

**LANGSHOTT, HORLEY, SURREY RH6 9LN**
**TEL: 01293 786680 FAX: 01293 783905**

The peace and seclusion of this beautiful Manor House belies its close proximity to London's Gatwick Airport, 8 minutes away by taxi or Hotel car. Geoffrey, Patricia and Christopher Noble offer the kind of welcome and hospitality seldom found in the world of airports and travel. The Manor becomes the perfect beginning or end to your holiday in Britain or is a safe haven for your car if you are flying abroad. Free car parking (2 weeks) and luxury courtesy car to Gatwick Airport are offered. Although Langshott Manor is only 8 minutes drive away the airport, the house is tucked away down a quiet country lane amidst 3 acres of beautiful gardens and ponds and offers its guests peace and seclusion. The property is not under the flight path. Hever Castle, Chartwell, Knole Park, Brighton Pavilion and many other properties are all within 30 minutes' drive. Central London is 30 minutes away via the Gatwick/Victoria Express. **Directions:** From A23 in Horley take Ladbroke Road (Chequers Hotel roundabout) to Langshott. The manor is three quarters of a mile (one kilometre) on the right. Price guide: Single from £105; double/twin from £135.

For hotel location, see maps on pages 490-496

# COMBE HOUSE HOTEL

**GITTISHAM, NR HONITON, DEVON EX14 0AD**
**TEL: 01404 42756 FAX: 01404 46004**

Tucked away in a glorious East Devon country estate at the head of a secluded valley, Combe House is a beautiful Elizabethan mansion crowned by tall, ornate chimneys and surrounded by sloping lawns, rhododendrons, magnolia's and cherry trees. The hotel commands extensive views over the Blackmore Hills as far as Exmoor and is a haven of peace and quiet, rich in ornate ceilings, oak panelling, flagged floors and mullioned windows. Personally run by owners John and Thérèse Boswell since 1970 the welcoming atmosphere of a large family house is enhanced with antiques, fine paintings, sculptures, warm colours and comfortable furniture. Fifteen spacious bedrooms have uninterrupted views over the lush countryside. The richly furnished main drawing room is hung with portraits of 18th century ancestors, the entrance hall is a superb example of Caroline grandeur, and the Boswell's interest in horseracing is recorded in an extensive collection of photographs on the walls of the hotel's bar. Excellent candlelit dinners are produced by Thérèse and two talented chefs in the two intimate dining rooms. Exeter, Sidmouth and Branscombe are within easy reach, there is golf at nearby Honiton and horse riding can be arranged. The hotel has dry-fly fishing rights on the River Otter. **Directions:** From the M5 junction 28 take A373, M5 junction 29 take A30, towards Honiton and then follow signs to Gittisham. Price guide: Single £65–£110; double/twin £99.50–£149.

For hotel location, see maps on pages 490-496

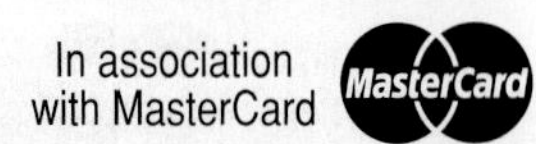

# The Wind In The Willows

**DERBYSHIRE LEVEL, GLOSSOP, DERBYSHIRE SK13 9PT**
**TEL: 01457 868001 FAX: 01457 853354**

"Not so much a hotel, more a delightful experience"wrote a guest of this charming, small, family-run hotel on the edge of the Peak District. It won the AA Greatest Courtesy and Care in the North of England award 1996/97. The Mother-and-Son team of Anne and Peter Marsh have added lavish care, attention to detail and a sincere courtesy to their recipe of antiques, Victorian bric-à-brac and delightful charm that is characteristic of The Wind in the Willows. If you don't know how it gets its name, stay there and read your bedside book! The marvellous scenery of the National Park is, literally, at the doorstep. All of the twelve, en suite bedrooms enjoy superb views, and all are full of character, even the newer ones, opened in 1995, having their share of antique furniture and traditional decor that embellishes the whole house. There are some very special features, too – huge antique mahogany beds, a Victorian style bath and individual touches created by Anne in various rooms. Anne also supervises in the kitchen from where delicious home-cooking is served to both the private dining room and the purpose-built meeting room. Many activities can be arranged locally, including pot-holing, horse riding, gliding and para/hang gliding. **Directions:** One mile east of Glossop on the A57, 400 yards down the road opposite the Royal Oak. Price guide: Single £65–£88; double/twin £85–£110.

12 rms · MasterCard · VISA · American Express · M 12 · 8

For hotel location, see maps on pages 490-496

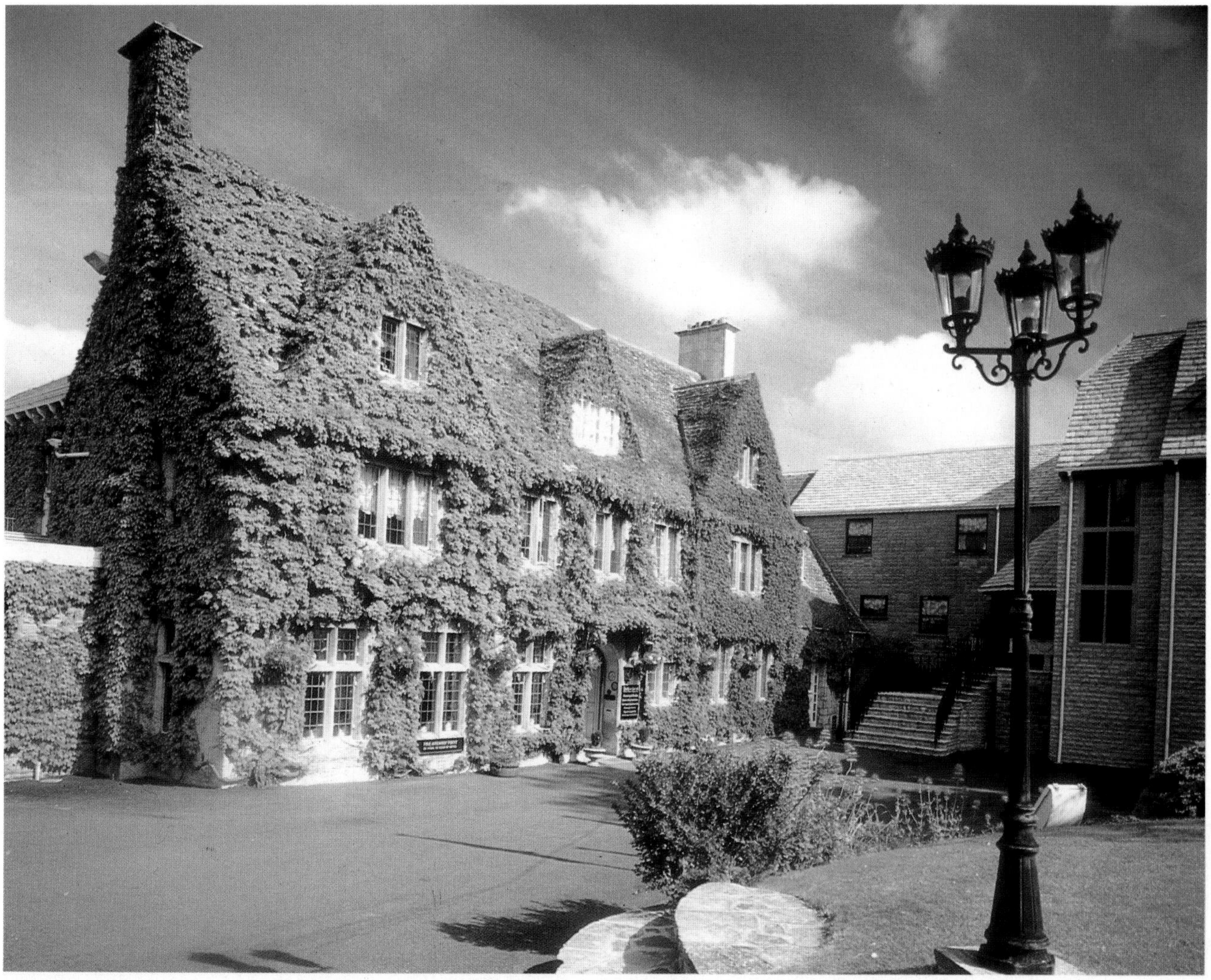

# HATTON COURT HOTEL

**UPTON HILL, UPTON ST LEONARDS, GLOUCESTER, GLOUCESTERSHIRE GL4 8DE**
**TEL: 01452 617412 FAX: 01452 612945 E-MAIL: Res@hatton-court.co.uk**

This old ivy-clad Cotswold manor is set in seven acres of beautifully maintained gardens and 30 acres of green pastures. Nestling in the hills of Upton St Leonards, it enjoys stunning views over the Severn Valley towards the Malvern Hills. Extensive refurbishment of the manor has sought to combine modern comfort and sophistication with 17th century charm and character. Lavishly furnished bedrooms, many featuring Jacuzzis, offer a host of amenities and a number of personal extras including fresh fruit, mineral water, home-made cookies and bathrobes. Carrington's, Hatton Court's restaurant, has delightful decor, panoramic views and gastronomic delights. Classical traditional dishes and food cooked in the modern French style are complemented by wines from some 140 bins. Riding, golf and dry skiing are available just minutes from the hotel. Places to visit nearby include the elegant spa towns of Bath and Cheltenham, the Wildfowl and Wetlands Trust at Slimbridge, Prinknash Abbey, Berkeley Castle and Stratford-upon-Avon. Special breaks are available and details of these can be supplied on request. A member of Hatton Hotels. Internet: http://www.hatton-hotels.com **Directions:** Hatton Court is located three miles south of Gloucester on the B4073 Painswick – Gloucester road, off the A46. Price guide: Single £90–£100; double/twin £105–£145.

For hotel location, see maps on pages 490-496

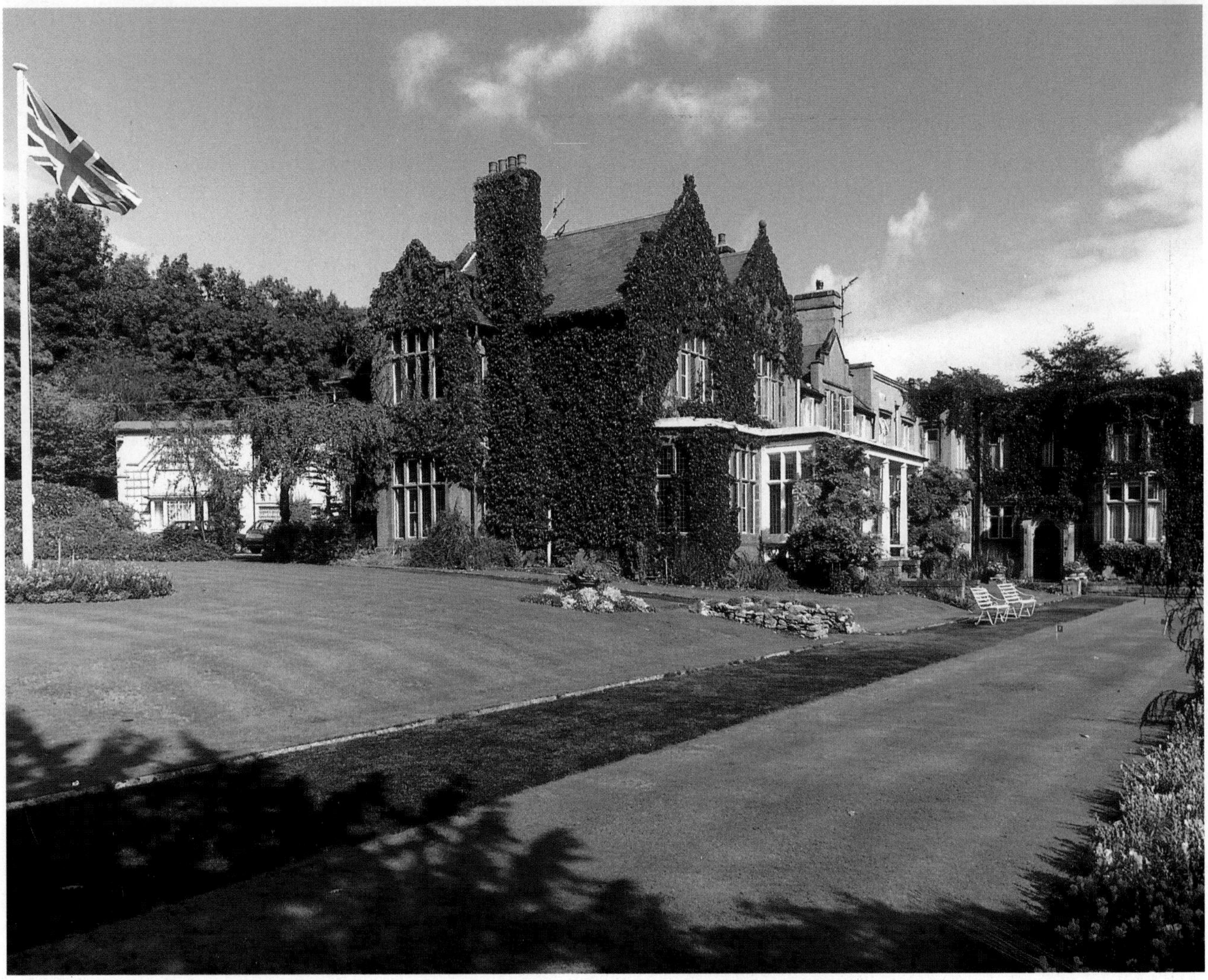

# GRAYTHWAITE MANOR

**FERNHILL ROAD, GRANGE-OVER-SANDS, CUMBRIA LA11 7JE**
**TEL: 015395 32001 FAX: 015395 35549**

This beautifully furnished, traditionally run country house has been owned and run by the Blakemore family since 1937 and extends a warm welcome to its guests. It enjoys a superb setting in eight acres of private landscaped gardens and woodland on the hillside overlooking Morecambe Bay. Each bedroom is decorated and furnished in the best of taste and many offer superb views across the gardens and bay to the Pennines beyond. Elegant, spacious lounges with fresh flowers and antiques provide an exclusive setting and log fires are lit to add extra cheer on chillier nights. The Manor enjoys an excellent reputation for its cuisine and guests can look forward to a six course dinner comprising carefully prepared dishes complemented by the right wine from the extensive cellar. A few miles inland from Grange-over-Sands are Lake Windermere and Coniston Water and some of the most majestic scenery in the country. Nearby are the village of Cartmel, Holker Hall, Levens Hall and Sizergh Castle. The area abounds with historic buildings, gardens and museums. **Directions:** Take M6 to junction 36 and then the A65 towards Kendal, followed by the A590 towards Barrow. At roundabout take B5277 to Grange-over-Sands and go through town turning right opposite the fire station into Fernhill Road. The hotel is on the left. Price guide: Single £45–£55; double/twin £80–£98.

For hotel location, see maps on pages 490-496

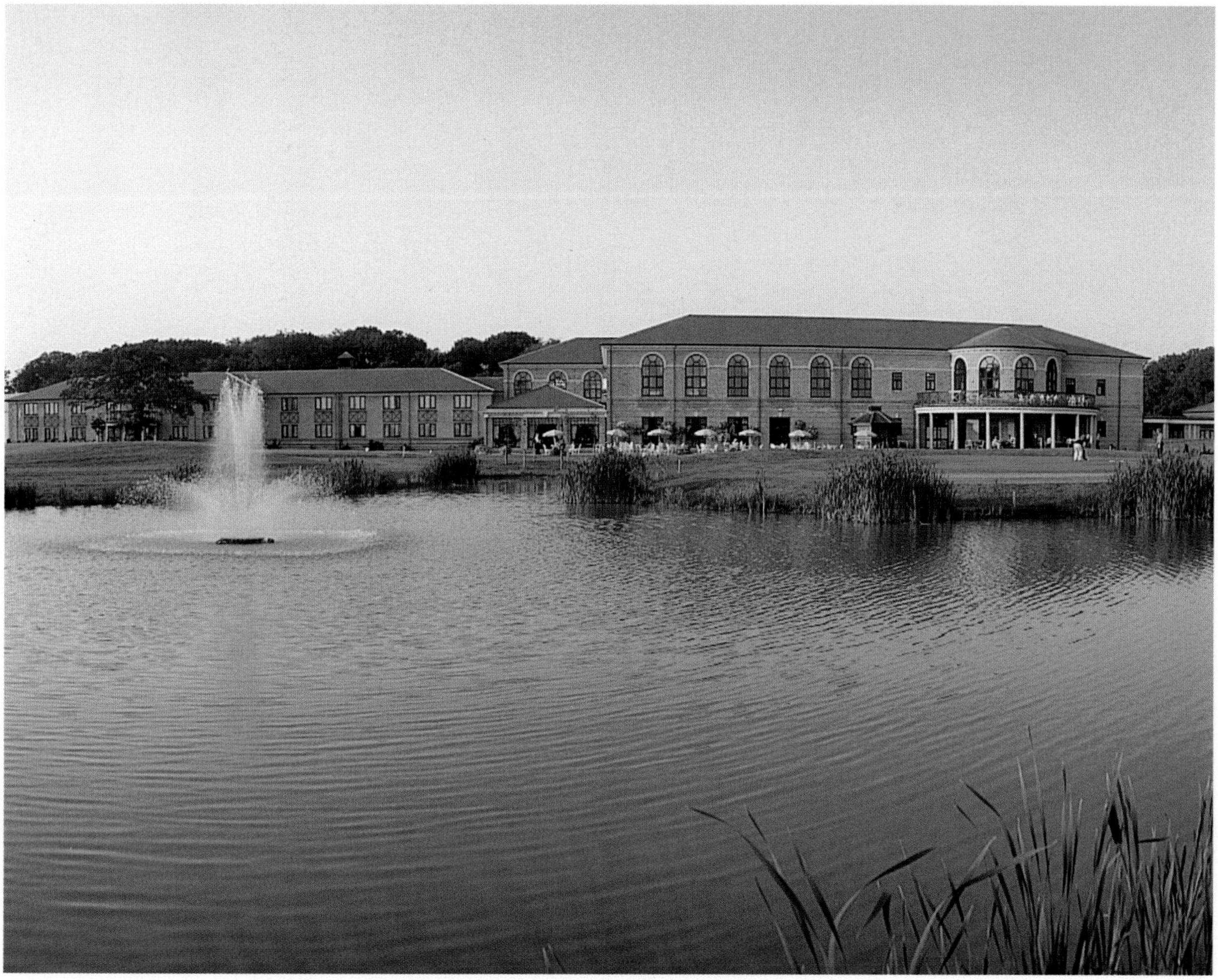

# Belton Woods

BELTON, NR GRANTHAM, LINCOLNSHIRE NG32 2LN
TEL: 01476 593200 FAX: 01476 574547

Set in the peaceful surroundings of beautiful rural Lincolnshire, Belton Woods, a modern hotel, has been furnished with all the characteristics of a country house, giving a feeling of space and tranquility, combining facilities for both business and leisure. Golfing enthusiasts are exceptionally well catered for – there are two excellent championship 18 hole golf courses, a testing 9 hole par 3 course, complemented by a first class golf centre. With a range of well appointed meeting/conference rooms, Belton Woods is able to cater for the smallest meetings to the larger conferences, for up to 275 delegates. Activities can be arranged such as archery, quad biking, karting and team building exercises. A magnificent Leisure Club offers a swimming pool, spa bath, sauna, gym, squash and tennis courts. There is also a hair and beauty salon. For the children there is an outdoor adventure playground as well as a supervised crèche. There is a choice of two restaurants, you can experience fine dining in the oak panelled surroundings of the Manor Restaurant or a delicious 'healthy option' the informal restaurant the Plus Fours, both catering for the everchanging needs of todays easting. Of interest nearby: Belton House, Belvoir Castle and Burghley House. **Directions:** From A1 (Gonerby Moor Services) take B1174–A607 and follow brown signs for Belton House. Price guide: Single £115; double/twin £125; suites £195.

For hotel location, see maps on pages 490-496

In association with MasterCard 

# MICHAELS NOOK

GRASMERE, CUMBRIA LA22 9RP

TEL: 015394 35496 FAX: 015394 35645

Built in 1859 and named after Michael the eponymous shepherd of Wordsworth's poem, Michael's Nook has long been established as one of Britain's leading country house hotels. Opened as a hotel in 1969 by Reg and Elizabeth Gifford, it overlooks Grasmere Valley and is surrounded by gardens and trees. The hotel's interior reflects Reg's appreciation of antique English furniture, rugs, prints and porcelain. There are two suites, and twelve individually designed bedrooms, all with en suite bathrooms. In the acclaimed restaurant, polished tables are set with fine Stuart crystal and Wedgewood china. The best ingredients are used to create dishes memorable for their delicate flavours and artistic presentation. The panelled Oak Room, with its stone fireplace and gilt furnishings, can be booked for private parties and executive meetings. Leisure facilities at the nearby Wordsworth Hotel are available to guests, as is free golf at Keswick Golf Club. Michael's Nook is, first and foremost, a home where comfort is the watchword. Awarded AA 1997 Best Hotel Restaurant in North England. **Directions:** Approaching Grasmere on the A591 from the south, ignore signs for Grasmere Village and continue to The Swan Hotel on the right. There turn sharp right and follow the lane uphill for 400 yds to Michael's Nook. Price guide (including 5 course dinner): Single from £130; double/twin £160–£300; suite £375.

14 rms MasterCard VISA AMERICAN EXPRESS M 30 10

For hotel location, see maps on pages 490-496

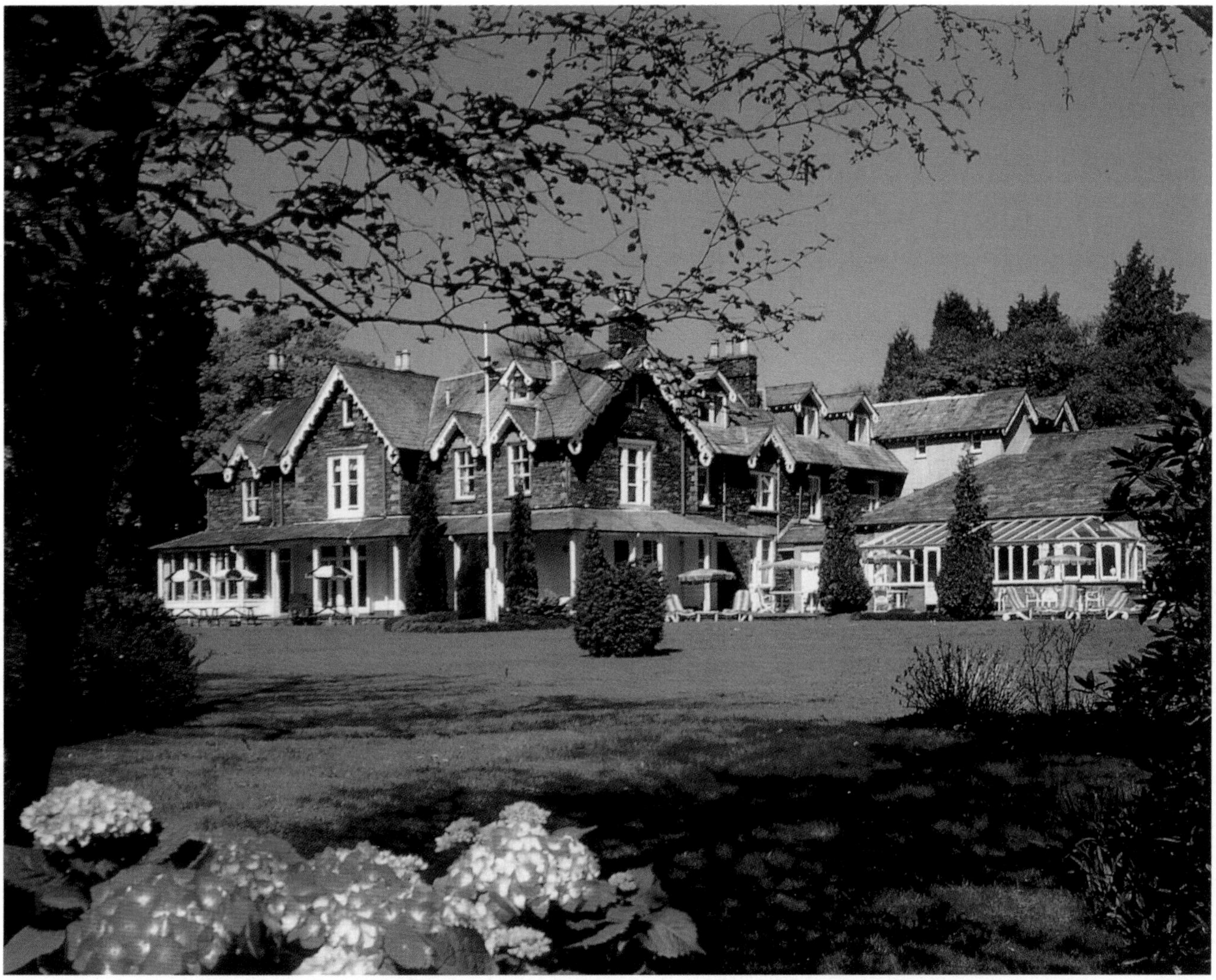

# THE WORDSWORTH HOTEL

**GRASMERE, NEAR AMBLESIDE, CUMBRIA LA22 9SW**
**TEL: 015394 35592 FAX: 015394 35765**

In the very heart of the English Lakeland, The Wordsworth Hotel combines AA 4 Star standards with the magnificence of the surrounding fells. Set in its own grounds in the village of Grasmere, the hotel provides first-class, year-round facilities for both business and leisure travellers. It has a reputaion for the high quality of its food, accommodation and hospitality. The comfortable bedrooms have well-equipped bathrooms, and there are two suites with whirlpool baths. 24-hour room service is available for drinks and light refreshments. Peaceful lounges overlook landscaped gardens, and the heated indoor pool opens on to a sun-trap terrace. There is a Jacuzzi, mini-gym, sauna and solarium. As well as a Cocktail Bar, the hotel has its own pub, "The Dove and Olive Branch", which has received accolades from The Good Pub Guide. In "The Prelude Restaurant" menus offer a good choice of dishes, prepared with skill and imagination from the freshest produce. The Wordsworth Hotel is a perfect venue for conferences, incentive weekends and corporate entertaining. Three function rooms are available with highly professional back-up. Lakeland's principal places of interest are all within easy reach. **Directions:** The hotel is located next to Grasmere village church. Price guide: Single £64–£80; double/twin £128–£165; suite £200–£210.

For hotel location, see maps on pages 490-496

# GRAYSHOTT HALL HEALTH FITNESS RETREAT

**HEADLEY ROAD, GRAYSHOTT, NEAR HINDHEAD, SURREY GU26 6JJ**
**TEL: 01428 604331 FAX: 01428 605463**

Grayshott Hall, with its 47 acres of gardens, woods and sweeping lawns, is set in a beautiful corner of rural England. Once the home of Victorian poet, Lord Tennyson, the house abounds with creature comforts and exudes a warm and friendly atmosphere conducive to total relaxation. On arrival, guests consult with a member of the medical team and a programme of treatments is devised to suit individual needs – whether these are to lose weight, start on a new fitness regime or simply relax and rejuvenate. Bedrooms range from tastefully decorated individually designed suites to stylish and comfortable doubles, twins or singles. Other main features of the Hall include a drawing room, two dining rooms, snooker room, smoking room, gym, exercise studio, spa, hydrotherapy suite and indoor swimming pool. There are two indoor tennis courts, while outside facilities include a tennis court, a badminton court and a 9 hole par 3 golf course. Lunch is taken in the dining room which offers a vast low fat buffet and during the evenings, following healthy cocktails, dinner includes delicious, nourishing dishes designed to satisfy the heartiest appetite. **Directions:** From M25 junction 10 take A3 to Hindhead and then turn right 500 yards after the traffic lights onto B3002. The Hall is 1½ miles after Grayshott Village. Price guide (per person): Single £165; double/twin £145. Prices include daily 40 minutes massage, food and exercise classes.

76 rms

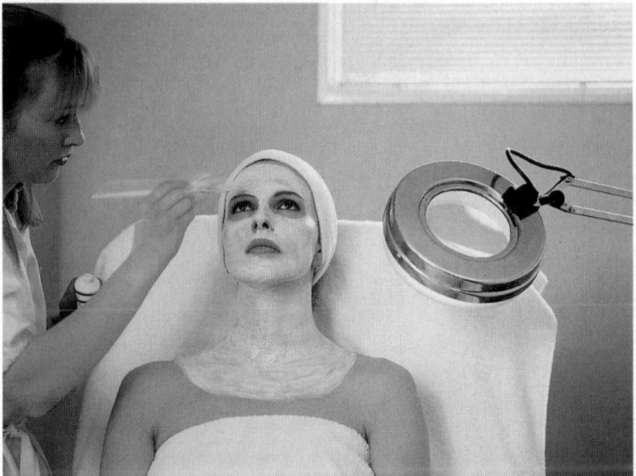



For hotel location, see maps on pages 490-496

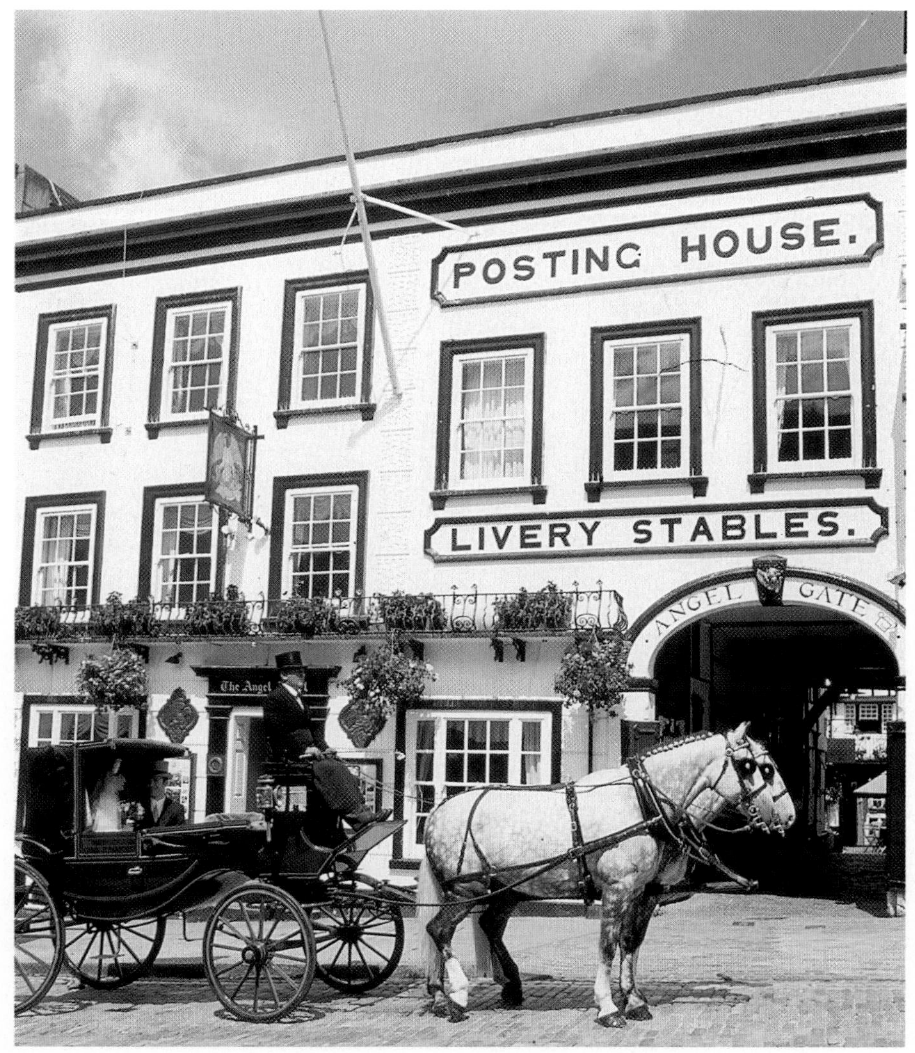


# THE ANGEL POSTING HOUSE AND LIVERY

91 THE HIGH STREET, GUILDFORD, SURREY GU1 3DP
TEL: 01483 564555 FAX: 01483 533770

The Angel, a delightful historic coaching inn on the old Portsmouth road, now a luxurious small hotel, has stood in Guildford High Street since the 16th century. This timber-framed building has welcomed many famous visitors, including Lord Nelson, Jane Austen and Charles Dickens. Today, with easy access to Gatwick, Heathrow, the M4, M3 and M25, The Angel is ideally placed for both business and pleasure. The galleried lounge with its oak-beamed Jacobean fireplace and 17th-century parliament clock is a welcome retreat from the bustle of the nearby shops. The No. 1 Angel Gate Restaurant, with its vaulted ceiling and intimate atmosphere, serves a wide choice of superb English and Continental cuisine together with fine wines and impeccable service. The charming bedrooms and suites, decorated with soft furnishings and fabrics, are all unique. Excellent communications, presentation facilities and 24-hour service make this a good choice for business meetings. Private dinners, buffets, dances and wedding receptions can also be catered for. **Directions:** From M3 junction 3 take the A322; or from M25 junction 10 take the A3. The Angel is in the centre of Guildford, within the pedestrian priority area – guests should enquire about vehicle access and parking when booking. Price guide (room only): Double/twin £135–£150; suite £180–£200.

For hotel location, see maps on pages 490-496

In association with MasterCard

# WEST LODGE PARK

**COCKFOSTERS ROAD, HADLEY WOOD, BARNET, HERTFORDSHIRE EN4 0PY**
**TEL: 0181 440 8311 FAX: 0181 449 3698**

West Lodge Park is a country house hotel which stands in 34 acres of Green Belt parklands and gardens. These include a lake and an arboretum with hundreds of mature trees. Despite the advantages of this idyllic setting, the hotel is only 1 mile from the M25 and within easy reach of London. Run by the Beale family for over 50 years, West Lodge Park was originally a gentleman's country seat, rebuilt in 1838 on the site of an earlier keeper's lodge. In the public rooms, antiques, original paintings and period furnishings create a restful atmosphere. All the bright and individually furnished bedrooms, many of which enjoy country views, have a full range of modern amenities. Well presented cuisine is available in the elegant restaurant. Residents enjoy free membership and a free taxi to the nearby David Lloyd leisure centre, which has excellent facilities. Hatfield House and St Albans Abbey are 15 minutes' drive. The hotel is credited with AA 4 stars and rosette, RAC 4 stars plus 3 merit awards and was the 1995 County Hotel of the Year in the Which? Hotel Guide. **Directions:** The hotel is on A111 one mile north of Cockfosters underground station and one mile south of junction 24 on M25. Price guide: Single £84.50–£105; double/twin from £130–£175; suites £195–£250.

For hotel location, see maps on pages 490-496

# HOLDSWORTH HOUSE

**HOLDSWORTH ROAD, HOLMFIELD, HALIFAX, WEST YORKSHIRE HX2 9TG**
**TEL: 01422 240024 FAX: 01422 245174**

Holdsworth House is a retreat of quality and charm standing three miles north of Halifax in the heart of Yorkshire's West Riding. Built in 1633, it was acquired by the Pearson family over 30 years ago. With care, skill and professionalism they have created a hotel and restaurant of considerable repute. The interior of the house, with its polished panelling and open fireplaces, has been carefully preserved and embellished with fine antique furniture and ornaments. The comfortable lounge opens onto a pretty courtyard and overlooks the herb garden and gazebo. The restaurant comprises three beautifully furnished rooms, ideally arranged for private dinner parties. Exciting modern English and continental cuisine is meticulously prepared and presented by Eric Claveau, complemented by a thoughtfully compiled wine list. The restaurant now has two AA Rosettes. Each cosy bedroom has its own style – from the four split-level suites to the two single rooms designed for wheelchair access. This is the perfect base from which to explore the Pennines, the Yorkshire Dales and Haworth – the home of the Brontë family. Closed at Christmas. **Directions:** From M1 junction 42 take M62 westbound to junction 26. Follow A58 to Halifax (ignore signs to town centre). At Burdock Way roundabout take A629 to Keighley; after 1½ miles go right into Shay Lane; hotel is one mile, on right. Price guide: Single £55–£85; double/twin £80–£95; suite £95–£120.

For hotel location, see maps on pages 490-496

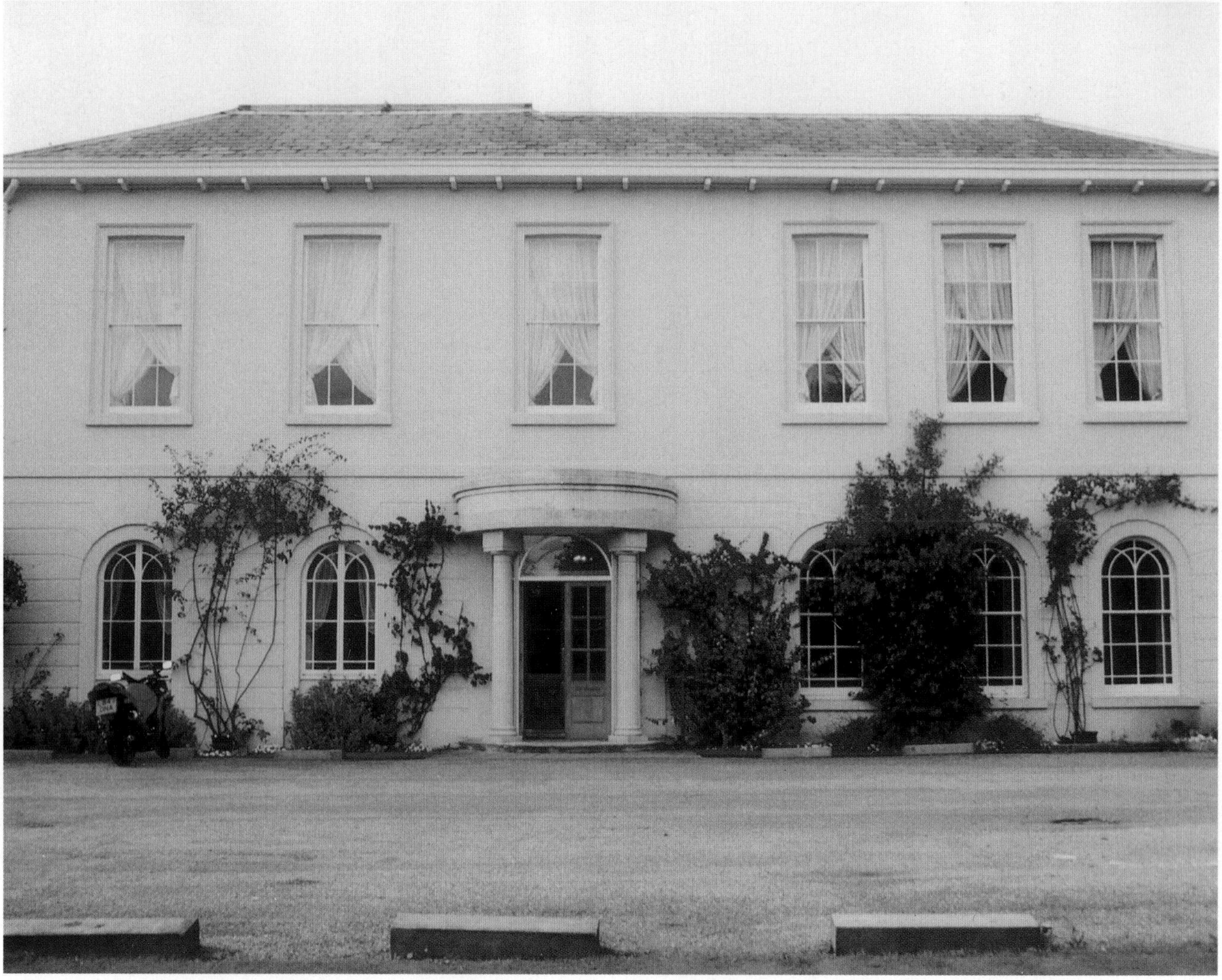

# THE MANOR OF GROVES HOTEL

**HIGH WYCH, SAWBRIDGEWORTH, HERTFORDSHIRE CM21 0LA**
**TEL: 01279 600777 FAX: 01279 600374**

The delightful name of this hotel conjures up a picture of a fine house and new arrivals are not disappointed when they see this splendid Georgian manor with its graceful facade. Standing in an estate of 150 acres, the facilities include a golf and country club as well as excellent conference facilities. The decor is in harmony with the Manor's past, the Loggia enchanting with its black and while tiled floor and palm trees. The lounge has a big fireplace and plump sofas. The bedrooms are rather grand, with drapes in flowery chintz, and all modern accessories. The opulent bathrooms are roomy, with an abundance of marble. Luxurious suites on two floors are in The Coach House. The bar is inviting, and the delightful green Colonnade Restaurant overlooks the gardens. The Manor is proud of its innovative cuisine and even more so of its fine wine list. There is an eighteen-hole golf course in the grounds, an open air pool, tennis courts and other opportunities for outdoor sport. Less active guests will enjoy strolling among the trees, beside the lakes or relaxing on the terrace. **Directions:** Leave M11 at Junction 7, taking A414, towards Harlow and Bishops Stortford, then A1184 through Sawbridgeworth, turning left at sign to High Wych. Right at Half Moon pub, then through gates 200 yards further on on left hand side. Price guide: Single £90–£105; double/twin £105–£130.

For hotel location, see maps on pages 490-496

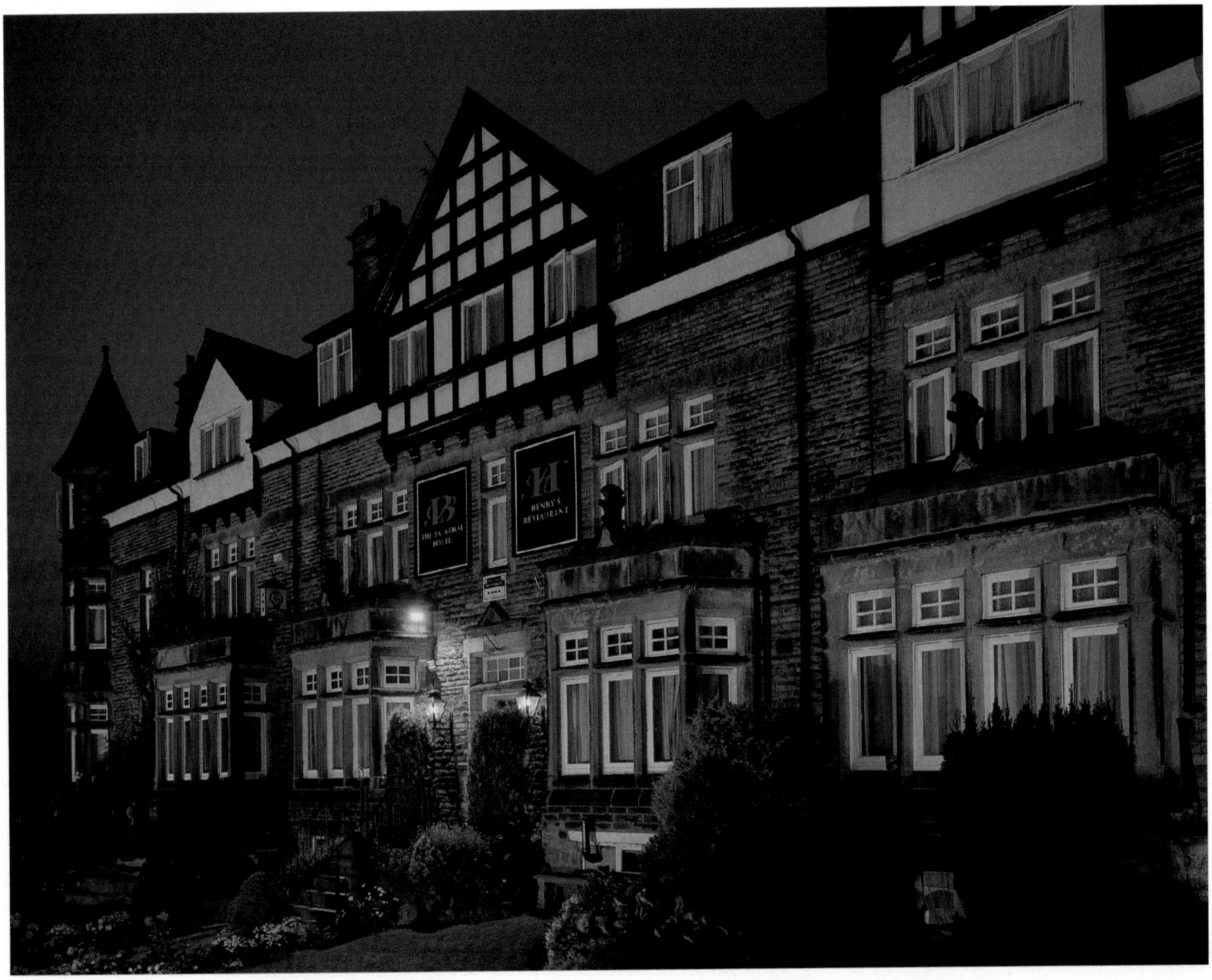

# THE BALMORAL HOTEL

**FRANKLIN MOUNT, HARROGATE, NORTH YORKSHIRE HG1 5EJ**
**TEL: 01423 508208 FAX: 01423 530652**

The Balmoral is a delightful privately owned individual hotel with an award winning garden, near the heart of the elegant spa town of Harrogate. All bedrooms are luxurious with individual decoration and furnishings offering the highest standards of comfort. Nine rooms have beautiful four-posters – each in a different style. For ultimate luxury, The Windsor Suite even boasts its own whirlpool bath. Guests enjoy the fascinating memorabilia on various themes throuhout the Hotel and they can relax in the exquisite Henry's Bar or enjoy a quiet drink in the cosy Snug before taking dinner in Henry's Restaurant. Henry's has a magical theme based on Houdini and enjoys a great reputation for conjuring up the finest modern English cuisine, complemented by an extensive list of predominantly New World wines. Guests can enjoy the use of the Academy – one of the finest Leisure, Health & Fitness Centres in the North, ten minutes from the Hotel. Special Spa Breaks throughout the year. Harrogate is famed for its antique and fashion shops, art galleries and Herriot country, and the many historic homes and castles in the area. **Directions:** From Harrogate Conference Centre, follow the Kings Road up, and the hotel is 1/2 mile on the right. Price guide: Single £80–£95; double/twin £95–£115; suites £115–£170. Special Breaks available.

For hotel location, see maps on pages 490-496

# THE BOAR'S HEAD HOTEL

**THE RIPLEY CASTLE ESTATE, HARROGATE, NORTH YORKSHIRE HG3 3AY**
**TEL: 01423 771888 FAX: 01423 771509**

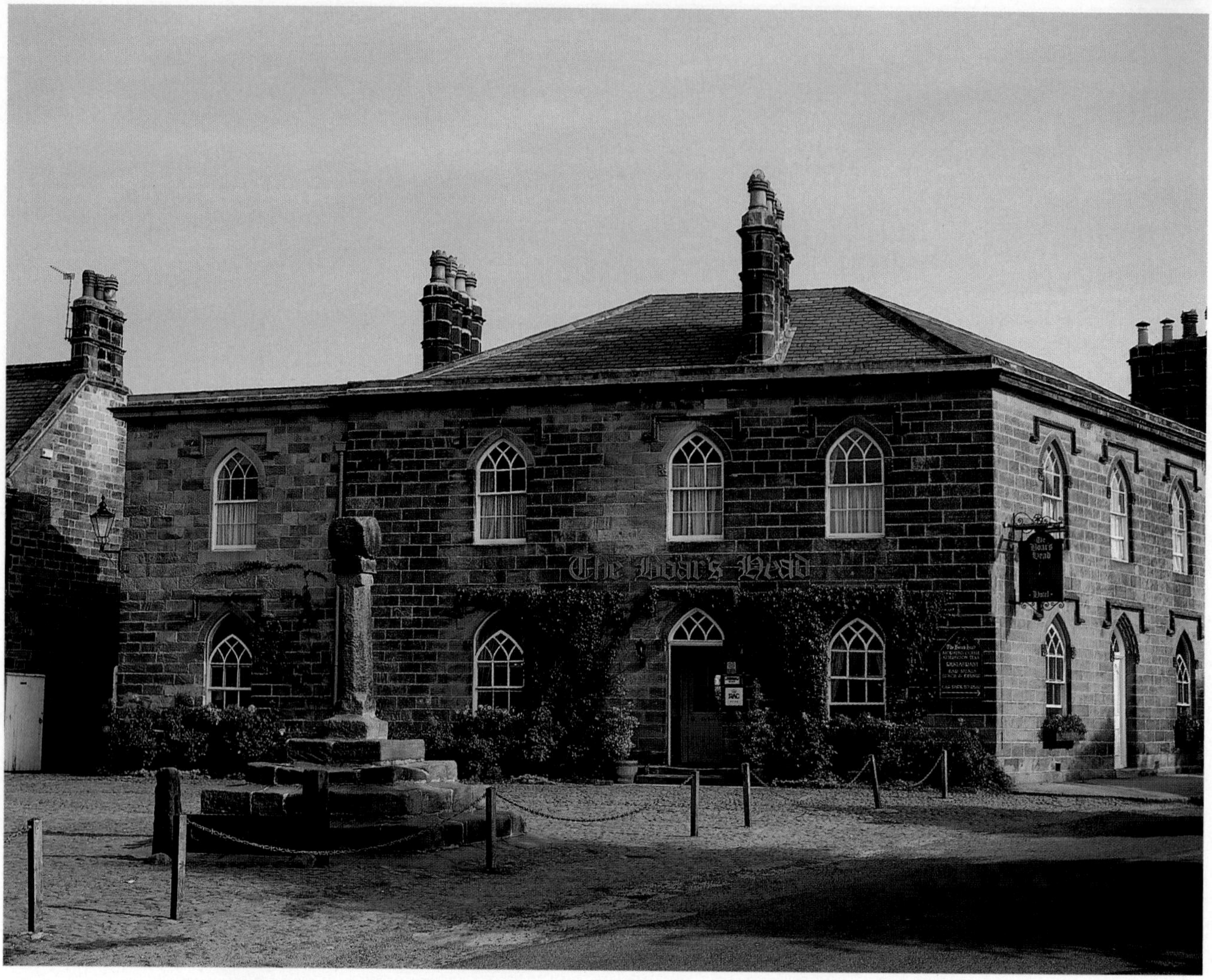

Imagine relaxing in a four star hotel at the centre of a historic 1700 acre private country estate in England's incredibly beautiful North Country. The Ingilby family who have lived in Ripley Castle for 28 generations invite you to enjoy their hospitality at The Boar's Head Hotel. There are 25 luxury bedrooms, individually decorated and furnished, most with king-size beds. The restaurant menu is outstanding, presented by a creative and imaginative kitchen brigade, and complemented by a wide selection of reasonably priced, good quality wines. There is a welcoming bar serving traditional ales straight from the wood, and popular bar meal selections. When staying at The Boar's Head, guests can enjoy complimentary access to the delightful walled gardens and grounds of Ripley Castle, which include the lakes and a deer park. A conference at Ripley is a different experience – using the idyllic meeting facilities available in the castle, organisers and delegates alike will appreciate the peace and tranquility of the location which offers opportunities for all forms of leisure activity outside meeting hours. **Directions:** Ripley is very accessible, just 10 minutes from the conference town of Harrogate, 20 minutes from the motorway network, and Leeds/Bradford Airport, and 40 minutes from the City of York. Price guide: Single £85–£105; double/twin £98–£120.

For hotel location, see maps on pages 490-496

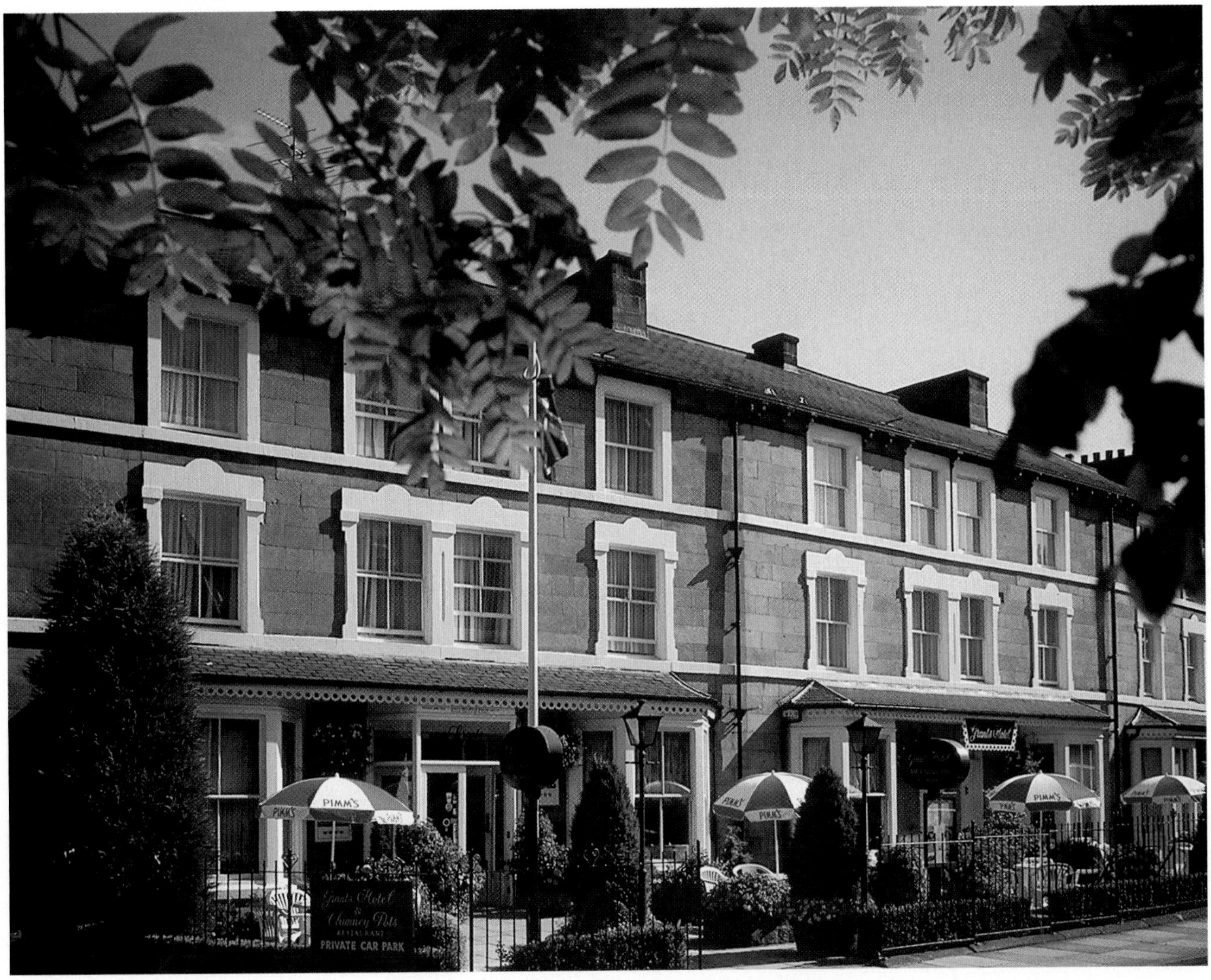

# GRANTS HOTEL

**SWAN ROAD, HARROGATE, NORTH YORKSHIRE HG1 2SS**
**TEL: 01423 560666 FAX: 01423 502550**

Towards the end of the last century, Harrogate became fashionable among the gentry, who came to 'take the waters' of the famous spa. Today's visitors have one advantage over their Victorian counterparts – they can enjoy the hospitality of Grants Hotel, the creation of Pam and Peter Grant. Their friendly welcome, coupled with high standards of service, ensures a pleasurable stay. All the bedrooms are attractively decorated and have en suite bathrooms. Downstairs, guests can relax in the comfortable lounge or take refreshments out to the terrace gardens. Drinks and light meals are available at all times from the cocktail bar, whereas dinner is a more formal occasion in the air-conditioned Chimney Pots restaurant. Cuisine is basically traditional rustic with a smattering of Oriental influence deliciously complemented by the homemade puddings – a blend which meets with the approval of local gourmets. Less than five minutes' walk from Harrogate's Conference and Exhibition Centre, Grants offers its own luxury meeting and syndicate rooms, the Herriot Suite. The Royal Pump Room Museum and the Royal Baths Assembly Rooms are nearby. Guests have free use of "The Academy Health and Leisure Club". **Directions:** Swan Road is in the centre of Harrogate, off the A61 to Ripon. Price guide: Single £96.50–£104; double/twin £104–£147; suites £157. Super value breaks available

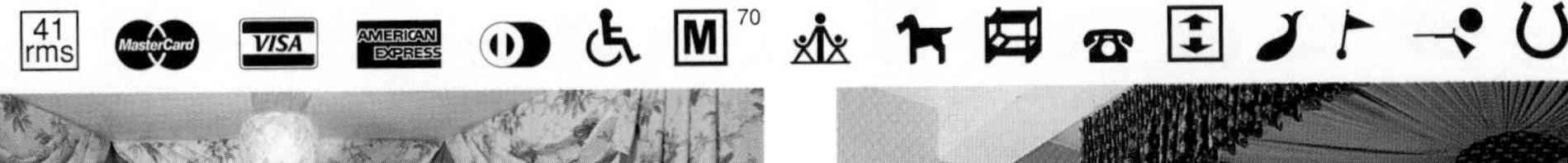

For hotel location, see maps on pages 490-496

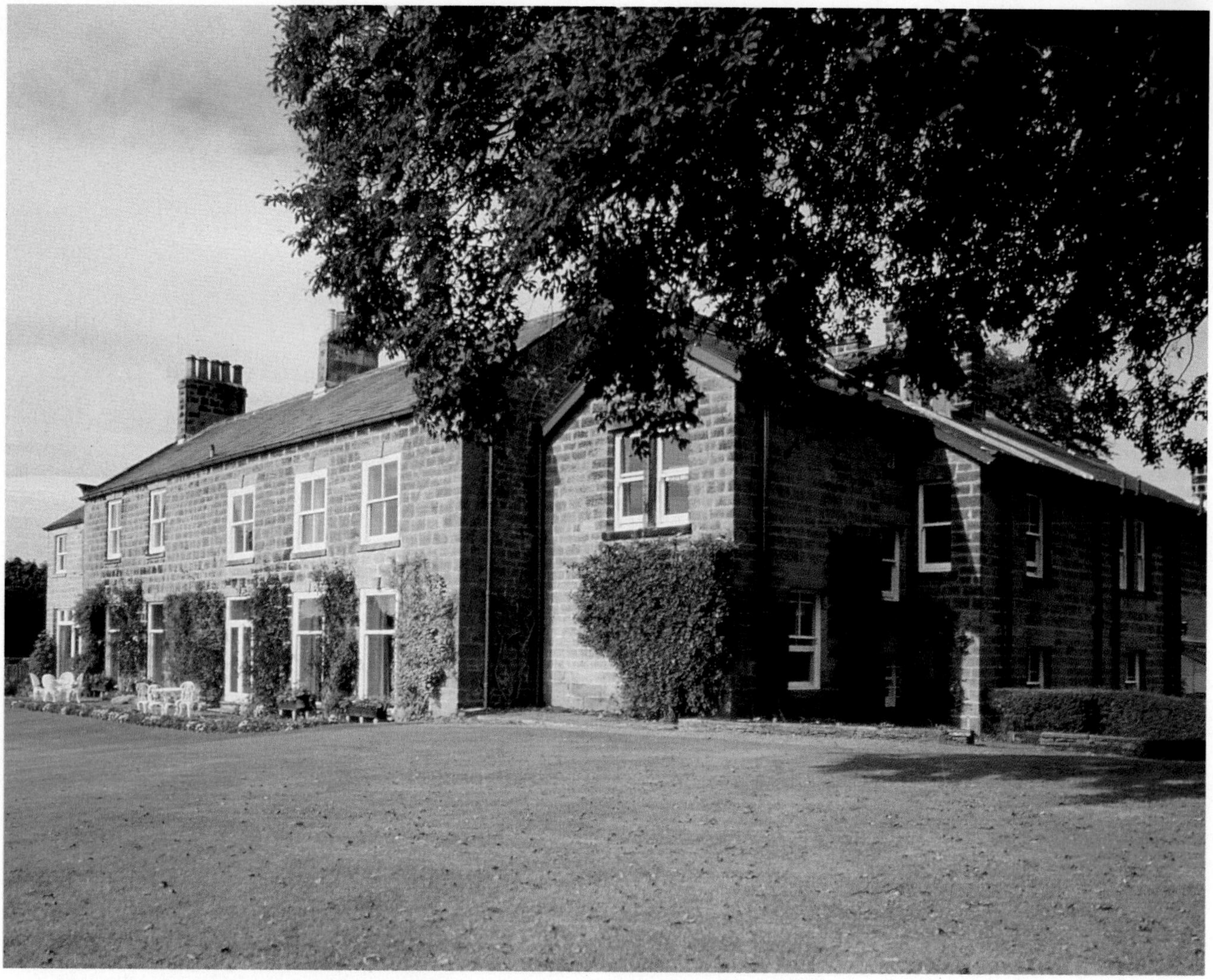

# Hob Green Hotel And Restaurant


**MARKINGTON, HARROGATE, NORTH YORKSHIRE HG3 3PJ**

**TEL: 01423 770031 FAX: 01423 771589**


Set in 870 acres of farm and woodland this charming 'country house' hotel is only a short drive from the spa town Harrogate and the ancient city of Ripon. The restaurant has an excellent reputation locally with only the finest fresh local produce being used, much of which is grown in the hotel's own garden. The interesting menus are complemented by an excellent choice of sensibly priced wines. All twelve bedrooms have been individually furnished and tastefully equipped to suit the most discerning guest. The drawing room and hall, warmed with log fires in cool weather, are comfortably furnished with the added attraction of fine antique furniture, porcelain and pictures. Situated in the heart of some of Yorkshire's most dramatic scenery guests can enjoy magnificent views of the valley beyond from all the main rooms. York is only 23 miles away. There is a wealth of cultural and historical interest nearby with Fountains Abbey and Studley Royal water garden and deer park a few minutes' drive. The Yorkshire Riding Centre is in Markington Village. Above all, Hob Green provides a tranquil and relaxing place to stay where your every comfort is catered for. **Directions:** Turn left signposted Markington off the A61 Harrogate to Ripon road, the hotel is one mile after the village on the left. Price guide: Single £80; double/twin £90–£99; suite £120.

For hotel location, see maps on pages 490-496

# RUDDING PARK HOUSE & HOTEL

**RUDDING PARK, FOLLIFOOT, HARROGATE, NORTH YORKSHIRE HG3 1JH**
**TEL: 01423 871350 FAX: 01423 872286**

Visitors to Harrogate will be delighted to find this splendid new hotel just 2 miles from the town centre. Rudding Park House, built in the early 19th century, is a fine conference and banqueting centre, and the new hotel has been brilliantly designed and built to harmonise with the original mansion. Its setting is superb, surrounded by 230 acres of parkland. The hotel has an elegant facade and entrance, approached by a sweeping driveway. A warm welcome awaits guests in the pleasant foyer, with its big fire place and easy chairs. The bedrooms are spacious, with contemporary cherry wood furniture, relaxing colour schemes, many modern accessories and lovely views over the estate. The needs of disabled guests have also been remembered. The Clocktower Bar & Brasserie, in the old Coaching Yard, are stylish, inviting and on sunny days they extend onto the terrace. The food is delicious and the wine list extensive. Leisure facilities are excellent – there is a private 18-hole golf course and golf academy on the estate, which has won accolades for its environmental sensitivity. 9000 new trees, lakes, roaming deer and bird watching hideaways have increased the estate's beauty. Croquet, fishing and riding are available close by. Directions: Rudding Park is accessible from the A1 north or south, via A661, being just off A658. Price guide: Single £99–£105; double/twin £129–£135; suite £195

50 rms 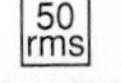      350      

For hotel location, see maps on pages 490-496

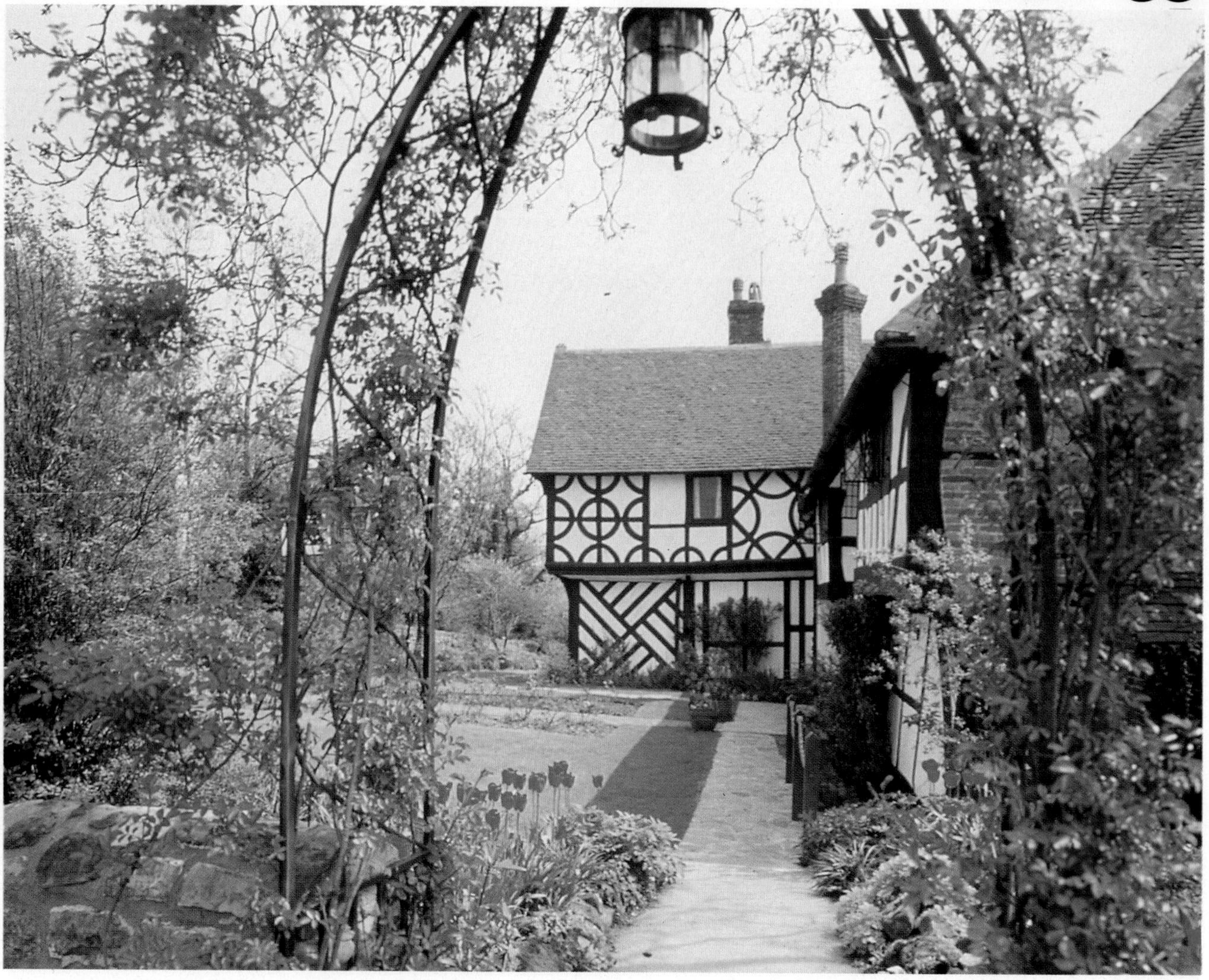

# LYTHE HILL HOTEL

**PETWORTH ROAD, HASLEMERE, SURREY GU27 3BQ**

**TEL: 01428 651251 FAX: 01428 644131 E-MAIL: lythehill@grayswood.co.uk**

Cradled by the Surrey foothills in a tranquil setting is the enchanting Lythe Hill Hotel. It is an unusual cluster of ancient buildings – parts of which date from the 14th century. While most of the beautifully appointed accommodation is in the more recently converted part of the hotel, there are five charming bedrooms in the Tudor House, including the Henry VIII room with a four-poster bed dated 1614! There are two delightful restaurants, the Auberge de France offers classic French cuisine in the oak-panelled room which overlooks the lake and parklands, and the 'Dining Room' has the choice of imaginative English fayre. An exceptional wine list offers over 200 wines from more than a dozen countries. Its situation, easily accessible from London, Gatwick and Heathrow. An excellent train service at Haslemere makes both central London and Portsmouth less than one hour away. National Trust hillside adjoining the hotel grounds provides interesting walking and views over the surrounding countryside. The area is steeped in history, with the country houses of Petworth, Clandon and Uppark to visit as well as racing at Goodwood and polo at Cowdray Park. Brighton and the south coast are only a few miles away. **Directions:** Lythe Hill lies about 1½ miles from the centre of Haslemere, east on the B2131. Price guide: Single from £99; double/twin from £115; suite from £138.

For hotel location, see maps on pages 490-496

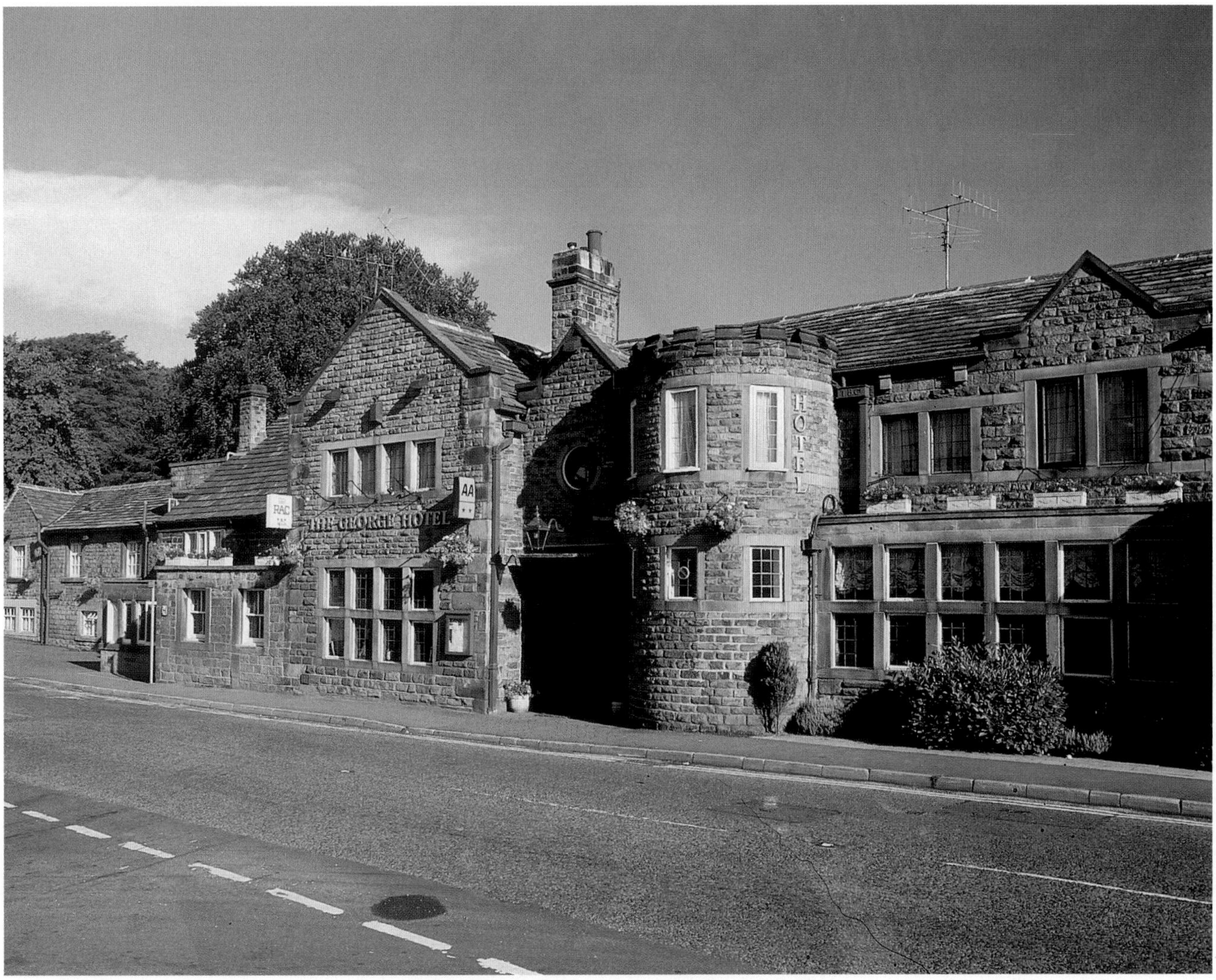

# GEORGE HOTEL

**MAIN ROAD, HATHERSAGE, DERBYSHIRE S32 1BB**
**TEL: 01433 650436 FAX: 01433 650099**

The George dates back to the end of the middle ages when it would have been an alehouse serving the packhorse road. Later it was well-known to Charlotte Brontë and it features anonymously in *Jane Eyre*. The present owner, an experienced hotelier, is ably backed by a team of professional senior personnel who guarantee guests a warm welcome and excellent personal service. In its latest hands the building has undergone extensive renovation. However, great care has been taken to preserve the character of the old inn and the stone walls, oak beams, open fires and antique furniture all remain as reminders of a distant age. The simple and pleasant bedrooms offer every modern amenity, including power showers and luxuriosuly enveloping bathsheets. There is well-equipped bar in which to relax and enjoy a drink before moving on to the brasserie-style restaurant with its regularly changed menu. Places of interest nearby include Chatsworth and Haddon Halls, Buxton and Bakewell. The area provides a host of recreational activities for the energetic and adventurous alike. There are opportunities for walking, potholing, hang-gliding, paragliding, cycling and golf. **Directions:** From the M1 Junction 29 take the A617 to Baslow, then the A623 and B6001 to Hathersage. The George is in the main street of the village. Price guide: Single £59.50–£69.50; double/twin £79.50–£99.50.

For hotel location, see maps on pages 490-496

# BEL ALP HOUSE

HAYTOR, NR BOVEY TRACEY, SOUTH DEVON TQ13 9XX
TEL: 01364 661217 FAX: 01364 661292

Peace and seclusion are guaranteed at the Bel Alp House with its spectacular outlook from the edge of Dartmoor across a rolling patchwork of fields and woodland to the sea, 20 miles away. Built as an Edwardian country mansion and owned in the 1920s by millionairess Dame Violet Wills, Bel Alp has been lovingly restored and the new owners Jack, Mary and Rachael Twist personal attention ensures their guests' enjoyment and comfort in the atmosphere of a private home. The set dinner is changed nightly, using only the best local produce, and the meals are accompanied by a well-chosen and comprehensive wine list. Of the eight en suite bedrooms, two still have their original Edwardian basins and baths mounted on marble plinths, and all bedrooms have views over the gardens. An abundance of house plants, open log fires and restful colours complements the family antiques and pictures to create the perfect environment in which to relax. Awarded an AA Rosette. Bel Alp is ideally situated for exploring Devon and parts of Cornwall: Plymouth, famed for Drake and the Pilgrim Fathers, Exeter with its Norman cathedral, and National Trust properties Castle Drogo and Cotehele Manor House are all within an hour's drive. **Directions:** Bel Alp is off the B3387 Haytor road, 2½ miles from Bovey Tracey. Price guide: Single £60; double/twin £120–£130.

8 rms

For hotel location, see maps on pages 490-496

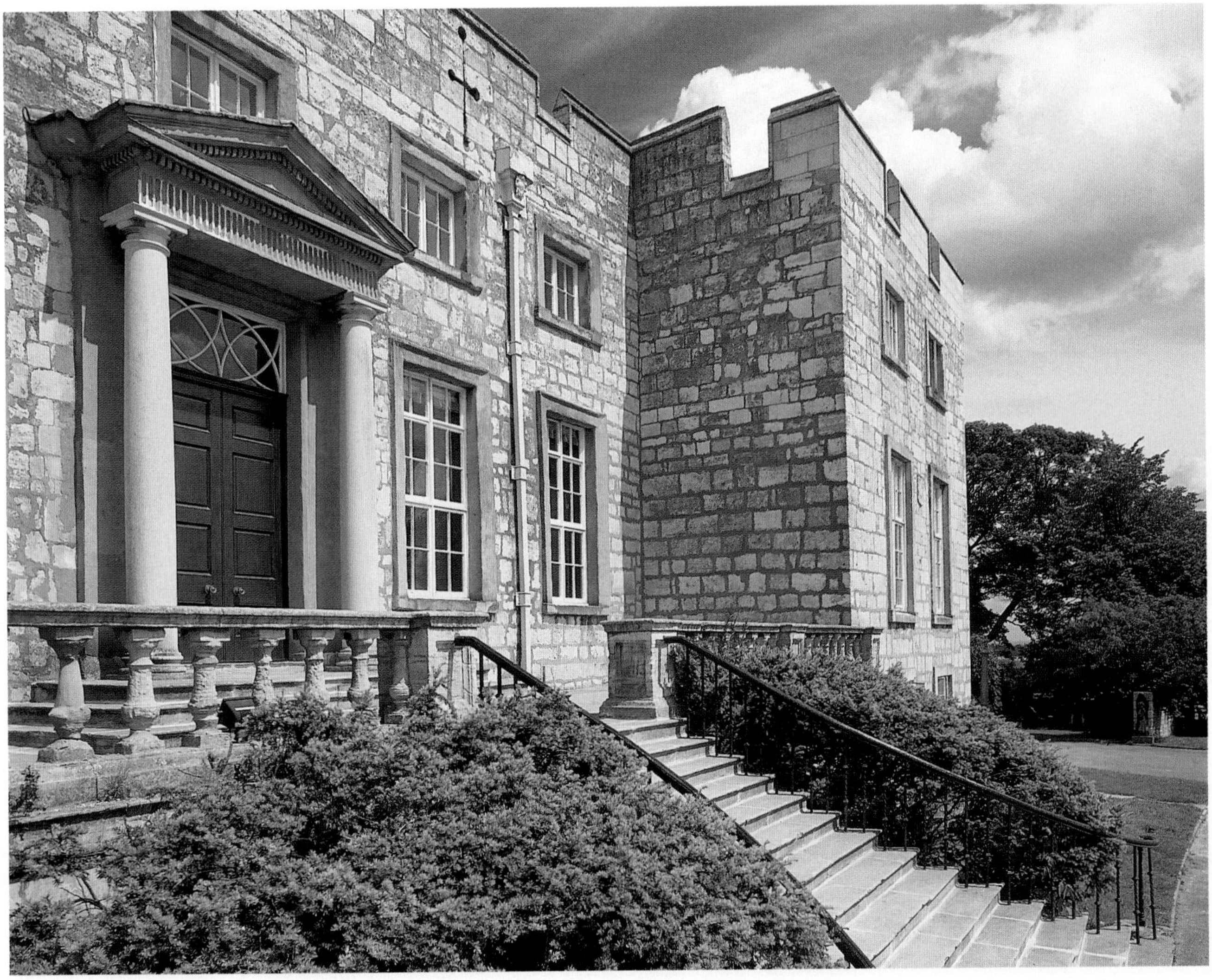

# HAZLEWOOD CASTLE

**PARADISE LANE, HAZLEWOOD, NEAR TADCASTER, NORTH YORKSHIRE LS24 9NJ**
**TEL: 01937 530530 FAX: 01937 530630**

Hazlewood Castle dates back to the late 13th century and was once a Knight's fortified residence. Standing on a limestone ridge in 77 acres of its own parkland, it is built of white limestone from the famous Thevesdale Quarry and enjoys an idyllic pastoral location. Extensive restoration work, along with some notable additions, has been carried out over the centuries and the castle has its own 13th century chapel. In September last year the castle opened as a luxurious country house hotel. Guests arrive in the courtyard and are greeted at the steps before being shown into the impressive Flemish Hall. There are nine beautifully furnished bedrooms in the main house and 12 similarly luxurious across the courtyard. The restaurant, set in the old dining room, offers an excellent menu. The cuisine is prepared by award-winning Chef Director John Benson-Smith, who also supervises the Hazlewood Cookery School, which is based at the castle. Yorkshire, with its rural villages, splendid beaches and magnificent countryside, offers a host of entertainment and leisure opportunities. Guests of Hazlewood Castle can take advantage of the its close proximity to York with its excellent shops and beautiful Minster, Leeds and Harrogate. **Directions:** Hazlewood Castle is just off the A64 east of A1 Leeds/York intersection. Price guide: Single £105; double/twin £145–£185; suites £185–£250.

21 rms MasterCard VISA AMERICAN EXPRESS M 120

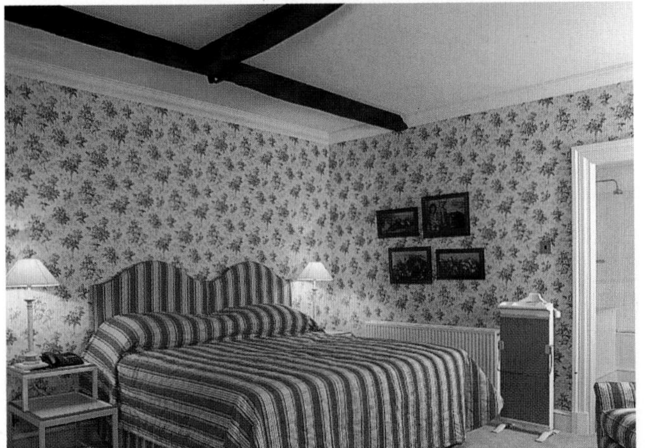

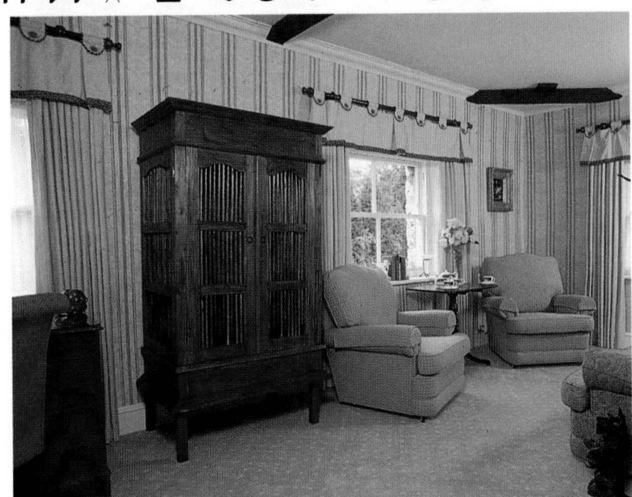

For hotel location, see maps on pages 490-496

# The Carlton Hotel

ALBERT STREET, HEBDEN BRIDGE, WEST YORKSHIRE HX7 8ES
TEL: 01422 844400 FAX: 01422 843117

The Carlton is an unusual town house hotel, centrally situated on the first and second floors of the old Co-operative Society building, dating from 1867. Following a full refurbishment of this Victorian emporium, The Carlton Hotel was able to continue serving the local community, while also attracting a much wider, international clientèle. A lift takes visitors from the entrance hall up to the elegant reception area where a friendly welcome waits. The 16 en suite bedrooms are individually appointed with attractive furnishings, satellite T.V. and hospitality bars. In the Hawkstones Restaurant imaginative menus combining European and traditionally English food are prepared daily by the kitchen team under the direction of head chef Earl McIniess. As an alternative to the restaurant a fine selection of hearty bar snacks are available daily in the Wragley Bar. Conference parties and banquets can be accommodated in the Hardcastle Suite. Situated at the head of the Calder Valley, Hebden Bridge is a thriving mill town, with many quaint antique and craft shops. The hotel is well placed for walkers to explore the Yorkshire Dales and nearby Howarth. Special weekend breaks available. **Directions:** Entering Hebden Bridge on the A646, turn down Hope Street, which runs into Albert Street. The hotel is on the left. Price guide: Single £49–£60; double/twin £65–£79.

For hotel location, see maps on pages 490-496

# THE PHEASANT

HAROME, HELMSLEY, NORTH YORKSHIRE YO6 5JG
TEL: 01439 771241/770416 FAX:01439 771744

The Pheasant, rich in oak beams and open log fires, offers two types of accommodation, some in the hotel and some in a charming, 16th century thatched cottage. The Binks family, who built the hotel and now own and manage it, have created a friendly atmosphere which is part of the warm Yorkshire welcome all guests receive. The bedrooms and suites are brightly decorated in an attractive, cottage style and all are complete with en suite facilities. Traditional English cooking is the speciality of the restaurant, many of the dishes prepared using fresh fruit and vegetables grown in the hotel gardens. During the summer, guests may chat or relax on the terrace overlooking the pond. The opening of a new indoor heated swimming pool is an added attraction. Other sporting activities available locally include swimming, riding, golf and fishing. York is a short drive away, as are a host of historic landmarks including Byland and Rievaulx Abbeys and Castle Howard of *Brideshead Revisited* fame. Also nearby is the magnificent North York Moors National Park. Dogs by arrangement. Closed Christmas, January and February. **Directions:** From Helmsley, take the A170 towards Scarborough; after 1/4 mile turn right for Harome. Hotel is near the church in the village. Price guide: Single £55–£65; double/twin £110–£130. (Including five-course dinner).

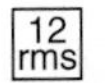

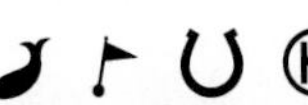

For hotel location, see maps on pages 490-496

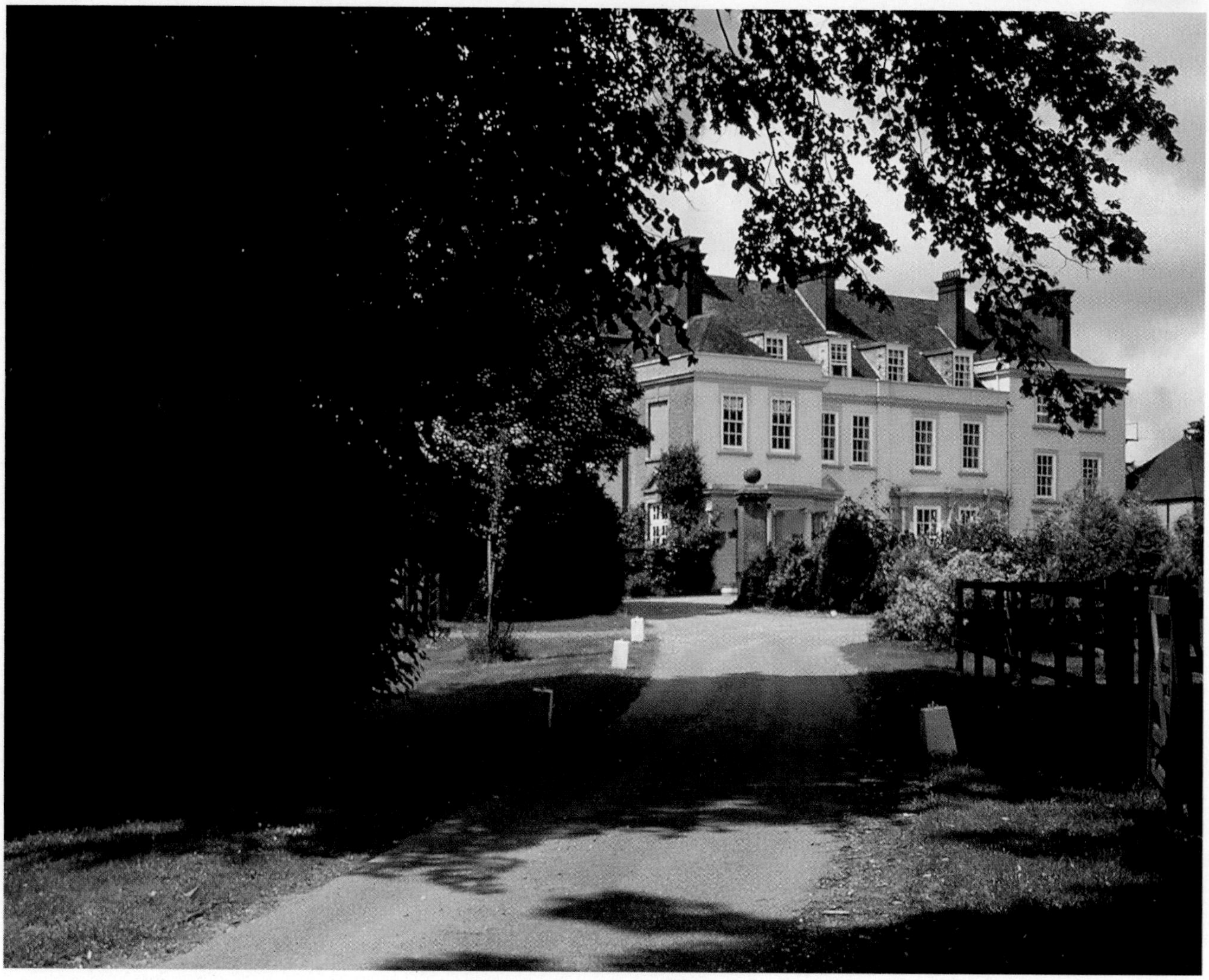

# Stocks

## STOCKS ROAD, ALDBURY, NR TRING, HERTFORDSHIRE HP23 5RX

## TEL: 01442 851 341 FAX: 01442 851 253

Set amidst 10,000 acres of National Trust property Stocks stands in 182 acres of beautiful parkland on the edge of the Chiltern Hills. This Georgian Mansion, built in 1773, boasts 18 individually furnished bedrooms most of which offer excellent views. The Tapestry Restaurant, with its intricate plasterwork and tapestries, offers fine dining from the à la carte & table d'hôte menus, whilst the Orangery Restaurant provides a more informal dining atmosphere. Guests have access to an excellent combination of leisure activities, comprising an outdoor heated swimming pool (May to September), reputedly the largest Jacuzzi in England, gymnasium, four all weather tennis courts, sauna, steam room, solarium and full size snooker table. On-site Riding and Livery Stables offer equine pursuits from show jumping lessons to hacking in Ashbridge Forest. Stocks Golf Club features a challenging parkland course (SSS 74) 7016 yards and a fully equipped pro-shop. A team of qualified PGA professionals will improve skill and add to pleasure. Local attractions include Woburn Safari Park, Whipsnade Zoo, Grand Union Canal and the Ridgeway Path. **Directions:** Leave M1 at J8 or M25 at J20 and head for Hemel Hempstead and Tring on A41. In Tring turn right towards Tring station. Aldbury is one mile past the station. Price guide: Single £60; double/twin £80–£100; suite £110

For hotel location, see maps on pages 490-496

# PHYLLIS COURT CLUB

MARLOW ROAD, HENLEY-ON-THAMES, OXFORDSHIRE RG9 2HT
TEL: 01491 574366 / 570528 FAX: 01491 410725

Founded in 1906 by the owner of the house and a group of friends and London businessmen, the Club has an intriguing history spanning six centuries and involving royal patronage. Phyllis Court occupies an unrivalled position on the banks of the Thames, and overlooking the Henley Royal Regatta course. Phyllis Court prides itself on retaining the traditions of its illustrious past while guests today who now stay in this fine historic residence can in modern times enjoy the highest standards of up to date hospitality. Oliver Cromwell slept here and he built the embankment wall; and it was here that William II held his first Royal Court. Years later, when the name Henley became synonymous with rowing, there came as patrons of the Royal Regatta Prince Albert, King George V and Edward, Prince of Wales. The character of the place remains unaltered in its hallowed setting, but the comfortable bedrooms, the restaurant, the "cellar" and the entire complement of amenities are of the latest high quality. What is more, they are available for all. Likely to be fully booked far ahead during the season. Ideal for meetings, functions and wedding parties. **Directions:** M40 junction 4 to Marlow or M4 junction 8/9 then follow signposts to Henley-on-Thames. Price guide: Single £77; twin/double £90.

For hotel location, see maps on pages 490-496

# NUTHURST GRANGE

## HOCKLEY HEATH, WARWICKSHIRE B94 5NL

**TEL: 01564 783972 FAX: 01564 783919 E-MAIL: 106220.1743@compuserve.com**

The most memorable feature of this friendly country house hotel is its outstanding restaurant. Chef-patron David Randolph and his team have won many accolades for their imaginative menus, described as 'English, cooked in the light French style'. Diners can enjoy their superb cuisine in one of the three adjoining rooms which comprise the restaurant and form the heart of Nuthurst Grange. The rest of the house is no less charming – the spacious bedrooms have a country house atmosphere and are appointed with extra luxuries such as an exhilarating air-spa bath, a trouser press, hairdryer and a safe for valuables. For special occasions there is a room furnished with a four-poster bed and a marble bathroom. There are fine views across the 7½ acres of landscaped gardens. Executive meetings can be accommodated at Nuthurst Grange – within a 12-mile radius of the hotel lie Central Birmingham, the NEC, Stratford-upon-Avon, Coventry and Birmingham International Airport. Sporting activities available nearby include golf, canal boating and tennis. **Directions:** From M42 exit 4 take A3400 signposted Hockley Heath (2 miles, south). Entrance to Nuthurst Grange Lane is ¼ mile south of village. Also, M40 (exit 16 – southbound only), take first left, entrance 300 yards. Price guide: Single £120; double/twin £140–£155; suite £165.

For hotel location, see maps on pages 490-496

Exclusive ·Hotels· U.K.

# South Lodge Hotel

**LOWER BEEDING, NR HORSHAM, WEST SUSSEX RH13 6PS**

**TEL: 01403 891711 FAX: 01403 891766 E-MAIL: inquiries@southlodgehotel.dial.iql.co.uk**

South Lodge is a magnificent country house hotel, which has successfully captured the essence of Victorian elegance. With one of the most beautiful settings in rural Sussex, unrivalled views may be enjoyed over the South Downs from the hotel's elevated position. The mansion was originally built by Frederick Ducane Godman, a 19th century botanist and explorer, and the hotel's wonderful 90 acre grounds are evidence of his dedication. Many original features have been preserved, wood panelling throughout the hotel and open fires in the reception rooms. The 39 individually designed bedrooms are luxuriously equipped with every modern day requirement. The Camillia Restaurant has menus which change with the seasons and are complemented by a wine list from many countries. The private rooms are perfect for both social and business functions. A variety of leisure facilities, including croquet, tennis and clay pigeon shooting, are available on site (shooting and archery by prior arrangement), also golf at South Lodge's two spectacular 18 hole championship courses just minutes from the hotel. Nearby attractions include Glyndebourne, Chartwell and the Royal Pavilion in Brighton. **Directions:** On A281 at Lower Beeding, south of Horsham. Gatwick airport 12 miles. Nearest motorway M23 junction 11. Price guide: Single from £120; double/twin from £145; suite from £265.

For hotel location, see maps on pages 490-496

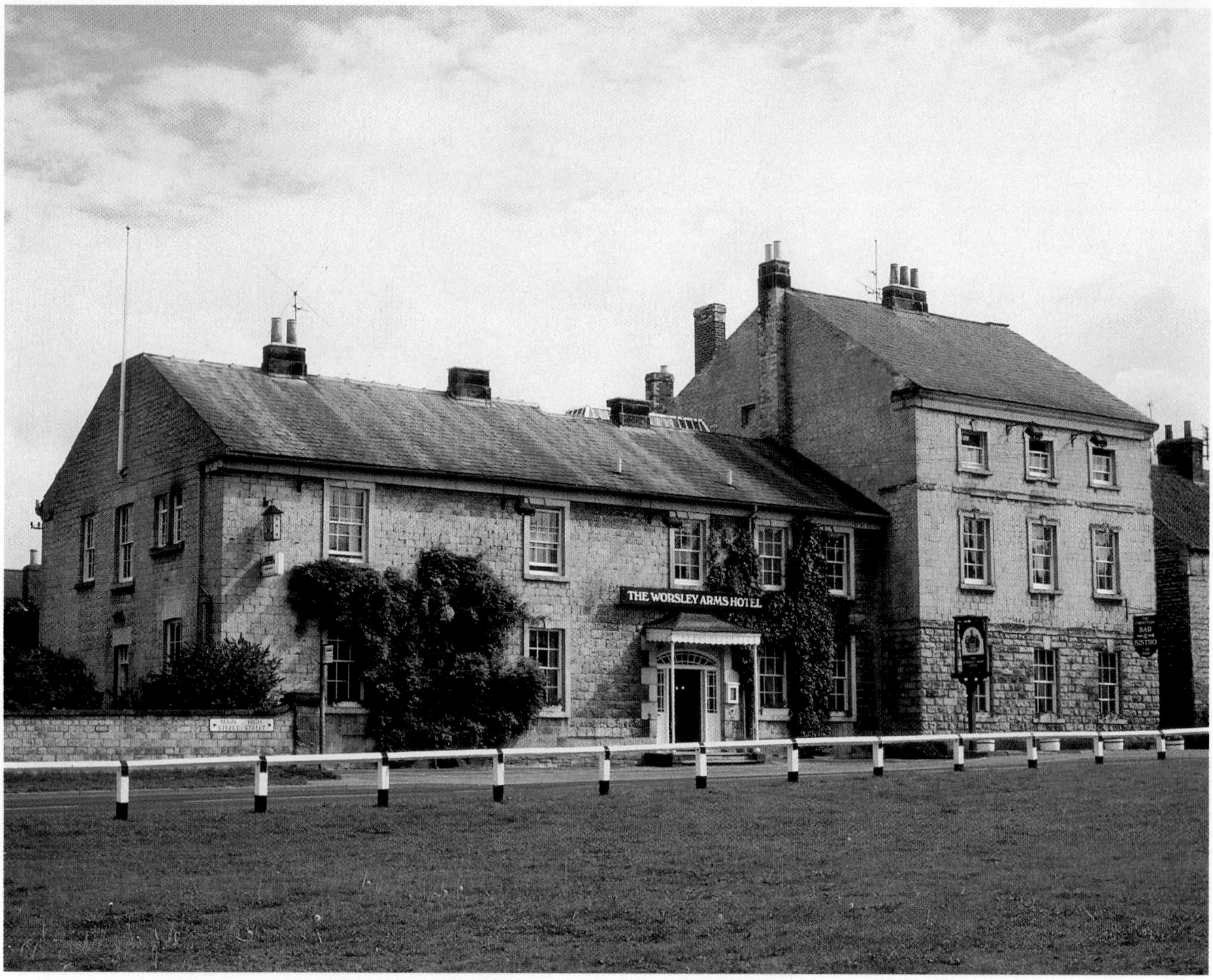

# THE WORSLEY ARMS HOTEL

**HOVINGHAM, YORK, NORTH YORKSHIRE YO6 4LA**
**TEL: 01653 628234 FAX: 01653 628130**

The Worsley Arms is an attractive stone-built Victorian coaching inn in the heart of Hovingham, a pleasant and unspoiled Yorkshire village with a history stretching back to Roman times. The hotel, which overlooks the village green and is set amid delightful gardens, was built in 1841 by the baronet Sir William Worsley and is now owned and personally run by Euan and Debbi Rodger. Hovingham Hall, the Worsley family and childhood home of the Duchess of Kent, is nearby. Elegant furnishings and open fires create a welcoming atmosphere. The spacious sitting rooms are an ideal place to relax over morning coffee or afternoon tea. The award-winning Restaurant (2 AA Rosettes) offers creatively prepared dishes, including game from the estate, cooked and presented with flair. The Cricketers Bistro (also 2 AA Rosettes) provides a more informal setting to enjoy modern cooking at its best. The en suite bedrooms range in size and are all prettily decorated with room service available. There is plenty to do nearby, including tennis, squash, jogging, golf and scenic walks along nature trails. Guests can explore the beauty of the Dales and the spectacular coastline or discover the historic abbeys, stately homes and castles nearby like Castle Howard just five miles away. **Directions:** Hovingham is on the B1257, eight miles from Malton and Helmsley. Price guide: Single £60–£80; double/twin £80–£90. Special breaks available.

For hotel location, see maps on pages 490-496

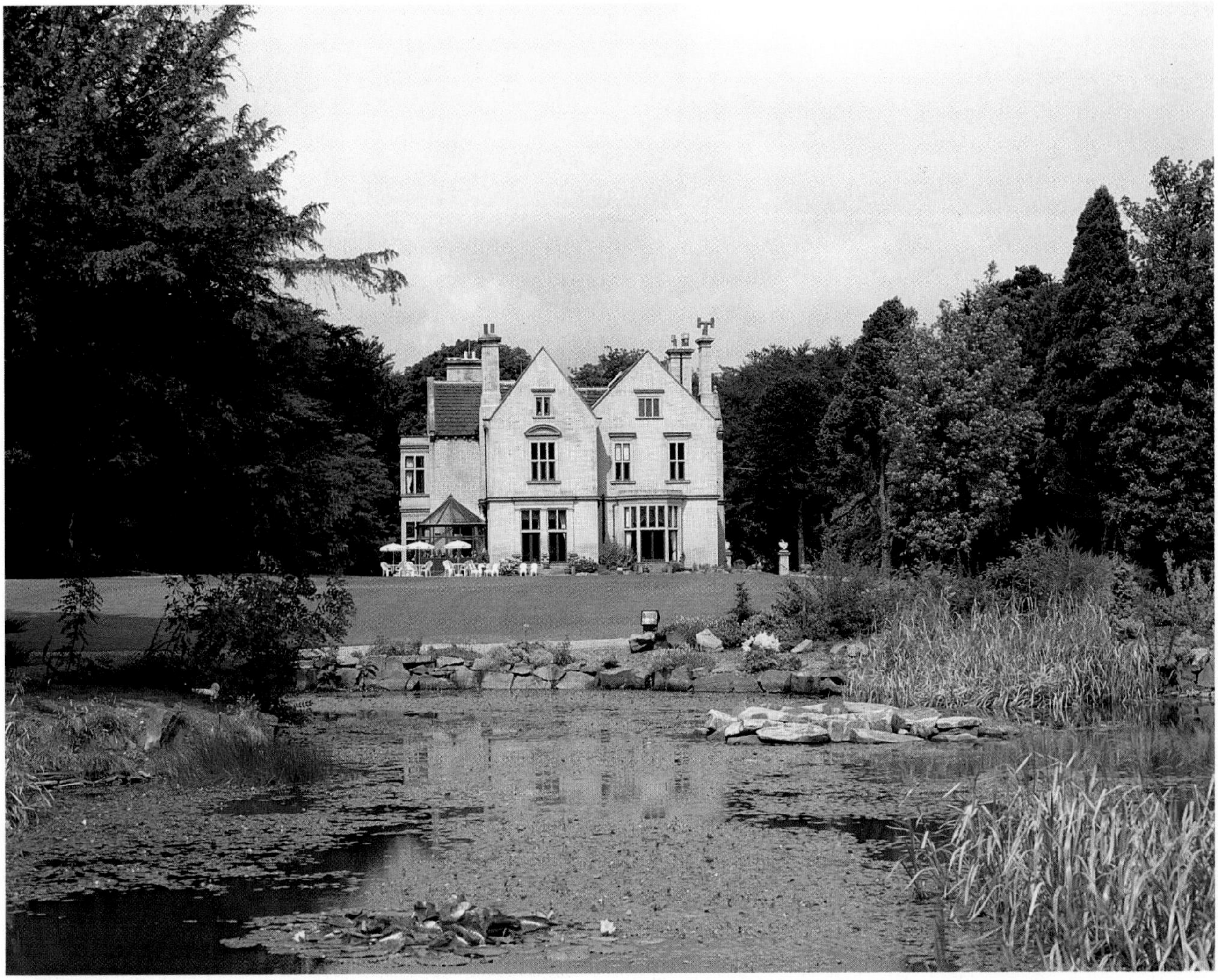

# BAGDEN HALL HOTEL & GOLF COURSE

**WAKEFIELD ROAD, SCISSETT, NR HUDDERSFIELD, WEST YORKSHIRE HD8 9LE**
**TEL: 01484 865330 FAX: 01484 861001**

Bagden Hall is set in 40 acres of parkland, yet less than 10 minutes from the M1. It was built in the mid-19th century by local mill owner George Norton as a home for his family, whose portraits still hang in the foyer. Lovingly restored by current owners the Braithwaite family, Bagden has been transformed into an elegant hotel. The grounds comprise magnificent lawns, superb landscaped gardens, a lake and an 18th century boathouse. Inside, the hotel has recently undergone a major programme of renovation and now has all the attributes one would expect of a modern hotel while retaining its original character. Each of the 17 bedrooms – one with four-poster – has en suite facilities. The oak-panelled lounge bar and conservatory have views over the lawns to the lake, an ideal setting for a drink before moving on to the Glendale Restaurant. Here traditional and modern English food with classical French influences is served amid tasteful surroundings. There is a fine wine list to complement the food. For golfers, there is a 9-hole par 3/4 golf course on site. Conference facilities are available. **Directions:** From south, leave M1 at junction 38, taking A637 towards Huddersfield. Take A636 to Denby Dale. From north, leave M1 at junction 39, taking A636 to Denby Dale. Hotel is 1/2 mile through Clayton West on left. Price guide: Single £65; double/twin £84–£110.

For hotel location, see maps on pages 490-496

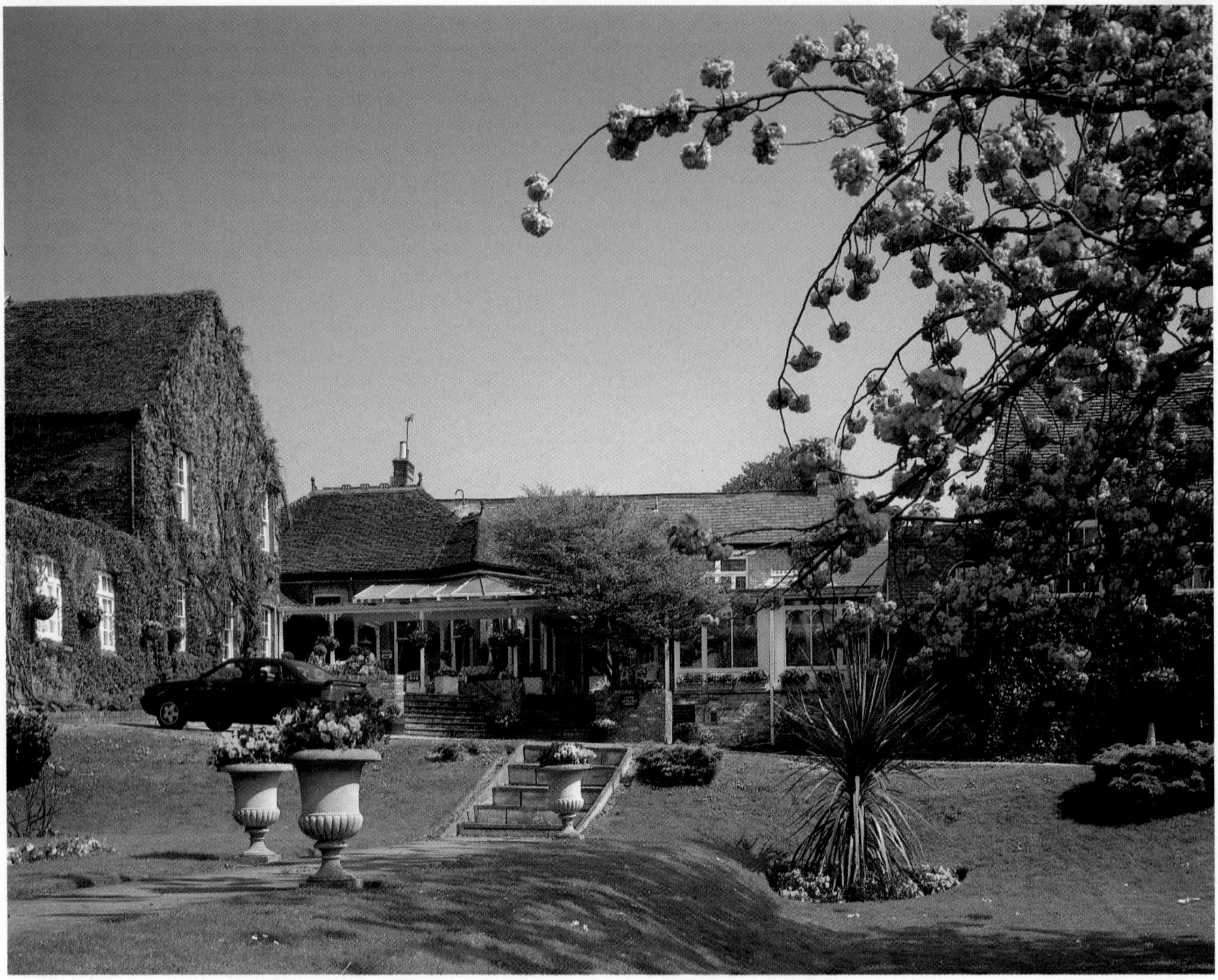

# The Old Bridge Hotel

1 HIGH STREET, HUNTINGDON, CAMBRIDGESHIRE PE18 6TQ
TEL: 01480 452681 FAX: 01480 411017

The Old Bridge Hotel is a handsome, 18th-century building standing on the banks of the River Ouse close to the centre of Huntingdon, a thriving market town and the birthplace of Oliver Cromwell, nowadays conveniently located on the egde of the motorway network. The hotel has been decorated in keeping with its original character. In the panelled dining room and main lounge, sumptuous fabrics, quality prints and beautiful furnishings impart a sense of elegance. Each of the 25 guest rooms is unique in its style and décor – all have been luxuriously appointed with every attention to detail, and with a full complement of facilities. The menu exemplifies modern British cooking at its best – dishes are interpreted with imagination and flair, and is balanced by an exceptional and award winning wine list. The same menu is also offered in the more informal setting of The Terrace which has a delightful series of murals painted by Julia Rushbury. Private parties or business lunches can be accommodated in the Cromwell Room and a fully integrated business centre is available for executive meetings. Guests can enjoy boating trips from the private jetty or visit nearby Cambridge, Ely and Newmarket. **Directions:** Situated off the A1 where it joins both the A1–M1 link and the M11/A14. The hotel is just off the inner ring road. Price guide: Single £79.50; double/twin £89.50–£139.50.

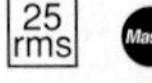

For hotel location, see maps on pages 490-496

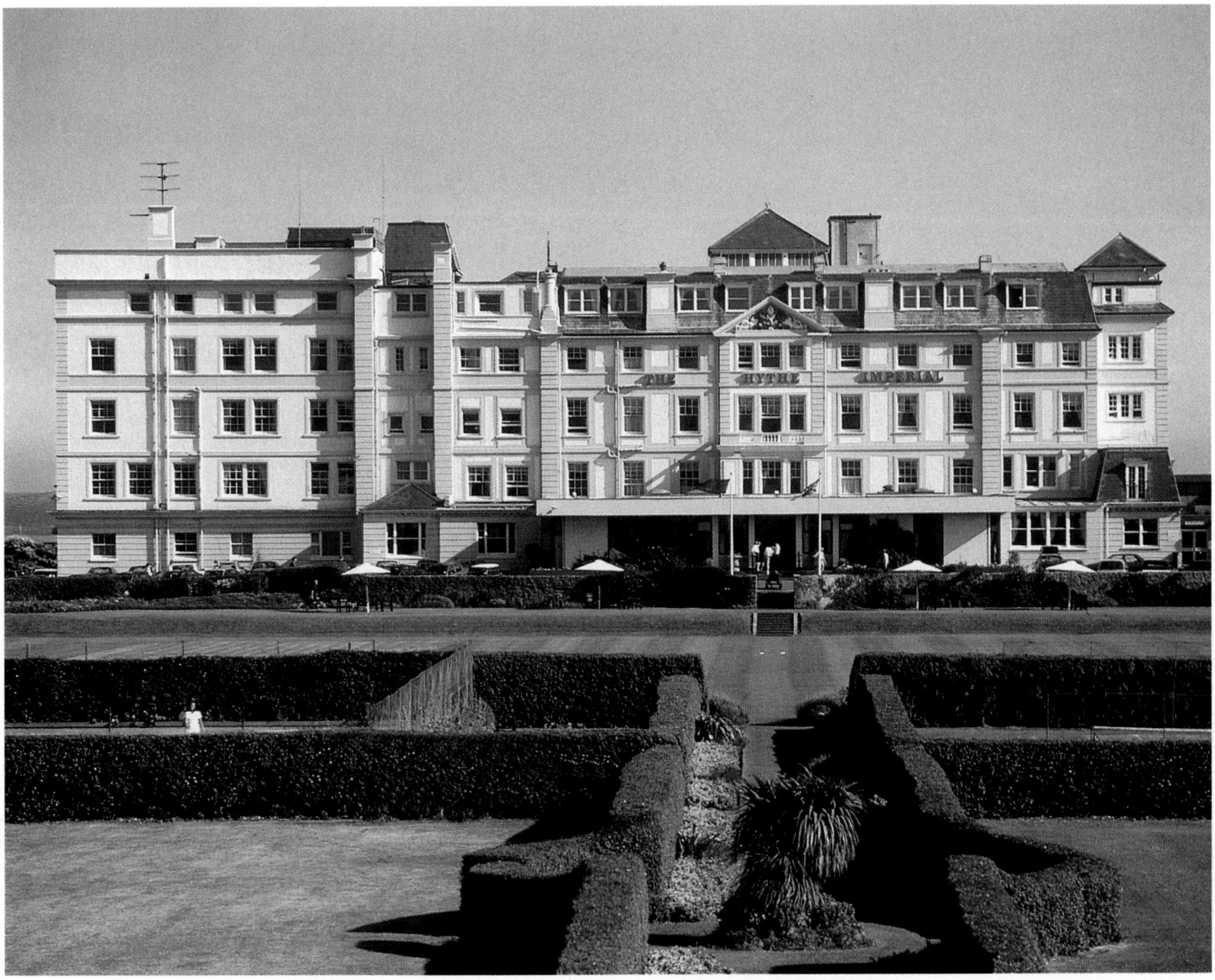

# THE HYTHE IMPERIAL

**PRINCE'S PARADE, HYTHE, KENT CT21 6AE**

**TEL: 01303 267441 FAX: 01303 264610**

The imposing Hythe Imperial stands majestically on the seafront of the historic Cinque Port of Hythe. Built in 1880, the hotel embodies the elegance of the Victorian age, combined with all the amenities expected by today's discerning visitor. All 100 en-suite bedrooms, suites and family rooms – some with four poster beds, half testers and Jacuzzis – enjoy wonderful views. The restaurant has an enviable reputation and has been awarded an AA Rosette for its cuisine. The hotel's 9-hole 18 tee links course, bounded by the Royal Military Canal, is a challenging test. There is also an extensive newly refurbished leisure centre with a heated pool, gymnasium, spa bath, steam and sauna rooms, squash, snooker tables and a bar and bistro. Outside are all-weather floodlit tennis courts, putting, croquet and bowls. Twelve fully equipped conference rooms and six syndicate rooms are available. Proximity to the Le Shuttle terminal and Channel ports makes the hotel an ideal base for visiting France as well as exploring the beautiful Kent countryside. Sailing and fishing locally and horseracing at Folkestone. Directions: From M20, exit at junction 11 onto A261 to Hythe. When in the town follow signs towards Folkestone and turn right into Twiss Road, opposite the Bell Inn, towards the seafront. Price guide: Single £98.50; double/twin £124–£144; Suite £164.

For hotel location, see maps on pages 490-496

# ROMBALDS HOTEL

**WEST VIEW, WELLS ROAD, ILKLEY, WEST YORKSHIRE LS29 9JG**
**TEL: 01943 603201 FAX: 01943 816586**

Ilkley Moor has been famous in song. Today the town is singing the praises of Rombalds Hotel, a lovely Georgian townhouse, on the edge the Moor and within walking distance of the town centre. Being slightly elevated, it has magnificent views over the countryside. The new owners, Colin and Jo Clarkson, are proud of its history, and the furnishings are appropriate to its 19th century architecture – an elegant facade with tall windows, and, inside, high ceilings, archways and fireplaces. The quiet and extremely comfortable bedrooms range from suites to the more compact with showers. The hotel is pristine throughout, following extensive redecoration. The lounge is a peaceful retreat, guests mingle in the bar while studying the extensive menu – an appetising buffet for those in a hurry or a superb à la carte selection to linger over. The diverse wine list includes some good half bottles. While business people may want to use the Rombalds' excellent conference and office facilities, others will enjoy Ilkley's intriguing Victorian shopping arcade or Harrogate's boutiques, visiting Fountains Abbey, Bolton Abbey, Castle Howard or Harewood House and exploring the Brontë and Herriot country. Sporting visitors are offered golf, tennis, fishing and riding. **Directions:** M1 Leeds exit, taking A65 to Ilkley. Leeds Airport 18 minutes. Price guide: Single £65–£85; double/twin £80–£105; Suites £95–£115.

For hotel location, see maps on pages 490-496

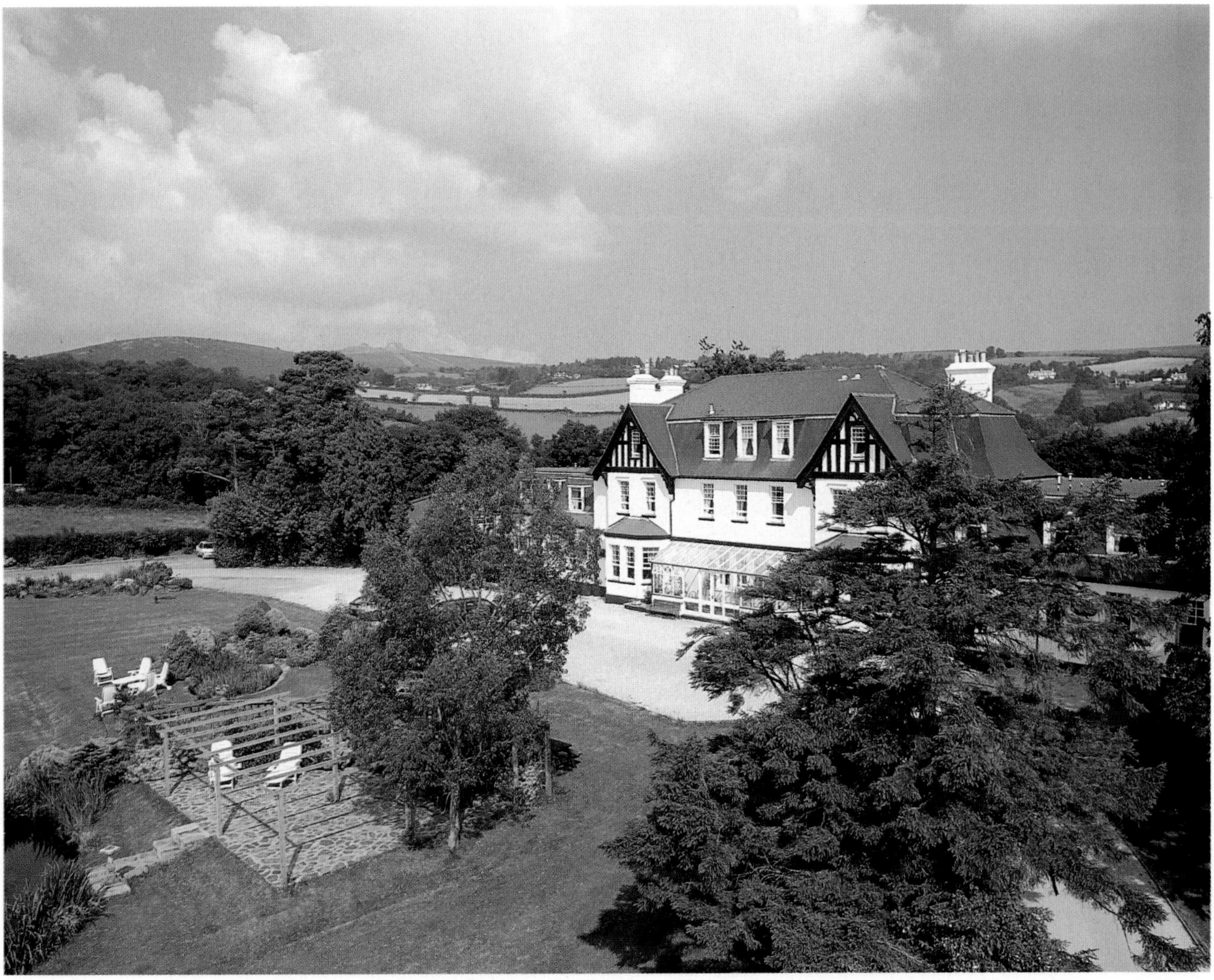

# ILSINGTON COUNTRY HOTEL

**ILSINGTON, NEWTON ABBOT, DEVON TQ13 9RR**
**TEL: 01364 661452 FAX: 01364 661307**

The Ilsington Hotel stands in ten acres of beautiful private grounds within the Dartmoor National Park. Run by charming owners, Howard and Karen Astbury, the delightful furnishings and friendly ambience offer a most comfortable environment in which to relax. Stylish bedrooms and suites all boast outstanding views across the rolling pastoral countryside and every comfort and convenience to make guests feel at home, including English toiletries. The distinctive candle-lit dining room is perfect for savouring the superb cuisine created by talented chefs from fresh local produce. The library is ideal for an intimate dining party or celebration whilst the Victorian conservatory is the place for morning coffee or a Devon cream tea. There is a fully equipped purpose built gymnasium, heated indoor pool, sauna and spa – also experienced masseurs. Some of England's most idyllic and unspoilt scenery surrounds Ilsington, with the picturesque villages of Lustleigh, Widecombe-in-the-Moor and Manaton all closeby. Footpaths lead from the hotel on to Dartmoor. Riding, fishing and many other country pursuits can be arranged. **Directions:** From M5 join A38 at Exeter following Plymouth signs. After approximately 12 miles exit for Moretonhampstead and Newton Abbot. At roundabout follow signs for Ilsington. Price guide: (including dinner) Single £80; double/twin £125.

For hotel location, see maps on pages 490-496

# BELSTEAD BROOK MANOR HOTEL

**BELSTEAD BROOK PARK, BELSTEAD ROAD, IPSWICH, SUFFOLK IP2 9HB**
**TEL: 01473 684241 FAX: 01473 681249**

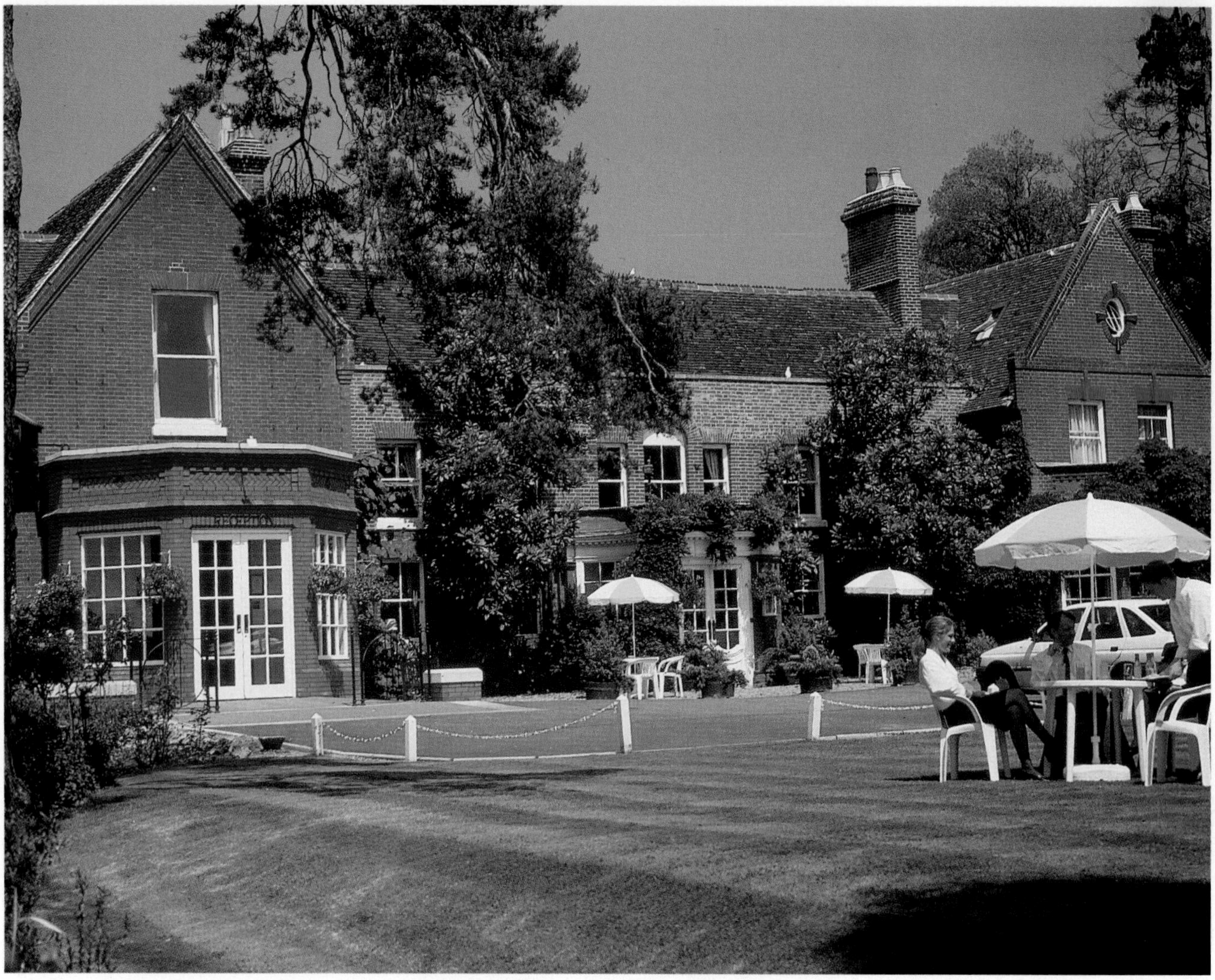

An oasis on the edge of Ipswich, Belstead Brook Manor Hotel is surrounded by eight acres of landscaped gardens and woodlands. It combines the charm and tranquillity of the original 16th century country house with every modern day comfort. Bedrooms are pleasantly furnished and many overlook the garden where resident peacocks stroll. A luxurious swimming pool with sauna, steam room, large Jacuzzi, separate pool for children and a well equipped gymnasium. The award winning restaurant offers a choice of menus, complemented by a comprehensive cellar. For weddings, conferences or banquets, the hotel offers private dining rooms and a choice of purpose built meeting and syndicate rooms to accommodate up to 130 guests or delegates. The hotel is an ideal base from which to explore the delights of Suffolk; These include Southwold, Aldeburgh, Woodbridge, the estuaries of the Deben and the Orwell, the wool towns of Lavenham and Long Melford and the countryside of the Stour Valley made famous by John Constable. **Directions:** At the A12/A14 interchange roundabout take the A1214 Ipswich West exit. Follow signs to Belstead. At the T junction at the bottom of the hill take a small lane signposted to Belstead Brook. The hotel is visible through trees on your left. Price guide: Double/twin £75–£85; suites £120.

For hotel location, see maps on pages 490-496

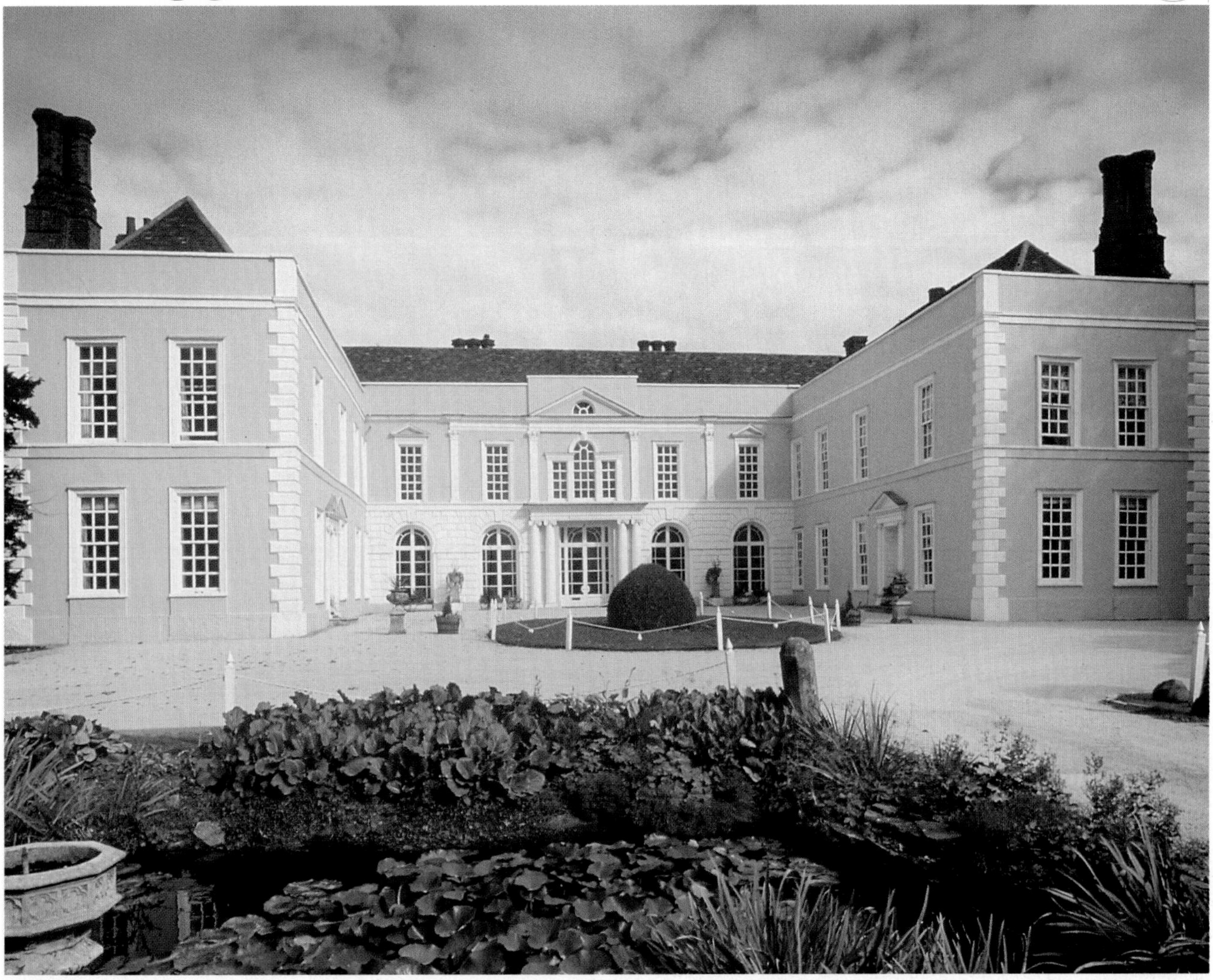

# HINTLESHAM HALL

**HINTLESHAM, IPSWICH, SUFFOLK IP8 3NS**
**TEL: 01473 652268 FAX: 01473 652463**

The epitome of grandeur, Hintlesham Hall is a house of evolving styles: its splendid Georgian façade belies its 16th-century origins, to which the red-brick Tudor rear of the hall is a testament. The Stuart period also left its mark, in the form of a magnificent carved-oak staircase leading to the north wing of the hall. The combination of styles works extremely well, with the lofty proportions of the Georgian reception rooms contrasting with the timbered Tudor rooms. The décor throughout is superb – all rooms are individually appointed in a discriminating fashion. Iced mineral water, toiletries and towelling robes are to be found in each of the comfortable bedrooms. The herb garden supplies many of the flavours for the well-balanced menu which will appeal to the gourmet and the health-conscious alike, complemented by a 300-bin wine list. Bounded by 175 acres of rolling countryside, leisure facilities include the Hall's own 18-hole championship golf course, gymnasium, saunas, steam room, spa bath, tennis, croquet and snooker. Guests can also explore Suffolk's 16th-century wool merchants' villages, its pretty coast, 'Constable country' and Newmarket. **Directions:** Hintlesham Hall is 4 miles west of Ipswich on the A1071 Sudbury road. Price guide: Single £85; double/twin £110; suite £210.

For hotel location, see maps on pages 490-496

# THE BORROWDALE GATES COUNTRY HOUSE HOTEL

**GRANGE-IN-BORROWDALE, KESWICK, CUMBRIA CA12 5UQ**
**TEL: 017687 77204 FAX: 017687 77254**

Built in 1860, Borrowdale Gates is surrounded on all sides by the rugged charm of the Lake District National Park. It affords panoramic views of the Borrowdale Valley and surrounding fells and nestles in two acres of wooded gardens on the edge of the ancient hamlet of Grange, close to the shores of Derwentwater. Tastefully decorated bedrooms offer every modern comfort and command picturesque views of the surrounding scenery. The comfortable lounges and bar, decorated with fine antiques and warmed by glowing log fires in cooler months, create the perfect setting in which to enjoy a drink and forget the bustle of everyday life. Fine food is served in the restaurant, with menus offering a wide and imaginative selection of dishes. The cuisine is complemented by a thoughtfully chosen wine list and excellent service. This Lakeland home is a haven of peace and tranquillity and is ideally located for walking, climbing and touring. There are also many places of literary and historical interest within easy reach, for example Wordsworth's birthplace in Cockermouth. The hotel is closed throughout January. **Directions:** M6 junction 40 A66 into Keswick. B5289 to Borrowdale. After four miles right into Grange over double hump back bridge. Price guide: Single £57–£78; double/twin £105–£150 (Including dinner). Special breaks available.

For hotel location, see maps on pages 490-496

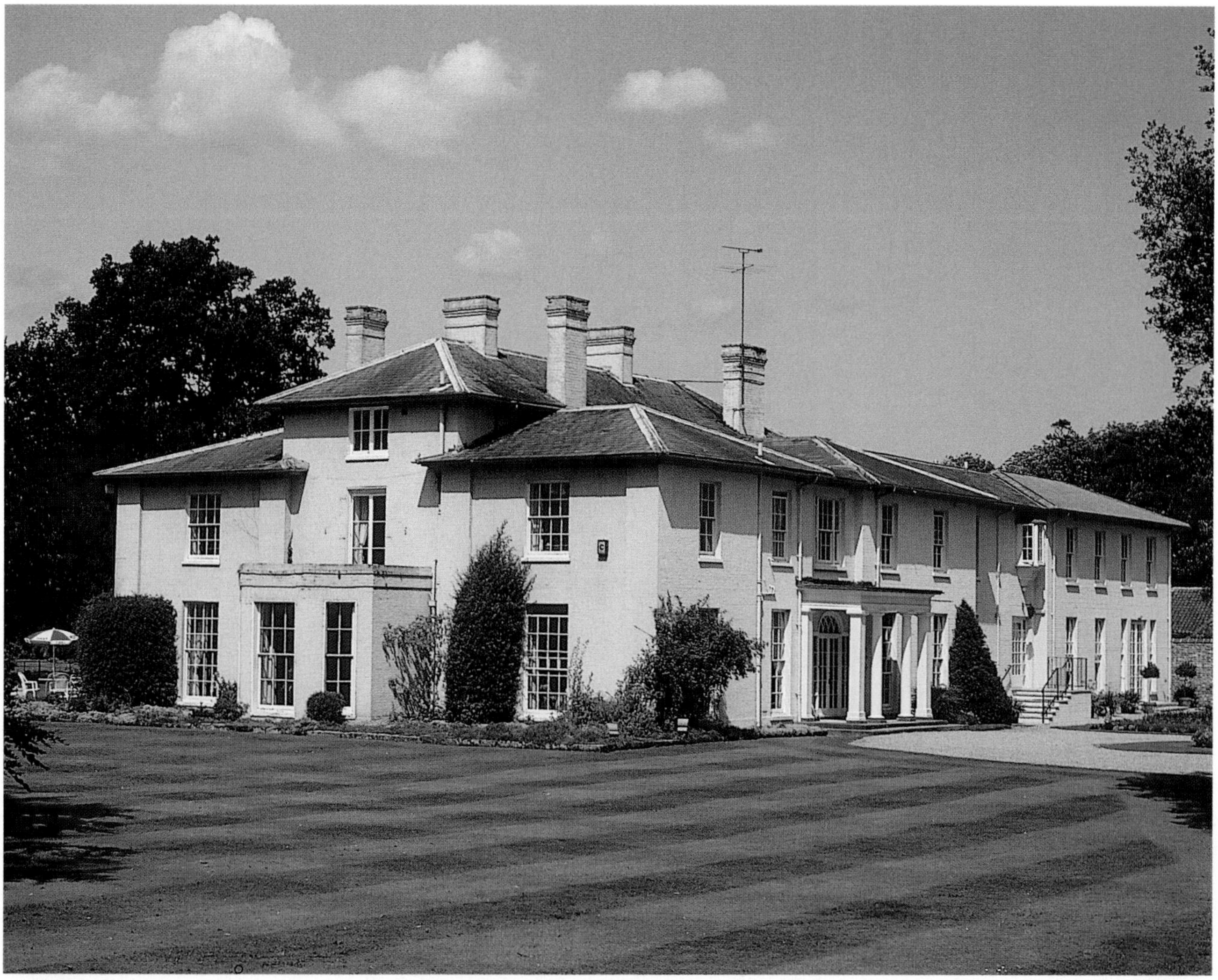

# Congham Hall

**GRIMSTON, KING'S LYNN, NORFOLK PE32 1AH**
**TEL: 01485 600250 FAX: 01485 601191**

Dating from the mid-18th century, this stately manor house is set in 40 acres of paddocks, orchards and gardens, including its own cricket pitch. The conversion from country house to luxury hotel in 1982 was executed with care to enhance the elegance of the classic interiors. Proprietors Christine and Trevor Forecast have, however, retained the atmosphere of a family home. Christine's particular forte is the herb garden and flower arranging, and her displays enliven the décor throughout, while the delicate fragrance of home-made pot-pourri perfumes the air. Winners of the Johansens Hotel Award for Excellence 1993. Light lunches available in the Bar, Lounge, Restaurant and Terrace. In the Orangery restaurant, guests can relish modern English cooking. The origin of many of the flavours is explained by the herb garden, with over 100 varieties for the chef's use. Even the most discerning palate will be delighted by the choice of wines. Congham Hall is an ideal base for touring the countryside of West Norfolk, as well as Sandringham, Fakenham races and the coastal nature reserves. **Directions:** Go to the A149/A148 interchange northeast of King's Lynn. Follow the A148 towards Sandringham/Fakenham/Cromer for 100 yards. Turn right to Grimston. The hotel is then 2½ miles on the left. Price guide: Single £85–£95; double/twin £115–£145; suites from £180.

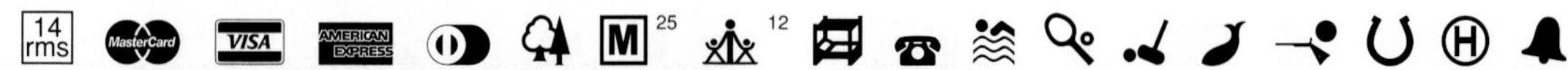

For hotel location, see maps on pages 490-496

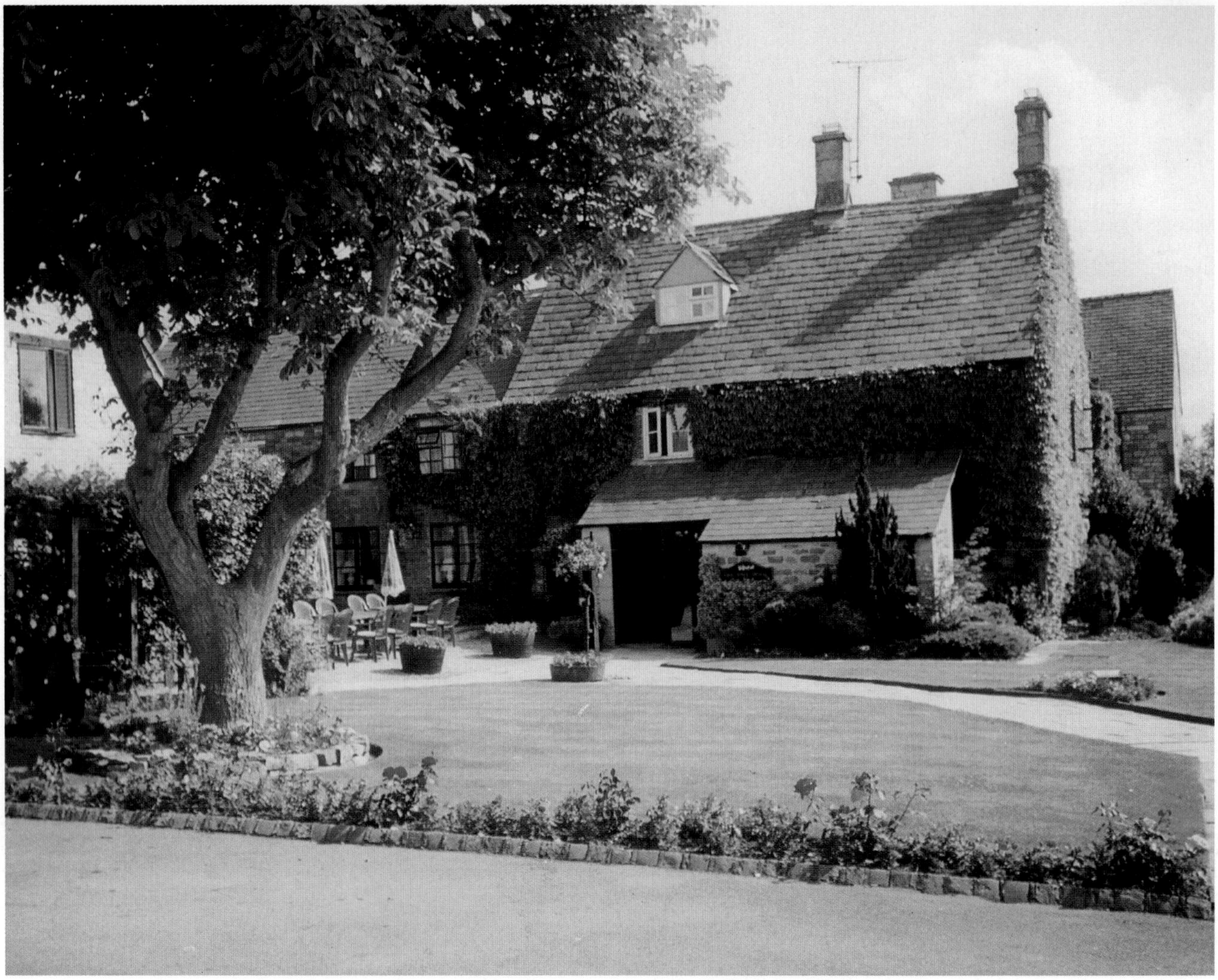

# MILL HOUSE HOTEL

**KINGHAM, OXFORDSHIRE OX7 6UH**
**TEL: 01608 658188 FAX: 01608 658492**

Superbly converted Cotswold stone Mill House listed in the *Domesday Book* and set in nine tranquil acres with its own trout stream in the heart of the Cotswolds between Burford, Chipping Norton and Stow-on-the-Wold. The 23 en suite bedrooms are all elegantly appointed and overlook the surrounding Cotswold countryside. There is a comfortable lounge with deep armchairs and sofas, and the bar features the ancient beamed ceiling and orginal bread ovens of the landfall flour mill. Open log fires are a feature throughout the winter; in summer, all rooms are enhanced by beautiful flower arrangements and fragrant pot-pourri. The heart of the hotel is the Marionette Room restaurant which provides cuisine of the highest standards. The menus are changed daily to take advantage of the very best of fresh, seasonal produce. With the whole of the Cotswolds within easy reach, the Mill House is the ideal base from which to explore: Broadway, Chipping Campden, Moreton-in-Marsh, the Slaughters and Bourton-on-the-Water are all within 30 minutes drive. The Mill House has AA 3 Stars and 2 Rosettes for food; RAC 3 Stars with Hospitality, Comfort and Restaurant Awards. **Directions:** South of Kingham village midway between Chipping Norton and Stow-on-the-Wold just off the B4450. Price guide: Single £65–£75; double/twin £100–£120.

For hotel location, see maps on pages 490-496

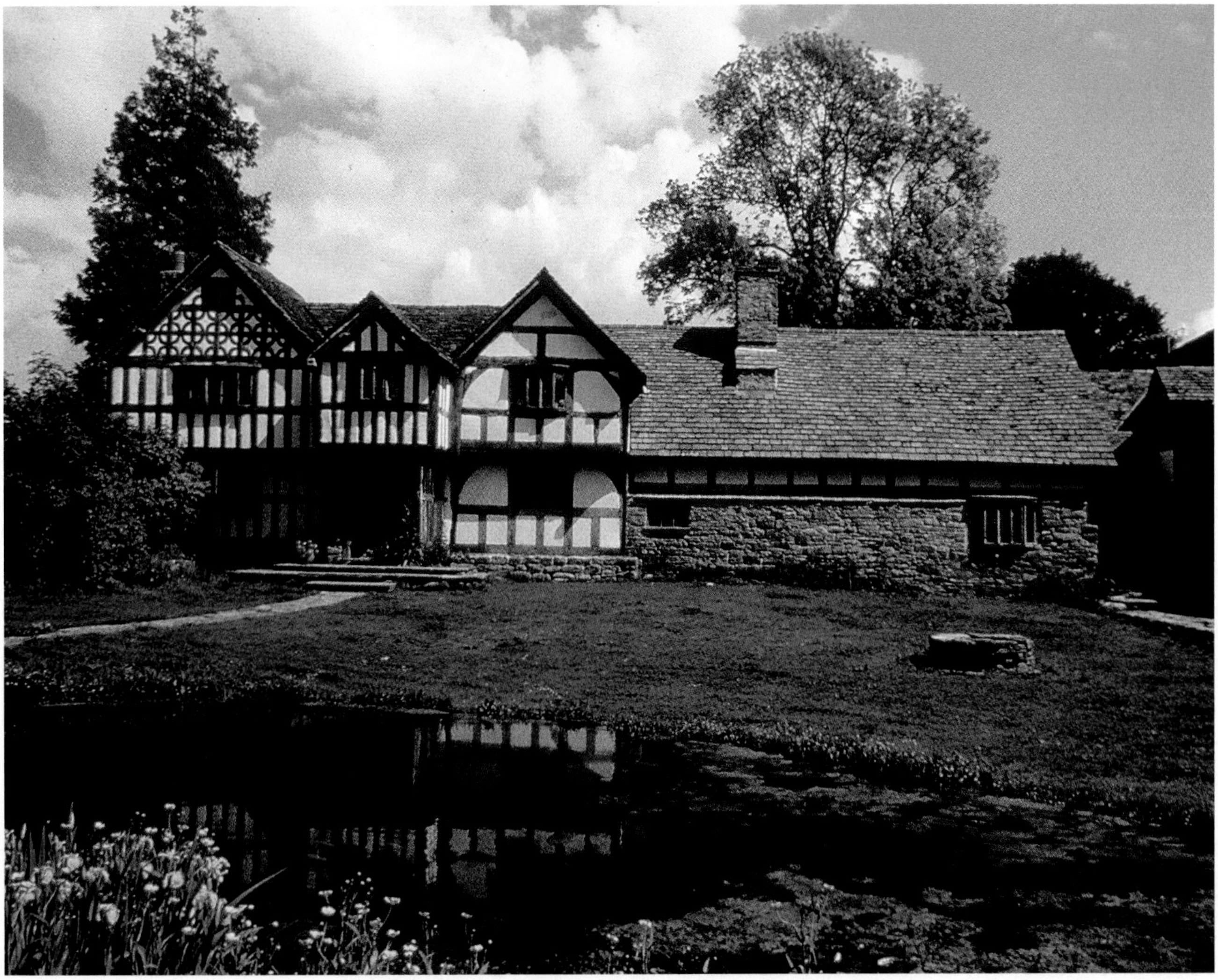

# PENRHOS COURT

KINGTON, HEREFORDSHIRE HR5 3LH
TEL: 01544 230720 FAX: 01544 230754

Penrhos was built in 1280, the year when Edward I, took Kington away from the Welsh. This unique farm building is set in six acres of grounds on the border of Herefordshire and Wales. Many years of devoted work by the owners have transformed Penrhos into a delightful small hotel, offering seclusion and high standards of comfort and service. Chef-patronne Daphne Lambert prepares the dishes served in the hotel's restaurant and over the years she has evolved her own style of cooking. She uses only fresh ingredients of the highest quality, preparing them in a way that does not mask the natural flavours nor strip the food of its nutritional value. The four-course meal, which changes every day, offers a choice for all tastes. All food served is organic and the restaurant is the first in the UK to be certified organic by the Soil Association. Many of the herbs, vegetables and fruit are grown in the garden next to the kitchen. Daphne's Cookery Courses run throughout the year and her project for The Penrhos School of Food & Health has been nominated for a Millennium Marque award. Penrhos is within reach of five golf courses and other activities include riding, hang-gliding and walking. Also nearby are Hay-on-Wye, the Wye Valley and Hereford. **Directions:** Half mile south of Kington on the A44. Price guide: Single £50–£90; double/twin £80–£100; suites £120.

For hotel location, see maps on pages 490-496

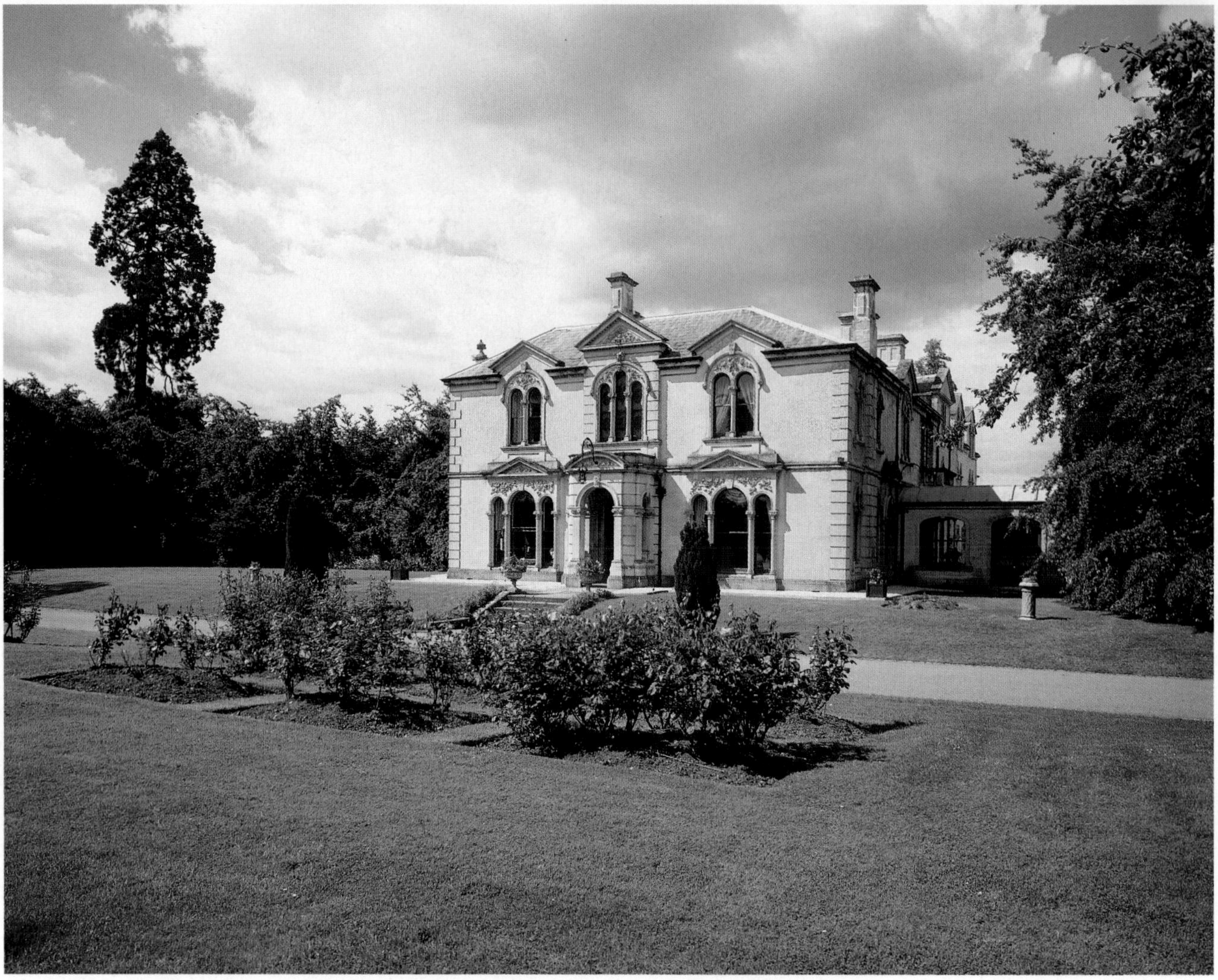

# BEECHFIELD HOUSE

**BEANACRE, MELKSHAM, WILTSHIRE SN12 7PU**
**TEL: 01225 703700 FAX: 01225 790118**

Beechfield House stands in a classical English landscape within an easy walk of the beautiful and historic National Trust village of Lacock with its winding streets of Gothic-arched grey-stone houses and half-timbered cottages. Built in 1878, this imposing, privately owned hotel is a fine example of late Victorian splendour and is surrounded by eight acres of secluded gardens and grounds. Each of the bedrooms is traditionally furnished to a high standard, combining the benefits and facilities of a hotel room with the atmosphere of a charming private country house. Well-defined colour schemes lend an uplifting brightness, particularly in the relaxing morning room, elegant drawing room and splendid dining room where a pianist entertains diners enjoying chef Geoffrey Bell's imaginative English cuisine. In a sheltered corner of the colourful, formal walled garden there is a heated swimming pool. Private functions and meetings can be accommodated. Four golf courses are in the vicinity and shooting, riding, hunting and fishing can be arranged. The Georgian city of Bath and the country houses of Bowood, Corsham Court and Longleat are close by. Beechfield House is closed between Christmas and New Year. **Directions:** From M4, exit at junction 4 and take A350 towards Melksham. The hotel is on the left one mile south of Lacock. Price guide: Single from £65; double/twin from £85.

For hotel location, see maps on pages 490-496

# RAMPSBECK COUNTRY HOUSE HOTEL

**WATERMILLOCK, LAKE ULLSWATER, NR PENRITH, CUMBRIA CA11 0LP**

**TEL: 017684 86442 FAX: 017684 86688**

A beautifully situated hotel, Rampsbeck Country House stands in 18 acres of landscaped gardens and meadows leading to the shores of Lake Ullswater. Built in 1714, it first became a hotel in 1947, before the present owners acquired it in 1983. Thomas and Marion Gibb, with the help of Marion's mother, Marguerite MacDowall, completely refurbished Rampsbeck with the aim of maintaining its character and adding only to its comfort. Most of the well-appointed bedrooms have lake and garden views. Three have a private balcony and the suite overlooks the lake. In the elegant drawing room, a log fire burns and French windows lead to the garden. Guests and non-residents are welcome to dine in the intimate candle-lit restaurant. Imaginative menus offer a choice of delicious dishes, carefully prepared by head chef Andrew McGeorge and his team. A good bar lunch menu offers light snacks as well as hot food. Guests can stroll through the gardens, play croquet or fish from the lake shore, around which there are designated walks. Lake steamer trips, riding, golf, sailing, wind-surfing and fell-walking are available nearby. Closed from the first week in January to mid-February. Dogs by arrangement only. **Directions:** Leave M6 at junction 40, take A592 to Ullswater. At T-junction at lake turn right; hotel is 1½ miles on left. Price guide: Single £55–£100; double/twin £95–£180; suite £180.

For hotel location, see maps on pages 490-496

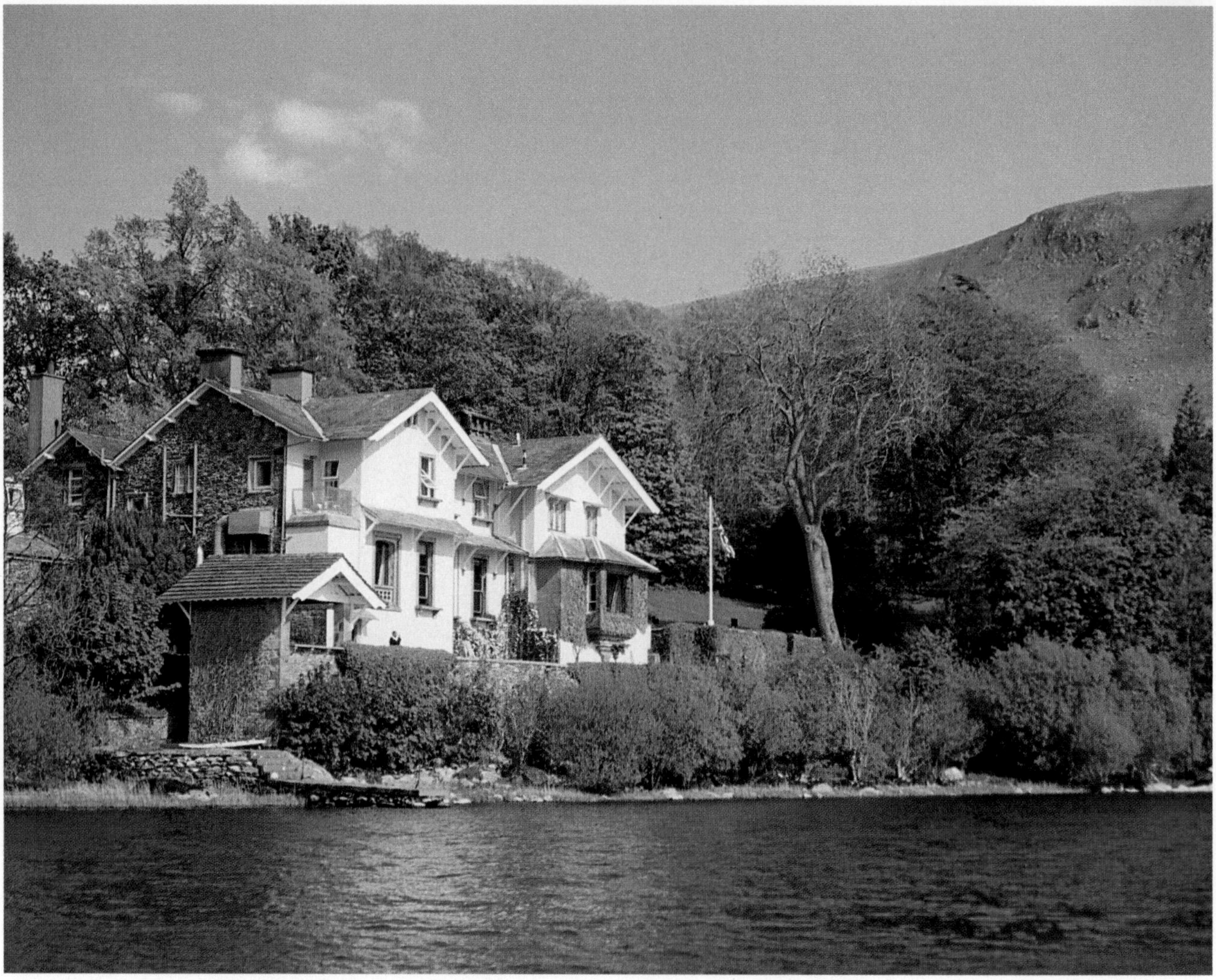

# SHARROW BAY COUNTRY HOUSE HOTEL

HOWTOWN, LAKE ULLSWATER, PENRITH, CUMBRIA CA10 2LZ
TEL: 017684 86301/86483 FAX: 017684 86349

Now in its 50th year, Sharrow Bay is known to discerning travellers the world over, who return again and again to this magnificent lakeside hotel. It wasn't always so. Francis Coulson arrived in 1948. He was joined by Brian Sack in 1952 and the partnership flourished, to make Sharrow Bay what it is today. Recently they have been joined by Nigel Lawrence and Nigel Lightburn who carry on the tradition. All the bedrooms are elegantly furnished and guests are guaranteed the utmost comfort. In addition to the main hotel, there are four cottages nearby which offer similarly luxurious accommodation. All the reception rooms are delightfully decorated. Sharrow Bay is universally renowned for its wonderful cuisine. The team of chefs led by Johnnie Martin and Colin Akrigg ensure that each meal is a special occasion, a mouthwatering adventure! With its private jetty and 12 acres of lakeside gardens Sharrow Bay offers guests boating, swimming, and fishing. Fell-walking is a challenge for the upwardly mobile. Sharrow Bay is the oldest British member of Relais et Châteaux. Closed in December and January. **Directions:** M6 junction 40, A592 to Lake Ullswater, into Pooley Bridge, then take Howtown road for 2 miles. Price guide: (including 7 course Dinner and full English Breakfast) Single £110–£260; double/twin £220–£350; suite £340–£350.

For hotel location, see maps on pages 490-496

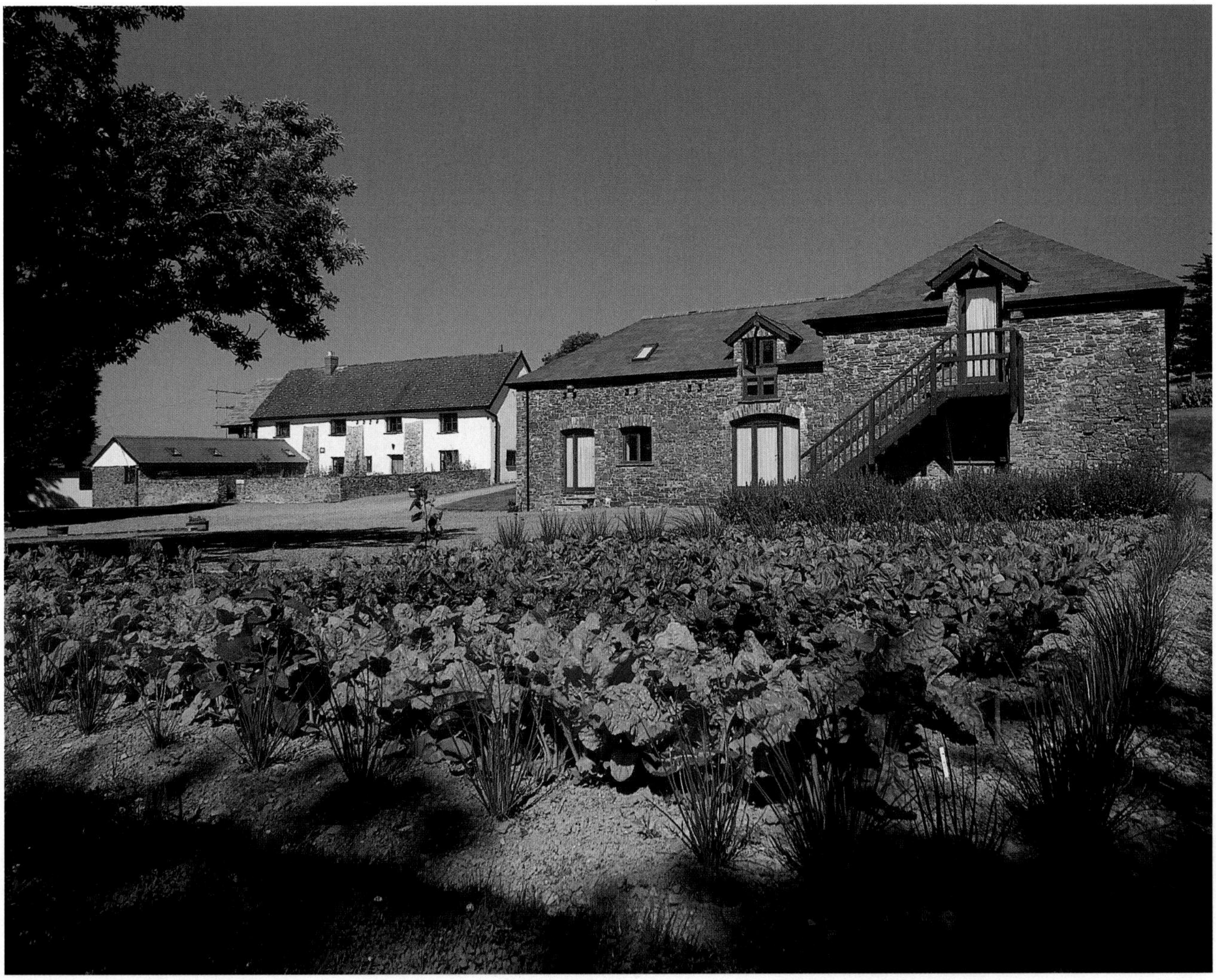

# PERCY'S AT COOMBESHEAD

**VIRGINSTOW, DEVON EX21 5EA**

**TEL: 01409 211236 FAX: 01409 211275 E-MAIL: percyscoomBESHEAD**

Percy's at Coombeshead is a sophisticated country cousin of Percy's, the restaurant with a Michelin Red M in North London. Both are renowned for their wonderful fresh salads, herbs and vegetables, and these are grown in abundance and in endless variety at Coombeshead – so the owners, Tina and Tony Bricknell-Webb, can truly boast that in their Devon hotel the salad on the table was in the ground a hour before! The Devon establishment, a 500 year old, 40 acre farm, is enchanting – a restaurant with rooms (all designated non smoking), accommodation is across the courtyard in the original stables, cleverly converted into eight delightful double bedrooms (all en suite) with lovely views across the countryside. The restaurant at Percy's can seat fifty lucky people, for the menus, ever changing, are inspired. Local fish, and game when appropriate, feature; the estate provides, tender peas, giant squash, chard, red mustard, every salad leaf and vegetable imaginable, including edible fungi, while neighbours bring in loganberries, plums and other soft fruit. The wine list reads very well and allows house and dessert wines to be ordered by the glass Country pursuits prevail – bird watching, riding, fishing, energetic walking – to work up an appetite for the next meal! **Directions:** M5, at Exeter A30 to Launceston, then A388 to Holsworthy. Percy's is signed at St Giles-on-the-Heath. Price guide: Single £39; doublt/twin £78

For hotel location, see maps on pages 490-496

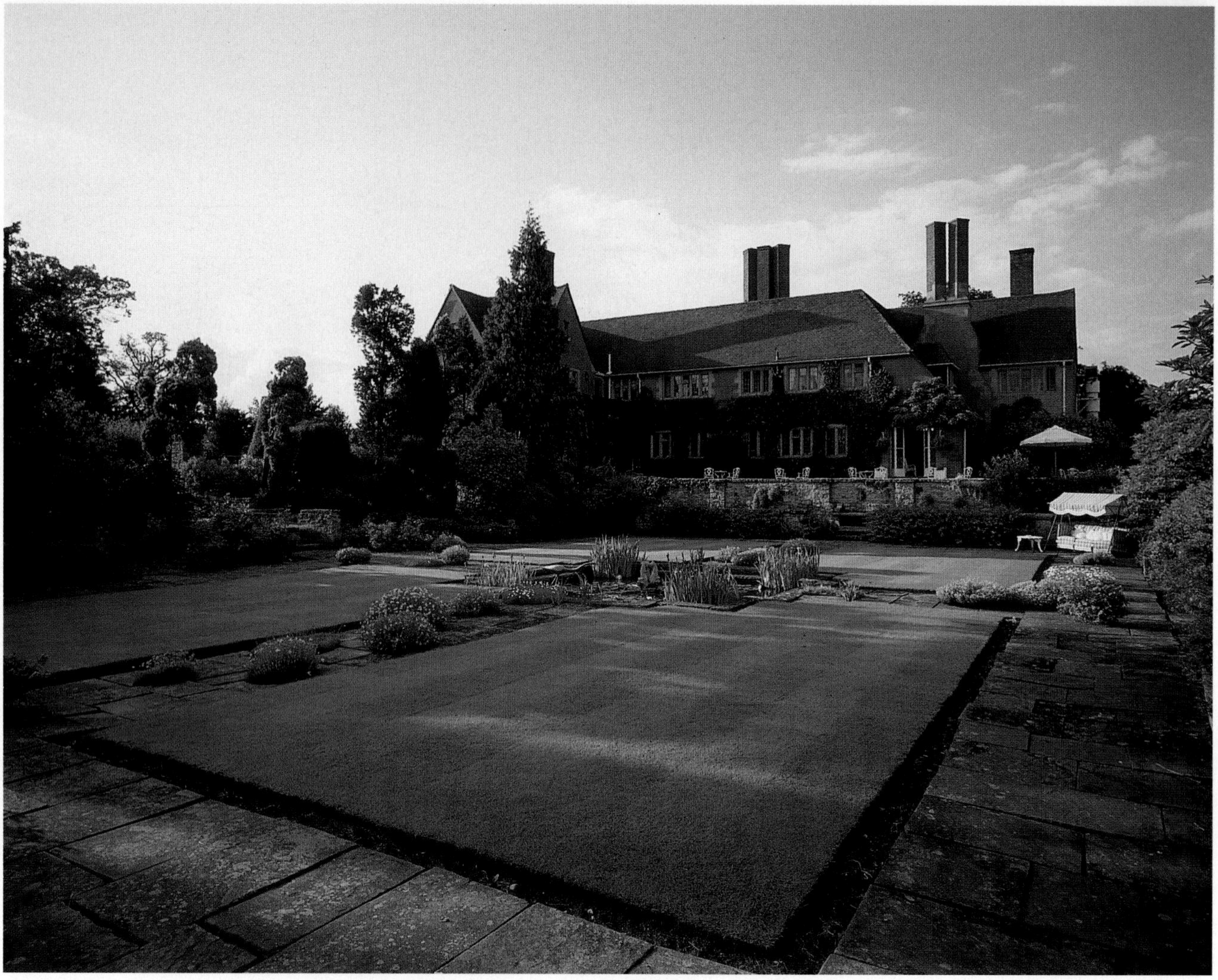

# MALLORY COURT

**HARBURY LANE, BISHOPS TACHBROOK, LEAMINGTON SPA, WARWICKSHIRE CV33 9QB**
**TEL: 01926 330214 FAX: 01926 451714 E-MAIL: Reception@Mallory.Co.UK**

Close to Stratford-upon-Avon in the heart of rural England, Mallory Court recreates the best traditions of an English country house by combining warm hospitality with exceptional comfort and superb cuisine. The hotel, built of mellow stone with leaded light windows, is an outstanding example of period architecture. It is set in 10 acres of magnificent landscaped gardens, complete with lawns, a formal rose garden and water gardens. The interiors are the essence of elegance and luxury, with beautiful reception rooms furnished with deep sofas, leather chesterfields, fine paintings and flowers. Drinks are served by the fireside or outside on the terrace during the warmer months. The spacious bedrooms are exquisitely and individually furnished, with views of the surrounding countryside adding to a sense of tranquillity. For the ultimate in luxury, the Bleinheim Suite boasts a magnificent two-tub bathroom and its own balcony. Reflecting the French classical style, a superb menu offers highly acclaimed cuisine. Memorable dishes are prepared under the personal supervision of Allan Holland, making extensive use of fresh herbs and vegetables from the hotel gardens. **Directions:** Mallory Court is located 2 miles south of Leamington Spa on Harbury Lane, just off the B4087 Bishops Tachbrook-Leamington Spa road, Harbury Lane runs from the B4087 towards the Fosse Way. Price Guide: single £125; Double/twin £185.

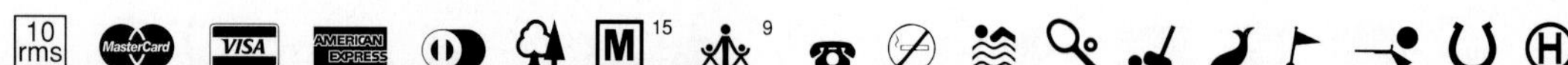

For hotel location, see maps on pages 490-496

# HOPE END HOTEL

**HOPE END, LEDBURY, HEREFORDSHIRE HR8 1JQ**
**TEL: 01531 633613 FAX: 01531 636366**

Hope End is a most romantic small hotel, set in 40 acres of restored 18th-century listed parkland. This very individual Georgian hotel provides total peace and an opportunity to enjoy an idle holiday amid rural surroundings. Formerly the childhood home of poet Elizabeth Barrett Browning, the building has been refurbished to offer discreet comfort. Eight en suite bedrooms are furnished with antiques and paintings, while the absence of TV ensures complete tranquillity. An extraordinary range of organic fruit, vegetables and herbs is grown in the walled kitchen garden. Free-range eggs, milk, yoghurt, local beef, lamb, fish and game in season are used in the kitchen. Fresh home-made bread is always available, along with a wide selection of farmhouse cheeses and the hotel's own spring water. Chef-patronne Patricia Hegarty prepares delicious dishes in the English country style to a high standard that has earned both national acclaim and 3 AA Rosettes. The wine list includes over 150 labels, with some rare vintages. Hope End is an ideal touring base as the Welsh Marches, Cotswolds and Malvern Hills are nearby. Ledbury itself is an interesting old market town with black and white houses. Closed from mid-December to early February. **Directions:** Two miles north of Ledbury, just beyond Wellington Heath. Price guide: Single £87; double/twin £123–£144.

For hotel location, see maps on pages 490-496

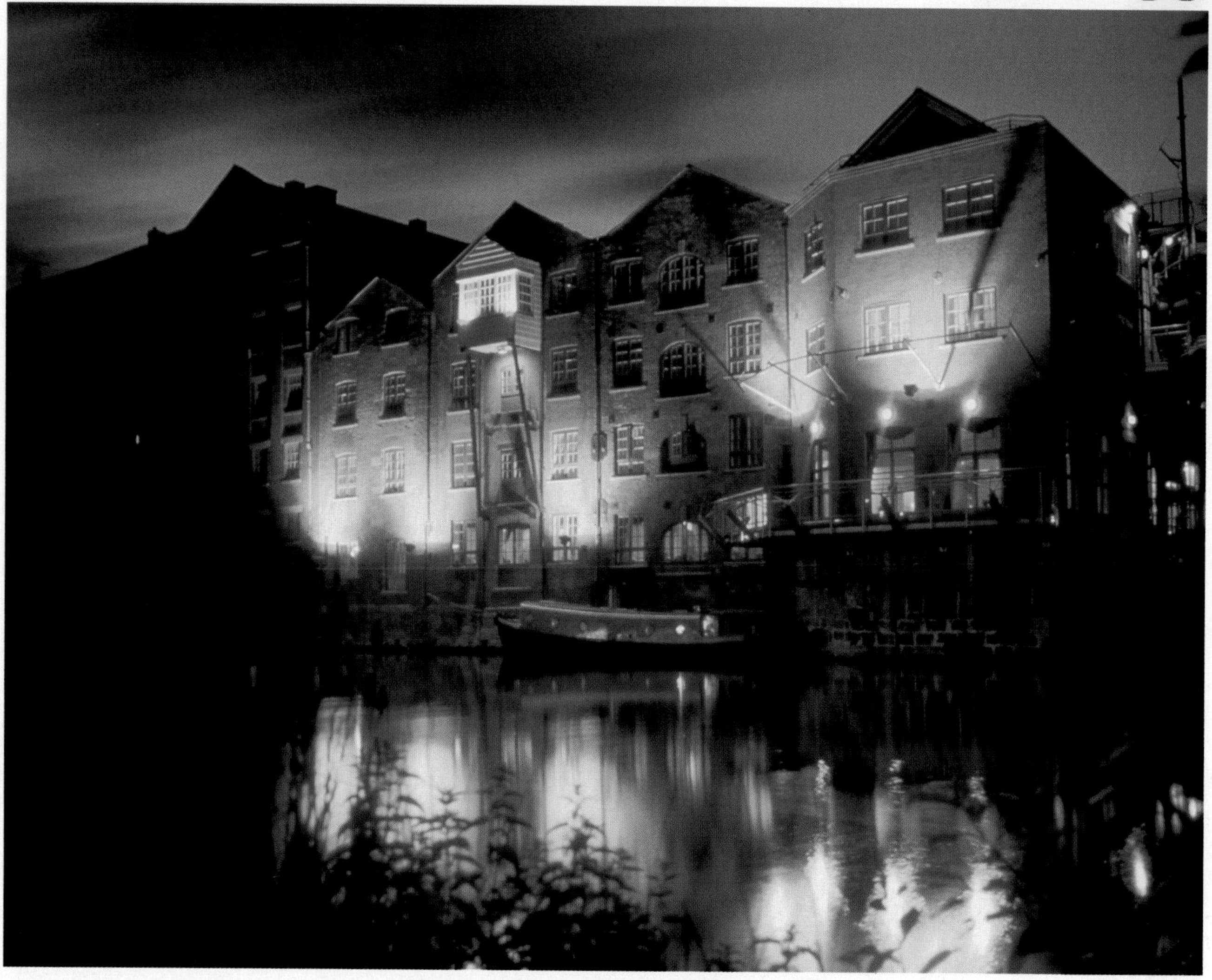

# 42 THE CALLS

42 THE CALLS, LEEDS, WEST YORKSHIRE LS2 7EW
TEL: 0113 244 0099 FAX: 0113 234 4100

This remarkable hotel is absolutely unique. Converted from an old riverside corn mill, it is run as a very personal and luxurious hotel by Jonathan Wix with General Manager Belinda Scott and a dedicated team of staff in a peaceful location in the centre of Leeds. Shops, offices and theatres are within a few minutes' walk. The bedrooms have been individually decorated and furnished, taking full advantage of the many original features from small grain shutes to massive beams, girders and old machinery. Each room has 10 channel TV, a fresh filter coffee machine, complimentry sweets and cordials, luxury toiletries, trouser press and hair dryer. Stereo CD players are fitted in all the bedrooms and a library of disks is available to guests. Every comfort has been provided with full-size desks, handmade beds and armchairs, a liberal scattering of eastern rugs and beautiful bathrooms. Inexpensive valet car parking and 24-hour room service are offered. Next door to the hotel is the simple but stylish Brasserie 44 and the superb Michelin Starred Pool Court at 42. **Directions:** M1 junction 46, follow signs to Harrogate, turn right by Tetley's Brewery. Go over Crown Point Bridge, then second left keeping the parish church on your left. Turn left again by Calls Landing and 42 will be directly in front of you. Price guide: Single £95–£145; double/twin £130–£150; suite £185–£260.

For hotel location, see maps on pages 490-496

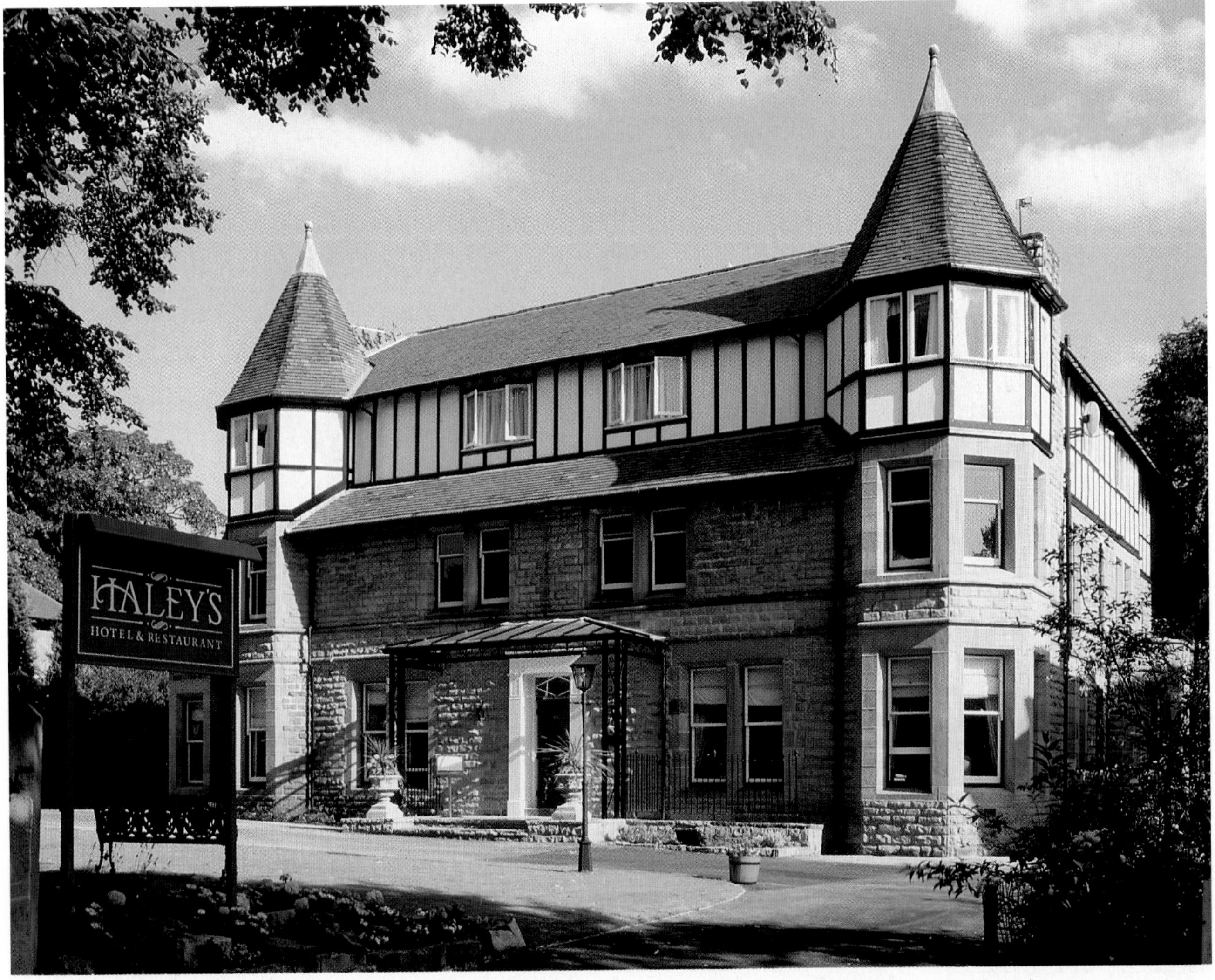

# HALEY'S HOTEL & RESTAURANT

**SHIRE OAK ROAD, HEADINGLEY, LEEDS, WEST YORKSHIRE LS6 2DE**
**TEL: 0113 278 4446 FAX: 0113 275 3342**

Just two miles from Leeds City Centre, yet set in a quiet leafy lane in the Headingley conservation area close to the cricket ground and the university, Haley's is truly the Country House Hotel in the City. Each of the 29 guest rooms offers the highest levels of comfort and is as individual as the fine antiques and rich furnishings which grace the hotel. A new edition to the existing accommodation is Bedford House, the elegant Victorian Grade II listed building next door which contains seven outstandingly furnished and beautifully equipped modern bedrooms, including two suites, one with its own private entrance. The Bramley Room and Library are popular venues for private meetings, lunch or dinner parties. Haley's Restaurant has an enviable reputation, holding two AA rosettes. An imaginative menu of modern English cuisine is accompanied by a fine wine list. Leeds offers superb shopping (including the newly opened Harvey Nichols). Opera North and the theatres combine with Haley's superb accommodation and food to provide entertaining weekends. Haley's is an independently owned member of Richard Branson's Virgin Hotel Collection. **Directions:** Two miles north of Leeds City Centre off the main A660 Otley Road – the main route to Leeds/Bradford Airport, Ilkley and Wharfedale. Price guide: Single £105–£120; double/twin £120–£140; suite £210–£220. Weekend rates from £85.

For hotel location, see maps on pages 490-496

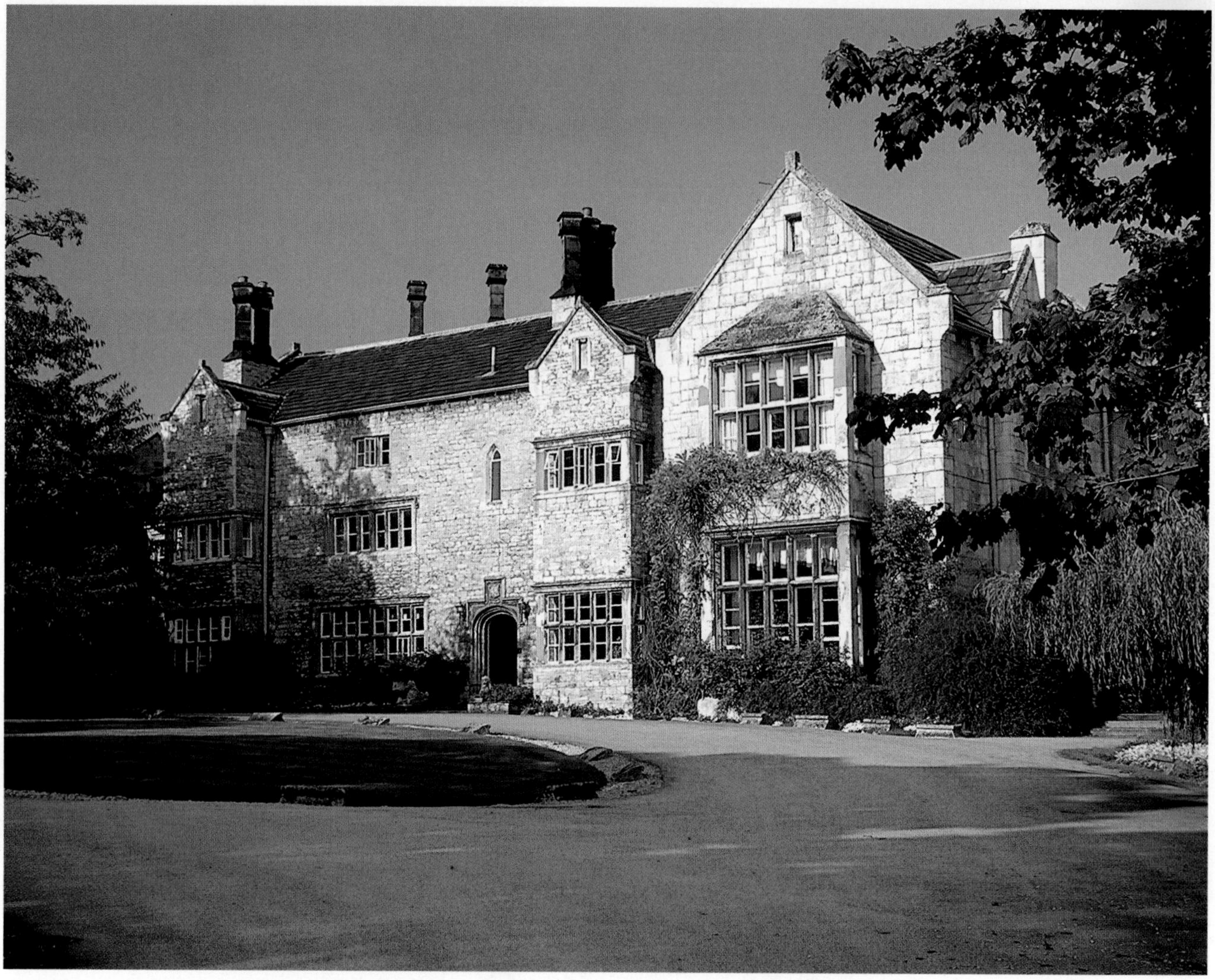

# MONK FRYSTON HALL

MONK FRYSTON, LEEDS, NORTH YORKSHIRE LS25 5DU
TEL: 01977 682369 FAX: 01977 683544

This mellow old manor house, with origins dating back to the time of William the Conqueror, is of great architectural interest. The mullioned and transom windows, and the family coat of arms above the doorway, are reminiscent of Monk Fryston's fascinating past. In 1954 the hall was acquired by the Duke of Rutland, who has since created an elegant contemporary hotel, while successfully preserving the strong sense of heritage and tradition. The bedrooms, ranging from cosy, to airy and spacious, all have private en suite bathrooms and are appointed to a high standard. A comprehensive menu offers a wide choice of traditional English dishes with something to suit all tastes. From the hall, the terrace leads to landscaped Italian gardens which overlook an ornamental lake and are a delight to see at any time of year. Wedding receptions and dinner-dances are catered for in the oak-panelled Haddon Room with its splendid carved fireplace. The Rutland Room makes a good conference venue. Monk Fryston Hall is an ideal choice for business people, tourists or those seeking a relaxing break. York is 16 miles, Leeds 14 miles and Harrogate 18 miles away. **Directions:** Three miles off A1, on the A63 towards Selby in the centre of Monk Fryston. Price guide: Single £72–£75; double/twin £98–£110.

For hotel location, see maps on pages 490-496

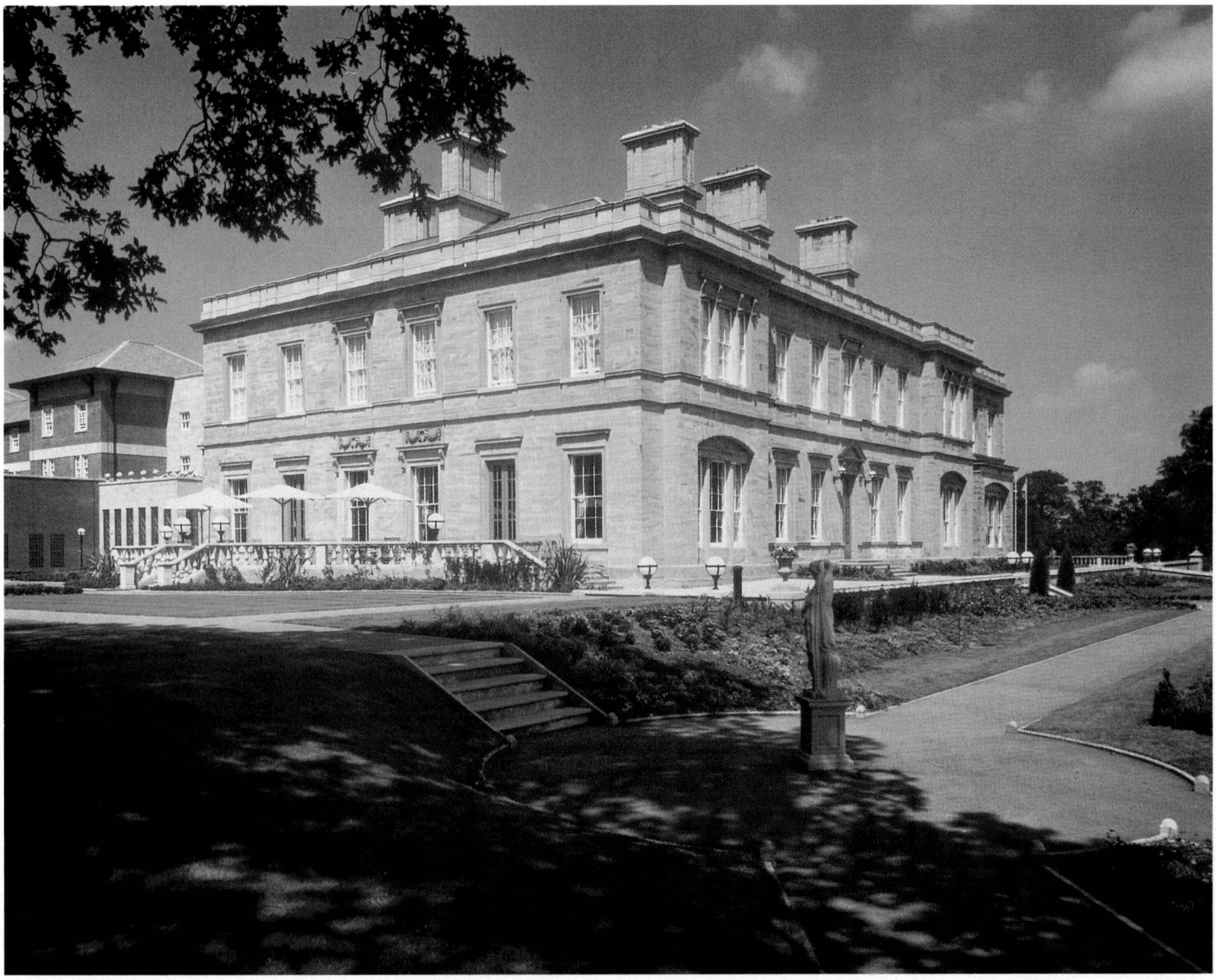

# OULTON HALL

ROTHWELL LANE, OULTON, LEEDS, WEST YORKSHIRE LS26 8HN
TEL: 0113 2821000 FAX: 0113 2828066

Oulton Hall stands majestically amid acres of woodland and rolling Yorkshire dales. Its 19th century formal gardens are on the English Heritage Register of Historic Gardens. A Grade II listed building, the Hall has a long and fascinating history. In 1850 it was re-built in the neoclassical style. Restored and extended as a 5-Star hotel with traditional character and unique charm it combines today the elegance of a Victorian mansion with impeccable service and the most modern facilities for business and leisure. These include 152 superb, en suite bedrooms complemented by 7 deluxe suites above the Great Hall. Guests can enjoy excellent cuisine in the intimate Brontë Restaurant, which pays decorative tribute to the great literary sisters, or comfortably relax in the softly furnished lounges or the panelled library. The conference facilities have been carefully constructed to a demanding professional standard and can accommodate up to 300 delegates. There is a large indoor swimming pool, Jacuzzi, sauna, steam room, solarium and a squash court. Adjacent to the hotel are the 9-hole and 18-hole Oulton Park golf courses. Shooting, fishing and riding are nearby. Special leisure breaks available. Directions: From M62, exit at junction 30 and take A642 north. After 2 miles, turn left at roundabout onto Rothwell Lane and the hotel is on the left. Price guide: Single from £130; double/twin from £150; suite £205–£245.

For hotel location, see maps on pages 490-496

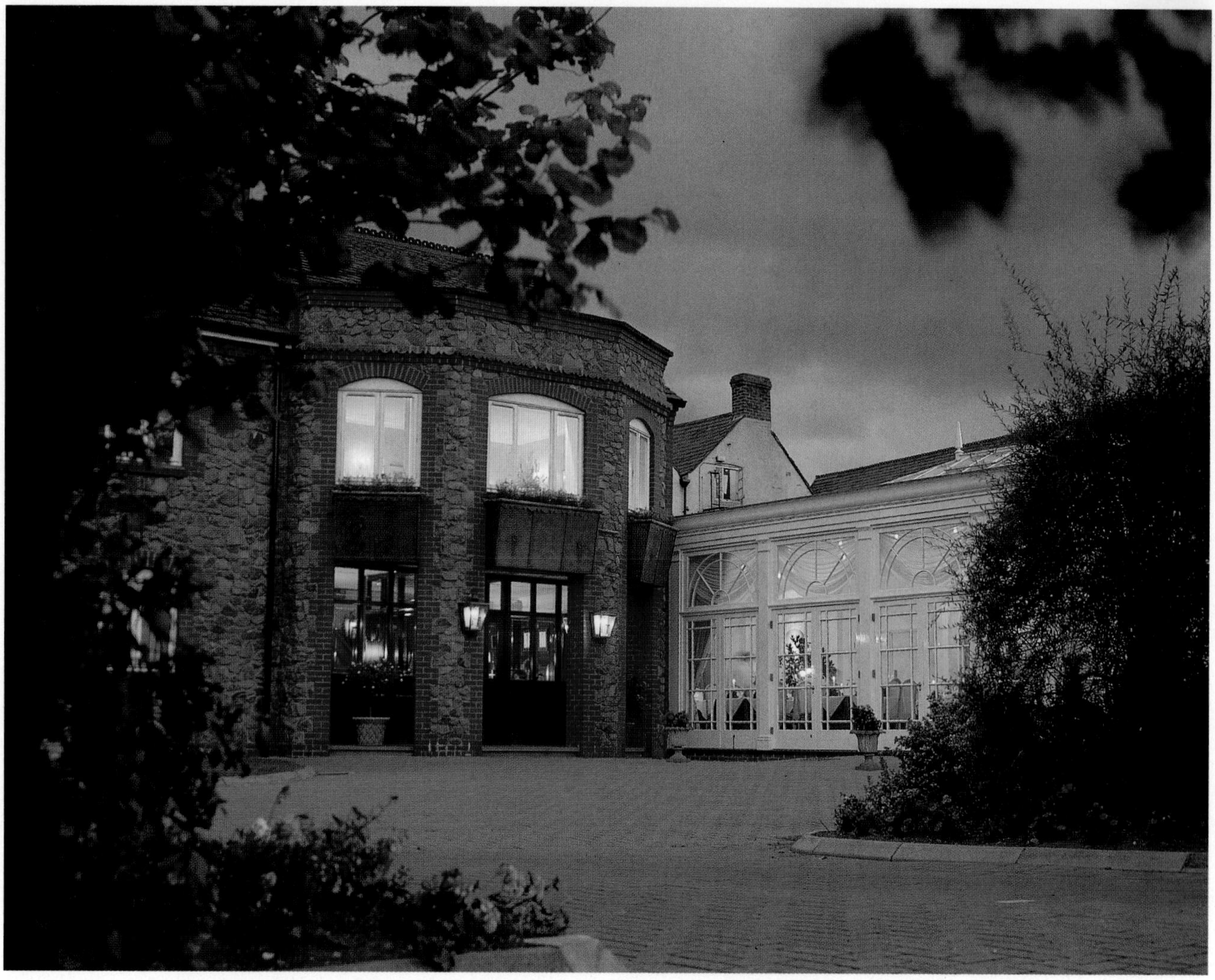

# QUORN COUNTRY HOTEL

**66 LEICESTER ROAD, QUORN, LEICESTERSHIRE LE12 8BB**
**TEL: 01509 415050 FAX: 01509 415557**

Originally Leicestershire's most exclusive private club, created around the original 17th century listed building, this award winning 4 star hotel is set in 4 acres of landscaped gardens. For the tenth consecutive year the hotel has received all 3 RAC merit awards for excellence in cuisine, hospitality and comfort and is also a recipient of the AA Rosette Award. The bedrooms are equipped to the very highest standard with attention given to every detail. Suitable for both the business traveller or for weekend guests seeking those extra 'touches' which help create the ideal peaceful retreat. Ladies travelling alone can feel reassured that their special needs are met and indeed exceeded. Particular emphasis is given to the enjoyment of food with a declared policy of using, whenever possible, the freshest local produce. Guests' stay will be enhanced by the choice of two different dining experiences. They can choose between the Shires Restaurant with its classical cuisine with a modern style or the Orangery Brasserie with its changing selection of contemporary dishes. **Directions:** Situated just off the A6 Leicester to Derby main road, in the bypassed village of Quorn (Quorndon), five miles from junction 23 of the M1 from North, junction 21A from South, East and West. Price Guide: Single £89; double/twin £99; suite £125.

For hotel location, see maps on pages 490-496

# LEWTRENCHARD MANOR

**LEWDOWN, NR OKEHAMPTON, DEVON EX20 4PN**
**TEL: 01566 783 256 FAX: 01566 783 332**

Nestling in the soft green Devon countryside just below Dartmoor, Lewtrenchard Manor is a beautiful 17th century grey stone manor house standing on the site of an earlier dwelling recorded in the Doomsday Book. Once the home of The Reverend Sabine Baring Gould, best remembered as a hymn writer and novelist, the Manor is rich in ornate ceilings, oak panelling, carvings and large open fireplaces. Personally run by owners James and Sue Murray the warm atmosphere of a large family house has been enhanced with the introduction of family antiques, fine paintings, warm colours and comfortable furniture. Nine spacious and light bedrooms have uninterrupted views through leaded windows over the peaceful countryside. The oak panelled dining room is the perfect setting in which to enjoy excellent dishes that combine superb flavour and delicacy with artistic presentation. There are lovely walks through the Lewtrenchard Estate, which also offers shooting and trout fishing nearby. Exeter, wild Dartmoor and quaint Devon villages are within easy reach and there are good facilities nearby for riding and golf. **Directions:** From Exeter and the M5 take A30 towards Okehampton and then join A386 for Tavistock. AT T-junction turn right and then left on to old A30 signposted to Bridestowe. Turn left at Lewdown for Lewtrenchard. Price guide: Single £80–£95; double/twin £110–£150; suite £145–£155.

9 rms · MasterCard · VISA · AMERICAN EXPRESS · M 50 · 8

For hotel location, see maps on pages 490-496

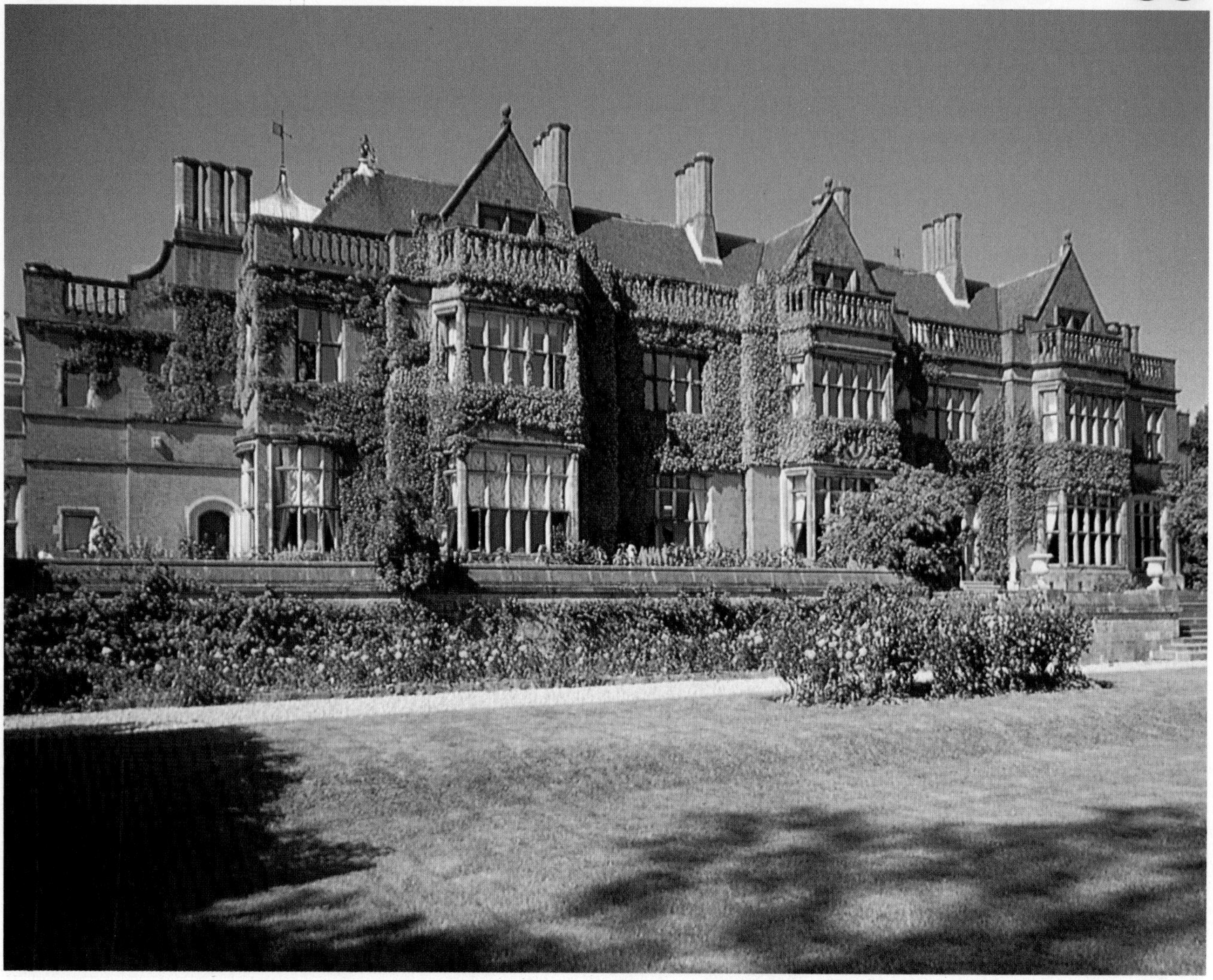

# HOAR CROSS HALL HEALTH SPA RESORT

**HOAR CROSS, NR YOXALL, STAFFORDSHIRE DE13 8QS**
**TEL: 01283 575671 FAX: 01283 575652**

Hoar Cross Hall is a health spa resort in a stately home hidden in the Staffordshire countryside with all the facilities of a 4 star hotel. Built in the 1860's it is a graceful listed residence. Today's guests want more than just to languish in beautiful surroundings they also wish to rejuvenate their mind and body. Water-based treatments are behind their successful philosophy; from hydro-therapy, baths and blitz jet douches, floatation therapy, saunas and steamrooms, to the superb hydrotherapy swimming pool, over 50 therapists pamper you with your choice of over 80 treatments. Peripheral activities are extensive. Partake of a full fitness assessment, a new hairstyle or venture into the 100 acres of woodlands and formal gardens. Play tennis, croquet and boules, or bicycle through the countryside. A Golf Academy with a PGA professional will teach you to play or improve your golf. Delight in the a la carte dining room where mouth watering dishes are served. Bedrooms and suites are exquisite with priceless views. Enjoy a day of relaxed luxury or a week of professional pampering. (minimum guest age is sixteen years). Price includes accommodation, breakfast, lunch, dinner, unlimited use of facilities and treatments according to length of stay. **Directions:** From Lichfield turn off A51 onto A515 towards Ashbourne. Go through Yoxall and turn left to Hoar Cross. Price guide (fully inclusive, see above): Single £118; double/twin £240.

For hotel location, see maps on pages 490-496

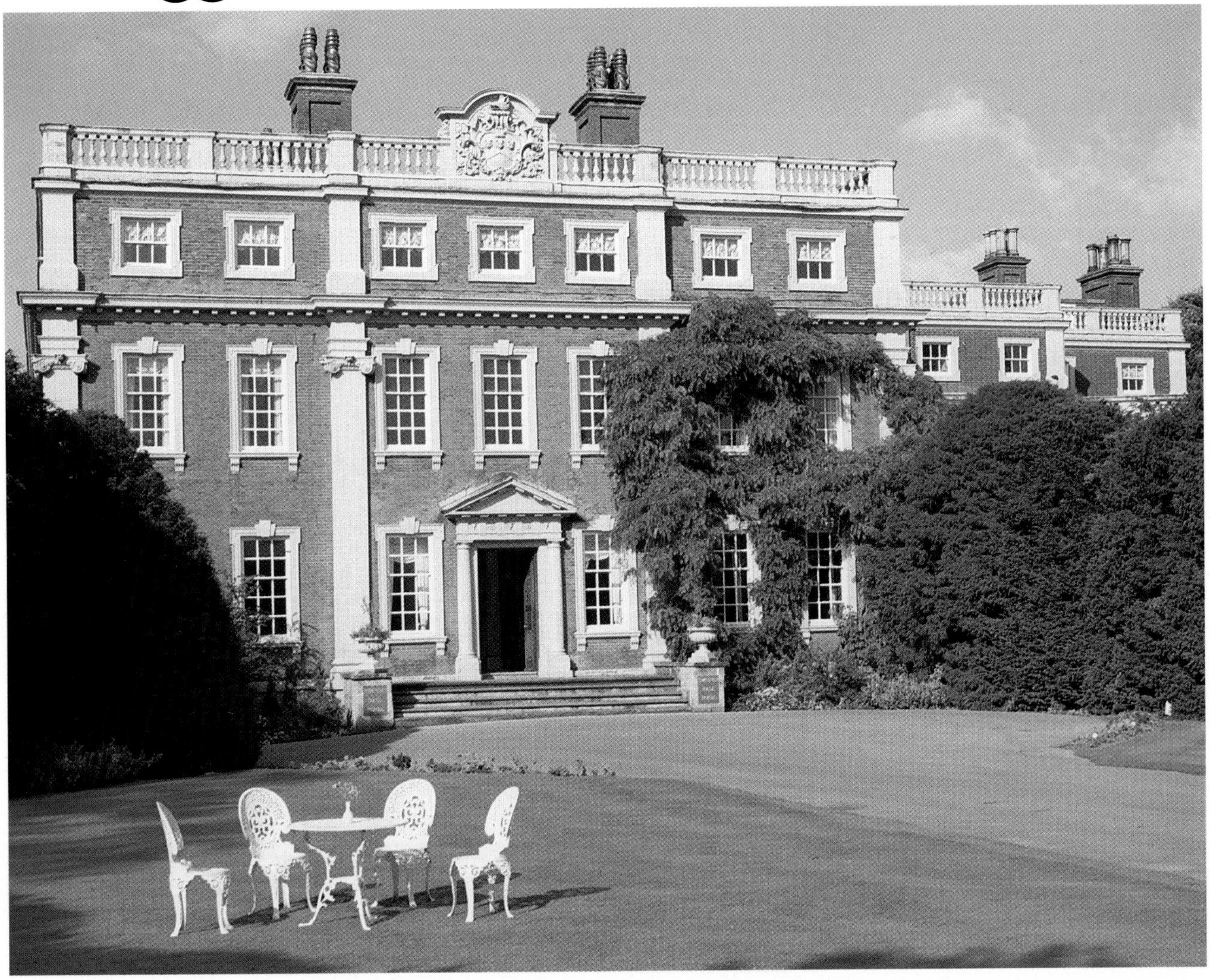

# SWINFEN HALL

SWINFEN, NR LICHFIELD, STAFFORDSHIRE WS14 9RS
TEL: 01543 481494 FAX: 01543 480341

Swinfen Hall is a luxurious country house hotel built in the mid-18th century under the supervision of local architect Benjamin Wyatt. The money lavished on this dream residence is evident today in Swinfen Hall's balustraded Minstrels' Gallery and superb stucco ceilings crafted by Italian artisans. Elsewhere, fine architectural touches include the splendid carved-wood lobby ceiling, plus magnificent panelling and tiled fireplaces perfect in every detail. Owned by Helen and Victor Wiser, Swinfen is expertly managed by Norman Wiser, who ensures a quality of service and hospitality befitting such a setting. In the restaurant and private dining room, guests can select from fresh fish, meat and local game (the breakfast menu is famed for its choice and value). A sun-filled banqueting hall with oak-panelled walls and magnificent Grinling Gibbons carvings is available for receptions and dinner dances. Bedrooms, decorated in pastel shades, are light, airy and comfortable, with period furnishings and modern conveniences including hospitality trays and hairdryers. Birmingham, and the International Airport are only 20 minutes away, and places to visit include Tamworth Castle and Lichfield Cathedral. **Directions:** Exit M42 at junctions 9 or 10. Swinfen Hall is set back from the A38, 2 miles south of Lichfield. Price guide: Single £80–£95; double/twin £95–£110; suite £120–£140.

# THE ARUNDELL ARMS


**LIFTON, DEVON PL16 0AA**
**TEL: 01566 784666 FAX: 01566 784494**


In a lovely valley close to the uplands of Dartmoor, the Arundell Arms is a former coaching inn which dates back to Saxon times. Its beautiful flagstone floors, cosy fires, paintings and antiques combine to create a haven of warmth and comfort in an atmosphere of old world charm. One of England's best-known sporting hotels for more than half a century, it boasts 20 miles of its own fishing on the Tamar and five of its tributaries. Guests also enjoy a host of other country activities, including hill walking and shooting. The hotel takes great pride in its elegant 3 AA Rosette restaurant, presided over by Master Chef Philip Burgess, formerly of L'Ecu de France in London. His gourmet cuisine, which includes traditional English and French dishes, has won the restaurant an international reputation. A splendid base from which to enjoy the wonderful surfing beaches nearby, the Arundell Arms is also well placed for visits to Tintagel and the historic houses and gardens of Devon and Cornwall. Boats can be hired in the fishing villages of Boscastle and Port Isaac. Only 45 minutes' from Exeter and Plymouth, it is also ideal for the business executive, reached by fast roads from all directions. A spacious conference suite is available. **Directions:** Lifton is approximately 1/4 mile off A30 2 miles east of Launceston and the Cornish Border. Price guide: Single £65-£70; double/twin £97-£110.

23 rms MasterCard VISA AMERICAN EXPRESS M 100

For hotel location, see maps on pages 490-496

# THE WOOLTON REDBOURNE HOTEL

**ACREFIELD ROAD, WOOLTON, LIVERPOOL, MERSEYSIDE L25 5JN**
**TEL: 0151 421 1500/428 2152 FAX: 0151 421 1501**

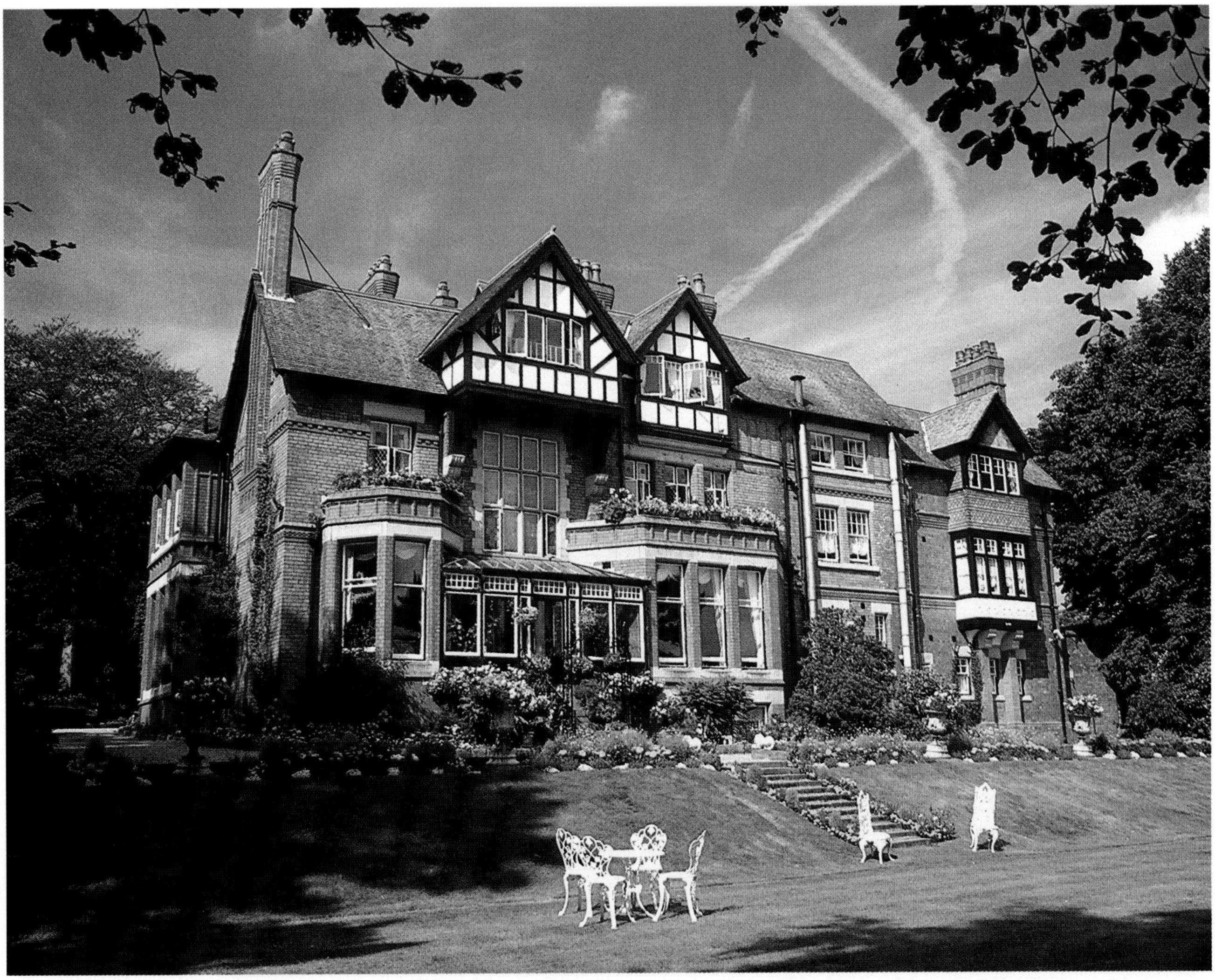

The Woolton Redbourne Hotel is a fine Grade II listed building which was built in the grand country house style by the great Victorian industrialist, Sir Henry Tate. Set amidst beautiful landscaped gardens and lawns, the hotel is a refuge of peace and tranquillity. Completely refurbished to original Victorian splendour by the Collins family, the Woolton Redbourne has quickly established itself as one of the region's foremost hotels. Whether for business or pleasure the hotel succeeds in creating a very homely atmosphere with highly personal and friendly service. The hotel is filled with intriguing Victorian antiques and each bedroom is delightfully decorated and furnished in period style. For those seeking the ultimate in comfort, the hotels seven suites are highly recommended. In the dining room an imaginative select table d'hôte is served. A full wine list is offered. The hotel caters for small business meetings and is just five miles from the city centre. **Directions:** At the end of the M62, junction 4, turn left onto the A5058. At third traffic lights turn left onto Woolton Road. The hotel is two miles on the left. Price guide: Single £60–£90; double/twin £86–£140; suite £150.

For hotel location, see maps on pages 490-496

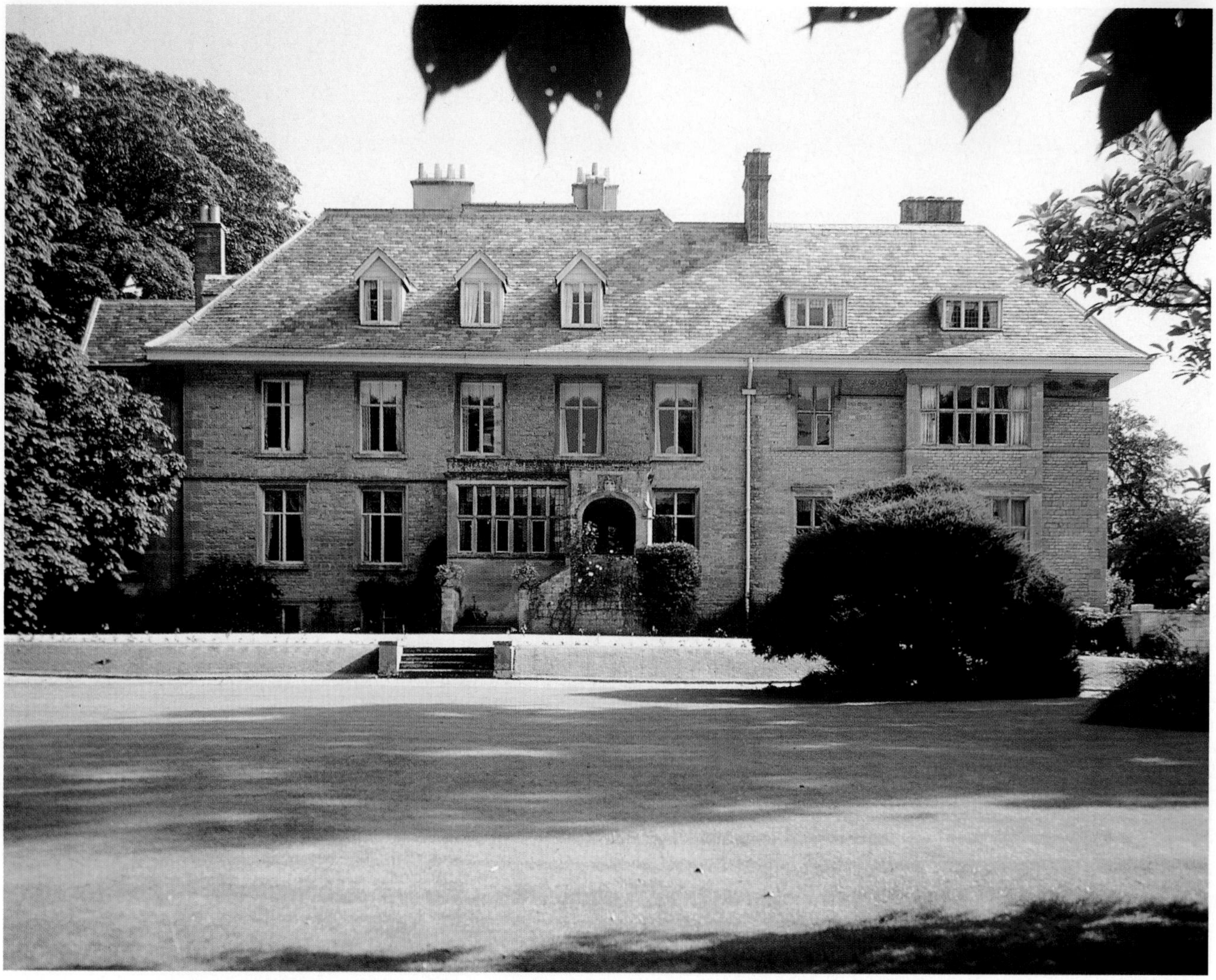

# LOWER SLAUGHTER MANOR

**LOWER SLAUGHTER, NR STOW-ON-THE-WOLD, GLOUCESTERSHIRE GL54 2HP**
**TEL: 01451 820456 FAX: 01451 822150**

One of the best kept secrets in the Cotswolds. This magnificent 17th century manor house has been transformed into one of the highest rated country house hotels in England. Egon Ronay rates it as one of the 10 best restaurants outside London with 2 stars. Flowers abound in all the elegant public rooms where fine antiques, works of art and blazing log fires in the winter add to the warm atmosphere. Exceptionally spacious bedrooms look out over stunning gardens. 500 wines from around the world and in particular California ensure Alan Dann's cuisine is accompanied with style. The emphasis is on warmth, exquisite food, comfort and service. There is an indoor heated swimming pool, all-weather tennis court, croquet lawn and putting green. The Manor is ideally located as a base from which to tour the Cotswolds and as an excellent venue for discreet meetings in the private Conference Suite. **Directions:** From the A429, follow the signs to The Slaughters; the Manor is on the right entering the village of Lower Slaughter. Price guide: Single £120–£300; double/twin £135–£300; suites £275–£350. All prices include English Breakfast and VAT. Room rates including Dinner from the à la carte menu are available.

For hotel location, see maps on pages 490-496

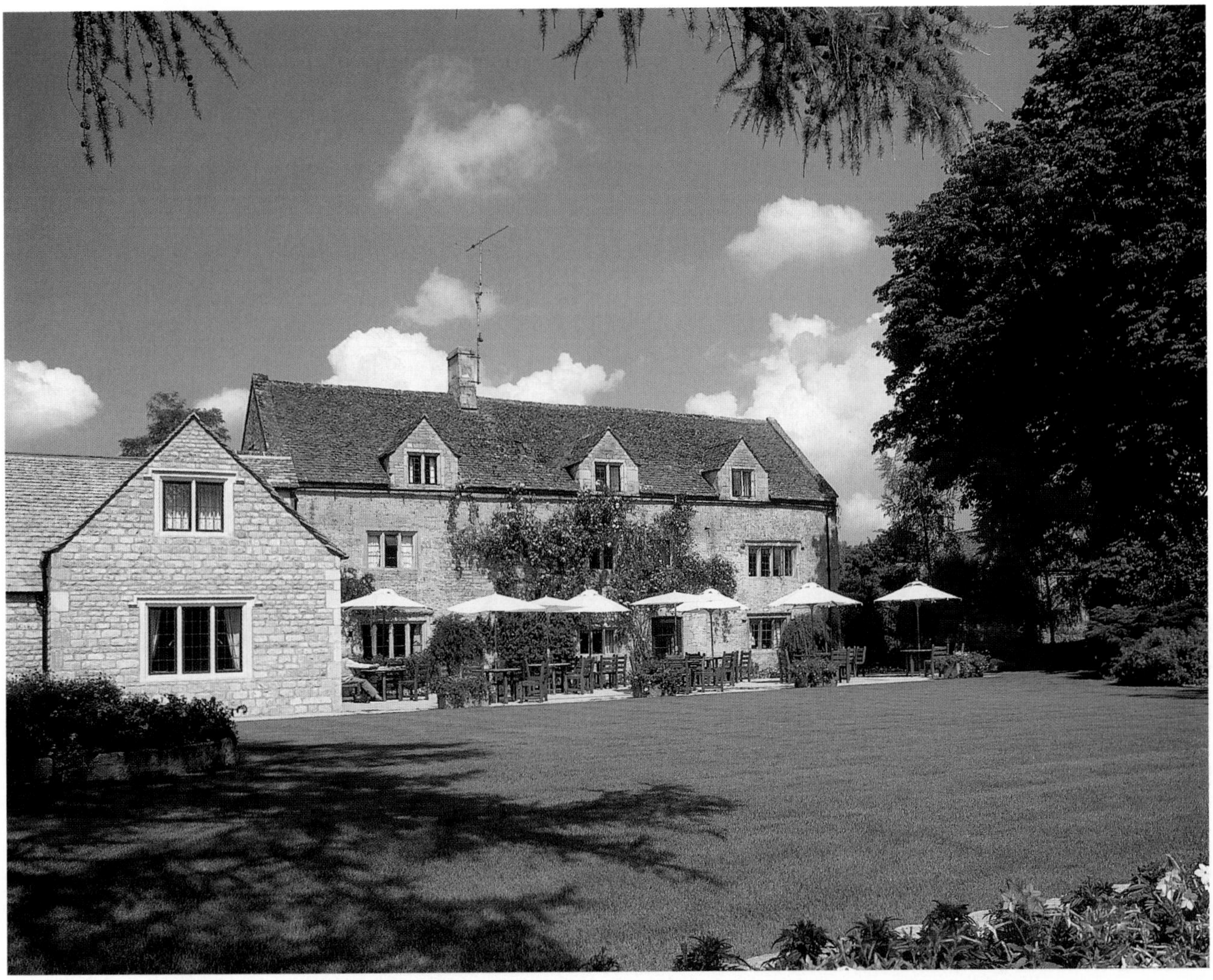

# WASHBOURNE COURT HOTEL

**LOWER SLAUGHTER, GLOUCESTERSHIRE GL54 2HS**
**TEL: 01451 822143 FAX: 01451 821045**

Now under the private ownership of Roy and Daphne Vaughan, together with Buckland Manor and Lower Slaughter Manor, the Washbourne Court Hotel is in the heart of the tranquil and beautiful Cotswold village of Lower Slaughter on the banks of the River Eye. The four acres of private gardens have been lovingly re-landscaped with lawns and many delightful features. With just twenty eight bedrooms, it has parts dating back to the 17th century. The recent additions to the hotel are a spacious new dining room and a further six guest rooms with comfortable and elegant furnishings blend in perfectly with the original building. Always full of freshly picked flowers and planted bowls, the hotel has the feel of a private house with the many personal touches. The modern English cuisine offers an abundance of fresh local produce, concentrating on good textures and intense flavours combined with outstanding presentation. Head Chef Martin White, who was previously Sous Chef at Buckland Manor, now oversees the running of the kitchen. Drinks, light lunches and traditional afternoon tea are also served on the garden terrace during Summer months. **Directions:** The hotel is situated 1/2 a mile from the main A429 Fosseway between Stow-on-the-Wold and Bourton-on-the-Water (signed To the Slaughters). Price guide (including dinner): Single from £155; double/twin £210–£235; suite £270.

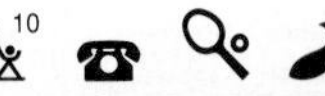

For hotel location, see maps on pages 490-496

# DINHAM HALL

**LUDLOW, SHROPSHIRE SY8 1EJ**
**TEL: 01584 876464 FAX: 01584 876019**

Built in 1792 Dinham Hall is situated in the historic town of Ludlow. It lies only 40 metres from the Castle which, having played an important part in England's history, today hosts the Shakespearian productions which form the major part of the annual Ludlow Festival. Dinham's enviable location provides its guests with the combination of ready access to the town and picturesque views over the open Shropshire countryside. There is a magnificent fireplace in the sitting room, with log fires in the winter. In the restaurant flowers help to provide a subtle atmosphere in which to enjoy prize-winning cuisine while the Merchant Suite, with its 14th century timbers, is an ideal setting for private dinners and meetings. During the summer afternoon teas are served on the terrace overlooking the walled garden. The décor of the bedrooms is a harmony of modern facilities and period design, a number of rooms having four-poster beds. The restaurant and many bedrooms command views over the gardens and Teme Valley to wooded hills. Guests may also enjoy a visit to Ludlow races or spend a few hours browsing in the town's antique shops. South Shropshire is one of the most beautiful parts of the country with Ludlow itself being one of the finest market towns. **Directions:** In the centre of Ludlow overlooking the castle. Price guide: Single £65–£75; double/twin £95–£125.

14 rms MasterCard VISA AMERICAN EXPRESS M 20

For hotel location, see maps on pages 490-496

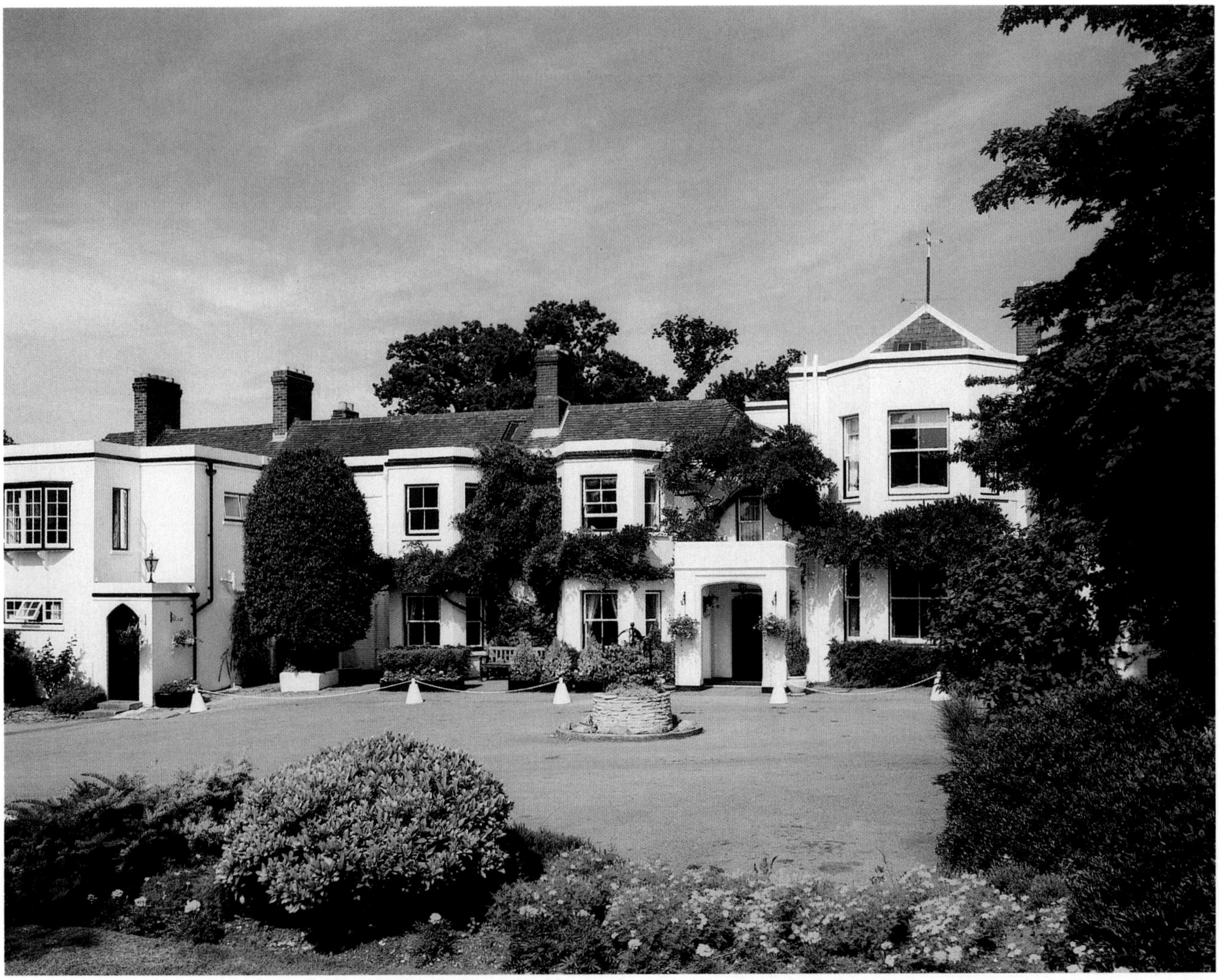

# PASSFORD HOUSE HOTEL

**MOUNT PLEASANT LANE, LYMINGTON, HAMPSHIRE SO41 8LS**

**TEL: 01590 682398 FAX: 01590 683494**

Set in nine acres of picturesque gardens and rolling parkland, the Passford House Hotel lies midway between the charming New Forest village of Sway and the Georgian splendour of Lymington. Once the home of Lord Arthur Cecil, it is steeped in history and the traditions of leisurely country life. Pleasantly decorated bedrooms include a number of de luxe rooms, while comfort is the keynote in the four public lounges. The hotel prides itself on the standard and variety of cuisine served in its delightful restaurant and the extensive menu aims to give pleasure to the most discerning of palates. Meals are complemented by a speciality wine list. The hotel boasts a superb leisure centre, catering for all ages and activities. In addition to two heated swimming pools, there is a multi-gym, sauna, solarium, pool table, croquet lawn, petanque and tennis court. Just a short drive away are Beaulieu, the cathedral cities of Winchester and Salisbury and ferry ports to the Isle of Wight and France. The New Forest area has five golf courses and, for those interested in riding, there are many stables and trekking centres. Milford-on-Sea, four miles away, is the nearest beach. **Directions:** At Lymington leave the A337 at the Tollhouse Inn, then take the first turning right and the hotel is on the right. Price guide: £75: double/twin £110–£135.

For hotel location, see maps on pages 490-496

# STANWELL HOUSE

HIGH STREET, LYMINGTON, HAMPSHIRE SO41 9AA
TEL: 01590 677123 FAX: 01590 677756

The Stanwell House Hotel is a fine example of Georgian architecture and great care has been taken in its restoration. Set on Lymington's fine wide High Street, which still hosts a Saturday market, it combines luxury with style, informal comfort and unobtrusive personal service. Along with 31 bedrooms, including 3 beautifully refurbished suites and 10 executive rooms, there is an intimate bar and bistro and a delightful conservatory leading onto a flower filled patio and charming walled garden. The stylish restaurant offers a cosmopolitan blend of bistro style along with a simpler table d'hôte menu accompanied by the finest wines from an incomparable list. Adjacent to the hotel, in a quiet courtyard off the street, is Elgars Cottage. This pretty period cottage is furnished to a very high standard and offers a full range of amenities. Guests are invited to use the services of the hotel. Lymington is a charming Regency town, close to the New Forest and the magnificent Solent with all its yachting facilities. There are opportunities for walking, riding and golf and river or sea fishing. Crossings by car ferry from Lymington to Yarmouth bring the Isle of Wight within a 30 minute journey. Directions: From the M27 Junction 1 through Lyndhurst and Brockenhurst. Price guide: Single £50–£75; double/twin £85–£110; suites £120–£140; Stanwell Cottage £500 per week for two people.

For hotel location, see maps on pages 490-496

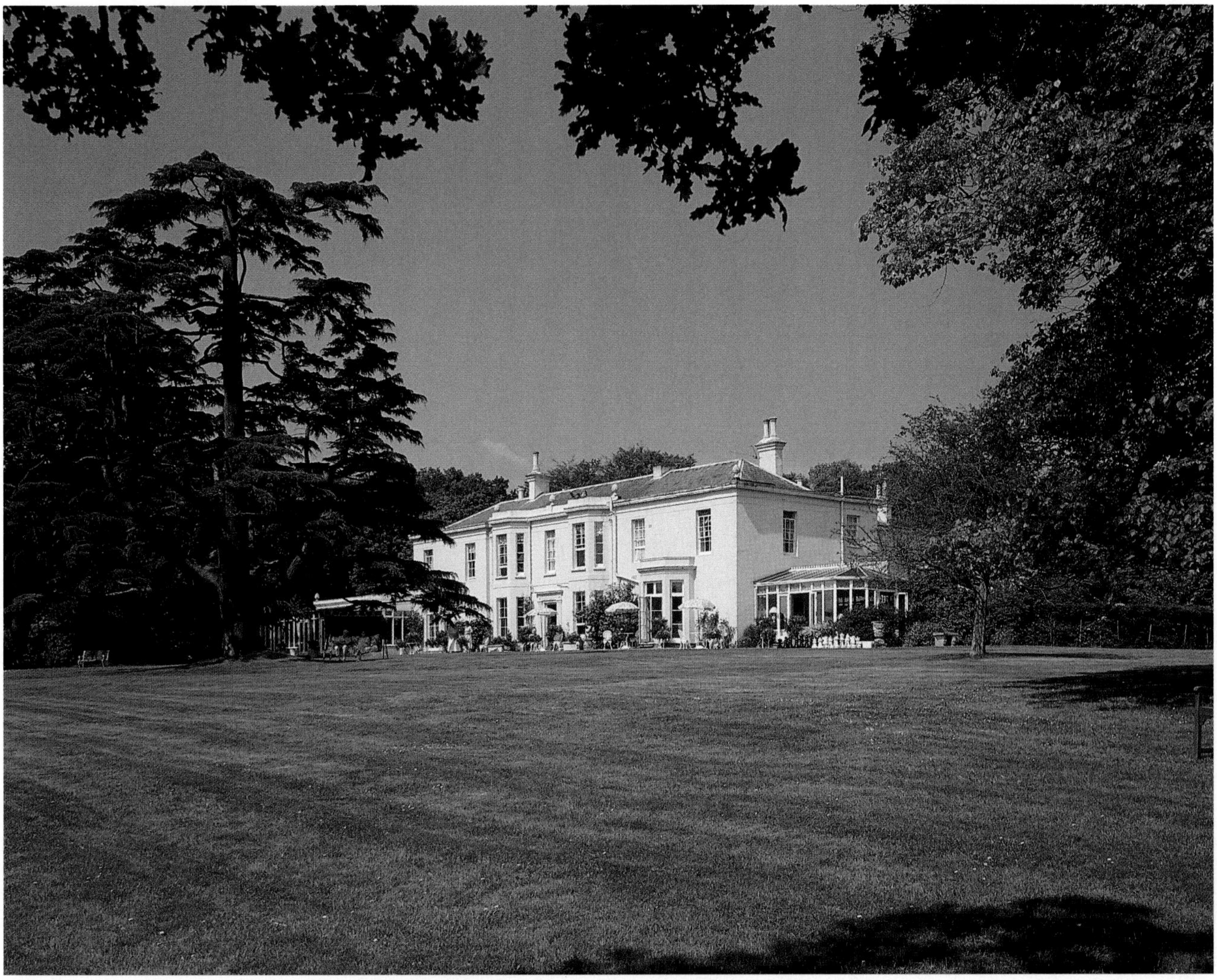

# Parkhill Hotel

**BEAULIEU ROAD, LYNDHURST, NEW FOREST, HAMPSHIRE SO43 7FZ**

**TEL: 01703 282944 FAX: 01703 283268**

Reached by a winding drive through glorious parkland from the scenic route between Lyndhurst and Beaulieu, Parkhill, situated in an elevated position with superb views across open forest and heathland, is perfect for a restful break or holiday and makes the ideal venue for special business meetings and small conferences, offering a charming New Forest remoteness coupled with an excellence of standards and service. Dining at Parkhill is very much an integral part of your overall pleasure. The award winning restaurant offers a most tranquil setting with fine views across the lawns, where deer can frequently be seen grazing. Cuisine is a delicious blend of modern and classical English cooking, where local fresh produce is used to create appetising menus, balanced by a carefully chosen and well-stocked cellar. Parkhill is also an ideal base for touring not only the delightful surrounding areas, but also the many places of interest which are all within easy driving distance, including Exbury Gardens, home to one of the world's finest collections of rhododendrons and azaleas, Broadlands, the old home of Lord Mountbatten, the *Mary Rose* in Portsmouth Dockyard, and the graceful cathedral cities of Salisbury and Winchester. **Directions:** From Lyndhurst take the B3056 toward Beaulieu; Parkhill is about 1 mile from Lyndhurst on your right. Price guide: Single £64.50–£71; double £99–£132; suite £140–£152.

For hotel location, see maps on pages 490-496

# CLIVEDEN

**TAPLOW, BERKSHIRE SL6 0JF**
**TEL: 01628 668561 FAX: 01628 661837**

Cliveden, Britain's only 5 Red AA star hotel that is also a stately home, is set in 376 acres of gardens and parkland, overlooking the Thames. As the former home of Frederick, Prince of Wales, three Dukes and the Astor family, Cliveden has been at the centre of Britain's social and political life for over 300 years. It is exquisitely furnished in a classically English style, with a multitude of oil paintings, antiques and *objets d'art.* The spacious guest rooms and suites are appointed to the most luxurious standards. One of the greatest pleasures of eating at Cliveden is in the choice of dining rooms and the scope of the menus. The French Dining Room, with its original Madame de Pompadour rococo decoration, is the finest 18th-century *boiserie* outside France. Alternatively, relish the Michelin-starred cuisine of chef Ron Maxfield in Waldo's Restaurant. The Pavilion offers a full range of health and fitness facilities and beauty therapies. Guests can ride Cliveden's horses over the estate or enjoy a leisurely river cruise on an Edwardian launch. Comprehensively equipped, the two secure private boardrooms provide self-contained business meeting facilities. Exclusive use of the hotel can be arranged. Cliveden's style may also be enjoyed at the Cliveden Town House, London and the Royal Crescent, Bath. **Directions:** Situated on B476, 2 miles north of Taplow. Price guide: Single £220; double/twin £245; suites from £398.

For hotel location, see maps on pages 490-496

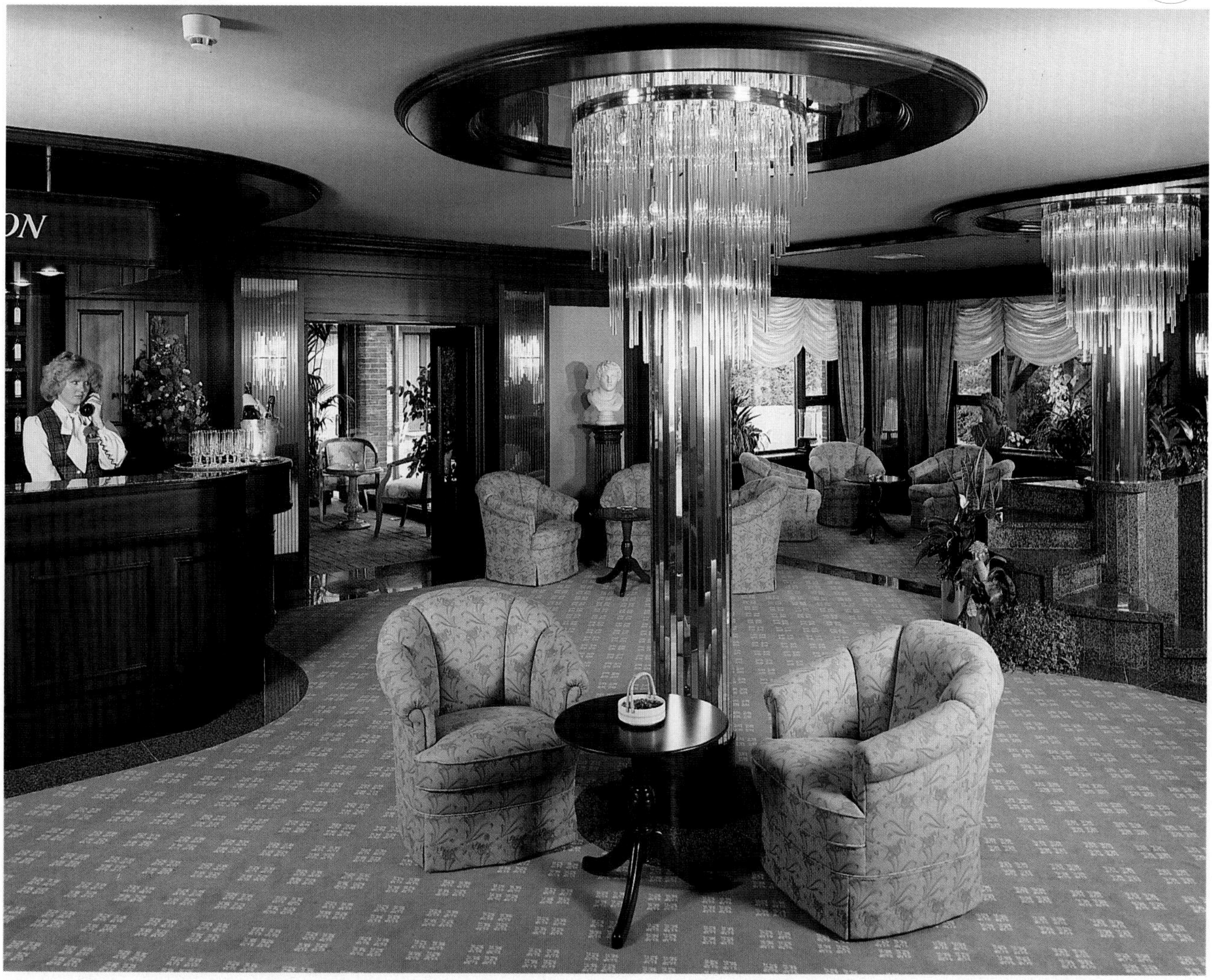

# FREDRICK'S HOTEL & RESTAURANT

**SHOPPENHANGERS ROAD, MAIDENHEAD, BERKSHIRE SL6 2PZ**
**TEL: 01628 635934 FAX: 01628 771054**

'Putting people first' is the guiding philosophy behind the running of this sumptuously equipped hotel and, indeed, is indicative of the uncompromising service guests can expect to receive. Set in two acres of grounds, Fredrick's overlooks the fairways and greens of Maidenhead Golf Club beyond. The immaculate reception rooms are distinctively styled to create something out of the ordinary. Minute attention to detail is evident in the 37 bedrooms, all immaculate with gleaming, marble-tiled bathrooms, while the suites have their own patio garden or balcony. A quiet drink can be enjoyed in the light, airy Wintergarden lounge before entering the air-conditioned restaurant. Amid the elegant décor of crystal chandeliers and crisp white linen, fine gourmet cuisine is served which has received recognition from leading guides for many years. Particularly suited to conferences, four private function rooms with full secretarial facilities are available. Helicopter landing can be arranged. Easily accessible from Windsor, Henley, Ascot, Heathrow and London. Closed 24 Dec to 3 Jan. **Directions:** Leave M4 at exit 8/9, take A404(M) and leave at first turning signed Cox Green/White Waltham. Turn into Shoppenhangers Road; Fredrick's is on the right. Price guide: Single £158–£178; double/twin £188–£208; suite £300.

For hotel location, see maps on pages 490-496

# CHILSTON PARK

## SANDWAY, LENHAM, NR MAIDSTONE, KENT ME17 2BE
## TEL: 01622 859803 FAX: 01622 858588

This magnificent Grade I listed mansion, one of England's most richly decorated hotels, was built in the 13th century and remodelled in the 18th century. Now sensitively refurbished, the hotel's ambience is enhanced by the lighting at dusk each day of over 200 candles. The drawing room and reading room offer guests an opportunity to relax and to admire the outstanding collection of antiques. The entire hotel is a treasure trove full of many interesting *objets d'art*. The opulently furnished bedrooms are fitted to a high standard and many have four-poster beds. Good, fresh English cooking is offered in each of Chilston's five dining rooms, where outstanding menus are supported by an excellent wine list. In keeping with the traditions of a country house, a wide variety of sporting activities is available, golf and riding nearby, fishing in the natural spring lake and punting. An Arcadian Hotel. **Directions:** Take junction 8 off the M20, then A20 to Lenham Station. Turn left into Boughton Road. Go over the crossroads and M20; Chilston Park is on the left. Price guide: Single £98–£170; double/twin £115–£185; suite £170–£210.

For hotel location, see maps on pages 490-496

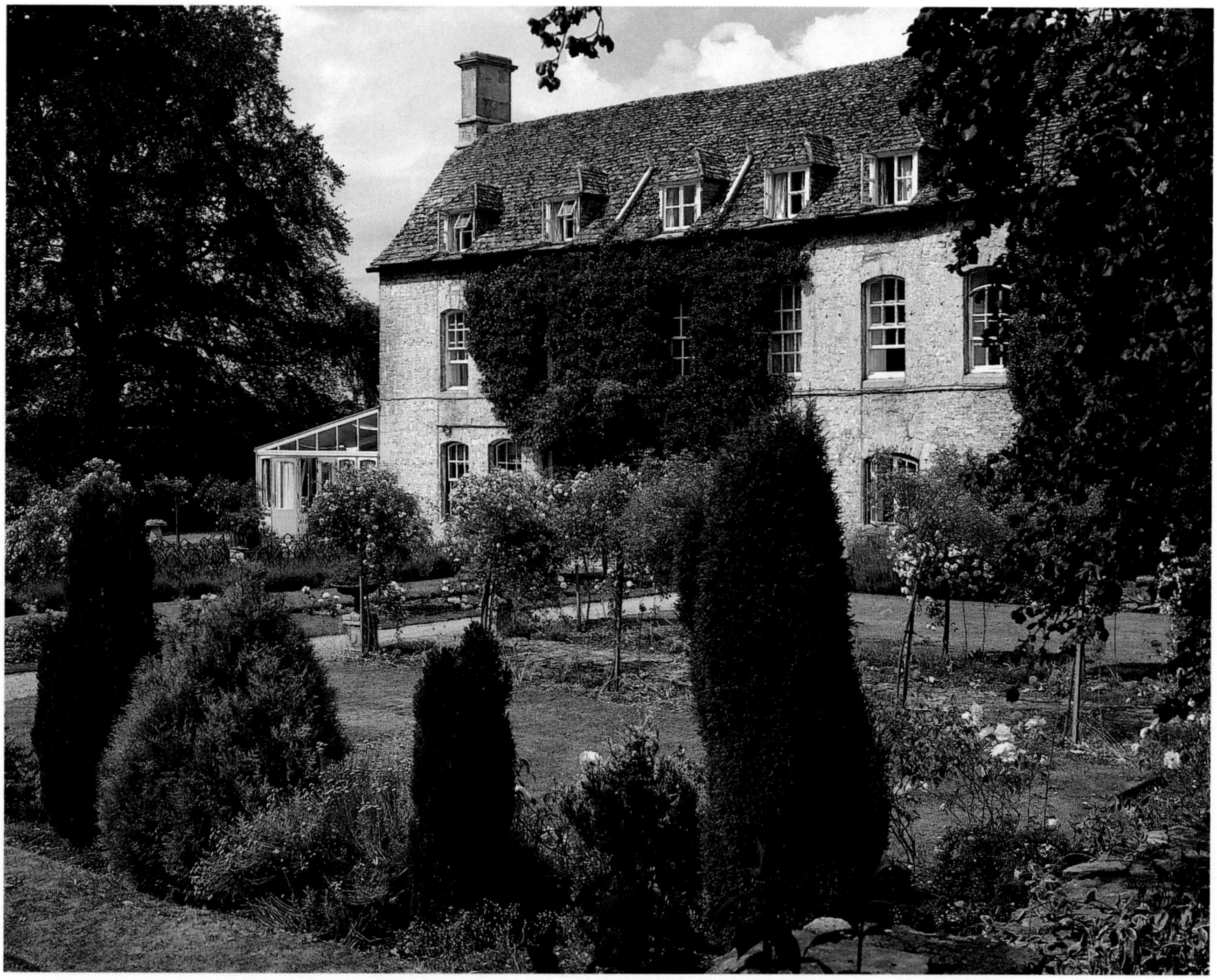

# CRUDWELL COURT HOTEL

**CRUDWELL, NR MALMESBURY, WILTSHIRE SN16 9EP**

**TEL: 01666 577194 FAX: 01666 577853 E-MAIL: Crudwellcrt@compuserve.com**

Crudwell Court is a 17th-century rectory, set in three acres of Cotswold walled gardens. The pretty, well-established grounds have lily ponds and a garden gate leading through to the neighbouring Saxon church of All Saints. Completely refurbished in recent years, the old rectory has been decorated with bright, cheery colours. Sunshine yellow in the sitting room, warm apricot in the drawing room and shades of buttercream and blue in the bedrooms lend a fresh feel to this hotel. Visitors enter through a flagstoned hall to discover rooms with comfortable seating and plenty of books to read. In the panelled dining room guests will find a weekly changing menu, which is best described as modern Anglo-French. Cooked to order, the meals are a feast for the eye as well as the palate. The restaurant has recently been extended by proprietor Nick Bristow into a new conservatory, which also takes private functions. Malmesbury has a magnificent Norman abbey church and a curious market cross. Nearby are the towns of Tetbury and Cirencester, the picturesque villages of Castle Combe and Lacock and numerous stately homes. **Directions:** Crudwell Court is on the A429. Travelling towards Cirencester, when you reach the village of Crudwell turn right (signposted Oaksey) opposite the Plough Inn, and the hotel is on the left. Price guide: Single £50; double/twin £90.

For hotel location, see maps on pages 490-496

# THE OLD BELL

**ABBEY ROW, MALMESBURY, WILTSHIRE SN16 0AG**
**TEL: 01666 822344 FAX: 01666 825145 E-MAIL: Woolley@cityscape.com.uk**

The Old Bell was established by the Abbot of Malmesbury during the reign of King John as a place to refresh guests who came to consult the Abbey's library. Situated at the edge of the Cotswolds, this Grade I listed building may well be England's most ancient hotel. Inside, the Great Hall boasts a medieval stone fireplace, while each bedroom is decorated and furnished with an individual style and character. In the main house a classic and imaginative menu exemplifies the best in English cooking, with meals ranging from four-course dinners complemented by fine wines in the Edwardian dining room, to informal snacks on the terrace. The Coach House features bedrooms styled on an oriental theme and many of these are suitable for families as interconnecting pairs of suites. Families are particularly welcomed at The Old Bell; there is no charge for children sharing parents' rooms and children's menus are available. The 'Den' is equipped with a multitude of toys and open every day. Malmesbury is only 30 minutes from Bath and is close to a number of other beautiful villages such as Castle Combe, Bourton-on-the-Water and Lacock. Other places of interest include the mysterious stone circle at Avebury and the Westonbirt Arboretum. **Directions:** Near the market cross in the centre of Malmesbury. Price guide: Single £70; double/twin £85–£135; suites £145–£160.

31 rms MasterCard VISA AMERICAN EXPRESS M 40

For hotel location, see maps on pages 490-496

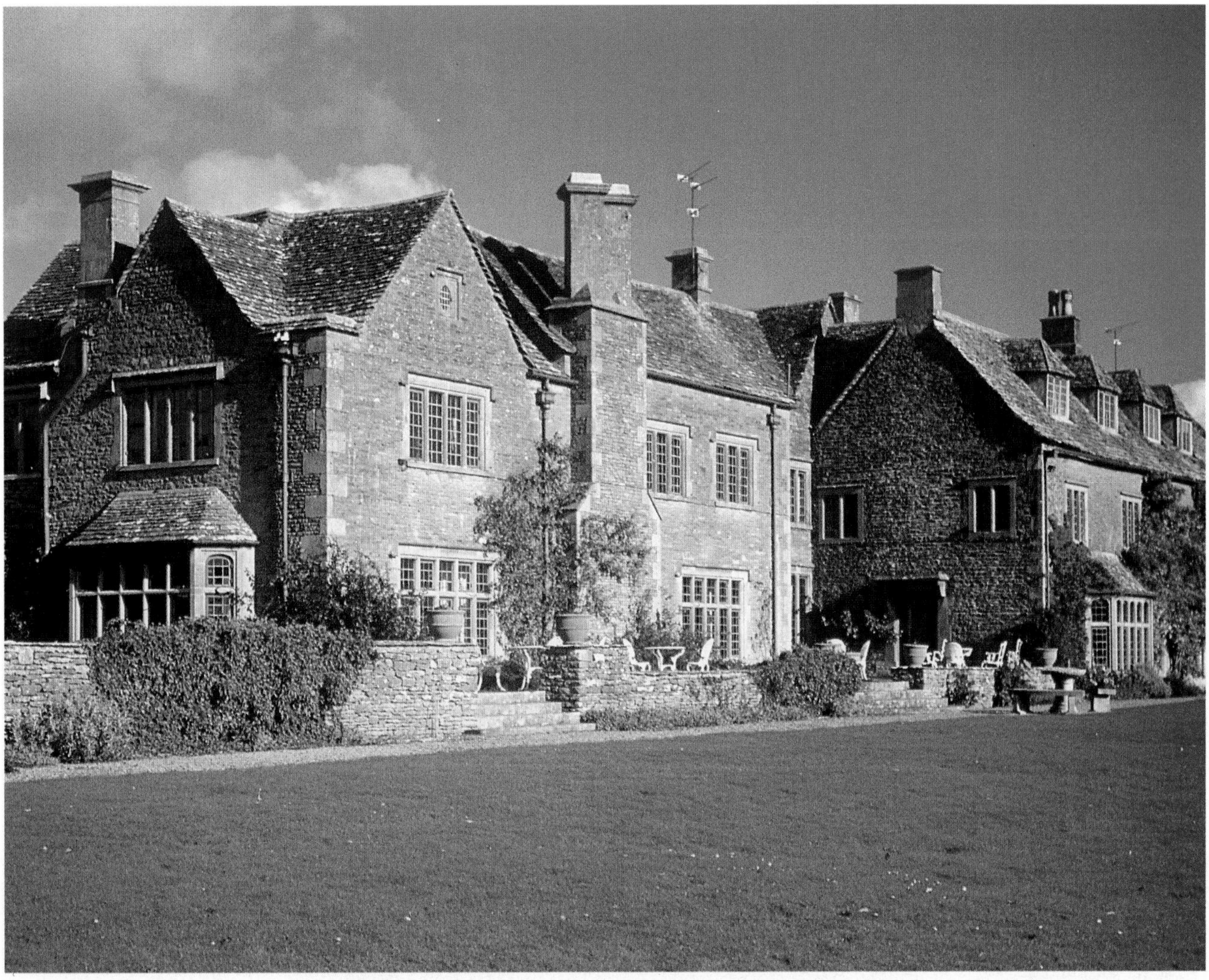

# WHATLEY MANOR

NR EASTON GREY, MALMESBURY, WILTSHIRE SN16 0RB
TEL: 01666 822888 FAX: 01666 826120

This Grade II listed manor, set around a central courtyard, stands in 12 acres of grounds running down to a peaceful stretch of the River Avon. Originally built in the 17th century, Whatley Manor was refurbished by a wealthy sportsman in the 1920s and many of the present buildings date from that period. While the hotel's interior is furnished to a high standard, an emphasis has always been placed on maintaining a relaxed, informal atmosphere, enhanced by pine and oak panelling, log fires and the effect of warm colours in the lounge and drawing room. The dining room similarly combines elegance with intimacy and it overlooks the gardens. Ten of the bedrooms are in the 'Courthouse'. Snooker and table-tennis facilities are provided in the original saddle rooms and there are also a sauna, a solarium and a Jacuzzi. Close for gardening enthusiasts is Hodges Barn at Shipton Moyne. With the Cotswolds, the cities of Bath and Bristol, Tetbury, Cirencester, Westonbirt Arboretum, Longleat, Stourhead Gardens and many places of historic interest nearby, Stays of 2 nights or longer are at a reduced tariff. **Directions:** The hotel is on the B4040 three miles west of Malmesbury. Price guide: Single £74–£84; double/twin £88–£120.

29 rms MasterCard VISA AMERICAN EXPRESS M 30

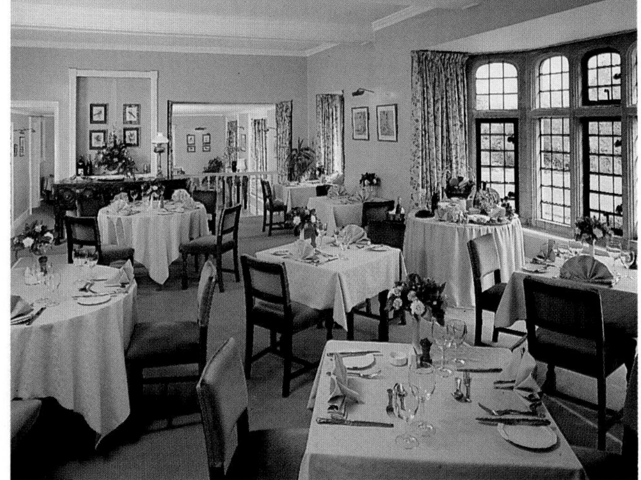

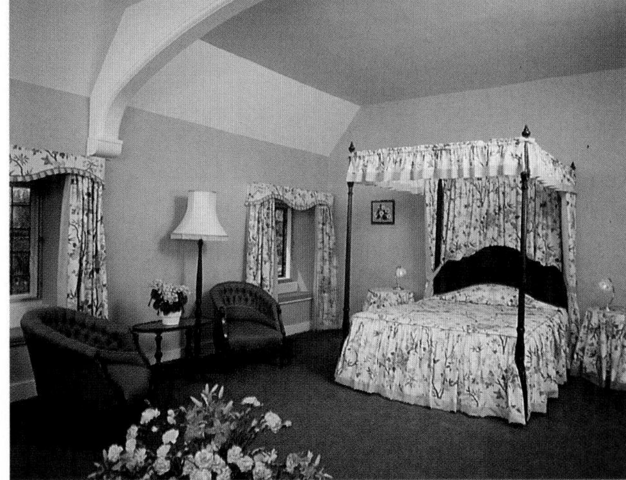

For hotel location, see maps on pages 490-496

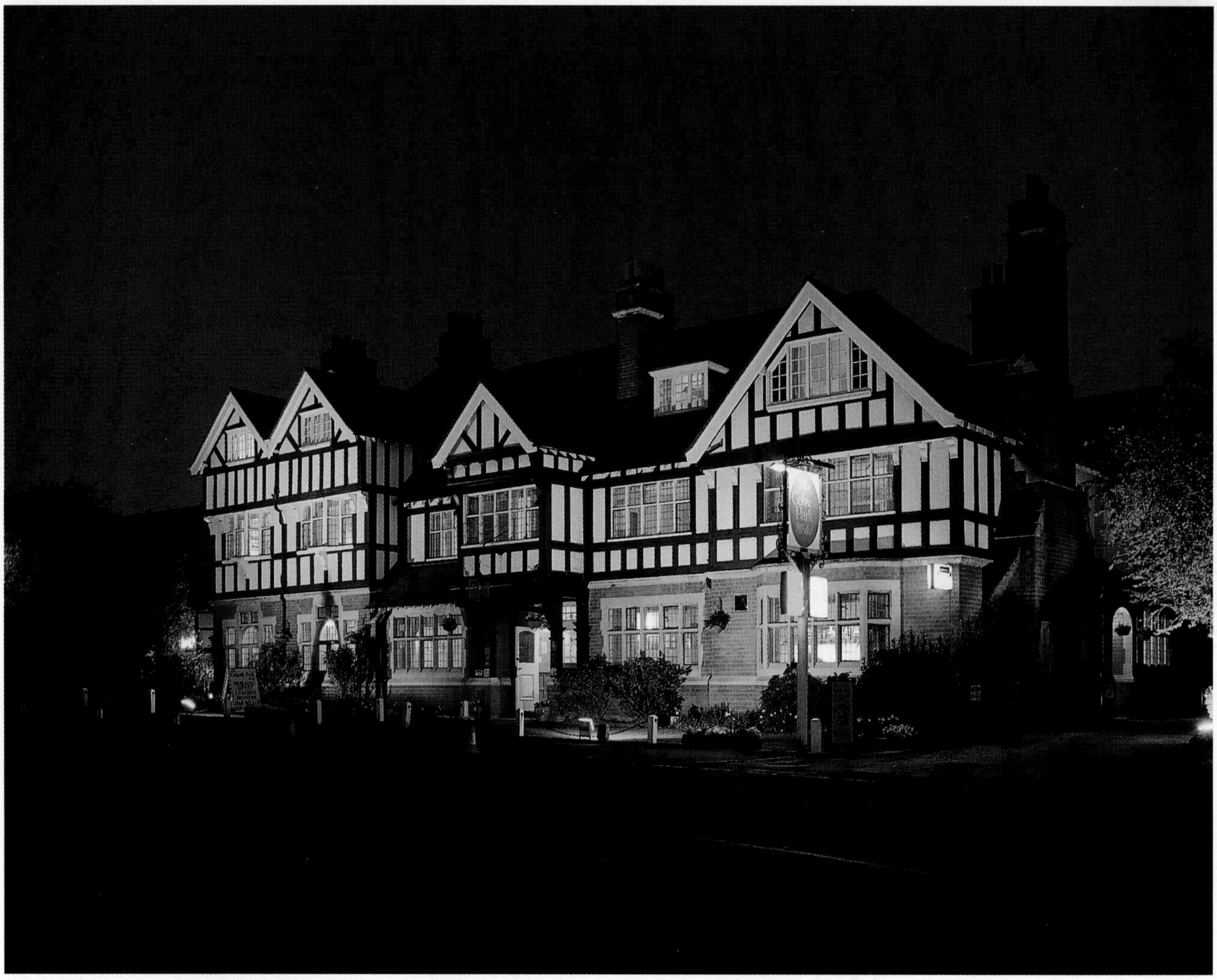

# THE COLWALL PARK HOTEL


**COLWALL, NEAR MALVERN, WORCESTERSHIRE WR13 6QG**

**TEL: 01684 540206 FAX: 01684 540847**


This delightful hotel is in the centre of the village, and set against a background of the Malvern Hills – to which it has direct access from its mature gardens. It also has the privilege of almost a private railway station, with two trains a day (just 2 hours from Paddington). The hotel is thriving under new management who have undertaken a thorough renovation of the hotel without spoiling its character. The bedrooms are pristine and comfortable and suites have been introduced – including one for families with an amusing children's bedroom. A bottle of the local Malvern water is always at hand. Residents enjoy the library (which can accomodate private dinners for 8 people), the first floor 'video' snug and the inviting panelled lounge bar where light meals are ordered from attentive waiters. The Edwardian Restaurant has table settings of delicate china and fine crystal. A pianist plays twice weekly. The kitchen is in the hands of a creative chef, offering table d'hôte and à la carte menus. Interesting international wines are listed. The ballroom, ideal for corporate events, leads onto the garden where wedding groups pose by the beautiful plane tree. Special breaks feature Cheltenham Races and the Motor Show. Hotel sports are boules and croquet. **Directions:** M5/J7, A442 then A449. Colwall village is on B4218 between Malvern and Ledbury. Price guide: Single £59.50–£69.50; double/twin £89.50–£105; suite £135 inc. champagne & flowers.

For hotel location, see maps on pages 490-496

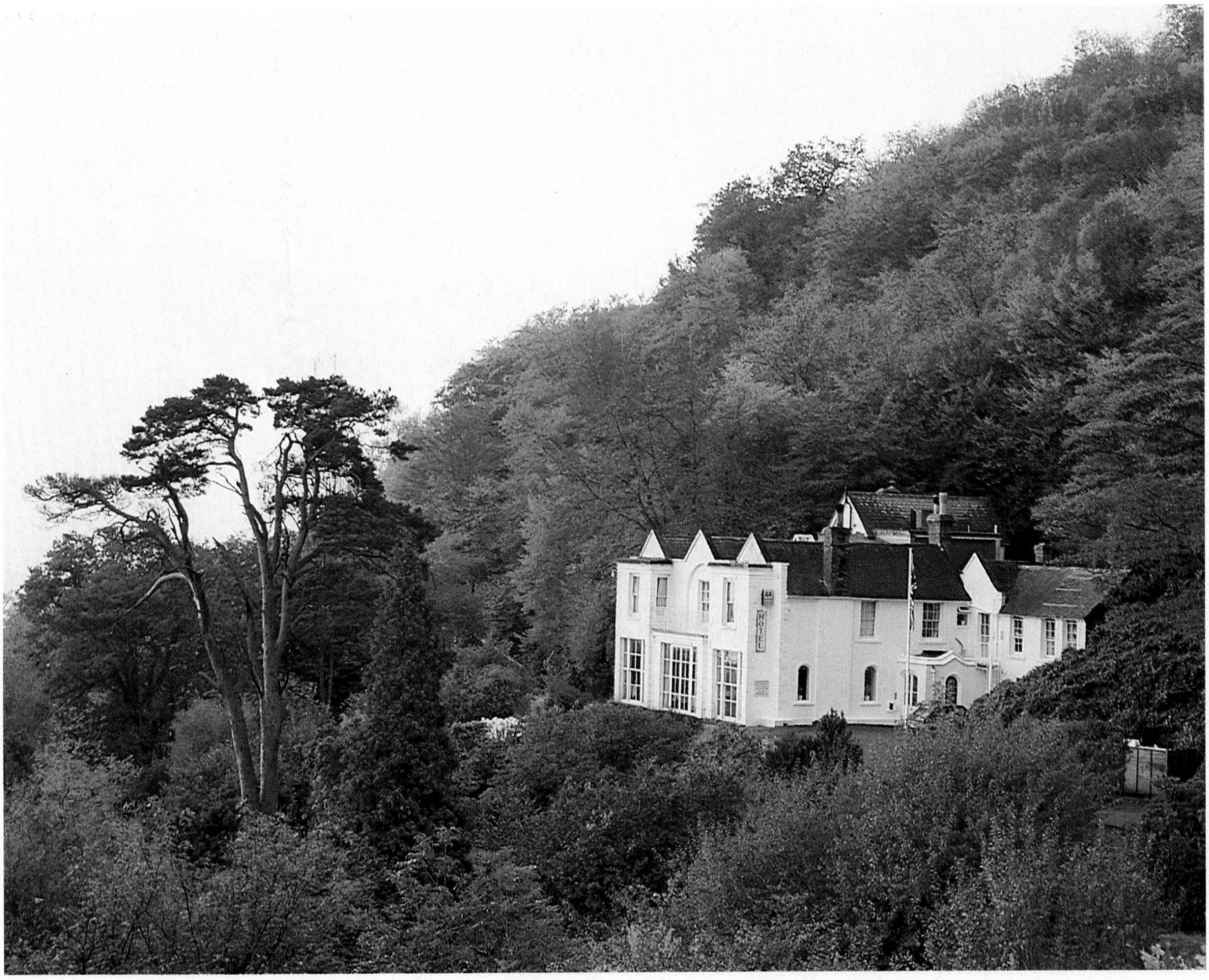

# THE COTTAGE IN THE WOOD

**HOLYWELL ROAD, MALVERN WELLS, WORCESTERSHIRE WR14 4LG**

**TEL: 01684 575859 FAX: 01684 560662**

The Malvern Hills once the home and inspiration for England's most celebrated composer Sir Edward Elgar, are the setting for The Cottage in the Wood. With its spectacular outlook across the Severn Valley plain this unique hotel won acclaim from the Daily Mail for the best view in England. The main house was originally the Dower House to the Blackmore Park estate and accommodation is offered here and in Beech Cottage, an old scrumpy house – and the Coach House. The cottage-style furnishings give an intimate and cosy impression and the smaller Coach House rooms have sun-trap balconies and patios. Owned and run by the Pattin family for over 10 years, the atmosphere is genuinely warm and relaxing. A regularly changing modern English menu is complemented by over 400 bins from the extensive cellar. If this causes any over-indulgence, guests can walk to the tops of the Malvern Hills direct from the hotel grounds. Nearby are the Victorian spa town of Great Malvern, the Three Counties Showground and the Cathedral cities of Worcester, Gloucester and Hereford. **Directions:** Three miles south of Great Malvern on A449, turn into Holywell Road opposite Gulf Rover dealer garage. Hotel is 250 yards on right. Price guide: Single £75; double/twin £89–£145. Bargain short breaks available.

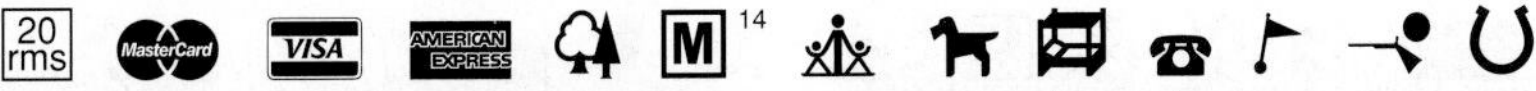

For hotel location, see maps on pages 490-496

In association with MasterCard

# The Stanneylands Hotel

**STANNEYLANDS ROAD, WILMSLOW, CHESHIRE SK9 4EY**
**TEL: 01625 525225 FAX: 01625 537282**

Privately owned and managed by Gordon Beech, Stanneylands is a handsome country house set in several acres of impressive gardens with an unusual collection of trees and shrubs. Some of the bedrooms offer lovely views over the gardens while others overlook the undulating Cheshire countryside. A sense of quiet luxury prevails in the reception rooms, where classical décor and comfortable furnishings create a relaxing ambience. In the restaurant, contemporary English cooking is prepared to a very high standard both in terms of composition and presentation, while live occasional music adds to the atmosphere. For meetings and parties, a private oak-panelled dining room can accommodate up to 60 people, while a larger suite is available for conferences and larger personal celebrations. The Stanneylands Hotel is conveniently located for tours of the rolling Cheshire plain or the more rugged Peak District, as well as the bustling market towns and notable industrial heritage of the area. Special corporate and weekend rates are available. **Directions:** Three miles from Manchester International Airport, Stanneylands is on a minor road which runs from the B5166 at Styal to the B5358 between Wilmslow and Handforth. Bear right on this road to find the hotel just after crossing the River Dean. Price guide: Single £89; double/twin £99–£125; suite £125.

For hotel location, see maps on pages 490-496

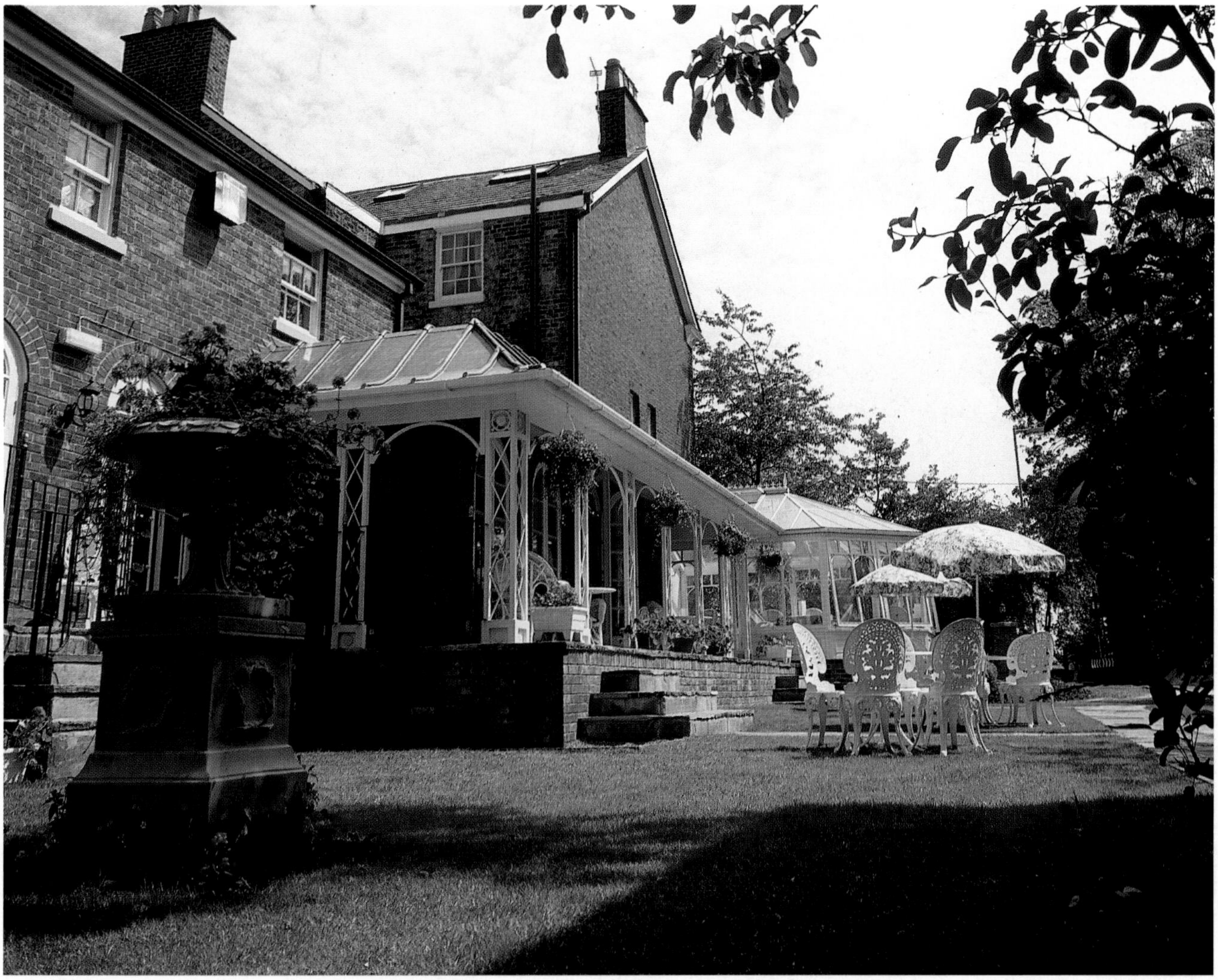

# ETROP GRANGE

**THORLEY LANE, MANCHESTER AIRPORT M90 4EG**
**TEL: 0161 499 0500 FAX: 0161 499 0790**

Hidden away near Manchester Airport lies Etrop Grange, a beautiful country house hotel and restaurant. The original house was built in 1780 and more than 200 years on has been lovingly restored. Today, the hotel enjoys a fine reputation for its accommodation, where the luxury, character and sheer elegance of the Georgian era are evident in every feature. The magnificent restaurant offers a well balanced mix of traditional and modern English cuisine, complemented by an extensive selection of fine wines. Attention to detail ensures personal and individual service. In addition to the obvious advantage of having an airport within walking distance, the location of Etrop Grange is ideal in many other ways. With a comprehensive motorway network and InterCity stations minutes away, it is accessible from all parts of the UK. Entertainment for visitors ranges from the shopping, sport and excellent nightlife offered by the city of Manchester to golf, riding, clay pigeon shooting, water sports and outdoor pursuits in the immediate countryside. Cheshire also boasts an abundance of stately homes, museums and historical attractions. **Directions:** Leave M56 at junction 5 towards Manchester Airport. Follow signs for Terminal 2. Go up the slip Road. At roundabout take first exit, take immediate left and hotel is 400yds on the right. Price guide: Single £78–£140; double/twin £90–£160; suites £120–£170.

For hotel location, see maps on pages 490-496

# THE IVY HOUSE HOTEL

**HIGH STREET, MARLBOROUGH, WILTSHIRE SN8 1HJ**

**TEL: 01672 515333 FAX: 01672 515338**

Owners David Ball and Josephine Scott and manager Julian Roff welcome you to this 18th century Grade II listed property overlooking Marlborough High Street. The original building contains period features in its reception and lounge areas overlooking the cobbled courtyard and sun terrace. The elegant Palladian style garden restaurant and the informal 'Options' bistro offer a choice of excellent dining. The recently appointed Beeches Wing provides additional accommodation of superior quality. Private parking is availables. The ancient sites of Silbury Hill, Stonehenge and Avebury are easily accessible by car, as are the stately homes of Bowood House, Corsham Court and Blenheim Palace and also Newbury Race Course. **Directions:** The hotel is in Marlborough High Street, just off the A4 Bath–London road. Price guide: Single £62–£72; double/twin £74–£99.

25 rms MasterCard VISA AMERICAN EXPRESS M 50

For hotel location, see maps on pages 490-496

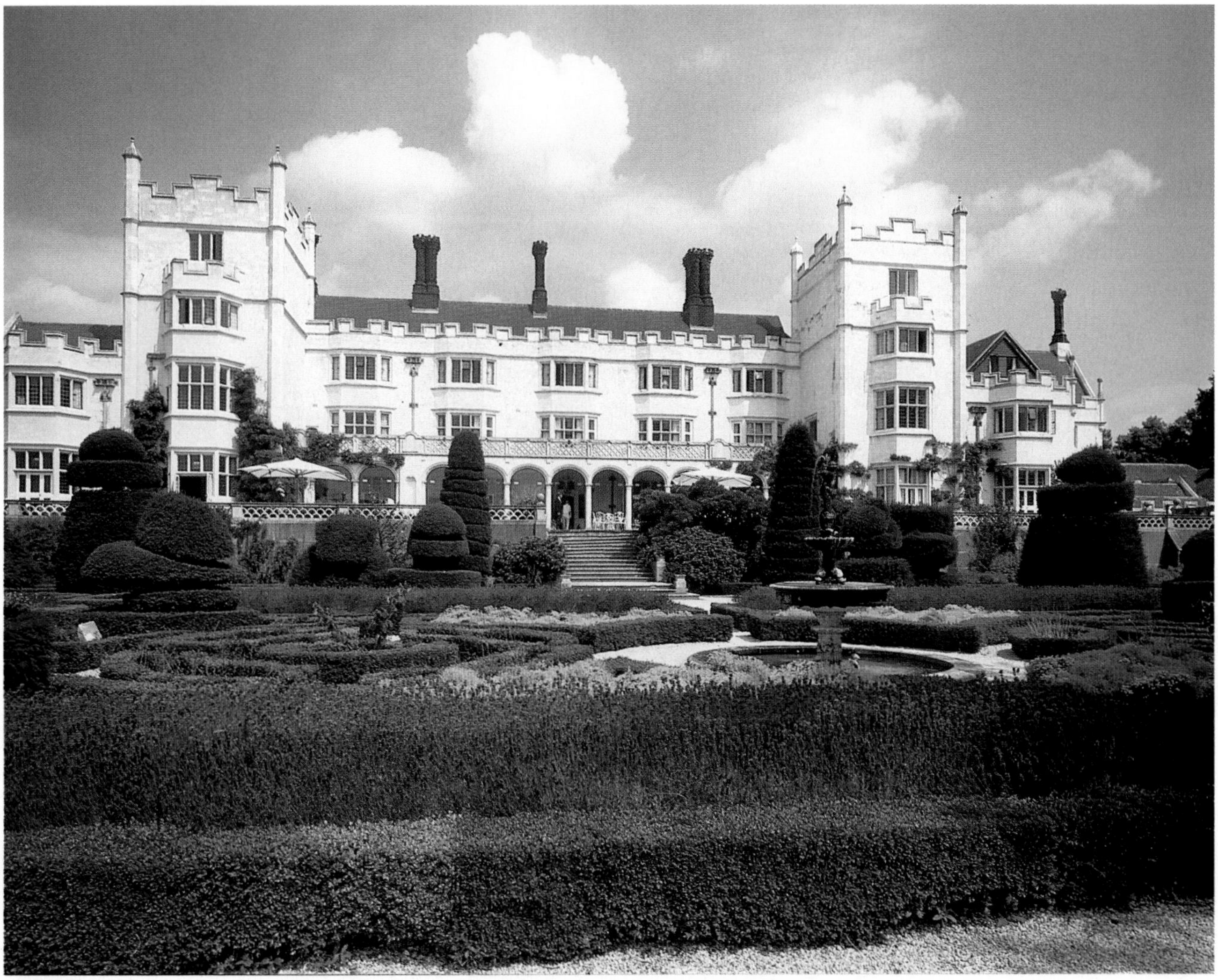

# DANESFIELD HOUSE

**HENLEY ROAD, MARLOW-ON-THAMES, BUCKINGHAMSHIRE SL7 2EY**

**TEL: 01628 891010 FAX: 01628 890408**

Danesfield House is set in 65 acres of gardens and parkland overlooking the River Thames and offering panoramic views across the Chiltern Hills. It is the third house since 1664 to occupy this lovely setting and it was designed and built in sumptuous style at the end of the 19th century. After years of neglect the house has been fully restored, combining its Victorian splendour with the very best modern hotel facilities. Among the many attractions of its luxury bedrooms, all beautifully decorated and furnished, are the extensive facilities they offer. These include two telephone lines (one may be used for personal fax), satellite TV,in-room movies, mini bar, trouser press, hair dryers, bath robes and toiletries. Guests can relax in the magnificent drawing room with its galleried library or in the sunlit atrium. There is a choice of two restaurants the Oak Room and Orangery Brasserie both of which offer a choice of international cuisine. The hotel also has six private banqueting and conference rooms. Leisure facilities include a swimming pool, croquet, tennis court and jogging and walking trails. Also within easy reach are Windsor Castle, Disraeli's home at Hughenden Manor, Milton's cottage and the caves of West Wycombe. **Directions:** Between the M4 and M40 on the A4155 between Marlow and Henley-on-Thames. Price guide: Single £135; double/twin £165; suites £195.

For hotel location, see maps on pages 490-496

# RIBER HALL

MATLOCK, DERBYSHIRE DE4 5JU
TEL: 01629 582795 FAX: 01629 580475 E-MAIL: info@riber-hall.co.uk

Enjoy pure tranquillity in the welcoming atmosphere of a bygone age in this historic Derbyshire country house, listed and starred in its class, dating from the 1400's. Recommended by all major hotel and restaurant guides, Riber Hall was recently nominated as one of "The most romantic hotels in Britain". Many original features have been preserved – magnificent oak beams, exposed stone work and period fireplaces. Acknowledged as a restaurant of distinction, English Classical, French Provincial cuisine – game when in season is served on bone china in elegant dining rooms. Superb wines, especially New World, are enjoyed in fine crystal glasses. Quietly located around an attractive courtyard, the bedrooms are appointed to a high standard with antiques throughout, including four poster beds, and many thoughtful extras. The tranquil setting can be appreciated in the secluded old wall garden and orchard which is full of bird life, whilst energetic guests can pit their skills against the tennis trainer ball machine on the all weather tennis court. Conferences, weddings, wedding receptions and small dinner parties are catered for to the highest standard. Nearby are Chatsworth House, Haddon Hall, Hardwick Hall and Calke Abbey; and the Peak National Park. **Directions:** 20 minutes from junction 28 of M1, off A615 at Tansley; 1 mile further to Riber. Price guide: Single £85; double/twin £105.

11 rms · MasterCard · VISA · AMERICAN EXPRESS · M 20 · 10

For hotel location, see maps on pages 490-496

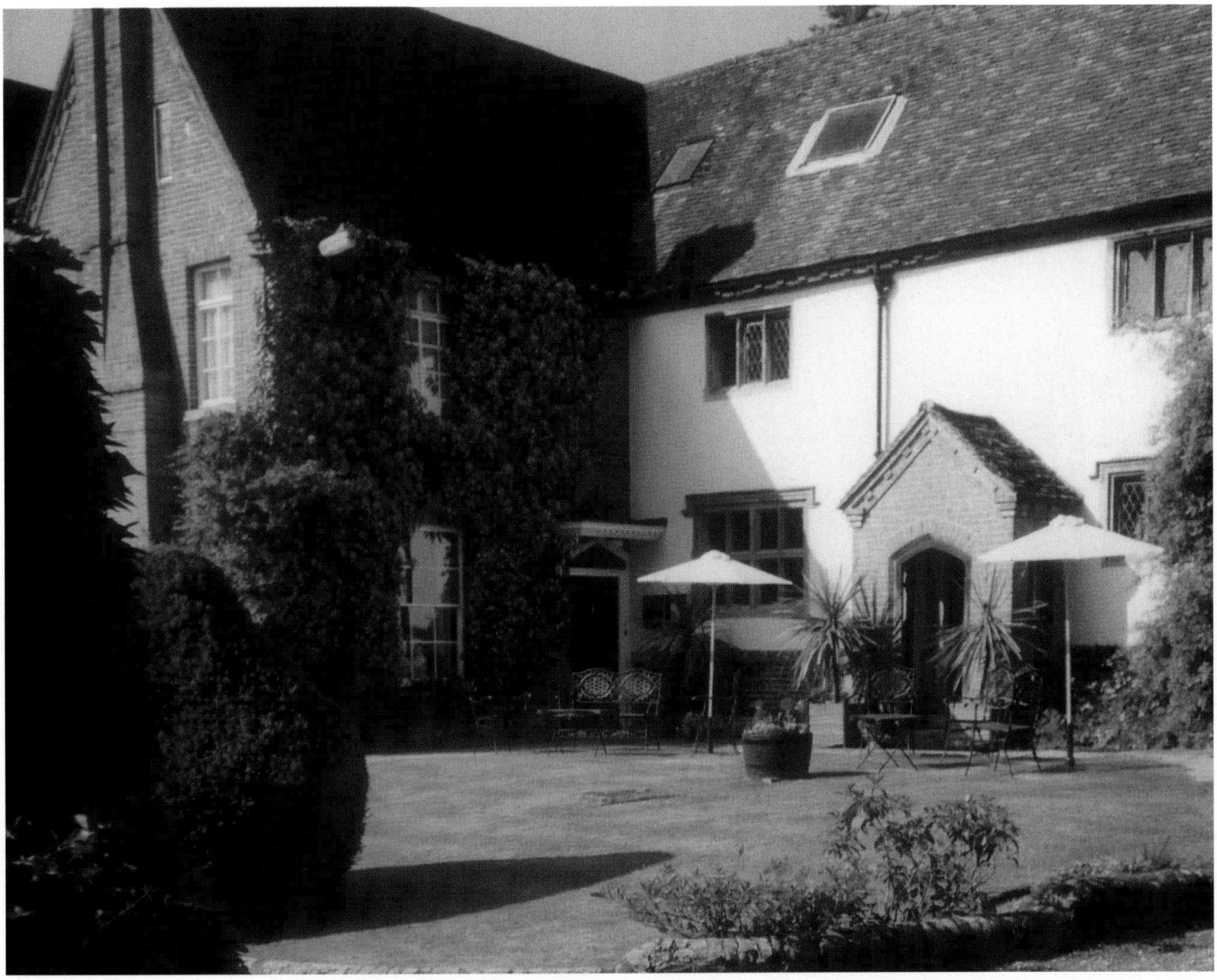

# FIFEHEAD MANOR

**MIDDLE WALLOP, STOCKBRIDGE. HAMPSHIRE SO20 8EG**
**TEL: 01264 781565 FAX: 01264 781400**

The foundations of this lovely Manor House date from the 11th century when it was owned by the wife of the Saxon Earl of Godwin whose son, King Harold, was killed at the Battle of Hastings. Today, Fifehead Manor offers all the comfort of a country house hotel but, with its barns and stables surrounded by acres of gardens, the historic atmosphere lingers. The beamed dining room with its lead-paned windows and huge open fireplace has a unique atmosphere illuminated by the light of flickering candles and a warmth generated by centuries of hospitality. It is believed to have been the main hall of the mediaeval manor and the remains of the Minstrels' Gallery can still be seen. The hotel's award winning cuisine is outstanding and the restaurant is featured in major guides in England and Europe. Local products are delivered daily. All 15 en suite bedrooms are individually furnished and have every amenity. Fifehead Manor is ideally situated for visiting Salisbury, Winchester, Stonehenge, Romsey Abbey, Broadlands and Wilton House. Golf, fishing, riding and motor racing at Thruxton are nearby. **Directions:** From M3, exit at junction 8 onto A303 to Andover. Then take A343 south for 6 miles to Middle Wallop. Price guide: Single from £60; double/twin from £80

For hotel location, see maps on pages 490-496

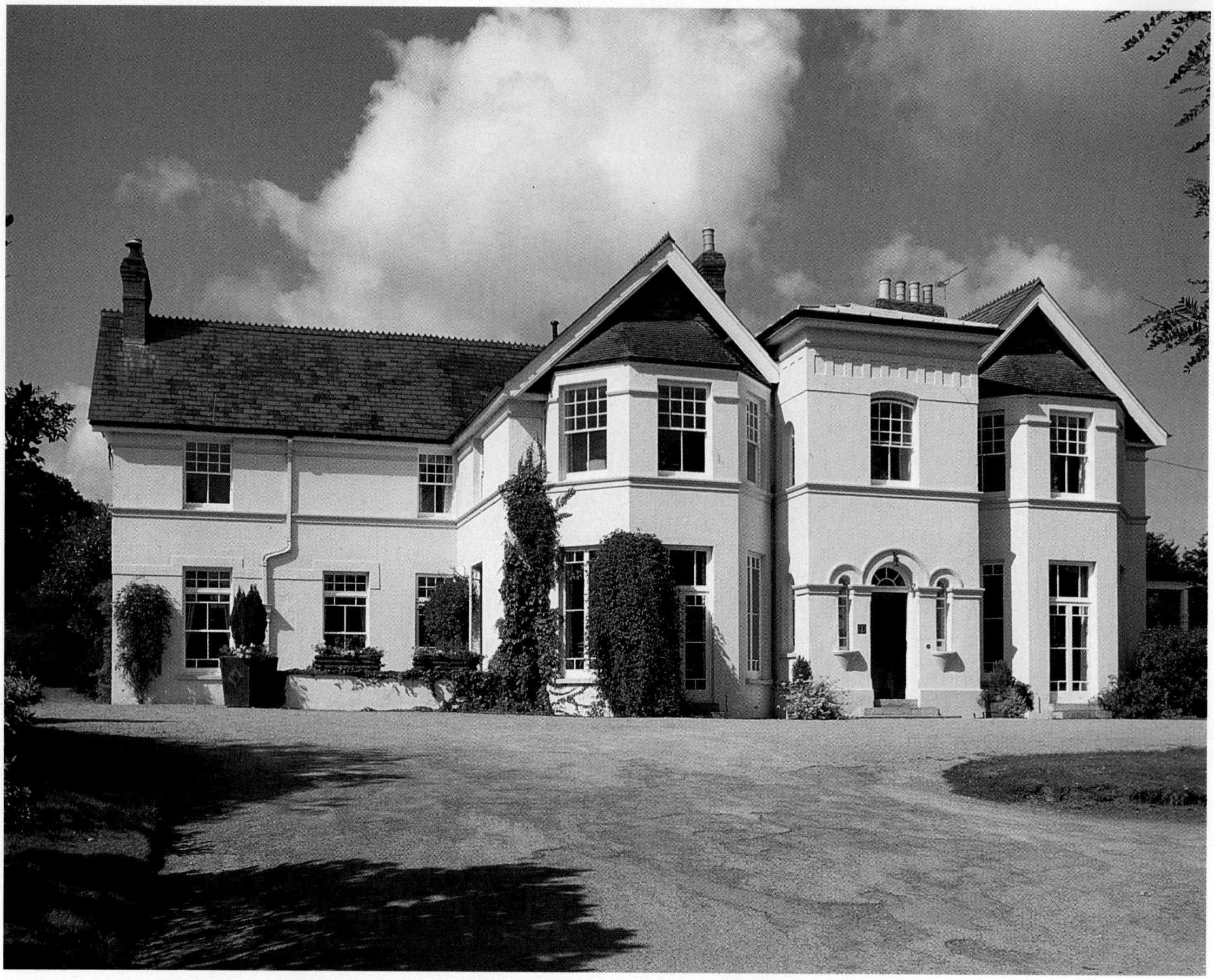

# Periton Park Hotel

**MIDDLECOMBE, NR MINEHEAD, SOMERSET TA24 8SW**
**TEL: 01643 706885 FAX: 01643 706885**

Some of the joys of staying in a small independent hotel are the individuality of the rooms, the interesting and varied food and the personal care and attention given to guests by its owners. Periton Park is just such a hotel which Richard and Angela Hunt run in an efficient, yet friendly way. Unusually perhaps today, the large bedrooms are very spacious and well appointed, with warm colours creating a restful atmosphere. From its secluded and quiet position guests may enjoy wonderful views of the Exmoor National Park in all directions and the early riser may well be rewarded by the sight of a herd of red deer grazing on the surrounding countryside. The wood panelled restaurant, with its double aspect views, is the perfect place to enjoy some of the best food on Exmoor. Fresh fish, local game, delicately cooked vegetables, local cheeses and Somerset wine have all helped the restaurant to achieve 2 AA Red Rosettes. Exmoor is very much for country lovers with miles of varied, unspoilt and breathtaking landscape. Riding is available from stables close to the hotel. Shooting is available in season. Internet: http://www.SmoothHound.co.uk/hotels/periton.html
**Directions:** Periton Park is situated off the A39 on the left just after Minehead, in the direction of Lynmouth and Porlock. Price guide: Single £65; double/twin £96.

For hotel location, see maps on pages 490-496

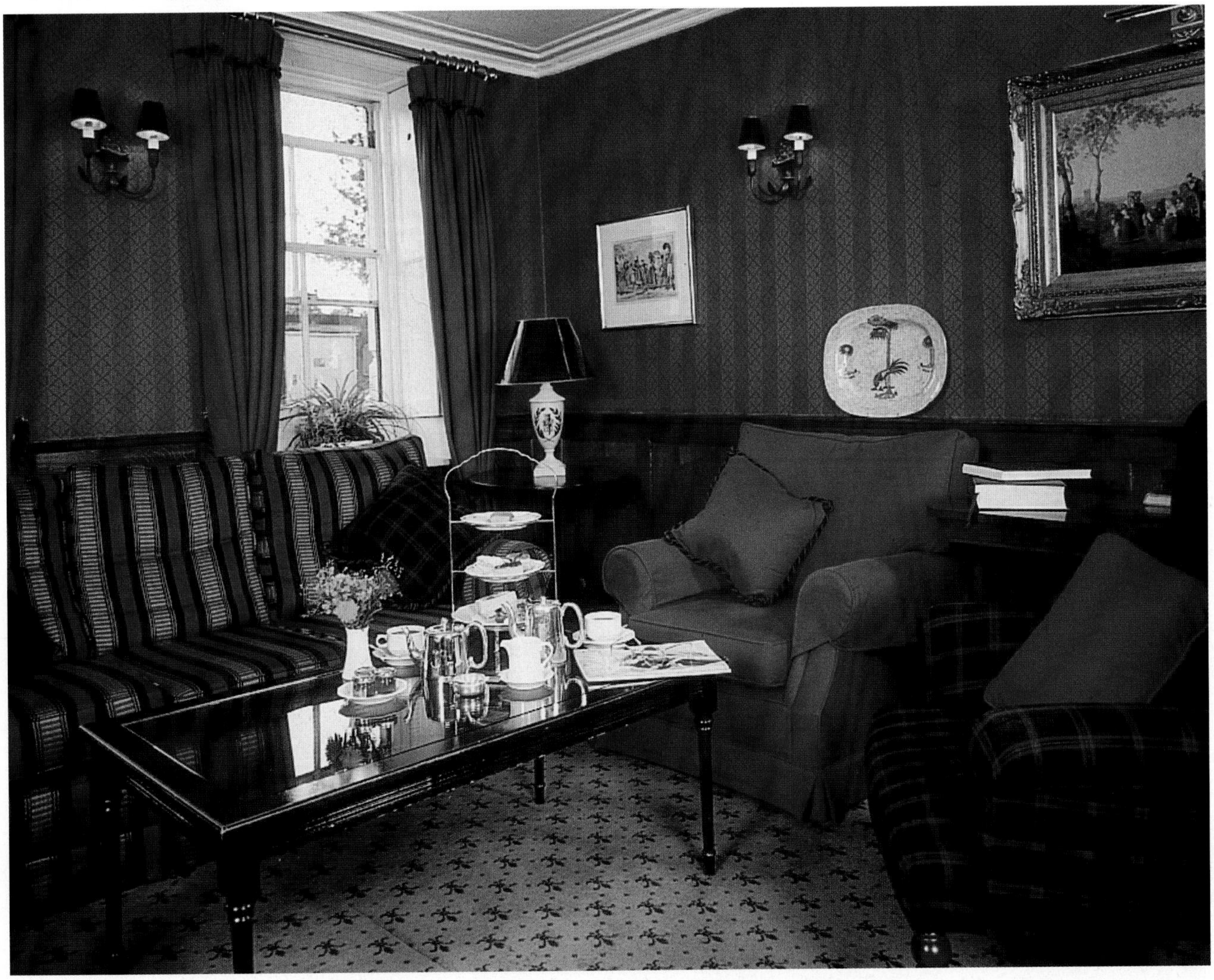

# THE ANGEL HOTEL

**NORTH STREET, MIDHURST, WEST SUSSEX GU29 9DN**
**TEL: 01730 812421 FAX: 01730 815928**

The Angel Hotel is a stylishly restored 16th century coaching inn which has earned widespread praise from its guests, the national press and guidebooks. Sympathetically renovated to combine contemporary comfort with original character, The Angel bridges the gap between town house bustle and country house calm. To the front, a handsome Georgian façade overlooks the High Street, while at the rear, quiet rose gardens lead to the parkland and ruins of historic Cowdray Castle. There are 28 bedrooms, all offering private bathrooms and modern amenities. Individually furnished with antiques, many rooms feature original Tudor beams. The hotel has been widely acclaimed for the quality of its food. For corporate guests the hotel offers two attractive meeting rooms, a business suite, presentation aids and secretarial services. Racegoers will find it very convenient for Goodwood and theatregoers for the internationally acclaimed Chichester Festival Theatre. The historic market town of Midhurst is well placed for visits to Petworth House, Arundel Castle and the South Downs. At present, the owners Nicholas Davies and Peter Crawford-Rolt are restoring another quite similar hotel in Salisbury. **Directions:** From the A272, the hotel is on the left as the town centre is approached from the east. Price guide: Single from £65–£95; double/twin from £75–£155.

For hotel location, see maps on pages 490-496

# THE SPREAD EAGLE HOTEL

SOUTH STREET, MIDHURST, WEST SUSSEX GU29 9NH
TEL: 01730 816911 FAX: 01730 815668

Dating from 1430, when guests were welcomed to the tavern here, The Spread Eagle with its emblem deriving from the time of the Crusades is one of England's oldest hotels. Throughout the centuries, including its years as a famous coaching inn, the influences of successive eras have been preserved both in the architecture and decorative features of the hotel. Heavy polished timbers, Tudor bread ovens and a series of Flemish stained-glass windows are among the many noteworthy features. Innovative cooking forms the basis of the meals, served in the dining room, with its huge, coppered inglenook fireplace and dark oak beams hung with traditional Sussex Christmas puddings. Colourful, co-ordinated fabrics and antique furnishings make for attractive bedrooms, all fully appointed. October 1997 will see the opening of the Aquila Health Spa. An outstanding facility offering a swimming pool, Scandinavian sauna, Turkish steam room, hot tub, fitness centre and a range of beauty treatments, aromatherapy and massage. The stately homes at Petworth, Uppark and Goodwood are all within a short drive, with Chichester Cathedral, the Downland Museum and Fishbourne Roman Palace among the many local attractions. Cowdray Park Polo Club is only 1 mile away. **Directions:** Midhurst is on the A286 between Chichester and Milford. Price guide: Single from £85; double/twin from £110.

39 rms · MasterCard · VISA · AMERICAN EXPRESS · M 60

For hotel location, see maps on pages 490-496

# MOORE PLACE HOTEL

**THE SQUARE, ASPLEY GUISE, MILTON KEYNES, BEDFORDSHIRE MK17 8DW**
**TEL: 01908 282000 FAX: 01908 281888**

This elegant Georgian mansion was built by Francis Moore in the peaceful Bedfordshire village of Aspley Guise in 1786. The original house, which is set on the village square, has been sympathetically extended to create extra rooms. The additional wing has been built around an attractive courtyard with a rock garden, lily pool and waterfall. The pretty Victorian-style conservatory restaurant, with its floral tented ceiling and festooned drapes, serves food that rates among the best in the area. Vegetarian options can always be found on the menus, which offer dishes prepared in the modern English style and balanced with a selection of fine wines. The 54 bedrooms are well appointed with many amenities, including a trouser press, hairdryer, welcome drinks and large towelling bath robes. Banquets, conferences and dinner parties can be accommodated in five private function rooms: all are decorated in traditional style yet are equipped with the latest audio-visual facilities. The hotel is close to Woburn Abbey, Silverstone, Whipsnade Zoo, Stowe and Milton Keynes. The convenient location and accessibility to the motorway network makes Moore Place Hotel an attractive choice, whether travelling on business or for pleasure. **Directions:** Only two minutes' drive from the M1 junction 13. Price guide: Single from £75; double/twin £95–£175; suite £175.

54 rms MasterCard VISA AMERICAN EXPRESS M 50

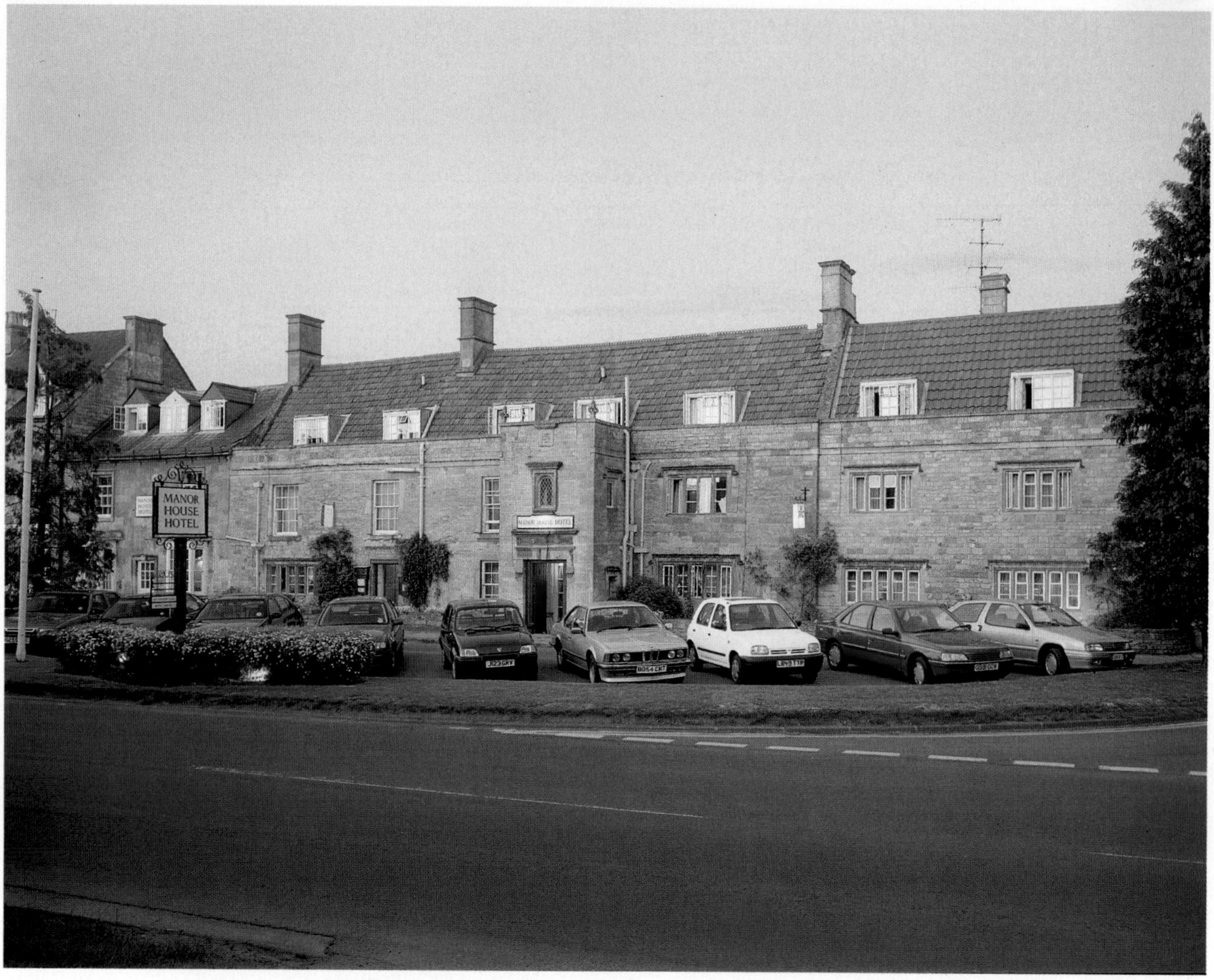

# The Manor House Hotel

**MORETON-IN-MARSH, GLOUCESTERSHIRE GL56 0LJ**
**TEL: 01608 650501 FAX: 01608 651481**

This former 16th-century manor house and coaching inn is set in beautiful gardens in the Cotswold village of Moreton-in-Marsh. The Manor House Hotel has been tastefully extended and restored, yet retains many of its historic features, among them a priest's hole and secret passages. The 39 well-appointed bedrooms have been individually decorated and furnished. The restaurant offers imaginative and traditional English dishes using only the freshest ingredients, accompanied by an expertly selected wine list. For the guest seeking relaxation, leisure facilities include an indoor heated swimming pool, spa bath and sauna. Sports enthusiasts will also find that tennis, golf, riding and squash can be arranged locally. The spacious conference facilities are set apart from the rest of the hotel. Modern business facilities, combined with the peaceful location, make this an excellent venue for executive meetings. It is also an ideal base for touring, with many attractions nearby, including Stratford-upon-Avon, Warwick and the fashionable centres of Cheltenham, Oxford and Bath. **Directions:** The Manor House Hotel is on the A429 Fosse Way near the junction of the A44 and A429 north of Stow, on the Broadway side of the intersection. Price guide: Single £65; double/twin £90–£125.

For hotel location, see maps on pages 490-496

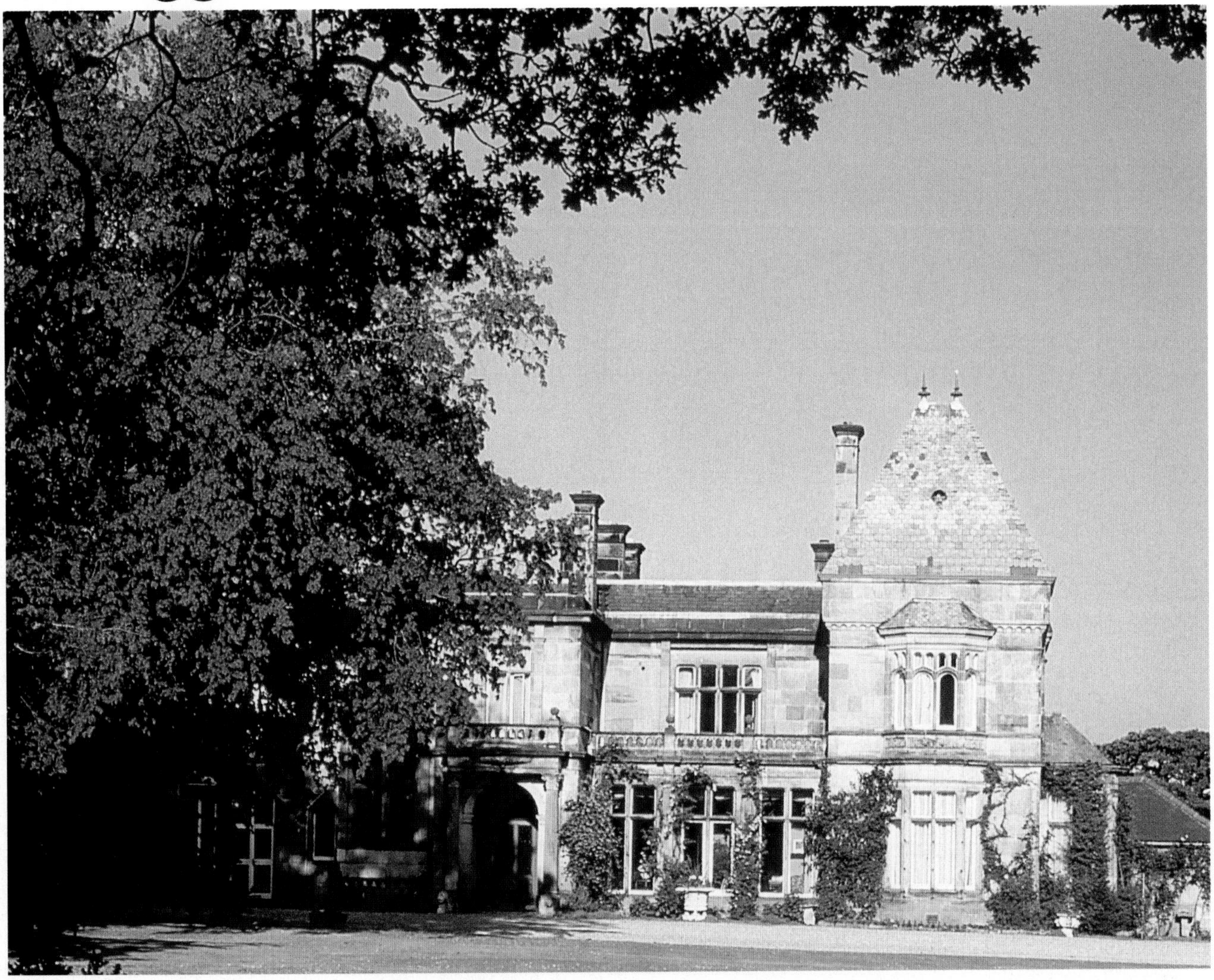

# ROOKERY HALL

WORLESTON, NANTWICH, NR CHESTER, CHESHIRE CW5 6DQ
TEL: 01270 610016 FAX: 01270 626027

Rookery Hall enjoys a peaceful setting where guests can relax, yet convenient for road, rail and air networks. The hotel also has a chauffeur driven Rolls Royce to take guests for local journeys or further afield. Within the original house are elegant reception rooms and the mahogany and walnut panelled restaurant, which is renowned for its cuisine. Dine by candlelight in the intimate dining room overlooking the lawns. Over 300 wines are in the cellar. Private dining facilities are available for meetings and weddings – summer lunches can be taken alfresco on the terrace. Companies can hire the hotel as their own "Country House", with leisure pursuits such as archery, clay pigeon shooting and off road driving available within the grounds. Tennis or croquet, fishing, golf and riding can be arranged. All of the bedrooms are individually designed and luxuriously furnished with spacious marbled bathroom many with views over fields and woodlands. Suites are available including the self contained stable block. Special breaks and Celebrations Packages are offered with Gourmet evenings in the restaurant and Jazz afternoons on the terrace. Ideally situated for historic Chester and North Wales. An Arcadian Hotel. **Directions:** From M6 junction 16 take A500 to Nantwich, then B5074 to Worleston. Price guide: Single £90–£160; double/twin £95–£200; suite £195–£260.

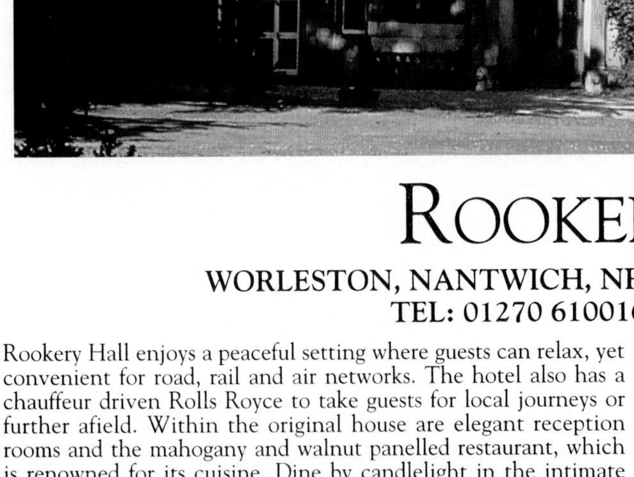

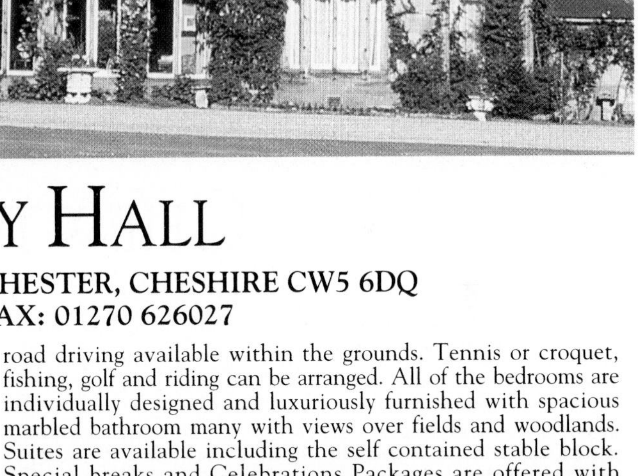

For hotel location, see maps on pages 490-496

# Chewton Glen

**CHEWTON GLEN, NEW MILTON, HAMPSHIRE BH25 6QS**
**TEL: 01425 275341 FAX: 01425 272310 E-MAIL: reservations@chewtonglen.com**

Chewton Glen, a shrine that merits many a pilgrimage, has a setting of lovely gardens, woodland and lawns. The original mansion was built in the short-lived Palladian style of the early 18th century and despite renovations it essentially retains the unique character of an English country house. There are antiques, paintings, memorabilia of the famous author, Captain Marryat, who lived there and wrote *Children of the New Forest* and *Mr Midshipman Easy*, and arrays of fresh flowers. Many bedrooms have balconies that give guests the chance to enjoy beautiful views of the surrounding parkland scenery. The menu in the Marryat Restaurant is a delicious harmony of the classical and the modern, gastronomically accompanied by a list of over 400 wines. The hotel has a health club with a magnificent swimming pool, and over 40 body and beauty treatments. There are excellent conference facilities. Among the other pursuits on hand are golf, tennis, snooker, shooting and riding. Places of interest nearby include Beaulieu, Broadlands, Exbury Gardens, The Solent, Kingston Lacy and Stonehenge. Internet: http://www.chewtonglen.com **Directions:** A35 from Lyndhurst toward Bournemouth.Turn left at Walkford (approx 10 miles after Lyndhurst). Turn left before roundabout, hotel is on the right. Price guide (room only rates): Double/twin £210–£325; suites £325–£450.

52 rms MasterCard VISA AMERICAN EXPRESS M 150 7

For hotel location, see maps on pages 490-496

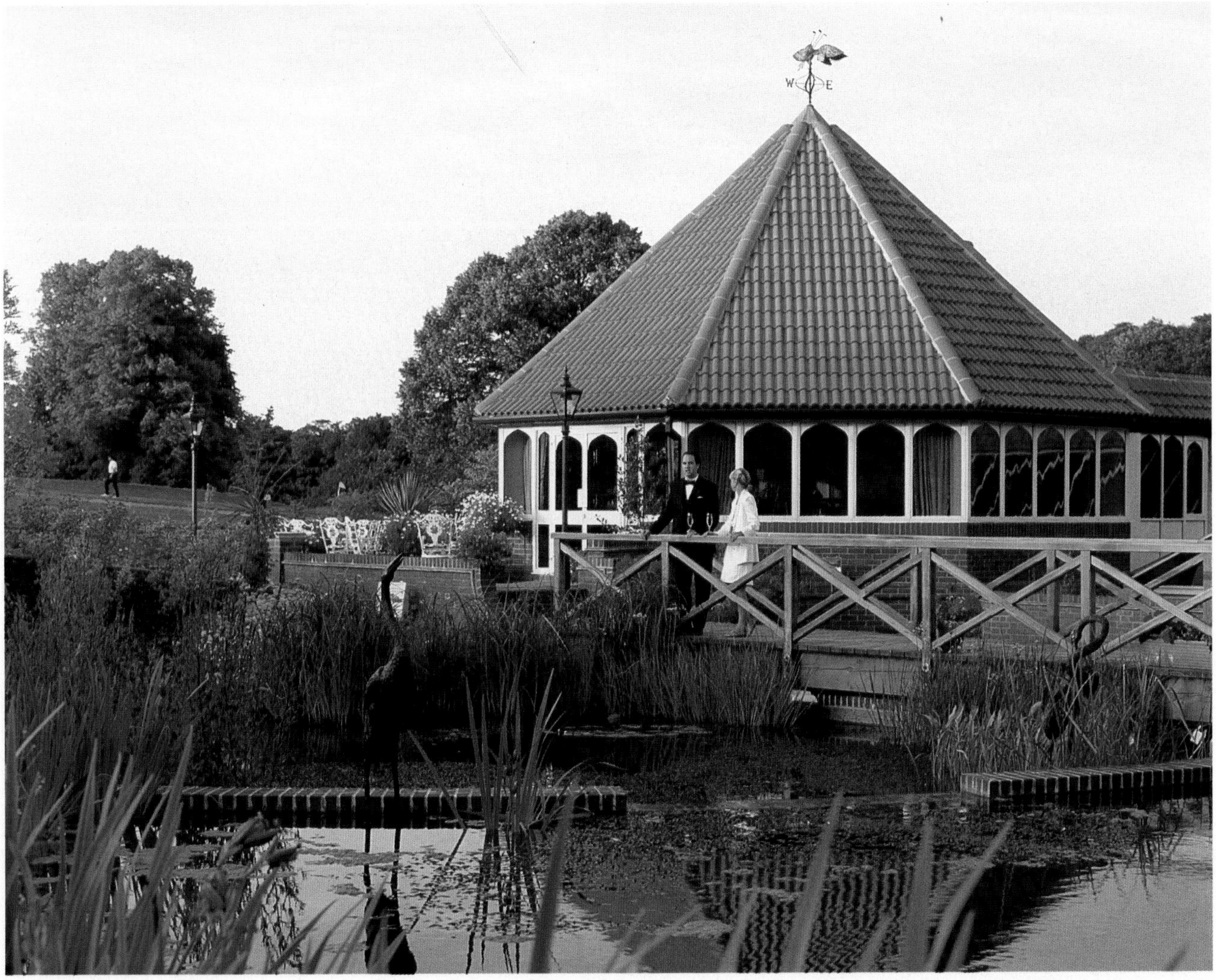

# Donnington Valley Hotel & Golf Course

**OLD OXFORD ROAD, DONNINGTON, NEWBURY, BERKSHIRE RG14 3AG**
**TEL: 01635 551199 FAX: 01635 551123 E-MAIL: 101317.506@compuserve.com**

Uncompromising quality is the hallmark of this hotel built in contrasting styles in 1991 with its own golf course. The grandeur of the Edwardian era has been captured by the interior of the hotel's reception area with its splendid wood-panelled ceilings and impressive overhanging gallery. Each individually designed bedroom has been thoughtfully equipped to guarantee comfort and peace of mind. In addition to the standard guest rooms Donnington Valley offers a number of non-smoking rooms, family rooms, superior executive rooms and luxury suites. With its open log fire and elegant surroundings, the Piano Bar is an ideal place to meet friends or enjoy the relaxed ambience of the Golf Bar. Guests lunch and dine in the Gallery Restaurant which offers fine international cuisine complemented by an extensive choice of wines and liqueurs. The golf course is the perfect place for a relaxing weekend or mixing business with pleasure. Special corporate golfing packages are offered and tournaments can be arranged. Purpose-built conference suites provide the flexibility to meet the demands of today's executive meeting. Donnington Castle, despite a siege during the Civil War, still survives for sight-seeing. **Directions:** Leave the M4 at junction 13, go south towards Newbury on A34, then follow signs for Donnington Castle. Price guide: Single from £95; double/twin from £110; suite from £130.

For hotel location, see maps on pages 490-496

# ELCOT PARK HOTEL AND COUNTRY CLUB

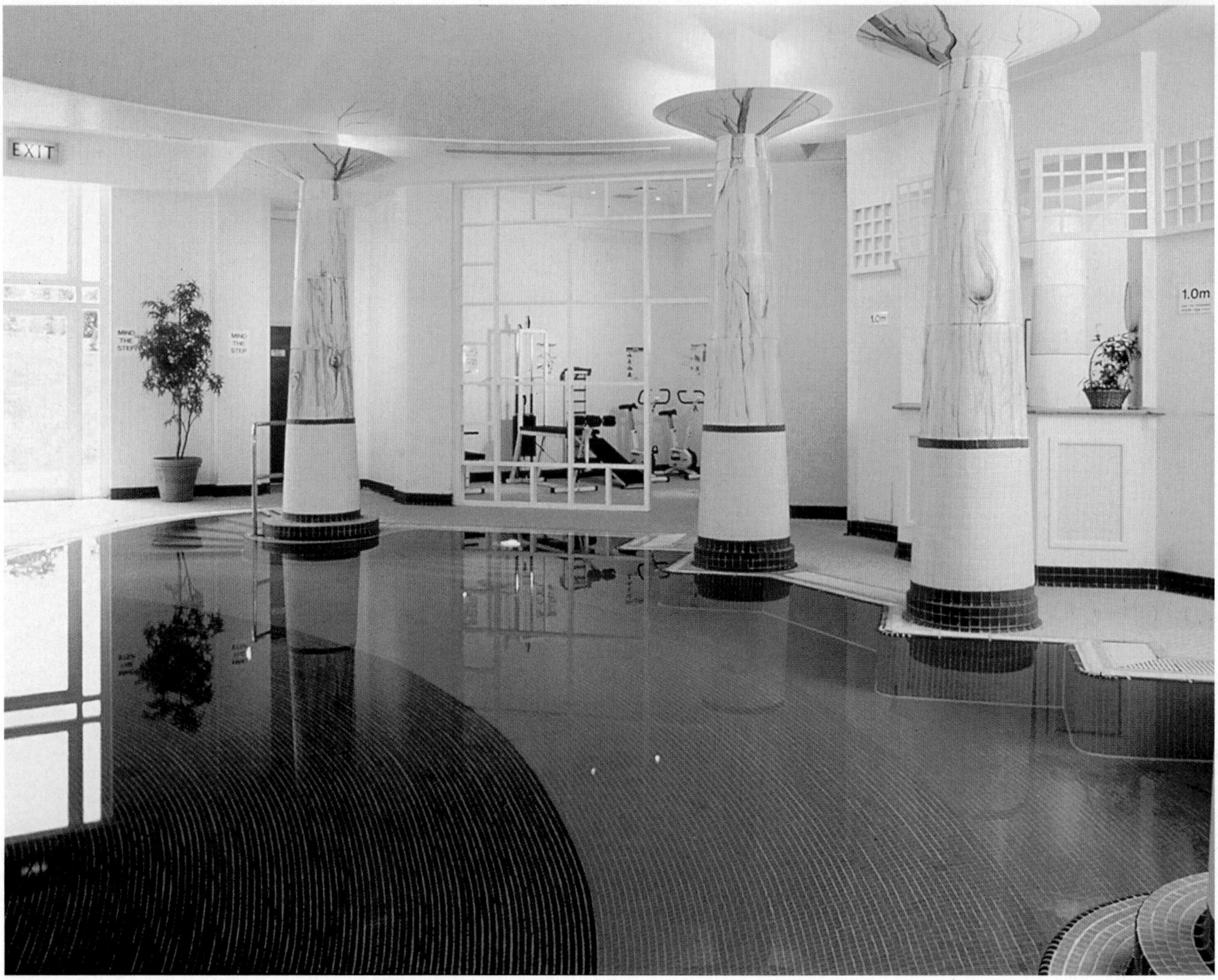

**NEAR NEWBURY, BERKSHIRE RG20 8NJ**

**TEL: 01488 658100 FAX: 01488 658288**


Elcot Park Hotel and Country Club, an ideal retreat for both pleasure and business, is set amid 16 acres of lovely woodland and landscaped gardens. Renowned as a first class conference venue, it offers comfortable accommodation and excellent, friendly service. The comfortable bedrooms include a full range of facilities, while fine English cuisine is served in the stylish setting of the Orangery restaurant. Guests can unwind in style at the hotel's indoor health and leisure suite. A host of excellent facilities include an indoor swimming pool, sauna, spa bath, solarium, gym, beauty room and trim trail and running track. For those wanting to venture beyond their immediate luxurious surroundings, there is no shortage of places of interest within easy reach – the old market town of Newbury; Watership Down, the beauty spot brought to fame by Richard Adams' book of the same name; and Highclere Castle housing "The Lord Carnarvon Racing Exhibition". Newbury Racecourse is also close by. The Summit Conference Centre, set apart from the hotel, contains four of the nine superbly equipped meeting rooms for business use. Directions: From junction 14 of the M4 turn south towards Hungerford. After 4 miles turn left at the T junction with the A4 towards Newbury. A further 4 miles along the A4 past the Kintbury Crossroads, Elcot is ½ mile up the next lane on the left. Price Guide: Single £95; double/twin £115; suites £130.

For hotel location, see maps on pages 490-496

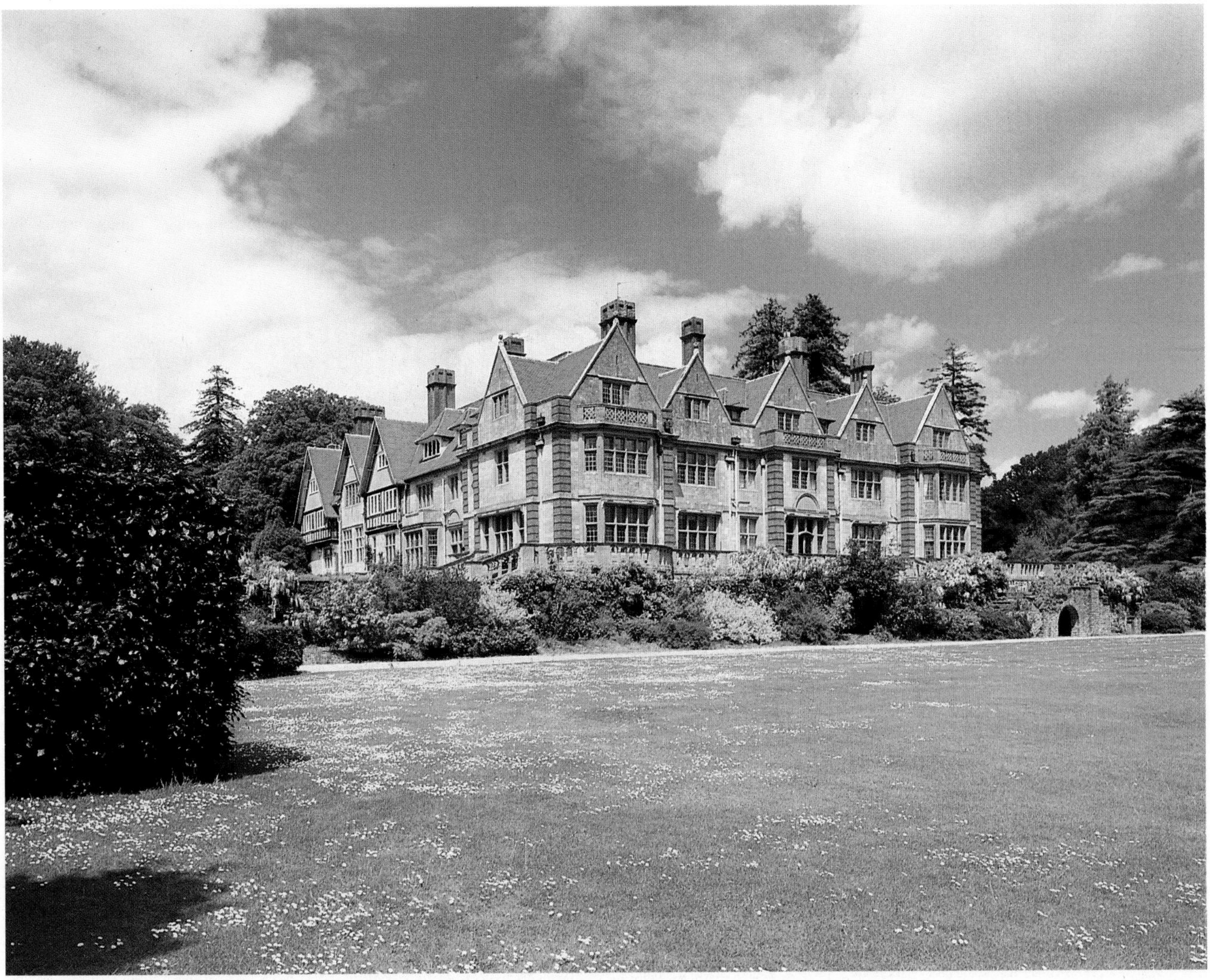

# HOLLINGTON HOUSE HOTEL

WOOLTON HILL, NR NEWBURY, BERKSHIRE RG20 9XA
TEL: 01635 255100 FAX: 01635 255075

Hollington House Hotel, one of England's foremost luxury country house hotels, opened in July 1992. The Elizabethan-style house, built in 1904, is set in 25 acres of Gertrude Jekyll woodland gardens, adjacent to 250 acres of private parkland. Prior to returning to the UK after an absence of 32 years, John and Penny Guy created and owned Burnham Beeches Hotel, near Melbourne, which became Australia's first Relais et Châteaux hotel. No expense has been spared in their successful endeavours to maintain similar standards of excellence here. The 20 individually designed bedrooms are furnished with antiques and paintings and have sumptuous bathrooms. Elegant reception rooms, an oak-panelled, galleried hall and private boardroom are among the many splendid features of the house. The Chef serves a modern style of cooking with flair and innovation, based on traditional English and French cuisine. Indoors there is a swimming pool and a full-size snooker table, outdoors a solar-heated swimming pool, a tennis court and a croquet lawn. The surrounding countryside offers opportunities for walking, shooting, hunting and horse-racing. Conference, wedding and weekend packages available. **Directions:** From M4 junction13 south of Newbury leave A343 Andover road, follow signs for Hollington Herb Garden. Price guide: Single from £95; spa feature room £175; kingsize double/twin £120; junior suite from £250.

20 rms MasterCard VISA AMERICAN EXPRESS M 60

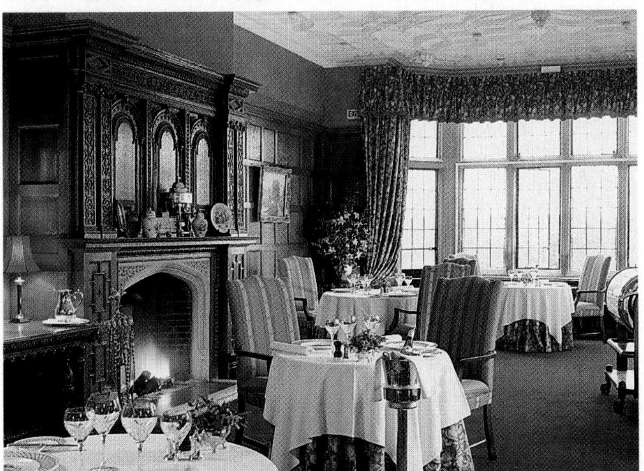

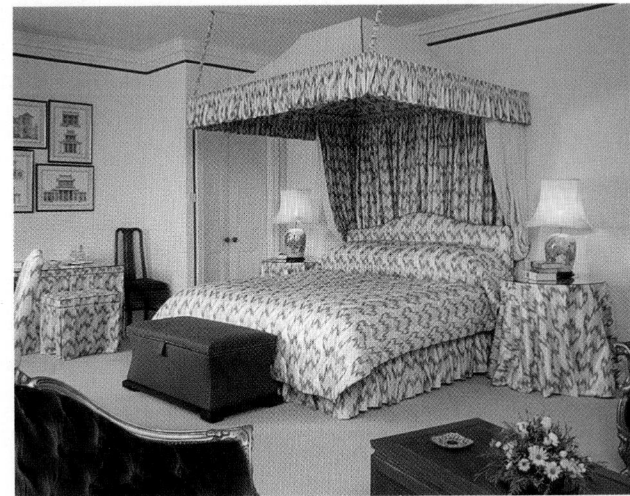

For hotel location, see maps on pages 490-496

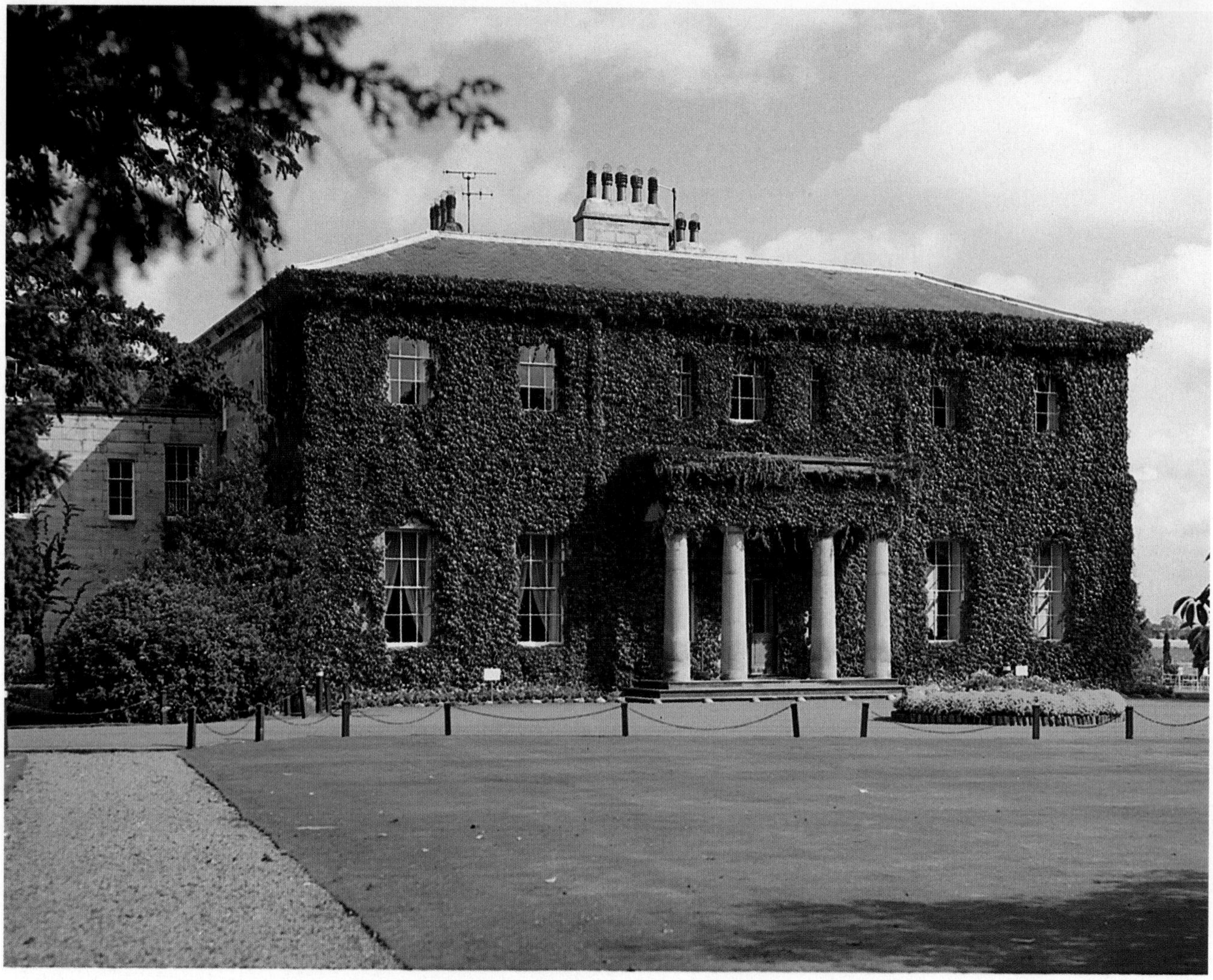

# LINDEN HALL HOTEL

LONGHORSLEY, MORPETH, NEWCASTLE-UPON-TYNE, NORTHUMBERLAND NE65 8XF
TEL: 01670 516611 FAX: 01670 788544

Ivy-clad, hidden away among 450 acres of fine park and woodland in mid-Northumberland, Linden Hall is a superb Georgian country house within easy reach of Newcastle-upon-Tyne. An impressive mile-long drive sweeps up to its main door where, upon entering, the visitor will discover a relaxed, dignified atmosphere enhanced by gracious marble hearths, antiques and period pieces. Those wishing to escape the urban stress will be delighted to find every fitness and relaxation requirement catered for on the 18 hole golf course or at the health and beauty spa. Beauty therapy treatments, fitness and steam room, swimming pool, sun terrace and solarium are all available on the premises. The 50 bedrooms are individually and elegantly furnished. Some rooms have four-poster beds; each has its own private bathroom, supplied with thoughtful extras. The Linden Tree Bar and Grill serves informal drinks and bar meals and the Dobson Restaurant, with panoramic views of the Northumberland coastline, serves delicious food, imaginatively prepared. Wedding receptions, banquets, dinner parties and business conferences can be held in comfort in any one of Linden Hall's conference and banqueting suites. **Directions:** From Newcastle take A1 north for 15 miles, then A697 toward Coldstream and Wooler. The hotel is 1 mile north of Longhorsley. Price guide: Single £97–£105; double/twin £125–£185; suite: £195.

For hotel location, see maps on pages 490-496

# Slaley Hall International Golf And Spa

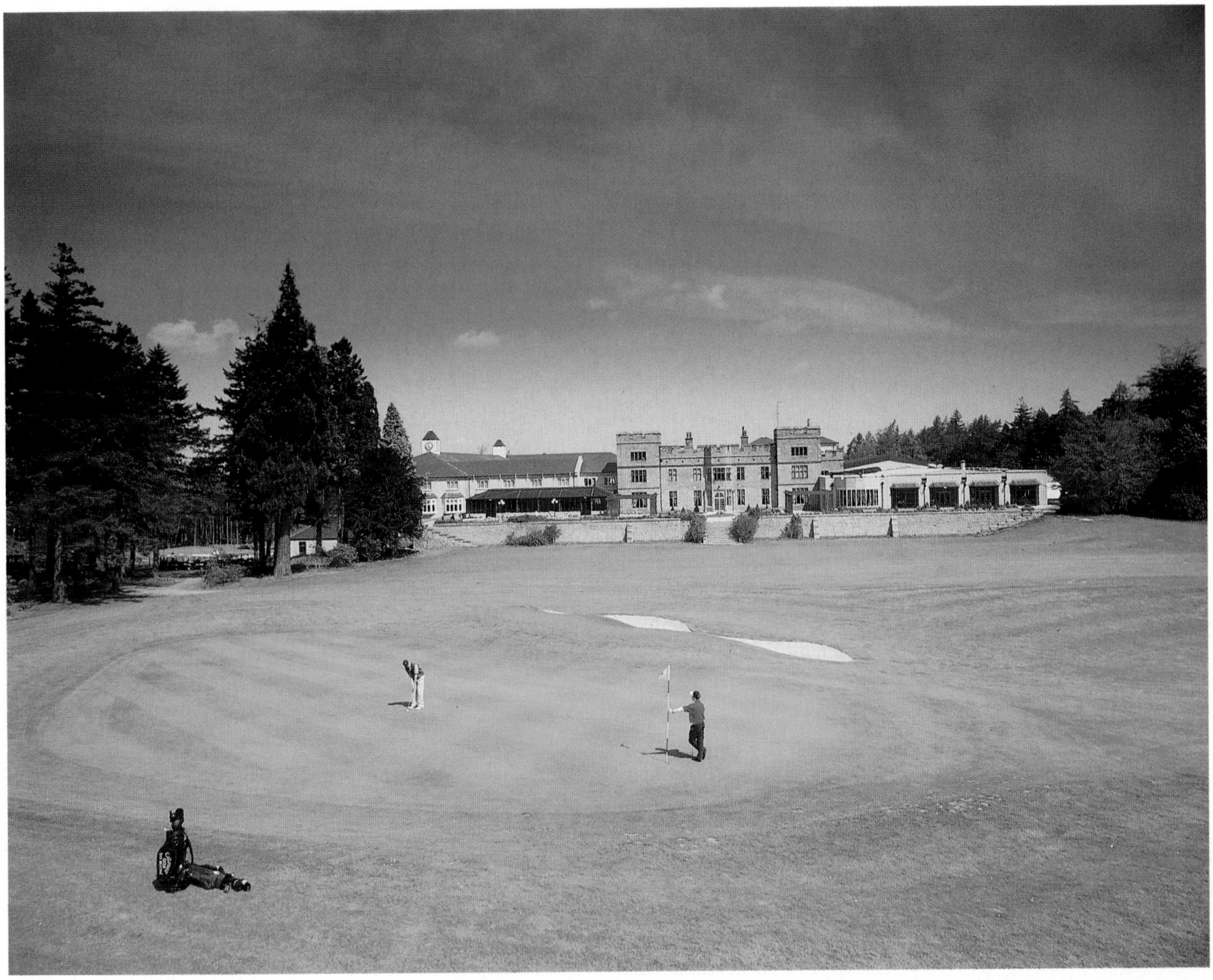

SLALEY, HEXHAM, NR NEWCASTLE-UPON-TYNE, NORTHUMBERLAND NE47 0BY

TEL: 01434 673350 FAX: 01434 673962

Set in a 1,000 acre estate in the heart of Northumberland, Slaley Hall International Hotel, Golf Resort and Spa is one of the UK's most splendid golfing locations. Formerly an Edwardian private residence, the five star country house hotel has 139 luxury bedrooms and 17 suites, many overlooking the golf course and picturesque landscape, and two superb restaurants, one of which specialises in local game and fish. The hotel's 18 hole championship standard golf course has played host to a number of major PGA European Tour. Hotel guests seeking more adventurous pursuits can participate in a range of outdoor activities including clay pigeon shooting and off road driving while Slaley Spa offers total relaxation and pampering with body and beauty treatments. The adjacent health and leisure club features a tempting pool set in tropical surroundings, saunas, steam rooms and gym. Slaley Hall also has a number of elegant conference and banqueting suites designed to accommodate groups of up to 400 guests. The hotel is 30 minutes drive from Newcastle city centre, rail station and international airport and close to the famous MetroCentre **Directions:** From Newcastle upon Tyne take A69 towards Hexham/Carlisle and then A68 south. Slaley Hall is signposted from the A68. Price guide: Single from £135; double/twin from £195; suites from £275

For hotel location, see maps on pages 490-496

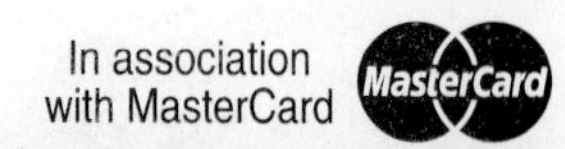

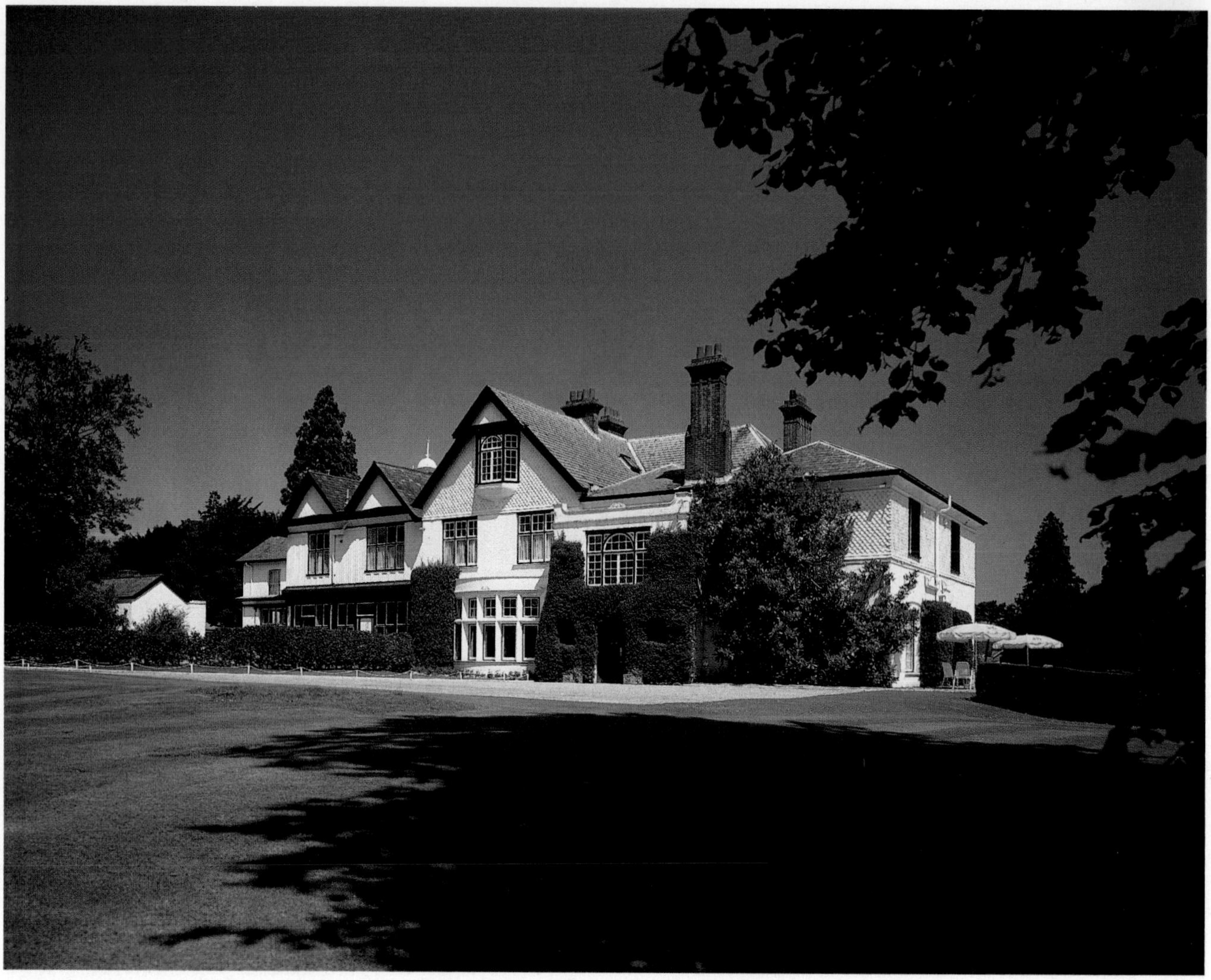

# SWYNFORD PADDOCKS HOTEL AND RESTAURANT

SIX MILE BOTTOM, NR NEWMARKET, SUFFOLK CB8 0UE
TEL: 01638 570234 FAX: 01638 570283

This graceful, classical white mansion standing in glorious gardens and idyllic countryside with racehorses grazing its pastures has a romantic history. In 1813 it was the scene of a passionate love affair between Lord Byron and the wife of the owner, Colonel George Leigh. Swynford was converted into a luxury hotel 20 years ago. It has a country house atmosphere with antique furniture, four-poster beds, open fires and attention to detail of times gone by. Each individually decorated, en suite bedroom has colour television, clock radio alarm, telephone, mini-bar, trouser press, hair dryer and tea and coffee making facilities. The lounge bar overlooks the gardens and the dining room offers an imaginative menu which is changed regularly to take advantage of the season's fresh produce. Awarded AA Rosette for food alongside The Romantic Hotel award 1997. There is a conference room for up to 20 delegates and a luxury marquee for private and special functions. Tennis, putting and croquet are within the grounds and arrangements can be made for guided tours of Newmarket with a behind the scenes look at the horseracing world. **Directions:** From M11, exit at junction 9 and take A11 towards Newmarket. After 10 miles join A1304 signposted Newmarket. Swynford Paddocks is on the left after 3/4 of a mile. Price guide: Single £85; double/twin £122–£143.

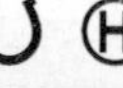

For hotel location, see maps on pages 490-496

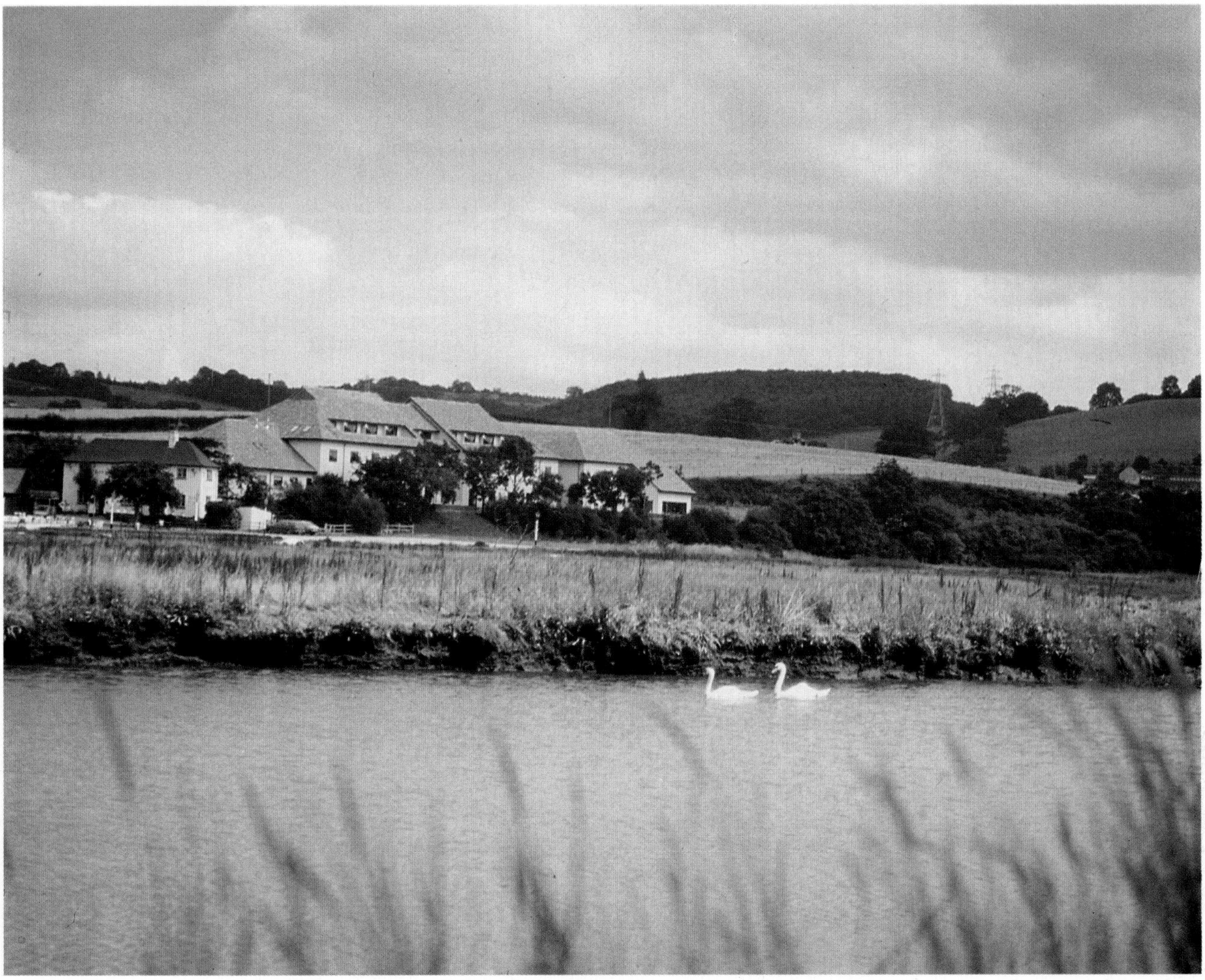

# PASSAGE HOUSE HOTEL

**KINGSTEIGNTON, NEWTON ABBOT, DEVON TQ12 3QH**

**TEL: 01626 55515 FAX: 01626 63336**

Overlooking the Teign Estuary, the Passage House Hotel has been designed to take advantage of the clear and panoramic views. Drawing inspiration from the natural beauty of the surrounding landscapes, the interior colour schemes are soft, muted shades of grey, blue and pink. The bedrooms provide every comfort, while the Penthouse rooms have a private terrace. The relaxing theme is continued in the reception rooms, with natural pale wood and mirrors enhancing the sense of space and light. Five-course table d'hôte and à la carte menus offer imaginatively prepared Devon recipes, using the freshest local fare, including Teign salmon and game. Throughout the hotel the service is extremely friendly and efficient. For active guests, there is a fully equipped leisure club, comprising indoor pool, hydro-spa, steam room, sauna, solarium and gymnasium. Sailing, water-skiing and golf are available locally. Racing fans should note that the hotel is located adjacent to Newton Abbot racecourse. The Devon heartland is rich in history – William of Orange was proclaimed King here on Guy Fawkes Day 1688. The rugged scenery of Dartmoor is only minutes from the hotel. Special rate breaks available. **Directions:** Turn off A380 onto A381, follow signs to racecourse. Turn left at mini-roundabout; hotel is first left. Price guide: Single £59; double/twin £75–£85; suite £125.

For hotel location, see maps on pages 490-496

# Redworth Hall Hotel & Country Club

## REDWORTH, NR NEWTON AYCLIFFE, COUNTY DURHAM DL5 6NL

TEL: 01388 772442 FAX: 01388 775112 CONFERENCE OFFICE FAX: 01388 775660

Redworth Hall, winner of the Pride of Northumberland 'Best Hotel 1996' award, is a 17th-century, tastefully converted manor house situated in 25 acres of woodland. There are 100 en suite bedrooms, several of which are suitable for guests who are disabled. The furnishings throughout range from antique to fine reproduction. The hotel's health club includes a heated indoor swimming pool, with a hoist for guests with disabilities, a spa bath, sunbeds, steam bath, squash courts, sauna, snooker tables, all-weather tennis courts and a fully equipped gymnasium. There is an indoor play area and an outdoor adventure playground for children. There are 16 function rooms which can accommodate from 3 to 300 guests, making the hotel ideal for conferences, training courses and weddings. Guests may choose between two restaurants: the elegant Blue Room offering innovative cuisine or the airy Conservatory which features a table d'hôte and contemporary à la carte menu. Redworth Hall, a Grand Heritage Hotel, has 4 stars AA, RAC, 5 Crowns Highly Commended ETB, 2 AA rosettes for food and service and has achieved the coveted Investor in People Standard. **Directions:** A1(M) exit 58, A68 to Corbridge, then A6072 to Bishop Auckland; hotel two miles on left. Price guide: Single £105–£125; double/twin £125–£160; four-poster £160.

For hotel location, see maps on pages 490-496

# BROOKDALE HOUSE RESTAURANT AND HOTEL

**NORTH HUISH, SOUTH BRENT, DEVON TQ10 9NR**
**TEL: 01548 821661 FAX: 01548 821606**

This Grade II listed Tudor Gothic mansion is hidden away in a sequestered valley with four acres of picturesque gardens, lawns and woodland. It was originally built in the mid 19th century as a rectory and recently has been sensitively restored and renovated to its former glory. Fine examples of moulded ceilings, Gothic windows and beautiful marble fireplaces have been retained. The hotel's bedrooms, tastefully decorated and furnished with antiques, offer every modern comfort and convenience. The restaurant is at the heart of Brookdale House and the à la carte menu enjoys an excellent reputation locally. The proprietors have concentrated on providing high quality food using local produce: additive free meat and fresh organically grown vegetables. The hotel, which prides itself on providing excellent and personal service, offers good facilities for small conferences of up to 40 people. Places of interest nearby include Dartmoor, Plymouth and Exeter, while leisure activities include riding, lawn tennis, hunting, fishing and walking. Dartington Hall is a short drive away, also Totnes and the Elizabethan Museum. **Directions:** Exit A38 at South Brent and follow signs to Avonwick. At Avon Inn turn right, then next left to North Huish. Price guide: Single £65; double/twin £100. Special breaks available.

For hotel location, see maps on pages 490-496

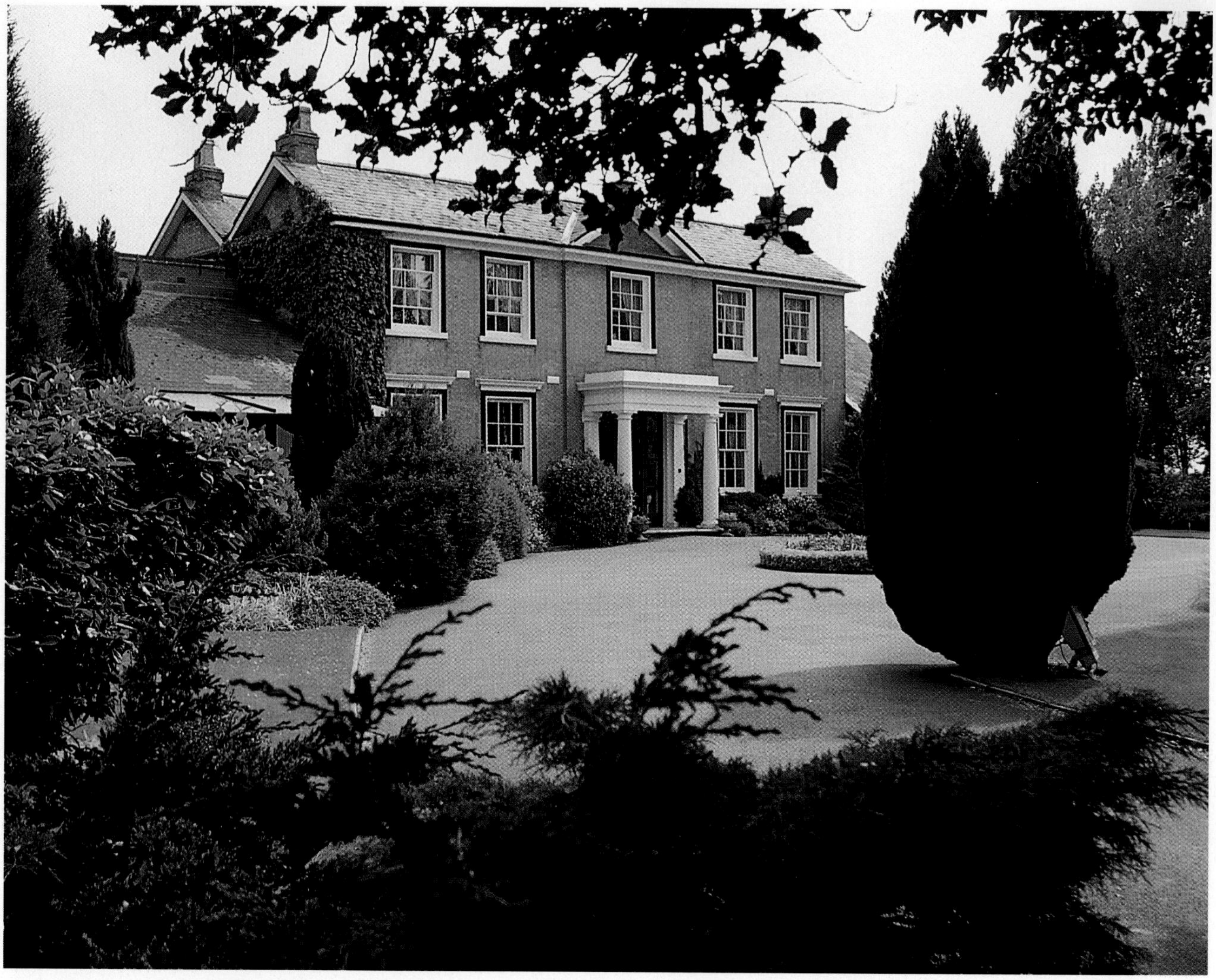

# PARK FARM COUNTRY HOTEL & LEISURE

**HETHERSETT, NORWICH, NORFOLK NR9 3DL**
**TEL: 01603 810264 FAX: 01603 812104**

Park Farm Hotel occupies a tranquil and secluded location in beautifully landscaped grounds south of Norwich, once the second greatest city in England. There are executive rooms for additional comforts, with four poster beds and Jacuzzi baths. Additional bedrooms have been sympathetically converted from traditional and new buildings to reflect the style of the six rooms available in the main house. A superb leisure complex to suit all ages has been carefully incorporated alongside the original Georgian house to include, heated swimming pool, sauna, steam room, solarium, spa bath, gymnasium and aerobics studio. The croquet lawn, putting green and hard tennis court are situated in the grounds. Associated with the hotel is a superb golf course. The delightful Georgian restaurant is renowned for high standards of cuisine and service, with a wide selection of dishes and fine choice of wines. Conference facilities cater for up to 120 candidates, (24 hour and daily delegate rates available). The Norfolk broads, the coast, Norwich open market, Castle museum and Cathedral are nearby. **Directions:** By road, just off A11 on B1172, Norwich Airport eight miles, Norwich rail station six miles and Norwich bus station five miles. There is a light aircraft landing strip and helipad in the grounds. Price guide: Single £65–£95; double/twin £90–£130; suite £130.

For hotel location, see maps on pages 490-496

# PETERSFIELD HOUSE HOTEL

**LOWER STREET, HORNING, NR NORWICH, NORFOLK NR12 8PF**
**TEL: 01692 630741 FAX: 01692 630745**

Petersfield House Hotel is set back from one of the most attractive reaches of the River Bure in the area known as the Norfolk Broads. The original property was built in the twenties on a prime site as a large private residence in two acres of gardens with its own moorings on a grassy bank of the river. Today it is a secluded family run hotel whose reputation is based on traditional comfort and hospitality. Guests can be sure of receiving personal attention at all times. The bedrooms are bright and welcoming – most rooms overlook the well-kept landscaped gardens which feature an ornamental pond, a putting green and a flintstone moon gate. Varied fixed-price and extensive à la carte menus are served in the restaurant where a list of over 60 wines provides an ideal accompaniment. Regular Saturday night dinner-dances are held with the hotel occupying one of the choicest positions on the Norfolk Broads. Sailing is the popular local pastime and open regattas are held in summer. Golf is within easy driving distance. Other local attractions include Norwich with its famous art gallery and "Ten Ancient Monuments" and Blickling Hall with its interesting furniture and gardens. **Directions:** From Norwich ring road, take A1151 to Wroxham. Cross bridge, turn right at Hoveton on A1062 to Horning; hotel is beyond centre of the village. Price guide: Single £60; double £75.

18 rms · MasterCard · VISA · AMERICAN EXPRESS · M 100

For hotel location, see maps on pages 490-496

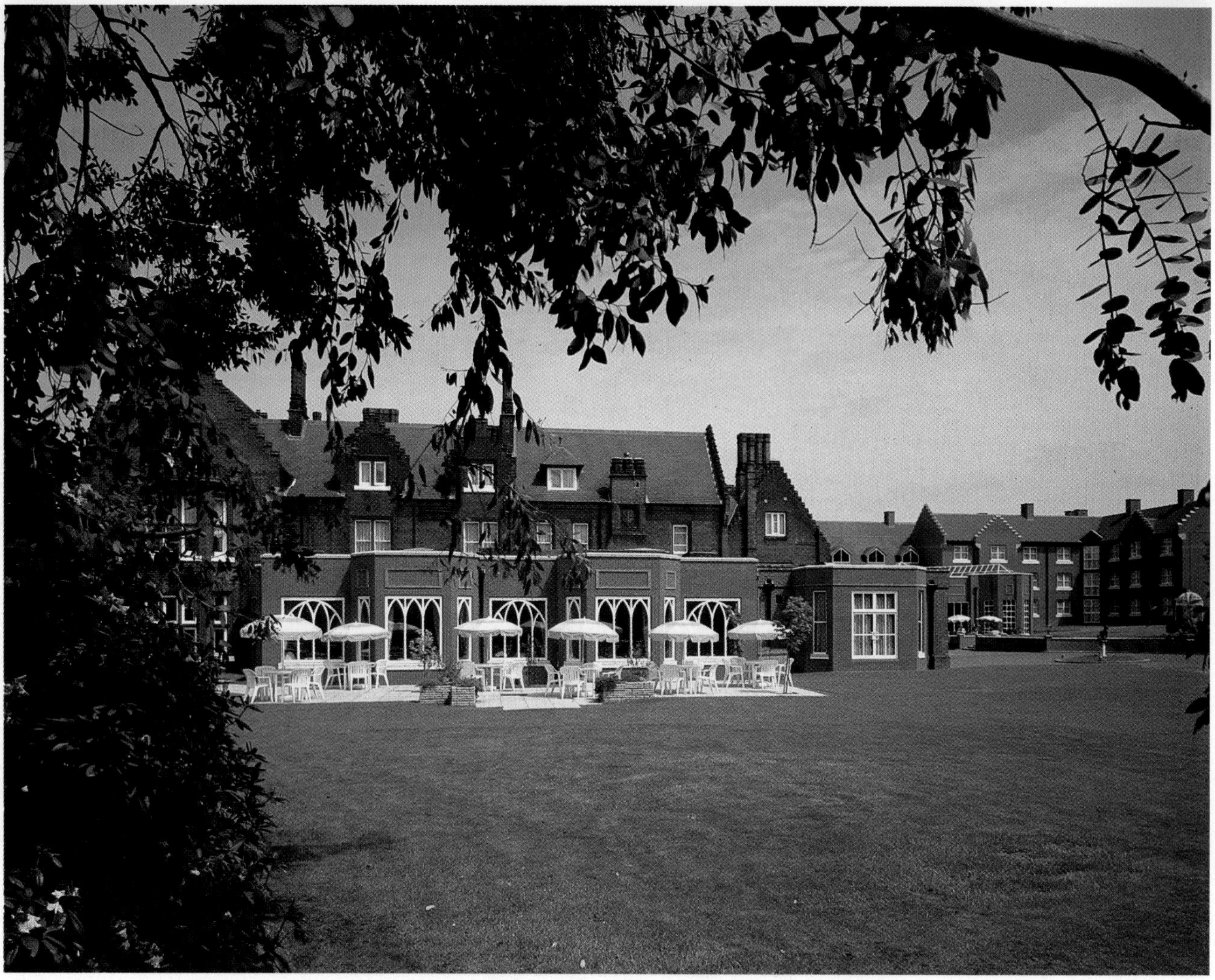

# SPROWSTON MANOR HOTEL

SPROWSTON PARK, WROXHAM ROAD, NORWICH, NORFOLK NR7 8RP
TEL: 01603 410871 FAX: 01603 423911

This imposing country house, built originally in 1559 and then largely rebuilt in the 19th century, stands at the end of an oak-lined driveway in 10 acres of grounds, just 3 miles from Norwich. The bedrooms, all en suite and some with four-posters, have views over the hotel's parkland setting and are spacious and comfortable. The hotel has two restaurants. In The Orangery lavishly draped Gothic arched windows provide the perfect atmosphere in which to enjoy the finest table d'hôte cuisine. The more traditional Manor Restaurant has been restored to classic splendour with mahogany columns, oil paintings and crystal chandeliers. The à la carte menu offers a good choice of dishes. The large health spa with indoor swimming pool and leisure club, with spa bath, pool bar, fitness studio, steam rooms and sauna, are open to hotel residents free of charge. Solarium and beauty salon are charged as taken. With its well-equipped conference rooms, the hotel is an excellent venue for social and business functions. Adjoining the hotel is the 18-hole Sprowston Park Golf Club, with floodlit driving range. The city of Norwich is rich with art and history, Sandringham, the Norfolk Broads and the Norfolk coast are all within easy reach. **Directions:** From Norwich, take the Wroxham Road (A1151) and follow signs to Sprowston Park. Price guide: Single £87–£125; double/twin £93–£125.

For hotel location, see maps on pages 490-496

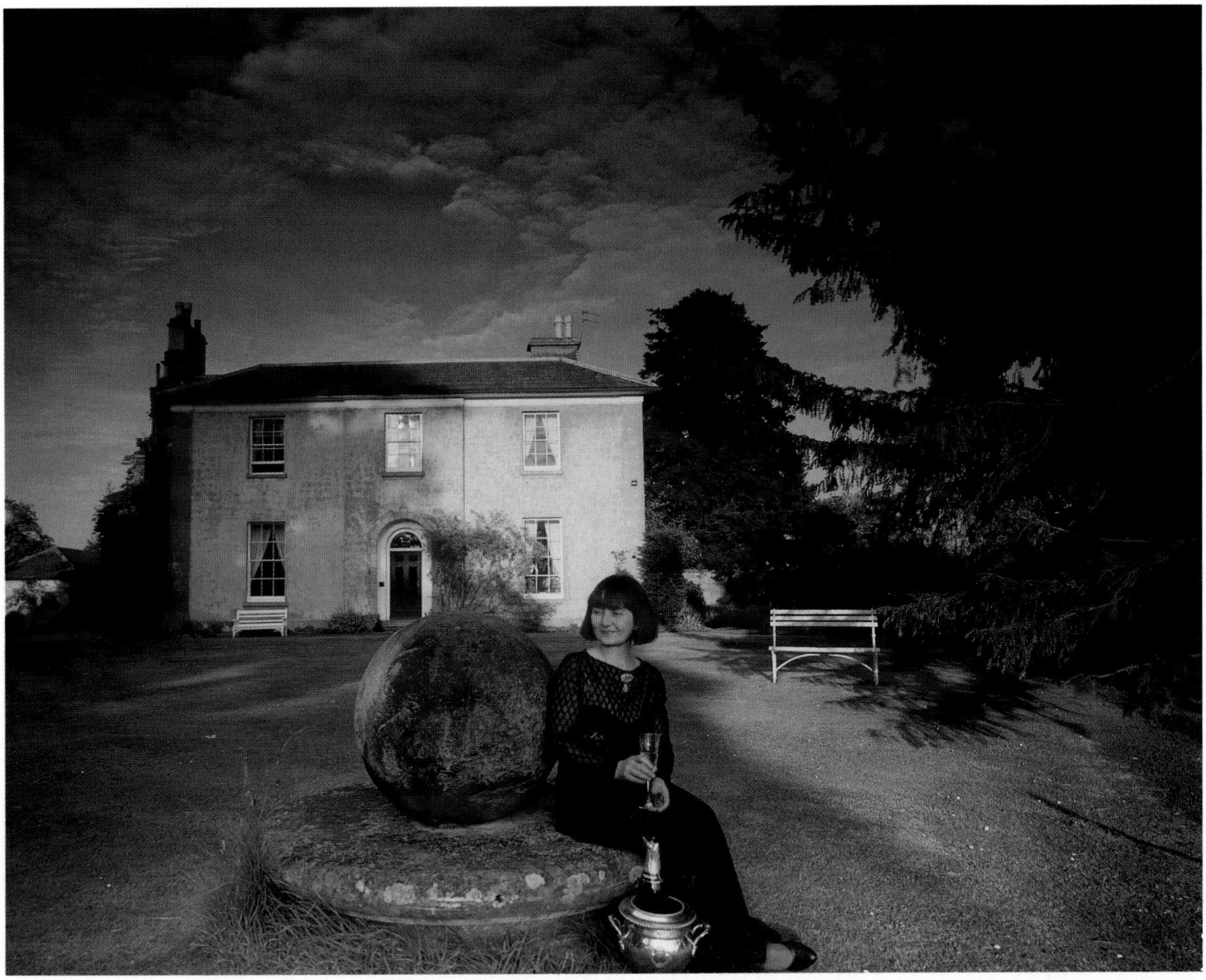

# LANGAR HALL

LANGAR, NOTTINGHAMSHIRE NG13 9HG
TEL: 01949 860559 FAX: 01949 861045

Set in the Vale of Belvoir, mid-way between Nottingham and Grantham, Langar Hall is the family home of Imogen Skirving. Epitomising "excellence and diversity" it combines the standards of good hotel-keeping with the hospitality and style of country house living. Having received a warm welcome, guests can enjoy the atmosphere of a private home that is much loved and cared for. The en suite bedrooms are individually designed and comfortably appointed. The public rooms feature fine furnishings and most rooms afford beautiful views of the garden, park and moat. Imogen and her kitchen team collaborate to produce an excellent, varied menu of modern British food. For the perfect start to the weekend it is worth booking early for a special Friday night break which sometimes combines a leisurely dinner with an entertaining in-house opera or theatre performance. Langar Hall is an ideal venue for small boardroom meetings. It is also an ideal base from which to visit Belvoir Castle, to see cricket at Trent Bridge, to visit students at Nottingham University and to see Robin Hood's Sherwood Forest. Dogs can be accommodated by arrangement. **Directions:** Langar is accessible via Bingham on the A52; or via Cropwell Bishop from the A46 (both signposted). The house adjoins the church and is hidden behind it. Price guide: Single £60–£95; double/twin £85–£150.

For hotel location, see maps on pages 490-496

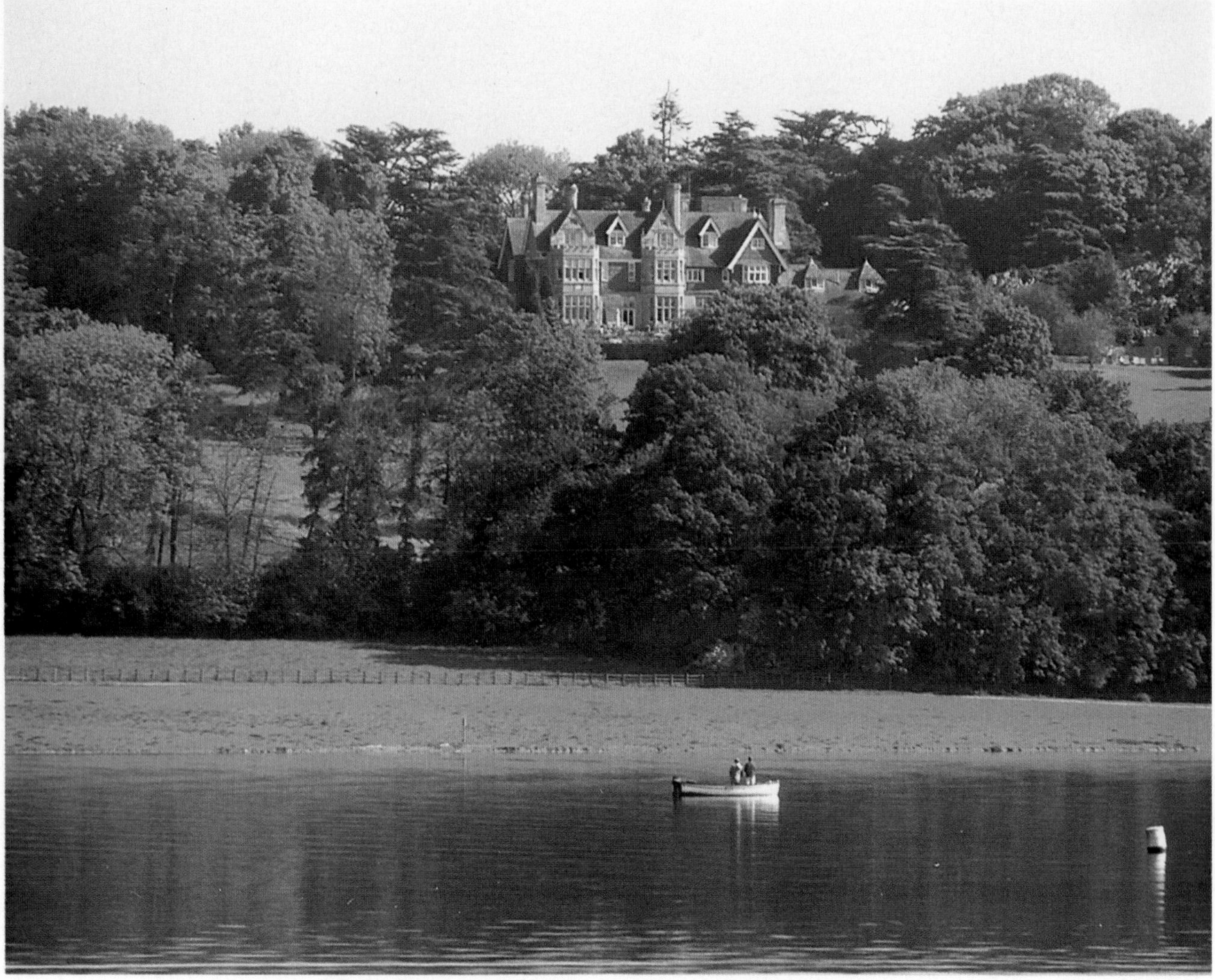

# HAMBLETON HALL

HAMBLETON, OAKHAM, RUTLAND LE15 8TH
TEL: 01572 756991 FAX: 01572 724721

Winner of Johansens Most Excellent Country Hotel Award 1996, Hambleton Hall, originally a Victorian mansion, became a hotel in 1979. Since then its renown has continually grown. It enjoys a spectacular lakeside setting in a charming and unspoilt area of Rutland. The hotel's tasteful interiors have been designed to create elegance and comfort, retaining individuality by avoiding a catalogue approach to furnishing. Delightful displays of flowers, an artful blend of ingredients from local hedgerows and the London flower markets colour the bedrooms. In the restaurant, the chef and his enthusiastic team offer a menu which is strongly seasonal. Grouse, Scottish ceps and chanterelles, partridge and woodcock are all available at just the right time of year, accompanied by the best vegetables, herbs and salads from the Hall's garden. The dishes are beautifully presented and supported by a list of interesting wines at reasonable prices. For the energetic there are lovely walks around the lake and opportunities for tennis and swimming, golf, riding, bicycling, trout fishing, and sailing. Burghley House and Belton are nearby, as are the antique shops of Oakham, Uppingham and Stamford. Hambleton Hall is a Relais et Châteaux member. **Directions:** In the village of Hambleton, signposted from the A606, 1 mile east of Oakham. Price guide: Single £140; double/twin £140–£280.

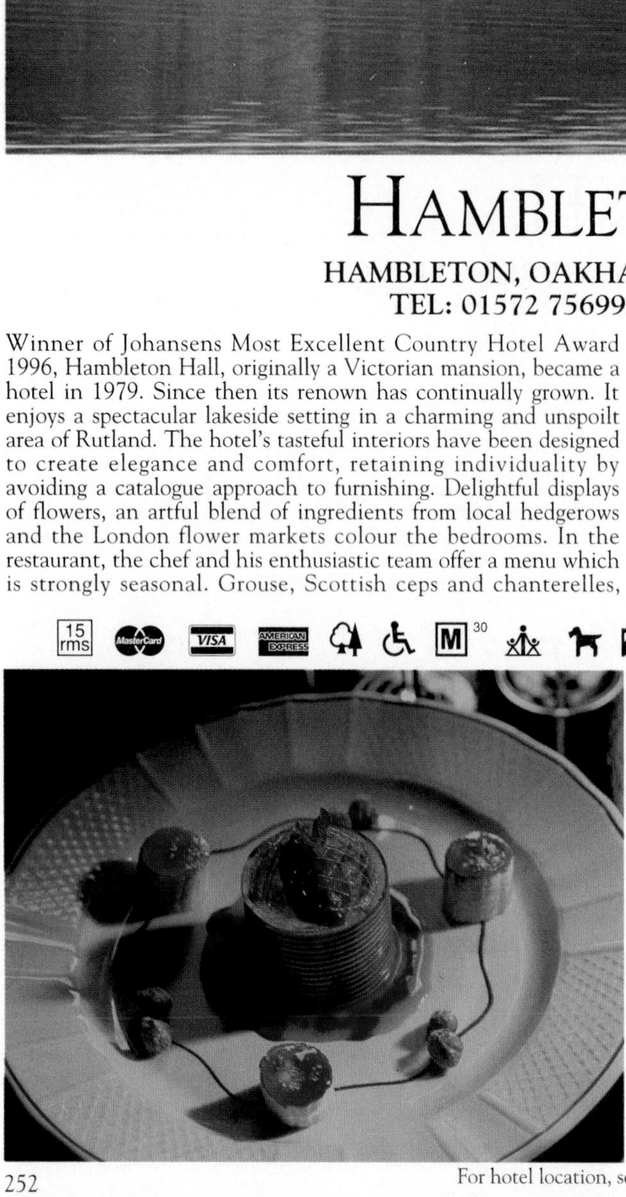

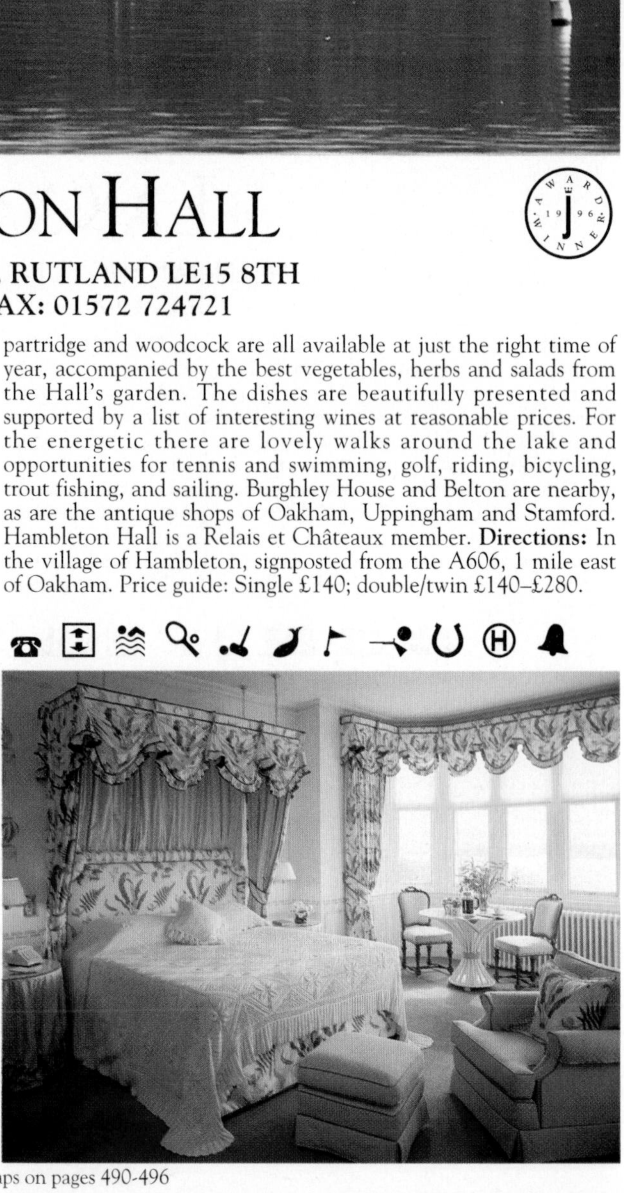

For hotel location, see maps on pages 490-496

# CHEVIN LODGE COUNTRY PARK HOTEL

**YORKGATE, OTLEY, WEST YORKSHIRE LS21 3NU**

**TEL: 01943 467818 FAX: 01943 850335 FREEPHONE RESERVATIONS 0500 340560**

A quite unique hotel – you would probably need to travel to Scandinavia to discover a similar hotel to Chevin Lodge. Built entirely of Finnish logs and surrounded by birch trees, it is set in 50 acres of lake and woodland in the beauty spot of Chevin Forest Park. The spacious, carefully designed bedrooms are furnished with pine and wicker and some have patio doors leading to the lakeside gardens. In addition, there are several luxury lodges tucked away in the woods, some with their own kitchen, which provide alternative accommodation to the hotel bedrooms. Imaginative and appetising meals are served in the beautiful balconied restaurant, which overlooks the lake. Chevin Lodge offers conference facilities in the Woodlands Suite which is fully equipped for all business requirements. There is a new Leisure Club with swimming pool, spa bath, sauna, solarium and gym. There is also a games room, all weather tennis court and jogging and cycling trails that wind through the woods. Leeds, Bradford and Harrogate are within 20 minutes' drive. Special weekend breaks are available. **Directions:** From A658 between Bradford and Harrogate, take the Chevin Forest Park road, then left into Yorkgate for Chevin Lodge. Price guide: Single £92–£108; double/twin £100–£120. Special breaks available.

For hotel location, see maps on pages 490-496

# LE MANOIR AUX QUAT' SAISONS

**GREAT MILTON, OXFORDSHIRE OX44 7PD**
**TEL: 01844 278881 FAX: 01844 278847**

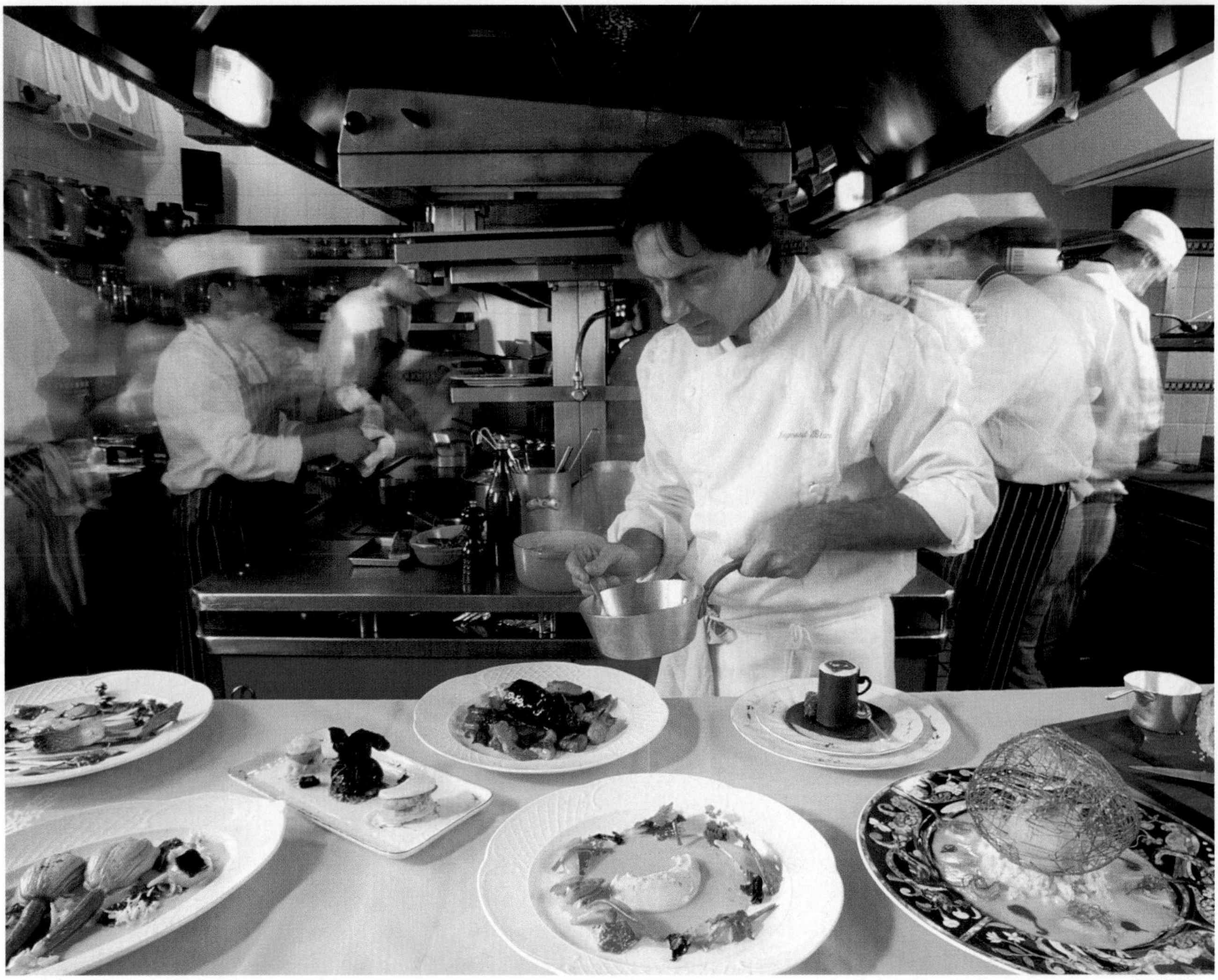

Situated in secluded grounds a few miles south of the historic city of Oxford in rural Cotswold countryside, the restaurant and the country house hotel of Le Manoir aux Quat' Saisons are among the finest in Europe. Le Manoir is the inspired creation of Raymond Blanc whose extraordinary cooking has received the highest tributes from all international guides to culinary excellence. The Times uniquely gives Blanc's cooking 10 out of 10 and rates it 'the best in Britain'. The atmosphere throughout is one of understated elegance while all nineteen bedrooms and suites offer guests the highest standards of comfort and luxury. Every need is anticipated, for service is a way of life here, never intrusive but always present.

For dedicated 'foodies', Raymond Blanc's highly successful cookery school, is a must. Five-day courses are run from October to April and participation is restricted to eight guests to ensure the highest level of personal tuition. Participants stay at Le Manoir and their partners are welcome to stay free of charge although their meals and drinks are charged separately. **Directions:** From London, M40 and turn off at junction 7 (A329 to Wallingford). From the North, leave M40 at junction 8 and follow signs to Wallingford (A329). After $1^1/_2$ miles, take second turning on right, Great Milton Manor. Price guide: Double/twin £195–£295; suites £360–£425.

For hotel location, see maps on pages 490-496

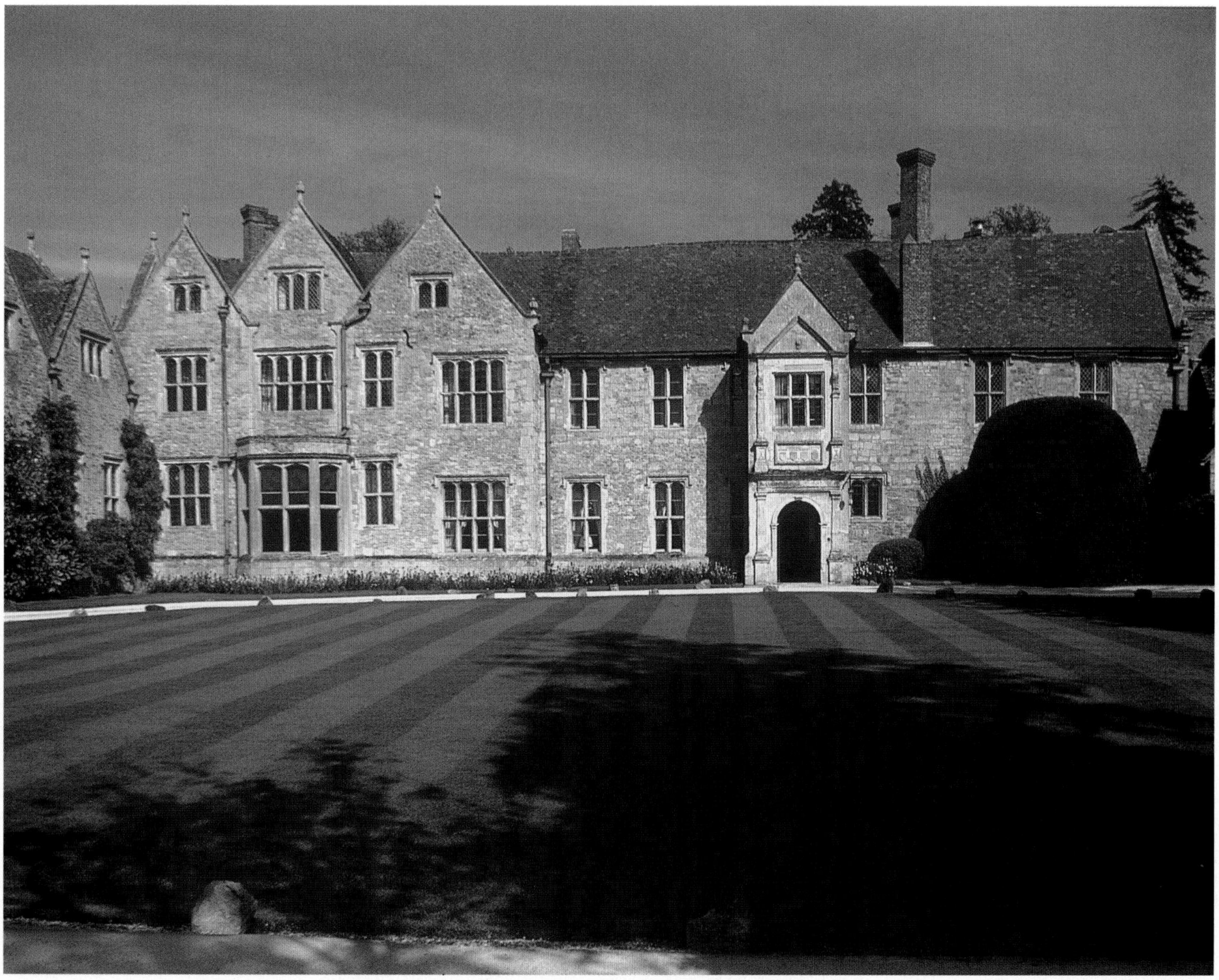

# STUDLEY PRIORY

**HORTON-CUM-STUDLEY, OXFORD, OXFORDSHIRE OX33 1AZ**

**TEL: 01865 351203 FAX: 01865 351613 USA/CANADA TOLL FREE: 800 437 2687**

Studley Priory, its exterior little altered since Elizabethan days, is conveniently located only 7 miles from both the main London–Oxford road and the dreaming spires of Oxford. There is a sense of timeless seclusion in the setting of 13 acres of wooded grounds with their fine views of the Cotswolds, the Chilterns and the Vale of Aylesbury. The bedrooms range from single rooms to the Elizabethan Suite, which has a half-tester bed dating from around 1700. Cots are available for young children. The restaurant, offering the best of English and French cuisine, provides a seasonally changing menu created from fresh local produce and complemented by an extensive and well-balanced wine list. Good conference facilities are available, and wedding parties and banquets can be accommodated. Studley Priory is ideally placed for visits to Blenheim Palace, the Manors of Waddesdon and Milton, Broughton Castle, the Great Western Museum of Railways and also horse-racing at Ascot, Newbury and Cheltenham. Clay pigeon shooting and many other activities can be arranged at the hotel. Riding facilities and the Studley Wood 18 hole golf course are nearby. **Directions:** From London leave M40 at J8. Follow A40 toward Oxford. Turn right for Horton-cum-Studley. Hotel is at the top of the hill. Price guide: Single £105–£135; double/twin £120–£175; suite £200–£250.

For hotel location, see maps on pages 490-496

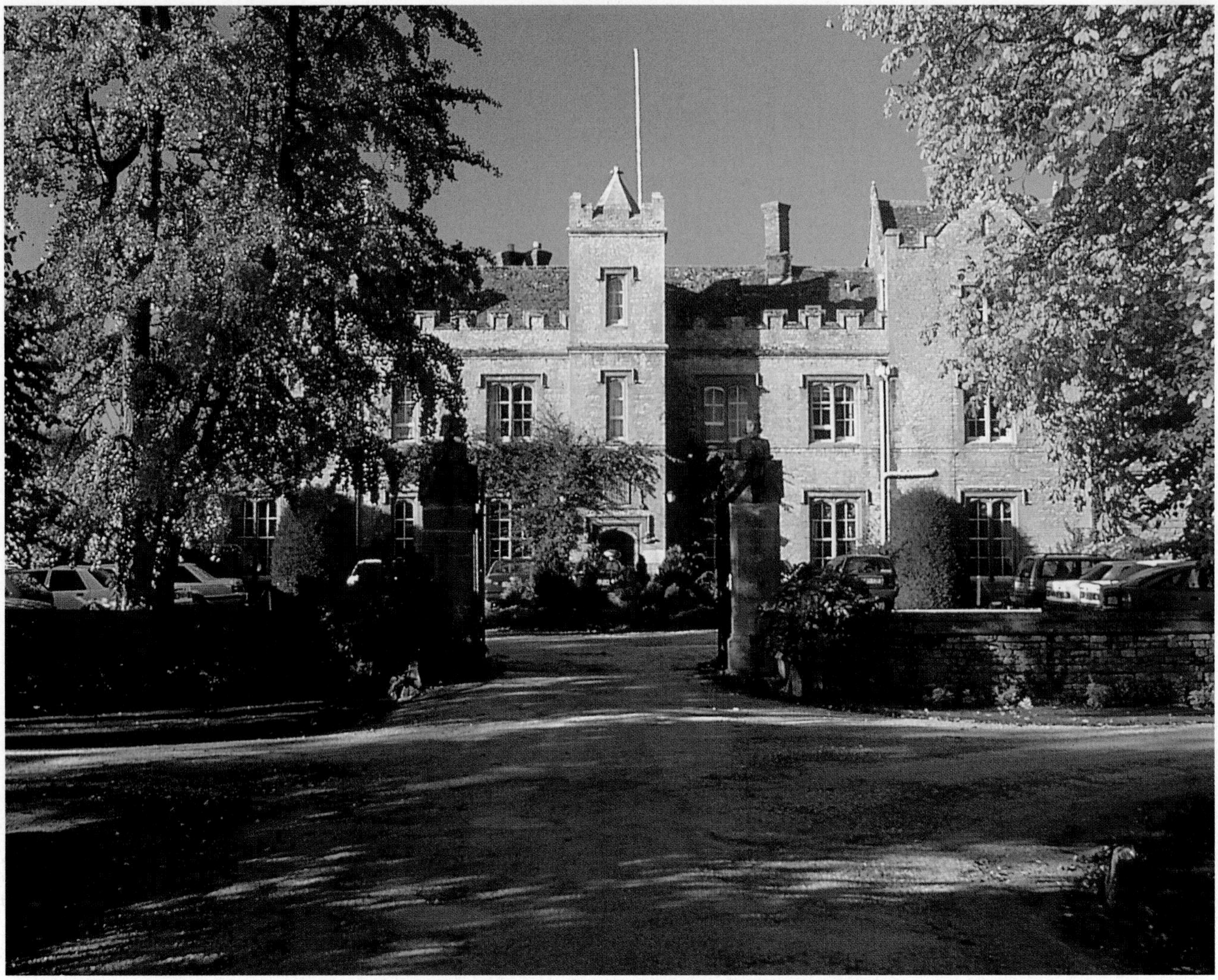

# WESTON MANOR

**WESTON-ON-THE-GREEN, OXFORDSHIRE OX6 8QL**
**TEL: 01869 350621 FAX: 01869 350901**

Imposing wrought-iron gates flanked by sculptured busts surmounting tall grey stone pillars lead into the impressive entrance to this delightful old manor house, the showpiece of the lovely village of Weston-on-the Green since the 11th century. The ancestral home of the Earls of Abingdon and Berkshire, and once the property of Henry VIII, Weston Manor stands regally in 13 acres of colourful gardens restored as a unique country house hotel of character. A peaceful retreat for visitors wishing to discover the delights of the surrounding Cotswold countryside and of Oxford, Woodstock, Blenheim Palace and Broughton Castle. Many of the Manor's 34 charming bedroom, including four in a cottage and 14 in the old coachhouse, retain antique furniture and all have garden views, private bathrooms and elegant suroundings. There is a squash court, croquet lawn and a secluded, heated outdoor swimming pool. Golf and riding are nearby. At the heart of the Manor is the restaurant, a magnificent vaulted and oak panelled Baronial Hall where delectable cuisine is served. Dining in such historic splendour is very much the focus of a memorable stay. Directions: From the M40, exit at junction 9 onto the A34. Leave A34 on 1st exit, towards Oxford. After approximately one mile turn right onto the B340. Weston Manor is on the left. Price guide: Single £97.50; double/twin £115; suite £155.

For hotel location, see maps on pages 490-496

# THE PAINSWICK HOTEL

**KEMPS LANE, PAINSWICK, GLOUCESTERSHIRE GL6 6YB**
**TEL: 01452 812160 FAX: 01452 814059**

Painswick stands high on a hill overlooking the beautiful rolling Cotswolds valleys – an old wool community of greystone buildings dating back to the 14th century. Medieval cottages mingle with elegant Georgian merchants' houses. There is one of the finest churches in the west and an ancient churchyard graced by 99 large clipped yew trees planted in 1792. Situated majestically in the centre of this architectural gem is the Palladian-style Painswick Hotel, built in 1790 and formerly the home of wealthy village rectors. The hotel's 20 en suite bedrooms have all modern amenities, fine fabrics, soft furnishings, antiques and objets d'art. Combined with the luxury toiletries, baskets of fruit, books and magazines provided for guests there is a distinct impression of staying in a comfortable private house. Delicious and tempting cuisine is served in the stylish dining room, making much use of locally reared Cotswold meat, wild Severn salmon, game, Vale of Evesham vegetables and fresh shellfish from a seawater tank. Quiet meals, wedding occasions and business meetings can be enjoyed in the private dining rooms. Resident dogs – visiting dogs only by arrangement. Directions: Exit M5 at junction 13 onto A419 and then left onto the A46 Stroud to Cheltenham road. Painswick is just north of Stroud and the hotel stands behind the church. Price guide: Single from £75; double/twin from £105.

For hotel location, see maps on pages 490-496

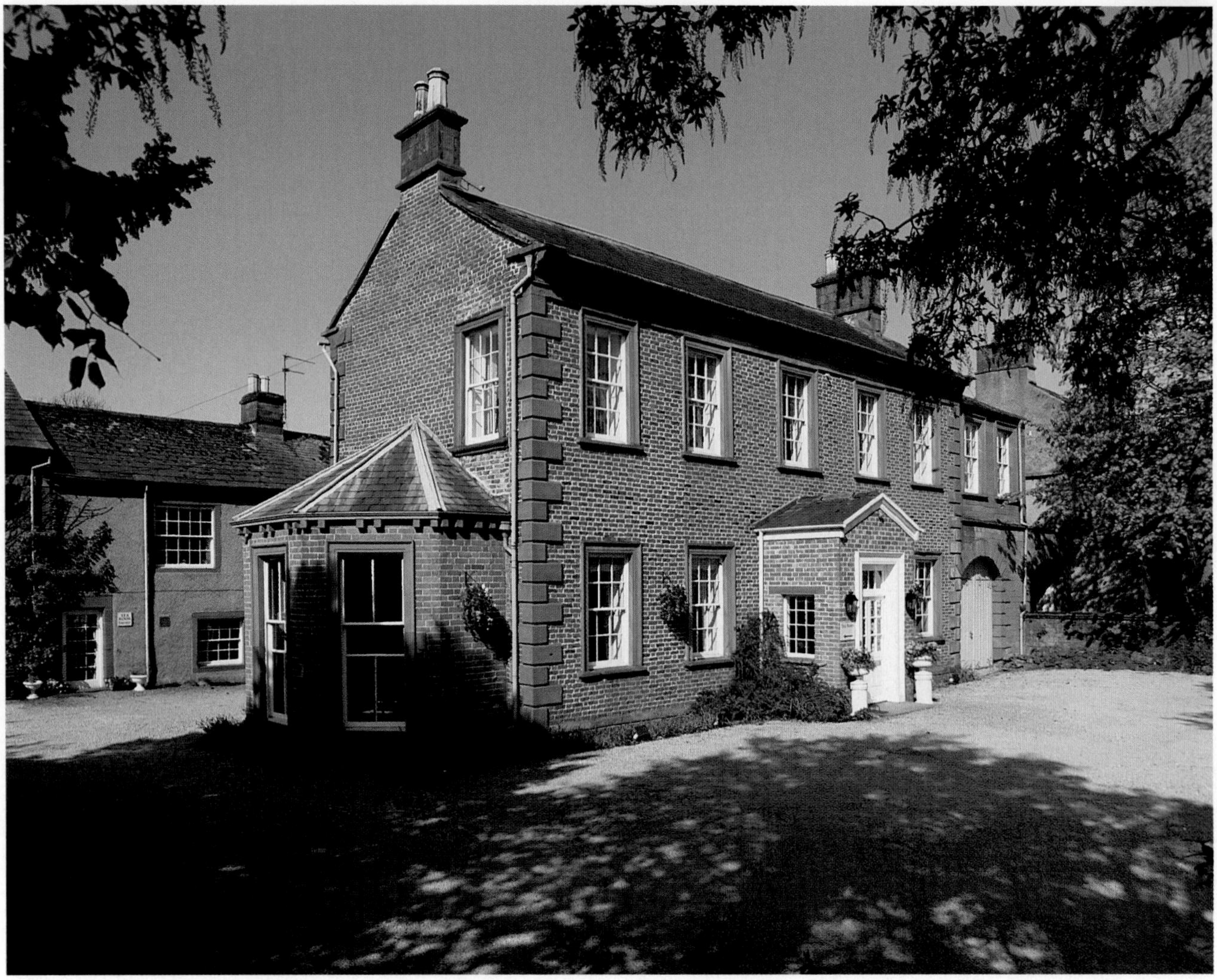

# TEMPLE SOWERBY HOUSE HOTEL

**TEMPLE SOWERBY, PENRITH, CUMBRIA CA10 1RZ**
**TEL: 017683 61578 FAX: 017683 61958 RESERVATIONS: 0800 146157**

Temple Sowerby House looks over at Cross Fell, the highest peak in the Pennines, noted for its spectacular ridge walk. This old Cumbrian farmhouse is set in two acres of gardens and guests are assured of peace and quiet. Geoffrey and Cécile Temple offer a warm, hospitable and friendly family service upon which the hotel prides itself. There are two dining rooms – the panelled room with its cosy atmosphere and the Rose Room which overlooks the garden. Delicious, home-cooked dishes might include a starter of a pithiviers of creamed wild mushrooms served with crisp salad leaves in a truffle and olive oil dressing, followed by tuna fillet served on a purée of spiced rhubarb wirh poppy seed vinegar, rounded off with iced chocolate parfait served with a white chocolate sauce. Individually furnished bedrooms all have private bathrooms. Four of the rooms are situated in the Coach House, just yards from the main house. During the winter, apéritifs are taken by the fireside, while in the summer, guests can sip drinks on the terrace and enjoy views across the fells. Lakes Ullswater and Derwentwater, the Borders, Scottish Lowlands, Hadrian's Wall and Yorkshire Dales are within easy reach by car. **Directions:** Temple Sowerby lies on the A66, seven miles from exit 40 of the M6, between Penrith and Appleby. Price guide: Single £60–£65; double/twin £85–£95. (Special breaks available)

For hotel location, see maps on pages 490-496

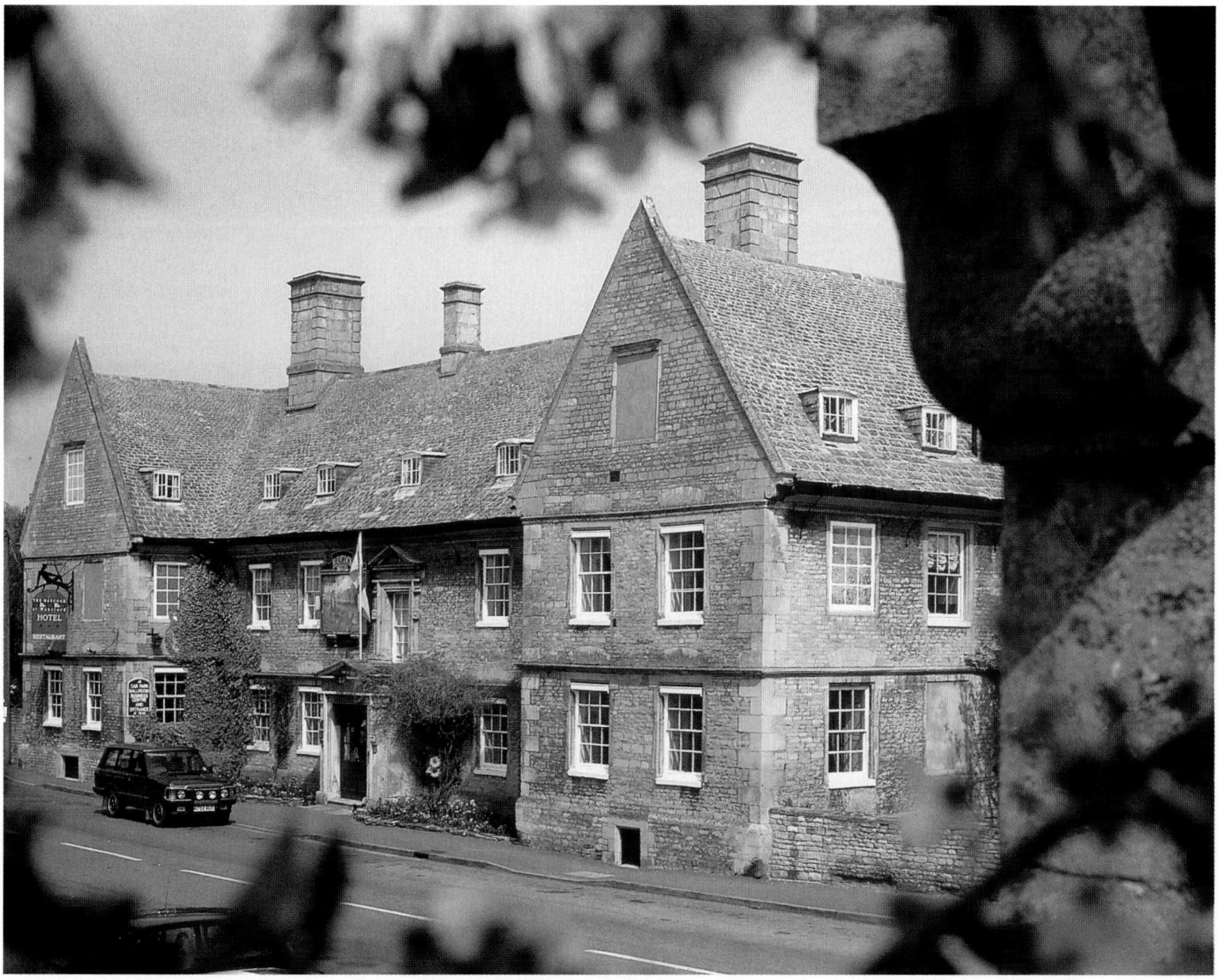

# THE HAYCOCK

WANSFORD-IN-ENGLAND, PETERBOROUGH, CAMBRIDGESHIRE PE8 6JA
TEL: 01780 782223 FAX: 01780 783031

The Haycock is a handsome old coaching inn of great charm, character and historic interest. It was host to Mary Queen of Scots in 1586 and Princess Alexandra Victoria, later Queen Victoria, in 1835. Overlooking the historic bridge that spans the River Nene, the hotel is set in a delightful village of unspoilt cottages. All the bedrooms are individually designed, equipped to the highest standards, and graced by Italian hand-painted furniture. The Tapestry Restaurant is renowned for the quality of its traditional English cooking, with dishes utilising the freshest possible ingredients. It is also famed for its outstanding wine list. A purpose-built ballroom, with lovely oak beams and its own private garden, is a popular venue for a wide range of events, from May Balls, wedding receptions and Christmas parties to the East Anglian Wine Festival. The Business Centre has also made its mark; it is well equipped with every facility required and offers the flexibility to cater for meetings, car launches, product seminars and conferences. Places of interest nearby include Burghley House, Nene Valley Railway, Elton Hall, Rutland Water and Peterborough Cathedral. An Arcadian Hotel. **Directions:** Clearly signposted on A1 a few miles south of Stamford, on A1/A47 intersection west of Peterborough. Price guide: Single £85–£115; double/twin room £115–£130; Four posters £140.

55 rms  M 200

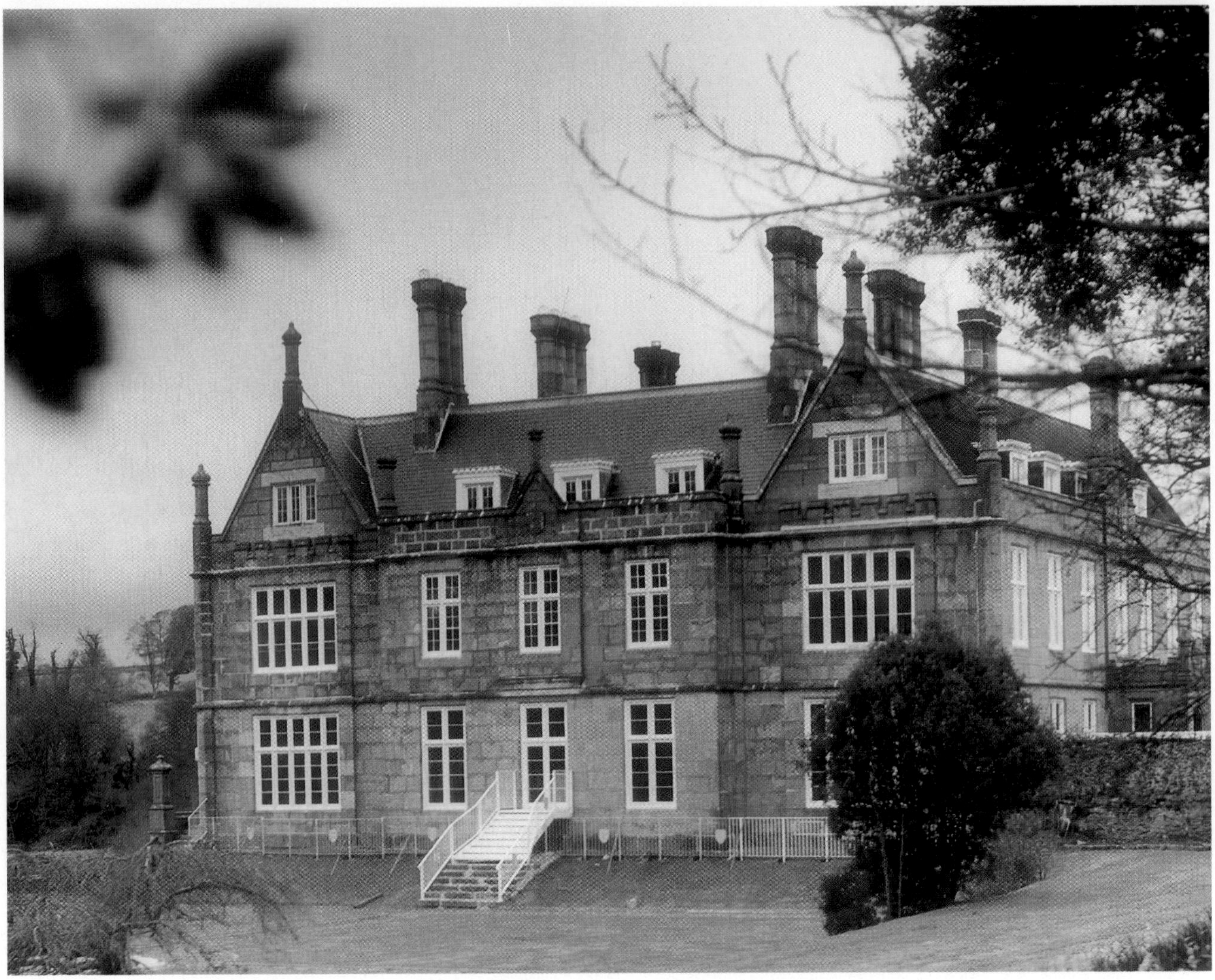

# KITLEY

**THE KITLEY ESTATE, YEALMPTON, PLYMOUTH, DEVON PL8 2NW**
**TEL: 01752 881555 FAX: 01752 881667**

This imposing Grade I listed country house hotel, built of silver grey Devonshire "marble", is situated in 300 acres of richly timbered parkland at the head of one of Yealm estuary's wooded creeks a few miles south-east of Plymouth. It is one of the earliest Tudor revival houses in England and has been splendidly restored to its former glory. Approached by a mile long drive through a magnificent private estate, Kitley is an oasis of quiet luxury, providing the highest standards in comfort, cuisine and personal service. A sweeping staircase leads to 19 spacious bedrooms and suites. Each has panoramic views over the estate and is richly appointed with furnishings designed to reflect the traditional elegance of the house whilst incorporating all modern facilities. The lounge area, with its huge open fireplace, and bar are stylish and relaxing. The restaurant is sumptuously decorated in burgundy and gold and provides the perfect atmosphere in which to enjoy the finest of cuisine – whatever the occasion. Guests can enjoy fishing in the private lake and golf, shooting and riding are nearby. **Directions:** A38, exit at the sign for the National Shire Horse Centre (A3121). Then turn right onto the A379. The hotel entrance is on the left after Yealmpton village. Price guide: Single from £65; double/twin from £75; suite from £130.

For hotel location, see maps on pages 490-496

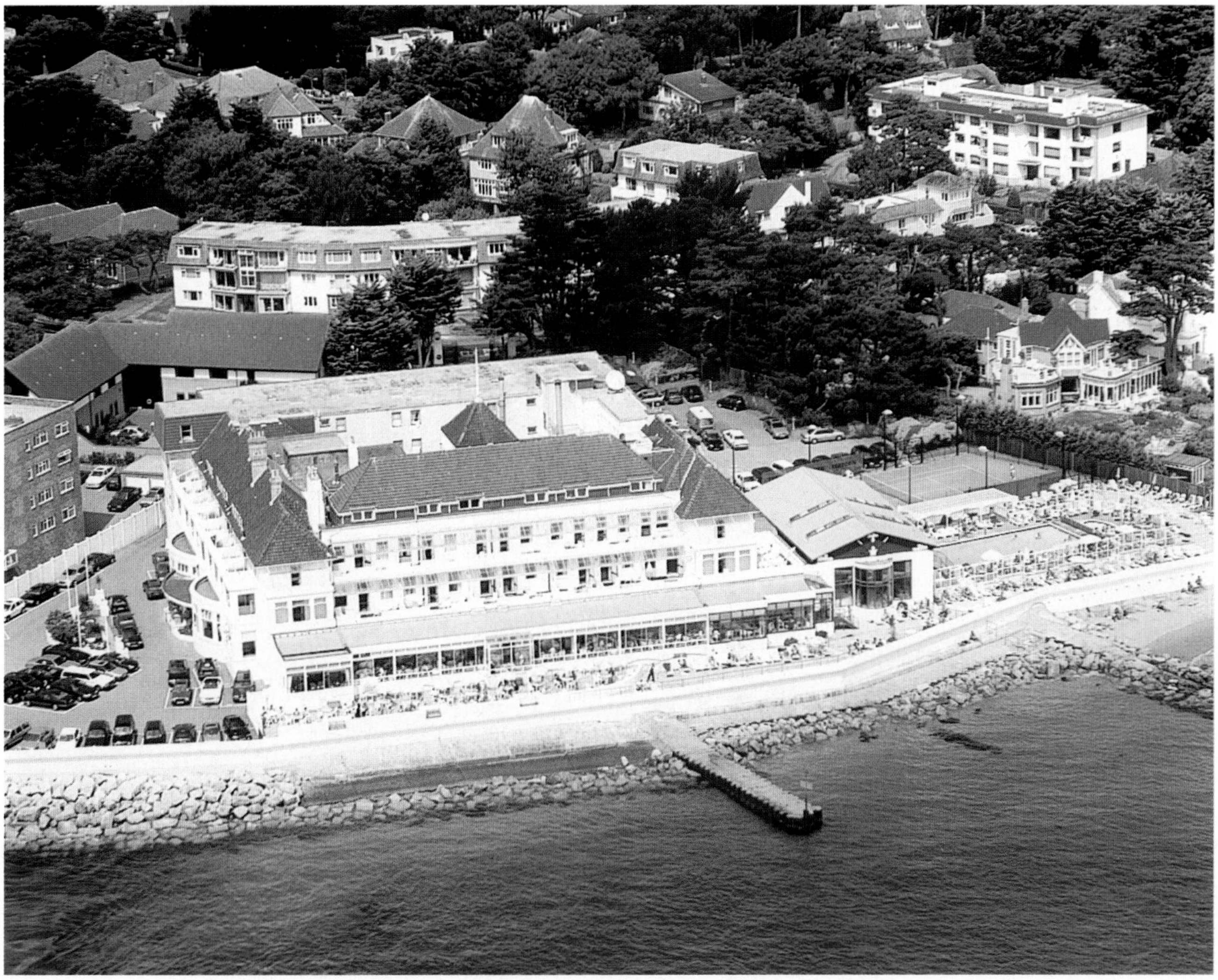

# THE HAVEN HOTEL

**SANDBANKS, POOLE, DORSET BH13 7QL**
**TEL: 01202 707333 FAX: 01202 708796**

The Haven Hotel is splendidly positioned at the sea's edge on the Sandbanks Peninsula at the mouth of Poole Harbour with its 18th century atmosphere, west of the superb sands of Bournemouth. With its mild climate and beach just on the doorstep, the hotel's setting is an ideal choice for those seeking relaxation and quieter pleasures. Behind the hotel's grand, modern facade there is comfort, style and ambience that reflects its AA and RAC four-star rating. Glorious sea views can be enjoyed from many of the 94 en suite bedrooms, all of which are decorated and furnished to a high standard. Excellent dinners are served in La Roche, a gourmet restaurant holding two rosettes, while there are further fine dining facilities in the Sea View restaurant and an attractive conservatory. Facilities of the hotel's sports and leisure club include indoor and outdoor heated pools, sauna, steam room, solarium, American hot tub, gymnasium, squash and tennis courts. There are a variety of comprehensively equipped meeting rooms. For the sports enthusiast, golf and sailing can be arranged. Local places of interest include Poole's historic harbour and nature reserve, delightful old inns and Brownsea Island, site of the first Boy Scout camp, Studland Bay, Corfe Castle and the Isle of Purbeck which can be reached by car ferry. **Directions:** From the A31 join the A338 to Bournemouth and follow the signs to Poole and Sandbanks. Price guide: Double £134–£190.

For hotel location, see maps on pages 490-496

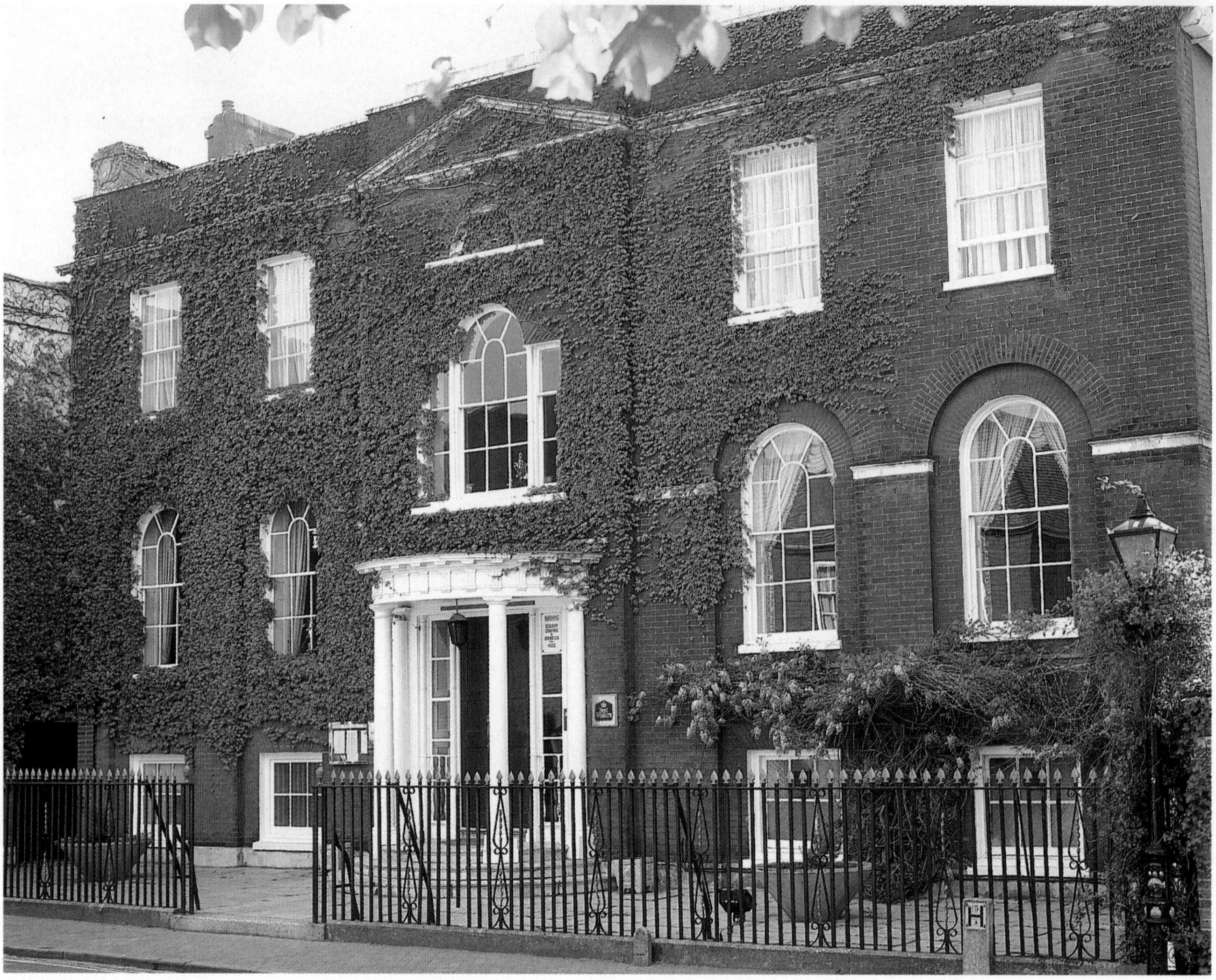

# THE MANSION HOUSE HOTEL AND DINING CLUB

**THAMES STREET, POOLE, DORSET BH15 1JN**
**TEL: 01202 685666 FAX: 01202 665709**

Poole has been a flourishing port and market town since the 13th century, and the Mansion House is one of its finest Georgian houses It is pleasantly secluded from the busy town in a quiet cobbled cul-de-sac close to St James' Church. New arrivals are instantly impressed by its graceful facade and the restrained luxury of the hall, with its marble pillars, chandelier and antiques. The drawing room is another charming reminder of a gracious era. The guest rooms have been beautifully decorated, with lovely floral prints, brass bedsteads and art deco lamps. Lots of little thoughtful extras create 'a home away from home'. Guests mingle in the smart Cocktail Bar, while deciding whether to dine in style in the elegant panelled Benjamin's Restaurant – gourmet cooking with traditional English dishes predominating – or relax in the more rustic JJ's Bistro, enjoying a delicious, less elaborate, meal. The hotel has a Dining Club and residents benefit from the special prices afforded to members. Golfers have good courses nearby, Parkstone for example; golf weekends and golf days organised by our in-house golfer. The port is fascinating and Corfe Castle is another local landmark. An ideal stopover for the Channel ferry. Directions: M3, M27, A 31, A349 and A350. Thames Street runs between The Quay and West Street by Poole Bridge. Follow signs to Channel Ferry. Price guide: Single £75–£82.50; double/twin £90–£125.

For hotel location, see maps on pages 490-496

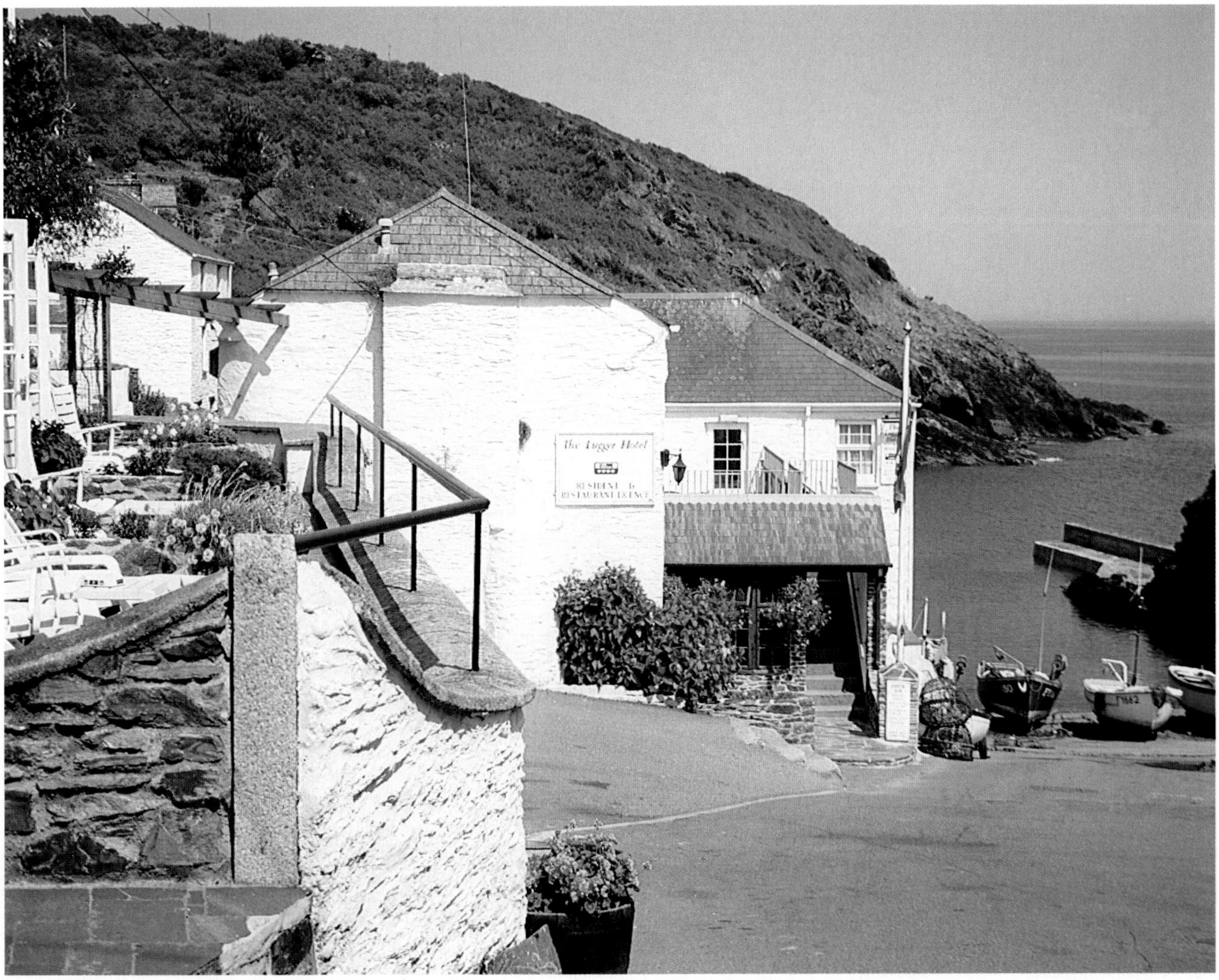

# THE LUGGER HOTEL

**PORTLOE, NR TRURO, CORNWALL TR2 5RD**
**TEL: 01872 501322 FAX: 01872 501691**

A 17th century inn by the sea – and reputed to have been the haunt of smugglers, it sits at the very water's edge in the picturesque fishing village of Portloe on the Cornish coast facing south. Situated in a conservation area in the heart of the beautiful Roseland Peninsula, this internationally renowned hotel is like a solid rock in a changing world. The Lugger has been in the Powell family for three generations during which, much thought and care have been taken to preserve its welcoming intimate atmosphere. There are 19 tastefully furnished bedrooms, all with en suite facilities as well as personal safes and refrigerators. A skilled team of chefs offers varied and exciting menus of English and Continental dishes in the attractive restaurant overlooking the cove. Local seafood is a speciality, with crab and lobster being particular favourites. The freshly made desserts on the sweet trolley, topped with clotted cream, are a delight to both the eye and the palate, whilst there is a wide choice of wines including Cornish wine from just a mile away. English Tourist Board 4 Crowns Highly Commended. Closed early November until late February. **Directions:** A390 from Plymouth, B3287 from St Austell to Tregony, then A3078 to Portloe. Price guide (including dinner): Single £75–£85; double/twin £150–£170.

For hotel location, see maps on pages 490-496

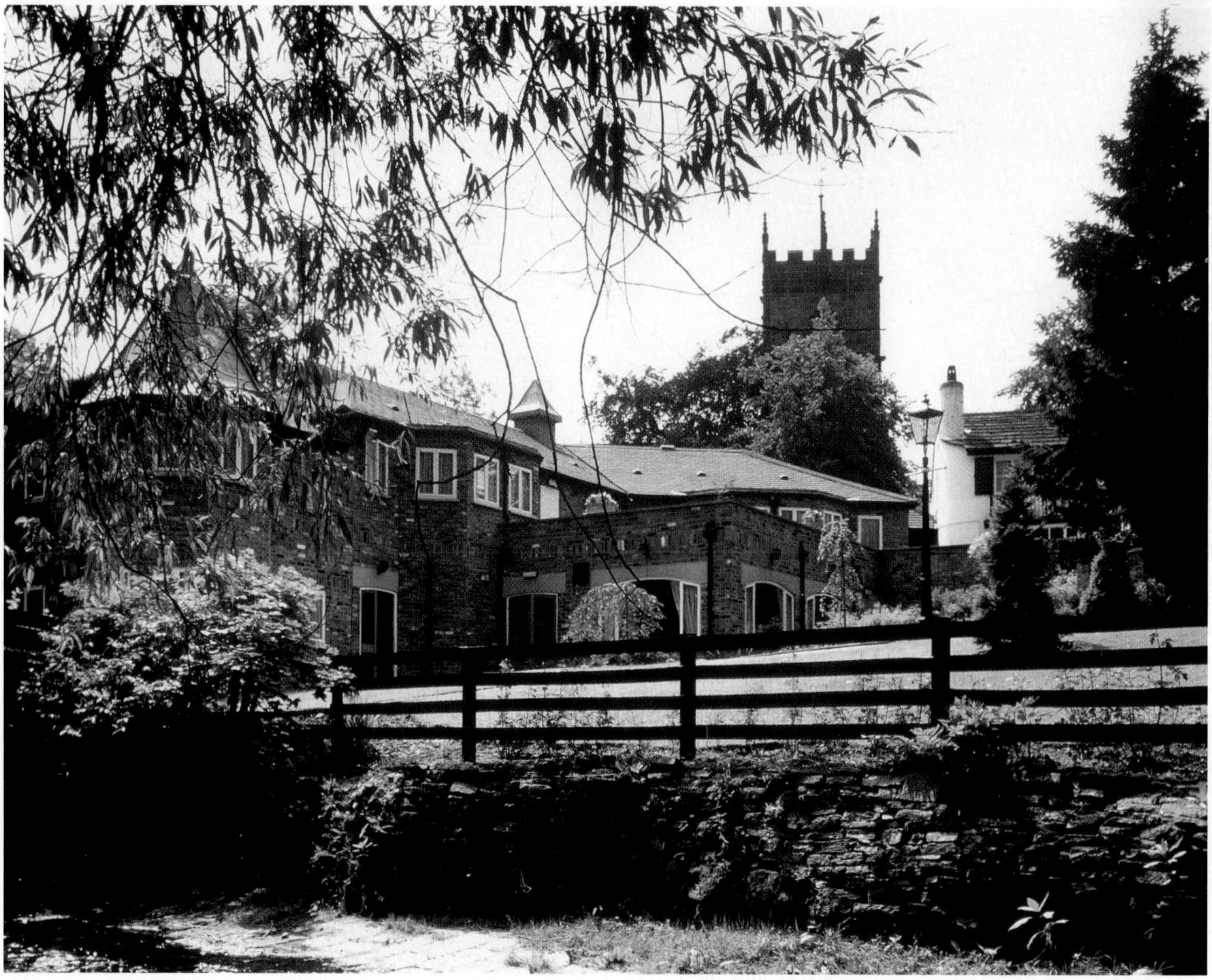

# The Bridge Hotel

PRESTBURY, CHESHIRE SK10 4DQ
TEL: 01625 829326 FAX: 01625 827557

The Bridge Hotel is situated in the centre of the village of Prestbury, one of the prettiest villages in the North West of England. Originally dating from 1626, The Bridge today combines the old world charm of an ancient and historic building with the comfort and facilities of a modern hotel, yet within easy reach of Manchester Airport and major motorways. The public rooms have retained much of the former inn's original character, with oak panelling and beams in the bar and reception area. The bedrooms, many of which overlook the River Bollin, are decorated to the highest standard, five of which are in the original building. In the attractive galleried dining room, table d'hôte and à la carte menus offer traditional English cuisine. There is an extensive selection of wines to accompany your meal. It is also the perfect place for business with three conference suites. While enjoying a quiet location, the hotel is convenient for Manchester, just 30 minutes away, and Manchester Airport. The Peak District National Park and Cheshire are nearby with Stately Homes including Chatsworth, Tatton Park and Capesthorne. **Directions:** In the centre of the village next to the church. Prestbury is on the A538 from Wilmslow to Macclesfield. Price guide: Single £75–£79; double/twin £82–£95; suites £115. Special weekend rates available.

For hotel location, see maps on pages 490-496

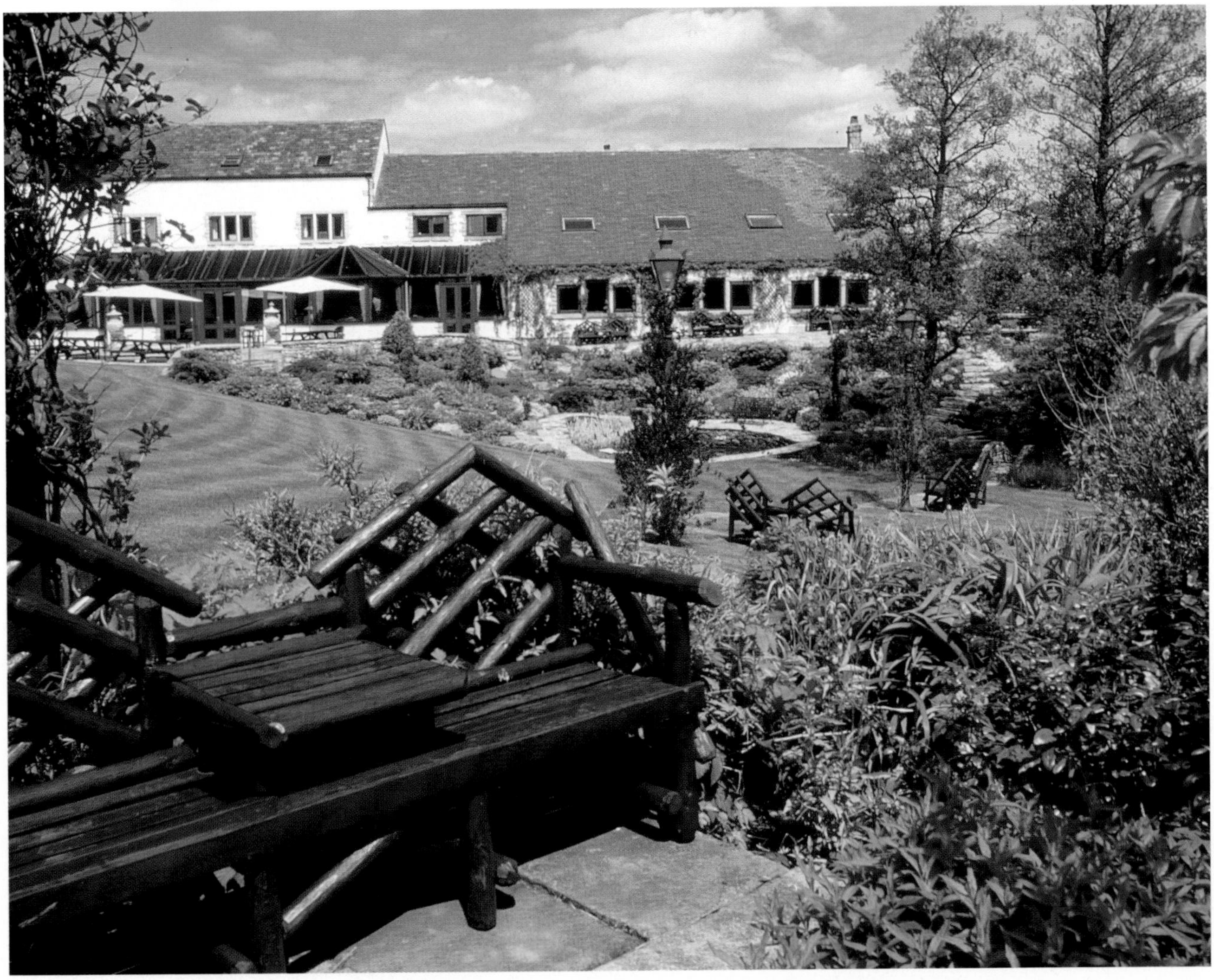

# THE GIBBON BRIDGE HOTEL

**NR CHIPPING, FOREST OF BOWLAND, LANCASHIRE PR3 2TQ**

**TEL: 01995 61456 FAX: 01995 61277**

This award-winning hotel, in the heart of Lancashire in the Forest of Bowland provides a welcoming and peaceful retreat. The area, a favourite of the Queen, is now famous for being recognised officially as the centre of the Kingdom! Created in 1982 by resident proprietor Janet Simpson and her late mother Margaret, the hotel buildings combine traditional architecture with interesting Gothic masonry. Individually designed, furnished and equipped to the highest standard, the eight bedrooms and twenty two suites include four poster, half tester and Gothic brass beds and Jacuzzi spa baths. The restaurant overlooks the garden and is renowned for traditional and imaginative dishes incorporating home-grown vegetables and herbs. The splendid garden bandstand is perfect for any musical repertoire or civil wedding ceremony. Inside the hotel elegant private rooms and lounges are available for dinner parties, receptions and executive meetings. Leisure facilities include a beauty salon, gymnasium, solarium, steam room, and all weather tennis court. Numerous sporting activities can be arranged locally. **Directions:** From the South: M6 Exit 31A, follow signs for Longridge. From the North: M6 Exit 32, follow A6 to Broughton and B5269 to Longridge – follow signs for Chipping – in the village turn right a T-junction, the hotel is ¾ miles on the right. Price guide: Single £70; double/twin £95; suite £130–£225.

For hotel location, see maps on pages 490-496

# NUTFIELD PRIORY

**NUTFIELD, REDHILL, SURREY RH1 4EN**
**TEL: 01737 822066 FAX: 01737 823321**

Built in 1872 by the millionaire MP, Joshua Fielden, Nutfield Priory is an extravagant folly embellished with towers, elaborate carvings, intricate stonework, cloisters and stained glass, all superbly restored to create an unusual country house hotel. Set high on Nutfield Ridge, the priory has far-reaching views over the Surrey and Sussex countryside, while being within easy reach of London and also Gatwick Airport. The elegant lounges and library have ornately carved ceilings and antique furnishings. Unusually spacious bedrooms – some with beams – enjoy views over the surrounding countryside. Fresh fruit is a thoughtful extra. The cloistered restaurant provides a unique environment in which to enjoy the high standard of cuisine, complemented by an extensive wine list. Conferences and private functions can be accommodated in the splendid setting of one of the hotel's 10 conference rooms. The Priory sports and leisure club, adjacent to the hotel, provides all the facilities for exercise and relaxation that one could wish for, including a swimming pool, sauna, spa, solarium, gym, steam room, beauty & hairdressing and billiard room. An Arcadian Hotel. **Directions:** Nutfield is on the A25 between Redhill and Godstone and can be reached easily from junctions 6 and 8 of the M25. From Godstone, the Priory is on the left just after the village. Price guide: Single £115–£125; double/twin £135–£155; suite from £250.

For hotel location, see maps on pages 490-496

# THE RICHMOND GATE HOTEL AND RESTAURANT

**RICHMOND HILL, RICHMOND-UPON-THAMES, SURREY TW10 6RP**

**TEL: 0181 940 0061 FAX: 0181 332 0354**

This former Georgian country house stands on the crest of Richmond Hill close to the Royal Park and Richmond Terrace with its commanding views over the River Thames. The 66 stylishly furnished en suite bedrooms combine every comfort of the present with the elegance of the past and include several luxury four-poster rooms and suites. Exceptional and imaginative cuisine, complemented by an extensive wine list offering over 100 wines from around the world is served in the sophisticated surroundings of 'Gates On The Park Restaurant'. Through the week a less formal alternative is available in the Bistro in the Victorian conservatory, overlooking the hotel's beautiful walled garden. Weddings, business meetings and private dining events can be arranged in a variety of rooms. Cedars Health and Leisure Club is accessed through the hotel and includes: 20 metre pool, 6 metre spa, sauna, steam room, aerobics studio, cardio-vascular and resistance gymnasia, health and beauty suite. Richmond is close to London and the West End yet in a country setting. The Borough offers a wealth of visitor attractions, including Hampton Court Palace, Syon House and Park and the Royal Botanic Gardens at Kew. Weekend breaks are inclusive of entry into one of the local attractions and are available from £140. **Directions:** Opposite the Star & Garter Home at the top of Richmond Hill. Price guide: Single £95–£122; double/twin £120–£144.

66 rms MasterCard VISA AMERICAN EXPRESS M 50

For hotel location, see maps on pages 490-496

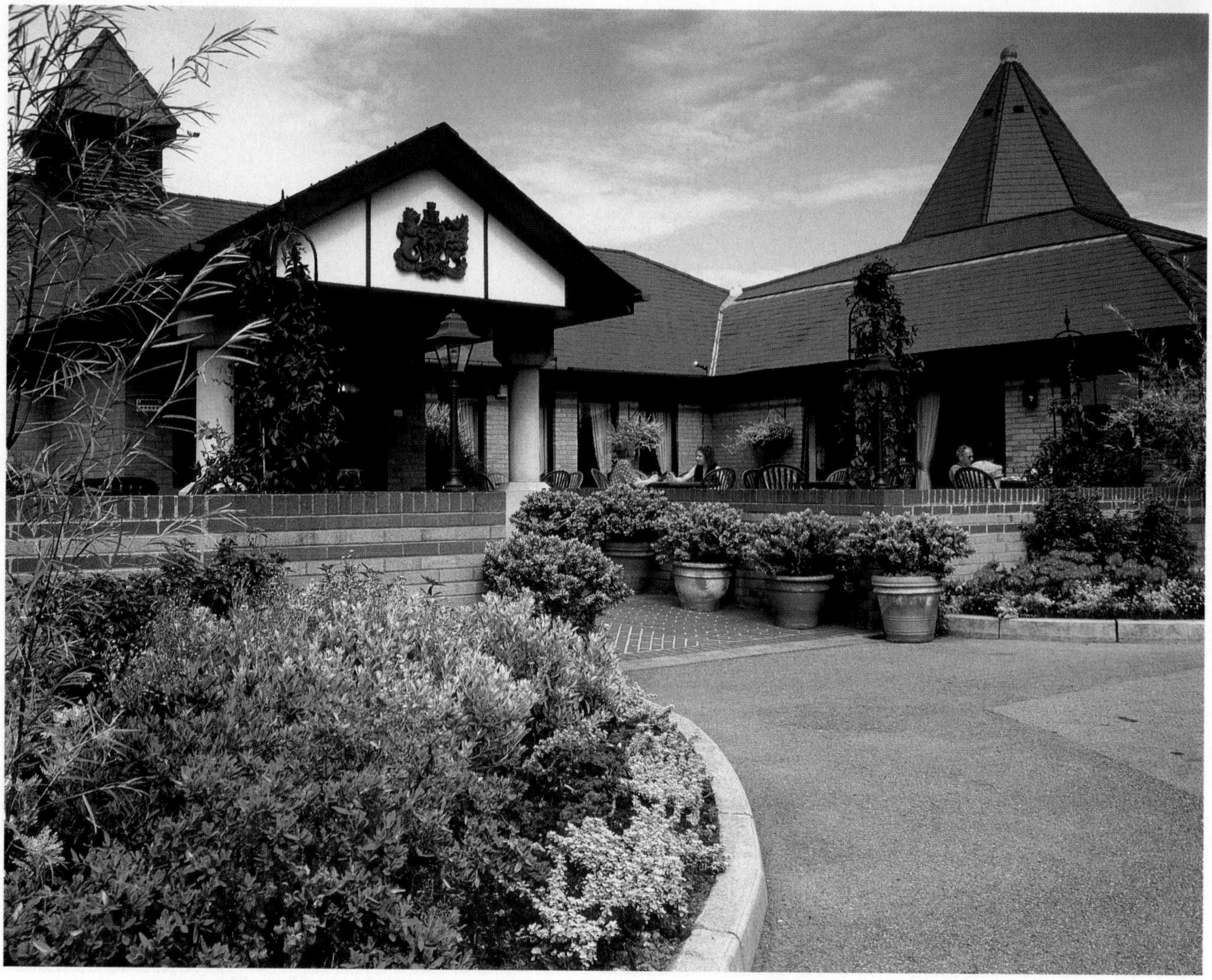

# Bridgewood Manor Hotel

**BRIDGEWOOD ROUNDABOUT, MAIDSTONE ROAD, CHATHAM, KENT ME5 9AX**
**TEL: 01634 201333 FAX: 01634 201330**

This spacious, purpose-built hotel situated on the edge of the historic city of Rochester has every modern facility that guests could wish for. Strategically placed near Ashford International Station between London and the Kent Channel Ports, Bridgewood has outstanding conference facilities, also a reputation that has earned it the award of four stars by the AA and RAC. Service is friendly and attentive and fine cuisine is served in the restaurant and in the Terrace Bar, complemented by a wide range of excellent wines. All the bedrooms are comfortable and equipped with colour satellite television, direct-dial telephone and hospitality tray. The leisure facilities include a indoor swimming pool, a spa bath, sauna and steam room, a gymnasium, hairdressers, solarium, beauty treatment room and full-size snooker table. Outside there is an all-weather tennis court and a putting green. Shooting and riding can be arranged. A short distance away are Rochester and Canterbury, Chatham Dockyard, Leeds Castle and Chartwell and the Tyland Wildlife Centre. **Directions:** From the M2, exit at junction 3 and take the A229 towards Rochester, Chatham and Walderslade. At Bridgewood Roundabout follow sign to Walderslade and Lordswood. The hotel entrance is 50 yards on the left along Walderslade Road. From M20, exit at junction 6 onto A229. Price guide: Single £90; double/twin £110.

For hotel location, see maps on pages 490-496

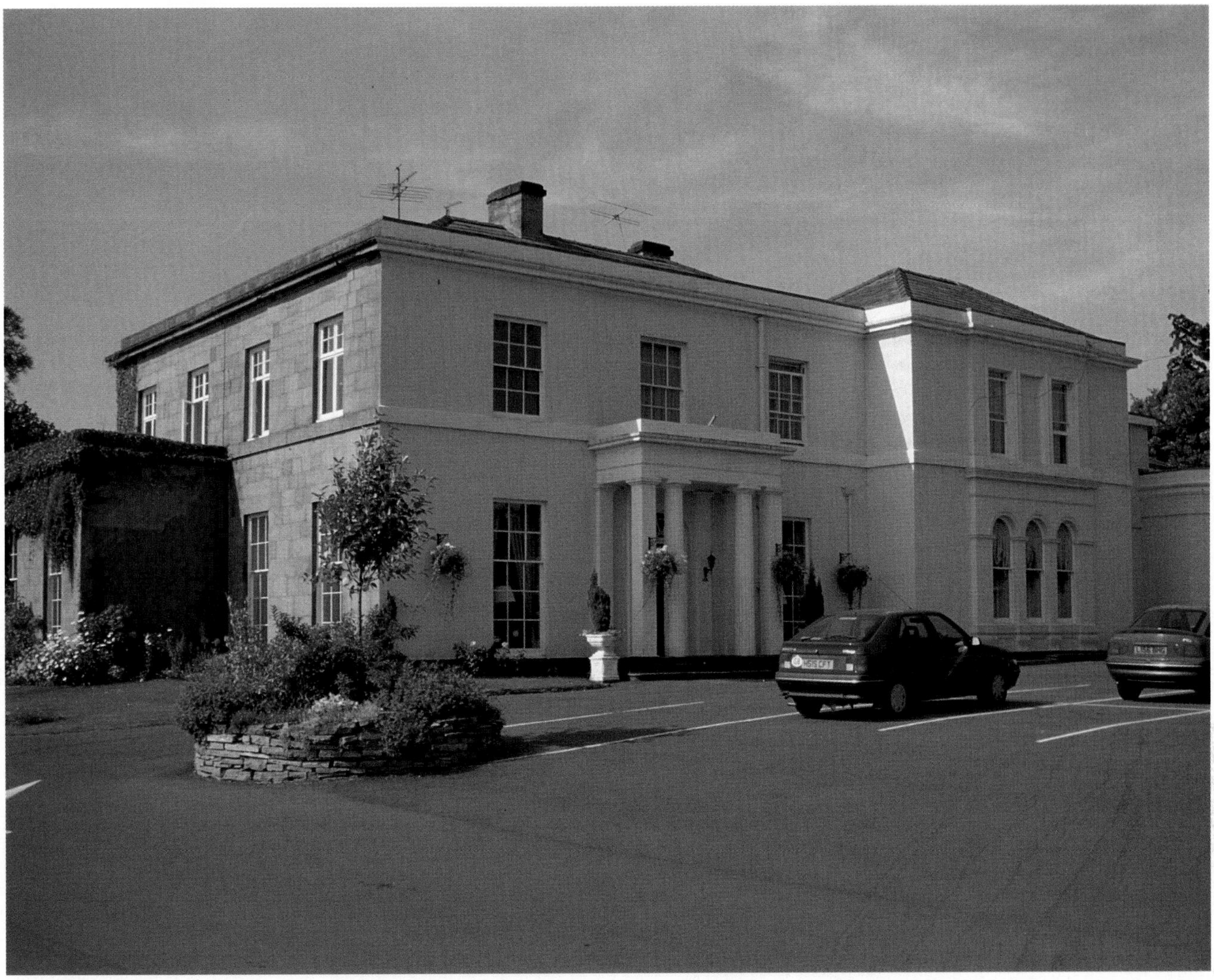

# THE CHASE HOTEL

**GLOUCESTER ROAD, ROSS-ON-WYE, HEREFORDSHIRE HR9 5LH**
**TEL: 01989 763161 FAX: 01989 768330**

The Chase Hotel, just a few minutes' walk from the centre of Ross-on-Wye, is a handsome Regency country house standing in pleasant grounds. Careful restoration of the interiors has recaptured the elegance and craftsmanship of the past. After an apéritif in the Chase Bar, guests are ushered into the dining room where the tall windows and voluminous drapes make a striking impression. Chef Ken Tait favours a modern British approach to cooking, with a distinct continental influence. He uses fine local produce, such as Herefordshire beef, game and fresh vegetables in combination, to create dishes that give an unexpected subtlety to traditional ingredients. When the bedrooms were renovated, great care was taken to preserve their original Georgian character: the effect was then softened with comfortable furniture and appealing fabrics. Unobtrusive, up-to-the-minute amenities have been provided in each room and en suite bathroom. The function suites can accommodate a host of events. The surrounding area offers an infinite variety of places to visit, including Hereford Cathedral, Symonds Yat, Monmouth and the Forest of Dean. **Directions:** From M50 exit 4 turn left at roundabout signposted Gloucester and right at first roundabout signposted 'Town Centre'. Hotel is ½ mile on left-hand side. Price guide: Single £65; double/twin £80; suite £110.

For hotel location, see maps on pages 490-496

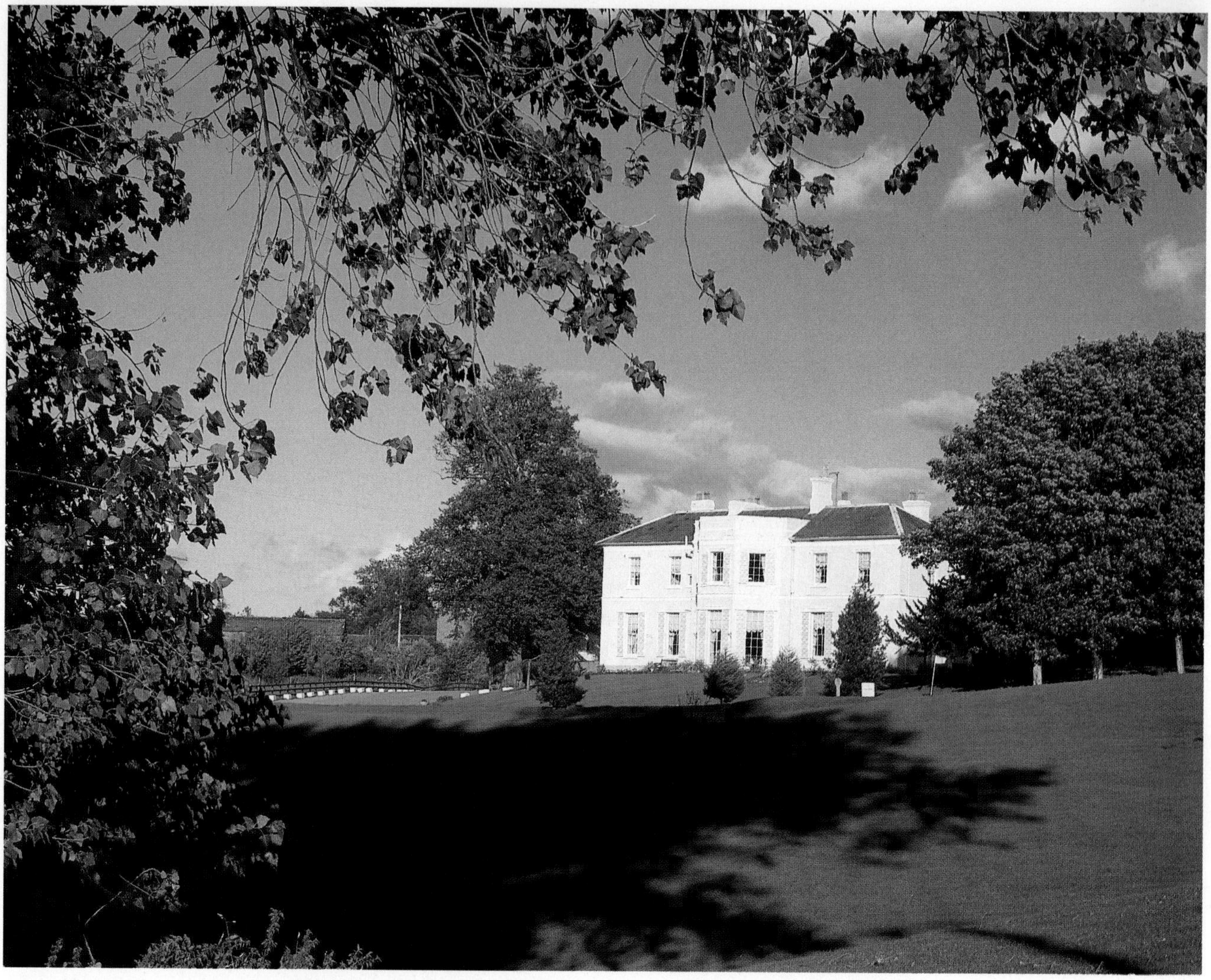

# PENGETHLEY MANOR

**NR ROSS-ON-WYE, HEREFORDSHIRE HR9 6LL**
**TEL: 01989 730211 FAX: 01989 730238**

The first Baron Chandos, a favourite of Mary I Queen of England is reputed to have acquired Pengethley Estate in 1544, and here he built the original Tudor house. Although much of the building was ravaged by fire in the early 19th century, some parts survived – notably the oak panelling in the entrance hall – and it was rebuilt as a Georgian manor house in 1820. The en suite bedrooms reflect the traditional character of a former nobleman's country home. Drawing on the best produce that rural Herefordshire can offer, the menu includes Wye salmon, prime Hereford beef and tender Welsh lamb. The manor's own vineyard flourish within the boundaries of the estate and the delicious product may be sampled in the restaurant. A complete vegetarian menu is available. Throughout their stay at Pengethley, guests will find the service always attentive, but never intrusive. Chandos House is a purpose-built conference suite which can cater for business and social events. For leisure, there is a snooker room, a well-stocked trout lake, a 9-hole golf improvement course and an outdoor heated pool. Riding and hot-air ballooning can be arranged. The Wye Valley and Welsh border are not very far away and the Malvern Hills are nearby. **Directions:** 4 miles from Ross-on-Wye, 10 miles from Hereford on the A49. Price guide: Single £75–£115; double/twin £120–£160.

For hotel location, see maps on pages 490-496

# BROOMHILL LODGE

**RYE FOREIGN, RYE, EAST SUSSEX TN31 7UN**
**TEL: 01797 280421 FAX: 01797 280402**

Imposing and ivy-bedecked, Broomhill is a dramatic mock-Jacobean construction towering above three green acres and dating back to the 1820s, when it was commissioned by a prominent local banker. Giving pleasing views over rolling East Sussex terrain, the hotel has been renovated with care by its owners to offer a standard of accommodation as impressive as the architecture. Relaxed, informal, yet unerringly professional, the management and staff have quickly established an elegant, comfortable and warm place to stay. All 12 rooms are equipped with en suite bath or shower rooms and all modern conveniences. A splendid new conservatory-style restaurant serves innovative cuisine expertly prepared. A fixed-price menu offers a wide choice (dinner £21.50) and a typical menu might include calamares, then venison with cranberries followed by chocolate torte. Special tariffs apply for bookings of two or more nights. The hotel has its own mini-gym and sauna. Sports available locally include windsurfing, sailing, angling, clay-pigeon shooting and golf on the famous links nearby. Hastings, Winchelsea, Rye itself, Romney Marsh and Battle Abbey are not far away and worth visiting. **Directions:** 1½ miles north of Rye on A268. Price guide: Single from £47; double/twin from £94.

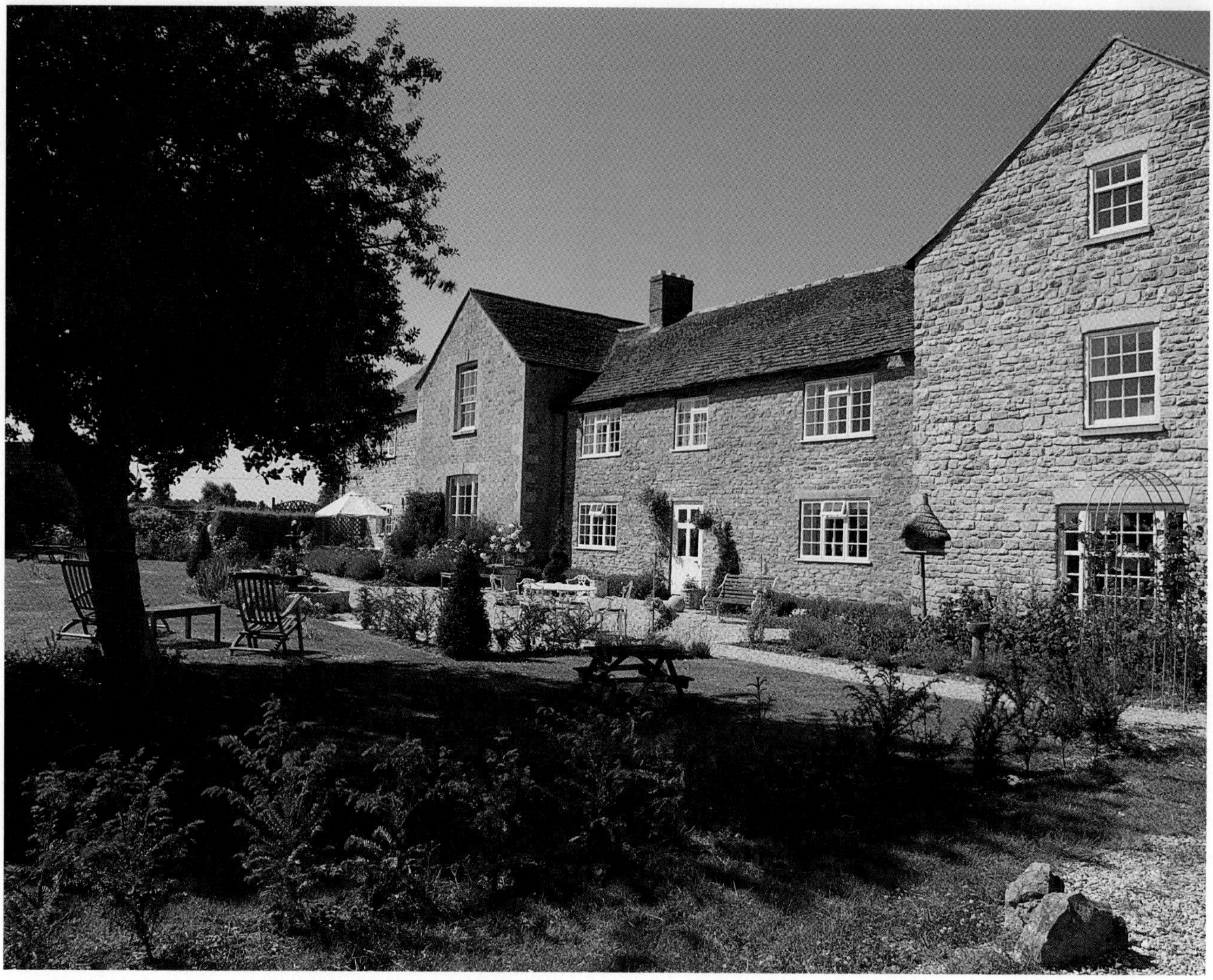

# BARNSDALE LODGE

**THE AVENUE, RUTLAND WATER, NR OAKHAM, RUTLAND, LEICESTERSHIRE LE15 8AH**
**TEL: 01572 724678 FAX: 01572 724961**

Situated in the heart of the ancient county of Rutland, amid unspoiled countryside, Barnsdale Lodge overlooks the rippling expanse of Rutland Water. Guests are invited to enjoy the hospitality offered by hosts The Hon. Thomas Noel and Robert Reid (who is also host at his sister hotel, Normanton Park). A restored 17th-century farmhouse, the atmosphere and style are distinctively Edwardian. This theme pervades throughout, from the courteous service to the furnishings – including chaises-longues and plump, upholstered chairs. The 29 en suite bedrooms, many of which are on the ground floor, including two superb rooms specifically designed for disabled guests, evoke a mood of relaxing comfort. A further 16 to be added for April 98. Traditional English cooking and fine wines are served. The chef makes all pastries and cakes as well as preserves. Elevenses, buttery lunches, afternoon teas and suppers may be enjoyed in the garden conservatory or courtyard. There are three conference rooms and facilities for wedding receptions and parties. A baby-listening service and safe play area are provided for children. Belvoir and Rockingham Castles and Burghley House are nearby. Rutland Water below offers a wide range of water sports, as well as being of interest to nature lovers, including an Aquatic and Butterfly Centre. **Directions:** Barnsdale Lodge is on the A606 Oakham–Stamford road. Price guide: Single £58; double/twin £75–£85; suite £90.

For hotel location, see maps on pages 490-496

# NORMANTON PARK HOTEL

NORMANTON PARK, RUTLAND WATER SOUTH SHORE, RUTLAND, LEICESTERSHIRE LE15 8RP
TEL: 01780 720315 FAX: 01780 721086

Situated alongside the famous 'submerged' church overlooking England's largest man-made reservoir, Normanton Park Hotel has been meticulously restored from its origins as the coach house to Normanton Park Hall. The Grade II listed hotel is set in four acres of grounds, which were landscaped in the 18th century and have one of the country's oldest Cedar of Lebanon trees. Many of the bedrooms overlook the lake, which provides fly and coarse fishing, boat hire, wind-surfing, kite-flying, cycling, walking and birdwatching. The Sailing Bar offers a warm welcome, and a good variety of meals, snacks and drinks is served throughout the day. Designed on an orangery theme, the delightful restaurant offers a gourmet's choice of both à la carte and reasonably priced Sunday lunch table d'hôte menus. The cocktail bar, decorated with ancient bellows and a blazing log fire in cooler months, makes a relaxing lounge area for guests. Many stately homes and National Trust properties are nearby and the A1 is easily accessible. Helicopters may be landed at Barnsdale Lodge, sister hotel to Normanton Park, and guests transferred from there. **Directions:** From the A1, take A606 at Stamford towards Oakham; turn along the south shore road towards Edith Weston. Price guide: Single £35; double/twin £75; suite/lake view £85.

For hotel location, see maps on pages 490-496

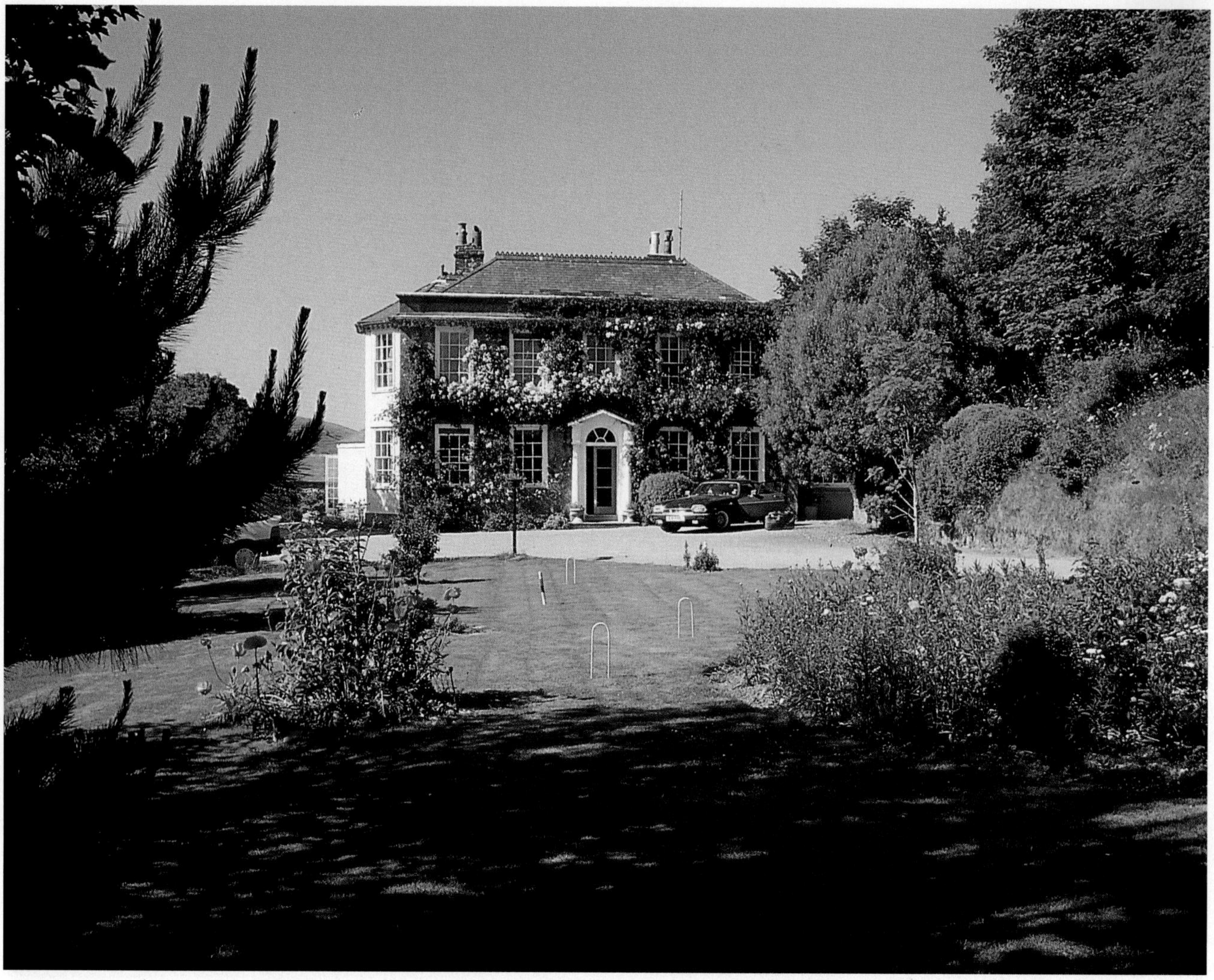

# Rose-in-Vale Country House Hotel

**MITHIAN, ST AGNES, CORNWALL TR5 0QD**
**TEL: 01872 552202 FAX: 01872 552700**

This 18th century Cornish manor house, tucked away in 11 acres of glorious gardens, woodlands and pasture in a wooded valley of great natural beauty, successfully blends the old with the new. It has an atmosphere and sense of timelessness – a world apart from the bustle of modern living. Restrained floral decor contrasts with dark mahogany throughout the elegant public rooms and tasteful bedrooms, many of which have outstanding views across the valley gardens. Three ground floor rooms have level access for the less able guest and the two Rose Suites have four-poster beds and separate sitting rooms. Chef Phillip Sims serves imaginative international cuisine in the intimate restaurant where sweeping, softly-draped bay windows overlook manicured lawns and flowerbeds. The gardens feature ponds with a collection of waterfowl, a secluded, heated swimming pool, croquet and badminton. The hotel can also provide a four-seater light aircraft for hire or for scenic coastal flights. The area is rich in National Trust properties and special walks, to and from the hotel, ensure that visitors see the best of the countryside. Six golf courses, horse riding, fishing, gliding, swimming and watersports are closeby. **Directions:** A30 through Cornwall. Two miles beyond Zelah turn right onto the B3284. Cross the A 307 and take the third left turn sign-posted Rose-in-Vale. Price guide: Single £49–£61; double/twin £100–£120; suite £140.

For hotel location, see maps on pages 490-496

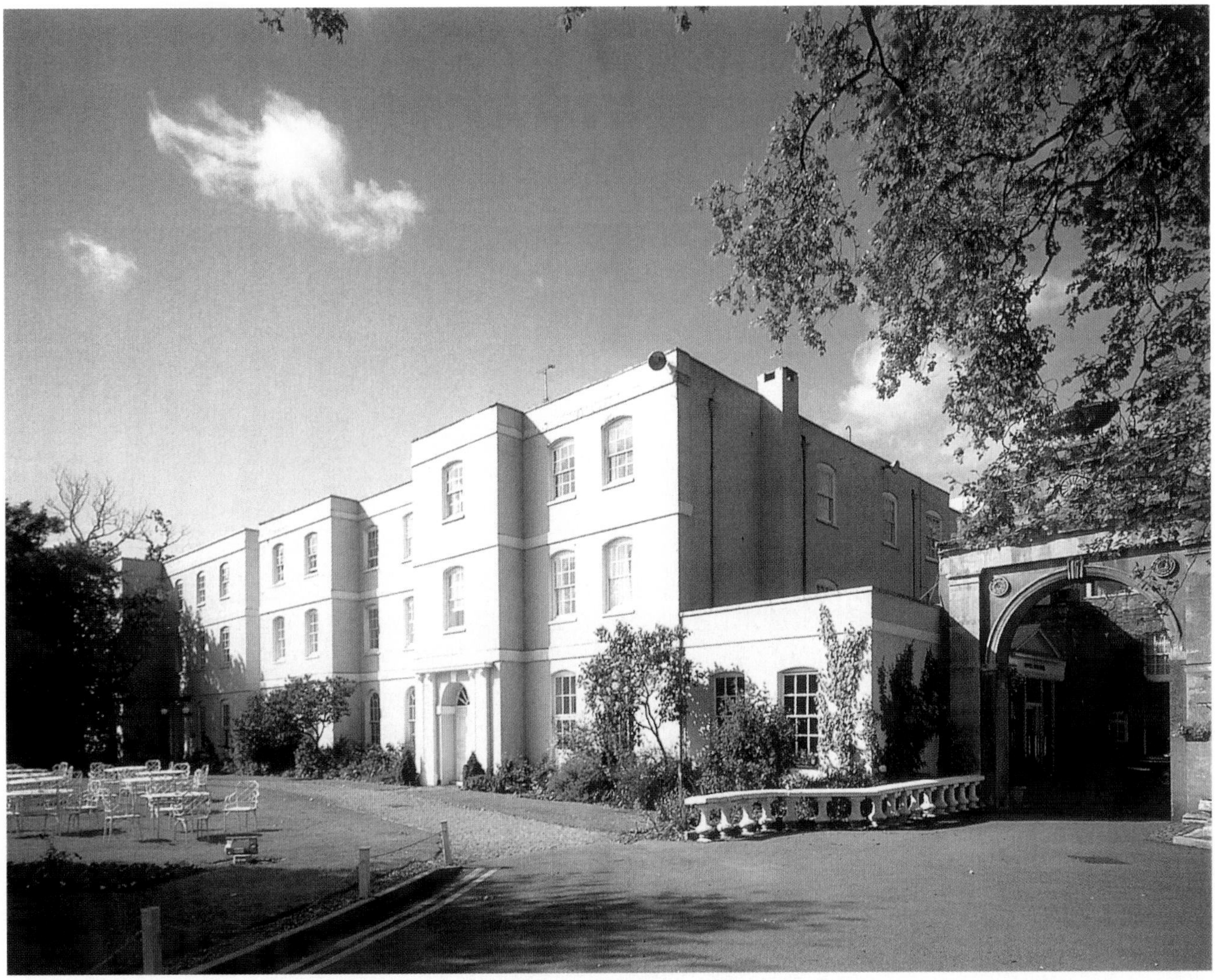

# SOPWELL HOUSE HOTEL & COUNTRY CLUB

COTTONMILL LANE, SOPWELL, ST ALBANS, HERTFORDSHIRE AL1 2HQ
TEL: 01727 864477 FAX: 01727 844741/845636

Once the country home of Lord Mountbatten, surrounded by a peaceful and verdant 11 acre estate, Sopwell House is an oasis just minutes away from the motorway and quickly reached by train from London. The classical reception rooms of the hotel reflect its illustrious past, and the grand panelled ballroom opens out onto the splendid terraces and gardens. The comfortable bedrooms, many with four-posters, are charming and equipped with all modern amenities. Dining is enchanting in the Magnolia Conservatory Restaurant amidst the trees after which it is named. Here guests enjoy superb English cooking and appreciate the fine wine list. More informal meals are served in Bejerano's Brasserie in the Country Club. Fifteen purpose-built meeting rooms form the business complex and the recent addition of the extensive conservatory lounge and bar, overlooking a new ornamental water terrace. Sopwell House is particularly proud of its Country Club & Spa, dedicated to health and relaxation. It has a fabulous pool, a full range of fitness facilities and a team of highly qualified beauty therapists. **Directions:** Close to M1, M10, M11 & A1(M). 22 miles from Heathrow. From A414 take A1081 toward St. Albans. Turn left at Mile House pub. Cross mini-roundabout. Hotel is ¼ mile on left. Price guide: Single from £104.75; double/twin from £136. Breakfast: Full English £9.95, Continental £7.75.

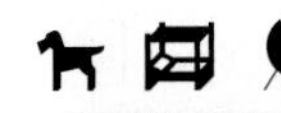

For hotel location, see maps on pages 490-496

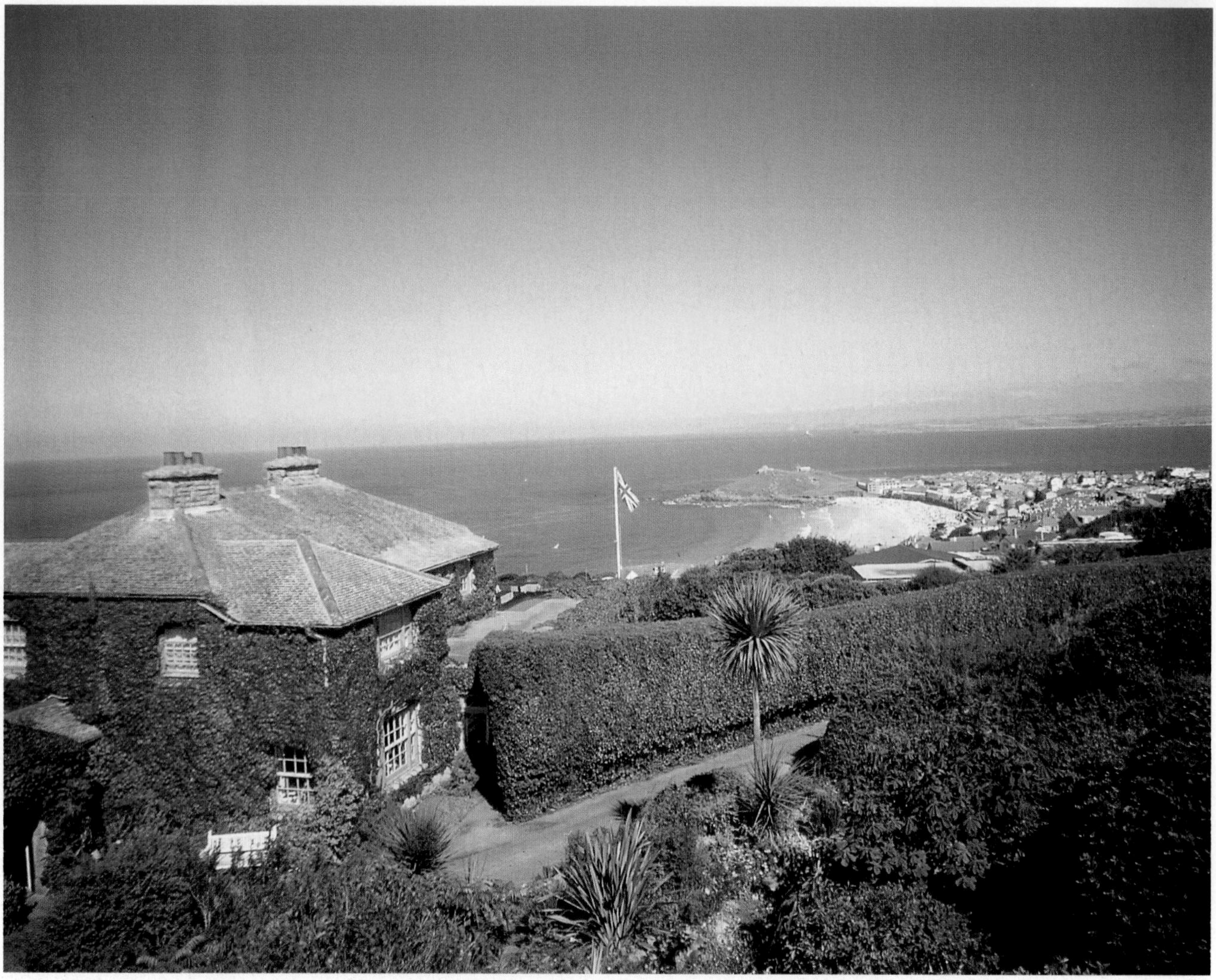

# THE GARRACK HOTEL

**BURTHALLAN LANE, ST IVES, CORNWALL TR26 3AA**
**TEL: 01736 796199 FAX: 01736 798955 FREEPONE: 0500 011 325**

This family-run hotel, secluded and full of character, ideal for a family holiday, is set in two acres of gardens with fabulous sea views over Porthmeor Beach, the St Ives Tate Gallery and the old town of St Ives. The bedrooms in the original house are in keeping with the style of the building. The additional rooms are modern in design. All rooms have private bathrooms and baby-listening facilities. Superior rooms have either four-poster beds or whirlpool baths. A ground-floor room has been fitted for guests with disabilities. Visitors return year after year to enjoy informal yet professional service, good food and hospitality. The restaurant specialises in seafood especially fresh lobsters. The wine list includes over 70 labels from ten regions. The lounges have books, magazines and board games for all, and open fires. The small attractive leisure centre contains a small swimming pool with integral spa, sauna, solarium and fitness area. The hotel has its own car park. Porthmeor Beach, just below the hotel, is renowned for surfing. Riding, golf, bowls, sea-fishing and other activites can be enjoyed locally. St Ives, with its harbour, is famous for artists and for the new St Ives Tate Gallery. Dogs by prior arrangement. **Directions:** A30–A3074–B3311–B3306. Go ½ mile, turn left at mini-roundabout, hotel signs are on the left as the road starts down hill. Price guide: Single £64–£68; double/twin £92–£134.

For hotel location, see maps on pages 490-496

# THE WELL HOUSE

**ST KEYNE, LISKEARD, CORNWALL PL14 4RN**
**TEL: 01579 342001 FAX: 01579 343891**

The West Country is one corner of England where hospitality and friendliness are at their most spontaneous, and nowhere more so than at The Well House, just beyond the River Tamar. New arrivals are entranced by their first view of this lovely Victorian country manor. Its façade wrapped in rambling wisteria and jasmine trailers is just one of a continuous series of delights including top-quality service, modern luxury and impeccable standards of comfort and cooking. The hotel is professionally managed by proprietor Nick Wainford, whose attention to every smallest detail has earned his hotel numerous awards, among them the AA 2 Red Stars. From the tastefully appointed bedrooms there are fine rural views, and each private bathroom offers luxurious bath linen, soaps and gels by Bronnley. Continental breakfast is served in bed – or a traditional English breakfast may be taken in the dining room. Chef Cameron Brown selects fresh, seasonal produce to create his superbly balanced and presented cuisine. Tennis, swimming and croquet are on site, and the Cornish coastline offers matchless scenery and walking territory. The Well House is a Pride of Britain member. **Directions:** Leave A38 at Liskeard, take A390 to town centre, then take B3254 south to St Keyne Well and hotel. Price guide: Single from £70; double/twin £95–£145; family suite £160

For hotel location, see maps on pages 490-496

# BOLT HEAD HOTEL

SOUTH SANDS, SALCOMBE, SOUTH DEVON TQ8 8LL
TEL: 01548 843751 FAX: 01548 843060

Bolt Head Hotel occupies a spectacular position overlooking Salcombe Estuary, where the mild climate ensures a lengthy holiday season. New improvements have ensured that guests can enjoy a fine range of modern comforts during their stay. The bedrooms are furnished to a high standard, all with good en suite bathrooms, and there are family suites available complete with a baby-listening service. The light and sunny lounge is ideal for relaxation, or guests may sit on the adjoining sun terrace with sweeping views of the sea. In the air-conditioned restaurant special care is taken to cater for all tastes. Both English and French cuisine are prepared, with freshly caught fish, lobster and crab delivered daily, as well as wholesome farm produce and local cheeses. Palm trees surround the heated outdoor swimming pool on the sunny terrace. There is a good golf course within a few miles. Riding, sailing and wind-surfing can be arranged. Sea fishing trips can be organised and private moorings are available. The hotel is adjacent to miles of magnificent National Trust cliff land at Bolt Head, including Overbecks, an unusual house and garden with rare plants. Dogs by arrangement. Closed mid-November to mid-March. **Directions:** Contact the hotel for directions. Price guide (including dinner): Single from £65; double/twin from £130; superior rooms available, as illustrated.

For hotel location, see maps on pages 490-496

# SOAR MILL COVE HOTEL

SOAR MILL COVE, SALCOMBE, SOUTH DEVON TQ7 3DS
TEL: 01548 561566 FAX: 01548 561223

Owned and loved by the Makepeace family who for nearly 20 years, have provided a special blend of friendly yet professional service. The hotel's spectacular setting is a flower-filled combe, facing its own sheltered sandy bay and entirely surrounded by 2000 acres of dramatic National Trust coastline. While it is perhaps one of the last truly unspoiled corners of South Devon, Soar Mill Cove is only 15 miles from the motorway system (A38). All the bedrooms are at ground level, each with a private patio opening onto the gardens, which in Spring or Summer provides wonderful alfresco opportunities. In winter, crackling log fires and efficient double glazing keeps cooler weather at bay. A strict "no conference policy" guarantees that the peace of guests shall not be compromised. Both the indoor and outdoor pools are spring-water fed, the former being maintained all year at a constant 88°F. Here is Keith Stephen Makepeace's award winning cuisine, imaginative and innovative, reflecting the very best of the West of England; fresh crabs and lobster caught in the bay are a speciality. Soar Mill Cove is situated midway between the old ports of Plymouth and Dartmouth. Closed 1 November to 9 February. Open for Christmas and New Year House Parties. **Directions:** A384 to Totnes, then A381 to Soar Mill Cove. Price guide: Single £65–£114; double/twin £130–£172.

For hotel location, see maps on pages 490-496

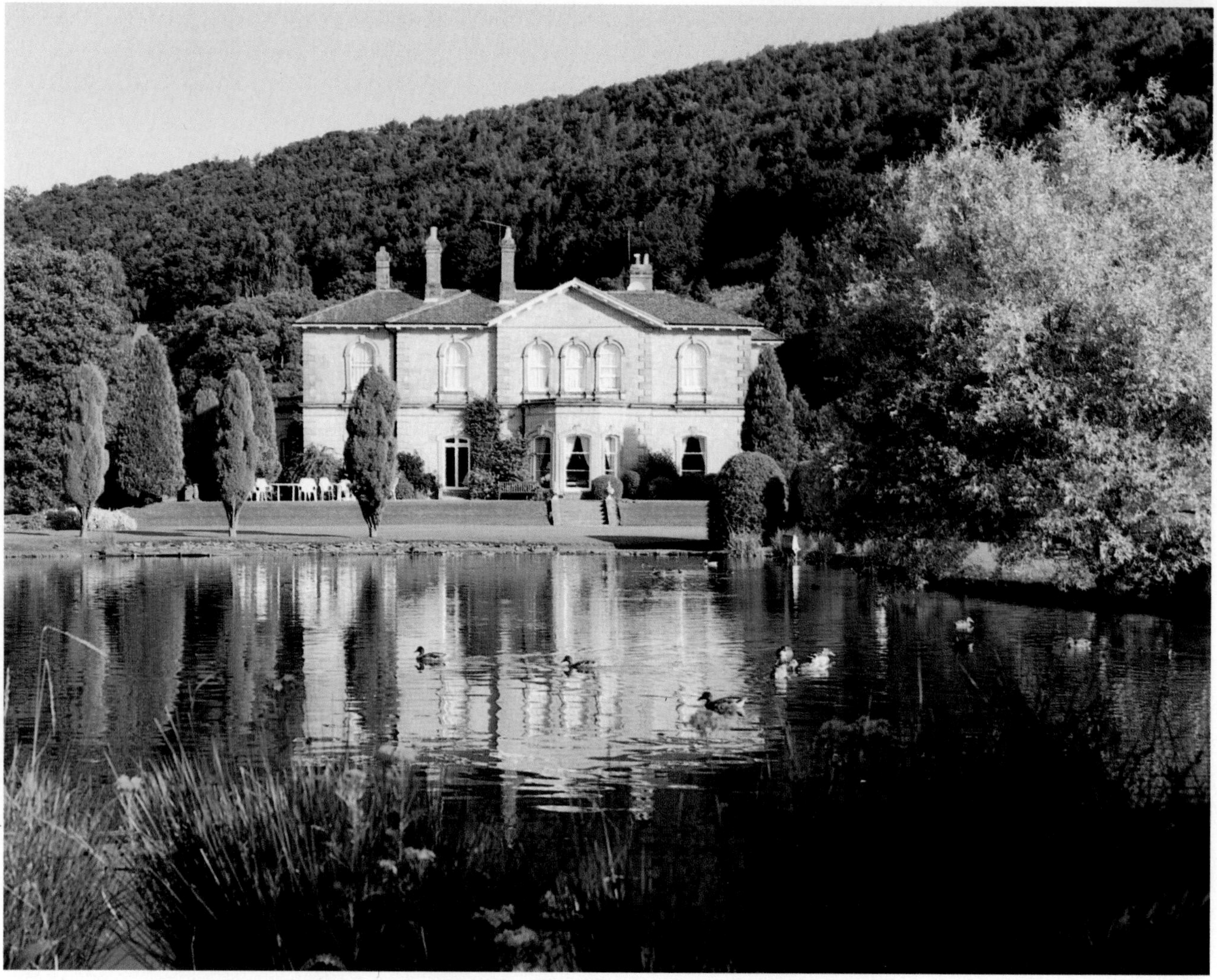

# HACKNESS GRANGE

**NORTH YORK MOORS NATIONAL PARK, SCARBOROUGH, NORTH YORKSHIRE YO13 0JW**
**TEL: 01723 882345 FAX: 01723 882391**

The attractive Georgian Hackness Grange country house lies at the heart of the dramatic North York Moors National Park – miles of glorious countryside with rolling moorland and forests. Set in acres of private grounds, overlooking a tranquil lake, home to many species of wildlife, Hackness Grange is a haven of peace and quiet for guests. There are charming bedrooms in the elegant courtyard which have enjoyed a delightful refurbishment last year, together with de luxe rooms in the main house. For leisure activites, guests can enjoy 9-hole pitch 'n' putt golf, tennis, private fishing on the River Derwent and an indoor heated swimming pool. Hackness Grange is an ideal meeting location for companies wishing to have exclusive use of the hotel for VIP gatherings. The attractive Derwent Restaurant with its quality décor and paintings, is the setting for lunch and dinner and you will enjoy creatively prepared delicious cuisine, which is partnered by a wide choice of international wines. When you choose to stay at Hackness Grange you will find you have chosen well – a peaceful and relaxing location with so much to see and do: for example, visit Great Ayton, birthplace of Captain Cook. **Directions:** Take A64 York road until left turn to Seamer on to B1261, through to East Ayton. and Hackness. Price guide: Single £80–£85; double/twin £120–£165; suite £185.

For hotel location, see maps on pages 490-496

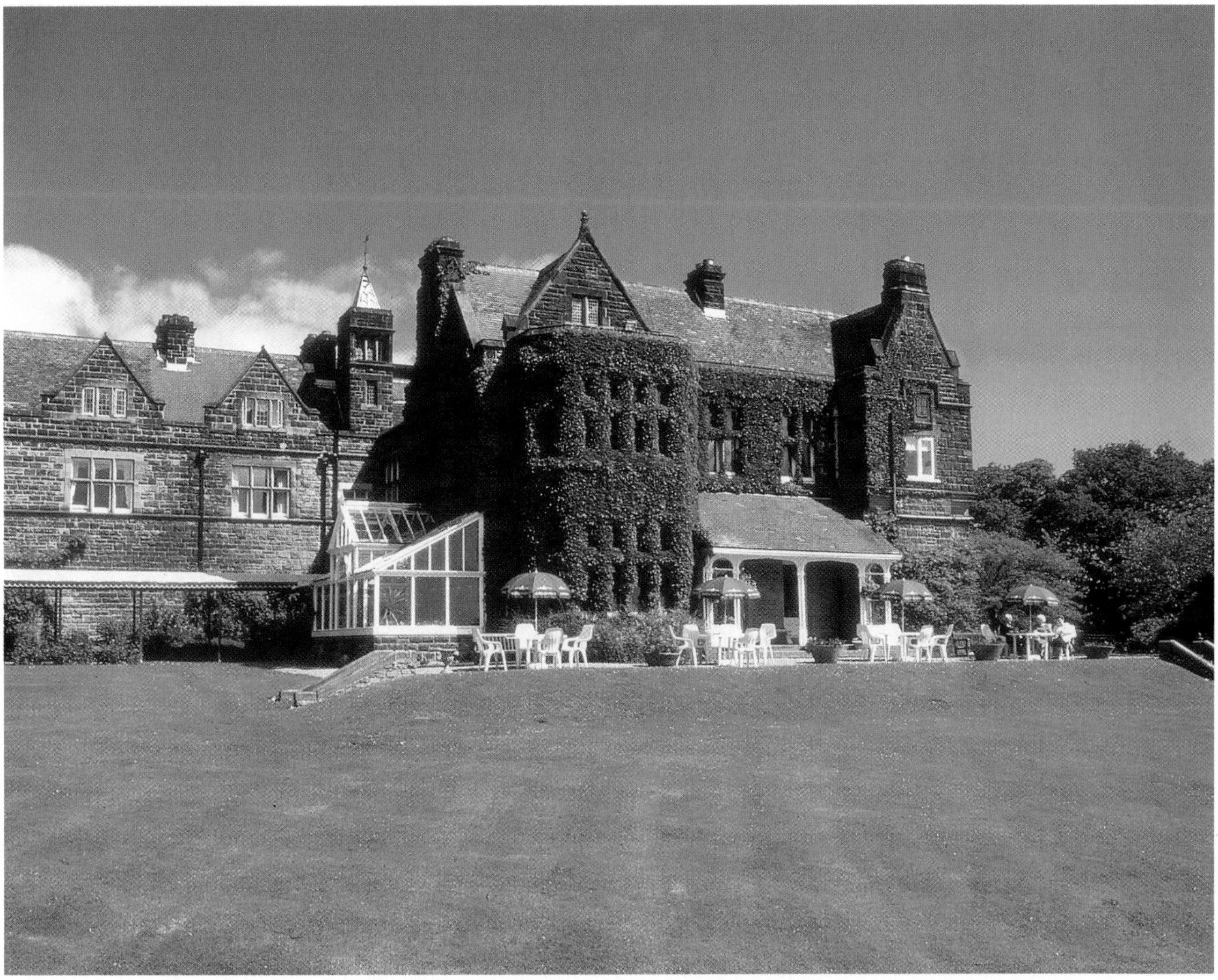

# Wrea Head Country Hotel

SCALBY, NR SCARBOROUGH, NORTH YORKSHIRE YO13 0PB

TEL: 01723 378211 FAX: 01723 355936

Wrea Head Country Hotel is an elegant, beautifully refurbished Victorian country house built in 1881 and situated in 14 acres of wooded and landscaped grounds on the edge of the North York Moors National Park just three miles from Scarborough. The house is furnished with antiques and paintings, and the oak-panelled front hall with its inglenook fireplace with blazing log fires in the winter, is very welcoming. All the bedrooms are individually decorated to the highest standards, with most having delightful views of the gardens. The elegant Four Seasons Restaurant is renowned for serving the best traditional English fare using fresh local produce and has an AA Rosette for outstanding cuisine. There are attractive meeting rooms, each with natural daylight, ideal for private board meetings and training courses requiring privacy and seclusion. Scarborough is renowned for its cricket, music and theatre. Wrea Head is a perfect location from which to explore the glorious North Yorkshire coast and country, and you can take advantage of special English Rose breaks throughout the year. **Directions:** Follow the A171 north from Scarborough, past the Scalby Village, until the hotel is signposted. Follow the road past the duck pond, and then turn left up the drive. Price guide: Single from £57.50–£75; double/twin from £95–£145; suite £165.

For hotel location, see maps on pages 490-496

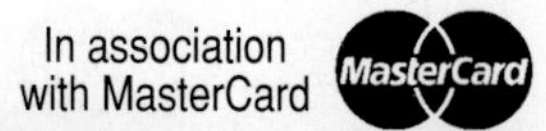

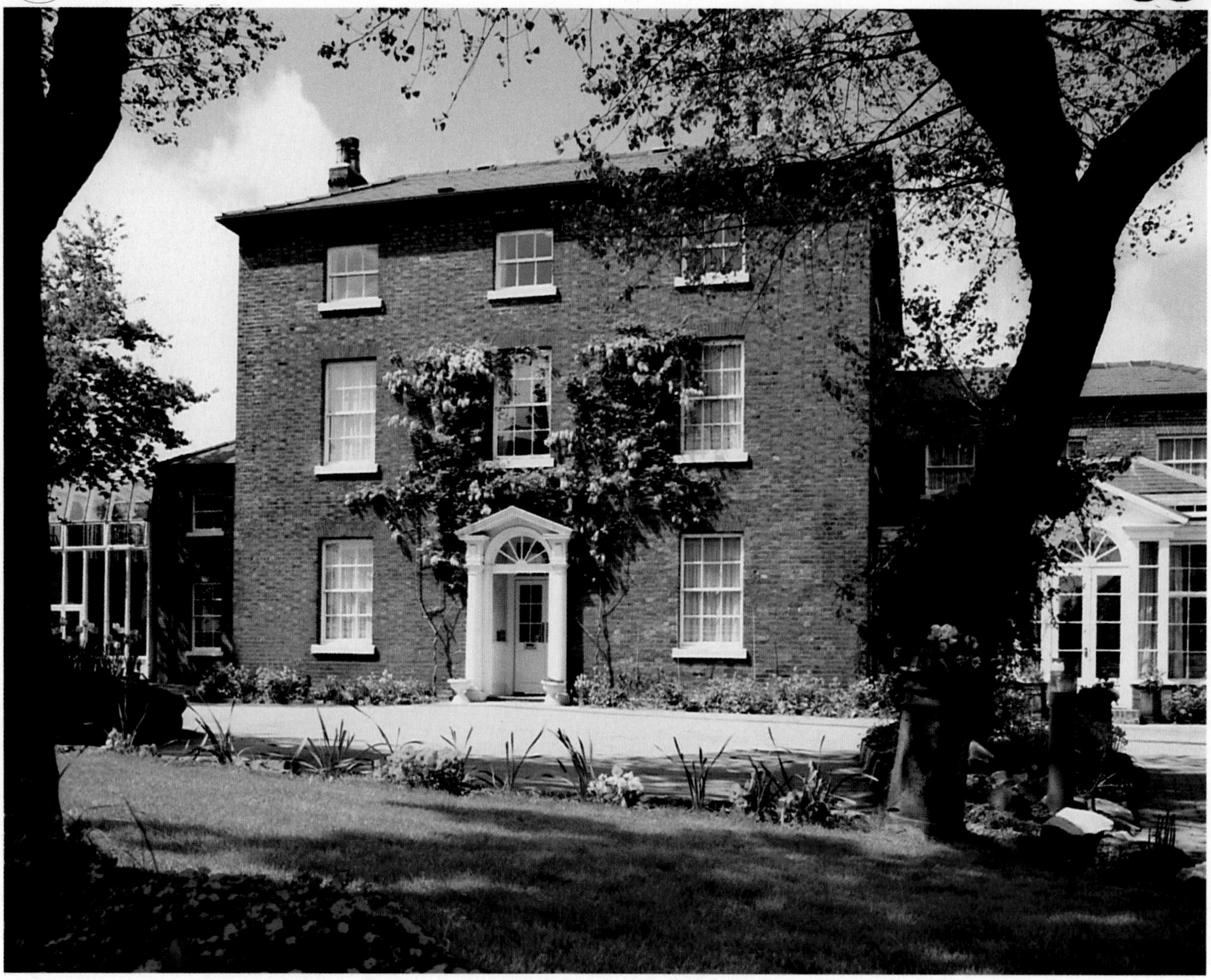

# CHARNWOOD HOTEL

**10 SHARROW LANE, SHEFFIELD, SOUTH YORKSHIRE S11 8AA**
**TEL: 0114 258 9411 FAX: 0114 255 5107**

The Charnwood Hotel is a listed Georgian mansion dating from 1780. Originally owned by John Henfrey, a Sheffield Master Cutler, it was later acquired by William Wilson of the Sharrow Snuff Mill. Restored in 1985, this elegant 'country house in town' is tastefully furnished, with colourful flower arrangements set against attractive décor. The bedrooms are decorated in a country style, with the Woodford suite designed specifically to meet the requirements of a family. Two dining rooms are available for experiencing the gourmet skills of the chef and his brigade. Dignified and formal, Henfrey's Restaurant offers cuisine to match the surroundings, while traditional English/French fare is the order of the day at Brasserie Leo. The Library is ideal for private dining or small meetings and larger functions are catered for in the Georgian Room and Coach House. While approximately a mile from Sheffield city centre, with its concert hall, theatre and hectic night-life, Charnwood Hotel is also convenient for the Peak District National Park. Meadowhall shopping centre and Sheffield Arena are nearby. **Directions:** Sharrow Lane is near the junction of London Road and Abbeydale Road, 1½ miles from city centre. Junction 33 from the M1. Price guide: Single £45–£90; double/twin £60–£100.

For hotel location, see maps on pages 490-496

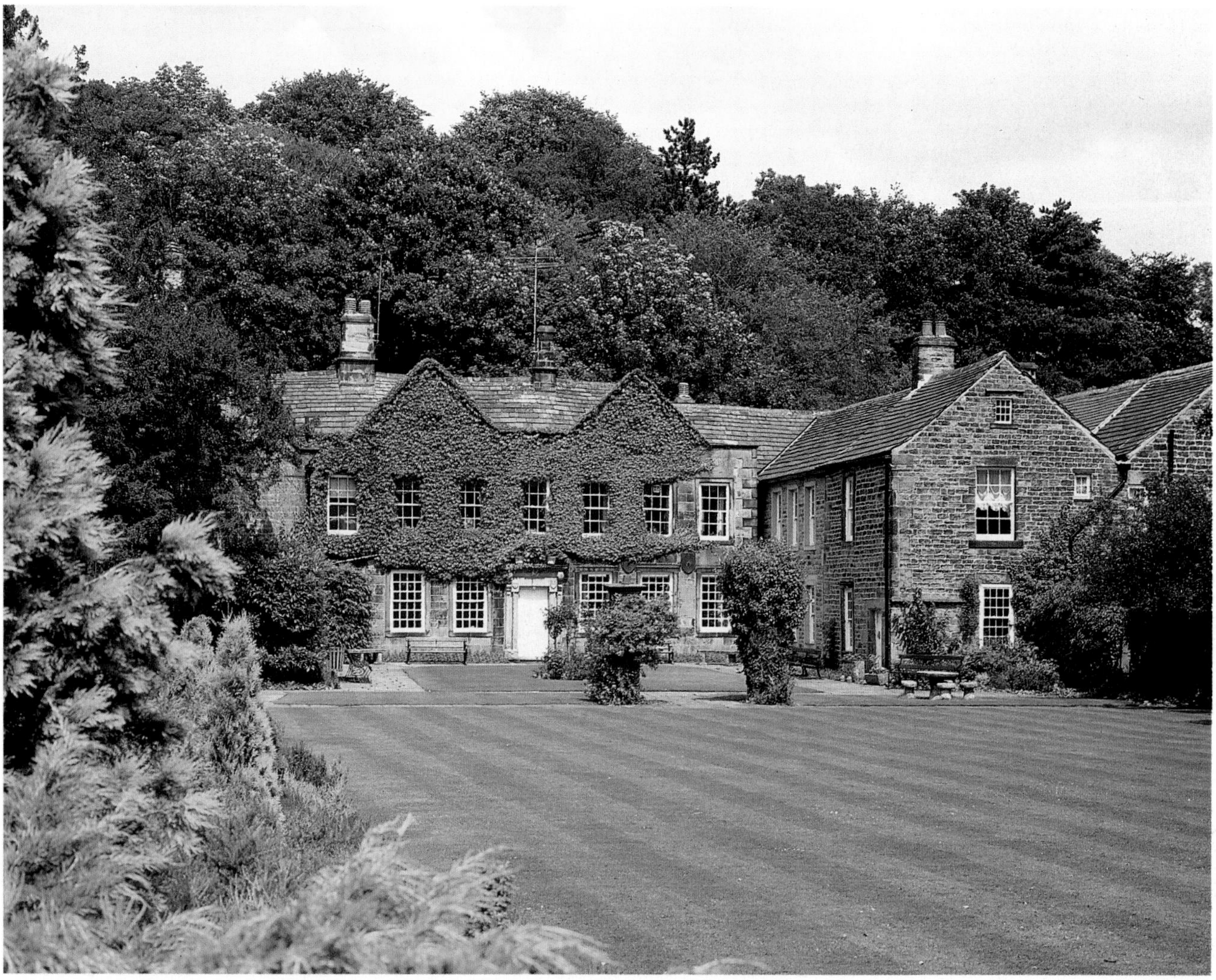

# WHITLEY HALL HOTEL

ELLIOTT LANE, GRENOSIDE, SHEFFIELD, SOUTH YORKSHIRE S35 8NR
TEL: 0114 245 4444 FAX: 0114 245 5414

Carved into the keystone above one of the doors is the date 1584, denoting the start of Whitley Hall's lengthy country house tradition. In the bar is a priest hole, which may explain the local belief that a tunnel links the house with the nearby 11th-century church. In the 18th century the house was a prestigious boarding school, with Gothic pointed arches and ornamentation added later by the Victorians. Attractively refurbished, Whitley Hall is now a fine hotel with all the amenities required by today's visitors. Stone walls and oak panelling combine with richly carpeted floors and handsome decoration. A sweeping split staircase leads to the bedrooms, all of which have en suite bathrooms. Varied yet unpretentious cooking is served in generous portions and complemented by a wide choice from the wine cellar, including many clarets and ports. Peacocks strut around the 30-acre grounds, which encompass rolling lawns, mature woodland and two ornamental lakes. Banquets and private functions can be held in the conference suite. **Directions:** Leave M1 at junction 35, following signs for Chapeltown (A629), go down hill and turn left into Nether Lane. Go right at traffic lights, then left opposite Arundel pub, into Whitley Lane. At fork turn right into Elliott Lane; hotel is on left. Price guide: Single £62–£78; double/twin £83–£105; suite £150

For hotel location, see maps on pages 490-496

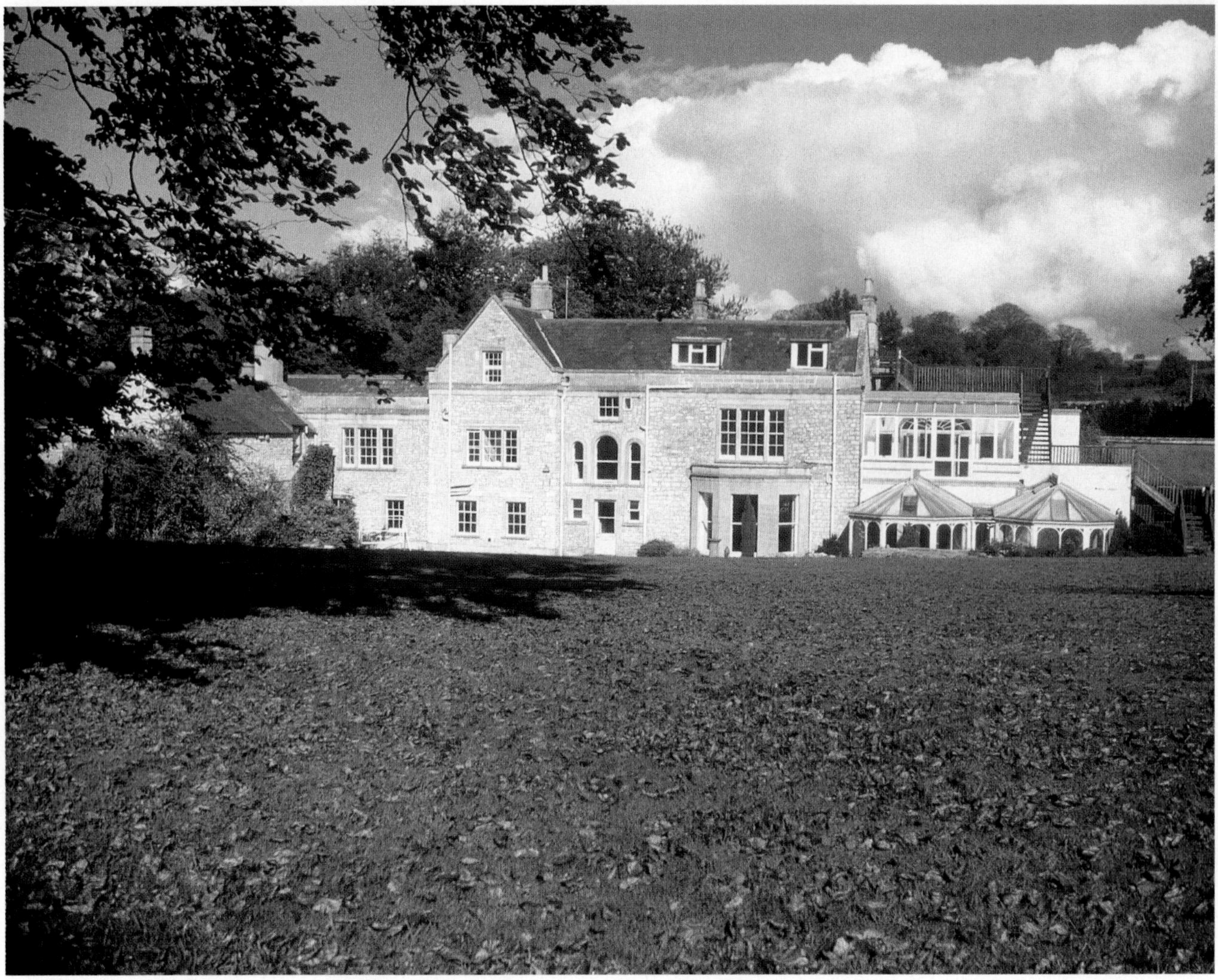

# CHARLTON HOUSE

**CHARLTON ROAD, SHEPTON MALLET, SOMERSET BA4 4PR**
**TEL: 01749 342008 FAX: 01749 346362**

This grand 17th century country manor, is now owned by Roger and Monty Saul, founders of the Mulberry Design Co. They have lovingly and skilfully created an exquisite hotel of the highest international standards without detracting from Charlton's own history and architecture. The reception rooms have wonderful proportions, and are not overwhelmed by the sumptuous furnishings, fine antiques, exotic flowers, brilliant rugs on polished floors, witty memorabilia and exciting paintings adorning their walls – veritable Aladdin's Caves! The bedrooms, some in the adjacent Coach House, are equally magical, totally luxurious and yet restful, with opulent bathrooms. Professional yet friendly staff play an important part both in the drawing room, with its marvellous intimate atmosphere, and in the dramatic dining room presided over by award-winning chef, Trevor Brookes. Fantastic cooking and sublime wines make every meal a sybaritic experience. The hotel prides itself on catering for "special occasions". Charlton House recreations include shove-halfpenny(!), croquet, a trout lake, tennis, a sauna and pool and strolling in the landscaped gardens. Nearby are Bath, Wincanton Races, sailing, golf, the Mendip Hills – and the Mulberry factory shop. Directions: A303, then A37 to Shepton Mallet. Take A361 towards Frome and find hotel drive on the right. Price guide: Single £95–£125; double/twin £110–£250; suite £185–£300.

For hotel location, see maps on pages 490-496

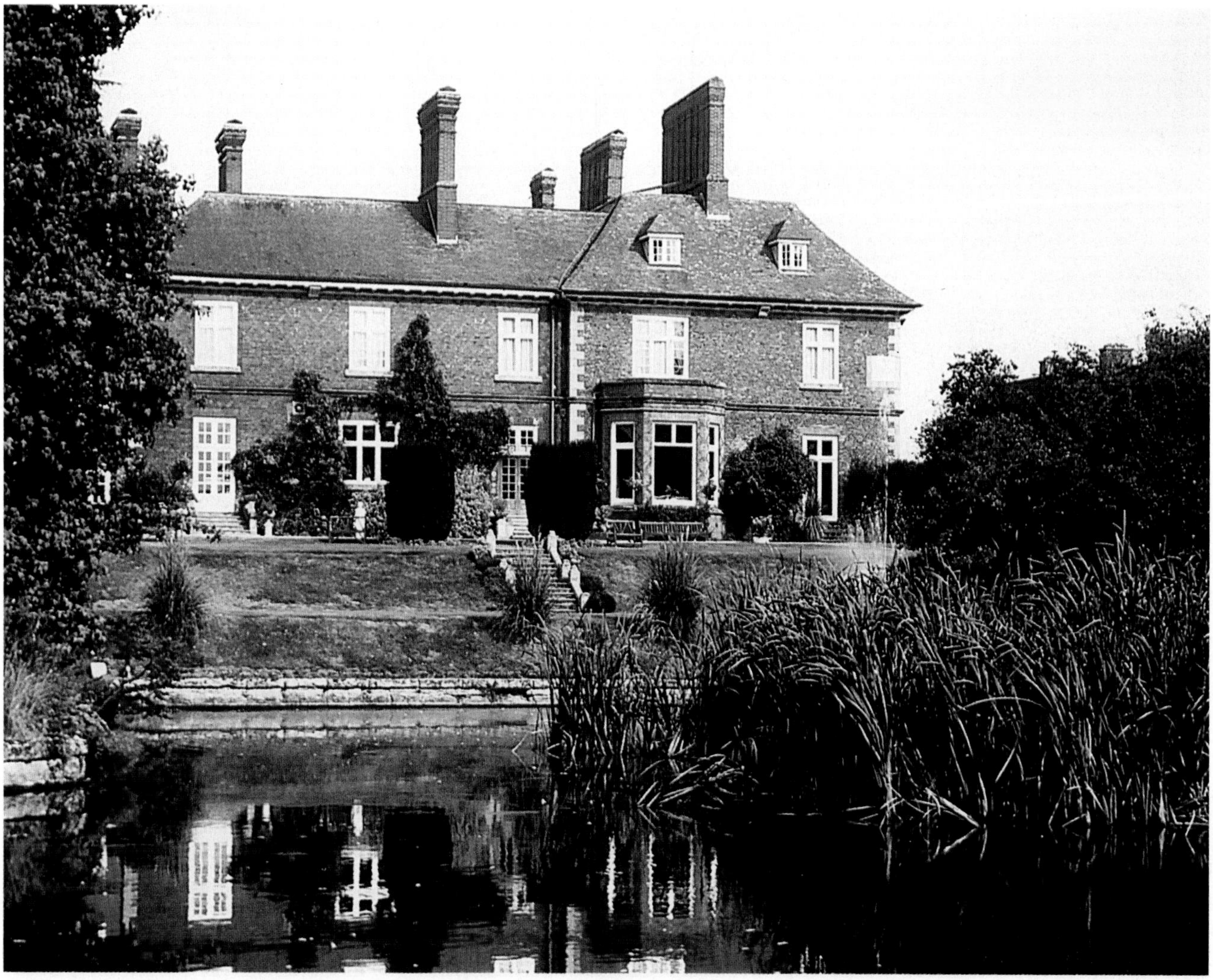

# ALBRIGHTON HALL HOTEL & RESTAURANT

**ALBRIGHTON, SHREWSBURY, SHROPSHIRE SY4 3AG**
**TEL: 01939 291000 FAX: 01939 291123**

Five minutes from the centre of the historic market town of Shrewsbury, ornamented by its pink-sandstone castle and superb black-and-white buildings, Albrighton Hall is a handsome 300 year-old house standing in 15 acres of secluded grounds with terraced gardens stepping down to a large ornamental pond which attracts a variety of wildlife. Careful restoration and sympathetic development have helped maintain the Hall's country house character. There is an abundance of rich panelling, open fires and fine paintings. The bedrooms, are individually styled and feature every modern facility from satellite television to a welcoming bottle of Mineral Water. Some have four-poster beds and most have stunning views over the gardens. The lounges are elegantly and comfortably furnished and decorated with appealing fabrics. Traditional and contemporary cuisine can be enjoyed in the Restaurant. Excellent leisure facilities include a heated indoor swimming pool, squash court, gymnasium and snooker room. Ludlow, the Midland Motor Museum, Ironbridge Gorge and Wyle Cop are within easy reach. **Directions:** Exit the M6 at junction 10a (if travelling from the north, exit junction 12). Follow the M54, A5 and A49 towards Whitchurch. Then join the A528 signposted Ellesmere. The hotel is one mile ahead. Price guide: Single £60–£85; double/twin £80–£95; suite £115–135

For hotel location, see maps on pages 490-496

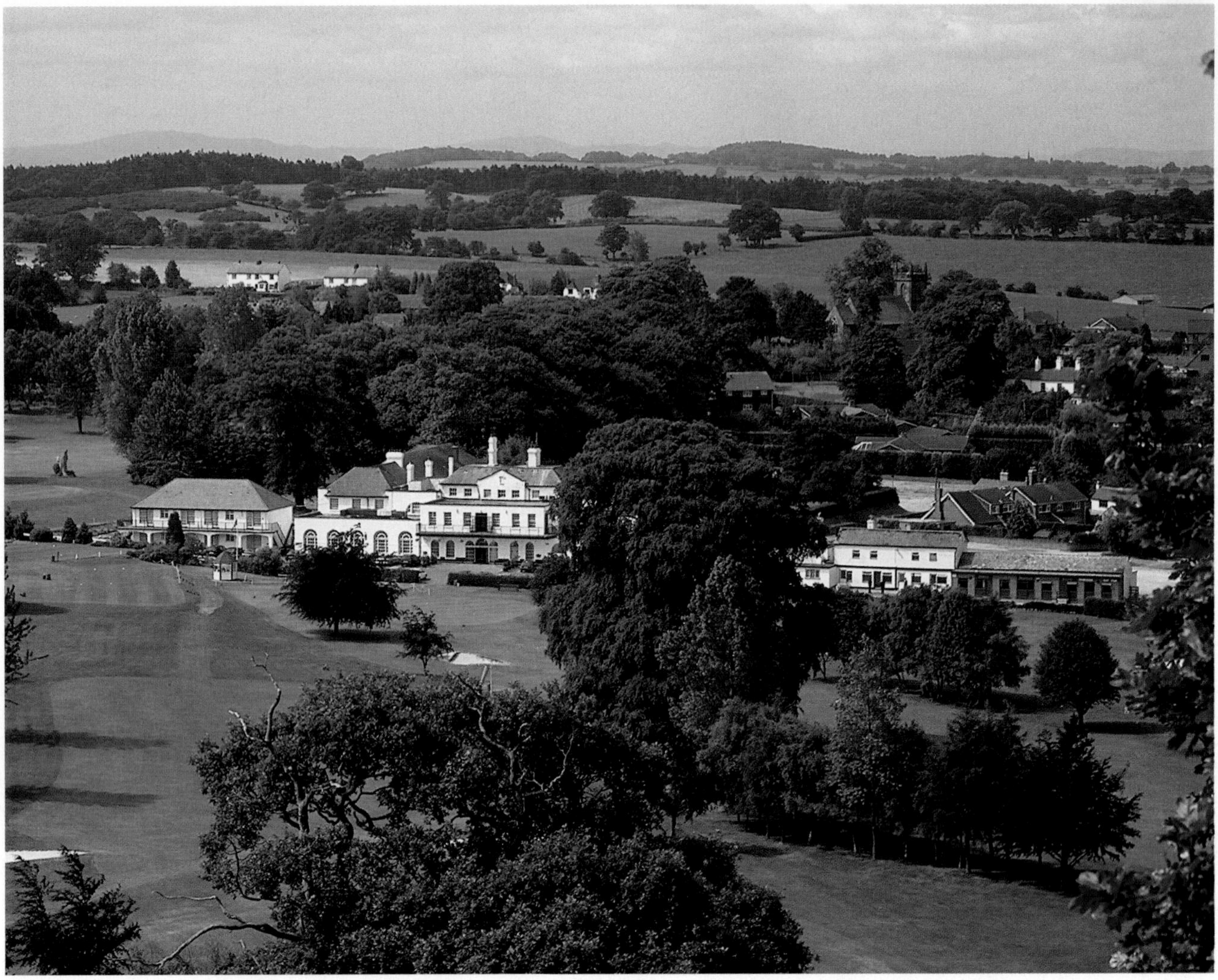

# HAWKSTONE PARK HOTEL

**WESTON-UNDER-REDCASTLE, SHREWSBURY, SHROPSHIRE SY4 5UY**
**TEL: 01939 200611 FAX: 01939 200311**

Hawkstone Park is a golfer's paradise. Set in 400 acres of idyllic Shropshire parkland the hotel is bounded on all sides by two contrasting 18-hole championship courses, on one of which British golfing star Sandy Lyle first learned the game. Supporting these courses is a 6-hole par 3 Academy Course, a driving range, practice area, and a purpose built Golf Centre. The top floor Terrace Room offers all-day bar and restaurant facilities with wonderful, panoramic views over the courses. The hotel's 65 en suite bedrooms, all newly refurbished rooms have tea and coffee making facilities, radio and satellite television, trouser press, iron and hairdryer. In the elegant restaurant which overlooks the landscaped gardens chef John Robinson offers a high standard of traditional British and classical French cuisine. There is a large, comfortable snooker room with two tables, a card room and private bar and a variety of comprehensively equipped meeting and conference rooms. Hawkstone Historic Park and Follies complements the Hotel and Golf courses situated on 400 acres of English Heritage designated Grade I landscape. Places of interest nearby include Shrewsbury Castle, ironbridge, Chester and Nantwich. Clay shooting, archery, croquet and hot-air ballooning are available. Directions: From M54, join A5 and then A49 north towards Whitchurch. Weston is signposted after approximately 11 miles. Price guide: Single/double/twin £75

For hotel location, see maps on pages 490-496

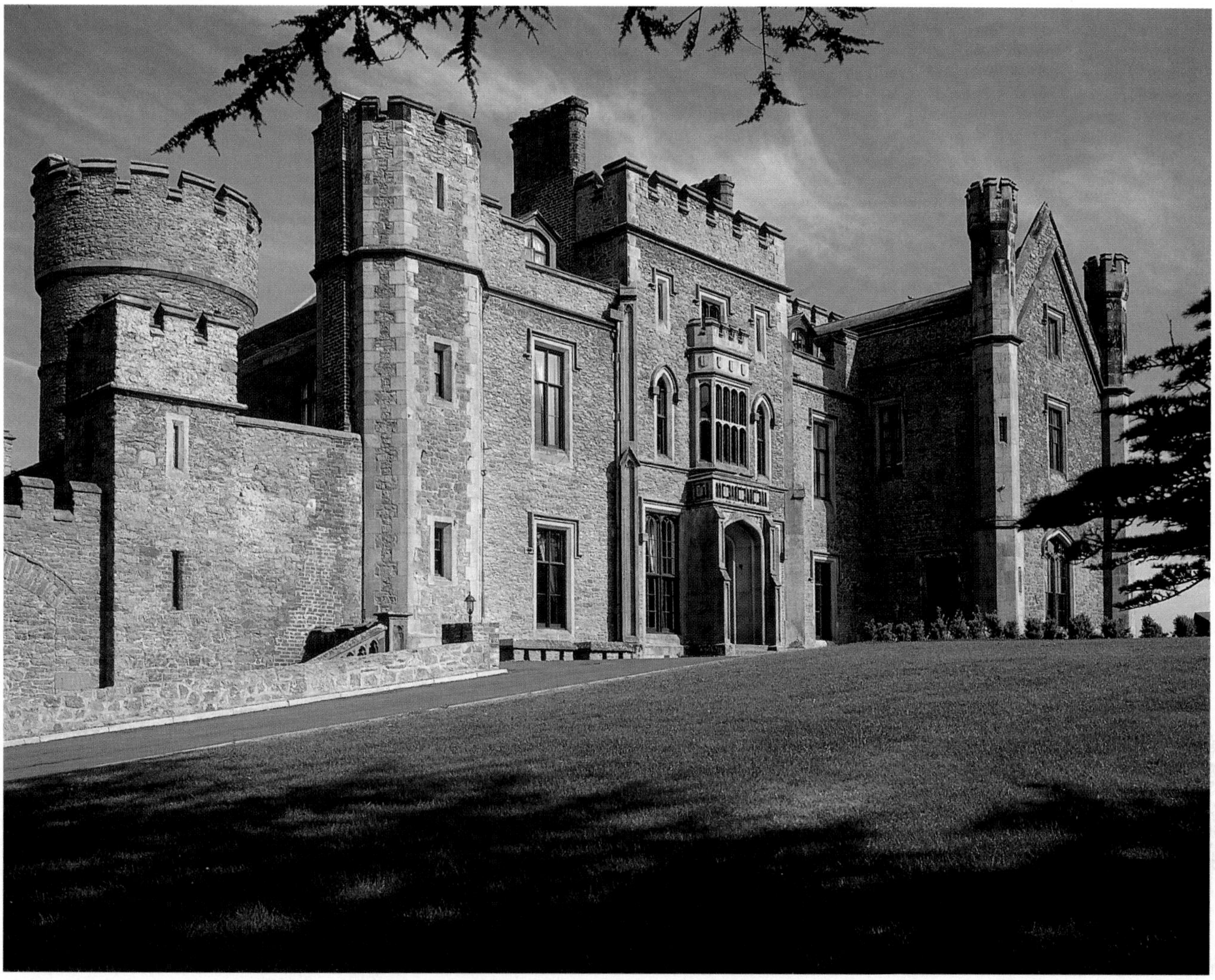

# Rowton Castle

**SHREWSBURY, SHROPSHIRE SY5 9EP**
**TEL: 01743 884044 FAX: 01743 884949**

Rowton Castle is mentioned in the Domesday Book and stands on the site of a Roman fort. Part of its large tower is reputed to date from the original castle. Residential parts date from 1696, with additions made in the early 19th century. Today it is a sympathetically restored and picturesque hotel set in 17 acres of formal gardens and grounds. From an armchair in the lounge guests are given wonderful views of the Welsh mountains through a spectacular avenue of lime trees. Each of the hotel's bedrooms has a unique charm and character and provides a full range of modern conveniences. The oak-panelled restaurant, centred on a 17th century carved oak fireplace, offers table d'hôte and à la carte menus in a setting which is ideal for important business entertaining, celebrations and intimate dinners. The Cardeston Suite can accommodate 150 delegates and has a separate reception room and bar. Privately owned leisure complex in grounds adjacent to hotel with extensive leisure facilities available to hotel guests. Places of interest nearby include Shrewsbury Castle, Ironbridge and Llangollen. Golf, shooting. fishing and croquet are available. Shrewsbury, Shropshire's thriving historic market town, is within 10 minutes' drive. **Directions:** Five miles from Shrewsbury on the A458 Welshpool road. Price guide: Single £55; double/twin £70–£135.

For hotel location, see maps on pages 490-496

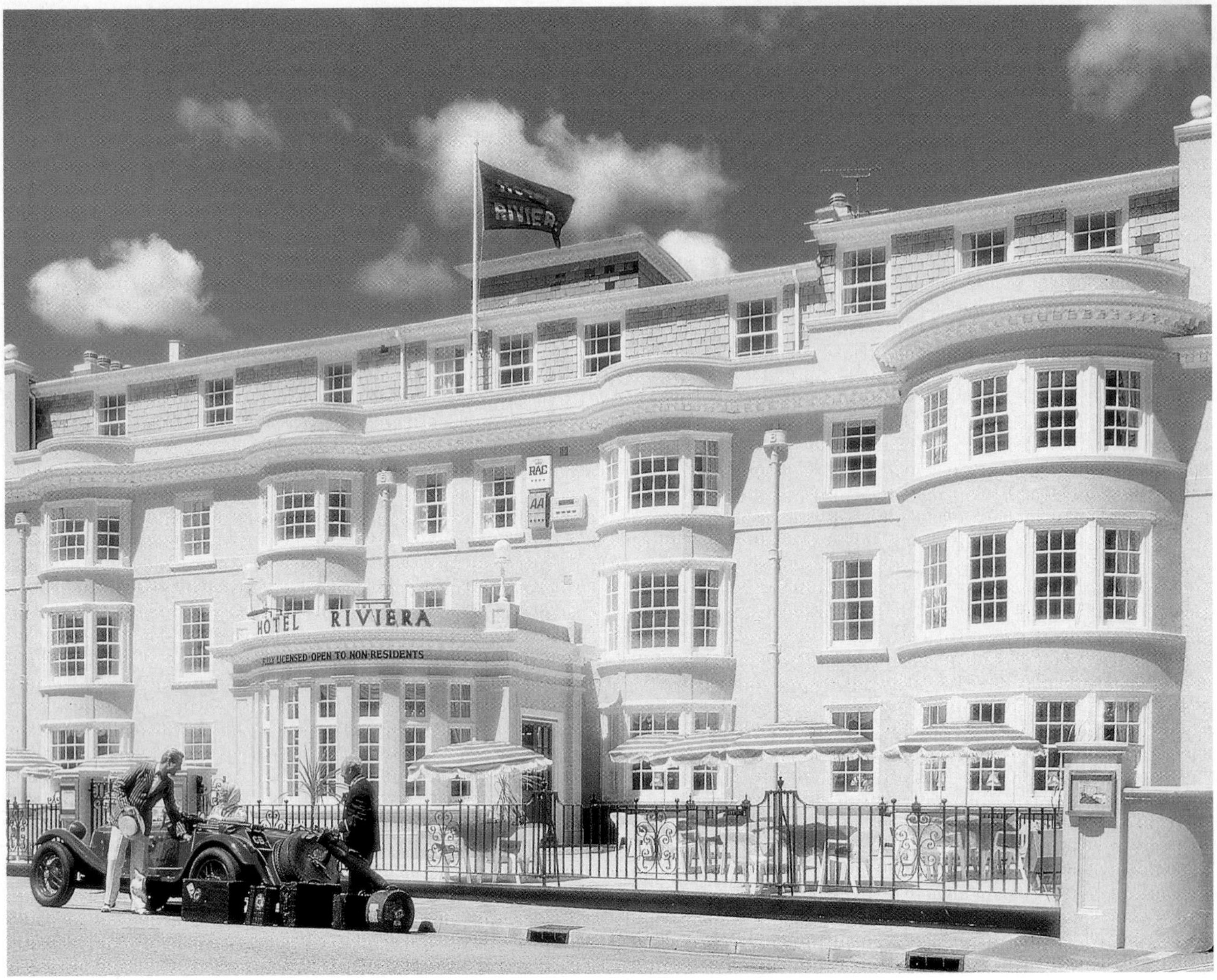

# HOTEL RIVIERA

**THE ESPLANADE, SIDMOUTH, DEVON EX10 8AY**
**TEL: 01395 515201 FAX: 01395 577775 E-MAIL: enquiries@hotelriviera.co.uk**

The Hotel Riviera is splendidly positioned at the centre of Sidmouth's esplanade, overlooking Lyme Bay. With its mild climate and the beach just on the doorstep, the setting mirrors the south of France and is the choice for the discerning visitor in search of relaxation and quieter pleasures. Behind the hotel's fine Regency façade lies an alluring blend of old-fashioned service and present-day comforts with a style and ambience that justly reflects its AA and RAC four-star rating. Glorious sea views can be enjoyed from the recently redesigned and refurbished en suite bedrooms, all of which are fully appointed and have many thoughtful extras like hairdryers, fresh flowers, bathrobes and complimentary toiletries. In the elegant bay-view dining room, guests are offered a fine choice of dishes from the extensive menus, prepared by French and Swiss trained chefs, with local seafood being a particular speciality. Arrangements can be made for guests to play golf, while bowls, croquet, tennis, putting, sailing and fishing are available nearby. Explore the many delightful villages of East Devon's rolling countryside and coastline, or just enjoy pottering around Sidmouth, with its enduring architectural charm. **Directions:** The hotel is situated at the centre of the esplanade. Price guide (including dinner): Single £75–£99; double/twin £132–£180; suite £178–£198.

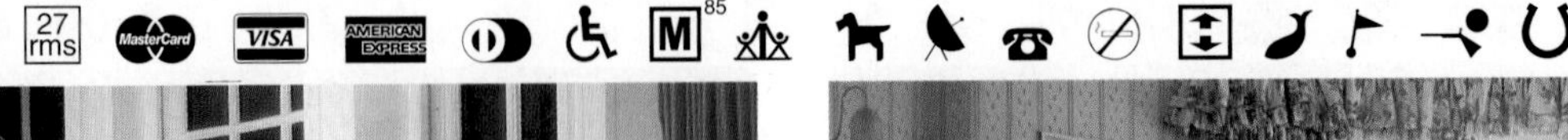

For hotel location, see maps on pages 490-496

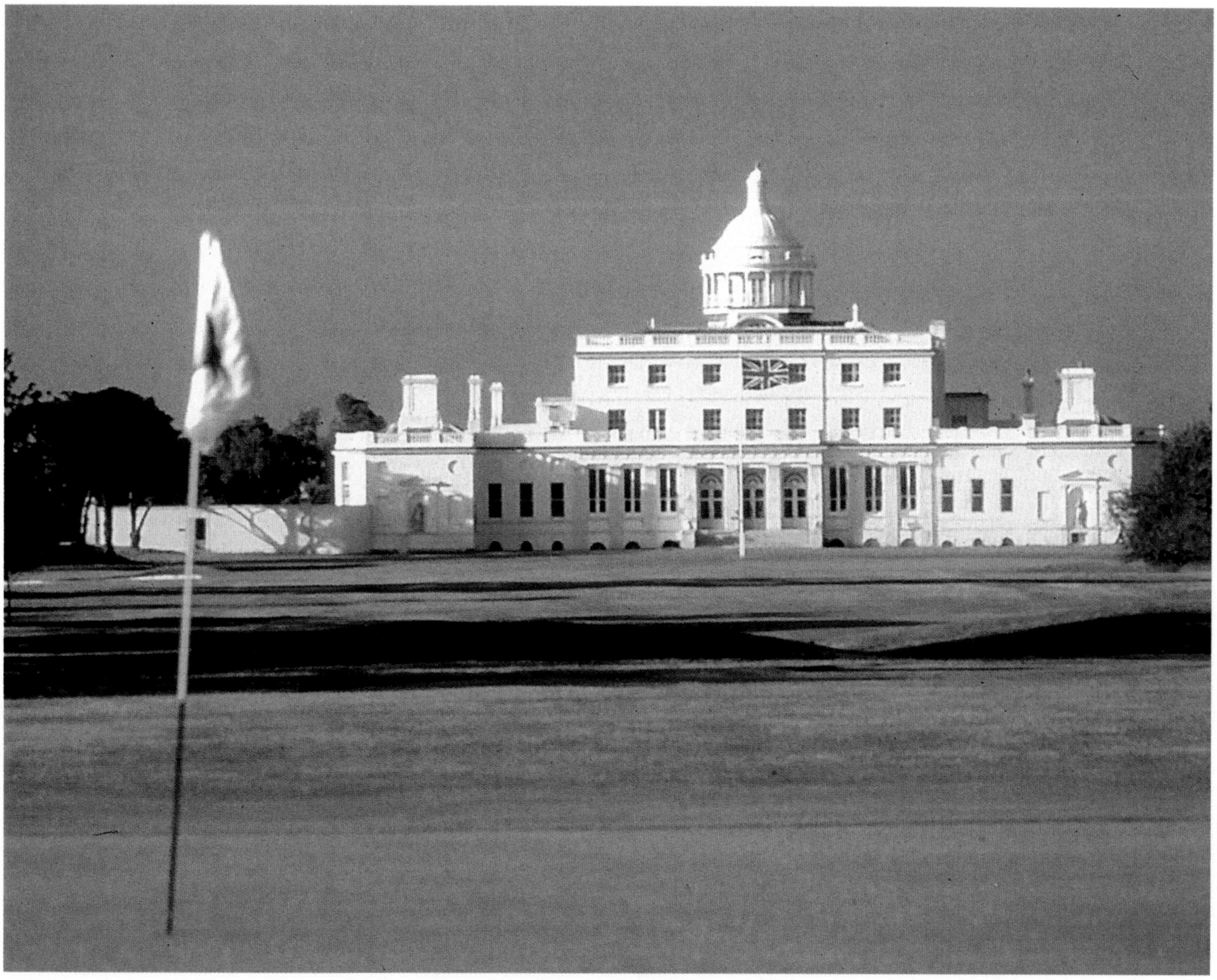

# STOKE PARK

**PARK ROAD, STOKE POGES, BUCKINGHAMSHIRE SL2 4PG**
**TEL: 01753 717171 FAX: 01753 717181**

This impressive Palladian mansion was built in 1791 and Capability Brown was responsible for the magnificent landscaped grounds. The Estate, featured in The Doomsday Book, can truly boast that Queen Elizabeth I and King Charles I slept here. It is the clubhouse of Stoke Poges Golf Club and also a splendid hotel, close to Heathrow, and only 30 minutes from London, wonderfully secluded and surrounded by extensive parkland. The interior is palatial, with fine tall ceilings, fine antiques and art with original etchings. The bedrooms are lavishly decorated, stunning exquisite fabrics and elegant period furniture. The bathrooms are luxurious with every possible 'extra'. The Golf Club shares its spacious drawing rooms and traditional President's Bar with residents. The Dining Room is classical and the menu lists great English and French dishes. The cellar is superb! Stoke Park has many well equipped meeting rooms, including the attractive Ballroom, quickly transformed into attractive venues for special celebrations. Special green fees are appreciated by golfing guests. Croquet and snooker are house sports, shooting and fishing nearby. Windsor, Ascot and Henley are in easy reach. **Directions:** From M4/J6 or M40/J2 take A344; at double roundabout at Farnham Royal take B416. Entrance is just over a mile on the right. Price guide: Single £275; suite £325.

For hotel location, see maps on pages 490-496

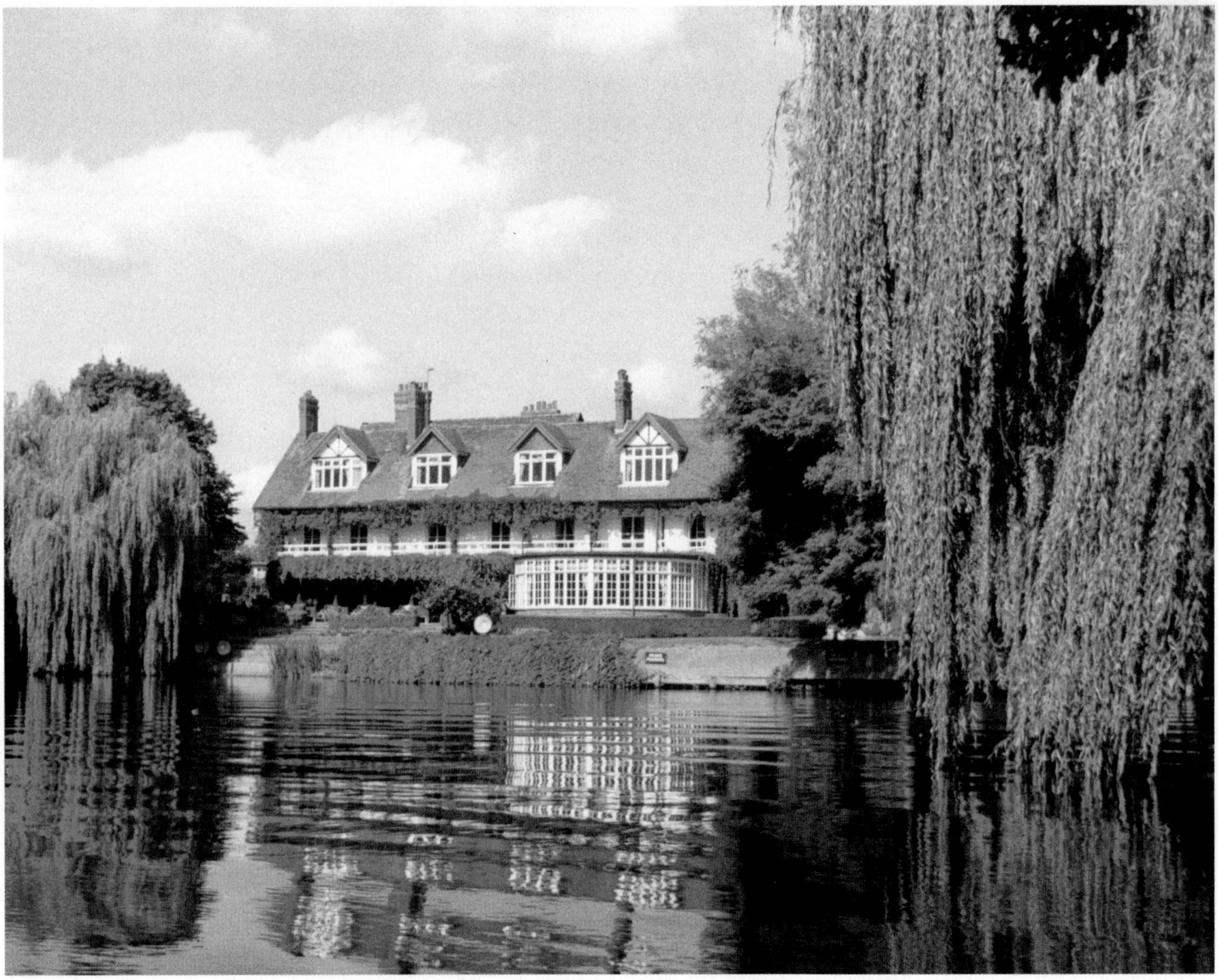

# The French Horn

**SONNING-ON-THAMES, BERKSHIRE RG4 OTN**
**TEL: 01734 692204 FAX: 01734 442210**

For over 150 years The French Horn has provided a charming riverside retreat from the busy outside world. Today, although busier on this stretch of the river, it continues that fine tradition of comfortable accommodation and outstanding cuisine in a beautiful setting. The hotel nestles beside the Thames near the historic village of Sonning. The well appointed bedrooms and suites are fully equipped with modern amenities and many have river views. The old panelled bar provides an intimate scene for pre-dinner drinks and the restaurant speciality, locally reared duck, is spit roasted here over an open fire. By day the sunny restaurant is a lovely setting for lunch, while by night diners can enjoy the floodlit view of the graceful weeping willows which fringe the river. Dinner is served by candlelight and the cuisine is a mixture of French and English cooking using the freshest ingredients. The French Horn's wine list is reputed to be amongst the finest in Europe. Places of interest include Henley, Stratfield Saye, Oxford, Blenheim Palace and Mapledurham. There are numerous golf courses and equestrian centres in the area. **Directions:** Leave the M4 at J8/9. Follow A404/M then at Thickets Roundabout turn left on A4 towards Reading for 8 miles. Turn right for Sonning. Cross Thames on B478. Hotel is on left. Price guide: Single £85–£125; double/twin £90–£145.

For hotel location, see maps on pages 490-496

# NORTHCOTE MANOR

**BURRINGTON AT PORTSMOUTH ARMS, TAW RIVER VALLEY, NORTH DEVON EX37 9LZ**
**TEL: 01769 560501 FAX: 01769 560770**

The Jacobean Northcote Manor is beautifully situated midway between Exeter and Dartmoor. The very special atmosphere pervading this 20 acre estate of lush woodland, sweeping lawns and landscaped gardens, owes much to its origins. Over 1000 years ago, the monks from nearby Tavistock Abbey worked and studied here. Henry VIII once owned it. Now under new ownership, Northcote Manor Country House Hotel and its new Restaurant provide a combination of warm hospitality, modern amenities, outstanding continental cuisine. The bedrooms are bright and well appointed all with en suite facilities, and the public rooms are spacious and elegant. Apart from an abundance of wildlife there are leisure facilities for all family members, including cycles for hire, tennis, croquet and plenty of benches on which to sit and revel in the atmosphere. Golf and fishing in the River Taw are minutes away. Riding can be arranged. Food is freshly prepared using organic meats and vegetables for which the area is well renowned. The breakfast table features muesli and preserves, fresh pressed juices as well as home-made sausages and bacon from the farm next door. **Directions:** About 25 miles from Exeter on the A377 at Portsmouth Arms turn into private drive. Do not enter Burrington Village. Price guide: Single from £74; double/twin from £128; suites from £139. (Including dinner). Family breaks.

For hotel location, see maps on pages 490-496

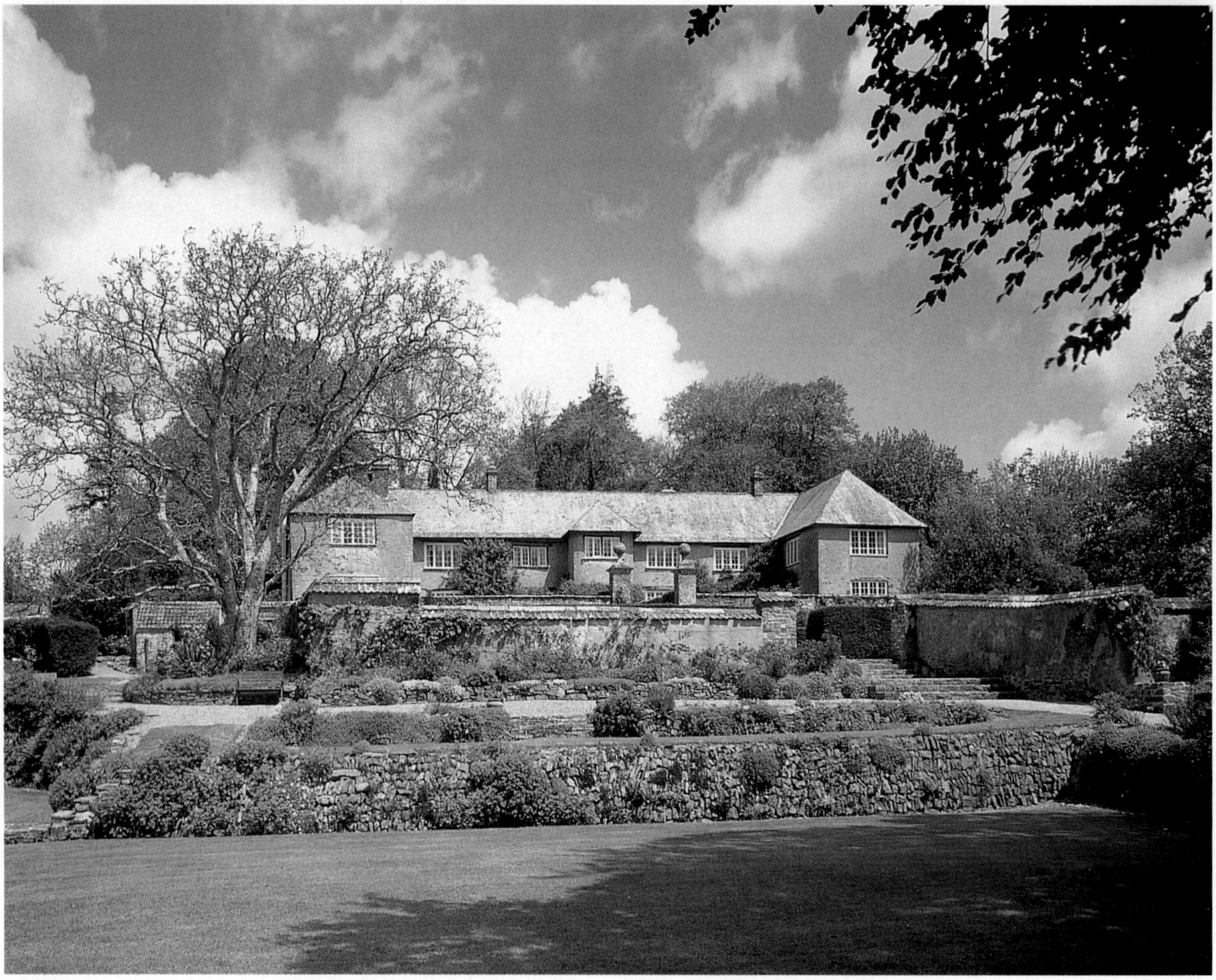

# Whitechapel Manor

**NR SOUTH MOLTON, NORTH DEVON EX36 3EG**
**TEL: 01769 573377 FAX: 01769 573797**

Built in 1575 by Robert de Bassett, pretender to the English throne, Whitechapel Manor a Grade I listed building is a vision of the past with terraced and walled gardens of manicured lawns, roses and clipped yew hedges offering peace and tranquility. The entrance hall has a perfect Jacobean carved oak screen. Elsewhere, William & Mary plasterwork and panelling along with painted overmantles have been preserved. The large bedrooms at the front overlooking the gardens and the smaller, cosy rooms which overlook the woodlands are thoughtfully appointed for comfort. The grounds teem with wildlife including numerous varieties of birds and the native Red Deer which are unique to Exmoor. The restaurant combines international flavours producing an exciting dining experience and is recognised as one of the best in the West Country. All around is tranquil, unspoilt countryside rising up to Exmoor National Park and the most dramatic coastline in England. Whitechapel is the ideal base from which to explore the moors, coast, ancient woodland valleys, Exmoor's villages and its wildlife. Also nearby are the RHS Gardens at Rosemoor, Dartington Crystal and many National Trust properties. **Directions:** Leave M5 at junction 27. Follow signs to Barnstaple. After 30 minutes turn right at roundabout to Whitechapel. Price guide: Single £70–£155; double/twin £110–£170. Special breaks and events all year round.

For hotel location, see maps on pages 490-496

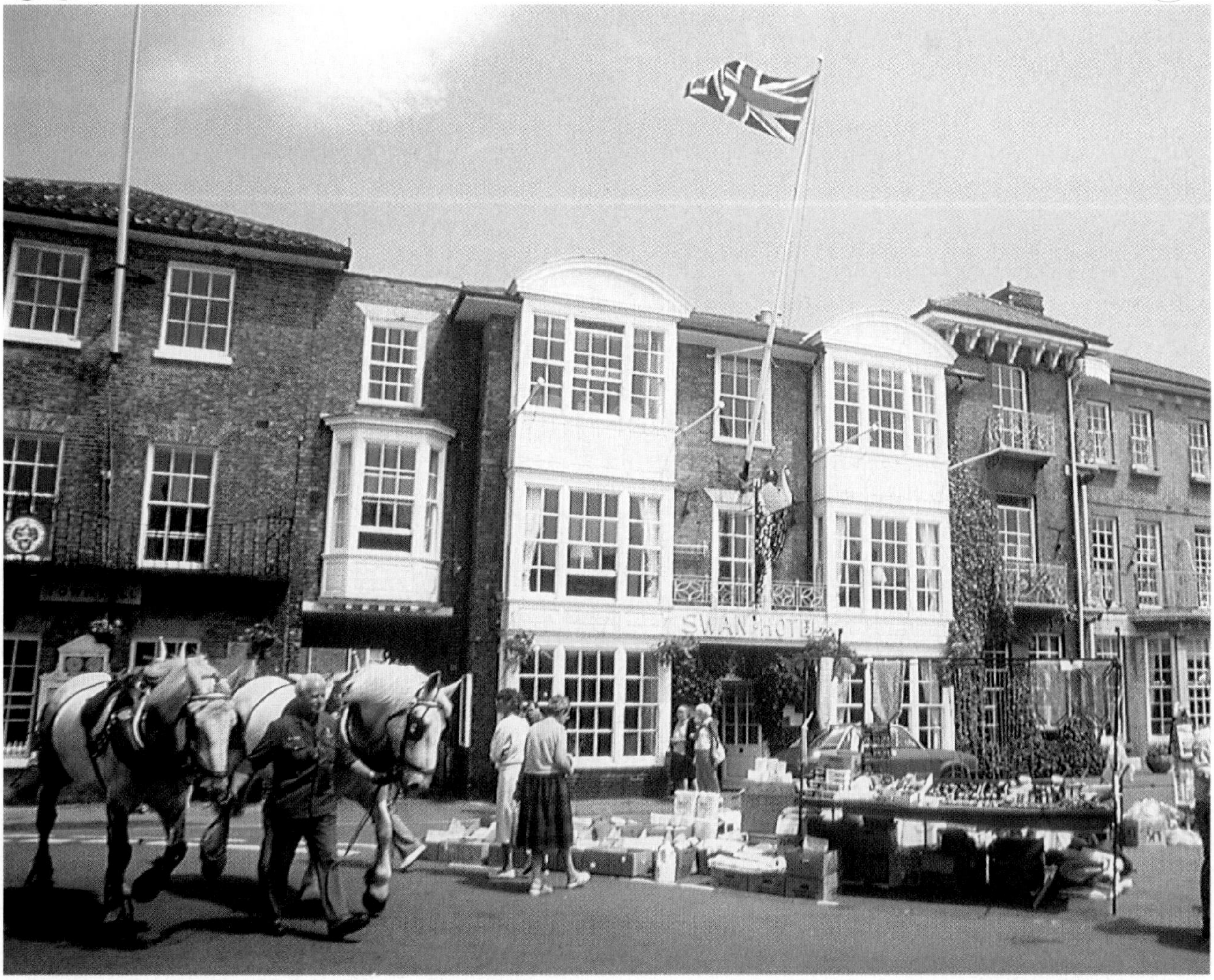

# THE SWAN HOTEL

MARKET PLACE, SOUTHWOLD, SUFFOLK IP18 6EG

TEL: 01502 722186 FAX: 01502 724800

Rebuilt in 1659, following the disastrous fire which destroyed most of the town, The Swan was remodelled in the 1820s, with further additions in 1938. The hotel provides all modern services while retaining its classical dignity and elegance. Many of the antique-furnished bedrooms in the main hotel offer a glimpse of the sea, while the garden rooms – decorated in a more contemporary style – are clustered around the old bowling green. The Drawing Room has the traditional character of an English country house and the Reading Room upstairs is perfect for quiet relaxation or as the venue for a private party. The daily menu offers dishes ranging from simple, traditional fare through the English classics to the chef's personal specialities. An exciting selection of wines is offered. Almost an island, Southwold is bounded on three sides by creeks, marshes and the River Blyth – making it a paradise for birdwatchers and nature lovers. Hardly changed for a century, the town, built around a series of greens, has a fine church, lighthouse and golf course. Music lovers flock to nearby Snape Maltings for the Aldeburgh Festival. Winner of Country Living Gold Award for the Best Hotel 1993/94. **Directions:** Southwold is off the A12 Ipswich–Lowestoft road. The Swan Hotel is in the town centre. Price guide: Single £40–£58; double/twin £86–£125; suite £145–£155.

For hotel location, see maps on pages 490-496

# The George Of Stamford

**ST MARTINS, STAMFORD, LINCOLNSHIRE PE9 2LB**
**TEL: 01780 755171 FAX: 01780 757070**

The George, a beautiful, 16th century coaching inn, retains the charm of its long history, as guests will sense on entering the reception hall with its oak travelling chests and famous oil portrait of Daniel Lambert. Over the years, The George has welcomed a diverse clientèle, ranging from highwaymen to kings – Charles I and William III were both visitors. At the heart of the hotel is the lounge, its natural stone walls, deep easy chairs and softly lit alcoves imparting a cosy, relaxed atmosphere, while the blazing log fire is sometimes used to toast muffins for tea! The flair of Julia Vannocci's interior design is evident in all the expertly styled, fully appointed bedrooms. Exotic plants, orchids, orange trees and coconut palms feature in the Garden Lounge, where a choice of hot dishes and an extensive cold buffet are offered. Guests may also dine alfresco in the courtyard garden. The more formal, oak-panelled restaurant serves imaginative but traditional English dishes and an award-winning list of wines. Superb facilities are incorporated in the Business Centre, converted from the former livery stables. Special weekend breaks available. **Directions:** Stamford is 1 mile from the A1 on the B1081. The George is in the town centre opposite the gallows sign. Car parking is behind the hotel. Price guide: Single from £72–£85; double/twin from £95–£115; suite £125–£160.

47 rms MasterCard VISA AMERICAN EXPRESS M 50

For hotel location, see maps on pages 490-496

# WHITEHALL

CHURCH END, BROXTED, ESSEX CM6 2BZ
TEL: 01279 850603 FAX: 01279 850385

Set on a hillside overlooking the delightful rolling countryside of north-west Essex is Whitehall, one of East Anglia's leading country hotels. While its origins can be traced back to 1151, the manor house is ostensibly Elizabethan in style, with recent additions tastefully incorporated. Traditional features such as beams, wide fireplaces and log fires blend well with the contemporary, fresh pastel shades and subtle-hued fabrics. A spectacular vaulted ceiling makes the dining room an impressive setting for dinner, with an à la carte or six-course set menu offering many a delicious bonne-bouche. For large private functions, the timbered Barn House is an ideal venue, where guests can enjoy the same high standards of cuisine found in the restaurant. Overlooked by the old village church is the attractive Elizabethan walled garden. Whitehall is only a short drive from London's most modern international airport at Stansted opened in 1989 and easily accessible from the M11 motorway, while Cambridge and Newmarket are only 30 minutes' drive away. **Directions:** Take junction 8 from the M11, follow Stansted Airport signs to new terminal building and then signs for Broxted. Price guide: Single £80; double/twin £110–£140.

25 rms MasterCard VISA AMERICAN EXPRESS M 120

For hotel location, see maps on pages 490-496

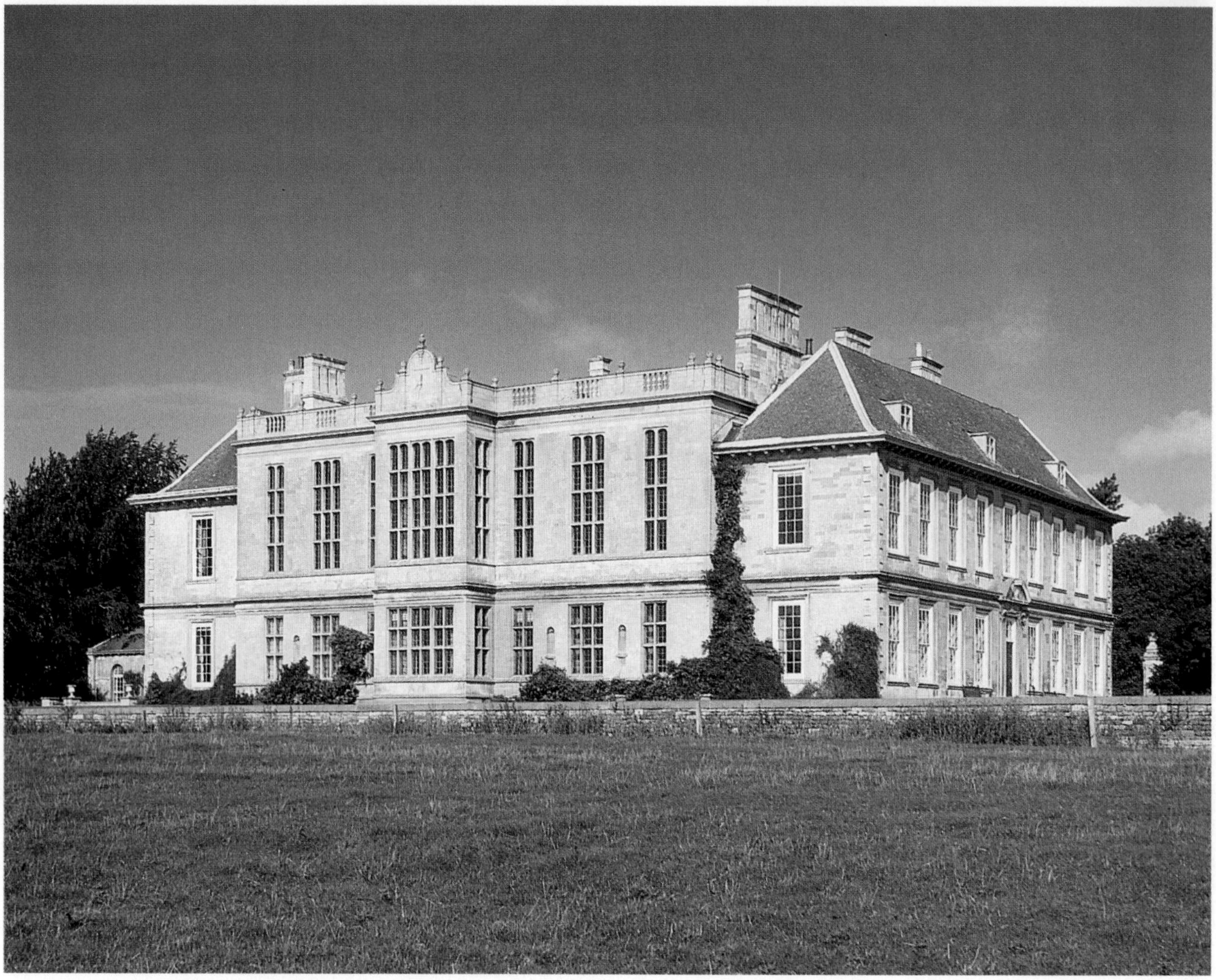

# STAPLEFORD PARK, AN OUTPOST OF THE CARNEGIE CLUB

**NR MELTON MOWBRAY, LEICESTERSHIRE LE14 2EF**

**TEL: 01572 787 522 FAX: 01572 787 651**

A Stately Home and Sporting Estate for House Guests. Casual luxury is the byword in this pre-eminent 16th century house, which was opened as a hotel in 1988. It was once coveted by Edward, The Prince of Wales, but his mother Queen Victoria forbade him to buy it for fear that his morals would be corrupted by the Leicestershire hunting society! Today, Stapleford Park offers resident hotel guests and club members supremely elegant surroundings and beautiful views over 500 acres of parkland. Described as "The Best Country House Hotel in the World" in Andrew Harper's Hideaway Report, it has received innumerable awards for its unique style and hospitality. The individually designed bedrooms have been created by famous names such as Tiffany, Wedgwood, Crabtree & Evelyn and Range Rover. An exclusive cottage with four themed bedrooms is also available. Excellent cuisine is carefully prepared to the highest standards and complemented by an adventurous and comprehensive wine list. There are a host of sporting pursuits including falconry, clay and game shooting, golf, riding, tennis and fishing. Convenient for Burghley Horse Trials. There are facilities for private dinners, weddings, receptions and conferences. An English Outpost of the Carnegie Club. **Directions:** Stapleford Park is only 1½ hours north of London, situated between the A1 and M1. Price guide: Double/twin £165-£245; suites from £250.

For hotel location, see maps on pages 490-496

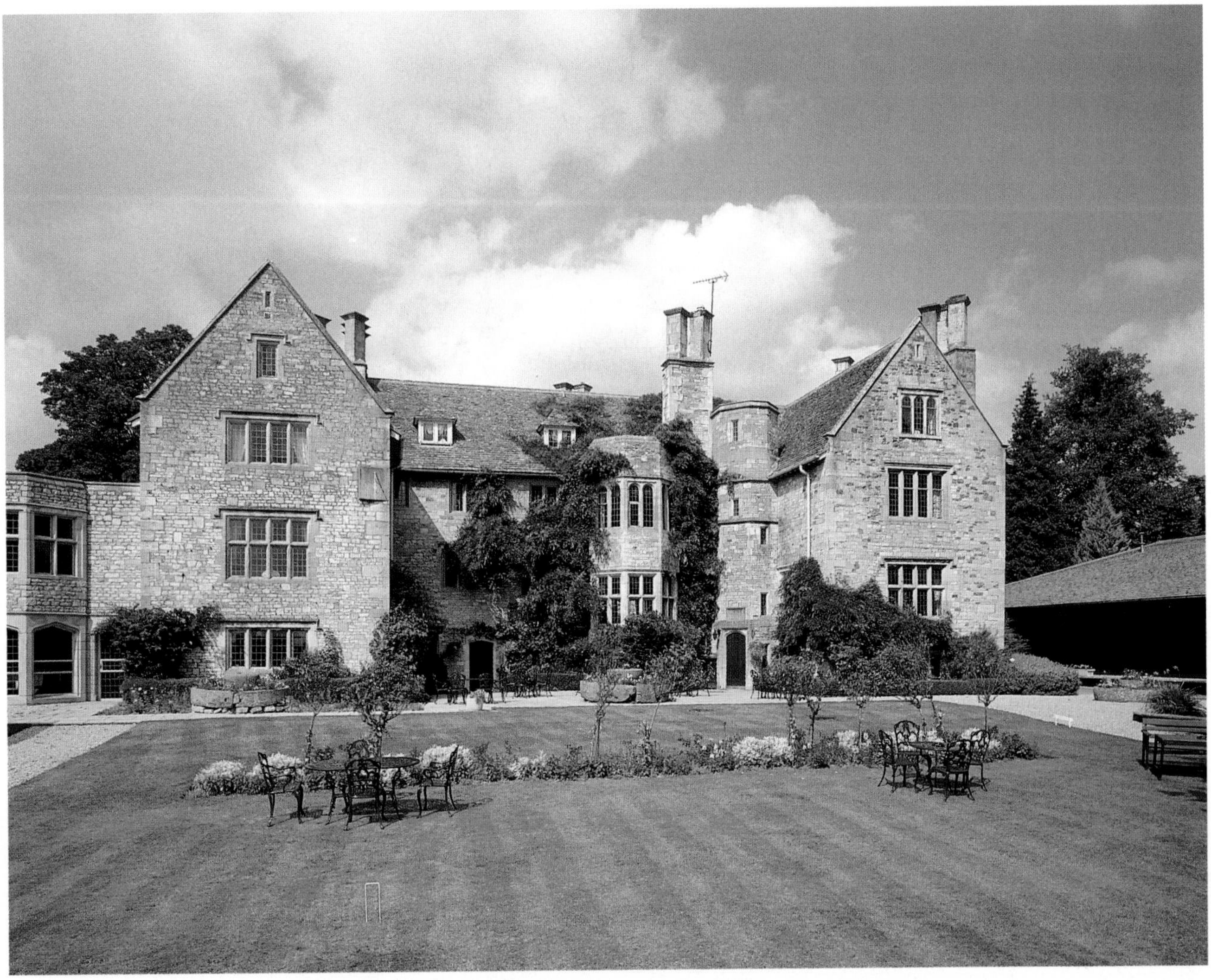

# STONEHOUSE COURT

**STONEHOUSE, GLOUCESTERSHIRE GL10 3RA**

**TEL: 01453 825155 FAX: 01453 824611**

This outstanding Grade II listed manor house is set in six acres of magnificent gardens on the edge of the Cotswolds. All of the bedrooms which have recently been totally refurbished are individually decorated, with many in the main house featuring original fireplaces and mullion windows. The highly acclaimed award winning John Henry Restaurant provides the perfect setting for either an intimate candlelit dinner, a family gathering or a formal business luncheon. The cuisine although primarily English has a rustic Mediterranean influence and is complemented by many fine wines. Outdoor pursuits include golf at Minchinhampton golf club, while activity days within the grounds can include laser shooting, archery, quad biking and team building exercises. The conference facilities at Stonehouse Court are designed for all styles of meetings, from informal to boardroom. The self-contained Caroline Suite is well suited to holding product launches, training courses and conferences and the oak-panelled Crellin Room ideal for small meetings or private dining. Nearby are Cheltenham, Berkeley Castle and Slimbridge Wildfowl Trust, also Cheltenham Races, polo at Cirencester or the Badminton horse trials. **Directions:** From junction 13 of the M5 Stonehouse Court is two miles on the A419 towards Stroud. Price guide: Single from £70; double/twin from £100

For hotel location, see maps on pages 490-496

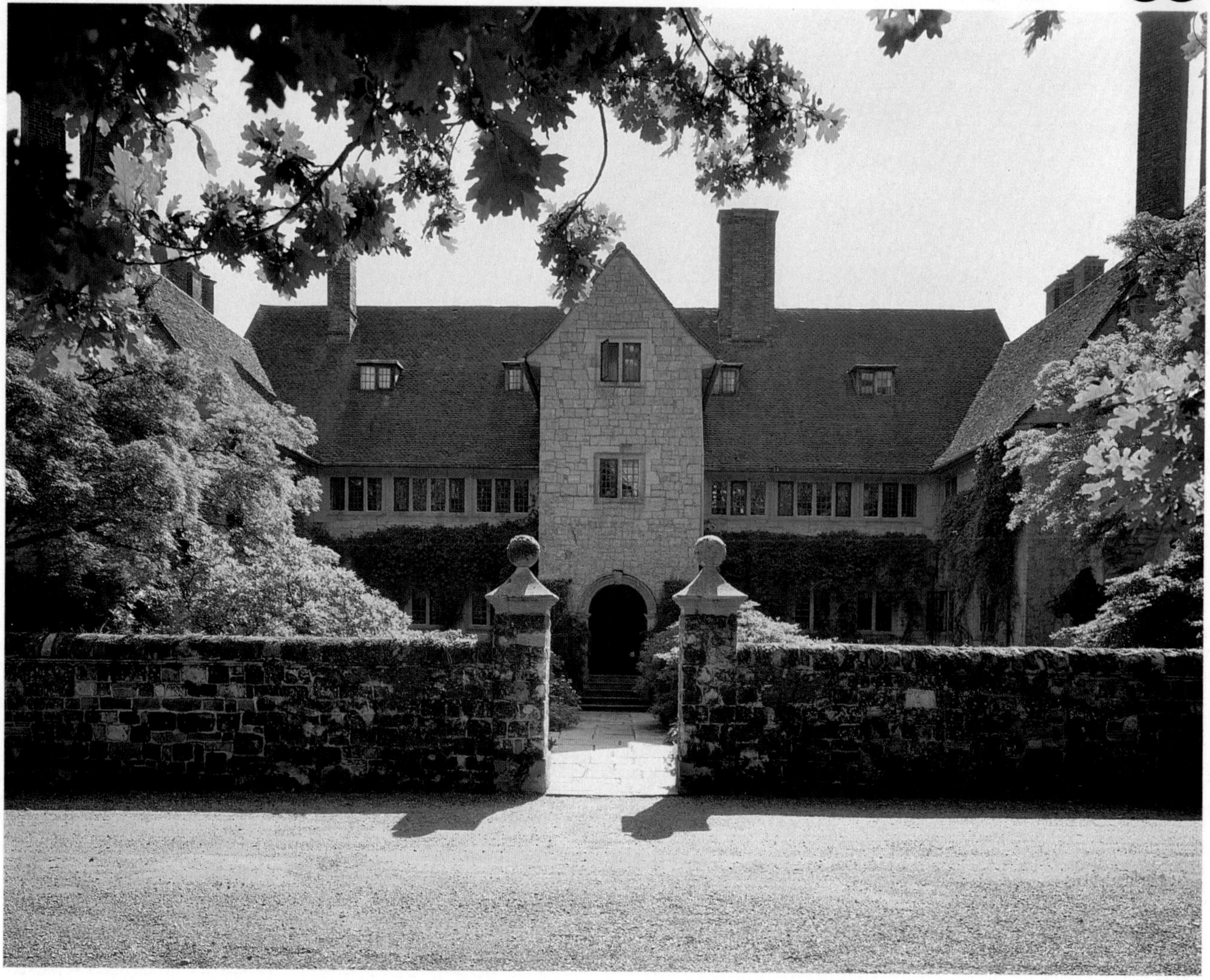

# LITTLE THAKEHAM

**MERRYWOOD LANE, STORRINGTON, WEST SUSSEX RH20 3HE**
**TEL: 01903 744416 FAX: 01903 745022**

One of the finest examples of a Lutyens Manor house, Little Thakeham is the home of Tim and Pauline Ractliff who have carefully preserved the feeling of a family home. Antiques, open log fires and a minstrel gallery all serve to enhance the authentic atmosphere of gracious living. There are two suites and seven bedrooms all furnished in character with the house. The restaurant, also open to non-residents, serves traditional English food based on local produce such as Southdown lamb and shellfish from the South Coast. The set menu changes daily and there is an excellent cellar. The surrounding gardens were created in the style of Gertude Jekyll and recently have been the subject of restoration. There is a heated swimming pool in the grounds. The famous country houses of Goodwood, Petworth and Arundel Castle are nearby, racing enthusiasts are well served with Goodwood, Fontwell Park and Plumpton. Antique collectors will not be disappointed, there are shops in Arundel, Petworth and Chichester. **Directions:** From Storrington, take B2139 to Thakeham. After about one mile turn right into Merrywood Lane. Hotel is 400 yards on left. Price guide: Single £105.75; double/twin from £164.50; suite from £223.25.

For hotel location, see maps on pages 490-496

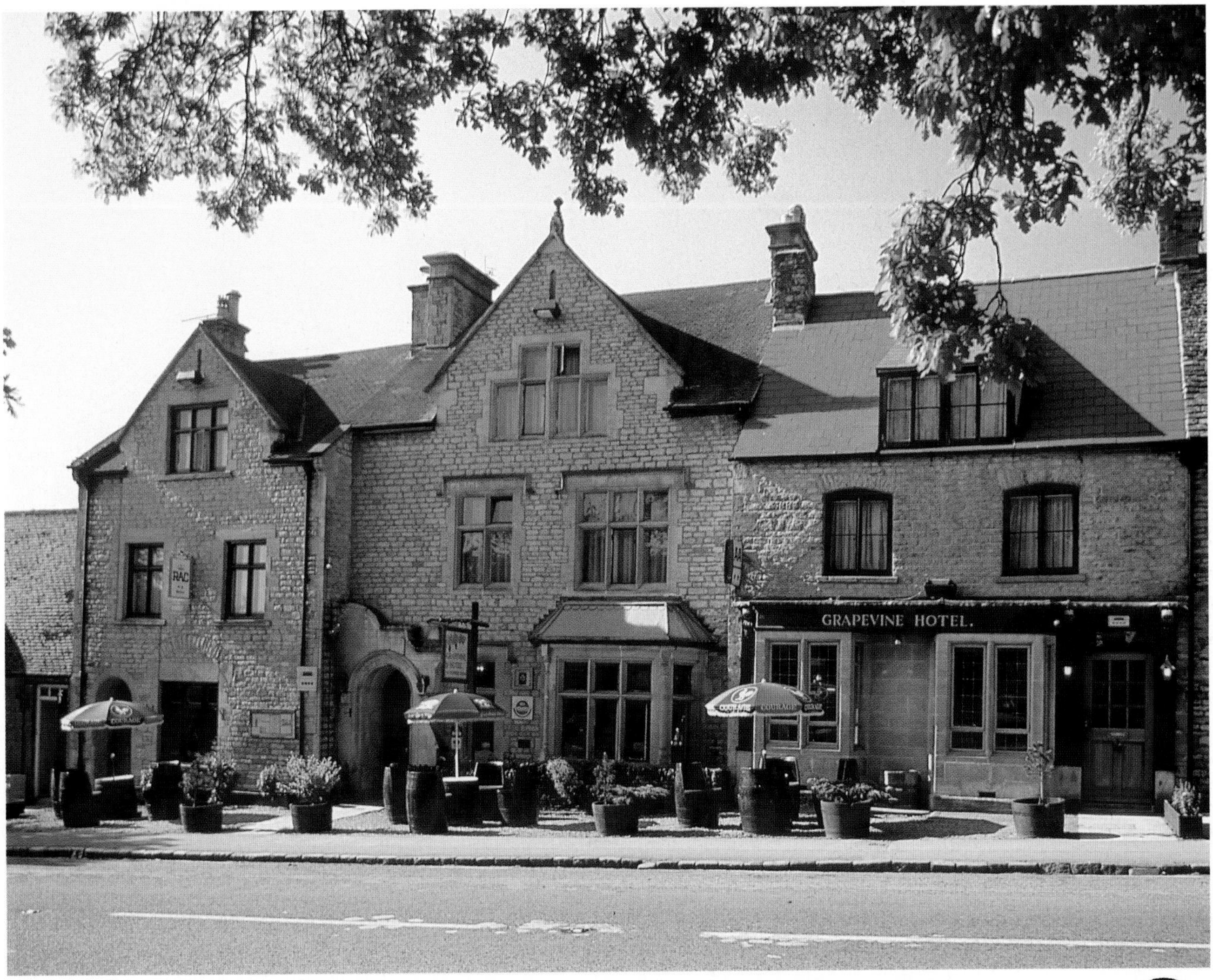

# THE GRAPEVINE HOTEL

**SHEEP STREET, STOW-ON-THE-WOLD, GLOUCESTERSHIRE GL54 1AU**
**TEL: 01451 830344 FAX: 01451 832278 E-MAIL: enquiries@vines.co.uk**

Set in the pretty town of Stow-on-the-Wold, regarded by many as the jewel of the Cotswolds, The Grapevine Hotel has an atmosphere which makes visitors feel welcome and at ease. The outstanding personal service provided by a loyal team of staff is perhaps the secret of the hotel's success. This, along with the exceptionally high standard of overall comfort and hospitality, earned The Grapevine the 1991 *Johansens Hotel Award for Excellence* – a well-deserved accolade. Beautifully furnished bedrooms, including six superb garden rooms across the courtyard, offer every facility. Visitors can linger over imaginative cuisine in the relaxed and informal atmosphere of the conservatory restaurant, with its unusual canopy of trailing vines. 2 AA rosettes awarded for food. Whether travelling on business or for pleasure, The Grapevine is a hotel that guests will wish to return to again and again. The local landscape offers unlimited scope for exploration, whether to the numerous picturesque villages tucked away in the Cotswolds or to the nearby towns of Oxford, Cirencester and Stratford-upon-Avon. Open over Christmas/New Year. Visit the Grapevine's Internet site: http://www.vines.co.uk **Directions:** Sheep Street is part of the A436 in the centre of Stow-on-the-Wold. Price guide: Single from £89; double/twin from £138.

For hotel location, see maps on pages 490-496

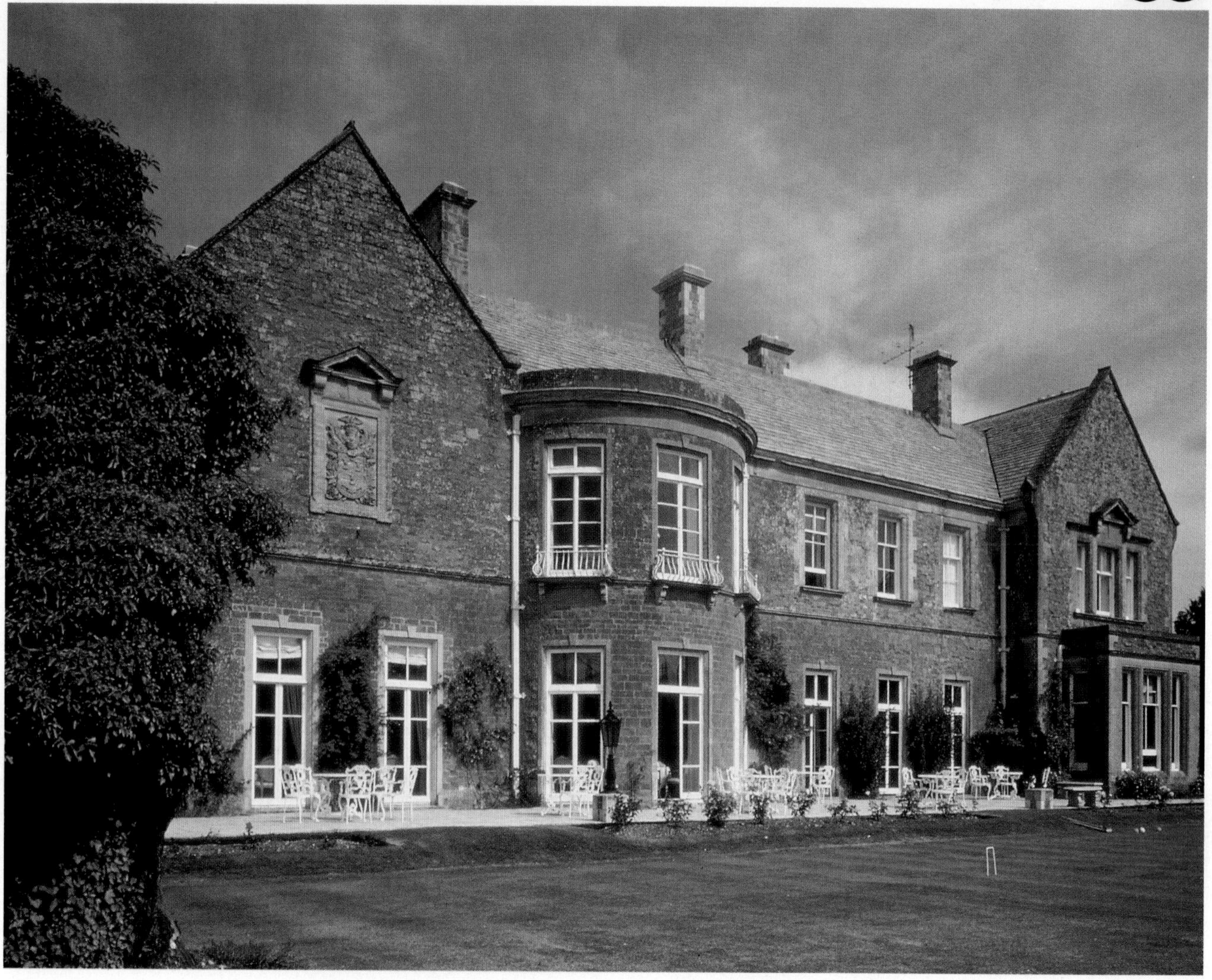

# WYCK HILL HOUSE

## WYCK HILL, STOW-ON-THE WOLD, GLOUCESTERSHIRE GL54 1HY

**TEL: 01451 831936 FAX: 01451 832243**

Wyck Hill House is a magnificent Cotswold mansion built in the early 1700s, reputedly on the site of an early Roman settlement. It is set in 100 acres of wooded and landscaped gardens, overlooking the beautiful Windrush Valley. The hotel has been elegantly restored and the bedrooms individually furnished to combine superb antiques with modern comforts. There is a suite with a large, antique four-poster bed, which is perfect for a honeymoon or for other special occasions. The cedar-panelled library is an ideal room in which to read, if you wish, and to relax with morning coffee or afternoon tea. The award-winning restaurant provides the highest standards of modern British cuisine from the freshest seasonally available local produce. The menus are complemented by a superb wine list. Wyck Hill House hosts several special events, including opera, travel talks, cultural weekends and a variety of theme activities. The hotel is an ideal base from which to tour the university city of Oxford and the Georgian city of Bath. Cheltenham, Blenheim Palace and Stratford-upon-Avon are just a short drive away. Special price 2-night breaks are available. **Directions:** One-and-a-half miles south of Stow-on-the-Wold on the A424 Stow–Burford road. Price guide: Single from £90; double/twin from £130; suite from £210.

For hotel location, see maps on pages 490-496

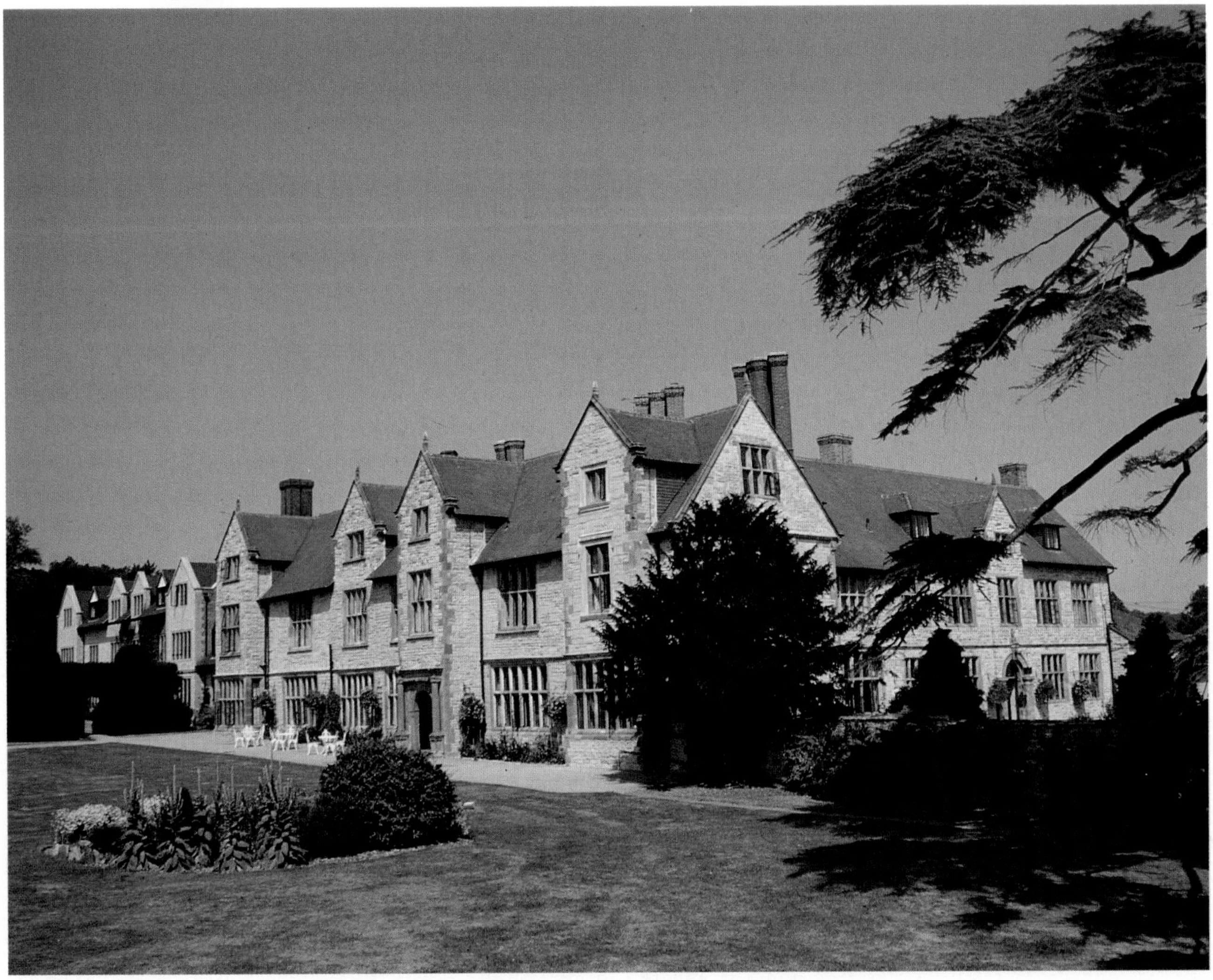

# BILLESLEY MANOR

**BILLESLEY, ALCESTER, NR STRATFORD-UPON-AVON, WARWICKSHIRE B49 6NF**

**TEL: 01789 279955 FAX: 01789 764145**

Three miles from Stratford-upon-Avon, Billesley Manor is set in 11 acres of delightful grounds with a typically English topiary garden and ornamental pond. Ten centuries of history and tradition welcome guests to this magnificent house in the heart of Shakespeare country. Billesley Manor has been extensively refurbished in recent years, blending old and new to create a hotel that is impressive, spacious and comfortable. Guests may stay in a suite, an oak-panelled four-poster room or one of the well-appointed modern rooms – all have a large bathroom and a good range of facilities. The panelled Tudor and Stuart Restaurants have won awards for their fine food and service, including 2 AA Rosettes. Billesley Manor is suitable for residential conferences and meetings, offering self-contained amenities and seclusion. In addition to the many on-site leisure activities, like the attractive sun patio, pool, mini-golf and tennis courts, weekend breaks can include hot-air ballooning, shooting and riding. The hotel is ideal for visiting the Royal Shakespeare Theatre, Warwick Castle, Ragley Hall and the Cotswolds. **Directions:** From M40 (exit 15) follow A46 towards Evesham and Alcester. Three miles beyond Stratford-upon-Avon turn right to Billesley. Price guide: Single £115; double/twin £165; suite £230.

For hotel location, see maps on pages 490-496

# Ettington Park

**ALDERMINSTER, STRATFORD-UPON-AVON, WARWICKSHIRE CV37 8BS**
**TEL: 01789 450123 FAX: 01789 450472**

The foundations of Ettington Park date back at least 1000 years. Mentioned in the *Domesday Book*, Ettington Park rises majestically over 40 acres of Warwickshire parkland, surrounded by terraced gardens and carefully tended lawns, where guests can wander at their leisure to admire the pastoral views. The interiors are beautiful, their striking opulence enhanced by flowers, beautiful antiques and original paintings. Amid these elegant surroundings guests can relax totally, pampered with every luxury. On an appropriately grand scale, the 48 bedrooms and superb leisure complex, comprising an indoor heated swimming pool, spa bath, solarium and sauna, make this a perfect choice for the sybarite. The menu reflects the best of English and French cuisine, served with panache in the dining room, with its elegant 18th century rococo ceiling and 19th century carved family crests. The *bon viveur* will relish the fine wine list. Splendid conference facilities are available: the panelled Long Gallery and 14th century chapel are both unique venues. Riding is a speciality, while clay pigeon shooting, archery and fishing can also be arranged on the premises. An Arcadian Hotel. **Directions:** From M40 junction 15 (Warwick) take A46, A439 signposted Stratford, then left-hand turn onto A3400. Ettington is five miles south of Stratford-upon-Avon off the A3400. Price guide: Single £125; double/twin from £175; suites from £245.

48 rms · MasterCard · VISA · American Express · M 65

For hotel location, see maps on pages 490-496

# SALFORD HALL HOTEL

**ABBOT'S SALFORD, NR EVESHAM, WORCESTERSHIRE WR11 5UT**
**TEL: 01386 871300 FAX: 01386 871301**

Between Shakespeare's Stratford-upon-Avon, the rolling Cotswolds and the Vale of Evesham is the Roman village of Abbot's Salford. Steeped in history, Salford Hall is a romantic Grade I listed manor house. It was built in the late 15th century as a retreat for the monks of Evesham Abbey and the imposing stone wing was added in the 17th century. Essentially unchanged, stained glass, a priest hole, exposed beams, oak panelling and original decorative murals are examples of the well-preserved features of the interior. The period charm is doubly appealing when combined with modern comforts, gracious furnishings, delicious food and an extensive selection of fine wines. Reflecting the past associations of the hall, the bedrooms are named after historical figures, and all are individually appointed with oak furniture and luxury fittings. Guests may relax in the Hawkesbury lounge, formerly a medieval kitchen, the conservatory lounge or on the sunny terrace within the walled flower garden. Facilities include snooker, a sauna and a solarium. Special weekends are arranged for hot-air ballooning, horse-racing, touring the Cotswolds, discovering Shakespeare and murder mysteries. Closed for Christmas. **Directions:** Abbot's Salford is 8 miles west of Stratford-upon-Avon on B439 towards The Vale of Evesham. Price guide: Single £75; double/twin £105–£140.

33 rms MasterCard VISA AMERICAN EXPRESS M 50

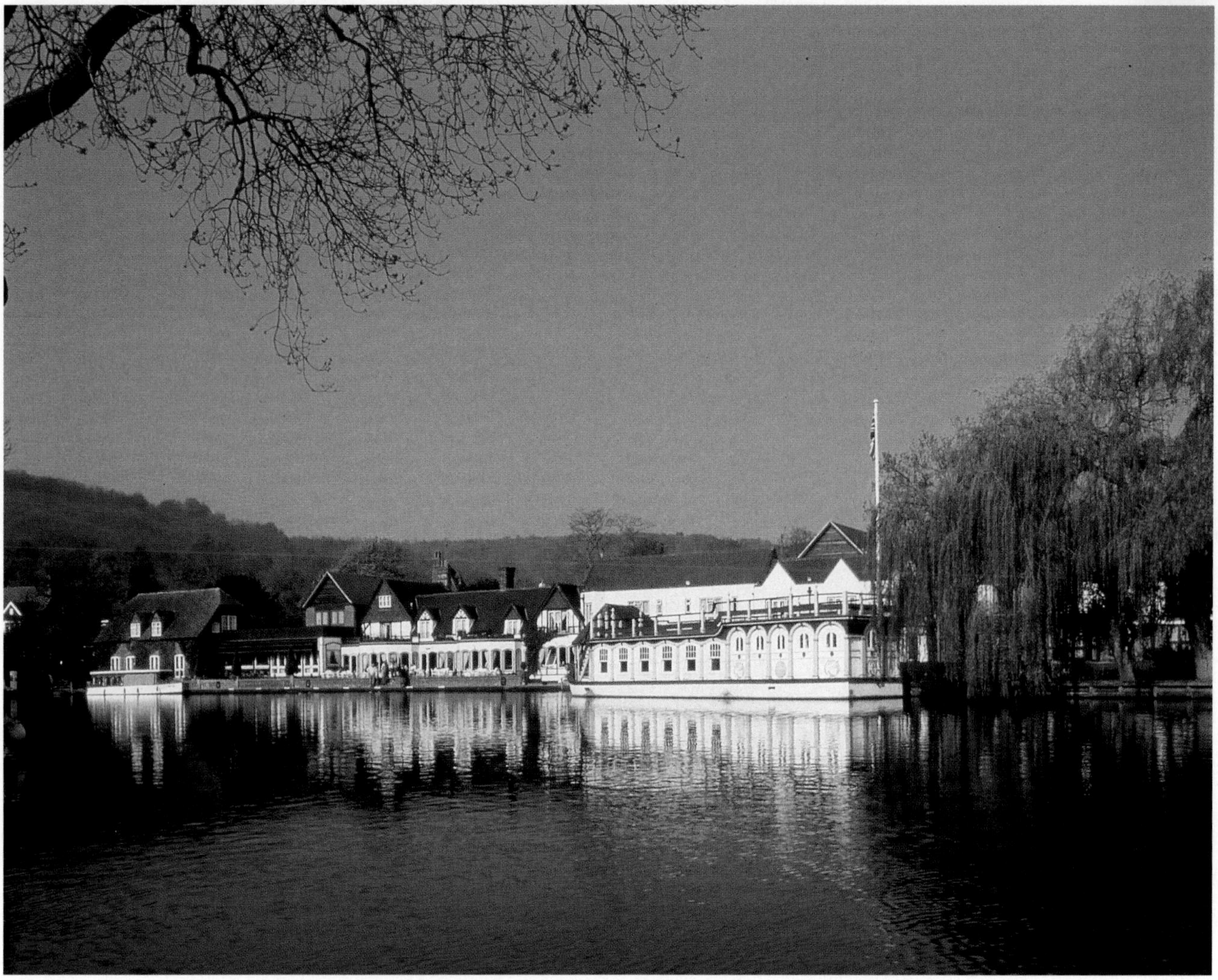

# THE SWAN DIPLOMAT


**STREATLEY-ON-THAMES, BERKSHIRE RG8 9HR**

**TEL: 01491 873737 FAX: 01491 872554**


In a beautiful setting on the bank of the River Thames, this hotel offers visitors comfortable accommodation. All of the 46 bedrooms, many of which have balconies overlooking the river, are appointed to high standards with individual décor and furnishings. The elegant Dining Room, with its relaxing waterside views, serves fine food complemented by a good choice of wines. Guests may also choose to dine in the informal Bar. Moored alongside the restaurant is the Magdalen College Barge, which is a stylish venue for meetings and cocktail parties. Business guests are well catered for – the hotel has six attractive conference suites. Reflexions Leisure Club is superbly equipped for fitness programmes and beauty treatments, with facilities that include a heated 'fit' pool; rowing boats and bicycles may be hired. Squash, riding and clay pigeon shooting can all be arranged. Special theme weekends are offered, such as bridge weekends. Events in the locality include Henley Regatta, Ascot and Newbury races, while Windsor Castle, Blenheim Palace, Oxford and London's airports are easily accessible. **Directions:** The hotel lies just off the A329 in Streatley village. Price guide: Single £57–£110; double/twin £87–£140.

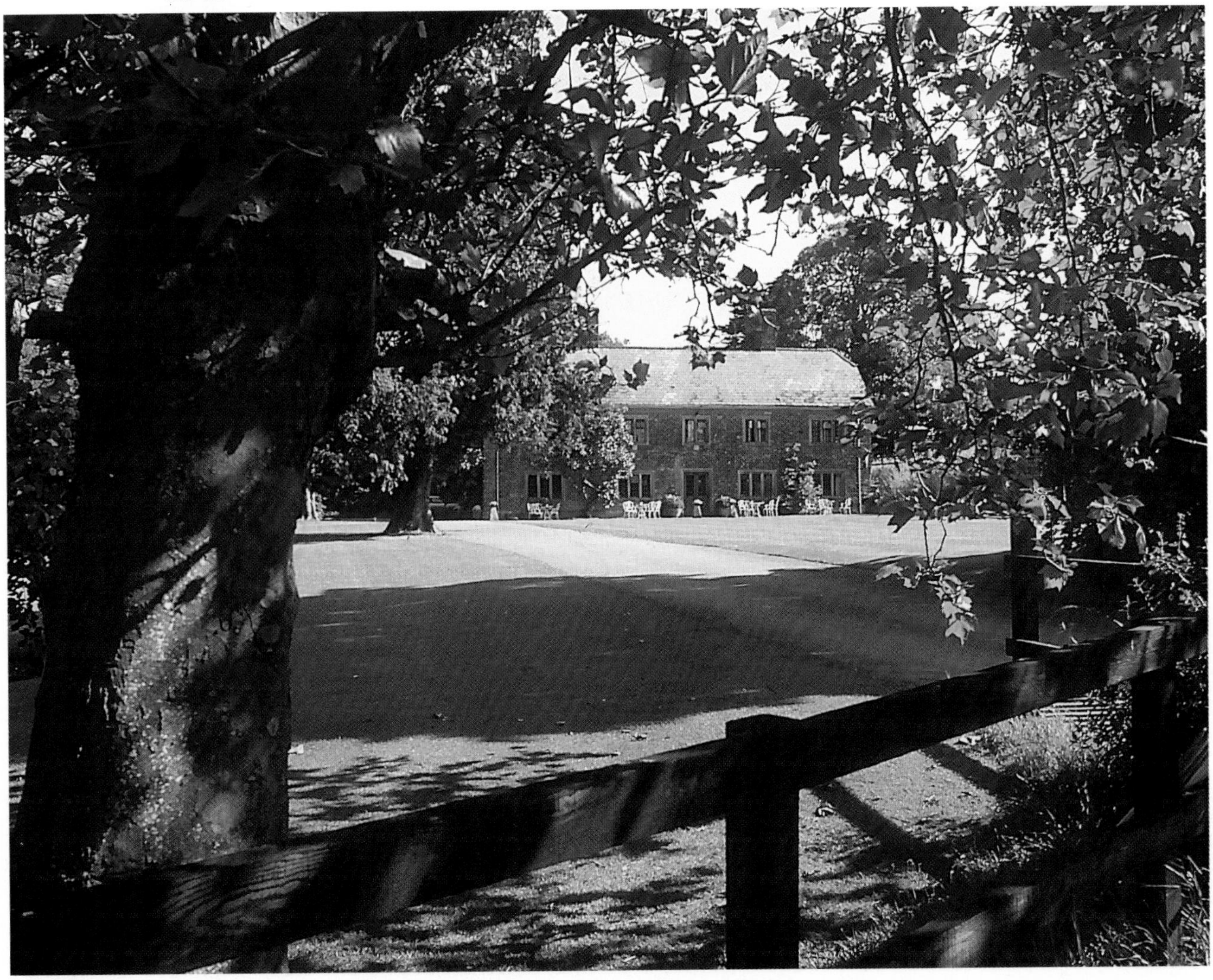

# PLUMBER MANOR

**STURMINSTER NEWTON, DORSET DT10 2AF**
**TEL: 01258 472507 FAX: 01258 473370**

An imposing Jacobean building of local stone, occupying extensive gardens in the heart of Hardy's Dorset, Plumber Manor has been the home of the Prideaux-Brune family since the early 17th century. Leading off a charming gallery hung with family portraits are six very comfortable bedrooms. The conversion of a natural stone barn lying within the grounds, as well as the courtyard building, has added a further ten spacious bedrooms, some of which have window seats overlooking the garden and the Develish stream. Three interconnecting dining rooms comprise the restaurant, where a good choice of imaginative, well-prepared dishes is presented, supported by a wide-ranging wine list. Chef Brian Prideaux-Brune's culinary prowess has been recognised by all the major food guides. Open for dinner every evening and Sunday lunch. The Dorset landscape, with its picture-postcard villages such as Milton Abbas and Cerne Abbas, is close at hand, while Corfe Castle, Lulworth Cove, Kingston Lacy and Poole Harbour are not far away. Riding can be arranged locally: however, if guests wish to bring their own horse to hack or hunt with local packs, the hotel provides free stabling on a do-it-yourself basis. Closed during February. **Directions:** Plumber Manor is two miles south west of Sturminster Newton on the Hazelbury Bryan road, off the A357. Price guide: Single from £70; double/twin £90–£130.

14

For hotel location, see maps on pages 490-496

# THE PEAR TREE AT PURTON

**CHURCH END, PURTON, SWINDON, WILTSHIRE SN5 9ED**
**TEL: 01793 772100 FAX: 01793 772369 E-MAIL: peartreepurton@msn.com**

Dedication to service is the hallmark of this excellent honey-coloured stone hotel nestling in the Vale of the White Horse between the Cotswolds and Marlborough Downs. Owners Francis and Anne Young are justly proud of its recognition by the award of the RAC's Blue Ribbon for excellence. Surrounded by rolling Wiltshire farmland, The Pear Tree sits majestically in seven-and-a-half acres of tranquil grounds on the fringe of the Saxon village of Purton, famed for its unique twin towered Parish Church and the ancient hill fort of Ringsbury Camp. Each of the 18 individually and tastefully decorated bedrooms and suites is named after a character associated with the village, such as Anne Hyde, mother of Queen Mary II and Queen Anne. All are fitted to a high standard and have satellite television, hairdryer, trouser press and a host of other luxuries. The award-winning conservatory restaurant overlooks colourful gardens and is the perfect setting in which to enjoy good English cuisine prepared with style and flair. Cirencester, Bath, Oxford, Avebury, Blenheim Palace, Sudeley Castle and the Cotswolds are all within easy reach. **Directions:** From M4 exit 16 follow signs to Purton and go through the village until reaching a triangle with Spar Grocers opposite. Turn right up the hill and the Pear Tree is on the left after the Tithe Barn. Price Guide: Single/double/twin £85; suite/4 poster £105.

For hotel location, see maps on pages 490-496

# TALLAND BAY HOTEL

**TALLAND-BY-LOOE, CORNWALL PL13 2JB**
**TEL: 01503 272667 FAX: 01503 272940**

This lovely old Cornish manor house, parts of which date back to the 16th century, enjoys a completely rural and unspoilt setting. The hotel is surrounded by over 2 acres of beautiful gardens with glorious views over the two dramatic headlands of Talland Bay itself. Bedrooms are individually furnished to a high standard, some having lovely sea views. Sitting rooms open to the south-facing terrace by a heated outdoor swimming pool. Dinner menus are imaginative and incorporate seafood from Looe, Cornish lamb and West Country cheeses. A choice of à la carte supplementary dishes changes with the seasons. Meals are complemented by a list of about 100 carefully selected wines. Leisure pursuits at the hotel include: swimming, putting, croquet, table tennis, sauna, painting courses and other special interest holidays. Talland Bay is a magically peaceful spot from which to explore this part of Cornwall – there are breathtaking cliff coastal walks at the hotel's doorstep, and many National Trust houses and gardens to visit locally – but most people come here just to relax and enjoy the view. This hotel provides old fashioned comfort in beautiful surroundings at exceptionally moderate prices. Resident owners: Barry and Annie Rosier. Closed January. **Directions:** The hotel is signposted from the A387 Looe–Polperro road. Price guide: Single £44–£79; double/twin £78–£158.

For hotel location, see maps on pages 490-496

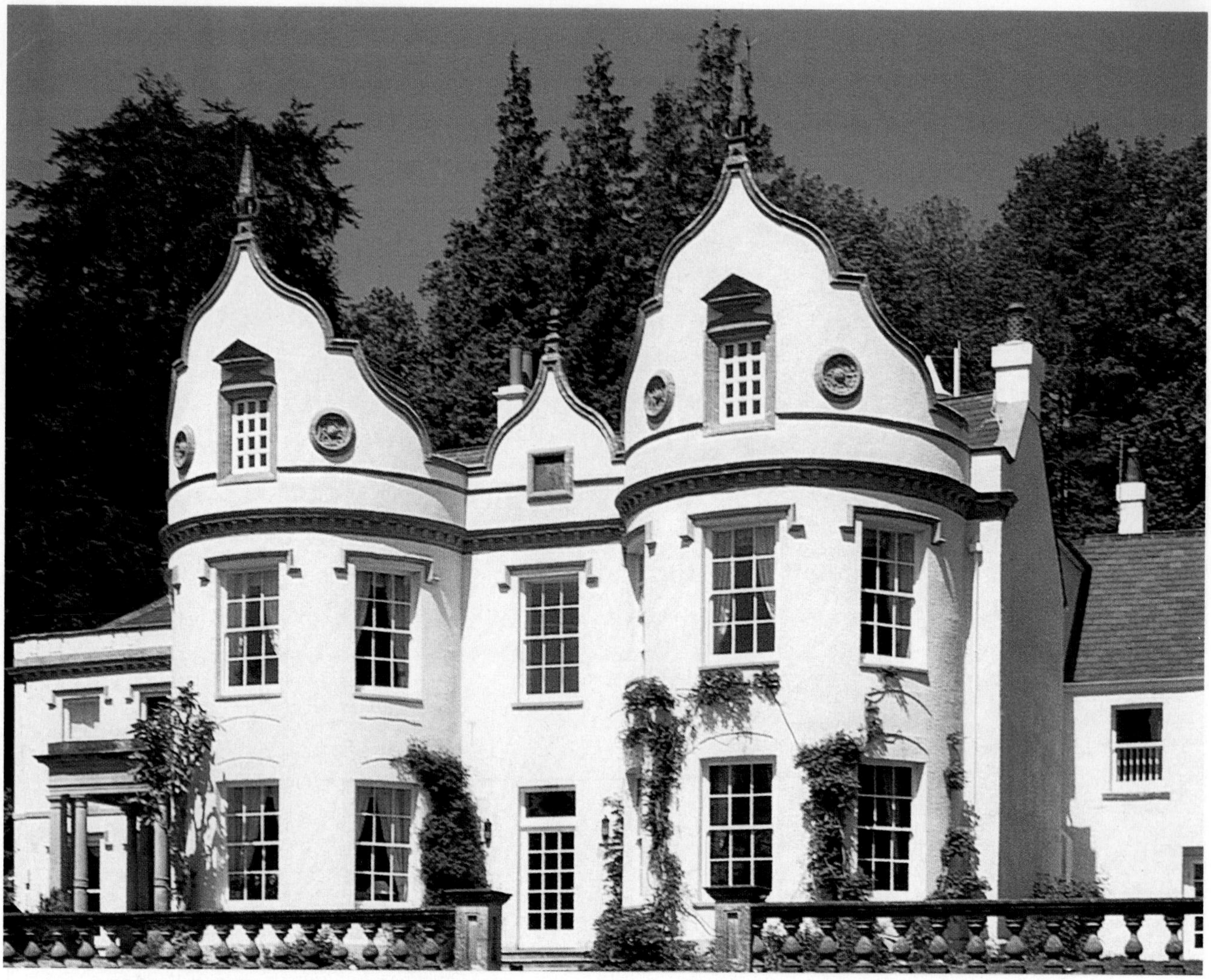

# Bindon Country House Hotel

**LANGFORD BUDVILLE, WELLINGTON, SOMERSET TA21 0RU**
**TEL: 01823 400070 FAX: 01823 400071**

This splendid baroque country house has a motto over the west wing door which although put there in the 1860s is appropriate today. 'Je trouve bien' is the perfect sentiment for this new hotel, albeit in an old setting. Mark & Lynn Jaffa have meticulously restored Bindon. It is tranquil and private, surrounded by seven acres of gardens and woodland. New arrivals immediatly have a feeling of well-being, as they respond to greetings from their hosts, and drop into sofas in the charming lounge. There are just twelve beautifully proportioned, luxurious bedrooms, all extremely comfortable with many 'extras' including robes in the well-designed bathrooms. The handsome panelled Jacobean bar is convivial and it is advisable to reserve a table in the Wellesley Restaurant, as its reputation is far flung. The graceful setting and excellent wines accompanying the exquisitely presented gourmet dishes make dining a memorable occasion. Country pursuits – fishing, riding, shooting and golf are nearby, and Bindon has its own pool, tennis court and croquet lawn. Wells Cathedral, stately homes and gardens are there to visit. **Directions:** M5/J26, drive to Wellington take A3187 to Langford Budville, through village, right towards Wiveliscombe, then right at junction. Pass Bindon Farm, and after 450 yards turn right. Price guide: Single from £75; double/twin £95–£145; suite from £100

12 rms MasterCard VISA AMERICAN EXPRESS M 50

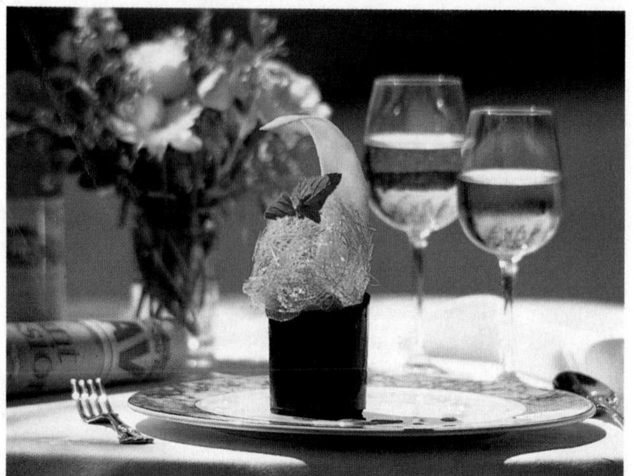

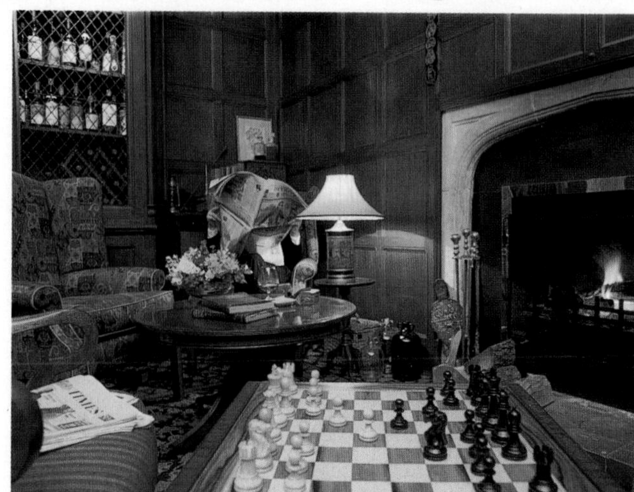

For hotel location, see maps on pages 490-496

# THE CASTLE AT TAUNTON

**CASTLE GREEN, TAUNTON, SOMERSET TA1 1NF**

**TEL: 01823 272671 FAX: 01823 336066 E-MAIL: reception@the-castle-hotel.com**

Winner of Johansens 1997 Town & City Award for Excellence, The Castle at Taunton is steeped in the romance of history. Once a Norman fortress, it has been welcoming travellers to the town since the 12th century. In 1685, the Duke of Monmouth's officers were heard "roystering at the Castle Inn" before their defeat by the forces of King James II at Sedgemoor. Shortly after, Judge Jeffreys held his Bloody Assize in the Great Hall of the Castle. Today the Castle lives at peace with its turbulent past but preserves the atmosphere of its ancient tradition. The Chapman family have been running the hotel for 47 years and in that time it has acquired a worldwide reputation for the warmth of its hospitality. Laurels in Egon Ronay, AA and the RAC also testify to the excellence of the Castle's kitchen and cellar. Located in the heart of England's beautiful West Country, the Castle is the ideal base for exploring a region rich in history. This is the land of King Arthur, King Alfred, Lorna Doone's Exmoor and the monastic foundations of Glastonbury and Wells. Roman and Regency Bath, Longleat House and the majestic gardens of Stourhead. Within easy driving distance of Taunton. **Directions:** Exit M5 junction 25 and follow signs for town centre. Alternatively from the south go by A303 and A358. Price guide: Single from £80; double/twin from £120; suites £195.

36 rms MasterCard VISA AMERICAN EXPRESS M 90

For hotel location, see maps on pages 490-496

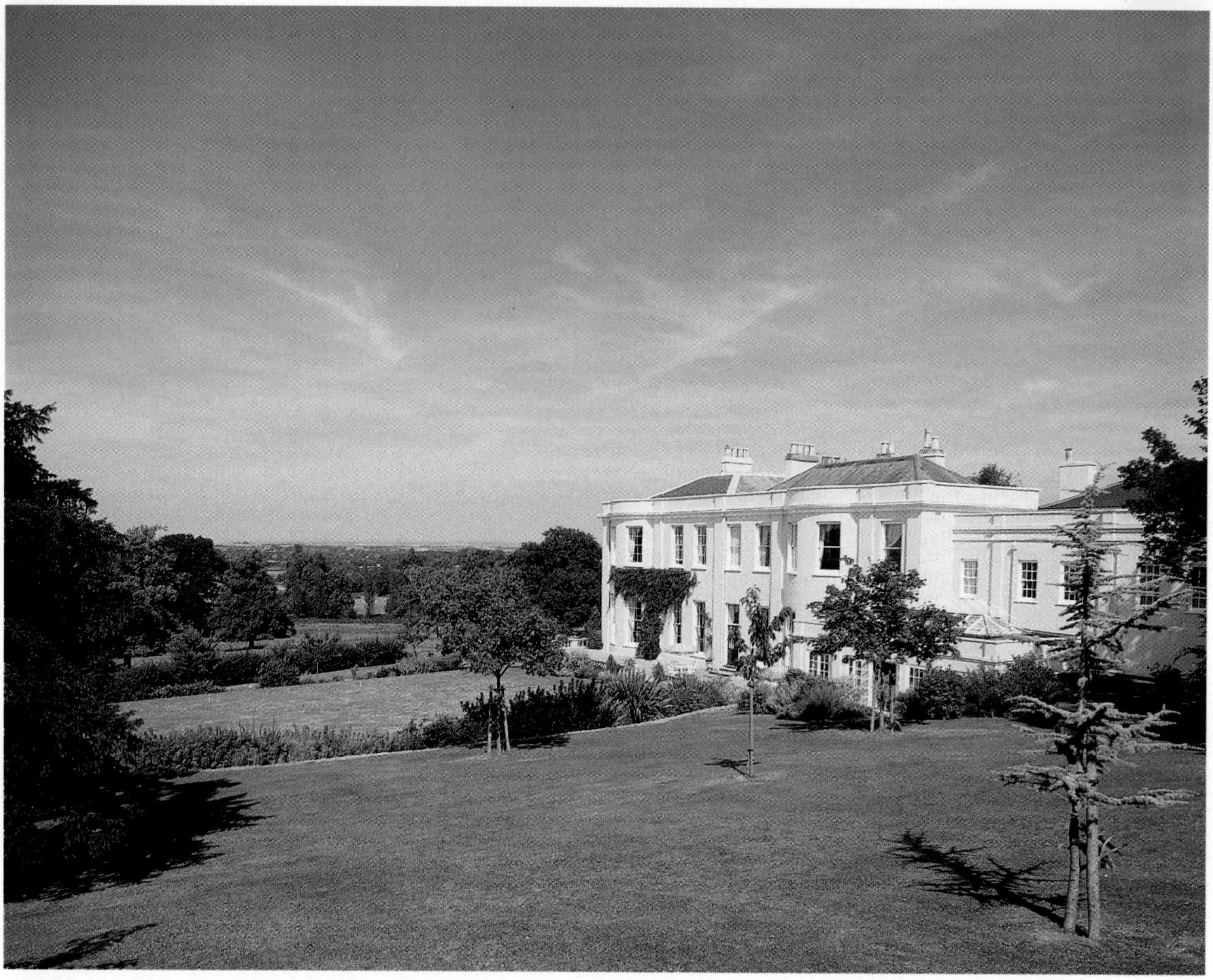

# Mount Somerset Country House Hotel

**HENLADE, TAUNTON, SOMERSET TA3 5NB**
**TEL: 01823 442500 FAX: 01823 442900**

This elegant Regency residence, awarded 2 Rosettes and 3 Red Stars, stands high on the slopes of the Blackdown Hills, overlooking miles of lovely countryside. The hotel is rich in intricate craftmanship and displays fine original features. Its owners have committed themselves to creating an atmosphere in which guests can relax, confident that all needs will be catered for. The bedrooms are sumptuously furnished and many offer excellent views over the Quantock Hills. Most of the luxurious en suite bathrooms have spa baths. Tea, coffee and home-made cakes can be enjoyed in the beautifully furnished drawing room, while in the evening the finest food and wines are served in the dining room. A team of chefs work together to create dishes to meet the expectations of the most discerning gourmet. The President's Health Club is close by and its pool and equipment can be used by hotel guests by arrangement. Somerset is a centre for traditional crafts and exhibitions of basket making, sculpture, wood turning and pottery abound. Places of interest nearby include Glastonbury Abbey and Wells Cathedral. **Directions:** At M5 exit at Junction 25 and join A358 towards Ilminster. Just past Henlade turn right at sign for Stoke St Mary. At T junction turn left, the hotel drive is 150 yards on the right. Price guide: Single from £75; double/twin £94–£120; suites £140–£160; 3 Course Luncheon from £15.95 and 4 Course Dinner from £24.50

23 rms

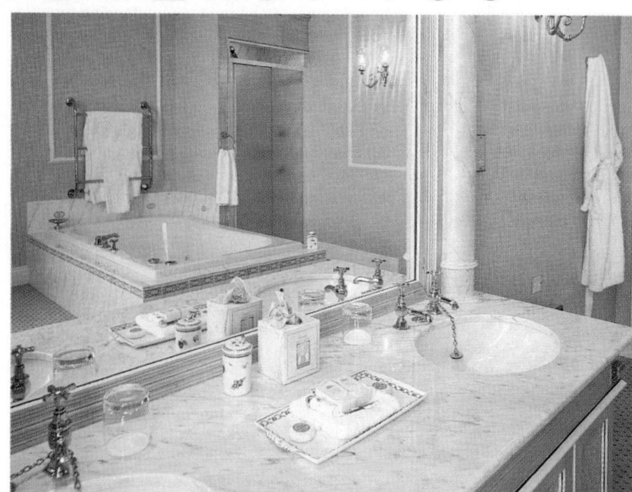



For hotel location, see maps on pages 490-496

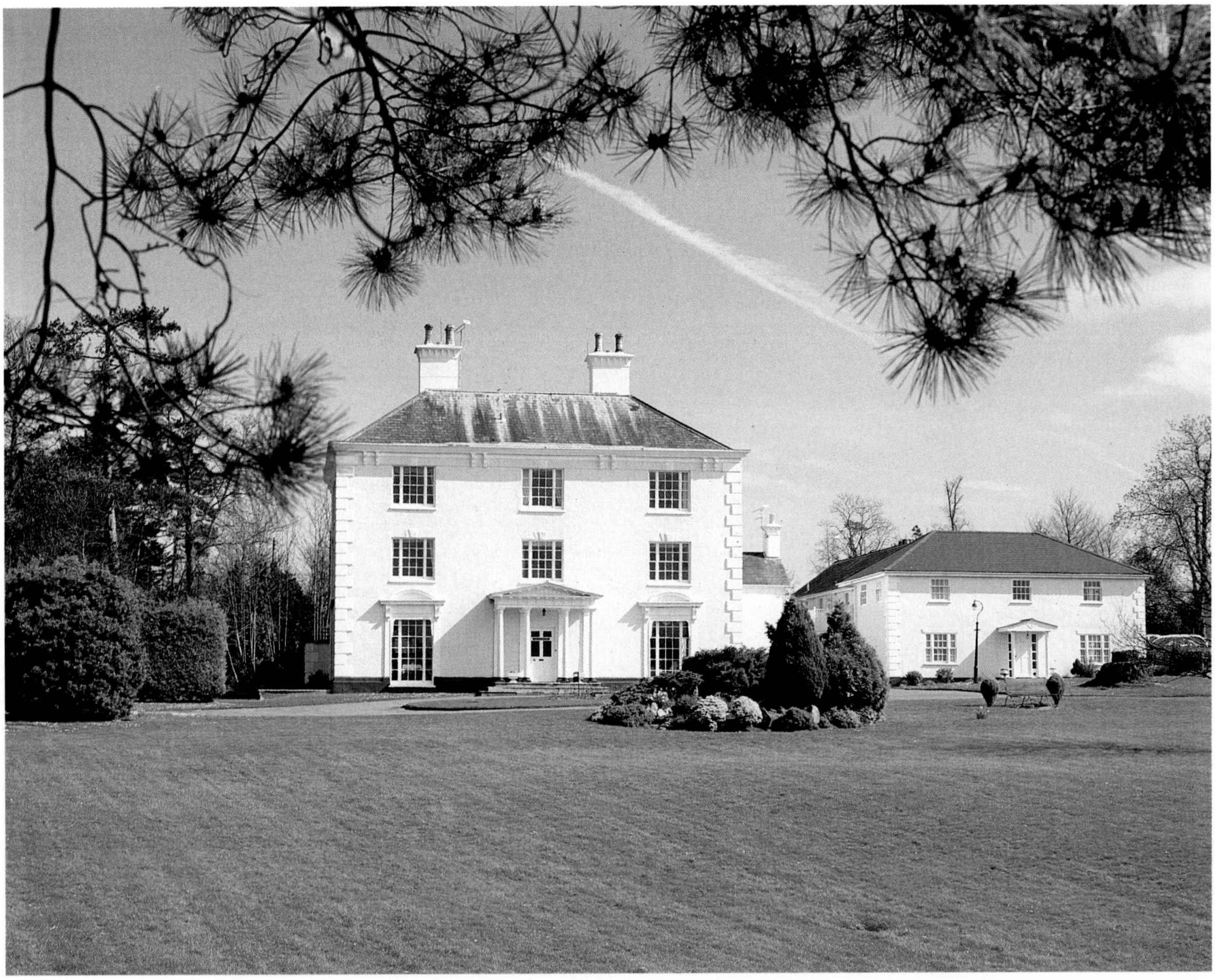

# RUMWELL MANOR HOTEL

**RUMWELL, TAUNTON, SOMERSET TA4 1EL**
**TEL: 01823 461902 FAX: 01823 254861**

Rumwell Manor Hotel, a magnificent Georgian Manor House, was built in 1805 by William Cadbury of Wellington. Standing in five acres of grounds, it looks south west across the peaceful Somerset countryside to the distant Blackdown Hills. The hotel's bedrooms are divided between the main house and the courtyard. All are individually decorated and furnished, although the main house bedrooms are superior in terms of their spaciousness and their spectacular views across the countryside. A full range of modern amenities is available in every bedroom. The beautifully proportioned public rooms provide an ideal environment in which to relax. The candlelit restaurant boasts an excellent range of imaginative dishes and there is a choice between table d'hôte and à la carte menus. An extensive wine list adds to the dining experience. The well stocked bar is the ideal place to sit. Guests of Rumwell Manor are given a warm and sincere welcome and an atmosphere of friendliness prevails throughout. Cheddar Gorge, the cathedrals of Exeter and Wells, the historic city of Bath, Exmoor, Glastonbury Abbey and Tor are just a few of the outings than can be enjoyed using Rumwell Manor as a base. **Directions:** Exit M5 junction 26. At next roundabout turn right onto A38 towards Taunton. The hotel drive is around three miles along on the right. Price guide: Single: £54–£65; double/twin £82–£110.

For hotel location, see maps on pages 490-496

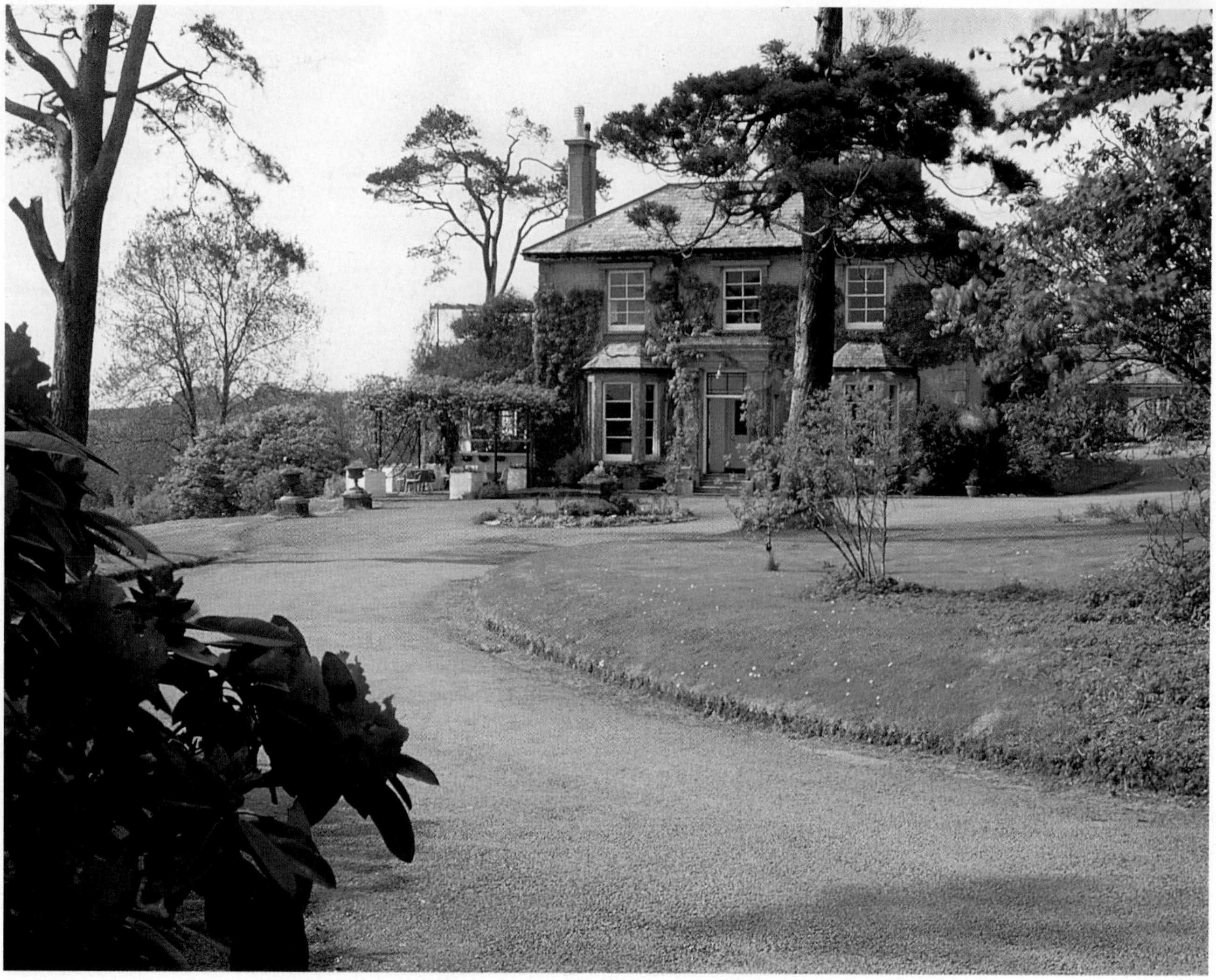

# THE HORN OF PLENTY

**GULWORTHY, TAVISTOCK, DEVON PL19 8JD**
**TEL: 01822 832528 FAX: 01822 832528**

Nestling in the foothills of Dartmoor and overlooking the Tamar Valley is The Horn of Plenty. Built by the Duke of Bedford, Marquess of Tavistock, nearly 200 years ago, this charming house exudes warmth and welcome. Its four acres of gardens are ablaze with camellias, azaleas and rhododendrons from early spring. Inside, the furnishings are designed for comfort rather than fashion. Throughout the hotel, the smell of fresh flowers competes with the tang of wood smoke from the log fires that burn in the colder winter months. The Coach House has been converted into six lovely en suite bedrooms, all of which are well equipped and have balconies overlooking the walled garden. The heart of The Horn of Plenty is the kitchen, where great thought is put into the taste, texture, contrast and harmony of the food prepared there, whilst the eating experience is enhanced by the surroundings of the restaurant with its beautiful view of the Tamar Valley. Places of interest nearby include Cotehele House and the old market town of Tavistock. The hotel is an ideal base for those interested in active pursuits such as golf, riding on Dartmoor, fishing, walking, sailing and canoeing. Breaks are available. **Directions:** At Tavistock take the A390 and after three miles turn right at Gulworthy Cross and follow the signs to the hotel. Price guide: Single £58–£78; double/twin £78–£98.

For hotel location, see maps on pages 490-496

# Madeley Court

**TELFORD, SHROPSHIRE TF7 5DW**

**TEL: 01952 680068 FAX: 01952 684275**

Madeley is a veritable gem of a residence. Its characteristic manor-house façade stands virtually unaltered since the 16th century when it was mainly built, while its interior has been recently expertly rejuvenated – with respect for its history – to provide accommodation suitable for all who stay there whether for pleasure or on business. Furnishings have been judiciously selected to enrich Madeley's period appeal: scatterings of fine fabrics, handsome antique pieces and elaborate fittings all accentuate the historic atmosphere, and ensure that every guest leaves with an indelible impression. Bedrooms, whether located in the old part of the Court or in the newer wing, are quiet and full of character; some offer whirlpool baths and views over the lake, all are en suite. At the heart of Madeley is the original 13th century hall, where the restaurant, awarded 2 coveted AA Rosettes is now located, serving inventive food of the highest standard, with a wine list to match. The Brasserie offers a more informal setting. Business meetings and private functions are happily catered for in the three rooms available. Places of interest nearby include: Ironbridge Gorge, Shrewsbury, Powys Castle and Weston Park. Directions: Four miles from junction 4 of M54; follow A442 then B4373. Signposted Dawley then Madeley. Price guide: Single £103.50; double/twin £122; historic £137.

For hotel location, see maps on pages 490-496

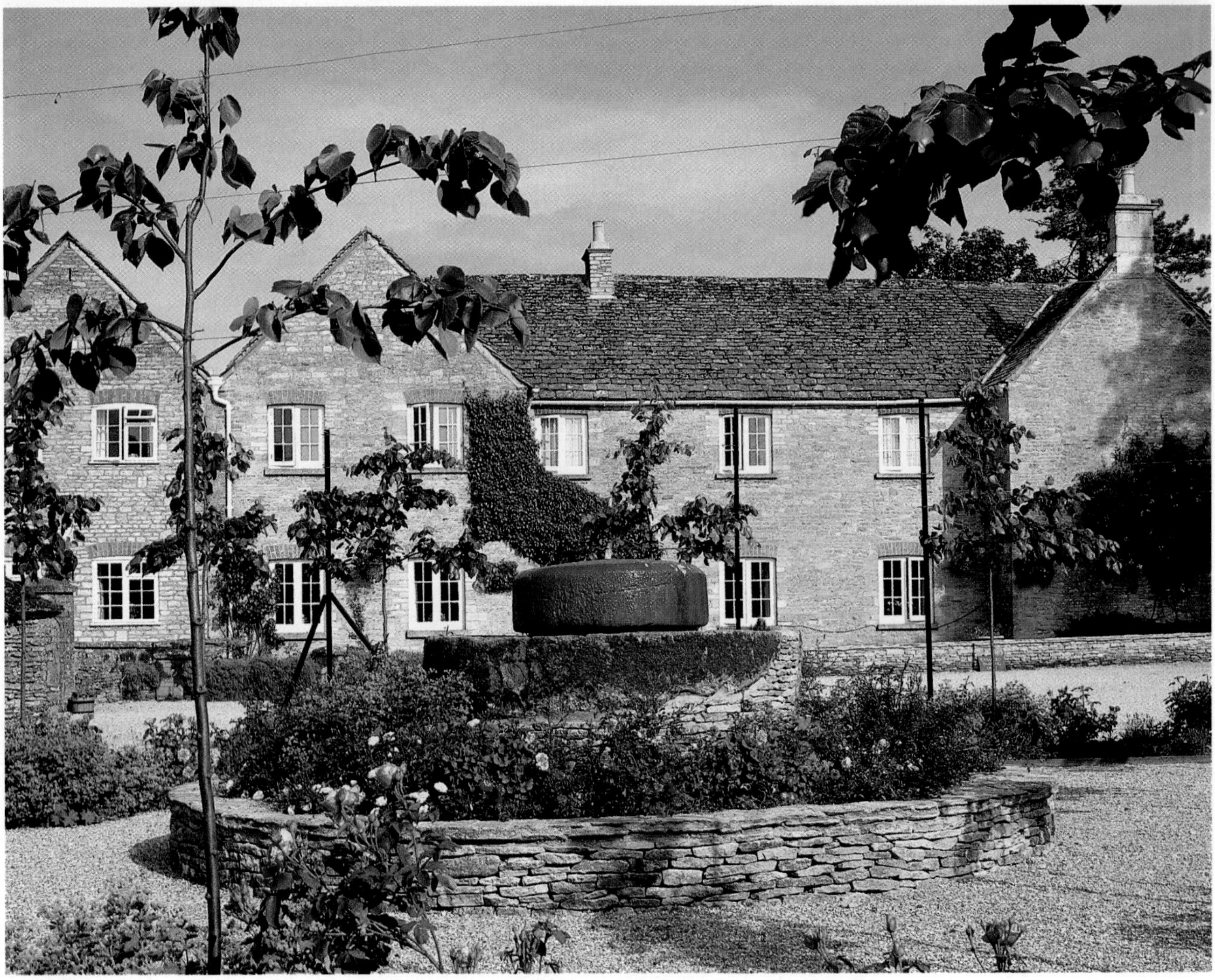

# Calcot Manor

**NR TETBURY, GLOUCESTERSHIRE GL8 8YJ**
**TEL: 01666 890391 FAX: 01666 890394**

This delightful old manor house, built of Cotswold stone, offers guests tranquillity amidst acres of rolling countryside. Calcot Manor is situated in the southern Cotswolds close to the historic town of Tetbury. The building dates back to the 15th century and was a farmhouse until 1983. Its beautiful stone barns and stables include one of the oldest tithe barns in England, built in 1300 by the Cistercian monks from Kingswood Abbey. These buildings form a quadrangle and the stone glistening in the dawn or glowing in the dusk is quite a spectacle. Calcot achieves the rare combination of professional service and cheerful hospitality without any hint of over formality. The atmosphere is one of peaceful relaxation. All the cottage style rooms are beautifully appointed as are the public rooms. Recent additions are a discreet conference facility and charming cottage providing nine family suites with the sitting areas convertible into children's bedrooms. At the heart of Calcot Manor is its elegant conservatory restaurant where dinner is very much the focus of a memorable stay. There is also the congenial Gumstool Bistro and bar offering a range of simpler traditional food and local ales. **Directions:** From Tetbury, take the A4135 signposted Dursley; Calcot is on the right after 3½ miles. Price guide: Double/twin £97–£145; family rooms £145; family suites £150.

For hotel location, see maps on pages 490-496

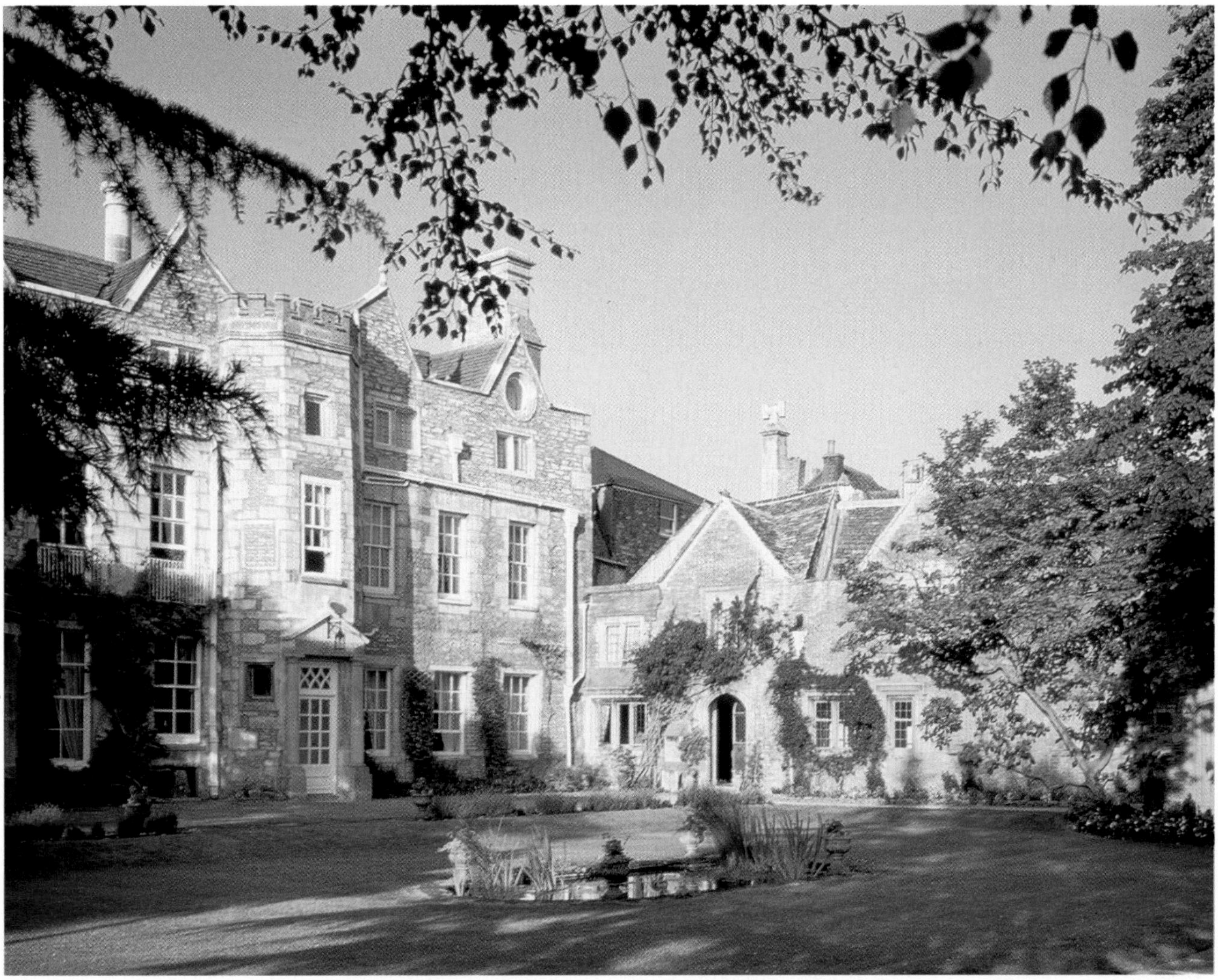

# The Close Hotel

LONG STREET, TETBURY, GLOUCESTERSHIRE GL8 8AQ

TEL: 01666 502272 FAX: 01666 504401 E-MAIL: hotel.reservations@virgin.co.uk

This distinctive town house, built over 400 years ago as a successful wool merchant's home, has been turned into a delightful hotel. It retains great character while boasting the facilities expected of a first class hotel. The Close is renowned for luxurious accomodation – individually styled bedrooms that are truly elegant, with hand painted bathrooms and antique furniture. The award winning cuisine, served in the stylish restaurant with its Adam style ceilings, is delicious, imaginative and well complemented by an outstanding wine list, including some excellent vintages. The restaurant overlooks a traditional Cotswold walled garden and in fine weather, you can take drinks or even dinner on the terrace. The Close offers a variety of rooms for conferences accomodating up to 24 guests. The hotel is extremely popular for wedding receptions and ceremonies and can be booked for exclusive use. Many famous sporting venues are close by, including Cheltenham Racecourse and Badminton House. Tetbury itself is a must for shoppers and antique lovers, while the Cotswolds are just on the doorstep. **Directions:** The Close is on Long Street, the main street of Tetbury which can be found on the A433 – minutes from the M4 and M5. Private parking is at the rear of the hotel in Close Gardens. Price guide: Single £75; double/twin £130.

For hotel location, see maps on pages 490-496

# THE SNOOTY FOX

MARKET PLACE, TETBURY, GLOUCESTERSHIRE GL8 8DD
TEL: 01666 502436 FAX: 01666 503479 E-MAIL: Res@snooty-fox.co.uk

This old coaching inn dating back to the 16th century is situated right in the heart of the quaint old market town of Tetbury. Built of mellow-hued stone, The Snooty Fox dominates the historic market place in the town centre. The hotel has been imaginatively refurbished by the owners, who have carefully maintained its considerable period character. There are 12 individual and charming en suite bedrooms which are decorated to convey the warm and homely atmosphere of a bygone age. All are well appointed and comfortable. The public areas and restaurant are steeped in history and are full of antiques and fine oil paintings. The prints that decorate the walls depict the hotel's long association with the famous Beaufort Hunt. The Snooty Fox is still a favourite meeting place for the local community of this famous royal town. Guests can choose either to dine in the elegant restaurant or to enjoy the splendid food from the bar menu. Facilities for executive meetings can be arranged and the hotel is the perfect destination for business and short breaks throughout the year. A member of Hatton Hotels. Internet: http://www.hatton-hotels.com **Directions:** The Snooty Fox is situated in the centre of Tetbury facing the market square. Price guide: Single from £65; double/twin from £90.

12 rms · MasterCard · VISA · AMERICAN EXPRESS · M 25

For hotel location, see maps on pages 490-496

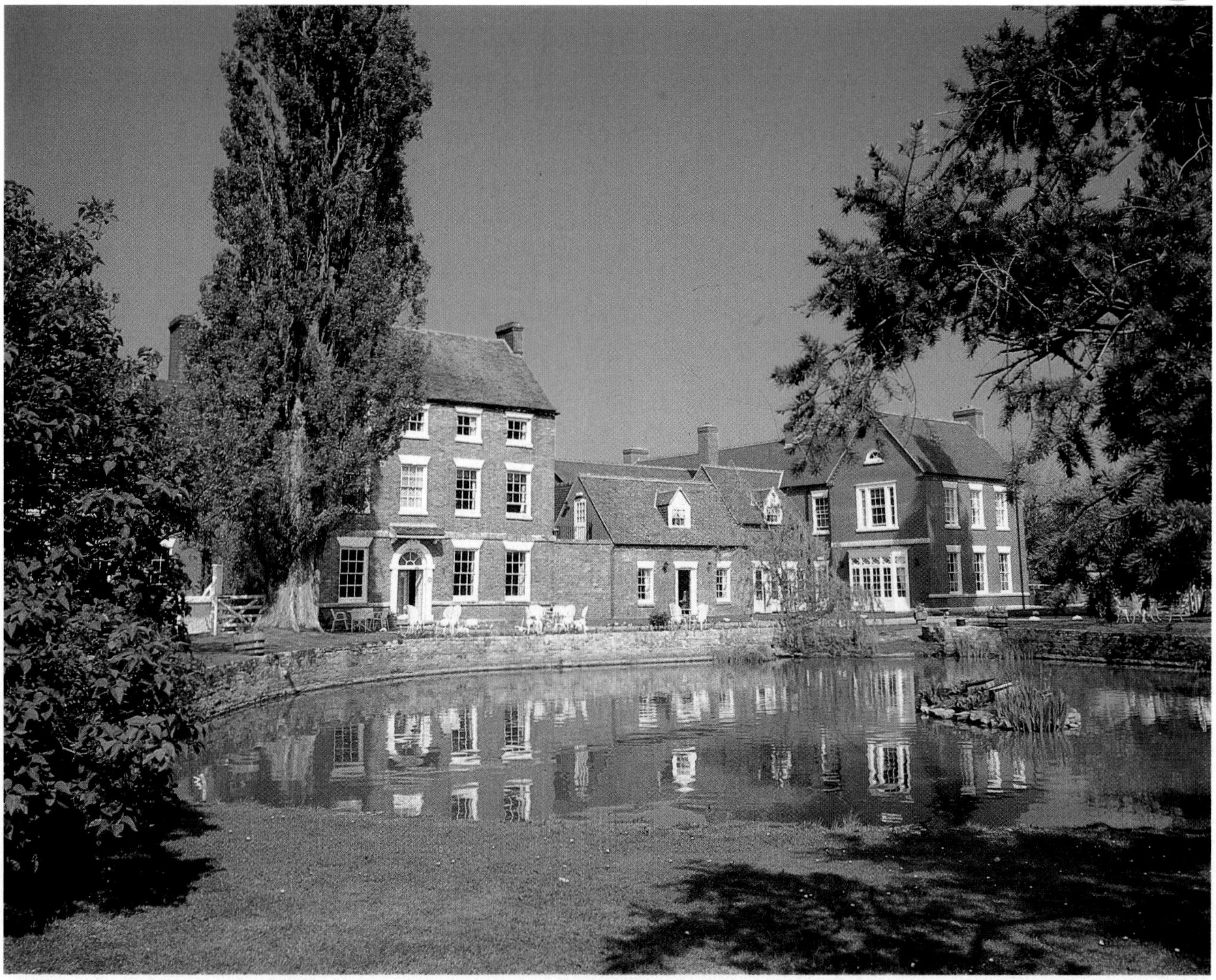

# CORSE LAWN HOUSE HOTEL

CORSE LAWN, NR TEWKESBURY, GLOUCESTERSHIRE GL19 4LZ
TEL: 01452 780479/771 FAX: 01452 780840

Though only 6 miles from the M5 and M50, Corse Lawn is a completely unspoiled, typically English hamlet in a peaceful Gloucestershire backwater. The hotel, an elegant Queen Anne listed building set back from the village green, stands in 12 acres of gardens and grounds, and still displays the charm of its historic pedigree. Visitors can be assured of the highest standards of service and cooking: Baba Hine is famous for the dishes she produces, while Denis Hine, of the Hine Cognac family, is in charge of the wine cellar. The service here, now in the hands of son Giles, is faultlessly efficient, friendly and personal. As well as the renowned restaurant, there are three comfortable drawing rooms, a large lounge bar, a private dining-cum-conference room for up to 45 persons, and a similar, smaller room for up to 20. A tennis court, heated swimming pool and croquet lawn adjoin the hotel, and most sports and leisure activities can be arranged. Corse Lawn is ideal for exploring the Cotswolds, Malverns and Forest of Dean. **Directions:** Corse Lawn House is situated on the B4211 between the A417 (Gloucester–Ledbury road) and the A438 (Tewkesbury–Ledbury road). Price guide: Single £70; double/twin £100; four-poster £120; suites £135. Good reductions for short breaks.

For hotel location, see maps on pages 490-496

# DALE HILL HOTEL AND GOLF CLUB

**TICEHURST, WADHURST, EAST SUSSEX TN5 7DQ**

**TEL: 01580 200112 FAX: 01580 201249**

Majestically situated in over 300 acres of beautiful grounds high on the Kentish Weald, Dale Hill is a superb ultra-modern hotel which combines the best in golfing facilities with the style and exclusiveness desired by discerning guests. Attractive decor, enhanced with soft coloured fabrics and carpeting, creates a summery impression all year. The 26 spacious en suite bedrooms are furnished to a high standard and offer every comfort and convenience. Golfers have the choice of two 18-hole courses, a gently undulating, 6,093 yards par 70 and a new, challenging championship-standard course designed by international star Ian Woosnam. Tuition is available from a PGA professional. Diners enjoy stunning views in a choice of restaurants where tempting dishes are complemented by an excellent wine list and service. A fully equipped health club has an attractive heated swimming pool and a range of health, beauty and fitness facilities. Dale Hill is only a short drive from elegant Tunbridge Wells with its world famous Pantiles shopping walk. Also nearby are medieval Scotney Castle, which dates back to 1380, Sissinghurst, a moated Tudor a castle with wonderful gardens, and 14th century Bodium Castle, a medieval fort. **Directions:** From the M25, junction 5, follow the A21 to Flimwell. Then turn right onto the B2087. Dale Hill Hotel is on the left. Price guide: Single from £58; double/twin £96–£136.

26 rms MasterCard VISA AMERICAN EXPRESS M 30

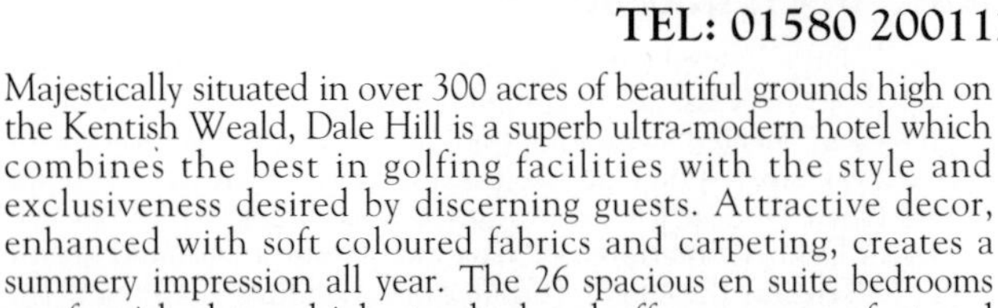

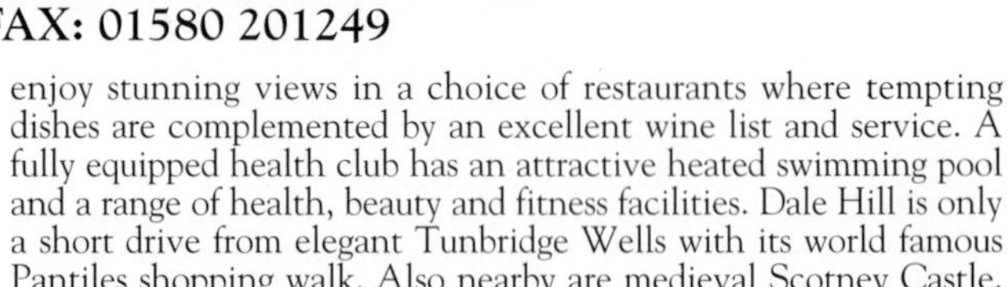

For hotel location, see maps on pages 490-496

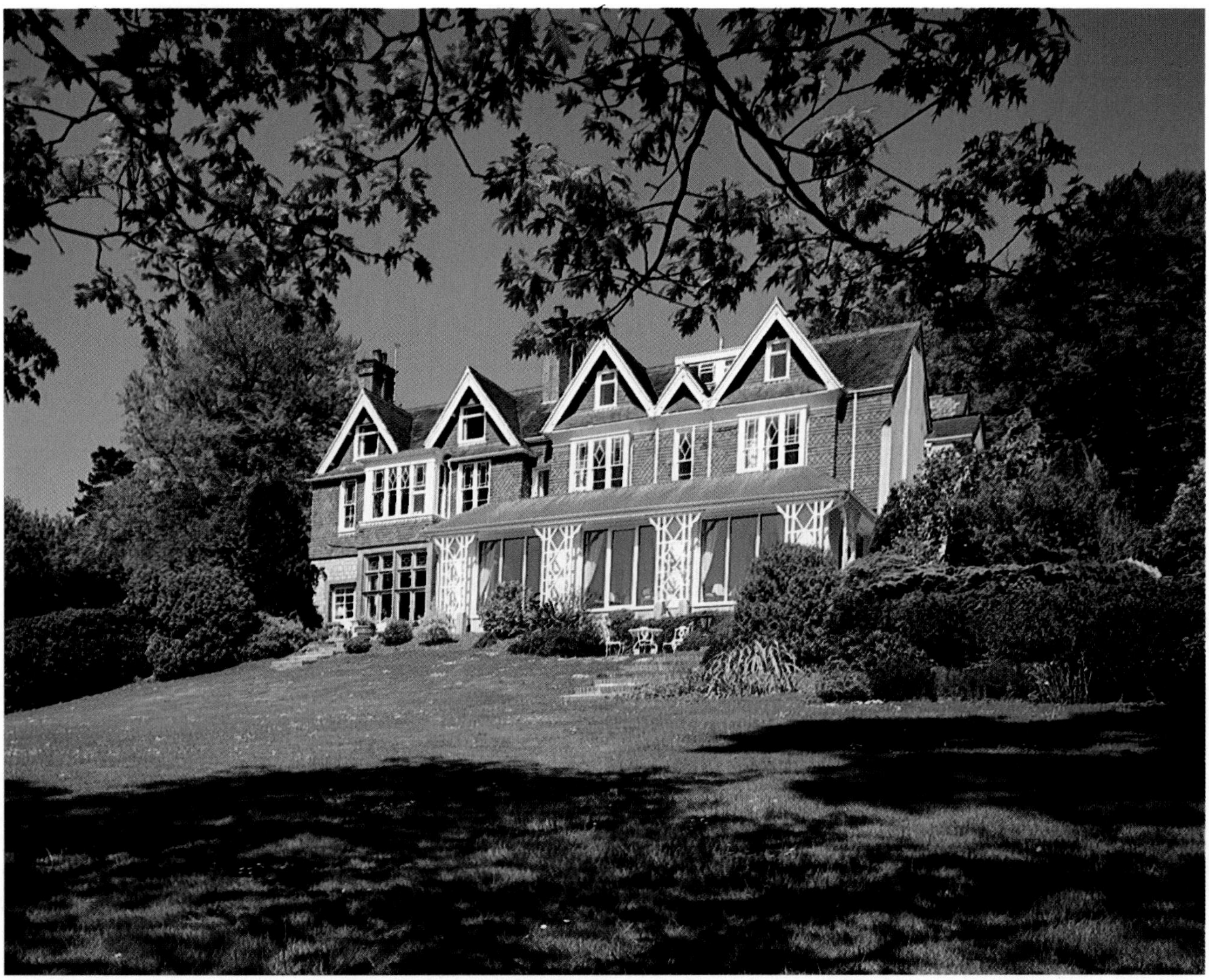

# Orestone Manor Hotel & Restaurant

ROCKHOUSE LANE, MAIDENCOMBE, TORQUAY, DEVON TQ1 4SX
TEL: 01803 328098 FAX: 01803 328336

Orestone Manor is an elegant Georgian building set in two acres of secluded gardens in an area of outstanding natural beauty overlooking Lyme Bay. Run by resident proprietors, the atmosphere is welcoming and relaxed. The Manor has been substantially extended since it was built in the early 19th century. The main lounge has a unique pitch-pine ceiling and some bedrooms feature gables. All the en suite bedrooms have a colour TV, direct-dial telephone and tea and coffee making facilities. All are individually furnished to a high standard, many with splendid sea views. Not only has Orestone Manor been ranked amoungst the top few in Torbay by the AA (1997), it is only one of two hotels there to be awarded two AA Rosettes (1997) for cuisine – for the fifth year in sucession. An imaginative menu changed daily always includes a vegetarian option. To enhance its growing reputation for fine food, the restaurant is non-smoking. There are five golf courses within seven miles, as well as sailing, horse-riding, tennis, squash and sailboarding. Dartmoor and many National Trust properties are nearby. Phone for details of special low-season breaks and Christmas and New Year packages. **Directions:** About three miles north of Torquay on A379 (formerly B3199) coast road towards Teignmouth. Price guide: Single from £70; double/twin from £110.

For hotel location, see maps on pages 490-496

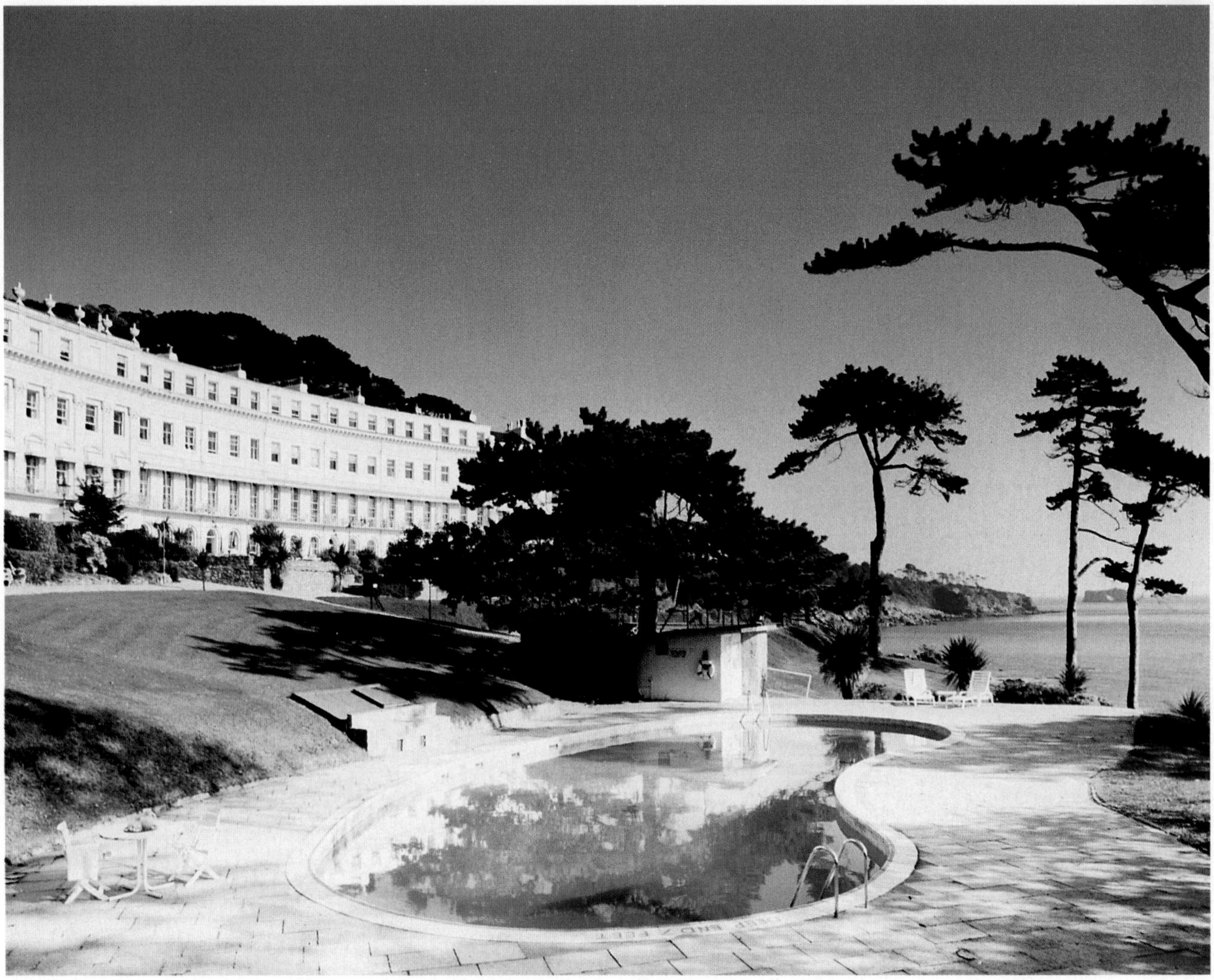

# The Osborne Hotel & Langtry's Restaurant

MEADFOOT BEACH, TORQUAY, DEVON TQ1 2LL
TEL: 01803 213311 FAX: 01803 296788

The combination of Mediterranean chic and the much-loved Devon landscape has a special appeal which is reflected at The Osborne. The hotel is the centrepiece of an elegant recently refurbished Regency crescent in Meadfoot, a quiet location within easy reach of the centre of Torquay. Known as a 'country house by the sea', the hotel offers the friendly ambience of a country home complemented by the superior standards of service and comfort expected of a hotel on the English Riviera. Most of the 25 bedrooms have magnificent views and are decorated in pastel shades. Overlooking the sea, Langtry's acclaimed award winning restaurant provides fine English cooking and tempting regional specialities, while the Brasserie has a menu available throughout the day. Guests may relax in the attractive 5-acre gardens and make use of indoor and outdoor swimming pools, gymnasium, sauna, solarium, tennis court and putting green – all without leaving the grounds. Sailing, archery, clay pigeon shooting and golf can be arranged. Devon is a county of infinite variety, with its fine coastline, bustling harbours, tranquil lanes, sleepy villages and the wilds of Dartmoor. The Osborne is ideally placed to enjoy all these attractions. **Directions:** The hotel is in Meadfoot, to the east of Torquay. Price guide: Single £55–£89; double/twin £78–£128; suite £98–£138.

For hotel location, see maps on pages 490-496

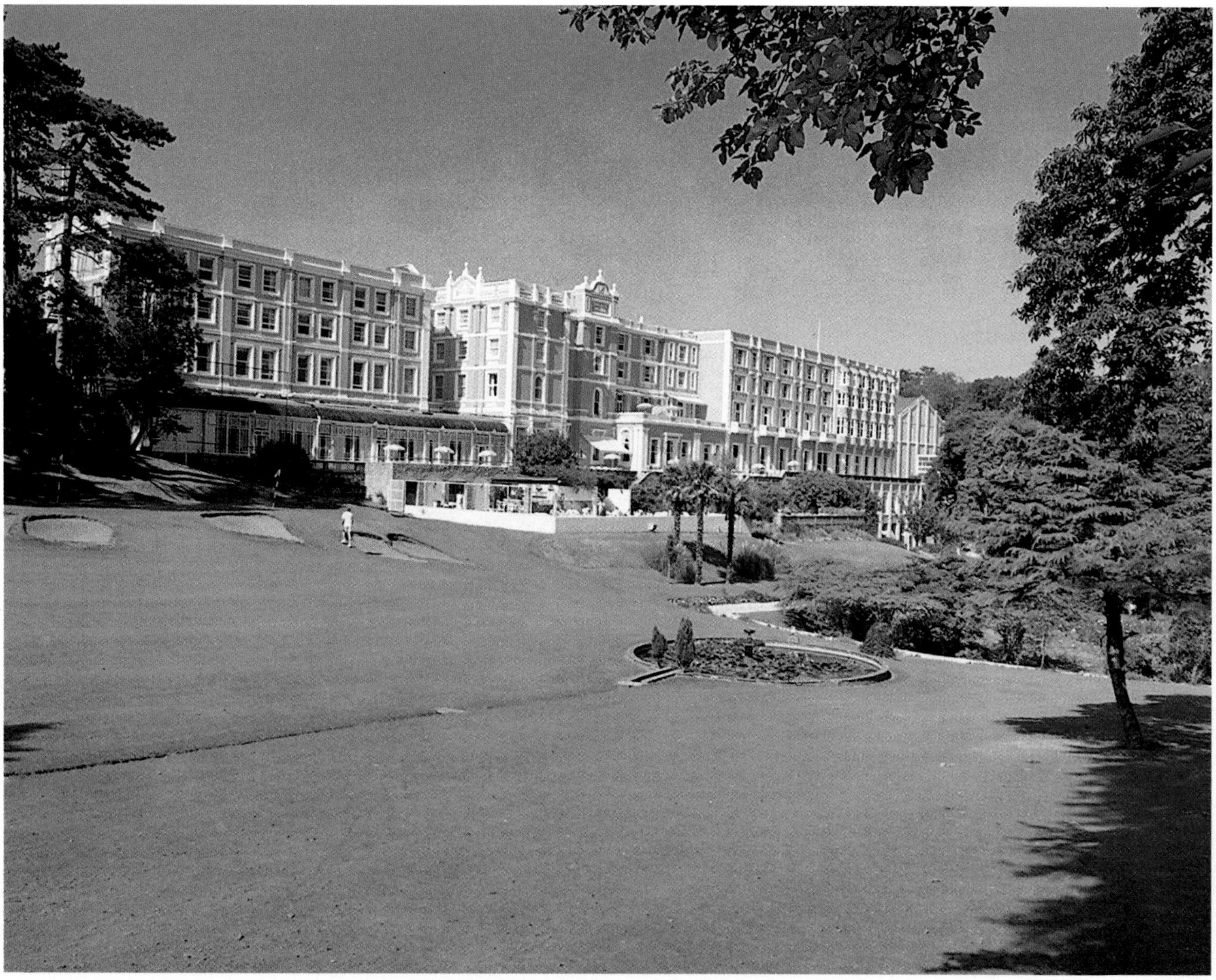

# THE PALACE HOTEL

**BABBACOMBE ROAD, TORQUAY, DEVON TQ1 3TG**
**TEL: 01803 200200 FAX: 01803 299899 E-MAIL: info@palacetorquay.co.uk**

Once the residence of the Bishop of Exeter, the privately owned Palace Hotel is a gracious Victorian building set in 25 acres of beautifully landscaped gardens and woodlands. The comfortable bedrooms are equipped with every modern amenity and there are also elegant, spacious suites available. Most rooms overlook the hotel's magnificent grounds. The main restaurant provides a high standard of traditional English cooking, making full use of fresh, local produce, as well as offering a good variety of international dishes. The cuisine is complemented by a wide selection of popular and fine wines. Light meals are also available from the lounge and, during the summer months, a barbecue and buffet are served on the terrace. A host of sporting facilities has made this hotel famous. These include a 9-hole championship golf course, indoor and outdoor swimming pools, two indoor and four outdoor tennis courts, two squash courts, saunas and snooker room. A children's nanny is available to give guests extra freedom to enjoy themselves. Places of interest nearby include Dartmoor, South Hams and Exeter. Paignton Zoo, Bygone's Museum and Kent's Cavern are among the local attractions. **Directions:** From seafront follow signs for Babbacombe. Hotel entrance is on the right. Price guide: Single £65–£75; double/twin £130–£150; suites £210–£250. Special breaks available.

For hotel location, see maps on pages 490-496

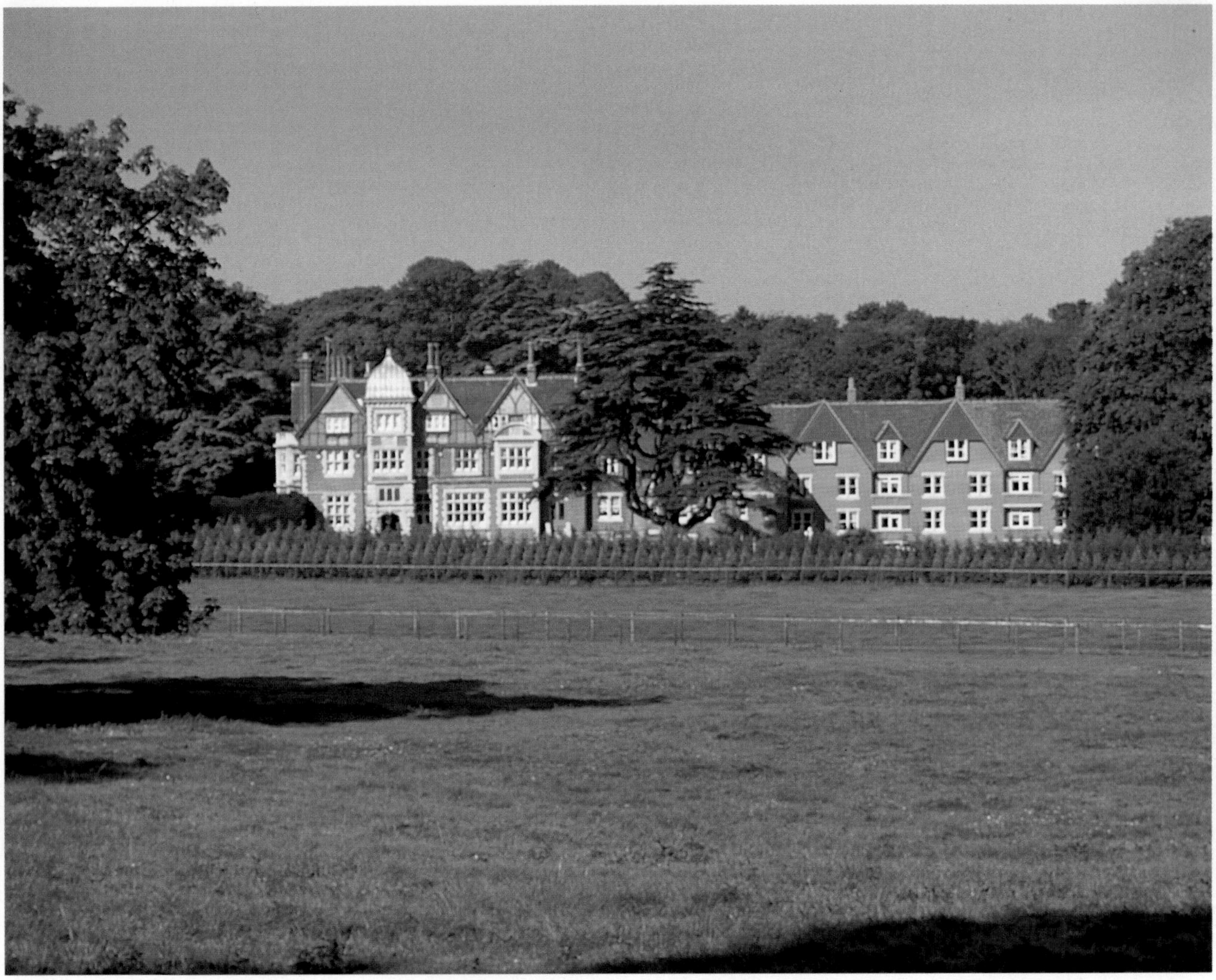

# PENDLEY MANOR HOTEL & CONFERENCE CENTRE

COW LANE, TRING, HERTFORDSHIRE HP23 5QY
TEL: 01442 891891 FAX: 01442 890687

The Pendley Manor was commissioned by Joseph Grout Williams in 1872. His instructions to architect John Lion were to build it in the Tudor style, reflecting the owner's interest in flora and fauna on the carved woodwork and stained glass panels. It stayed in the Williams family for three generations, but in 1987 the Manor was purchased by an independent hotel company, Craydawn Ltd. A refurbishment programme transformed it to its former glory and today's guests can once again enjoy the elegance and beauty of the Victorian era. The bedrooms are attractively furnished and well equipped, while the cuisine is appealing and well presented. Pendley Manor offers flexible conference facilities for up to 200 people. For indoor recreation a snooker room with a full size table has been added to the amenities. On its estate, which lies at the foot of the Chiltern Hills, sporting facilities include tennis courts, gymnasium, snooker room with full size table, games rooms, buggy riding, laser shooting, archery and hot air balloon rides. Places of interest nearby include Woburn, Winslow Hall, Chenies Manor, Tring Zoological Museum and Dunstable Downs. **Directions:** Take Tring exit from new A41 and from roundabout take road marked Berkhamsted and London. Then take first turn on left. Price guide: Single £90; double/twin £120–£130; suites £150.

74 rms MasterCard VISA AMERICAN EXPRESS M 220

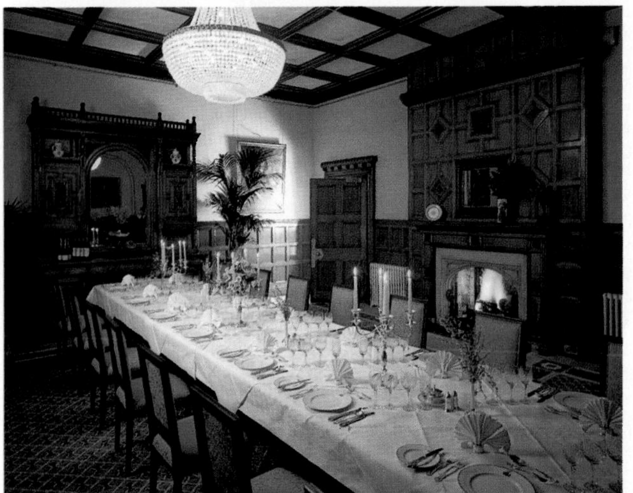

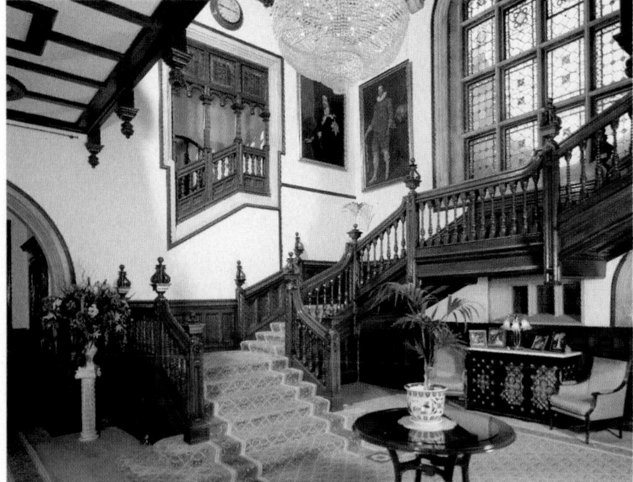

For hotel location, see maps on pages 490-496

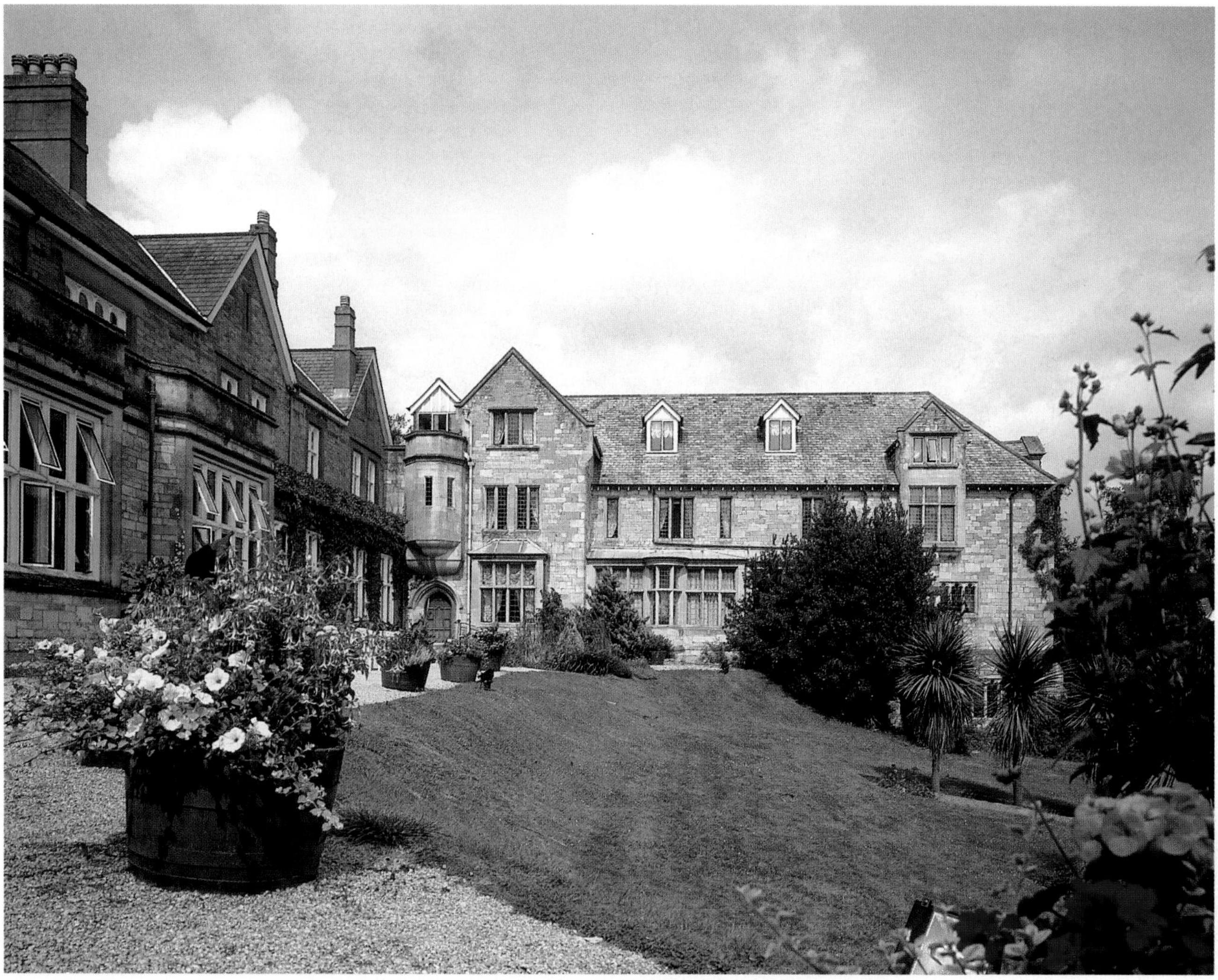

# Alverton Manor

**TREGOLLS ROAD, TRURO, CORNWALL TR1 1XQ**
**TEL: 01872 276633 FAX: 01872 222989**

Alverton Manor is situated on an eminence in the cathedral city of Truro. It was built over 150 years ago. In recent years it has been beautifully renovated as a modern hotel. It is an impressive sight on its hillside setting with fine period sandstone walls, attractive mullioned windows and original Cornish Delabole slate roof proudly defending its right to be a Grade II listed building of special historical interest. It is outstandingly comfortable in a discreet, elegant way. Each bedroom has been individually designed to provide a special and unique ambience from the intimate to the grand and all are furnished with the amenities visitors expect from a modern, luxury hotel. The spacious dining room is renowned for the excellent modern style English cuisine served and has been recognised by Egon Ronay and awarded two AA Rosettes. Numerous places of interest nearby include Falmouth, the Seal Sanctuary at Gweek, several heritage sites and many magnificent gardens and properties of the National Trust. There are opportunities for playing golf, shooting, riding, fishing, gliding, sailing and surfing. Dogs by arrangement. Special weekend breaks available. **Directions:** From St Austell, continue on A390 and the hotel is on the right as you approach the first major roundabout on entering Truro. Price guide: Single £65; double/twin £110–£120; suite £140.

For hotel location, see maps on pages 490-496

# HOTEL DU VIN & BISTRO

**CRESCENT ROAD, ROYAL TUNBRIDGE WELLS, KENT TN1 2LY**
**TEL: 01892 526455 FAX: 01892 512044**

**This hotel is scheduled to open in November 1997. The publishers therefore do not base their recommendation on an inspection visit in this case, although the reputation of the owners would suggest that this establishment will offer very high standards similar to those earned at their other property, Hotel du Vin in Winchester.** The formula remains the same, a unique combination of sophistication and informality, meticulous attention to the authenticity of the decorations and enthusiastic hosts who mingle with the guests. In Tunbridge Wells the Grade II sandstone mansion dates back to 1762 and, although in the centre of the town, it has spectacular views over Calverley Park. The ambience is inviting. The bedrooms will have antiques, fine linen, splendid colour schemes and amusing memorabilia. Gerard Basset, European Sommelier of the Year, is to be behind the Burgundy Bar and another innovation is the Havana Room, complete with a billiard table and a wide range of cigars. The appealing Bistro will have an imaginative menu, interesting wine list and reasonable prices. Guests can work up their appetites visiting the many castles, gardens and stately homes in the vicinity, shopping in the Pantiles or playing golf nearby. **Directions:** From M25 take A21 to Tunbridge Wells. The hotel has a drive and excellent parking facilities. Price guide: Single /double/twin £75.

31 rms MasterCard VISA AMERICAN EXPRESS M 100

For hotel location, see maps on pages 490-496

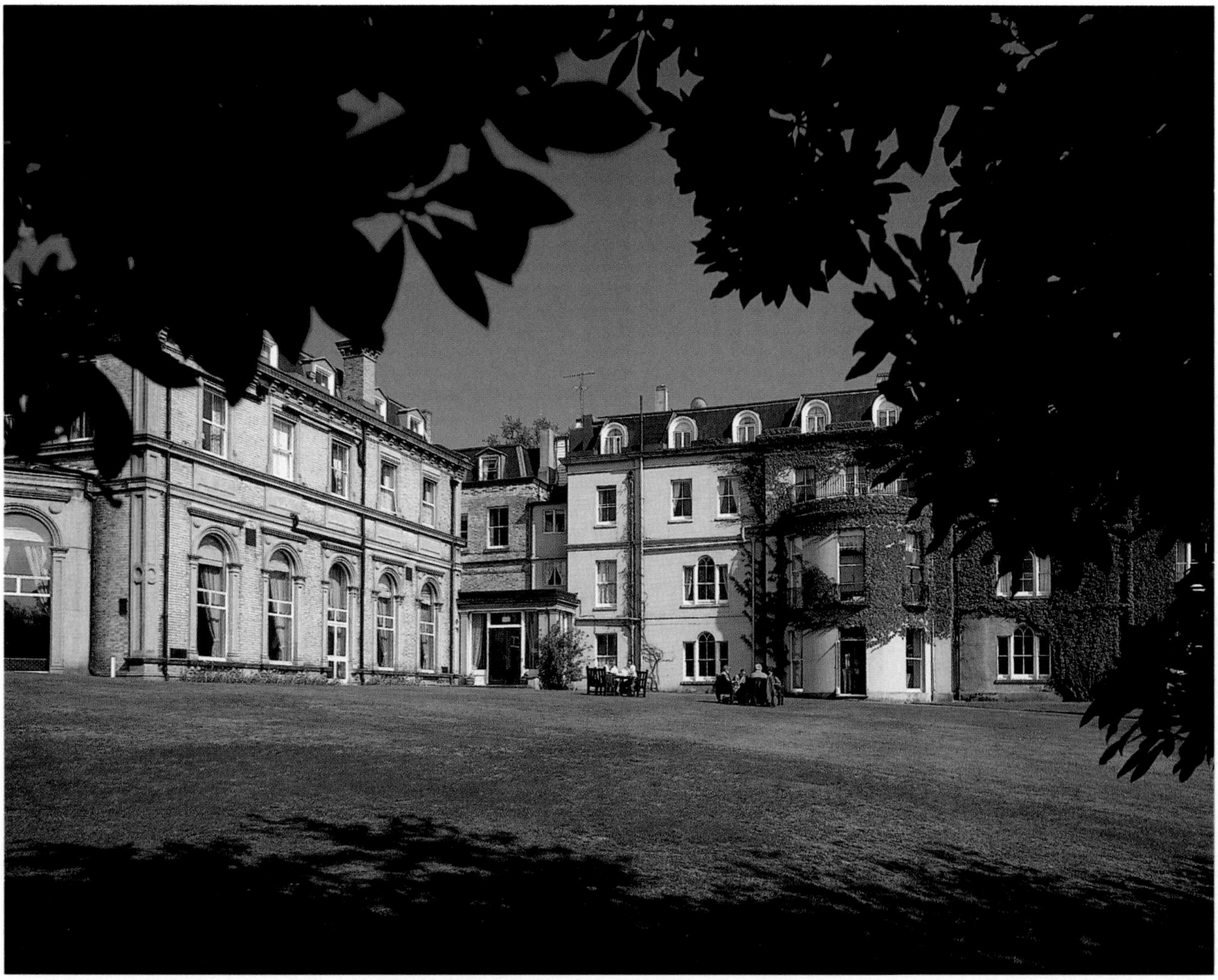

# THE SPA HOTEL

MOUNT EPHRAIM, ROYAL TUNBRIDGE WELLS, KENT TN4 8XJ
TEL: 01892 520331 FAX: 01892 510575

The Spa was originally built in 1766 as a country mansion, with its own parkland, landscaped gardens and two beautiful lakes. A hotel for over a century now, it retains standards of service reminiscent of life in Georgian and Regency England. All the bedrooms are individually furnished and many offer spectacular views. Above all else, The Spa Hotel prides itself on the excellence of its cuisine. The grand, Regency-style restaurant features the freshest produce from Kentish farms and London markets, complemented by a carefully selected wine list. Within the hotel is Sparkling Health, a magnificent health and leisure centre which is equipped to the highest standards. Leisure facilities include an indoor heated swimming pool, a fully equipped state-of-the-art gymnasium, cardiovascular gymnasium, aerobics dance studio, steam room, saunas, sunbeds, beauty clinic, hairdressing salon, flood-lit hard tennis court and $^{1}/_{2}$ mile jogging track. The hotel is perfectly positioned for exploring the castles, houses and gardens of Kent and Sussex. Special weekend breaks are offered, with rates from £70 per person per night – full details available on request. **Directions:** Facing the common on the A264 in Tunbridge Wells. Price guide (excluding breakfast): Single £79–£84; double/twin £94–£105; suites £115– £140.

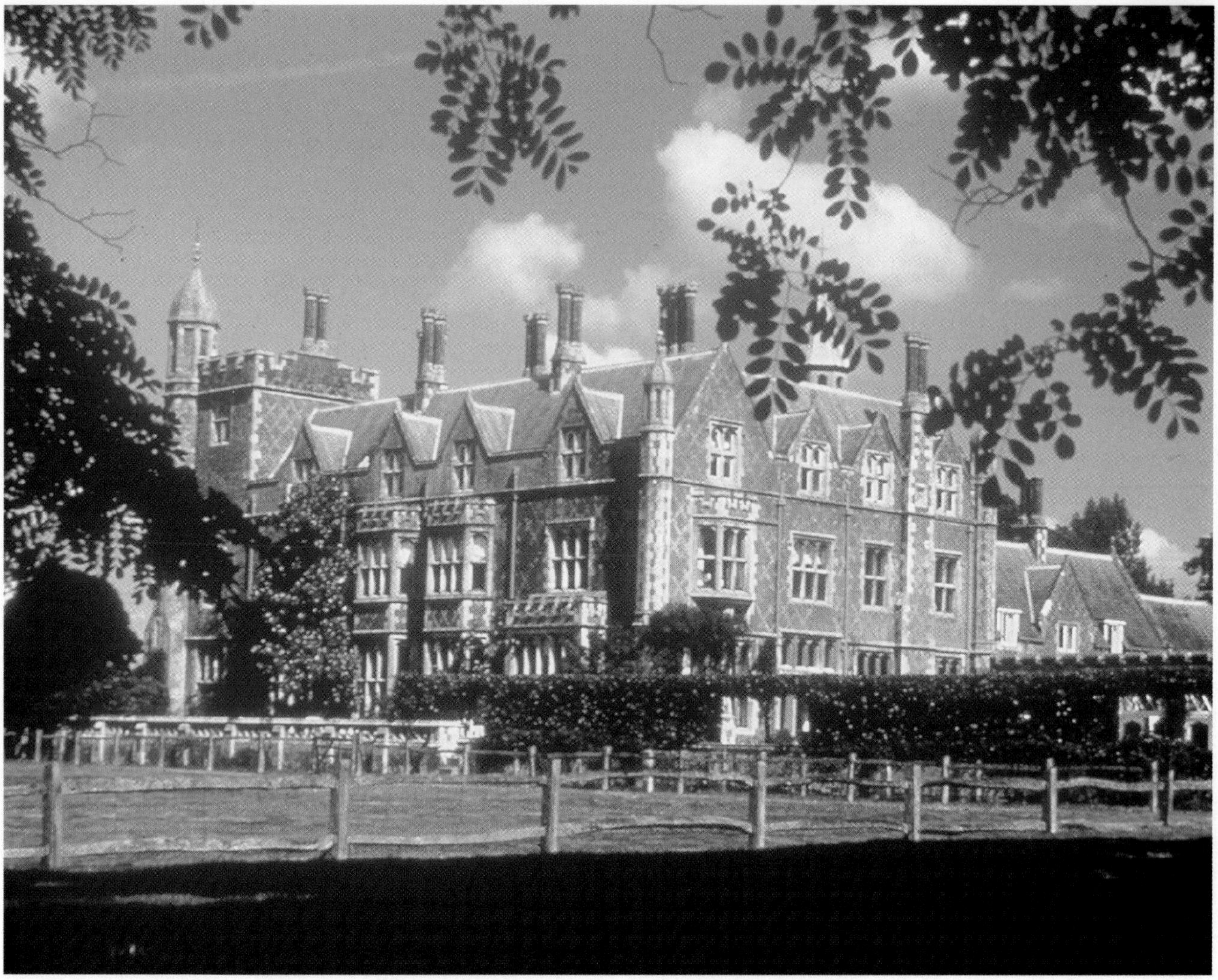

# HORSTED PLACE SPORTING ESTATE AND HOTEL

**LITTLE HORSTED, NR UCKFIELD, EAST SUSSEX TN22 5TS**
**TEL: 01825 750581 FAX: 01825 750240**

Horsted Place enjoys a splendid location amid the peace of the Sussex Downs. This magnificent Victorian Gothic Mansion, which was built in 1851, overlooks the East Sussex National golf course and boasts an interior predominantly styled by the celebrated Victorian architect, Augustus Pugin. In former years the Queen and Prince Philip were frequent visitors. Guests today are invited to enjoy the unobtrusive but excellent service offered by a committed staff. The bedrooms in this lovely hotel are luxuriously decorated and furnished and offer every modern day comfort. Dining at Horsted is guaranteed to be a memorable experience. Chef Allan Garth offers a number of fixed priced and seasonally changing menus with his eclectic style of cooking. The Horsted Management Centre is a suite of air-conditioned rooms which have been specially designed to accommodate theatre-style presentations and training seminars or top level board meetings. Places of interest nearby include Royal Tunbridge Wells, Lewes and Glyndebourne. For golfing enthusiasts there is the added attraction of the East Sussex National Golf Club, one of the finest golf complexes in the world. **Directions:** The hotel entrance is on the A26 just short of the junction with the A22, two miles south of Uckfield and signposted towards Lewes. Price guide: Double/twin £90; suites from £200.

For hotel location, see maps on pages 490-496

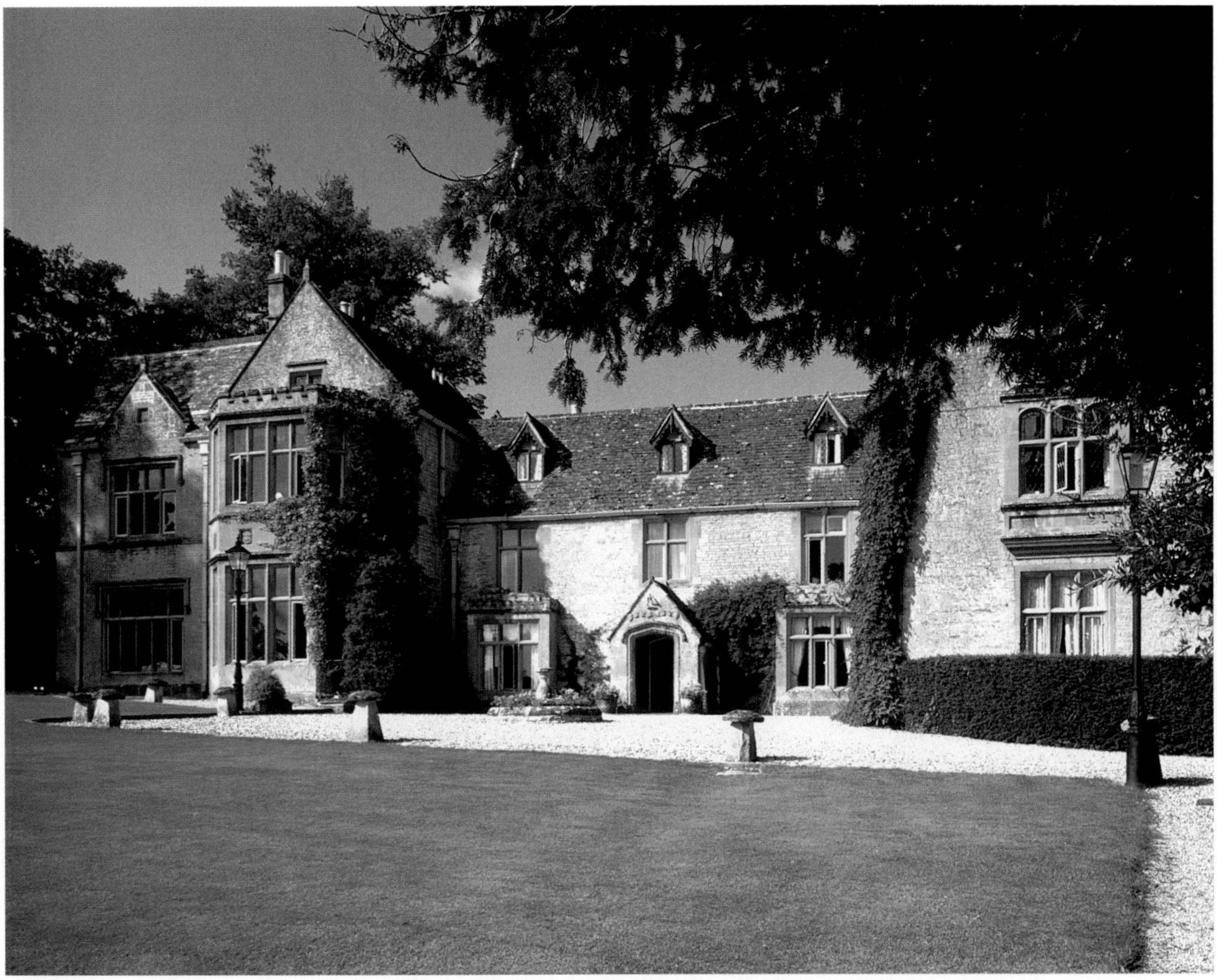

# LORDS OF THE MANOR HOTEL

UPPER SLAUGHTER, NR BOURTON-ON-THE-WATER, CHELTENHAM, GLOUCESTERSHIRE GL54 2JD

TEL: 01451 820243 FAX: 01451 820696

Situated in the heart of the Cotswolds, on the outskirts of one of England's most unspoiled and picturesque villages, stands the Lords of the Manor Hotel. Built in the 17th century of honeyed Cotswold stone, the house enjoys splendid views over the surrounding meadows, stream and parkland. For generations the house was the home of the Witts family, who historically had been rectors of the parish. It is from these origins that the hotel derives its distinctive name. Charming, walled gardens provide a secluded retreat at the rear of the house. Each bedroom bears the maiden name of one of the ladies who married into the Witts family: each room is individually and imaginatively decorated with traditional chintz and period furniture. The reception rooms are magnificently furnished with fine antiques, paintings, traditional fabrics and masses of fresh flowers. Log fires blaze in cold weather. The heart of this English country house is its dining room, where truly memorable dishes are created from the best local ingredients. Nearby are Blenheim Palace, Warwick Castle, the Roman antiquities at Bath and Shakespeare country. **Directions:** Upper Slaughter is 2 miles west of the A429 between Stow-on-the-Wold and Bourton-on-the-Water. Price guide: Single from £95; double/twin £125–£245.

For hotel location, see maps on pages 490-496

# THE LAKE ISLE

16 HIGH STREET EAST, UPPINGHAM, RUTLAND, LEICESTERSHIRE LE15 9PZ
TEL: 01572 822951 FAX: 01572 822951

This small personally run restaurant and town house hotel is situated in this pretty market town of Uppingham, dominated by the famous Uppingham School and close to Rutland Water. The entrance to the building, which dates back to the 18th century, is via a quiet courtyard where a wonderful display of flowering tubs and hanging baskets greets you. In winter sit in the bar where a log fire burns or relax in the upstairs lounge which overlooks the High Street. In the bedrooms, each named after a wine growing region in France, and all of which are en suite, guests will find fresh fruit, home-made biscuits and a decanter of sherry. Those in the courtyard are cottage-style suites. Under the personal direction of chef-patron David Whitfield the restaurant offers small weekly changing menus using fresh ingredients from far afield. There is an extensive wine list of more than 300 wines ranging from regional labels to old clarets. Special 'Wine Dinners' are held throughout the year, enabling guests to appreciate this unique cellar. Burghley House, Rockingham and Belvoir Castles are within a short drive. **Directions:** Uppingham is near the intersection of A47 and A6003. The hotel is on the High Street and is reached on foot via Reeves Yard and by car via Queen Street. Price guide: Single £47–£52; double/twin £65–£75; suite £75–£85.

12 rms

For hotel location, see maps on pages 490-496

# The Nare Hotel


**CARNE BEACH, VERYAN-IN-ROSELAND, TRURO TR2 5PF**

**TEL: 01872 501279 FAX: 01872 501856**


The Nare Hotel overlooks the fine sandy beach of Gerrans Bay, facing south, and is sheltered by The Nare and St Mawes headlands. In recent years extensive refurbishments have ensured comfort and elegance without detracting from the country house charm of this friendly hotel. All the bedrooms are within 100 yards of the sea, many with patios or balconies to take advantage of the outlook. While dining in the restaurant, with its colour scheme of soft yellow and green, guests can enjoy the sea views from three sides of the room. Local seafoods such as lobster, and delicious home-made puddings, served with Cornish cream, are specialities, complemented by an interesting range of wines. The Nare is one of the only AA 4 Star hotels in the South West with a rosette for its food. Surrounded by sub-tropical gardens and National Trust land, the peaceful seclusion of The Nare is ideal for lazing or for exploring the coastline and villages of the glorious Roseland Peninsula and is also central for many of Cornwall's beautiful houses and gardens including the famous Heligan. Guests arriving by train can be met by prior arrangement at Truro. Christmas and New Year house parties. **Directions:** Follow road to St Mawes; 3 miles after Tregony Bridge turn left for Veryan. The hotel is 1 mile from Veryan. Price guide: Single £56–£130; double/twin £112–£230; suite £186–£442.

For hotel location, see maps on pages 490-496

# THE SPRINGS HOTEL

NORTH STOKE, WALLINGFORD, OXFORDSHIRE OX10 6BE
TEL: 01491 836687 FAX: 01491 836877

The Springs is a grand old country house which dates from 1874 and is set deep in the heart of the beautiful Thames valley. One of the first houses in England to be built in the Mock Tudor style, it stands in six acres of grounds. The hotel's large south windows overlook a spring fed lake from which it takes its name. Many of the luxurious bedrooms and suites offer beautiful views over the lake and lawns, while others overlook the quiet woodland that surrounds the hotel. Private balconies provide patios for summer relaxation. The Lakeside restaurant has an intimate atmosphere inspired by its gentle décor and the lovely view of the lake. The restaurant's menu is changed regularly to take advantage of fresh local produce and seasonal tastes. A well stocked cellar of carefully selected international wines provides the perfect accompaniment to a splendid meal. Leisure facilities include the swimming pool, a putting green, sauna and touring bicycles. A new 18 hole golf course is due to open April '98. Oxford, Blenheim Palace and Windsor are nearby and the hotel is convenient for racing at Newbury and Ascot and the Royal Henley Regatta. Directions: From the M40, take exit 6 onto the B4009, through Watlington to Benson; turn left onto A4074 towards Reading. After $^1/_2$ mile go right onto B4009. The hotel is $^1/_2$ mile further, on the right. Price guide: Single from £82; double/twin £115–£150; suite from £150.

30 rms MasterCard VISA AMERICAN EXPRESS M 50

For hotel location, see maps on pages 490-496

# HANBURY MANOR

**WARE, HERTFORDSHIRE SG12 0SD**
**TEL: 01920 487722 FAX: 01920 487692**

An outstanding hotel, Hanbury Manor combines palatial grandeur with the most up-to-date amenities. Designed in 1890 in a Jacobean style, the many impressive features include elaborately moulded ceilings, carved wood panelling, leaded windows, chandeliers, portraits and huge tapestries. These create an elegant and comfortable environment. The three dining rooms vary in style from the formal Zodiac Restaurant to the informal Vardon Restaurant. All the cuisine is under the inspired guidance of Executive Chef Robert Gleeson. The health club includes a 17m indoor swimming pool, spa bath, resistance gymnasium, cardiovascular suite, dance studio, crèche, sauna and steam rooms. Professional treatments include herbal wraps, aromatherapy, mineral baths and massage, while specialists can advise on a personal fitness programme. There is an 18-hole golf course *par excellence* designed by Jack Nicklaus II, host to the 1997 Alamo English Open. Outdoor pursuits include shooting, archery, horse-riding and hot-air ballooning. Ideal for conferences, ten rooms offer versatile business meetings facilities, with fax, photocopying, secretarial services and full professional support available. Stansted Airport is 16 miles away. **Directions:** On the A10 25 miles north of London and 32 miles south of Cambridge. Price guide: Single/double/twin from £160; suites £260–£460.

96 rms · 100

For hotel location, see maps on pages 490-496

In association with MasterCard

# THE PRIORY HOTEL

**CHURCH GREEN, WAREHAM, DORSET BH20 4ND**
**TEL: 01929 551666 FAX: 01929 554519**

Dating from the early 16th century, the one-time Lady St Mary Priory has for hundreds of years offered sanctuary to travellers. In Hardy's Dorset, 'far from the madding crowd', it placidly stands on the bank of the River Frome in four acres of immaculate gardens. Steeped in history, The Priory has undergone a sympathetic conversion to a hotel which is charming yet unpretentious. Each bedroom is distictively styled, with family antiques lending character and many rooms have views of the Purbeck Hills. A 16th century clay barn has been transformed into the Boathouse, consisting of two spacious luxury suites at the river's edge. Tastefully furnished, the drawing room, residents' lounge and intimate bar together create a convivial atmosphere. The Greenwood Dining Room is open for breakfast and lunch, while splendid dinners are served in the vaulted stone cellars. There are moorings for guests arriving by boat. Dating back to the 9th century, the market town of Wareham has more than 200 listed buildings. Corfe Castle, Lulworth Cove, Poole and Swanage are all close by with superb walks and beaches. **Directions:** Wareham is on the A351 to the west of Bournemouth and Poole. The hotel is beside the River Frome at the southern end of the town near the parish church. Price guide: Single £75–£115; double/twin £105–£185; suite £215.

19 rms

For hotel location, see maps on pages 490-496

# BISHOPSTROW HOUSE

**WARMINSTER, WILTSHIRE BA12 9HH**

**TEL: 01985 212312 FAX: 01985 216769 E-MAIL: Bishopstrow_House_Hotel@msn.com**

Bishopstrow House is the quintessential Georgian mansion. It combines the intimacy of a grand country hotel retreat with all the benefits of modern facilities and the luxury of the new Ragdale spa, offering a superb range of beauty, fitness and relaxation therapies in addition to Michaeljohn's world class hair styling. A Grade II listed building, Bishopstrow House was built in 1817 and has been sympathetically extended to include indoor and outdoor heated swimming pools, a high-tech gymnasium and a sauna. The attention to detail is uppermost in the Library, Drawing Room and Conservatory with their beautiful antiques and Victorian oil paintings. Grandly furnished furnished bedrooms are festooned with fresh orchids and some have opulent marble bathrooms and whirlpool baths. The Mulberry Restaurant serves skilfully prepared modern British food, with lighter meals available in the Mulberry Bar and the Conservatory which overlooks 27 acres of gardens. There is fly–fishing on the hotel's private stretch of the River Wylye, golf at five nearby courses, riding, game and clay-pigeon shooting. Longleat House, Wilton House, Stourhead, Stonehenge, Bath, Salisbury and Warminster are within easy reach. **Directions:** Bishopstrow House is south–east of Warminster on the B3414 from London via the M3. Price guide: Single from £85; double/twin from £145–£215.

For hotel location, see maps on pages 490-496

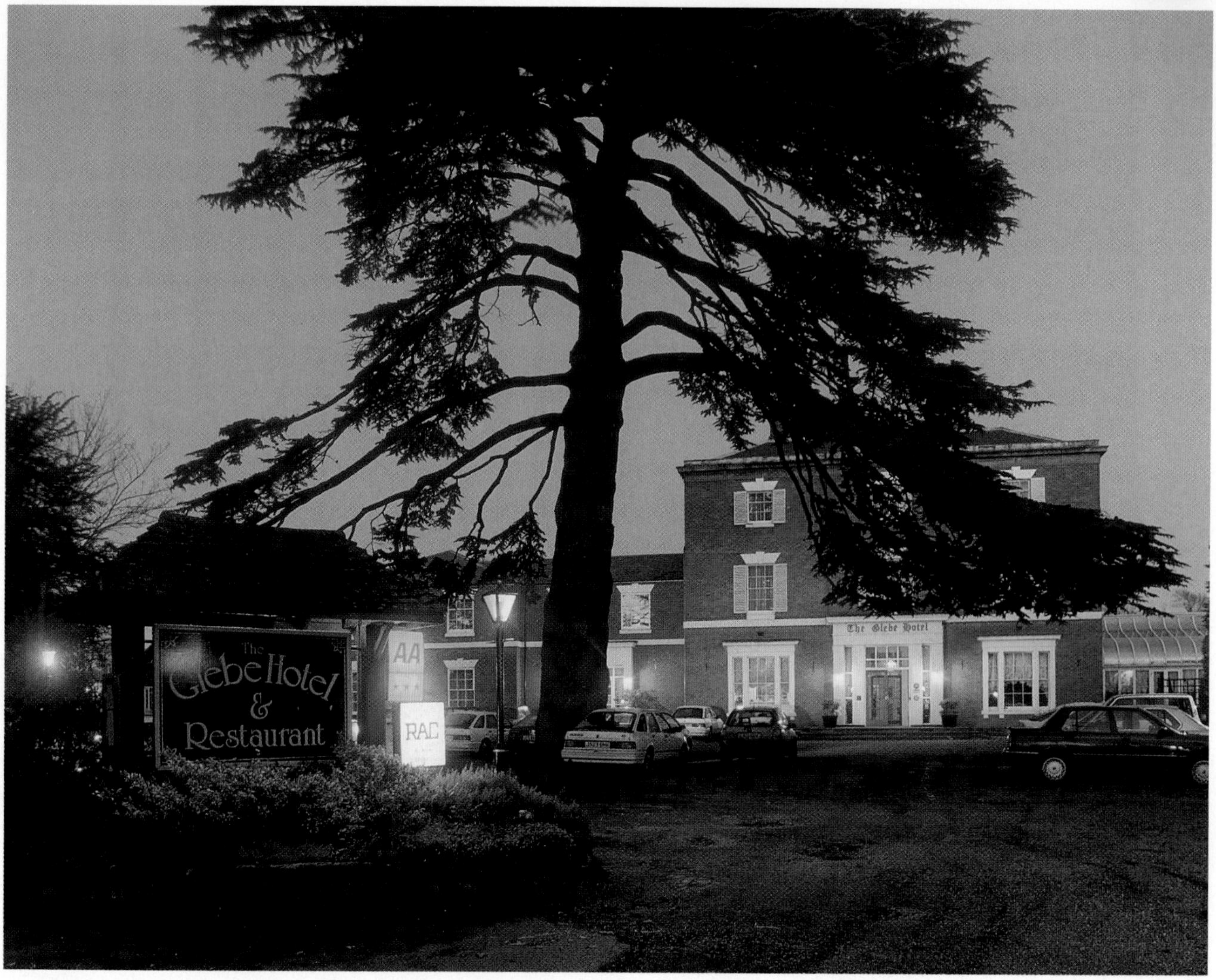

# THE GLEBE AT BARFORD

**CHURCH STREET, BARFORD, WARWICKSHIRE CV35 8BS**
**TEL: 01926 624218 FAX: 01926 624625**

"Glebe" means belonging to the Church, which explains why this beautiful Georgian country house is in a unique and quiet position next to the church in Barford, one of the most attractive villages in Warwickshire. It is a Grade II listed building, dating back to 1820, with an unusual central atrium, and surrounded by landscaped gardens. The bedrooms are spacious, comfortable and peaceful. They have all the accessories expected by today's travellers, and opulent bathrooms in marble with golden fittings. There is a pleasant lounge where guests can relax at teatime, and the bar is inviting. The restaurant is in an elegant, conservatory, green plants adding cool colour. There are excellent table d'hôte and à la carte menus. The wine list is extensive. The Glebe is a ideal venue for private celebrations and corporate events as it has several well-equipped conference rooms – the Bentley Suite seats 120 people for a banquet and the Directors Suite, with leather armchairs, is ideal for a discreet strategy meeting. Guests appreciate the Glebe Leisure Club with a pool, gymnasium and spa facilities. They can play croquet in the garden, or tennis and golf nearby. **Directions:** M40 exit Junction 15 A429 signed Barford & Wellesbourne. Turning left at mini-roundabout, the hotel is on the right just past the church. Price guide: Single £90; double/twin £110; suite £140

For hotel location, see maps on pages 490-496

# LINTON SPRINGS

**SICKLINGHALL ROAD, WETHERBY, WEST YORKSHIRE LS22 4AF**
**TEL: 01937 585353 FAX: 01937 587579**

Set in 14 acres of beautiful parkland, Linton Springs is an elegant country house hotel which successfully combines the grace of an English period mansion with modern day comforts. The house was built in the late 1700s as a shooting lodge for the nearby Harewood Estate. It has undergone extensive restoration work in recent times and boasts tasteful décor and furnishings throughout. The attractive and spacious bedrooms all feature oak panelling and are equipped with every modern amenity to ensure the highest level of comfort and convenience. Meals are served in the Gun Room Restaurant and excellent traditional English cuisine is complemented by a fine wine list. The menu features "special" dishes which are changed daily. The Linton Suite is an ideal setting for special occasions, while The Terrace Room and Boardroom provide privacy for business meetings and private dining. For sporting guests, there is a 250 yard golf driving range and all weather tennis court within the grounds. There are also eight golf courses within a 20 minute drive. Nearby attractions include Leeds, York with its famous minster and the spa town of Harrogate. **Directions:** From A1 go through Wetherby towards Harrogate on the A661. After quarter of a mile turn left to Sicklinghall and the hotel is one mile on the left. Price guide: Single: £65–£70; double/twin £85–£90; suites £105–£110.

For hotel location, see maps on pages 490-496

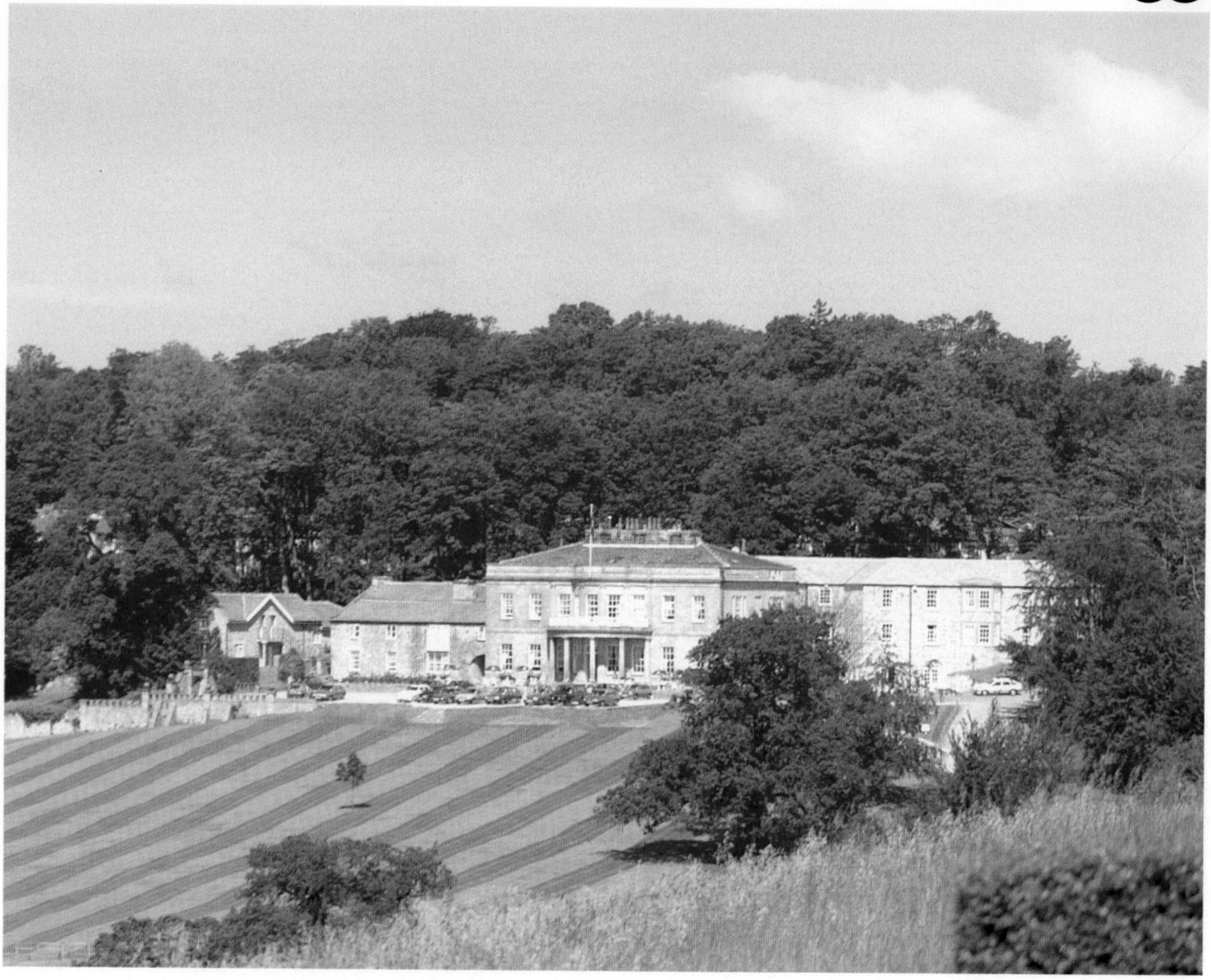

# WOOD HALL

TRIP LANE, LINTON, NR WETHERBY, WEST YORKSHIRE LS22 4JA
TEL: 01937 587271 FAX: 01937 584353

Off the A1 about 15 miles due west of York, built of stone from the estate, Wood Hall is an elegant Georgian house overlooking the River Wharfe. Its grounds, over 100 acres in all, are approached along a private drive that winds through a sweep of parkland. The sumptuously furnished drawing room and the oak-panelled bar, with its gentlemen's club atmosphere, lead off the grand entrance hall. Superb floral displays, gleaming chandeliers and immaculately designed interiors hint at the careful attention that has been lavished on Wood Hall. Gastronomes will relish the excellent à la carte menu, which combines contemporary Anglo-French style with attractive presentation. The mile-long private stretch of the Wharfe offers up trout and barbel to the keen angler, while miles of walks and jogging paths encompass the estate. There is a leisure club including a swimming pool, spa bath, steam room, gymnasium, solarium and treatment salon. Near to the National Hunt Race-course at Wetherby, York, Harrogate, Leeds, the Dales and Harewood House are only a short distance away. An Arcadian Hotel. **Directions:** From Wetherby, take the A661 towards Harrogate. Take turning for Sicklinghall and Linton, then left for Linton and Wood Hall. Turn right opposite the Windmill public house; hotel is 1½ miles further on. Price guide: Single £110–£150; double/twin £120–£160; suite £175.

For hotel location, see maps on pages 490-496

# OATLANDS PARK HOTEL

**146 OATLANDS DRIVE, WEYBRIDGE, SURREY KT13 9HB**
**TEL: 01932 847242 FAX: 01932 842252**

Records of the Oatlands estate show that Elizabeth I and the Stuart kings spent time in residence in the original buildings. The present mansion dates from the late-18th century and became a hotel in 1856: famous guests included Émile Zola, Anthony Trollope and Edward Lear. The hotel stands in acres of parkland overlooking Broadwater Lake, with easy access to Heathrow, Gatwick and central London. Although it caters for the modern traveller, the hotel's historic character is evident throughout. The accommodation ranges from superior rooms to large de luxe rooms and suites. The elegant, high-ceilinged Broadwater Restaurant is the setting for creative à la carte menus with dishes to suit all tastes. A traditional roast is served every Sunday lunchtime. The professional conference team, six air conditioned meeting rooms and up-to-date facilities include video conferencing. Theme evenings, such as Henry VIII banquets, are a speciality. Many sporting and leisure activities can be arranged, including golf, archery and shooting. There is a new fitness room. **Directions:** From M25 junction 11, follow signs to Weybridge. Follow A317 through High Street into Monument Hill to mini-roundabout. Turn left into Oatlands Drive; hotel is 50 yards on left. Price guide: Single £100–£110; double/twin £130–£145; suite £120–£150. Special Break rate: Single £47.50; double/twin £75–£85.

128 rms · MasterCard · VISA · AMERICAN EXPRESS · M 200

For hotel location, see maps on pages 490-496

# Moonfleet Manor

**FLEET, WEYMOUTH, DORSET BT3 4ED**
**TEL: 01305 786948 FAX: 01305 774395**

Overlooking Chesil Bank, a unique feature of the Dorset coast, Moonfleet Manor is both a luxury hotel and a family resort. The owners have applied the same flair for design evident in their other properties, Woolley Grange and the Old Bell at Malmesbury. The use of a variety of unusual antiques and objects from around the world lends a refreshing and individual style to this comfortable and attractive hotel. The bedrooms are beautifully decorated and furnished and a range of amenities ensures that guests enjoy standards of maximum comfort and convenience. An enthusiastic and attentive staff works hard to ensure that guests feel at home, whatever their age. Moonfleet's dining room, whose décor and style would do credit to a fashionable London restaurant, offers an excellent and varied menu based on fresh local produce but bringing culinary styles from around the world. Facilities at the hotel include an indoor swimming pool with squash and tennis courts for the more energetic. Key places of interest nearby include Abbotsbury, Dorchester, Corfe Castle and Lulworth Cove, while in Weymouth itself the Sea Life Park, The Deep Sea Adventure and The Titanic Story. Directions: Take the B3157 Weymouth to Bridport Road, then turn off towards the sea at the sign for Fleet. Price guide: Single £40-£70; double/twin £60-£150; suite from £130.

41 rms MasterCard VISA AMERICAN EXPRESS M 90

For hotel location, see maps on pages 490-496

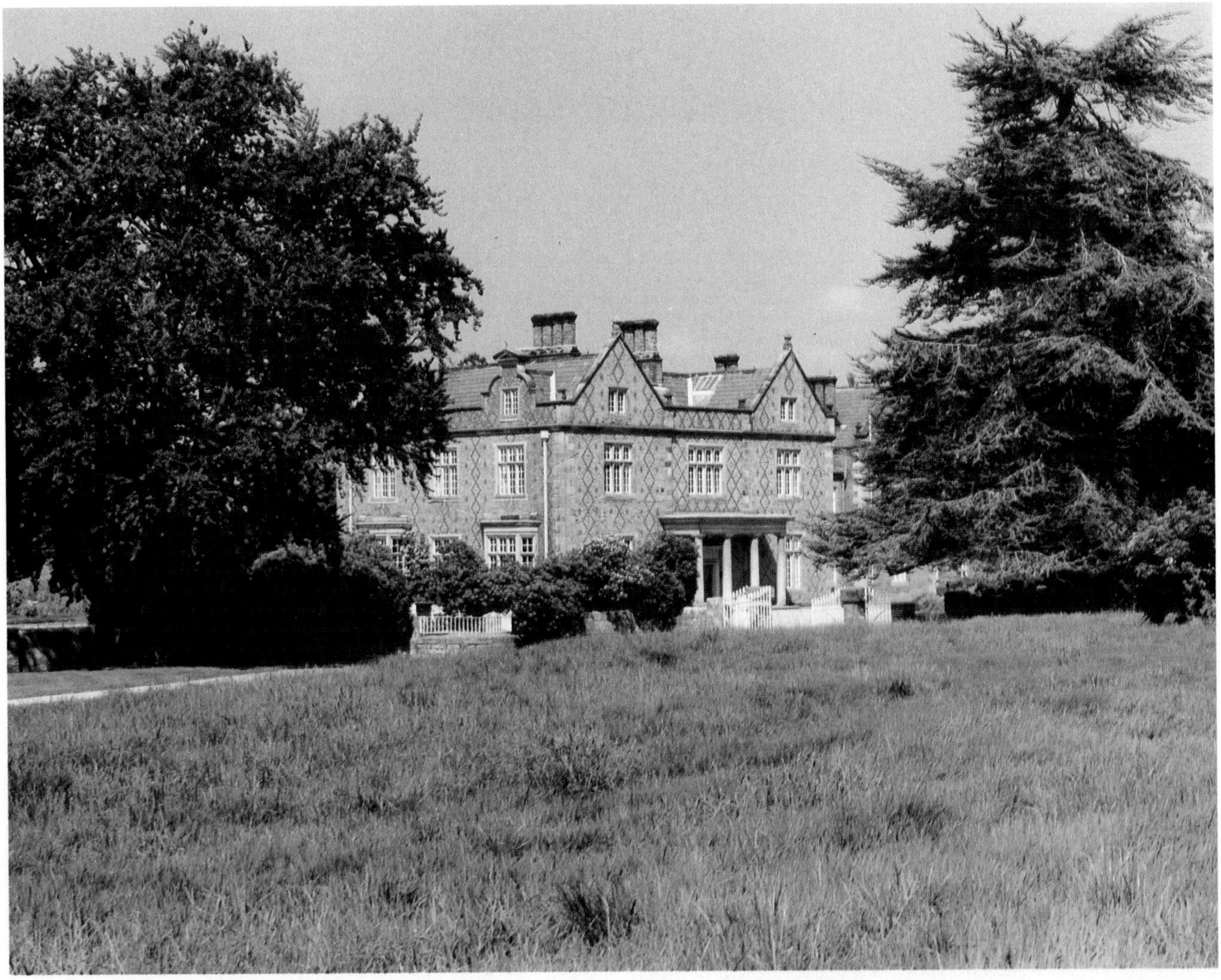

# WILLINGTON HALL HOTEL

**WILLINGTON, NEAR TARPORLEY, CHESHIRE CW6 0NB**
**TEL: 01829 752321 FAX: 01829 752596**

Built by Cheshire landowner Charles Tomkinson, Willington Hall was converted into a hotel by one of his descendants in 1977. Set in 17 acres of woods and parkland, the hotel affords wonderful views across the Cheshire countryside towards the Welsh mountains. There are both formally landscaped and 'wild' gardens, which create a beautiful backdrop for the handsome architectural proportions of the house. The hotel is a comfortable and friendly retreat for those seeking peace and seclusion. Under the personal supervision of Ross Pigot, Willington Hall has acquired a good reputation with local people for its extensive bar meals and à la carte restaurant, along with friendly and attentive service. The menus offer traditional English cooking, with dishes such as roast duckling with black cherry sauce. It is an ideal location for visiting the Roman city of Chester, Tatton Park, Beeston Castle and Oulton Park racetrack. North Wales is easily accessible from Willington Hall. The hotel is closed on Christmas Day. **Directions:** Take the A51 from Tarporley to Chester and turn right at the Bull's Head public house at Clotton. Willington Hall Hotel is one mile ahead on the left. Price guide: Single £44–£56; double/twin £78–£82.

For hotel location, see maps on pages 490-496

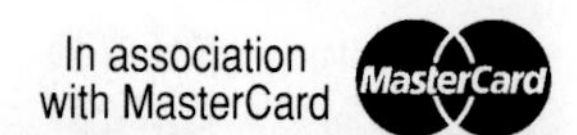

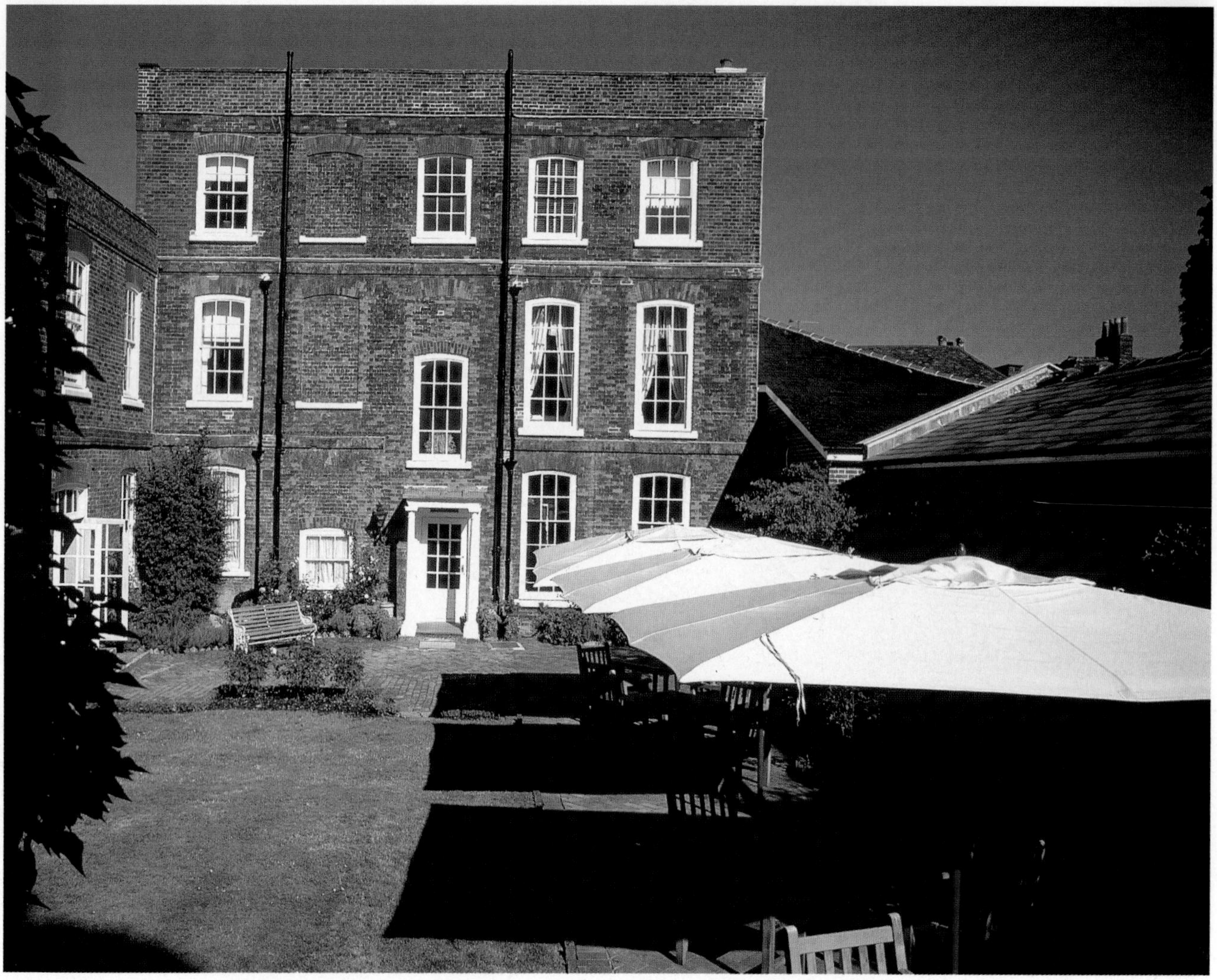

# HOTEL DU VIN & BISTRO

SOUTHGATE STREET, WINCHESTER, HAMPSHIRE SO23 9EF
TEL: 01962 841414 FAX: 01962 842458

Relaxed, charming and unpretentious are words which aptly describe the stylish and intimate Hotel du Vin & Bistro. This elegant hotel is housed in one of Winchester's most important Georgian buildings, dating back to 1715. It is jointly run by Gerard Basset, perhaps the UK's most famous sommelier, and Robin Hutson, whose successful career includes experience in other similarly fine hotels. The 23 individually decorated bedrooms feature superb beds made up with crisp, Egyptian cotton and offer every modern amenity, including trouser press, mini bar and and CD players. Each bedroom is sponsored by a wine house whose vineyard features in its decorations. Bathrooms boasting power showers, oversized baths and fluffy towels and robes add to guests' sense of luxury and comfort. Quality food cooked simply with fresh ingredients is the philosophy behind the Bistro, where an excellent and reasonably priced wine list is available. There are also 2 function rooms available for special occasions. A welcoming and enthusiastic staff cater for every need. The hotel is a perfect base for exploring England's ancient capital, famous for its cathedral, its school and antique shops. The New Forest is a short drive away. **Directions:** M3 to Winchester. Southgate Street leads from the City centre to St. Cross. Price guide: Single/double/twin £75–£105; suite £165.

23 rms MasterCard VISA AMERICAN EXPRESS M 30

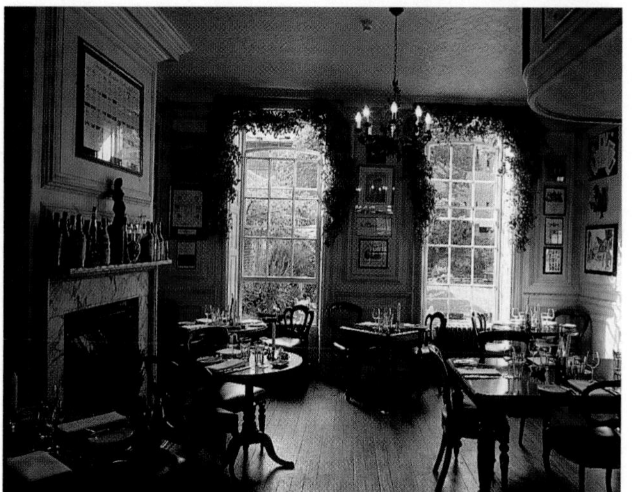

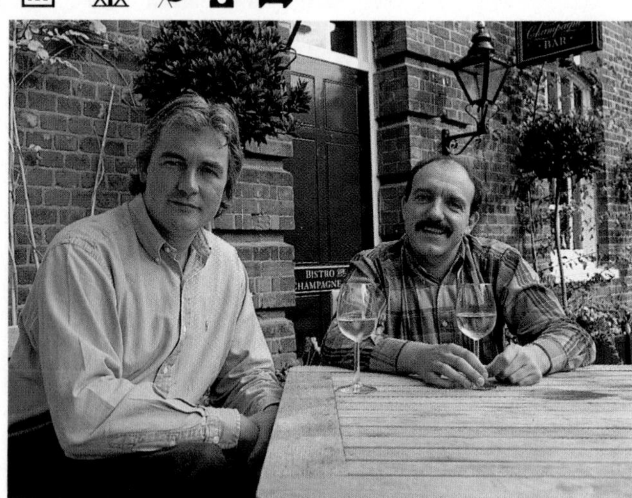

For hotel location, see maps on pages 490-496

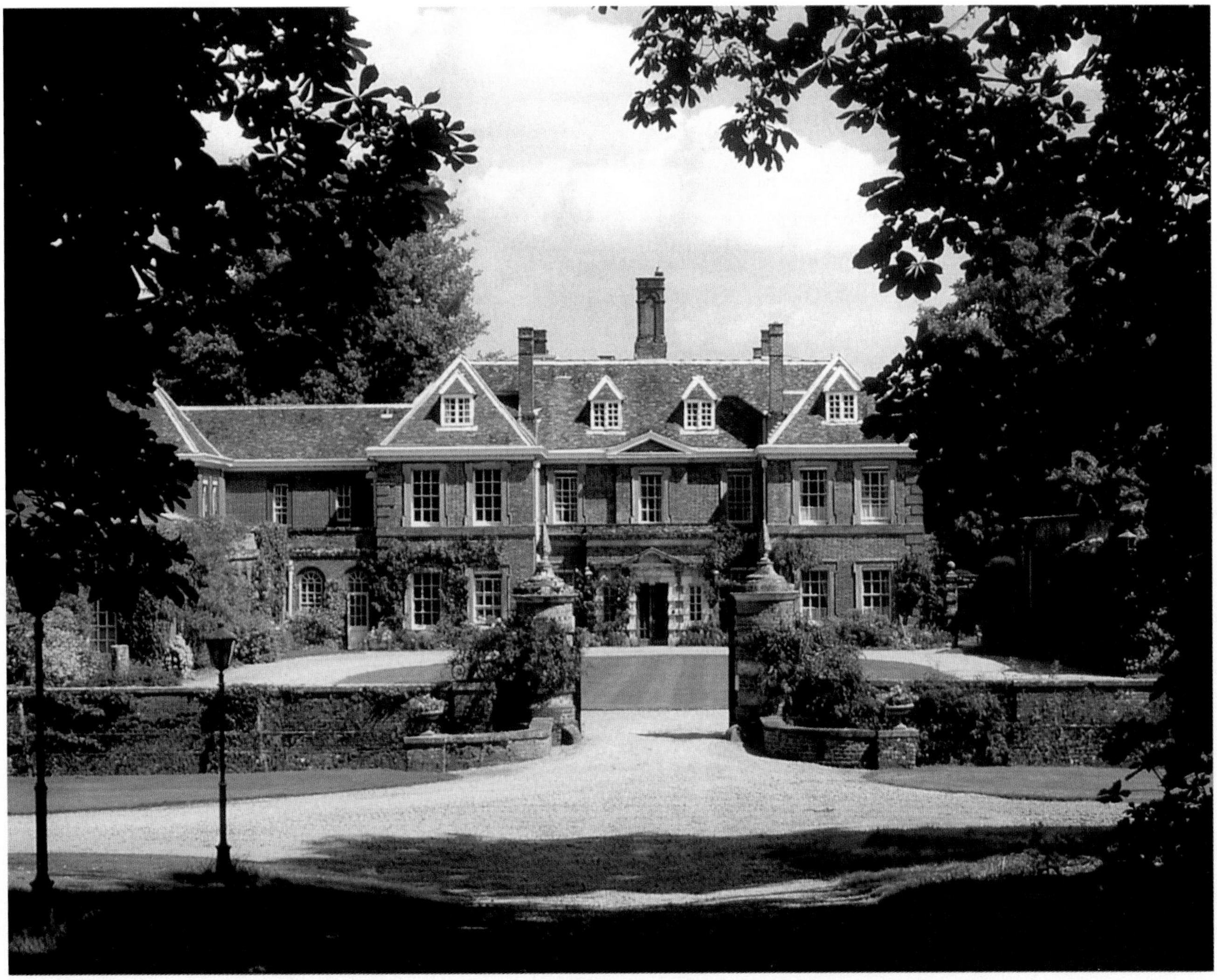

# LAINSTON HOUSE HOTEL

**SPARSHOLT, WINCHESTER, HAMPSHIRE SO21 2LT**
**TEL: 01962 863588 FAX: 01962 776672**

The fascinating history of Lainston House is well documented, some of its land having been recorded in the *Domesday Book* of 1087. Set in 63 acres of superb downland countryside, this graceful William and Mary country house has been sympathetically restored to create a beautiful hotel with a stately home atmosphere. From the individually designed bedrooms to the main reception rooms, elegant and comfortable furnishings are the hallmark of Lainston House. Freshly prepared food, attentive service and views over the lawn make the restaurant one of the most popular in Hampshire. Facilities are available for small meetings in the Mountbatten Room or larger functions in the recently converted 17th century Dawley Barn. The charming grounds hold many surprises – an ancient chapel, reputedly haunted by the legendary Elizabeth Chudleigh, an 18th century herb garden and a dovecote. Historic Winchester is only 2½ miles south, while Romsey Abbey, Salisbury and the New Forest are a short drive away. Other local activities include riding, country walking and good trout fishing on the River Test at nearby Stockbridge. **Directions:** Lainston House is well signposted off the B3049 Winchester–Stockbridge road, at Sparsholt 2½ miles from Winchester. Price guide: Single from £95; double/twin from £135; suite from £245.

For hotel location, see maps on pages 490-496

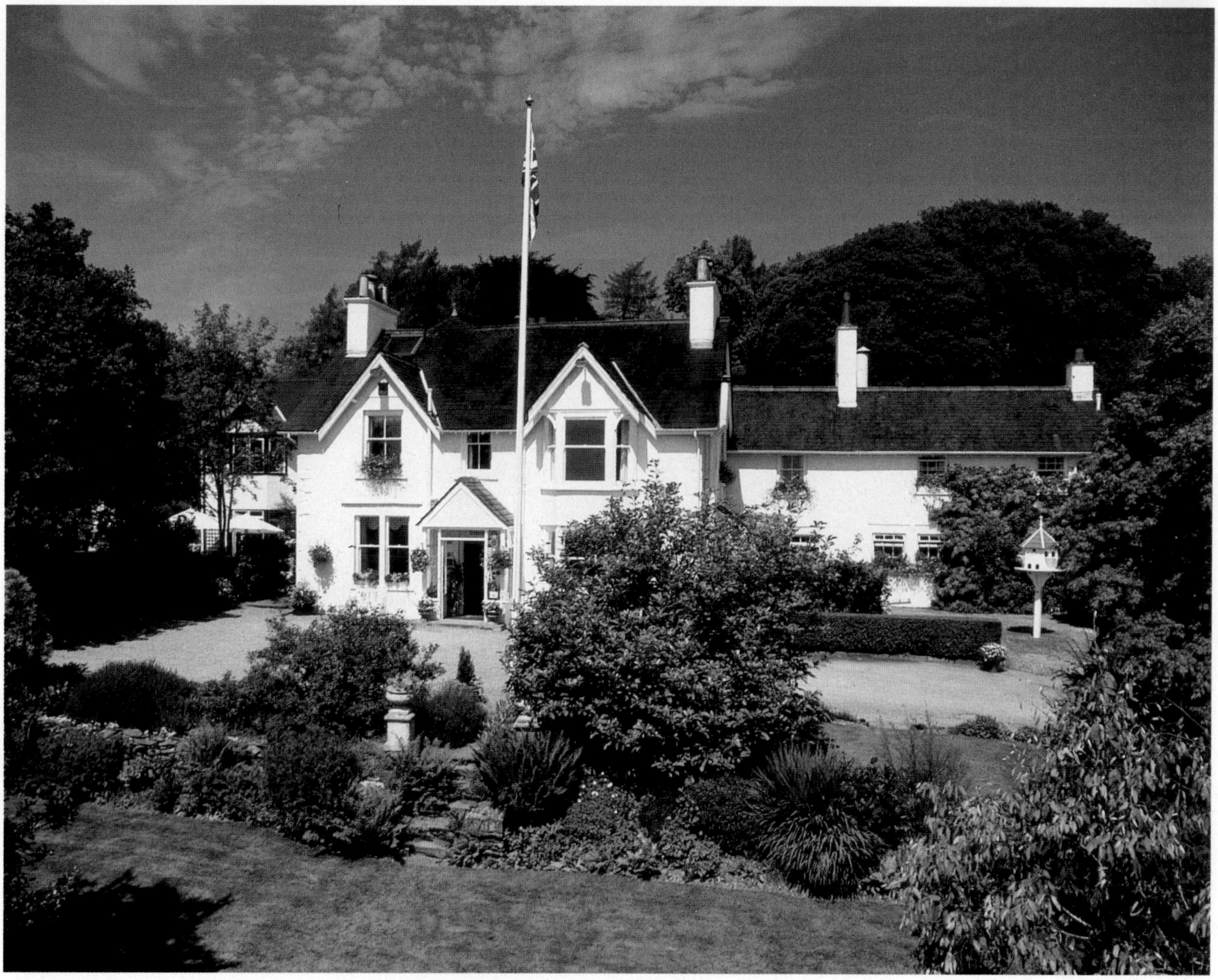

# GILPIN LODGE

CROOK ROAD, NEAR WINDERMERE, CUMBRIA LA23 3NE
TEL: 015394 88818 FREEPHONE: 0800 269460 FAX: 015394 88058

Gilpin Lodge is a small, friendly, elegant, relaxing country house hotel set in 20 acres of woodlands, moors and country gardens 2 miles from Lake Windermere, yet just 12 miles from the M6. The original building, tastefully extended and modernised, dates from 1901. A profusion of flower arrangements, picture-lined walls, antique furniture and log fires in winter are all part of John and Christine Cunliffe's perception of hospitality. The sumptuous bedrooms (5 new in 1997) all have en suite bathrooms and every comfort. Some have four-poster beds, split levels and whirlpool baths. The exquisite food, created by a team of 7 chefs, has earned 3 rosettes from the AA. The award-winning wine-list contains 175 labels from 13 different countries. The beautiful gardens are the perfect place in which to muse while savouring the lovely lakeland scenery. Windermere golf course is ½ a mile away. There's almost every kind of outdoor activity imaginable. Guests have free use of a nearby private leisure club. This is Wordsworth and Beatrix Potter country and nearby there are several stately homes, gardens and castles. Lancashire Life Lake District Hotel of the year 1996-97, English Tourist Board 4 crowns De Luxe, AA 3 red stars. **Directions:** M6 exit 36. A591 Kendal bypass then B5284 to Crook. Price guide: Single £75–£100; double/twin £90–£140. Dinner inclusive and year-round short-break rates available.

For hotel location, see maps on pages 490-496

# LAKESIDE HOTEL ON LAKE WINDERMERE

**LAKESIDE, NEWBY BRIDGE, CUMBRIA LA12 8AT**
**TEL: 015395 31207 FAX: 015395 31699**

Lakeside Hotel offers you a unique location on the water's edge of Lake Windermere. It is a classic, traditional lakeland hotel offering four star facilities and service. All the bedrooms are en suite and enjoy individually designed fabrics and colours, many of the rooms offer superlative views of the lake. Guests may dine in either the award-winning Lakeview Restaurant or Ruskin's Brasserie, where extensive menus offer a wide selection of dishes including Cumbrian specialities. The Lakeside Conservatory serves drinks and light meals throughout the day – once there you are sure to fall under the spell of this peaceful location. Berthed next to the hotel there are cruisers which will enable you to explore the lake from the water and there is also a water ski school. Guests are given free use of the Cascades Leisure Club at Newby Bridge. The hotel offers a fully equipped conference centre and many syndicate suites allowing plenty of scope and flexibility. Most of all you are assured of a stay in an unrivalled setting of genuine character. The original panelling and beams of the old coaching inn create an excellent ambience, whilst you are certain to enjoy the quality and friendly service. **Directions:** From M6 junction 36 join A590 to Newby Bridge, turn right over bridge towards Hawkshead; hotel is one mile on right. Price guide: Single £95–£135; double/twin £140–£160; suites £180–£210.

72 rms

For hotel location, see maps on pages 490-496

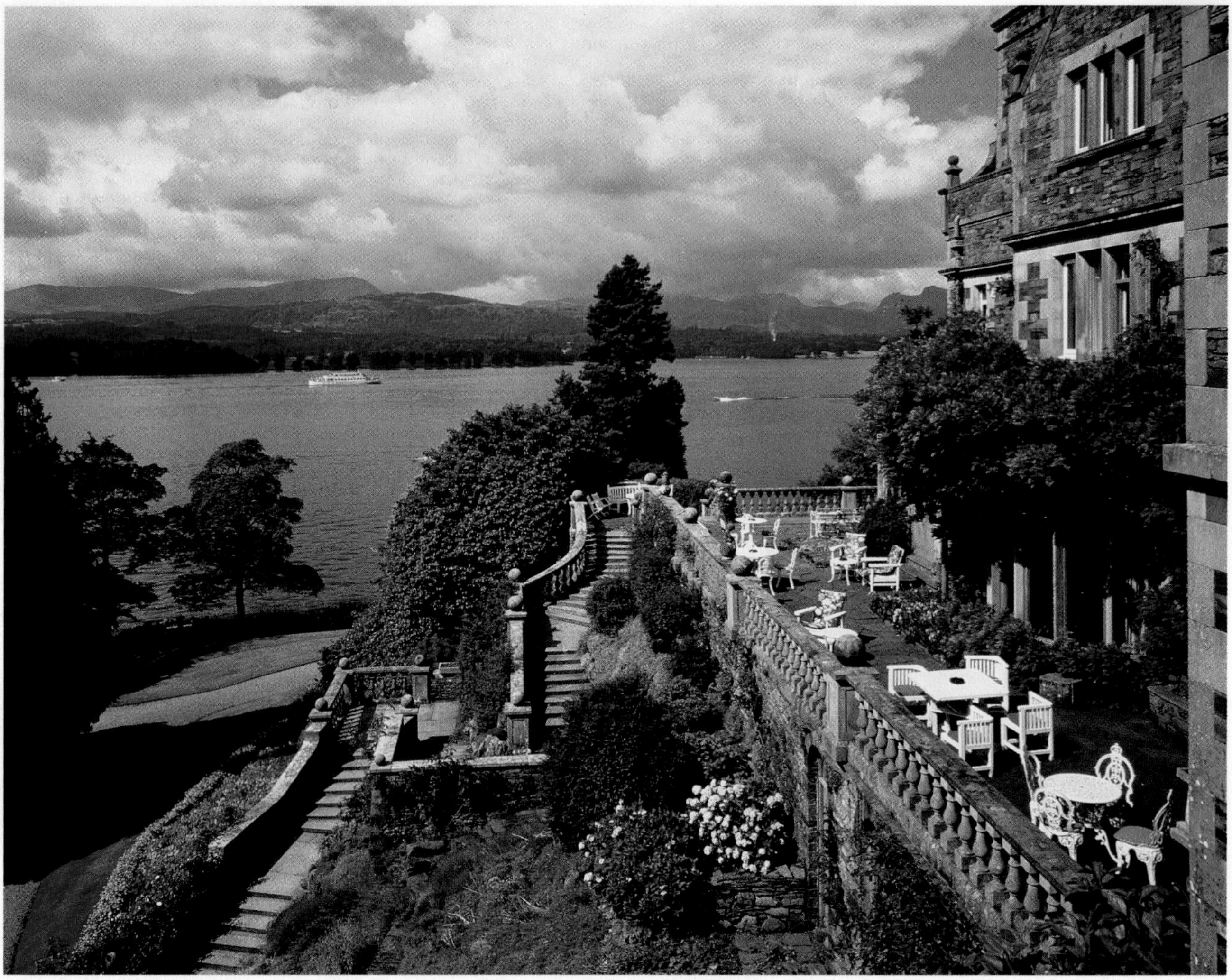

# LANGDALE CHASE

**WINDERMERE, CUMBRIA LA23 1LW**
**TEL: 015394 32201 FAX: 015394 32604**

Langdale Chase stands in five acres of landscaped gardens on the shores of Lake Windermere, with panoramic views over England's largest lake to the Langdale Pikes beyond. Visitors will receive warm-hearted hospitality in this well-run country home, which is splendidly decorated with oak panelling, fine oil paintings and ornate, carved fireplaces. A magnificent staircase leads to the well-appointed bedrooms, many overlooking the lake. One unique bedroom is sited over the lakeside boathouse, where the traveller may be lulled to sleep by the gently lapping waters below. For the energetic, there is a choice of water-skiing, swimming or sailing from the hotel jetty. Guests can stroll through the gardens along the lake shore, in May the gardens are spectacular when the rhododendrons and azalias are in bloom. Being pampered by attentive staff will be one of the many highlights of your stay at Langdale Chase. The variety of food and wine is sure to delight the most discerning diner. Combine this with a panoramic tableau across England's largest and loveliest of lakes and you have a truly unforgettable dining experience. **Directions:** Situated on the A591, three miles north of Windermere, two miles south of Ambleside. Price guide: Single from £50–£65; double/twin from £90–£160; suite £160.

For hotel location, see maps on pages 490-496

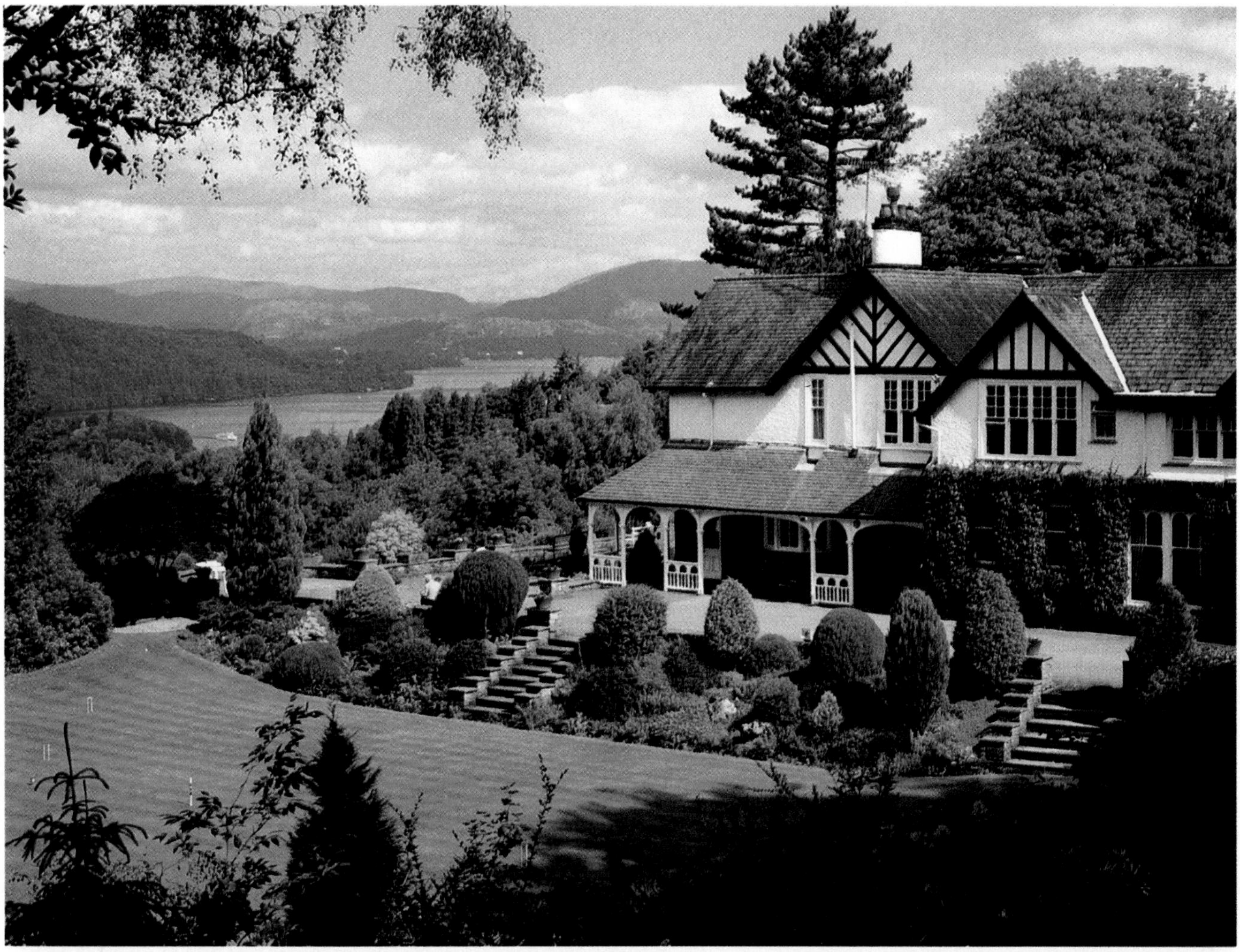

# LINTHWAITE HOUSE HOTEL

CROOK ROAD, BOWNESS-ON-WINDERMERE, CUMBRIA LA23 3JA
TEL: 015394 88600 FAX: 015394 88601

Situated in 14 acres of gardens and woods in the heart of the Lake Distict, Linthwaite House overlooks Lake Windermere and Belle Island, with Claiffe Heights and Coniston Old Man beyond. Here, guests will find themselves amid spectacular scenery, yet only a short drive from the motorway network. The hotel combines stylish originality with the best of traditional English hospitality. The superbly decorated bedrooms, all en suite, offer glorious views. The comfortable lounge is the perfect place to unwind and there is a fire on winter evenings. In the restaurant, excellent cuisine features the best of fresh, local produce, accompanied by a fine selection of wines. Within the hotel grounds, there is a 9-hole putting green and a par 3 practice hole. Fly fishermen can fish for brown trout in the hotel tarn. Guests have complimentary use of a private swimming pool and lesiure club nearby, while fell walks begin at the hotel's front door. The area around Linthwaite abounds with places of interest: this is Beatrix Potter and Wordsworth country, and there is much to interest the visitor. **Directions:** From the M6 junction 36 follow Kendal by-pass (A590) for 8 miles. Take B5284 Crook Road for 6 miles. 1 mile beyond Windermere Golf Club, Linthwaite House is signposted on left. Price guide: Single £90–£130; double/twin £80–£180; suite £210.

# Oakley Court

**WINDSOR ROAD, WATER OAKLEY, NR WINDSOR, BERKSHIRE SL4 5UR**
**TEL: 01753 609988 FAX: 01628 37011 E-MAIL: oaklyct@atlas.co.uk**

The turreted towers of Oakley Court rise majestically over the banks of the Thames, where this handsome mansion has stood since 1859. The waterside location enables the hotel to offer a unique range of boating facilities, from a champagne picnic hamper for two on a chauffeured punt to a gastronomic feast for a hundred on a steamboat. The hotel's grandeur is quite awe-inspiring. Restored to their original splendour, the entrance hall, library and drawing room feature elaborate plasterwork, fresh flowers and elegant furnishings. An antique billiard table in the games room is kept in pristine condition. Many of the bedrooms have views over the river or the 35-acre gardens. Gourmet cuisine is prepared by a skilled team, under Chef Murdo Macsween, and is served with finesse in the candle-lit Le Boulestin Restaurant, or in Boaters for lighter, less formal dining. Private dining can be arranged in the superbly equipped conference and banqueting suites. Activities organised for corporate parties include archery, laser clay pigeon shooting and falconry. There is a 9-hole par 3 golf course and 2 tennis courts on site and the hotel has its own gym, sauna, solarium, indoor swimming pool and beauty treatments. Windsor Castle, Eton and Ascot are nearby, and Heathrow is 20 minutes' drive. **Directions:** Situated just off the A308, between Windsor and Maidenhead. Price guide: Single £130–£160; double/twin £130–£185; suites £275–£395.

113 rms · MasterCard · VISA · AMERICAN EXPRESS · M 150

For hotel location, see maps on pages 490-496

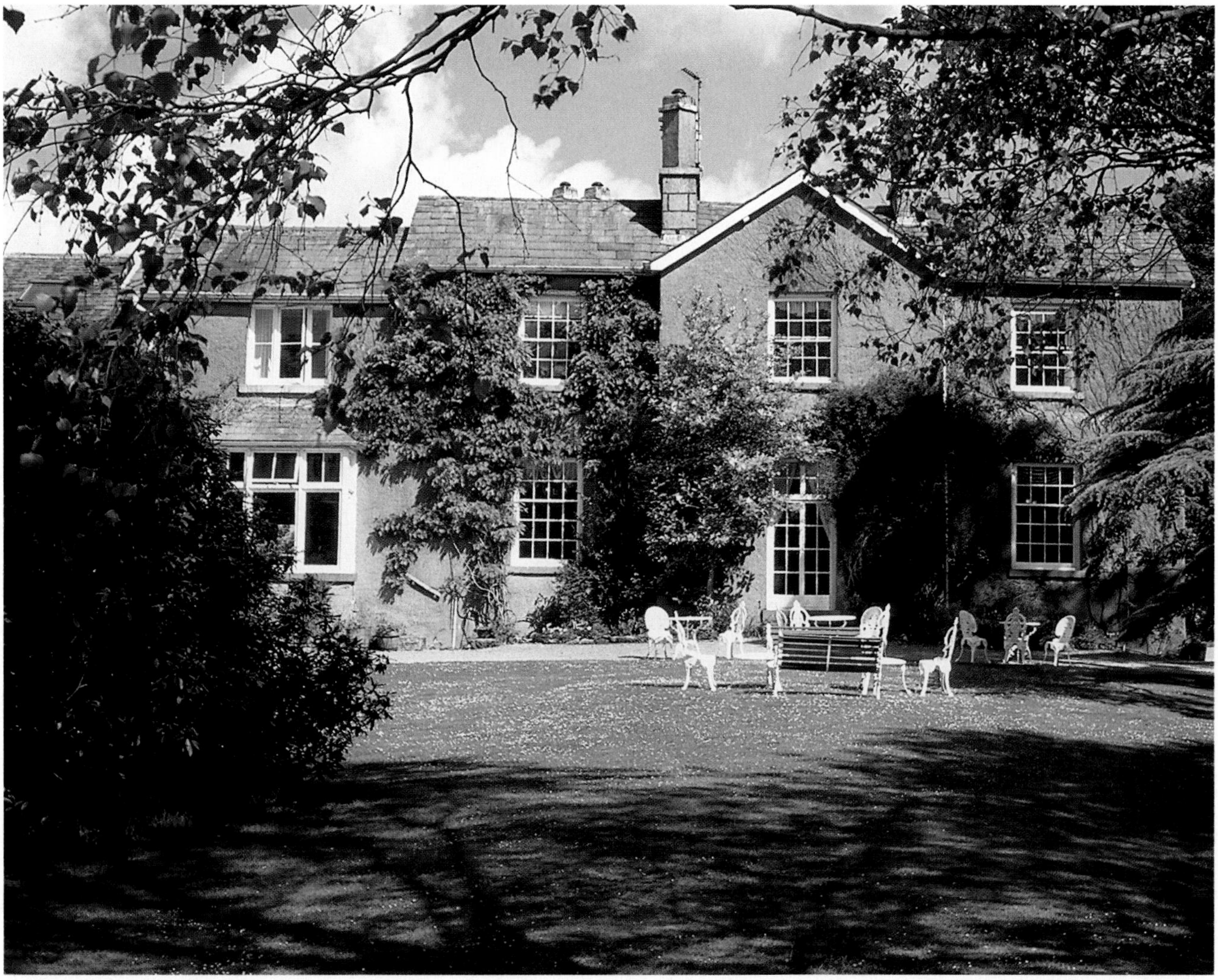

# THE OLD VICARAGE COUNTRY HOUSE HOTEL

CHURCH ROAD, WITHERSLACK, NR GRANGE-OVER- SANDS, CUMBRIA LA11 6RS

TEL: 015395 52381 FAX: 015395 52373 E-MAIL: hotel@old–vic.demon.co.uk

Near to the lakes...far from the crowds, this lovely old, family-run historic house offers the tranquil timeless atmosphere that reflects the calm and beauty of the surrounding countryside. The delightful, mature garden is stocked with many interesting plants and part of it is left natural for wild flowers, unusual orchids, butterflies, dragonflies and birds. An all-weather tennis court in a delightful setting is for guests' use. Also guests have free use of the nearby Cascades Leisure Club. In the old house, each of the comfortable bedrooms has its own particular character yet with all the modern facilities. The Orchard House, close by, is set beside an ancient damson orchard and has particularly well-equipped, spacious rooms each with its own woodland terrace. With top culinary awards, the well-planned menus include interesting, good quality locally-produced specialities. Diets can, of course, easily be catered for. Lake District National Park, Winderemere, Wordsworth Heritage, Sizergh Castle (NT), world famous topiary gardens at Levens Hall. **Directions:** From M6 junction 36, follow A590 to Barrow. After 6 miles turn right into Witherslack, then first left after the telephone box. Price guide: Single £59–£79; double £98–£158. Bargain Breaks all year.

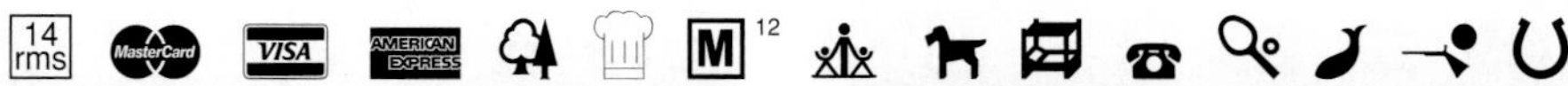

For hotel location, see maps on pages 490-496

# LANGLEY HOUSE HOTEL

**LANGLEY MARSH, WIVELISCOMBE, SOMERSET TA4 2UF**
**TEL: 01984 623318 FAX: 01984 624573**

Conveniently located not far from the M5 junction 26, Langley House is a 16th century retreat set in four acres of beautifully kept gardens on the edge of the pretty Somerset town of Wiveliscombe. Modifications in Georgian times have invested this small, cosy hotel with a unique period charm, which explains its enduring popularity. Owners Peter and Anne Wilson have excelled in making Langley House a relaxed and comfortable place to stay. The eight bedrooms, all en suite, are individually decorated, with direct-dial telephone, TV and radio. Most have peaceful garden views and personal touches throughout including fresh flowers and mineral water, books and hot-water bottles. Discreet good taste has been exercised in furnishing the public rooms with pastel sofas, traditional rugs, china and glass, antiques and paintings. (Langley House won the Wedgwood/British Tourist Authority Interior Design Award). In the beamed restaurant, Peter Wilson serves critically acclaimed cuisine and has been awarded a Michelin Red M. The wine list carries over 200 wines. Places of interest nearby include Exmoor, and famous gardens Knightshayes, Stourhead and Hestercombe. **Directions:** Wiveliscombe is 10 miles from Taunton on B3227. Langley House is half a mile north, signposted Langley Marsh. Price guide: Single £72.50–£75; double/twin £95–£125.

8 rms MasterCard VISA AMERICAN EXPRESS M 20

For hotel location, see maps on pages 490-496

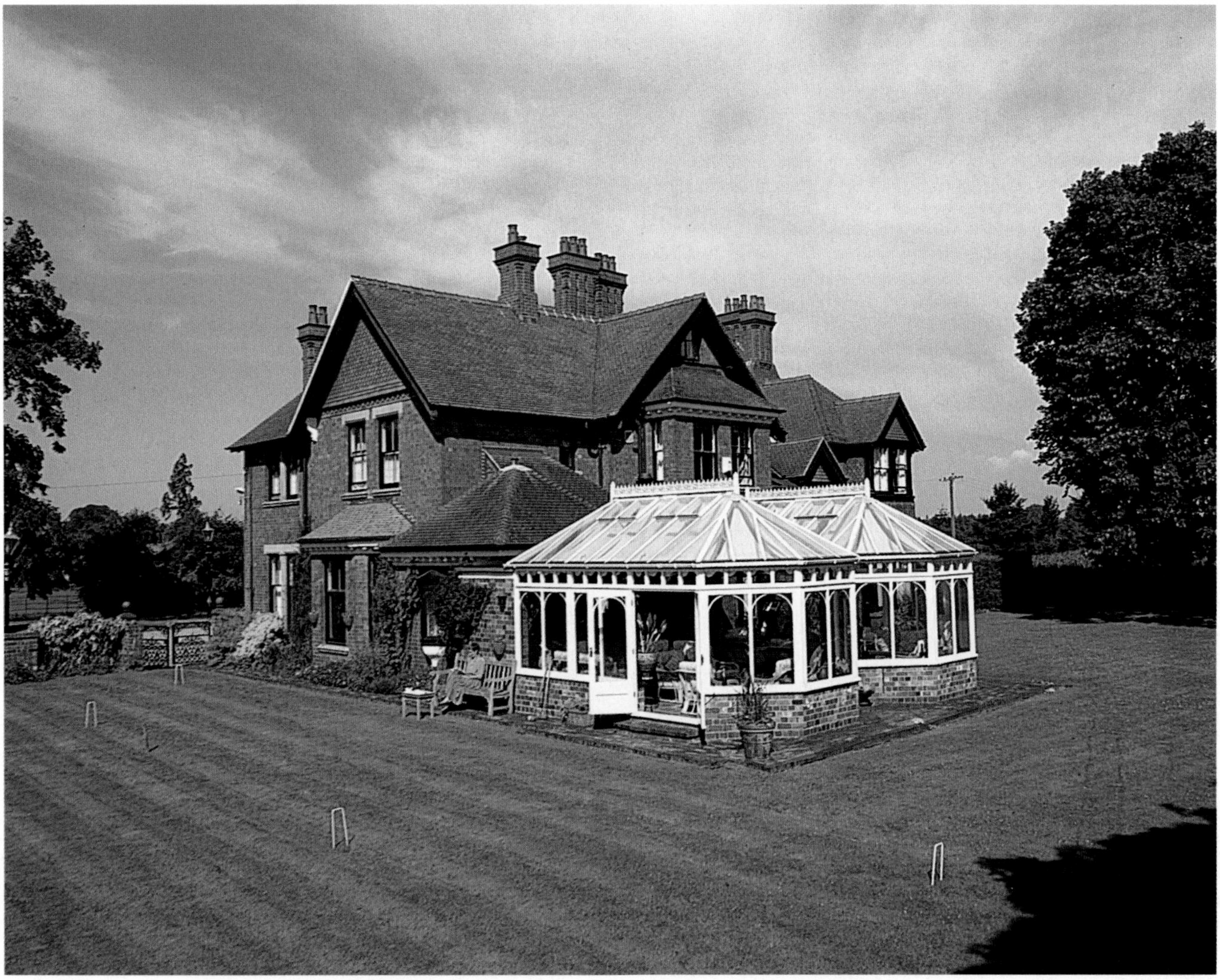

# THE OLD VICARAGE HOTEL

**WORFIELD, BRIDGNORTH, SHROPSHIRE WV15 5JZ**

**TEL: 01746 716497 FAX: 01746 716552**

Standing in 2 acres of mature grounds, this Edwardian parsonage has been lovingly transformed into a delightful country house hotel. Awards abound – Michelin Red M for food, 3 AA Rosettes for food – English Tourist Board De Luxe Hotel and RAC 3 Merit Awards. The Old Vicarage offers guests an opportunity to enjoy a peaceful retreat in countryside of outstanding beauty. The spacious bedrooms are sensitively furnished in Victorian and Edwardian styles to complement the period features of the house. Four Coach House rooms offer complete luxury and comfort – and the Leighton suite has been specially designed with the disabled guest in mind. The daily changing menu features the best of local produce and the award-winning cheeseboard and wine cellar will complete a wonderful evening. Local attractions include the world famous Telford's Ironbridge Gorge Museum complex, the Severn Valley preserved steam railway and the splendour of the border towns and villages. Half price golf is available at Worfield Golf Club. Two-day breaks available from £72.50 per person per day, which includes free Passport Tickets to Ironbridge Gorge. **Directions:** Eight miles west of Wolverhampton, one mile off A454, eight miles south of junction 4 of M54. Price guide: Single £72.50–£97.50; double/twin £110–£155.

For hotel location, see maps on pages 490-496

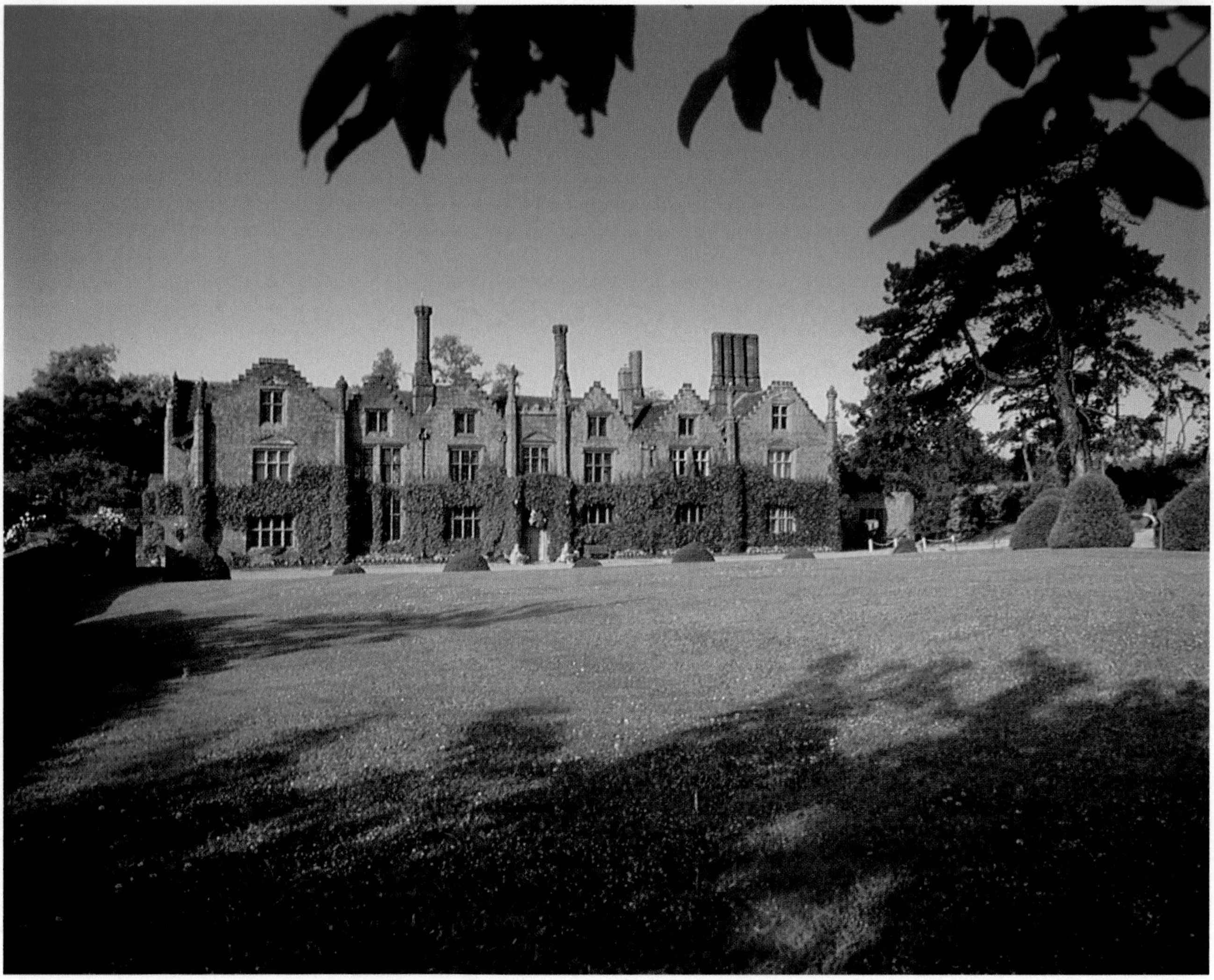

# SECKFORD HALL

**WOODBRIDGE, SUFFOLK IP13 6NU**
**TEL: 01394 385678 FAX: 01394 380610**

Seckford Hall dates from 1530 and it is said that Elizabeth I once held court there. The hall has lost none of its Tudor grandeur. Furnished as a private house with many fine period pieces, the panelled rooms, beamed ceilings, carved doors and great stone fireplaces are displayed against the splendour of English oak. Local delicacies such as the house speciality, lobster, feature on the à la carte menu. The original minstrels gallery can be viewed in the banqueting hall, which is now a conference and function suite designed in keeping with the general style. The Courtyard area was converted from a giant Tudor tithe barn, dairy and coach house. It now incorporates ten charming cottage-style suites and a modern leisure complex, which includes a heated swimming pool, exercise machines, solarium and spa bath. The hotel is set in 34 acres of tranquil parkland with sweeping lawns and a willow-fringed lake, and guests may stroll about the grounds or simply relax in the attractive terrace garden. There is a 18-hole golf course, where equipment can be hired, and a gentle walk along the riverside to picturesque Woodbridge, with its tide mill, antiques shops, yacht harbours and the rose-planted grave of Edward Fitzgerald. Constable country and the Suffolk coast are nearby. **Directions:** Remain on the A12 Woodbridge bypass until the blue-and-white hotel sign. Price guide: Single £79–£115; double/twin £110–£135; suite £125–£150.

For hotel location, see maps on pages 490-496

# THE FEATHERS HOTEL

**MARKET STREET, WOODSTOCK, OXFORDSHIRE OX20 1SX**
**TEL: 01993 812291 FAX: 01993 813158**

The Feathers is a privately owned and run country house hotel, situated in the centre of Woodstock, a few miles from Oxford. Woodstock is one England's most attractive country towns, constructed mostly from Cotswold stone and with some buildings dating from the 12th century. The hotel, built in the 17th century, was originally four separate houses. Antiques, log fires and traditional English furnishings lend character and charm. There are only 16 bedrooms, all of which have private bathrooms and showers. Public rooms, including the drawing room and study, are intimate and comfortable. The small garden is a delightful setting for a light lunch or afternoon tea and guests can enjoy a drink in the cosy courtyard bar, which has an open fire in winter. The antique-panelled restaurant is internationally renowned for its fine cuisine, complemented by a high standard of service. The menu changes daily and offers a wide variety of dishes, using the finest local ingredients. Blenheim Palace, seat of the Duke of Marlborough and birthplace of Sir Winston Churchill, is just around the corner. The Cotswolds and the dreaming spires of Oxford are a short distance away. **Directions:** From London leave M40 at junction 8; from Birmingham leave at junction 9. Take A44 and follow signs to Woodstock. The hotel is on the left. Price guide: Single £88; double/twin £105–£155; suite £195–£250.

For hotel location, see maps on pages 490-496

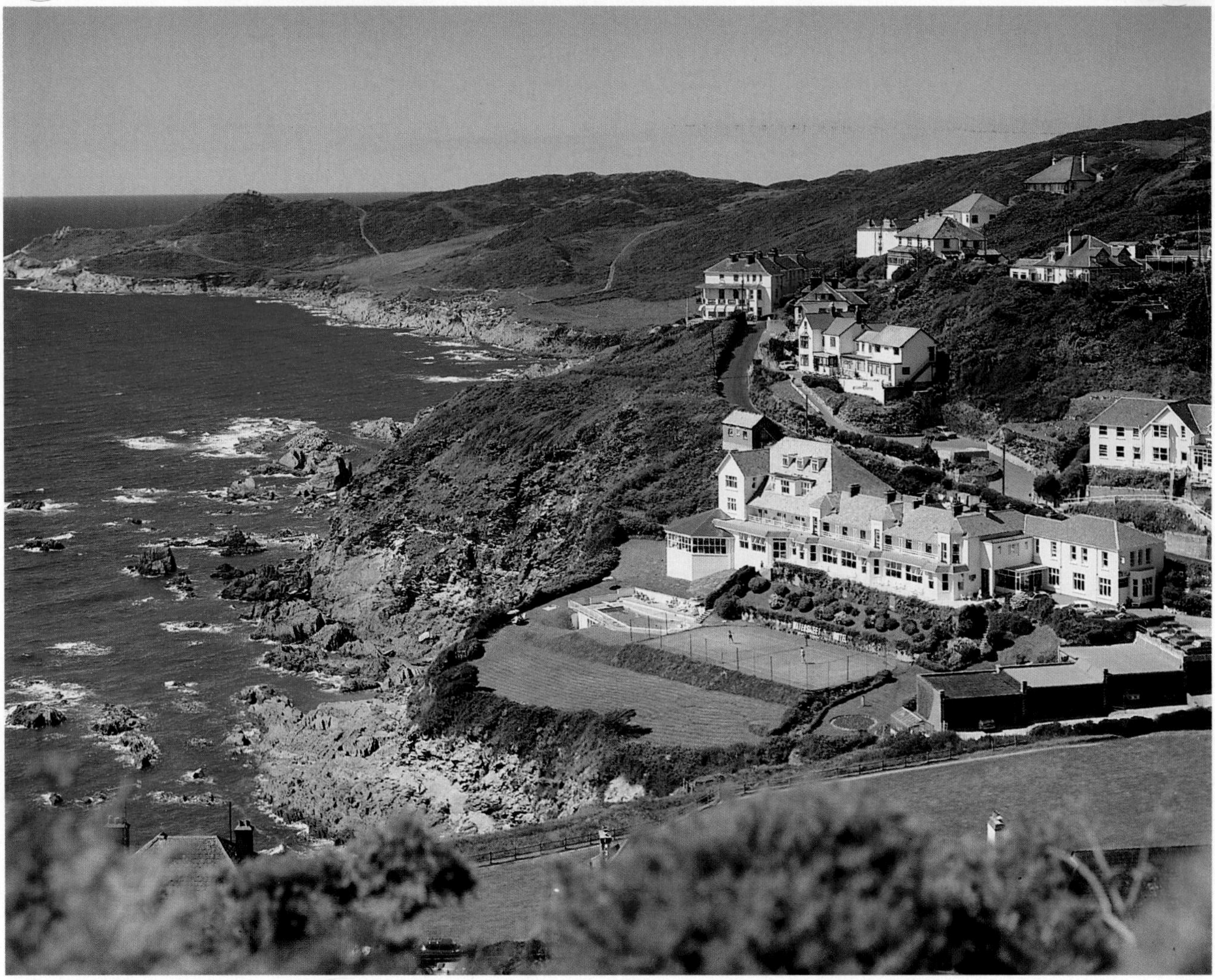

# WATERSMEET HOTEL

**MORTEHOE, WOOLACOMBE, DEVON EX34 7EB**
**TEL: 01271 870333 FAX: 01271 870890**

Watersmeet personifies the comfortable luxury of a country house hotel. Majestically situated on The National Trust's rugged North Atlantic coastline the hotel commands dramatic views across the waters of Woolacombe Bay past Hartland Point to Lundy Island. The gardens reach down to the sea and nearby steps lead directly to the beach. Attractive decor, combined with soft coloured fabrics, creates a summery impression all year round. The main bedrooms look out to sea and guests can drift off to sleep to the sound of lapping waves or rolling surf. Morning coffee, lunch and afternoon tea can be served in the relaxing comfort of the lounge, on the terrace or by the heated outdoor pool. The splendid new indoor pool and spa is a favourite with everyone. Tempting English and international dishes are served in the award winning Watersmeet Restaurant where each evening candles flicker as diners absorb a view of the sun slipping below the horizon. The hotel has been awarded two AA Rosettes for cuisine and all three RAC Merit awards for excellent hospitality, restaurant and comfort. There is a grass tennis court and locally surfing, riding, clay pigeon shooting and bracing walks along coastal paths. Open February to December. **Directions:** From M5, J27, follow A361 towards Ilfracombe, turn left at roundabout and follow signs to Mortehoe. Price guide (including dinner): Single £55–£92; double/twin £90–198.

For hotel location, see maps on pages 490-496

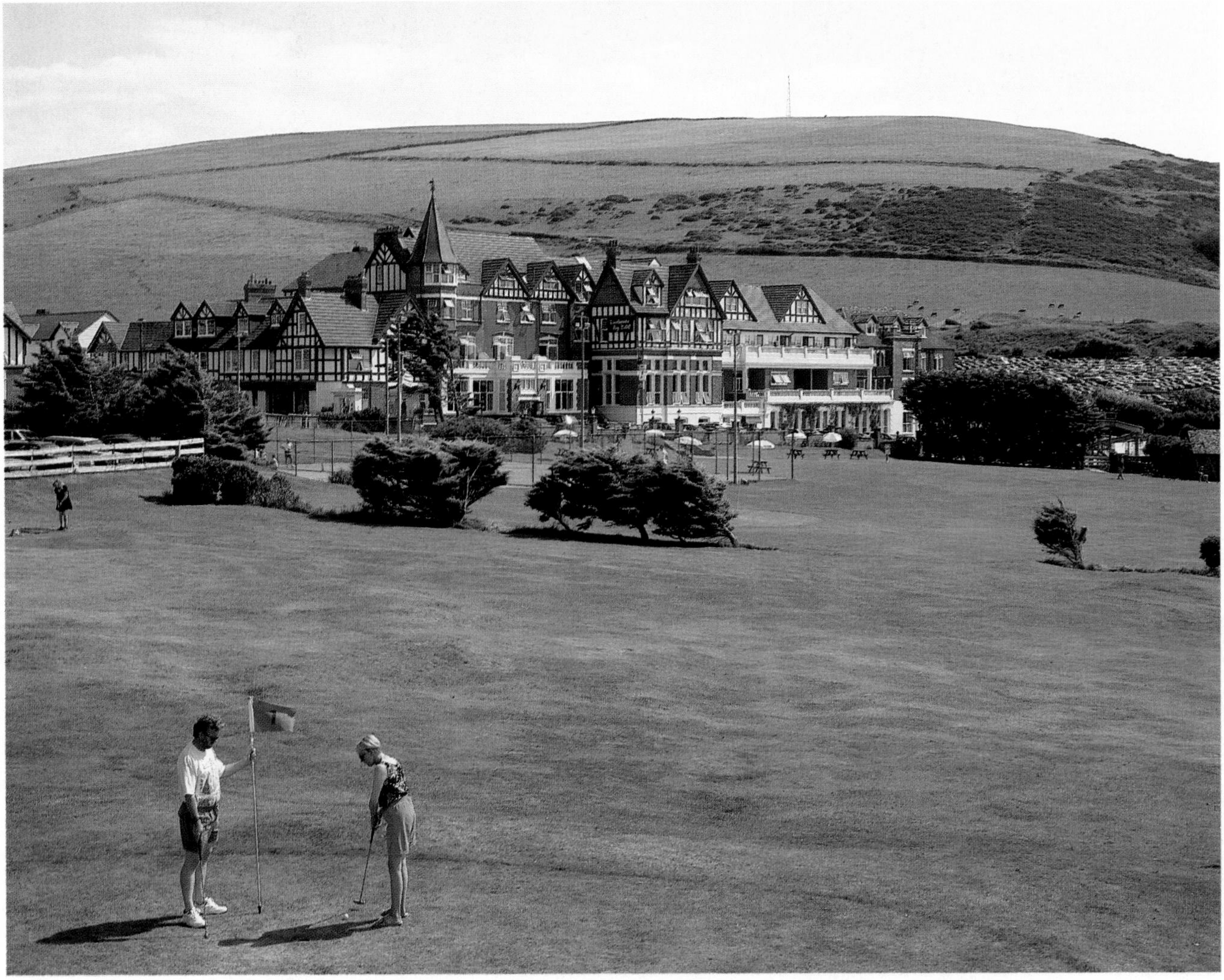

# WOOLACOMBE BAY HOTEL

**SOUTH STREET, WOOLACOMBE, DEVON EX34 7BN**
**TEL: 01271 870388 FAX: 01271 870613**

Woolacombe Bay Hotel stands in 6 acres of grounds, leading to three miles of golden sand. Built by the Victorians, the hotel has an air of luxury, style and comfort. All rooms are en suite with satellite TV, baby listening, ironing centre, some with a spa bath or balcony. Traditional English and French dishes are offered in the dining room. Superb recreational amenities on site include unlimited free access to tennis, squash, indoor and outdoor pools, billiards, bowls, croquet, dancing and films, a health suite with steam room, sauna, spa bath with heated benches and high impulse shower. Power-boating, shooting and riding can be arranged, and preferential rates are offered for golf at the Saunton Golf Club. New "Hot House" aerobics studio, cardio vascular weights room, solariums, massage and beautician. However, being energetic is not a requirement for enjoying the qualities of Woolacombe Bay. Many of its regulars choose simply to relax in the grand public rooms and in the grounds, which extend to the rolling surf of the magnificent bay. A drive along the coastal route in either direction will guarantee splendid views. Exmoor's beautiful Doone Valley is an hour away by car. ETB 5 Crowns Highly Commended. Closed January. **Directions:** At centre of village, off main Barnstaple–Ilfracombe road. Price guide (including dinner): Single £70–£90; double/twin £140–£180.

61 rms MasterCard VISA AMERICAN EXPRESS M 350

# THE GEORGE HOTEL

QUAY STREET, YARMOUTH, ISLE OF WIGHT PO41 0PE
TEL: 01983 760331 FAX: 01983 760425

This historic 17th century Town House is superbly located just a few paces from Yarmouth's ancient harbour. Built for Admiral Sir Robert Holmes, a former governor of the island, it once welcomed Charles II through its doors. With the cosy ambience of a well-loved home, The George is the perfect place for self-indulgence. Beautifully furnished and well-equipped bedrooms complement the luxurious surroundings. Enjoy either the 3 AA rosette cuisine in the elegant restaurant or opt for a more informal à la carte meal in the lively brasserie with its lovely sea views. the excellent cellar contains particularly good claret. The hotel has its own private beach and there is no shortage of leisure opportunities in the near vicinity, including world class sailing on the Solent. Yarmouth remains the gateway to the downs and villages of the West Wight and there are countless opportunities to make the most of this area of outstanding natural beauty by walking, hiking or enjoying a host of other country pursuits, golf too. Historic places of interest include Carisbrook Castle and Osborne House. **Directions:** From the M3, exit at junction 1 and take the A377 to Lymington and then the ferry to Yarmouth. Alternatively, ferry services run regularly to the island from Southampton and Portsmouth. The A3054 leads direct to Yarmouth. Price guide: Single £80–£90; double/twin £110–140.

17 rms MasterCard VISA AMERICAN EXPRESS M 30

For hotel location, see maps on pages 490-496

# THE GRANGE HOTEL

1 CLIFTON, YORK, NORTH YORKSHIRE YO3 6AA
TEL: 01904 644744 FAX: 01904 612453

Set near the ancient city walls, 4 minutes' walk from the famous Minster, this sophisticated Regency town house has been carefully restored and its spacious rooms richly decorated. Beautiful stone-flagged floors in the corridors of The Grange lead to the classically styled reception rooms. The flower-filled Morning Room is welcoming, with its blazing log fire and deep sofas. Double doors between the panelled library and drawing room can be opened up to create a dignified venue for parties, wedding receptions or business entertaining. Prints, flowers and English chintz in the bedrooms reflect the proprietor's careful attention to detail. The Ivy Restaurant has an established reputation for first-class gastronomy, incorporating the best in French and country house cooking. The Dom Ruinart Seafood bar has two murals depicting racing scenes. The Brasserie is open for lunch and dinner until after the theatre closes in the evening. For conferences, a computer and fax are available as well as secretarial services. Brimming with history, York's list of attractions includes the National Railway Museum, the Jorvik Viking Centre and the medieval Shambles. **Directions:** The Grange Hotel is on the A19 York–Thirsk road, 1/2 mile from the centre on the left. Price guide: Single £99; double/twin £108–£160; suites £190.

30 rms MasterCard VISA AMERICAN EXPRESS M 50

For hotel location, see maps on pages 490-496

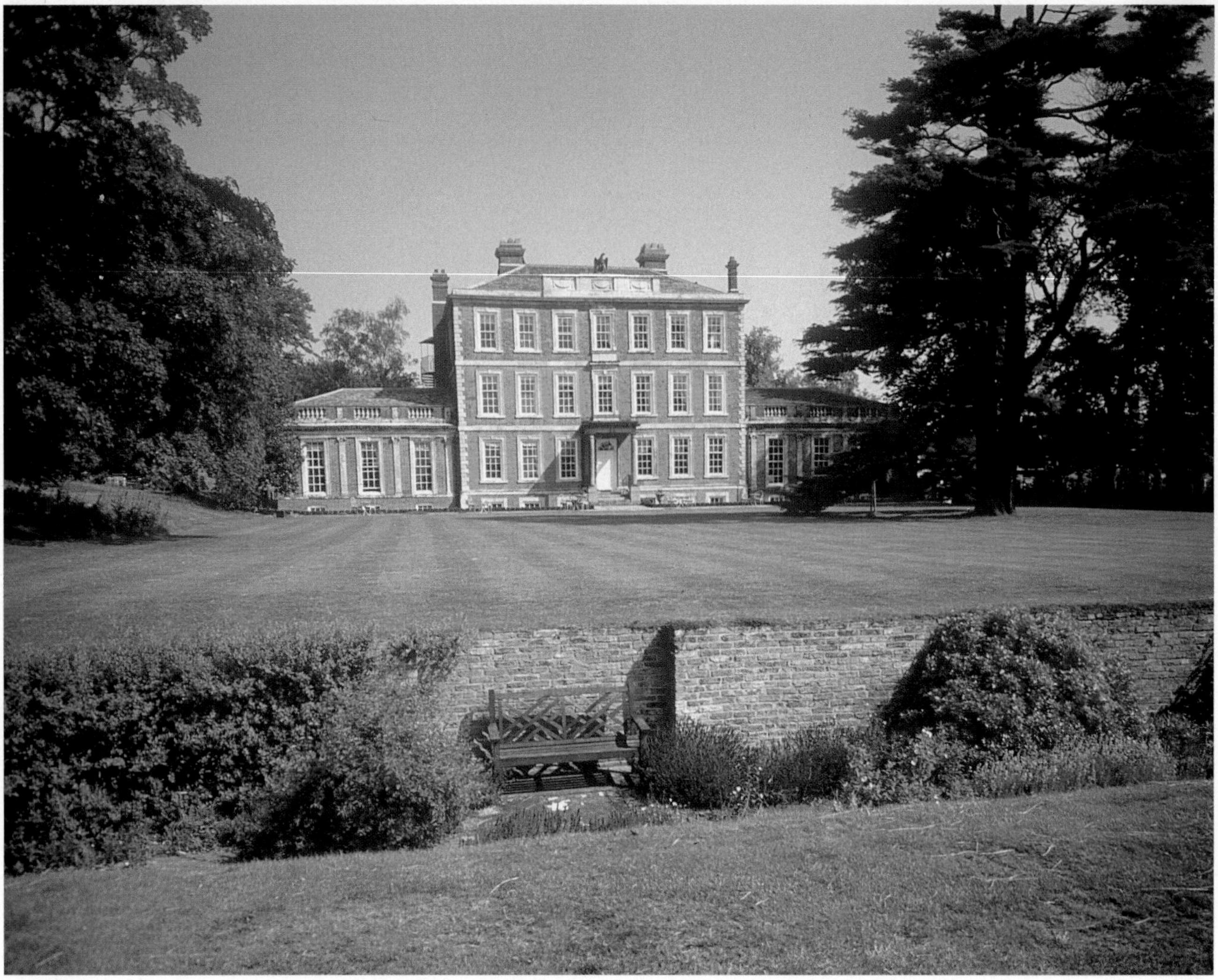

# MIDDLETHORPE HALL

**BISHOPTHORPE ROAD, YORK YO2 1QB**
**TEL: 01904 641241 FAX: 01904 620176**

Middlethorpe Hall is a delightful William III house, built in 1699 for Thomas Barlow, a wealthy merchant, and it was for a time the home of Lady Mary Wortley Montagu, the 18th-century writer of letters. The house has been immaculately restored by Historic House Hotels who have decorated and furnished it in its original elegance and style. There are beautifully designed bedrooms and suites in the main house and in the adjacent classical courtyard. The restaurant offers the best in contemporary English cooking which has 3 rosettes from the AA. Middlethorpe stands in 26 acres of parkland where guests can wander and enjoy the walled garden, the white garden, the lake and the original ha ha's. The hotel overlooks York Racecourse – known as the 'Ascot of the North' – and the medieval city of York with its fascinating museums, restored streets and world-famous Minster is only 2 miles away. From Middlethorpe you can visit Yorkshire's famous country houses, like Castle Howard, Beningbrough and Harewood, the ruined Abbeys of Fountains and Rievaulx and explore the magnificent Yorkshire Moors. Helmsley, Whitby and Scarborough are nearby. **Directions:** Take A64 (T) off A1 (T) near Tadcaster, follow signs to York West, then smaller signs to Bishopthorpe. Price guide: Single £95–£110; double/twin £131–£199; suite from £165–£215.

For hotel location, see maps on pages 490-496

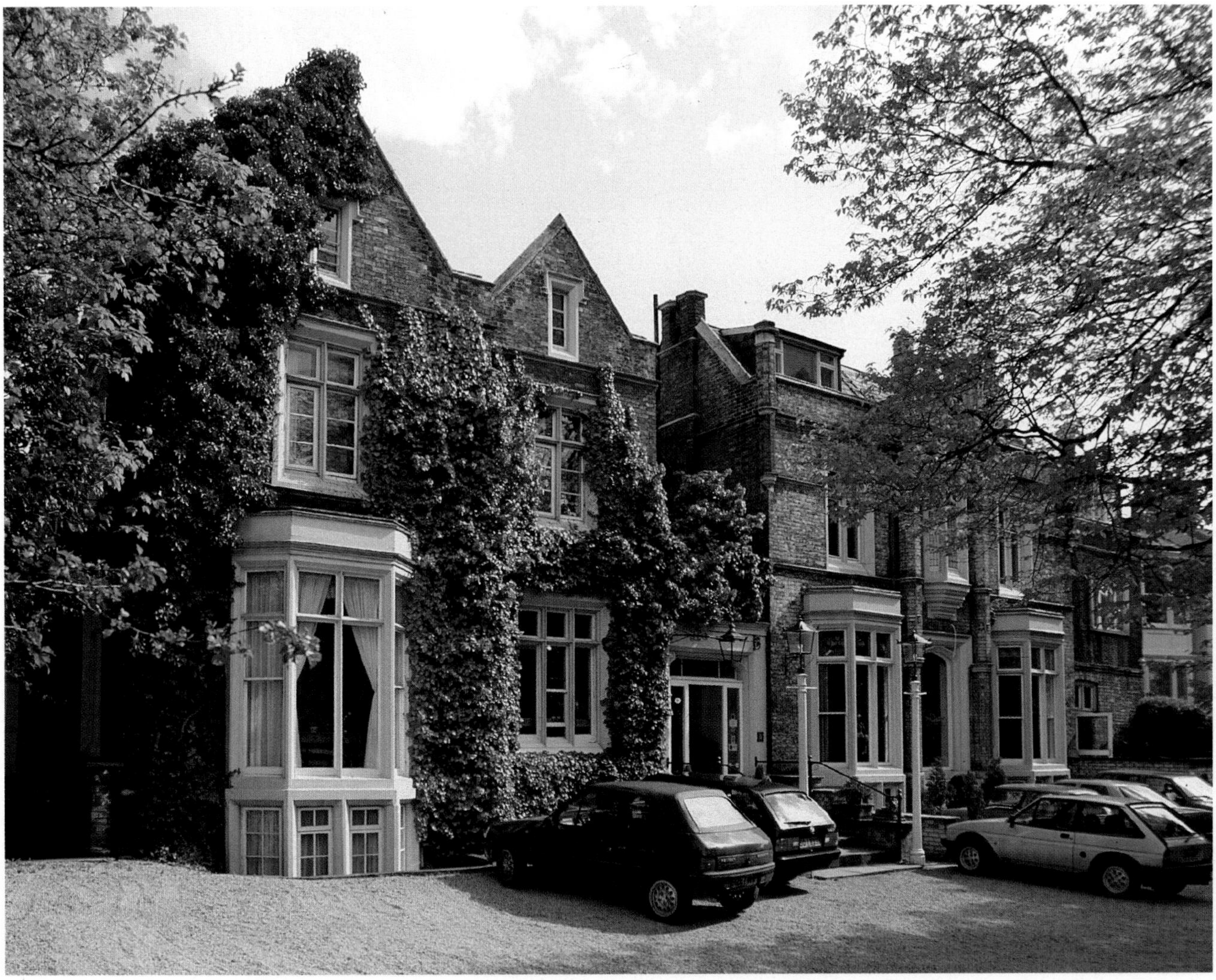

# MOUNT ROYALE HOTEL

**THE MOUNT, YORK, NORTH YORKSHIRE YO2 2DA**
**TEL: 01904 628856 FAX: 01904 611171**

Two elegant William IV houses have been restored to their former glory to create the Mount Royale Hotel, which is personally run by the Oxtoby family. Comfortable bedrooms are furnished with imagination, all in an individual style. Each of the garden rooms opens onto the garden and has its own verandah. Downstairs, the public rooms are filled with interesting items of antique furniture, *objets d'art* and gilt-framed paintings. To the rear of the building, overlooking the gardens, is the restaurant, where guests can enjoy the best of traditional English cooking and French cuisine. Amenities include a snooker room with a full-sized table, steam room, sauna, solarium and Phytomer treatment centre. With a delightful English garden and heated outdoor pool, the one acre grounds are a peaceful haven just minutes from York's centre. York is a historic and well-preserved city, famous for its Minster and medieval streets. Also within walking distance is York racecourse, where the flat-racing season runs from May to October. Lovers of the great outdoors will find the Yorkshire Dales and North York Moors a 45-minute drive away. Only small dogs by arrangement. **Directions:** From A64, turn onto the A1036 signposted York. Go past racecourse; hotel is on right before traffic lights. Price guide: Single £70–£90; double/twin £90–£120; suites £120.

For hotel location, see maps on pages 490-496

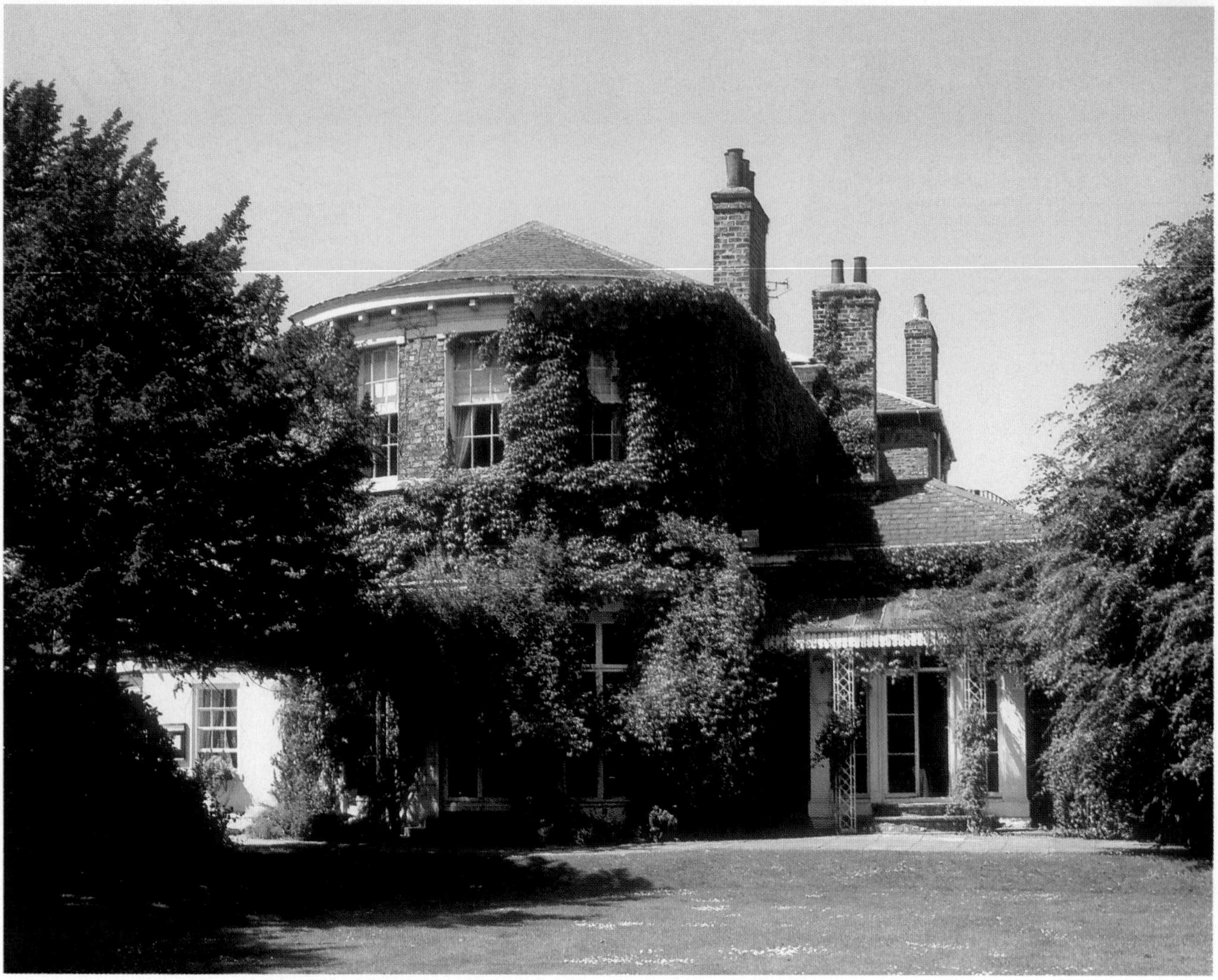

# YORK PAVILION HOTEL

**45 MAIN STREET, FULFORD, YORK, NORTH YORKSHIRE YO1 4PJ**
**TEL: 01904 622099 FAX: 01904 626939**

Originally a Georgian farm house, the York Pavilion has been extended and converted into a gracious and charming country house hotel. Open fireplaces, deep armchairs and sofas invite visitors to relax. Much of the ground floor is flagged in York Stone. The 34 bedrooms are individually styled and combine traditional furnishings with modern comfort. Each room has a private bathroom, writing desk, satellite television with teletext, radio, direct-dial telephone, hairdryer and tea and coffee making facilities. Some have four-poster beds. The attractive restaurant overlooks mature gardens and chef David Spencer has gained an enviable reputation for fine cuisine. His weekly changing House menus are complemented with an extensive selection of wines. There are conference facilities for up to 150 delegates. A large marquee is available for additional conference use or for wedding or private functions. York Pavilion is 2 miles from the city centre with its many attractions. Fulford championship golf course and York racecourse are a five minute drive away. Shooting, fishing and riding can be arranged. Directions: From the A1 follow A64 outer ring road and turn onto A39 at the York/Selby junction. The hotel is 1/4 mile on the right heading towards York. Price guide: Single £84-£98; double/twin £106-£126. Special breaks available.

For hotel location, see maps on pages 490-496

# *Johansens Recommended Hotels in* Wales

*Magnificent scenery, a rich variety of natural, cultural and modern leisure attractions, and the very best accommodation awaits the Johansens visitor to Wales.*

Wales, like Caesar's Gaul, can be divided into three parts – South Wales, Mid Wales and North Wales. These parts are determined by physical geography, mountain groups which break up the country east-west and are fissured by narrow valleys. These lock a large part of the population into small settlements – not dissimilar from those others built around markets and staging posts along the drovers routes – fostering a strong sense of community. The Celtic folk that the Romans encountered were a civilised and artistic people whose sense of design and skills in oratory were greatly admired. These Celtic origins are still apparent today in the language that is spoken by 250,000 – understood by many more – and to be seen everywhere in Wales.

South Wales' industrial past is now enshrined in museums – like Big Pit, the Rhondda Heritage Park and the Industrial and Maritime Museum in Cardiff Bay. For the industrial valleys have been greened again and now house commuter villages for people who work in the new high-tech and service industries along the M4 and the Heads of the Valleys Roads. The old ports that declined with coal and steel are being revived as marinas, with an imaginative mix of commercial and social development.

Nowhere is this more so than in Cardiff Bay, the former dockland of the capital city. Here a modern maritime city is being catered to compare with any in the world – the centre piece of which is a barrage from Queen Alexandra Dock to Penarth. But the city already has so much to commend it – more parkland per head of population than any other city in the UK and a graceful civic centre modelled on Lutyens' plans for New Delhi.

Swansea is a modern city which over the last 25 years has regenerated a lunar landscape left by 200 years of metal processing in the Lower Swansea Valley into a great green lung in which are set a mixture of commercial and leisure developments. It has also created an attractive marina from its disused dockland. And on its western door-step it has an Area of Outstanding Natural Beauty, the Gower Peninsula.

Carmarthen and Pembrokeshire have lovely beaches, cosy coves, lush pastures and plump hills into which are set golf courses to please the eye and to challenge the handicap. The area boasts fantastic fishing, wonderful walks and watersports galore – and two fantastic parks at Pembrey and Oakwood offering a wide range of attractions and amusements.

Mid Wales is a marvellous land beyond those blue remembered hills – a rolling, round green country with a silver filigree of rivers and lakes. Buttressed to the north by Cader Idris and to the south by the Brecon Beacons, this lovely hilly region is threaded by rivers and streams and old drovers roads that simply invite exploration – whether on foot, horseback or mountain bike. The land looks and leans towards the west, to the 75 miles long crescent of Cardigan Bay with its magnificent Heritage Coast studded with small ports.

North Wales has mountains offering bracing walks or pre-Everest training, a coast that holds charms for the sailor, the water-sports enthusiast or the sunbather. It has rivers, lakes and forest in which walkers, anglers, mountain-bikers and wild water canoeists can lose themselves and each other. It has castles galore – fine examples built by Welsh lords and by Edward I.

But Wales' greatest asset is its people and the welcome they give the friendly visitor – Croeso I Cymru, Welcome to Wales.

For more information about Wales, please contact:–

**Wales Tourist Board**
**Brunel House**
**2 Fitzalan Road**
**Cardiff**
**Wales CF2 1UY**
**Tel: 01222 475226**

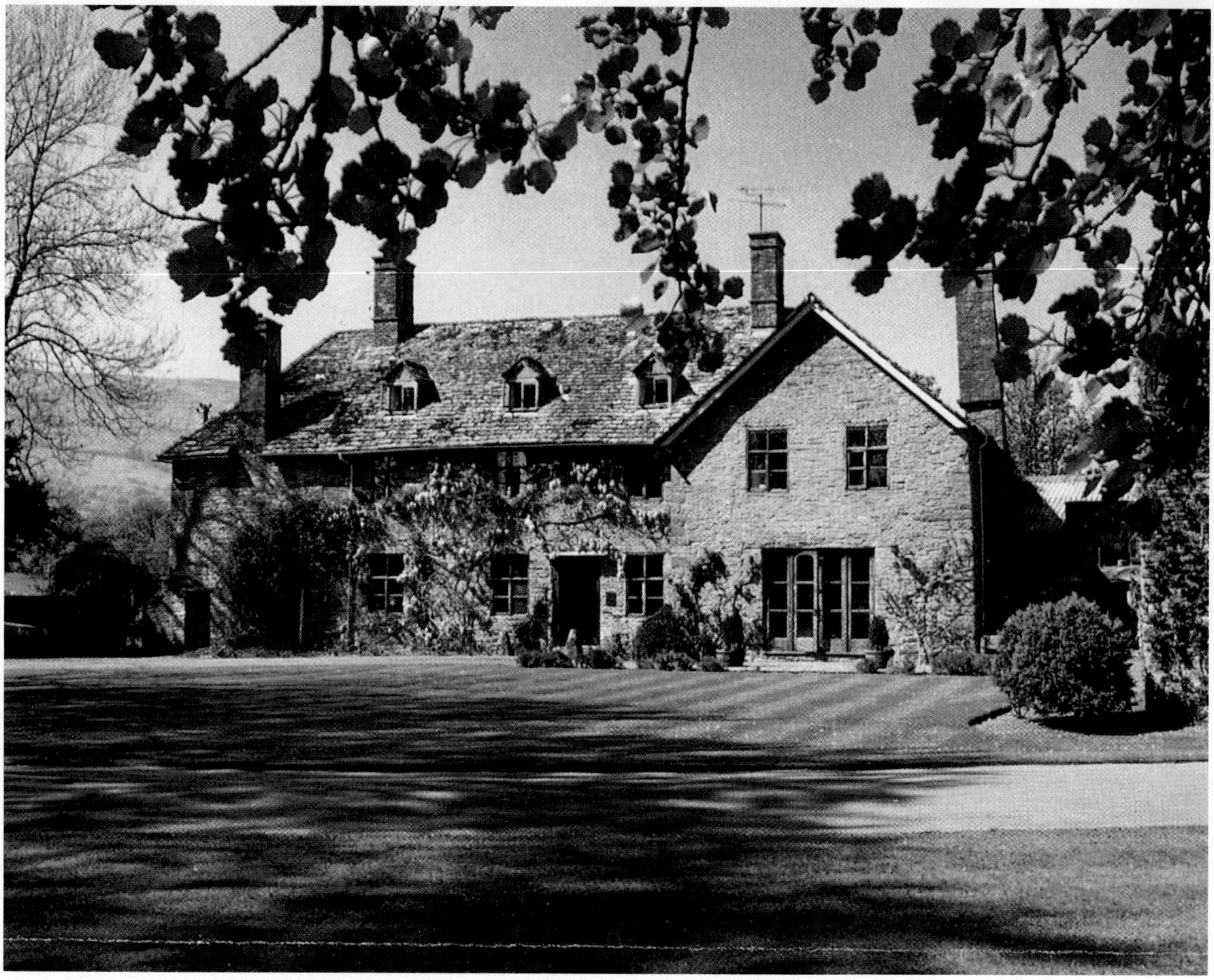

# ALLT-YR-YNYS HOTEL

**WALTERSTONE, HEREFORDSHIRE HR2 0DU**
**TEL: 01873 890307 FAX: 01873 890539**

Allt-yr-Ynys straddles the border that runs between England and Wales – with rural Herefordshire on one side and the Black Mountains on the other. The original manor house on this site belonged to the estate of Robert Cecil, a Knight of the Court during the reign of King Henry II; however, the buildings that comprise today's hotel date from 1550. Many of the authentic features have been preserved, typically the moulded ceilings, oak panelling and massive oak beams. The bedrooms, some of which are situated in the converted outbuildings, have been beautifully appointed to complement their period character. Delicious British cooking features on the menu, and the chef can also prepare 'special dishes for special occasions' to cater for private functions of up to 100 people. In the bar, adjacent to the Jacuzzi and indoor heated pool, there is an ancient, horse-powered cider press. An undercover clay pigeon range is in the grounds, with all equipment – shotguns, cartridges and tuition. There are four golf courses within the vicinity. **Directions:** Midway between Abergavenny and Hereford, turn off A465 by Pandy Inn. Turn right at Green Barn crossroads as signposted to Walterstone. Price guide: Single £60; double/twin £75 –£95.

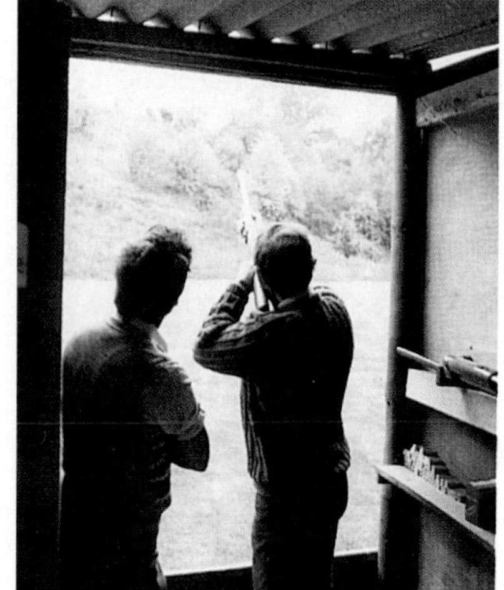

For hotel location, see maps on pages 490-496

# LLANSANTFFRAED COURT HOTEL

LLANVIHANGEL GOBION, ABERGAVENNY, GWENT NP7 9PA
TEL: 01873 840678 FAX: 01873 840674

Llansantffraed Court is a perfect retreat from the fast pace of modern life. This elegant Georgian-style country house hotel, part of which dates back to the 14th century, is set in spacious grounds on the edge of the Brecon Beacons and the Wye Valley. Guests are welcomed with warmth and provided with the highest level of personal, yet unobtrusive service. Most of the tastefully decorated and luxuriously furnished bedrooms offer views over the hotel's garden. While one has a four poster bed, others feature oak beams and dormer windows. An excellent reputation is enjoyed by the restaurant, which offers menus reflecting the changing seasons and the availability of fresh local produce. Exquisite cuisine is complemented by a fine wine list. Afternoon tea can be taken in the lounge, with guests warming themselves in front of the blazing log fire during the cooler months and savouring the views of the South Wales countryside. A range of excellent facilities is available for functions, celebrations and meetings. Llansantffraed Court is an ideal base for exploring the diverse history and beauty of this area and there are plenty of opportunities to take advantage of energetic or relaxing pursuits, including, golf, trekking, walking, and salmon and trout fishing. **Directions:** Off the old A40 Abergavenny to Raglan road. Price guide: Single £68–£80; double/twin £85–£95; suites £155.

21 rms MasterCard VISA AMERICAN EXPRESS M 120

For hotel location, see maps on pages 490-496

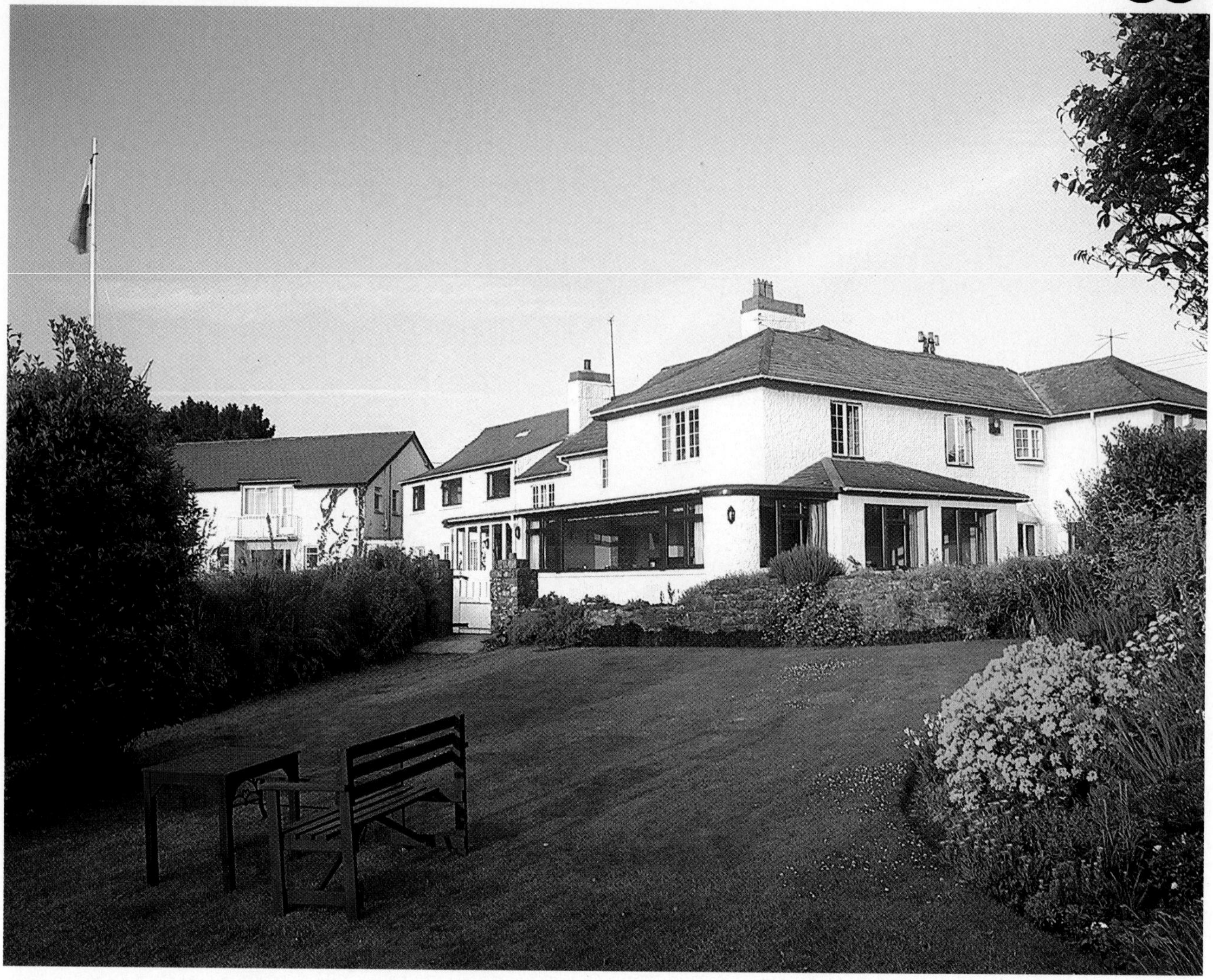

# PORTH TOCYN COUNTRY HOUSE HOTEL

**ABERSOCH, PWLLHELI, GWYNEDD LL53 7BU**
**TEL: 01758 713303 FAX: 01758 713538**

This is a rare country house seaside hotel – family owned for three generations, the first of whom had the inspiration to transform a row of miners' cottages into an attractive low white building, surrounded by enchanting gardens, with glorious views over Cardigan Bay and Snowdonia. The Fletcher-Brewer family has created a unique ambience that appeals to young and old alike. Children are welcome – the younger ones have their own sitting room and high tea menu. Nonetheless, Porth Tocyn's charm is appreciated by older guests, with its Welsh antiques,and delightful, comfortable sitting rooms. Most of the pretty bedrooms have sea views, some are family orientated, and three on the ground floor are ideal for those with mobility problems. All have en suite bathrooms. Enjoy cocktails in the intimate bar, anticipating a fabulous meal, for dining at Porth Tocyn is a memorable experience every day of the week (the menu changes continually). Scrumptious dishes and mellow wines are served in great style on antique tables. Lunch is informal, on the terrace or by the pool. Glorious beaches, water sports, golf, tennis, riding and exploring the coast provide activities for all ages. **Directions:** The hotel is 2 miles from Abersoch on the Sarn Bach road. Watch for bi-lingual signs – Gwesty/hotel – then the hotel name. Price guide: Single £43.50; double/twin £67–£104.

For hotel location, see maps on pages 490-496

# CONRAH COUNTRY HOUSE HOTEL

RHYDGALED, CHANCERY, ABERYSTWYTH, CEREDIGION SY23 4DF
TEL: 01970 617941 FAX: 01970 624546

One of Wales' much loved country house hotels, the Conrah is tucked away at the end of a rhododendron-lined drive, only minutes from the spectacular rocky cliffs and sandy bays of the Cambrian coast. Set in 22 acres of rolling grounds, the Conrah's magnificent position gives views as far north as the Cader Idris mountain range. Afternoon tea and Welsh cakes or pre-dinner drinks can be taken at leisure in the quiet writing room or one of the comfortable lounges, where antiques and fresh flowers add to the relaxed country style. The acclaimed restaurant uses fresh local produce, together with herbs and vegetables from the Conrah kitchen garden, to provide the best of both classical and modern dishes. The hotel is owned and run by the Heading family who extend a warm invitation to guests to come for a real 'taste of Wales', combined with old-fashioned, high standards of service. For recreation, guests may enjoy a game of table-tennis in the summer house, croquet on the lawn or a walk around the landscaped gardens. The heated swimming pool and sauna are open all year round. Golf, Pony-trekking and sea fishing are all available locally, while the university town of Aberystwyth is only 3 miles away. Closed Christmas. **Directions:** The Conrah lies 3 miles south of Aberystwyth on the A487. Price guide: Single £61–£88; double/twin £88–£110.

20 rms MasterCard VISA AMERICAN EXPRESS M 60 5

For hotel location, see maps on pages 490-496

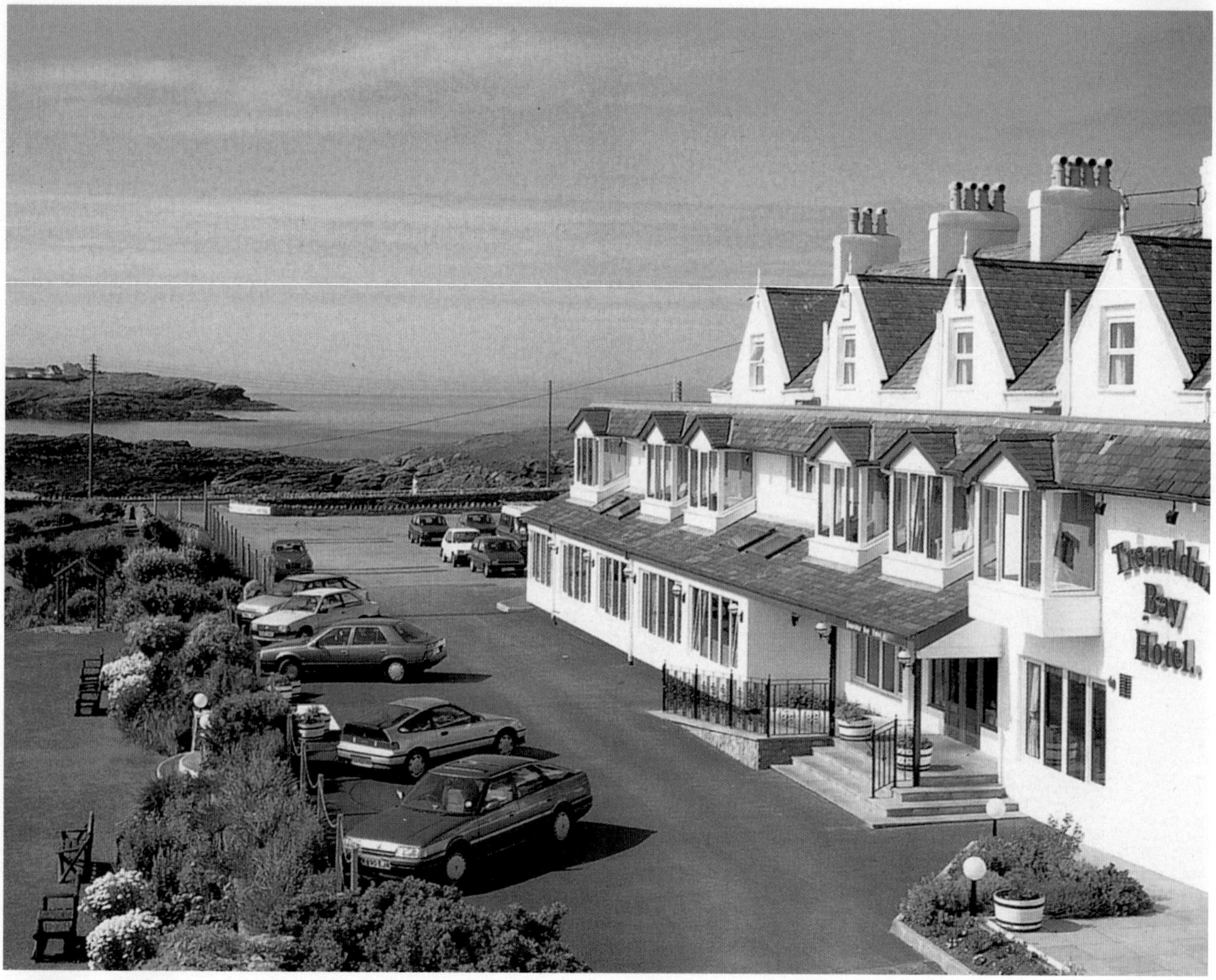

# TREARDDUR BAY HOTEL

LON ISALLT, TREARDDUR BAY, NR HOLYHEAD, ANGLESEY LL65 2UN
TEL: 01407 860301 FAX: 01407 861181

This seaside hotel enjoys a magnificent location on the Anglesey coast, overlooking Trearddur Bay and close to a medieval chapel dedicated to the nun St Brigid. An extensive refurbishment programme in recent years has given the hotel a completely new look. Many of the spacious bedrooms, all of which are en suite, have panoramic views over the bay. All are furnished to a high standard. There are also nine studio suites, including one with four-poster bed. The comfortable lounge is the perfect place to relax and read the papers over morning coffee or afternoon tea. Before dinner, enjoy an apéritif in one of the hotel bars. Superb views apart, the hotel restaurant enjoys a reputation for excellent food – including locally caught fish and seafood – complemented by fine wines. Table d'hôte and à la carte menus offer a good choice of dishes. For those who find the Irish Sea too bracing, the hotel has an indoor pool. The beach is just a short walk away and there is an 18-hole golf course nearby. Anglesey is a haven for watersports enthusiasts and birdwatchers. Places of interest include Beaumaris Castle and the Celtic burial mound at Bryn Celli Ddu. Snowdonia is a little further afield. **Directions:** From Bangor, take A5 to Valley crossroads. Turn left onto B4545 for 3 miles, then turn left at garage. Hotel is 350 yards on right. Price guide: Single £70; double/twin £100–£110; studio suite £120–£140.

For hotel location, see maps on pages 490-496

# PALÉ HALL

**PALÉ, LLANDDERFEL, BALA, GWYNEDD LL23 7PS**
**TEL: 01678 530285 FAX: 01678 530220**

Palé Hall, a privately owned Victorian mansion, is nestled amongst 150 acres of parkland on the edge of the Snowdonia National Park. The house was built in 1870 for Mr Henry Robertson (a Scottish gentleman) who instructed his architects to spare no expense. Undoubtedly one of the most impressive buildings in Wales, notable guests included Queen Victoria, who described the house as enchanting and stayed. Other guests included Winston Churchill and many other famous people. The house contains stunning interiors and exquisite features of a magnificent entrance hall with its galleried staircase, plus the boudoir with its hand-painted ceiling, marble fireplaces and bar. The comfortable lounges (including a non-smoking lounge) enable quiet relaxation and contemplation. Each of the 17 suites are individually decorated and contain en suite bathrooms, TV, hospitality tray and luxury toiletries, plus a magnificent view of the surrounding scenery. The restaurant offers fine dishes and is complemented by an extensive cellar. Facilities for the pursuit of a number of outdoor activities are available; walking, riding, fishing, shooting, golf or white-water rafting. **Directions:** Palé Hall is situated off the B4401 Corwen to Bala road, four miles from Llandrillo. Price guide (including breakfast and dinner): Single £89–£130; double/twin £135–£195

For hotel location, see maps on pages 490-496

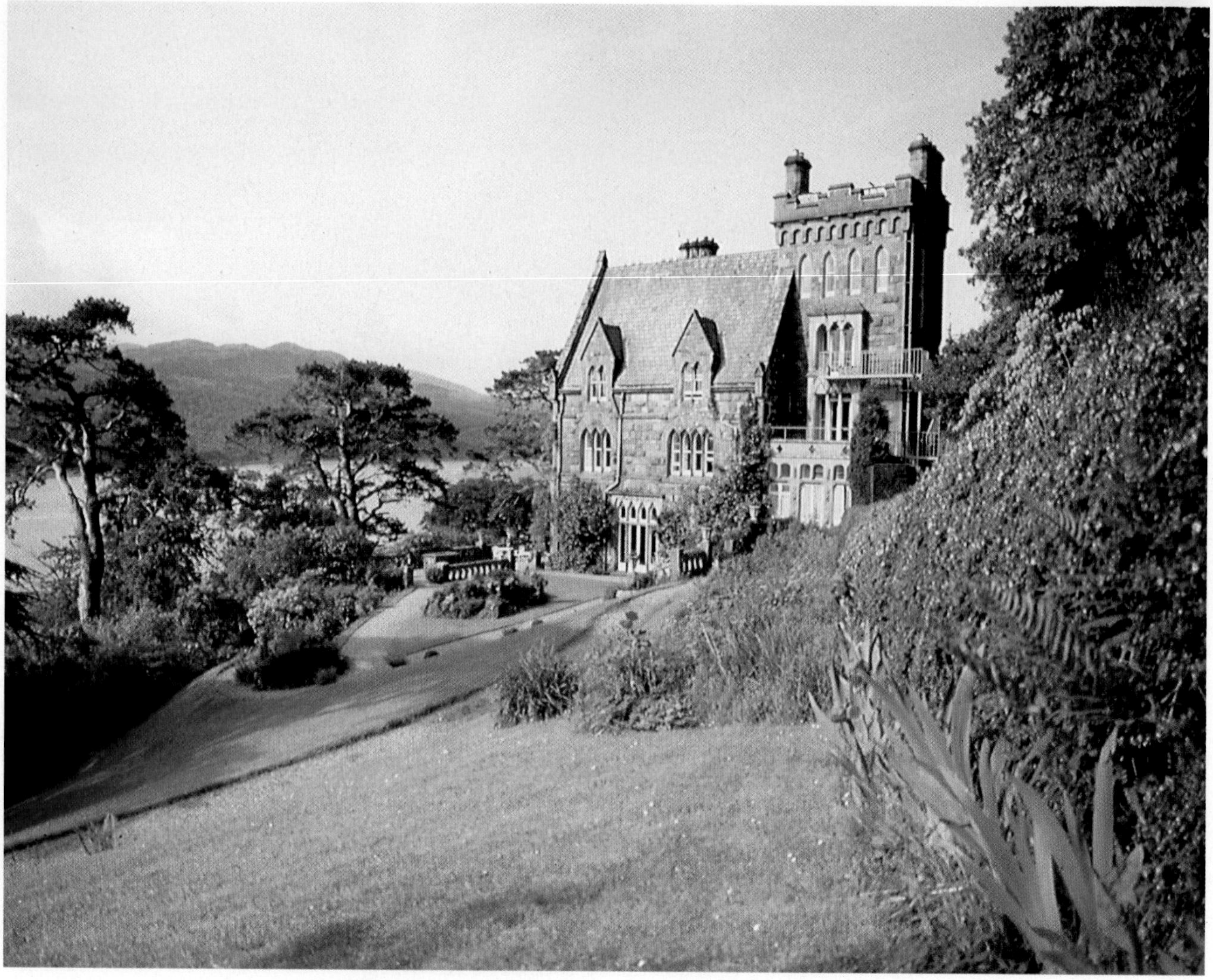

# BONTDDU HALL

**BONTDDU, NR BARMOUTH, GWYNEDD LL40 2SU**
**TEL: 01341 430661 FAX: 01341 430284**

The beautiful Southern Snowdonia National Park is the perfect setting for Bontddu Hall, a superb example of Victorian Gothic architecture. It stands high up, surrounded by extensive grounds. Graceful archways, tall windows, high beamed ceilings, handsome portraits and big fireplaces add to the elegance of the spacioous reception rooms. The Hall has a civil wedding licence. The comfortable bedrooms are named after visiting Prime Ministers of bygone times. Period furniture and Victorian-style wallpapers add to the country-house ambience (the bathrooms are modern). The Lodge houses four rooms, with balconies looking across to the mountains. Guests mingle in the panelled bar before adjourning to the Mawddach Restaurant which overlooks the Estuary. They enjoy succulent Welsh Mountain Lamb, Meironnydd Salmon, Barmouth Lobster and other local dishes – superbly cooked and presented in classic style. Connoisseurs appreciate the fine wines, ports and malts listed. Bontddu Hall is an ideal centre for exploring the region, with its lakes, mountains and beaches, old gold and silver mines and famous castles and narrow gauge railway climbing Snowdon. Water sports, tennis and golf are close by. **Directions:** The hotel is on the A496 midway between Dolgellau and Barmouth. Price guide: Single £65; double/twin £95–£120; suite £150.

20 rms

For hotel location, see maps on pages 490-496

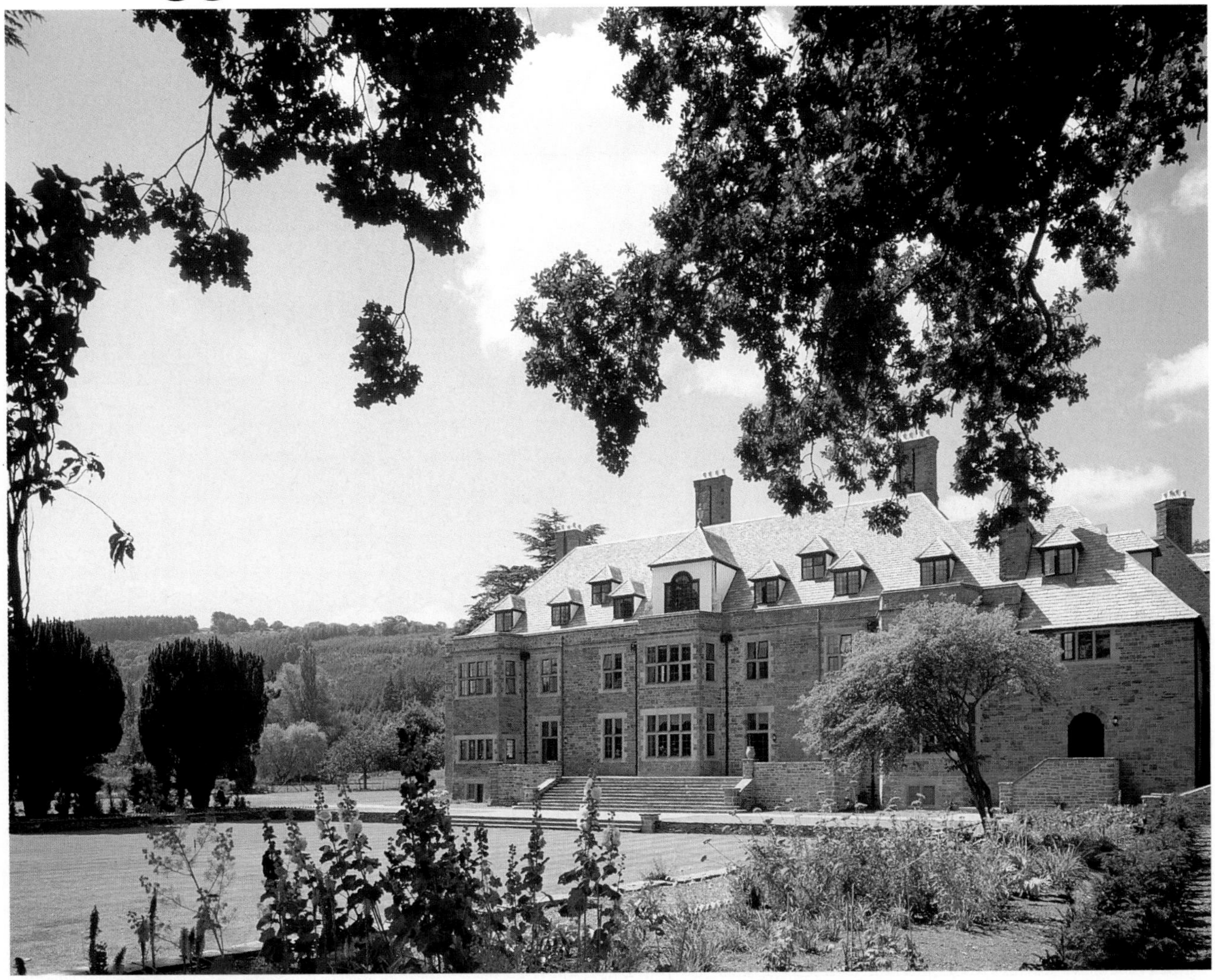

# LLANGOED HALL

LLYSWEN, BRECON, POWYS, WALES LD3 0YP
TEL: 01874 754525 FAX: 01874 754545

The history of Llangoed Hall dates back to 560 AD when it is thought to have been the site of the first Welsh Parliament. Inspired by this legend, the architect Sir Clough Williams-Ellis, transformed the Jacobean mansion he found here in 1914 into an Edwardian country house. Situated deep in a valley of the River Wye, surrounded by a walled garden, the hotel commands magnificent views of the Black Mountains and Brecon Beacons beyond. The rooms are warm and welcoming, furnished with antiques and oriental rugs and, on the walls, an outstanding collection of paintings acquired by the owner, Sir Bernard Ashley. Head Chef Ben Davies makes eating at Llangoed one of the principal reasons for going there. Classic but light, his Michelin starred menus represent the very best of modern cuisine, complemented by a cellar of more than 300 wines. Tennis and croquet are available on site, and nearby there is golf, fishing, riding, shooting, and some of the best mountain walking and gliding in Britain. For expeditions, there are the Wye Valley, Hay-on-Wye and its bookshops, the border castles, Hereford and Leominster. Children over 8 are welcome. The hotel is a member of Welsh Rarebits and Small Luxury Hotels of the World. **Directions:** The hotel is 9 miles west of Hay, 11 miles north of Brecon on the A470. Price guide: Single £100; double/twin £165–£215; suite £215–£315.

23 rms                

For hotel location, see maps on pages 490-496

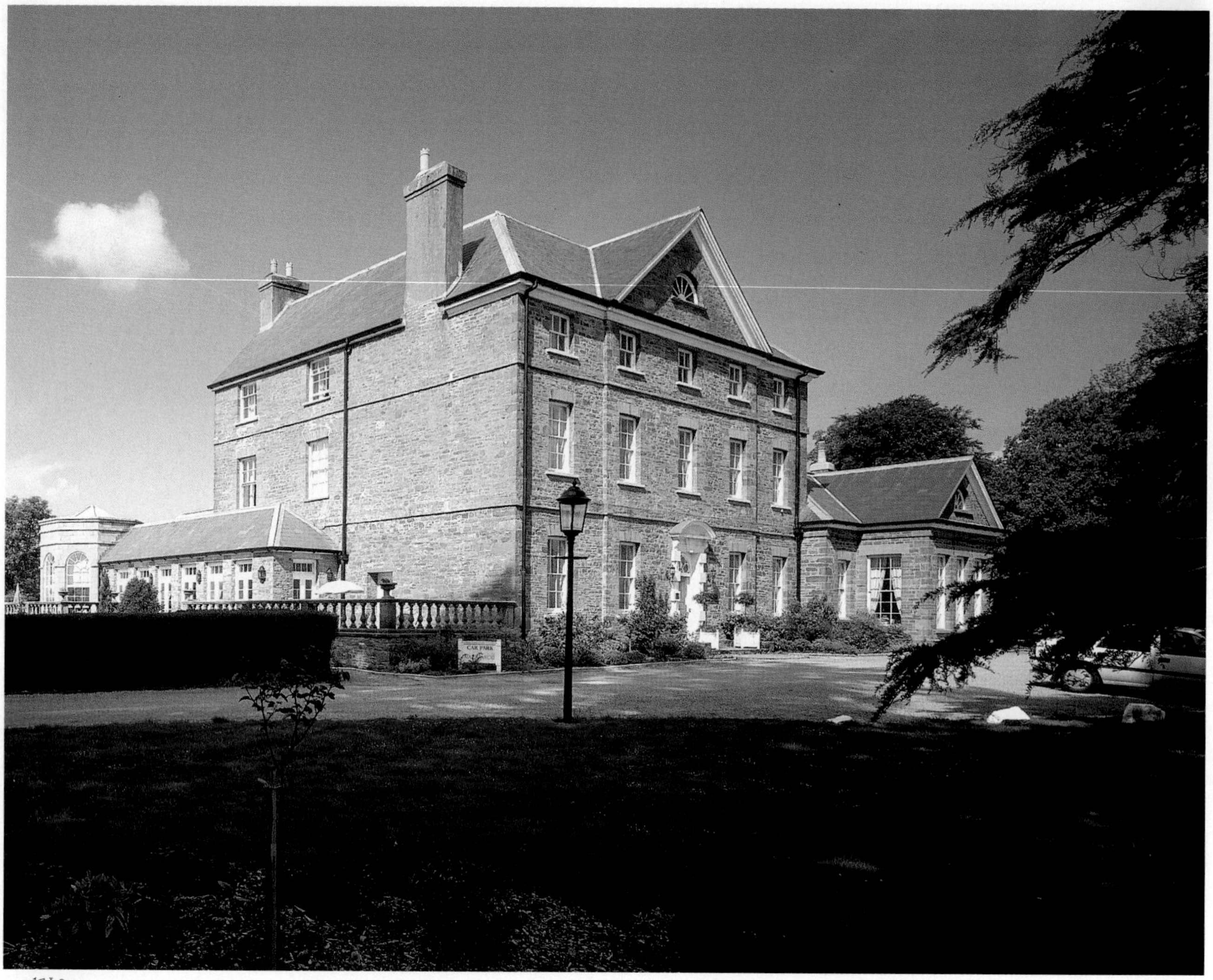

# PETERSTONE COURT

LLANHAMLACH, BRECON, POWYS LD3 7YB
TEL: 01874 665387 FAX: 01874 665376

Set in a tiny village on the eastern edge of the mysterious Brecon Beacons National Park, Peterstone is a carefully restored Georgian manor, swathed in history which can be traced back to the time of William the Conqueror. It was voted the best new hotel in Wales by the AA in 1992 and amongst a string of awards the hotel has collected merits from the RAC and the Welsh Tourist Board. There are just 12 guest bedrooms at the court, eight beautifully proportioned period style rooms in the main house, and four split level rooms in the former stable that have all the things you expect to find and many you don't, such as tape players, video players and a welcoming decanter of sherry. Intimate parties and special occasions can be accommodated in one of the two small private rooms. The surrounding countryside has an abundance of walks, one of which starts at the end of the hotel drive and goes along the river and the canal back into Brecon. Alternatively, or perhaps even after all the walking, there is in the hotel basement a fully equipped health club, with gymnasium, sauna, solarium and Jacuzzi. In the grounds are an outdoor heated pool, croquet and putting. **Directions:** Peterstone Court is located in the village of Llanhamlach, on the A40, three miles east of Brecon. Price guide: Single £79.50; double/twin £95–£130. Short breaks available all year round.

For hotel location, see maps on pages 490-496

# Coed-y-Mwstwr Hotel

**COYCHURCH, NEAR BRIDGEND, MID GLAMORGAN CF35 6AF**
**TEL: 01656 860621 FAX: 01656 863122**

Coed-y-Mwstwr is a country mansion of Victorian origin set in 17 acres of mature woodland, which is also home to an abundance of wildlife – kestrels, woodpeckers and buzzards all nest here, with foxes, rabbits and badgers never far away. Much thought has gone into ensuring that the décor and furnishings are in keeping with the style of the house. High ceilings, chandeliers and large fireplaces feature in the elegant public rooms. The 23 luxurious bedrooms all have en suite facilities and wonderful views. The elegant oak-panelled restaurant enjoys a good reputation locally and offers a blend of traditional and modern cuisine, with both table d'hôte and à la carte menus with an AA Rosette. The wine list has more than 80 wines. Private functions for up to 130 people may be held in the Hendre Suite. In addition, there are two private dining rooms. A heated outdoor swimming pool and all-weather tennis court are available for guests' use. For golfers, Royal Porthcawl and Southerndown courses are 10 minutes' drive from the hotel. The beautiful Gower and Pembrokeshire coastline and Brecon Beacons National Park are within easy reach. Open all year. **Directions:** Leave M4 at junction 35, take A473 towards Bridgend for 1 mile, turn right into Coychurch. At filling station turn right and follow signs uphill. Price guide: Single £85; double/twin £125; suite £140.

23 rms MasterCard VISA AMERICAN EXPRESS M 140

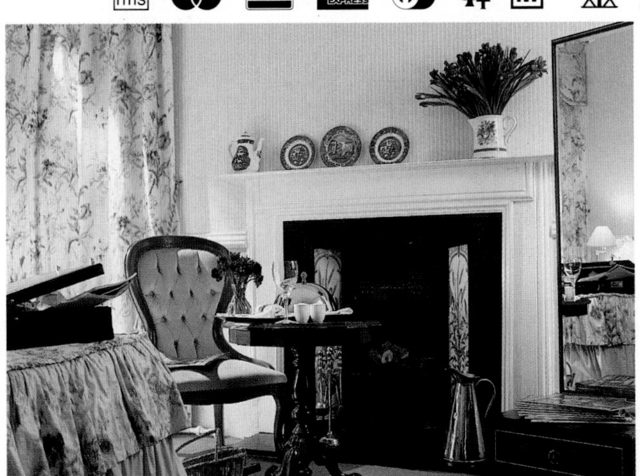

For hotel location, see maps on pages 490-496

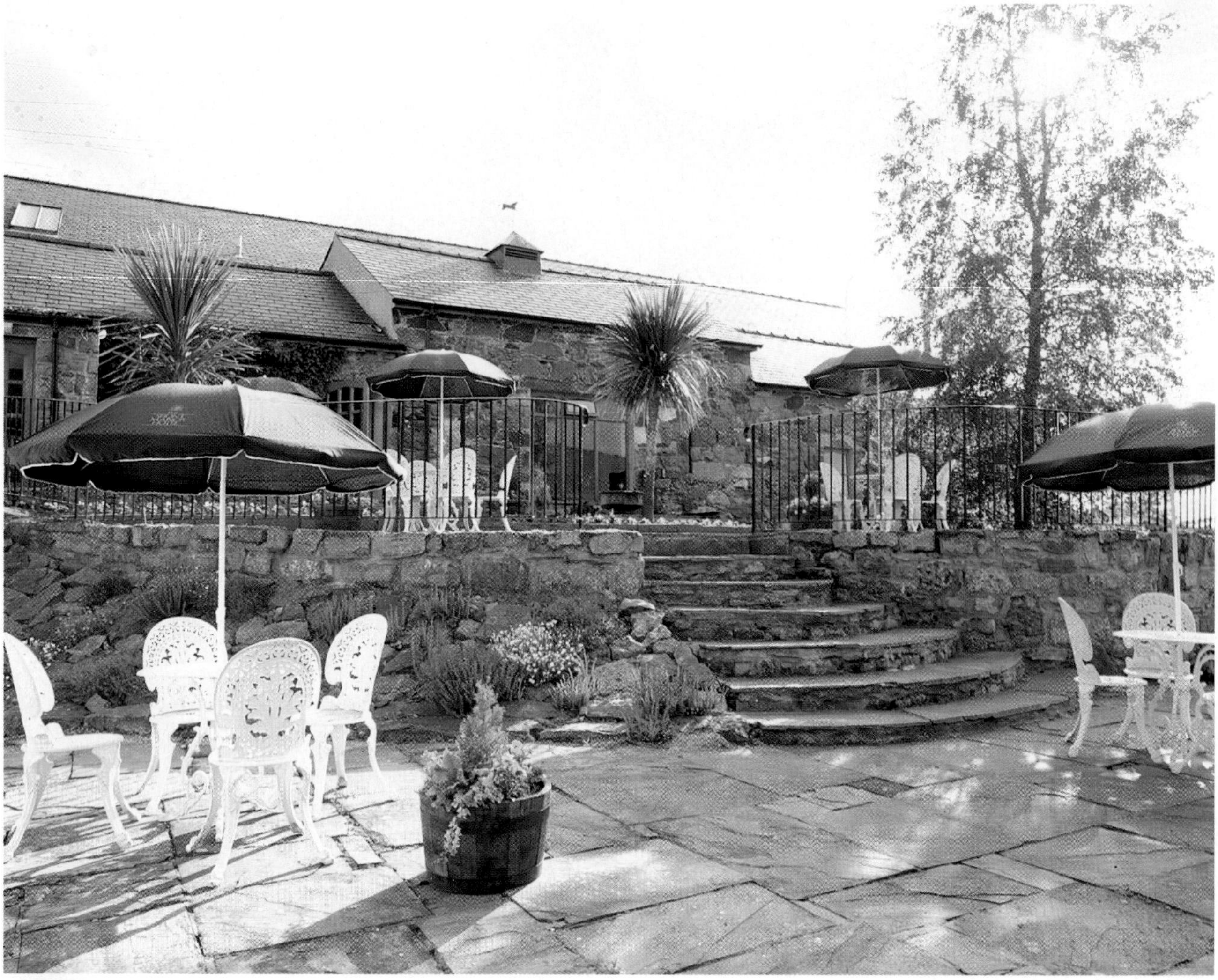

# GWESTY SEIONT MANOR HOTEL

**LLANRUG, CAERNARFON, GWYNEDD LL55 2AQ**
**TEL: 01286 673366 FAX: 01286 672840**

Set in 150 acres of parkland amid the majestic scenery of Snowdonia, Seiont Manor has been stylishly remodelled from original rustic buildings to create a unique luxury hotel offering guests every comfort. The oak-panelled bar and library, with its collection of leather-bound volumes, provide the perfect environment for relaxing with a drink before dinner. For lovers of good food, the excellent restaurant, overlooking the hotel's lake and grounds, serves classic French cuisine as well as superb local dishes, all prepared from the best ingredients. Each of the 28 bedrooms, with furnishings from around the world, is comfortable and spacious and has en suite facilities. The hotel is an ideal venue for conferences, functions, weddings and meetings of up to 100 people. A heated pool housed in the Victorian-style 'chapel' takes pride of place among the leisure facilities, which also include a sauna, solarium, multi-gym, aromatherapy and reflexology treatments. Mountain bikes and a jogging track are available for guests' use and there is fishing for salmon and trout in the river. Caernarfon golf course, with its stunning views over the Menai Straits, is nearby, as are the Snowdonia Mountain Range, Ffestiniog Mountain Railway and Caernarfon Castle. **Directions:** 3 miles from Caernarfon on the A4086. Price guide: Single £79; double/twin £125–£160.

For hotel location, see maps on pages 490-496

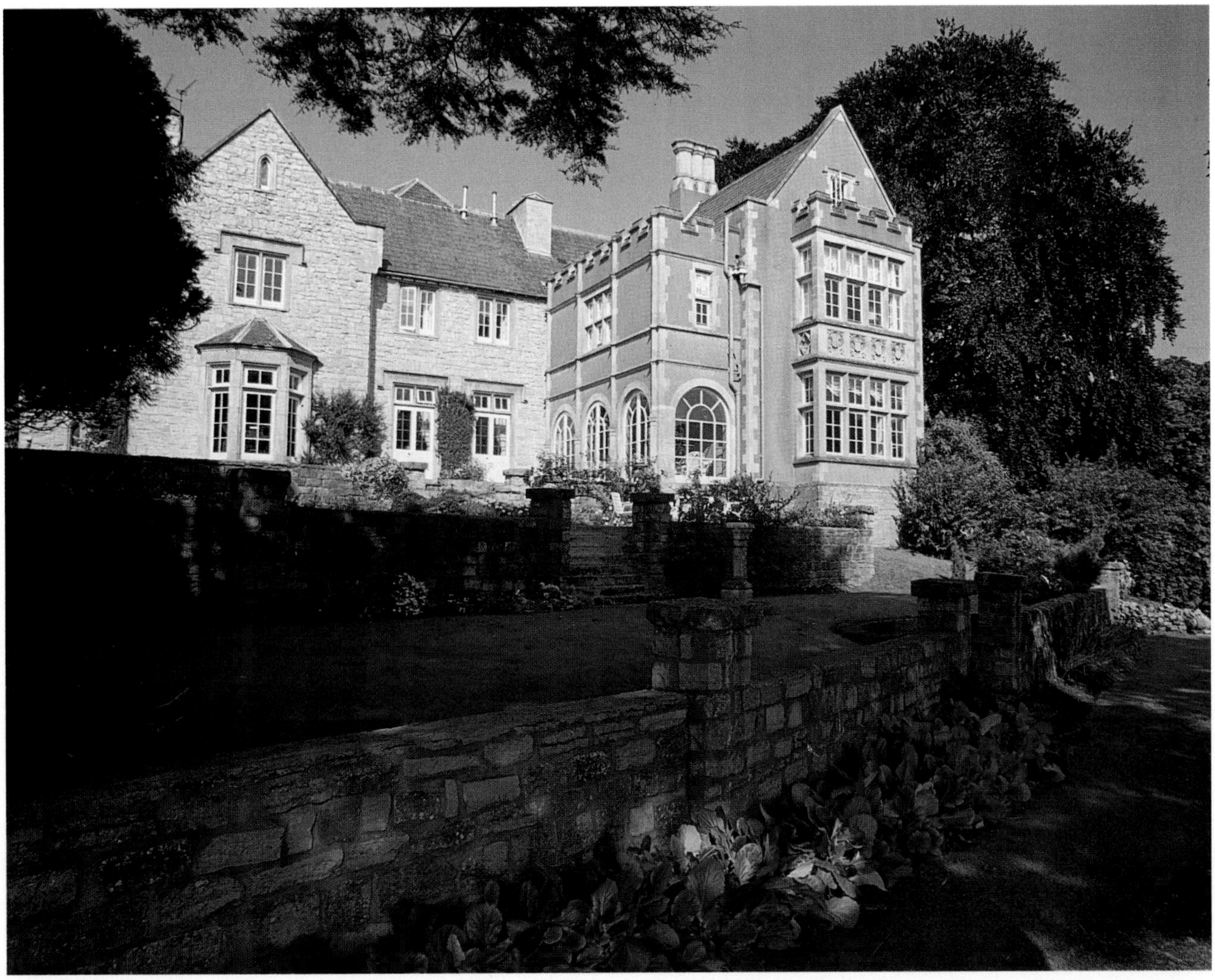

# EGERTON GREY COUNTRY HOUSE HOTEL

**PORTHKERRY, NR CARDIFF, VALE OF GLAMORGAN CF62 3BZ**
**TEL: 01446 711666 FAX: 01446 711690**
**E-MAIL:** info@egertongrey.co.uk **INTERNET:** www.egertongrey.co.uk

A distinguished former rectory dating from the early-19th century, Egerton Grey is tucked away in seven acres of gardens in a secluded, wooded valley in the Vale of Glamorgan. Visitors can enjoy glorious views towards Porthkerry Park and the sea beyond. The interior design complements the architectural features of the house. The Edwardian drawing room has intricate plaster mouldings, chandeliers, an open fireplace and oil paintings. A quiet library overlooks the garden. All of the immaculately presented bedrooms are extremely comfortable, and several have Victorian baths and brasswork. Original Cuban mahogany panelling and candle-lit tables create an air of intimacy in the main restaurant. High-quality cuisine is presented with finesse on bone china, and wine is served in Welsh Royal Crystal glasses. Riding and sailing can be arranged and there is a pitch-and-putt course a short stroll away by the sea. The Welsh Folk Museum, Castle Coch and Cardiff Castle are nearby. **Directions:** From M4 junction 33, take A4050; follow airport signs for 10 miles. Take A4226 towards Porthkerry; after 400 yards turn into lane between two thatched cottages, hotel is at end of lane. Price guide: Single £60–£95; double/twin £90–£120.

For hotel location, see maps on pages 490-496

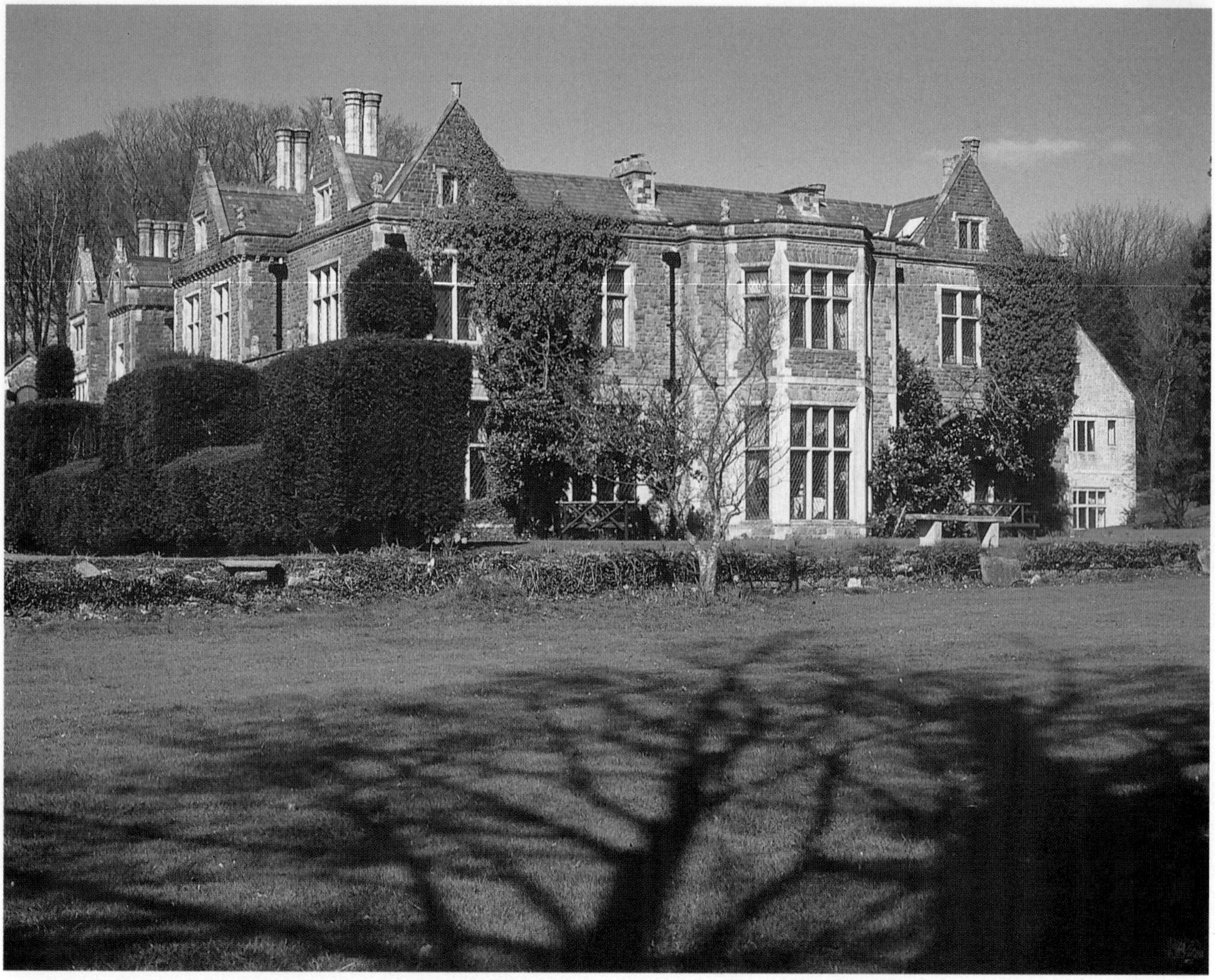

# MISKIN MANOR COUNTRY HOUSE HOTEL

**MISKIN, MID-GLAMORGAN CF72 8ND**
**TEL: 01443 224204 FAX: 01443 237606**

Although its history dates back to the 11th century, Miskin Manor first became a hotel only in 1986, following extensive restoration and refurbishment. Set amid 20 acres of undisturbed parkland, criss-crossed with streams, peace and seclusion are guaranteed. The uncommonly spacious reception rooms have fine fireplaces, panelled walls and elaborate plasterwork ceilings, all enhanced by rich drapery and comfortable furniture. All of the bedrooms have en suite bathrooms and full facilities. In the 1920s, one of the de luxe suites was occupied by the Prince of Wales (later King Edward VII), a room which is now aptly named the Prince of Wales suite. First-class Welsh cuisine is served in the AA red rosette awarded restaurant and complemented by a comprehensive wine list. Within the grounds is the popular sports and leisure club, Frederick's, which guests can use. It comprises three squash courts, badminton court, indoor heated swimming pool, gymnasium, snooker, spa, sauna, solarium, beautician, bistro and crèche. Celebrations, conferences and all functions can be catered for at Miskin Manor, with reliable, professional support assured. Corporate activites can be held on site. **Directions:** From junction 34 of the M4, towards Llantrisant. Drive is one mile on the north side of the motorway. Price guide: Single from £80; double/twin £100; suite £175.

For hotel location, see maps on pages 490-496

# SOUGHTON HALL COUNTRY HOUSE HOTEL

NORTHOP, NR MOLD, FLINTSHIRE CH7 6AB
TEL: 01352 840811 FAX: 01352 840382

Built as a Bishops Palace in 1714, Grade I Soughton Hall set in beautiful landscaped gardens amidst 150 acres of parkland is approached via a spectacular half mile avenue of limes. Beautiful antique furniture adorns a house of unique history and architecture. With just 12 authentic bedrooms and the personal welcome of the Rodenhurst family, a memorable stay is assured. The hotel is also ideal for business use with a boardroom that is second to none. 1997 featured the opening of a country inn within the old coach house and stables, a listed building of immense historical and architectural interest also. It features a beer parlour specialising in serving many real ales from local breweries and an informal wine and steak bar within the original haylofts. Special three day packages are available to include dinner in either the hotel restaurant (past awards include Welsh Restaurant of the Year) or the inn. Within the surrounding parkland is an 18-hole championship golf course. Golfing holidays are available. From the hotel, excursions can be made into North Wales and historic Chester. An exclusive, full-colour guide to selected holiday drives in the area is provided. **Directions:** From the M56 take the A55 towards North Wales, then the A5119 to Northop. Cross the traffic lights; the hall is one mile along the road on the left. Price guide: Single/double/twin £100–£150.

12 rms MasterCard VISA AMERICAN EXPRESS M 22 12

For hotel location, see maps on pages 490-496

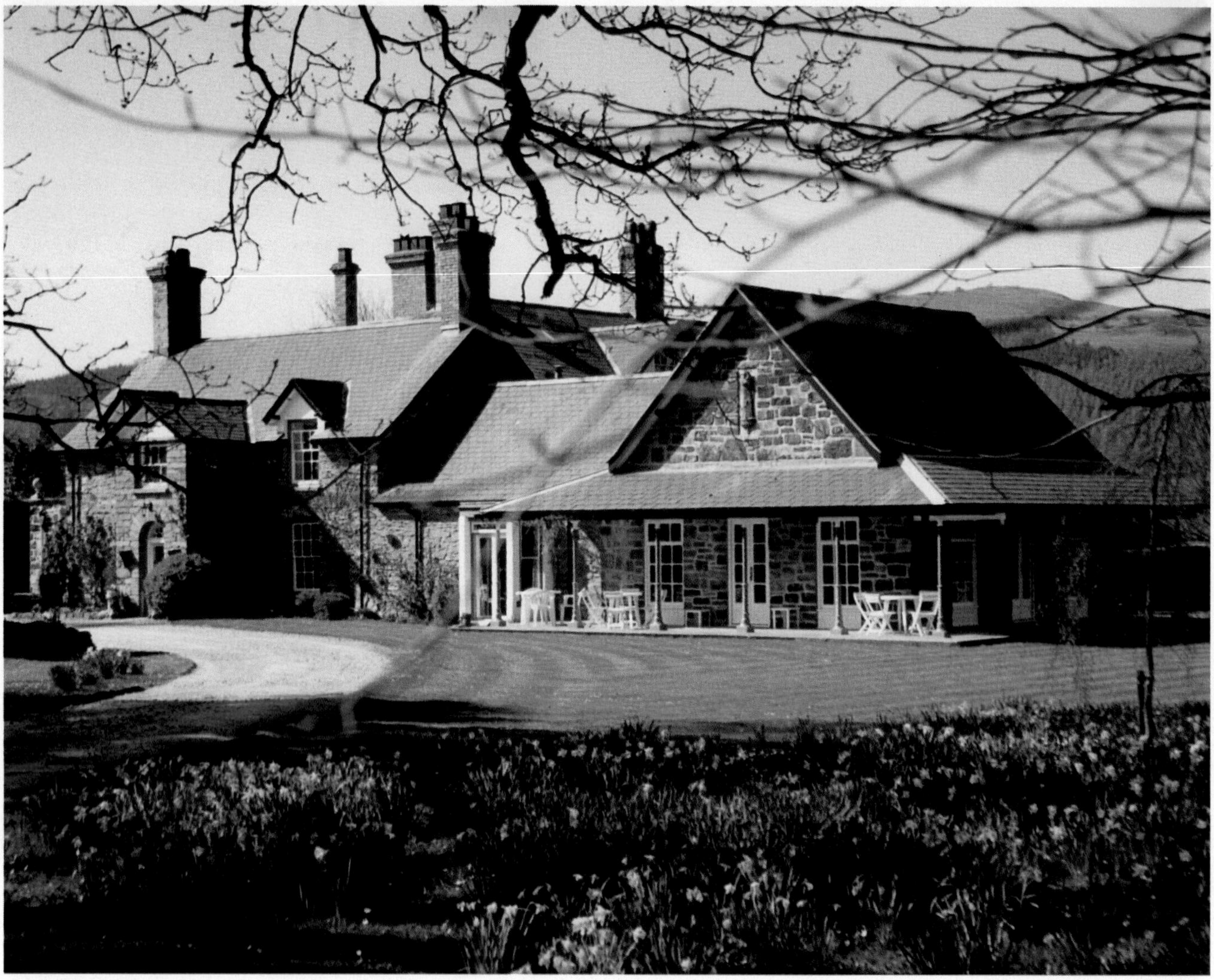

# TYDDYN LLAN COUNTRY HOUSE HOTEL

**LLANDRILLO, NR CORWEN, DENBIGHSHIRE LL21 0ST**
**TEL: 01490 440264 FAX: 01490 440414**

Tyddyn Llan is an elegant Georgian country house situated amid breathtaking scenery in the Vale of Edeyrnion. Owned and run by Peter and Bridget Kindred, the hotel is a quiet oasis in an area of outstanding natural beauty at the foot of the Berwyn Mountains. There are 10 bedrooms, all individual in style and elegantly furnished with antiques and period furniture. Each enjoys views of the gardens and the mountains beyond and has a bathroom en suite. The hotel is proud of the reputation it has established for the quality of the food served in the restaurant. Inventive and frequently changing menus feature dishes using fresh local ingredients and herbs from the kitchen garden. A carefully selected wine list complements the cuisine. In the gardens, guests may enjoy a game of croquet and tea is served on fine days. The hotel has rights to four miles of fly-fishing on the River Dee. Keen walkers can trace the ancient Roman road, Ffordd Gam Elin, which traverses the Berwyn Mountains. Here naturalists will find many different species of birds and wild flowers. Tyddyn Llan is well placed for exploring nearby Snowdonia, and the Roman city of Chester is only 35 miles away. **Directions:** Llandrillo is midway between Corwen and Bala on the B4401, four miles from the A5 at Corwen. Price guide (bed and breakfast): Single £64–£70; double/twin £98–£110.

For hotel location, see maps on pages 490-496

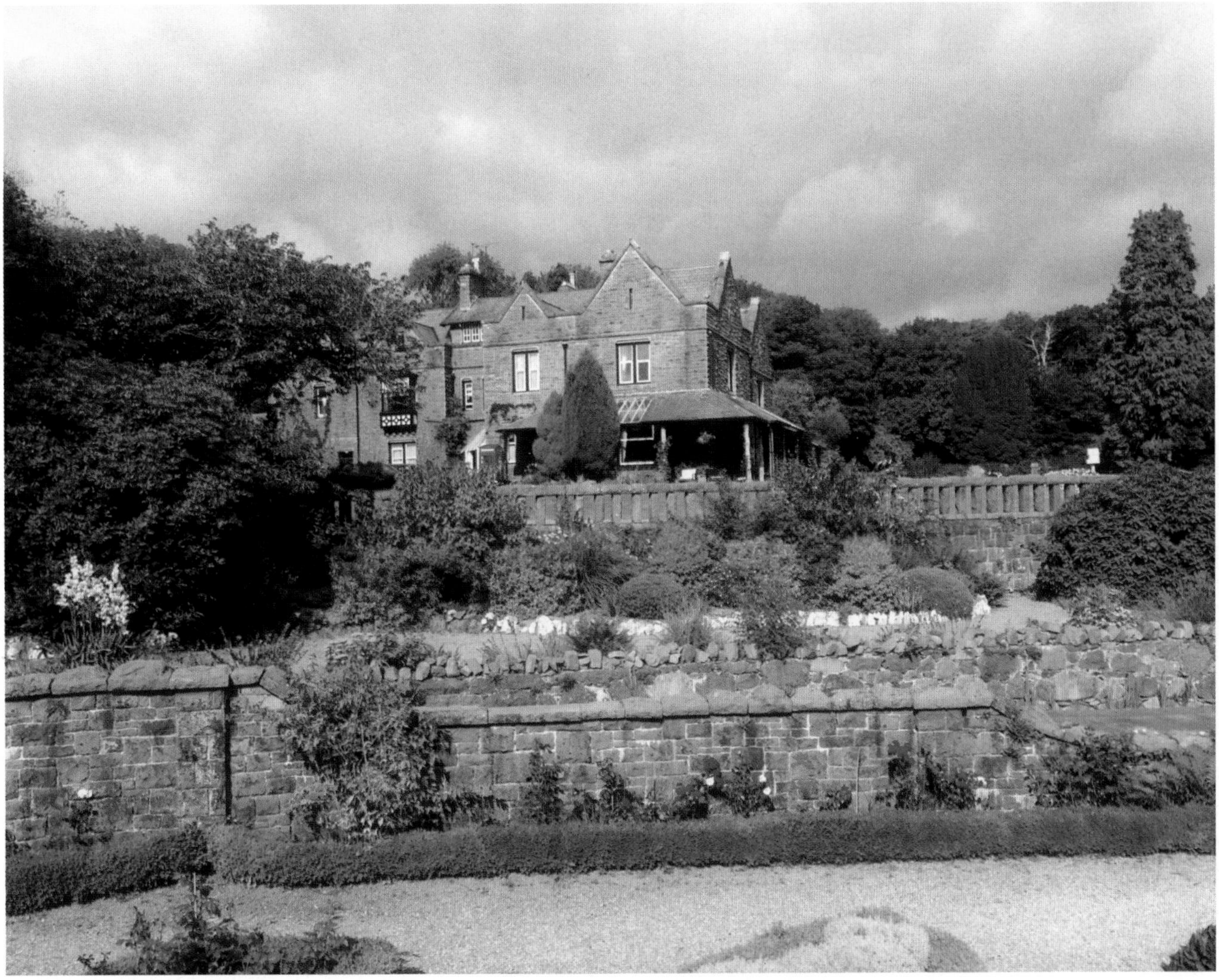

# BRON EIFION COUNTRY HOUSE HOTEL

**CRICCIETH, GWYNEDD LL52 0SA**
**TEL: 01766 522385 FAX: 01766 522003**

This magnificent baronial mansion stands within five acres of glorious gardens and woodlands, yet only minutes from the sea. It was built by the millionaire slate owner John Greaves whose master craftsmen carved the spectacular pitch and Oregon pine panelled hallway, minstrels gallery and vaulted ceiling. The Conservatory Restaurant, which overlooks the floodlit gardens serves innovative cuisine, complemented by a superb selection of wines. All 19 bedrooms are en suite and are individually decorated, offering king-sized and four-poster beds, or you could choose a standard or de luxe room. The gardens provide interesting walks, from the stone walled terraces to the secluded herb garden. Perhaps you would like to laze on the verandah overlooking the lawns which abound in a variety of wildlife. Golf, shooting, riding and fishing are all nearby. A short car drive will take you to the pretty villages of Criccieth, Porthmadog or the Italiante village of Portmeirion. The rugged beauty of the mountains of Snowdonia, together with castles, stately homes, Lloyd George's Museum and Ffestiniog Railway are all closeby. **Directions:** The hotel is on the A497 on the outskirts of Criccieth and stands at the top of a tree-lined drive, nestled in Woodland. Price guide: Single £59–£74; double/twin £88–£120. De luxe supplement £15 per room per night.

For hotel location, see maps on pages 490-496

# GLIFFAES COUNTRY HOUSE HOTEL

**CRICKHOWELL, POWYS NP8 1RH**

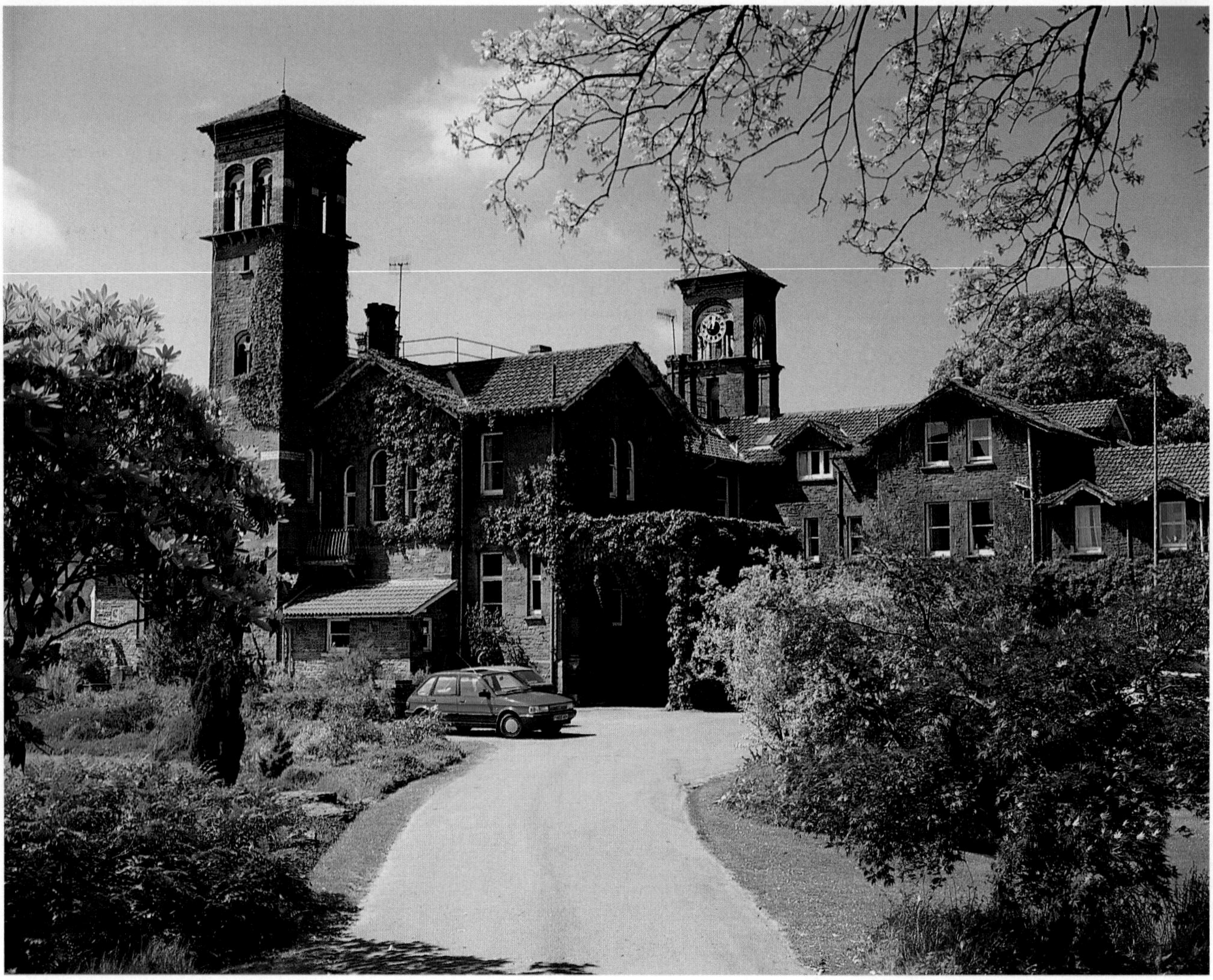

**TEL: 01874 730371 FAX: 01874 730463 FREEPHONE: 0800 146719**

Visitors may be surprised to discover a hotel featuring distinctive Italianate architecture midway between the Brecon Beacons and the Black Mountains. Gliffaes Country House Hotel is poised 150 feet above the River Usk and commands glorious views of the surroundings hills and valley. The elegantly furnished, Regency style drawing room is an ideal place to relax and leads to a large sun room and on to the terrace, from which guests may enjoy the magnificent scenery. In addition to a panelled lounge, there is a billiard room with a full-size table. An informal atmosphere prevails in the dining room, a wide choice from an imaginative menu covering the best of National dishes and Mediterranean specialities created by a talented team led by Head Chef, Mark Coulton. The Gliffaes fishery includes every type of water, from slow-flowing flats to fast-running rapids, on $2\frac{1}{2}$ miles of the River Usk renowned for its wild brown trout and salmon fishing. The 33 acre hotel grounds have rare trees and shrubs as well as lawns for putting and croquet. There are two Golf courses within reach. Riding can be arranged nearby. Now open throughout the year. **Directions:** Gliffaes is signposted from the A40, $2\frac{1}{2}$ miles west of Crickhowell. Price guide: Single £37.75–£72; double/twin £75.50–£111.50.

For hotel location, see maps on pages 490-496

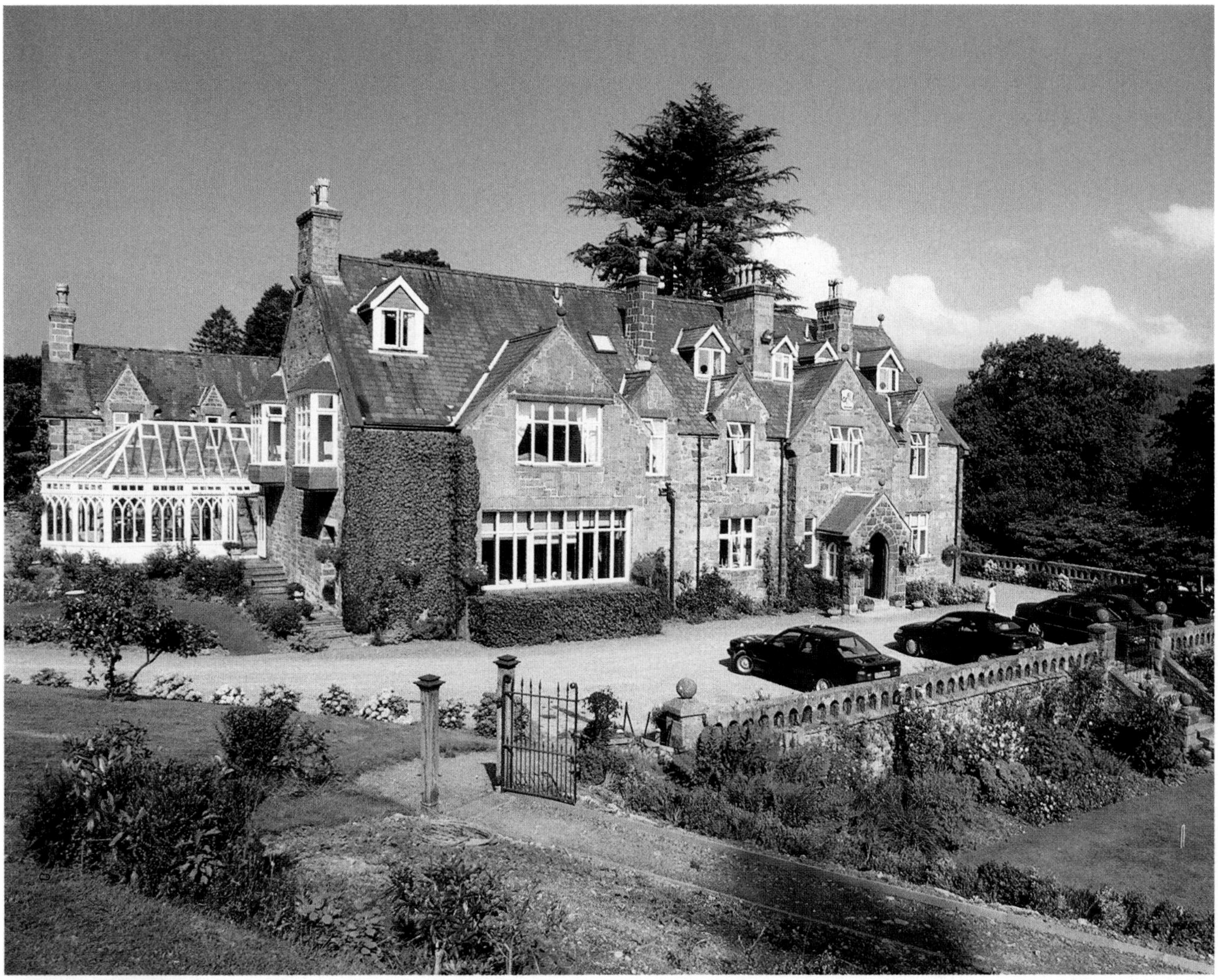

# PENMAENUCHAF HALL

**PENMAENPOOL, DOLGELLAU, GWYNEDD LL40 1YB**

**TEL: 01341 422129 FAX: 01341 422787**

The splendour of Cader Idris and the Mawddach Estuary forms the backdrop for this handsome Victorian mansion which is an exceptional retreat. Set within the Snowdonia National Park, the 21-acre grounds encompass lawns, a formal sunken rose garden, a water garden and woodland. The beautiful interiors feature oak and mahogany panelling, stained-glass windows, log fires in winter, polished Welsh slate floors and freshly cut flowers. There are 12 luxurious bedrooms, some with four-poster and half-tester beds, and all with interesting views. In the Gothic-style conservatory restaurant, guests can choose from an imaginative menu prepared with the best seasonal produce and complemented by an extensive list of wines. An elegant panelled dining room can be used for private dinners or meetings. Penmaenuchaf Hall is perfect for a totally relaxed holiday. For recreation, guests can fish for trout and salmon along ten miles of the Mawddach River, or take part in a range of water sports. They can also enjoy scenic walks, visit sandy beaches and historic castles and take trips on narrow-gauge railways. **Directions:** The hotel is off the A493 Dolgellau–Tywyn road, about two miles from Dolgellau. Price guide: Single £50–£95; double/twin £95–£150.

For hotel location, see maps on pages 490-496

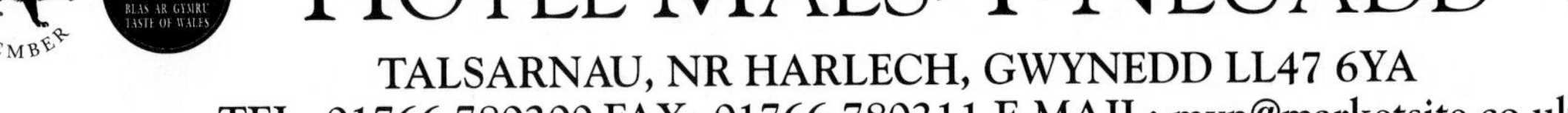

# HOTEL MAES-Y-NEUADD

**TALSARNAU, NR HARLECH, GWYNEDD LL47 6YA**

**TEL: 01766 780200 FAX: 01766 780211 E-MAIL: myn@marketsite.co.uk**

This part-14th century house, built of granite and slate, is cradled by eight acres of landscaped mountainside. As a much-loved hotel it has been run by the Horsfall and Slatter families since 1981. Peace and tranquillity are all-pervasive, whether relaxing in the pretty, beamed lounge or reclining in a leather Chesterfield in the bar while enjoying an apéritif. Talented chefs create delicious English and Welsh dishes using fresh produce such as lamb, fish and a variety of Welsh farmhouse cheeses, along with vegetables and herbs from the kitchen garden. As an alternative dining venue for special occasions and parties, dinner can be provided on the world famous Ffestiniog railway. The hotel produces its own oils and vinegars which are stylishly presented for sale. Spring and autumn breaks are available. The bedrooms vary in style, from early beams and dormers to later Georgian elegance with full-length windows. For golfers, the Royal St David's Golf Course is located three miles away. Nearby attractions include the Italianate village of Portmeirion, slate caverns, beautiful beaches, Snowdonia, Edward I's castle at Harlech and the Ffestiniog railway. USA toll-free reservations: 1-800 635 3602. **Directions:** Hotel is $3^1/_2$ miles north of Harlech, off the B4573, signposted at the end of the lane. Price guide: Single £72; double/twin £152–£203. (Including dinner)

16 rms

For hotel location, see maps on pages 490-496

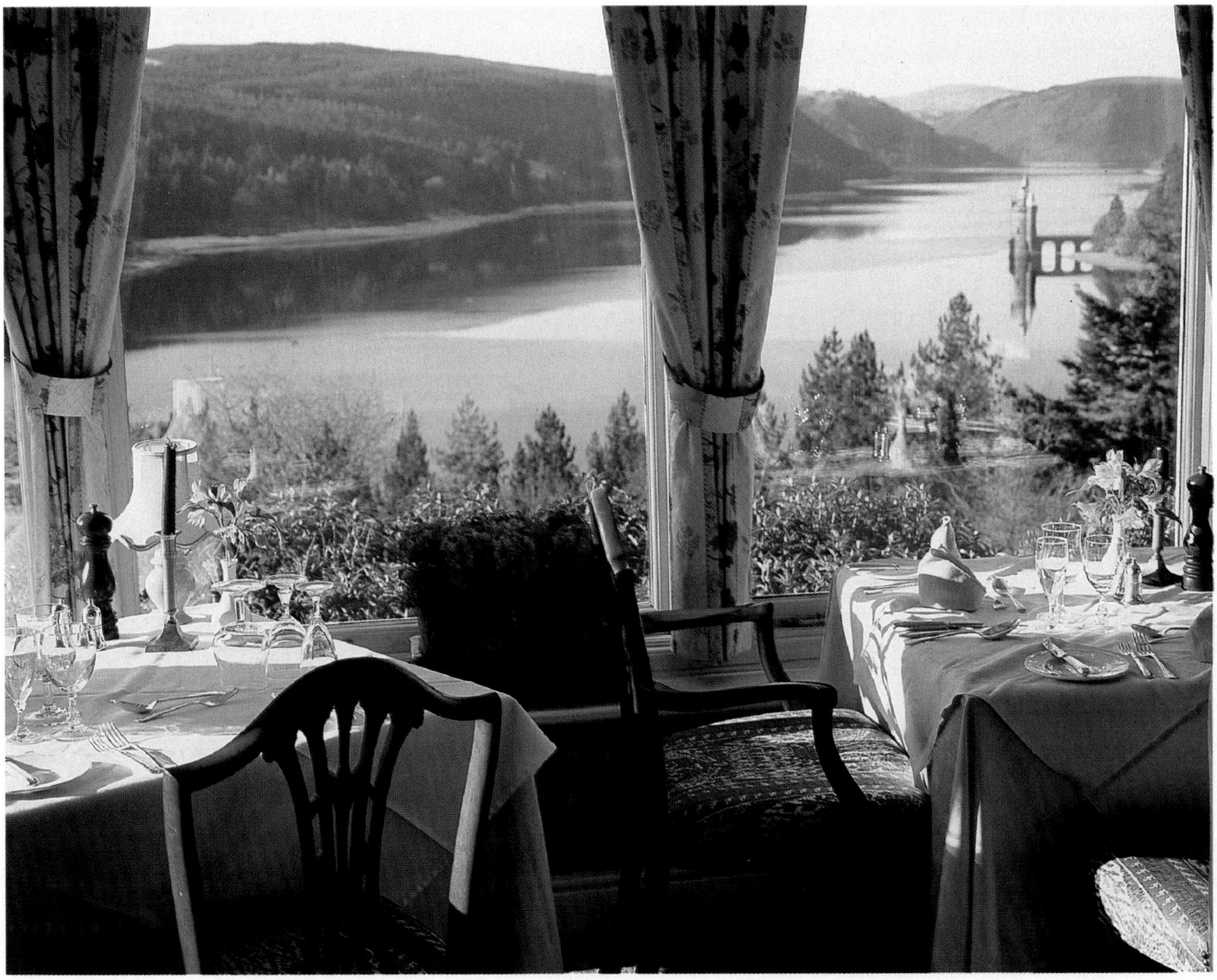

# LAKE VYRNWY HOTEL

**LAKE VYRNWY, LLANWDDYN, MONTGOMERYSHIRE SY10 0LY**
**TEL: 01691 870 692 FAX: 01691 870 259**

Situated high on the hillside within the 24,000 acre Vyrnwy Estate the hotel commands breathtaking views of mountains, lakes and moorland. It is also surrounded by lawns, an abundance of rhododendrons, woods and meadowlands. Built in 1860 its heritage has been maintained for well over a hundred years as a retreat for all lovers of nature and fine dining. There are 37 bedrooms all individually furnished and decorated, many with antiques and some with special features such as Jacuzzis, balconies, four-posters or suites. There are also dedicated meeting and private dining facilities. The award-winning candle-lit restaurant has a seasonally changing menu. Everything from the marmalade to the *petits fours* at dinner are created in the Vyrnwy kitchens. Its own market garden provides many of the seasonal herbs, fruits, vegetables and flowers. The hotel owns some of Wales' best fishing together with some 24,000 acres of sporting rights. Other pursuits include sailing, cycling, tennis, quad trekking and some beautiful walking trails. Also an RSPB sanctuary, the estate provides a wealth of wildlife and represents true peace and tranquillity. **Directions:** From Shrewsbury take the A458 to Welshpool, then turn right onto B4393 just after Ford (signposted to Lake Vyrnwy 28 miles). Price guide: Single from £68; double/twin from £88–£150; suite £132.

For hotel location, see maps on pages 490-496

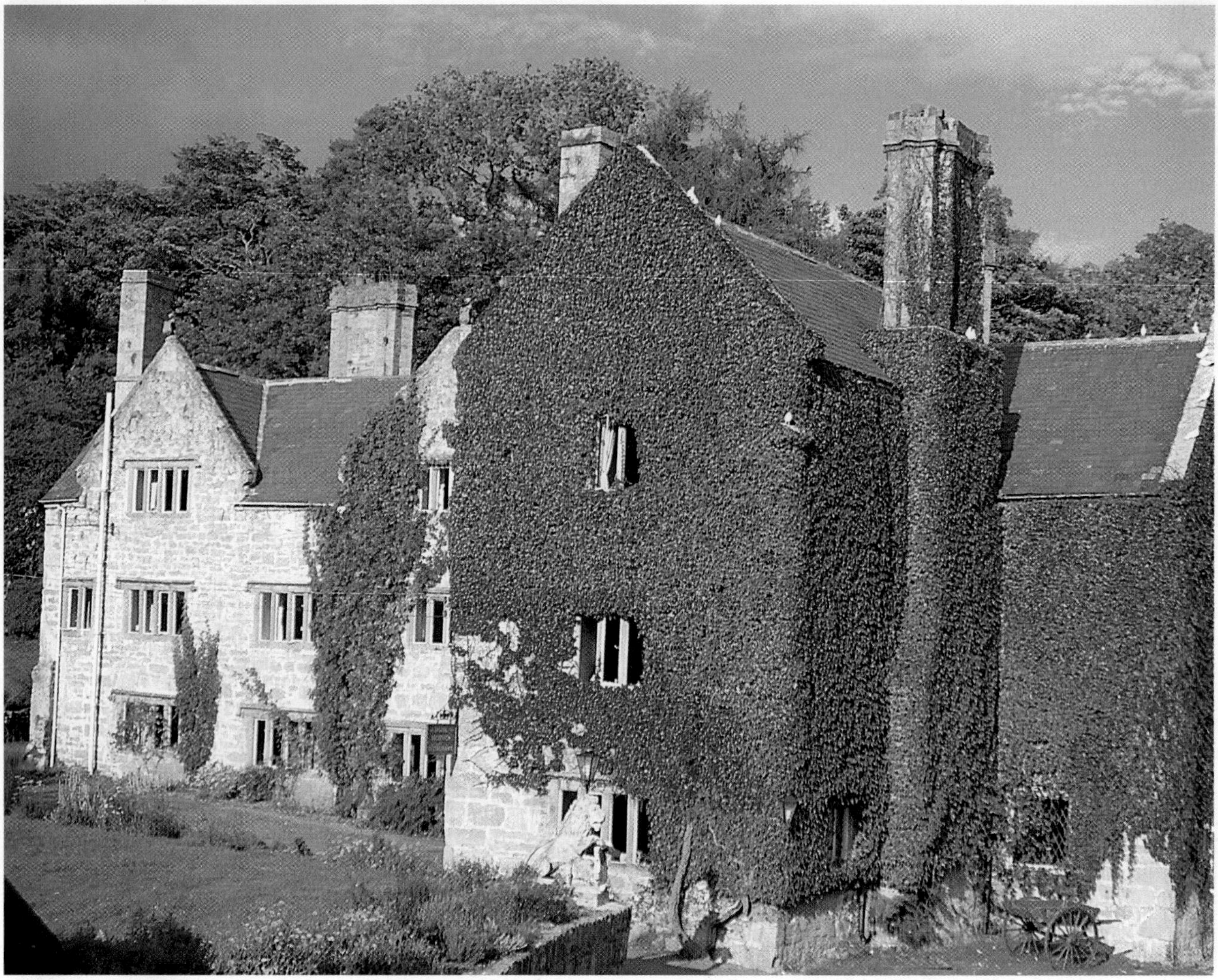

# BODIDRIS HALL

LLANDEGLA, WREXHAM, DENBIGHSHIRE LL 11 3AL
TEL: 01978 790434 FAX: 01978 790335

Ivy-clad Bodidris Hall, amid the wild hills, forests and moorlands of North Wales, is steeped in history and legend. A fortified building has stood on the site since two Crusaders were granted the estate by their Prince, Gryffydd ap Madoc, as a reward for valour. It later became the Tudor hunting lodge of Lord Robert Dudley, controversial favourite of Elizabeth I. The Hall still harbours many historical features inside its thick, grey-stone walls, including a former prison cell, a priest hole and a narrow staircase on which duels were fought. Spacious bedrooms, some with four-poster beds, are individually designed with magnificent views over 50 acres of rugged countryside, landscaped lawns and the Hall's own trout filled pond that is a haven for wildfowl. The heavily beamed bar with its mullion windows is welcoming with nooks that beckon you to relax and unwind, and the intimate restaurant with its excellent British and Continental cuisine features a huge open fireplace built to roast a whole lamb. The Hall is excellent value for money and an ideal base for exploring North Wales, or enjoying walks on nearby Offa's Dyke. Riding, cycling, pony trekking, trout fishing, archery, clay pigeon and driven shooting are available. Directions: Bodidris Hall is ½ mile off the main A5104 Chester-Corwen road, 2 miles west of the junction with the A525. Price guide: Single £80–£99; double/twin £96–£140.

For hotel location, see maps on pages 490-496

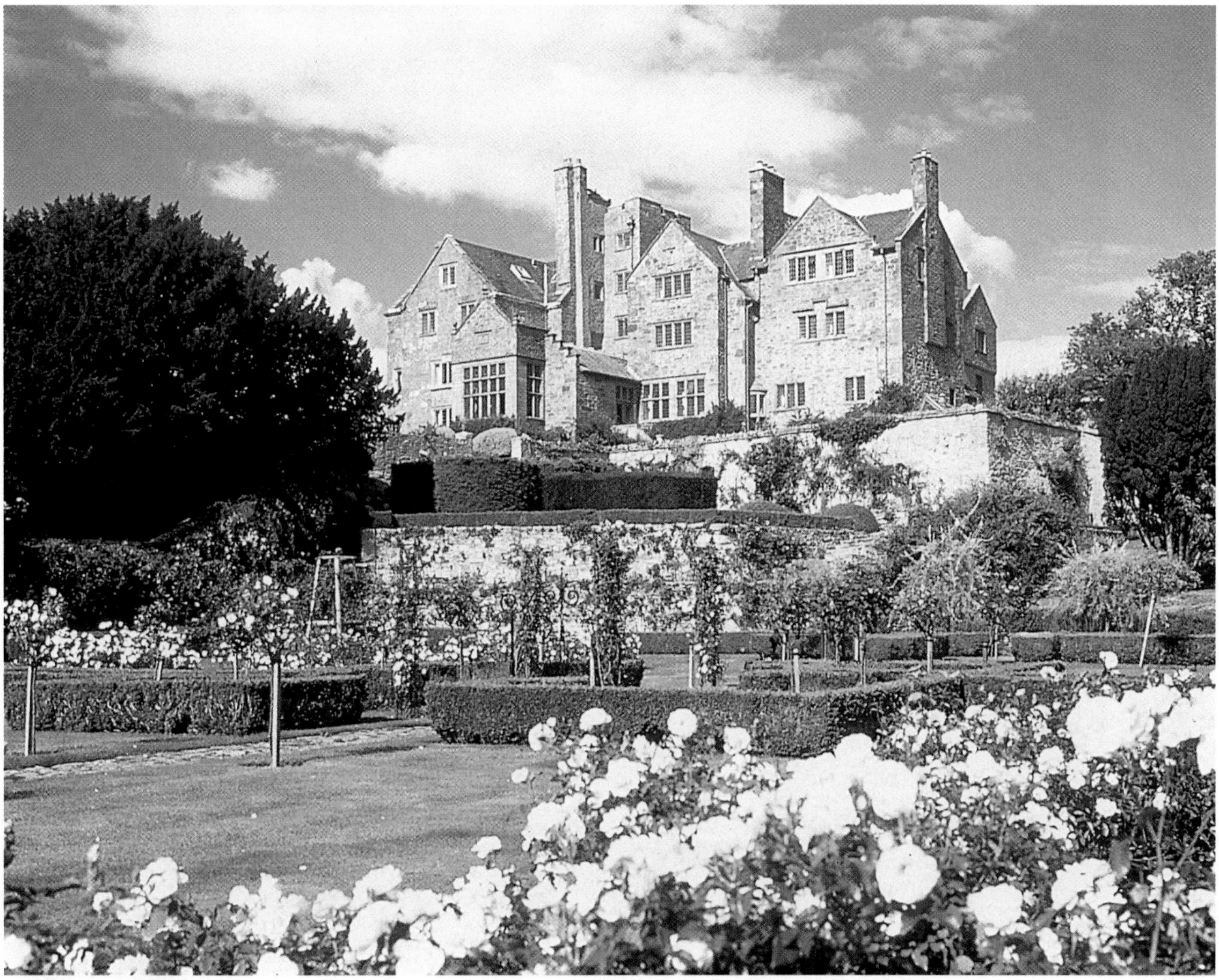

# BODYSGALLEN HALL

**LLANDUDNO LL30 1RS**

**TEL: 01492 584466 FAX: 01492 582519**

Bodysgallen Hall, owned and restored by Historic House Hotels, lies at the end of a winding drive in 200 acres of wooded parkland and beautiful formal gardens. Magnificent views encompass the sweep of the Snowdonia range of mountains, and the hotel looks down on the imposing medieval castle at Conwy. This Grade I listed house was built mainly in the 17th century, but the earliest feature is a 13th century tower, reached by a narrow winding staircase, once used as a lookout for soldiers serving the English kings of Conwy and now a safe place from which to admire the fabulous views. The hotel has 19 spacious bedrooms in the house and 16 delightful cottage suites in the grounds. Two of the finest rooms in the house are the large oak-panelled entrance hall and the first floor drawing room, both with splendid fireplaces and mullioned windows. Head chef is Mike Penny, who produces superb dishes using fresh local ingredients. The Bodysgallen Spa comprises a spacious swimmng pool, steam room, sauna, solaria, gym, beauty salons, restaurant and bar. The hotel is ideally placed for visiting the many historic castles and stately homes in North Wales. Famous golf courses adorn the coastline. **Directions:** On the A470 one mile from the intersection with the A55. Llandudno is a mile further on the A470. Price guide: Single £85–£105; double/twin £125–£180; suite £145–£210.

For hotel location, see maps on pages 490-496

# ST TUDNO HOTEL

**PROMENADE, LLANDUDNO, GWYNEDD LL30 2LP**
**TEL: 01492 874411 FAX: 01492 860407**

Without doubt one of the most delightful small hotels to be found on the coast of Britain, St Tudno Hotel, a former winner of the *Johansens Hotel of the Year Award for Excellence,* certainly offers a very special experience. The hotel, which has been elegantly and lovingly furnished with meticulous attention to detail, offers a particularly warm welcome from owners, Martin and Janette Bland, and their caring and friendly staff. Each beautifully co-ordinated bedroom has been individually designed with many thoughtful extras provided to ensure guests' comfort. The bar lounge and sitting room, which overlook the sea, have an air of Victorian charm. Regarded as one of Wales' leading restaurants, the air-conditioned Garden Room has won three AA Rosettes for its excellent cuisine. This AA Red Star hotel has won a host of other awards, including *Best Seaside Resort Hotel in Great Britain, Welsh Hotel of the Year,* national winner of the AA's *Warmest Welcome Award* and even an accolade for having the *Best Hotel Loos in Britain*! St Tudno is ideally situated for visits to Snowdonia, Conwy and Caernarfon Castles, Bodnant Gardens and Anglesey. Golf, riding, swimming and dry-slope skiing and tobogganing can be enjoyed locally. **Directions:** On the promenade opposite the pier entrance and gardens. Price guide: Single from £70; double/twin £90–£160; suite £250

20 rms

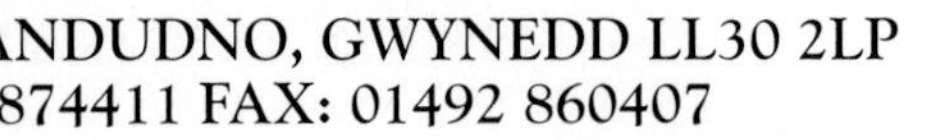

For hotel location, see maps on pages 490-496

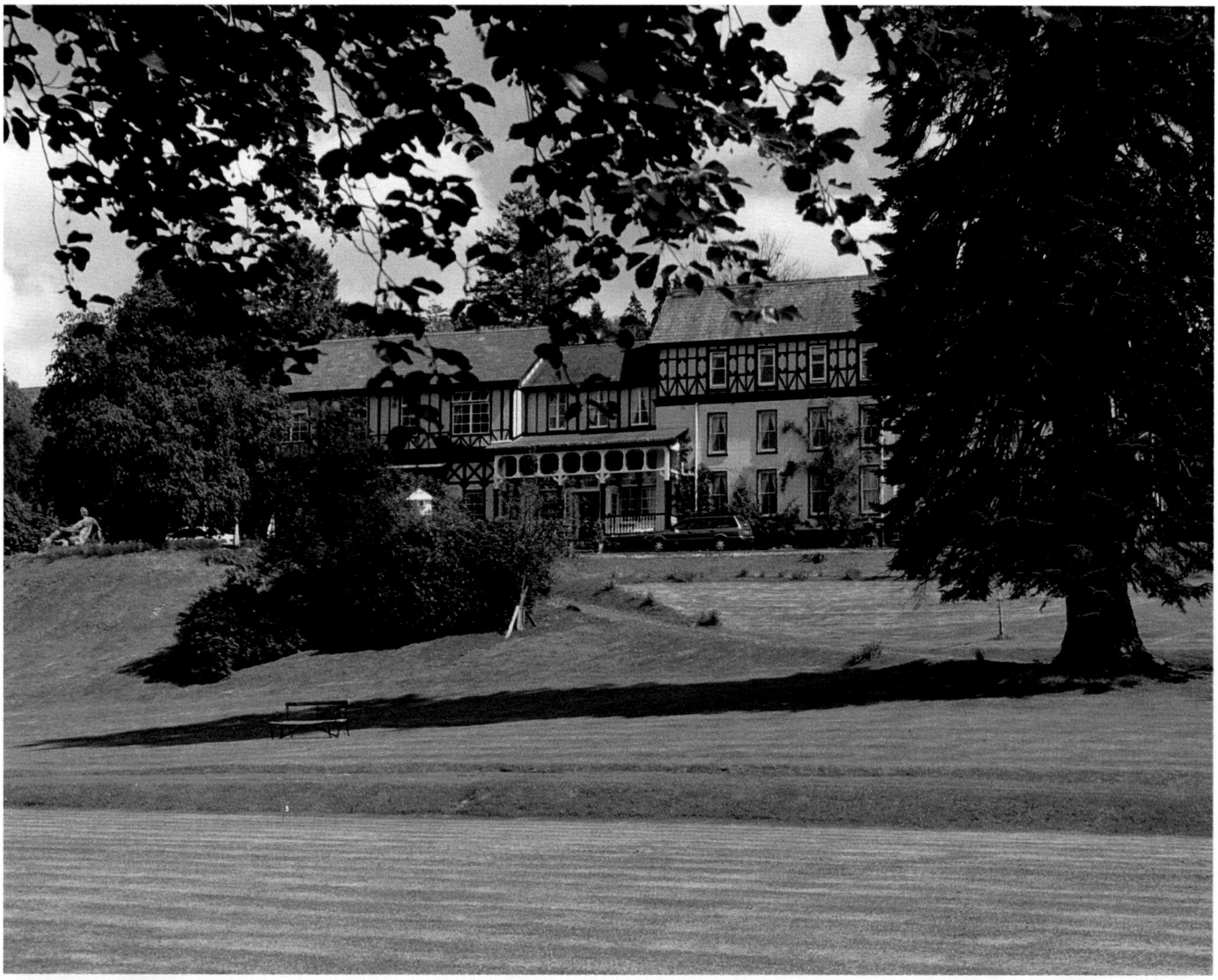

# THE LAKE COUNTRY HOUSE

LLANGAMMARCH WELLS, POWYS LD4 4BS

TEL: 01591 620202 FAX: 01591 620457

A welcoming Welsh Country house set in its own 50 acres with rhododendron lined pathways, riverside walks and a large well stocked trout lake. Within the hotel, airy rooms filled with fine antiques, paintings and fresh flowers make this the perfect place to relax. Delicious homemade teas are served everyday beside log fires. From the windows ducks and geese can be glimpsed wandering in the gardens which cascade down to the river. In the award winning restaurant, fresh produce and herbs from the gardens are used for seasonal Country House menus, complemented by one of the finest wine lists in Wales. Each of the supremely comfortable bedrooms or suites with beautifully appointed sitting rooms are furnished with the thoughtful attention to details seen throughout the hotel. Guests can fish for trout or salmon on the four miles of river which runs through the grounds, and the 3 acre lake regularly yields trout of five pounds and over. The grounds are a haven for wildlife: herons, dippers and kingfishers skim over the river, there are badgers in the woods and swans and waterfowl abound. There is a large billiard room in the hotel and a 9 hole par three golf course, tennis court, croquet lawn and putting green. AA 3 Red star – RAC Blue Ribbon. **Directions:** From the A483, follow signs to Llangammarch Wells and then to the hotel. Price guide: Single £80; double/twin £120–£165; suite from £165.

For hotel location, see maps on pages 490-496

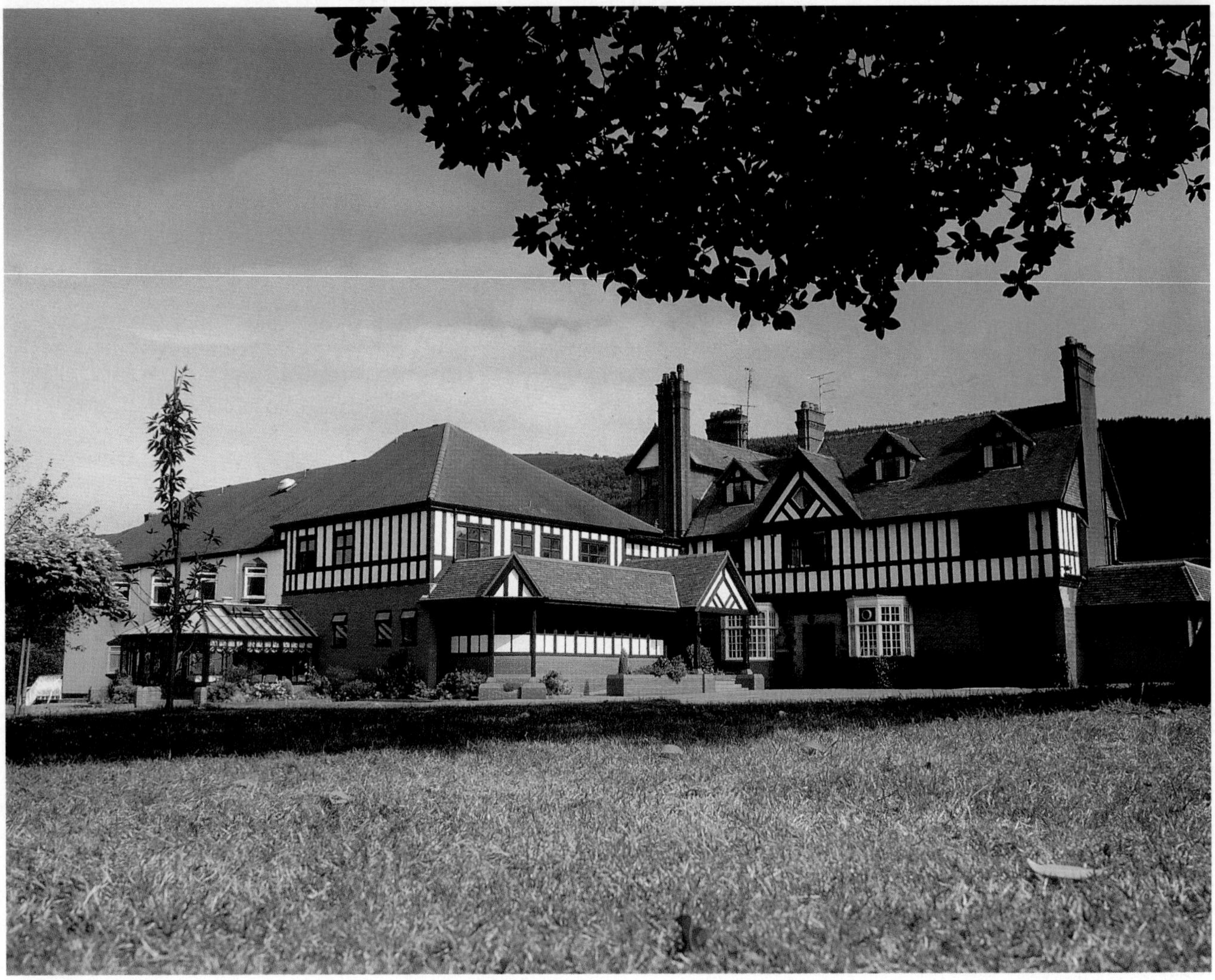

# BRYN HOWEL HOTEL AND RESTAURANT

**LLANGOLLEN, DENBIGHSHIRE LL20 7UW**
**TEL: 01978 860331 FAX: 01978 860119**

Bryn Howel, set in the magnificent Vale of Llangollen, was built in 1896. Although the hotel has been extended and regularly refurbished over the years, great care has been taken to preserve the original character and unique features of the building and its red brickwork, mullioned windows, oak panelling and intricate plaster mouldings still remain. The hotel is run by a brother and sister team, members of the Lloyd family who have owned the hotel for 30 years. They pride themselves on providing the highest standards of both comfort and service. Well appointed bedrooms, with a full range of modern amenities, offer splendid views of the surrounding countryside. Delicious food, featuring Dee salmon, Welsh lamb and local game and poultry, is served in the Cedar Tree Restaurant, winner of many awards for its tempting cuisine. Alternatively, guests may dine in the intimacy of the Oak Room. The hotel's leisure facilities include a sauna and solarium. Reduced fees for the nearby golf club are available to residents, who may also enjoy free game fishing on a five mile stretch of the River Dee. Places of interest nearby include the historic city of Chester and town of Shrewsbury. Bryn Howel is closed at Christmas. **Directions:** On the A539 (three miles from Llangollen) between Llangollen and the A483. Price guide: Single £44–£79; double/twin £88–£125; suite £120–£155.

For hotel location, see maps on pages 490-496

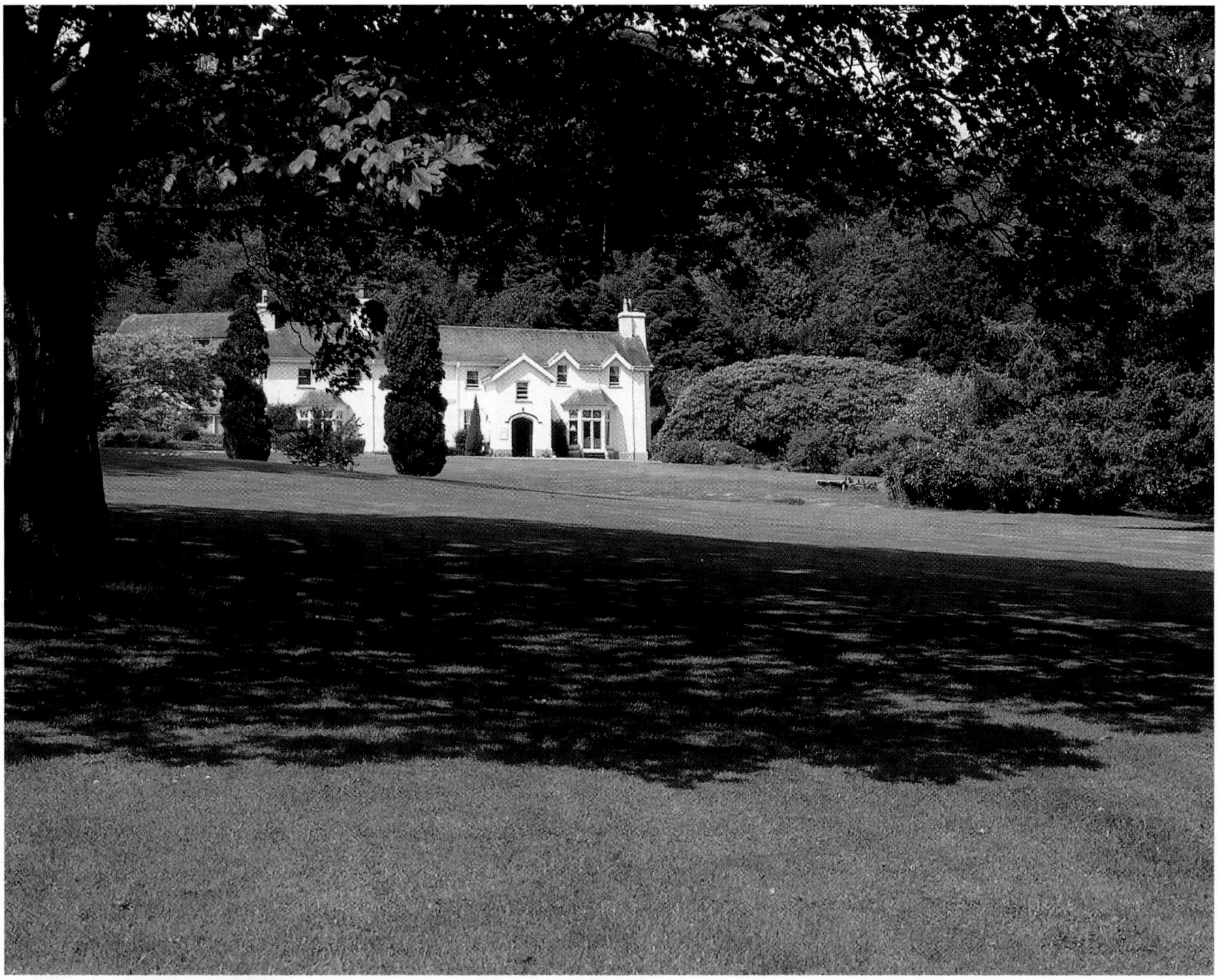

# YNYSHIR HALL

EGLWYSFACH, MACHYNLLETH, POWYS SY20 8TA
TEL: 01654 781209 FAX: 01654 781366

Once owned by Queen Victoria, Ynyshir Hall is a captivating Georgian manor house that perfectly blends modern comfort and old-world elegance. Its 12 acres of picturesque, landscaped gardens are set alongside the Dovey Estuary, one of Wales' most outstanding areas of natural beauty and the hotel is surrounded by the Ynyshir Bird Reserve. Hosts Rob and Joan Reen offer guests a warm welcome and ensure a personal service, the hallmark of a good family-run hotel. Period furniture and opulent fabrics enhance the eight charming bedrooms. The suites are particularly luxurious and, along with a four-poster room and ground floor room, are popular with many guests. The interiors are exquisitely furnished throughout with comfortable sofas, antiques, contemporary colour schemes, oriental rugs and many original paintings. These works of art are the creation of Rob, an established and acclaimed artist. Local seafood, game, and vegetables from the kitchen garden are used to create superb English, French and Welsh dishes. Dogs by prior arrangement. In 1402 in Machynlleth the patriot Owen Glendower was crowned Prince of Wales. Another local landmark is Cader Idris, Wales' second most popular mountain. **Directions:** Off the main road between Aberystwyth and Machynlleth. Price guide: Single £85–£105; double/twin £100–£140; suite £165.

For hotel location, see maps on pages 490-496

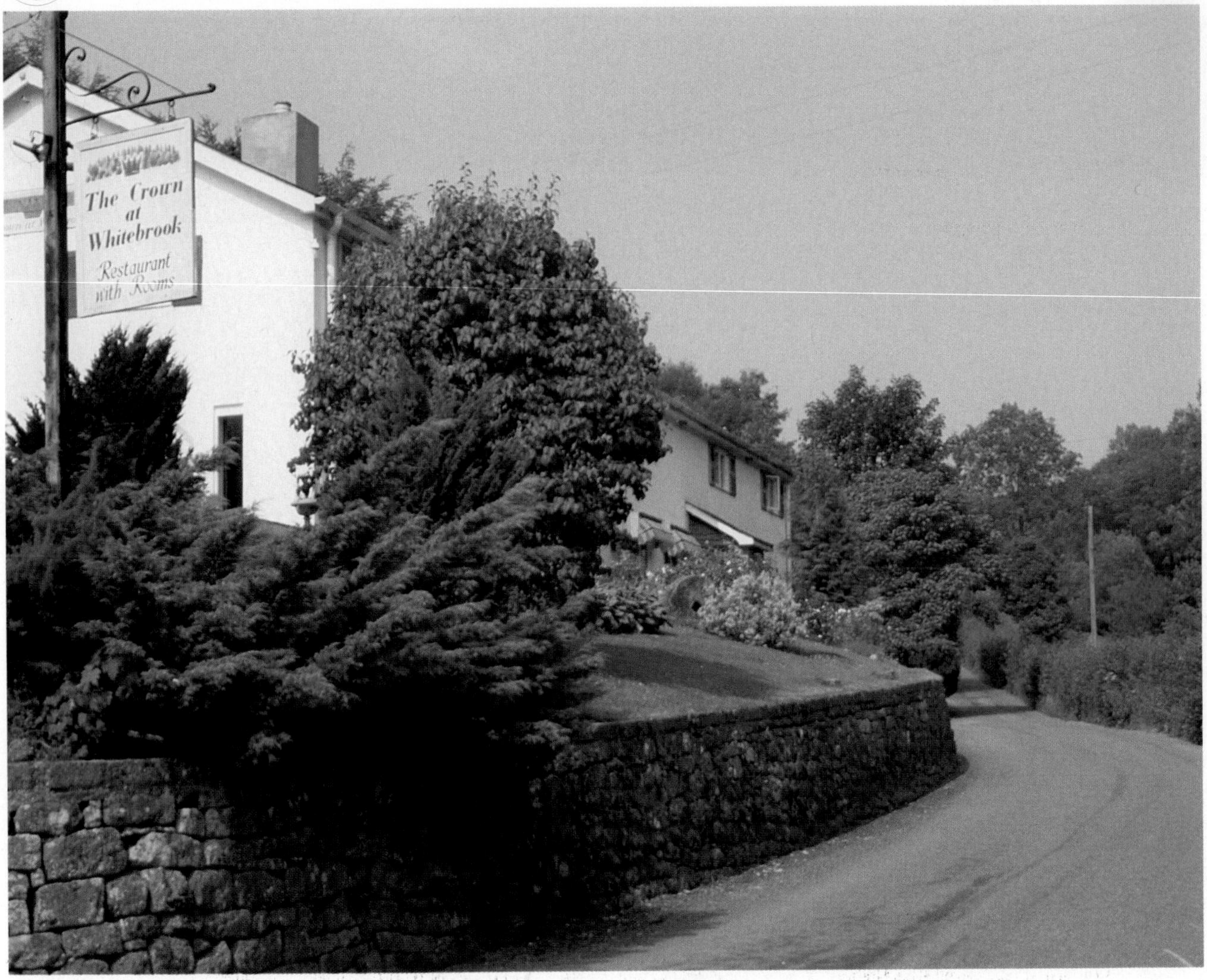

# THE CROWN AT WHITEBROOK

WHITEBROOK, MONMOUTH, GWENT NP5 4TX
TEL: 01600 860254 FAX: 01600 860607

A romantic auberge nestling deep in the Wye Valley, a designated area of outstanding natural beauty, The Crown is ideally situated for those seeking peace and tranquillity. Located up the wooded Whitebrook Valley on the fringe of Tintern Forest and only one mile from the River Wye, this is a place where guests can enjoy spectacular scenery. Roger and Sandra Bates offer their visitors a genuinely friendly welcome. Guests can relax in the cosy lounge and bar. The Manor Room, features ash furniture, hand-made locally. Sandra Bates' cooking has earned the Restaurant several awards, as well as recommendations from other guides. Dishes include local Welsh lamb and Wye salmon cooked with a classical French influence, followed by a choice of delicious home-made puddings and a selection of British farm cheeses. Most dietary requirements can be catered for as all food is freshly cooked to order. There is an extensive wine list. Tintern Abbey, Chepstow Castle and the Brecon Beacons National Park are nearby. **Directions:** Whitebrook is situated between the A466 and the B4293 approximately five miles south of Monmouth. Price guide: Single £39.50–£50; double/twin £53–£81.

For hotel location, see maps on pages 490-496

# THE CELTIC MANOR HOTEL & GOLF CLUB

BLAS AR GYMRU TASTE OF WALES

COLDRA WOODS, NEWPORT, GWENT NP6 2YA
TEL: 01633 413000 FAX: 01633 412910/410284

Consistently acknowledged as one of the finest hotels in Wales, this refurbished Victorian manor house is set on the edge of over one thousand acres of rolling Welsh hills. Spacious bedrooms are elegantly furnished with comfort in mind. Sports enthusiasts will enjoy a choice of excellent leisure facilities. The golf complex comprises two 18-hole championship courses designed by Robert Trent-Jones Snr, American style clubhouse, Ian Woosnam Golf Academy and two tier driving range. Two exclusive health and fitness clubs with the very latest cardio-vascular exercise equipment, aerobics, swimming, sauna, steam room, Jacuzzi, beauty treatments and solarium. Three fine restaurants: Dining Terrace, overlooking the 18th green; The Patio Brasserie in the picturesque conservatory and Hedleys, benefit from the culinary skills of twice winner of the title, Welsh Chef of the Year, Trefor Jones and his team. An ancient woodland walk winds through Coldra Woods, with its rare flora and fauna. Activity weekends can be arranged for parties, including murder mysteries and hot-air ballooning. Nearby are Tintern Abbey, the Wye Valley and the castles at Chepstow, Caerphilly and Cardiff. **Directions:** Leave M4 at junction 24; hotel is 400 yards along the A48 towards Newport on the right-hand side. Price guide: Single/double/twin £95–£105; suite £125–£150.

For hotel location, see maps on pages 490-496

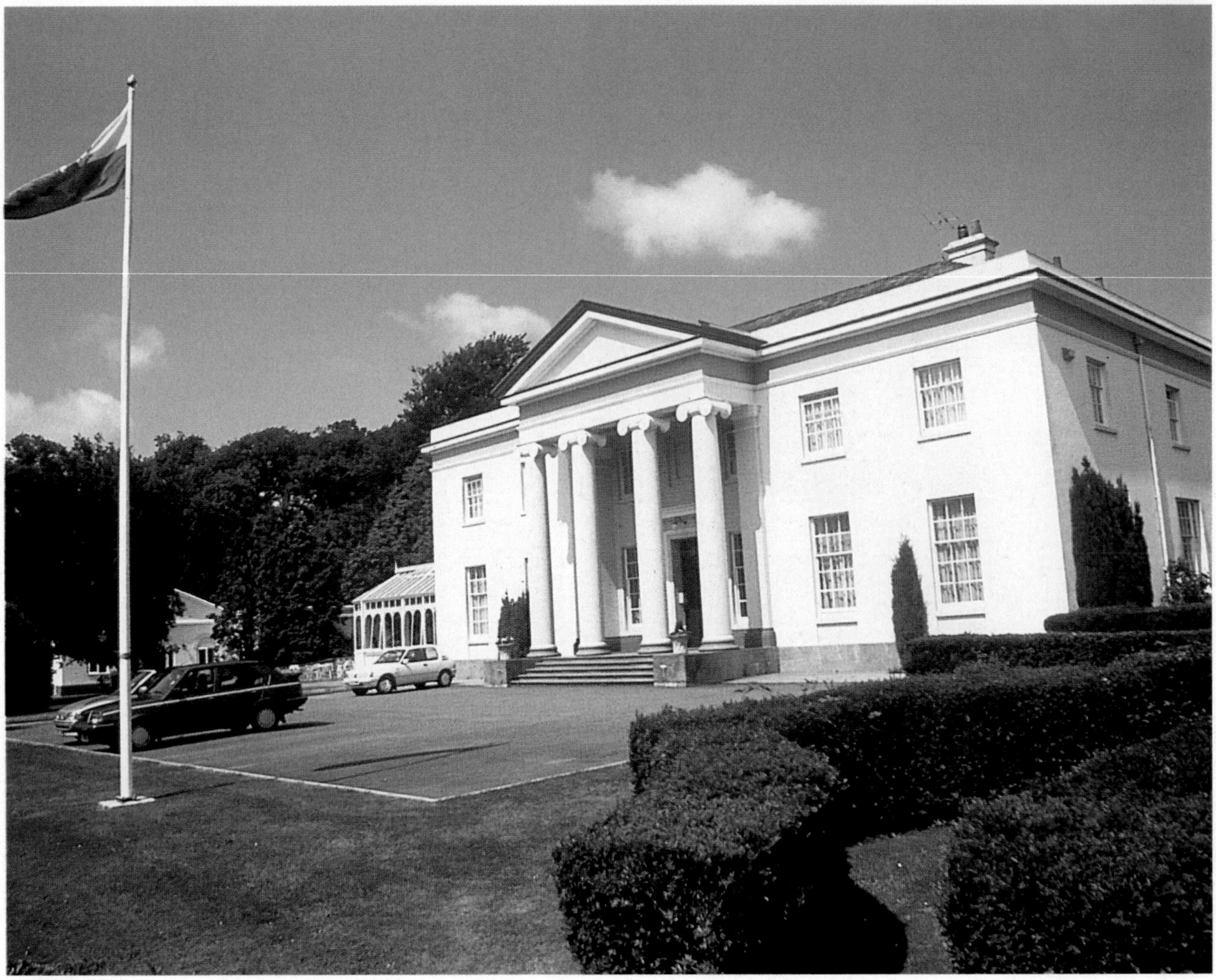

# THE COURT HOTEL AND RESTAURANT

**LAMPHEY, NR TENBY, PEMBROKESHIRE SA71 5NT**
**TEL: 01646 672273 FAX: 01646 672480**

This magnificent Georgian mansion, with its classical Ionic colonade, is idyllically situated in acres of grounds bordered by the beautiful Pembrokeshire National Park and just one mile from some of Britain's finest coastal scenery and beaches. Warm, friendly and efficient service is enriched by comfortable furnishings and decor. All bedrooms are en suite and have every convenience. The purpose-built Coach House studios situated in the courtyard provide the extra space required by families or visiting business executives. The restaurant has a prestigious AA Rosette. Traditional flavours and local produce, includes such pleasures as Teifi salmon and Freshwater Bay lobster. Lighter meals and snacks can be taken in the elegant conservatory. The wide range of facilities in the leisure centre includes an indoor heated swimming pool, Jacuzzi, sauna, solarium and a gymnasium. There are aerobics classes, massage and a beautician by appointment. Golf, sailing and fishing are nearby and the hotel's private yacht is available for charter. Well worth a visit is picturesque Tenby, the cliffside chapel of St Govan's, the Bishops Palace at Lamphey and Pembroke's impressive castle. Directions: From M4, exit at junction 49 onto the A48 to Carmarthen. Then follow the A477 and turn left at Milton Village for Lamphey. Price guide: Single £59-£72; double/twin £75-£125; suite £85–£125. Special rates available for short breaks.

For hotel location, see maps on pages 490-496

# THE HOTEL PORTMEIRION

**PORTMEIRION, GWYNEDD LL48 6ET**
**TEL: 01766 770228 FAX: 01766 771331**

Portmeirion is a magical, private Italianate village, designed by the renowned architect Sir Clough Williams-Ellis. The unique avant-garde complex was started in 1925 and completed in the 1970s. It enjoyed a celebrated clientèle from the start – writers such as George Bernard Shaw, H G Wells, Bertrand Russell and Noel Coward were habitués. It is set in 120 acres of beautiful gardens and woodland, including two miles of tranquil sandy beaches, and provides accommodation for visitors either in the village or in the main hotel. The Hotel Portmeirion, originally a mansion house, has been sensitively restored, retaining striking features from the past, such as the Victorian Mirror Room. The bedrooms are furnished to the highest standards, 14 rooms being in the hotel and 23 rooms and suites in the village. The restaurant offers the best French and Welsh cooking, the seasonal menu relying on fresh, locally produced ingredients. AA Hotel of the Year Wales 1996. Swimming and tennis are available within the grounds as well as golf at Porthmadog (with complimentary green fees), and sailing is close at hand. The Ffestiniog and Snowdon mountain railways, slate caverns and Bodnant Gardens are nearby. Conference facilities can accommodate up to 100 people. Closed 5th January to 7th February. **Directions:** Portmeirion lies off the A487 between Penrhyndeudrath and Porthmadog. Price guide: Single £80–£125; double/twin £90–£135; suite £110–£175.

For hotel location, see maps on pages 490-496

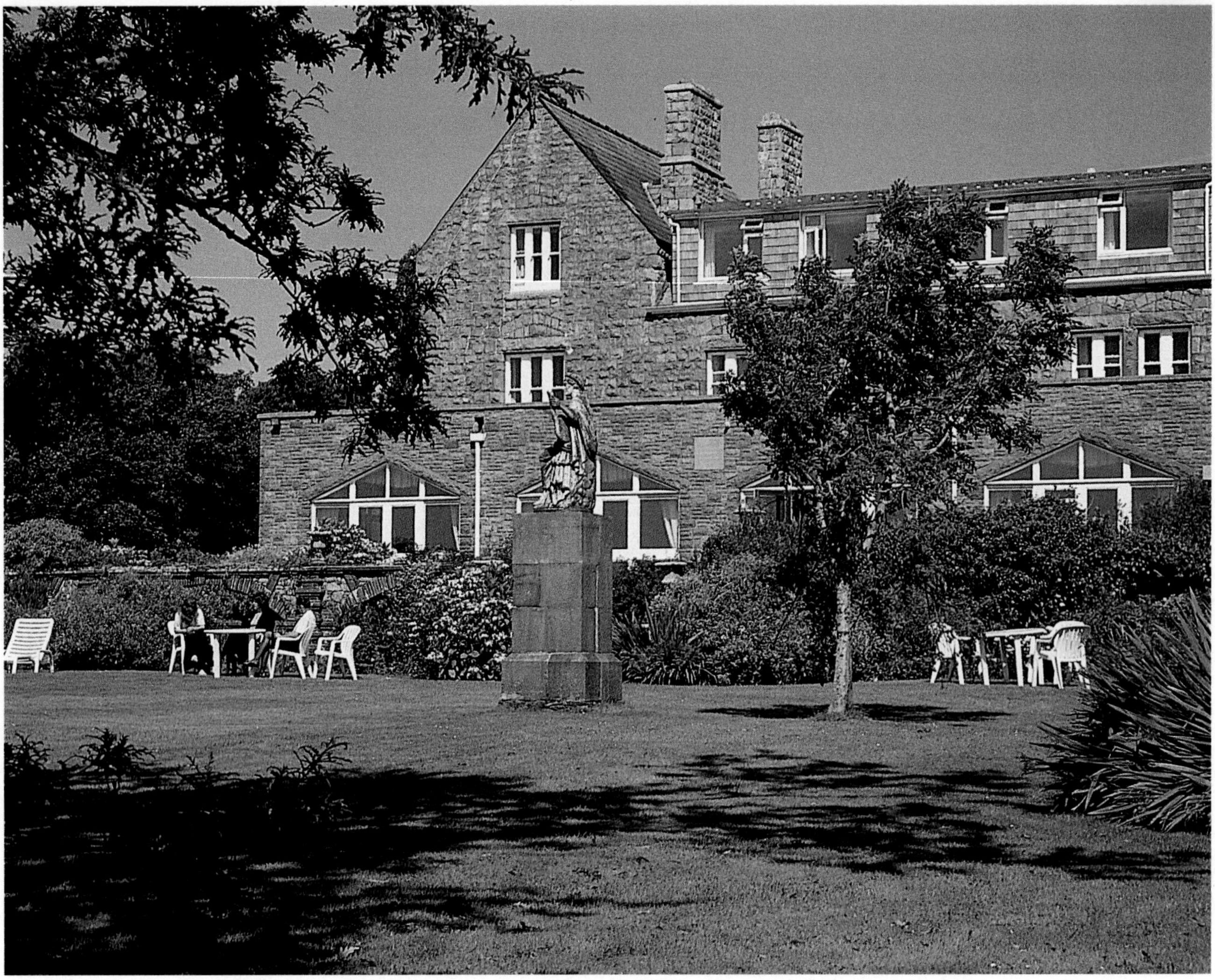

# WARPOOL COURT HOTEL

ST DAVID'S, PEMBROKESHIRE SA62 6BN
TEL: 01437 720300 FAX: 01437 720676

Originally built as St David's Cathedral Choir School in the 1860s, Warpool Court enjoys spectacular scenery at the heart of the Pembrokeshire National Park, with views over the coast and St Bride's Bay to the islands beyond. First converted to a hotel 40 years ago, the Court has undergone extensive refurbishments over the last two years. All 25 comfortably furnished bedrooms have en suite facilities with half having glorious sea views. The hotel restaurant enjoys a splendid reputation. Imaginative menus, including vegetarian, offer a wide selection of modern and traditional dishes. Local produce, including Welsh lamb and beef, is used whenever possible, with crab, lobster, sewin and sea bass caught just off the coast. Salmon and mackerel are smoked on the premises and a variety of herbs are grown. The hotel gardens are ideal for a peaceful stroll or an after-dinner drink on a summer's evening. There is a covered heated swimming pool (open April to end of October) and all-weather tennis court in the grounds. A path from the hotel leads straight on to the Pembrokeshire Coastal Path, with its rich variety of wildlife and spectacular scenery. Boating and watersports are available locally. St David's Peninsula offers a wealth of history and natural beauty and has inspired many famous artists. **Directions:** The hotel is signposted from St David's town centre. Price guide: Single £70–£86; double/twin £98–£162.

For hotel location, see maps on pages 490-496

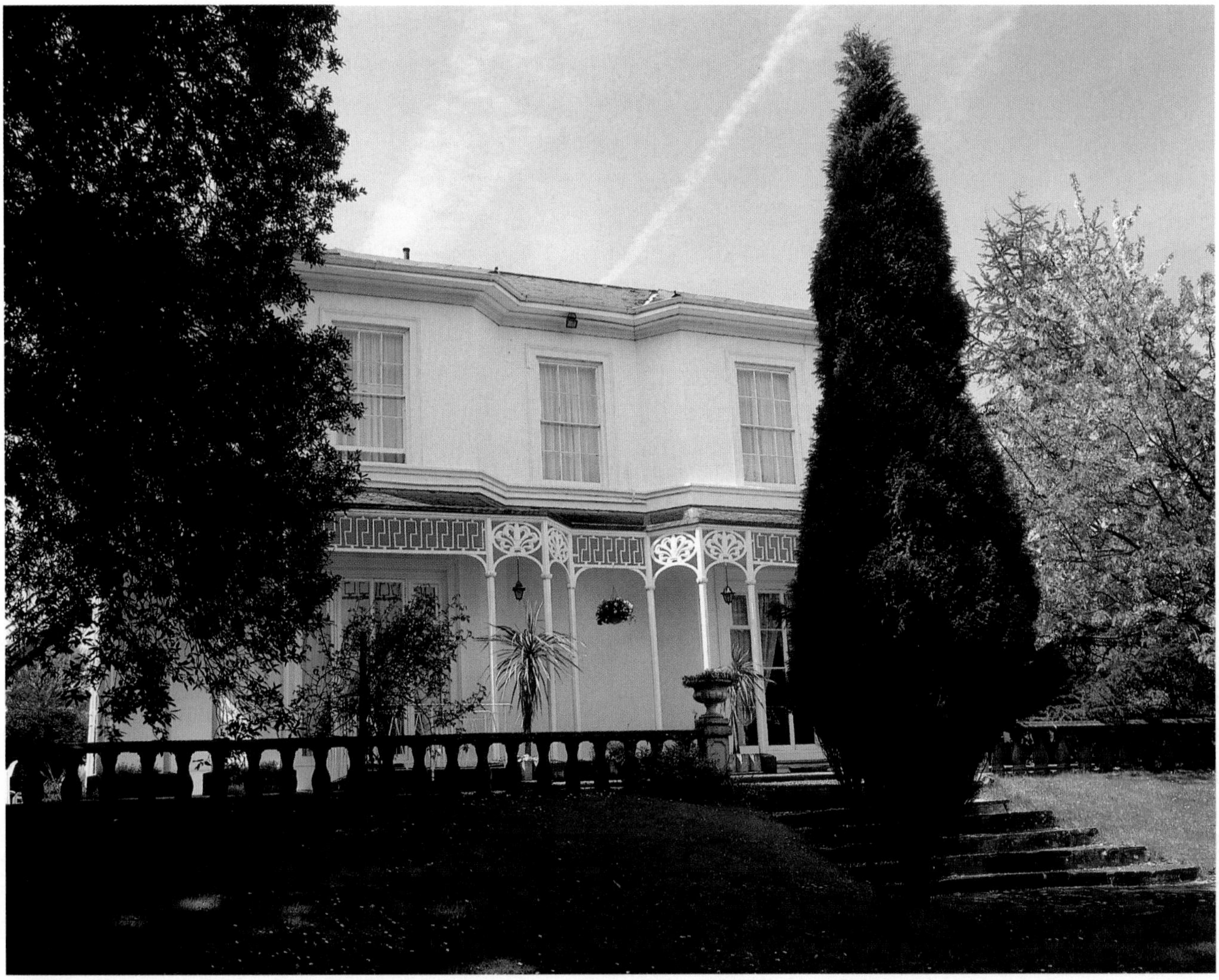

# NORTON HOUSE HOTEL AND RESTAURANT

NORTON ROAD, MUMBLES, SWANSEA SA3 5TQ
TEL: 01792 404891 FAX: 01792 403210

This elegant Georgian hotel, set in gardens near the shore of Swansea Bay, provides a comfortable and peaceful base from which to explore the countryside of South Wales. Resident proprietors Jan and John Power have earned a reputation for offering attentive, friendly service. The bedrooms all have private amenities, four of the more spacious rooms have four-poster beds, the majority are smaller rooms in a newer wing. The restaurant overlooks the terrace and gardens. The emphasis is on local produce and traditional flavours with starters such as 'bara lawr' – mushrooms filled with laverbread, cockles and bacon followed by main courses which include 'cig oen mewn pasteiod' – best end of Welsh lamb coated in a duxelle of mushrooms, cooked in puff pastry and served with a minted gravy. Golf and riding can be arranged. The hotel has conference facilities for up to 20 people. The unspoiled Gower Peninsula is nearby, with its sandy bays and rugged cliffs. Mumbles village is a short walk away, while the city of Swansea is alive with galleries, theatres, a good shopping centre, its famous market and the maritime quarter. **Directions:** Leave the M4 at junction 42, take A483 to Swansea, then A4067 alongside Swansea Bay. A mile beyond the Mumbles sign, the hotel is signposted on the right-hand side. Price guide: Single £60–£65; double/twin £80.

For hotel location, see maps on pages 490-496

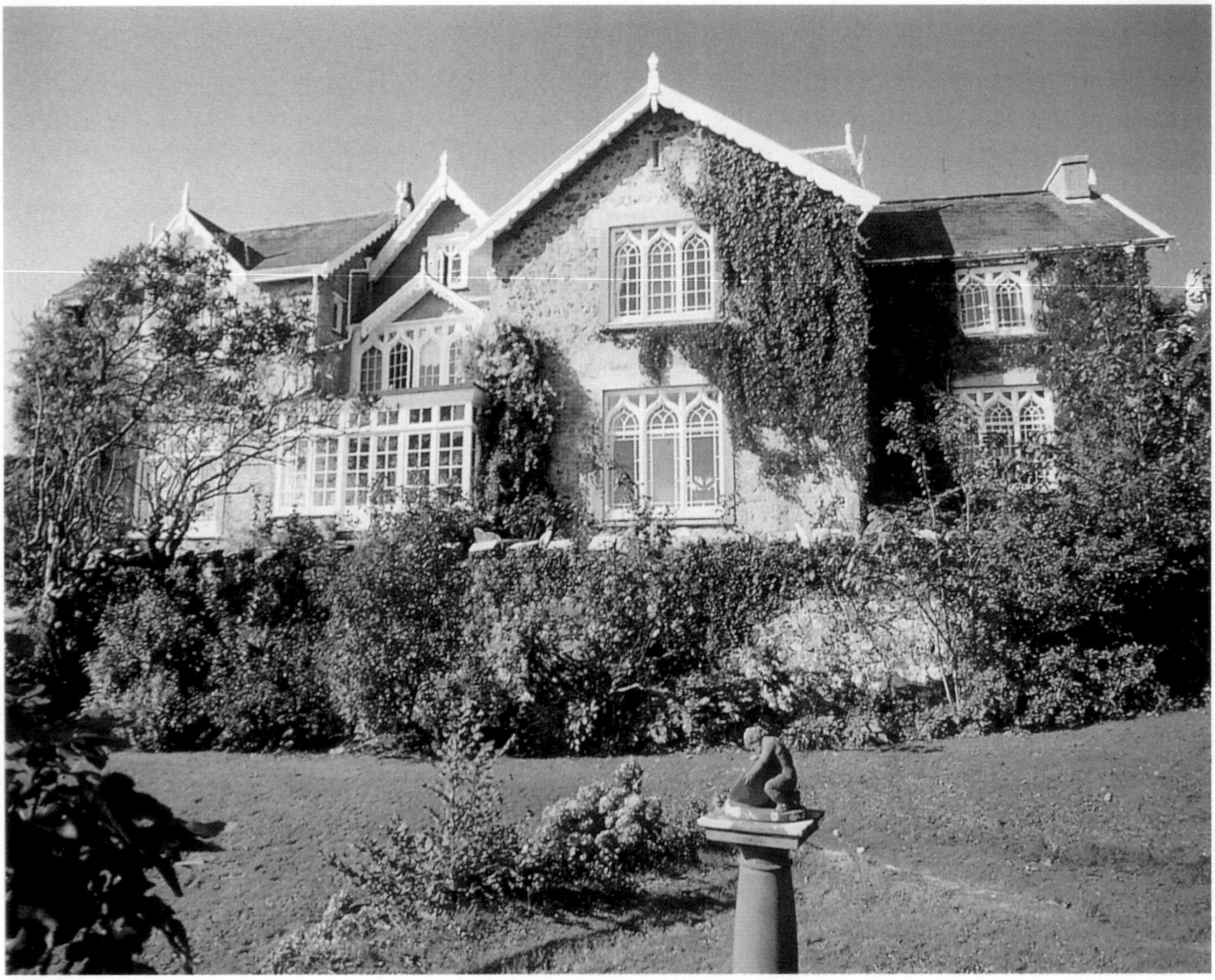

# PENALLY ABBEY

**PENALLY, TENBY, PEMBROKESHIRE SA70 7PY**
**TEL: 01834 843033 FAX: 01834 844714**

Penally Abbey, a beautiful listed Gothic-style mansion, offers comfort and hospitality in a secluded setting by the sea. Standing in five acres of gardens and woodland on the edge of Pembrokeshire National Park, the hotel overlooks Carmarthen Bay and Caldey Island. The bedrooms in the main building and in the adjoining coach house are well furnished, many with four-poster beds. The emphasis is on relaxation – enjoy a late breakfast and dine at leisure. Fresh seasonal delicacies are offered in the candle-lit restaurant, with its chandeliers and colonnades. Guests can enjoy a game in the snooker room or relax in the elegant sunlit lounge, overlooking the terrace and gardens. In the grounds there is a wishing well and a ruined chapel – the last surviving link with the hotel's monastic past. Water-skiing, surfing, sailing, riding and parascending are available nearby. Sandy bays and rugged cliffs are features of this coastline, making it ideal for exhilarating walks or simply building sandcastles on the beach. As the rates include the cost of dinner, this friendly hotel offers splendid value for money. **Directions:** Penally Abbey is situated adjacent to the church on Penally village green. Price guide (including dinner): Single £96; double/twin £146–£162.

For hotel location, see maps on pages 490-496

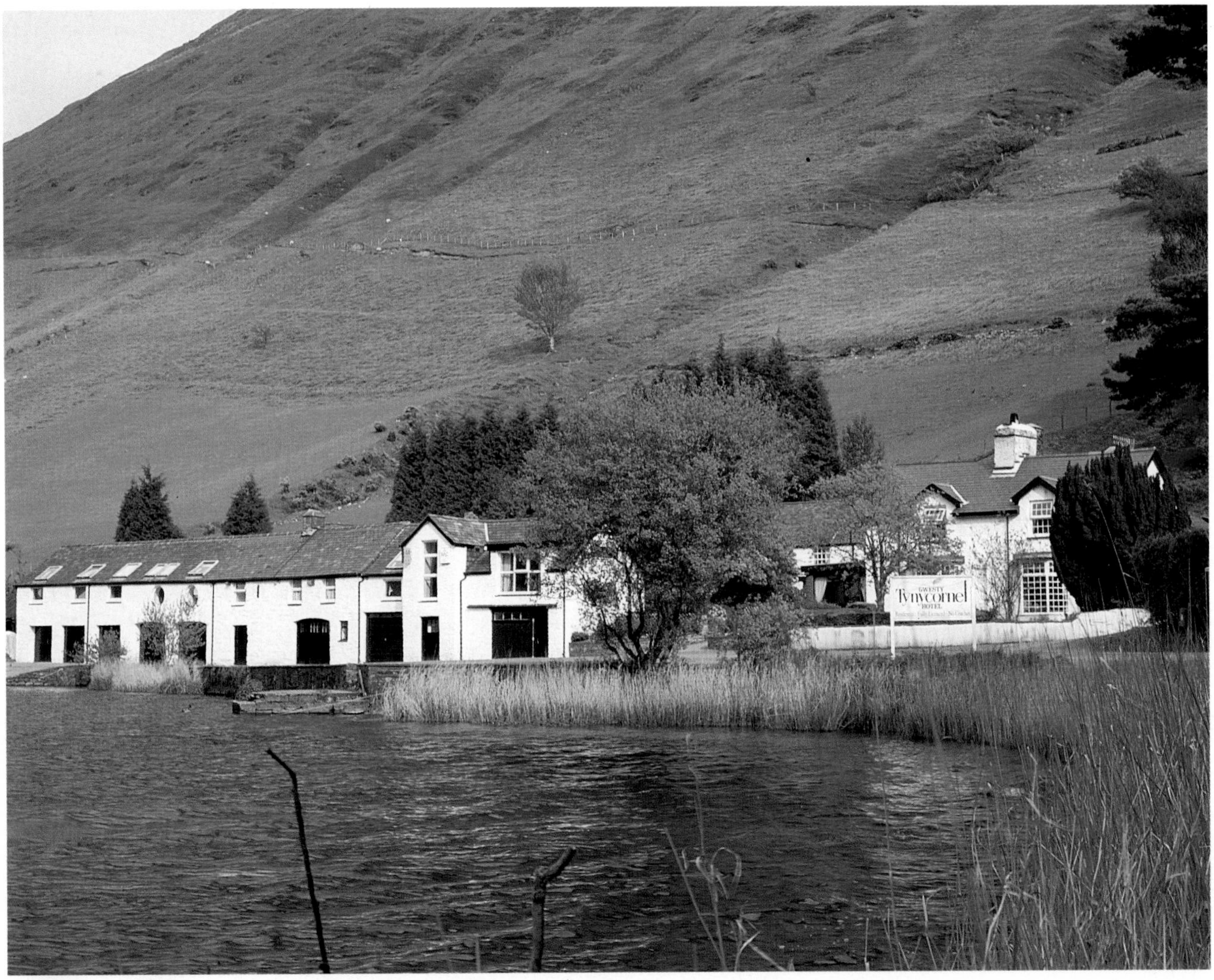

# TYNYCORNEL HOTEL

**TAL-Y-LLYN, TYWYN, GWYNEDD LL36 9AJ**
**TEL: 01654 782282 FAX: 01654 782679**

Situated in the magnificent Snowdonia National Park, Tynycornel Hotel overlooks its own 222-acre lake, whose waters reflect the grandeur of Cader Idris. Originally constructed as a farmhouse in the 16th century, the hotel has been extensively and sensitively refurbished so that none of the original ambience has been lost. The spacious lounge has views over the lake, with comfortable furniture, fine antiques, original prints and a blazing fire in winter. The 17 pretty bedrooms, all with bathrooms including two luxury suites, enjoy lakeside or garden views. The restaurant offers a high standard of cuisine and the set-price menu changes daily. Within the grounds there is a sauna and solarium. Tynycornel is an angler's paradise – wild brown trout, salmon and sea trout fishing are readily available – and the hotel is equipped with 10 petrol-powered boats and provides tackle hire, freezing facilities and a drying room. The stunning landscape offers many opportunities for those interested in birdwatching, walking and photography. Snowdonia and mid-Wales are steeped in history and a wide variety of leisure pursuits can be enjoyed, including scenic golf at Dolgellau. **Directions:** Tal-y-llyn is signposted from the main A487 Machynlleth-Dolgellau road. The hotel is on the lake shore. Price guide: Single £47; double/twin £94; suite £114.

17 rms  M 30

For hotel location, see maps on pages 490-496

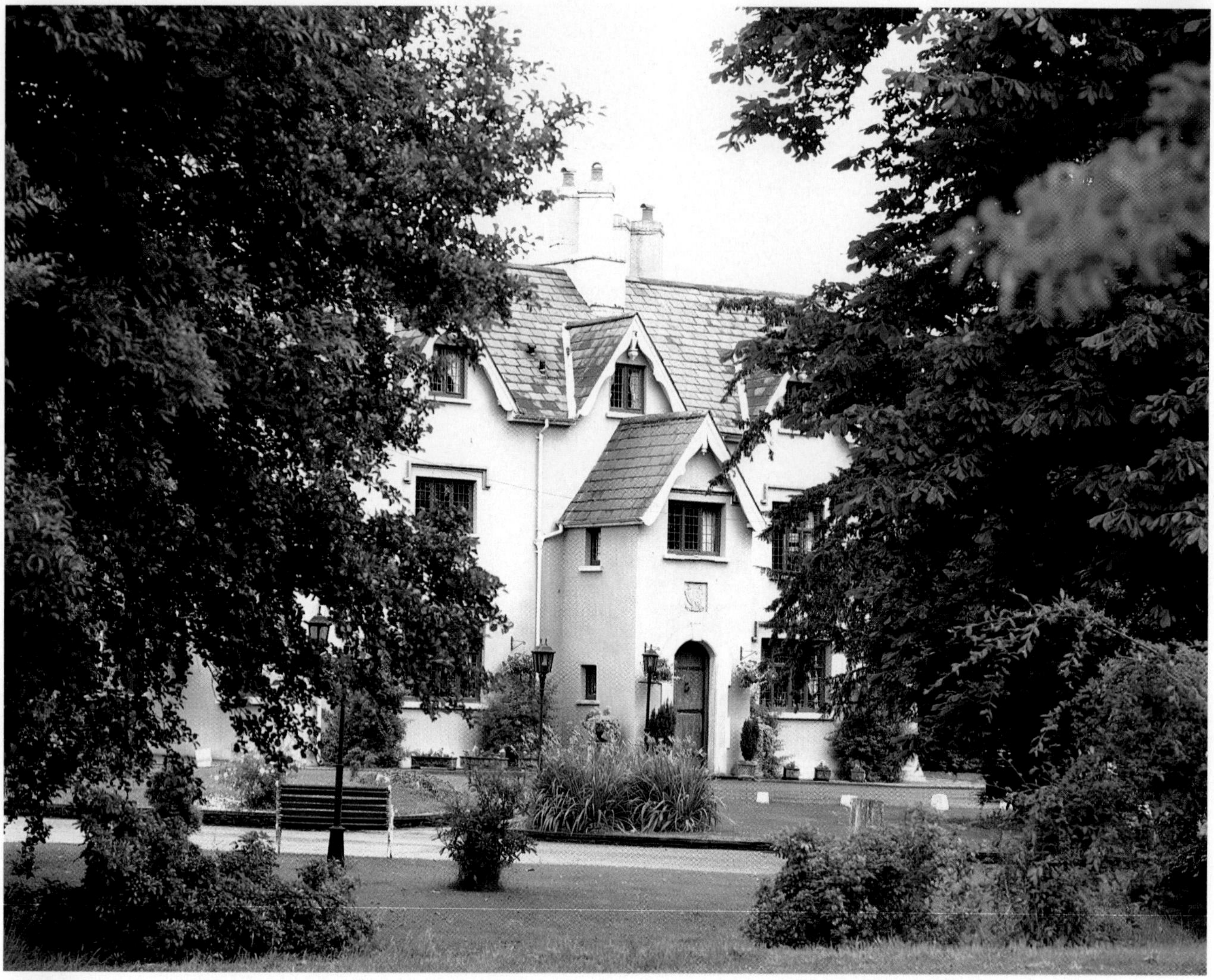

# THE CWRT BLEDDYN HOTEL

**LLANGYBI, NEAR USK, GWENT, SOUTH WALES NP5 1PG**
**TEL: 01633 450521 FAX: 01633 450220**

Set in 17 acres of wooded grounds, this 14th century manor house, not far from the Roman town of Caerleon, is the perfect location from which to explore the Wye Valley and Forest of Dean. The hotel is a fine example of the traditional and the modern under one roof. Carved panelling and huge fireplaces in the lounge lend an air of classic country-house comfort. The 36 en suite bedrooms are spacious and offer guests every amenity, and most have wonderful views over the surrounding countryside. Cwrt Bleddyn's restaurant is renowned for its French-influenced cuisine, with both à la carte and table d'hôte menus. There is a good choice of vegetarian dishes. Light meals are also served in the hotel's country club. Here, extensive leisure facilities include an indoor heated swimming pool, sauna, solarium, steam room and beauty salon. Alternatively, guests may just wish to stroll and relax in the grounds. Nearby is the local beauty spot of Llandegfedd, with its 434-acre reservoir. The hotel is open all year round. Private dining/function rooms are available. **Directions:** From Cardiff/Bristol, leave M4 at junction 25. Hotel is 3 miles north of Caerleon on the road to Usk. From the Midlands, take M5, then A40 to Monmouth. Turn off A449, through Usk, over stone bridge, then left towards Caerleon for 4 miles. Price guide: Single £85; double/twin £105.

For hotel location, see maps on pages 490-496

# Johansens Recommended Hotels in Scotland

*Myths and mountains, lochs and legends – Scotland's stunning scenic splendour acts as a magnet for visitors from all over the globe. Superb as it is, Scotland's charismatic charm is more than just visual.*

Rich in history and heritage this ancient nation can trace its origins back over 14 centuries when the 'Scots' tribe from Ireland who had carved out their new Kingdom of Dalriada from land held by the Picts in the 5th Century, eventually gave their name to the united nation of Picts and Scots - Scotland.

Prehistoric sites can be found in almost every corner of Scotland, including the outer islands (Orkney has a particularly rich concentration of bronze age ruins), and ancient standing stones have long been a fascination for curious visitors.

Several new archaeological attractions have opened recently, including Kilmartin House in Argyll. Close to Dunadd, the ancient capital of Dalriada, - the birthplace of Scotland, Kilmartin House brings 6000 years of history to life with imaginative audio visual displays, exhibitions and a range of prehistoric artefacts from Argyll, the original 'coastline of the Gael' (Earraghaidheal in Gaelic).

Across the country in Grampian region, Archeolink at Oyne, around 25 miles north of Aberdeen, is a £4 million interpretative centre which looks set to become a major visitor attraction for the north east. Situated in 40 acres around Berry Hill, an iron age enclosure, the Centre applies state-of-the-art technology to Aberdeenshire's wealth of Stone Circles, Symbol Stones and ancient hill forts.

Far from being stuck in the past, Scotland boasts cosmopolitan cities throbbing with life and vitality. Vibrant arts and culture, magnificent architecture, superb shopping and exciting night-life are all there to be enjoyed.

Getting around is easy with a modern transport infrastructure and communications befitting a nation whose sons invented the telephone, television and tarmacadam! Indeed, air, rail and ferry links are on the increase and competitive economy fares have encouraged many new visitors, but don't worry, beyond the city boundaries space, peace and tranquillity are still the order of the day and you don't have to go far off the beaten track to find solitude and wilderness.

The glorious natural environment remains one of Scotland's most attractive features offering endless options for sports, including walking, cycling, sailing, riding and climbing.

The home of golf and the Highland games, Scotland is an outdoor enthusiast's dreamland. But you don't have to be active to appreciate this wealth of natural brilliance.

Travelling by car is simple and enjoyable; and where but Scotland would you find main roads bordering world-famous beauty spots, such as Loch Lomond and Loch Ness?

You can take your car by ferry to most of Scotland's numerous islands and a new Irish ferry service to Campbeltown has opened up the Kintyre Peninsula - an area of outstanding natural beauty.

Kintyre's coastline, characteristically for Scotland's west coast, is riveted with ruined ramparts and crowned with castellations. The stone walls bear witness to Argyll's bloody past, for this area has seen numerous battles, often between rival clans, with a massacre at Dunaverty Castle on a scale more heinous than Glencoe.

For all their feuding, the clans gave Scotland some of its most recognisable icons. Kilts, bagpipes, Highland Games and dancing - all survived and flourished despite the ban imposed following the Jacobite defeat at Culloden in 1746. Scotland's relationship with England these days is more cordial. The historic 'Stone of Destiny' - the stone which pillowed Jacob's head as he dreamed his dream, later became the property of the migrating Celtic tribe who eventually settled in Scotland in AD498 - was stolen from Scone by Edward I of England in 1296.

Seven hundred years later the Government of Great Britain returned this ceremonial seat for the inauguration of Scots' Kings to Scotland and it can now be seen on display in Edinburgh Castle.

The lavish history and heritage of the oldest Kingdom in Europe is matched by its majestic landscapes and superlative scenery. Friendly and welcoming, the Scots are proud of their country and you'll find them eager to share its many delights and attractions.

For more information on Scotland, please contact:-

**The Scottish Tourist Board**
**23 Ravleston Terrace**
**Edinburgh**
**EH4 3EU**
**Tel: 0131 332 2433**

In association with MasterCard

# ARDOE HOUSE HOTEL AND RESTAURANT

**SOUTH DEESIDE ROAD, BLAIRS, ABERDEEN AB12 5YP**
**TEL: 01224 867355 FAX: 01224 861283 US TEL: (800) 2236764**

Built in 1874 by a local manufacturer for his wife, the majestic, tall turreted Ardoe House is designed in the Scottish Baronial style favoured by Queen Victoria for Balmoral Castle, 40 miles upstream. Just ten minutes drive from Aberdeen city centre, the hotel stands high and hidden away with magnificent views over the River Dee and open countryside. Guests approaching along the shrub lined drive can be forgiven for feeling that they are approaching a fairytale castle, particularly as day turns to night and floodlights illuminate the solid, silver granite walls. Ardoe House has the style and charm of an elegant country mansion with all modern comforts. Rich oak panelling, high, ornate ceilings and stained glass windows abound. The Grand Hall reception area is truly grand, the richly decorated and furnished public rooms truly relaxing and there are various small secluded areas where guests can privately enjoy a glass of malt whisky. Every bedroom has a pleasant and comfortable atmosphere and whatever your taste in cuisine, the fare available in the hotel's award-winning restaurant will more than match expectations. Ardoe House is ideally situated for touring Royal Deeside and the surrounding Grampian region. **Directions:** Leave Aberdeen on the A92 south and join the B9077 Deeside Road at the Bridge of Dee. Price guide: Single £85–£145; double/twin £120–£165; suite £160–£220.

71 rms · 220

For hotel location, see maps on pages 490-496

# THAINSTONE HOUSE HOTEL & COUNTRY CLUB

**INVERURIE, ABERDEENSHIRE AB51 5NT**
**TEL: 01467 621643 FAX: 01467 625084**

An avenue of tall, whispering beech and sycamore trees culminates at a gracious portal leading into the grandeur of the galleried reception area of this historic Palladian mansion. Standing resplendent in 40 acres of lush meadowland, surrounded by richly wooded valleys, heather-clad moors and a magnificent series of castles, Thainstone House offers visitors the opportunity to enjoy the style of a bygone area, combined with all the modern comforts of a first-class hotel. Rebuilt in the 19th century after being torched by 18th century Jacobites, the hotel radiates a relaxed ambience and a regal atmosphere confirmed by the elegance of its public rooms. Superb meals can be enjoyed in the sumptuous Georgian restaurant. Informally, you can dine in Cammie's Bar with its lighthearted charm. All the bedrooms have been created for comfort and restfulness. There is even a welcoming decanter of sherry and a tray of shortbread awaiting arrivals. Extensive leisure facilities include a trimnasium and a heated swimming pool designed in the style of an ancient Roman bath. Outdoor activities range from golf and fishing to clay pigeon shooting and falconry. Walkers can tramp the famed Grampian castle and whisky trails. **Directions:** From Aberdeen, take A96 towards Inverurie and turn left at Thainstone Mart roundabout. Price guide: Single £85; double/twin £110; suite £180.

48 rms        250           

For hotel location, see maps on pages 490-496

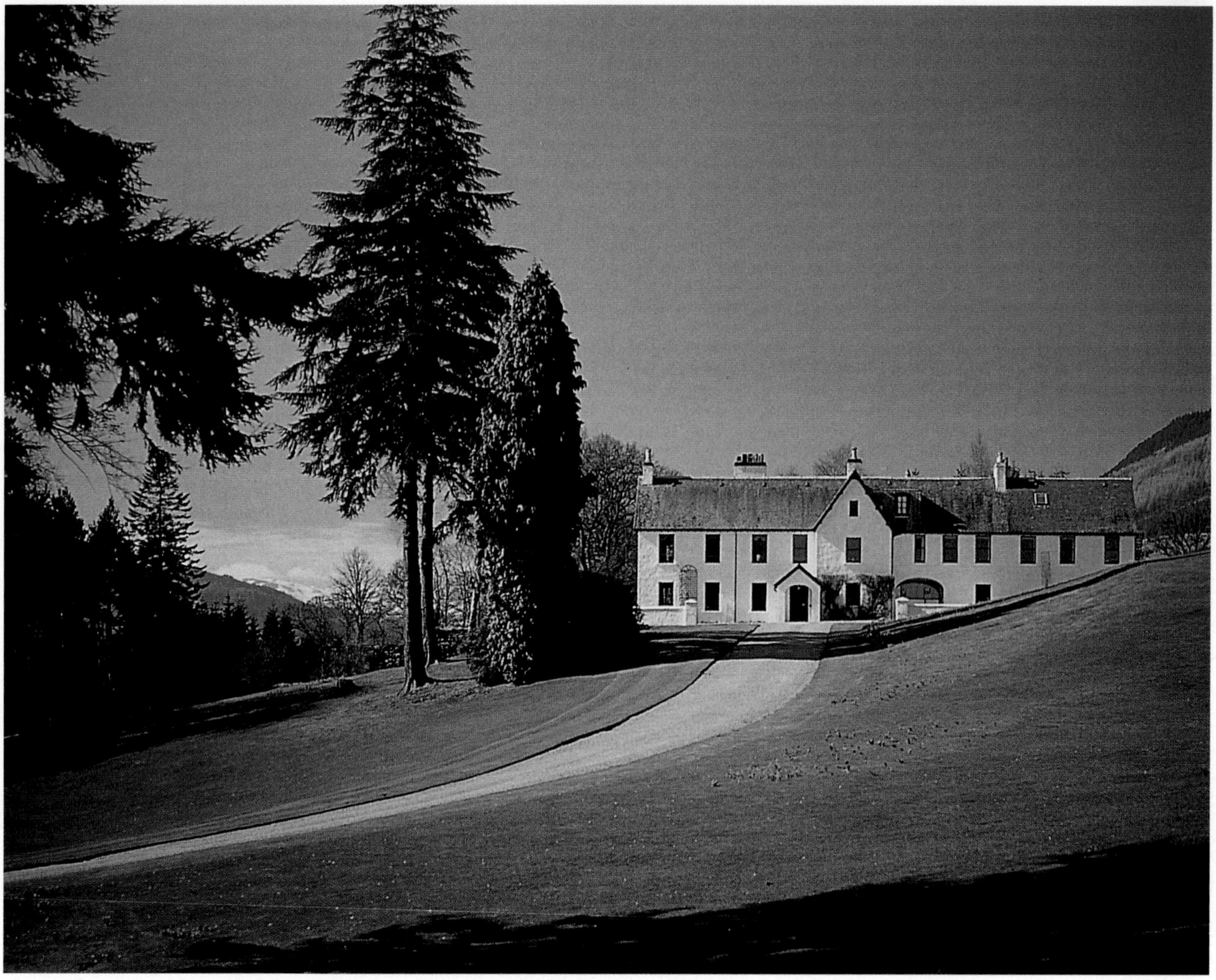

# FARLEYER HOUSE HOTEL

**ABERFELDY, PERTHSHIRE PH15 2JE**

**TEL: 01887 820332 FAX: 01887 829430 E-MAIL: 100127@compuserve.com**

Farleyer House, whose pedigree dates from the 16th century, stands amid mature woodland overlooking the Tay Valley. The hotel has won the *Good Food Guide* Tayside Restaurant of the Year 1990 & 1996 award for its wonderful cuisine, and is highly praised in the most prestigious food guides. The four-course dinner is always delicious with wines to match. A more relaxed and informal meal may be enjoyed in the new Scottish Bistro where the blackboard menu offers an outstanding choice. The house has a lengthy history, dating back to the 16th century. It has a warm luxurious feel with soft-pile carpets, full-bodied drapes, clusters of paintings and scattered *'objets d'art'*. Deer-stalking, fishing, riding, sailing and water sports can be arranged and there is a 6-hole practice golf course in the grounds. The nearby Kenmore Club with its indoor pool and leisure facilities is available for guests. The central location makes this hotel a perfect base for touring the countryside and historic towns of Scotland. Dogs are accommodated separately from the main house and strictly by prior arrangement. **Directions:** Drive through Weem on the B846 past Castle Menzies and Farleyer is on the Kinloch– Rannoch road. Price guide: Single £75–£105; double/twin £150–£195.

For hotel location, see maps on pages 490-496

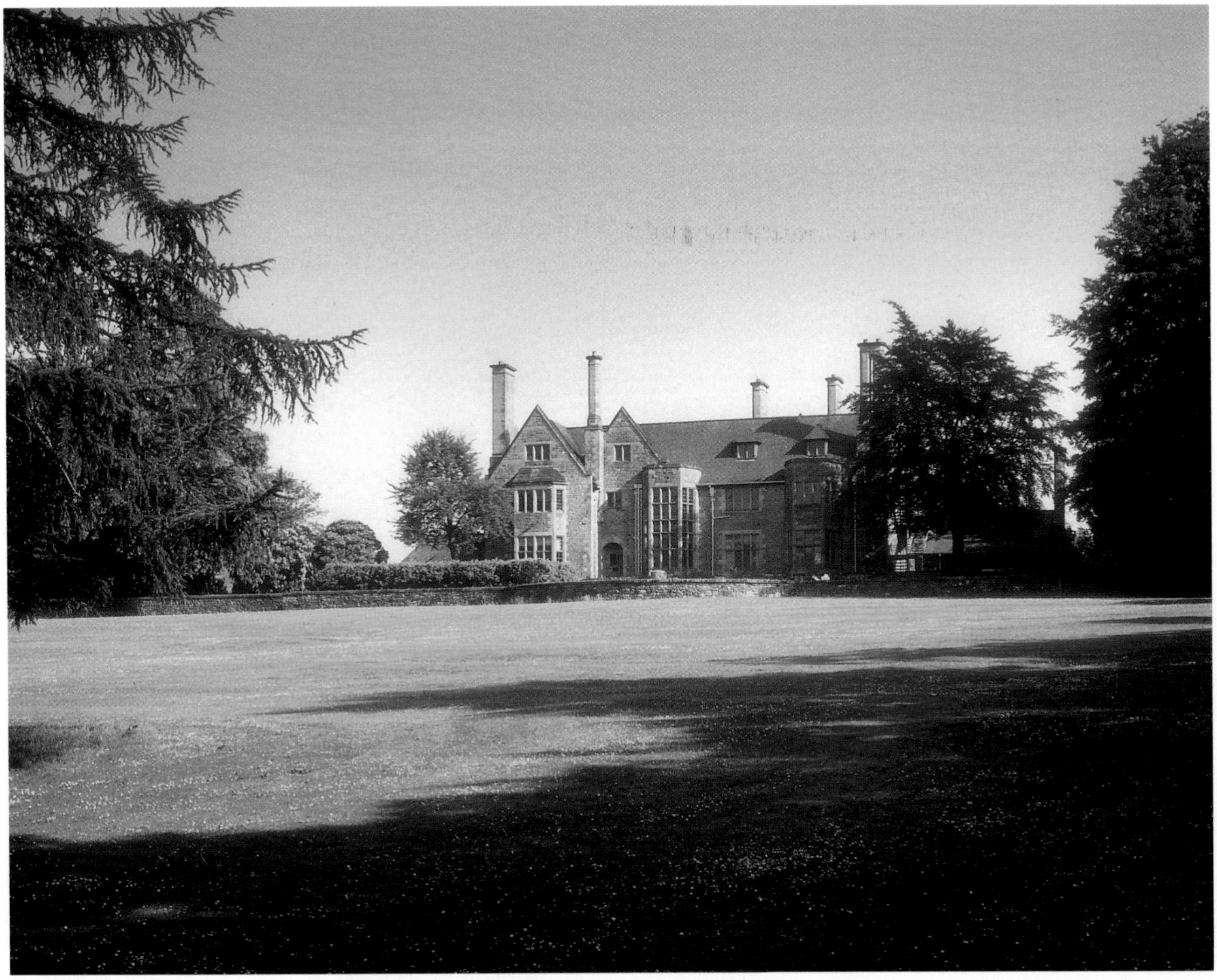

# THE GEAN HOUSE

**GEAN PARK, ALLOA, NR STIRLING FK10 2HS**
**TEL: 01259 219275 FAX: 01259 213827**

The Gean House was commissioned in 1910 by Alexander Forrester-Paton, a leading industrialist, as a wedding present for his eldest son. Fully restored and beautifully furnished, this architecturally significant house is surrounded by parkland. The elegant reception hall has a minstrels gallery, an inglenook fireplace and fine views of the nearby Ochil Hills. In the south-facing, walnut-panelled dining room – a non-smoking room overlooking the rose garden – guests enjoy the recognised gourmet cuisine. A splendid breakfast menu is also offered and room service is available. With its wide doors and absence of steps on the ground floor, the hotel is particularly suitable for guests with disabilities. Facilities for business meetings and conferences are also available. Only ten minutes drive from Stirling town centre, there is much to enjoy locally – walks in the Ochils, fishing, boating, golf – St Andrews and Gleneagles are forty minutes drive away. Shopping for hand-knit, fine woollens and cashmeres is a popular past-time. **Directions:** Alloa via Kincardine Bridge and A907 from east, or via same road west from Stirling; park entrance is on the B9096 Tullibody Road. Price guide: Single £80; double/twin £120–£140.

For hotel location, see maps on pages 490-496

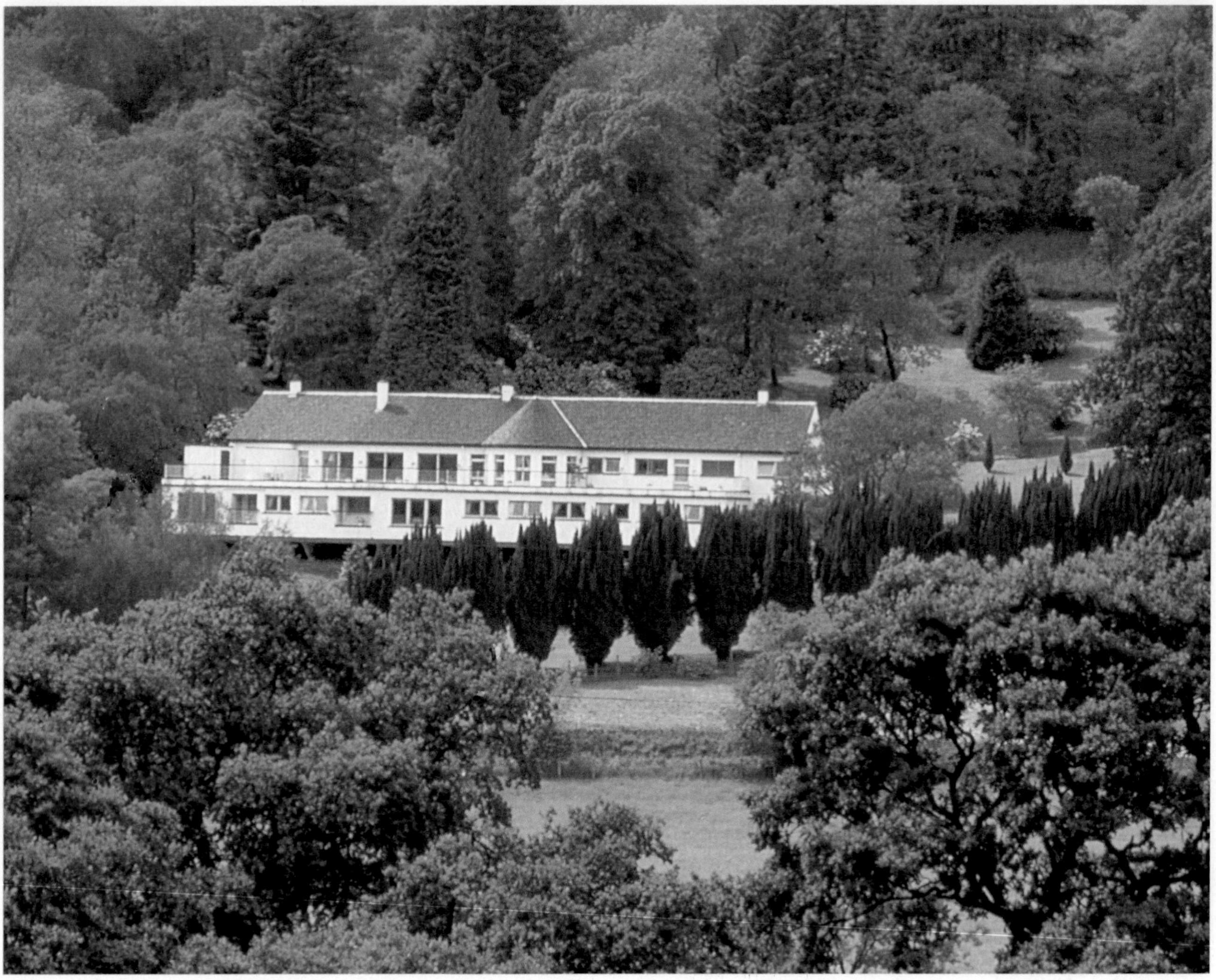

# Invercreran Country House Hotel

**GLEN CRERAN, APPIN, ARGYLL PA38 4BJ**
**TEL: 01631 730 414 FAX: 01631 730 532 E-MAIL: invercreran@dial.pipex.com**

The outstanding setting of Invercreran House is one of the many reasons for its popularity. Surrounded by mountains, it stands in 25 secluded acres of shrub gardens and woodland, overlooking the mature trees and meadows of Glen Creran. Guests can stroll through the grounds towards the River Creran which flows through the glen. Viewed from the outside, it is surprising to discover that the hotel has only nine guest bedrooms. The interiors, reception rooms and bedrooms alike are spacious. In the large lounge there is a free-standing fireplace where logs burn beneath a copper canopy. The Kersley family are involved in all aspects of the day-to-day running of the house. Their son Tony, the master chef, prepares delicious dishes that emphasise the full flavour of fresh Scottish game, fish, vegetables and soft fruits. Meals are served in the semi-circular, marble-floored dining room. Invercreran House is well positioned for touring the Western Highlands, offering easy access to Oban, Fort William and Glencoe. Closed November to early March. Internet: http://www.invercreran.com **Directions:** Hotel is off the A828 Oban–Fort William road, 14 miles north of Connel Bridge, 18 miles south of Ballachulish Bridge. Travelling to Invercreran at the head of Loch Creran, stay on the minor road going north east into Glen Creran; hotel is 3/4 mile on left. Price guide: Single £67.50; double/twin £100–£145; suite £150–£160.

For hotel location, see maps on pages 490-496

# BALCARY BAY HOTEL

**AUCHENCAIRN, NR CASTLE DOUGLAS, DUMFRIES & GALLOWAY DG7 1QZ**
**TEL: 01556 640217 FAX: 01556 640272**

The hotel takes its name from the bay on which it stands, in an area of Galloway that is romantic in its isolation and which was once full of intrigue. Heston Isle, the hide-out of 17th century smugglers, fronts the hotel's view across the Solway coast and the Cumbrian Hills beyond. Originally owned by a shipping firm, the hotel was known to harbour illegal loot in its secret underground passages. Nowadays, Scottish hospitality at Balcary Bay includes the provision of modern facilities with a traditional atmosphere. It offers local delicacies such as lobsters, prawns and salmon imaginitavely prepared, plus the reasurring intimacy of a family-run hotel. Despite its northerly aspect, Galloway benefits from the Gulf Stream and enjoys a mild and long holiday season. The area has great coastal and woodland walks. Closed from mid November to early March. Nearby are several 9 and 18 hole golf courses at Colvend, Kirkcudbright, Castle Douglas, Southerness and Dumfries. There are also salmon rivers and trout lochs, sailing, shooting, riding and birdwatching facilities. The area abounds with National Trust historic properties and gardens. **Directions:** Located off the A711 Dumfries–Kirkcudbright road, two miles out of Auchencairn on the Shore Road. Price guide: Single £54; double/twin £96–£108. Seasonal short breaks and reduced inclusive rates for 3 and 7 nights.

For hotel location, see maps on pages 490-496

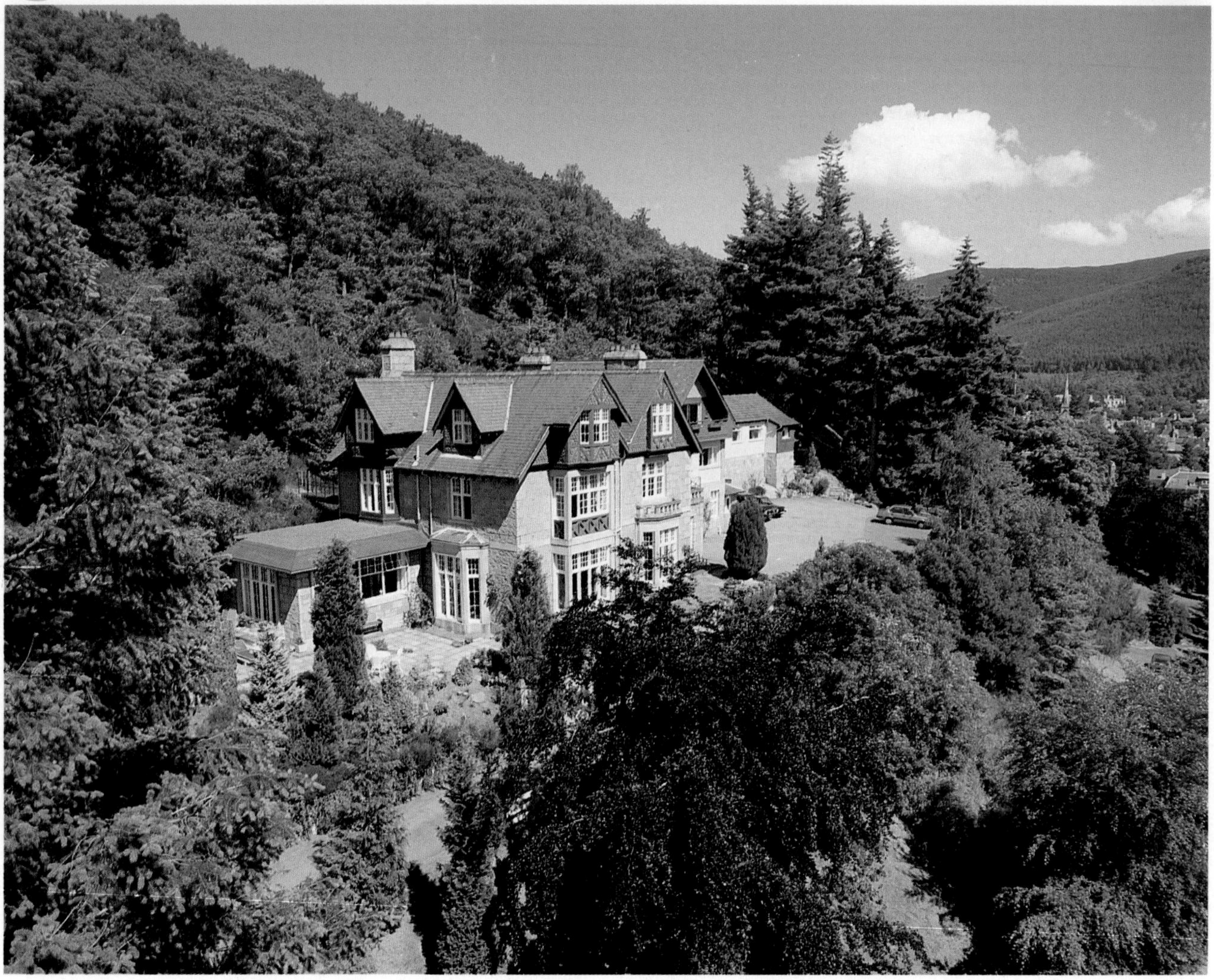

# DARROCH LEARG HOTEL

**BRAEMAR ROAD, BALLATER, ABERDEENSHIRE AB35 5UX**
**TEL: 013397 55443 FAX: 013397 55252**

Four acres of leafy grounds surround Darroch Learg, sited on the side of the rocky hill which dominates Ballater. The hotel, which was built in 1888 as a fashionable country residence, offers panoramic views over the golf course, River Dee and Balmoral Estate to the fine peaks of the Grampian Mountains. Oakhall, an adjacent mansion built in Scottish baronial style and adorned with turrets, contains five of the 18 bedrooms ideal for private groups. All are individually furnished and decorated, providing every modern amentity. The reception rooms in Darroch Learg are similarly elegant and welcoming, a comfortable venue in which to enjoy a relaxing drink. Log fires create a particularly cosy atmosphere on chilly nights. The beautifully presented food has been awarded 3AA Rosettes. A wide choice of wines complements the cuisine, which is best described as modern and Scottish in style. To perfect the setting, there is a wonderful outlook south towards the hills of Glen Muick. The wealth of outdoor activities on offer include walking, riding, mountain-biking, loch and river fishing, gliding and ski-ing. Ballater itself is interesting with an old ruined Kirk and ancient Celtic stones.A few miles away stands Balmoral Castle, the Highland residence of the British sovereign. **Directions:** At the western edge of Ballater on the A93. Price guide: Single £45; double/twin £75–£110.

18 rms · MasterCard · VISA · AMERICAN EXPRESS · M 35

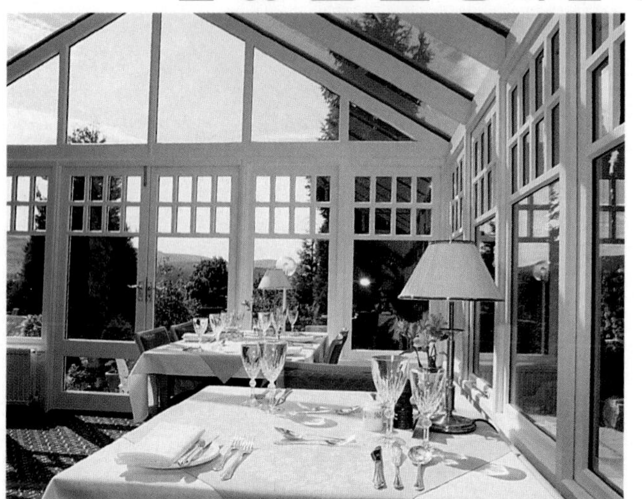

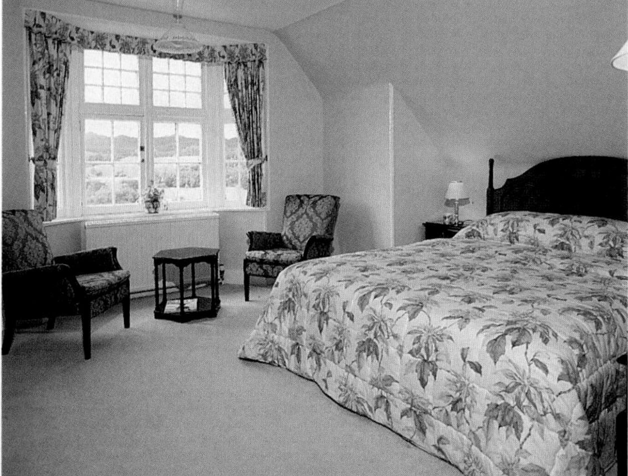

For hotel location, see maps on pages 490-496

# ARISAIG HOUSE

**BEASDALE, BY ARISAIG, INVERNESS-SHIRE PH39 4NR**
**TEL: 01687 450622 FAX: 01687 450626**

Princely redwoods rising above the sudden abundance of Arisaig's oak and rhododendron declare your journey done: now it is time to relax and enjoy the hospitality offered by your hosts, the Smither family. Natural light floods into the house, streaming through tall windows into the inner hall to warm the oak staircase and cast a gleam across polished furniture. The chef's epicurean offerings – supported by a lineage of fine château bottlings – give promise of the restoration of body and soul. Comprising game in season, crisp local vegetables, fruits de mer and pâtisserie baked daily, the cuisine is always a gastronomic delight. High above the ponticum and crinodendrons, the 14 spacious bedrooms afford a magnificent vista of mountains, sea and ever-changing sky. On some days, the clink of billiard balls or the clunk of croquet from the beautiful grounds are the only sounds to thread their way across the rustle of a turning page. On other days guests are hard to find, taking trips on ferries to Skye and the Inner Hebrides or discovering the landscape that has barely changed since Bonnie Prince Charlie's passage through these parts many years ago. Closed early November to mid-March. Arisaig House is a Relais et Châteaux member. **Directions:** Three miles from Arisaig village on the A830 Mallaig road. Price guide : Single £65; double/twin £80–£90.

14 rms MasterCard VISA AMERICAN EXPRESS M 12 10

For hotel location, see maps on pages 490-496

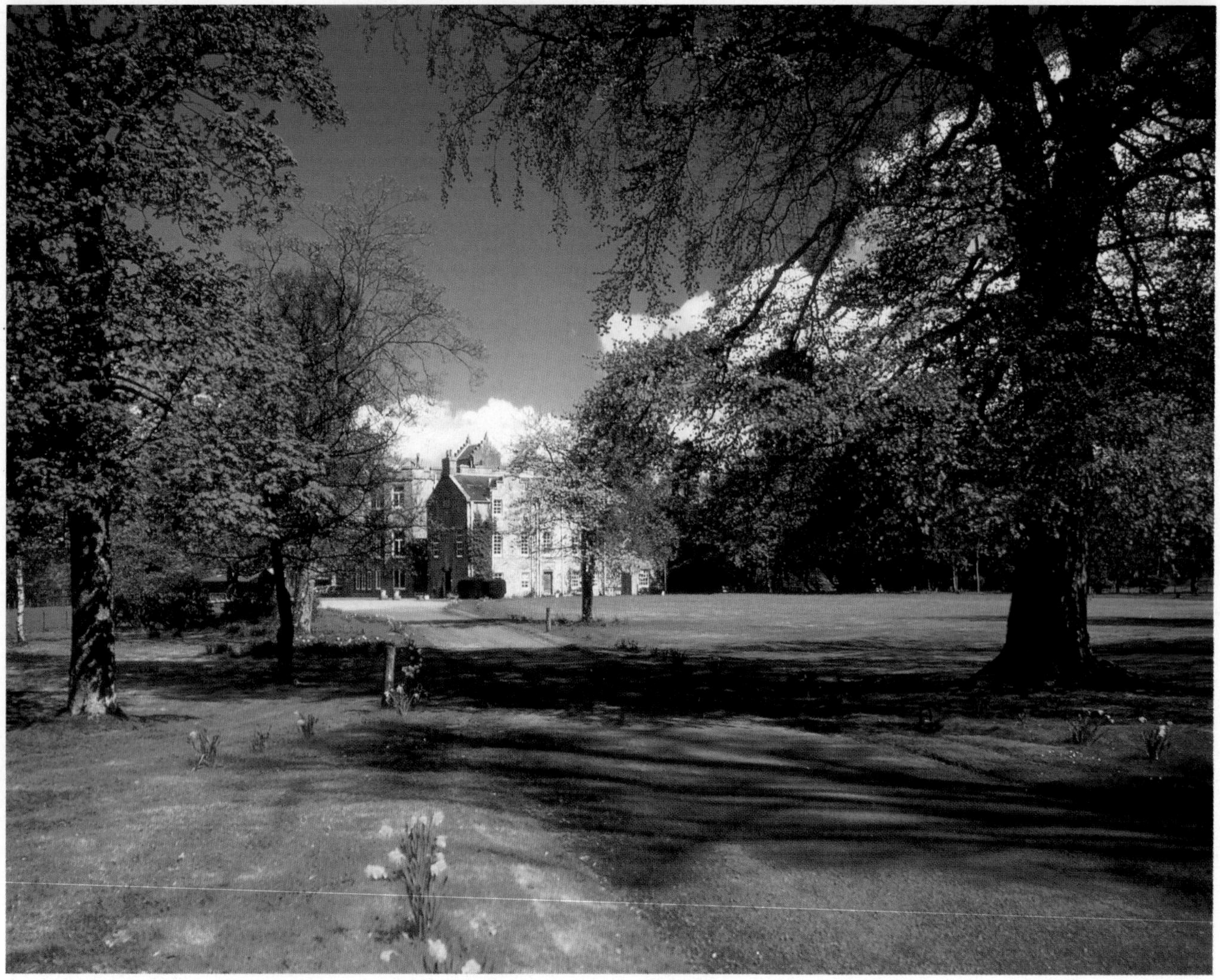

# SHIELDHILL


**QUOTHQUAN, BIGGAR, LANARKSHIRE ML12 6NA**
**TEL: 01899 220035 FAX: 01899 221092**


Set amongst the rolling hills and farmlands of the Upper Clyde Valley lies Shieldhill, a historic castle-style country house hotel offering true Scottish hospitality. The ancestral home of the Chancellor family for more than 700 years. The 'old keep', turreted roof and secret staircase are all romantic reminders of a past age. Individually designed, spacious bedrooms all boast king, queen, twin or four poster beds and en suite facilities and the reception rooms are similarly sumptuous. A welcoming bistro bar, the Gun Room, is the perfect place to enjoy a pre-dinner drink before moving on to the Chancellor Restaurant to sample the creations of head chef, Trevor Williams. The imaginative menu served in this characterful dining room, uses the best fresh fish, meat, game and vegetables. Shieldhill has a permanent marquee ideal for up to 200 wedding guests or dancers. There are also good facilities for meetings and conferences. The surrounding area offers opportunities for walking and golf, while clay pigeon shooting and trout fishing can be arranged. Glasgow, Edinburgh and Carlisle are all within easy reach. **Directions:** From Biggar take B7016 (signposted Carnwath), after 2 miles turn left into Shieldhill Road. The hotel is one and a half miles on the right. Price guide: Single £68–£89; double/twin £104–152; suite £152.

For hotel location, see maps on pages 490-496

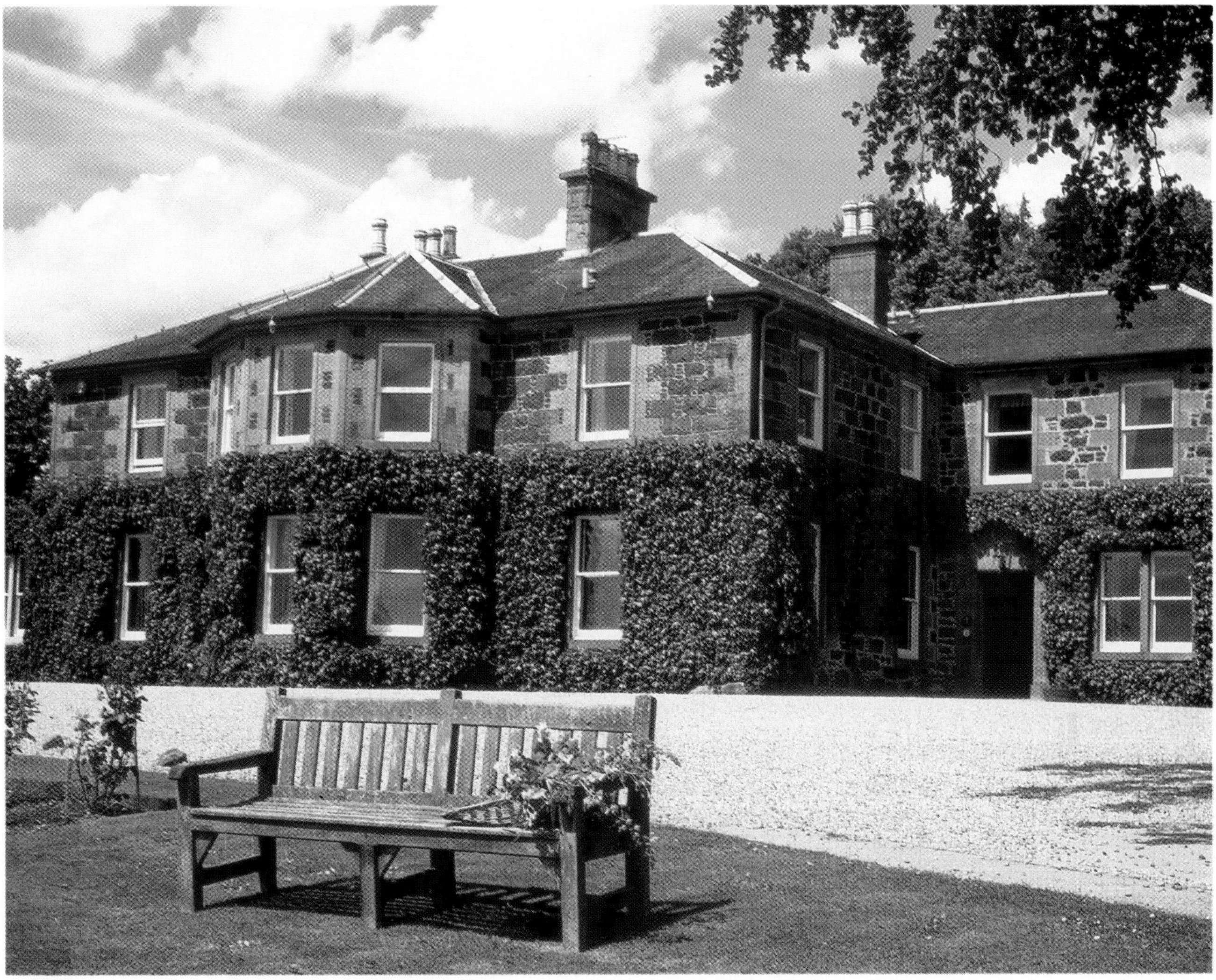

# KINLOCH HOUSE HOTEL

**BY BLAIRGOWRIE, PERTHSHIRE PH10 6SG**
**TEL: 01250 884237 FAX: 01250 884333**

Winner of the 1994 Johansens Country Hotel Award, Kinloch House is an elegant example of a Scottish country home built in 1840. Set in 25 acres, including a magnificent walled garden, and wooded parkland grazed by Highland cattle, it offers panoramic views to the south over Marlee Loch to the Sidlaw Hills beyond. It has a grand galleried hall with an ornate glass ceiling and fine paintings and antiques in the reception rooms. Chef Bill McNicoll and his team have established Kinloch House as one of the top dining venues in Scotland and his daily changing menus are complemented by the very extensive wine list. The cocktail bar, which stocks over 140 malt whiskies, is adjacent to the conservatory and is a focal point of the hotel. In August 1997 a fully equipped Health and Fitness Centre was opened for the exclusive use of guests. David and Sarah Shentall offer a warm personal welcome to all their guests, whether they come simply to enjoy the beauty of the area, or to take advantage of the local pursuits of golf, hill walking, fishing and shooting. For the sightseer, Glamis Castle, Scone Palace and Blair Castle are among the area's attractions. 3 AA Rosettes and 3 AA Red Stars. Closed at Christmas. **Directions:** The hotel is 3 miles west of Blairgowrie, off the A923 Dunkeld road. Price guide (including dinner): Single £88; double/twin £178–£215.

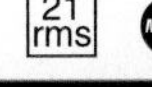

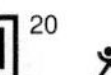

For hotel location, see maps on pages 490-496

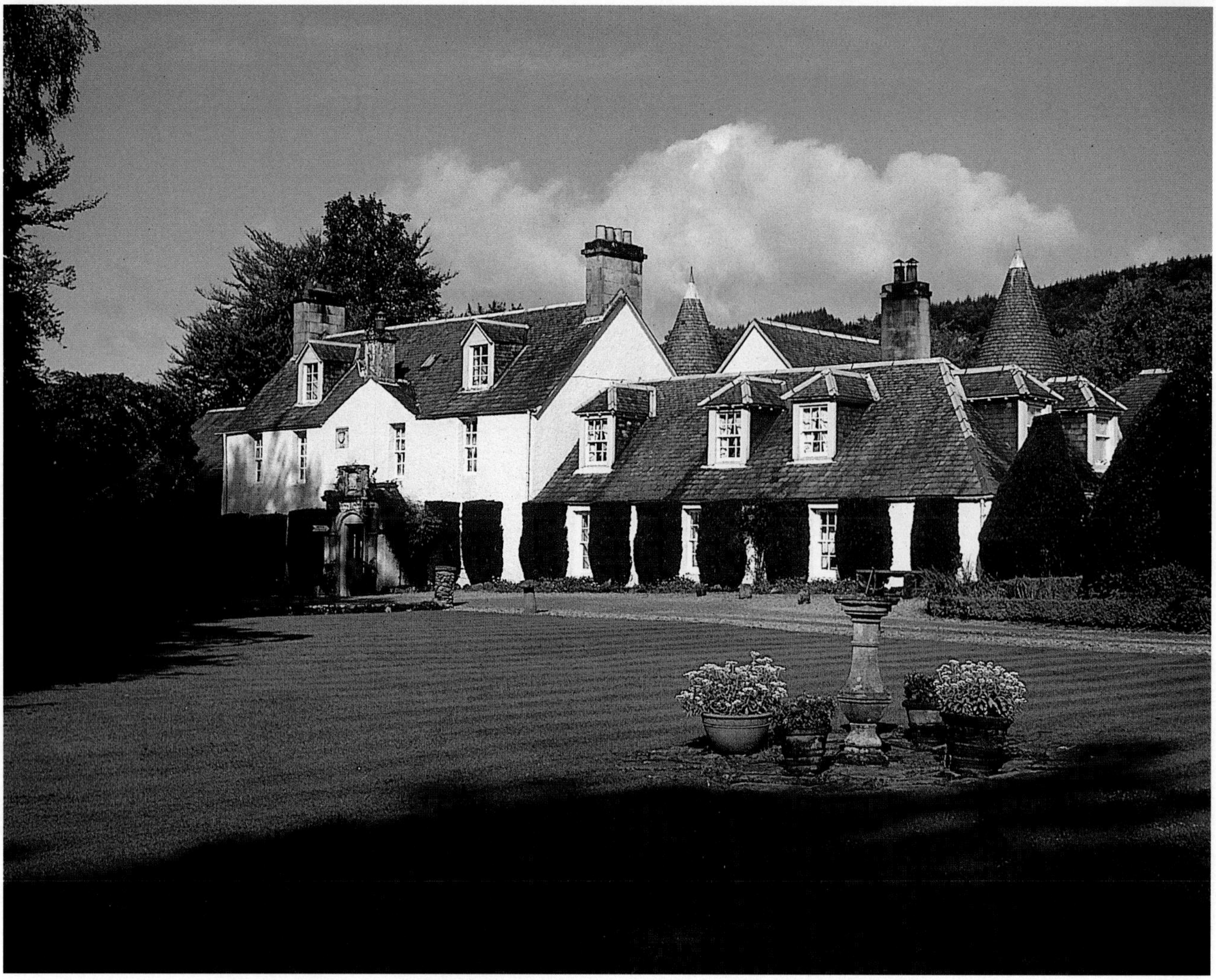

# ROMAN CAMP HOTEL

**CALLANDER, PERTHSHIRE FK17 8BG**
**TEL: 01877 330003 FAX: 01877 331533**

Roman Camp Hotel, originally built in 1625 as a hunting lodge for the Dukes of Perth, takes its name from a nearby Roman encampment. Reminiscent of a French château, the hotel's turrets house a myriad of period features, including a tiny chapel, linenfold wood panelling and ornate moulded ceilings. Set on the banks of the River Teith, the hotel is surrounded by 20 acres of superb grounds including a listed walled garden where herbs and flowers are grown for the hotel. The public rooms, drawing room, sun lounge and library are characterised by grand proportions, antique furnishings and fine views over the river and gardens. The bedrooms are individually and most becomingly furnished. A richly painted ceiling, depicting traditional Scottish designs, is a unique feature of the restaurant, where the thoughtfully compiled menu is accompanied by a long and tempting wine list. Guests are welcome to fish free of charge on the private stretch of the river, while all around there are plenty of interesting walks. Callander is an ideal tourist centre for Central Scotland. Within easy reach are the Trossachs, Doune Motor Museum and Aberfoyle. Dogs are welcome by prior arrangement. **Directions:** Approaching Callander on the A84, the entrance to the hotel is between two cottages in Callander's main street. Price guide: Single £65–£95; double/twin from £89–£145; suite £129–£160.

For hotel location, see maps on pages 490-496

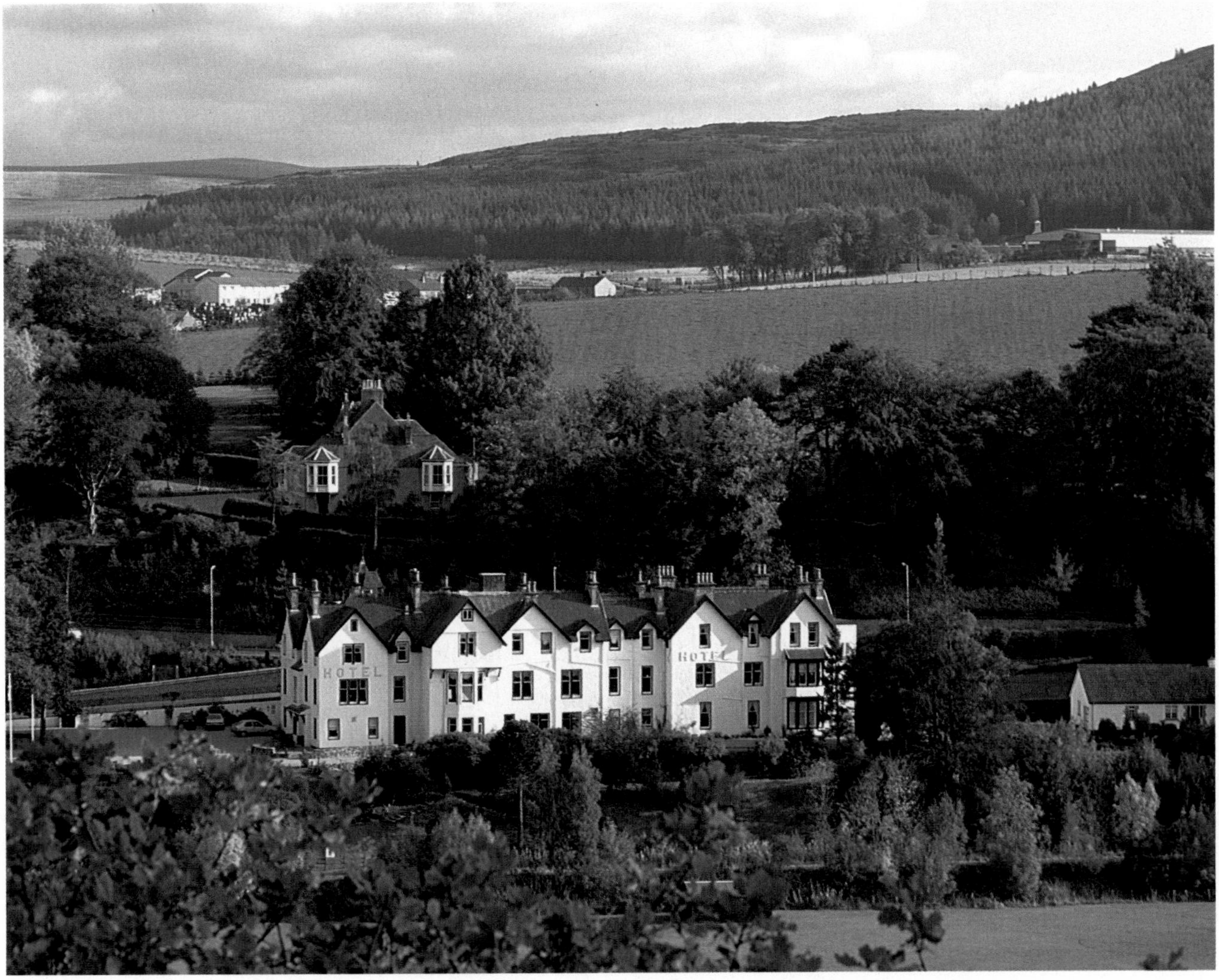

# CRAIGELLACHIE HOTEL

**CRAIGELLACHIE, BANFFSHIRE AB38 9SR**
**TEL: 01340 881204 FAX: 01340 881253**

Overlooking the River Spey, with direct access to the Speyside Walk, Craigellachie Hotel is located in the centre of Scotland's famous Malt Whisky and Castle Trails, in one of the most picturesque villages in Moray. This Victorian hotel opened in 1893 and has recently undergone a meticulous restoration to incorporate all the amenities of a first-class hotel while retaining the charm and elegance of a Scottish country house. Many of the 30 individually designed bedrooms overlook the River Spey and several have a view of the local landmark, Thomas Telford's slender iron bridge. The Ben Aigan and Rib Room have firmly established a good reputation for their innovative treatment of traditional Scottish recipes. Only fresh local produce is used in the preparation of dishes, which are always beautifully presented and accompanied by an extensive wine list. After dinner, guests can choose from a wide selection of 300 malt whiskies. Craigellachie specialises in personalised packages including traditional Scottish Christmas and New year events. Sporting holidays can include golf with private tuition, salmon and trout fishing, deer stalking, game shooting, falconry and pony-trekking. There is also a sauna & solarium and an old-fashioned games room. **Directions:** Just off A95 between Grantown-on-Spey (24 miles) and Elgin (12 miles). Price guide: Single £55–£94; double/twin £109–£130.

For hotel location, see maps on pages 490-496

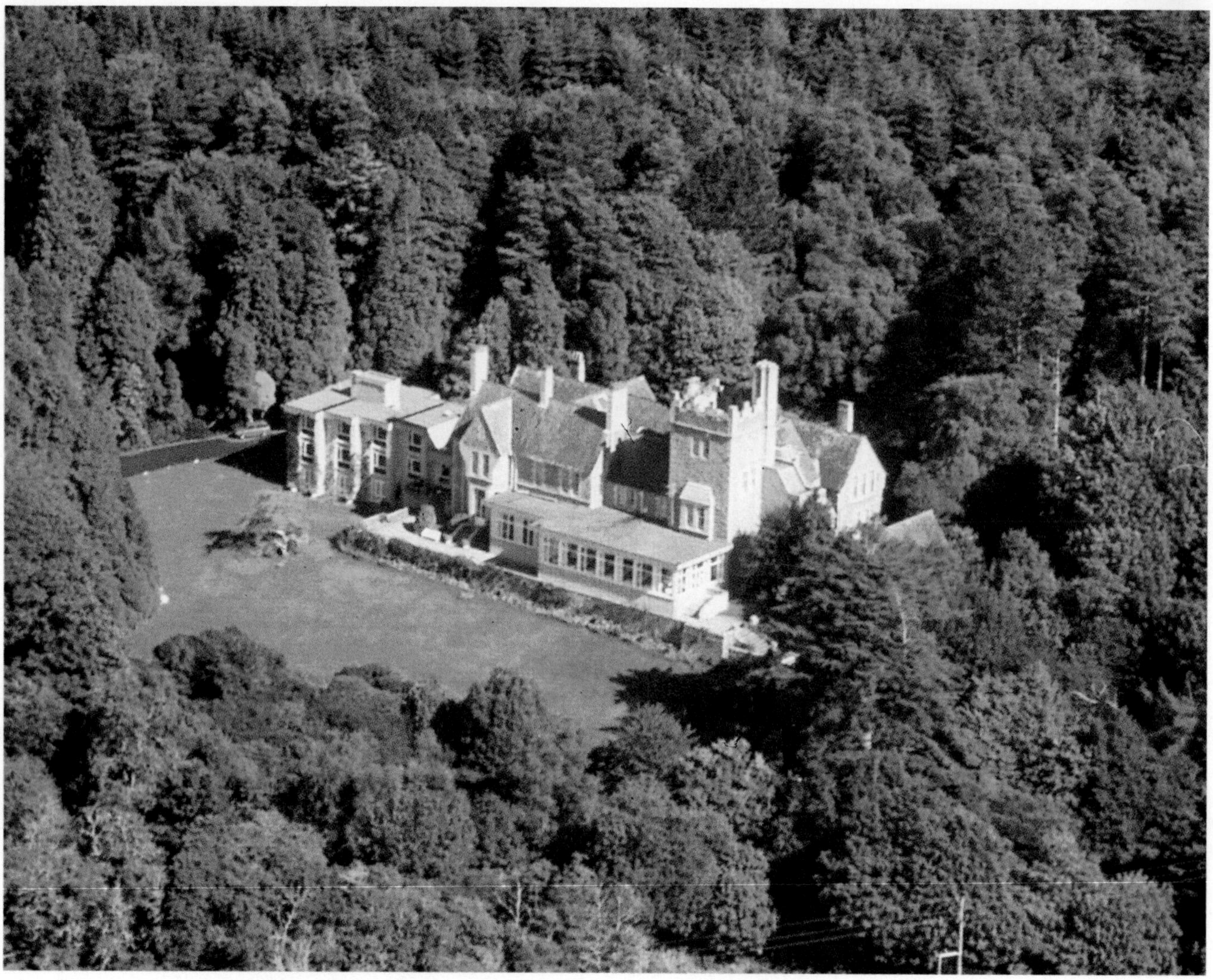

# Baron's Craig Hotel

**ROCKCLIFFE BY DALBEATTIE, KIRKCUDBRIGHTSHIRE DG5 4QF**
**TEL: 01556 630225 FAX: 01556 630328**

Baron's Craig Hotel stands in wooded country overlooking Solway and Rough Firth, a tidal inlet biting deep into tree-covered and heathered hills. Thanks to the mild climate, the 9 acre grounds are ablaze with colour throughout much of the holiday season, especially in May, when masses of rhododendrons are in bloom. An imposing granite edifice, Baron's Craig was built in 1880 and harmoniously extended more recently. The 22 bedrooms have en suite facilities, both bath and shower; all have colour TV, radio, direct-dial telephone and baby-listening service. Tea and coffee making facilities are in all rooms for the convenience of guests but room service is available too. The original character of the building has been retained, with furnishings chosen to complement the period style. Excellent international cooking is augmented by a comprehensive wine list. Only three minutes from the hotel is a safe beach for swimming, while there is abundant scope for golf, fishing, boating, sailing and walking nearby. Among the local attractions are Castle Douglas, New Abbey, Glen Trool and Kirkcudbright. The owner, Alberto Capaccioli, offers a warm welcome to all guests. Closed from November to Easter. **Directions:** Rockcliffe is a small village just off the A710 south of Dalbeattie. Price guide: (including breakfast) Single £55–£62; double/twin £45–£54 (per person). Reductions for stays of three days or more.

For hotel location, see maps on pages 490-496

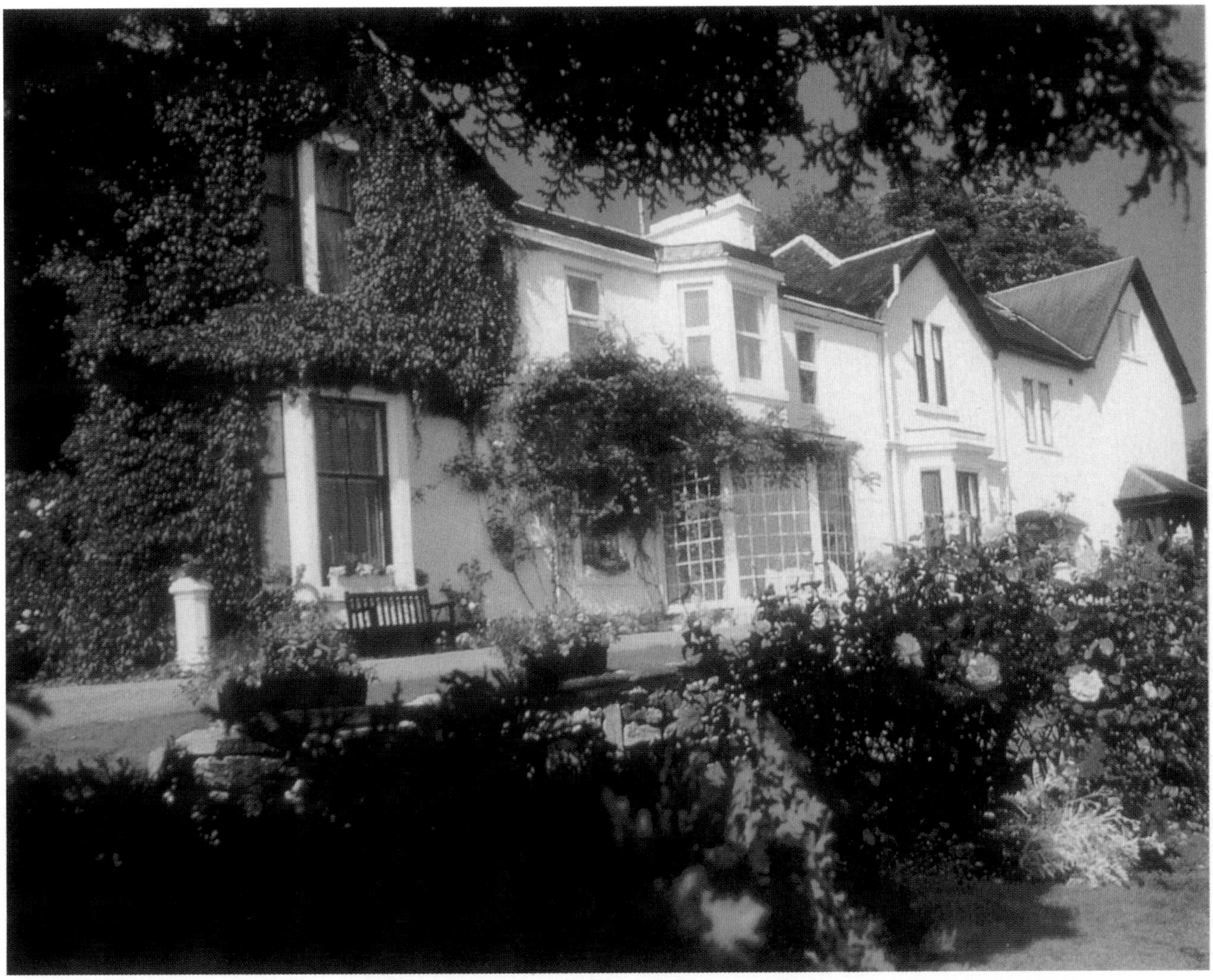

# ENMORE HOTEL

**MARINE PARADE, KIRN, DUNOON, ARGYLL PA23 8HH**
**TEL: 01369 702230 FAX: 01369 702148 E-MAIL: enmorehotel@btinternet.co**

Known as the jewel on the Clyde, the waterfront town of Dunoon on the Cowal peninsula is often regarded as the gateway to the Western Highlands yet only 3/4 hour from Glasgow airport. Enmore Hotel is an attractive house, built in 1785 as a summer retreat for a wealthy cotton merchant. It has since been fully restored by owners David and Angela Wilson. Pretty country wallpaper and bright fabrics characterise the bedrooms, with fluffy towelling robes and flowers among the extras. One of the bedrooms has a water bed and an invigorating whirlpool bath and another has a four-poster bed with a Jacuzzi. In the restaurant, the emphasis is on the use of fresh, local produce to create traditional Scottish dishes. Typical choices may include Arbroath smokies, haggis soup, kippers or steak served in a Drambuie and cream sauce. Chef-patron David Wilson offers a five-course table d'hôte menu each evening. Two international-standard squash courts are available. Dunoon is well equipped with recreational amenities, including bowling, tennis, sailing and a championship golf course. **Directions:** Kirn is on the A815, north-west of Dunoon (A885). A car-ferry crosses to and from Gourock across the Firth of Clyde. Price guide: Single £35–£65; double/twin £40–£69.

For hotel location, see maps on pages 490-496

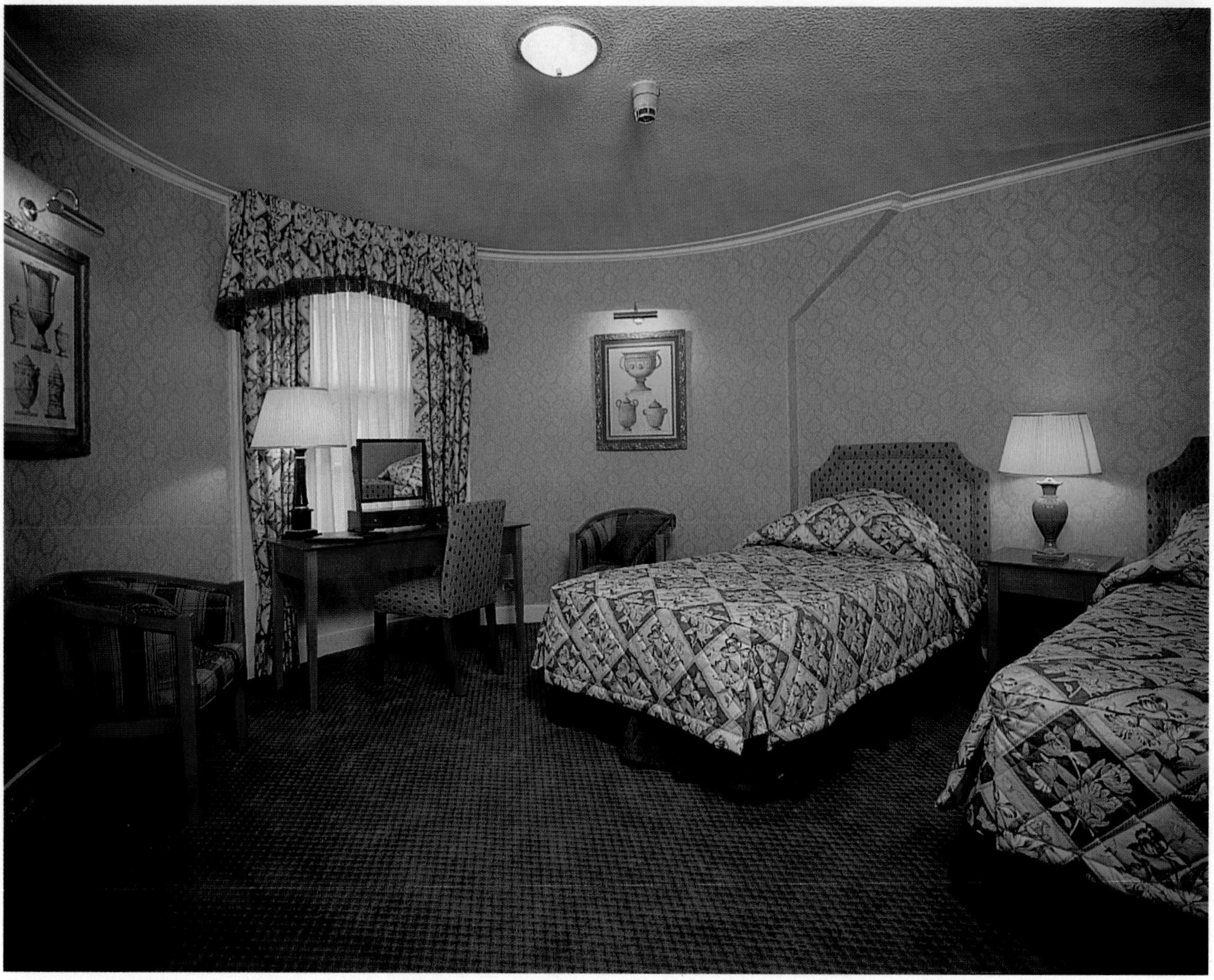

# The Albany Townhouse Hotel

**39 ALBANY STREET, EDINBURGH EH1 3QY**
**TEL: 0131 556 0397 FAX: 0131 557 6633**

Visitors to Edinburgh will welcome The Albany, an exceptional new hotel which has been created out of three Georgian town houses in the centre of the city. With just twenty-one rooms, regular guests will soon become known to the staff, and feel they have come 'home'. The high moulded ceilings, tall windows and other features of the era have been retained. The hand of a top designer is evident throughout in the choice of traditional wallpapers, furnishings and fabrics – yet all todays comforts (including high-tec plugs) can be found in the bedrooms, and the bathrooms are pristine and well-lit. 19th century elegance is the theme of the reception rooms, and the tranquil drawing room is an ideal meeting place. The well stocked, inviting bar and Haldanes restaurant are in the experienced hands of Mr & Mrs George Kelso who have returned to Edinburgh from Ardsheal House where they won many accolades for their inspired interpretation of Scottish and European dishes. The Albany is close to The Castle, The Scottish Whisky Heritage, the Edinburgh Playhouse and Jenners for shopping. The hotel staff will arrange access to any sports or leisure facilities sought by guests. Albany Street is just a few minutes walk from the railway and bus stations, and 30 minutes from the airport. Multi-storey parking is close by. Price guide: Single £65–£85; double/twin £125–£200.

For hotel location, see maps on pages 490-496

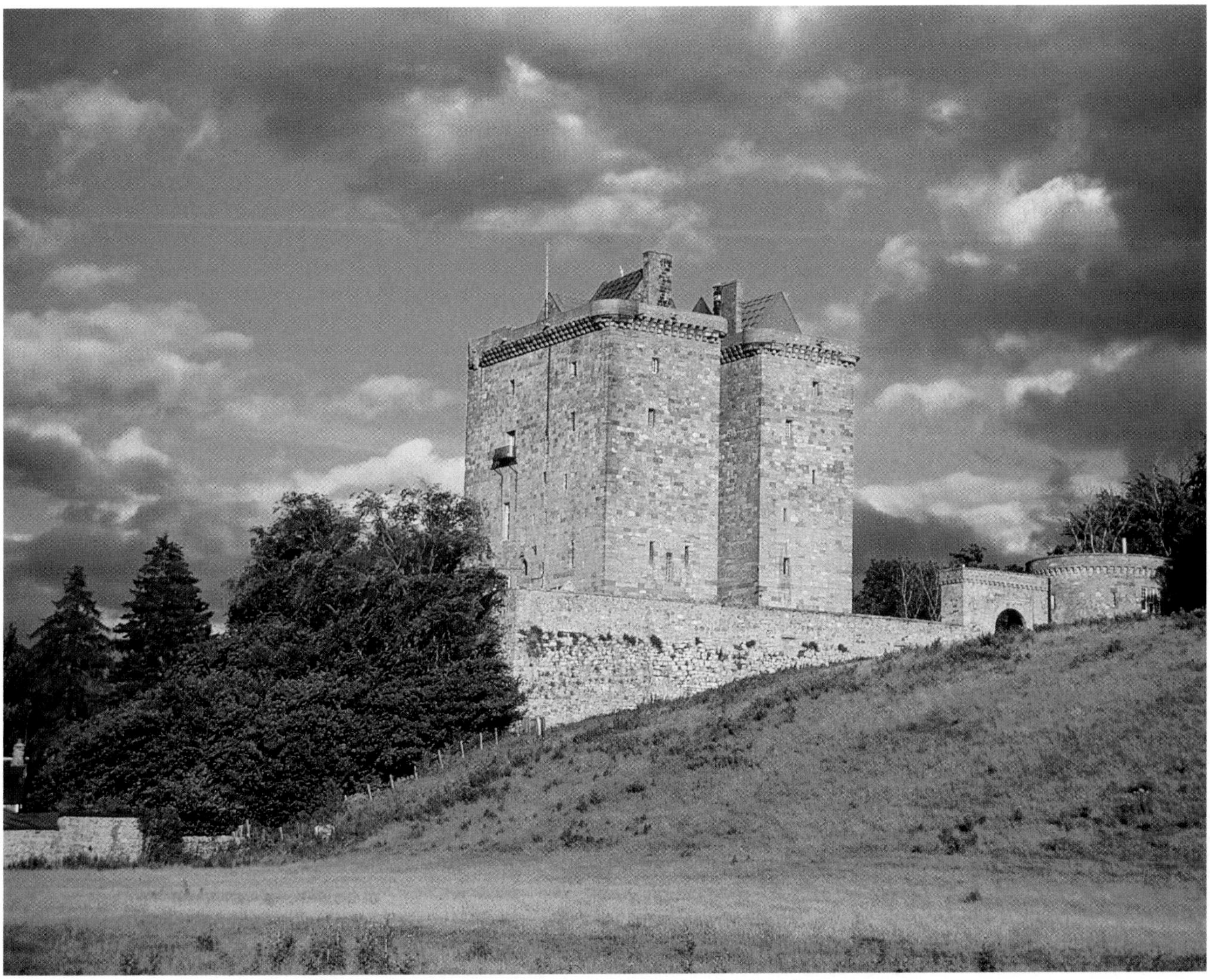

# Borthwick Castle

**BORTHWICK, NORTH MIDDLETON, MIDLOTHIAN EH23 4QY**

**TEL: 01875 820514 FAX: 01875 821702**

To the south of Edinburgh, off the A7, stands historic Borthwick Castle Hotel, a twenty minute drive from Scotland's capital. Built in 1430 by the Borthwick family, this ancient stronghold has witnessed many of the great events of Scotland's history at first hand. Notably, the safe keeping of Mary Queen of Scots following her wedding to the Earl of Bothwell and a forceful visitation by Oliver Cromwell in 1650. At Borthwick Castle there are 10 bedchambers, each with en suite facilities and five with four-poster beds. In the evening, guests dine in the magnificent setting of the candle-lit Great Hall where a four-course set menu is prepared by the chef. The cooking is traditional Scottish, serving fresh local produce. A comprehensive wine list is complemented by a fine selection of malt whiskies. While the castle caters for banquets of up to 65 guests, it especially welcomes those in search of that intimate dinner for two. In either case, the experience is unforgettable. Open from March to January 3rd. **Directions:** 12 miles south of Edinburgh on the A7. At North Middleton, follow signs for Borthwick. A private road then leads to the castle. Price guide: Single £80–£165; double/twin £95–£190.

For hotel location, see maps on pages 490-496

# CHANNINGS

## SOUTH LEARMONTH GARDENS, EDINBURGH EH4 1EZ
## TEL: 0131 315 2226 FAX: 0131 332 9631

Channings is located on a quiet cobbled street only 10 minutes' walk from the centre of Edinburgh, with easy access to the host of shops on Princes Street and the timeless grandeur of Edinburgh Castle. Formerly five Edwardian town houses, the original features have been restored with flair and consideration and the atmosphere is like that of an exclusive country club. Guests can relax in one of the lounges with coffee or afternoon tea. For those who like to browse, the hotel has an interesting collection of antique prints, furniture, *objets d'art*, periodicals and books. The Brasserie (AA Rosette) offers varied menus from a light lunch to full evening meals. Five ground floor suites provide versatile accommodation for corporate requirements, small seminars and presentations, while both the Kingsleigh Suite and oak-panelled library make an ideal venue for cocktail parties and private dinners. At the rear of the hotel is a terraced, patio garden. Special weekend breaks are available throughout the year and offer good value. Closed for Christmas. **Directions:** Go north-west from Queensferry Street, over Dean Bridge on to Queensferry Road. Take third turning on right down South Learmonth Avenue, turn right at end into South Learmonth Gardens. Price guide: Single £90–£102; double/twin £120–£150.

For hotel location, see maps on pages 490-496

# DALHOUSIE CASTLE

**EDINBURGH, BONNYRIGG EH19 3JB**
**TEL: 01875 820153 FAX: 01875 821936**

For over 700 years Dalhousie Castle has stood in beautiful countryside, in bygone times a stronghold, today providing warm Scottish hospitality. Restoration has woven history back into the sandstone walls whilst retaining elegant characteristics of the past. There are fascinating reminders of a rich and turbulent history, such as the Vaulted Dungeon Restaurant, now a delightful and unique setting in which to enjoy classical French and traditional Scottish 'Castle Cuisine'. Sumptuous fabrics and furnishings give the bedrooms an exclusive atmosphere. Five carefully renovated function rooms provide an excellent location for conferences, meetings, banquets and weddings. Parking and a helicopter landing site in the grounds. Only 20 minutes drive from Edinburgh city centre and just 14 miles from the airport. The hotel holds the Scottish Tourist Board's 5 Crowns Highly Commended classification. Taste of Scotland approved. Dalhousie Castle prides itself on the high quality of the personal service received by all its guests. Outdoor activities include mini-highland games, falconry, clay pigeon shooting and riding. Three golf courses are nearby and championship courses half an hour's drive away. **Directions:** from Edinburgh A7 south, through Lasswade and Newtongrange. Right at junction onto B704 and hotel is ¼ mile. Price guide: Single £90–£120; double £110–£210.

For hotel location, see maps on pages 490-496

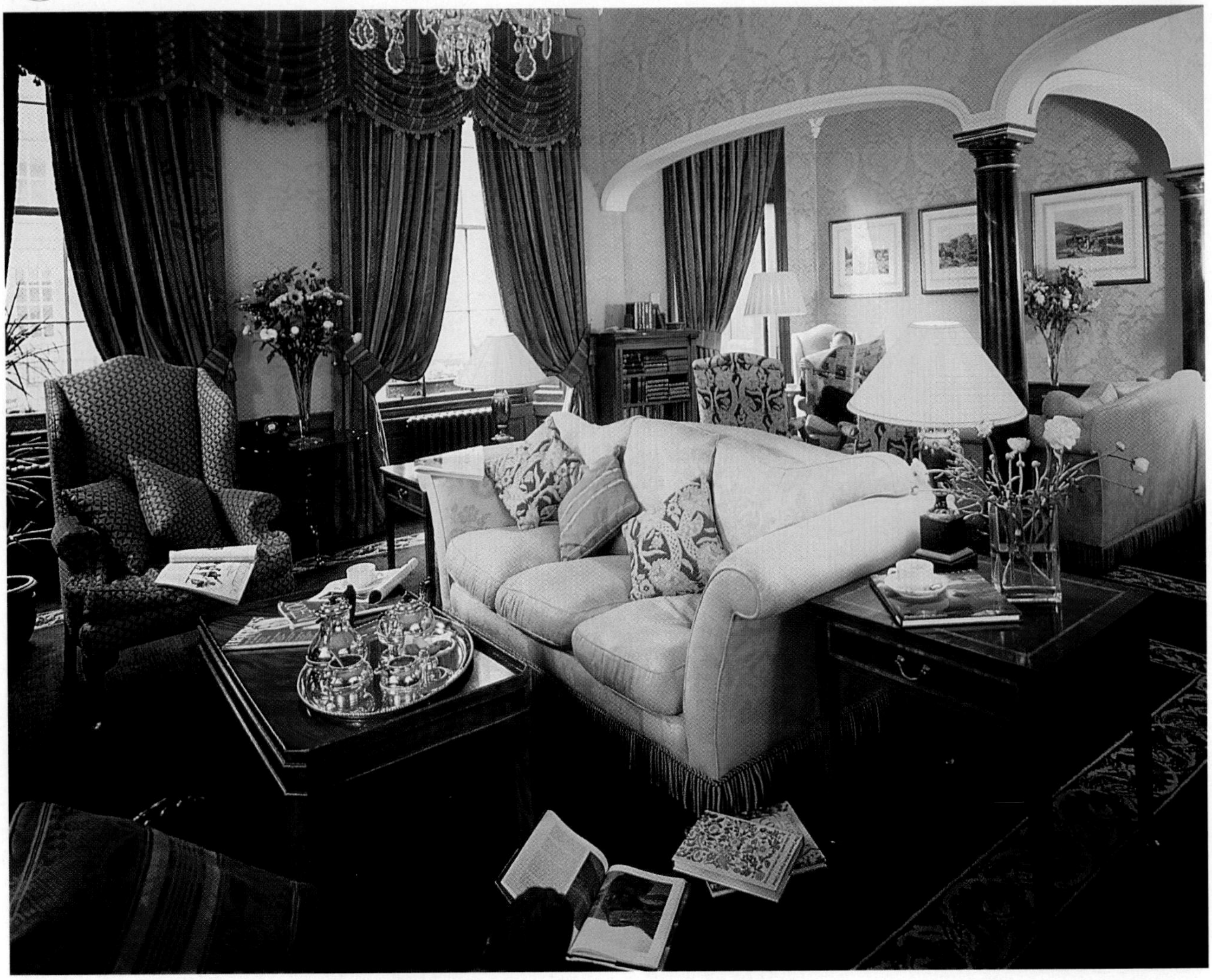

# THE HOWARD

34 GREAT KING STREET, EDINBURGH EH3 6QH
TEL: 0131-557 3500 FAX: 0131-557 6515

Since its conversion from private residence to hotel, The Howard has been sumptuously appointed throughout and offers a service to match the surroundings. The original character of this Georgian town house still prevails. The 15 bedrooms, including two suites, are beautifully furnished with antiques, while the drawing room centres on an elaborate crystal chandelier. The Oval and Cumberland suite offers quiet and elegant surroundings for either meetings or private dining, accommodating 12–30 guests. The Howard is an integral part of the largest classified historical monument in Britain: Edinburgh's New Town. Having a private car park to the rear, The Howard is a superb city centre base from which to explore Edinburgh's cultural heritage, being in close proximity to such monuments as Edinburgh Castle, the Palace of Holyrood and the Royal Mile. Equally it is just minutes from much of the city's business community. **Directions:** Travelling east on Princes Street, take the third left into Frederick Street and turn right into George Street. Take the next left into Hanover Street, go through three sets of lights then turn right into Great King Street. Hotel is on the left. Price guide: Single £110; double £195; suite £275.

15 rms MasterCard VISA AMERICAN EXPRESS M 45

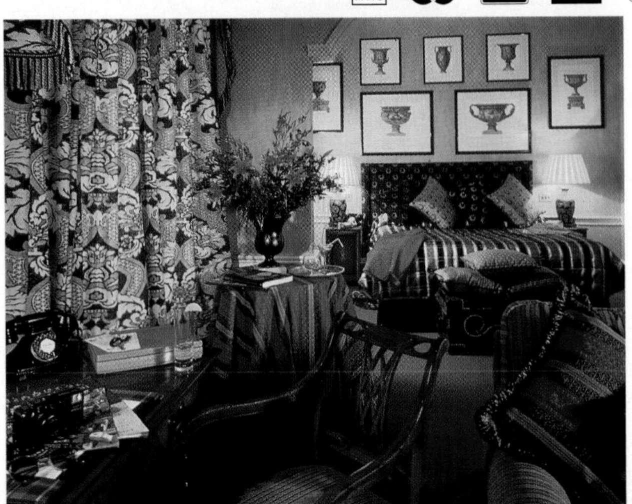

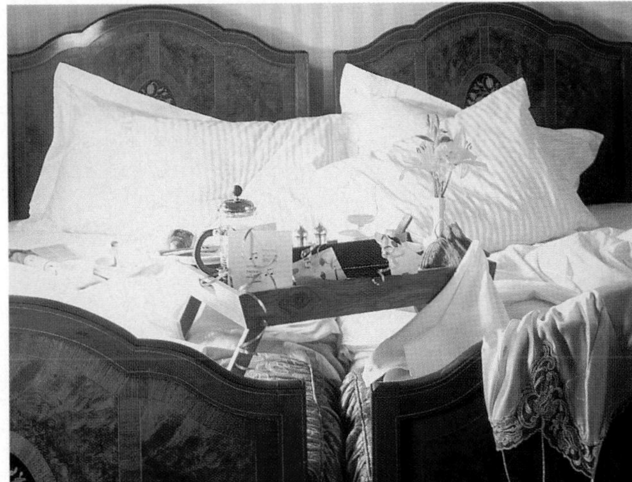

For hotel location, see maps on pages 490-496

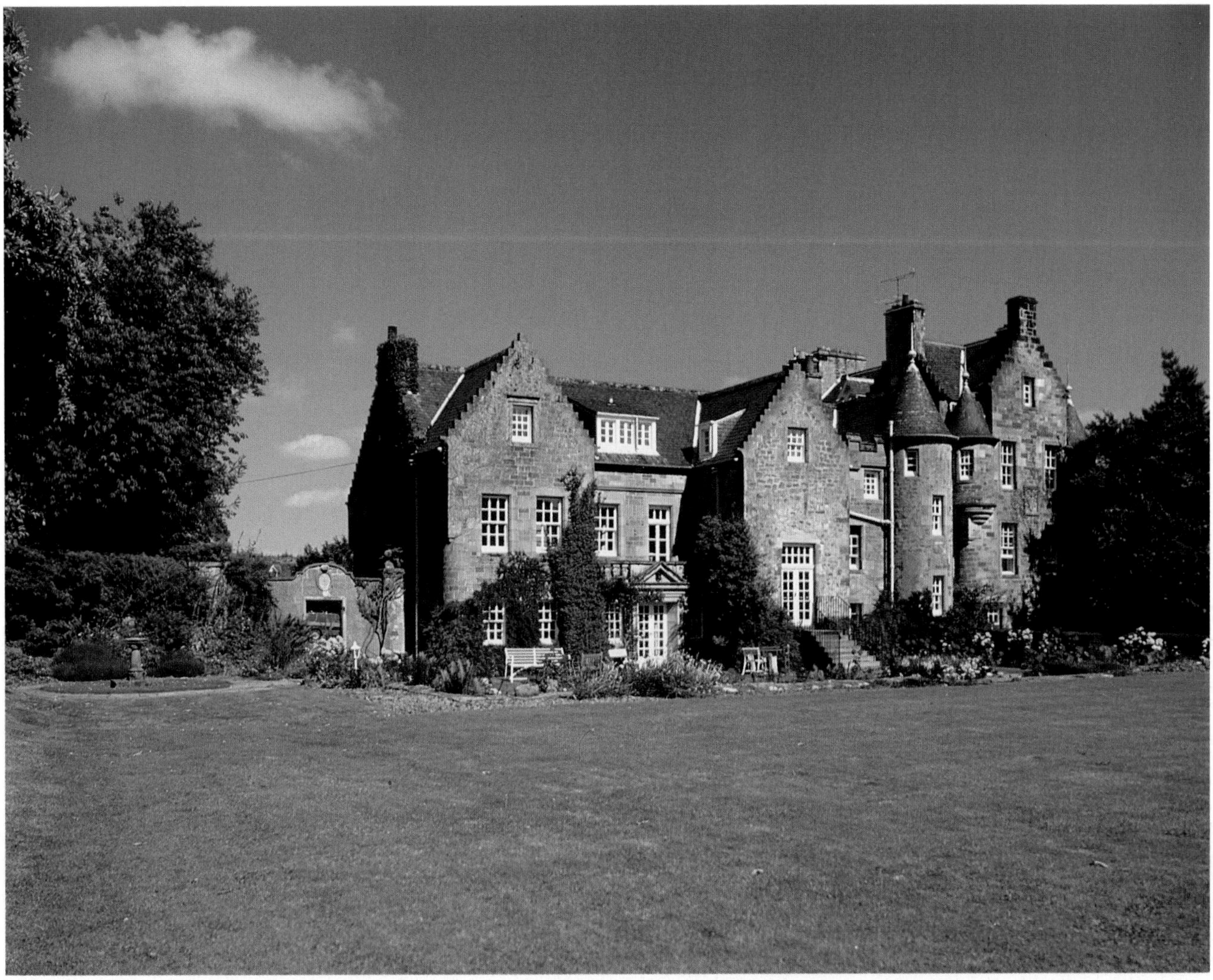

# JOHNSTOUNBURN HOUSE


**HUMBIE, NR EDINBURGH, EAST LOTHIAN EH36 5PL**

**TEL: 01875 833696 FAX: 01875 833626**


Dating from 1625, Johnstounburn House stands at the foot of the Lammermuir Hills, only 15 miles south of Edinburgh. Today it is a superb country house hotel. Set amid lawns and parklands in a private estate, its grounds feature imposing yew hedges, an orchard, a patio rose garden and a herbaceons walled garden. Upon entering the house, guests will sense the depth of Scottish heritage preserved here. Refurbishments have enhanced the historical features while enabling guests to enjoy modern comforts. Of the 20 well-appointed bedrooms, 11 are in the house and nine in the tastefully converted coach house. There is a spacious cedar-panelled lounge where an open fire will warm you on chilly days. In the 18th-century, pine-panelled dining room, chef Bryan Thom prepares sumptuous fare from the finest Scottish produce. In the grounds, guests can enjoy clay pigeon shooting, off-road and all terrain vehicle driving and fishing in a trout-filled pond. There is also a "fairway course" where the golfer can practise. Muirfield and Gullane are among 15 golf courses nearby. Tantallon Castle, Abbotsford and Traquair House are a short drive away. **Directions:** From Edinburgh take A68 through Dalkeith and Pathhead to Fala. Turn left through Fala $1\frac{1}{2}$ miles to T-junction; the hotel is on your right. Price guide: Single £110; double/twin £145–£195; suite £195.

For hotel location, see maps on pages 490-496

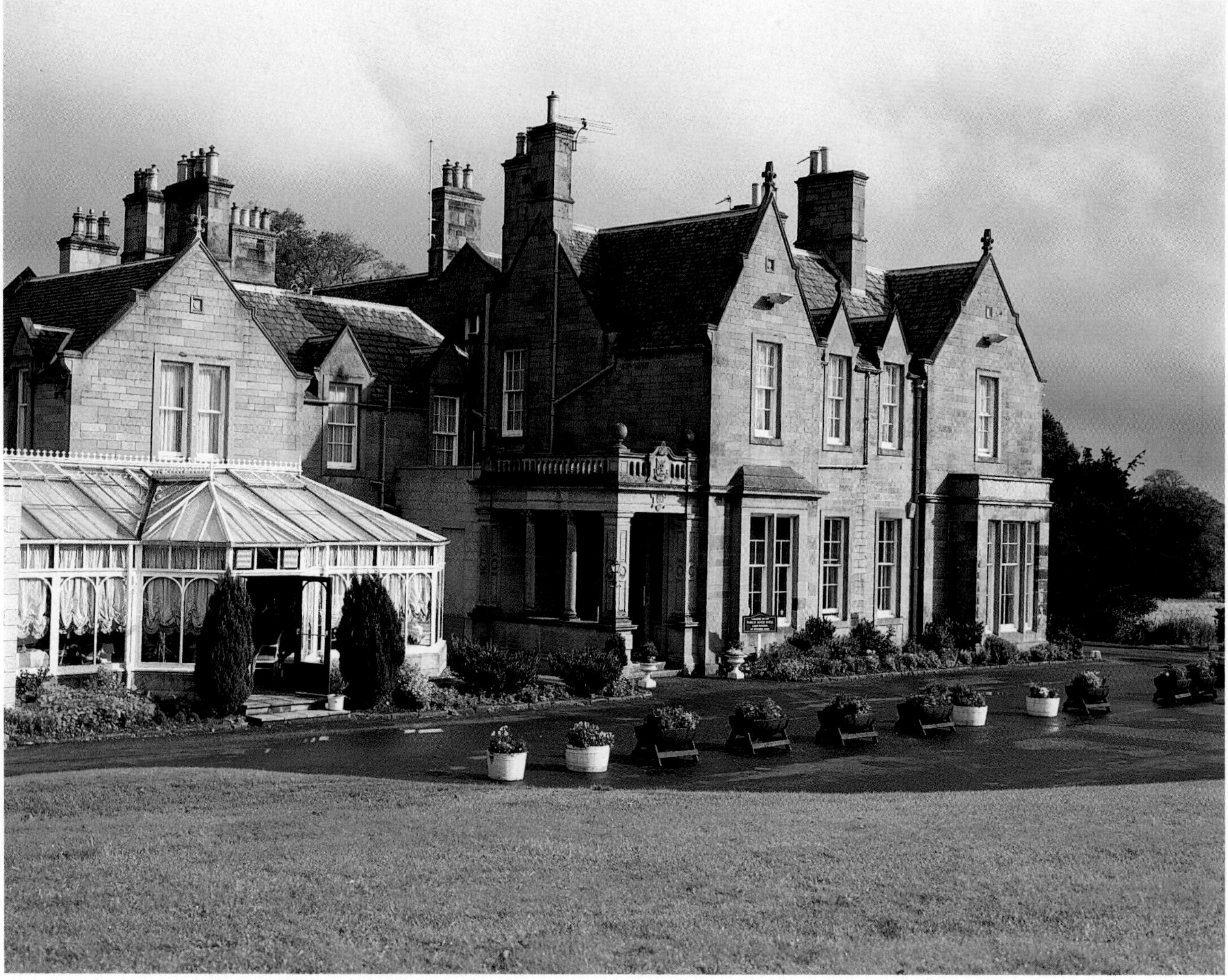

# THE NORTON HOUSE HOTEL

**INGLISTON, EDINBURGH EH28 8LX**
**TEL: 0131 333 1275 FAX: 0131 333 5305**

This Victorian mansion, dating back to 1861, is a part of the Virgin Hotel Collection. Situated in 55 acres of mature parkland, Norton House combines modern comforts with elegance. The 47 en suite bedrooms are bright and spacious, with many facilities, including a video channel and satellite TV. Influenced by the best Scottish and French traditions, the menu offers a balanced choice. Moments away, through leafy woodlands, a former stable block has been converted into The Gathering Bistro and Bar, where drinks and snacks are available to family and friends. Set in a walled garden, it is an ideal venue for the barbecues which are a regular feature in the summer months. The Patio, Veranda and Usher Room lend a sense of occasion to small gatherings, while the Linlithgow Suite can cater for large-scale events such as banquets, weddings and conferences. Norton House is conveniently 1 mile from Edinburgh Airport and 6 miles from the city centre, it is also a base from which to explore the Trossachs, Borders and Lothians. **Directions:** From Edinburgh take A8 past airport and hotel is ½ mile on left. From Glasgow, follow M8 to junction 2, take the first exit off the roundabout following signs for Ratho, take the first left, then left again following the signs to Ratho, then turn left at the top of the hill where hotel is signposted. Price guide: Single £110–£180; double/twin £140–£160; suite from £180.

For hotel location, see maps on pages 490-496

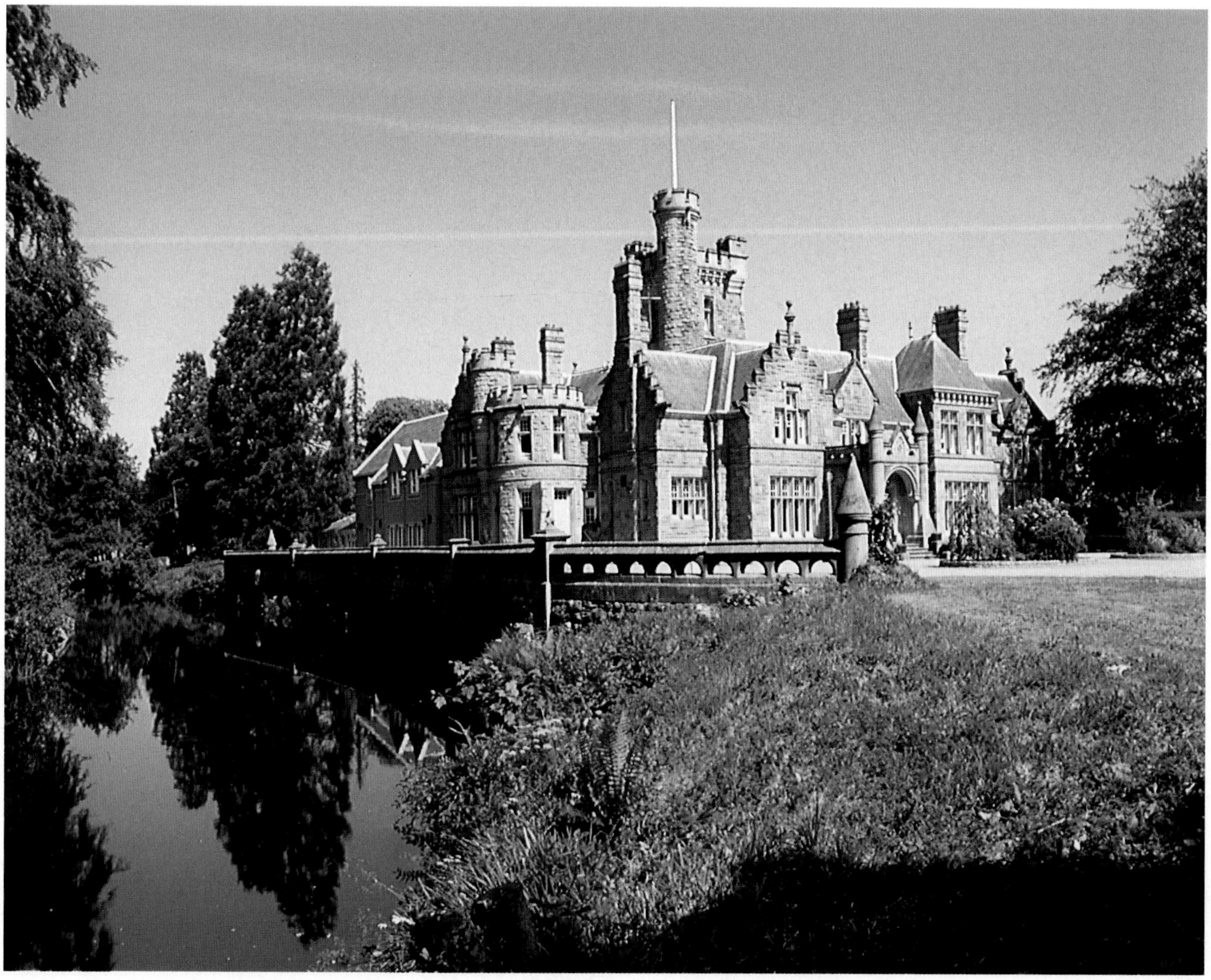

# Mansion House Hotel

**THE HAUGH, ELGIN, MORAY IV30 1AW**
**TEL: 01343 548811 FAX: 01343 547916**

Set within private woodland and overlooking the River Lossie stands the grand Mansion House Hotel. This former baronial mansion is only a minute's walk from the centre of the ancient city of Elgin. A welcoming entrance hall boasts oak-panelled walls, fresh flowers and many antique curiosities. Its majestic staircase leads to the well appointed bedrooms, featuring four-poster beds and welcoming glasses of sherry. The Piano Lounge is an ideal place to relax before entering the elegant restaurant. Here the cuisine is creative, delicious and beautifully presented. The "Wee Bar" is in the centre of the house, well placed next to the Snooker Room, while a unique collection of whiskies gives the name to the Still Room. A purpose built function room, called the Haugh Room, has its own entrance, bar, cloakrooms, and dance area. Guests at the hotel are invited to use the Country Club facilities which include a swimming pool, gymnasium, spa, steam room, sauna and sun bed. Complementing this is the Beauty Spot, which provides a multitude of unisex services. There is a choice of ten golf courses within ten miles, the opportunity to fish on the Spey and unlimited water sports in Findhorn Bay. **Directions:** In Elgin, turn off the main A96 road into Haugh Road. The hotel is at the end of this road by the river. Price guide: Single £75–£95; double/twin £110–£150; suite £200

For hotel location, see maps on pages 490-496

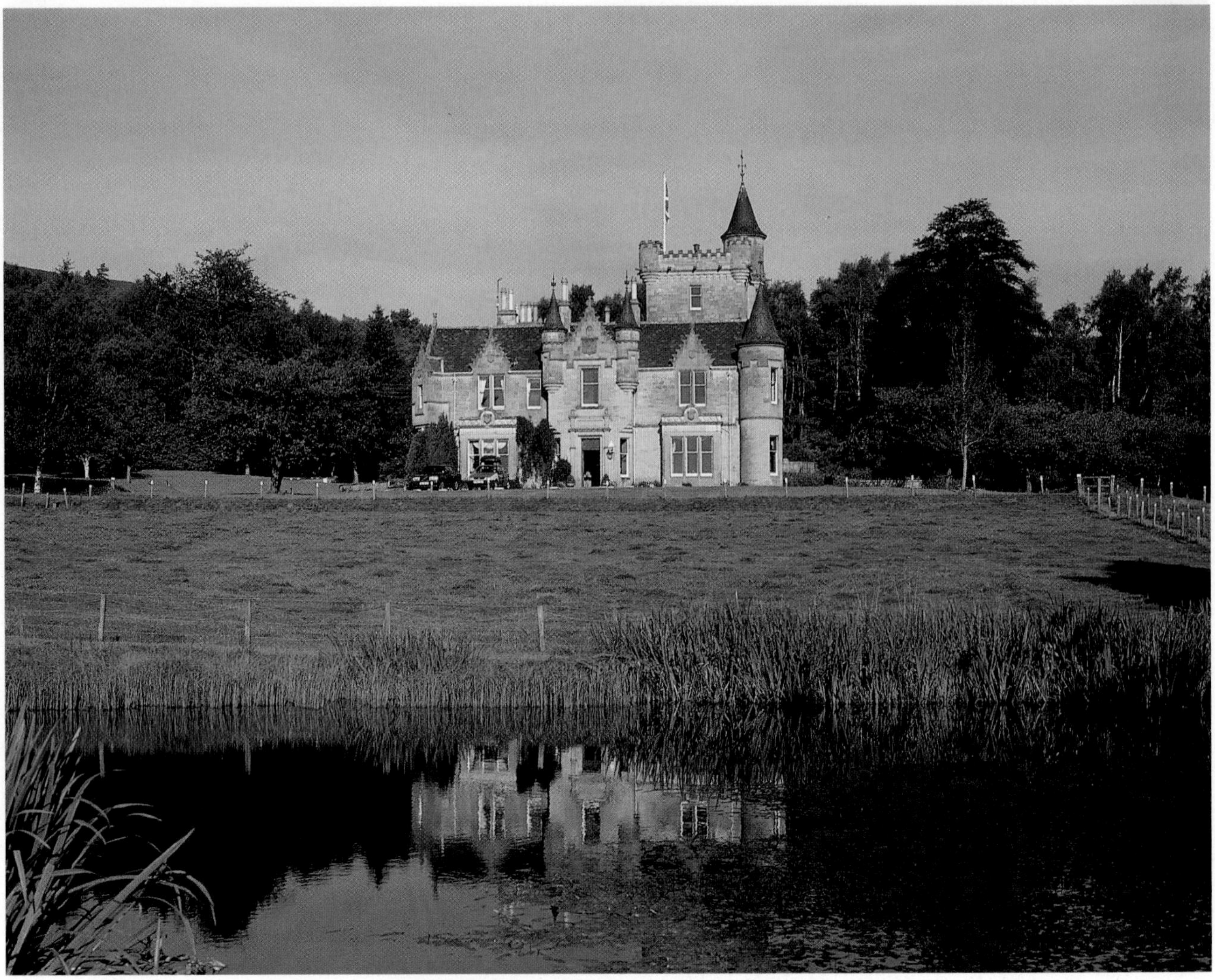

# ROTHES GLEN

**ROTHES, BY ELGIN, MORAYSHIRE AB38 7AQ**

**TEL: 01340 831254 FAX: 01340 831566 E-MAIL: 101516.1660@Compuserve.com**

Situated at the head of the Glen of Rothes and surrounded by acres of parkland where pedigree Highland cattle graze, this comfortable old country mansion offers the warmest of welcomes. Designed similarly to Balmoral castle in 1893 for the wealthy Dunbar shipping family, Rothes Glen provides spectacular views from every window and turret over the beautiful Spey Valley and distant, heather-clad Banffshire hills. Every bedroom is equipped to the highest standard. Rothes Glen is noted for its fine food. The best of Scottish beef and venison are a feature of the menus, together with freshly caught Spey salmon and fish and shellfish from the Moray Firth, for which the hotel has been awarded 2 AA rosettes. There is an extensive wine list and a good selection of Speyside malts and the Fountain Patio is an idyllic sun spot on which to sit and sample them on a warm summer evening. In the hotel grounds there is a putting green, croquet and a quarter acre lochan which is stocked with brown trout. Elgin, with its ancient ruined cathedral, and the bustling resort of Lossiemouth, with their challenging golf courses, are only short drives away, as is 13th century Pluscarden Abbey, 14th century Balvenie Castle, the many whisky distilleries and the sandy shores and picturesque fishing villages of the Moray Firth. **Directions:** Rothes Glen is on the A941, 6 miles south of Elgin. Price guide: Single £65–£90; double/twin £95-£130; suite £110–£150.

For hotel location, see maps on pages 490-496

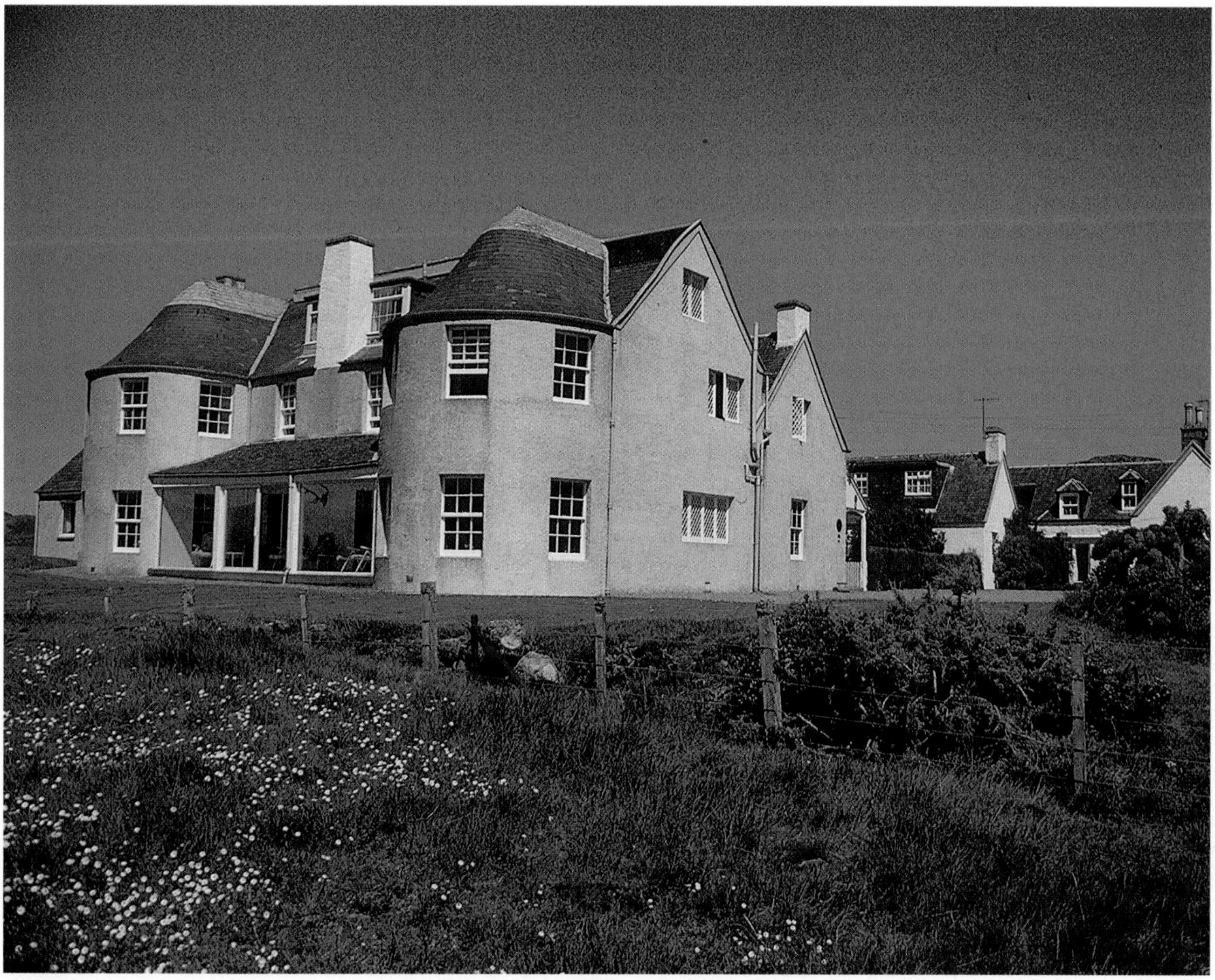

# KNOCKIE LODGE HOTEL

WHITEBRIDGE BY FORT AUGUSTUS, INVERNESS-SHIRE, IV1 2UP

TEL: 01456 486276 FAX: 01456 486389 US TOLL FREE: 1 800 635 3603

Built originally as a shooting lodge in 1789, Knockie Lodge stands not far from Loch Ness, 25 miles south of Inverness, in an area of outstanding natural beauty and total peace and quiet. It is now very much the home of Nicholas Bean and Louise Dawson. With its 10 spotlessly clean bedrooms, each comfortably and individually furnished, its drawing and dining rooms filled with antique furniture and family paintings, the billiard room and, of course, superb food prepared from a wide range of local produce, guests at Knockie Lodge can be assured of a real welcome and a very relaxed and hospitable atmosphere. For the brown trout fly-fisherman, there is excellent fishing on two lochs close to the house. It is also possible, by arrangement, to cast for salmon on Loch Ness or in the local salmon rivers. Other activities on offer locally include deerstalking in the autumn, bird-watching, sailing, ponytrekking and hill-walking. Knockie Lodge Hotel prides itself on its deserved awards: the AA 2 Red Stars and 2 Red rosettes for food and service, and the STB 3 Crowns De Luxe. The hotel is open from the end of April until the end of October and welcomes children aged ten and above. Those wishing to make reservations from the USA can telephone 1-800-635 3603. **Directions:** Knockie Lodge Hotel is situated eight miles north of Fort Augustus on the B862. Price guide: Single: £60; double/twin: £100–£160.

For hotel location, see maps on pages 490-496

In association with MasterCard 

# ALLT-NAN-ROS HOTEL

ONICH, FORT WILLIAM, INVERNESS-SHIRE PH33 6RY
TEL: 01855 821210 FAX: 01855 821462 E-MAIL: 106021.2552@compuserve.com

Situated on the north shore of Loch Linnhe, Allt-nan-Ros Hotel (Gaelic for 'Burn of the Roses') was originally built as a Victorian shooting lodge. It has been tastefully upgraded by its resident proprietors, the MacLeod family, and it offers both a high standard of comfort and exceptional views of the surrounding mountains and lochs. The design of the hotel takes advantage of its southerly aspect and all bedrooms and public rooms overlook the loch. Quality furnishings and a full range of amenities are provided in all the bedrooms, while the superior rooms available all incorporate a bay window. In the traditionally furnished lounges, dining room and bar a country house atmosphere prevails and guests are invited to relax and enjoy the lovely views. The cuisine served in the splendid restaurant is influenced by modern and French styles, but also adapts traditional Scottish recipes to today's tastes. A comprehensive and reasonably priced wine list includes wines from all around the world. Lying midway between Ben Nevis and Glencoe, the hotel is located in an area of unsurpassed scenery and history. Among the many local activities are climbing, walking, touring the towns and islands, sailing, fishing or taking a trip on the steam trains. **Directions:** Ten miles south of Fort William on the main A82. Price guide: Single £35–£55; double/twin £70–£110; suites £76–£130.

For hotel location, see maps on pages 490-496

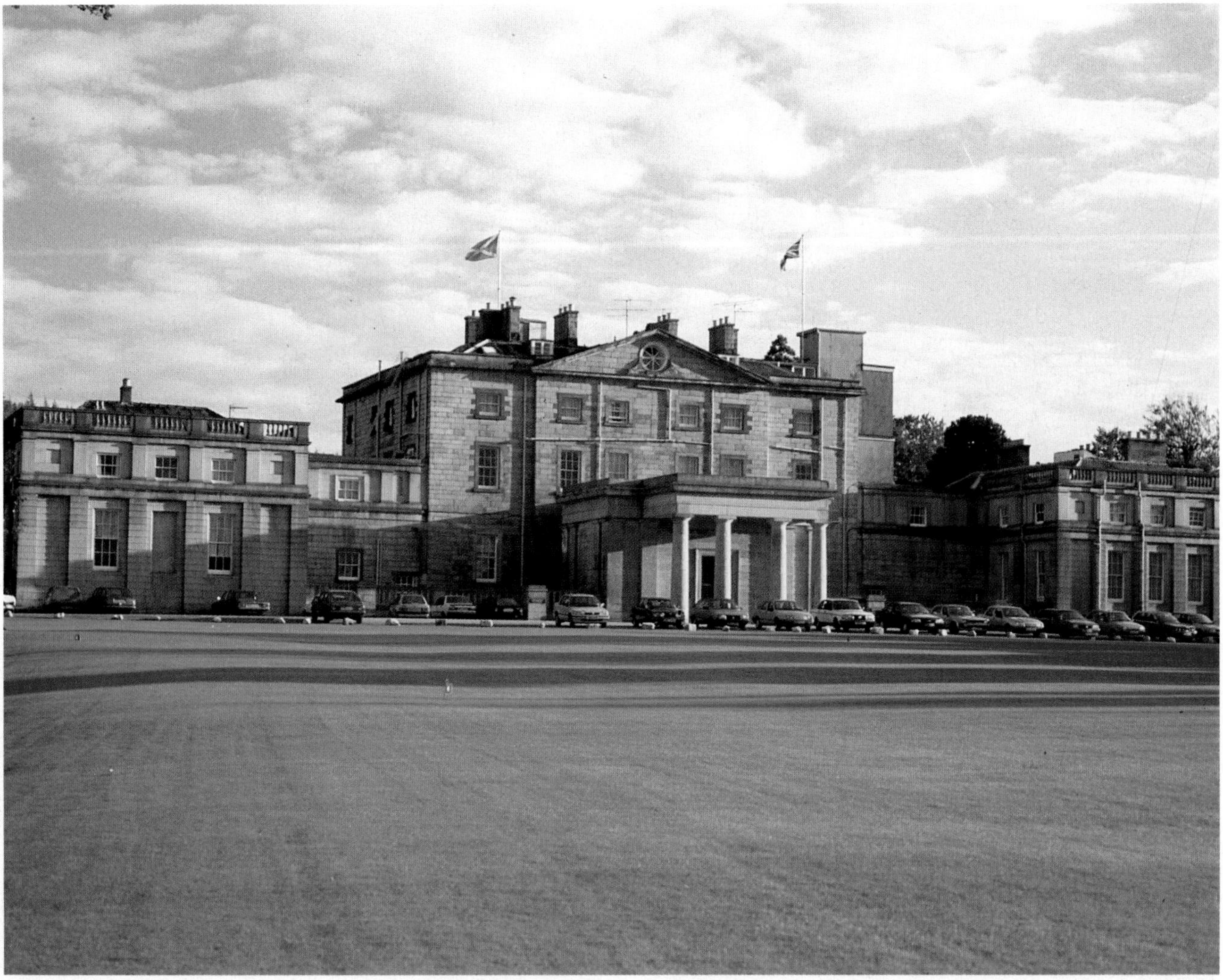

# CALLY PALACE HOTEL

GATEHOUSE OF FLEET, DUMFRIES & GALLOWAY DG7 2DL
TEL: 01557 814341 FAX: 01557 814522

Set in over 100 acres of forest and parkland, on the edge of Robert Burns country, this 18th-century country house has been restored to its former glory by the McMillan family, the proprietors since 1981. On entering the hotel, guests will initially be impressed by the grand scale of the interior. Two huge marble pillars support the original moulded ceiling of the entrance hall. All the public rooms have ornate ceilings, original marble fireplaces and fine reproduction furniture. Combine these with grand, traditional Scottish cooking and you have a hotel *par excellence*. The 56 en suite bedrooms have been individually decorated. Some are suites with a separate sitting room; others are large enough to accommodate a sitting area. An indoor leisure complex, completed in the style of the marble entrance hall, includes heated swimming pool, Jacuzzi, saunas and solarium. The hotel has an all-weather tennis court, a putting green, croquet, and a lake for private fishing or boating. Also, for exclusive use of hotel guests is an 18-hole golf course, par 70, length 5,500 yards set around the lake in the 150 acre grounds. Special weekend and over-60s breaks are available out of season. Closed January and February. **Directions:** Sixty miles west of Carlisle, 1-1½ miles from Gatehouse of Fleet junction on the main A75 road. Price guide: (including dinner): Single £70; double/twin £114–£140.

For hotel location, see maps on pages 490-496

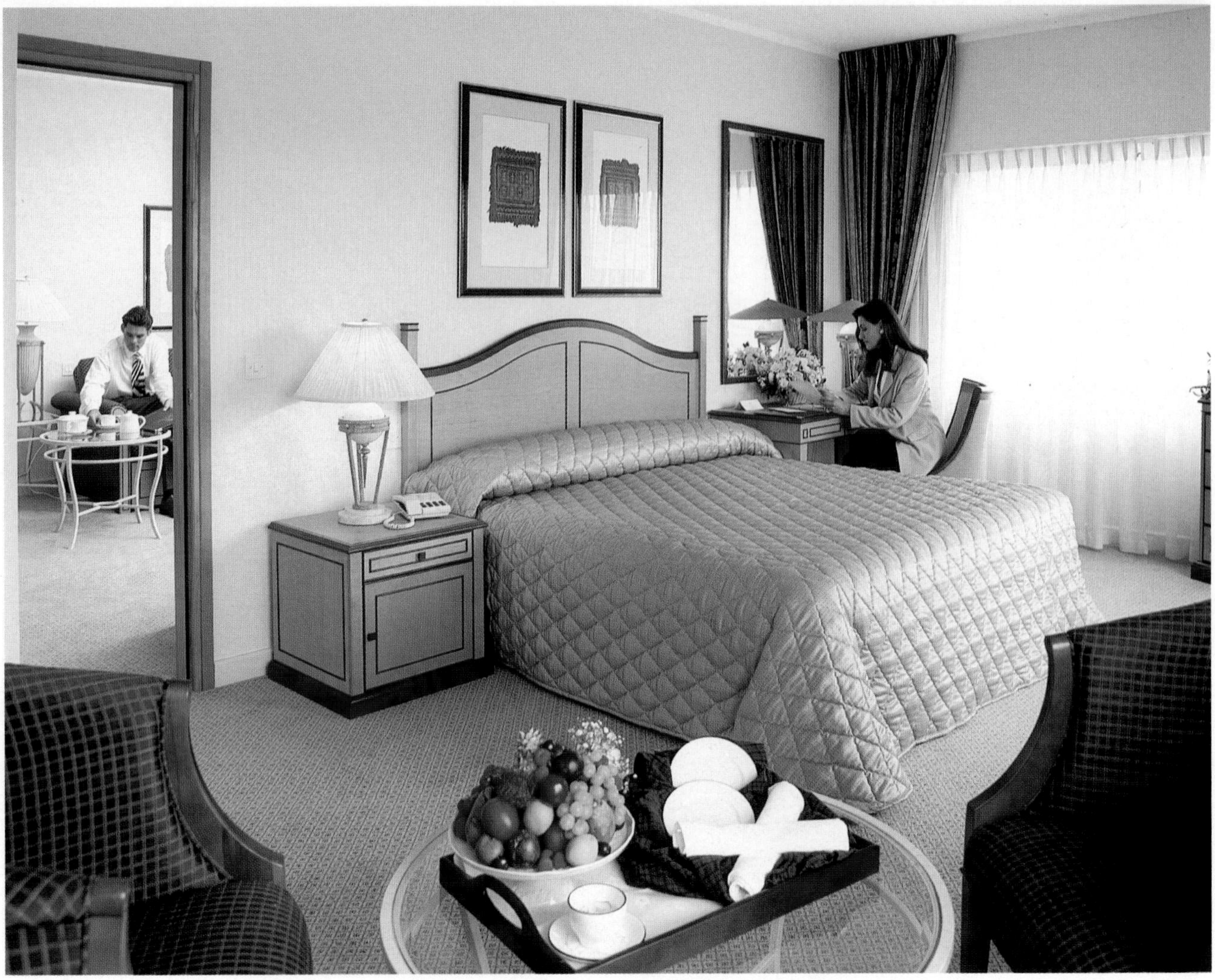

# THE BEARDMORE HOTEL

**BEARDMORE STREET, CLYDEBANK, SCOTLAND G81 4SA**
**TEL: 0141 9516000 FAX: 0141 9516018**

This light, modern and spacious hotel stands in extensive grounds on the north bank of the River Clyde, eight miles from the city centre of Glasgow on the road to Loch Lomond. It shares this stunning location with the renowned HCI International Medical Centre, enabling both establishments to benefit from world class facilities. The hotel's bedrooms are larger than most and offer air conditioning, tea and coffee-making facilities and 30 channel TV. Guests can enjoy a drink in the large lounge bar before moving on to sample the delights of the brasserie style buffet served in the Waterhouse Restaurant at both lunch and dinner overlooking the river. The Symphony Room, a special occasion restaurant which was voted Scotland's Restaurant of the Year in 1996 (Taste of Scotland Macallan Award) is open on Friday and Saturday only. Fine food and wine is complemented by a professional but unobtrusive service. The hotel's excellent conference centre features a 170-seater auditorium, nine smaller meeting rooms and a boardroom for senior managers. Guests can enjoy the hotel's leisure facilities, which include a pool, sauna, spa and gym, at any time. **Directions:** From Glasgow M8, at Junction 19 take A814, follow signs for Clydebank Ind. Eastate, turn right in to Beardmore St, hotel on left. Price guide: Single £90; double/twin £90; suites £200.

For hotel location, see maps on pages 490-496

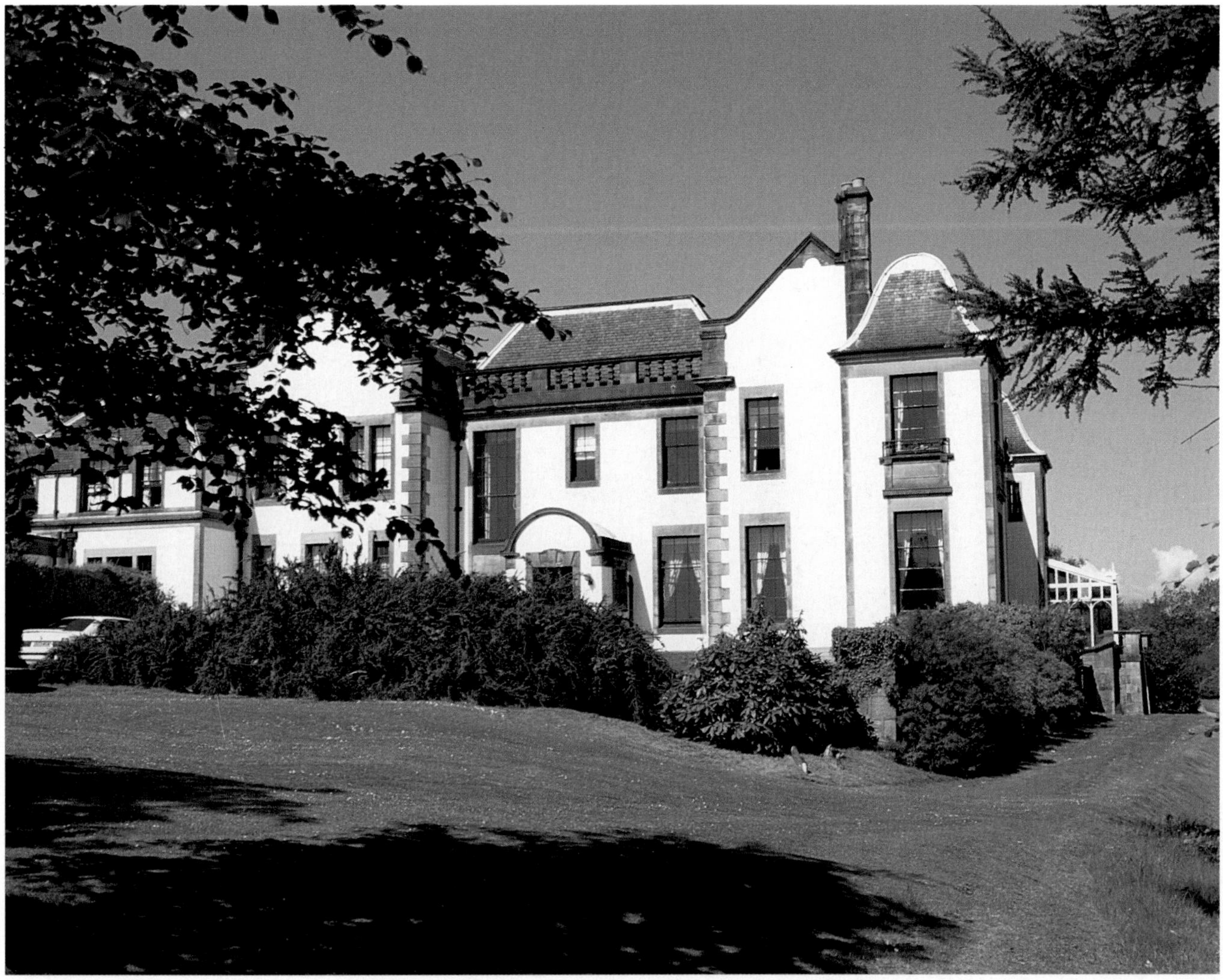

# GLEDDOCH HOUSE

**LANGBANK, RENFREWSHIRE PA14 6YE**
**TEL: 01475 540711 FAX: 01475 540201**

Once the home of a Glasgow shipping baron, Gleddoch House stands in 360 acres, with dramatic views across the River Clyde to Ben Lomond and the hills beyond. The individually appointed bedrooms all have en suite facilities and some have four-poster beds. Executive rooms and suites and family rooms are also available. There are also self-catering lodges on the estate. Other amenities include a range of meeting rooms to cater for up to 120 delegates theatre style. The Restaurant is renowned for its award-winning modern Scottish cuisine and is complemented by a comprehensive wine list. On the estate a series of activities are available such as golf, clay pigeon shooting, archery and off-road driving, making Gleddoch an ideal venue to host corporate events. Additionally the equestrian centre caters for all levels, from trekking to pony rides and individual tuition. Gleddoch's location offers an experience of a bygone era yet amid the sophistication that today's traveller requires. A range of short breaks, golfing packages and gourmet events are available throughout the year. Glasgow Airport is only 10 minutes drive away and the City Centre 20 minutes. **Directions:** M8 towards Greenock; take B789 Langbank/ Houston exit. Follow signs to left and then right after ½ mile; hotel is on left. Price guide: Single £95; double/twin £140; suite £175.

For hotel location, see maps on pages 490-496

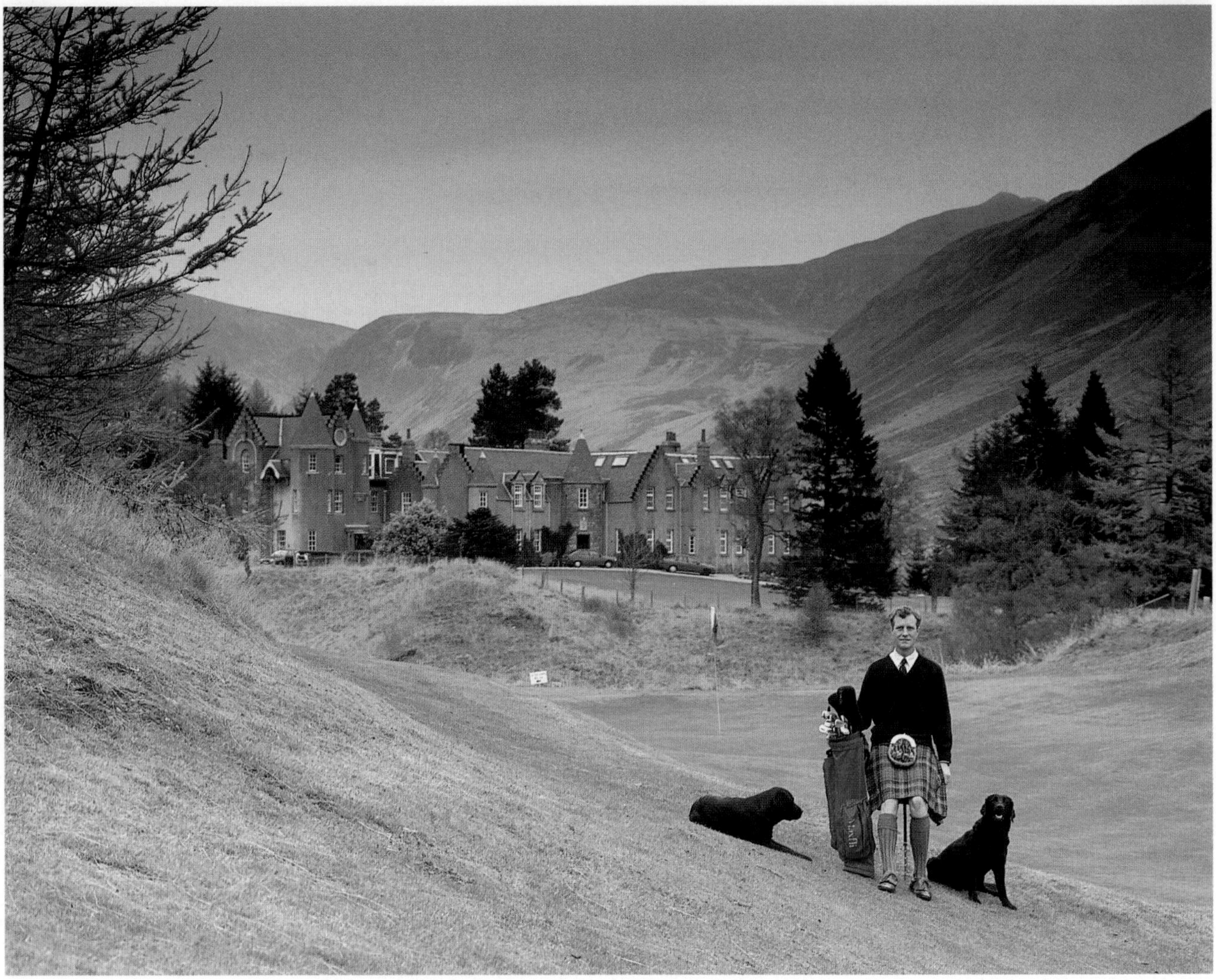

# Dalmunzie House

SPITTAL O'GLENSHEE, BLAIRGOWRIE, PERTHSHIRE PH10 7QG
TEL: 01250 885224 FAX: 01250 885225

Dalmunzie House is beautifully tucked away high in the Scottish Highlands, 18 miles north of Blairgowrie and 15 miles south of Braemar. Standing in its own mountainous 6,000-acre sporting estate, it is run by Simon and Alexandra Winton. Guests come to enjoy the relaxed family atmosphere which, together with unobtrusive service and attention, ensures a comfortable stay. The bedrooms are individual in character, some with antiques, others romantically set in the turrets of the house, all tastefully decorated. Delicately cooked traditional Scottish fare is created from local ingredients fresh from the hills and lochs. The menu changes daily and meals are served in the dining room, accompanied by wines from the well-stocked cellar. Among the sporting activities available on site are golf (the 9-hole course is one of the highest in Britain) and shooting for grouse, ptarmigan and black game. Other country pursuits include river and loch fishing, clay pigeon shooting, mountain biking and stalking for red deer. Pony-trekking can be organised locally. Glenshee Ski Centre is 6 miles away: it offers cross-country and downhill skiing. Closer to home, the hotel games room provides more sedate pastimes for all the family. Closed late November to 28 December. Special winter/Skiing Rates. **Directions:** Dalmunzie is on the A93 at the Spittal O'Glenshee, south of Braemar. Price guide: Single £33–£57; double/twin £52–£92.

For hotel location, see maps on pages 490-496

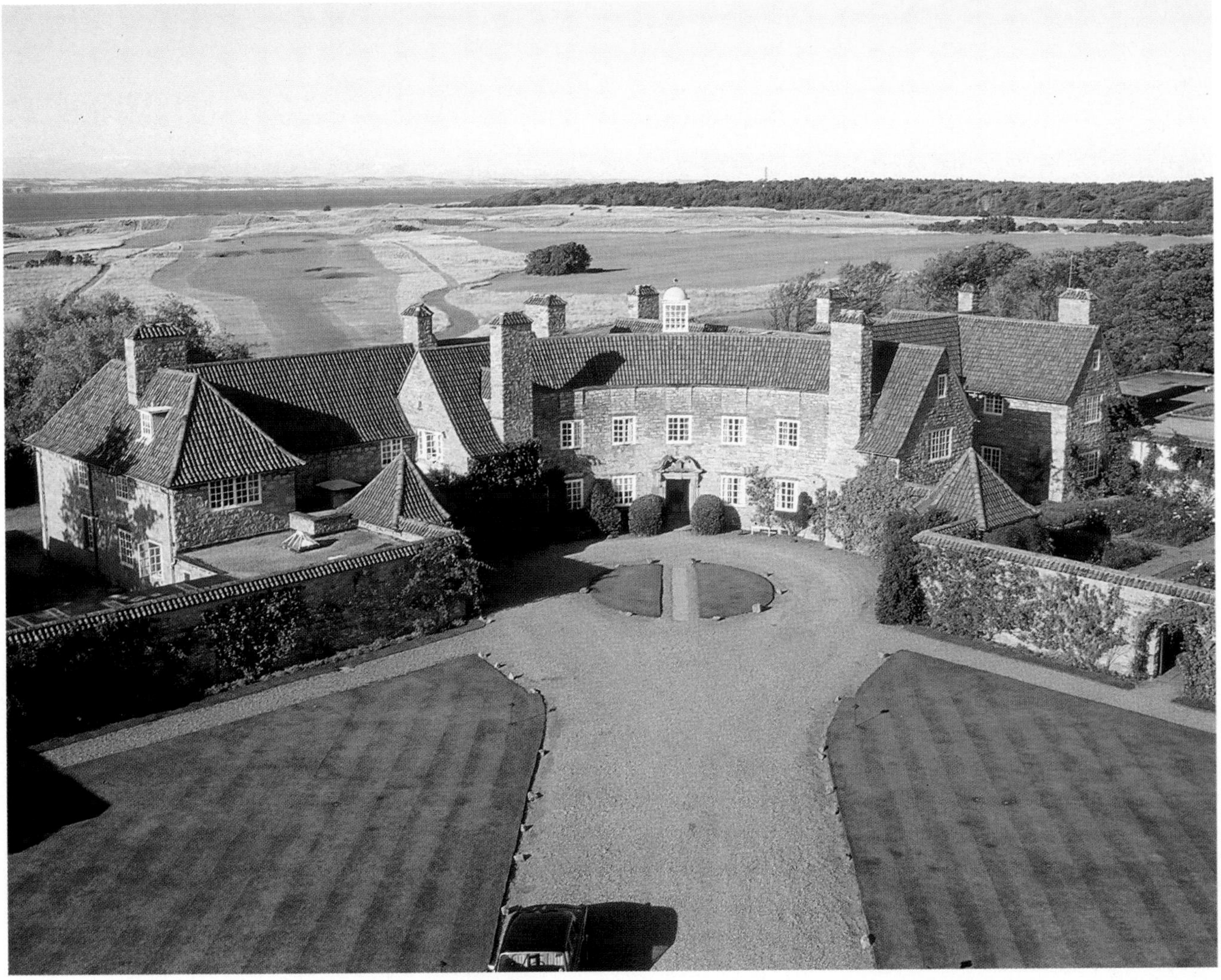

# GREYWALLS

**MUIRFIELD, GULLANE, EAST LOTHIAN EH31 2EG**
**TEL: 01620 842144 FAX: 01620 842241**

Greywalls, neighbouring Muirfield golf course, the home of the Honourable Company of Edinburgh Golfers, was designed by Sir Edwin Lutyens. King Edward VII was a frequent visitor. The hotel is a beautiful crescent shaped building made of warm, honey coloured stone from the local quarry. A delightful garden, believed to be the work of Gertrude Jekyll, provides secret enclaves where guests can escape to enjoy a good book and savour the delightful scents of roses and lavender. The hotel's bedrooms, all of varying size and design, are individually furnished and include many fine antiques. Downstairs is the peaceful panelled library, Edwardian tea room and small bar stocked with a selection of excellent brandies and whiskies. Hearty breakfasts of porridge, kippers from Achiltibuie, tasty sausages and freshly made croissants make an ideal start to the day while dinner is an outstanding feast provided by dedicated chefs. East Lothian has excellent golf courses, including Muirfield, where The Open is held regularly. Beautiful sandy beaches are within easy reach, along with nature reserves, ruined castles, villages, market towns and stately homes. The hotel is closed from November through to March. **Directions:** On A198 from city bypass which links to the M8, M9 and M90. Price guide: Single £95; double/twin £170–£190.

For hotel location, see maps on pages 490-496

# BUNCHREW HOUSE HOTEL


**INVERNESS, SCOTLAND IV3 6TA**

**TEL: 01463 234917 FAX: 01463 710620**


This splendid 17th century Scottish mansion, owned by Stewart and Lesley Dykes, is set amidst 20 acres of landscaped gardens and woodlands on the shores of Beauly Firth. Guests can enjoy breathtaking views of Ben Wyvis and the Black Isle, while just yards from the house the sea laps at the garden walls. Bunchrew has been carefully restored to preserve its heritage, while still giving its guests the highest standards of comfort and convenience. A further schedule of refurbishment began in 1995. The luxury suites are beautifully furnished and decorated to enhance their natural features. The elegant panelled drawing room is the ideal place to relax at any time, while during the winter log fires lend it an added appeal. In the candle-lit restaurant the traditional cuisine includes prime Scottish beef, fresh lobster and langoustines, locally caught game and venison and freshly grown vegetables. A carefully chosen wine list complements the menu. Local places of interest include Cawdor Castle, Loch Ness, Castle Urquhart and a number of beautiful glens. For those who enjoy sport there is skiing at nearby Aviemore, sailing, cruising and golf. **Directions:** From Inverness follow signs to Beauly, Dingwall on the A862. One mile from the outskirts of Inverness the entrance to Bunchrew House is on the right. Price guide: Single £65–£95; double/twin £90–£140; suites £105–£120.

For hotel location, see maps on pages 490-496

# CULLODEN HOUSE HOTEL

INVERNESS, INVERNESS-SHIRE IV1 2NZ

TEL: 01463 790461 FAX: 01463 792181 FROM USA TOLL FREE FAX 1 800 373 7987

A majestic circular drive leads to the splendour of this handsome Georgian mansion, battle headquarters of Bonnie Prince Charlie 252 years ago. Three miles from Inverness this handsome Palladian country house stands in 40 acres of beautiful gardens and peaceful parkland roamed by roe deer. Princes past and present and guests from throughout the world have enjoyed the hotel's ambience and hospitality. Rich furnishings, sparkling chandeliers, impressive Adam fireplaces and ornate plaster reliefs add to the grandness of the hotel's luxurious, high-ceilinged rooms. The bedrooms are appointed to the highest standard many having four-poster beds and Jacuzzis. Four non-smoking suites are in the Pavilion Annex which overlooks a three-acre walled garden. In the Dining Room guests can savour superb cuisine prepared by chef Michael Simpson, who trained at the Gleneagles Hotel and the Hamburg Conference Centre. There is an outdoor tennis court and indoor sauna and sunbed facilities. Shooting, fishing and pony-trekking can be arranged, while nearby are Cawdor Castle, the Clava Cairns Bronze Age burial ground and Culloden battlefield. AA 4 stars, Scottish Tourist Board 5 crowns de luxe. **Directions:** Take A96 going east from Inverness and turn right to Culloden. Price guide: Single £135–£170; double/twin £190–£220; suite: £220–£250.

28 rms · 40 · 10

For hotel location, see maps on pages 490-496

# KINGSMILLS HOTEL

## CULCABOCK ROAD, INVERNESS, INVERNESS-SHIRE IV2 3LP

TEL: 01463 237166 FAX: 01463 225208

Built in the capital of The Highlands in 1785, this historic hotel has been extended and it offers guests both comfort and elegance. It is only a mile from the town centre, in three acres of gardens, adjacent to Inverness Golf Course. There is a choice of attractively appointed bedrooms, all with modern amenities. In addition to the standard rooms, as pictured below, there are seven beautifully furnished suite-style rooms, also family rooms with bunk beds and six self-catering villas. The Leisure Club incorporates a heated swimming pool, spa bath, steam cabin, sauna, sunbeds, mini-gym and pitch-and-putt. Hairdressing facilities are also provided. Throughout the year exceptionally good value is offered by special breaks which include local seasonal attractions. Golf, fishing, skiing, riding and pony-trekking can all be enjoyed nearby and arranged as part of an activity holiday. Christmas, Easter and New Year packages are also available. The Kingsmills Hotel is well placed for visiting the Highlands, Loch Ness, the Whisky Trail, Culloden battlefield and Cawdor Castle. USA representative – Thomas McFerran, telephone toll free: 1-800-215 443 7990. **Directions:** Turn left off A9 signposted Kingsmills and Culcabock. Turn right at the first roundabout, left at the second and the hotel is on the left just past the golf course. Price guide: Single £100–£135; double/twin £135–£170; suite £145.

79 rms MasterCard VISA AMERICAN EXPRESS M 80

For hotel location, see maps on pages 490-496

# MONTGREENAN MANSION HOUSE HOTEL

**MONTGREENAN ESTATE, KILWINNING, AYRSHIRE KA13 7QZ**
**TEL: 01294 557733 FAX: 01294 850397**

Set in 48 acres of wooded gardens, Montgreenan commands views towards Ailsa Craig and the Arran Hills, which make a spectacular sight at sunset. The history of the estate dates back to 1310, and the present mansion house was built in 1817 by Dr Robert Glasgow. The original features, including marble and brass fireplaces, decorative ceilings and plasterwork, have been retained. A family home until 1980, the hotel has a friendly atmosphere. The bedrooms are well appointed with antique and reproduction furniture and one of the bedrooms has a Jacuzzi bath. The elegant dining room, with burgundy-and-gold tapestried chairs, is the setting for dinner. Gourmet cooking features fresh Scottish salmon, lobster, game and Ayrshire beef. To accompany your meal, choose from 200 fine vintages. Whatever the occasion, there are good facilities for conferences and entertaining. In addition to the 5-hole golf course on site, over 30 courses, including those at Royal Troon and Turnberry, are within 45 minutes' drive. Special rates available. **Directions:** Glasgow and Prestwick Airport are only 30 minutes' drive away. 19 miles south of Glasgow, 4 miles north of Irvine. From Irvine take A736 towards Glasgow for 4 miles. Turn left at Torranyard Inn; hotel entrance is 2 minutes from there. Price guide: Single £70; double/twin £110–£146.

21 rms · MasterCard · VISA · American Express · M 100

For hotel location, see maps on pages 490-496

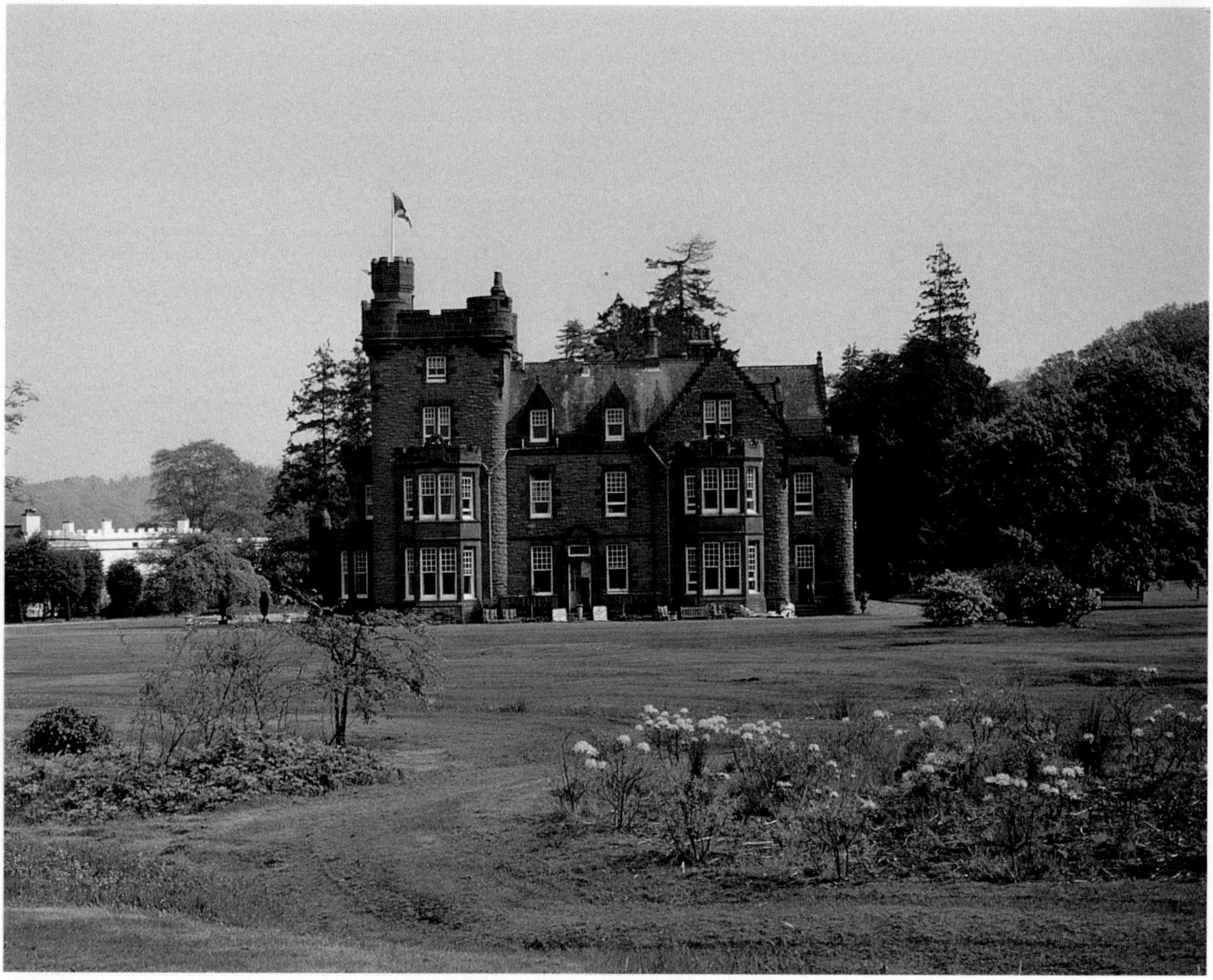

# Isle Of Eriska

**LEDAIG, BY OBAN, ARGYLL PA37 1SD**
**TEL: 01631 720371 FAX: 01631 720531**

Isle of Eriska was built in 1884, towards the end of the Scots Baronial period. Its imposing exterior of grey granite and red sandstone stands as a living monument to a bygone age. Inside, no two bedrooms are the same in size or outlook and each is named after one of the neighbouring Hebridean islands. With its bay window and chintz covered furniture, the Drawing Room is the perfect place to relax while there can be no better place than the library to enjoy a drink from the selection of malt whiskies. Internationally acclaimed standards of cuisine are meticulously maintained in the dining room, the garden supplying a wide range of herbs, vegetables and soft fruits. For energetic guests there are various pursuits, tennis on an all weather court, clay pigeon shooting and nature trails. Croquet and the golf putting green are available for those who prefer leisurely pursuits. In addition, there is now a golf course facility, fitness suite and indoor swimming pool. Oban is 20 minutes away by car and from here steamers ply to and from the islands. **Directions:** From Edinburgh and Glasgow, drive to Tyndrum, then A85 towards Oban. At Connel proceed on A828 for four miles to north of Benderloch. Thereafter follow signs to Isle of Eriska. Price guide: Single £160; double/twin £195–£230.

For hotel location, see maps on pages 490-496

# Western Isles Hotel

**TOBERMORY, ISLE OF MULL, ARGYLL PA75 6PR**
**TEL: 01688 302012 FAX: 01688 302297**

Poised above Tobermory Harbour, the Western Isles Hotel combines friendly hospitality with breathtaking views over an ever-changing vista of mountain and sea. An appetite sharpened by the fresh sea air is certain to be sated in the elegant restaurant, with its spectacular outlook over the Sound of Mull. Special diets and vegetarians are well catered for with some notice. The lounge has an atmosphere of grace and comfort, while the conservatory, with a bar and magnificent views across the harbour, is delightful on scented summer evenings. The bedrooms are spacious. Off Mull's coast is the holy island of Iona, while Fingal's Cave can be seen on Staffa. Special rates for Easter and New Year. If bringing a dog, please say when booking and bring a basket/bed for it. **Directions:** Travelling to Mull is so pleasurable that it should be considered part of the holiday. On booking, contact ferry operators Caledonian MacBrayne, The Pier, Gourock; or ring 016315 62285 and book the Oban–Craignure ferry (40 minutes). There is an hourly Lochaline–Fishnish ferry, also. Oban is on the A82/A85 from Glasgow (two hours) or the A85 from Perth. At Craignure, turn right off ferry; Tobermory is 40 minutes' drive. A warm welcome awaits! Price guide: Single £37–£95; double/twin £74–£169.

For hotel location, see maps on pages 490-496

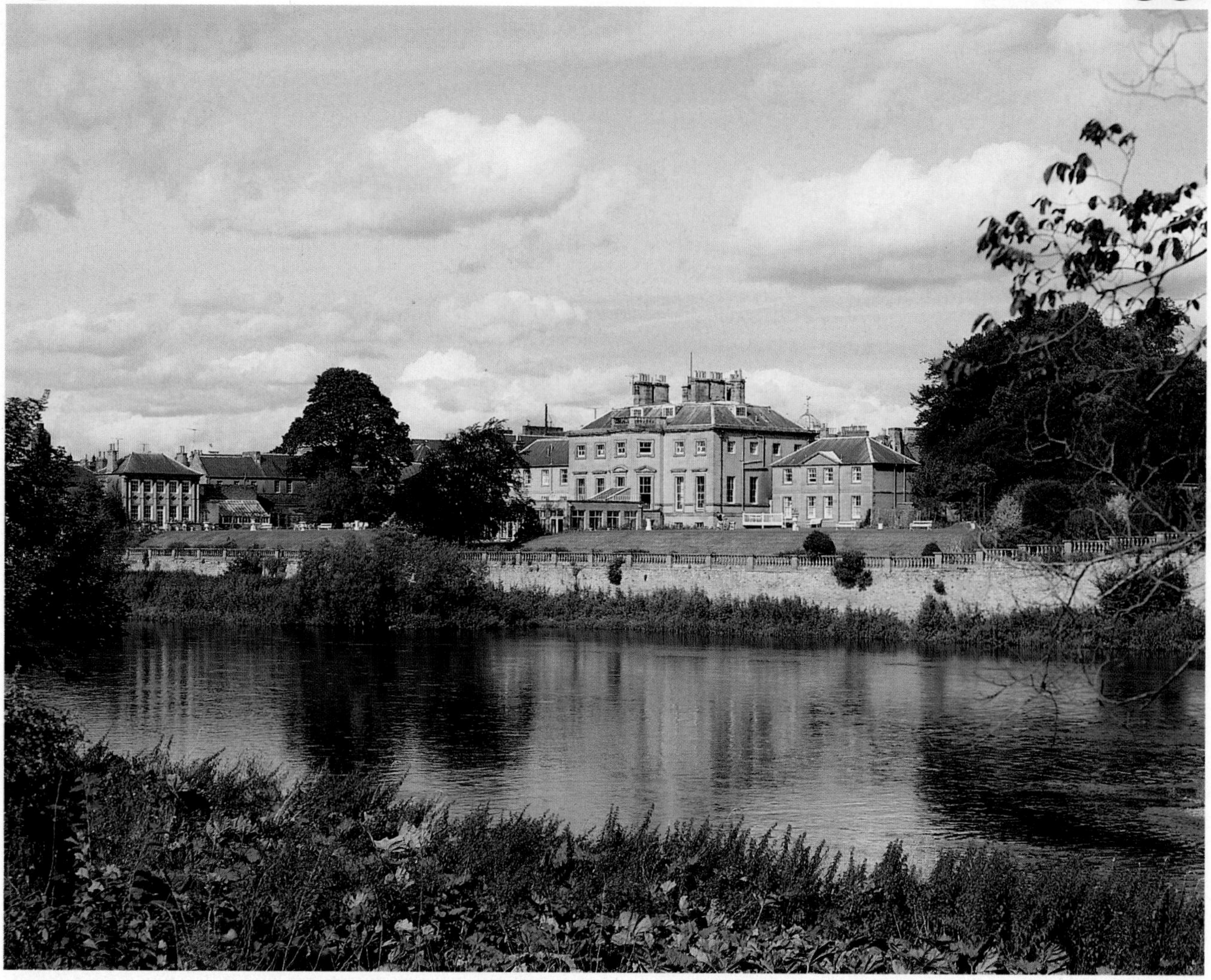

# EDNAM HOUSE HOTEL

**BRIDGE STREET, KELSO, ROXBURGHSHIRE TD5 7HT**
**TEL: 01573 224168 FAX: 01573 226319**

Overlooking the River Tweed, in 3 acres of gardens, Ednam House is one of the region's finest examples of Georgian architecture. This undulating, pastoral countryside was immortalised by Sir Walter Scott. Ednam House has been owned and managed by the Brooks family for over 65 years, spanning four generations. Although the grandiose splendour may seem formal, the warm, easy-going atmosphere is all-pervasive. The lounges and bars are comfortably furnished and command scenic views of the river and grounds. All 32 bedrooms are en suite, individually decorated and well equipped. In the elegant dining room which overlooks the river, a blend of traditional and creative Scottish cuisine, using fresh local produce, is served. The wine list is very interesting and reasonably priced. Ednam House is extremely popular with fishermen, the Borders being renowned for its salmon and trout. Other field sports such as stalking, hunting and shooting can be arranged as can riding, golfing and cycling. Local landmarks include the abbeys of Kelso, Melrose, Jedburgh and Dryburgh. Closed Christmas and New Year. **Directions:** From the south, reach Kelso via A698; from the north, via A68. Hotel is just off market square by the river. Price guide: Single from £50; double/twin £69–£97.

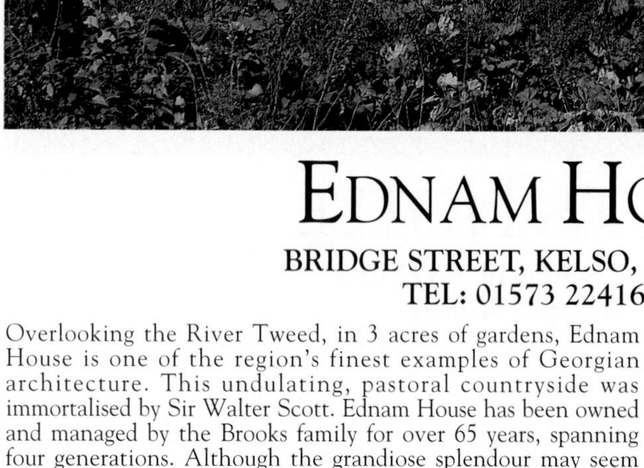

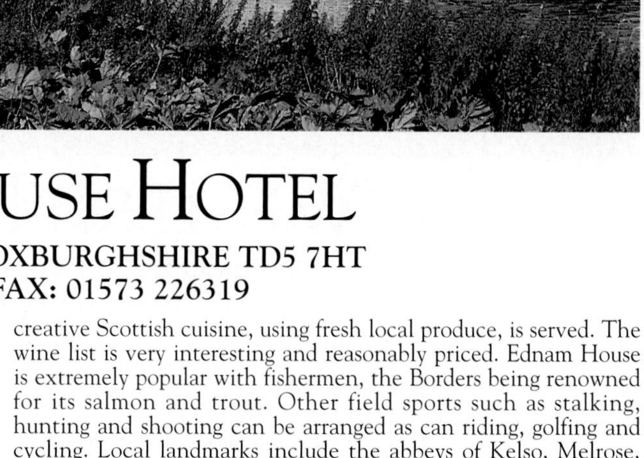

For hotel location, see maps on pages 490-496

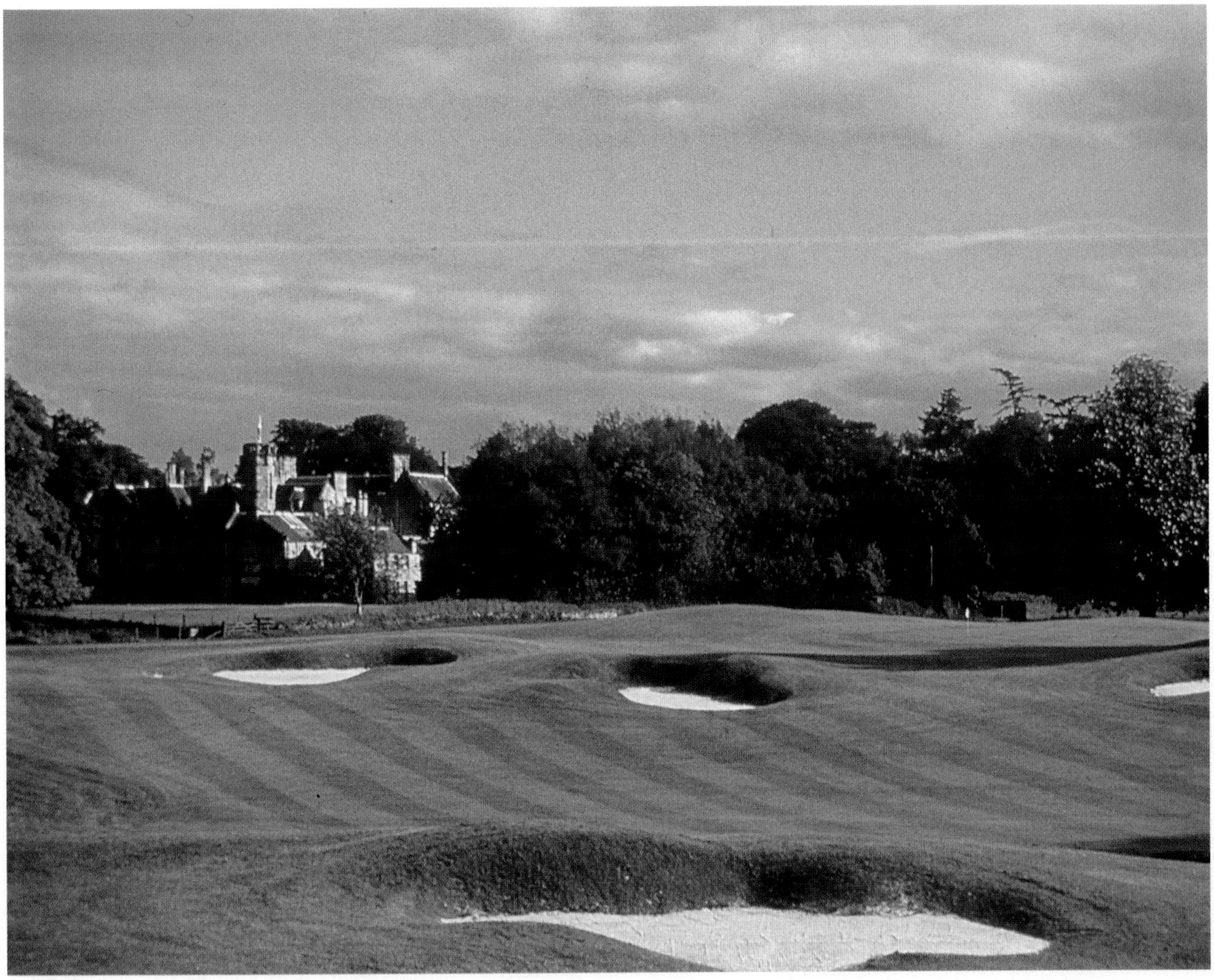

# Sunlaws House Hotel & Golf Course

KELSO, ROXBURGHSHIRE TD5 8JZ
TEL: 01573 450331 FAX: 01573 450611

Converted by its owners, the Duke and Duchess of Roxburghe, into a luxury hotel of character and charm, Sunlaws House is situated in over 200 hundred acres of rolling grounds on the bank of the River Teviot. There are 22 bedrooms, including four poster rooms and suites, and like the spacious reception rooms, they are furnished with care and elegance. The menu, which is changed daily, reflects the hotel's position at the source of some of Britain's finest fish, meat and game – salmon and trout from the waters of the Tweed, or grouse, pheasant and venison from the Roxburghe estate – complemented with wines from the Duke's own cellar. Fine whiskies are served in the Library Bar, with its log fire and leather-bound tomes. The Beauty Clinique *Elixir* brings to guests the régimes of Decleor, Paris. Surrounding the hotel is the magnificent Roxburghe Golf Course, designed by Dave Thomas. This parkland course is the only championship standard golf course in the Scottish Borders. A full sporting programme can be arranged, including fly and coarse fishing, and falconry. The shooting school offers tuition in game and clay shooting. Seven great country houses are within easy reach including Floors Castle, the home of the Duke and Duchess of Roxburghe. **Directions:** The hotel is at Heiton, just off the A698 Kelso–Jedburgh road. Price guide: Single £98; double/twin £145; suite £185–£230.

For hotel location, see maps on pages 490-496

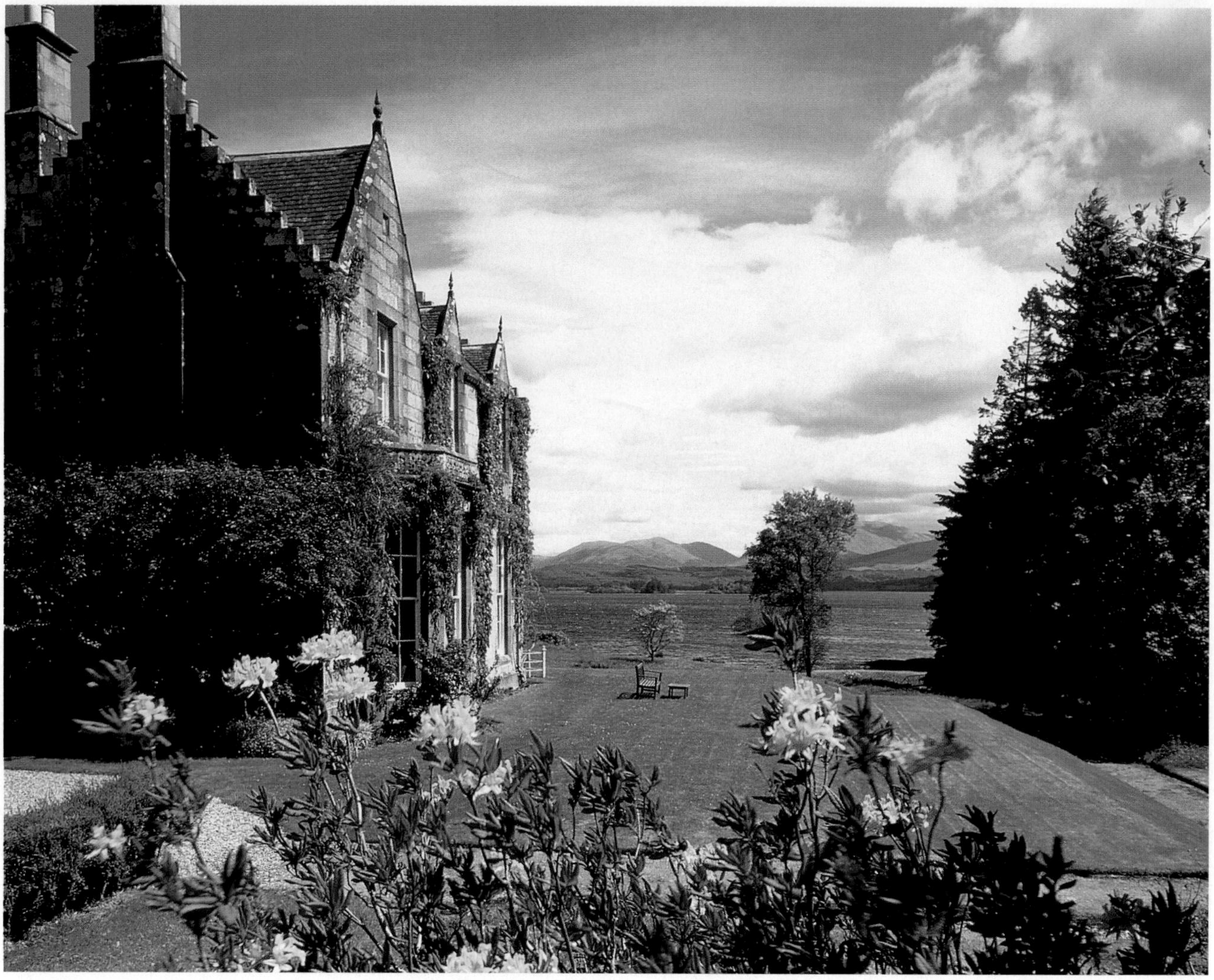

# ARDANAISEIG

**KILCHRENAN BY TAYNUILT, ARGYLL PA35 1HE**
**TEL: 01866 833333 FAX: 01866 833222**

This romantic small luxury hotel, built in 1834, stands alone in a setting of almost surreal natural beauty at the foot of Ben Cruachan. Directly overlooking Loch Awe and surrounded by wild wooded gardens, Ardanaiseig is evocative of the romance and history of the Highlands. Skilful restoration has ensured that this lovely old mansion has changed little since it was built. The elegant drawing room has log fires, bowls of fresh flowers, superb antiques, handsome paintings and marvellous views of the islands in the Loch and of faraway mountains. The traditional library, sharing this outlook, is ideal for post-prandial digestifs. The charming bedrooms are peaceful, appropriate to the era of the house, yet equipped thoughtfully with all comforts. True Scottish hospitality is the philosophy of the Ardanaiseig Restaurant, renowned for its inspired use of fresh produce from the Western Highlands. The wine list is magnificent. Artistic guests enjoy the famous 100 acre Ardanaiseig gardens and nature reserve, filled with exotic shrubs and trees brought back from the Himalayas over the years. Brilliant rhododendrons and azaleas add a riot of colour. The estate also offers fishing, boating, tennis and croquet (snooker in the evenings) and exhilarating hill or lochside walks. **Directions:** Reaching Taynuilt on A85, take B845 to Kilchrenan. Price guide: Single £42–£80; double/twin £84–£160.

15 rms MasterCard VISA AMERICAN EXPRESS M 28 8

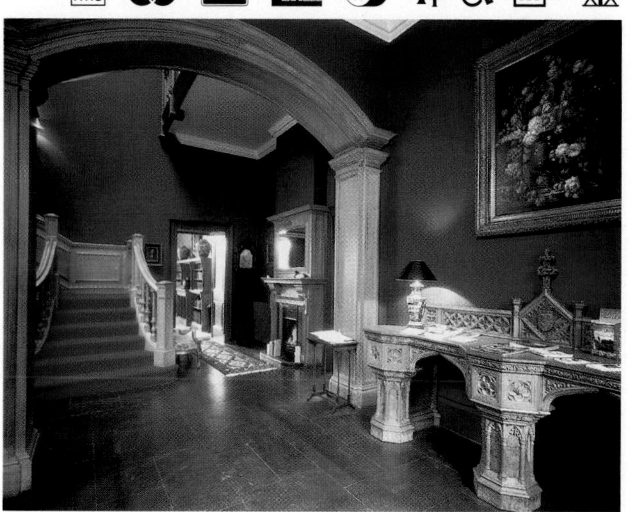

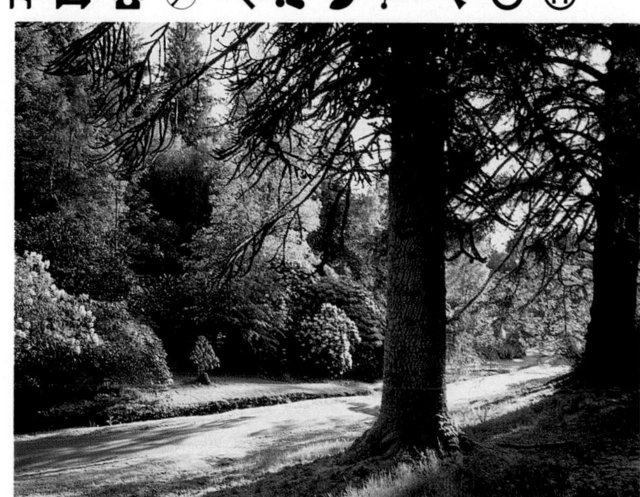

For hotel location, see maps on pages 490-496

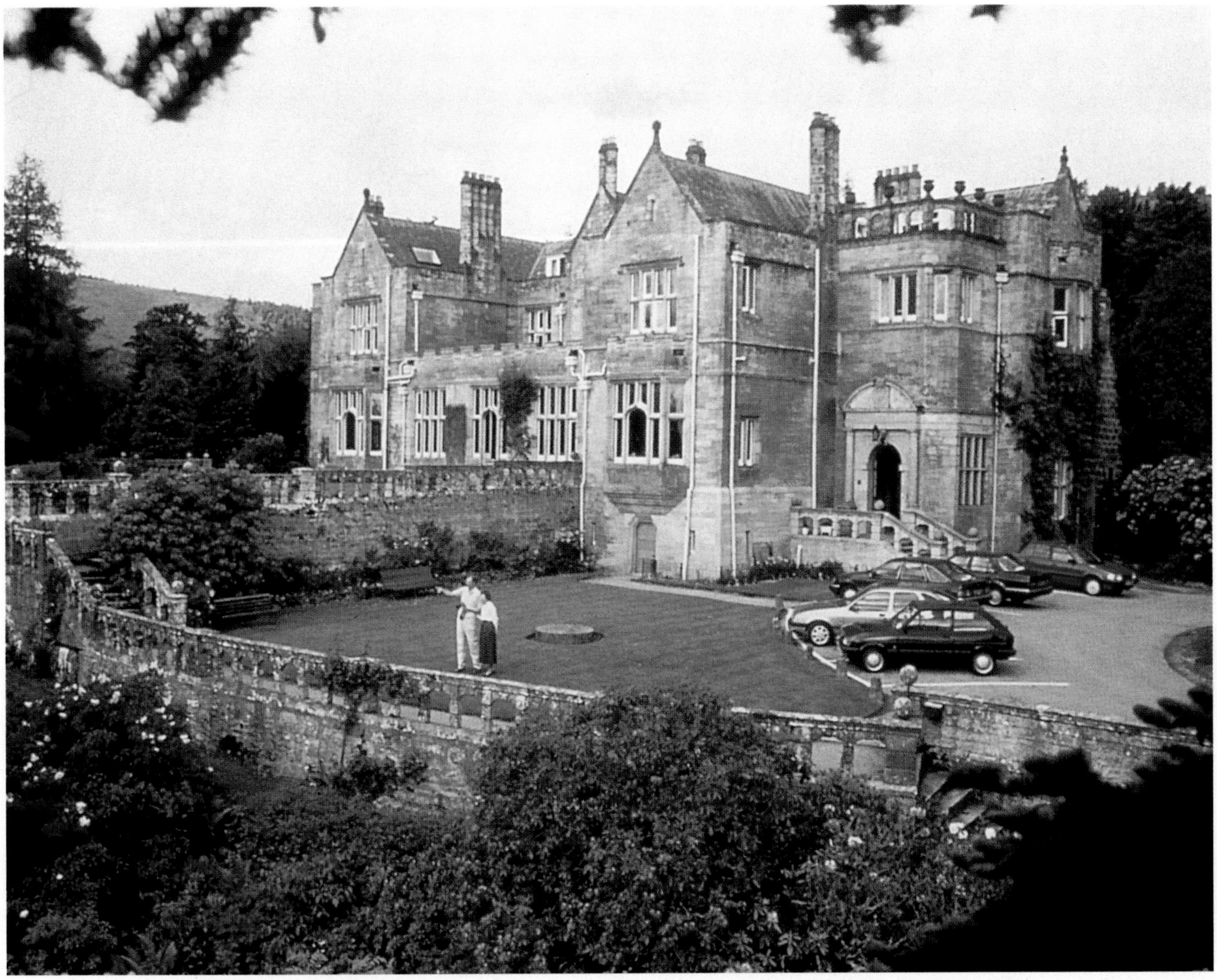

# KILDRUMMY CASTLE HOTEL

**KILDRUMMY, BY ALFORD, ABERDEENSHIRE AB33 8RA**
**TEL: 019755 71288 FAX: 019755 71345**

In the heart of Donside near to the renowned Kildrummy Castle Gardens, and overlooking the ruins of the original 13th century castle from which it takes its name, Kildrummy Castle Hotel offers a rare opportunity to enjoy the style and elegance of a bygone era combined with all the modern comforts of a first-class hotel. Recent improvements have not detracted from the turn-of-the century interior, featuring the original wall tapestries and oak-panelled walls and high ceilings. The bedrooms, some with four-poster beds, all have en suite bathrooms. All have been refurbished recently to a high standard. The hotel restaurant was runner-up for Johansens 1996 Restaurant Award. Chef Kenneth White prepares excellent menus using regional produce that includes local game and both fish and shellfish from the Moray Firth. Kildrummy Castle is ideally located for touring Royal Deeside and Balmoral, the Spey Valley, Aberdeen and Inverness, while the surrounding Grampian region has more castles than any other part of Scotland – 8 of the National Trust for Scotland's finest properties are within an hour's drive of the hotel. Also within an hour's drive are more than 20 golf courses. Visitors can discover the 'Scotch Whisky Trail' and enjoy a tour of some of Scotland's most famous distilleries. **Directions:** Off the A97 Ballater/Huntly road, 35 miles west of Aberdeen. Price guide: Single £75–£80; double/twin £120–£150.

For hotel location, see maps on pages 490-496

# CROMLIX HOUSE

**KINBUCK, BY DUNBLANE, PERTHSHIRE FK15 9JT**
**TEL: 01786 822125 FAX: 01786 825450**

The Cromlix estate of some 3,000 acres in the heart of Perthshire is a relaxing retreat. Built as a family home in 1874, much of the house remains unchanged including many fine antiques acquired over the generations. Proprietors David and Ailsa Assenti are proud of their tradition of country house hospitality. The individually designed bedrooms and spacious suites have recently been redecorated with period fabrics to enhance the character and fine furniture whilst retaining the essential feeling of a much loved home. Unpretentious, restful and most welcoming, the large public rooms have open fires. In the restaurant, the finest local produce is used, including game from the estate, lamb and locally caught salmon. Cromlix is an ideal venue for small conferences and business meetings, and there is a charming chapel – the perfect setting for weddings. Extensive sporting and leisure facilities include trout and salmon fishing and game shooting in season. Challenging golf courses within easy reach include Rosemount, Carnoustie and St Andrews. The location is ideal for touring the Southern Highlands, with Edinburgh and Glasgow only an hour away. **Directions:** Cromlix House lies four miles north of Dunblane, north of Kinbuck on B8033 and four miles south of Braco. Price guide: Single £95–£125; double/twin £145–£200; suite with private sitting room £185–£280.

For hotel location, see maps on pages 490-496

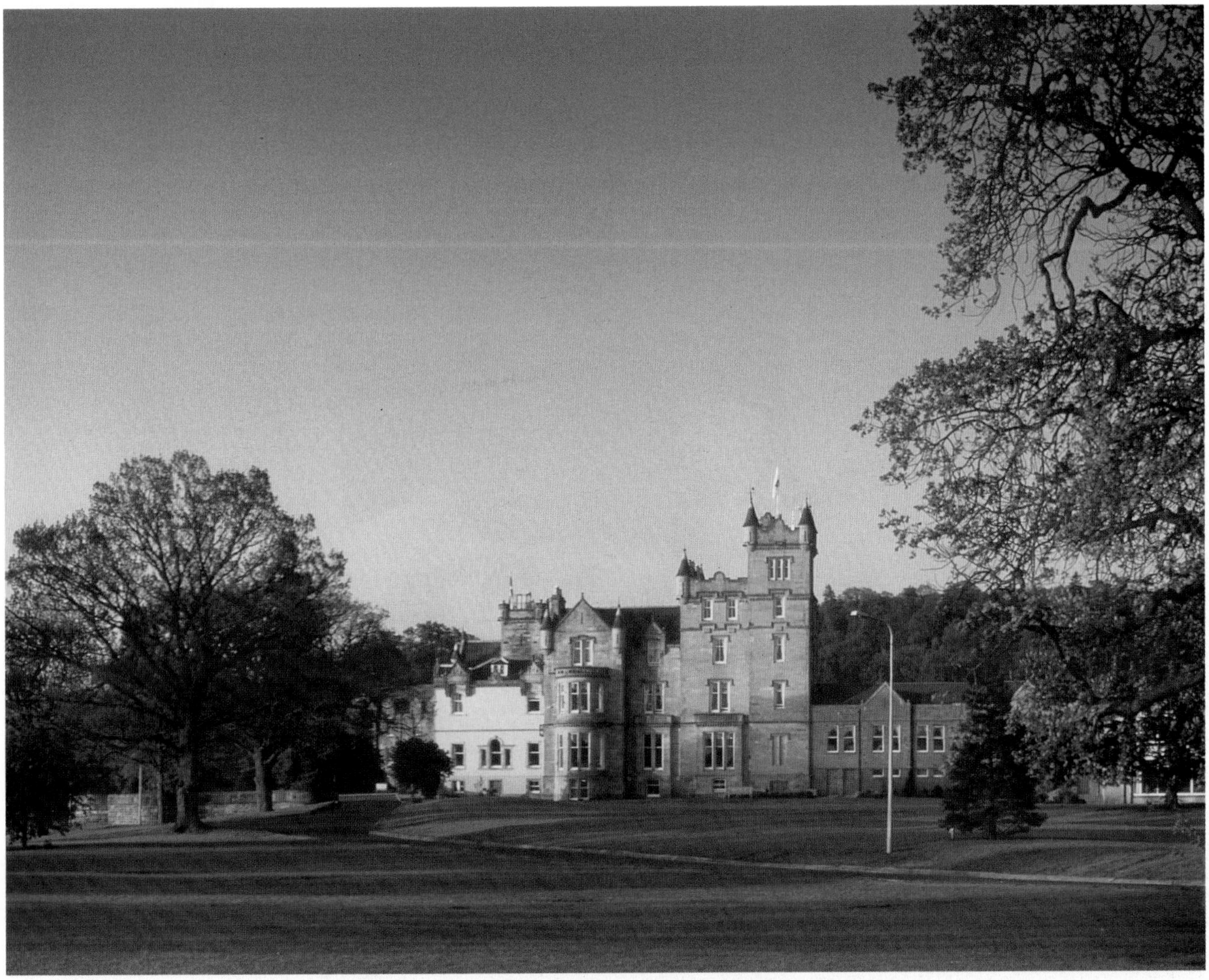

# CAMERON HOUSE

LOCH LOMOND, DUNBARTONSHIRE G83 8QZ
TEL: 01389 755565 FAX: 01389 759522

The splendour and location of this impressive baronial house has lured many famous visitors, from Dr Johnson and the Empress Eugénie to Sir Winston Churchill. Standing in over 100 acres of green lawns and wooded glades leading down to the shores of Loch Lomond, Cameron House offers luxurious accommodation and superlative recreational amenities. The indoor leisure club includes squash, badminton and aerobic facilities, three beauty treatment rooms, a games room with three full-size snooker tables and a state-of-the-art gymnasium. For children there is a games room, toddlers' pool, crèche and a children's club. Outside, another sporting world unfolds, with professional tennis coaching, 9-hole golf, clay pigeon shooting, archery, off-road driving, sailing, cruising and wind-surfing available. Each of the bedrooms and the five opulent suites is furnished in soft colours that complement the beautiful views from the windows. Guests can dine in the intimate Georgian Room or the Smollets Restaurant both overlooking the loch. The conference, banqueting and function facilities are second to none and Glasgow, with its museums, art galleries and theatres, is less than 30 minutes' drive away. **Directions:** Cameron House is on the southern banks of Loch Lomond, via the A82 from Glasgow. Price guide: Single £135–£140; double/twin £175–£185; suite £275–£400.

For hotel location, see maps on pages 490-496

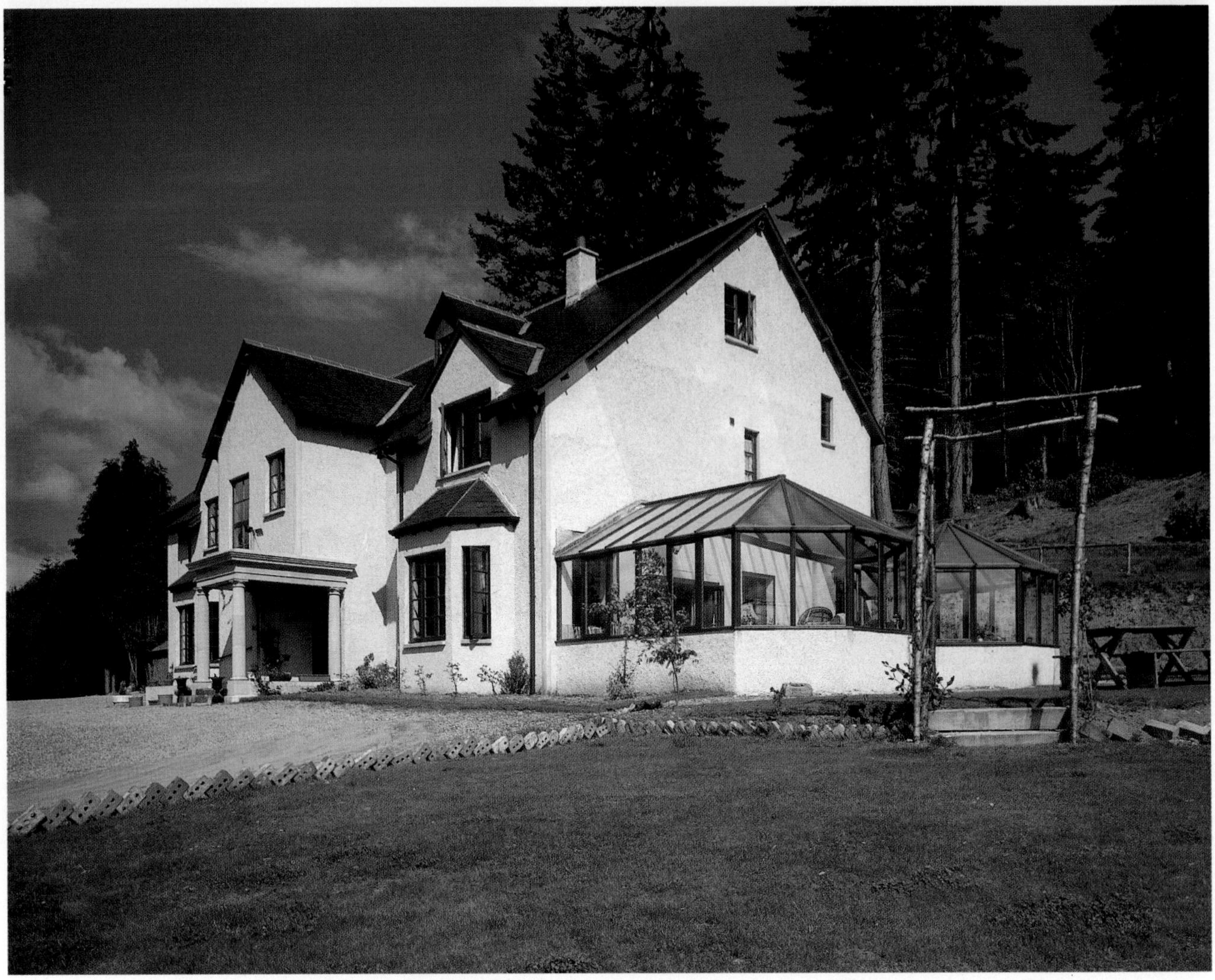

# CRAIGDARROCH HOUSE HOTEL

**FOYERS, LOCH NESS SIDE, INVERNESS-SHIRE IV1 2XU**
**TEL: 01456 486 400 FAX: 01456 486 444**

Situated in 35 acres of woodland on the southern hillside shore of Loch Ness, Craigdarroch House looks over Loch Ness and the mountainous Highlands beyond. Craigdarroch incorporates all the facilities expected in a prestigious country hotel. Owners David and Kate Munro have taken great care to recreate an air of history. High ceilings and open log fires combined with traditional soft furnishings help to create the ambience of a 19th century Highland Lodge. Most of the bedrooms, some with four-poster beds, and all the public rooms enjoy panoramic views. There is a family bedroom and also one specially adapted for disabled guests. The lounge bar, aptly named the "Malt Shop", has over 50 malt whiskies and the restaurant offers a wide choice of cuisine expertly prepared from local produce by chef Andrew Munro. Local places of interest include Loch Ness Visitors Centre, Fort Augustus, Inverness, Culloden battlefield and a number of beautiful glens. Golf, fishing, shooting and riding are nearby. Directions: From Inverness take the B862 towards Dores and then the B852 signposted Foyers. From Fort Augustus take the B862 to just beyond the village of Whitebridge and then the B852. Price guide: Single £50-£80; double £100-£120.

For hotel location, see maps on pages 490-496

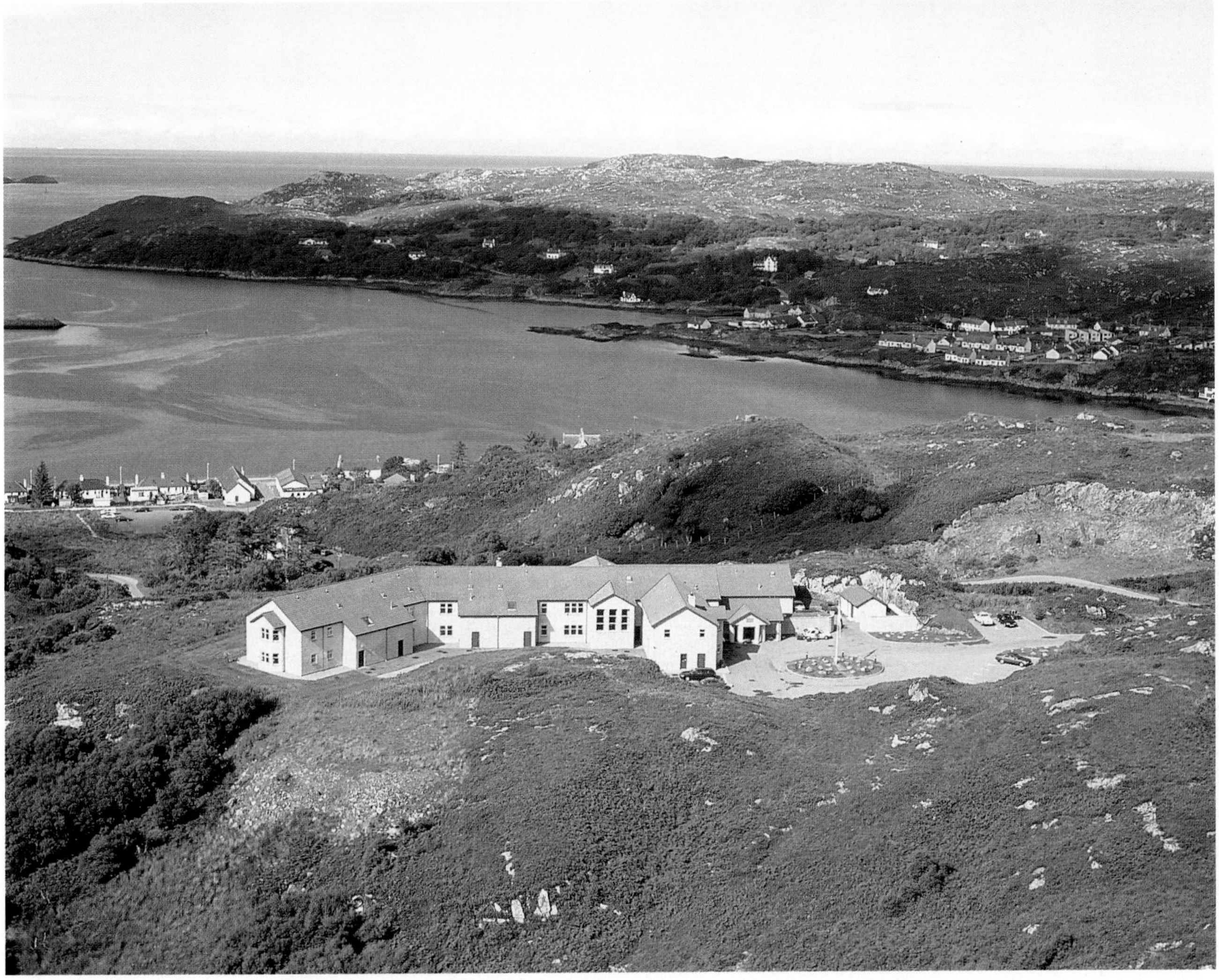

# INVER LODGE HOTEL

**LOCHINVER, SUTHERLAND IV27 4LU**
**TEL: 01571 844496 FAX: 01571 844395**

The Highlands have a unique appeal for those who appreciate country pursuits and magnificent landscapes. The Inver Lodge Hotel not only meets these criteria, but also offers luxurious accommodation. From Inverness Airport it is two hours drive through dramatic Highland landscapes, the Lodge stands above the fishing village of Lochinver, with spectacular views across Inver Loch to the Western Isles. A warm welcome awaits new arrivals in the reception hall, and the Residents Lounge has a big fireplace and comfortable chairs. The spacious bedrooms, each named after a loch or mountain, have magnificent views. Beautifully decorated, with period furniture, and providing every modern amenity, they have extra big beds, coffee tables and an aura of serenity. The handsome Cocktail Bar stocks the Lodge's own malt whisky. In the traditional Dining Room, discerning guests feast on local fish, lobsters, wild salmon and Highland beef and imbibe excellent wines. The Lodge has 10 rods on local rivers and access to deer forests Ornithologists study innumerable wild birds, while country lovers explore the waterfalls, sub-tropical gardens and castles. Children enjoy the loch's sandy beach. Golf, climbing and snooker provide other diversions. **Directions:** A9 north to Dornoch, left onto A949, then A837 to Lochinver. Price guide: Single £80–£120; double/twin £120–£200.

For hotel location, see maps on pages 490-496

# KIRROUGHTREE HOUSE

**NEWTON STEWART, WIGTOWNSHIRE DG8 6AN**
**TEL: 01671 402141 FAX: 01671 402425**

Winner of the Johansens Most Excellent Service Award 1996 Kirroughtree House is situated in the foothills of the Cairnsmore of Fleet, on the edge of Galloway Forest Park. The hotel stands in eight acres of landscaped gardens, where guests can relax and linger over the spectacular views. This striking mansion was built by the Heron family in 1719 and the oak-panelled lounge with open fire place reflects the style of that period. From the lounge rises the original staircase, from which Robert Burns often recited his poems. Each bedroom is well furnished – guests may choose to spend the night in one of the hotel's spacious deluxe bedrooms with spectacular views over the surrounding countryside. Many guests are attracted by Kirroughtree's culinary reputation – only the finest produce is used to create meals of originality and finesse. This is a good venue for small conferences. Pitch-and-putt, lawn tennis and croquet can be enjoyed in the grounds. Residents can play golf on the many local courses and also have use of our sister hotel's new exclusive 18-hole course at Gatehouse of Fleet. Trout and salmon fishing can be arranged nearby, as can rough shooting and deer stalking during the season. Closed 3 January to mid February. **Directions:** The hotel is signposted one mile outside Newton Stewart on the A75. Price guide: Single £60–£85; double/twin £100–£124; suite £140.

For hotel location, see maps on pages 490-496

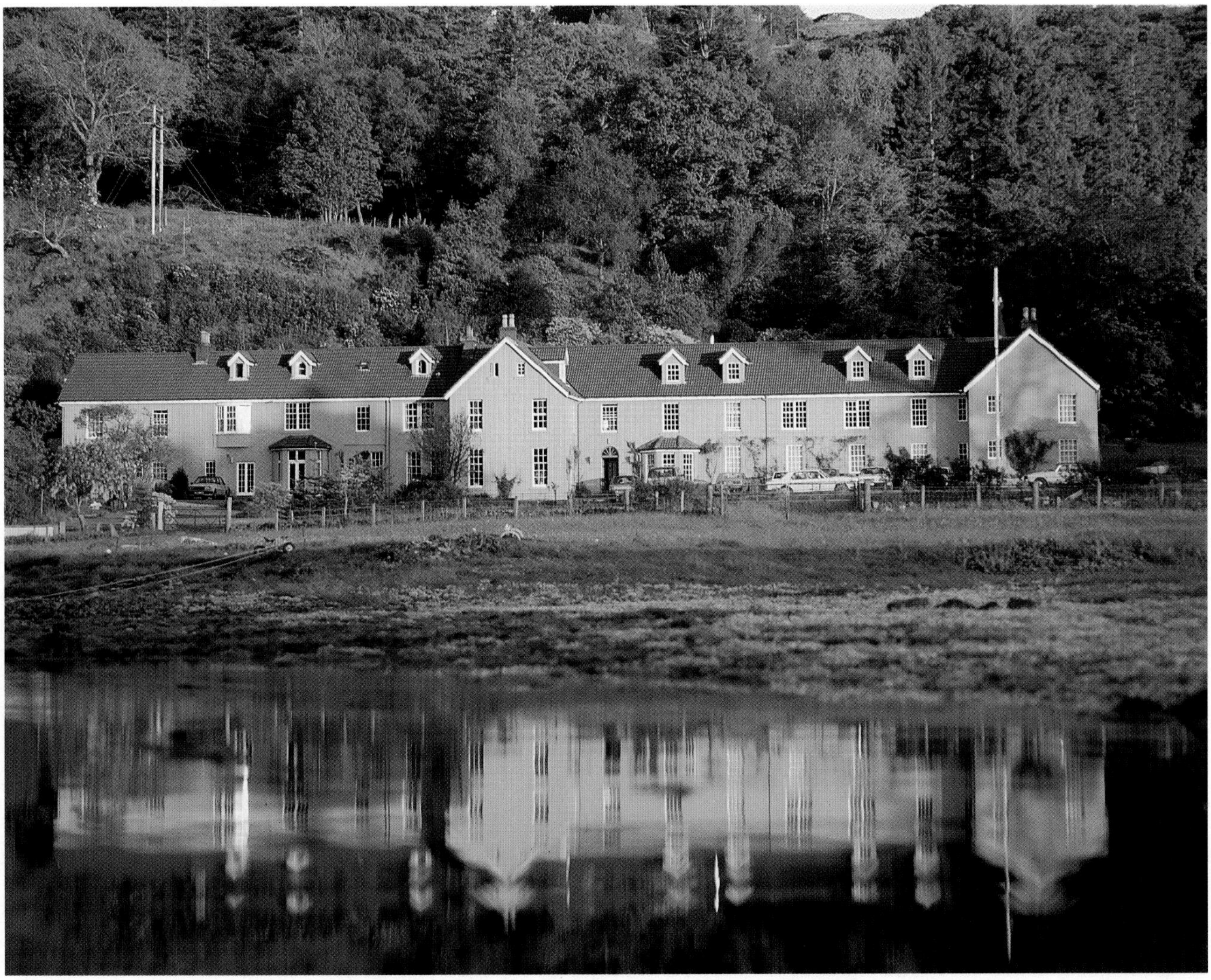

# KNIPOCH HOTEL

BY OBAN, ARGYLL PA34 4QT
TEL: 01852 316251 FAX: 01852 316249

Six miles south of Oban lies Knipoch, an elegant Georgian building with a history dating from 1500, set halfway along the shore of Loch Feochan wit, an arm of the sea stretching 4 miles inland. Wildlife is abundant in this area – rare birds of prey, deer and otters can often be seen. The hotel is owned and personally run by the Craig family, who go out of their way to ensure that their guests enjoy their stay. All the bedrooms are fully equipped and offer splendid views either of the loch or the surrounding hills. High standards of cooking are proudly maintained here. The daily menu features many Scottish specialities, prepared with imaginative flair. Not only is the choice of wines extensive – there are over 350 labels – but the list is informative too. Guests are given a copy to peruse at leisure rather than to scan hurriedly before ordering. In addition, the bar stocks a wide range of malt whiskies. Sporting activities available locally include fishing, sailing, yachting, golf, tennis, pony-trekking and skiing. A traditional Scottish event, the Oban Highland Games, is particularly renowned for its solo piping competition. The Knipoch Hotel makes a good base from which to visit the Western Isles and explore the spectacular scenery of the area. Closed mid-November to mid-February. **Directions:** On the A816, 6 miles south of Oban. Price guide: Single £40–£75; double/twin £80–£150; suite £195–£250

17 rms

# CRINGLETIE HOUSE HOTEL

**PEEBLES EH45 8PL**
**TEL: 01721 730233 FAX: 01721 730244**

This distinguished mansion, turreted in the Scottish baronial style, stands in 28 acres of beautifully maintained gardens and woodland. Designed by Scottish architect David Bryce, Cringletie was built in 1861 for the Wolfe Murray family, whose ancestor, Colonel Alexander Murray, accepted the surrender of Quebec after General Wolfe was killed. All of the bedrooms have fine views and many have been redesigned with attractively co-ordinated curtains and furnishings. The splendid panelled lounge has an impressive carved oak and marble fireplace, a painted ceiling and many oil portraits. The imaginative cooking, prepared with flair, attracts consistently good reports. The range and quality of fruit and vegetables grown in the 2-acre walled garden make this the only Scottish garden recommended in Geraldene Holt's *The Gourmet Garden*, which includes some of Britain's most distinguished hotels. On-site facilities include a new hard tennis court, croquet lawn and putting green. Golf can be played at Peebles and fishing is available by permit on the River Tweed. Convenient for visiting Edinburgh, Cringletie is a good base from which to discover the rich historic and cultural heritage of the Borders. Closed 2 January to 7 March. **Directions:** The hotel is on the A703 Peebles–Edinburgh road, 2½ miles from Peebles. Price guide: Single £60; double/twin £105–£115.

For hotel location, see maps on pages 490-496

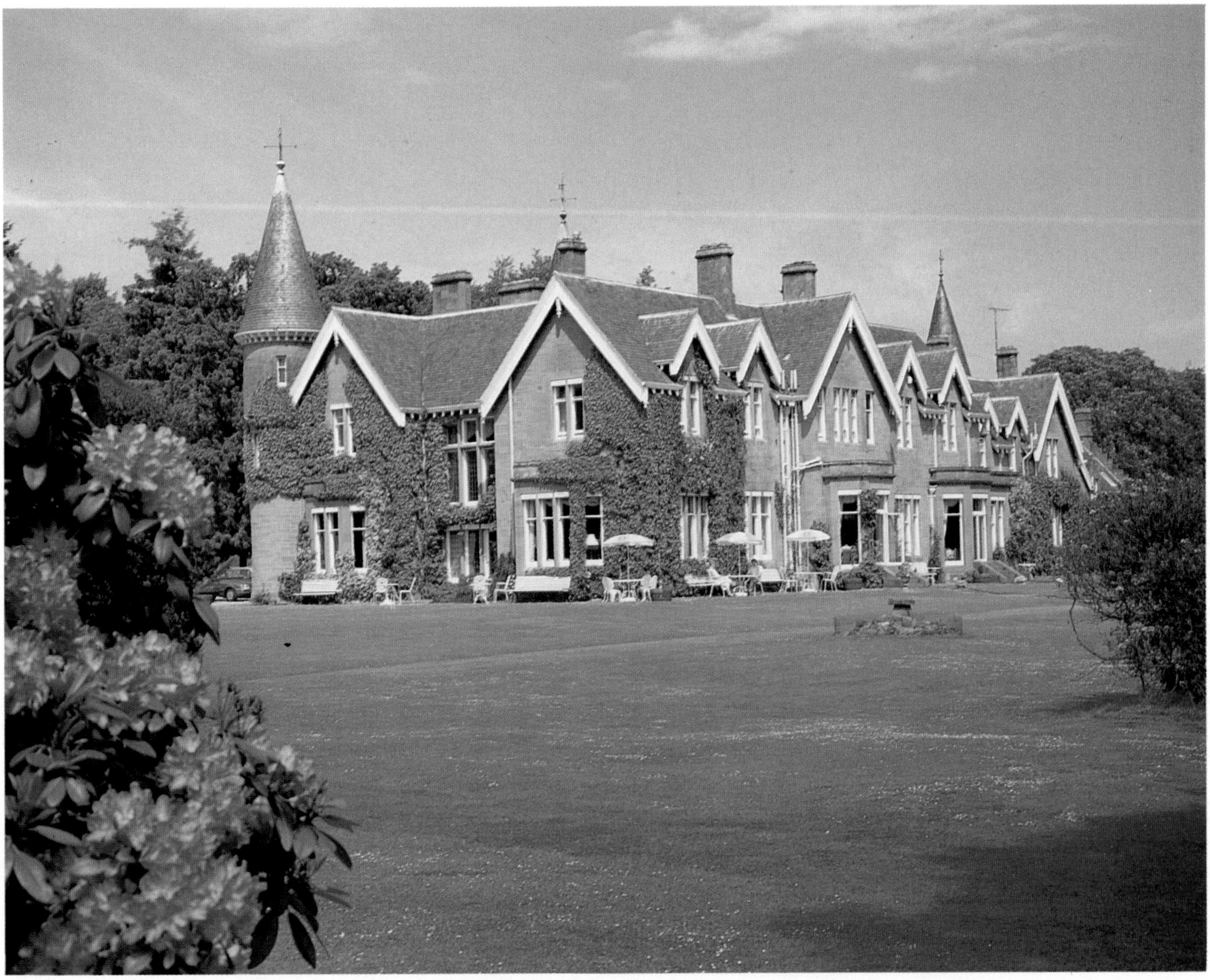

# BALLATHIE HOUSE HOTEL

**KINCLAVEN, STANLEY, PERTH, PERTHSHIRE PH1 4QN**
**TEL: 01250 883268 FAX: 01250 883396**

Set in an estate overlooking the River Tay, Ballathie House Hotel offers Scottish hospitality in a house of character and distinction. Dating from 1850, this mansion has a French baronial façade and handsome interiors. Overlooking lawns which slope down to the riverside, the drawing room is an ideal place to relax with coffee and the papers, or to enjoy a malt whisky after dinner. The premier bedrooms are large and elegant, while the standard rooms are designed in a cosy, cottage style. On the ground floor there are several bedrooms suitable for guests with disabilities. Local ingredients such as Tay salmon, Scottish beef, seafoods and piquant soft fruits are used by chef Kevin MacGillivray to create menus catering for all tastes. The hotel has two rosettes for fine Scottish cuisine. Activities available on the estate include trout and salmon fishing and clay pigeon shooting. The Sporting Lodge adjacent to the main house is designed to accommodate sporting parties. The area has many good golf courses. Perth, Blairgowrie and Edinburgh are within an hour's drive. STB 4 Crowns De Luxe. Dogs in certain rooms only. **Directions:** From A93 at Beech Hedges, signposted for Kinclaven and Ballathie, or off the A9, 2 miles north of Perth take the Stanley Road. The hotel is 8 miles north of Perth. Price guide: Single £60–£95; double/twin £115–£180; suite £160–£200.

For hotel location, see maps on pages 490-496

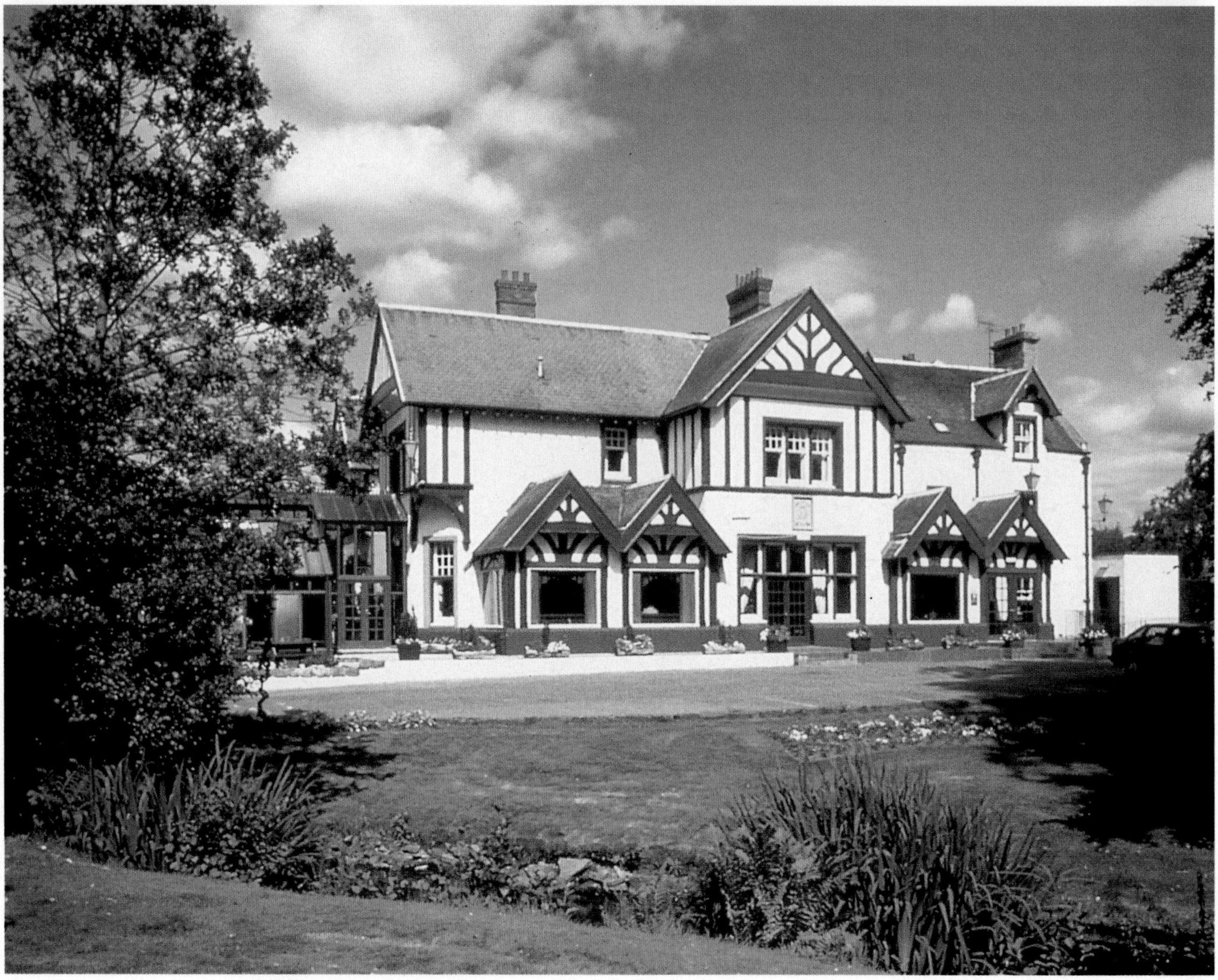

# HUNTINGTOWER HOTEL

**CRIEFF ROAD, PERTH, SCOTLAND PH1 3JT**
**TEL: 01738 583771 FAX: 01738 583777**

When staying at this splendid country house, guests soon forget that they are just 5 minutes from the busy city of Perth. Once the home of wealthy millowners, and mentioned in Sir Walter Scott's Ivanhoe, it has an ambience of gracious living. There is a delightful burn in the four acre grounds which surround the hotel and ensure privacy and quiet, so valued by people today. Huntingtower has splendid Victorian interiors, with high ceilings and elaborate panelling. Tartan carpeting brightens the entrance hall and staircase. The bedrooms are also evocative of its past, with elaborate chintz drapes and period furniture. They are all individually decorated and have well designed bathrooms. The handsome bar is well stocked, an ideal rendezvous for evening drinks at the end of a long day. The Restaurant is quite formal, but the menu covers a spectrum of traditional Scottish dishes through to French regional specialities. Superb wines are listed. The charming Conservatory, overlooking the gardens, is a more relaxed brasserie restaurant. The Huntingtower Suite, opening onto the gardens, is ideal for corporate functions or private celebrations. Marvellous golf, shooting and fishing are nearby, and it is easy to travel to Edinburgh, Glasgow and St Andrews or set off to tour the Highlands. **Directions:** The hotel is west of Perth, 500 yards off the A9 dual carriageway. Price guide: Single £71.50; double/twin £90; suite £95

For hotel location, see maps on pages 490-496

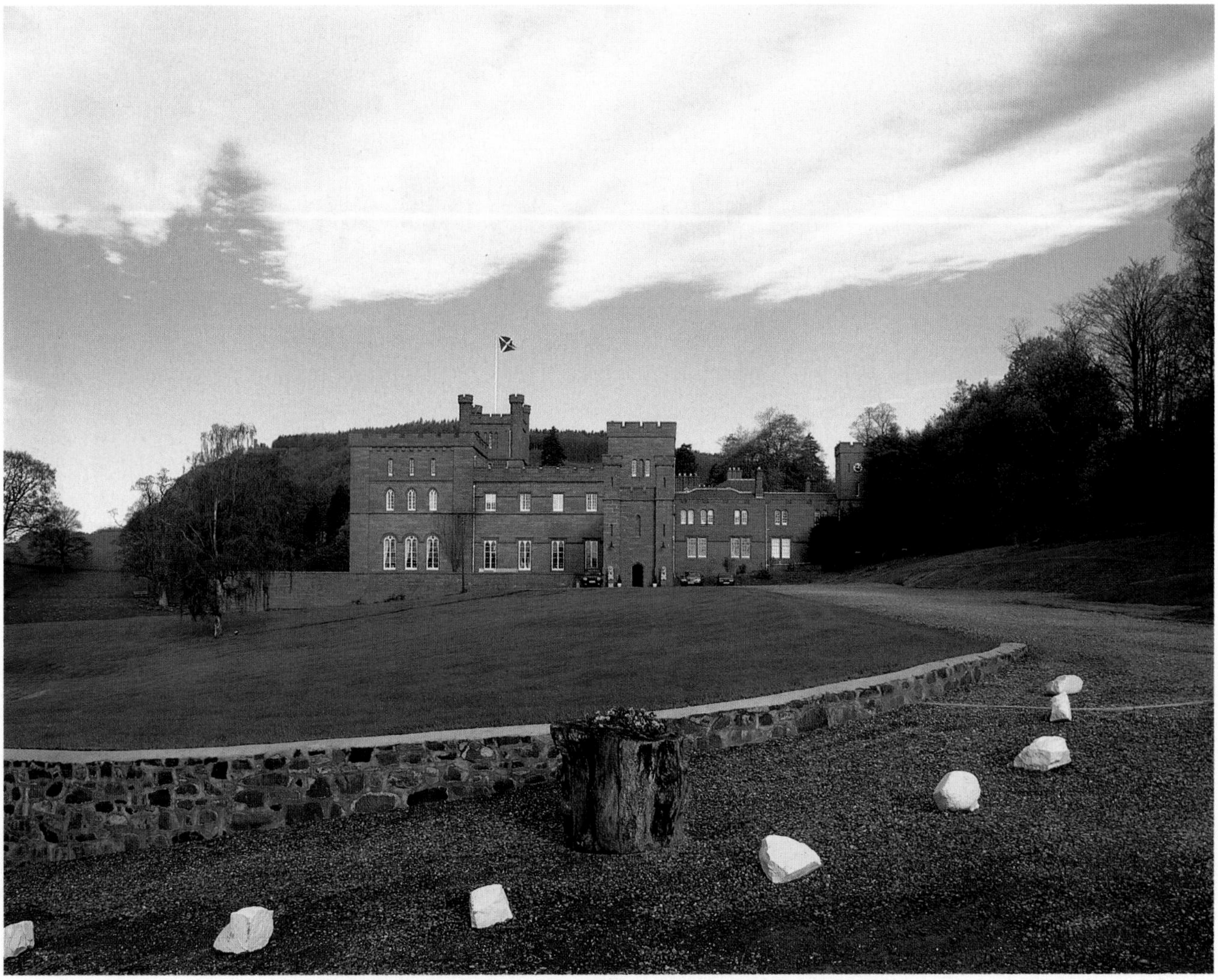

# KINFAUNS CASTLE

**NR PERTH, PERTHSHIRE**

**TEL: 01738 620777 FAX: 01783 620778**

Kinfauns Castle stands impressively in 26 acres of parkland adorned with rare trees. The castle, built for Lord Gray in 1820 is located immediately off the A90 motorway and two miles from Perth. The new Directors, Mr and Mrs James A. Smith, made a commitment to the restoration of the wonderful building the historical home of the Earls Gray and Moray. Mr Smith, born not far away, was until recently Vice-President of Hilton International for Central Asia. The sixteen suites and rooms are individually decorated and reflect the quality comfort and ambience one expects in a luxury Country House. The public rooms have their original decor in the rich style of the 19th century. One particular lounge bar feature is the decorative dragon head and tail from a Hilton Hotel in the Far East. Jeremy Wares who leads the Gold Medal Award Winning Brigade serves excellent traditional Scottish and Continental cuisine in the elegant Library Restaurant. The area abounds with castles and ancient sites: Scone Palace and Glamis, the birthplace of the Queen Mother. The hotel has its own fishing beat on the River Tay. Golf, shooting and riding are easily available. Recently awarded Scottish Tourist Board 5 Crowns De Luxe. **Directions:** The hotel is one miles from Perth on the A90. Price guide: Single £95; double £140; suite £240.

For hotel location, see maps on pages 490-496

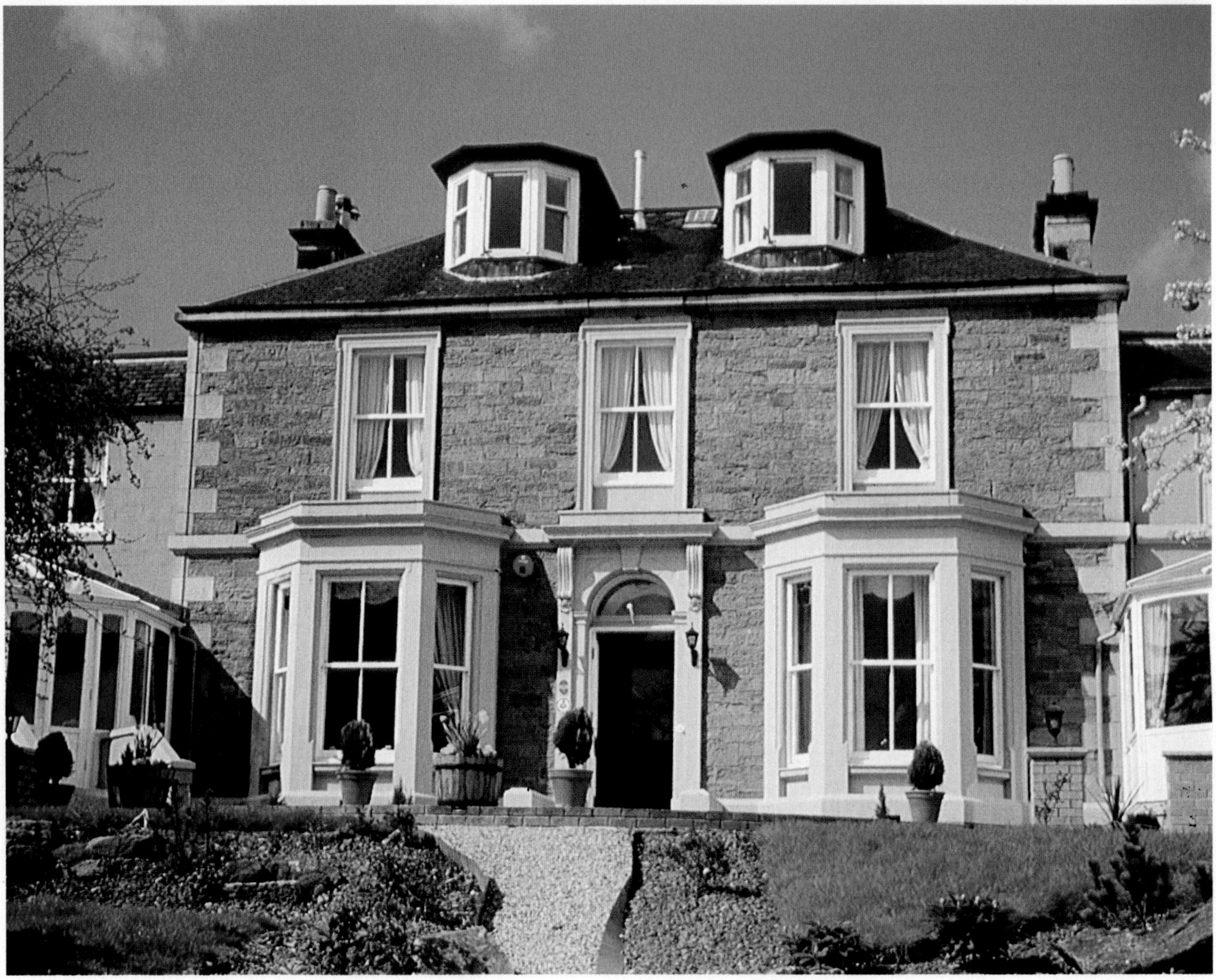

# PARKLANDS HOTEL & RESTAURANT

**ST LEONARD'S BANK, PERTH, PERTHSHIRE PH2 8EB**
**TEL: 01738 622451 FAX: 01738 622046 E-MAIL: 100414.1237@COMPUSERVE.COM**

The Parklands Country Hotel and Restaurant, which overlooks Perth's South Inch Park, has benefited from an extensive programme of improvements. The hotel, with its classic lines, was formerly the home of John Pullar, who was Lord Provost of the City of Perth from 1867 to 1873. The 14 bedrooms all have en suite facilities and are immaculate. Each has been individually decorated to high standards under the personal supervision of proprietor Allan Deeson. In the main restaurant the accent is on light, traditional Scottish food. A choice of table d'hôte menus' is available at both lunchtime and dinner. The boardroom opens off the hotel's entrance and overlooks the hotel gardens. It is a perfect venue for small private lunches or dinners or for business meetings and seminars, and has a large mahogany table and all the latest audio-visual equipment. Perth is a Royal Burgh of great age on the Tay Estuary, at the entrance to Strath Earn and Strath More, full of historical buildings, rich in story and legend. Interesting places to visit locally include Scone Palace and Blair Castle. **Directions:** From the M90 head towards the station; Parklands is on the left at the end of the park. Price guide: Single £70–£107; double/twin £80–£140.

For hotel location, see maps on pages 490-496

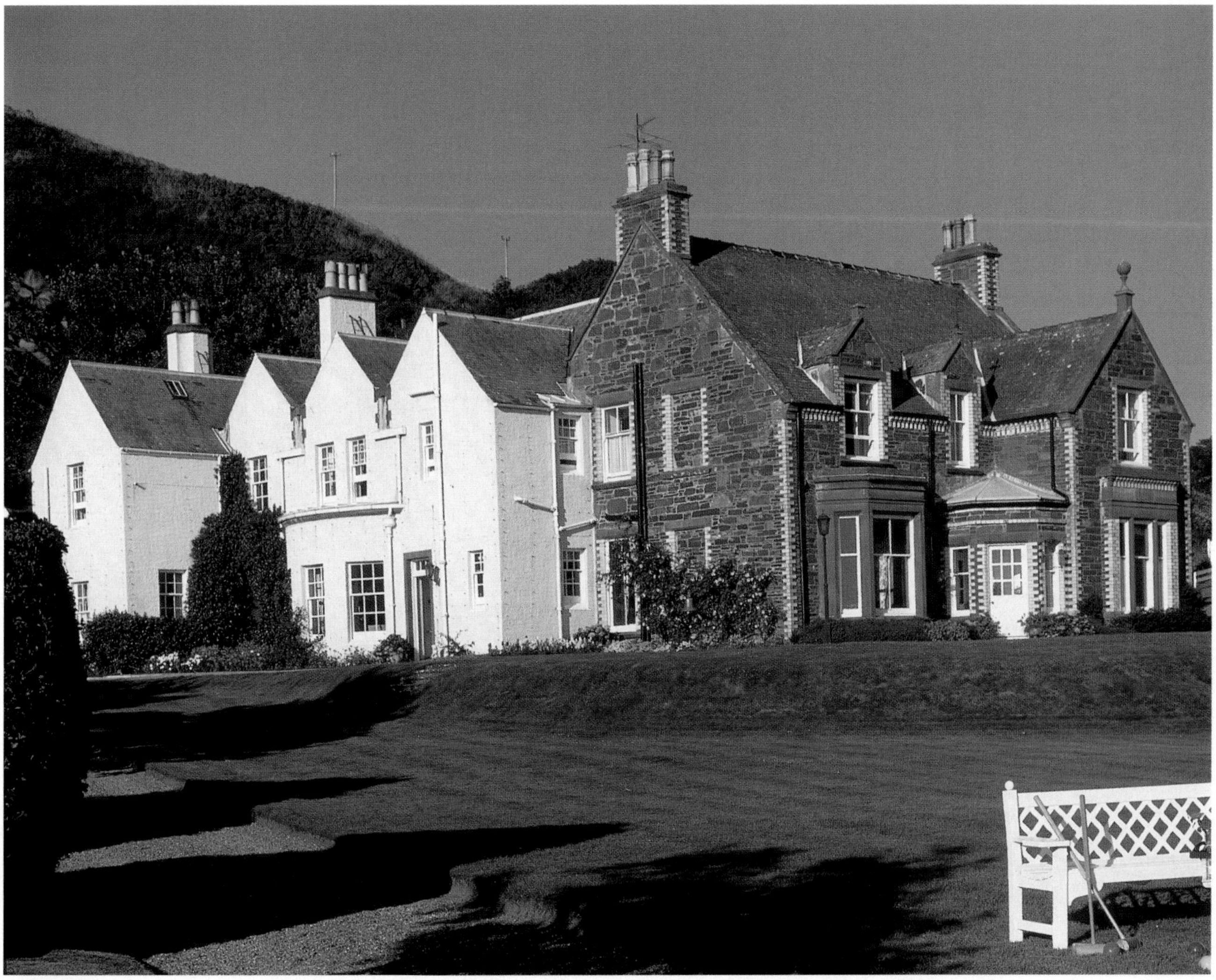

# Knockinaam Lodge

**PORTPATRICK, WIGTOWNSHIRE DG9 9AD**

**TEL: 01776 810471 FAX: 01776 810435**

On the beautiful West Coast of Scotland, surrounded on three sides by sheltering cliffs, lies Knockinaam. This delightful Lodge is perfectly situated to allow guests to enjoy magnificent views of the distant Irish coastline and to marvel at the stupendous sunsets and the changing moods of the sea and sky. In this atmosphere of timelessness and tranquillity Sir Winston Churchill held a secret meeting here with General Eisenhower during the Second World War. Cheerful colour schemes and fabrics have been chosen for the comfortable en suite bedrooms, while the public rooms are warm and cosy and during cooler months residents can relax in front of their lovely open log fires. The AA 3 Rosette restaurant offers a daily changing menu of superb international cuisine, complemented by an extensive wine list of over 400 wines. There are also 114 single malt scotch whiskies for lovers of fine malts. Due to the mild climate there are many famous gardens within easy reach of Knockinaam. There are several excellent golf courses close to the hotel. All inclusive low season rates are available from November until mid-December and from January 5th until Easter. **Directions:** On the A77 to Portpatrick look out for the roadside signpost to the hotel. Price guide (inclusive of dinner and VAT): Single £95–£125; double/twin £80–£125 pp.

For hotel location, see maps on pages 490-496

# RUFFLETS COUNTRY HOUSE AND RESTAURANT

**STRATHKINNESS LOW ROAD, ST ANDREWS, FIFE KY16 9TX**
**TEL: 01334 472594 FAX:01334 478703 E-MAIL: rufflets@standrews.co.uk**

One of the oldest country house hotels in Scotland, Rufflets has been privately owned and managed by the same family since 1952 and extends a friendly and personal service to its guests. Over the years the original turreted house, built in 1924, has been tastefully extended and upgraded to the optimum level of luxury and comfort. It faces south and overlooks ten acres of beautifully landscaped gardens. The hotel's 25 en suite bedrooms are individually designed, using a blend of contemporary and antique furnishings. Three of them are located in the charming Rose Cottage within the grounds of Rufflets. A well stocked kitchen garden supplies fresh herbs, vegetables and fruit for the award-winning restaurant. Featured on the menus are the finest quality Scottish beef, lamb, venison and East Neuk seafood. A carefully selected wine list is available to complement the cuisine. The hotel now has 2 AA rosettes and the AA courtesy and Care Award for Scotland 1996/97. St Andrews is famous for its university and its golf courses and among the many places of interest nearby is the British Golf Museum. Other local features well worth a visit include Falkland Palace, Kellie Castle and Crail Harbour. **Directions:** Rufflets is situated $1\frac{1}{2}$ miles west of St Andrews. Price guide: Single £65–£80; double/twin £120–£170. Seasonal prices.

25 rms MasterCard VISA AMERICAN EXPRESS M 30 15

For hotel location, see maps on pages 490-496

# ST ANDREWS GOLF HOTEL

**40 THE SCORES, ST ANDREWS, FIFE KY16 9AS**
**TEL: 01334 472611 FAX: 01334 472188**

St Andrews Golf Hotel stands tall and handsomely on the coast road of the old town with commanding views of St Andrews Bay and the vast, world famous links. Fashioned from two solid, grey stone Victorian houses the hotel is family owned and extends friendly and personal true Scottish hospitality to guests. The interior decor of warm browns and deep greens, rich oak panelling and beautifully framed scenic and golfing prints enhance the comfortable ambience. All 22 luxuriously draped bedrooms are individually designed and have every modern amenity. Most enjoy panoramic sea views. The elegant bar opens onto a patio and small garden, an ideal place for pre-dinner aperitifs prior to sampling the cuisine provided by chef Colin Masson in his award-winning restaurant. Featured on the menus are the finest quality Scottish meats, pheasant and East Neuk seafood. More casual eating can be enjoyed throughout the day in the bistro bar. St Andrews is not only famous for its golf courses but also for its early 15th century university, predated in Britain only by Oxford and Cambridge, and the ruined splendour of a 15th century cathedral and 14th century castle. Among the many places of interest nearby are the British Golf Museum and Crail Harbour. **Directions:** From the M90, exit at junction 8 and take the A91 east to St Andrews. Price guide: Single £78–£86; double/twin £130–£145; suites £165.

For hotel location, see maps on pages 490-496

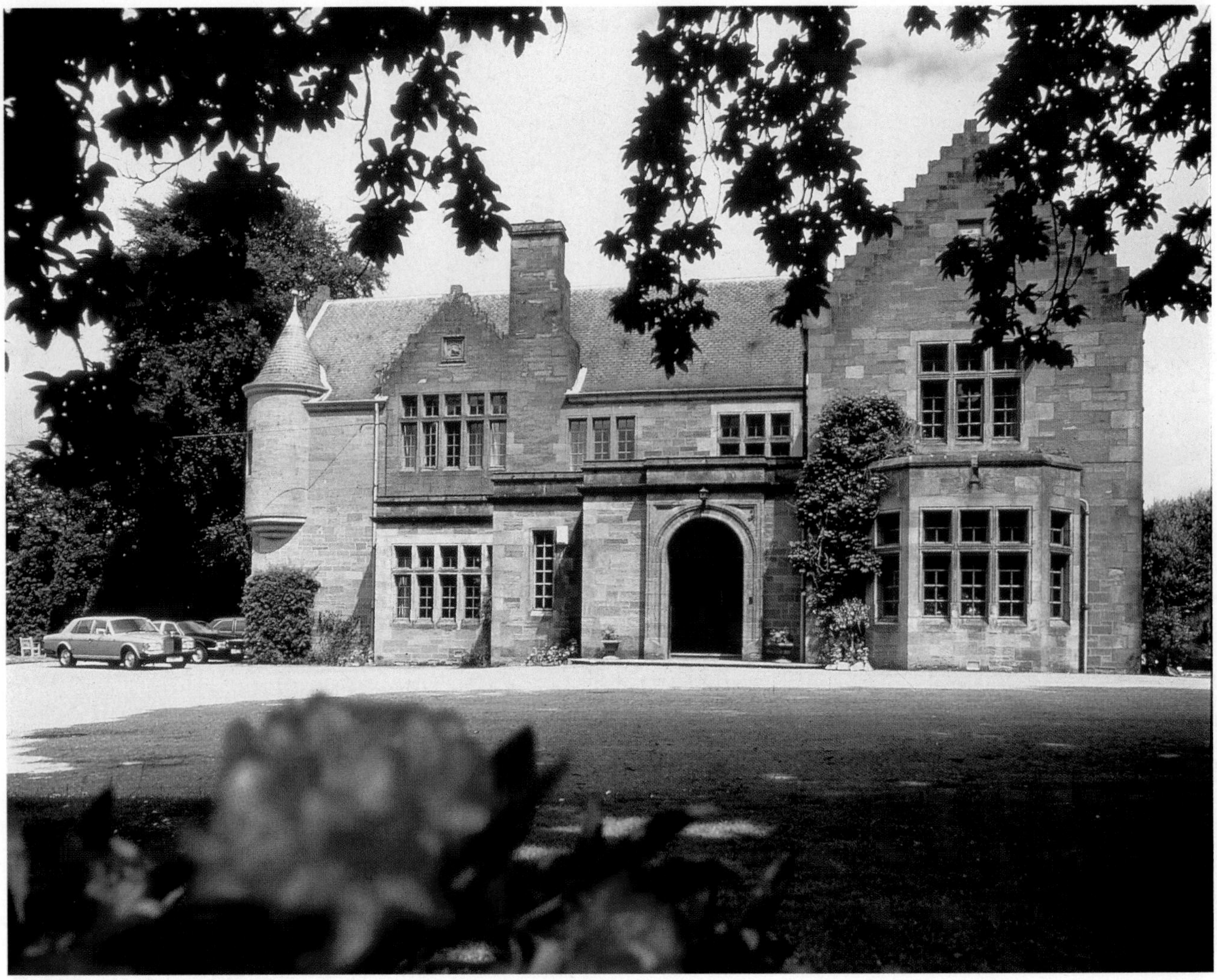

# MURRAYSHALL HOUSE HOTEL AND GOLF COURSE

**SCONE, PERTHSHIRE PH2 7PH**
**TEL: 01738 551171 FAX: 01738 552595**

The Murrayshall Country House Hotel is set in 300 acres of undulating parkland and wooded hillside, with views sweeping across to the Grampians. Entering the hotel through the arched front door, visitors are welcomed by a friendly team of staff. The Old Masters' Restaurant, hung with Dutch 16th and 17th century oil paintings, is a visual delight, well suited to complement the artistry of the hotel's chef. Chef takes advantage of the abundance of local produce, creating menu's and dishes which have a Scottish flavour, with a hint of Modern French Cuisine. The Old Master's Restaurant has retained two AA rosettes. The bedrooms have been designed to suit the varied demands of holiday-makers, honeymooners and fishermen, golfers and business travellers alike. With its own club house and bar, there is an 18-hole golf course adjacent to the hotel, where a golf professional is available to give lessons. The Murrayshall offers special residential golf tuition courses. Guests may play croquet and bowls on the premises or follow one of the published walks that start from the hotel. Dogs by arrangement. Off season rates begin from £48 for dinner, bed and breakfast. **Directions:** Signposted a mile out of Perth on A94. Price guide: Single £80–£85; double/twin £120–£130; suites £135–£150.

For hotel location, see maps on pages 490-496

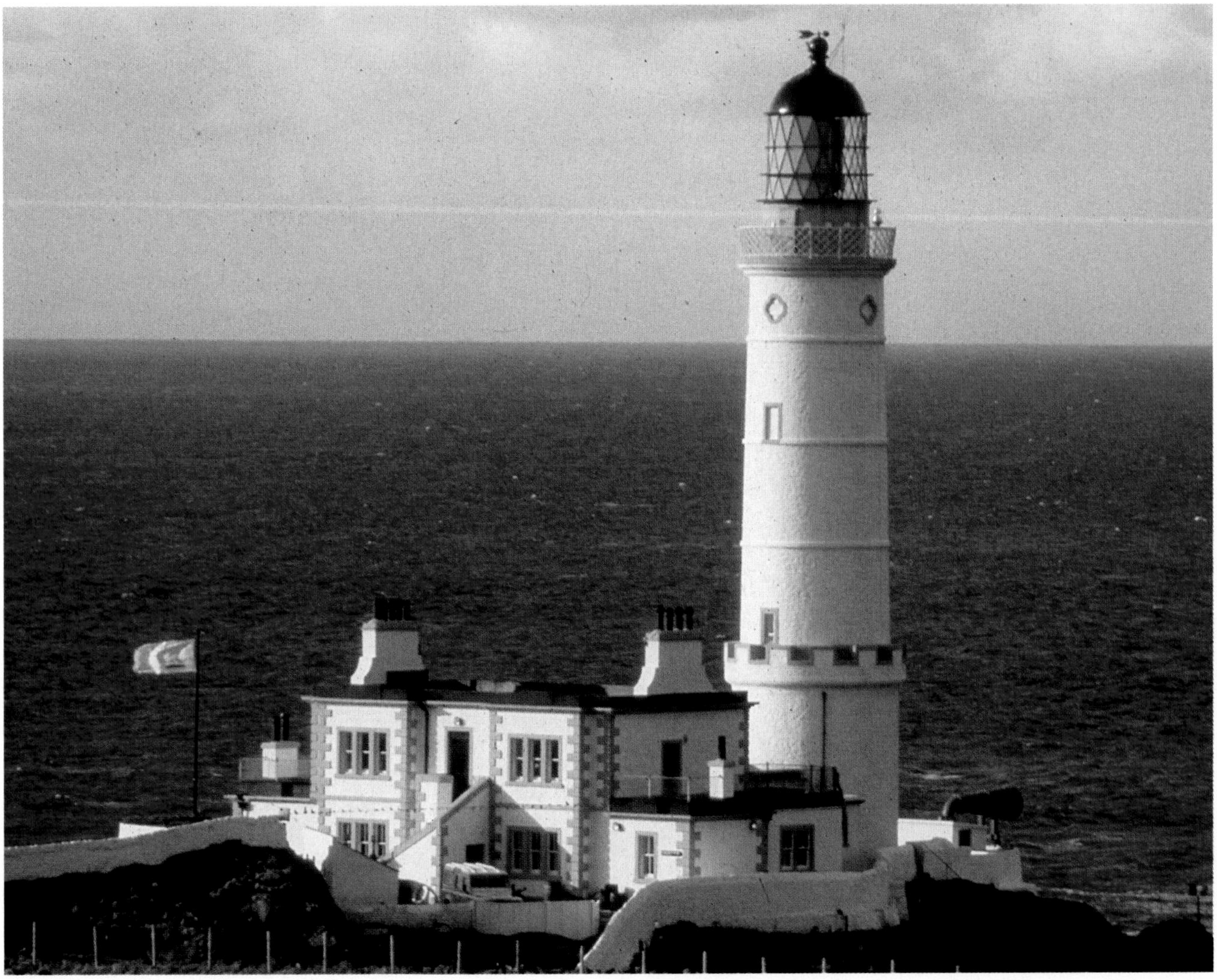

# CORSEWALL LIGHTHOUSE HOTEL

**STRANRAER, SCOTLAND DG9 OQG**
**TEL: 01776 853220 FAX: 01776 854231**

The charm and romance of a 19th century lighthouse have been combined with every modern day comfort to create this unique and delightful luxury hotel and restaurant. Remaining a listed building of national importance, with a light still beaming a warning for ships approaching the mouth of Loch Ryan, the Corsewall Lighthouse Hotel promises its guests the ultimate in peace and relaxation. Extensive restorations have taken place to provide eight charming bedrooms, all equipped with a full range of amenities. The restaurant features flickering candlelight and a blazing log fire, and the menu caters for a wide variety of tastes including local beef, lamb, seafood and vegetarian dishes. Savour a plump breast of duck, gently pan-fried and masked in peach and cherry sauce, or perhaps one of the Corsewall House specialities such as roasted loin of lamb, scented with garlic and rosemary and served with a rich pickled walnut sauce. Within the hotel's 20-acre grounds and further afield can be found some of Scotland's most spectacular coastline, along with unique rock forms, seals, birds, deer and a wide variety of flora. Outdoor activities available by arrangement include golf, horseriding, windsurfing, sailing and day trips to Ireland, Directions: The hotel is located 15 minutes from Stranraer. Take A718 signposted to Kirkcolm and then the B738 to Corsewall and the Lighthouse. Price guide: Double/twin £50–£85.

For hotel location, see maps on pages 490-496

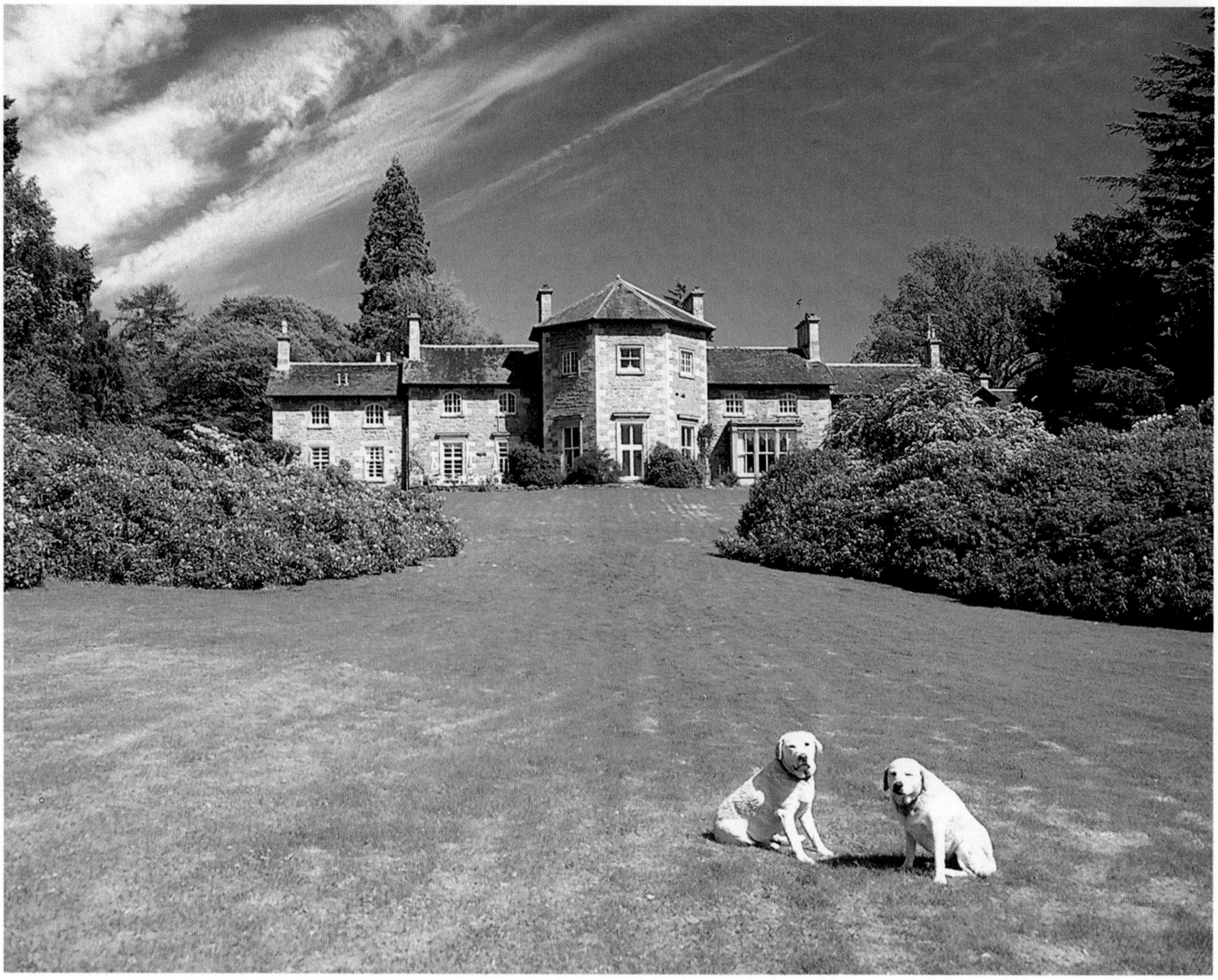

# COUL HOUSE HOTEL

**CONTIN, BY STRATHPEFFER, ROSS-SHIRE IV14 9EY**
**TEL: 01997 421487 FAX: 01997 421945**

Coul House is a handsome country mansion in secluded grounds with magnificent, uninterrupted views. Owners Martyn and Ann Hill have a reputation for their friendly, personal service and high standards, both of food and accommodation. Refurbishments of the decor and furnishings have enhanced the lovely interiors. All bedrooms are en suite, individually designed and each has a colour television, clock radio, trouser press, hairdryer, iron and hospitality tray. One has a four-poster bed. There are three elegant lounges with log burning fires, a cocktail bar and a Kitchen Bar where there is regular evening entertainment. A piper entertains during summer months. In the dining room guests can savour "Taste of Scotland" cuisine such as fresh salmon and venison. Conferences and private functions can be accommodated. A cruise on Loch Ness or a sailing trip to to the Summer Isles can be arranged while nearby are Cawdor Castle, Culloden battlefield, fishing, pony-trekking, shooting and golf. The hotel has its own 9 hole pitch and putt course. Numerous routes lead to lovely glens. **Directions:** From the south, bypassing Inverness, continue on A9 over Moray Firth Bridge and after 5 miles take second exit at roundabout onto A835. Follow to Contin. The hotel is 1/2 mile along a private drive to the right. Price guide (including dinner): Single £61.50–£85.25; double/twin £99–£166.50; suite £129–£186.50.

20 rms M 50

For hotel location, see maps on pages 490-496

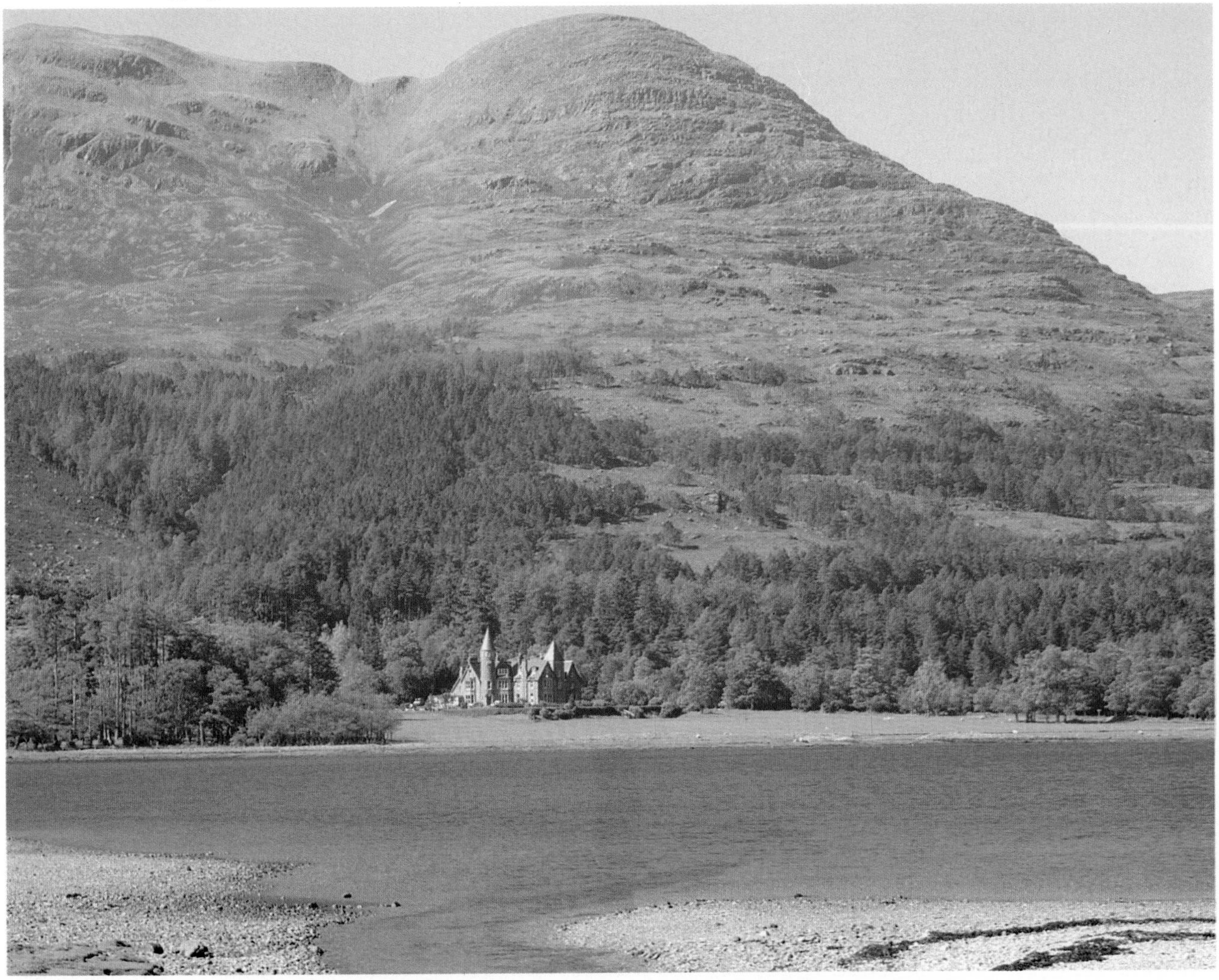

# LOCH TORRIDON HOTEL

TORRIDON, BY ACHNASHEEN, WESTER-ROSS IV22 2EY
TEL: 01445 791242 FAX: 01445 791296

The Loch Torridon Hotel is gloriously situated at the foot of wooded mountains on the shores of the loch which gives it its name. The hotel was built as a shooting lodge for the first Earl of Lovelace in 1887 in a 58 acre estate containing formal gardens, mature trees and resident Highland cattle. David and Geraldine Gregory, formerly of the Kinlochbervie Hotel, acquired the hotel in March 1992. They brought with them an excellent reputation for their brand of Highland hospitality and good cooking. A phased upgrading of the property has been completed to enhance the impact of the interiors and provide every comfort. Chef Ged Boylan, from Cameron House, Loch Lomond, has brought with him a reputation for innovation and uses only the finest of local ingredients from the lochs and hills. The hotel was chosen as the Best New Three Star Hotel in Scotland by the AA Inspector for 1993 and awarded two Rosettes for its food. Dinner is served between 7.15pm and 8.30pm. A starter of scallop and langoustine terrine or quail filled with a vegetable and raisin farce could be followed by a pan fried halibut with mushroom crust or loin of Scottish lamb in a spinach mousse with a thyme scented jus. **Directions:** Ten miles from Kinlochewe on the A896. Do not turn off to Torridon village. Price guide: Single £50–£90; double/twin £110–£230; suites £220–£250.

For hotel location, see maps on pages 490-496

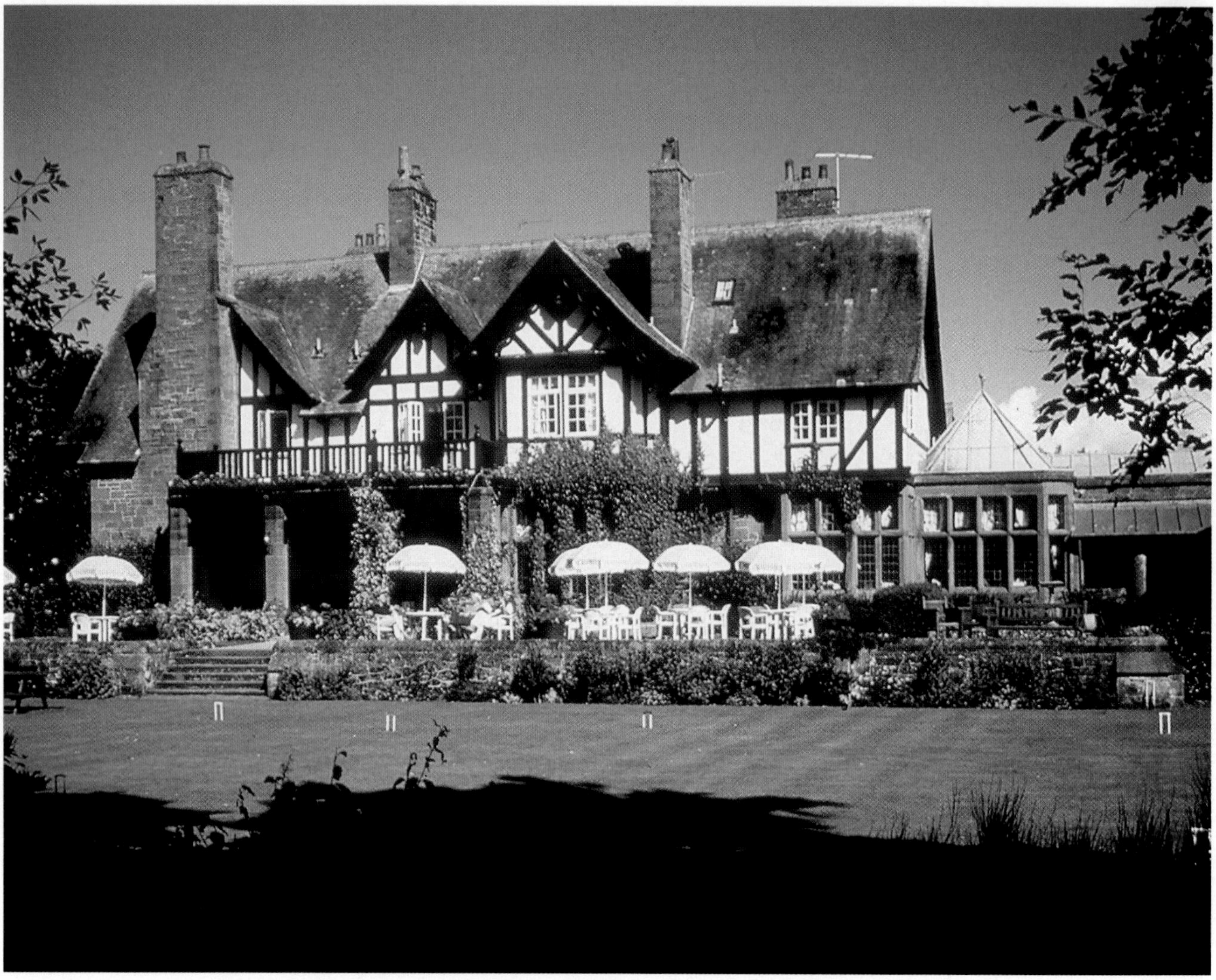

# Piersland House Hotel

**CRAIGEND ROAD, TROON, AYRSHIRE KA10 6HD**
**TEL: 01292 314747 FAX: 01292 315613**

This historic listed house, built for the grandson of Johnnie Walker, founder of the Scottish whisky brand, is as attractive inside as out. All the public rooms are spacious and inviting, with original features such as oak panelling and a frieze of Jacobean embroidery. Retaining their original charm, the bedrooms are formally decorated in a period style with soft colourings. Afternoon cream teas are served on the verandah overlooking the beautiful gardens. The landscaped grounds include an oriental garden. Guests can enjoy classically prepared gourmet dishes and continental-style cooking in the warm, intimate atmosphere of our two restaurants. The wine list is compiled from labels supplied by one of Scotland's oldest-established wine firms. For golfers, venue of the British Open 1997, Royal Troon, is situated across the road. Turnberry, Old Prestwick and numerous championship courses are nearby. Ayr, the county town and birthplace of Robert Burns, our national poet, and Culzean Castle, Seat of the Kennedy Clan are also close at hand. Glasgow, Edinburgh and the beautiful island of Arran are easily accessible, as are Loch Lomond and the Trossachs. **Directions:** The hotel is just off the A77 on the B749, beside Royal Troon Golf Club. Price guide: Single £62.50–£82.50; double/twin £110–£140.

For hotel location, see maps on pages 490-496

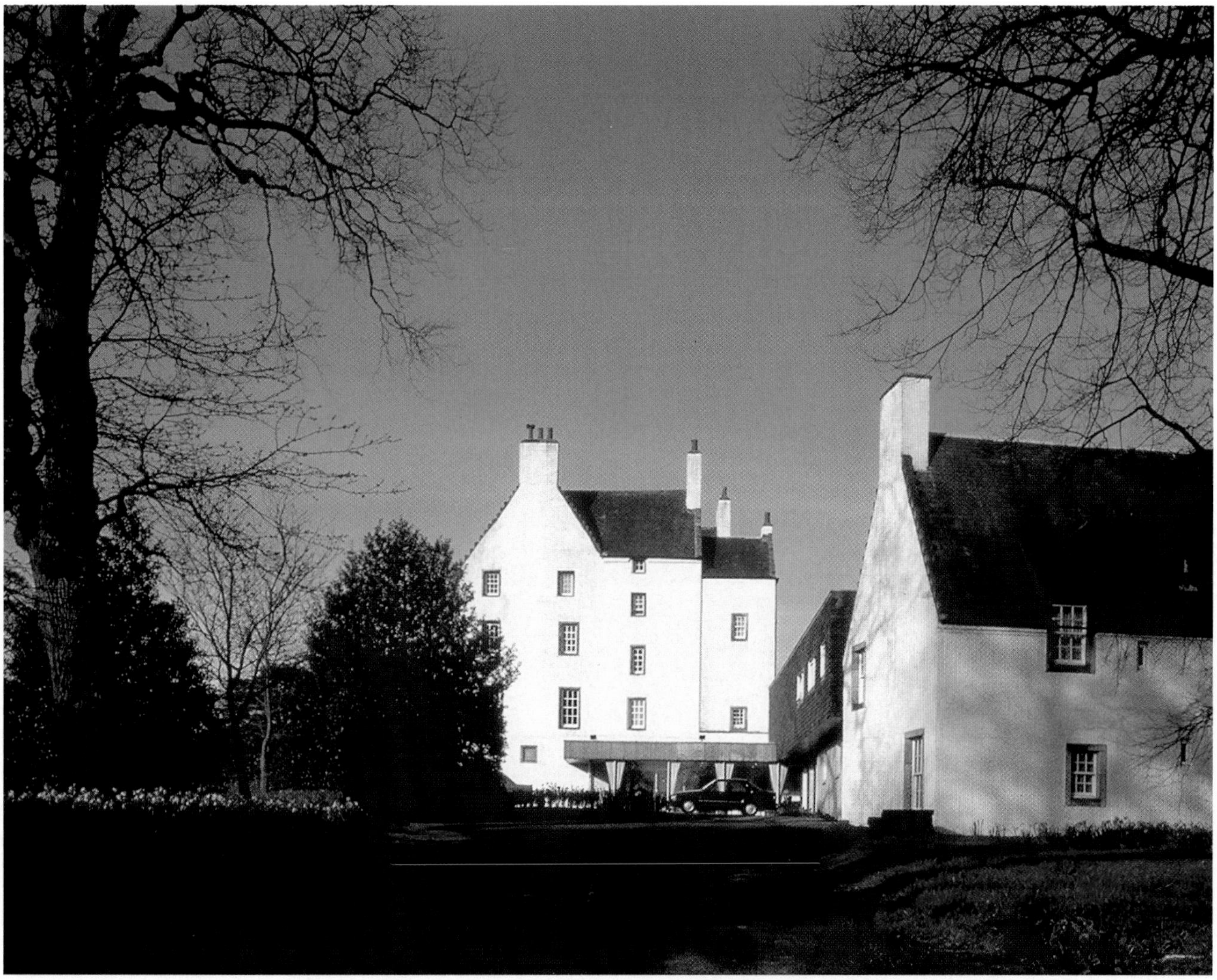

# HOUSTOUN HOUSE

**UPHALL, WEST LOTHIAN, SCOTLAND EH52 6JS**
**TEL: 01506 853831 FAX: 01506 854220**

Houstoun House is a beautiful and unspoilt example of a 17th century Scottish laird's house. The fine gardens were laid out in the 1700s and include a great cedar tree which was grown from seed brought from the Lebanon by one of the early lairds. The 20 acres of gardens and woodland are adjacent to Uphall Golf Course where guests can play by arrangement. The house is divided into three distinct buildings – the Tower, containing the dining rooms and vaulted bars; the Woman House, a 16th century manor house joined to the Tower by a stone-flagged courtyard; and The Steading, formerly the estate factor's house. Bedrooms all offer a range of modern facilities and overlook the historic gardens. The standard bedrooms are mostly modern in style, while the traditional bedrooms are generally larger and feature antique furnishings. Executive bedrooms are all non-smoking and elegantly decorated and furnished. Houstoun House enjoys an excellent reputation for its cuisine, with the best of Scottish and international dishes served in wood-panelled dining rooms situated in the old Drawing Room, the Library and the Great Hall. **Directions:** From M8 junction 3 (Livingston), turn right at first roundabout and follow signs for Broxburn – A89 left at traffic lights on A899 to Uphall. Price guide: Single £105 double/twin £140

For hotel location, see maps on pages 490-496

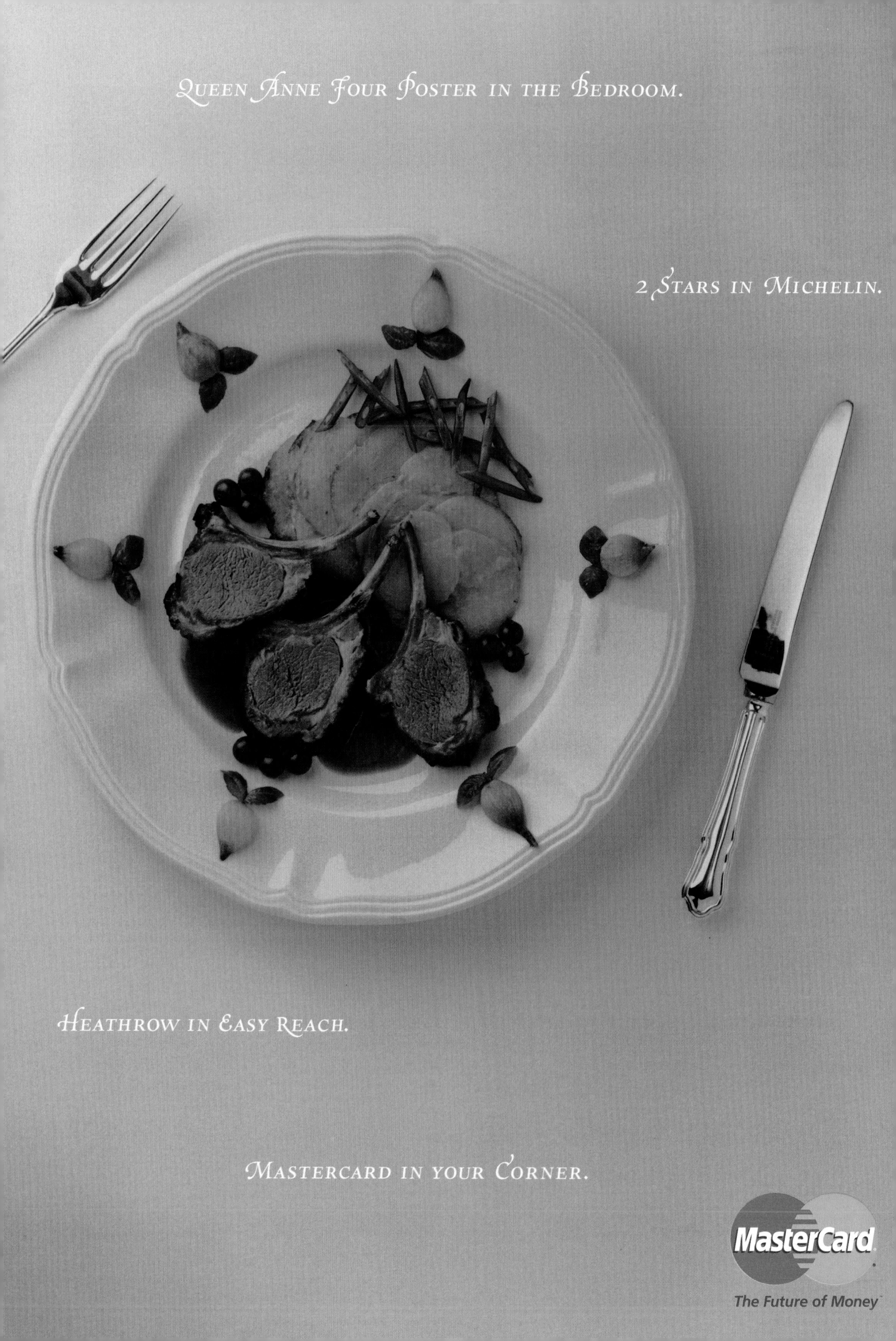
Queen Anne Four Poster in the Bedroom.
2 Stars in Michelin.
Heathrow in Easy Reach.
Mastercard in your Corner.
MasterCard
The Future of Money

# Johansens Recommended Hotels in Ireland

*Celtic treasures and legends, medieval architecture, racecourses and golf courses, great art collections and a richness of literature are all to be found amongst the green landscapes of Ireland.*

While Ireland's number of annual visitors has been breaking its own newly-created record each year in the present decade making it the fastest growing tourism destination in Europe, it is the performance of Irish golf which stands out as the greatest success story of all. Golf has become the Republic's flagship product among a multiplicity of attractions and leisure pursuits which now account for a yearly visitor number which considerably exceeds that of the resident population.

The great historic golf courses of Ireland are well known internationally, Portmarnock, Royal Dublin, Ballybunion and Waterville being formidable among them as links challenges of world standard, while the parkland contrast is confidently provided on the verdant fairways of such as Woodbrook, Mullingar or Headford. In Ireland it is virtually impossible to be more than 20 miles away from a golf course, and every town or village of more than a thousand souls has a course of its very own. The 1990's have seen the development of even more new courses to cater for increasing international demand, and several world status professionals have brought their individual design talents to their construction.

It is the hidden gems, however, when stumbled upon which regularly compel their discoverers to speak of them in whispers, and the scenic, rugged countryside along the Atlantic seaboard provides Ireland's greatest source of such lesser-known treasures. Six of these courses have now come together to form a unique western golfing challenge group known as West Coast Links. Set in the purity of an unspoiled environment and amid the distinct Celtic culture and natural warmth of the rural community, their aim is to ensure that the visitor's golfing holiday will be both invigorating and memorable.

Much of Ireland's history is preserved in the architecture and ancient monuments of many of the towns and villages around the country and an association, Heritage Towns of Ireland, can assist the visitor in achieving the most comprehensive experience during a visit.

In addition to the many beautiful forest parks, Ireland has three internationally recognised national parks. Killarney National Park is perhaps the best known with Muckross House and Gardens as the centrepiece of this magnificent lakeside park. Connemara National Park in Letterfrack is set amid the wild rugged beauty so typical of the West of Ireland, and Glenveagh National Park in County Donegal has a beautiful castle and gardens.

The ancient history of Northern Ireland is comparable to that of the Greeks and Egyptians with the old tales of derring do, bravery and romance of the ancient Celts brought back to life at museums and centres including the Navan Centre of Armagh and the Tower Museum of Derry City.

Visitors to Ireland who make the journey north are inevitably surprised by "how different it is", or "how tidy it is", or "how rural it is". And this is what they enjoy.

Northern Ireland has made a name for itself as a place where welcomes are genuine and the land unspoilt. The last great outdoors playground for western Europe, this part of the island of Ireland remains top favourite among those in the know.

Wild salmon and trout anglers are tempted here by some of the world's best rivers. The Foyle system stands out as one of the best but the Bann, Bush, Erne and Melvin are other rivers and lakes teeming with indigenous sonnghan and dollaghan trout.

Similarly, golfers from the four corners return year after year to the freedom of the great links courses of the north coast. Both Royal Portrush and Royal County Down feature time after time in the world's top ten list of courses which is an indication of the quality available here.

And walkers, ramblers, watersports enthusiasts and other outdoor lovers know Northern Ireland's secret charms and are attracted back again and again.

But it's not all blustery outdoors. With the warmth of the fire in an Ulster bar surrounded by music and friends you will wish never to have to leave. The top class restaurants will seduce you as they have top food connoisseurs from around the world.

The fun of a good night's entertainment with live music, traditional Irish, jazz, rock or classical will help make any stay very memorable and can be enjoyed in most parts of the north.

Ultimately, you'll find an ancient culture here which was already 2,000 years old when St Patrick arrived from Britain 1,500 years ago.

Northern Ireland is special. Once visitors make their way here, they are sure to find what they are looking for – even if they didn't know what they were looking for in the first place!

**Heritage Towns of Ireland**
**City Hall**
**Main Street**
**Cashel**
**Co Tipperary**
**Tel: 00 353 62 62068**

**West Coast Links**
**Teach Sonas**
**Rinville West**
**Oranmore**
**Co Galway**
**Ireland**
**Tel: 00 353 91 794500**

For more information about Ireland and Northern Ireland please contact:

**The Irish Tourist Board**
**Bord Failte**
**Baggot Street Bridge**
**Dublin 2**
**Tel: 00 353 1 676 5871**

**Northern Ireland Tourist Board**
**St Anne's Court**
**59 North Street**
**Belfast BT1 1NB**
**Tel: 01232 246609**

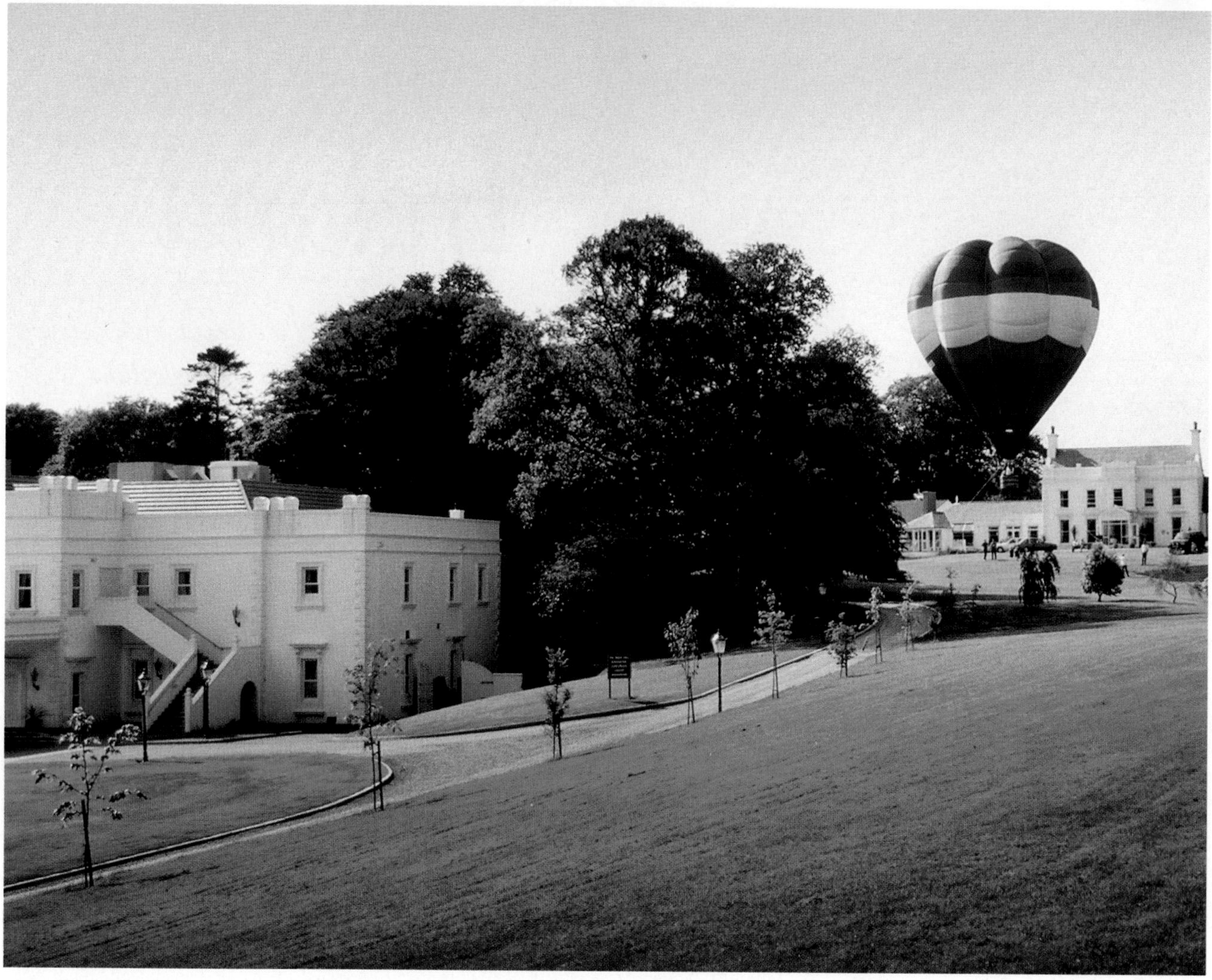

# GALGORM MANOR

**BALLYMENA, CO ANTRIM BT42 1EA**
**TEL: 01266 881001 FAX: 01266 880080**

This converted gentleman's residence is set amidst some of Northern Ireland's most beautiful lush scenery, with the River Maine running less than 100 yards from the main entrance. Most of the comfortable en suite bedrooms offer spectacular views of the surrounding countryside. The Dining Room offers a choice of table d'hôte or à la carte menus with local produce used wherever possible. For lighter eating there is a full bar menu in the Gillies Bar. There are six self-catering cottages available in the grounds which are perfect for weekend breaks or the longer stay. The Manor offers a varied choice of meeting rooms, all with the most modern facilities. Its estate includes 12 stables, a show jumping course and an eventing cross-country practice area, so there is plenty of scope for the equestrian enthusiast. Clay pigeon shooting is also available and there are opportunites to play golf on some of the best links courses in Ireland. Galgorm Manor is perfectly located for touring Northern Ireland. The lovely Antrim Coast, including the Giant's Causeway, is only a short drive away. **Directions:** Follow the A42 towards Ballymena. Shortly after passing Galgorm Castle on the right, turn left at Galgorm towards Cullybackey. Galgorm Manor is halfway between Galgorm and Cullybackey. Price guide: Single £99; double/twin £120; suites £135.

For hotel location, see maps on pages 490-496

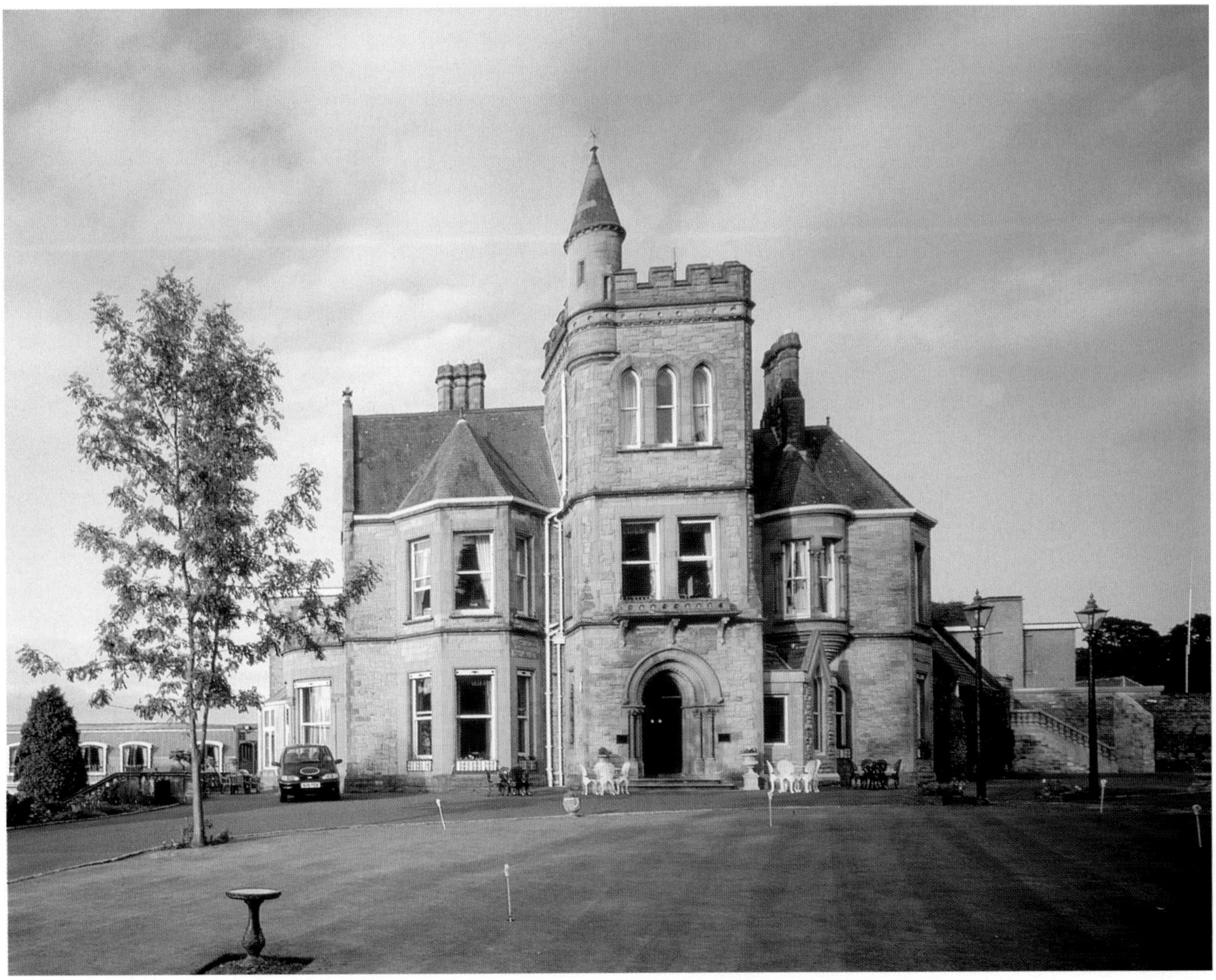

# CULLODEN HOTEL

BANGOR ROAD, HOLYWOOD, CO DOWN, N. IRELAND BT18 OEX
TEL: 01232 425223 FAX: 01232 426777 E-MAIL: res.cull@hastingshotels.com

Standing in 12 acres of beautifully secluded gardens on the wooded slopes of Holywood overlooking Belfast Lough and the County Antrim coastline is the magnificent and palatial Culloden Hotel. Once an official palace for the Bishops of Down it is a magnificent example of 19th-century Baronial Architecture and is Northern Ireland's only five star hotel. Antique furniture, valuable paintings, elegant plasterwork ceilings and Louis XV chandeliers give it a unique elegance. All modern amenities have been blended to this background to make the Culloden an excellent hotel. The bedrooms have magnificent views over the gardens and coast, and the sumptuous, 900 square feet "Palace Suite" boasts the finest four-poster bedroom in Ireland. As well as superb cuisine in the award-winning Mitre Restaurant, informal dining is available in the Cultra Inn situated in the grounds. The hotel has a range of leisure facilities and guests have full use of the Elysium private health spa whose state-of-the-art facilities are complemented by a splendid octagonal-shaped ozone pool. There are 10 golf courses nearby, including the Royal Belfast where an exclusive arrangement for tee-off times is available for Culloden guests. Directions: The Culloden Hotel is six miles east of Belfast city centre on the A2 towards Bangor. Price guide: Single £120; double/twin £150; suite £350.

87 rms MasterCard VISA AMERICAN EXPRESS M 500

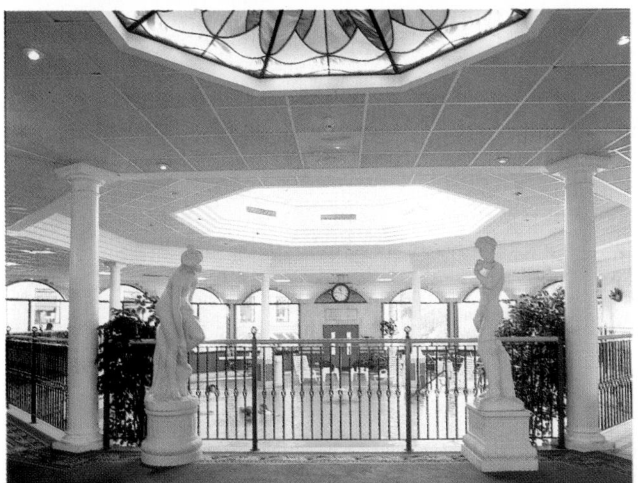

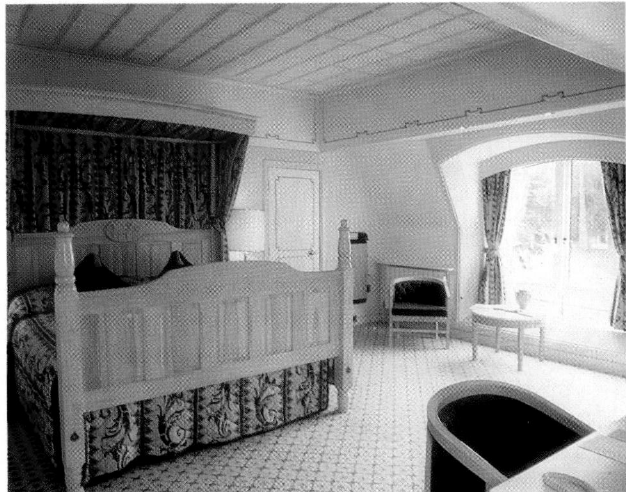

For hotel location, see maps on pages 490-496

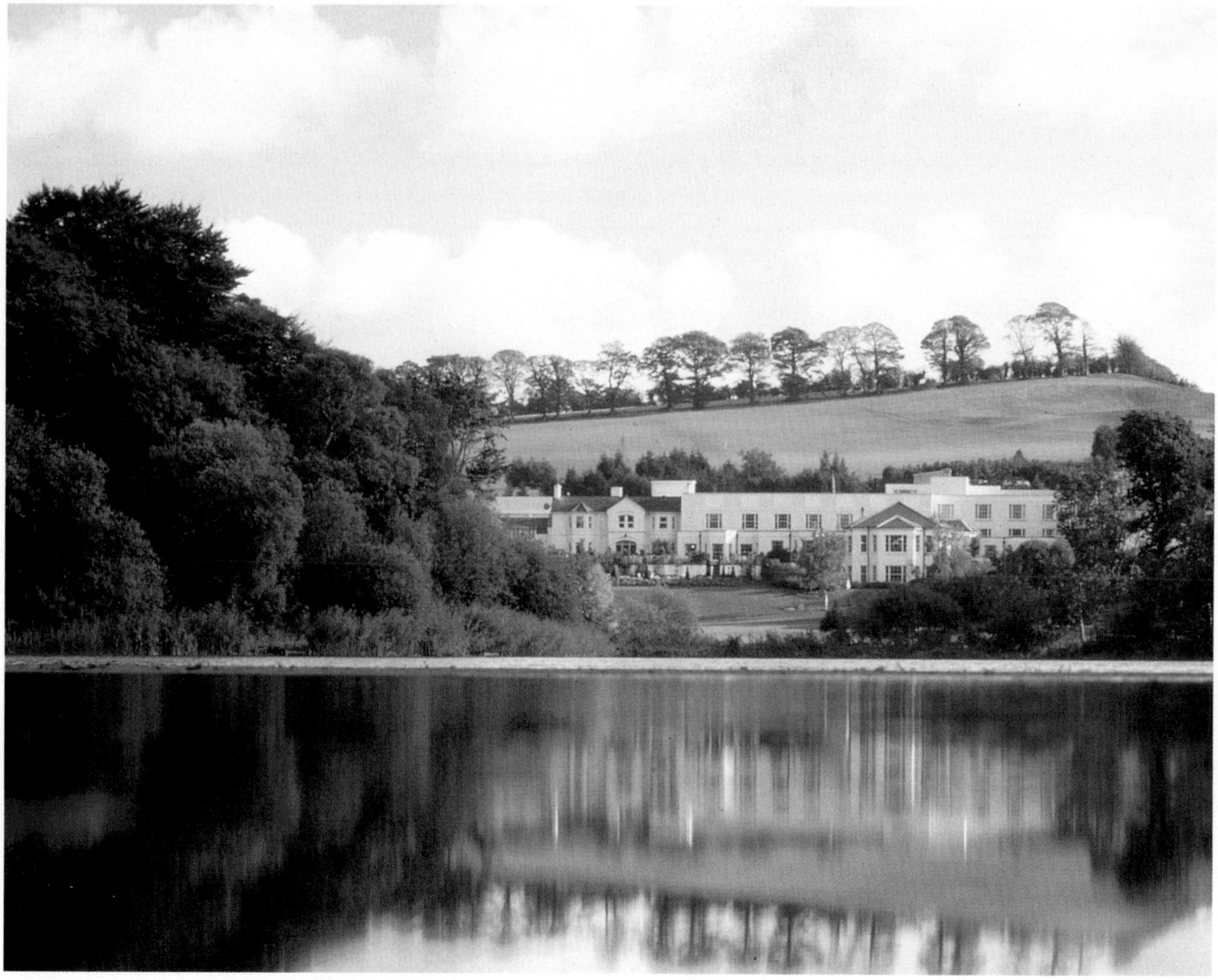

# NUREMORE HOTEL

**CARRICKMACROSS, CO MONAGHAN, IRELAND**

**TEL: 00 353 42 61438 FAX: 00 353 42 61853**

Set in 200 acres of glorious countryside on the fringe of Carrickmacross, the Nuremore Hotel has been extensively renovated. It offers guests all-round enjoyment, a vast array of activities and facilities and all that is best in a first-class country hotel. The bedrooms are well appointed and attractively designed to create a generous sense of personal space. Lunch and dinner menus, served in a spacious and elegant dining room, emphasise classic European cooking, with French and Irish dishes featured alongside. For sport, fitness and relaxation, guests are spoiled for choice by the range of amenities. A major feature is the championship-length, par 73, 18-hole golf course designed by Eddie Hackett to present an exciting challenge to beginners and experts alike. Maurice Cassidy has been appointed as resident professional and is on hand to give tuition. Riding nearby in Carrickmacross. The leisure club has a superb indoor pool, modern gymnasium, squash and tennis courts, sauna, steam room and whirlpool bath. Meetings, conferences and seminars held here are guaranteed a professional support service. Dublin is 90 minutes' drive away, while Drogheda and Dundalk are nearby for shopping. **Directions:** The hotel is on the main N2 road between Dublin and Monaghan. Price guide: Single IR£80–IR£100; double/twin IR£120–IR£140; suite IR150.

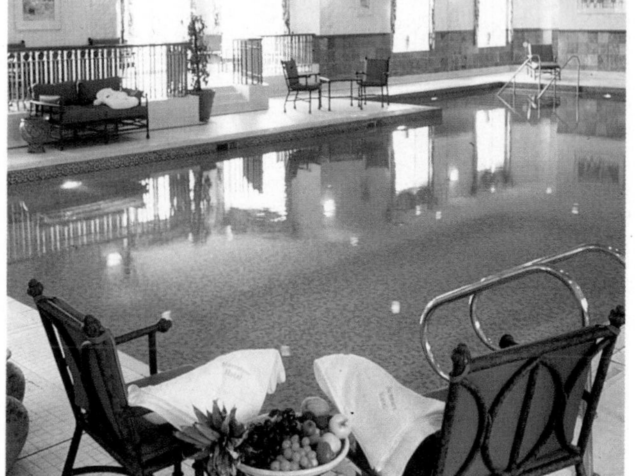

For hotel location, see maps on pages 490-496

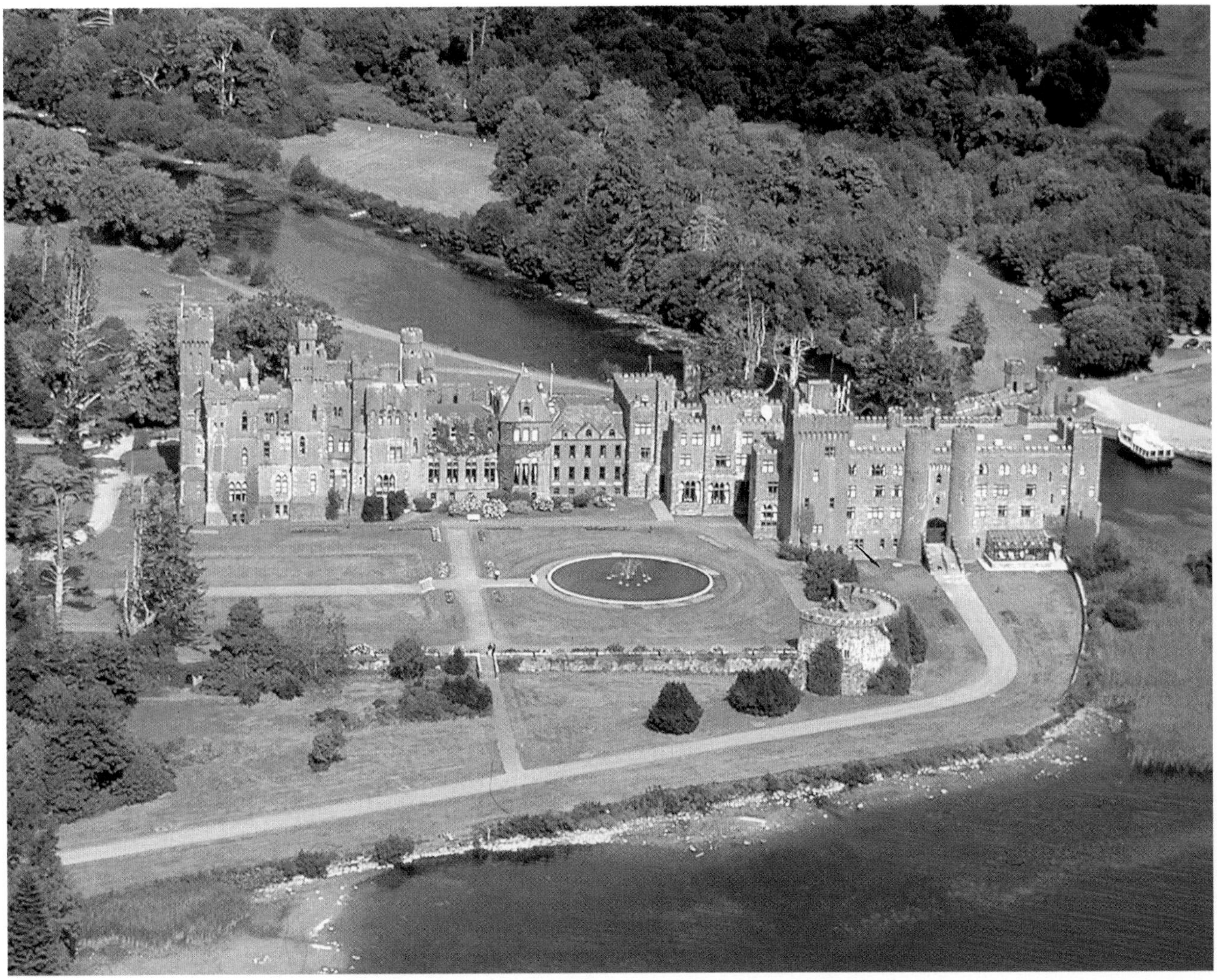

# ASHFORD CASTLE

CONG, CO MAYO
TEL: 00 353 92 46003 FAX: 00 353 92 46260

Ashford Castle is set on the northern shores of Lough Corrib amidst acres of beautiful gardens and forests. Once the country estate of Lord Ardilaun and the Guinness family, it was transformed into a luxury hotel in 1939. The castle's Great Hall is lavishly decorated with rich panelling, fine period pieces, *objets d'art* and masterpiece paintings. Guest rooms are of the highest standards and many feature high ceilings, enormous bathrooms and delightful lake views. The main dining room offers superb continental and traditional menus, while the gourmet restaurant, The Connaught Room, specialises in excellent French cuisine. Before and after dinner in the Dungeon Bar guests are entertained by a harpist or pianist. Ashford Castle offers a full range of country sports, including fishing on Lough Corrib, clay pigeon shooting, riding and an exclusive 9-hole golf course. The hotel has just added a health centre comprising a whirlpool, sauna, steam room, fully equipped gymnasium and conservatory. Ashford is an ideal base for touring the historic West Ireland, places like Kylemore Abbey and Westport House, Sligo and Drumcliffe Churchyard, the burial place of W.B. Yeats. **Directions:** 30 minutes from Galway on the shore of Lough Corrib, on the left when entering the village of Cong. Price guide: Single/twin/double IR£127–IR£270; suite IR£300–IR£475.

For hotel location, see maps on pages 490-496

# RENVYLE HOUSE HOTEL

**CONNEMARA, CO GALWAY**
**TEL: 00 353 95 43511 FAX: 00 353 95 43515 E-MAIL: renvyle@iol.ie**

Renvyle House Hotel has occupied its rugged, romantic position on Ireland's west coast for over four centuries. Set between mountains and sea on the unspoilt coast of Connemara, this hardy, beautiful building with its superlative views over the surrounding countryside is just an hour's drive from Galway or Sligo. Originally constructed in 1541, Renvyle has been an established hotel for over 100 years, witnessing in that time a procession of luminaries through its doors – attracted them Augustus John, Lady Gregory, Yeats and Churchill, drawn no doubt by an atmosphere as warm and convivial then as it is today. Renvyle now welcomes visitors with turf fires glowing in public areas, wood-beamed interiors and comfortable, relaxed furnishings in the easy rooms. The bedrooms too are comfortably appointed and all have been refurbished in the past three years. In the dining room, meals from a constantly-changing menu are served with emphasis on local fish and Renvyle lamb. In the grounds activities include tennis, croquet, riding, bowls and golf. Beyond the hotel, there are walks in the heather-clad hills, or swimming and sunbathing on empty beaches. **Directions:** On the N59 from Galway turn right at Recess, take the Letterfrack turning to Tully Cross and Renvyle is signposted. Price guide: Single IR£40–IR£100; double/twin IR£80–IR£160.

For hotel location, see maps on pages 490-496

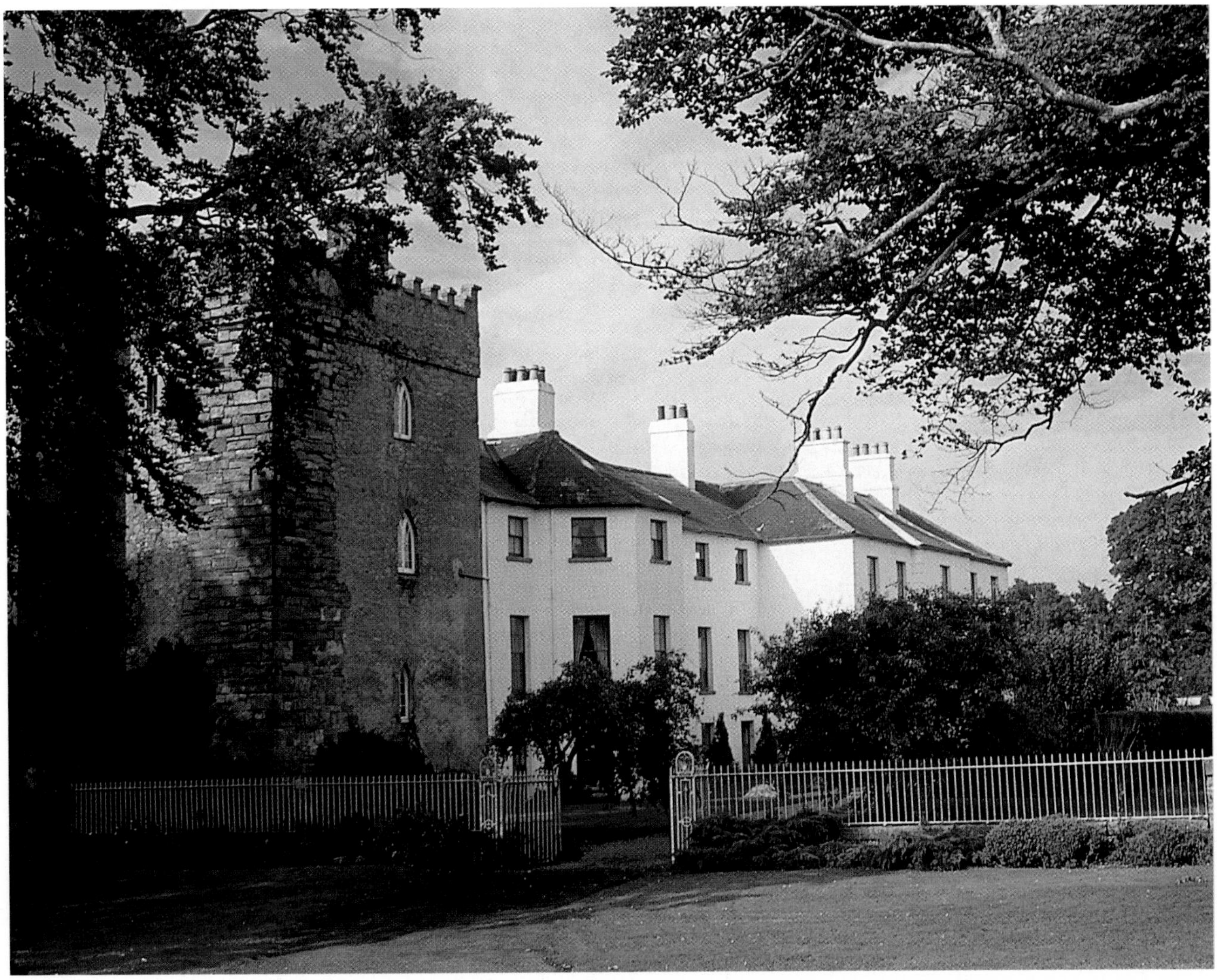

# BARBERSTOWN CASTLE

**STRAFFAN, CO KILDARE**

**TEL: 00 353 1 6288157 FAX: 00 353 1 6277027**

Barberstown Castle was one of the first great Irish country houses to open up its splendour to the outside world. The Castle was built in the early 13th century by Nicholas Barby, a heritage that embraces over 750 years of Irish history. The restaurant at Barberstown is renowned for its creative food and has received the RAC Restaurant Award for 1996/97 and also two Rosettes from the AA for 1996/97. Each of the en suite bedrooms has been decorated in an individual style and dedicated to the ordinary and extraordinary people who have lived within its walls. The Castle received Hospitality and Comfort Awards from the RAC for 1995. Golf can be arranged at The Kildare Country Club and at several other courses nearby. Expert equestrian tuition as well as hunting, racing, tennis, gym, squash and clay pigeon shooting are all available in the area. Coarse, trout and salmon fishing on the River Liffey, ghillies available. For the less active, relax in an atmosphere of pure calm and tranquillity, deep in the heart of County Kildare. **Directions:** Barberstown Castle is 30 minutes drive from Dublin City centre and 30 minutes drive from the airport. It is an ideal first or last stop on your country house tour of Ireland. South on the N7 take the turn for Straffan at Kill. Travelling west on N4 take the turn for Straffan at Maynooth. Price guide: Single IR£65–IR£85; double/twin IR£121–IR£130; suite IR£175.

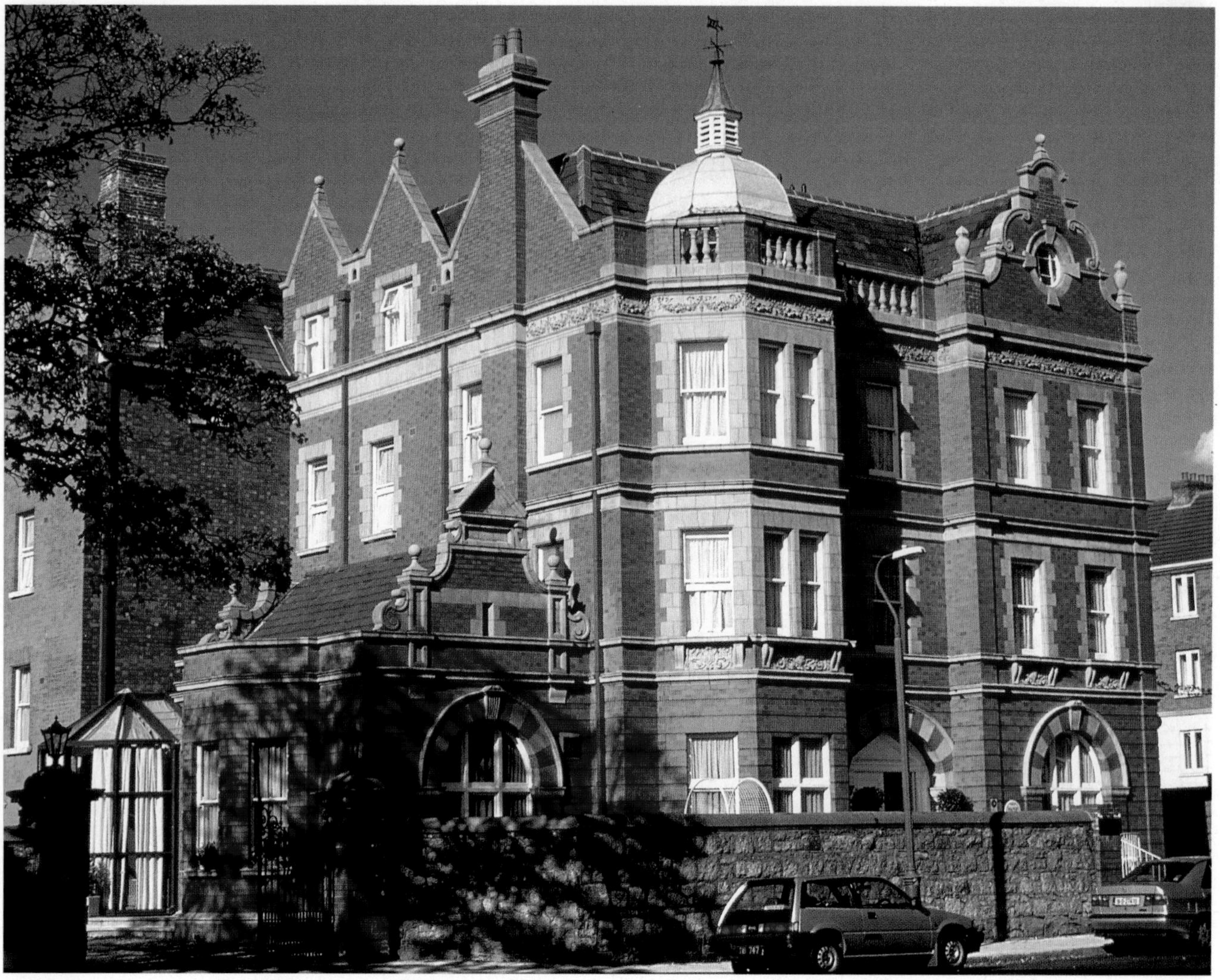

# THE HIBERNIAN HOTEL

**EASTMORELAND PLACE, BALLSBRIDGE, DUBLIN 4**

**TEL: 00 353 1 668 7666 FAX: 00 353 1 660 2655 E-MAIL: info@hibernianhotel.ie**

In bustling downtown Dublin, the Hibernian Hotel is a magnificent architectural feat constructed just before the turn of the century in the commercial heart of the city. Refurbished and reopened in 1993 as a grand townhouse hotel, The Hibernian now prides itself on the elegance, style and warmth of service it can offer visitors to this vibrant metropolis: the hotel has a unique blend of modern ease and bygone atmosphere. David Butt, the general manager, is ably assisted by a professional team who ensure that the needs of both business and holiday guests are met quickly and efficiently. Luxury prevails at The Hibernian in soft furnishings, rich fabrics and deep upholstery; in each of the 40 individually designed bedrooms and suites. En suite bathrooms with a full range of toiletries are standard, as are fax/modem points, drinks facilities, individually controlled thermostats and hairstyling appliances. In the Patrick Kavanagh Room the young virtuoso chef, David Foley, creates menus full of gastronomic dishes, from locally caught, artfully interpreted seafood to modern cuisine classics and fine wines to accompany them. The hotel makes an ideal base from which to explore the city. **Directions:** Turn right from Mespil Road into Baggot Street Upper, then left into Eastmoreland Place; The Hibernian is on the left. Price guide: Single IR£110; double/twin IR£145; suite IR£180.

For hotel location, see maps on pages 490-496

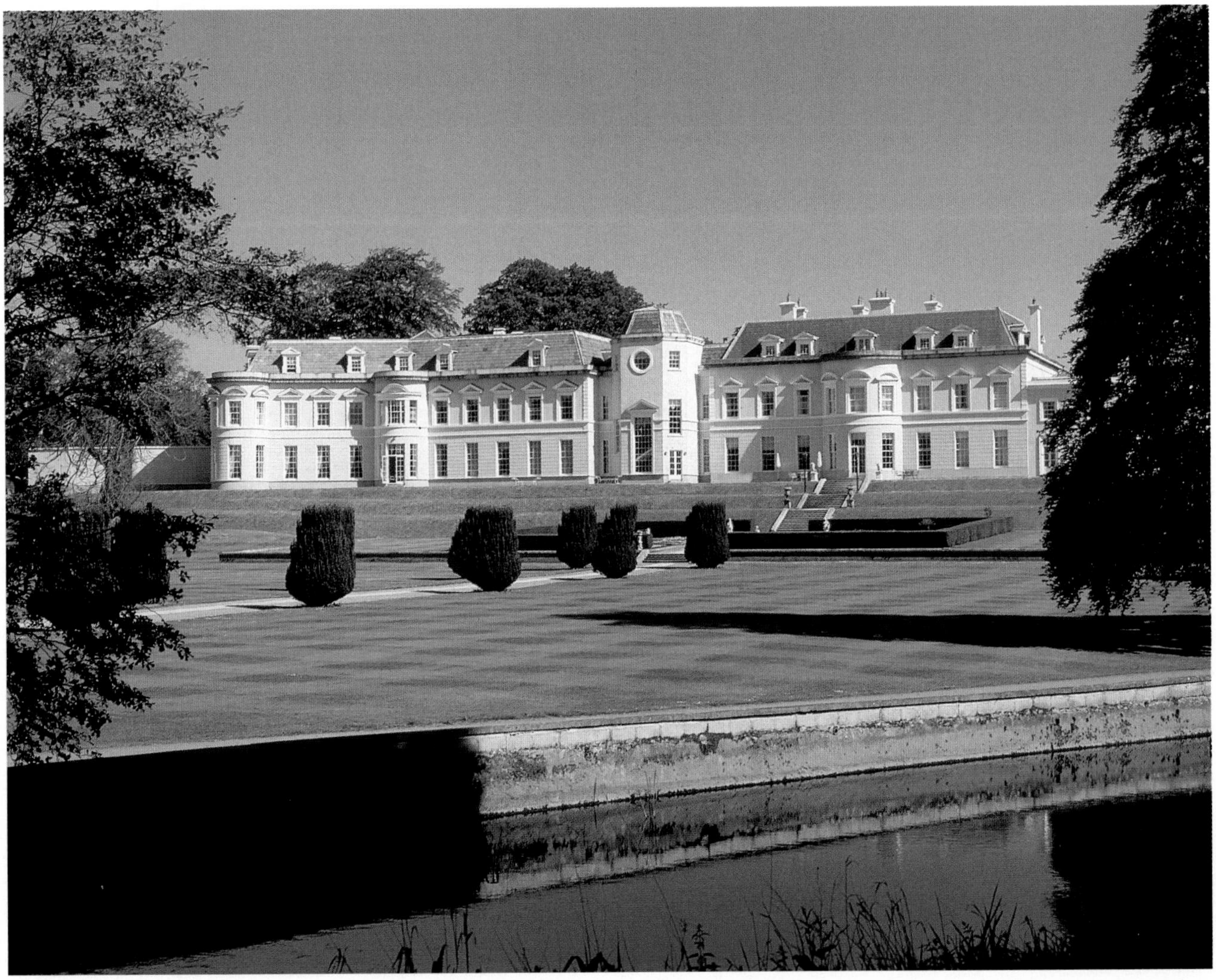

# THE KILDARE HOTEL & COUNTRY CLUB

## AT STRAFFAN, CO KILDARE

TEL: 00 353 1 601 7200 FAX: 00 353 1 601 7299

Straffan House is one of Ireland's most elegant 19th century manor houses, set in 330 acres of beautiful countryside and overlooking the River Liffey. Just 17 miles from Dublin this is an international world class resort with its graceful reception rooms, totally luxurious bedrooms and palatial en suite bathrooms, also a superb leisure club with a sybaritic indoor pool. The public areas of the hotel are a treasure trove of contemporary paintings and works of art. There are excellent conference areas for business meetings, while corporate entertaining is dominated by facilities which include the Arnold Palmer course which is the venue for The Smurfit European since 1995, indoor tennis and squash courts, a gymnasium, clay target shooting, fishing and riding, croquet. Formal entertaining, meeting in the bar followed by a magnificent meal in the prestigious Byerley Turk Restaurant, with table d'hôte and à la carte menus complemented by an extensive wine list, is effortless, The Legend Bar and Restaurant in the Country Club offer less formality. The Arnold Palmer Room is available for gala functions and conferences at the Clubhouse. **Directions:** Leave Dublin on N7 driving south for 17 miles. Straffan is signposted on the left. Price guide: Double/twin IR£280–IR£350; suite IR£450–£1,000. Conference rates on request.

For hotel location, see maps on pages 490-496

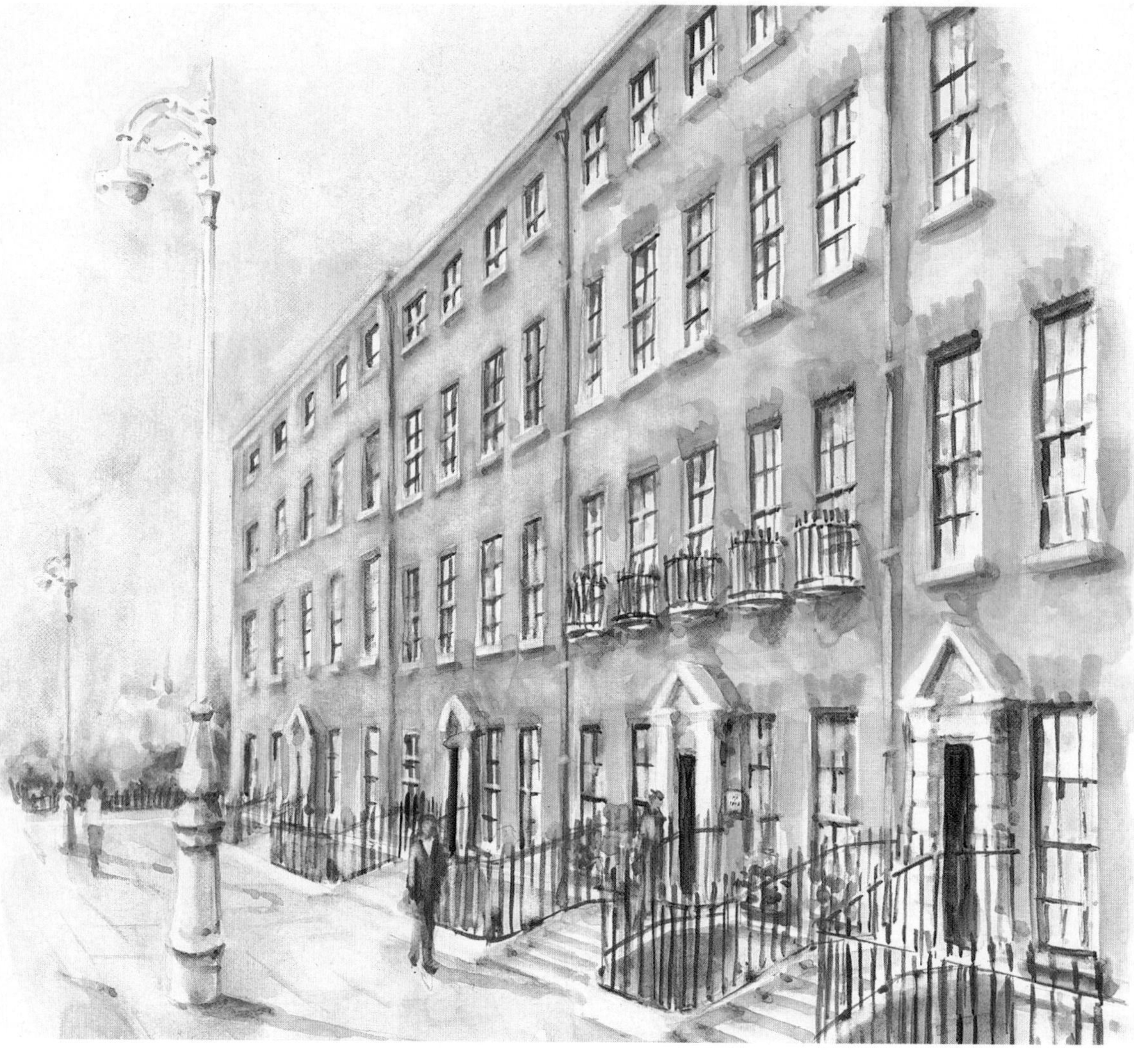

# THE MERRION HOTEL

**UPPER MERRION STREET, DUBLIN 2, IRELAND**
**TEL: 00 353 1 603 0600 FAX: 00 353 1 603 0700**

Dublin has an élite new hotel. The Merrion is the city's latest landmark. It has been imaginatively and brilliantly conceived, four superb Grade I Georgian terrace houses meticulously restored. There is also an elegant new Garden Wing. The interior decorations are impressive, authentically reflecting the Georgian era by the choice of wall colours, specially commissioned fabrics and well researched antiques. By contrast, a private collection of 20th century art is displayed throughout the hotel, and the neo-classic stairwell has a series of contemporary murals. Every guest room is luxurious, some situated in the Garden Wing, with views over the two gardens – delightful with box hedges, statuary and fountains, approached from the drawing rooms in summer. The Merrion offers a choice of two handsome bars, the larger a fascinating 18th cellar, the other more intimate, and two restaurants, the legendary Restaurant Patrick Guilbaud in a dramatic new setting, and the Mornington Restaurant, offering traditional dishes with an Irish influence. The Merrion has a state-of-the-art meeting and private dining facility, perfect for hosting banquets. Guests relax in The Tethra Spa, which has an 18m pool, gymnasium and salons for pampering. **Directions:** City Centre. The hotel has valet parking. Price guide: Single IR£190–IR£230; double/twin IR£210–IR£255; suite IR£460–IR£650

For hotel location, see maps on pages 490-496

# PORTMARNOCK HOTEL AND GOLF LINKS

**STRAND RD, PORTMARNOCK, CO. DUBLIN, IRELAND**
**TEL: 00 353 1 846 0611 FAX: 00 353 1 846 2442**

This magnificent hotel is a golfer's paradise for it is on the new golf links designed by Bernhard Langer in 1995. It also has two famous championship courses in the vicinity, Portmarnock Golf Club and the Royal Dublin Golf Club. The mansion was the home of the Jameson whiskey family, and has been transformed into a magnificent hotel. The Jamesons hosted many prestigious visitors, and in its new guise the guest book is once again filling with distinguished names. Skilled restoration has rediscovered the beauty of the reception rooms. Extensions to the hotel have been carefully designed to blend with the old house, and today big picture windows look out onto the course. The charming bedrooms have modern comforts and efficient bathrooms. Executive Suites have balconies overlooking Dublin Bay, and the Jameson Suites have four-posters. Guests mingle in the traditional drawingroom, on the terrace or in the inviting bar before feasting in the elegant restaurant which has an excellent wine list. The smart Golf Clubhouse is adjacent to the hotel, and the atmosphere is more relaxed. It has a pleasant bar where players review the day's round. The informal restaurant is very popular. When not golfing, visitors fish or explore the delights of Dublin. **Directions:** Follow signs to Portmarnock from Dublin airport or city centre. Price guide: Single IR£125; double/twin IR£195; suite IR£300

For hotel location, see maps on pages 490-496

# MARLFIELD HOUSE

GOREY, CO WEXFORD
TEL: 00 353 55 21124 FAX: 00 353 55 21572

Staying at Johansens Awards winning Marlfield House is a memorable experience. Set in 34 acres of woodland and gardens, this former residence of the Earl of Courtown preserves the Regency lifestyle in all its graciousness. Built in 1820 it is recognised as one of the finest country houses in Ireland, and is supervised by its welcoming hosts and proprietors, Raymond and Mary Bowe and their daughter Margaret. The State Rooms have been built in a very grand style and have period fireplaces where open fires burn even in the cooler weather. All of the furniture is antique and the roomy beds are draped with sumptuous fabrics. The bathrooms are made of highly polished marble and have large freestanding bathtubs. There is an imposing entrance hall, luxurious drawing room and an impressive curved Richard Turner conservatory. The kitchen's gastronomic delights have earned it numerous awards. Located two miles from fine beaches and Courtown golf club, the house is central to many touring high points: Glendalough, Waterford Crystal and Powerscourt Gardens and the medieval city of Kilkenny. Closed mid-December to mid-January. **Directions:** On the Gorey–Courtown road, just over a mile east of Gorey. Price guide: Single from IR£85; double/twin IR£165–IR£176; suites from IR£210–IR£440.

For hotel location, see maps on pages 490-496

# SHEEN FALLS LODGE

**KENMARE, CO. KERRY, IRELAND**

**TEL: 00 353 64 41600 FAX: 00 353 64 41386 E-MAIL: sheenfalls@iol.ie**

You could be forgiven for expecting a magic carpet instead of a plane to land you at Sheen Falls Lodge – one of the Emerald Isle's most romantic and luxurious hotels. Standing amidst a vast estate of green countryside and well kept gardens, with the sparkling Sheen River tumbling down the falls. The Lodge is a magnificent mansion, built in the attractive local stone, with a slate roof, and the interior of this prestigious hotel is evocative of the past, with its country house ambience. The Library, with traditional leather furniture, holds many fine books and the spacious lounges have warm colour schemes, log fires and generous sofas. Flowers, lovely antiques and memorabilia enhance the atmosphere. The guest rooms are exquisite, luxuriously appointed, and decorated in soft restful shades. They have opulent bathrooms. Dining here starts with the privilege of touring the extensive wine cellar with the sommelier to select a great vintage to accompany a magnificent meal – local salmon, lobster or duck perhaps. Riding, tennis, croquet, fishing, shooting and billiards are 'house' sports The Lodge also has a superb fitness centre, with indoor heated swimming pool. Nearby are several excellent golf courses, marvellous walking, bikes to hire and deep sea fishing can be arranged. **Directions:** The hotel is signed from the junction of N70 and N71 at Kenmare. Helipad. Price guide: Deluxe Room IR£165–IR£245; suite IR£281–IR£386

For hotel location, see maps on pages 490-496

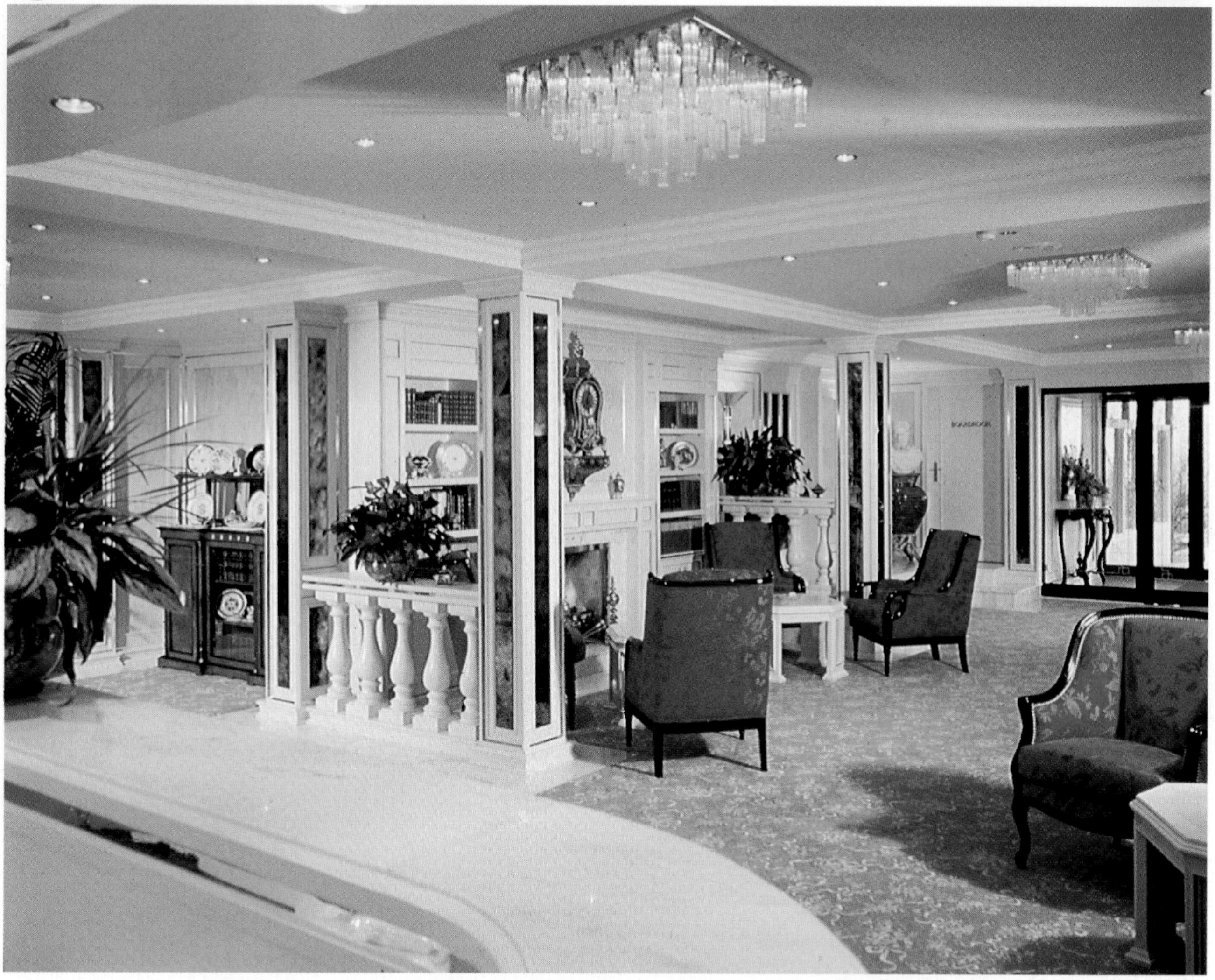

# AGHADOE HEIGHTS HOTEL

**AGHADOE, KILLARNEY, CO KERRY**
**TEL: 00 353 64 31766 FAX: 00 353 64 31345**

In the heart of beautiful County Kerry overlooking stunning panoramic views of the lakes and mountains of Killarney, stands the Aghadoe Heights Hotel, sister hotel to Fredrick's of Maidenhead. It reflects owner Fredrick Losel's influence: rich tapestries, crystal chandeliers, paintings and antiques. Much attention has been given to the bedrooms. The furniture is of mahogany, ash or cherry wood, with soft drapes and deep carpets. Excellent cuisine and fine wines are served in the rooftop restaurant. Chef Robin Suter uses the freshest local ingredients to create innovative dishes. Three function rooms offer good conference facilities. A leisure club includes an indoor pool, Jacuzzi, sauna, plunge pool, solarium, fitness room and now by appointment a massage and beauty treatment service in the hotel. Aghadoe Heights is a good departure point for tours of Kerry or for playing south-west Ireland's premier golf courses, such as Killarney, Waterville and Ballybunion. The hotel has its own stretch of river for salmon and trout fishing and there is also a tennis court within the eight acre gardens. Pony-trekking, lake and sea fishing are also offered locally. **Directions:** The hotel is ten miles south of Kerry Airport, three miles north of Killarney. It is situated off the N22 Tralee road. Price guide: Single IR£90–IR£130; double/twin IR£125–IR£185; suite IR£185–£235.

For hotel location, see maps on pages 490-496

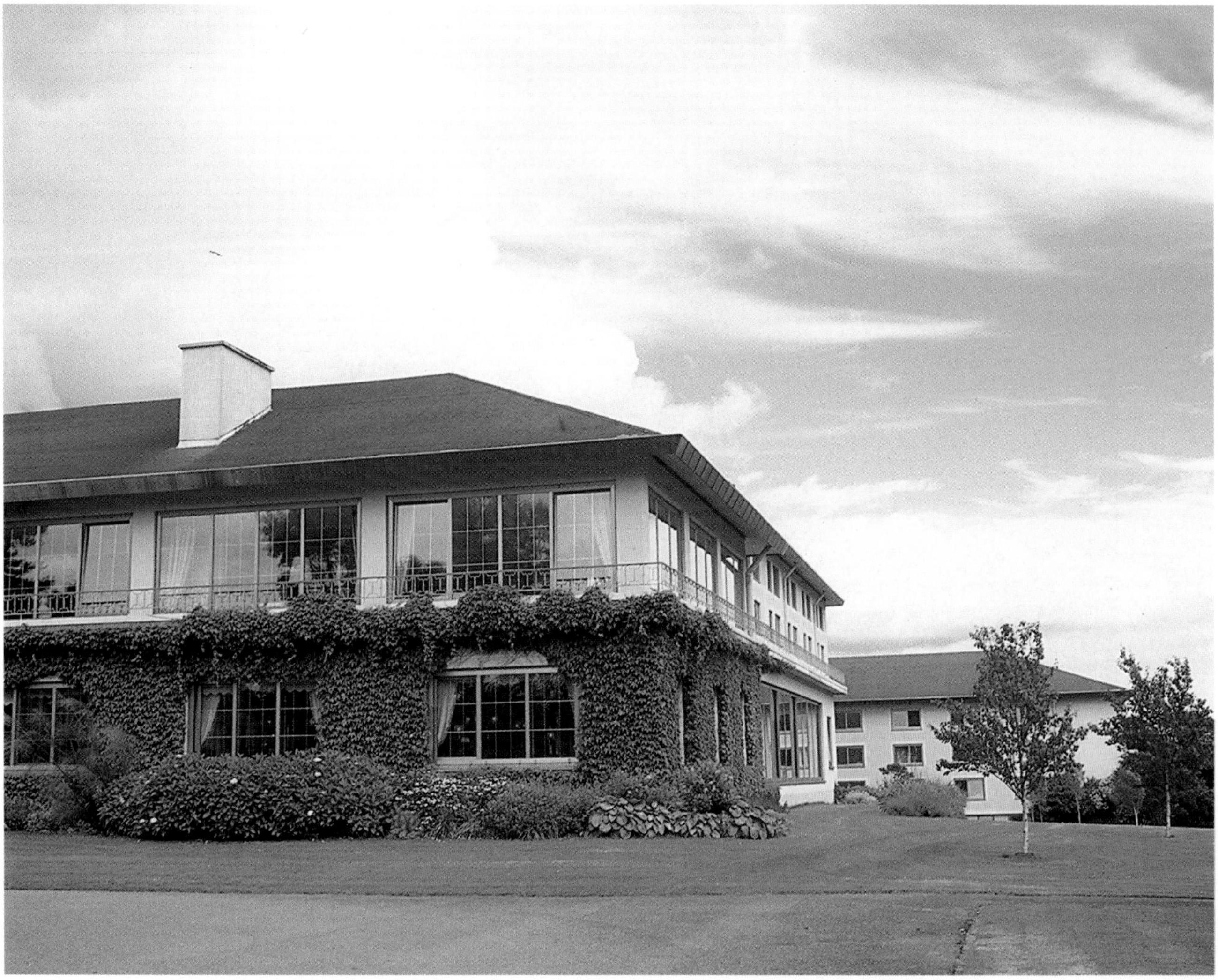

# Dunloe Castle

**KILLARNEY, CO. KERRY, IRELAND**
**TEL: 00 353 64 44111 FAX: 00 353 64 44583**

Dunloe Castle is a 20th century building on the site of an old Norma fortress. It is a magnificent hotel ideal for all guest but of special interest to gardners and golfers! It stands in an extensive estate which is categorised as one of "The Distinguished Gardens of Ireland", with fascinating trees and shrubs from all parts of the globe. It is also in the orbit of many famous golf courses, with one opposite the gate. The reception hall is traditional, designed to be an ideal rendezvous, and the spacious lounge has graceful chairs and big bowls of flowers. It looks across to the spectacular Gap of Dunloe. The attractive bedrooms and mini-suites are provided with the amenities expected by today's traveller. They are decorated in pleasant colours, very comfortable and look out over the gardens. Guests gather in the well stocked bar, perhaps sampling Irish whiskey or Guinness, before dining well on local specialities in the stylish dining room. The Park Restaurant has its own bar, and is ideal for private celebrations or corporate functions, following meetings held in the well equipped conference centre. The Leisure Centre has a splendid pool and sauna. Other facilities include indoor tennis, riding, fishing on the River Laune and a jogging trail. **Directions:** The Castle is 6 miles from Killarney on R562. Price guide: Single IR£88–IR£108; double/twin IR£110–IR£142; suite IR£200

For hotel location, see maps on pages 490-496

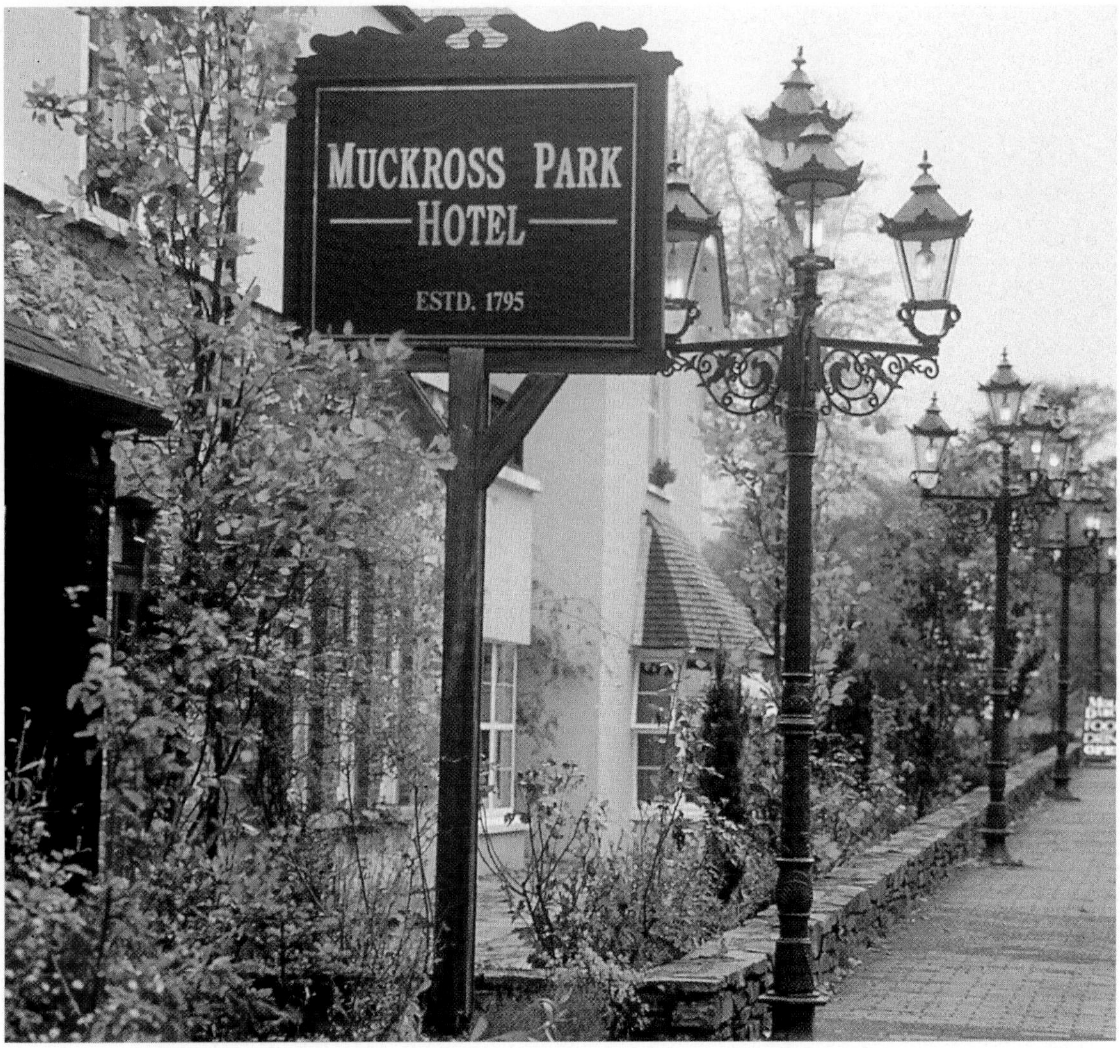

# MUCKROSS PARK HOTEL

MUCKROSS, KILLARNEY, CO KERRY

TEL: 00 353 64 31938 FAX: 00 353 64 31965 – FROM USA TOLL FREE 800 223 6510

Muckross Park stands in the heart of beautiful County Kerry surrounded by the 25,000 acre Killarney National Park with its lakes, mountains and peaceful gardens with giant rhododendrons and tropical plants. It is a redevelopment of an 18th century hotel with stone wall interiors, wooden panelling and exposed beams. Fine antiques and paintings, deep carpets and glittering chandeliers combine the luxurious ambience of a traditional country house with the comfort of a modern four star hotel. All the en suite bedrooms are charmingly old-world. Each has satellite television, direct dial telephone, trouser press and hair dryer. Innovative cuisine and fine wines are served in the bright, sunny Blue Pool Restaurant which looks out over two acres of landscaped gardens that lead down to the hotel's river frontage. Adjacent to the hotel is Molly's, a famous, award-winning traditional Irish pub and restaurant, where bare wooden floors, beamed ceilings, open fires and live entertainment recreate the pleasures of bygone days. Muckross Park is a good base from which to tour Kerry, to explore Killarney National Park, or play south west Ireland's premier golf courses. Boating, fishing, tennis, clay pigeon shooting, riding and hill walking can all be arranged. **Directions:** The hotel is $2^1/_2$ miles south of Killarney on N71 towards Kenmare. Price guide: Single IR£80; double/twin IR£120; suite IR£180–IR£250.

For hotel location, see maps on pages 490-496

# RADISSON ROE PARK HOTEL AND GOLF RESORT

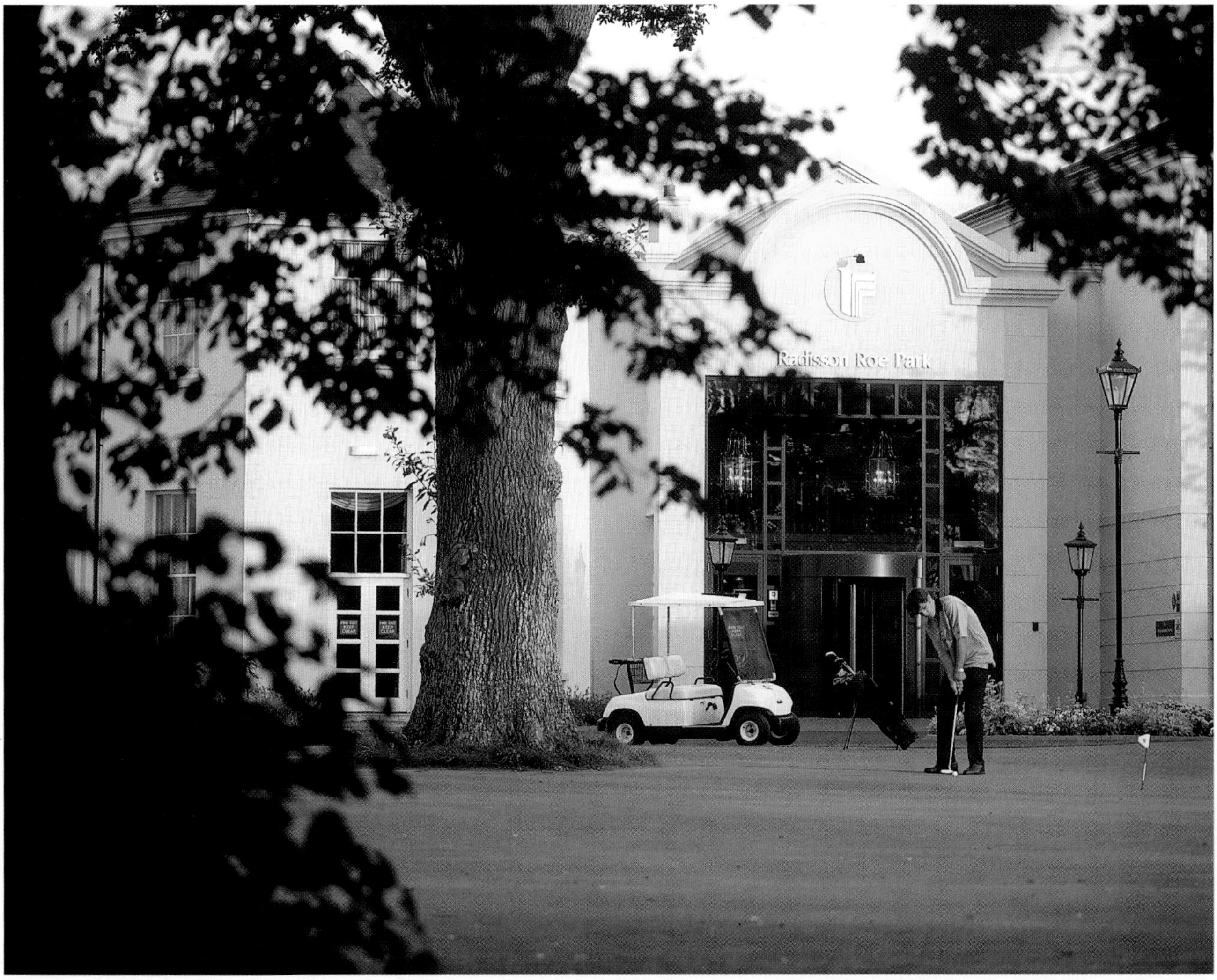

ROE PARK, LIMAVADY, CO LONDONDERRY BT49 9LB

TEL: 015047 22212 FAX: 015047 22313

About 50 miles north-west of Belfast, situated amidst the beautiful Roe Valley countryside with mountains to the south and Lough Foyle and the sea to the north, Radisson Roe Park Hotel brings together the atmosphere and elegance of the historic Irish country house with the best of today's international hotel facilities. Guests enjoy bedrooms whose furnishings include everything from satellite television and a trouser press to an iron, also tea and coffee making facilities. Fresh seafood from Donegal's Atlantic coast, succulent lamb from the hill farms of the Sperrins, the finest game and poultry and tempting desserts are enhanced by outstanding presentation in the Courtyard Restaurant. Golfers can practise on the hotel's driving range, or enjoy 18 holes on the hotels own championship parkland course, whilst tuition is available from the resident PGA professional. A fully equipped leisure club has a heated swimming pool and a wide range of health, beauty and fitness facilities. Radisson Roe Park is the ideal base from which to discover some of the best countryside in Ireland. The legendary Giant's Causeway and Glenveagh National Park are short distances away. Benone Strand's award-winning beach is close to the hotel and there is fishing at nearby Roe Valley Country Park. Directions: On the A2 road, 16 miles from Londonderry and one mile from Limavady. **Price guide:** Single £75–£90; double/twin £90–£130; suite £120–£150.

For hotel location, see maps on pages 490-496

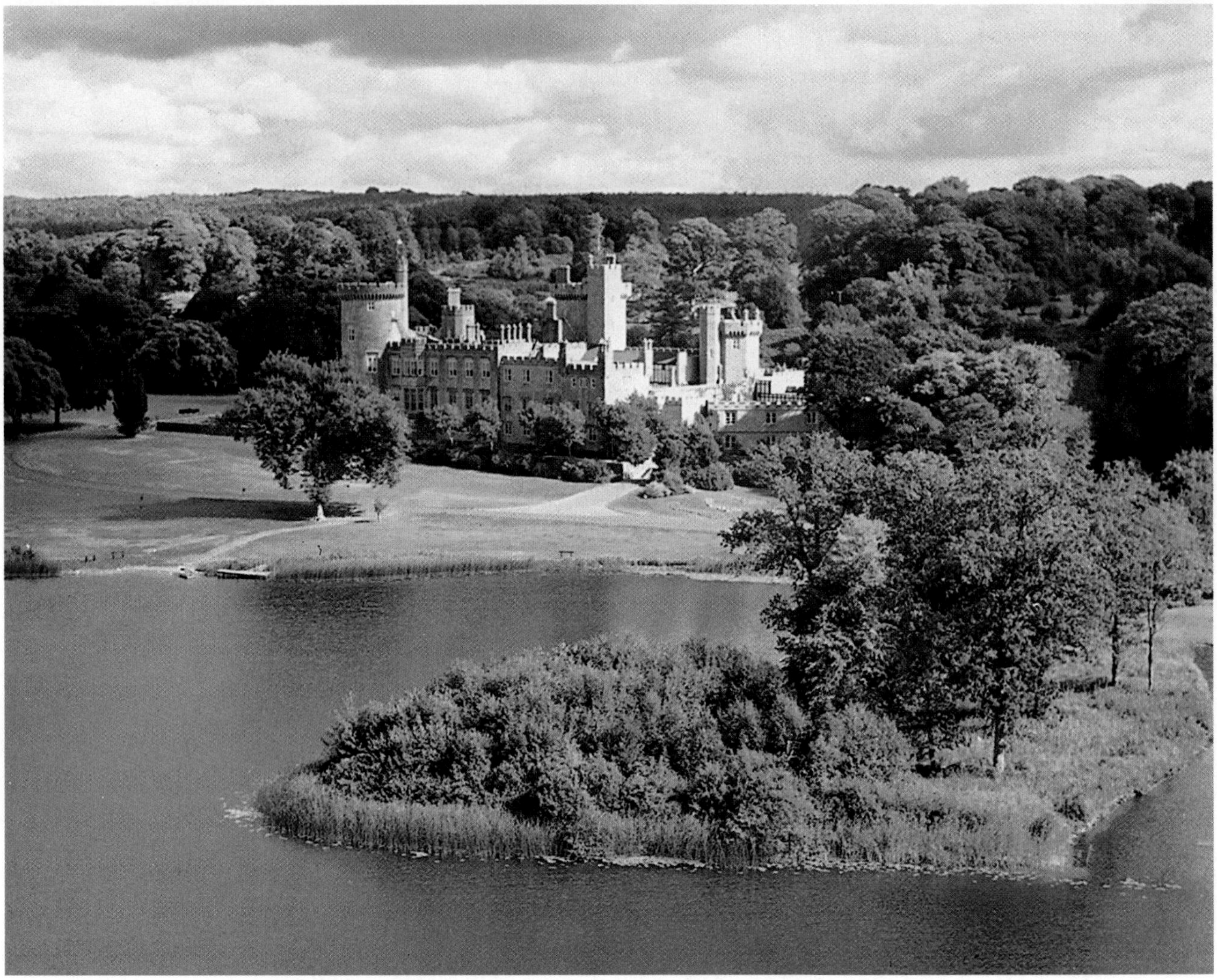

# DROMOLAND CASTLE

**NEWMARKET-ON-FERGUS, SHANNON AREA, CO CLARE**
**TEL: 00 353 61 368144 FAX: 00 353 61 363355 TELEX: 70654**

Dromoland Castle, just 8 miles from Shannon Airport, is one of the most famous baronial castles in Ireland, dating from the 16th century. Dromoland was the ancestral seat of the O'Briens, direct descendants of Irish King Brian Boru. Priceless reminders of its past are everywhere: in the splendid wood and stone carvings, magnificent panelling, oil paintings and romantic gardens. The 73 en suite guest rooms and suites are all beautifully furnished. Stately halls and an elegant dining room are all part of the Dromoland experience. The new Dromoland International Centre is one of Europe's most comprehensive conference venues, hosting groups of up to 450. Classical cuisine is prepared by award-winning chef David McCann. Fishing, 18 hole golf, clay pigeon shooting and Full Health and Beauty Centre are all available on the Estate. While activities nearby include horse riding and golf on some of Ireland's other foremost courses. The castle is an ideal base from which to explore this breathtakingly beautiful area. Dromoland Castle is a Relais et Châteaux member. **Directions:** Take the N18 to Newmarket-on-Fergus, go two miles beyond the village and the hotel entrance is on the right-hand side. Price guide: Double/twin IR£127–IR£270; suite IR£355–IR£700.

For hotel location, see maps on pages 490-496

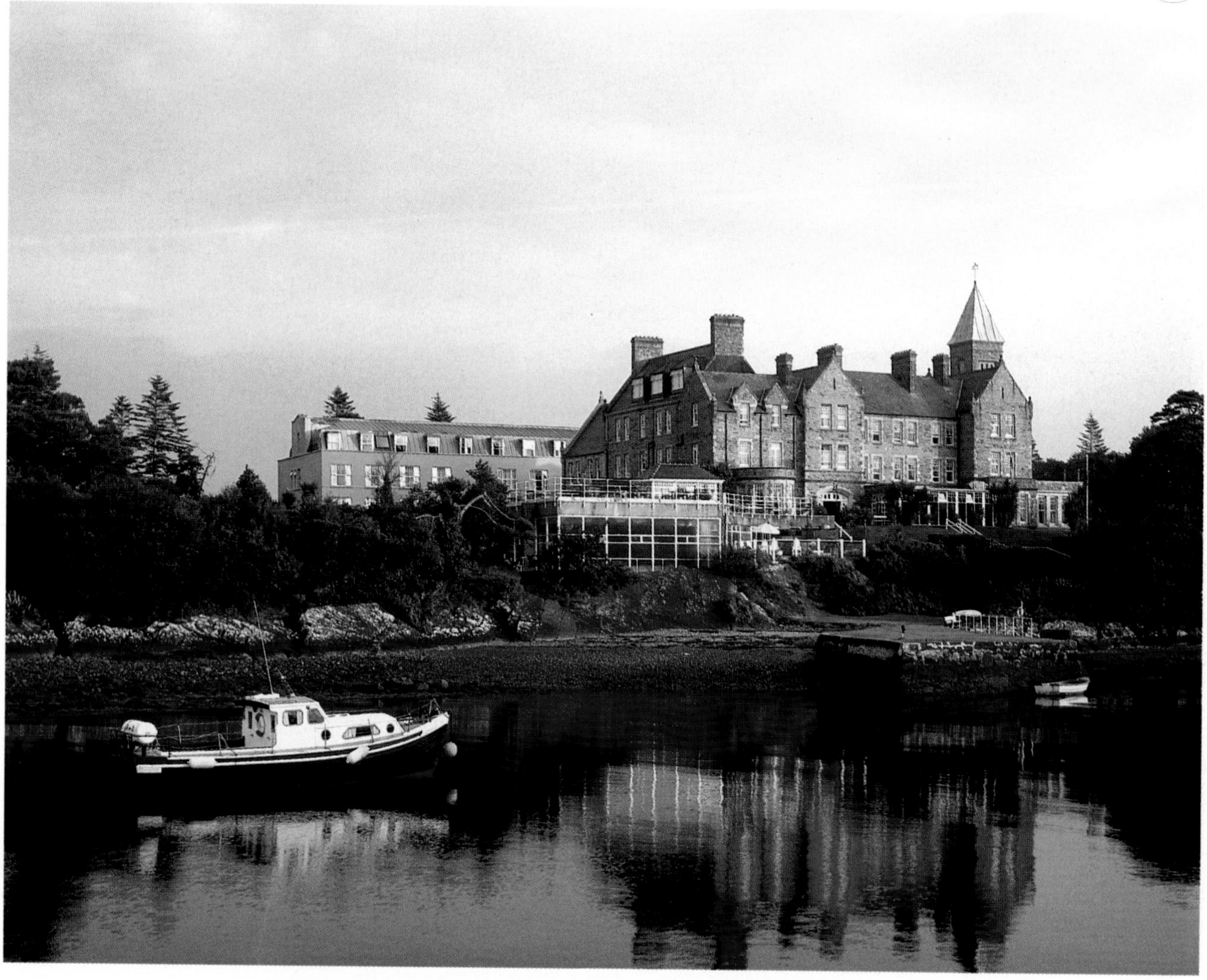

# PARKNASILLA HOTEL

GREAT SOUTHERN HOTEL, PARKNASILLA, CO.KERRY, IRELAND
TEL: 00 353 64 45122 FAX: 00 353 64 45323

County Kerry has an equitable climate from the warm Gulf Stream. Parknasilla is a splendid Victorian mansion surrounded by extensive parkland and subtropical gardens leading down to the sea shore. New arrivals appreciate the graceful reception rooms which, like the luxurious bedrooms, look out on the mountains, across the verdant countryside or down to Kenmare Bay. Wonderful damask and chintz harmonize with the period furniture, and thoughtful 'extras' have been provided. The bathrooms are lavishly appointed. George Bernard Shaw's many visits are reflected in the names of the inviting Doolittle Bar and the elegant Pygmalion Restaurant. The sophisticated menus – always including fish fresh from the sea – and the long international wine list will be enjoyed by the most discerning guests. Corporate activities and private celebrations are hosted in the traditional Shaw Library or handsome Derryquin Suite. Leisure facilities abound – a private 9 hole golf course (with challenging championship courses close by), tennis, riding, fishing, water sports, sailing, clay pigeon shooting and archery. Parknasilla has seven recommended walks through the estate and its own motor yacht for cruises round the coast. Indoors there is a superb pool, sauna, steam room, Jacuzzi and outdoor hot tub. **Directions:** The hotel is south west of Killarney off the N70. Price guide: Single IR£88.50–103.50; double/twin IR£143–167; suite (room only) IR£230

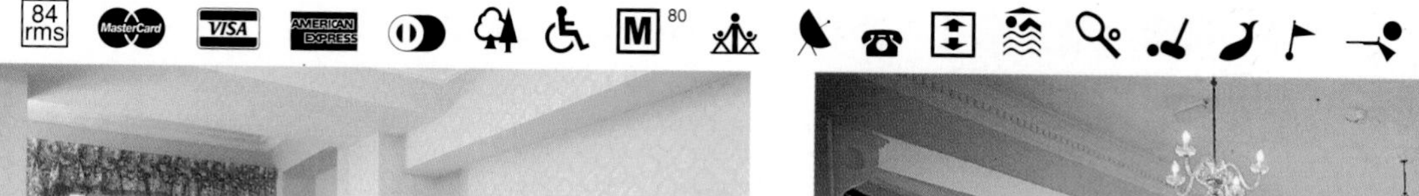

For hotel location, see maps on pages 490-496

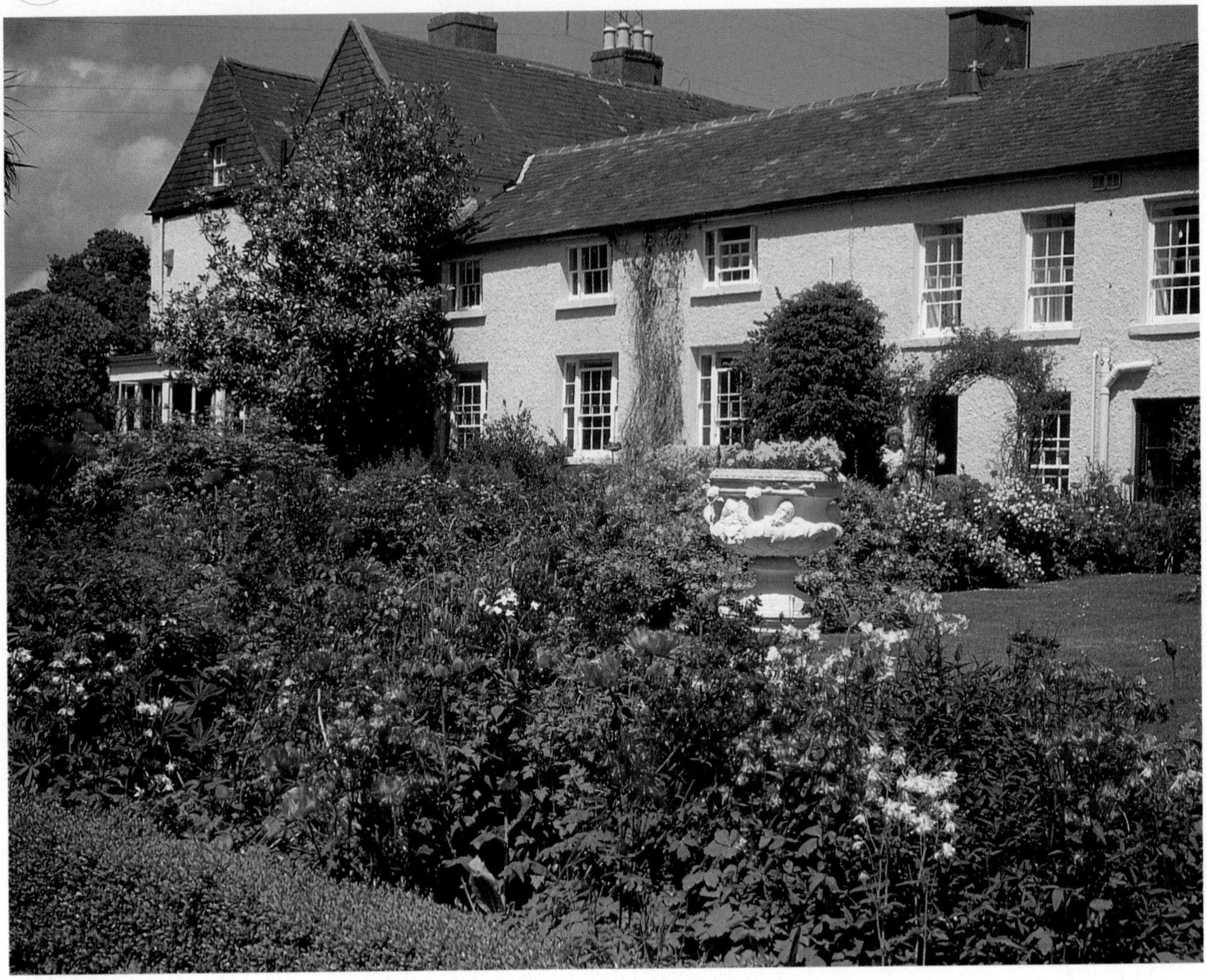

# HUNTER'S HOTEL

NEWRATH BRIDGE, RATHNEW, CO WICKLOW
TEL: 00 353 404 40106 FAX: 00 353 404 40338 E-MAIL: hunters@indigo.ie

Hunter's Hotel, one of Ireland's oldest coaching inns, has been established since the days of post horses and carriages. Run by the Gelletlie family for five generations, the hotel has a long-standing reputation for hospitality, friendliness and excellent food. The restaurant is known for its roast joints, its locally caught fish and its home-grown vegetables. The hotel gardens above the river are a delightful scene for enjoying afternoon lunch or dinner. All the reception rooms retain the character of bygone days with antique furniture, open fires, fresh flowers and polished brass. Most of the 16 attractive en suite bedrooms have lovely views. Hunter's is an ideal base from which to visit Mount Usher gardens, Powerscourt Gardens, Russborough House, Glendalough, Killruddery House, Avondale House and the other attractions of Co. Wicklow, "The Garden of Ireland", where a Garden Festival is held each year in May/June. Local amenities include fifteen 18 hole golf courses within half an hour's drive, most notably Druid's Glen and the highly regarded European. Horse riding and hill walking are other pursuits which can be arranged. **Directions:** Take N11 to Rathnew; turn left just before village on Dublin side. Price guide: Single IR£45–IR£70; double/twin IR£90–IR£120.

For hotel location, see maps on pages 490-496

# KELLY'S RESORT HOTEL

ROSSLARE, CO. WEXFORD, IRELAND
**TEL: 00 353 53 32114 FAX: 00 353 53 32222**

Situated beside the long, sandy beach at Rosslare, Kelly's is very much a family hotel, now managed by the fourth generation of Kellys. With a firm reputation as one of Ireland's finest hotels, based on a consistently high standard of service, Kelly's extends a warm welcome to its guests, many of whom return year after year. The public rooms are tastefully decorated and feature a collection of carefully selected paintings. All bedrooms have been refurbished and extended in the last three years and have en suite facilities. The hotel restaurant is highly regarded for its superb cuisine, served with great attention to detail. An extensive wine list includes individual estate wines imported directly from France. To complement Chef Aherne's fine cuisine we have now opened a new french Bar/Bistro "La Marine", which is an inspired assemblage of design and offers the ideal venue for pre-dinner drinks. Ireland's Egon Ronay Hotel of the Year 1995. For exercise and relaxation, guests have the use of the hotel's new Aqua Club, with two swimming pools and a range of water and health facilities including hydro massage, 'swimming lounge', plunge pool and hot tub, also a beauty salon. Golfers have courses at Rosslare and Wexford, which has an excellent shopping centre. Places of interest nearby include the Irish National Heritage Park at Ferrycarrig. **Directions:** Follow signs to Rosslare. Price guide: Single IR£70; double/twin IR£110–IR£130.

99 rms MasterCard VISA AMERICAN EXPRESS M 20

For hotel location, see maps on pages 490-496

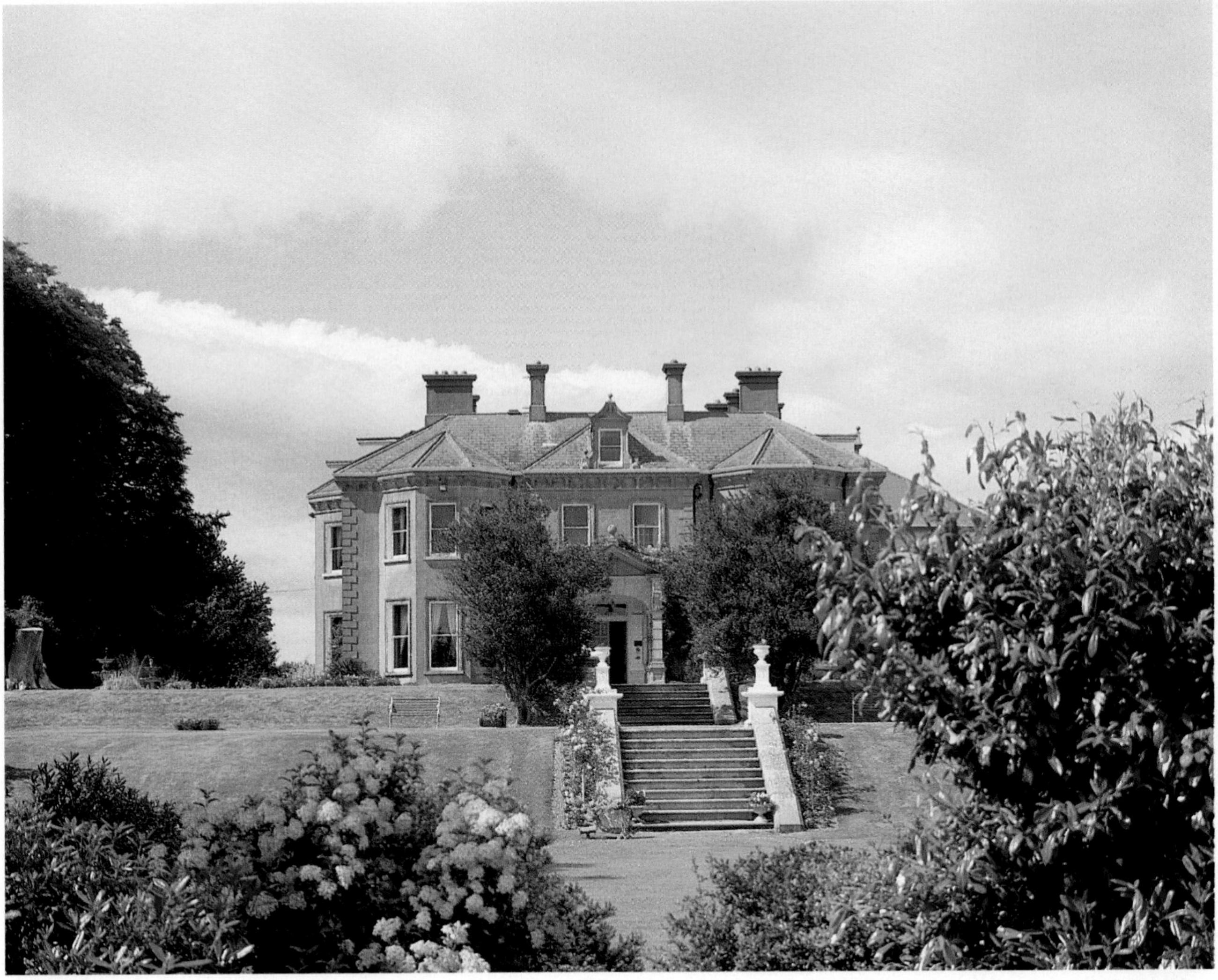

# TINAKILLY HOUSE HOTEL

RATHNEW, WICKLOW, CO WICKLOW

TEL: 00 353 404 69274 FAX: 00 353 404 67806


Less than an hour's drive from Dublin, romantic hideaway Tinakilly House stands on seven acres of beautifully landscaped gardens overlooking the Irish Sea. Tinakilly was built by Captain Halpin, the man who, as Commander of the *Great Eastern*, laid the transatlantic telegraph cables in the 1860s. Tinakilly is now a luxury country house and restaurant, where owners William and Bee Power create a house-party atmosphere for guests. The bedrooms, including three suites, are a perfect blend of Victorian splendour and modern comfort and most offer breathtaking views. Superb country house cooking is augmented by an excellent wine cellar. Open all year round, Tinakilly offers special short break packages to take advantage of the many wonderful gardens, touring (Ballykissangel), and historic attractions of County Wicklow. Top class golf courses including European Club and Druid's Glen, venue for 1998 Irish Open, are nearby. Business meetings are welcome. A brochure, suggesting a variety of sporting pursuits and evening entertainment is available. A Small Luxury Hotel of the World, Tinakilly is also an AA Red Star, ITB 4 Star, RAC Blue Ribbon hotel. **Directions:** Take N11 from Dublin to Rathnew village. Hotel is 500 metres outside the village. Dublin 29 miles; Dunlaoighaire ferryport 20 miles. Price guide: Single IR£100–108; double/twin IR£120–170; suite IR£200–220.

40 rms

For hotel location, see maps on pages 490-496

# *Johansens Recommended Hotels in the* Channel Islands

*With a wealth of wonderful scenery, magnificent coastlines, historic buildings, natural and man-made attractions plus mouthwatering local produce, the Channel Islands provide a memorable destination that's distinctly different.*

**ALL OF THE JOHANSENS RECOMMENDED ESTABLISHMENTS IN THE CHANNEL ISLANDS ARE ABLE TO MAKE FAVOURABLE TRAVEL ARRANGEMENTS FOR YOU.**

Jersey and Guernsey offer VAT free shopping, the official language is English, passports are not required and both islands can be reached by sea from Poole or any one of about 30 airports in Britain and Europe.

And don't forget the other islands. Herm has dazzling beaches, Sark lives in a rural timewarp without traffic and Alderney's cobbled streets, pretty cottages and Victorian forts are another world again.

## JERSEY

The largest and most southerly of the Channel Islands, Jersey measures only nine miles by five and is just fourteen miles from the French coast. The island slopes from north to south, creating dramatic differences between the high cliffs of the north and broad sandy bays of the south.

Jersey was originally part of Normandy. When William the Conqueror invaded England, it came under English rule until 1204, when King John lost Normandy to France.

The Islanders were given a choice – stay with Normandy or remain loyal to the English Crown. They chose England and gained rights and privileges which to this day are subject not to the British Parliament, but only to the reigning monarch.

The French influence is still strong however, and visitors are often surprised to find the names of streets and villages in French. The granite architecture of the farms and manor houses has a Continental feel too, and in rural areas, you may still hear farmworkers speaking in the local 'patois' or dialect.

Food is also something for which Jersey is renowned. It has an excellent choice of restaurants serving everything from simple family meals to gourmet dishes. Shellfish and fresh fish are the specialities of the Island and lobster, crab, seafood platter, bass and Jersey plaice feature on many menus. The annual Good Food Festival, held in early summer, is a must for food lovers.

History enthusiasts can trace the Island's development from prehistory to the present day through a variety of different sites. The Channel Islands were the only part of the British Isles to be occupied by the Germans during World War II and there are reminders all over Jersey.

For a small island, Jersey boasts more than its fair share of fascinating museums where the emphasis is very definitely 'hands on' history. Jersey Museum in St Helier; The Hamptonne Country Life Museum; and the new Maritime Museum which opened in July 1997.

You're never far from Jersey's spectacular coastline – all 50 miles of it – but the interior of the Island is worth exploring too. The largely rural landscape is criss-crossed by a network of narrow country roads, some of which have recently been designated as 'Green Lanes', where priority is given to walkers, cyclists and horseriders.

But the cultural attractions of Jersey can never eclipse the Island's natural beauty. Every bend in the lane, every turn in the coast path reveals a new view to be savoured and enjoyed.

## GUERNSEY

Guernsey, somewhat smaller than its sister island, supports a successful, self-sufficient economy which mixes finance, horticulture and, of course, tourism – all within a total area of 25 square miles. Its charming little capital, St Peter Port, rises in tiers above the quaysides of the busy harbour where the colourful banners of yachts of all nations flutter in the sunshine. Needless to say, delicious seafood features prominently on the menus, though all tastes are catered for by the chefs of many nationalities who have settled in the island.

Guernsey offers enormous variety within its relatively small size. The south coast comprises high cliffs, covered, in springtime, with a profusion of colourful flowers, at the foot of which nestle beautiful little sandy coves.

A network of cliff paths provides splendid walking all the way from St Peter Port to Pleinmont Point in the far south west corner of the island. These paths stretch for a total distance of some 25 miles, one spectacular seaview succeeding the other all the way. Inland, high-banked country lanes lead past old granite farmhouses and tiny fields, where the local breed of cows, famed for their superb cream, contentedly graze.

The west and north coasts comprise a series of sweeping sandy beaches where rocky outcrops are dotted with little pools, teaming with sea life, which provide hours of fascination for youngsters.

Guernsey's heritage provides a fascinating choice of subjects to study during a holiday. The island is girded with fortifications dating back to prehistoric times, and of paramount interest is Castle Cornet, dating from the 13th to 17th centuries, which dominates the harbour of St Peter Port and contains imaginatively conceived maritime and other museums. Other fortifications include 18th century coastal defence towers and the many substantial bunkers, tunnels and towers constructed by the occupying German forces during the second World War, a number of which have now been skilfully refurbished.

And it is this feeling of bygone ages which, coupled with the highest modern standards, prove so great an attraction to visitors to the island.

For further information, please contact:

Jersey Tourism
38 Dover Street, London, W1X 3RB
Tel: 0171 493 5278

Guernsey Tourist Board
PO Box 23, St Peter Port, Guernsey, GY1 3AN
Tel: 01481 723557 (24 hrs); 01481 723552

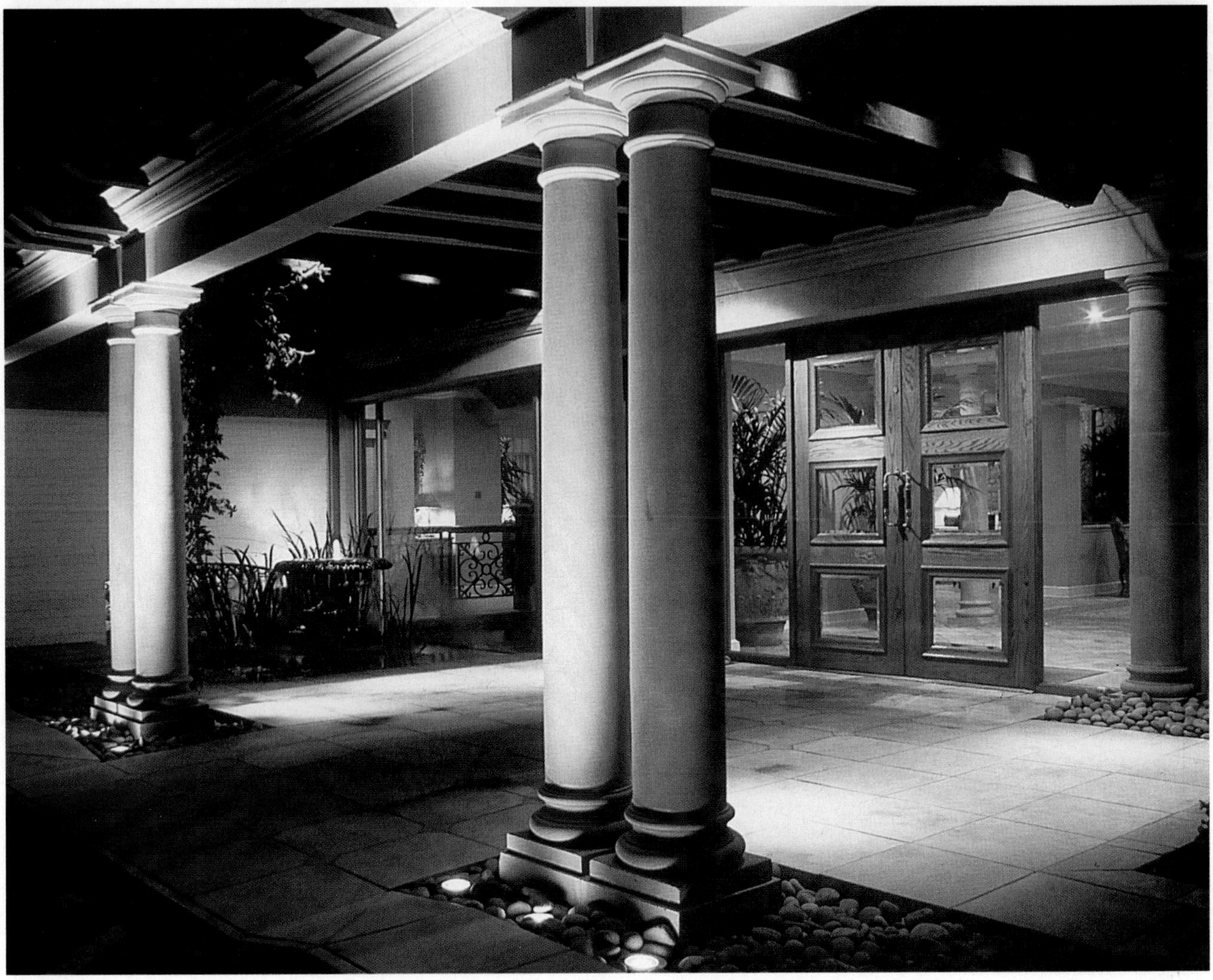

# THE ATLANTIC HOTEL

LA MOYE, ST BRELADE, JERSEY JE3 8HE
TEL: 01534 44101 FAX: 01534 44102 E-MAIL: atlantic@itl.net

A major refurbishment programme in 1994 has transformed this modern building into one with classical warmth and style internally. Privately owned and supervised, every aspect of the four-star service matches its location overlooking the five-mile sweep of St Ouen's Bay. Situated in three acres of private grounds alongside La Moye Golf Course, there is something here for everyone. General Manager, Simon Dufty and his team provide the highest standards of welcome and service. The 50 bedrooms are furnished in the style of the 18th century and like the public rooms, all have co-ordinated colours and fabrics. All have picture windows with views of the sea or the golf course. There are luxury suites and garden studios within the hotel as well. The award-winning restaurant, beautifully situated overlooking the open air pool and terrace, specialises in modern British cooking created by Head Chef, Tom Sleigh. For the more energetic guest, or those wishing to lose excess calories, The Atlantic has extensive indoor health and leisure facilities in The Palm Club including an indoor ozone treated pool. The hotel is an ideal spot from which to walk on the beach or coast paths, to play golf, go riding or just relax. There are comprehensive meeting facilities. **Directions:** Off a private drive off the A13 at La Pulente, two miles from the airport. Price guide: Single £95; double/twin £120; suite £190.

For hotel location, see maps on pages 490-496

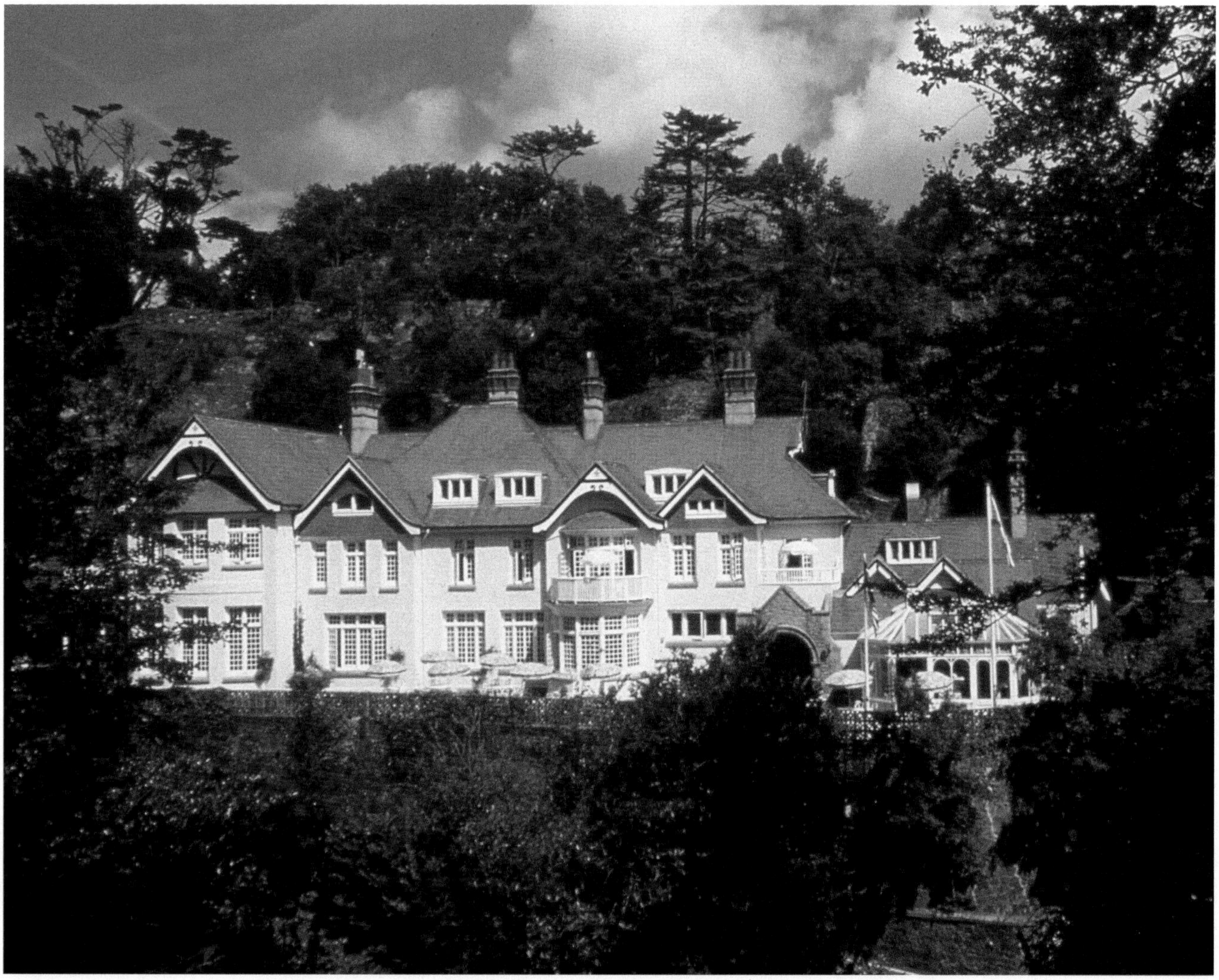

# CHATEAU LA CHAIRE


**ROZEL BAY, JERSEY JE3 6AJ**

**TEL: 01534 863354 FAX: 01534 865137**


Nestling on the Rozel Valley's sunny slopes is Château La Chaire, an elegantly proportioned Victorian house surrounded by terraced gardens. Built in 1843, the Château has been enhanced and transformed into a luxurious hotel providing its guests with a superb blend of superior comfort, service and cuisine. Each of the bedrooms has been furnished to the highest standards and offers an impressive array of personal comforts many en suite bathrooms feature Jacuzzis. The same attention to detail is evident in the public rooms, such as the splendid rococo lounge. The atmophere throughout the hotel is enhanced by the exceptional personal service that its residents receive. Both adventurous and traditional dishes can be enjoyed in the oak panelled setting of La Chaire restaurant. Seafood is a speciality, but there is plenty of choice to cater for all tastes. Awarded 3AA Red Stars and 2 AA Rosettes. A few minutes from the hotel is the picturesque Rozel Bay, a bustling fishing harbour with safe beaches close by. The island's capital, St Helier, is just six miles away. Local tours, golf, fishing and riding are among the many leisure activities that the hotel's staff will be happy to arrange for guests. **Directions:** The hotel is signposted off the main coastal road to Rozel Bay, six miles north east of St Helier. Price guide: Single from £59 ; double/twin from £85; suites from £155.

For hotel location, see maps on pages 490-496

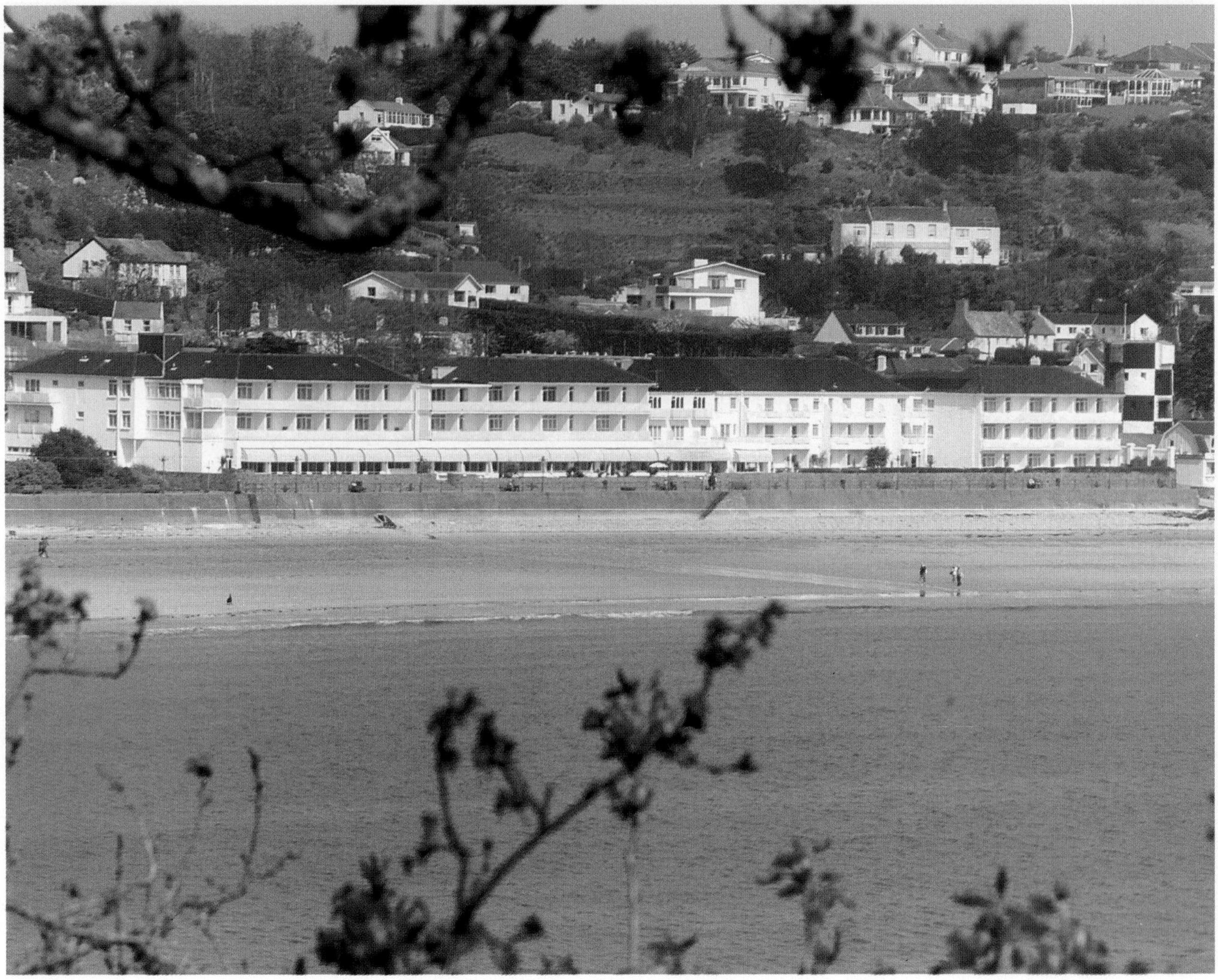

# HOTEL L'HORIZON

**ST BRELADE'S BAY, JERSEY, JE3 8EF, CHANNEL ISLANDS**
**TEL: 01534 43101 FAX: 01534 46269**

A premier hotel in the Channel Islands, L'Horizon is situated on Jersey's lovely St Brelade's Bay. Its south facing position ensures that the hotel enjoys many hours of sunshine. A variety of reception areas provides guests with a choice of environments in which to sit and relax. Comfortable and spacious bedrooms provide every modern amenity and many enjoy a wonderful view across the bay. All sea facing bedrooms have balconies. There are two restaurants, each noted for its individual style, the traditional and elegant Crystal Room and the intimate Grill Room. L'Horizon has won many international accolades and its menus are compiled from the best fresh Jersey produce and from speciality ingredients from the world's top markets.In summer, relax and sip your favourite cocktails enjoying the panoramic views from the terrace. Guests are invited to take advantage of the superb facilities of the Club L'Horizon, which include a mini gym, large swimming pool, steam room, sauna and hairdressing salon. Activities available nearby are swimming, walking, and golf. There are two 18-hole golf courses on the island. Seafarers can go on boat trips round the island or across to Guernsey, Alderney, Herm, Sark, even France **Directions:** In the heart of St Brelade's Bay, ten minutes from the airport. Price guide: Single from £110; double/twin from £160. Special breaks available.

For hotel location, see maps on pages 490-496

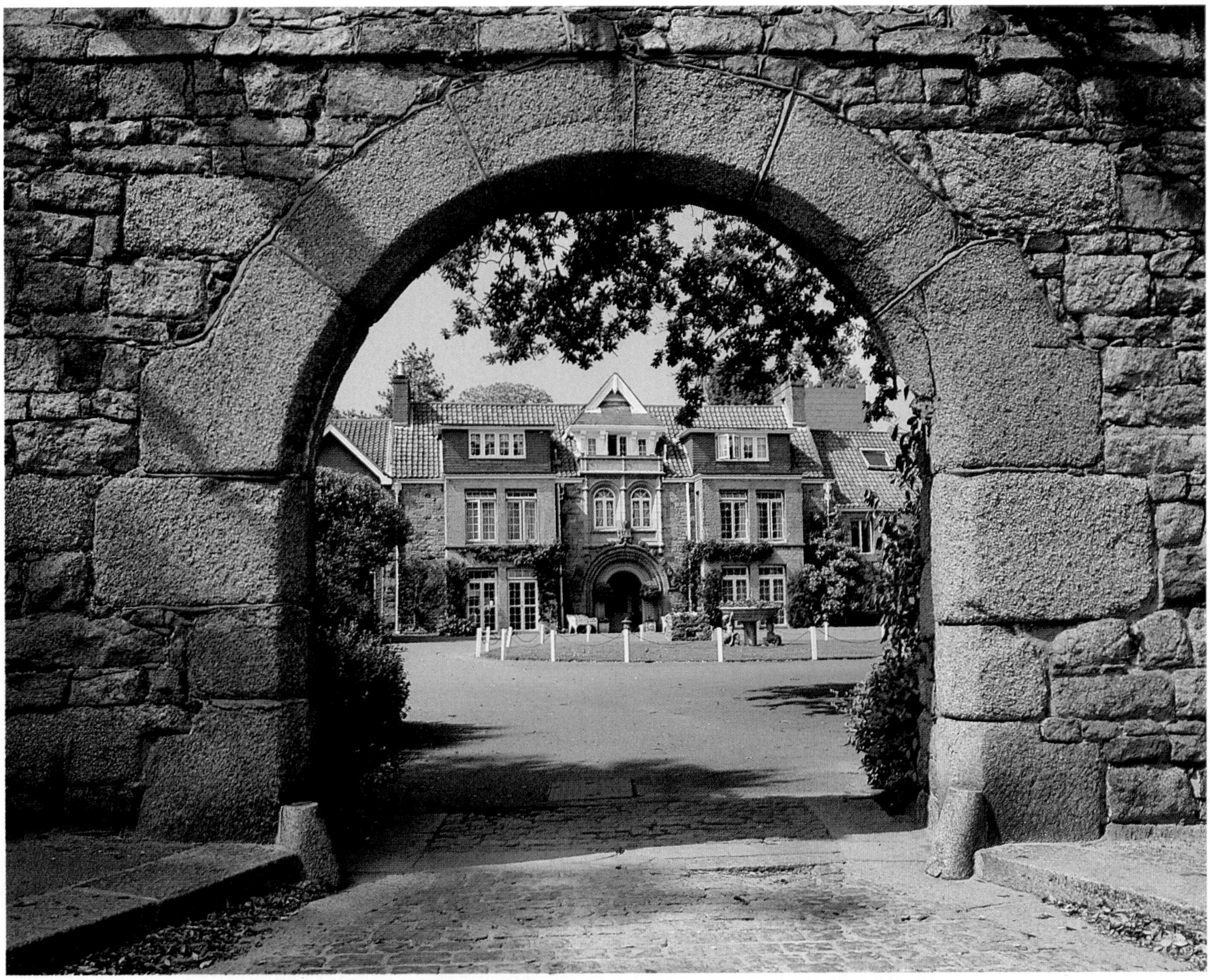

# LONGUEVILLE MANOR

**ST SAVIOUR, JERSEY JE2 7WF**

**TEL: 01534 25501 FAX: 01534 31613 E-MAIL: longman@itl.net**

Three generations of the Lewis family have welcomed guests to Longueville Manor for more than forty years. For their endeavours, Longueville was deservedly named the 1991 Egon Ronay Hotel of the Year and its standards remain at their zenith. Set in 15 acres at the foot of its private wooded valley, the manor has stood here since the 13th century. Nowadays, in the comfort of exquisitely decorated rooms and surrounded by beautiful floral displays, fine antique furnishings and elegant fabrics, guests are pampered by attentive staff. The ancient, oak-panelled dining room sports an array of silver trophies awarded for excellent cuisine. Many of the fruits, vegetables, herbs and flowers are grown in the walled kitchen gardens, which include hothouses to provide fresh produce that would otherwise be out of season. Wines from all over the world are stocked in the expertly managed cellars. Each bedroom is individually decorated with flair and imagination – separate sitting areas have books, magazines, flowers and fresh fruit. By the heated swimming pool, a bar and service area offer a special alfresco menu in the summer months. Beyond this, a stream trickles down a hillside into a lake, with black swans and mandarin ducks completing the picture. **Directions:** On the A3, one mile from St Helier. Price guide: Single from £115; double/twin £150; suite £275.

For hotel location, see maps on pages 490-496

## Johansens Recommended Inns With Restaurants in Great Britain & Ireland

### *ENGLAND*

**Amberley,Near Arundel** – The Boathouse Brasserie, Houghton Bridge, Amberley, BN18 9LR. Tel: 01798 831059

**Ambleside (Great Langdale)** – The New Dungeon Ghyll Hotel, Great Langdale, Ambleside, LA22 9JY. Tel: 015394 37213

**Appleby-In-Westmorland** – The Royal Oak Inn, Bongate, Appleby-In-Westmorland, CA16 6UN. Tel: 017683 51463

**Ashbourne (Hognaston)** – Red Lion Inn, Main Street, Hognaston, Ashbourne, DE6 1PR. Tel: 01335 370396

**Askrigg (Wensleydale)** – The Kings Arms Hotel And Restaurant, Market Place, Askrigg-In-Wensleydale, Askrigg-In-Wensleydale, DL8 3HQ. Tel: 01969 650258

**Badby Nr Daventry** – The Windmill At Badby, Main Street, Badby, NN11 6AN. Tel: 01327 702363

**Bassenthwaite Lake** – The Pheasant Inn, Bassenthwaite Lake, CA13 9YE. Tel: 017687 76234

**Beckington Nr Bath** – The Woolpack Inn, Beckington, BA3 6SP. Tel: 01373 831244

**Belford** – The Blue Bell Hotel, Market Place, Belford, NE70 7NE. Tel: 01668 213543

**Blakeney** – White Horse Hotel, 4 High Street, Blakeney, Holt, NR25 7AL. Tel: 01263 740574

**Boroughbridge** – The Crown Hotel, Horsefair, Boroughbridge, YO5 9LB. Tel: 01423 322328

**Bourton-On-The-Water** – The Old Manse, Victoria Street, Bourton-On-The-Water, GL54 2BX. Tel: 01451 820082

**Bridport (West Bexington)** – The Manor Hotel, West Bexington, Dorchester, DT2 9DF. Tel: 01308 897616

**Brixham (Churston Ferrers)** – Ye Olde Churston Court Inn, Churston Ferrers, TQ5 0JE. Tel: 01803 842186

**Broadway** – The Broadway Hotel, The Green, Broadway, WR12 7AA. Tel: 01386 852401

**Burford** – The Lamb Inn, Sheep Street, Burford, OX18 4LR. Tel: 01993 823155

**Burford** – Cotswold Gateway Hotel, Cheltenham Road, Burford, OX18 4HX. Tel: 01993 822695

**Burnham Market** – The Hoste Arms Hotel, The Green, Burnham Market, PE31 8HD. Tel: 01328 738777

**Burnley (Fence)** – Fence Gate Inn, Wheatley Lane Road, Fence, BB12 9EE. Tel: 01282 618101

**Burnsall (Skipton)** – The Red Lion, By the bridge at Burnsall, BD23 6BU. Tel: 01756 720204

**Burton Upon Trent (Branston)** – The Old Vicarage Restaurant, Main Street, Branston, Burton Upon Trent, DE14 3EX. Tel: 01283 533222

**Burton Upon Trent (Sudbury)** – Boar's Head Hotel, Lichfield Road, Sudbury, DE6 5GX. Tel: 01283 820344

**Calver,Nr Bakewell** – The Chequers Inn, Froggatt Edge, S30 1ZB. Tel: 01433 630231

**Camborne** – Tyacks Hotel, 27 Commercial Street, Camborne, TR14 8LD. Tel: 01209 612424

**Cambridge** – Panos Hotel & Restaurant, 154-156 Hills Road, Cambridge, CB2 2PB. Tel: 01223 212958

**Carlisle (Talkin Tarn)** – The Tarn End House Hotel, Talkin Tarn, Brampton, CA8 1LS. Tel: 016977 2340

**Castle Ashby** – The Falcon Hotel, Castle Ashby, Northampton, NN7 1LF. Tel: 01604 696200

**Castle Combe** – The Castle Inn, Castle Combe, SN14 7HN. Tel: 01249 783030

**Castle Donington** – Donington Manor Hotel, High Street, Castle Donington, DE74 2PP. Tel: 01332 810253

**Cheltenham (Birdlip)** – Kingshead House Restaurant, Birdlip, GL4 8JH. Tel: 01452 862299

**Chester (Tarporley)** – Wild Boar Hotel & Restaurant, Whitchurch Road, Near Beeston, Tarporley, CW6 9NW. Tel: 01829 260309

**Chester (Tarporley)** – The Swan Hotel, 50 High Street, Tarporley, CW6 0AG. Tel: 01829 733838

**Chipping Campden (Broad Campden)** – The Noel Arms, High Street, Chipping Campden, GL55 6AT. Tel: 01386 840317

**Cirencester (Coln St-Aldwyns)** – The New Inn, Coln St-Aldwyns, GL7 5AN. Tel: 01285 750651

**Cirencester (Meysey Hampton)** – The Masons Arms, Meysey Hampton, GL7 5JT. Tel: 01285 850164

**Clavering (Stansted)** – The Cricketers, Clavering, CB11 4QT. Tel: 01799 550442

**Cleobury Mortimer** – The Redfern Hotel, Cleobury Mortimer, DY14 8AA. Tel: 01299 270 395

**Cleobury Mortimer** – Crown At Hopton, Hopton Wafers, Cleobury Mortimer, DY14 0NB. Tel: 01299 270372

**Clovelly** – New Inn Hotel, High Street, Clovelly, EX39 5TQ. Tel: 01237 431303

**Colchester** – The Red Lion Hotel, High Street, Colchester, CO1 1DJ. Tel: 01206 577986

**Crowborough** – Winston Manor, Beacon Road, Crowborough, TN6 1AD. Tel: 01892 652772

**Dartmouth** – The Victoria Hotel, Victoria Road, Dartmouth, TQ6 9RT. Tel: 01803 832572

**Dorchester-On-Thames** – The George Hotel, High Street, Dorchester-On-Thames, OX10 7HH. Tel: 01865 340404

**Dulverton (Exbridge)** – The Anchor Country Inn & Hotel, Exbridge, TA22 9AZ. Tel: 01398 323433

**East Witton (Wensleydale)** – The Blue Lion, East Witton, DL8 4SN. Tel: 01969 624273

**East Grinstead (Felbridge)** – The Woodcock Inn & Restaurant, Woodcock Hill, Felbridge. Tel: 01342 325859

**Eccleshall** – The George Hotel, Eccleshall, ST21 6DF. Tel: 01785 850300

**Egton** – The Wheatsheaf Inn, Egton, YO21 1TZ. Tel: 01947 895271

**Eton/Windsor** – The Christopher Hotel, High Street, Eton, Windsor, SL4 6AN. Tel: 01753 852359

**Evesham (Offenham)** – Riverside Restaurant And Hotel, The Parks, Offenham Road, WR11 5JP. Tel: 01386 446200

**Exmoor (Withypool)** – The Royal Oak Inn, Withypool, Emoor National Park, TA24 7QP. Tel: 01643 831506/7

**Eyam (Foolow)** – The Bulls Head Inn, Foolow, Eyam, Hope Valley, S32 5QR. Tel: 01433 630873

**Falmouth (Constantine)** – Trengilly Wartha Country Inn & Restaurant, Nancenoy, Constantine, Falmouth, TR11 5RP. Tel: 01326 340332

**Fordingbridge (New Forest)** – The Woodfalls Inn, The Ridge, Woodfalls, Fordingbridge, SP5 2LN. Tel: 01725 513222

**Fulbeck (Lincoln)** – Hare & Hounds, The Green, Fulbeck, NG32 3SS. Tel: 01400 272090

**Goathland** – Mallyan Spout Hotel, Goathland, YO22 5AN. Tel: 01947 896486

**Godalming** – Inn On The Lake, Ockford Road, Godalming, GU7 1RH. Tel: 01483 415575

**Goring-On-Thames** – The Leatherne Bottel Riverside Inn & Restaurant, The Bridleway, Goring-On-Thames, RG8 0HS. Tel: 01491 872667

**Grimsthorpe (Bourne)** – The Black Horse Inn, Grimsthorpe, Bourne, PE10 0LY. Tel: 01778 591247

**Grindleford** – The Maynard Arms, Main Road, Grindleford, S32 2HE. Tel: 01433 630321

**Halifax/Huddersfield** – The Rock Inn Hotel, Holywell Green, Halifax, HX4 9BS. Tel: 01422 379721

**Handcross (Slaugham)** – The Chequers At Slaugham, Slaugham, RH17 6AQ. Tel: 01444 400239/400996

**Harrogate (Killinghall)** – The Low Hall Hotel, Ripon Road, Killinghall, Harrogate, HG3 2AY. Tel: 01423 508598

**Harrogate (Ripley Castle)** – The Boar's Head Hotel, Ripley, Harrogate, HG3 3AY. Tel: 01423 771888

**Hatherleigh** – The George Hotel, Market Street, Hatherleigh, EX20 3JN. Tel: 01837 810454

**Hathersage** – The Plough Inn, Leadmill Bridge, Hathersage, S30 1BA. Tel: 01433 650319

**Haworth** – Old White Lion Hotel, Haworth, Keighley, BD22 8DU. Tel: 01535 642313

**Hay-On-Wye** – Rhydspence Inn, Whitney-On-Wye, HR3 6EU. Tel: 01497 831262

**Hayfield (High Peak)** – The Waltzing Weasel, New Mills Road, Birch Vale High Peak, Hayfield, SK22 1BT. Tel: 01663 743402

**Helmsley** – The Feversham Arms Hotel, Helmsley, YO6 5AG. Tel: 01439 770766

**Helmsley** – The Feathers Hotel, Market Place, Helmsley, YO6 5BH. Tel: 01439 770275

**Henley (Ibstone)** – The Fox Country Hotel, Ibstone, HP14 3GG. Tel: 01491 638289

**Hinkley (Nr Leicester)** – Barnacles Restaurant, Watlins Street, LE10 3JA. Tel: 01455 633220

**Honiton (Wilmington)** – Home Farm Hotel, Wilmington, EX14 9JQ. Tel: 01404 831278

**Kirkby Lonsdale** – Whoop Hall Inn, Burrow-With-Burrow, Kirkby Lonsdale, LA6 2HP. Tel: 015242 71284

**Knutsford** – Longview Hotel And Restaurant, 51/55 Manchester Road, Knutsford, WA16 0LX. Tel: 01565 632119

**Ledbury** – Feathers Hotel, High Street, Ledbury, HR8 1DS. Tel: 01531 635266

**Leek (Blackshaw Moor)** – The Three Horseshoes Inn & Restaurant, Buxton Road, Blackshaw Moor, ST13 8TW. Tel: 01538 300296

**Leominster (Stoke Prior)** – Wheelbarrow Castle, Stoke Prior, Leominster, HR6 0NB. Tel: 01568 612219

**Long Melford** – The Countrymen, The Green, Long Melford, CO10 9DN. Tel: 01787 312356

**Ludlow (Brimfield)** – The Roebuck, Brimfield. Tel: 01584 711230

**Lynmouth** – The Rising Sun, Harbourside, Lynmouth, EX35 6EQ. Tel: 01598 753223

**Maidenhead** – Boulters Lock Hotel, Boulters Island, Maidenhead, SL6 8PE. Tel: 01628 21291

**Maidstone (Ringlestone)** – Ringlestone Inn, 'Twixt' Harrietsham and Wormshill, ME17 1NX. Tel: 01622 859900

**Maidstone (Warren Street)** – The Harrow At Warren Street, Warren Street, ME17 2ED. Tel: 01622 858727

**Malmesbury** – The Horse And Groom Inn, Charlton, SN16 9DL. Tel: 01666 823904

**Mells Nr Bath** – The Talbot Inn at Mells, High Street, Mells, BA11 3PN. Tel: 01373 812254

**Milton Keynes (Stony Stratford)** – The Different Drummer, High Street, Stony Stratford, MK11 1AH. Tel: 01908 564733

**Minchinhampton (Hyde)** – The Ragged Cot, Hyde, Minchinhampton, GL6 8PE. Tel: 01453 884643/731333

**Montacute** – The King's Arms Inn & Restaurant, Montacute, TA16 6UU. Tel: 01935 822513

**Moretonhampstead** – The White Hart Hotel, The Square, Moretonhampstead, TQ13 8NF. Tel: 01647 440406

**Newark (Barnby-in-the-Willows)** – The Willow Tree, Barnby-in-the-Willows, Newark, NG24 2SA. Tel: 01636 626613

**Newbury (Kingsclere)** – The Swan Hotel, Swan Street, Kingsclere, RG20 5PP. Tel: 01635 298314

**Newby Bridge** – The Swan Hotel, Newby Bridge, LA12 8NB. Tel: 015395 31681

**Norwich (Rackheath)** – The Garden House Hotel, Salhouse Road, Rackheath, Norwich, NR13 6AA. Tel: 01603 720007

**Nottingham** – Hotel Des Clos, Old Lenton Lane, Nottingham, NG7 2SA. Tel: 01159 866566

**Oakham** – The Whipper-In Hotel, The Market Place, Oakham, Rutland, LE15 6DT. Tel: 01572 756971

**Onneley** – The Wheatsheaf Inn At Onneley And La Puerta Del Sol Restaurante Español, Barhill Road, Onneley, CW3 9QF. Tel: 01782 751581

**Oxford (Banbury)** – Holcombe Hotel, High Street, Deddington, OX15 0SL. Tel: 01869 338274

**Oxford (Middleton Stoney)** – The Jersey Arms, Middleton Stoney, OX6 8SE. Tel: 01869 343234

**Oxford (Minster Lovell)** – The Mill & Old Swan, Minster Lovell, OX8 5RN. Tel: 01993 774441

**Oxford (Stanton St John)** – The Talkhouse, Wheatley Road, Stanton-St-John, OX33 1EX. Tel: 01865 351648

**Padstow** – The Old Custom House Hotel, South Quay, Padstow, PL28 8ED. Tel: 01841 532359

**Pelynt,Nr Looe** – Jubilee Inn, Pelynt, PL13 2JZ. Tel: 01503 220312

**Petworth (Coultershaw Bridge)** – Badgers, Coultershaw Bridge, Petworth, GU28 0JF. Tel: 01798 342651

**Petworth (Sutton)** – White Horse Inn, Sutton, RH20 1PS. Tel: 01798 869 221

**Pickering** – The White Swan, The Market Place, Pickering, YO18 7AA. Tel: 01751 472288

**Port Gaverne** – The Port Gaverne Hotel, PL29 3SQ. Tel: 01208 880244

**Porthleven (Nr Helston)** – The Harbour Inn, Commercial Road, Porthleven, TR13 9JD. Tel: 01326 573876

**Preston (Goosnargh)** – Ye Horn's Inn, Horn's Lane, Goosnargh, PR3 2FJ. Tel: 01772 865230

**Reepham (Norwich)** – The Old Brewery House Hotel, Market Square, Reepham, Norwich, NR10 4JJ. Tel: 01603 870881

**Rugby (Easenhall)** – The Golden Lion Inn of Easenhall, Easenall, CV23 0JA. Tel: 01788 832265

**Saddleworth (Delph)** – The Old Bell Inn Hotel, Huddersfield Road, Delph, Saddleworth, OL3 5EG. Tel: 01457 870130

**Settle (Clapham)** – The New Inn Hotel, Clapham, LA2 8HH. Tel: 015242 51203

**Sevenoaks** – The Royal Oak, High Street, Sevenoaks, TN14 5PG. Tel: 01732 451109

**Shaftesbury (Motcombe)** – The Coppleridge Inn, Motcombe, Shaftesbury, SP7 9HW. Tel: 01747 851980

**Sherborne (West Camel)** – Walnut Tree, West Camel, BA22 7QW. Tel: 01935 851292

**Shipton-Under-Wychwood** – The Shaven Crown Hotel, High Street, Shipton Under Wychwood, OX7 6BA. Tel: 01993 830330

**Shipton-Under-Wychwood** – The Lamb Inn, Shipton-Under-Wychwood, OX7 6DQ. Tel: 01993 830465

**Shrewsbury (Nesscliffe)** – The Nesscliffe, Nesscliffe, Shrewsbury, SY4 1DB. Tel: 01743 741430

**Southport (Formby)** – Tree Tops Country House Restaurant & Motel, Southport Old Road, Formby, L37 0AB. Tel: 01704 879651

**St Mawes** – The Rising Sun, The Square, St Mawes, TR2 5DJ. Tel: 01326 270233

**Stafford (Ingestre)** – The Dower House, Ingestre Park, Great Haywood, ST18 0RE. Tel: 01889 270707

**Stow-On-The-Wold** – The Royalist Hotel, Digbeth Street, Stow-On-The-Wold, GL54 1BN. Tel: 01451 830670

**Stow-On-The-Wold (Bledington)** – The Kings Head Inn & Restaurant, The Green, Bledington, OX7 6XQ. Tel: 01608 658365

**Stow-on-the-Wold (Oddington)** – The Horse and Groom, Upper Oddington, Moreton-in-Marsh, GL56 0XH. Tel: 01451 830584

**Stratford-upon-Avon** – The Coach House Hotel & Cellar Restaurant, 16/17 Warwick Road, Stratford-upon-Avon, CV37 6YW. Tel: 01789 204109 / 299468

**Telford (Norton)** – The Hundred House Hotel, Bridgnorth Road,Norton, Nr Shifnal, Telford, TF11 9EE. Tel: 01952 730353

**Thelbridge** – Thelbridge Cross Inn, Thelbridge, EX17 4SQ. Tel: 01884 860316

**Thornham** – The Lifeboat Inn, Ship Lane, Thornham, PE36 6LT. Tel: 01485 512236

**Thorpe Market** – Green Farm Restaurant And Hotel, North Walsham Road, Thorpe Market, NR11 8TH. Tel: 01263 833602

**Tintagel (Trebarwith Strand)** – The Port William, Trebarwith Strand, PL34 0HB. Tel: 01840 770230

**Torbryan Nr Totnes** – The Old Church House Inn, Torbryan, Ipplepen, TQ12 5UR. Tel: 01803 812372

**Torquay (Kingskerswell)** – The Barn Owl Inn, Aller Mills, Kingskerswell, TQ12 5AN. Tel: 01803 872130

**Totnes (Staverton)** – The Sea Trout Inn, Staverton, TQ9 6PA. Tel: 01803 762274

**Troutbeck (Near Windermere)** – The Mortal Man Hotel, Troutbeck, LA23 1PL. Tel: 015394 33193

**Tunbridge Wells** – The Royal Wells Inn, Mount Ephraim, Tunbridge Wells, TN4 8BE. Tel: 01892 511188

**Upton-Upon-Severn,Nr Malvern** – The White Lion Hotel, High Street, Upton-Upon-Severn, WR8 0HJ. Tel: 01684 592551

**Weobley** – Ye Olde Salutation Inn, Market Pitch, Weobley, HR4 8SJ. Tel: 01544 318443

**West Witton (Wensleydale)** – The Wensleydale Heifer Inn, West Witton, Wensleydale, DL8 4LS. Tel: 01969 622322

**Whitewell** – The Inn At Whitewell, Forest Of Bowland, Clitheroe, BB7 3AT. Tel: 01200 448222

**Worcester (Knightwick)** – The Talbot, Knightwick, Worcester, WR6 5PH. Tel: 01886 821235

**Worcester (Severn Stoke)** – The Old Schoolhouse, Severn Stoke, Worcester, WR8 9JA. Tel: 01905 371368

**Worthing (Bramber)** – The Old Tollgate Restaurant And Hotel, The Street, Bramber, Steyning, BN44 3WE. Tel: 01903 879494

**Wroxham** – The Barton Angler Country Inn, Irstead Road, Neatishead, NR12 8XP. Tel: 01692 630740

**Yattendon** – The Royal Oak Hotel, Yattendon, Newbury, RG18 0UG. Tel: 01635 201325

**York (Easingwold)** – The George at Easingwold, Market Place, Easingwold, York, YO6 3AD. Tel: 01347 821698

**York (Thorganby)** – The Jefferson Arms, Main Street, YO4 6DB. Tel: 01904 448316

### WALES

**Chepstow** – The Castle View Hotel, 16 Bridge Street, Chepstow, NP6 5EZ. Tel: 01291 620349

**Llanarmon Dyffryn Ceiriog** – The West Arms Hotel, Llanarmon D C, LL20 7LD. Tel: 01691 600665

**Llandeilo (Rhosmaen)** – The Plough Inn, Rhosmaen, Llandeilo, SA19 6NP. Tel: 01558 823431

**Ruthin** – Ye Olde Anchor Inn, Rhos Street, Ruthin, LL15 1DX. Tel: 01824 702813

**Welshpool** – The Royal Oak Hotel & Restaurant, Welshpool, SY7 7DG. Tel: 01938 552217

**Welshpool (Berriew)** – The Lion Hotel And Restaurant, Berriew, SY21 8PQ. Tel: 01686 640452

## SCOTLAND

**Banchory (Royal Deeside)** – Potarch Hotel, By Banchory, Royal Deeside, AB31 4BD. Tel: 013398 84339

**Blair Atholl** – The Loft Restaurant, Golf Course Road, Blair Atholl, PH18 5TE. Tel: 01736 481377

**Blairgowrie (Glenisla)** – The Glenisla Hotel, Kirkton of Glenisla, By Alyth, PH11 8PH. Tel: 01575 582223

**Isle Of Skye (Eilean Iarmain)** – Hotel Eilean Iarmain or Isle Ornsay Hotel, Sleat, IV43 8QR. Tel: 01471 833332

**Isle Of Skye (Uig)** – Uig Hotel, Uig, Isle Of Skye, IV51 9YE. Tel: 01470 542205

**Moffatt** – Annandale Arms Hotel, High Street, Moffatt, DG10 9HF. Tel: 01683 220013

**Pitlochry** – The Moulin Hotel, Moulin, By Pitlochry, PH16 %EW. Tel: 01796 472196

**Powmill (Nr Kinross)** – Whinsmuir Country Inn, Powmill, By Dollar, FK14 7NW. Tel: 01577 840595

## IRELAND

**Crawfordsburn Co Down Northern Ireland** – The Old Inn, Crawfordsburn, Crawfordsburn, BT19 1JH. Tel: 01247 853255

## CHANNEL ISLANDS

**Jersey (Gorey)** – The Moorings Hotel, Gorey Pier, Jersey, JE3 6EW. Tel: 01534 853633

**Jersey (St Brelade)** – Sea Crest Hotel and Restaurant, Petit Port, St Brelade, JE3 8HH. Tel: 01534 46353

# Johansens Recommended Country Houses in Great Britain & Ireland

## ENGLAND

**Alcester (Arrow)** – Arrow Mill Hotel And Restaurant, Arrow, B49 5NL. Tel: 01789 762419

**Alston** – Lovelady Shield Country House Hotel, Nenthead Road, Alston, CA9 3LF. Tel: 01434 381203

**Appleton-Le-Moors** – Appleton Hall, Appleton-Le-Moors, YO6 6TF. Tel: 01751 417227

**Arundel (Burpham)** – Burpham Country House Hotel, Old Down, Burpham, BN18 9RV. Tel: 01903 882160

**Ashbourne** – The Beeches Farmhouse, Waldley, Doveridge, DE6 5LR. Tel: 01889 590288

**Ashbourne (Grindon)** – Porch Farmhouse, Grindon, ST13 7TP. Tel: 01538 304545

**Ashwater** – Blagdon Manor Country Hotel, Ashwater, EX21 5DF. Tel: 01409 211224

**Atherstone** – Chapel House, Friars' Gate, Atherstone, CV9 1EY. Tel: 01827 718949

**Bakewell (Rowsley)** – East Lodge Country House Hotel, Rowsley, Matlock, DE4 2EF. Tel: 01629 734474

**Bakewell (Rowsley)** – The Peacock Hotel at Rowsley, Rowsley, DE4 2EB. Tel: 01629 733518

**Bamburgh** – Waren House Hotel, Waren Mill, Bamburgh, NE70 7EE. Tel: 01668 214581

**Barwick Village (Nr Yeovil)** – Little Barwick House, Barwick Village, BA22 9TD. Tel: 01935 423902

**Bath** – Bloomfield House, 146 Bloomfield Road, Bath, BA2 2AS. Tel: 01225 420105

**Bath** – Apsley House, 141 Newbridge Hill, Bath, BA1 3PT. Tel: 01225 336966

**Bath** – Eagle House, Church Street, Bathford, BA1 7RS. Tel: 01225 859946

**Bath** – Paradise House, Holloway, Bath, BA2 4PX. Tel: 01225 317723

**Bath** – Oldfields, 102 Wells Road, Bath, BA2 3AL. Tel: 01225 317984

**Bath (Bradford-On-Avon)** – Widbrook Grange, Trowbridge Road, Bradford-On-Avon, BA15 1UH. Tel: 01225 864750 / 863173

**Bath (Norton St Philip)** – Bath Lodge Hotel, Norton St Philip, Bath, BA3 6NH. Tel: 01225 723040

**Bath (Woolverton)** – Woolverton House, BA3 6QS. Tel: 01373 830415

**Belper (Shottle)** – Dannah Farm Country Guest House, Bowman's Lane, Shottle, DE56 2DR. Tel: 01773 550273 / 630

**Bibury** – Bibury Court, Bibury , GL7 5NT. Tel: 01285 740337

**Bideford (Northam)** – Yeoldon House Hotel, Durrant Lane, Northam, EX39 2RL. Tel: 01237 474400

**Biggin-By-Hartington** – Biggin Hall, Biggin-By-Hartington, Buxton, SK17 0DH. Tel: 01298 84451

**Blackpool (Singleton)** – Mains Hall Hotel & Brasserie, Mains Lane, Little Singleton, FY6 7LE. Tel: 01253 885130

**Blockley (Chipping Campden)** – Lower Brook House, Blockley, GL56 9DS. Tel: 01386 700286

**Bolton (Edgworth)** – Quarlton Manor Farm, Plantation Road, Edgeworth,Turton, Bolton, BL7 0DD. Tel: 01204 852277

**Bonchurch (Isle of Wight)** – Peacock Vane Hotel, Bonchurch, PO38 1RJ. Tel: 01983 852019

**Bournemouth** – Langtry Manor, Derby Road, East cliff, Bournemouth, BH1 3QB. Tel: 01202 553887

**Bourton-On-The-Water** – Dial House Hotel, The Chestnuts, High Street, Bourton-On-The-Water, GL54 2AN. Tel: 01451 822244

**Bridgnorth** – Cross Lane House Hotel, Astley Abbots, Bridgnorth, WV16 4SJ. Tel: 01746 764887

**Bristol (Chelwood)** – Chelwood House, Achelwood, BS18 4NH. Tel: 01761 490730

**Broadway (Willersey)** – The Old Rectory, Church Street, Willersey, Broadway, WR12 7PN. Tel: 01386 853729

**Brockenhurst** – Thatched Cottage Hotel & Restaurant, 16 Brookley Road, Brockenhurst, SO42 7RR. Tel: 01590 623090

**Brockenhurst** – Whitley Ridge & Country House Hotel, Beaulieu Road, Brockenhurst, SO42 7QL. Tel: 01590 622354

**Cambridge (Melbourn)** – Melbourn Bury, Melbourn, Cambridgeshire, SG8 6DE. Tel: 01763 261151

**Canterbury (Boughton under Blean)** – The Garden Hotel, 167-169 The Street, Boughton under Blean, Faversham, ME13 9BH. Tel: 01227 751411

**Carlisle** – Number Thirty One, 31 Howard Place, Carlisle, CAI 1HR. Tel: 01228 597080

**Carlisle (Crosby-On-Eden)** – Crosby Lodge Country House Hotel, High Crosby, Crosby-On-Eden, Carlisle, CA6 4QZ. Tel: 01228 573618

**Cartmel** – Aynsome Manor Hotel, Cartmel, Grange-Over-Sands, LA11 6HH. Tel: 015395 36653

**Chagford** – Easton Court Hotel, Easton Cross, Chagford, TQ13 8JL. Tel: 01647 433469

**Cheddar (Axbridge)** – The Oak House Hotel, The Square, Axbridge, BS26 2AP. Tel: 01934 732444

**Cheltenham (Charlton Kings)** – Charlton Kings Hotel, Charlton Kings, Cheltenham, GL52 6UU. Tel: 01242 231061

**Cheltenham (Withington)** – Halewell, Halewell Close, Withington, GL54 4BN. Tel: 01242 890238

**Chichester (Apuldram)** – Crouchers Bottoms, Birdham Road, Apuldram, PO20 7EH. Tel: 01243 784995

**Chichester (Charlton)** – Woodstock House Hotel, Charlton, PO18 0HU. Tel: 01243 811666

**Chippenham** – Stanton Manor, Stanton Saint Quinton, SN14 6DQ. Tel: 01666 837552

**Chipping Campden (Broad Campden)** – The Malt House, Broad Campden, GL55 6UU. Tel: 01386 840295

**Clearwell** – Tudor Farmhouse Hotel & Restaurant, High Street, Clearwell, GL16 8JS. Tel: 01594 833046

**Coalville (Greenhill)** – Abbots Oak, Greenhill, Coalville, LE67 4UY. Tel: 01530 832 328

**Colchester (Frating)** – Hockley Place, Rectory Road, Frating, Colchester, CO7 7HG. Tel: 01206 251703

**Combe Martin (East Down)** – Ashelford, Ashelford, East Down, EX31 4LU. Tel: 01271 850469

**Crediton (Coleford)** – Coombe House Country Hotel, Coleford, Crediton, EX17 5BY. Tel: 01363 84487

**Dartmoor (Nr Two Bridges)** – Prince Hall Hotel, Two Bridges, Dartmoor, PL20 6SA. Tel: 01822 890403

**Dedham Vale (Nayland)** – Gladwins Farm, Harpers Hill, Nayland, CO6 4NU. Tel: 01206 262261

**Diss** – Salisbury House, Victoria Road, Diss, IP22 3JG. Tel: 01379 644738

**Dorchester (Lower Bockhampton)** – Yalbury Cottage Hotel, Lower Bockhampton, Dorchester, DT2 8PZ. Tel: 01305 262382

**Dover (Temple Ewell)** – The Woodville Hall, Temple Ewell, Dover, CT16 1DJ. Tel: 01304 825256

**Dover (West Cliffe)** – Wallett's Court, West Cliffe, St. Margaret's-at-Cliffe, CT15 6EW. Tel: 01304 852424

**Dronfield** – Manor House Hotel & Restaurant, High Street, Old Dronfield, SY18 6PY. Tel: 01246 413971

**Dulverton** – Ashwick Country House Hotel, Dulverton, TA22 9QD. Tel: 01398 323868

**Dunster** – The Exmoor House Hotel, West Street, Dunster, TA24 6SN. Tel: 01643 821268

**Enfield (London)** – Oak Lodge Hotel, 80 Village Road, Bush Hill Park, Enfield, EN1 2EU. Tel: 0181 360 7082

**Evesham (Harvington)** – The Mill At Harvington, Anchor Lane, Harvington, Evesham, WR11 5NR. Tel: 01386 870688

**Exeter (Dunchideock)** – The Lord Haldon Hotel, Dunchideock, EX6 7YF. Tel: 01392 832483

**Exford (Exmoor)** – The Crown Hotel, Exford, Exmoor National Park, TA24 7PP. Tel: 01643 831554/5

**Fakenham (Weekly Let)** – Vere Lodge, South Raynham, Fakenham, NR21 7HE. Tel: 01328 838261

**Falmouth (Mawnan Smith)** – Trelawne Hotel-The Hutches Restaurant, Mawnan Smith, TR11 5HS. Tel: 01326 250226

**Fenny Drayton (Leicestershire)** – White Wings, Quaker Close, Fenny Drayton, CV13 6BS. Tel: 01827 716100

**Fressingfield (Diss)** – Chippenhall Hall, Fressingfield, Eye, IP21 5TD. Tel: 01379 588180 / 586733

**Gatwick (Charlwood)** – Stanhill Court Hotel, Stanhill, Charlwood, RH6 0EP. Tel: 01293 862166

**Glossop** – The Wind In The Willows, Derbyshire Level, Glossop, SK13 9PT. Tel: 01457 868001

**Golant by Fowey** – The Cormorant Hotel, Golant, Fowey, PL23 1LL. Tel: 01726 833426

**Grasmere (Rydal Water)** – White Moss House, Rydal Water, Grasmere, LA22 9SE. Tel: 015394 35295

**Great Snoring** – The Old Rectory, Great Snoring, Fakenham, NR12 0HP. Tel: 01328 820597

**Hadleigh (Nedging)** – The Old Rectory, Nedging. Tel: 01449 740745

**Hampton Court (Hampton Wick)** – Chase Lodge, 10 Park Road, Hampton Wick, Kingston Upon Thames, KT1 4AS. Tel: 0181 943 1862

**Hamsterley Forest (Near Durham)** – Grove House, Hamsterley Forest, DL13 3NL. Tel: 01388 488203

**Harrogate** – The White House, 10 Park Parade, Harrogate, HG1 5AH. Tel: 01423 501388

**Hawes (Upper Wensleydale)** – Simonstone Hall, Hawes, DL8 3LY. Tel: 01969 667255

**Hawes (Wensleydale)** – Rookhurst Georgian Country House Hotel, West End, Gayle, Hawes, DL8 3RT. Tel: 01969 667454

**Haytor (Dartmoor)** – Bel Alp House, Haytor, TQ13 9XX. Tel: 01364 661217

**Helford River (Gillan)** – Tregildry Hotel, Gillan Manaccan, Helston, TR12 6HG. Tel: 01326 231378

**Helston** – Nansloe Manor, Meneage Road, Helston, TR13 0SB. Tel: 01326 574691

**Hereford (Fownhope)** – The Bowens Country House, Fownhope, HR1 4PS. Tel: 01432 860430

**Hereford (Ullingswick)** – The Steppes, Ullingswick, HR1 3JG. Tel: 01432 820424

**Honiton (Yarcombe)** – The Belfry Country Hotel, Yarcombe, EX14 9BD. Tel: 01404 861234

**Hope (Castleton)** – Underleigh House, Off Edale Road, Hope, Hope Valley, S33 6RF. Tel: 01433 621372

**Keswick (LakeThirlmere)** – Dale Head Hall Lakeside Hotel, Thirlmere, Keswick, CA12 4TN. Tel: 017687 72478

**Keswick (Newlands)** – Swinside Lodge Hotel, Grange Road, Newlands, Keswick, CA12 5UE. Tel: 017687 72948

**Keswick-On-Derwentwater** – Grange Country House Hotel, Manor Brow, Keswick-On-Derwentwater, CA12 4BA. Tel: 017687 72500

**Kingsbridge (Chillington)** – The White House, Chillington, Kingsbridge, TQ7 2JX. Tel: 01548 580580

**Kirkby Lonsdale** – Hipping Hall, Cowan Bridge, Kirkby Lonsdale, LA6 2JJ. Tel: 015242 71187

**Lavenham** – Lavenham Priory, Water Street, Lavenham, Sudbury, CO10 9RW. Tel: 01787 247404

**Leominster** – Lower Bache, Kimbolton, HR6 0ER. Tel: 01568 750304

**Lifton (Sprytown)** – The Thatched Cottage Country Hotel And Restaurant, Sprytown, Lifton, PL16 0AY. Tel: 01566 784224

**Lincoln** – D'Isney Place Hotel, Eastgate, Lincoln, LN2 4AA. Tel: 01522 538881

**Lincoln (Washingborough)** – Washingborough Hall, Church Hill, Washingborough, Lincoln, LN4 1BE. Tel: 01522 790340

**Looe (Talland Bay)** – Allhays Country House. Tel:

– Talland Bay, Looe, PL13 2JB, COUNTRY HOUSE. Tel:

**Looe (Widegates)** – Coombe Farm, Widegates, PL13 1QN. Tel: 01503 240223

**Ludlow (Diddlebury)** – Delbury Hall, Diddlebury, Craven Arms, SY7 9DH. Tel: 01584 841267

**Ludlow (Overton)** – Overton Grange Hotel, Overton, Ludlow, SY8 4AD. Tel: 01584 873500

**Luton (Little Offley)** – Little Offley, Hitchin, SG5 3BU. Tel: 01462 768243

**Lydford (Vale Down)** – Moor View House, Vale Down, Lydford, EX20 4BB. Tel: 01822 820220

**Lyme Regis (Charmouth)** – Thatch Lodge Hotel, The Street, Charmouth, DT6 6PQ. Tel: 01297 560407

**Lymington (Hordle)** – The Gordleton Mill Hotel, Silver Street, Hordle, SO41 6DJ. Tel: 01590 682219

**Lynton** – Hewitt's Hotel, North Walk, Lynton, EX35 6HJ. Tel: 01598 752293

**Maidstone (Boughton Monchelsea)** – Tanyard, Wierton Hill, Boughton Monchelsea, ME17 4JT. Tel: 01622 744705

**Malton** – Newstead Grange, Norton-On-Derwent, Malton, YO17 9PJ. Tel: 01653 692502

**Matlock (Dethick)** – The Manor Farmhouse, Dethick, Matlock, DE4 5GG. Tel: 01609 534246

**Middlecombe (Minehead)** – Periton Park Hotel, Middlecombe, TA24 8SW. Tel: 01643 706885

**Middleham (Wensleydale)** – Millers House Hotel, Middleham, Wensleydale, DL8 4NR. Tel: 01969 622630

**Midsomer Norton (Bath)** – The Old Priory, Church Square, Midsomer Norton, Bath, BA3 2HX. Tel: 01761 416784

**Minchinhampton** – Burleigh Court, Minchinhampton, GL5 2PF. Tel: 01453 883804

**Minehead** – Channel House Hotel, Church Path, Minehead, TA24 5QG. Tel: 01643 703229

**Minehead (Exmoor)** – The Beacon Country House Hotel, Beacon Road, Minehead, TA24 5SD. Tel: 01643 703476

**Morchard Bishop** – Wigham, Morchard Bishop, EX17 6RJ. Tel: 01363 877350

**New Romney (Littlestone)** – Romney Bay House, Coast Road, Littlestone, New Romney, TN28 8QY. Tel: 01797 364747

**North Walsham** – Beechwood Hotel, Cromer Road, North Walsham, NR28 0HD. Tel: 01692 403231

**North Walsham** – Elderton Lodge Hotel & Restaurant, Gunton Park, Thorpe Market, NR11 8TZ. Tel: 01263 833547

**Norwich** – The Beeches Hotel & Victorian Gardens, 4-6 Earlham Road, Norwich, NR2 3DB. Tel: 01603 621167

**Norwich (Coltishall )** – Norfolk Mead Hotel, Coltishall, Norwich, NR12 7DN. Tel: 01603 737531

**Norwich (Drayton)** – The Stower Grange, School Road, Drayton, NR8 6EF. Tel: 01603 860210

**Norwich (Hethel)** – The Moat House, Rectory Lane, Hethel, Norwich, NR14 8HD. Tel: 01508 570149

**Norwich (Old Catton)** – Catton Old Hall, Lodge Lane, Catton, Norwich, NR6 7HG. Tel: 01603 419379

**Norwich (Thorpe St Andrew)** – The Old Rectory, 103 Yarmouth Road, Thorpe St Andrew, Norwich, NR7 0HF. Tel: 01603 700772

**Nottingham (Ruddington)** – The Cottage Country House Hotel, Ruddington, Nottingham, NG11 6LA. Tel: 01159 846882

**Oswestry** – Pen-y-Dyffryn Country Hotel, Rhydycroesau, SY10 7JD. Tel: 01691 653700

**Oulton Broad** – Ivy House Farm, Ivy Lane, Oulton Broad, Lowestoft, NR33 8HY. Tel: 01502 501353

**Owlpen** – Owlpen Manor, GL11 5BZ. Tel: 01453 860261

**Oxford (Kingston Bagpuize)** – Fallowfields, Kingston Bagpuize With Southmoor, OX13 5BH. Tel: 01865 820416

**Peterborough (Southorpe)** – Midstone House, Southorpe, Stamford, PE9 3BX. Tel: 01780 740136

**Porlock Weir** – The Cottage Hotel, Porlock Weir, Porlock, TA24 8PB. Tel: 01643 863300

**Porthleven (Nr Helston)** – Tye Rock Hotel, Loe Bar Road, Porthleven, TR13 9EW. Tel: 01326 572695

**Portsmouth** – The Beaufort Hotel, 71 Festing Road, Portsmouth, PO4 0NQ. Tel: 01705 823707

**Pulborough** – Chequers Hotel, Church Place, Pulborough, RH20 1AD. Tel: 01798 872486

**Redditch (Ipsley)** – The Old Rectory, Ipsley Lane, Redditch, B98 0AP. Tel: 01527 523000

**Ross-On-Wye (Glewstone)** – Glewstone Court, HR6 6AW. Tel: 01989 770367

**Rye** – White Vine House, High Street, Rye, TN31 7JF. Tel: 01797 224748

**Saham Toney (Thetford)** – Broom Hall, Richmond Road, Saham Toney, Thetford, IP25 7EX. Tel: 01953 882125

**Saunton** – Preston House Hotel, Saunton, Braunton, EX33 1LG. Tel: 01271 890472

**Seavington St Mary, Nr Ilminster** – The Pheasant Hotel, Seavington St Mary, TA19 0QH. Tel: 01460 240502

**Sedgeford (Weekly Let)** – The Sedgeford Estate, Bordering Royal Estate, Sedgeford, PE36 5LT. Tel: 01485 572855

**Sheffield (Chapeltown)** – Staindrop Lodge, Lane End, Chapeltown, Sheffield, S30 4HH. Tel: 0114 284 6727

**Sherborne** – The Eastbury Hotel, Long Street, Sherborne, DT9 3BY. Tel: 01935 813131

**Shipton Under Wychwood** – The Shaven Crown Hotel, High Street, Shipton Under Wychwood, OX7 6BA. Tel: 01993 830330

**Simonsbath (Exmoor)** – Simonsbath House Hotel, Simonsbath, Exmoor, TA24 7SH. Tel: 01643 831259

**South Molton** – Marsh Hall Country House Hotel, South Molton, EX36 3HQ. Tel: 01769 572666

**St. Ives (Cambridge)** – Olivers Lodge Hotel & Restaurant, Needingworth Road, St. Ives, PE17 4JP. Tel: 01480 463252

**St Ives (Trink)** – The Countryman At Trink Hotel & Restaurant, Old Coach Road, St Ives, TR26 3JQ. Tel: 01736 797571

**St Mawes (Ruan Highlanes)** – The Hundred House Hotel, Ruan Highlanes, TR2 5JR. Tel: 01872 501336

**Stamford (Ketton)** – The Priory, Church Road, Ketton, Stamford, PE9 3RD. Tel: 01780 720215

**Stamford (Tallington)** – The Old Mill, Mill Lane, Tallington, Stamford, PE9 4RR. Tel: 01780 740815

**Staverton (Nr Totnes)** – Kingston House, Staverton, Totnes, TQ9 6AR. Tel: 01803 762 235

**Stevenage (Hitchin)** – Redcoats Farmhouse Hotel & Restaurant, Redcoats Green, SG4 7JR. Tel: 01438 729500

**Stonor (Henley-on-Thames)** – The Stonor Arms, Stonor, RG9 6HE. Tel: 01491 638345

**Stow-On-The-Wold (Kingham)** – Conygree Gate Hotel, Kingham, OX7 6YA . Tel: 01608 658389

**Stratford-upon-Avon (Loxley)** – Glebe Farm House, Loxley, CV35 9JW. Tel: 01789 842501

**Sudbury** – Tarantella Hotel & Restaurant, Sudbury Hall, Melford Road, Sudbury, CO10 6XT. Tel: 01787 378879

**Sutton Coldfield** – Marston Farm Country Hotel, Bodymoor Heath, Sutton Coldfield, B76 9JD. Tel: 01827 872133

**Taunton (Fivehead)** – Langford Manor, Fivehead, Taunton, TA3 6PH. Tel: 01460 281674

**Taunton (Lydeard St.Lawrence)** – Higher Vexford House, Higher Vexford, Lydeard St.Lawrence, TA4 3QF. Tel: 01984 656267

**Tewkesbury (Kemerton)** – Upper Court, Kemerton, GL20 7HY. Tel: 01386 725351

**Tintagel (Trenale)** – Trebrea Lodge, Trenale, Tintagel, PL34 0HR. Tel: 01840 770410

**Titchwell** – Titchwell Manor Hotel, Titchwell, Brancaster, King's Lynn, PE31 8BB. Tel: 01485 210221

**Truro** – The Royal Hotel, Lemon Street, Truro, TR1 2QB. Tel: 01872 270345

**Uckfield** – Hooke Hall, High Street, Uckfield, TN22 1EN. Tel: 01825 761578

**Venn Ottery (Near Ottery St. Mary)** – Venn Ottery Barton, Venn Ottery, Ottery St. Mary, EX11 1RZ. Tel: 01404 812733

**Wareham (East Stoke)** – Kemps Country House Hotel & Restaurant, East Stoke, Wareham, BH20 6AL. Tel: 01929 462563

**Warwick (Claverdon)** – The Ardencote Manor Hotel & Country Club, Lye Green Road, Claverdon, CU35 8LS. Tel: 01926 843111

**Wells** – Glencot House, Glencot Lane, Wookey Hole, BA5 1BH. Tel: 01749 677160

**Wells** – Beryl, Wells, BA5 3JP. Tel: 01749 678738

**Whitby** – Dunsley Hall, Dunsley, Whitby, YO21 3TL. Tel: 01947 893437

**Wimborne Minster** – Beechleas, 17 Poole Road, Wimborne Minster, BH21 1QA. Tel: 01202 841684

**Wincanton (Holbrook)** – Holbrook House Hotel, Wincanton, BA9 8BS. Tel: 01963 32377

**Winchelsea** – The Country House At Winchelsea, Hastings Road, Winchelsea, TN36 4AD. Tel: 01797 226669

**Windermere** – Braemount House Hotel, Sunny Bank Road, Windermere, LA23 2EN. Tel: 015394 45967

**Windermere** – Quarry Garth Country House Hotel, Windermere, LA23 1LF. Tel: 015394 88282

**Windermere (Bowness)** – Fayrer Garden House Hotel, Lyth Valley Road, Bowness-On - Windermere, LA23 3JP. Tel: 015394 88195

**Woodbridge** – Wood Hall Hotel & Country Club, Shottisham, Woodbridge, IP12 3EG. Tel: 01394 411283

**York (Escrick)** – The Parsonage Country House Hotel, Escrick, York, YO4 6LF. Tel: 01904 728111

**Yoxford** – Hope House, High Street, Yoxford, Saxmundham, IP17 3HP. Tel: 01728 668281

## *WALES*

**Aberdovey** – Plas Penhelig Country House Hotel, Aberdovey. Tel: 01654 767676

**Abergavenny (Glangrwyney)** – Glangrwyney Court, Glangrwyney, NP8 1ES. Tel: 01873 811288

**Abergavenny (Govilon)** – Llanwenarth House, Govilon, Abergavenny, NP7 9SF. Tel: 01873 830289

**Abergavenny (Llanfihangel Crucorney)** – Penyclawdd Court, Llanfihangel Crucorney, Abergavenny, NP7 7LB. Tel: 01873 890719

**Betws-y-Coed** – Tan-y-Foel, Capel Garmon, LL26 0RE. Tel: 01690 710507

**Brecon (Three Cocks)** – Old Gwernyfed Country Manor, Felindre, Three Cocks, Brecon, LD3 0SU. Tel: 01497 847376

**Caernarfon** – Ty'n Rhos Country House, Llanddeiniolen, Caernarfon, LL55 3AE. Tel: 01248 670489

**Cardigan (Cilgerran)** – The Pembrokeshire Retreat, Rhosygilwen Mansion, Cilgerran, SA43 2TW. Tel: 01239 841387

**Conwy** – Berthlwyd Hall Hotel, Llechwedd, LL32 8DQ. Tel: 01492 592409

**Conwy** – The Old Rectory, Llansanffried Glan Conwy, Nr Conwy, Colwyn Bay, LL28 5LF. Tel: 01492 580611

**Dolgellau (Ganllwyd)** – Dolmelynllyn Hall, Ganllwyd, Dolgellau, LL40 2HP. Tel: 01341 440273

**Harlech (Llanbedr)** – Aber Artro Hall, Llanbedr, LL45 2PA. Tel: 01341 241374

**Tenby (Waterwynch Bay)** – Waterwynch House Hotel, Waterwynch Bay, Tenby, SA70 8TJ. Tel: 01834 842464

**Tintern** – Parva Farmhouse and Restaurant, Tintern, Chepstow, NP6 6SQ. Tel: 01291 689411

## *SCOTLAND*

**Ballater,Royal Deeside** – Balgonie Country House, Braemar Place, Royal Deeside, Ballater, AB35 5NQ. Tel: 013397 55482

**Blairlogie (Nr Stirling)** – Blairlogie House, Blairlogie by Stirling, FK9 5QE. Tel: 01259 761441

**Dalbeattie** – Auchenskeoch Lodge, By Dalbeattie, DG5 4PG. Tel: 01387 780277

**Dalbeattie** – Broomlands House, Haugh Road, Dalbeattie, DG5 4AR. Tel: 01556 611463

**Dingwall (Highlands)** – Kinkell House, Easter Kinkell, By Dingwall, IV7 8HY. Tel: 01349 861270

**Drumnadrochit (Loch Ness)** – Polmaily House Hotel, Drumnadrochit, Loch Ness, IV3 6XT. Tel: 01456 450343

**Edinburgh** – No 22, Murrayfield Gardens, Edingburgh, EH12 6DF. Tel: 0131 337 3569

**Fife (Kettlebridge)** – Chapel House, Kettlebridge, KY15 7TU. Tel: 01337 831790

**Fintry (Stirlingshire)** – Culcreuch Castle Hotel, Fintry, Loch Lomond, G63 0LW. Tel: 01360 860555

**Fort William** – Ashburn House, 5 Achintore Road, Fort William, PH33 6RQ. Tel: 01397 706000

**Glasgow (Stewarton)** – Chapletoun House, Stewarton, KA3 3ED. Tel: 015604 82696

**Grantown-on-Spey** – Ardconnel House, Woodlands Terrace, Grantown-on-Spey, PH26 3JU. Tel: 01479 872104

**Huntley (Bridge of Marnoch)** – The Old Manse of Marnoch, Bridge of Marnoch, By Huntley, AB54 5RS. Tel: 01466 780873

**Inverness** – Culduthel Lodge, 14 Culduthel Road, Inverness, IV2 4AG. Tel: 01463 240089

**Isle Of Harris** – Ardvourlie Castle, Aird amhulaidh, Isle Of Harris, HS3 3AB. Tel: 01859 502307

**Isle Of Mull** – Killiechronan, Killiechronan, PA72 6JU. Tel: 01680 300403

**Kentallen Of Appin** – Ardsheal House, Kentallen Of Appin, PA38 4BX. Tel: 01631 740227

**Killiecrankie,By Pitlochry** – The Killiecrankie Hotel, Killiecrankie, By Pitlochry, PH16 5LG. Tel: 01796 473220

**Kinlochbervie** – The Kinlochbervie Hotel, Kinlochbervie, By Lairg, IV27 4RP. Tel: 01971 521275

**Kinross (Cleish)** – Nivingston House, Cleish, By Kinross, KY13 7LS. Tel: 01577 850216

**Moffat** – Well View Hotel, Ballplay Road, Moffat, DG10 9JU. Tel: 01683 220184

**Nairn (Auldearn)** – Boath House, Auldearn, Nairn, IV12 5TE. Tel: 01667 454896

**Oban** – The Manor House Hotel, Gallanch Road, Oban, PA34 4LS. Tel: 01631 562087

**Oban** – Dungallen House Hotel, Gallanach Road, Oban, PA34 4PD. Tel: 01631 563799

**Old Meldrum (By Aberdeen)** – Meldrum House, Old Meldrum, AB57 0AE. Tel: 01651 872294

**Perth** – Dupplin Castle, Dupplin Estate, By Perth, PH2 0PY. Tel: 01738 623224

**Perth (Guildtown)** – Newmiln Country House, Newmiln Estate, Guildtown, Perth, PH2 6AE. Tel: 01738 552364

**Pitlochry** – Dunfallandy House, Logierait Road, Pitlochry, PH16 5NA. Tel: 01796 472648

**Port Appin** – Druimneil, Port Appin, PA38 4DQ. Tel: 01631 730228

**Port Of Menteith** – The Lake Hotel, Port Of Menteith, FK8 3RA. Tel: 01877 385258

**Strathtummel (By Pitlochry)** – Queen's View Hotel, Strathtummel, By Pitlochry, PH16 5NR. Tel: 01796 473291

**Tongue (Sutherland)** – Borgie Lodge Hotel, Skerray, By Tongue, Sutherland, KW14 7TH. Tel: 01641 521332

## *IRELAND*

**Annalong (Co Down N.Ireland)** – Glassdrumman Lodge Country House & Restaurant, 85 Mill Road, Annalong, BT34 4RH. Tel: 013967 68451

**Caragh Lake Co Kerry** – Caragh Lodge, Caragh Lake. Tel: 00 353 66 69115

**Carragh Lake Co Kerry** – Ard-Na-Sihde. Tel: 00 353 66 69105

**Cashel Co Tipperary** – Cashel Palace Hotel, Cashel. Tel: 00 353 62 62707

**Dublin** – Aberdeen Lodge, 53-55 Park Avenue, Ailesbury Road. Tel: 00 353 1 2838155

**Kilkee Co Clare** – Halpins Hotel & Vittles Restaurant, Erin Street, Kilkee. Tel: 00 353 65 56032

**Killarney Co Kerry** – Earls Court House, Woodlawn Junction, Muckross Road. Tel: 00 353 64 34009

**Letterkenny (Co Donegal)** – Castle Grove Country House, Ramelton Road, Letterkenny. Tel: 010 353 745 1118

**Portaferry (Co Down N Ireland)** – Portaferry Hotel, The Strand, Portaferry, BT22 1PE. Tel: 012477 28231

**Riverstown,Co Sligo** – Coopershill House, Riverstown. Tel: 00 353 71 65108

**Skibbereen Co.Cork** – Liss Ard Lake Lodge, Skibbereen . Tel: 00 353 28 22365

**Sligo,Co Sligo** – Markree Castle, Colooney. Tel: 00 353 71 67800

**Wicklow,Co Wicklow** – The Old Rectory, Wicklow Town. Tel: 00 353 404 67048

## *CHANNEL ISLANDS*

**Guernsey (Castel)** – Hotel Hougue Du Pommier, Hougue Du Pommier Road, Castel, GY5 7FQ. Tel: 01481 56531

**Guernsey (Fermain Bay)** – La Favorita Hotel, Fermain Bay, GY4 6SD. Tel: 01481 35666

**Guernsey (St Martin)** – Bella Luce Hotel & Restaurant, La Fosse, St Martin, Guernsey. Tel: 01481 38764

**Jersey (St Aubin)** – Hotel La Tour, Rue de Croquet, St Aubin, Jersey, JE3 8BR. Tel: 01534 43770

# Johansens Recommended Hotels Europe

## *AUSTRIA*

**Altaussee** – Landhaus Hubertushof, Puchen, A-8992 Altaussee, Steiermark. Tel: 00 43 36 22 71 28 080

**Bad Gastein** – Hotel & Spa Haus Hirt, Kaiserhofstrasse, 14, Bad Gastein. Tel: 43 64 34 27 97 48

**Bregenz** – Deuring Schlössle, Ehre-Guta-Platz 4, A-6900, Bregenz. Tel: 43 55 74 47800-80

**Dürnstein** – Hotel Schloss Dürnstein, A-3601, Dürnstein. Tel: 43 2711 351

**Igls** – Schlosshotel Igls, Viller Steig 2, A-6080 Igls, Tirol. Tel: 43 512 3786 79

**Igls** – Sporthotel Igls, Hilberstrasse 17, A-6080 Igls, Tirol. Tel: 512 37 86 79

**Innsbruck** – Romantik Hotel Schwarzer Adler, Kaiserjägerstrasse 2, A-6020, Innsbruck. Tel: 43 512 561697

**Kitzbühel** – Romantik Hotel Tennerhof, A-6370, Kitzbühel, Griesenauweg 26. Tel: 43 53566 318170

**Klagenfurt** – Hotel Palais Porcia, Neuer Platz 13, A-9020, Klagenfurt. Tel: 43 463 51 159030

**Kötshach-Mauthen** – Landhaus Kellerwand, A-9640 Kötshach-Mauthen, Mauthen 24. Tel: 43 47 15 37 816

**Lech** – Sporthotel Kristiania, Omesberg 331, A-6764 Lech/Arlberg. Tel: 43 55 83 35 50

**Pörtschach Am Wörther See** – Hotel Schloss Leonstain, Hauptstrasse 228, Pörtschach Am Wörther See. Tel: 43 4272 2823

**Salzburg** – Hotel Altstadt Radisson SAS, Rudolfskai 28 / Judengasse 15, A-5020, Salzburg. Tel: 43 662 8485716

**Salzburg** – Hotel Auersperg, Auerspergstrasse 61, A-5021, Salzburg. Tel: 43 662 8894455

**Salzburg** – Hotel Schloss Mönchstein, Mönchsberg Park A-5020, 26-Joh A-5020, City Center, Salzburg. Tel: 43 662 84 85 59

**Salzburg** – Schloss Haunsperg, A-5411, Oberalm bei Hallein, Salzburg. Tel: 00 43 62 45 85 680

**Schwarzenberg im Bregenzerwald** – Romantik-Hotel Gasthof Hirschen, Hof 14, A-6867, Schwarzenberg. Tel: 43 55 12/29 44 20

**Seefeld in Tyrol** – Hotel Klosterbräu, A-6100, Seefeld/Tirol. Tel: 43 5212 3885

**St Wolfgang am See** – Romantik Hotel im Weissen Rössl, A-5360, St Wolfgang am See, Salzkammergut. Tel: 43 61 38 23 06 41

**Vienna** – Hotel im Palais Schwarzenberg, Schwarzenbergplatz 9, A-1030, Vienna. Tel: 43 1 798 4714

**Zürs** – Thurnhers Alpenhof, A-6763, Zürs/Arlberg. Tel: 43 5583 3330

## *BELGIUM*

**Antwerp** – Firean Hotel, Karel Oomsstraat 6, B-2018 Antwerp. Tel: 00 32 3238 11 68

**Antwerp** – Hotel Rubens, Oude Beurs 29, B-2000 Antwerp. Tel: 00 32 32 26 95 82

**Bruges** – Die Swaene, Steenhouwersdijk, B-8000, Bruges. Tel: 32-50- 33 66 74

**Bruges** – Hotel de Orangerie, Kartuizerinnenstraat10, B-8000, Bruges. Tel: 00 32 50 33 30 16

**Bruges** – Hotel Hansa, N. Desparsstraat 11, B-8000, Bruges. Tel: 32 50 33 42 05

**Bruges** – Hotel Prinsenhof, Ontvangersstraat 9, B-8000, Bruges. Tel: 32-50- 34 23 21

**Bruges** – Romantik Pandhotel, Pandreitje 16, B-8000, Bruges. Tel: 32 50 34 05 56

**Brussels** – L'Amigo, 1-3 Rue L'Amigo, B-1000, Brussels. Tel: 32 2 513 52 77

**Brussels** – Stanhope Hotel, 9 Rue du Commerce, B-1000, Brussels. Tel: 32 2 512 17 08

**Lanaken** – La Butte Aux Bois, Paalsteenlaan 90, 3B-620 Lanaken. Tel: 32 89 72 16 47

**Malmédy** – Hostellerie Trôs Marets, Route Des Trôs Marets, B-4960, Malmédy. Tel: 32-80- 33 79 10

**March-En-Famenne** – Château d'Hassonville, Marche-En-Famenne, 6900. Tel: 32 84 31 60 27

**Stervoort** – Scholteshof, Kermstraat 130, B-3512, Stevoort. Tel: 32 11 25 43 28

**Vieuxville** – Château de Palogne, Route du Palogne 3, B-4190, Vieuxville. Tel: 32 86 21 38 76

## *BRITISH ISLES*

**Ashburton** – Holne Chase Hotel, Nr Ashburton, Devon TQ13 7NS. Tel: 44 1364 631471

**Ashford** – Eastwell Manor, Boughton Lees, Ashford, Kent TN25 4HR. Tel: 44 1233 219955

**Berwick upon Tweed** – Tillmouth Park, Cornhill-On-Tweed, Nr Berwick, Northumberland TD12 4UU. Tel: 44 1890 882255

**Chester** – The Chester Grosvenor, Eastgate, Chester, Cheshire, CH1 1LT. Tel: 44 1244 313246

**Chester** – Crabwall Manor, Whitebrook, Monmouth, Gwent NP5 4TX. Tel: 44 1600 860254

**Coventry,Berkswell** – Nailcote Hall, Nailcote Lane, Berkswell, Warwickshire. Tel: 44 1203 470720

**Exford** – The Crown Hotel, Exford, Exmoor, National Park, Somerset TA24 7PP. Tel: 44 1643 831554/5

**Gatwick** – South Lodge Hotel, Lower Beeding, Nr Horsham, West Sussex RH13 6PS. Tel: 44 1403 891711

**Haslemere** – Lythe Hill Hotel, Petworth Road, Haslemere, Surrey. Tel: 44 1428 644131

**Jersey** – The Atlantic Hotel, La Moye, St Brelade, Jersey. Tel: 44 1534 44102

**Lake Ullswater** – Sharrow Bay Country House Hotel, Howtown, Lake Ullswater, Penrith, Cumbria. Tel: 44 1684 86349

**London, Mayfair** – The Ascott Mayfair, 49 Hill Street, London W1. Tel: 44 171 499 0705

**London, Knightsbridge** – The Beaufort, 33 Beaufort Gardens, Knightsbridge, London SW2 1PP. Tel: 44 171 589 2834

**London, Knightsbridge** – Basil Street Hotel, Basil Street, London SW3 1AH. Tel: 44 171 581 3693

**London, Knightsbridge** – Beaufort House Apartments, 45 Beaufort Gardens, London SW3 1PN. Tel: 44 171 584 6532

## Johansens Recommended Hotels Europe continued

**London, South Kensington** – Blakes Hotel, 33 Roland Gardens, London SW7 3PF. Tel: 44 171 373 0442

**London, Knightsbridge** – The Cadogan, Sloane Street, London SW9X 1SG. Tel: 44 171 2450994

**London, Wimbledon Common** – Cannizaro House, West Side, Wimbledon Common, London SW19 4UE. Tel: 44 181 879 7338

**London, Knightsbridge** – The Cliveden Town House, 26 Cadogan Gardens, London SW3 2RP. Tel: 44 171 730 0236

**London** – The Dorchester, Park Lane, Mayfair, London W1A 2HJ. Tel: 44 171 409 0114

**London, Chelsea** – Draycott House Apartments, 10 Draycott Avenue, Chelsea, London SW3 3AA. Tel: 44 171 225 3694

**London, Holland Park** – The Halcyon, 81 Holland Park, London W11 3RZ. Tel: 44 171 229 5816

**London, Kensington** – Harrington Hall, 5-25 Harrington Gardens, London SW7 4JW. Tel: 44 171 396 9090

**London** – The Hempel, Hempel Garden Square, 31-35 Craven Hill Gardens, London W2 3EA. Tel: 44 171 402 4666

**London** – The Leonard, 15 Seymour Street, London W1H 5AA. Tel: 44 171 935 6700

**London** – The Milestone, 1-2 Kensington Court, London W8 5DL. Tel: 44 171 917 1010

**London South Kensington** – Number Sixteen, 16 Sumner Place, London SW7 3EG. Tel: 44 171 584 8615

**London,Kensington** – Pembridge Court Hotel, 34 Pembridge Gardens, London W2 4DX. Tel: 44 171 727 4982

**Lynmouth** – The Rising Sun, Harbourside, Lynmouth, Devon EX35 6EQ. Tel: 44 1598 753223

**Maidenhead, Taplow** – Cliveden, Taplow, Berkshire SL6 OJF. Tel: 44 1628 661837

**Salcombe** – Soar Mill Cove, Salcombe, South Devon TQ7 3DS. Tel: 44 1548 561566

**Southwold** – The Swan, Market Place, Southwold, Suffolk IP18 64G. Tel: 44 1502 722186

**Streatley-On-Thames, Reading** – Swan Diplomat, Streatley-On-Thames, Reading, Berkshire RG8 9HR. Tel: 44 1491 872554.

**Wallingford, North Stoke** – The Springs Hotel, North Stoke, Wallingford, Oxfordshire OX10 6BE. Tel: 44 1491 836877

**Woodbridge** – Seckford Hall, Woodbridge, Suffolk IP13 6NU. Tel: 44 1394 380610

**York** – The Grange, 1 Clifton, York, North Yorkshire YO3 6AA. Tel: 44 1904 644744

### CYPRUS

**Paphos** – The Annabelle, P.O. Box 401, Paphos. Tel: 357 62 45 502

### CZECH REPUBLIC

**Prague** – Hotel Sieber, Slezska 55, CZ-130 00, Prague. Tel: 422 24 25 00 27

### DENMARK

**Fanø** – Sønderho Kro, Kroplasden 11, Sønderho DK-6720, Fanø. Tel: 45 75 16 43 85

**Hornbaek** – Havreholm Slot, 4 klosterrisvej, Havreholm, DK-3100 Hornbaek. Tel: 45 4975 8023

**Nyborg** – Hotel Hesselet, Christianslundsvej 119, DK-5800 Nyborg. Tel: 45 65 31 29 58

### FRANCE

**Arles Le Sambuc** – **Le** Mas de Peint, Le Sambuc, F-13200 Arles. Tel: 33 90 4 97 22 20

**Avallon** – Château de Vault de Lugny, 11 Rue de Château, F-89200, Avallon. Tel: 33 3 86 34 16 36

**Baix** – La Cardinale et Sa Residence, Quai du Rhône, F-07210 Baix. Tel: 33 4 75 85 82 07

**Biarritz** – Hôtel du Palais, F-64200 Biarritz, Avenue de L'Impératrice. Tel: 33 5 59 41 67 99

**Cannes** – Hôtel Savoy, 5 Rue François Einesy, F-6400, Cannes. Tel: 33 4 93 68 25 59

**Cannes** – Star Clippers, Fred Olsen Travel, Fred Olsen House, White House Road, Ipswich, Suffolk. Tel: 44 1473 292200

**Chambéry-le-Vieux** – Château de Candie, Rue du Bois de Candie, F-73000 Chambéry-le-Vieux. Tel: 33 47 99 66 310

**Chamonix** – Le Hameau Albert 1er, 119 Impasse du Montenvers, F-74402, Chamonix-Mont Blanc. Tel: 33 4 50 55 95 48

**Champigné** – Chateau des Briottieres, F-49330, Champigné. Tel: 33 2 41 42 01 55

**Chênehutte-Les-Tuffeaux** – Le Prieuré, F-49350, Chênehutte-Les-Tuffeaux, Saumur. Tel: 33 2 41 67 92 24

**Connelles** – Le Moulin de Connelles, 39 Route d'Amfreville-Sous-Les-Monts, F-27430, Connelles. Tel: 33 2 32 59 21 83

**Courchevel** – Hotel Annapurna, F-73120, Courchevel, 1850. Tel: 33 4 79 08 15 31

**Courchevel** – Hôtel des Trois Vallées, BP 22, F-73122, Courchevel, Cedex. Tel: 33 4 79 08 17 98

**Courchevel** – Le Byblos des Neiges, BP 98, F-73122, Courchevel. Tel: 33 4 79 00 98 01

**Deauville** – Hôtel Royal, Boulevard Cornuché, F-14800, Deauville, Calvados. Tel: 33 2 31 98 66 34

**Divonne-Les-Bains** – Grand Hôtel de Divonne, Avenue des Thermes, F-1220, Divonne-Les-Bains. Tel: 33 4 50 40 34 24

**Elincourt-Sainte-Marguerite** – Château de Bellinglise, F-60157 Elincourt-Sainte-Marguerite, Oise. Tel: 33 3 44 96 03 00

**Épernay** – Hostellerie La Briqueterie, 4 Route de Sézanne, Vinay F-51530, Epernay. Tel: 33 3 26 59 92 10

**Eze Village** – Château Eza, Rue de la Pise, F-6360, Eze Village. Tel: 33 4 93 41 16 64

**Gérardmer** – Hostellerie Les Bas Rupts et Son Chalet Fleuri, F-88400 Gérardmer, Vosges. Tel: 33 29 63 00 40

**Gressy-en-France** – Le Manoir de Gressy, F-77410, Gressy-en-France, Seine et Marne. Tel: 33 1 60 26 45 46

**Honfleur** – La Cháumiere, Route du Littoral, F-14600, Honfleur. Tel: 33 2 31 89 59 23

**Honfleur** – La Ferme Saint Siméon, Rue Adolphe-Marais, F-14600, Honfleur. Tel: 33 2 31 89 48 48

**Honfleur** – Le Manoir du Butin, Phare du Butin, F-14600, Honfleur. Tel: 33 2 31 89 59 23

**Langeais** – Château de Rochecotte, Saint Patrice, F-37130 Langeais. Tel: 33 2 47 96 90 59

**Les Issambres** – Villa Saint Elme, Corniche des Issambres, F-83380 Les Issambres. Tel: 33 4 94 49 63 18

**Lyon** – La Tour Rose, 22 Rue de Boeuf, F-69005, Lyon. Tel: 33 4 78 42 26 02

**Méribel** – L'Antarès, Le Belvédère, F-73550, Méribel les Allues. Tel: 33 4 79 23 28 18

**Monestier** – Château des Vigiers, F-24240 Monestier. Tel: 33 5 53 61 50 20

**Montlouis-sur-Loire** – Château de la Bourdaisière, F-37270 Montlouis-sur-Loire. Tel: 33 2 47 45 09 11

**Mougins** – Hôtel de Mougins, 205 Avenue du Golf, F-06250 Mougins. Tel: 33 4 92 92 17 08

**Nice** – Hôtel Westminster, Promanade des Anglais, F-06000 Nice. Tel: 33 4 93 82 45 35

**Paris** – Hôtel Buci Latin, 34 Rue de Buci, F-75006, Paris. Tel: 33 1 4329 6744

**Paris** – Hôtel de Crillon, 10 Place de la Concorde, F-75008, Paris. Tel: 33 1 4471 1502

**Paris** – Hôtel de L'Arcade, 9 Rue de L'Arcade, F-75008, Paris. Tel: 33 1 40 07 03 07

**Paris** – Hôtel L'Horset Opera, 18 Rue d'Antin, F-75002, Paris. Tel: 33 1 42 66 55 54

**Paris** – Hôtel Vernet, 25 rue Vernet, F-75008, Paris. Tel: 33 1 44 31 85 69

**Paris** – Hôtel Westminster, 13 Rue de la Paix, F-75002, Paris. Tel: 33 1 4260 3066

**Paris** – L'Hôtel Pergolese, 3 Rue Pergolèse, F-75116, Paris. Tel: 33 1 45 00 12 11

**Paris** – Relais St Germain, 9 Carrefour de L'Odéon, F-75006, Paris. Tel: 33 1 46 33 45 30

**Propriano/Corsica** – Grand Hotel Miramar, Route de la Corniche, F-20110, Propriano, Corsica. Tel: 00 33 4 95 76 13 14

**Roquebrune Cap-Martin/Monaco** – Grand Hotel Vista Palace, Route de la Grande Corniche, F-06190 Roquebrune/Cap-Martin. Tel: 33 4 93 35 18 94

**Sciez sur Léman** – Château de Coudrée, Domaine de Coudrée, Bonnatrait, F-74140 Sciez sur Léman. Tel: 33 4 50 72 57 28

**Serre-Chevalier** – L'Auberge du Choucas, 5220, Monetier-Les-Bains, Serre-Chevalier F-1550. Tel: 33 4 92 24 51 60

**St Paterne** – Château de Saint Paterne, F-72610 Saint Paterne. Tel: 33 2 3329 16 71

**St Paul** – Mas d'Artigny, Route de la Colle, F-6570, Saint-Paul. Tel: 33 4 93 32 95 36

**St Rémy** – Domaine de Valmouriane, Petite route des Baux, F-13210, Saint Remy de provence. Tel: 33 4 90 92 37 32

**St-Rémy-de-Provence** – Château des Alpilles, Route Départementale 31, Ancienne route du Grés, F-13210, St-Rémy-de-Provence. Tel: 33 4 90 92 45 17

**St Tropez** – Hôtel Byblos, Avenue Paul Signac, F-83990, St Tropez. Tel: 33 4 94 56 68 01

**St Tropez** – Hôtel Sube, 15 Quai Suffren, F-83390, St Tropez. Tel: 33 4 94548908

**St Tropez** – Hôtel Villa Belrose, Boulevard des Crêtes, La Grande Bastide, F-83580 Gassin. Tel: 33 4 94 55 97 98

**Strasbourg** – Hôtel Regent Petite France, 5 rue des Moulins, 67000, Strasbourg. Tel: 33 3 88 76 43 76

### GERMANY

**Bad Herrenbald** – Mönchs Posthotel, D-76328, Bad Herrenbald. Tel: 49 70 83 74 41 22

**Berlin** – Grand Hotel Esplanade Berlin, Lützowufer 15, D-10785 Berlin. Tel: 00 49 302651171

**Cologne** – Hotel Cristall, Ursulaplatz 9-11, D-50668, Cologne. Tel: 00 49 221 16 300

**Cologne** – Hotel im Wasserturm, Kaygasse 2, D-50676. Tel: 49 221 20088 88

**Dresden** – Bülow Residenz, Rähnitzgasse 19, D-1097, Dresden. Tel: 49 351 8003100

**Friedrichsruhe** – Wald & Schlosshotel, D-74639 Friedrichsruhe/Zweiflingen. Tel: 49 7941 61468

**Garmisch Partenkirchen** – Reindl's Partenkirchner Hof, Bahnhofstasse 15, Garmisch Partenkirchen. Tel: 49 8821 73401

**Munich** – Hotel Königshof, Karlsplatz 25, D-80335, Munich. Tel: 49 89 5513 6113

**Murnau** – Alpenhof Murnau, Ramsachstrasse 8, D-82418, Murnau. Tel: 49 8841 5438

**Niederstotzingen** – Schlosshotel Oberstotzingen, Stettener Strasse 35-37, D-89168, Niederstotzingen. Tel: 49 7325 10370

**Oberwesel/Rhein** – Burghotel Auf Schönburg, D-55430, Oberwesel/Rhein. Tel: 49 67 44 16 13

**Rothenburg ob der Tauber** – Hotel Eisenhut, Herrngasse 3-7, D-91541. Tel: 49 9861 7 05 45

**Rüdesheim am Rhein** – Jagdschloss Niederwald, Auf Dem Niederwald 1, D-65385 Rüdesheim am Rhein. Tel: 49 67 22 47970

**Schlangenbad** – Parkhotel Schlangenbad, Rheingauer Strasse 47, D-65388, Schlangenbad. Tel: 49 61 29 41 420

**Wassenberg** – Hotel Burg Wassenberg, Kirchstrasse 17, D-41849 Wassenberg. Tel: 49 2432 949100

**Wertheim-Bettingen** – Schweizer Stuben, Geiselbrunnwre, D-97877 Wertheim-Bettingen. Tel: 49 9342 307155

### GREECE

**Athens** – Andromeda, 22 Timoleontos Vassou Street, GR-115 21, Athens. Tel: 30 1 6466361

**Crete** – Elounda Bay Palace, GR-721 00 Aghios Nikolaos, Crete. Tel: 00 30 84141783

**Crete** – Elounda Beach, GR-721 00, Aghios Nikolaos, Crete. Tel: 30 841 41 375

### HUNGARY

**Budapest** – Hotel Gellért, St.Gellért Tér 1, H-1111, Budapest. Tel: 36 1 166 6631

### ICELAND

**Reykjavik** – Hótel Borg, Posthusstraeti 11, P.O Box 200, 121 Reykjavik. Tel: 354 551 14 20

### ITALY

**Assisi** – Le Silve di Armenzano, I-06081, Loc Armenzano, Assisi. Tel: 39 75 801 90 05

**Bordighera** – Hotel Parigi, Lungomare Argentina 18, I-18012 Bordighera IM. Tel: 39 184 260 421

**Breuil-Cervinia** – Hotel Bucaneve, Piazza Jumeaux 10, I-11021, Breuil-Cervinia. Tel: 39 166 948308

**Cogne** – Romantik Hotel Miramonti, Avenue Cavagnet 31, I-11012, Cogne. Tel: 39 165 749378

**Como** – Albergo Terminus, Lungo Lario Trieste, I-14-22100, Como. Tel: 39 31 302550

**Como** – Hotel Villa Flori, Via per Cernobbio, I-12 - 22100, Como. Tel: 39 31 570379

**Cortona** – Relais Il Falconiere, Frazione San Martino, I-52044, Cortona AR. Tel: 39 575 612927

**Etna** – Hotel Villa Paradiso Dell' Etna, Via per Viagrande 37, SG La Punta, I-95030 CT. Tel: 39 741 3861

**Ferrara** – Ripagrande Hotel, Via Ripagrande 21, I-44100, Ferrara. Tel: 39 532 764377

**Fié Allo Scilari** – Romantik Hotel Turm, Piazza Della Chiesa 9, Fié Allo Scilari, Bolzano. Tel: 39 471 725474

**Florence** – Romantik Hotel J &J, Via Mezzo 20, I-50121 Florence. Tel: 39 55 240282

**Gargonza-Monte San Savino** – Residence Castello Di Gargonza, I-52048 Monte San Savino, Arezzo. Tel: 39 575 847 054

**Giardini Naxos** – Hellenia Yachting Hotel, Via Jannuzzo 41, I-Giardini Naxos MS. Tel: 39 942 54310

**Isla d'Ischia** – La Villarosa, via G.Gigante 5, I-80077 Porto d'Ischia, Naples. Tel: 39 81 99 24 25

**Isola d'Elba** – Hotel Villa Ottone, Localitá Ottone, I-57037 Portoferraio, Isola d'Elba. Tel: 39 565 93 3257

**Lago Garda** – Grand Hotel Fasano, I-25083, Gardone Riviera, Lake Garda. Tel: 39 365 290 221

**Madonna Di Campiglio** – Hotel Lorenzetti, Via Dolomiti Di Campiglio 119, I-38084 Madonna Di Campiglio TN. Tel: 39 465 44 14104

**Maratea** – Romantik Hotel Villa Cheta Elite, I-85041 Acquafredda di Maratea. Tel: 39 973 878 135

**Marling/Meran** – Romantic Hotel Oberwirt, St Felixweg 2, I-39020, Marling/Meran. Tel: 39 473 44 71 30

**Messina,Sicily** – Museo Albergo Atelier Sul Mare, via Cesare Battisti, Castel di Tusa Me, Sicily. Tel: 39 921 334 283

**Milan** – Regency Hotel, Via Arimondi 12, I-20155 Milan. Tel: 39 2 39217734

**Mira** – Villa Margherita, Via Nazionale 416/417, I-30030 Mira, Venezia. Tel: 39 41 42 65 838

**Nova Levante** – Posthotel Weisses Rössl, Via Carezza 30, I-39036, Nova Levante BZ, Dolomites. Tel: 39 471 613390

**Pievescola** – Hotel Relais La Suvera, I-53030 Pievescola, Siena. Tel: 39 577 960 220

**Porto Ercole** – Il Pellicano, Hotel in Porto Ercole, Aeralita Cala Dei Santi, Porto Ercole GR. Tel: 39 564 833418

**Positano** – Romantik Hotel Poseidon, Via Pasitea 148, I-84017, Positano. Tel: 39 89 87 58 33

**Rome** – Hotel Farnese, Via Alessandro Farnese, 30 Anglo Viale Giulio Cesare I-00192, Rome. Tel: 39 6 321 51 29

**Rome** – Romantik Hotel Barocco, Piazza Barberini, 9 I-00187, Rome. Tel: 39 6 485994

**San Candino** – Parkhotel Sole Paradiso, Via Haunold 8, San Candino BZ. Tel: 39 474 913 193

**Saturnia** – Terme Di Saturnia Hotel, I-58050, Saturnia, Grosseto. Tel: 39 564 601266

**Savignone** – Hotel Palazzo Fieschi, Piazza Della Chiesa 14, Savignone GE I-16010. Tel: 39 10 936821

**Selva Val Gardena** – Hotel Sochers Resort Club, I-39048, Selva Val Gardena. Tel: 39 471 793537

**Sestri Levante** – Grand Hotel Villa Balbi, Viale Rimembranza 1, I-16039, Sestri Leuante. Tel: 39 185 482459

**Sicily** – Romantic Hotel Villa Ducale, Via Leonardo Da Vinci 60, I-98039 Taormina, Sicily. Tel: 39 942 28710

**Sorrento** – Grand Hotel Cocumella, Via Cocumella 7, I-80065 Sant'Agnello, Sorrento. Tel: 39 81 878 3712

**Sorrento** – Grand Hotel Excelsior Vittoria, Piazza Tasso 24, Sorrento-Napoli. Tel: 39 81 87 71 206

**South Tyrol Mauls** – Romantik Hotel Stafler, Mauls 10, I-39040 Freienfeld. Tel: 39 472 77 1094

**South Tyrol Meran** – Castel Rundegg, Via Scena 2, I-39020, Meran. Tel: 39 473 237200

**Taormina** – Villa Fabbiano, Via Pirandello 81, I-98039 Taormina ME. Tel: 39 942 23732

**Taormina Mare** – Hotel Villa Sant' Andrea, Via Nazionale 137, I-98030, Taormina Mare. Tel: 00 39 942 24838

**Venice** – Hotel Cipriani,Palazzo Vendramin & Il Palazzetto, Giudecca 10, 30133, Venice. Tel: 39 041 520 39 30

**Venice** – Hotel Metropole, San Marco- Riva Degli Schiavoni 4149, I-30122 Venice. Tel: 39 41 52 23 679

**Venice Lido** – Albergo Quattro Fontane, 30126, Lido di Venezia. Tel: 39-41 5260726

**Venice** – Villa Condulmer, 31020 Zerman Di Mogliani Veneto, Treviso. Tel: 39 41 45 71 34

### LATVIA

**Riga** – Hotel de Rome, Kalkuiela 28, LV 1050, Riga. Tel: 37 1 722 82 51

### LIECHTENSTEIN

**Vaduz** – Parkhotel Sonnenhof, Mareestrasse 29, FL-9490 Vaduz. Tel: 41 75 232 0053

### LUXEMBOURG

**Berdorf** – Parc Hotel, 16 Rue De Grundhof, L-6550, Berdorf. Tel: 352 790223

## MONACO

**Monte-Carlo** – Hotel Hermitage, Square Beaumarchais BP277, MC 98005. Tel: 33 92 16 38 52

## NETHERLANDS

**Amsterdam** – Hotel Ambassade, Herengracht 341, NL-1016 AZ, Amsterdam. Tel: 31 20 624 5321

**Bergambacht** – Hotel De Arendshoeve, Molenlaan 14, NL-2861, LB Bergambacht. Tel: 31 182 35 1155

**Bosch en Duin** – De Hoefslag, Vossenlaan 28, NL-3735, Bosch en Duin. Tel: 31 30 228 5821

**Drunen** – Hotel De Duinrand, Steergerf 2, NL-5151, RB Drunen. Tel: 31 416 374 919

**Oisterwijk** – Hotel Restaurant de Swaen, De Lind 47, NL-5061 HT Oisterwijk. Tel: 31 135 28 58 60

**Ootmarsum** – Hotel de Wiemsel, Winhofflaan 2, NL-7631 HX, Ootmarsum. Tel: 31 541 293 295

**Vooburg** – Restaurant-Hotel Savelberg, Oosteinde 14, NL-2271 EH, Vooburg. Tel: 31 70 387 7715

## NORWAY

**Balestrand** – Kvikne's Hotel, N-5850, Balestrand. Tel: 00 47 57 69 15 02

**Oslo** – First Hotel Bastion, Postboks 27, Sentrum, Skippergaten 7, 0152 Oslo. Tel: 47 22 33 11 80

**Voss** – Fleischers Hotel, N-5700, Voss. Tel: 47 56 51 22 89

## PORTUGAL

**Agueda** – Hotel Palacio Agueda, Quinta da Borralha, P-3750, Agueda. Tel: 351 34 60 19 76

**Coimbra** – Hotel Quinta das Lagrimas, Santa Clara, P-3040 Coimbra. Tel: 351 39 44 16 95

**Faro** – La Réserve, Santa Bárbara de Nexe, P-8000 Faro, Algarve. Tel: 351 89 90402

**Faro** – Monte do Casal, Cerro do Lobo, Estoi P-8000 Faro, Algarve. Tel: 351 89 91341

**Lagos** – Romantik Hotel Vivenda Miranda, Porto de Mós, P-8600 Lagos, Algarve. Tel: 351 82 760 342

**Lisbon** – As Janelas Verdes, Rua das Janelas Verdes 47, P-1200, Lisbon. Tel: 351 1 39 68 144

**Madeira** – Quinta Da Bela Vista, Caminho Do Avista Navios,4, P-9000, Funchal-Madeira. Tel: 351 91 765090

**Sintra** – Hotel Palacio de Seteais, Rua Barbosa de Bocage,10, Setais, P-2710 Sintra. Tel: 351 1 923 42 77

**Sintra** – Quinta de Sao Thiago, Estrâda de Moserrate, Sintra P-2710. Tel: 351 1 923 43 29

## SLOVENIA

**Bled** – Hotel Vila Bled, Cesta Svobode 26, SL-4260, Bled. Tel: 386 64 741 320

## SPAIN

**Barcelona** – Hotel Claris, Pau Claris 150, E-8009, Barcelona. Tel: 34 3 215 79 70

**Ibiza** – Pikes, San Antonio De Portmany, Isla De Ibiza, Balearic Islands. Tel: 34 71 34 23 12

**Jerez de la Frontera** – Montecastillo Hotel & Golf Club, Ctra. de Arcos, E-11406 Jerez, Cadiz. Tel: 34 56 15 12 09

**Madrid** – Villa Real, Plaza De Las Cortes 10, Madrid E-28014. Tel: 34 1420 25 47

**Mallorca** – Hotel Vistamar De Valldemosa, Ctra. Valldemosa, Andratx, Km 2 E-07170 Valldemosa, Mallorca. Tel: 34 71 61 25 83

**Mallorca** – Read's, Ca'n Moragues, E-07320 Santa Marta, Mallorca. Tel: 34 71 140 762

**Marbella** – Hotel Puente Romano, P.O Box 204, E-29600, Marbella. Tel: 34 52 77 57 66

**Marbella** – Marbella Club Hotel, Boulevard Principe Alfonsoe von Hohenlohe s/n, E-29600, Marbella. Tel: 34 5 282 98 84

**Marbella** – Hotel Rincon Andaluz, Crta de Cádiz,km 173, E-29680, Marbella. Tel: 34 5 281 4180

**Marbella/Estepona** – Las Dunas Suites, Ctra de Cádiz Km163.5, E-29689 Marbella-Estepona, Malaga. Tel: 34 5 279 48 25

**Oviedo** – Hotel de la Reconquista, Gil de Jaz 16, E-33004 Oviedo, Principado de Asturias. Tel: 34 8524 1166

**Salamanca** – Residencia Rector, Rector Esparabé, 10-Apartado 399, E-37008 Salamanca. Tel: 34 23 21 40 08

**Seville** – Casa De Carmona, Plaza de Lasso 1, E-41410 Carmona, Seville. Tel: 34 54 19 01 89

**Tenerife** – Gran Hotel Bahia Del Duque, E-38660 Adeje, Costa Adeje, Tenerife South. Tel: 34 22 74 69 25

**Tenerife** – Hotel Botánico, Avda. Richard J. Yeoward 1, Urb Botánico, E-238400 Puerto de la Cruz, Tenerife. Tel: 34 22 38 15 04

**Tenerife** – Hotel Jardin Tropical, Calle Gran Bretana, E-38670 Costa Adeje, Tenerife, Canary Islands. Tel: 1 34 34 22752844

## SWEDEN

**Åre** – Hotell Åregården, Box 6, S-83013, Åre. Tel: 46 647 17960

**Aspa Bruk** – Aspa Herrgård, S-696 93, Aspa Bruk. Tel: 46 583 50150

**Båstad** – Buena Vista, Tarravägen 5, S-269, 35 Båstad. Tel: 46 431 791 00

**Borgholm** – Halltorps Gästgiveri, S-387 92, Borgholm. Tel: 46 485 85001

**Eskilstuna** – Sundbyholms Slott, S-635 08, Eskilstuna. Tel: 46 16 96578

**Gothenburg** – Hotel Eggers, Drottningtorget, Box 323 S-401 25, Gothenburg. Tel: 46 31 15 42 43

**Lagan** – Toftaholm Herrgård, Toftaholm P.A., S-34014, Lagan. Tel: 46 370 44045

**Söderköping** – Romantik Hotel Söderköpings Brunn, Skönbergagatan 35, Box 44 S-614 21, Söderköping. Tel: 46 121 139 41

**Stockholm** – Hotell Diplomat, Strandvägen 7C, Box 14059 S-10440, Stockholm. Tel: 46 8 783 66 34

**Svartå** – Svartå Herrgård, S-69393 Svartå. Tel: 46 585 500 03

**Tällberg** – Romantik Hotel Åkerblads, S-793 70, Tällberg. Tel: 46 247 50652

**Tanndalen** – Hotel Tanndalen, S-84098, Tanndalen. Tel: 46 684 220020

**Tanumshede** – Tanums Gestgifveri, S-45700, Tanumshede. Tel: 46 525 29571

**Tommarp** – Karlaby Kro, S-27293, Tommarp. Tel: 46 414 204 73

**Vikbolandet** – Mauritzbergs Slott, S-61031, Vikbolandet. Tel: 46 125 50104

## SWITZERLAND

**Château d'Oex** – Hostellerie Bon Accueil, CH-1837, Chateau d'Oex. Tel: 41 26 924 5126

**Glion** – Hotel Victoria, CH-1823, Glion. Tel: 41 21 963 1351

**Gstaad** – Grand Hotel Park, CH-3780, Gstaad. Tel: 41 30 44 414

**Kandersteg** – Royal Hotel Bellevue, CH 3718, Kandersteg. Tel: 41 33 675 88 80

**Lucerne** – Romantik Hotel Wilden Mann, Bahnhofstrasse 30, CH 6000, Lucerne 7. Tel: 41 210 16 29

**Saas Fee** – Romantik Hotel Beau-Site, CH-3906, Saas Fee. Tel: 41 27 958 1565

**Zouz** – Posthotel Engiadina, Via Maistra, Zous. Tel: 41 81 85 43 303

## TURKEY

**Alanya** – Hotel Grand Kaptan, Oba Göl Mevkii, 7400, Alanya. Tel: 90 242 514 0092

**Kalkan** – Hotel Villa Mahal, P.K 4 Kalkan, 7960, Antalya. Tel: 90 242 844 2122

# Johansens Recommended Hotels North America

## CANADA

**Canada (British Columbia),** Dashwood Manor, 1 Cook Street, Victoria, British Columbia V8V-3W6. Tel: 001 250 383 1763

**Canada (Jackson's Point),** The Briars, 55 Hedge Road, RR 1, Jackson's Point, Ontario LOE ILO. Tel: 001 905 722 3271

## CARRIBBEAN

**Caribbean (Antigua),** Star Clippers, Fred Olsen Travel, Fred Olsen House, White House Road, Ipswich IP1 5LL. Tel: 01473 292200

**Caribbean (St Vincent),** Petit St Vincent Resort, The Grenadines, St Vincent, West Indies. Tel: 001 809 458 8801

**Caribbean (Bermuda),** Lantana, Sandys, SBBX. Tel: 001 441 234 0141

**Caribbean (Bermuda),** The Newstead Hotel, 27 Harbour Road, Paget PG02. Tel: 001 1 441 236 6060

**Caribbean (Bermuda),** Surf Side Beach Club, 90 South Shore, Warwick. Tel: 001 441 236 7100

## UNITED STATES OF AMERICA

**Arizona (Sedona),** Canyon Villa Inn, 125 Canyon Circle Drive, Sedona, Arizona 86351. Tel: 001 520 284 1226

**Arizona (Tucson),** Tanque Verde Ranch, 14301 East Speedway Boulevard, Tucson, Arizona 85748. Tel: 001 520 296 6275

**California (Eureka),** Carter House, 301 L Street, Eureka, California 95501. Tel: 001 800 404 1390

**California (Yosemite National Park),** Château du Sureau, 48688 Victoria Lane, PO Box 577, Oakhurst, California 93644. Tel: 001 209 683 6860

**California (Hollywood),** Château Marmont, 8221 Sunset Boulevard, Hollywood, California 90046-2413. Tel: 001 213 656 1010

**California (Healdsburg),** Madrona Manor, 1001 Westside Road, Healdsburg, California 95448. Tel: 001 707 433 4231

**California (Pacific Grove),** The Martine Inn, 255 Oceanview Boulevard, Pacific Grove, California 93950. Tel: 001 408 373 3388

**California (Mill Valley),** Mountain Home Inn, 810 Panoramic Highway, Mill Valley, California 94941. Tel: 001 415 381 9000

**California (San Francisco),** Nob Hill Lambourne, 725 Pine Street, San Francisco, California 94108. Tel: 001 415 433 2287

**California (Muir Beach),** Pelican Inn, Highway 1, Muir Beach, California 94965. Tel: 001 415 383 6000

**California (Nevada City),** Red Castle Inn Historic Lodgings, 109 Prospect Street, Nevada City, California 95959. Tel: 001 916 265 5135

**California (Sacramento),** The Sterling Hotel, 1300 H Street, Sacramento, California 95826. Tel: 001 916 448 1300

**California (Hopland),** Thatcher Inn, 13401 South Highway 101, Hopland, California 95449. Tel: 001 707 744 1890

**Connecticut (New Preston),** The Boulders, East Shore Road, Route 45, Connecticut 06777. Tel: 001 860 868 0541

**Connecticut (Old Saybrook),** Saybrook Point Inn & Spa, 2 Bridge Street, Old Saybrook, Connecticut 06475. Tel: 001 860 395 2000

**Connecticut (Mystic),** Steamboat Inn, 73 Steamboat Wharf, Mystic, Connecticut 06355. Tel: 001 860 536 8300

**Connecticut (Washington),** The Mayflower Inn, 118 Woodbury Road, Washington, Connecticut 06793. Tel: 001 860 868 9466

**Florida (Lake Wales),** Chalet Suzanne, 3800 Chalet Suzanne Drive, Lake Wales, Florida 33853–7060. Tel: 001 941 676 6011

**Florida (Key West),** The Marquesa, 600 Fleming Street, Key West, Florida 33040. Tel: 001 305 292 1919

**Florida (Miami Beach),** The Richmond, 1757 Collins Avenue, Miami Beach, Florida 33139. Tel: 001 305 538 2331

**Georgia (Macon),** 1842 Inn, 353 College Street, Macon, Georgia 31201. Tel: 001 912 741 1842

**Georgia (Savannah),** Foley House Inn, 14 West Hull, Chippewa Square, Savannah, Georgia 31401. Tel: 001 912 232 6622

**Georgia (Savannah),** The Jesse Mount House, 209 West Jones Street, Savannah, Georgia 31401. Tel: 001 912 236 1774

**Georgia (St. Simons Island),** Little St Simons Island, PO Box 21078, Little St Simons Island, Georgia. Tel: 001 912 638 7472

**Illinois (Chicago),** The Whitehall Hotel, 105 East Delaware Place, Chicago, Illinois 60611. Tel: 001 312 573 6208

**Indiana (Indianapolis),** Canterbury Hotel, 123 S Illinois Street, Indianapolis, Indiana 46225. Tel: 001 317 634 3000

**Louisiana (Napoleonville),** Madewood Plantation House, 4250 Highway 308, Napoleonville, Louisiana 70390. Tel: 001 504 369 7151

**Maine (Prouts Neck),** Black Point Resort, 510 Black Point Road, Prouts Neck, Scarborough, Maine 04074. Tel: 001 207 883 4126

**Maine (Bar Harbor),** Breakwater 1904, 45 Hancock Street, Bar Harbor, Maine 04609. Tel: 001 207 288 2313

**Maine (Cape Elizabeth),** Inn By The Sea, 40 Bowery Beach Road, Cape Elizabeth, Maine 04017. Tel: 001 207 799 3134

**Maine (Greenville),** The Lodge at Moosehead Lake, Upon Lily Bay Road, Box 1167, Greenville, Maine 04441. Tel: 001 207 695 4400

**Maine (Kennebunkport),** Old Fort Inn, 8 Old Fort Avenue, PO Box MI, Kennebunkport, Maine 04046 Tel: 001 207 967 5353

**Maryland (Taneytown),** Antrim 1844, 30 Trevanion Road, Taneytown, Maryland 21787. Tel: 001 410 756 6812

**Maryland (St Michaels),** The Inn at Perry Cabin, 308 Watkins Lane, St Michaels, Maryland 21663. Tel: 001 410 745 2200

**Massachusetts (Cambridge),** A Cambridge House, 2218 Massachusetts Avenue, Cambridge, Massachusetts 02140–1836. Tel: 001 617 491 6300

**Massachusetts (Chatham),** The Captain's House Inn, 369-377 Old Harbor Road, Chatham, Massachusetts 02633. Tel: 001 508 945 4569

**Massachusetts (Deerfield),** Deerfield Inn, 108 Old Main Street, Deerfield, Massachusetts 01342. Tel: 001 413 774 5587

**Massachusetts (Boston),** The Eliot, 370 Commonwealth Avenue, Boston, Massachusetts 02215. Tel: 001 617 267 1607

**Massachusetts (Stockbridge),** The Inn At Stockbridge, 30 East Street North, Route 7, Box 618, Stockbridge, Massachusetts 01262. Tel: 001 413 298 3337

**Massachusetts (Chatham),** Pleasant Bay Village Resort, PO Box 772, Route 28, Chatham, Massachusetts 02633. Tel: 001 508 945 1133

**Massachusetts (Cape Cod),** Wedgewood Inn, 83 Main Street, Yarmouth Port, Massachusetts 02675. Tel: 001 508 362 5157

**Massachusetts (Eastham),** The Whalewalk Inn, 220 Bridge Road, Eastham, Massachusetts 02642. Tel: 001 508 255 0617

**Massachusetts (Lenox),** Wheatleigh, Hawthorne Road, Lenox, Massachusetts 01240. Tel: 001 413 637 0610

**Michigan (Petoskey),** Staffords Perry Hotel, Bay at Lewis Street, Petoskey, Michigan 49770. Tel: 001 616 347 4000

**Mississippi (Natchez),** Monmouth Plantation, 36 Melrose Avenue, Natchez, Mississippi 39120. Tel: 001 601 442 5852

**New Hampshire (Jackson),** Inn at Thorn Hill, Thorn Hill Road, Jackson, New Hampshire 03846. Tel: 001 603 383 4242

**New York (New York),** The Kitano New York, 66 Park Avenue at 38th Street, New York, New York 10016. Tel: 001 212 885 7000

**New York (New York),** The Lowell, 28 East 63rd Street, New York , New York 10021-8088. Tel: 001 212 838 1400

**New York (Dover Plains),** Old Drovers Inn, Old Route 22, Dover Plains, New York 12522. Tel: 001 914 832 9311

**New York (New York),** The Peninsula New York, 700 Fifth Avenue at 55th Street, New York, New York 10019. Tel: 001 212 247 2200

**New York (Ithaca),** The Rose Inn, 813 Auburn Road, Route 34, PO Box 6576, Ithaca, New York 14851. Tel: 001 607 533 7905

**North Carolina (Pittsboro),** The Fearrington House, 2000 Fearrington Village Center, Pittsboro, North Carolina 27312. Tel: 001 919 542 2121

**North Carolina (Lake Toxaway),** The Greystone Inn, Lake Toxaway, North Carolina 28747. Tel: 001 704 966 4700

**North Carolina (Waynesville),** The Swag Country Inn, 2300 Swag Road, North Carolina 28786. Tel: 001 704 926 0430

**Pennsylvania (South Sterling),** The French Manor, Huckleberry Road (Route 191), South Sterling, Pennsylvania 18460. Tel: 001 717 676 3311

**Pennsylvania (Farmington),** Nemacolin Woodlands Resort & Spa, Route 40E, Farmington, Pennsylvania 15437. Tel: 001 412 329 6195

**Rhode Island (Newport),** Cliffside Inn, 2 Seaview Avenue, Newport, Rhode Island 02840. Tel: 001 401 847 1811

**South Carolina (Summerville),** Woodlands Resort & Inn, 125 Parsons Road, Summerville, South Carolina 29483. Tel: 001 803 875 2600

**Vermont (Manchester Village),** 1811 House, PO Box 39, Route 7A, Manchester Village, Vermont 05254. Tel: 001 802 362 1811

**Vermont (Goshen),** Blueberry Hill, 32 Forest Rd, Goshen, Vermont 05733. Tel: 001 802 247 6735

**Vermont (Shelburne),** The Inn at Shelburne Farms, 102 Harbor Road, Shelburne, Vermont 05482. Tel: 001 802 985 8686

**Vermont (Stowe),** The Mountain Road Resort, PO Box 8, Stowe, Vermont 05672. Tel: 001 802 253 4566

**Vermont (Chittenden),** Mountain Top Inn & Resort, Mountain Top Road, Chittenden, Vermont 05737. Tel: 001 802 483 2311

**Vermont (Barnard),** Twin Farms, Barnard, Vermont 05031. Tel: 001 802 234 9999

**Vermont (West Townshend),** Windham Hill Inn, West Townshend, Vermont 05359. Tel: 001 802 874 4080

**Virginia (Keswick),** Keswick Hall, 701 Club Drive, Keswick, Virginia 22947. Tel: 001 804 979 3440

**Virginia (White Post),** L'Auberge Provençale, Route 340, White Post, Virginia 22663. Tel: 001 540 837 1375

**Virginia (Alexandria),** Morrison House, 116 South Alfred Street, Alexandria, Virginia 22314. Tel: 001 703 838 8000

**Virginia (Paris),** The Ashby Inn & Restaurant, 692 Federal Street, Paris, Virginia 20130. Tel: 001 540 592 3900

**Washington (Seattle),** Inn at the Market, 86 Pine, Seattle, Washington 98101. Tel: 001 206 443 3600

**Washington (Seattle),** Sorrento Hotel, 900 Madison Street, Seattle, Washington 98104-9742. Tel: 001 206 622 6400

**Washington (Winthrop),** Sun Mountain Lodge, Patterson Lake Road, Winthrop, Washington 98862. Tel: 001 509 996 2211

**Washington (Orcas Island),** Turtleback Farm Inn, Crow Valley Road, East Sound, Orcas Island, Washington 98245. Tel: 001 360 376 4914

**Wyoming (Jackson Hole),** The Alpenhof Lodge, Teton Village, Jackson Hole, Wyoming 83025. Tel: 001 307 733 3242

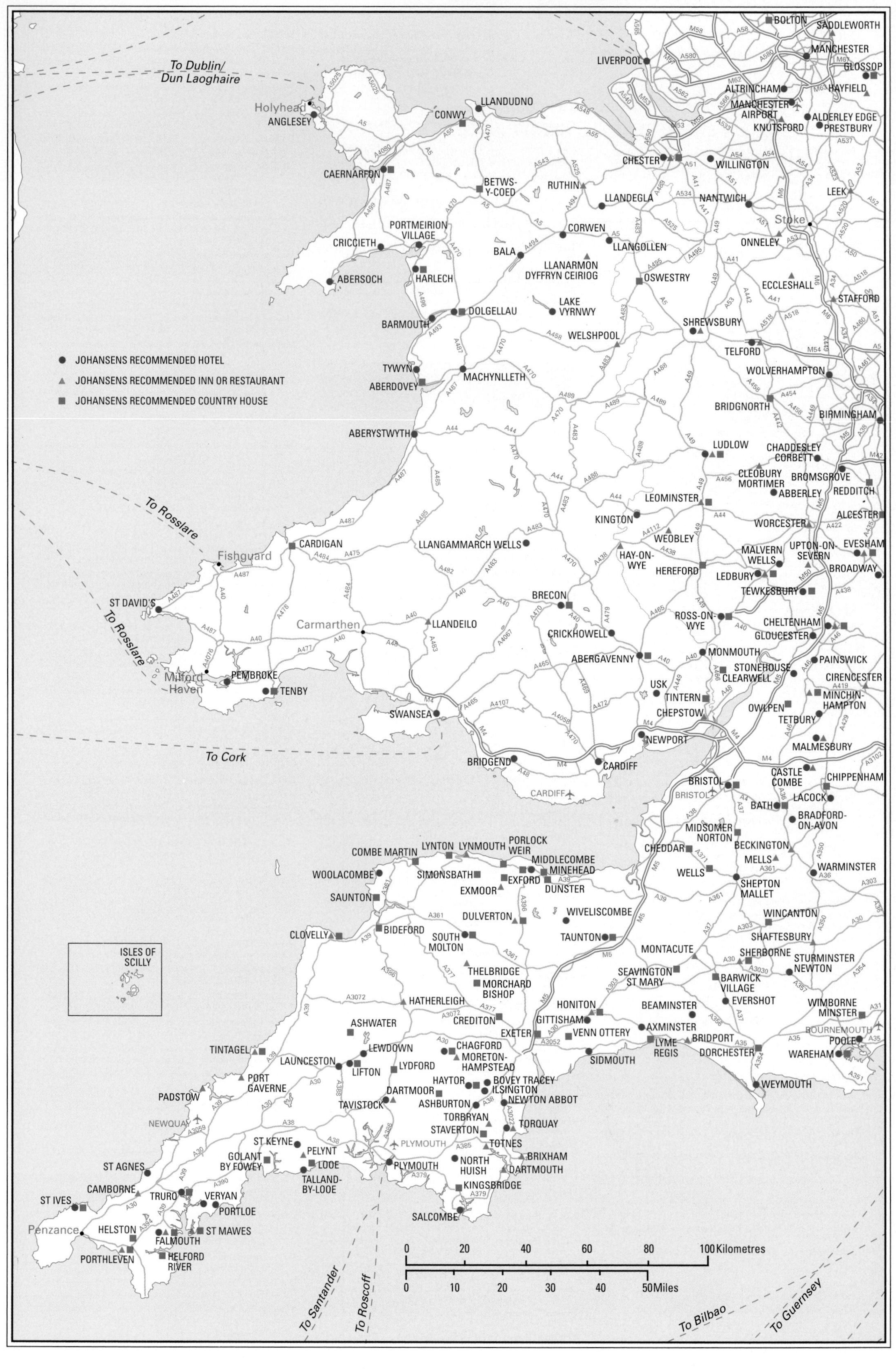

● JOHANSENS RECOMMENDED HOTEL
▲ JOHANSENS RECOMMENDED INN OR RESTAURANT
■ JOHANSENS RECOMMENDED COUNTRY HOUSE
To Dublin/
Dun Laoghaire
To Rosslare
To Rosslare
To Cork
To Santander
To Roscoff
To Bilbao
To Guernsey
Holyhead
ANGLESEY
LLANDUDNO
CONWY
CAERNARFON
BETWS-
Y-COED
RUTHIN
LLANDEGLA
PORTMEIRION
VILLAGE
CRICCIETH
ABERSOCH
HARLECH
BALA
CORWEN
LLANGOLLEN
LLANARMON
DYFFRYN CEIRIOG
OSWESTRY
LAKE
VYRNWY
DOLGELLAU
BARMOUTH
WELSHPOOL
SHREWSBURY
TYWYN
ABERDOVEY
MACHYNLLETH
ABERYSTWYTH
LIVERPOOL
BOLTON
SADDLEWORTH
MANCHESTER
GLOSSOP
ALTRINCHAM
HAYFIELD
MANCHESTER
AIRPORT
KNUTSFORD
ALDERLEY EDGE
PRESTBURY
CHESTER
WILLINGTON
NANTWICH
LEEK
Stoke
ONNELEY
ECCLESHALL
STAFFORD
TELFORD
WOLVERHAMPTON
BRIDGNORTH
BIRMINGHAM
LUDLOW
CHADDESLEY
CORBETT
CLEOBURY
MORTIMER
BROMSGROVE
ABBERLEY
REDDITCH
LEOMINSTER
KINGTON
WORCESTER
ALCESTER
WEOBLEY
LLANGAMMARCH WELLS
HAY-ON-
WYE
HEREFORD
MALVERN
WELLS
UPTON-ON-
SEVERN
EVESHAM
BROADWAY
LEDBURY
TEWKESBURY
CARDIGAN
Fishguard
ST DAVID'S
Carmarthen
LLANDEILO
BRECON
CRICKHOWELL
ROSS-ON-
WYE
CHELTENHAM
GLOUCESTER
ABERGAVENNY
MONMOUTH
PAINSWICK
STONEHOUSE
CLEARWELL
CIRENCESTER
USK
TINTERN
MINCHIN-
HAMPTON
Milford
Haven
PEMBROKE
TENBY
SWANSEA
CHEPSTOW
OWLPEN
TETBURY
NEWPORT
MALMESBURY
BRIDGEND
CARDIFF
CARDIFF
CASTLE
COMBE
CHIPPENHAM
BRISTOL
BRISTOL
LACOCK
BATH
BRADFORD-
ON-AVON
MIDSOMER
NORTON
BECKINGTON
CHEDDAR
MELLS
WARMINSTER
WELLS
SHEPTON
MALLET
COMBE MARTIN
LYNTON
LYNMOUTH
PORLOCK
WEIR
MIDDLECOMBE
MINEHEAD
WOOLACOMBE
SIMONSBATH
EXFORD
DUNSTER
EXMOOR
SAUNTON
DULVERTON
WIVELISCOMBE
WINCANTON
CLOVELLY
BIDEFORD
SOUTH
MOLTON
TAUNTON
SHAFTESBURY
MONTACUTE
SHERBORNE
STURMINSTER
NEWTON
ISLES OF
SCILLY
THELBRIDGE
MORCHARD
BISHOP
SEAVINGTON
ST MARY
BARWICK
VILLAGE
EVERSHOT
HATHERLEIGH
HONITON
BEAMINSTER
WIMBORNE
MINSTER
CREDITON
GITTISHAM
ASHWATER
AXMINSTER
BOURNEMOUTH
EXETER
VENN OTTERY
BRIDPORT
POOLE
TINTAGEL
CHAGFORD
MORETON-
HAMPSTEAD
LYME
REGIS
DORCHESTER
WAREHAM
LAUNCESTON
LEWDOWN
LIFTON
LYDFORD
SIDMOUTH
PORT
GAVERNE
HAYTOR
BOVEY TRACEY
ILSINGTON
WEYMOUTH
PADSTOW
DARTMOOR
TAVISTOCK
ASHBURTON
NEWTON ABBOT
NEWQUAY
TORBRYAN
STAVERTON
TORQUAY
ST KEYNE
PELYNT
PLYMOUTH
TOTNES
BRIXHAM
GOLANT
BY FOWEY
LOOE
PLYMOUTH
NORTH
HUISH
DARTMOUTH
ST AGNES
TALLAND-
BY-LOOE
CAMBORNE
KINGSBRIDGE
ST IVES
TRURO
VERYAN
PORTLOE
SALCOMBE
Penzance
HELSTON
FALMOUTH
ST MAWES
PORTHLEVEN
HELFORD
RIVER
0 20 40 60 80 100 Kilometres
0 10 20 30 40 50 Miles

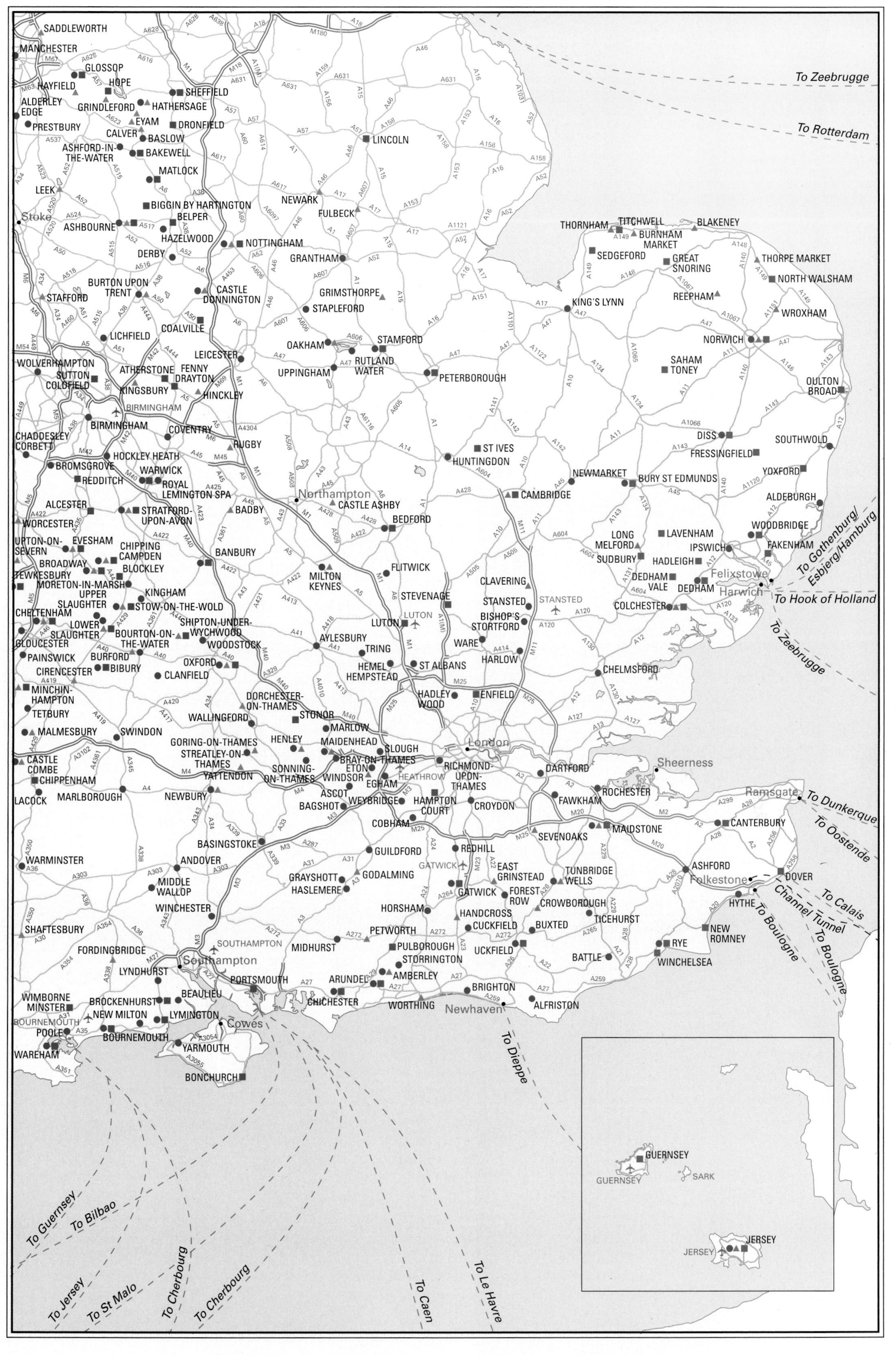

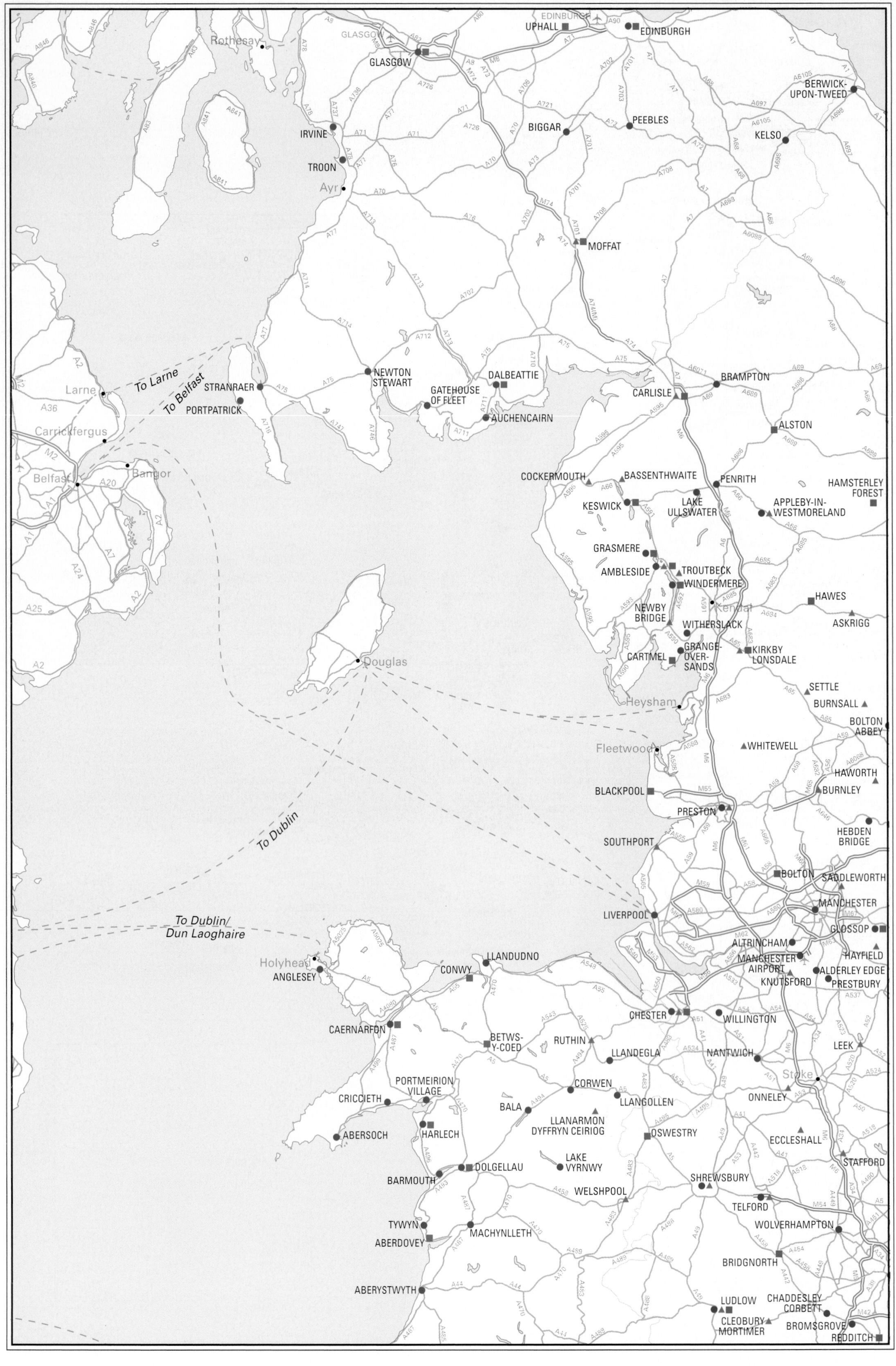

UPHALL
EDINBURGH
Rothesay
GLASGOW
BERWICK-UPON-TWEED
IRVINE
BIGGAR
PEEBLES
KELSO
TROON
Ayr
MOFFAT
To Larne
To Belfast
Larne
STRANRAER
PORTPATRICK
NEWTON STEWART
GATEHOUSE OF FLEET
DALBEATTIE
AUCHENCAIRN
CARLISLE
BRAMPTON
ALSTON
Carrickfergus
Belfast
Bangor
COCKERMOUTH
BASSENTHWAITE
PENRITH
HAMSTERLEY FOREST
KESWICK
LAKE ULLSWATER
APPLEBY-IN-WESTMORELAND
GRASMERE
AMBLESIDE
TROUTBECK
WINDERMERE
Kendal
HAWES
ASKRIGG
NEWBY BRIDGE
WITHERSLACK
CARTMEL
GRANGE-OVER-SANDS
KIRKBY LONSDALE
Douglas
SETTLE
BURNSALL
BOLTON ABBEY
Heysham
WHITEWELL
Fleetwood
HAWORTH
BLACKPOOL
BURNLEY
PRESTON
To Dublin
SOUTHPORT
HEBDEN BRIDGE
BOLTON
SADDLEWORTH
MANCHESTER
LIVERPOOL
GLOSSOP
To Dublin/ Dun Laoghaire
ALTRINCHAM
HAYFIELD
MANCHESTER AIRPORT
ALDERLEY EDGE
KNUTSFORD
PRESTBURY
Holyhead
ANGLESEY
LLANDUDNO
CONWY
CHESTER
WILLINGTON
CAERNARFON
BETWS-Y-COED
RUTHIN
LLANDEGLA
NANTWICH
LEEK
Stoke
PORTMEIRION VILLAGE
CORWEN
CRICCIETH
LLANGOLLEN
ONNELEY
BALA
LLANARMON DYFFRYN CEIRIOG
OSWESTRY
ECCLESHALL
ABERSOCH
HARLECH
STAFFORD
LAKE VYRNWY
BARMOUTH
DOLGELLAU
SHREWSBURY
WELSHPOOL
TELFORD
TYWYN
ABERDOVEY
MACHYNLLETH
WOLVERHAMPTON
BRIDGNORTH
ABERYSTWYTH
LUDLOW
CHADDESLEY CORBETT
CLEOBURY MORTIMER
BROMSGROVE
REDDITCH

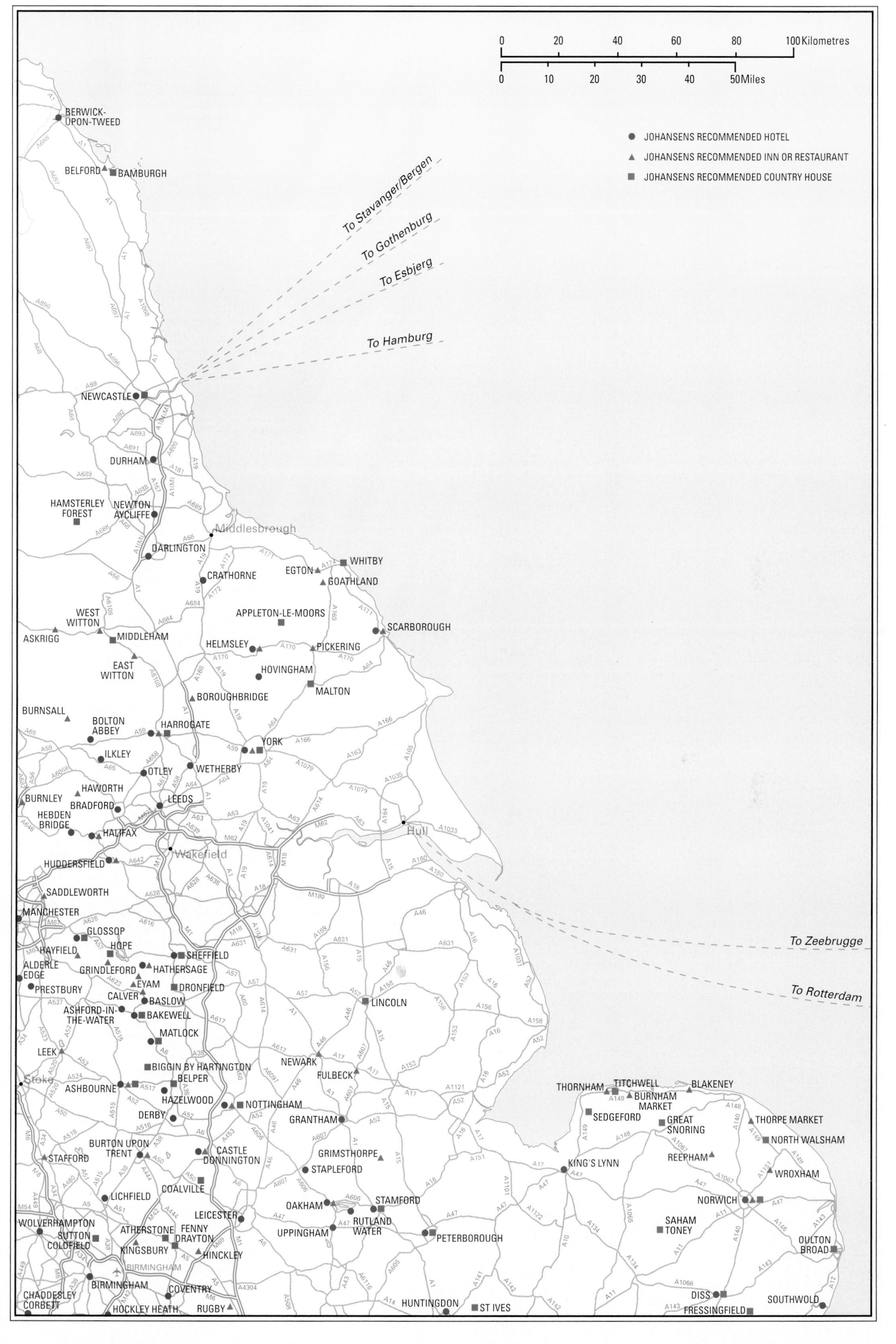

0 20 40 60 80 100 Kilometres
0 10 20 30 40 50 Miles
JOHANSENS RECOMMENDED HOTEL
JOHANSENS RECOMMENDED INN OR RESTAURANT
JOHANSENS RECOMMENDED COUNTRY HOUSE
To Stavanger/Bergen
To Gothenburg
To Esbjerg
To Hamburg
To Zeebrugge
To Rotterdam
BERWICK-UPON-TWEED
BELFORD
BAMBURGH
NEWCASTLE
DURHAM
HAMSTERLEY FOREST
NEWTON AYCLIFFE
Middlesbrough
DARLINGTON
CRATHORNE
EGTON
WHITBY
GOATHLAND
APPLETON-LE-MOORS
SCARBOROUGH
WEST WITTON
ASKRIGG
MIDDLEHAM
HELMSLEY
PICKERING
EAST WITTON
HOVINGHAM
MALTON
BOROUGHBRIDGE
BURNSALL
BOLTON ABBEY
HARROGATE
YORK
ILKLEY
OTLEY
WETHERBY
HAWORTH
BURNLEY
BRADFORD
LEEDS
HEBDEN BRIDGE
HALIFAX
Hull
Wakefield
HUDDERSFIELD
SADDLEWORTH
MANCHESTER
GLOSSOP
HAYFIELD
HOPE
SHEFFIELD
ALDERLEY EDGE
GRINDLEFORD
HATHERSAGE
EYAM
DRONFIELD
PRESTBURY
CALVER
BASLOW
LINCOLN
ASHFORD-IN-THE-WATER
BAKEWELL
MATLOCK
LEEK
BIGGIN BY HARTINGTON
NEWARK
Stoke
BELPER
FULBECK
ASHBOURNE
HAZELWOOD
NOTTINGHAM
THORNHAM
TITCHWELL
BLAKENEY
BURNHAM MARKET
DERBY
GRANTHAM
SEDGEFORD
GREAT SNORING
THORPE MARKET
NORTH WALSHAM
BURTON UPON TRENT
CASTLE DONNINGTON
GRIMSTHORPE
REEPHAM
STAFFORD
STAPLEFORD
KING'S LYNN
WROXHAM
LICHFIELD
COALVILLE
STAMFORD
NORWICH
OAKHAM
RUTLAND WATER
LEICESTER
SAHAM TONEY
WOLVERHAMPTON
ATHERSTONE
FENNY DRAYTON
UPPINGHAM
PETERBOROUGH
SUTTON COLDFIELD
KINGSBURY
HINCKLEY
OULTON BROAD
BIRMINGHAM
COVENTRY
CHADDESLEY CORBETT
HOCKLEY HEATH
RUGBY
HUNTINGDON
ST IVES
DISS
SOUTHWOLD
FRESSINGFIELD

Scrabster
KINLOCHBERVIE
TONGUE
Stornoway
LOCHINVER
Tarbert
ISLE OF HARRIS
Ullapool
ISLE OF SKYE
ELGIN
NAIRN
STRATHPEFFER
DINGWALL
TORRIDON
INVERNESS
INVERNESS
DRUMNADROCHIT
GRANTOWN-ON-SPEY
LOCH NESS SIDE
ISLE OF SKYE
Ardvasar
FORT AUGUSTUS
Mallaig
BEASDALE
FORT WILLIAM
GLENSHEE
BLAIR ATHOLL
KILLIECRANKIE
STRATHTUMMEL
PITLOCHRY
KENTALLEN OF APPIN
ABERFELDY
APPIN
Lochaline
BLAIRGOWRIE
ISLE OF ERISKA
PORT APPIN
ISLE OF MULL
OBAN
SCONE
PERTH
KILCHRENAN
CALLANDER
PORT OF MENTETH
KINBUCK
KINROSS
BLAIRLOGIE
POWMILL
ALLOA
FINTRY
LOCH LOMOND
DUNOON
EDINBURGH
UPHALL
EDINBURGH
Rothesay
GLASGOW
GLASGOW
BIGGAR
PEEBLES
IRVINE
TROON
Ayr
MOFFAT
Coleraine
Londonderry

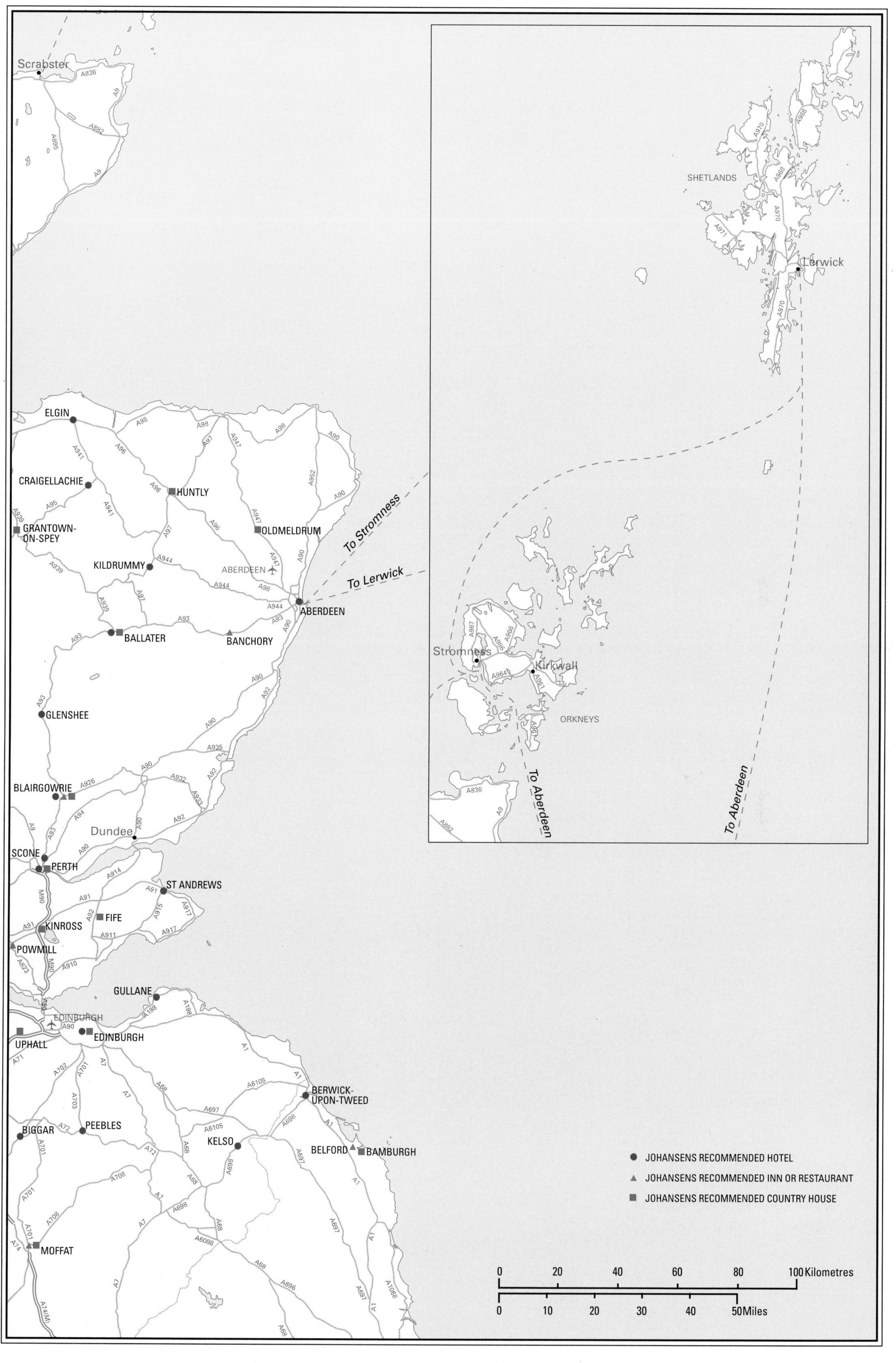
Scrabster
SHETLANDS
Lerwick
ELGIN
CRAIGELLACHIE
HUNTLY
GRANTOWN-ON-SPEY
OLDMELDRUM
KILDRUMMY
ABERDEEN
To Stromness
To Lerwick
BALLATER
BANCHORY
GLENSHEE
BLAIRGOWRIE
Dundee
SCONE
PERTH
ST ANDREWS
FIFE
KINROSS
POWMILL
GULLANE
EDINBURGH
UPHALL
BERWICK-UPON-TWEED
PEEBLES
BIGGAR
KELSO
BELFORD
BAMBURGH
MOFFAT
Stromness
Kirkwall
ORKNEYS
To Aberdeen
To Aberdeen
JOHANSENS RECOMMENDED HOTEL
JOHANSENS RECOMMENDED INN OR RESTAURANT
JOHANSENS RECOMMENDED COUNTRY HOUSE
0 20 40 60 80 100 Kilometres
0 10 20 30 40 50 Miles

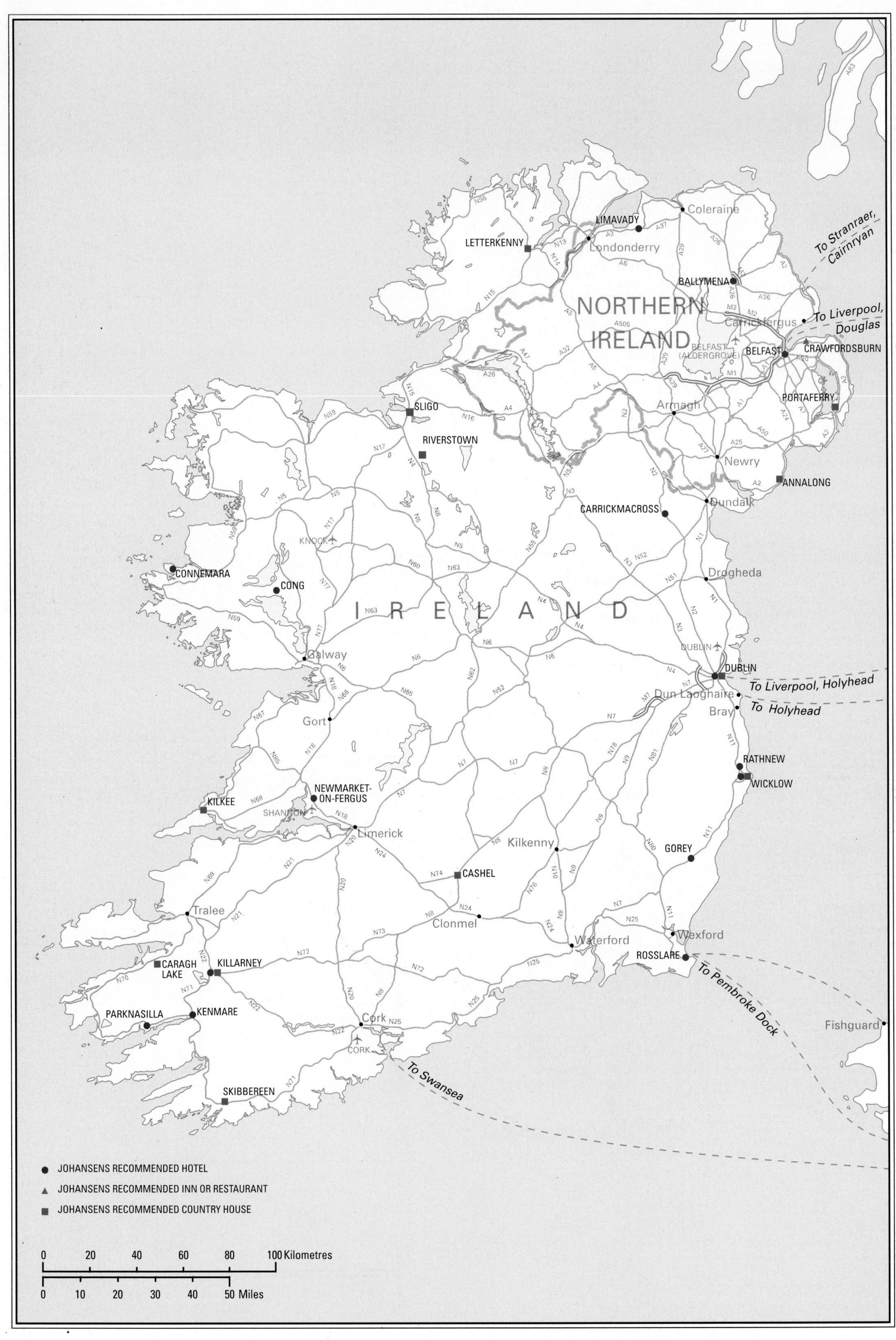

NORTHERN IRELAND
IRELAND
LIMAVADY
Coleraine
LETTERKENNY
Londonderry
To Stranraer, Cairnryan
BALLYMENA
Carrickfergus
To Liverpool, Douglas
BELFAST (ALDERGROVE)
BELFAST
CRAWFORDSBURN
PORTAFERRY
SLIGO
Armagh
RIVERSTOWN
Newry
ANNALONG
Dundalk
CARRICKMACROSS
KNOCK
CONNEMARA
CONG
Drogheda
Galway
DUBLIN
DUBLIN
To Liverpool, Holyhead
Dun Laoghaire
Bray
To Holyhead
Gort
RATHNEW
WICKLOW
NEWMARKET-ON-FERGUS
KILKEE
SHANNON
Limerick
Kilkenny
GOREY
CASHEL
Tralee
Clonmel
Wexford
Waterford
ROSSLARE
CARAGH LAKE
KILLARNEY
To Pembroke Dock
Fishguard
PARKNASILLA
KENMARE
Cork
CORK
To Swansea
SKIBBEREEN
JOHANSENS RECOMMENDED HOTEL
JOHANSENS RECOMMENDED INN OR RESTAURANT
JOHANSENS RECOMMENDED COUNTRY HOUSE
0 20 40 60 80 100 Kilometres
0 10 20 30 40 50 Miles

## 1998 Johansens Recommended Hotels listed by region

*To enable you to use your 1998 Johansens Recommended Hotels Guide more effectively the following pages of indexes contain a wealth of useful information about the hotels featured in the guide. As well as listing the hotels alphabetically by region and by county, the indexes also show at a glance which hotels offer certain specialised facilities.*

***The indexes are as follows:***

- By region
- By county
- With a heated indoor swimming pool
- With a golf course on site
- With shooting arranged
- With salmon or trout fishing on site
- With health/fitness facilities
- With childcare facilities
- With conference facilities for 250 delegates or more
- Relais et Châteaux members
- Small Luxury Hotels of the World members
- Pride of Britain members
- Exclusive Hotels members
- Taste of Wales members
- Welsh Gold Collection members
- Arcadian Hotels members
- Johansens Preferred Partners
- Hotels accepting the Johansens Privilege Card

### *LONDON*



### *ENGLAND*

## 1998 Johansens Recommended Hotels by region continued



### WALES



### SCOTLAND



### IRELAND



### CHANNEL ISLANDS

## 1998 Johansens Recommended Hotels by county

## 1998 Johansens Recommended Hotels by county continued

### IRELAND



### CHANNEL ISLANDS



## Hotels with a heated indoor swimming pool

***Swimming pools at these hotels are open all year round***

### ENGLAND



### WALES



### SCOTLAND



### IRELAND



### CHANNEL ISLANDS



## Hotels with golf

***Hotels with golf on site***

### ENGLAND



### WALES



### SCOTLAND



### IRELAND



## Hotels with shooting

***Shooting on site, to which guests have access, can be arranged***

### ENGLAND

## Hotels with shooting continued

### WALES



### SCOTLAND



## Hotels with fishing

*Guests may obtain rights to fishing within the hotel grounds*

### ENGLAND



### WALES



### SCOTLAND



### IRELAND



## Hotels with health/fitness facilities

*At the following hotels there are health/fitness facilities available*

### LONDON



### ENGLAND



### WALES



### SCOTLAND



### IRELAND



### CHANNEL ISLANDS



## Hotels with childcare facilities

***Comprehensive childcare facilities are available, namely crèche, babysitting and organised activities for children of all ages***

### LONDON



### ENGLAND



### SCOTLAND



### IRELAND



## Hotels with conference facilities

***These hotels can accommodate theatre-style conferences for 250 delegates or over***

### LONDON



### ENGLAND

*WALES*



*SCOTLAND*



*IRELAND*



## Relais et Châteaux members



## Small Luxury Hotels of the World members



## Pride of Britain members



## Exclusive Hotels UK members



## Taste of Wales members



## Welsh Gold Collection members



## Arcadian Hotels members



## Johansens Preferred Partners



## Hotels Accepting the Johansens Privilege Card

***10% discount, room upgrade where available, VIP service at participating establishments. Full Terms & Conditions available on request.***

*LONDON*



*ENGLAND*



*WALES*



*SCOTLAND*



*IRELAND*



# Play the role of Hotel Inspector

*At the back of this book you will notice a quantity of Guest Survey forms. If you have had an enjoyable stay at one of our recommended hotels, or alternatively you have been in some way disappointed, please complete one of these forms and send it to us FREEPOST.*

*These reports essentially complement the assessments made by our team of professional inspectors, continually monitoring the standards of hospitality in every establishment in our guides. Guest Survey reports also have an important influence on the selection of nominations for our annual awards for excellence.*

# PREFERRED PARTNERS

Preferred partners are those organisations specifically chosen and exclusively recommended by Johansens for the quality and excellence of their products and services for the mutal benefit of Johansens members, readers and independent travellers.

MasterCard International

Knight Frank International

Dunhill Tobacco of London Ltd

Halliday Meecham

Hildon Ltd

Moët & Chandon Champagne

Honda UK Ltd

Classic Malts of Scotland

Lakesure Ltd in association with Charter Insurance Ltd

PACIFIC DIRECT LIMITED

Pacific Direct

NPI

# Guest Survey Report

Your own Johansens 'inspection' gives reliability to our guides and assists in the selection of Award Nominations

Name/location of hotel: ______________________ Page No: __________

Date of visit: ______________________

Name & address of guest: ______________________

______________________ Postcode: __________

1J6

| *Please tick one box in each category below:* | *Excellent* | *Good* | *Disappointing* | *Poor* |
|---|---|---|---|---|
| Bedrooms | | | | |
| Public Rooms | | | | |
| Restaurant/Cuisine | | | | |
| Service | | | | |
| Welcome/Friendliness | | | | |
| Value For Money | | | | |

**PLEASE return your Guest Survey Report form!**

Occasionally we may allow other reputable organisations to write with offers which may be of interest.
If you prefer not to here from them, tick this box ☐

To: Johansens, FREEPOST (CB264), 175-179 St John Street, London EC1B 1JQ


# Guest Survey Report

Your own Johansens 'inspection' gives reliability to our guides and assists in the selection of Award Nominations

Name/location of hotel: ______________________ Page No: __________

Date of visit: ______________________

Name & address of guest: ______________________

______________________ Postcode: __________

1J6

| *Please tick one box in each category below:* | *Excellent* | *Good* | *Disappointing* | *Poor* |
|---|---|---|---|---|
| Bedrooms | | | | |
| Public Rooms | | | | |
| Restaurant/Cuisine | | | | |
| Service | | | | |
| Welcome/Friendliness | | | | |
| Value For Money | | | | |

**PLEASE return your Guest Survey Report form!**

Occasionally we may allow other reputable organisations to write with offers which may be of interest.
If you prefer not to here from them, tick this box ☐

To: Johansens, FREEPOST (CB264), 175-179 St John Street, London EC1B 1JQ

# Order Coupon

**To order Johansens guides, simply indicate which publications you require by putting the quantity(ies) in the boxes provided. Choose you preferred method of payment and return this coupon (NO STAMP REQUIRED). You may also place your order using FREEPHONE 0800 269397 or by fax on 0171 251 6113.**

❑ I enclose a cheque for £______________ payable to Johansens.

❑ I enclose my order on company letterheading, please invoice me. (UK companies only)

❑ Please debit my credit/charge card account (please tick)

❑ MASTERCARD ❑ VISA ❑ DINERS ❑ AMEX ❑ SWITCH

Switch Issue Number

Card No

Signature ______________________ Expiry Date ________________

Name (Mr/Mrs/Miss) ________________________________

Address ________________________________

________________________ Postcode ________________

*(We aim to despatch your order within 10 days, but please allow 28 days for delivery)*

**Post free to: Johansens, FREEPOST (CB264), 43Millharbour, London E14 9TR**

*Occasionally we may allow reputable organisations to write to you with offers which may interest you. If you prefer not to hear from them, tick this box* ❑

save £10

| | PRICE | QTY | TOTAL |
|---|---|---|---|
| The Collection of 4 Johansens Guides *+ Recommended Hotels & Inns – North America FREE* ~~£53.80~~ | £43.80 | | |
| The Collection in a Presentation Boxed Set ~~£58.80~~ *+ Recommended Hotels & Inns – N. America FREE* | £48.80 | | |
| The 2 CD ROMS ~~£49.90~~ | £39.00 | | |
| Recommended Hotels – Great Britain & Ireland 1998 | £18.95 | | |
| Recommended Country Houses and Small Hotels – GB & Ireland 1998 | £10.95 | | |
| Recommended Inns with Restaurants – GB & Ireland 1998 | £9.95 | | |
| Recommended Hotels – Europe 1998 | £13.95 | | |
| Recommended Hotels – North America 1998 | £9.95 | | |
| Historic Houses Castles & Gardens, Published and mailed to you in March 1998 | £6.95 | | |
| CD ROM – Hotels, Country Houses & Inns Great Britain & Ireland 1998 with Historic Houses Castles & Gardens | £29.95 | | |
| CD ROM – Recommended Hotels & Inns N. America and Recommended Hotels Europe 1998 | £19.95 | | |
| 1998 Privilege Card – *10% discount, room upgrade when available. VIP Service at participating establishments* | | | FREE |
| The Independent Traveller – *Johansens newsletter including many special offers* | | | FREE |
| Postage & Packing *UK: £4 – or £2 for single orders and CD-Roms Outside UK: Add £5 – or £3 for single orders and CD-Roms* | | | |
| **TOTAL** | **£** | | |

**CALL THE JOHANSENS CREDIT CARD ORDER SERVICE FREE ☎ 0800 269397**

**PRICES VALID UNTIL 31/08/98** **2J2**


# Order Coupon

**To order Johansens guides, simply indicate which publications you require by putting the quantity(ies) in the boxes provided. Choose you preferred method of payment and return this coupon (NO STAMP REQUIRED). You may also place your order using FREEPHONE 0800 269397 or by fax on 0171 251 6113.**

❑ I enclose a cheque for £______________ payable to Johansens.

❑ I enclose my order on company letterheading, please invoice me. (UK companies only)

❑ Please debit my credit/charge card account (please tick)

❑ MASTERCARD ❑ VISA ❑ DINERS ❑ AMEX ❑ SWITCH

Switch Issue Number

Card No

Signature ______________________ Expiry Date ________________

Name (Mr/Mrs/Miss) ________________________________

Address ________________________________

________________________ Postcode ________________

*(We aim to despatch your order within 10 days, but please allow 28 days for delivery)*

**Post free to: Johansens, FREEPOST (CB264), 43Millharbour, London E14 9TR**

*Occasionally we may allow reputable organisations to write to you with offers which may interest you. If you prefer not to hear from them, tick this box* ❑

save £10

| | PRICE | QTY | TOTAL |
|---|---|---|---|
| The Collection of 4 Johansens Guides *+ Recommended Hotels & Inns – North America FREE* ~~£53.80~~ | £43.80 | | |
| The Collection in a Presentation Boxed Set ~~£58.80~~ *+ Recommended Hotels & Inns – N. America FREE* | £48.80 | | |
| The 2 CD ROMS ~~£49.90~~ | £39.00 | | |
| Recommended Hotels – Great Britain & Ireland 1998 | £18.95 | | |
| Recommended Country Houses and Small Hotels – GB & Ireland 1998 | £10.95 | | |
| Recommended Inns with Restaurants – GB & Ireland 1998 | £9.95 | | |
| Recommended Hotels – Europe 1998 | £13.95 | | |
| Recommended Hotels – North America 1998 | £9.95 | | |
| Historic Houses Castles & Gardens, Published and mailed to you in March 1998 | £6.95 | | |
| CD ROM – Hotels, Country Houses & Inns Great Britain & Ireland 1998 with Historic Houses Castles & Gardens | £29.95 | | |
| CD ROM – Recommended Hotels & Inns N. America and Recommended Hotels Europe 1998 | £19.95 | | |
| 1998 Privilege Card – *10% discount, room upgrade when available. VIP Service at participating establishments* | | | FREE |
| The Independent Traveller – *Johansens newsletter including many special offers* | | | FREE |
| Postage & Packing *UK: £4 – or £2 for single orders and CD-Roms Outside UK: Add £5 – or £3 for single orders and CD-Roms* | | | |
| **TOTAL** | **£** | | |

**CALL THE JOHANSENS CREDIT CARD ORDER SERVICE FREE ☎ 0800 269397**

**PRICES VALID UNTIL 31/08/98** **2J2**

# Guest Survey Report

Your own Johansens 'inspection' gives reliability to our guides and assists in the selection of Award Nominations

Name/location of hotel: ______________________________ Page No: __________

Date of visit: ______________________________

Name & address of guest: ______________________________

______________________________ Postcode: __________

1J6

| *Please tick one box in each category below:* | *Excellent* | *Good* | *Disappointing* | *Poor* |
|---|---|---|---|---|
| Bedrooms | | | | |
| Public Rooms | | | | |
| Restaurant/Cuisine | | | | |
| Service | | | | |
| Welcome/Friendliness | | | | |
| Value For Money | | | | |

**PLEASE return your Guest Survey Report form!**

Occasionally we may allow other reputable organisations to write with offers which may be of interest.
If you prefer not to here from them, tick this box ☐

To: Johansens, FREEPOST (CB264), 175-179 St John Street, London EC1B 1JQ


# Guest Survey Report

Your own Johansens 'inspection' gives reliability to our guides and assists in the selection of Award Nominations

Name/location of hotel: ______________________________ Page No: __________

Date of visit: ______________________________

Name & address of guest: ______________________________

______________________________ Postcode: __________

1J6

| *Please tick one box in each category below:* | *Excellent* | *Good* | *Disappointing* | *Poor* |
|---|---|---|---|---|
| Bedrooms | | | | |
| Public Rooms | | | | |
| Restaurant/Cuisine | | | | |
| Service | | | | |
| Welcome/Friendliness | | | | |
| Value For Money | | | | |

**PLEASE return your Guest Survey Report form!**

Occasionally we may allow other reputable organisations to write with offers which may be of interest.
If you prefer not to here from them, tick this box ☐

To: Johansens, FREEPOST (CB264), 175-179 St John Street, London EC1B 1JQ

# Order Coupon

**To order Johansens guides, simply indicate which publications you require by putting the quantity(ies) in the boxes provided. Choose you preferred method of payment and return this coupon (NO STAMP REQUIRED). You may also place your order using FREEPHONE 0800 269397 or by fax on 0171 251 6113.**

❑ I enclose a cheque for £______________ payable to Johansens.
❑ I enclose my order on company letterheading, please invoice me. (UK companies only)
❑ Please debit my credit/charge card account (please tick)
❑ MASTERCARD ❑ VISA ❑ DINERS ❑ AMEX ❑ SWITCH

Switch Issue Number

Card No

Signature ______________ Expiry Date ______________

Name (Mr/Mrs/Miss) ______________

Address ______________

______________ Postcode ______________

*(We aim to despatch your order within 10 days, but please allow 28 days for delivery)*

**Post free to: Johansens, FREEPOST (CB264), 43Millharbour, London E14 9TR**

*Occasionally we may allow reputable organisations to write to you with offers which may interest you. If you prefer not to hear from them, tick this box* ❑

save £10

| | PRICE | QTY | TOTAL |
|---|---|---|---|
| The Collection of 4 Johansens Guides *+ Recommended Hotels & Inns – North America FREE* ~~£53.80~~ | £43.80 | | |
| The Collection in a Presentation Boxed Set ~~£58.80~~ *+ Recommended Hotels & Inns – N. America FREE* | £48.80 | | |
| The 2 CD ROMS ~~£49.90~~ | £39.00 | | |
| Recommended Hotels – Great Britain & Ireland 1998 | £18.95 | | |
| Recommended Country Houses and Small Hotels – GB & Ireland 1998 | £10.95 | | |
| Recommended Inns with Restaurants – GB & Ireland 1998 | £9.95 | | |
| Recommended Hotels – Europe 1998 | £13.95 | | |
| Recommended Hotels – North America 1998 | £9.95 | | |
| Historic Houses Castles & Gardens, Published and mailed to you in March 1998 | £6.95 | | |
| CD ROM – Hotels, Country Houses & Inns Great Britain & Ireland 1998 with Historic Houses Castles & Gardens | £29.95 | | |
| CD ROM – Recommended Hotels & Inns N. America and Recommended Hotels Europe 1998 | £19.95 | | |
| 1998 Privilege Card – *10% discount, room upgrade when available. VIP Service at participating establishments* | | | FREE |
| The Independent Traveller – *Johansens newsletter including many special offers* | | | FREE |
| Postage & Packing *UK: £4 – or £2 for single orders and CD-Roms Outside UK: Add £5 – or £3 for single orders and CD-Roms* | | | |
| **TOTAL** | **£** | | |

**CALL THE JOHANSENS CREDIT CARD ORDER SERVICE FREE ☎ 0800 269397**

**PRICES VALID UNTIL 31/08/98** **2J2**


# Order Coupon

**To order Johansens guides, simply indicate which publications you require by putting the quantity(ies) in the boxes provided. Choose you preferred method of payment and return this coupon (NO STAMP REQUIRED). You may also place your order using FREEPHONE 0800 269397 or by fax on 0171 251 6113.**

❑ I enclose a cheque for £______________ payable to Johansens.
❑ I enclose my order on company letterheading, please invoice me. (UK companies only)
❑ Please debit my credit/charge card account (please tick)
❑ MASTERCARD ❑ VISA ❑ DINERS ❑ AMEX ❑ SWITCH

Switch Issue Number

Card No

Signature ______________ Expiry Date ______________

Name (Mr/Mrs/Miss) ______________

Address ______________

______________ Postcode ______________

*(We aim to despatch your order within 10 days, but please allow 28 days for delivery)*

**Post free to: Johansens, FREEPOST (CB264), 43Millharbour, London E14 9TR**

*Occasionally we may allow reputable organisations to write to you with offers which may interest you. If you prefer not to hear from them, tick this box* ❑

save £10

| | PRICE | QTY | TOTAL |
|---|---|---|---|
| The Collection of 4 Johansens Guides *+ Recommended Hotels & Inns – North America FREE* ~~£53.80~~ | £43.80 | | |
| The Collection in a Presentation Boxed Set ~~£58.80~~ *+ Recommended Hotels & Inns – N. America FREE* | £48.80 | | |
| The 2 CD ROMS ~~£49.90~~ | £39.00 | | |
| Recommended Hotels – Great Britain & Ireland 1998 | £18.95 | | |
| Recommended Country Houses and Small Hotels – GB & Ireland 1998 | £10.95 | | |
| Recommended Inns with Restaurants – GB & Ireland 1998 | £9.95 | | |
| Recommended Hotels – Europe 1998 | £13.95 | | |
| Recommended Hotels – North America 1998 | £9.95 | | |
| Historic Houses Castles & Gardens, Published and mailed to you in March 1998 | £6.95 | | |
| CD ROM – Hotels, Country Houses & Inns Great Britain & Ireland 1998 with Historic Houses Castles & Gardens | £29.95 | | |
| CD ROM – Recommended Hotels & Inns N. America and Recommended Hotels Europe 1998 | £19.95 | | |
| 1998 Privilege Card – *10% discount, room upgrade when available. VIP Service at participating establishments* | | | FREE |
| The Independent Traveller – *Johansens newsletter including many special offers* | | | FREE |
| Postage & Packing *UK: £4 – or £2 for single orders and CD-Roms Outside UK: Add £5 – or £3 for single orders and CD-Roms* | | | |
| **TOTAL** | **£** | | |

**CALL THE JOHANSENS CREDIT CARD ORDER SERVICE FREE ☎ 0800 269397**

**PRICES VALID UNTIL 31/08/98** **2J2**